WITHDRAWN

NORTH DAKOTA
STATE UNIVERSITY
MAY 29 1981
SERIALS DEPT.
LIBRARY

The Bowker Annual

THE BOWKER ANNUAL
OF LIBRARY & BOOK TRADE INFORMATION

26TH EDITION · 1981

Compiled & Edited by
FILOMENA SIMORA

Consulting Editor
Frank Schick

Sponsored by
The Council of National Library
& Information Associations, Inc.

R. R. BOWKER COMPANY
NEW YORK & LONDON

Published by R. R. Bowker Co.
1180 Avenue of the Americas, New York, N.Y. 10036
Copyright © 1981 by Xerox Corporation
All rights reserved
International Standard Book Number 0-8352-1343-9
International Standard Serial Number 0068-0540
Library of Congress Catalog Card Number 55-12434
Printed and Bound in the United States of America

No copyright is claimed for articles in this volume prepared by U.S. Government employees as part of their official duties. Such articles are in the public domain and can be reproduced at will.

Contents

Preface ix

PART 1
REPORTS FROM THE FIELD

NEWS REPORTS
LJ News Report, 1980. *Noël Savage* 3
SLJ News Report, 1980. *Bertha M. Cheatham* 33
PW News Report, 1980. *John F. Baker* 42

SPECIAL REPORTS
Library Networking in the United States, 1980. *Henriette D. Avram* 46
The Decision Information Display System (DIDS). *Curtis L. Fritz* 52
President Carter's Message to Congress on Libraries (Reprint) 56

FEDERAL AGENCIES
Federal Information Centers Program. *Donald R. Knenlein* 60
United States International Communication Agency. *Donald C. Hausrath* ... 67
The Copyright Office: Developments in 1980. *Susan Robinson* 73
The National Commission on Libraries and Information Science.
    Toni Carbo Bearman and *Douglas S. Price* 78
Depository Library Program. *Bernadine Abbott Hoduski* 82

FEDERAL LIBRARIES
Library of Congress. *James W. McClung* 85
The Center for the Book in the Library of Congress. *John Y. Cole* 90
National Library of Medicine. *Robert B. Mehnert* 93
Technical Information Systems/National Agricultural Library.
    Eugene M. Farkas 98

NATIONAL ASSOCIATIONS
American Library Association. *Peggy Sullivan* 102
American National Standards Committee Z-39 and International Organization
    for Standardization TC 46. *James L. Wood* and *Robert W. Frase* 107
Association of American Publishers. *Gregory V. Gore* 112

Association of Research Libraries, Office of Management Studies.
  Maxine K. Sitts 120

PART 2
LEGISLATION, FUNDING, AND GRANTS

Legislation Affecting Librarianship in 1980.
  Eileen D. Cooke and *Carol C. Henderson* 127
Legislation Affecting Publishing in 1980. *Washington Staff, AAP* 141
Legislation Affecting the Information Industry, 1980. *Robert S. Willard* 147

FUNDING PROGRAMS AND GRANT-MAKING AGENCIES
Council on Library Resources, Inc. *Nancy E. Gwinn* 153
Library Services and Construction Act 162
Elementary and Secondary Education Act, Title IV, Part B—Instructional
  Materials and School Library Resources. *Beatrice Simmons* 173
Higher Education Act, Title II-A, College Library Resources.
  Beth A. Phillips and *Frank A. Stevens* 176
Higher Education Act, Title II-B, Library Education.
  Frank A. Stevens and *Janice Owens* 179
Higher Education Act, Title II-B, Library Research and Demonstration Program.
  Adrienne Chute 184
Higher Education Act, Title II-C, Strengthening Research Library Resources.
  Frank A. Stevens 189
National Endowment for the Humanities Support for Libraries, 1980 192
National Science Foundation Support for Information Science Research.
  Sarah N. Rhodes 195
National Historical Publications and Records Commission 201

PART 3
LIBRARY EDUCATION, PLACEMENT, AND SALARIES

Guide to Library Placement Sources. *Margaret Myers* 209
Recent Library Personnel Surveys. *Margaret Myers* 223
Placements and Salaries, 1979: Wider Horizons. *Carol L. Learmont* 231
The Information Profession: An Occupational Survey. *Anthony Debons* 246
Accredited Library Schools 249
Library Scholarship Sources 252
Library Scholarship and Award Recipients, 1980 254

PART 4
RESEARCH AND STATISTICS

LIBRARY RESEARCH AND STATISTICS

Research on Libraries and Librarianship in 1980: An Overview. *Mary Jo Lynch*. 263

Recent Developments in Library Statistical Activities. *Susanne Henderson* .. 267

Characteristics of the U.S. Population Served by Libraries. *Nadine Edles* ... 270

Number of Libraries in the United States and Canada 272

Public and Academic Library Acquisition Expenditures 274

Health Sciences Libraries in the United States: Survey III, 1979.
Susan Crawford and *Alan M. Rees* 279

NCES Survey of College and University Libraries, 1978–1979.
Theodore Samore 287

Academic Library Buildings in 1980.
Barbara Livingston, Bette-Lee Fox, and *Deborah Waithe* 304

Public Library Buildings in 1980.
Barbara Livingston, Bette-Lee Fox, and *Deborah Waithe* 310

BOOK TRADE RESEARCH AND STATISTICS

U.S. Book Title Output—A One Hundred-Year Overview.
Dorothy B. Hokkanen 324

Book Title Output and Average Prices, 1980 Preliminary Figures.
Chandler B. Grannis 329

Book Sales Statistics: Highlights from AAP Annual Survey, 1979.
Chandler B. Grannis 336

U.S. Consumer Expenditures on Books in 1979. *John P. Dessauer* 338

Prices of U.S. and Foreign Published Materials. *Sally F. Williams* 340

Number of Book Outlets in the United States and Canada 354

Book Review Media Statistics 355

PART 5
INTERNATIONAL REPORTS AND STATISTICS

INTERNATIONAL REPORTS

Frankfurt Book Fair, 1980. *Herbert R. Lottman* 359

International and Comparative Librarianship: A Current Assessment.
Josephine Riss Fang 366

IFLA: Some Highlights of the 1980 Conference. *Josephine Riss Fang* 375

Library Services in India. *D. R. Kalia* 377

The Protocol to the Florence Agreement. *Robert W. Frase* 381

viii / CONTENTS

INTERNATIONAL STATISTICS
U.S. Book Exports and Imports and International Title Output.
    Chandler B. Grannis 384
British Book Production, 1980. 388

PART 6
REFERENCE INFORMATION

BIBLIOGRAPHIES
The Librarian's Bookshelf. *Carol S. Nielsen* 397
Basic Publications for the Publisher and the Book Trade. *Jean R. Peters* 407

DISTINGUISHED BOOKS
Literary Prizes, 1980 415
Notable Books of 1980 426
Best Young Adult Books of 1980 427
Best Children's Books of 1980 429
Best Sellers of 1980: Hardcover Fiction and Nonfiction. *Daisy Maryles* 431

PART 7
DIRECTORY OF ORGANIZATIONS

DIRECTORY OF LIBRARY AND RELATED ORGANIZATIONS
National Library and Information-Industry Associations,
    United States and Canada 439
State, Provincial, and Regional Library Associations 504
State Library Agencies 515
State School Library Media Associations 519
State Supervisors of School Library Media Services 525
International Library Associations 529
Foreign Library Associations 538

DIRECTORY OF BOOK TRADE AND RELATED ORGANIZATIONS
Book Trade Associations, United States and Canada 549
International and Foreign Book Trade Associations 555

CALENDAR, 1981–1982 562

CUMULATIVE INDEX, 1977–1981 565

DIRECTORY OF U.S. AND CANADIAN LIBRARIES 627

Preface

Networking, the Decision Information Display System (DIDS), the Federal Information Centers Program, the United States International Communication Agency (successor to USIA), recent library personnel surveys, and the Protocol to the Florence Agreement are just some of the topics covered in this, the twenty-sixth, edition of the *Bowker Annual*.

For the second year, the *Bowker Annual* includes the information industry in its coverage of developments and issues of interest to libraries and the book trade. Reports on the Federal Information Centers Program and on legislation affecting the information industry are now counted among the annually updated reports, and such articles as the report on the Decision Information Display System (DIDS)—the system developed by the federal government to facilitate access to and utilization of federal statistical data—and a report on a survey of information professionals are among the special features of this new edition.

Other special features include a report on the status of library networking in the United States, a report on the worldwide library program of the United States International Communication Agency, and another on the Depository Library System. The complete text of President Carter's message to Congress on libraries also is reprinted in the Special Reports section of Part 1.

"Recent Library Personnel Surveys" is a feature article in Part 3, together with a separate report focusing on the University of Pittsburgh survey of information professionals. Featured in Part 4 are reports on the recently completed survey of health sciences librarians and on the NCES survey of college and university libraries, as well as a 100-year overview of book title output. Also there are "Research on Libraries and Librarianship" and "Recent Developments in Library Statistical Activities," two annually updated features.

This year's international coverage includes a report on the Protocol to the Florence Agreement, an overview of international librarianship, and a status report on library services in India. Rounding out the international coverage is the annually updated International Statistics section.

These are just some of the highlights of the 1981 edition. The temptation to comment on each of the annual features, reviews of legislation and grants, statistical analyses and surveys, bibliographies, literary commendations, and directories is great, but we hope this brief introduction to the new edition will interest our readers in discovering its contents further on their own. A five-year cumulative index is included with this volume to help readers in becoming acquainted with its contents as well as that of the preceding four editions.

We wish to thank all those who contributed articles and information for the *Bowker Annual* this year. We appreciate their cooperation in meeting our deadlines at a time of year when demands on contributors' time are particularly heavy.

Part 1
Reports from the Field

News Reports

LJ NEWS REPORT, 1980

Noël Savage
Associate News Editor, *Library Journal*

The nation's economy was the one issue to grab the attention of Americans of all classes in 1980. The deepening recession pushed President Carter out of office and ushered in what looks to be a much sterner conservatism than Carter's. Republicans have taken up the reins of power all across the land.

Long before the national election, libraries were busy registering voters (Baltimore County, Maryland), opening meeting rooms to politicians (Portage, Michigan), and countering voter apathy with programs stressing the importance of voting (Tucson, Arizona). The Minneapolis Public Library brought in top-ranking government people for lectures, "town meetings," and tours aimed at giving people a real feel for city, state, and national politics.

Stimulated in part by their activity in the political process at 1979's White House Conference on Libraries and Information Services (WHCOLIS), libraries worked hard to keep people informed about the issues and the candidates. The Detroit Public Library set up a public information center at Republican Convention headquarters. Some 100 volunteer reference librarians, backed up by NEXUS and DIALOG terminals, kept delegates and media people up to date on fast-breaking action and fielded reference questions. Following Detroit's precedent-setting example, Enoch Pratt established an information center for reporters covering the presidential debate in Baltimore. The space shortage did not permit an on-site library operation at Democratic Convention headquarters, but New York City libraries provided a Library-on-Call information telephone service.

When the votes were tallied, Reagan had it by a landslide. The election brought out animosities toward doves, candidates of the liberal persuasion, and Cuban refugees. South Dakota lifted a ban against shooting mourning doves and also shot down "dove" George McGovern. Few Democrats survived the unexpected Republican sweep of the nation.

Hostility towards America's newest immigrants (the new wave of Cubans) was reflected in the Florida vote banning the use of public funds for bilingual materials. This vote could impair library service to Dade County's many ethnic communities. Dade County librarians have been reaching out to the new influx of Cuban and Haitian refugees, often volunteering their free time. The Miami Dade Public Library brought Spanish materials to the refugee processing centers and beefed up collections at five library outlets serving ethnic enclaves. Those five libraries were about the only buildings spared in the riots that followed the acquittal of four white policemen accused of murdering a black insurance salesman.

Note: Reprinted from *Library Journal*, January 15, 1981.

When 13,000 Cubans were dumped at Fort McCoy, Wisconsin's Winding Rivers Library System asked for state aid. Undaunted by the governor's refusal to address this "federal problem," Winding Rivers gave what it could in materials and human resources and publicized the Cubans' plight. Donations poured in from all over. An airline transported Spanish newspapers from Miami free.

One of the big questions for libraries on election eve was whether the "great conservative revolt" would indeed wipe out the tax support most libraries depend upon. Out of the many states and localities to weigh the question, Massachusetts alone voted for drastic tax reform. Librarians, teachers, union people, and politicians had warned against Proposition 2½, but new (higher) tax assessments delivered mere days before the election turned the vote.

Reagan's reign is expected to bring out a new stress on protecting the nation from its enemies. Following his election, the stock market had heavy trading in defense stocks and bonds. New in the nation is a begrudging acceptance of the possibility of war and the need for preparing for it. This mood was reflected in ALA-N.Y. when resolutions urging libraries to widely disseminate information about the draft (and alternatives to it) and about disarmament passed without debate. Prominent in the ALA resolutions was a serious questioning of the power of the press in America and new recognition of the dangers inherent in that power.

During the Reagan years, the warm liaisons with China (no longer "Red China") that started in the Nixon era are expected to continue. Chances are that hostility toward Russia will continue unless that nation pulls out of Afghanistan and thus poses less of a threat to the rich oil lands almost every nation has a stake in.

Bowing to wishes of the U.S. State Department, ALA did not send a delegation of U.S. librarians to Moscow as a follow-up to the 1979 American-Soviet seminar that had opened the door to potentially fruitful exchanges on both sides of the border. As with the boycott of the Moscow Olympics, it's difficult to say which nation lost out.

The tight economy threatens to undermine America's public institutions. New in the nation is the premium put on "privatized" services and the low regard with which "public" services are held. Financially ailing libraries have had to learn the dynamics of professional and political assertiveness in order to compete for shrinking tax dollars. Working against them are citizen groups which maintain that money supporting "public institutions" like libraries should be rechanneled to more "essential" services.

The lingering recession is taking a human toll: People of all classes are queuing up at unemployment lines, and the "welfare syndrome" is spreading. The tight job market has made employers (libraries among them) more demanding than ever. Job mobility is cramped for all but the highly skilled. Reflected in the faces of Americans are unrealized hopes and a lack of hope. Violence is on the upsurge; human tragedy is getting front-page coverage from newspapers out to make a profit. There is a blaring focus on law and order amidst chaos.

But libraries are addressing society's ills today and taking important steps to help people get a new understanding of the nation's cities, its prisons, and its many nationalities. Among the notable expressions of these concerns: a Rutgers Conference on Literature and the Urban Experience; an NEH project to bring humanities behind the bars of a Baltimore Penitentiary; Chicago's Dial Law information service for both English- and Spanish-speaking; and California's multiethnic I&R service.

Libraries are also helping people deal with the economy crunch by disseminating consumer information about money management (Gary, Indiana). They're training senior citizens to design programs for their own communities (Brooklyn, New York). They're pioneering in the delivery of medical consumer education (Tulsa, Oklahoma).

They're reaching out to the handicapped with workshops for blind parents, story hours for handicapped kids (Tustin, California), and prime time TV captioning for the deaf (Salt Lake County System).

When Chicago was held in the grip of three back-to-back strikes by transit workers, teachers, and firemen, Chicago Public opened its doors wider and reached out with programs to alleviate strike-related problems. Fayetteville, North Carolina, built up a foreign language resource center serving people who speak Vietnamese, Laotian, Japanese, Korean, German, Spanish, Kirundi, and many other foreign tongues. Public libraries are no longer "the best kept secret in town."

FEDERAL LIBRARY $$

Thanks to the spadework done at WHCOLIS, federal library aid prospects improved substantially in 1980. Breaking with tradition, the Office of Management and Budget nixed the cutbacks HEW had recommended and instead restored funding to ESEA IV-B for school libraries (up from HEW's $90,000,000 to $171,000,000) and Title I, LSCA (up from $56,900,000 to $62,500,000). HEW, in turn, asked for more money for research libraries and for interlibrary cooperation.

The new stress on cooperation and building up the nation's research libraries was reflected in the just authorized Higher Education Act. HEA II-A was redefined to include resource-sharing networks as well as basic grants for college book buying. Funding provided under HEA II-A: $10 million for 1981, $30 million a year for 1982–1984, and $35 million for 1985.

HEA II-B has been expanded to a three-part program of career training, research, and demonstration programs at funding levels of $10 million for 1981, $30 million for each of the next two years, and $35 million for 1985. Written into law is the need for providing opportunity to the disadvantaged and minorities, much in keeping with concerns voiced at WHCOLIS.

HEA for the Strengthening of Research Library Programs will go up from the current $6 million to $10 million in 1981 and $15 million for each of the following five years.

There were setbacks, too. The Local Public Works Program, which has been building libraries, was not authorized by Congress. But the Public Works and Economic Development Act did make it.

Signaling the start of sterner austerity by the federal government were cutbacks affecting the Library of Congress and new funding threats to the nation's medical library network. The low prestige of NCLIS led to the cancellation of its 1980 budget, an action rescinded at the last moment. NCLIS may face new funding threats for the plain and simple reason that Carter has reappointed Charles Benton to the top post at NCLIS and Reagan cannot unseat him.

THE ROLLBACK ROLL CALL

The possible consequences of tax revolt loomed large in the minds of librarians in Arizona, Nevada, Oregon, South Dakota, Utah, Michigan, Montana, Arkansas, California, and Massachusetts. Relatively benign tax measures made it in Montana and Arkansas. But the passage of Proposition 2½ spells real trouble for Massachusetts libraries, particularly urban libraries; Boston and Chelsea could lose up to 75 percent of their tax revenue.

For Montana, Initiative 86 indexes tax bills to keep pace with inflation; it could undermine support to academe. The Arkansas vote bars court-ordered property reassessments. This tax curb won't hurt Arkansas libraries, but they really lost out when the new state constitution (lifting limitations on library taxes) went down to defeat. Californians, wise to the real impact of Proposition 13, nixed the inviting "Jaws" of Proposition 9, which would have curbed state personal and sales taxes.

Massachusetts voted three-to-two for Proposition 2½; it mandates gradual reductions to "2½ percent of full and fair cash values" and will result in property tax rollbacks in the 40 percent range. Unlike California, Massachusetts has no surplus to "bail out" libraries and other municipal services, and the competition for shrinking tax dollars will be keen. Library closings, staff layoffs, and curtailments in services are inevitable. Some libraries announced cutbacks mere hours after the crucial vote. Tragically, this funding crisis follows on the heels of a successful ten-year fight to push state aid up to its current $6.7 million level. State aid that could have upgraded library service in the Bay State now seems destined to be used to help libraries survive.

California, too, faces a hard year ahead: The last of the state surplus is going fast, and there is a deepening fiscal crisis in that state. Libraries have yet to recover from the ravages of Proposition 13: library staff statewide has dropped 18 percent since 1979; library outlets are down 22 percent; and hours of service are cut back 23 percent.

In 1980 the California library community campaigned mightily for a precedent-setting bill that would have mandated state responsibility for "basic" library service and indexed it to keep pace with inflation. SB 958, scaled down so as not to take too big a bite out of the state's budget, got the unanimous approval of the legislature, but Governor Jerry Brown vetoed it at the last minute. There is a deep-rooted bipartisan support for SB 958, however, and California's stalwart library community will try again in 1981.

THE UPSURGE IN STATE AID

The library community is counting on states to shoulder more of the funding burden and, in the process, to equalize service. Monitoring steady growth in state library aid, the Urban Libraries Council reported that 46 states gave $166,458,228 to libraries and networks last year, an increase of $12,344,352. Taken together, states now pay for 13 percent of library expenditures; ULC's goal is to have them assume 50 percent of the funding load.

Spotlighting the big contributors, ULC applauds New York and its $37,000,000 library budget. West Virginia is highest in per capita support at $3.61, followed by Georgia at $2.47. The national average in per capita aid is 82 cents, up 5 cents.

Maryland's library leaders have made $6.50 per capita their next target. That state has forward-looking legislation that gives more to the poorer communities and expects more of wealthier ones. Also on the books is compensation to libraries designated as regional centers; Enoch Pratt gets $2 million for doubling as the state library.

Arizona wants to bring state grant aid from $550,000 to $750,000. Arizona also gives county and metropolitan libraries $300,000 to share.

New benchmarks in state aid were logged: Virginia upped biennium aid from $5,215,995 to $9 million. South Carolina brought library aid up 50 percent and liberalized it to give local government free rein. Oklahoma gave $400,000 more last year and also provided new funding to make libraries energy efficient and accessible to the handicapped.

In 1979 Montana started channeling coal severance tax revenue to libraries; this added up to $380,000 for 1980. Pennsylvania reformed its law to enable the legislature to appropriate more money to libraries; $750,000 was released immediately for a $9,768,000 total for 1980.

Alabama legislators boosted state aid 12 percent (to $3 million) despite stern opposition from the governor, but he later cut aid to all agencies 7 percent. Wisconsin's governor made clear his reluctance in signing legislation that makes the state match local funding indexed at 11.25 percent for a $5,147,200 total. His gripe—the state may not be able to honor its commitment in the hard years ahead.

Oregon took one on the chin when the legislature cut the state library budget 15 percent; budgets for staff, books, and services were pared back. Operations like the Pacific Northwest Bibliographic Center are endangered.

ACTION AT THE LOCAL LEVEL

Public libraries rely on the property tax for a lion's share of their revenue. This funding source is commonly disparaged because it doesn't keep pace with inflation as would a sales tax. But a North Carolina survey (1974 to 1979) found libraries far in the lead, averaging budget increases of 80.3 percent, while inflation rose 40 percent.

The unpopular property tax supports many libraries like the thriving Arlington Heights Memorial Library (Illinois) at the tune of $23 per capita. This library, the fourth largest in Illinois, gets by with a $1.7 million budget. It has a new building to house its 320,000 volumes and a circulation of 870,720.

To fight off dangers posed by tax-cutting proposals, libraries formed new alliances. Friends of the Buffalo and Erie County Library joined hands with union people to fight a proposal to force county government to "live within its means." The voting majority agreed that the county couldn't afford to withdraw support from libraries and other "nonmandated services" that enrich the life of the community.

Militant antitax citizen groups and the media backing them were no match for Pennsylvania's Cambria County Library, which had 51 churches behind it; a 61 percent majority nixed a bid to abolish the tax supporting the library.

Maryland's Harford County Library got unions, management, community organizations, newspapers, and politicians to help it prevent a second tax rollback. An informed public voted down a tax cut, thus preventing losses in tax income of 30 percent and up.

Libraries are gaining the savvy they need to win an election. South Carolina's Richland County Public Library ran a public relations campaign that pushed its budget up 24 percent to $1.9 million.

There's new recognition of the value of getting through to political candidates. After the Maine Library Association got Democrats to put a statement backing libraries in their platform, it decided to go after Republicans, too. Starting in 1982, MLA will be selective about which candidate to endorse. Indiana got both parties to include libraries in their respective platforms.

Libraries carried many an election last year. Majority votes (70 percent and up) in two counties served by Oklahoma's Pioneer Multicounty Library pushed its revenue up one-third, for over $4 million total.

Five difficult years of prodding Missouri's legislature to lift the ceiling on library taxes paid off for three districts that won out in elections. For the Springfield-Green County Library the positive vote ended years of deficit spending and brought in money desperately needed for books and salaries. SGCL had hired a consultant to devise a campaign strategy; it concentrated on people identified as "undecided" instead of wasting time on "library opponents in areas farthest away from the library."

Setting an important precedent for other libraries wiped out by Proposition 13, California's Berkeley Public Library went after the two-thirds majority vote it needed to create a tax to support itself. Thanks to a high-powered "Keep the Libraries Alive" campaign and the leadership of BPL's feisty Regina Minudri, the vote was two-to-one in favor of a tax that gives Berkeley assured funding for ten years, with annual increases of 7 percent indexed to keep pace with inflation. Berkeley's Proposition E, the first tax measure to make it since Jarvis Jaws, gives BPL a budget of $2.4 million, close to what it had before Proposition 13.

The Cleveland Public Library went after a second five-year tax levy to support operations and its ambitious building expansion. The tactic that won over the voters: CPL said that its "good management and operating efficiency" would enable it to grow with less tax support. CPL's 14 new and renovated branches gave glowing testimony to that growth. With the new levy in its pocket, CPL put a record $2 million into acquisitions primarily for the branches.

When the tax revolt came to Casa Grande, Arizona, the library fought for a sales tax to cover the shortfall and was rewarded for its good work with a 19 percent budget increase.

Vigo County, Indiana, found itself short of revenue when the state's Tax Control Board (which monitors spending) cut its budget request $173,000; but the library appealed to tax commissioners and had restored all but $70,000. The library has enough of a budget to boost salaries and looks to expanded service in its brand-new building.

Libraries hard hit by Proposition 13 fallout showed that they could survive. Long Beach, California, rented its garden space for weddings and funeral ceremonies (without the body). It realized great profits with the first in a prospective chain of stores that will sell books, ethnic clothing, and stationery. Volunteers and an OCLC connection also helped ease Long Beach's manpower shortage.

Kern County, California, took decisive steps towards recovery by consolidating its reference department, implementing the LIBRIS ordering system, merging its services with Los Angeles County's, and hooking into the databases of RLIN, DIALOG, and ORBIT. In 1980 Kern County added 24 staff positions, doubled McNaughton and paperback purchases, and bought 44,000 new books and 80 films.

San Bernardino, California, realized a 60 percent increase in its funding base, counting in a 10 percent budget boost, grants, and hours of volunteer service.

When the tax revolt of 1979 put its iron grip on Prince George's County, Maryland, the library expanded service despite massive manpower losses. In 1980 the county cut just about every other department, but gave the library $75,000 in recognition for its "good management."

In some places, libraries are clearly high on the list of priorities. On the eve of the opening of a $3 million headquarters expansion, the budget of Forsyth County, North Carolina, went up 30 percent. Hennepin, Minnesota, struck gold again in 1980 with an 18 percent increase that brings its budget to $10,532,381.

Fund raising can bring in big money. Buffalo and Erie County raised $26,000 in its first book sale. The Mideastern Michigan Library Cooperative's Durand Memorial Library raised $1,300 thanks to a 24-hour Cut-a-Thon put on by a local beauty salon; proceeds went to Durand's newest branch. Idaho State University publicizes book fund donations by printing coupons in the *ISU Outlook*; it rakes in about $1,000 a year. Providence, Rhode Island, got Senator Claiborne Pell to kick off its effort to raise $135,000, primarily for books.

Foundation aid and gifts can make major contributions. New York Public's Research Libraries has another challenge grant ($1.6 million) to match. Over the years NEH grants to NYPL have totaled over $9 million and have generated over $17 million in matching funds. The University of Tennessee at Chattanooga has received $828,000 from the Lyndhurst Foundation to upgrade its collection and facilities. James Thomason has given $1,250,000 to the library bearing his name at South Carolina's Presbyterian College.

BUILDING AMERICA'S LIBRARIES

The faltering economy has made voters more selective, and it often takes an aggressive campaign to muster the votes needed to put a library construction bond issue over the top. In many cases, people are putting their vote behind the library service they've been getting.

Among the many bonds to get the nod: $22 million to build a new central library in Orlando, Florida; $15 million for a main library project in Anchorage, Alaska; $10,430,000 to build three new regional libraries and renovate Virginia's Fairfax County Library; $4.5 million to expand the New Mexico Junior College (Hobbs); and $3.5 million to build in Iowa City.

Shirley, New York, has a record of regularly turning down school budgets and bond proposals, but it went for a $1.7 million bond issue for the Mastics-Moriches-Shirley Community Library. The Garfield County Library System in New Castle, Colorado, will build five new branches thanks to a sales tax referendum that will generate $1.7 million. It needs to grow to accommodate the spurt in population brought on by the booming oil shale industry.

The responsibility for building public libraries rests squarely on the shoulders of localities, but money also comes from state and federal sources. At last count six states had funding for library construction projects on the books, but this money often gets sidelined. Florida cut off the flow of building dollars despite a four-year record that showed that a mere $1.3 million in state aid generated $18 million in local giving. West Virginia had to transfer building money to other library programs when the state library budget dropped 21.6 percent. In California, academic libraries have had to pit themselves against the regional storage facilities that are currently getting top priority.

All the hard work that went into preparing the state for WHCOLIS paid off when North Carolina legislators decided to invest $1 million in library construction. Georgia will be building more libraries thanks to its newly revitalized aid program. And in 1981 New York legislators will weigh a proposal to channel major funding into library construction.

LSCA Title II hasn't provided construction money for years. But libraries will be built with federal funds from the just-renewed Public Works Act and from new antirecession programs expected. Revenue sharing has built 83 libraries for Mississippi. NEH put its funding behind eight library construction projects last year for still another form of federal aid.

The largesse of the Fleishman foundation made construction projects possible for three Nevada libraries. San Bernardino, California, used a combination of Community Development funds and LSCA Title I to build and stock a library for Mexican-Americans.

The economy crunch has prompted academe to think smaller; only a handful of new building projects top the $1 million mark. The University of North Dakota took advantage of a predicted slump in the construction industry and got a price 24 percent under the architect's estimate. The Baltimore County Public Library capitalized on the construction slump, too.

URBAN DECLINE

The plight of the urban library came into new prominence last year. Even before the fateful vote that made tax support to Massachusetts libraries shrink, Boston Public had been hit with a 10 percent cutback that threatened jobs, hours, and book buying.

Urban libraries in California were spared the worst ravages of Proposition 13, but the Massachusetts tax rollback will affect urban libraries most.

Denver Public tried for a meager 4 percent increase (for a budget of $8.2 million), but tight-fisted city fathers turned it down. DPL flatly refused to sacrifice its book budget and instead threw the spotlight on its budget plight by closing branches, curtailing service, and cutting staff. The fight isn't over yet; DPL wants $1 million for books.

The budgets of urban libraries have been inching up too slowly to recoup lost ground. The Free Library of Philadelphia's 3.4 percent increase enabled it to restore a few positions, but made no appreciable dent in the 246 positions lost to date. Philadelphia brought in Lowell Martin to help it scale down operations while "maintaining certain principles of service." In the last five years, Philadelphia's book budget dropped 5 percent (from $1.7 million to $1.6 million); compared with nine other large city libraries, FLP was doing better than most.

Revenue from the city brought Chicago Public's budget up 15.3 percent, but the library still had to give up 57 positions to make up for salary increases and the city's failure to carry over expenses. CPL's total budget from city, state, and federal sources (including $2,882,807 to bring on 300 new CETA employees) added up to $42 million. The priorities for the city were jobs to bring in automation, children's services, and branch service. The union representing CPL staffers protested job shrinkage (down from 1,700 to 1,430 since 1977) and threatened to seek a "budget amendment" to restore the 57 "core staff positions."

The Louisville Free Library faced the new decade with a 12.95 percent budget increase it will never see reflected in books or services thanks to rising costs for guards (up 27 percent), social security (up 12.8 percent), supplies (up 30 percent), and an outlay of $50,000 for a 3M theft detection system.

In New York City a civic watchdog group that calls itself the Citizens Budget Commission demanded that funds for libraries and other "frills" be diverted to more essential services like police cars and garbage trucks. Taking the side of libraries, the Five Borough Library Users Council draped black cloth over NYPL's famous lions to call attention to fiscal gloom. In the past decade, NYPL's Branch System lost 350 full-time staffers and half its hours of service. Things will get worse when the last of the CETA people go. Also to be faced is an expected 53 percent loss in LSCA that has been used to bolster the ailing library system.

The steady exodus of people from the inner city to the suburbs poses another threat to urban libraries. When Buffalo and Erie County, New York, made its comeback, "public service" got top priority. The upshot: libraries in outlying areas were restored while city library facilities had to be bypassed.

In 1980 Cuyahoga County gained ground in its battle for a larger share of the county intangibles tax. Cuyahoga's gain ($660,000) was Cleveland's loss ($530,000). County commissioners decided that Cuyahoga deserved more of the take because of the migration of people to its domain. Cuyahoga will try for more again next year.

Atlanta Public opened its new library, designed by Marcel Breuer, amid political bickering that underscored the library's miserably poor budget. Refusing to accept defeat, Denver Public prodded the city for $23.5 million to expand its present cramped quarters. Chicago Public will have to move out of its current headquarters by 1984. It intends to tap state, local, and private sources for the funding to make its central library the keystone of a multiuse facility in the South Loop section of Chicago.

The Urban Libraries Council has teamed up with the National Citizens Emergency Committee to Save Our Public Libraries in a national effort to alert the American public to the funding problems of libraries, particularly urban institutions. They're placing ads in magazines like *People* and *Time*.

Libraries in England have been living under the shadow of disaster for some time. Their strategies for survival hold lessons for libraries in the United States. In England the closing of libraries is stoically regarded as a "management decision to improve service."

How England's libraries absorbed their losses: Book budgets fell 30 percent on the average; AV buying stopped; fines went up and new charges were imposed; vacancy freezes and early retirements were common. Job mobility came to a virtual standstill, but there was a new emphasis on training to enable staffers to take on more duties.

One indication of how bad things are in England: In the space of two years, funding to the Commonwealth Institute Library and Resource Center plummeted from £44,240 to £20,000. The center will cease to function as a lending service, although it intends to beef up reference and information service.

WEATHERING THE ENERGY CRUNCH

War in the oil empires reinforced fears of oil shortages. Libraries have had to budget for long-range energy saving and spiraling fuel bills. Rate increases granted Southwest California's utility doubled energy prices for people living in desert communities. The Palm Springs Public Library's fuel bills leapt $15,000 over budget, but the library gained new visibility by offering people refuge from the heat. When the heat wave last summer didn't let up, Oklahoma libraries stayed open and expanded services.

In the winter months, libraries across the nation turned down thermostats and looked for ways to conserve. Waterbury, Connecticut's, Cooperative Library Service brought in a specialist who urged each and every library to hire both an energy consultant and a qualified maintenance man.

One school of thought holds that libraries need not switch to solar, but can live with existing systems; timers for heating units, better furnaces, and more efficient light bulbs are among the measures advocated. Fine tuning worked for Chicago Public, which racked up big savings with devices like thermal chimney caps and automatic stack dampers. Even all-electric libraries were able to cut back by rearranging hours, eliminating electric doors, and putting in system controls.

The switch to solar has steadily been gaining momentum. Ohio's Stark County District Library, New Mexico's Thomas Branigan Memorial Library, and Drew University's archives building (Madison, New Jersey) were among the many institutions which have gone the solar route.

Some architects are specializing in solar. One such is Harry Russell who designed the Jefferson Township Library, a new solar-heated library in New Jersey. He criticized other architects for too often sticking with traditional HVAC technologies instead of going with the solar revolution.

Hyattsville, Maryland's, new Surattsville branch benefited from the largesse of the National Association of Plumbing-Heating-Cooling Contractors, which installed a solar water system free to give its apprentices experience.

Nashua, New Hampshire's, all-electric library will stop worrying about energy bills when it plugs into a hydroelectric power plant the city will build.

In this era of dwindling energy sources, the future of the bookmobile is uncertain. Steep repair bills and shrinking usage were enough to derail New Rochelle, New York's, bookmobile.

But bookmobiles are alive and well in places like Minneapolis and Clinton-Essex,

New York, and in the counties of Howard and Montgomery in Maryland. Los Angeles bookmobiles are a hit with various ethnic enclaves; they carry multilingual staffers and books in five languages. Book vans in Buffalo and Erie County, New York, are important, not only to rural hamlets but also to the city's urban redevelopment projects.

Oshkosh, Wisconsin, found bookmobile demand to be soaring more than ever because people can't afford to drive their own cars as often to the library; its bookmobiles get a price break at city pumps. Bookmobile clientele now include many women newly returned to the work force as well as retirees.

Bookmobiles can be a highly visible weapon in the battle for the library dollar; it wasn't until the District of Columbia library sidelined its bookmobile that people noticed DCPL's serious budget dilemma. The upshot: When DCPL faced a $2.8 million cutback, outcries from the public and the press prodded the mayor to restore $1.5 million.

Alternatives to bookmobiles are being tried. New York's Southern Tier Library System put small reading centers at its busiest bookmobile stops. Kiosks are doing a thriving business in places like Montgomery County, Maryland; Case County, Missouri; and Youngstown and Mahoning County, Ohio. Essex County, England, has a traveling cabin that works like a kiosk with wheels.

Consciousness raising in the area of energy has become a national concern even though the nation still lacks a concrete energy policy. Some libraries, however, are pioneering in consumer education. In an address to Congress, President Carter saluted Denver Public for creating a consumer and environmental information clearinghouse that disseminates information from a number of federal agencies. The president said, "We should not create new delivery systems when libraries, with strong community bases, can do the job." Montana plans to make libraries across the state into energy centers. The National Endowment for the Humanities' "Courses by Newspaper" project involved 11 libraries in teaching people about energy.

Among the many energy programs to make headlines last year: the traveling "Rural Energymobile" of Minnesota's Traverse des Sioux Library; Baltimore County's workshop on wood-burning stoves; and Pawtucket, Rhode Island's, program to show energy entrepreneurs how to play the stock market.

THE FUTURE IS IN TECHNOLOGY

Cynicism about the promise of new technology is rapidly fading in the face of mounting evidence that electronic gadgetry will enhance the exchange of information and shape the destiny of society and its institutions. Soaring interlibrary loan demand brought on by OCLC technology reinforced the notion that libraries will be part of the technological revolution, but could be outpaced by it.

There were new developments in 1980 that showed libraries more of what technology could do. Among them: on-line interfaces linking OCLC with the circulation systems of CLSI, DataPhase, and ULISYS; document delivery service on line via Lockheed's DIALORDER; and a CATV and library circulation connection that transforms TV sets into on-line catalog terminals (Lexington, Virginia).

In Orange County, California, library terminals take a patron through an interactive learning experience in the sciences. For the visually handicapped there are faster Kurzweil talking machines and closed-circuit TV enlargers. The United States, Canada, France, Germany, and England are developing communications systems that transmit information direct to homes. Fiber optics technology could speed up telecommunications and bring costs down; Houston Public already uses fiber optics cables to transmit bibliographic information to a computer center.

When the faltering Universal Serials and Book Exchange (USBE) asked for a prescription for survival, the Council on Library Resources urged it to make greater use of new technology to streamline service and curb rising costs. Libraries of all sizes are counting on new technology to cut staff and costs.

The unnerving frequency with which technological gadgetry in traveling road shows can bomb out suggests that current optimism about the swift emergence of a brave new technological world is too rosy a view. Libraries, it is argued, will have a place in a world of machines. As SOLINET director Lee Handley put it, they'll be needed more than ever to assure "free, unbiased access to information."

Computers are helping libraries today and will do more for them tomorrow. The University of Pittsburgh launched a pioneering computer simulation experiment to teach library managers to use computers to make sounder network decisions. OCLC has been working out an algorithm to show libraries how to figure out the exact number of terminals to install for maximum information access. The viability of public access terminals in homes and supermarkets as well as in libraries is being researched.

Providing consumer guidance to libraries shopping for new technology has become a major concern for professional associations. Overflow crowds came to conference programs to learn more about microcomputers (ASIS), on-line circulation (ALA), MEDLARS III (Medical LA), and the OCLC/RLIN wars (Special LA).

The problems technology can create for people received new attention in 1980. The National Institute for Occupational Safety and Health opened a probe into the health hazards faced by people who do long stints at video terminals. Some unions are making the hazards of terminal duty a contract issue, and libraries could one day be held accountable for failing to do enough to reduce this kind of work stress.

The slogan "information is power" was the hallmark of many a conference in the United States, Canada, and Europe last year. Although there wasn't much meat to many of the prolonged discussions that ensued, potential stakeholders were clearly stating their positions. They see in technology the makings of a second industrial revolution that could provide a way out for countries hard hit by the lingering economy slump. Information producers had their own "Chautauqua"—a hearing before members of Congress. They urged the government to subsidize the production of information and drop regulatory controls so that this new industry could indeed thrive.

Participants (mostly industry heavies) invited to the "closed session" Information Agenda for the 1980's Colloquium in New York prior to ALA also argued for a mutually profitable interface between government and industry. But the concern was voiced that the information revolution could (inadvertently or purposely) enlarge the gap between the information poor and the information rich. And it could create a new elite of technocrats who could and would control what is known and what is not known.

The impact technology is having on libraries even today has sparked more debate about fees. At issue is how much fees for information access will cost all of society in the long run.

The White House Conference on Libraries backed "free access, without charge to the individual, to information in public and publicly supported libraries." The Library Association of Australia endorsed free and open access to all library services, including automation. Its reasoning: All of society suffers when access barriers exist. On the other hand, ALA's members are deeply divided on the issue, and fees are still hotly debated.

Advances in technology have forced a new questioning of the legitimacy of access barriers. When OCLC's interlibrary loan machinery created unprecedented demand, Columbus, Ohio, and Rochester, New York, started charging to discourage borrowers outside their respective regions. To many, fees make sense if they prevent overuse.

Acceptance is also growing for charging the consumer for on-line search services. But some libraries view on-line searching as just another library reference tool. One such is the Minneapolis Public Library, which promotes its on-line reference service heavily and does a booming business. Seattle provides the funding ($30,000) to enable its library to offer the public free access to Lockheed's ERIC, Grants, Energyline, and other popular data bases. Traffic averages 70 searches a month.

State funding brought Lockheed terminals to eight Connecticut libraries and put them in a position to be Lockheed brokers. Not unexpectedly, Greenwich (which serves a wealthy community) opted for fees. But instead of mindlessly following the Greenwich example, Westport set a different precedent by deciding to charge only when a particular search requires time or staff help in excess of that traditionally (and manually) given free.

THE REVOLUTION IN CATALOGING

January 1 signaled the adoption of the much debated second edition of the *Anglo-American Cataloguing Rules* by LC, the British Library, and the national libraries of Canada and Australia. There were new arguments on both sides of the issue as the deadline for the switch approached. One new study (Arlene Dowell, University of North Carolina) concluded that the changeover would be far less costly than had been feared. But the opposing camp maintained that time and money would be saved by postponing *AACR 2* again.

On the whole, there was a begrudging acceptance of the inevitable, even relief that the new code's time had finally come. *AACR 2* institutes run nationwide by ALA's Resources and Technical Services Division, helped prepare the way, as did the comprehensive briefings provided by the British Library.

The University of Illinois jumped the gun and started applying the code early to avoid a January 1 overload. OCLC plans to shut down for a few days to convert to *AACR 2*.

Less fuss was made over Dewey 19. Almost all national libraries went with Dewey early; only the British Library waited until the new year.

There is new skepticism about using COM (Computer Output Microfilm) in large-scale cataloging. One reason: COM technology reportedly can't keep pace with large-scale cataloging output. COM, nonetheless, is viewed by some as a cost-effective first step towards on-line cataloging; it takes care of the onerous task of retrospretrive conversion. You can build an on-line catalog with the COM master tape as well as adapt it for circulation, acquisitions, and resource sharing. Chicago Public started out with COM, and then went on line with the DataPhase system.

Despite the advent of fully on-line systems, there's still a demand for COM. SOLINET has been doing a thriving business producing COM CATS for its members. NELINET intends to do the same. Cuyahoga County got OCLC to do its retrospective conversion and reported savings of up to $235,000 in catalog maintenance since it switched.

There are alternatives in cataloging other than COM and OCLC. Jefferson County, Colorado, built its own on-line interactive public access catalog (Jeffcat), and a neighboring library (Littleton) opted to piggyback. Other inexpensive cataloging options include the MINIMARC system (that relies on regularly updated MARC microform records of LC cataloging), MARCFICHE, and INMAGIC, a software package developed by Warner Eddison Associates. Informatics is developing the software that will link its MINIMARC with RLIN to permit "search only" access to RLIN records not in MINIMARC.

Indications are that the time of the bulky, cumbersome card catalog is long gone. Pikes Peak found a surprising majority of its patrons favored on-line access over manual. Public access terminals are being tried at such places as Northwestern, the Stephen Austin University (Texas), and the Salt Lake County Public Library, to mention only a few.

But Enoch Pratt in Baltimore won't go the way of the public access terminal if systems planner Joseph Cavanaugh has his way. In his opinion, most on-line circulation systems (with the exception of the Carnegie-Mellon BROWSE system) are inadequately designed for patron access. He's skeptical that people will take to on-line access, and if they do, he argues, "the brutal economics of public hardware in public libraries" indicates that libraries will have more problems than they bargained for. People, he noted, don't even use the card catalog today.

ON-LINE CIRCULATION

Staff and money shortages are making on-line circulation systems mandatory for most medium and large libraries; even small libraries are automating, sometimes by sharing a system. The on-line revolution has stimulated resource sharing between libraries of all types and sizes.

There is new recognition today of the importance of briefing both patrons and staffers about new technology being adopted. Weber County, Utah's, "Meet the Computer" week showed taxpayers how much money ($500,000) its CLSI would save in five years. Chicago Public's *Data Processing News* bulletin was only a first step in a broadgauge publicity campaign about automation both in CPL branches and in the regional library network for the blind that CPL oversees. Battelle, incidentally, has the job of designing a circulation system for LC's national library network for the blind.

A growing number of states are investing heavily in on-line circulation. Alabama put its money behind CLSI. Wyoming went with Cincinnati Electronics' CLASSIC system. North Carolina picked DataPhase for a statewide system that will handle a whole range of functions: circulation, cataloging, acquisitions, statistics, and inventory.

Illinois is investing $1.4 million a year in an intrasystem circulation system that will be the basis of a statewide resource-sharing network. The Greater Vancouver Library Federation got $3 million to build a provincewide on-line circulation and cataloging system.

In the United States, federal dollars are also going into on-line circulation. A Public Works Act grant brought ULISYS (Vancouver, B.C.'s, Universal Library Systems) to Eugene, Oregon. LSCA helped create the nation's first interstate, intertype library circulation system: Cincinnati Electronics will interconnect all kinds of libraries in an area lying both in Illinois (River Bend Library System) and Iowa. Libraries in Wisconsin can get LSCA money to hire a consultant to help them pick a circulation system.

Many libraries today plan from the outset to link systems for circulation, cataloging, and other functions. The DataPhase system at Oral Roberts interconnects with the library's COM catalog and acquisitions systems as well as with OCLC. When it moves into its new $4 million central library, Aurora, Colorado, will link its CLSI system with its Baker and Taylor LIBRIS acquisitions system and OCLC. The interfaces available from circulation vendors now enable libraries to update and retrieve from OCLC the full bibliographic record.

The sharing of a circulation system is a growing trend. Two New Orleans colleges (Xavier University and Loyola) went in together on a CLSI neither could afford alone.

Some libraries are sharing in order to make money on their automation investment. California's Anaheim Public Library has a growing number of libraries that are paying to piggyback on its SCI (Systems Control, Inc.) system. When its DataPhase is up and running, Chicago Public intends to contract with the 200 or so special, academic, and institutional libraries affiliated with the Chicago Library System.

Sharing in another way, Michigan's Lakeland Library Cooperative bought a copy of Hennepin County's data base to get a headstart on catalog conversion. Columbus, Ohio, has been selling its data-base records, too.

The on-line revolution has done much to bring about new cooperative configurations and more resource sharing. Spokane County has a multitype network based on ULISYS. To promote resource sharing with neighboring public, county, and federal libraries, the University of District of Columbia Library attached an automatic answering device to its CLSI.

Public libraries in the Denver and Jefferson County area established a cooperative structure (IRVING) to help them coordinate decision making on new technology. For starters, they're working out standards with the end goal of interfacing their different circulation systems.

Libraries have become smarter shoppers, and their new vigilance has prompted vendors to sharpen service. Shortly after a band of its users started complaining, CLSI expanded its troubleshooting service with a round-the-clock telephone diagnostic service. One presumably unhappy CLSI customer (Austin, Texas) stopped paying for its three-year-old LIBS 100, and CLSI threatened to yank it out. When Canada's Geac nailed contracts with Yale and several Connecticut regional library systems, it exported a service center to serve them. Cincinnati Electronics has plans for "field service for the whole country" for its circulation system.

Competition among vendors stepped up in 1980. DataPhase sued CLSI for its "anticompetitive" sales tactics, and the temporary injunction it won forced CLSI to tone down its hard sell. An appeals court lifted the injunction, however, and ordered a speedy trial to find out which firm was telling the truth.

A "bigger and better" debate waxed as competing vendors jockeyed for position in a fast-moving market. Gaylord noted pointedly that its 96-terminal system at New York's Queens Borough Public Library is bigger than the giant at Baltimore County that BCPL was heavily promoting as the "nation's biggest."

CLSI remains the front runner, with revenues up 40 percent, 400 users, and new sales coming in thanks to its new touch-sensitive terminals. But as the circulation systems of other vendors prove themselves, CLSI's domination will be challenged.

NETWORK STEPS AND PITFALLS

The foundations of the now emerging national library network were laid in the last decade. OCLC's bibliographic enterprise grew into a de facto national network. The Research Libraries Group made strong progress towards building a specialized network for the research library community and developing products for other, allied libraries. RLG came into direct competition with OCLC. Meanwhile, the regional service organizations that had come into being primarily to broker OCLC services showed a new willingness to broker for RLG as well. The Southeastern Library Network took the first steps toward harnessing the technology that would put it in position to compete with OCLC. Hostilities between the two organizations reached a peak and then subsided when SOLINET and OCLC joined hands and agreed to collaborate. This new union could pose a threat to other fast-growing regionals like the New England Library Network and AMIGOS. Meanwhile, libraries with their own data bases are getting the technology to move into today's crowded marketplace.

This fast-developing network scene differs markedly from the overarching superstructure envisioned by the National Commission on Libraries and Information Science (NCLIS) before the various network pieces were visible. The national library network has become a businesslike enterprise; many regional and state organizations, as well as commercial firms and large libraries and library systems, have a stake in it. Special libraries have complained that they've been cut off from network planning; in 1980 NCLIS named a task force to give them a chance to sketch their network future, and they're doing it now.

CLR put major funding into a Bibliographic Service Development Program aimed at bringing about coordination among the major bibliographic utilities. LC established communication channels via its Network Development Office, Network Technology Group, and Network Advisory Committee.

But these efforts to usher in a new era of coordination were stymied by "turf problems"; the major utilities refused to cooperate. There was a serious questioning of the validity of interlocking their separate bibliographic data bases. Resistance grew to the notion of having any single entity—LC, CLR, or NCLIS—shape network development. Access questions were raised by the steady flow of foundation dollars to the Research Libraries Group, a network made up primarily of private (not public) institutions. These questions were given a new insistence by a reluctance in academe to sharing its treasures (or even agreeing to a standardized fee structure) in the face of spiraling interlibrary loan demand. CLR's efforts to forge cooperative alliances were viewed by some as a front for building up the private research libraries at the potential expense of publicly controlled institutions. Serious concerns about prospective curbs in funding to library networks were raised when Ronald Reagan won the presidential election; all during his campaign he stressed the need for cutting back "soft" public services and building up defense instead.

Notable progress in cooperation was logged in 1980, however. The CONSER (Conversion of Serials) project grew. LC and the research libraries developed an interactive authority file that will be available nationwide. RLG and the Washington Library Network teamed up on a shared authority system that will enable their data bases to communicate with each other. LC and RLIN created a data base of Oriental titles to which OCLC will have access. And OCLC and RLG jointly studied the feasibility of setting up public access terminals in all kinds of settings, not just libraries. At year's end, RLG struck up a new alliance with Canada's UTLAS (University of Toronto Library Automation System) to develop products and services for RLG member libraries. UTLAS made clear its intention to compete with the three library automation systems in the United States. [See the report on the status of library networking in the United States in 1980 by Henriette Avram in the Special Reports section of Part 1—*Ed.*]

RLG'S ASCENT

With the steady flow of foundation dollars into its coffers, the Research Libraries Group (RLG) achieved new "economic equilibrium" in 1980. Expecting to get out of the red with as few as 23 members, RLG came close to that mark at year's end when membership climbed to 22. RLG counted its combined holdings at 57.8 million and purchasing power at $35.4 million.

Among the prestigious institutions to join RLG (and thus replace OCLC with RLIN): Pennsylvania State, Northwestern, New York University, Brown, Cornell, Princeton, Dartmouth, Rutgers, the University of Pennsylvania, Brigham Young, Tulane, Harvard's Fine Arts Department, and the state universities of Iowa, Michigan, and Colorado. New York Public, Columbia, Harvard, and Yale founded RLG. Harvard dropped out and was replaced by Stanford.

RLG has been selling itself as a "partnership" of research libraries dedicated to resolving common problems in collection development, management, access, and preservation. One of the consortium's most powerful drawing cards is the Research Libraries Information Network (RLIN), which can provide members with an on-line catalog of their own holdings as well as *AACR2* support, up and running subsystems for acquisitions and interlibrary loan, and patron access to on-line catalogs. To make itself even more attractive to prospective members, RLG offered small grants to defray the cost of connecting with RLIN. The Hewlett Foundation supplied $300,000 for this purpose.

The defection of state universities to RLG prompted regional library networks dependent on them to voice concern about the loss of valuable shared resources. But RLG quickly reassured them that the state universities would remain active in their regions and not sever their linkages. Taking a most conciliatory stance, RLG promised the regional library networks access to RLIN, but did not specify how.

RLG had in 1979 set a precedent for linkages with regional networks when it offered a "partnership" to the California Library Authority for Systems and Services to broker the bibliographic services RLG develops in cooperation with WLN. But RLG seems to be shying away from having regional service organizations (like SOLINET) be its middlemen. RLG broke off a contractual arrangement with the Bibliographic Center for Research, seemingly preferring to provide services direct to new members in the Denver area.

RLG seems to want to protect the solid footing it has achieved as an organization for the nation's big research libraries. This special status as a gathering of peers assures its future and makes RLIN impervious to threats from up and coming bibliographic utilities. OCLC, on the other hand, is quite vulnerable to the encroachment of RLIN and of libraries and regional organizations with the technology to compete.

Seeking to broaden clientele in 1980, RLG tried for smaller libraries with a new membership category; the State University of New York at Binghamton became its first "associate member." Specialized institutions like art libraries and museums can become RLG "special members"; they're particularly active in indexing and cataloging projects.

Establishing an organizational identity became a prime target for RLG in 1970. It improved visibility with a logo symbolizing the consortium, new publications, and exhibits at ALA and other national organizations.

Despite RLG's forceful campaign, many academic libraries won't switch, because they believe that RLIN remains unproven, while OCLC sports a proven track record and is less costly.

Seeking to discourage the defection of academic libraries to the RLG camp, OCLC has been adamant in its opposition to dual memberships. But the pressure for linkages between the two utilities has mounted, with most of it coming from the research library community. The Association of Research Libraries (ARL) and the Technical Services Directors of Large Research Libraries were among those to speak out. A tersely worded statement about detente announced negotiations for cooperation among OCLC, RLG, and WLN, but no real progress has been visible.

The competition of RLG, coupled with new resourcefulness by libraries and library networks in utilizing records in the OCLC data base, prompted OCLC to try to introduce new restrictions on third party use. At often tumultuous hearings on the issue, OCLC was accused of aspiring to monopoly by trying to stifle the exchange of information. In the end, OCLC came down on the side of "cooperation" and adopted a most liberal third party use policy that endorsed "no restrictions . . . provided that third party use benefits participating libraries, networks, and OCLC." But "for profit" organizations will have to live with the restrictions OCLC imposes or pay royalties.

The great debate about third party use did show the library community the many benefits to be reaped through the ingenious sharing and repackaging of OCLC records.

OCLC concentrated on countering competition from RLIN; it established a Research Library Advisory Committee and made site visits to ARL libraries. Seeking to solidify its foothold in RLIN country, OCLC set up a service center in Portland to serve Oregon, Washington, and British Columbia. OCLC beefed up its ILL subsystem and introduced "search enhancements" to improve access to its 6.6 million item data base. But the recession made it scuttle an idea for providing the Geac circulation system nationwide. OCLC tried selling libraries on its discounts on Lockheed and other in-demand data bases. Seeking out a new clientele altogether, OCLC pioneered in transmitting information (*The Source*) direct to people's TV screens.

The decade ahead could be a most decisive one. Founding father Frederick Kilgour stepped down and handed the reins to Rowland Brown as OCLC prepared to move into its new $25.7 million home by 1981. In the 13 years Kilgour was at the helm, OCLC evolved from a modest one-state entity into an international network serving 2,300 libraries in the United States, and Canada, and Europe. Its assets add up to $53 million, making it the undisputed leader today.

The Pacific Northwest's Washington Library Network doesn't want to go national, but has been exporting its wares and encouraging replication of its system in other parts of the nation and the world. Illinois wants to use WLN software for a prospective statewide bibliographic network. Seeking to prevent a scrap over proper participant representation in governance (as OCLC faced in 1979), WLN adopted a multistate governance structure in keeping with its spread into new terrain both in the United States and abroad.

In the years ahead, America's major utilities will face new competition from libraries in the United States and abroad that have developed sophisticated automation. The just signed contract between RLG and UTLAS puts the latter in direct competition with WLN. UTLAS will produce catalogs for some RLG members, starting with New York Public. UTLAS also nailed the first Canadian sale of computerized library support products to Japan when it contracted with Maruzen, Ltd., for an expected $1 million in sales of UTLAS products and services.

Earlier in the year, the New York Public Library Branch System decided to build upon the 16-year effort that created its Systems Analysis and Data Processing Organization. SADPO had been a top contender as the bibliographic system for RLG, but was edged out by Stanford's BALLOTS. Looking to a bright (possibly statewide) future, NYPL renamed its on-line system LIONS (Library Information and Online Network).

The British Columbia Union Catalog could become a major bibliographic utility, too; a Ringgold study urged it to stop buying from UTLAS and to develop into a multitype service center for its region. Harvard, Boston Public, and the University of Chicago have the automation that puts them in a position to barter.

Northwestern has started selling its NOTIS software. The University of Illinois' sophisticated Library Computer System made great strides in 1980 as it spread statewide.

REGIONALS COME OF AGE

It now looks as if regional service organizations that have served solely as middlemen for OCLC will evolve into network utilities themselves. While proclaiming their loyalty to OCLC, the Southeastern Library Network and New England Library Network moved ahead with ambitious plans to get into the business of helping their respective regions chart their technological future. Preaching a new gospel, the two regionals eschewed any monopolistic desires and instead emphasized that today's market is competitive and libraries should shop around.

Taking the lead among regionals, SOLINET announced a Regional Support System that will use WLN software and Burroughs hardware to build an on-line bibliographic data base made up of member records and MARC backfiles. The goal of RSS is to give SOLINET members a whole range of computer-based services and to establish linkages with other utilities as well as WLN, LC, and state and regional networks.

SOLINET flatly denies wanting to usurp OCLC territory. OCLC proclaimed its support for the project and the "co-responsibility" it signaled. But the two organizations were clearly at loggerheads when OCLC refused to let SOLINET connect all its communications lines to the telecommunications processor OCLC installed at SOLINET headquarters. In the end, SOLINET and OCLC made their peace in a memorandum of understanding that paves the way for new cooperation in the development of products and services.

Other regionals moved decisively in 1980. In keeping with its newly adopted "online computer-based strategy," NELINET will provide such products as on-line catalogs and circulation systems to its members. Rhode Island asked NELINET to map its statewide automation future.

AMIGOS set out to do for ten Southwest academic libraries what RLG has done for the nation's research libraries: establish a bibliographic data base for its new Council of Academic Libraries. Taking a step toward an international network, AMIGOS established a beachhead in Latin America at Mexico's Universidad Iberoamericana. Proclaiming its "public interest," AMIGOS got most of its members behind a new interloan code more liberal than ALA's.

Opening a door to the private sector, the Pennsylvania Library Information Network (PALINET) contracted with Baker & Taylor for a tape management service to assure that OCLC honors its warranty. The arrangement gives B&T the opportunity to inch into territory the regionals have staked out for themselves and gives libraries still another automation alternative.

At this time regional organizations are set to enter into more open competition with state or multistate operations: The high performance of OCLC's interlibrary loan subsystem prompted the State University of New York/OCLC user group to question anew the advisability of pumping state money into New York's slow-moving, hierarchical interloan network. In response, NYSILL stakeholders emphasized that the two systems are "complementary" and that linkages between them are most desirable. Meanwhile, SUNY/OCLC started selling services to corporate libraries for the first time.

The new assertiveness of regional organizations caught the eye of state library chiefs who apparently don't want to be cut out of the action. The Western Council of State Library Agencies brought state library people, librarians, and network people to a "planning retreat" that gave the council itself responsibility for overseeing resource sharing and the spread of technology in the region.

Responding to the needs of the region's small but special libraries, state librarians from the Southwest asked SOLINET to find a way to let small libraries join. SOLINET itself responded with a "consortium membership" that allows two or more libraries to share a membership.

OCLC kept an eye on the performance of the regionals, and when one (the Michigan Library Consortium) seemed to be faltering, it offered to set up a service center to assure that OCLC clients not be let down. The underlying message, it seemed, was that regional service organizations (that get most of their revenue from OCLC) could be replaced.

THE PRESSURE FOR MULTITYPE

Government at the national, state, and local levels clearly favors library cooperation, particularly multitype cooperation, and scorns duplication of effort. In all, 31 states channel dollars to library networks. Oklahoma Governor George Nigh urged more school/library cooperation, while pointedly noting that while he's in charge, state dollars will not build libraries or rescue projects running out of federal aid.

California's response to the new stress on sharing was to put $250,000 of LSCA into school/library cooperation. Meanwhile, California's Library Authority for Systems and Services (CLASS) is developing into a diversified multitype serving 300 member libraries in five states. Seed money for CLASS itself was provided by an accumulation of LSCA dollars.

Iowa decided to channel more LSCA into cooperative projects having "greater statewide impact," such as its IOWA Library Information Teletype Exchange (I-LITE) and OCLC conversion projects.

New Mexico turned down a proposal for $1.4 million computerized library network, but the legislature was all for paying out $165,000 to bring OCLC to 14 libraries. This mini-network is an important first step toward New Mexico's blueprint for a Coordinated Library System.

Alabama appointed a state-level committee to chart multitype trails. Illinois continued to lead the way and planned to get state money for a new era of multitype cooperation. Indiana made library history by channeling its first state dollars ($450,000) to Area Library Services Authorities (ALSAs).

New York has invested heavily in cooperation, and it's now concentrating on integrating school libraries into its many overlapping networks of public, special, and academic libraries. Besides sharing resources and technology, New York network activity pioneered new direct service to people: telephone reference and homework hotlines for the downstate area via New York's INTERSHARE project.

Despite efforts by states to channel money into cooperation, funding is still tight and there have been territorial scraps over the money that is available. Colorado upped its support of its seven library systems 15 percent ($803,071), but the largest one, the Central Colorado Library System, demanded more of the take. CCLS argued that the current distribution formula penalized it for serving the largest proportion of the population.

At year's end, members of New York's Public Library System Directors Organization (PULISDO) voiced the concern that library systems in New York would lose state aid when the new U.S. census showed them to be serving fewer people. Some did.

But the slumping economy has been a powerful force in bringing about cooperation, too. Proposition 13 prodded city and county libraries to seriously consider merger. Public libraries in Los Angeles and Long Beach, California, joined the Metropolitan Cooperative Library System, making it one of the nation's biggest.

But the money crunch proved to be too much for the debt-ridden Niagara Regional Library System in Ontario; it had to close shop and terminate the service it had provided to 24 libraries and their 450,000 patrons.

The province of Alberta gave a strong forward push to cooperation by boosting aid to cooperatives $1.62 per capita to $5. Noting increasing cooperation with five Pacific Northwest states across the border, Alberta made plans to build a provincewide library network that will harness new technology. Overall library aid to Alberta libraries went up 60 percent in 1980.

ALA's Association of Specialized and Cooperative Library Agencies set up a clearinghouse to keep track of multitypes. Seeing the future in multitypes, Sue Martin of Johns Hopkins said, "There's a critical mass" for multitype cooperation; Maryland has six network links and plans even more.

Looking at one of the most problematic elements in cooperation, ASCLA workshops tackled "the human aspect of cooperation."

THE COPYRIGHT WARS

Copyright became a hot issue again in 1980. The information industry won its battle against the National Periodicals Center (and the copyright threat it embodies). Congress won't fund an NPC operation unless there's more of a consensus for it in the library/industry community.

The Association of American Publishers sued Connecticut's Gnomon firm for copyright violation on a massive scale, and when it won the case AAP threatened to step up surveillance everywhere. One target named: special libraries that are purportedly ignoring AAP's still faltering Copyright Clearance Center, while the publishers themselves are subsidizing CCC.

Music publishers cracked down on churches and their choirs for "wanton defiance" of the law of copyright as it applies to musical scores. A religious publication, in turn, advised church people to get around copyright restrictions by using an opaque projector to share scores.

The enforcement efforts of publishers stirred the ire of educators and librarians, who formed a coalition to fight back. This Ad Hoc Committee on Copyright urged the Copyright Office to deny copyright to those publishers that post "exaggerated" warnings of copyright restrictions in libraries and schools. The Copyright Office refused on the grounds that it lacked jurisdiction and suggested that publishers who do this are acting in "good faith."

The producers of today's data banks are becoming increasingly edgy about copyright. They're concerned about the loss of their property rights, not only through piracy but even through inadvertent granting of rights in situations where these rights are still ill defined by law.

This decade looks to be a decisive one in the area of copyright. David Ladd succeeded Barbara Ringer as Register of Copyrights. King Research, Inc., will survey libraries, publishers, and patrons to determine if the new copyright law has indeed "balanced the rights of creators of copyrighted works and the needs of users." The conclusions reached will figure heavily in the report the Register is slated to make to Congress in 1983. [For a report on the 1980 activities of the Copyright Office, see the Federal Agencies section of Part 1—*Ed.*]

A 1977 King study found most photocopying by libraries to be within boundaries set by law, and warned publishers not to expect much revenue from this source. A study by Gary Byrd (University of Missouri-Kansas City) found academic and health science libraries to be strictly adhering to the law. When the five-copy "fair use" limit is reached, most libraries either buy the periodical or refuse the request. Thanks to the copyright law, librarians are more aware of gaps in their journal holdings.

The issue of copyright will take on international implications as governments decide whether the sharing of information is to their best advantage. The International Federation of Library Associations (IFLA) endorsed "unconstrained flow of bibliographic records internationally as essential to research and scholarship worldwide."

But some countries are wary of the implications of large-scale sharing. At the White House Conference, Canada's Bernard Ospry said that his nation had its own identity to preserve and would not want to jeopardize it by naively sharing with big nations that could dominate it. There was a new questioning in the United States, too, about the wisdom of freely providing access to America's information stores. But America's information industry was criticized for failing to capitalize on developments in technology abroad. In contrast, China's effort to catch up with the West drew attention. China clearly wants to have the technology it needs to become a part of the world's technological marketplace.

China dominated the international library scene last year. Simmons will welcome the first (mainland) Chinese scholars to come to the United States for advanced training in librarianship. Ohio University Library's Southeast Asia Librarian-Intern Program attracted the attention of UNESCO, which has offered it unexpected funding. Chinese publishers and librarians toured the United States. China wants to catch up on ground lost during the repressive Cultural Revolution; it's building up libraries and training librarians at a furious pace.

New associations for Asian librarians are sprouting up. Among those just launched: the Asian/Pacific American Librarians Association (New York) and the Chinese-Canadian Librarians Association (Thunder Bay, Ontario).

The eight-year-old Chinese-American Librarians Association is going strong, with 300 members, 5 chapters, and a publication.

THE MARKET FOR LIBRARIANS

The library job market did not open up in 1980, and prospects look grim for any significant improvement in the decade ahead. There are fewer professionals working in libraries today because of a combination of factors: skyrocketing personnel costs, leaner budgets, mandatory layoffs, and the elimination of jobs by attrition. Libraries in Denver and Contra Costa, California, consolidated positions to make up for staff shortages and "improve efficiency." Libraries that had to cut book budgets (Buffalo and Erie County, New York) laid off or redeployed their acquisitions people. Some particularly hard-hit libraries are trying to make a go of it with manpower down one-third (District of Columbia Public Library).

The shortage of library posts gave momentum to a minor exodus of librarians from the public to the private sector. Library associations responded to this trend with programs on alternate library careers.

The Illinois Library Association ran a preconference on a new hybrid: the freelance librarian who provides service for a fee.

Meanwhile, the private sector absorbed a few library professionals like Los Angeles County's Carol Moss (who went to a law firm) and the New England Library Board's Sally Roberts (now with a publisher). June Fleming abandoned the top post at the Palo Alto Library to become assistant city manager. And automated circulation vendors hired several more librarians.

For the seasoned professional, the easy job mobility of years past is long gone, but some men and women made important career moves: Harrison Bryan (National Librarian of Australia); Arthur Curley (NYPL Research Libraries); Lee Handley (SOLINET); James Skipper (Midwest Region Library Network); Donald Simpson (Center for Research Libraries); Kevin Flaherty (Michigan Library Consortium); Edward O'Neill (Case Western Reserve); Bernard Franckowiak (University of Denver); Richard Halsey (State University of New York at Albany); Samuel Carrington (Rice); Robert

Croneberger (Memphis/Shelby County Public Library); David Walsh (California Polytechnic); and Billy Wilkinson (University of Maryland).

Women advanced to new prominence, too, although they are still clearly outnumbered and outdistanced by men. But there were notable exceptions. Toni Carbo Bearman won out in the stiff competition for the top NCLIS post vacated by Al Trezza, who's now in charge of a network study at LC. Ruth Tighe left NCLIS to spend a year in Saipan as consultant to the government of the Northern Marianas. Shirley Echelman left the Medical Library Association to head up the Association of Research Libraries.

Other top appointments included: Joleen Bock (dean, University of Guam); Elaine Sloan (dean, Indiana University); Margaret Chisholm (acting director, University of Washington Library School); Joanne Euster (director, San Francisco State); Nancy McAdams (associate director, University of Texas at Austin); Yen-Tsai Feng (Harvard College librarian); Patricia Senn Breivik (director, Auraria Libraries, Denver); Constance Cooke (director, Queens Borough, New York, Library), Agnes Griffen (director, Montgomery County Library, Maryland); and Nancy Bolt (public libraries chief, Maryland Department of Education).

FACING THE JOB SHORTAGE

Library associations responded to the plight of the job hunter with conference placement centers and joblines. The New England Library Board broadened the geographic reach of its jobline; the Association of College and Research Libraries launched one. The Medical Library Association ran workshops to help people sharpen their job hunting skills, starting with the résumé.

There is a new focus on internships much in keeping with library schools' current interest in the two-year degree. Two ALA divisions (AALS and ACRL) urged every major research library to have an internship for the beginning librarian. The Council on Library Resources has forwardlooking programs to train tomorrow's library leaders; in 1980 it launched an ambitious new program of recruitment and training expected to cost $1,750,000. The State University of New York instituted a management internship program for both faculty and line staffers.

Library professionalism became a cause célèbre in Massachusetts when A. J. Rineer fought the governor's attempt to give his job (state librarian) to a political ally, making it into a patronage plum. Rineer was finally ousted, but the man who now fills his shoes is a young, competent professional librarian: James Fish.

Many libraries have been trying to keep their personnel costs down by adhering to federal antiinflation guidelines. But there was renewed concern in 1980 about the poverty wages librarians often get. Library associations in Massachusetts and Connecticut upped to $12,000 the bare minimum salary they would endorse and found that employers respected it. ALA was urged to take a stand, too, but backed off for fear of possible antitrust violations. The average beginning salary for 1979 M.L.S. graduates was $13,127.

The economy crunch has, on the whole, dampened progress in improving the wages and mobility of female librarians. It's a different story for women in special libraries, who are still moving up and logging salary increases greater than men. Fighting against salary bias in a "female profession," librarians at California State University got statistics to prove a discriminatory pay scale; CSU academics responded by sharing with librarians their own cost of living increases.

Libraries tried to make up for staff shortages. Haverhill, Massachusetts', all-electric library curbed fuel bills and wiped out a backlog of projects thanks to a flextime schedule. Broward County, Florida, found success with a pool of "will call" staffers for emergencies. The Bibliographic Center for Research in Denver offered access to its new "people resources bank" for a price.

Staff and money shortages engendered a new emphasis on in-service staff training. The District of Columbia Public Library developed a librarywide training program that also serves as a career ladder. Two Maryland library systems (Prince George's and Montgomery counties) used LSCA to hire consultants to run workshops that reached over 1,000 staffers. Each of Indiana's seven library districts benefited from librarian/trustee meetings covering such topics as the problem patron, library cooperation, and hiring and firing procedures.

Staff exchange was utilized to upgrade staff competencies. Hennepin County, Minnesota, and Columbus, Ohio, exchanged staffers with specific expertise: know-how in AV and technology. Chicago went international with a new exchange, and Columbus went after a faculty resident wise to new technology.

CETA SHRINKAGE

Libraries that have relied heavily on Comprehensive Employment and Training Act employees had to face up to withdrawal of the last of their CETA people in 1980. The plight of New York's Brooklyn Public Library was compounded by a hiring freeze and city funding cutbacks that crippled the library system. Chicago Public transferred staff, cut hours, and reduced programming to counter CETA losses and the elimination of positions by attrition; taken together, these added up to a 22 percent drop in personnel. But in 1981 Chicago got the promise of 300 new CETA employees.

CETA withdrawal pains stem from the refusal (or inability) of city government to assume funding responsibility for people CETA brings into the workforce. The shirking of funding responsibility has been a pitfall with revenue sharing, too. Once federal money comes in, local government tends to withdraw its support—and likes it that way.

An example of more positive thinking comes from Seattle, which boosted library funding 16.7 percent ($8,618,000 total) to bring its CETA people into the permanent staff as well as to expand library service. Incidentally, when federal funding ran out, the state picked up the tab for the statewide service to the handicapped provided by Seattle.

THE VOLUNTEER BOOM

In California many libraries wouldn't have been able to provide even the most marginal service without volunteers; statewide volunteer use climbed 282 percent. In the first year of crisis, Ventura County received 13,170 hours of service worth $54,260. Some were contributed by retired librarians who staffed a senior citizens center for the Long Beach Public Library.

Volunteers have provided libraries all around the country with the extra manpower that enables them to eliminate backlogs and do their jobs better. A growing trend is the staffing of kiosk libraries entirely with volunteers; Baltimore County has four such operations. When the Chester Public Library in Illinois discovered a rare book cache, volunteers put 700 hours into restoring the unique collection.

More libraries today are budgeting for a full-scale volunteer program headed up by a coordinator. Columbus, Ohio, has a highly integrated program; in 1979 its volunteers and volunteens contributed 16,000 hours worth $84,000.

Volunteers can be found in offbeat places: the 51st Squadron at Lowry Air Force did the dogwork that brought DataPhase to Denver faster. Inmates at Iowa State Penitentiary wiped out a processing backlog for the state library; some of them now want to be librarians.

Friends contribute to libraries, too. Columbus and Minneapolis consider them to be part of their volunteer army and recognize them as such. In one year Friends of Libraries USA mushroomed from 100 to 511 members. ALA has welcomed the organization as an affiliate.

RANK AND FILE INVOLVEMENT

Unions last year took aggressive action that brought them into new prominence. The longest strike in library history shut down the Public Library of Youngstown and Mahoning County for three months; striking librarians and nonpros won retroactive salary increases and the promise of wage reopeners in 1981. Metro Toronto Library Board assistants set a precedent with the first strike ever by Toronto municipal library workers; their action, wholeheartedly supported by the union of library professionals, shut down the library. At Boston Public staffers walked out when their paychecks were withheld; their union got an injunction that prodded the city to pay up fast.

The Association of Research Libraries scrutinized unions unsympathetically and found no strong evidence that unions benefit either librarians or libraries. ARL noted that unions often bring about "adversary relationships between management and staff"; and usher in "rigid work rules." Looking to the future, ARL pegged multicampus centralized bargaining as the trend to watch.

There is growing evidence that libraries in trouble are turning more than ever before to their staff for answers. District of Columbia Public Library employees—line staffers as well as supervisors—devised better ways of managing the library in the face of massive manpower losses. California's Long Beach Public Library heeded a city directive to get its staff in on management assessment and found that this kind of participative management bolstered sagging morale. But Proposition 13 blues still got to nearly everyone; Long Beach had to set up a "work stress" unit for the growing numbers of city employees suffering from battle fatigue.

STATE LIBRARIES TODAY

Strong leadership at the state agency level has brought about dramatic library development in California, Maryland, Illinois, Washington, West Virginia, New York, and Florida. In 1980 major changes in command occurred in a number of state agencies currently at the crossroads. Gary Strong succeeds Ethel Crockett as California state librarian. California's Contra Costa County librarian, Clarence Walters, took up the helm in Connecticut. Elliot Shelkrot got the top post in Pennsylvania. Jim Nelson took the helm in Kentucky. David Reich stepped down as Massachusetts bureau chief just as that state agency faced a serious threat. The bureau has not yet been realigned in Massachusetts' reorganization of government departments. There is uncertainty about whether it would be best to put the Library Bureau with education or to merge the bureau and the state library (which serves as the library of the legislature).

CRISIS IN EDUCATION

In 1980 some library schools painted a surprisingly rosy picture of job opportunity, particularly in private industry. Simmons proclaimed itself the "only school in the U.S. granting 200 or more degrees . . . with 95 percent placement." It contended that in just one year's time job openings leaped up 130 percent all over the United States.

Library schools stressed the great demand for M.L.S. grads who had specialized in areas (science, technology, business, and language) that academe is counting on heavily. The University of Illinois library school actively recruited undergraduate science majors.

Simmons and the University of Texas at Austin became the latest to adopt new names (adding information science) to stress their new emphasis on all aspects of librarianship and information science. With the same intention, the University of California at Berkeley changed its M.L.S. into a M.L.I.S. (Masters of Library and Information Studies).

Most ALA-accredited schools sent an educator to Columbia's invitational conference on the two-year M.L.S. Three schools that have tried it heartily endorsed the two-year affair. But there was a serious questioning of the real merit of the program and of its impact on students (especially minorities), who would have to pay more for their M.L.S. and yet have no guarantee of getting a higher salary or even nailing a job in a library. Privately supported library schools said that they couldn't chance the two-year M.L.S. because they would end up pricing themselves out of the market.

The University of California-Los Angeles is a fervent backer of the two-year degree it has developed. Louisiana State currently favors the extended M.L.S., but it has definitely decided against an integrated core structure of six-credit-hour courses because this lacks the flexibility of the three-credit-hour format. The University of North Carolina-Chapel Hill, on the other hand, launched a two-year M.L.S. that starts with a 12-hour block of courses and goes on to a three-hour course framework research methodology and an internship.

ALA's handling of the accreditation process came under serious criticism in 1980 for too often failing to assure quality in library education. The Association of American Library Schools gave strong focus to a research study that found it doesn't take much to get reaccredited.

Indiana University's Herbert White (himself a Committee on Accreditation site visitor) scorned COA teams for being "apologists rather than monitors" and for "retreating from an insistence on excellence" in a myopic effort to save floundering schools. He urged COA to "involve more practitioners, students, and nonlibrarians in the accreditation process."

In 1980 COA accredited Ball State University's new program and reaccredited those of the University of Alabama, Hawaii, Iowa, and South Carolina.

New in a year marked by criticism of library schools were efforts to upgrade the competencies of educators. The Council on Library Resources put money behind a program to update faculty members from three New York library schools. The University of Texas at Austin and Birmingham Polytechnic exchanged educators and stressed the need for more sabbaticals.

Dipping enrollments, coupled with scanty institutional support, has prompted some library schools to drop out of continuing education. This trend is expected to accelerate if the two-year degree catches on.

The University of Michigan, on the other hand, put itself firmly behind continuing education when it launched a statewide program that provided CEU credit. The University of Utah teamed up with the Shawnee Library System in a correspondence course aimed at reaching more practicing librarians. The University of Missouri trained thousands of social workers to make more use of technology and their libraries in solving casework problems. The University of Southern California's Norris Medical Library got into developing continuing education for practicing physicians. Library associations, state and regional as well as national, are taking a dominant position as providers of continuing education.

ALA put its money behind the Continuing Education Center that its Standing Committee on Library Education (SCOLE) endorsed. But there was early criticism that ALA was more interested in making money than in improving education nationwide.

Meanwhile, ALA divisions moved strongly into education, too. The Library and Information Technology Association (LITA) went national with a workshop series on automation. RTSD capitalized on the conversion to *AACR 2* with a nationwide and profitable series of workshops. ALA's Machine-Assisted Reference Section (MARS), one unit clearly in orbit with membership topping 2,200, eyed a possible national role in educating end users as well as librarians.

SLA now has on its staff a coordinator to oversee its integrated program of continuing education courses. MLA has long been a trend setter with its certification program. Last year the two associations made library history with a Joint Continuing Education Program providing CEU credit. ASIS teamed up with SLA in conference education and also strengthened its regional and local educational offerings.

Seeking to improve its certification program, MLA cracked down on regional library groups that abruptly cancel CEU courses; they have to pay MLA penalties.

The Continuing Library Education Network Exchange (CLENE) picked a logo for its voluntary education service, added nontraditional education to programs it counts as worthy of "recognition certificates," and ran institutes to help states plan for certification. CLENE has drawn criticism for being too liberal in its definition of educational experiences.

Says CLENE, 41 states use LSCA to provide library continuing education; 14 states fund their own programs; and 11 more plan to get into certification. The American College Testing Program runs for CLENE a national registry of everyone's CE credits. According to CLENE, employers are now counting in CE credits when they evaluate prospective employees.

LIBRARY ASSOCIATIONS

A new era of interassociational cooperation dawned as national library and information associations linked education programs, lined up back-to-back conferences, and eyed other ways of pooling resources and saving money. ASIS brought together a conclave of the chiefs of large and small national associations to "get the library act together." The Medical LA and the Special LA formed a committee to explore joint action in legislation and programming. MLA and the Canadian Health Libraries Association signed a bilateral cooperative agreement.

The big national associations have been fighting inflation by regularly upping their dues. ALA, SLA, and ASIS did it again in 1980, but in a stunning upset MLA's membership voted down a dues increase. The MLA vote may be the first indication of new and stronger resistance to dues hikes. MLA is clearly in trouble and must now weigh what services to scuttle; a planned headquarters expansion is out.

Despite repeated headquarters groans about its "dues problems," things are looking good for ALA, which has a new headquarters building nearing completion, a thriving publication program, and undeveloped land worth $2 million. ALA will link its 1982 annual conference with that of the Pennsylvania Library Association as an experiment. ALA's latest poll of membership priorities points to slackening interest in a socially activist role for ALA members, a result not surprising if you consider the way the slumping economy and the deprivations it has wrought dominate the hearts and minds of Americans.

The only cloud on ALA's horizon is the growing strength of its divisions and their hankering for more independence. At ALA-N.Y., there was a proposal to break up the national meeting into three regionals. Meanwhile, the Association of College and Research Libraries and the American Association of School Librarians flexed their muscles with national conferences that attracted thousands. ACRL will take its second conference to Minneapolis in 1981; AASL wants to do it again in Portland in 1983. The lure of the regional meetings is the specialized focus they provide to people who are uninterested in ALA politics and who can't afford the high price of attending a national conference (over $700).

Biennial regional/national meetings by ALA divisions seem to be the wave of the future. But still to be resolved are the threats these conclaves could pose to the national organization.

State and regional library organizations are maturing. High grade conference programming is now common for many state organizations: New York, Indiana, Illinois, and California are prime examples. Now attention is being paid by them to special constituencies: NYLA has expanded its section for special libraries.

Mergers are creating new organizations with great ambitions. The California Academic and Research Libraries grew out of a merger of the Northern and Southern Chapters of ALA/ACRL and the California Library Association's Chapter of Academic and Research Libraries. If all goes well, CARL could bridge the split existing (in California) between ARL members and the rest of the academic library community.

WOMEN'S RIGHTS

The battle for ERA continued into the new decade. ALA marched for ERA in Chicago, but Illinois nixed ratification. ALA is firmly behind the boycott of non-ERA states; Midwinter will not return to Chicago unless Illinois goes with ERA. ALA established a $10,000 kitty to support its chapters in the ERA battle; some members (Ed Holley was one) complained that this commitment helped make dues go up.

Women's rights became a dominant issue at ALA's New York Conference: The membership voted to add "discrimination and sexual harassment" to the list of complaints SCMAI would investigate, reminded COA (Committee on Accreditation) to require affirmative action reports in its accreditation procedures, and endorsed the establishment of "continuing coalitions" with occupational organizations (such as unions) in which women predominate.

ALA's Task Force on Women rechristened itself the SRRT Feminist Task Force. The ERA Task Force raised $2,465 selling ERA buttons at ALA-New York; another $4,142 came in through the checkoff option on ALA membership forms. But the task force maintains that ALA must give it more money if headway is to be made in the struggle for equality.

INTELLECTUAL FREEDOM

At year's end a New York Appeals Court found the Island Trees school guilty of infringing on the constitutional rights of students. The ruling sends the case, which dates back to 1976 when 11 "objectionable" books were yanked from library shelves, back to court for trial.

That a school board can come down on the side of access was demonstrated by Mt. Diablo, California's, board, which refused to ban *Ms.* magazine despite strong community pressure. It compromised by requiring students to get their parents' blessing to check out *Ms.*

Other censorship cases made headlines in 1980. Fundamentalists marched on the Virginia Beach Public Library to protest the presence of a gay rights journal; VBPL appeased them by tucking the publication in "community information" files. North

Carolina's Columbus County Public Library weathered public outcry (coupled with threats of abolishing tax support for the library) concerning "sexual filth" in Judy Blume's *Wifey*. Library trustees bucked county commissioners and even the attorney general by refusing to deny youngsters access to the book unless parents specifically requested it. Maryland's Fairfax County library struck a political nerve during the primaries when it bought 88 copies of an anti-Kennedy book (*Teddy Bare*) published by a Bircher affiliate; Kennedy supporters cried foul.

Davis County, Utah's, embattled librarian Jeanne Layton won the coveted Downs award for her costly ($33,000) battle against censorship: The book that triggered the controversy was David DéLillo's *Americana*. She's back at the job she was ousted from, and contributions are streaming in. The Freedom to Read Foundation is matching every $1 with $2 for a $10,000 maximum.

IFC created lamentable ill will during ALA-N.Y. by putting its program on school censorship in the same time frame as meetings of three major divisions: AASL, ALSC, and YASD. IFC issued a public apology after the three divisions got council to pass a resolution to prevent another such "breach of organizational integrity."

The new *Library Bill of Rights* has provisions liberalizing use of library meeting rooms. Despite earlier fears that the more liberal *Bill* would tempt some radical groups to abuse library facilities, it seems that individual libraries are holding their own. After a KKK disruption, North Carolina's Forsyth County Library came out with a model meeting room policy that endorses "free access," but clearly bars disruption. Oklahoma City's standard practice of inspecting exhibits foiled a Hare Krishna attempt to pass off the cult's craftsmanship as "native Indian art."

Taking a stand against racism, the South African Library Association renounced apartheid and regrouped as the South African Institute for Librarianship and Information Science.

SECURITY IN LIBRARIES

Recent studies have pegged library security problems. A statewide Illinois study found disruptive or threatening behavior to be a common occurrence both for medium-sized and big city libraries; violent crime was reported growing, too. A New Hampshire research team came up with these disturbing statistics in a random sample of 100 libraries: Over 80 percent reported intentional book damage; 31 percent, vandalism in the parking lot; 59 percent, verbal abuse to staff; and 50 percent, intentional equipment damage. Ohio State University pegged the annual costs of fixing mutilated periodicals at $13,860 to $23,100, but it found that damages dropped after OSU launched a public relations campaign to educate patrons.

Libraries are coping with crime in the stacks in a variety of ways. Electronic security is the most common approach. New York's Rochester Public Library started shopping when it counted its losses at $34,000 annually (15 percent of its acquisitions budget). St. Louis found its Tattletale System worth the investment when losses dropped from 20 percent to 6. Pennsylvania's Westminster College might scrap its honor system and go electronic thanks to the eight "investigative journalists" who sneaked out 139 books before they got nailed by a security guard; they were charged with theft.

Worcester, Massachusetts, tightened security with a new closed stacks policy that permits only closely supervised browsing. Worcester also prosecuted rubbish people it caught stealing. Kankakee, Illinois, stopped one thief; library director Neal Ney chased the culprit out of the library and finally wrestled him to the ground in a nearby parking lot.

Professional thieves were on the move again in 1980. Academic libraries with eighteenth-century travel and exploration books locked them up when they got wise to a wave of theft. The Northern Virginia Community College found itself to be a clearinghouse for stolen goods when most of the books in the 100 cartons it got from a warehouse turned out to be stolen.

Reports of OCLC terminal snatching are starting to mount; Illinois Benedictine College beefed up security after pros got through locked doors and tucked its terminal in to a van.

In response to spiraling theft problems, ACRL's Rare Books Section started collecting data on rare book thefts with the aim of improving existing theft alert and recovery nationwide. R. R. Bowker launched a monthly (*Stolen Art Alert*) to help keep track of the latest art heists. ALA warned libraries to be wary of possible mail fraud if a firm solicits advance payment and offers substantial discounts in exchange for prompt prepayment; it published all 45 imprints used by the indicted Frank Gille.

Libraries continued to gain legal backup in their battle against crime: Wisconsin came out with a tough library theft law modeled on the state shoplifting statute. South Carolina was among the growing number of states to pass laws that give library staffers liability protection should they decide to detain a thief.

Delinquent patrons make library collections shrink, too. Many of the libraries that have taken a hard line on overdues are recouping losses in a big way. Tactics include threatening letters, mailgrams, action by collection agencies, and actual prosecution. Chicago Public launched an extensive campaign when losses in a three-year period were pegged at $2 million; threatening letters alone brought back $34,200 worth of strayed materials plus $12,000 in fines and reimbursements.

CPL is among the growing number of libraries to screen patrons more carefully by demanding more identification. Robeson County, North Carolina, defends this stance as "a matter of life and death for the book budget." Faculty members at America's colleges can be the worst scofflaws of all; the University of North Carolina at Chapel Hill made no headway with them until it resorted to fines despite objections.

The customary mailing of overdue notices can be expensive. Cleveland Public scrapped this practice when it found that these reminders don't bring books back faster. CPL will depend on its new circulation system to peg delinquents who will then be barred.

Soft persuaders such as fine moratoriums work for some libraries. Washington, D.C., celebrated National Library Week by dropping fines; area libraries got back 18,000 books worth $500,000. New Rochelle, New York, was forgiving, too, but it still charged delinquents $2 for every overdue book.

Libraries, often at the urging of their staff organizations, are more squarely facing up to the librarian's nightmare: the problem patron. LC's union filed a grievance to get the library to run classes to teach staffers how to deal with "prima donnas from Congress" and other problematic patrons. Enoch Pratt was among the many libraries all over the United States to ask specialists to tell their staffers how to deal sanely with trouble.

Arson is definitely on the upswing, and libraries are targets because they're public institutions and are vulnerable to attack when closed. A wave of vandalism in Garfield Heights, Ohio, ended with the torching of the library. Vandals were blamed for two San Diego burnouts; North Claremont's library was set afire to cover up a robbery.

Natural disaster can also wreck a library. Lightning started the fire that destroyed Virginia's Scottsville Library. Torrential rains shut down ten Los Angeles branches and sidelined bookmobiles for over a week. Mount St. Helen's eruption dumped ash in Washington and shut down many libraries. But it was business as usual for some in that area: Librarians wore surgical masks, collected clothing for victims, and answered hundreds of questions.

Library preservation is starting to get the national and international attention it requires if libraries are to make any headway in their seemingly futile efforts to save deteriorating books and films. This attention ranges from state-level colloquiums (Oklahoma) to regional and national conservation programs. The National Endowment for the Humanities expanded its conservation programs with a new "national campaign to save endangered humanities resources." ARL put Pamela Darling in charge of its program to help research libraries deal with mounting preservation problems. The Western Council of State Libraries has been coordinating a regional effort.

Seeing worldwide information access as a not far off goal, the Council on Library Resources backed work in conservation by the International Federation of Library Associations (IFLA).

THE WHCOLIS MANDATE

Giving WHCOLIS top priority, Carter appointed an interagency task force in the Office of the President to review the WHCOLIS recommendations. The ground gained after WHCOLIS need not be lost when Reagan assumes command. In his report to Congress, Carter had urged that funding be provided to undergird library networking and resource sharing, to fortify the nation's urban and research libraries, and to address such concerns as illiteracy, geographic barriers to information access, and international cooperation. But Carter reminded libraries that much of the work that lies ahead will have to be done by libraries. [The complete text of President Carter's report is reprinted in the Special Reports section of Part 1—*Ed.*]

Taking positive action, delegates who came to Minneapolis to organize an Ad Hoc Committee on Implementation of the WHCOLIS Resolutions decided that the committee become an ongoing effort. It appointed a steering committee to carry forward the task of implementing the WHCOLIS recommendations and organizing citizen support for libraries.

There was also forward action at the state level. In Indiana the entire delegation to WHCOLIS now serves as an Advisory Committee on Libraries and Information Services. New Hampshire delegates are working together with the legislature on a blueprint for library development in that state. And North Carolina spelled out its goals.

A permanent political action group, The National Citizens for Public Libraries, is drawing library supporters, too. The difficult task that lies ahead is making the WHCOLIS vision a reality in the face of pressures brought on by the nation's recession.

SLJ NEWS REPORT, 1980

Bertha M. Cheatham
Associate Editor, *School Library Journal*

School media specialists concerned with annual funding allocations under Title IV-B of the Elementary and Secondary Education Act (now under the newly created Department of Education) are aware that some of their "friends" in the House and Senate have been ousted and more fiscally conservative legislators have been elected to fill their positions. Commenting on the election results and their implications for school media specialists, Alice Fite, executive secretary of the American Association of School Librarians (AASL), remarked, "There was mourning in the ALA headquarters" the day the election results were announced. "Just when AASL has reached the point of working with supporting legislators, we'll have to begin again and develop new strategies."

Fite spoke for many librarians who have had to contend with staff cutbacks, job consolidations, restricted budgets, and communities with diminishing tax bases. On the eve of the election, ten states were facing tax incentives drawn to the pattern of California's devastating 1979 Proposition 13, which caused extensive rollbacks in library hours and services.

Librarians in Oregon and Michigan who faced major tax-cut measures that would impact on their budgets relaxed a bit. But in Massachusetts, a plan (Proposition 2½) to limit property taxes to 2½ percent of real value was passed by voters. This means a 26 percent cut in the state's budget, and it will have destructive effects on municipal services including public libraries. Massachusetts has no surplus to turn to as California did. Cities such as Boston plan to hike the income and sales taxes to make up the difference. But that may be too late for the public service employees and municipal workers who will find themselves without jobs.

There were indications that voters in Arizona, Nebraska, Nevada, Ohio, South Dakota, and Utah are aware of the losses in government services because of regulations limiting spending—they rejected 1981 tax-cut measures. And last summer California voters turned down Proposition 9, which would have cut income taxes—it was evident that California's surplus funds were just a stopgap measure, and that these taxpayers are beginning to revolt against the results of their tax revolts.

The election fallout resulted in the loss of library supporters Majority Whip John Bradamas (Indiana) and Senator Jacob Javits (New York), who (with Edward Kennedy) coauthored the proposed National Library Act. Republicans will control all Senate committees. Eileen Cooke, director of the American Library Association's (ALA) Washington office, in assessing the changes in Congress, said, "It's a new ball game in terms of dealing with two different parties controlling the House and Senate. There will be no way to override a veto."

What this will mean for such legislation as Carter's youth bill reauthorizing Title IV-A of the Comprehensive Employment and Training Act (CETA) and the president's

Note: Adapted from *School Library Journal*, December 1980.

Author's Note: This report covers some of the major national news affecting library funding and support in 1980. Events and issues in related fields such as education are touched on, and developments in areas such as copyright and intellectual freedom, technology, and the publishing industry are briefly discussed.

request for an appropriation of $2 billion is speculation at this juncture. The bill includes a provision for vocational education for disadvantaged youth in junior and senior high schools and vocational schools. The House version requires school site councils (parents, young adults, teachers, community leaders, and representatives of industry) to monitor the schools' programs; the Senate calls for a district-level "advisory" council without direct authority over school officials.

Young adult librarians and teachers who, through outreach and dropout programs, have waged a losing battle to stem the rise in functional illiteracy have watched the progress of the youth bill—now it may get lost in the reshuffling of congressional power.

Librarians had good reason to monitor state and local election campaigns this year. The 1979 cutbacks in local services experienced in California were still fresh in mind and similar tax revolts threatened to sweep across the country; many librarians mobilized citizen support to prevent repeats of this initiative.

California survived Proposition 13, but just barely. A report issued early in the year told of phasing out library facilities: in 1978 there were 3,857 library branches and bookmobile outlets. This was narrowed down to 3,245 in 1979, and to 3,027 in 1980. Professional staff positions in the state dropped 18 percent in a two-year period, and in some libraries, volunteers have been recruited to fill professional positions. Weekend and evening service hours have been eliminated in many systems.

There was a cause for celebration in Berkeley, however. Librarians joined forces with the Friends of the Library to effectively campaign for important legislation to restore $2.4 million to the library budget.

Regina Minudri, Berkeley Public Library's (BPL) director, and Berkeley librarians were commended by the ALA Council for waging a vigorous "Keep Libraries Alive" campaign, which resulted in a 29,899 to 13,200 vote in favor of the referendum. Now BPL is working to restore service schedules and add to the book collection. The book budget was upped $40,000 after the vote.

Librarians in Massachusetts took another approach. To get more state aid, the governor was sent a library card from every public library and received numbers of letters and phone calls. The aid was increased by $1.9 million. In South Carolina, the state aid was raised 50 percent largely due to alert librarians who championed the increase in funding.

Media support was a big factor in Cleveland's two-to-one vote to renew a second-year tax levy to support the public library. The campaign tactic here was to show what it would cost the average household each year: $6.20. This year's levy, which was lower than the previous year's, also impressed the voters.

The 64 resolutions of the White House Conference on Libraries and Information Services (WHCLIS) provided another means of keeping library issues and concerns before state and national legislators. The final WHCLIS report was sent to President Carter in March; his report was forwarded to Congress in late September. There was a flurry of excitement among the school media specialists who attended the first National Conference of the American Association of School Librarians in Louisville, Kentucky, when they heard that this report had been hand delivered to their conference by a White House aide. The excitement quickly diminished after portions of the report were read by Charles Benton, chairman of the National Commission on Libraries and Information Science. It was evident that the report contained very little pertaining specifically to services to children and young adults. Carter (who left office in January 1981) promised to initiate new legislation in such areas as barriers to information access for the handicapped and disadvantaged, library networking and resource sharing, urban libraries and research libraries as centers for resource networks, and the funding for new information technologies. After all the years of hard work and planning (remember all those pre-White House Conferences?), it is to be hoped that the next president will endorse the report and that its resolutions will be acted upon.

In the fall, a committee of 91 delegates met in Minneapolis, Minnesota, to develop means of implementing the resolutions coming out of the WHCLIS. The delegates, professionals and laypersons known as a "Committee of 114" (actually there are 118 possible state delegates who attended WHCLIS), heard F. James Rutherford, assistant secretary for Education Research and Improvement, U.S. Department of Education, urge them to "keep the pressure on" for more federal support for libraries. But, he warned, "I don't think you can look forward to a quick and dramatic infusion of federal dollars." To get the message across, he urged unity of efforts. "Separately, you won't be able to speak with a single voice. Washington won't hear you."

ALA AND YOUTH DIVISIONS

Good-bye Palmer House! This was the comment ALA members uttered at the 1980 ALA Midwinter Meeting in Chicago. But the ALA membership overturned a council vote to boycott the Palmer House hotel until Illinois ratified the Equal Rights Amendment (ERA). ALA will recognize the contractual agreement with Palmer House for Midwinter Meetings scheduled until 1984. After that, if Illinois still has not ratified ERA, Midwinter Meetings will be held in Washington, D.C.

The ALA/Social Responsibilities Round Table (SSRT) Task Force on Women is working with other organizations to see that ERA is ratified. The group, now renamed the Feminist Task Force, has picked up ALA members' support and is becoming more visible in ALA. Their resolution calling for free child-care services at annual conferences and Midwinter Meetings did not get council approval, but will be reintroduced at 1981 Midwinter for reconsideration.

The council approved, despite objections from some divisional councilors, a $5 membership fee for students. However, the resolution requires a mail vote approval by membership and will not immediately affect divisions.

Over the years, ALA's divisions have been seeking more autonomy from ALA in terms of managing their own budgets. The success of AASL's Louisville Conference presented some problems for AASL's directors, who had asked for their own savings and checking accounts. No ALA funds had been used to produce the conference, they maintain, and reason that they ought to be able to invest the funds generated. It is an issue that faces all divisions that produce surplus funds and will continue to confront the ALA Council and Executive Board.

In holding its first national conference, AASL chose to go it alone, without involving the Association for Library Service to Children (ALSC) or the Young Adult Services Division (YASD) in the program. Many of the concurrent workshops and lectures dealt with issues that also concerned public librarians serving youth—intellectual freedom, access, accountability, resource sharing, and more. The 2,500 in attendance—school media specialists, supervisors, administrators, and exhibitors—left the three-day conference with praise for a smoothly run, informative, and enjoyable meeting. It drew many non-ALA members, and many members who had never attended an ALA Annual Conference because of the travel restrictions set by school principals and boards that are not reimbursing educational or library-associated travel expenses.

In late October, the ALA Executive Board approved another AASL national conference scheduled for 1982. The site will be in the Southwestern region of the United

States. AASL's successful conference venture has provided a model to its youth divisions, a model of an effective way to bring programs to nonmembers of ALA. It seems destined to influence future program plans for all ALA divisions.

The youth divisions are exploring ways in which to work together on programs, committee efforts, legislation, networking, and other areas to advance youth concerns. At the 1980 Midwinter Meeting, the three incoming presidents met with interested members to determine the feasibility of working together on cooperative ventures. This exploratory meeting generated much interest from active members who, while wanting to retain their identities as separate divisions, realize the advantage in uniting efforts to support mutual interests that come before ALA's Council.

PROGRAMS AND SERVICES

Preschoolers were the target audience of many library programs this year. The audience for children's programs grows younger and younger; programs for infants are now popular. New York Public Library's Early Childhood Center held a series of programs on "The Effects of Current Political Decisions on Children, Parents, and Educators." The rights of children and child abuse are still among the most important topics of such programs for parents and those who work with young children.

In Seattle, a van is provided by Seattle Public Library to service licensed daycare facilities with books and materials. The users of the Center for Discovery of the Public Library of Columbus & Franklin County (PLCFC), Ohio, are handicapped and disadvantaged children who are offered skills activities. PLCFC also cooperates with cable television companies (via a two-way video system hookup) to broadcast live programs from the center. The thematic programs, which are produced by the library staff and volunteers, are broadcast bimonthly and include segments with puppet shows, stories, crafts, community talent, and special guests.

Backed by a grant from the Louise Brown Foundation, the 26 branches of Cuyahoga County (Ohio) Public Library are bolstering their puppet collections. Under the direction of the library's puppet center, custom puppet stages have been built for the branches. Funds are also available for the creation and presentation of new puppet shows, puppetry workshops for children, and a performance at a spring festival.

Bilingual programs are now a "must" because of the influx of Cubans, Haitians, and other refuges from the world's troubled areas. "Saving the Past/Guardando El Pasado" is the theme of a unique bilingual program conducted by the Houston Public Library. Patrons of four branches shared family photographs, letters, and other documents to learn how to appreciate family history. The funding for the program came from the National Endowment for the Humanities (NEH).

And in Tucson, an ambitious cultural program, "Sonoran Heritage," funded by NEH in 1977, ended in September. Children who participated attended a "Utopia" workshop, and their drawings of their versions of cities of the future were exhibited in a branch library.

INTELLECTUAL FREEDOM

Every year for the past five years, the *Island Trees Union Free School District* (New York) case has made the news. The long-standing controversy and legal battle, which stems from a March 1976 removal of nine books from the school library by members of the school board, has not yet been resolved. In October, the U.S. Court of Appeals for the Second Circuit in New York City decided two to one to send the *Pico* v. *Board of Education* case back to a lower court for trial. The majority opinion of the decision concluded that the school board's removal of books it deemed "anti-American, anti-Christian, anti-Semitic [sic] and just plain filthy," was "an unusual and irregular intervention in the school libraries' operation by persons not routinely concerned with their contents." Judge Charles P. Sifton also wrote that the board's main concern was not to "cleanse the libraries of all titles containing materials insulting to religious groups or that distort history"; rather it was an effort to "express an official policy with regard to God and country of uncertain and indefinite content which is to be ignored by pupils, librarians and teachers at their peril."

At an October 30 meeting, the school board's lawyer, George W. Lipp, Jr., announced plans to fight the appeal that reversed a lower court's ruling (in 1979) that the board's policy was "misguided" but did not infringe on First Amendment rights.

No one openly opposed the board at the meeting, but one parent was concerned about the school superintendent's comment that he personally reviews and approves lists of proposed library books. "I review several hundred titles a year," said Walf H. Oglesby, "and I do it religiously." We do not practice censorship here; we practice wise selection.

Another long-fought First Amendment case, *Bicknell* v. *Vergennes Union High School* (Vermont), involved the school board's removal of *The Wanderers* from the high-school library and its restrictions of *Dog Day Afternoon*. The board also froze library acquisitions. The reason? The books were "obscene and vulgar." This could have an "adverse effect" on students. The Freedom to Read Foundation of ALA granted funds to aid librarian Elizabeth Phillips and student plaintiffs in fighting the case. The Second Circuit Court of Appeals upheld the district's ban.

Other cases involving book censorship:

Zykan v. *Warsaw Community School Corporation* (Indiana), where an amicus brief has been filed by ALA's Freedom to Read Foundation, the National Council of Teachers of English, and the Indiana Council of Teachers of English asking that the U.S. Court of Appeals for the Seventh Circuit review District Judge Allen Sharp's ruling that Warsaw students' First Amendment rights were not violated. The case, which began in 1977, involved the burning of 40 copies of *Values Clarification* by a senior citizens' group and the dismissal of a teacher. The school board ordered the removal of five books from the curriculum (*The Stepford Wives*, *Growing Up Female in America*, *Go Ask Alice*, *The Bell Jar*, and *Values Clarification*); cancelled seven English courses (one was Black Literature); and passed resolutions calling for removal of "all objectionable" material from classrooms.

Ms. Magazine, which was ordered reinstated in the Nashua, New Hampshire, school board in 1979, is a target for censorship in other school libraries because of its advertisements and feature articles. In the Mt. Diablo Unified School District Libraries in California, a group called Citizens for the Improvement of Public Schools attacked *Ms.* for its "obscene and pornographic" content. Its use in an English class in Ygnacio Valley High School was disputed. Eventually, the board voted three to two that *Ms.* was to be used only at the high-school level, that it was to be put on the restricted reserve shelf, and that students using it must have a written request signed by a parent and by the teacher making the assignment.

School librarians in Sampson County, Clinton, North Carolina, voted unanimously to remove *Jaws* from the elementary and middle-school libraries because of a parent's complaints about the book's language.

Judy Blume's novels *Blubber* and *Wifey* came under fire in two communities. In Bethesda, Maryland, *Blubber* can be used only under the direct guidance of a teacher. A parent complained about a word (bitch) and the "cruelty and nastiness" in the story of a fat girl who is tormented by her classmates. During this hassle, the press (*Washington Post*) reported that Montgomery County Public Libraries (Rockville, Maryland) had added 110 copies of the book to its collection.

A controversy involving *Wifey* made headlines nationwide when a reporter wrote that the book was banned in the Columbus County Public Library (North Carolina). Library Director Amanda Bible corrected the report and explained that Blume's *Wifey* did make a stir when a parent found it in the hands of her 12-year-old daughter. The library's board of trustees backed Bible's refusal to remove the book, and in the end the library board (which had voted unanimously to have it removed on receiving the complaint) passed a motion to restrict its use to children over 18. Now, parents in Columbus who choose to restrict their children's reading can request that they be issued a card indicating restricted circulation.

Davis County (Utah) librarian Jeanne Layton, fired in 1979 over a dispute about the book *Americana*, returned to her job early this year when the civil service commission found she was fired without cause. Her suit against the county commissioner and others is still pending, however. She charged them with violating her right and the First Amendment rights of the community residents to read controversial literature.

The recent rise of Christian fundamentalists in the United States indicates that more trouble is ahead for librarians who adhere to the tenets of intellectual freedom. The fundamentalists' attacks on secular humanism received wide coverage during the election campaign when they vowed to oust officials they felt endorsed the philosophy.

In the year ahead, we will see more attacks by groups belonging to the Moral Majority, which has claimed several hundred thousand members in the last year.

TECHNOLOGY

The year saw many libraries joining networks, establishing computerized services, and installing the latest in audiovisual equipment. Now that they have become more knowledgeable about technology, school library media center specialists and academic librarians are acquiring advanced technology at a rapid pace—perhaps too rapidly for the traditionalists. A case in point: Clarkson College in Potsdam, New York, is creating a new $4-million computerized complex, the Educational Resource Center, in which students will have access to resources via computer. In two years, college officials expect to do away with all volumes of reference books and the wooden card catalog. This information will all be transferred to microfiche. Storing books was an expensive and space consuming process, and the school wanted more than just a new building. According to Clarkson's president, Robert A. Plaine, "Books can be too slow." He said that it is possible to disseminate information without waiting for books to be published. And, the assistant dean of arts and sciences said, "Youngsters, today, in the first grade may never get involved with a book . . . not books as we know them." Not surprisingly, the president conceded that some faculty members have balked at this library (?) of the future.

The Dataphase and on-line circulation system of the Stephen F. Austin University of Nacogdoches, Texas, provides access terminals that replace the traditional card catalog. Students can use one of 15 terminals to locate books. It's so popular and efficient, the school intends to close its card catalog and have all new acquisitions available through the automated system.

Anaheim Public Library (California) has a computerized library circulation system to update its overdue book procedures. The installation of wands, video display terminals, and an automated circulation control system enables library clerks to instantly access the patron's record of overdue fines as well as to verify names and addresses.

EDUCATION

Perhaps because of the blitz of television spot announcements about the benefits of schools, the American public ranked schools second to the church on a list of American institutions in which they had a great deal of confidence. In the 1980 Gallup poll of adults 18 years of age and older, the church garnered 42 percent of the top responses and public schools received 28 percent, as compared with 14 percent for the national government and 13 percent for big business. The survey, as in past years, listed lack of discipline as the biggest problem of the public schools.

Discipline

A recent report from the American Association of School Administrators, *Student Discipline: Problems and Solutions*, lists the most serious problems as student smoking, insubordination, use of marijuana, and use of alcohol. To combat persistent discipline problems (which are also cited as a cause for teachers' leaving the profession), some Cincinnati high schools have set up discipline committees that include staff, parents, community leaders, and high-school students. In-school suspension centers have been organized in ten Indianapolis high schools and in some junior highs. The centers advise teachers on how to handle behavioral problems and how to provide guidance for students.

Strikes

Higher salaries were the target of teachers' strikes. In September, teachers and school employees in nine states walked out—in Philadelphia the strike lasted more than a week.

When Chicago was hit with a succession of strikes—public transit, teachers, firemen—the Chicago Public Library (CPL) staff volunteered to assist in operating the city's 24-hour emergency switchboard. The "Recess Fair," which provided a series of educational programs and tutors for idle school children during the January teachers' strike, was another service CPL provided.

Politics

On the national scene, the National Education Association (NEA), which backed President Carter in 1979 and was rewarded when he pushed through the legislation that created a separate Department of Education, endorsed Carter's reelection. Its 1.8 million members were urged to vote for the Carter-Mondale ticket. The National Education Association has become increasingly and visibly political. "Our ultimate goal is to have the federal government carry one-third of the cost of public education," said Kenneth F. Melley, NEA's political affairs director. And NEA's competitor, the American Federation of Teachers (AFT), also leaned toward Carter.

Bilingual Education

Proposed major changes in the guidelines for bilingual education, mandated by the federal government, hit flak from education groups such as AFT, which opposed the imposition of specific programs in local school district curricula. Under the new rules, foreign children will be instructed in English if they are already conversant in

English; those who speak their native language better *must* be taught in both languages. Educators claim that the proposal will require the hiring of many bilingual teachers and that existing teachers will have to learn a variety of foreign languages. Bilingual education is an unresolved issue, and the outcome will affect school media specialists who must find appropriate materials to supplement such instruction.

Trends

San Diego's plan to "pay" students for attending school: Memorial Junior High School trustees unanimously approved a plan to lure truant students back to school. The 886-student school, which had lost $132,000 in state attendance funds, offers students a card stamped 25¢ for each day they attended school the previous month. A perfect attendance would add up to $5, which could be spent on school-related items such as library fines, gym clothes, paper, etc. A follow-up news report said that the "pay" plan, still in its early stages, has cut the truancy rate in half.

North Carolina School of Science and Mathematics offers free rooms and meals to 150 eleventh-grade students who have been tested and found gifted with potential for high achievement. Along with studying advanced algebra and calculus, the students practice writing skills in seminar groups and relax with the school's four microcomputers.

COPYRIGHT

Publishers went after a photocopying business this year and won an out-of-court settlement. A civil complaint against the Gnomon Corporation of Cambridge, Massachusetts, charged that the company routinely made multiple copies of textbook materials without permission from publishers and sold compilations of photocopied chapters to students for a profit. The seven publishers—Basic Books, CBS, McGraw-Hill, Princeton University Press, Nelson Hall, Prentice-Hall, and John Wiley & Sons—are all members of the Association of American Publishers (AAP), which vows to monitor such commercial photocopying services and institute action against companies that violate the copyright laws.

Advocates for women's right to assume higher positions in the library profession can record Barbara Ringer's career of trailblazing. In May, this pioneer, the highly respected register of copyrights, retired after 30 years of service to the Copyright Office and Library of Congress (LC). In 1972, she had to fight for the position after the former librarian of Congress, Quincy Mumford, bypassed her to appoint someone else to the post. She eventually won her complaint of sex bias and racial discrimination (because of her request for an investigation of racial discrimination at LC) through a Civil Service Commission determination. Her successor, David L. Ladd, was appointed register after an extensive search. [See the report on the 1980 activities of the Copyright Office in the Federal Agencies section of Part 1—*Ed.*]

THE BOOK INDUSTRY

Publishers, hard hit by inflationary costs, had many problems to iron out this year. While continuing to cut back staff positions and lists, they found adult book sales were steadily dropping and huge book inventories were possible liabilities.

The competition for book dollars was further complicated by an Internal Revenue Service (IRS) ruling that companies had to comply with a *Thor Power Tool Company* v. *The Commissioner of Internal Revenue* decision, issued on January 16, 1979, that involved spare-parts inventories. The Supreme Court held that the valuation of warehouse stock could not be reduced for tax purposes unless it was disposed of or sold at reduced prices. Internal Revenue Service officials claimed this applied to books as well as other merchandise. Publishers, who will no longer be able to mark down titles, are asking for a change in this ruling. Some have already asked their authors to buy their own unsold books at reduced prices in an effort to reduce inventory. Because they will not be able to indicate the actual value of the inventories for tax purposes, publishers predict that titles will go out of print sooner; that first and second printings will be smaller, causing an increase in book prices; that contracts for scholarly books will decrease because they sell slowly and have remained on backlists over a long period.

As of January 1, 1981, Harcourt Brace Jovanovich, Inc., expects to abandon the practice of allowing bookstores to return trade books for full credit. It is the first publisher to restrict liberal return privileges. The rate of such returns can reach from 35 to 50 percent of the books shipped to bookstores.

Publishers forecast a lowering of book production. Librarians, already experiencing unfilled book orders because titles are put out of print so rapidly, will have greater difficulty in ordering from reduced backlists.

AND, THE NEXT YEARS . . .

In 1980, as the decade changed, the library community tried to look into the future and prepare for it. A pre-ALA seminar brought together experts in the fields of information and communications technology with leaders in American library service, but their discussions held in closed session have not yet been published by ALA. The brief reports offered at the first session of the 1980 ALA conference suggested that the seminar's discussion concentrated heavy attention on technology's uses to storage and research but gave only glancing consideration to library services to the general public or the young. Then, AASL's first national conference looked ahead with the theme "The '80s and Beyond," but got no further into the future of school library services than the commitment of a second national AASL conference in 1982. The year-old cabinet-level Department of Education, which promised closer attention to library concerns, did not have the support of the newly elected Republican administration and may not survive under Reagan. His campaign promises of reduced federal support for locally controlled public services chill the hope that existing education and library programs can be maintained or extended without renewed struggles.

There are now only 19 years left before the twenty-first century. At the end of the first year of the 1980s only one thing is certain: The next few years in library service to children and young adults are not going to be easy. This calls for the redoubling of efforts by librarians serving the young to keep attention focused on the library service needs of youth in our society.

PW NEWS REPORT, 1980

John F. Baker

Editor-in-Chief, *Publishers Weekly*

1980 was a remarkable year in publishing history—one that may well come to be regarded as something of a watershed year, in which many of the book world's assumptions, relationships, and approaches of long standing began to be decisively altered.

THE SLOW CASH FLOW

It was a year, for a start, of considerable economic hardship for many publishers, one in which inflation continued at a steady and unacceptably high level and the cost of borrowing money rose at some points to over 20 percent. Cash flow became a serious problem all along the line from author to bookseller. The controversial *Thor Power Tool* decision, in which heavy discounting of inventory for tax purposes was disallowed by the IRS and the decision upheld by the Supreme Court, was held also to apply to publishers' backlist books—a particularly hard blow at sci-tech and professional publishers that print books in small runs and sell them over a long period, as well as to the more literary houses that struggle to keep quality titles in print. Efforts to have the ruling ameliorated for publishers failed in Washington, though there was some hope as the year ended that matters might improve in 1981. In any case, the impact seemed to vary greatly from publisher to publisher, and although there was some speedier remaindering, and a limited amount of premature pulping of old titles, and a great deal of complaining, the full impact seemed not yet to have been felt in 1980.

PUBLISHERS AND BOOKSELLERS

Prices of books continued to rise sharply with the increased cost of materials, salaries, and freight charges, and at the American Booksellers Association convention in Chicago in June, long-simmering discontents among many smaller independent booksellers rose to the surface. At a series of later regional meetings, and later in a letter circulated to publishers, they complained of discrimination against them in publishers' discount policies, which were held to favor the large chains. Apparently in response to such protest, before year's end a number of publishers announced major changes in their discount and returns policies. Harcourt Brace Jovanovich went furthest, announcing a flat no-returns policy coupled with much higher discounts—though initial reaction from booksellers and wholesalers indicated that for many this might be too drastic a solution. Crown, Scribner's, and Oxford University Press all announced more tempered approaches: higher discounts beginning at a lower purchase level, and a graduated penalty system for returns above a certain level, the two factors designed to reward careful buying. These won more general approval. A number of such readjustments were promised for 1981.

Note: Reprinted from *Publishers Weekly*, March 13, 1981, where the article was entitled "News and Trends: A Time of Far-Reaching Change."

THE ADVANCE OF PAPERBACKS

Meanwhile, there were increasing signs that the traditional relationships between hardcover and paperback books were breaking down. A *PW* survey prepared during 1980 (but published just after the end of the year) showed that the mix between hardcovers and paperbacks in bookstores was tilting decisively in favor of the latter, with predictions of 70 percent of stock in paper before the decade is out. Many hardcover publishers began launching new lines of trade paperbacks, sometimes for new books, sometimes as a way of reviving old ones after mass market paperback licenses had reverted. (A prime example was Holt, Rinehart and Winston's republication of Norman Mailer's *The Naked and the Dead* in its own new trade paperback line, after the license for the NAL paperback version expired.) In his Bowker lecture, delivered in November, Oscar Dystel, retired president of Bantam, warned paperback publishers to expect more of the same and added that "paperback companies have bankrolled hardcover publishers for too long, and I believe that trip is about over." Bantam itself announced it would publish best-selling author Clive Cussler in hardcover, NAL put Erica Jong's latest into a trade paperback version, Crown promised a new novel in trade paper, St. Martin's planned to do its own mass market edition of Gordon Liddy's *Will*. Mass paperback companies continued to publish more and more "originals"—usually genre novels with strong women's interest—as their lead titles, and to buy fewer and fewer of the "middle" sort of books on which hardcover companies depend heavily for subsidiary rights income. The bidding fever for the blockbuster novels so characteristic of recent years seemed to have subsided somewhat, though Bantam did pay $3.2 million for Judith Krantz's *Princess Daisy*—and inspired long pieces in the *New Yorker* and the *New York Times* that in effect deplored today's publishing as a money-mad branch of show business.

THE CONGLOMERATE SCENE

The pace of conglomeratization—or the swallowing up of publishing houses by large corporations essentially involved in other lines of work—slowed in 1980, and there even seemed to be signs of a reverse trend, with corporate owners selling off publishing arms that did not seem to accord ideally with their own operations, to other owners that did. RCA's sale of the Random House operation—including, of course, Knopf, Pantheon, and Ballantine—to the Newhouse newspaper chain, for a sum estimated at between $65 million and $70 million—was a case in point. And William Collins divided its U.S. branches: the dictionary division to Simon & Schuster; the Bible division to an Iowa Falls Bible operation; and its children's division, under the name Philomel, to Putnam. Bertelsmann of West Germany bought out its Italian partner's share in Bantam to make its ownership complete. On a lighter note, Doubleday relived earlier publishing history by buying a baseball team, the New York Mets, for $21 million.

THE YEAR OF THE CHINESE

On the international front, it was the year of the Chinese. For several months, beginning a little before ABA and running well into the summer, delegates from the Chinese publishing industry seemed to be omnipresent. Deals were arranged with McGraw-Hill, Van Nostrand Reinhold, and Indiana University Press to publish titles originating in China, mostly of an artistic or scientific nature. And *PW* published a major study, by Herbert Lottman, of the Chinese industry—as well as a comprehensive look at publishing in Brazil and new looks at Scandinavian and German publishing. Mexico City held its first book fair and immediately launched a bid to become the new Latin American center of Spanish-language publishing. The Moscow Book Fair caused a flurry by revoking the visas of both Winthrop Knowlton of Harper & Row and Robert Bernstein of Random House for supposedly anti-Soviet sentiments; both are, of course, strong and vocal supporters of freedom to publish.

LEGAL HASSLES

On the legal front, there were some decidedly unsettling decisions. Frank Snepp, former CIA operative who wrote a Random House book, *Decent Interval*, based on his experiences in Vietnam, was held to have violated a CIA secrecy oath in writing the book, and in a decision upheld 6–3 by the Supreme Court, was ordered to pay back his very considerable royalties to the government. Later in the year, Snepp submitted the text of a novel he had written to the CIA for prior censorship, under protest, promising to sue if changes were demanded. In fact, only one minor change was asked, which he agreed to make. In another case that much disturbed publishers and authors alike, Doubleday author Gwen Davis, who had been successfully sued for libel by Paul Bindrim on the grounds that she libeled him in a novel called *Touching*, was in turn sued by her publisher for the damages awarded against them. A number of authors protested, and later in the year Davis and Doubleday reached an out-of-court settlement on the matter. In an apparently related case, a New York State police official who claimed he was libeled in another novel, *.44*, lost his suit against the authors, suggesting that *Bindrim* was not about to be accepted widely as a precedent. A suit by seven publishers, coordinated by the Association of American Publishers, was launched against a major photocopying mill, Gnomon, and won a consent decree that declared that permission of copyright owners must be obtained to make multiple copies. There was a promise of further such suits in 1981.

THE PROBLEMS WITH PRIZES

1980 was also the year of TABA—the first and last year of TABA, in fact, because the organizers of the American Book Awards decided their acronym sounded too much like a soft drink, and resolved not use it any more. They held an elaborate audiovisual awards ceremony in May in New York, jointly hosted by William F. Buckley, Jr., and John Chancellor, and with a host of celebrity presenters—but never an author in sight to pick up a prize from among the bewildering range of category awards. The show achieved some TV exposure, but was generally agreed to have been overlong and insufficiently author-oriented. The awards, which currently get by without an acronym, are by no means dead, however—despite the opposition of some authors and publishers to the selection process and the tone—and under Esther Margolis, who left Bantam early in the year to form her own publishing house, will reappear (albeit in different form) in 1981. Meanwhile, the National Book Critics Circle decisively stepped into the breach as the book awards ceremony to beat.

SHRINKING HOUSES—AND LISTS

There were various moves during the year to consolidate and contract existing publishing operations. Harper & Row consolidated both its Lippincott and Crowell divisions into a new Harper trade division, with resulting staff cuts; Harcourt Brace Jovanovich cut its New York trade editorial staff; New York Times Company reorganized its book operations, including Times Books (and early in 1981 the latter cut its list, reduced staff, and vowed to concentrate more on *Times*-originated material); at Macmillan, chairman Raymond Hagel was forced out and a group of new executives, including Albert Litewka, formerly of Baker & Taylor, took over the book operations; and Werner Mark Linz moved from Seabury to form his own Crossroad Press, which was later absorbed into the Thomson organization; and the Atlantic Monthly Press was bought by a Boston realtor who shortly closed the company's New York office.

SALES FOR THE YEAR

And how was business? As always, publishing statistics tend to appear slowly and erratically; but at year's end the AAP's bulletin on domestic sales, compiled from reports by a representative but obviously not comprehensive 85 publishers, showed an upturn in dollar sales in all categories, ranging from a high of 35.7 percent for children's paperbacks to a low of 1.5 percent for el-hi texts and materials; adult hardcovers were up 17.5 percent, trade paperbacks 28 percent, and mass market paperbacks 8.2 percent. Unit sales were not reported, and the figures will reflect higher book prices to a considerable degree. It seemed clear, however, that in many areas book sales were staying ahead of inflation, in some cases very considerably ahead. Reports from booksellers canvassed by *PW* during the year tended to bear this out. Many agreed that last spring was the low point of the year, and a time of considerable anxiety, but that things picked up in the fall and for many the Christmas season was better than expected.

Note: For 1980 news from Washington, D.C., see "Legislation Affecting the Publishing Industry" in Part 2—*Ed.*

Special Reports

LIBRARY NETWORKING IN THE UNITED STATES, 1980

Henriette D. Avram
*Director for Processing Systems, Networks and Automation Planning,
Library of Congress*

An overview of library networking by necessity involves so many organizations and individuals, and touches on so many issues and divergent points of view, that there is no way to describe all activities succinctly but adequately. It is even more difficult to take stock of the state of affairs on an annual basis. Although many of the components of the library networking picture have been reported in previous volumes of the *Bowker Annual*, they are briefly discussed here in order to place these activities in context with others.

By 1980, library networking in the United States had left its infancy well behind and had advanced to a level of maturity where its impact on library organization, budgets, procedures, and services was recognized and accepted. It does not follow that all the issues have been resolved or that the implications of the emerging technology on present configurations and planned developments are fully comprehended. Much remains to be accomplished. Hopefully, the future can be approached in such a way that consensus can be achieved through coordination at all levels of development.

THE NETWORK ADVISORY COMMITTEE

The Network Advisory Committee (NAC)[1] had its beginning in April 1976 when senior representatives from major network organizations were invited to attend a meeting at the Library of Congress (LC) to discuss networking activities and to explore ways in which a more cohesive nationwide system might be developed. At that time, a proliferation of network and network-related organizations already existed with little attempt being made to coordinate activities. The participants concluded that the meeting was worthwhile and that the group should continue to meet. By the end of the first full year (April 1977) the committee had produced its planning paper, *Toward a National Library and Information Service Network: The Library Bibliographic Component.*[2] The primary recommendations of that report were acted on as follows: (1) work on specifications for an authority control system and for a bibliogrpahic data base configuration combined to become one project, known as the Nationwide Data Base Design Project. The Library of Congress (LC) Network Development Office assumed responsibility for the defined background tasks for this project, with funding provided by the National Commission on Libraries and Information Science (NCLIS); (2) investigation of governance issues was approached by a NAC subcommittee, which wrote a work statement to be incorporated in a request for proposal for a full study of these issues; (3) initial design work for the architecture of the network was performed by a task force of technical experts, the Network Technical Architecture Group.

In 1978, the Council on Library Resources (CLR) received funding for its Bibliographic Services Development Program (BSDP). This development created some confusion in subsequent NAC meetings as to the relationship of NAC and its activities to BSDP. In late 1979, a new statement of objectives was formulated by NAC, in which its role was defined as a forum that the major segments of the information community could use for identifying issues and making recommendations concerning nationwide networking. Other objectives included advising the Librarian of Congress on the role of LC in nationwide networking and providing input to CLR for its BSDP program.

In March 1980, NAC held its first forum meeting with the ownership and distribution of bibliographic data as the topic for discussion. The committee concluded that bibliographic information must be made widely available without discouraging the legitimate economic incentives of those providing the services. It also recommended that funding be found to support a study (1) to identify the creators, modifiers, and possessors of machine-readable bibliographic data, (2) to seek their endorsement of the meeting results, (3) to determine their plans to make data available and their requirements for compensation for their data, and, based on the above, (4) to establish a satisfactory mechanism for sharing bibliographic data.

In its forum meeting in October 1980, NAC tackled the problems of governance of a nationwide network. The governance issue was approached from three points of view: legislation, the private sector, and what will evolve over time. The committee decided that public meetings should be held at the midwinter and annual conferences of the American Library Association in 1981 to discuss the results of the forums on governance and ownership and distribution of bibliographic data.

The Network Advisory Committee has no enforcement power. Nevertheless, it is at present the only forum in which representatives from all segments of the information community discuss networking issues.[3]

THE BIBLIOGRAPHIC SERVICES DEVELOPMENT PROGRAM

The efforts of NAC and its various subordinate groups provided the basis for a program formulated by CLR and submitted to several major foundations in this country for funding. In 1978, funds in excess of $5 million were received from seven private foundations and the National Endowment for the Humanities in support of BSDP. The goals of the program are: "(1) To provide effective bibliographic services for all who need them, (2) To improve the nature and quality of bibliographic products, and (3) To stabilize the costs of many bibliographic processes in individual libraries."[4] A management committee to provide overall direction for program development and a program committee to define program plans and projects and to recommend courses of action were established.

Several major activities have been undertaken within BSDP to date:

1. Based on the assumption that it was cost beneficial and effective to link computer-based bibliographic systems via telecommunications, NAC's Technical Architecture Group had specified the general requirements for a communications facility[5] and had submitted a proposal to CLR to fund the development of detailed specifications. However, the BSDP Program Committee felt it desirable to conduct a study to evaluate the economic and service impact of various linking alternatives. The study focused on three library operations: interlibrary loan, shared cataloging of current monographs, and reference searching. The work, performed by Battelle Columbus Laboratories, is now completed[6] and recommends that LC, Ohio College Li-

brary Center, Inc. (OCLC), the Research Libraries Information Network (RLIN), and the Washington Library Network (WLN) develop on-line links using automatic translation of requests and responses. This recommendation supports the assumptions underlying the activities of the Network Technical Architecture Group. The report also recommends that two committees be formed to work on communications and applications standards, respectively.

    2. In September 1979, CLR sponsored a meeting of individuals who either had experience in or had given thought to the inclusion of an authority system in bibliographic processing. The participants agreed that a single consistent name authority file should be built with multi-institutional cooperation and made available to the nation's libraries. It was further agreed that the file should be built by a small group of large research libraries, that LC should manage the bibliographic aspects of the cooperative effort, and that RLIN, the facility chosen to house the data base, should manage the technical aspects. A task force was established to provide detailed requirements for such areas as data collection, file maintenance, on-line and off-line access, standards, financing, and management. This project has become known as the Name Authority File Service (NAFS). Concurrent with this effort, in March 1980, a grant was awarded to the Research Libraries Group (RLG)[7] and WLN to develop and redesign internal authority systems and to design and test the necessary systems modules to share authority data in an on-line mode. Travel funds were also provided for LC to participate in the project. The project has become known as the WLN/RLG/LC Linked Authority System Project (LASP). The procedures to be implemented for LASP are the same as those required for NAFS. The participation of RLG, WLN, and LC in the NAFS task force should guarantee the coordination of both of these efforts into one integrated system. LC's name authority file is considered the base file for LASP and NAFS.

    3. OCLC and RLG were funded to investigate public access to bibliographic data bases in an on-line mode. As part of this effort, a meeting was held with staff from organizations actively planning catalogs for public use.

    4. BSDP has undertaken a variety of activities in support of standards. A joint committee on bibliographic standards with representation from several organizations, including LC and the bibliographic utilities, was formed. The committee assists LC in the selection of cataloging options, interpretation of cataloging rules, and so forth. Position papers have been written by consultants on institution identification codes and detailed bibliographic holdings statements. These position papers will be submitted to the appropriate American National Standard Institute (ANSI) Z39 subcommittees. Funds administered by RLG will be used to assist in the work required to establish an application-level protocol. This work will also be submitted to the Z39 subcommittee responsible for that effort. A MARC format review committee was established to work with LC on its review of the MARC communications format.

THE LIBRARY OF CONGRESS

    LC's involvement in networking can be said to have begun with the MARC pilot project in 1965 and continued throughout the development and operation of its MARC Distribution Service. Its networking efforts became more formalized after the completion of the NCLIS program document[8] and the subsequent study funded by NCLIS to define the role of LC in this evolving network, conducted with contractual support by LC.[9] The results of the latter report, briefly summarized, stated that if LC continued and expanded its MARC services and made the data available both off-line and on-line, the requirements for machine-readable records for the community would be satisfied to a large extent. The report also recommended that LC assume the responsibility of a coordinating body in an attempt to bring the many disparate networking efforts together into a more cohesive whole.

LC responded to this latter recommendation by establishing the Network Development Office and calling the first meeting of NAC in 1976. In addition to its continuing supporting role as secretariat to NAC, the Network Development Office has been active in many network-related projects, nationally and internationally. These have included (1) standards activities, for example, protocol and character set development; (2) design activities, for example, network architecture design, data base design; and (3) the coordination of the various LC units involved and itself participating in the LASP and NAFS projects. Much of this activity has been documented as a series of planning papers.[10]

To further support nationwide networking, LC's Processing Services has instituted several projects to test the concept of cooperative cataloging by centers of responsibility. To date, the concentration has been on name authorities. In most cases, the participating organization searches various tools (e.g., the LC name authority file in the OCLC data base, the *National Union Catalog*, the *National Union Catalog: Pre 1956 Imprints*, and *Name Headings with References*) to obtain an LC heading. If the heading is not found, it is established by the participating organization and submitted to LC to be verified against the LC files and modified as required. The record for the heading is then communicated to the organization, added to the LC files, and distributed via the MARC distribution services.

The Government Printing Office and Northwestern University, for its African material, are participants in the name authority cooperative project and, in addition, send their bibliographic records to LC for distribution through the MARC service.

Working toward the cooperative building of a consistent nationwide data base, Processing Services has also defined a national level MARC record for the various forms of materials and for authorities. The aim is to seek agreement on the mandatory and optional data elements to be included in a record when it is to be contributed to a nationwide data base.

To date, the LC system is available on-line for searching to only a few libraries in the United States, as part of research studies such as the Northwestern Africana Project, the Government Printing Office project, and the RLG/LC computer-to-computer linking project. LC continues to study various alternatives to present to Congress in order to obtain approval for participation in the nationwide library network in an on-line mode. This must be accomplished in a way that will not impact LC's own requirements and its service to Congress.

OPERATIONAL NETWORK ORGANIZATIONS

The operational network structure in the United States, which evolved over the past decade, is principally made up of two types of organizations—bibliographic utilities and service centers. The bibliographic utilities house computer-based files and provide products and services from this data. The service centers broker the services of the utilities to their member libraries, normally operating within a state or multistate region. (An exception to this is FEDLINK, which is a service center to federal libraries in all fifty states and the U.S. territories.) Currently, responding to the needs of their members for additional services of a more local nature, for example, circulation or regional union catalogs, and to the desire to link regional systems to other regional or national systems, several service centers are at different stages in the planning and/or development of their own automated systems.

It appears that there has been a "settling down" in the growth of the number of utilities, OCLC, RLIN, and WLN having been the only ones on the U.S. scene for some time. The University of Toronto Library Automation System (UTLAS) is a viable fourth, but has not been considered in this paper because it is home-based in Canada, although it has a charter to conduct business in the United States.

The products and services offered by the utilities are in some cases the same, for example, computer-produced catalog cards, and search services, and in other cases different, for example, not all utilities have a subject searching capability, produce book-form or microform catalogs, or perform serial check-in. Each utility includes LC MARC bibliographic records in its data base, although not all include records for all forms of material. OCLC is the only utility to date that offers its users access to the LC MARC name authority file, although WLN includes an authority system that contains many LC authority files. The LC subject headings have been keyed for use on the WLN system. At the present time, none of the utilities has the capability to share resources with any other utility, although some current activity in this direction is described in the BSDP section of this paper.

OCLC, with the largest customer base, is a nationwide network serving all sizes and types of libraries. RLIN is also nationwide in scope, with its main interest in research libraries. WLN, on the other hand, has confined its growth to libraries of any size or type within the northwest region.

Although OCLC has more serious competition from the other utilities, it is still the major system in terms of number of members and economic stability. Its financial position has permitted the expending of resources for a new facility, enhancement of existing software, implementation of new services, and a significant research and development program. This program operates an experimental Videotex system, which interfaces a home television screen through a telephone to such data bases as the catalog of a county library, an encyclopedia, and local community information. OCLC also makes a general information program, The Source,[11] available to libraries. In the past year, OCLC has accelerated its marketing effort internationally, with concentration principally in Western Europe. It is interested in mounting the MARC files of various national bibliographic agencies, for example, UK MARC from the British Library, in addition to having organizations in other countries input directly into the OCLC system. Cataloging data from other countries, with location of the material in some cases, would then be available to OCLC members.

WLN and RLIN continue to concentrate on building systems with procedures to control the quality and content of the records in order to provide a consistent on-line catalog. Both organizations are involved with the implementation of an authority control system and are part of the CLR authority projects to build an integrated authority file to be made available to the nation's libraries.

An interesting development on the networking scene this past year has been the possibility of SOLINET and OCLC's establishing a mutual support corporation (MSC). SOLINET started out in 1973 with the intent of replicating OCLC. It was decided that this was not feasible at that time and therefore SOLINET has acted as a service center broker of OCLC services to its membership. However, the intent to operate an automated system for its members remained. This past year, SOLINET purchased its own hardware and the WLN software system with the intent to develop the SOLINET Regional Support System (RSS), an on-line union catalog with automated authority control, and the capability to provide on-line catalogs, subject access, and so forth. A cooperative effort with OCLC appeared to be the most effective means of operation. This would permit SOLINET to expand on the OCLC services rather than having to implement services already available from OCLC as well as new ones. SOLINET and OCLC are attempting to establish MSC as a legal entity with its own board of directors, but no staff. The board of directors would make policy to be carried out through contracts with OCLC and SOLINET. SOLINET and OCLC would both contribute assets to MSC. The effect should foster cooperation and reduce or remove competition. It is possible that other regional networks could form similar mutual support corporations with a bibliographic utility or such corporations could be developed among or between the bibliographic utilities themselves. As network configurations continue to evolve, it seems that it would be cost-effective for the various regional systems to coordinate activities and thus share in the cost of development of regional automated systems.

Today, it is still the case that the members of one bibliographic utility do not have access to the data, the products, or the services of any other utility, unless they have the resources to join more than one utility. The technology is in place to link the computer-based services and thus expand the data, products, and services available. There is little question that access to an enlarged data base would decrease costly duplication in cataloging, expand interlibrary loan availability, and in general increase resource sharing of materials, products, and services. There are certain technical problems still requiring resolution such as the development of application-level protocol and the capability to handle the queries and responses across systems. These, however, are not the major impediments to a distributed network by linking through a telecommunications facility. The difficult issues are legal, economic, and governing. These need to be resolved before such a linked system can become a reality.

NOTES

1. The name of the Network Advisory Committee was changed from the Network Advisory Group in mid-1977 when the Librarian of Congress established the committee to advise the library on matters relating to networking.
2. Network Advisory Group, *Toward a National Library and Information Service Network: The Library Bibliographic Component*, prelim. ed. (Washington, D.C.: Library of Congress, June 1977).
3. For a more complete account of the activities of the Network Advisory Committee see Lenore S. Maruyama, *Nationwide Networking and the Network Advisory Committee*. Forthcoming.
4. C. Lee Jones, "Bibliographic Service Development Program," in *National Planning for Bibliographic Control: Minutes of the Ninety-fourth Meeting, May 10–11, 1979, Cambridge, Massachusetts* (Washington, D.C.: Association of Research Libraries, 1979), p. 4.
5. Network Technical Architecture Group, *Message Delivery System for the National Library and Information Service Network: General Requirements*, Network Planning Paper, no. 4 (Washington, D.C.: Library of Congress, 1978), p. 57.
6. *Linking the Bibliographic Utilities: Benefits and Costs*. (Columbus, Ohio: Battelle Columbus Laboratories, September 15, 1980), p. 169 and appendices.
7. The Research Libraries Group is a consortium of research libraries that owns the Research Libraries Information Network and uses it as a computer-based facility.
8. *Toward a National Program for Library and Information Services: Goals for Action*. (Washington, D.C.: National Commission on Libraries and Information Science, 1975), p. 106.
9. Lawrence F. Buckland, *The Role of the Library of Congress in the Evolving National Network: A Study Commissioned by the Library of Congress Network Development Office and Funded by the National Commission on Libraries and Information Science* (Washington, D.C.: Library of Congress, 1978), p. 141. For sale by Superintendent of Documents, U.S. Government Printing Office.
10. Network Planning Papers, nos. 1–6. (Washington, D.C.: Library of Congress), 1978–1980.
11. The Source is an information system of the Source Telecomputing Corporation providing current news items, stock market information, electronic mail, and access to various information banks.

THE DECISION INFORMATION DISPLAY SYSTEM (DIDS)

Office of Federal Statistical Policy and Standards
Office of Management and Budget, Executive Office of the President

Curtis L. Fritz
Program Manager

The Decision Information Display System (DIDS) is a cooperative interagency program for the application of information technology in the federal statistical community. The program management structure includes a steering committee comprised of representatives of the 26 participating agencies, who also fund the program, and a full-time program management staff in the Office of Federal Statistical Policy and Standards (OFSPS), formerly in the Department of Commerce but reassigned as of April 1, 1981, to the Office of Management and Budget in the Executive Office of the President. The program has two major goals: (1) to improve issues analysis, policy formulation, decision making, and program management, primarily at the national level; and (2) to improve the effectiveness of access to federal statistics by all sectors.

Approximately $750,000,000 is spent each year by federal agencies in collecting and processing economic, social, and demographic statistics. In the past, difficulty of data access and nonstandardization among agencies have severely limited use of this rich data resource. However, recently developed computerized information technology has made possible the development of the Decision Information Display System, which, utilizing four particular technologies (interactive color graphics, spatial display, data integration and management, and data telecommunications), represents new dimensions in statistics utilization at a reasonable cost.

DIDS is an attempt to adapt and apply modern technology from the physical sciences to the social sciences operating environment. Specifically, it attempts to facilitate analysis of statistical data relevant to persistent national policy issues such as inflation, unemployment, foreign trade, energy usage, and taxation. One of the significant features of this system is the ability to rapidly and graphically cross-correlate data from various source agencies. It thereby has the potential to greatly facilitate access to federal statistics and serve as a stimulus and a vehicle for standardization efforts among statistical agencies for subnational data.

HISTORY OF THE PROGRAM

Under a White House initiative and through the joint efforts of NASA and the Census Bureau, a pilot system was demonstrated in June 1978 at the White House and at the Capitol building that displayed socioeconomic and demographic data by a computer-driven color graphics interactive terminal. Reaction to the demonstration (including that of the president) was positive, and the decision was made to mount a one-year demonstration project, jointly funded and participated in by 15 federal agencies.

During that first one-year period of demonstration and experimentation, the system was enchanced with the addition of data from several agencies, and with the development of additional data manipulation and display features. The system has been demonstrated to dozens of agencies and hundreds of people—to both federal and local government, and to private industry. Both the executive and legislative branches of the federal government participate in and have access to the system. Different users have tested for correlations between pollution factors and death rates from various causes; depicted geographic distribution of federal funds; seen regional differences in infant mortality rates, purchase of imported cars, women in the work force, hospital beds per capita, Vietnam veterans' residence preference, population growth or loss rates, property tax rates, value of exports, unemployment rates, ethnic distribution, fresh water usage rates, and so forth.

The second year of the interagency program has seen the development of a fulltime host operating system with a special graphics terminal and an economical "smart" terminal system for remote access. In June 1979, a downtown terminal was installed at the Department of Commerce headquarters building to provide more ready access to the system. This, in turn, was replaced by a common-access pilot Remote Terminal System (RTS), which is designed to serve as a node in a system network of agencies and is also the precursor for a stand-along system in nonfederal sectors.

Thus, the goal of an operational capability and practicable multiple remote access is at hand. In addition, the definitive demonstration projects at other levels of government attest to the success of the outreach efforts.

SYSTEM COMPONENTS

The physical system is comprised of hardware, software, and data files.

The host computer is a DEC VAX 11/780 minicomputer with .5 megabytes of core and three RP06 large disc drives of 176 megabytes each. Rack-mounted with the VAX is a special graphics terminal device driver developed by DeAnza Corporation to DIDS specifications. Hard-wired to the host system is a black-and-white CRT alphanumeric terminal (VT 100), a 19-inch high-resolution (512 x 512) color television monitor (Conrac), and an image camera (Dunn). Also available at the host system is a Xerox 6500 color copier and several A/N terminals for on-line development.

The Remote Terminal System (RTS) consists of a DEC LSI 11/23 minicomputer with 128 K words, three RL01 disc drives of 5.2 megabytes each, the rack-mounted DeAnza terminal device driver, a hard-wired Conrac high-resolution monitor, and a VT 100. Also hard-wired to the RTS is a large-screen (ADVENT) projection system in a remote conference room. This common-access RTS is connected to the host system by a dedicated 9600 baud data link. A second RTS is temporarily installed at a state capital site as a demonstration project.

The software for the host system and RTS consists of modules for creating both statistical and cartographic data files, search menu creation and display, file retrieval and display, file computation and segmentation, image manipulation, communications, and utilities. Most (80–90 percent) of the applications software is written in Fortran-IV with the remainder in machine code.

The data files in the demonstration data base consist of approximately 5,000 statistical data elements from 20 different federal statistical source agencies. Subjects include census of population, census of housing, county business patterns, veterans demographics and benefits, water resources, federal funding, air and water quality, energy consumption, health resources, motor vehicles, finances, coal production, mortality rates, and others.

The cartographic data bases consist of digitized boundary files for the U.S. states, counties, congressional districts, and standard metropolitan statistical area census tracts, and worldwide country boundries.

HOW THE SYSTEM WORKS

Because a program objective of the system was to provide users with a direct analytical tool, a design criterion was that the system be user-friendly. This was accomplished by adopting a menu-driven rather than a procedural approach. This means the user need not learn a new "language" nor indeed know much of anything about computers or computer programming. In this mode, the user is presented with a list of numbered options in plain English on a screen. The user selects an option by entering the corresponding one- or two-digit number on the keyboard. A successive set of options on a "sub menu" list automatically appears on the screen. This interactive procedure continues until the final selection is made and the resulting graphic presentation of data is flashed on the color television monitor.

A typical user session follows the following sequence of menu presentation and user selection after logging onto the system.

Geography

The user selects the geographic base he/she wants to address. The choices are: The United States by counties, by states, or by congressional districts; an individual state by county; an individual metropolitan area; or the world by countries.

Function

The user selects the system function that is desired (e.g., display a single variable; bivariate display; or variable computation).

Data Selection

Source Agency: The user selects from a list of agencies that have entered data in the system (e.g., HUD, HHS, Census, VA, Geological Survey).

File: The user selects from the list of files that have been loaded on the system from the selected agency (e.g., federal grants or sectoral engery usage).

Subfile: The user selects a subfile within the main file that had been selected (e.g., education grants).

Data Element: The user selects the specific data element for display (e.g., total dollar grants, number of grants, number of recipients, 1978, or 1979).

Display

After selection of the specific data element, the data for the selected geography are displayed on the color monitor in choropleth map form. The geographic entities (e.g., counties or census tracts) are categorized by color into five classes based on approximate equal-occurrence frequency distribution. (The whole process takes less than one minute). The user can then call for a photographic hard copy (two minutes) or color film exposure (ten seconds) of the image shown on the color monitor.

IMAGE MANIPULATION

Once an image has been displayed, the user can call up, on the alphanumeric screen, a list of options for analytical manipulation of the image. These options include:

Data class changes
    from two to nine classes (univariate)
    from 2×2 to 5×5 classes (bivariate)
    equal occurrence frequency distribution
    equal value range between classes
    nested means
    standard deviation from national means

uniform percentage distribution
favorable/unfavorable frequency distribution
user-set class boundaries

Color selection by user from 64-color palette for any or all data classes

Zoom on any area in three steps, 2×, 4×, 8×

Highlight geographic areas falling in any one or successive data classes

OTHER CAPABILITIES

System capabilities and features are developed in response to user suggestions and requests on line. Presently, the user can exercise the following features:

Compute and display a new variable file by arithmetic operation on two variables from any or different agencies. For example, derive the per capita allocation of federal funds for each of the 3,041 counties, or determine the percentage gain or loss in unemployment rate by county between May and June.

Composite index-variable construction, equal or weighted, for any number of variables in the interagency data base.

Bivariate display of any two variables for the same geographic base. For example, education levels achieved versus income levels; or ischemic heart disease mortality rates versus water hardness.

Display bivariate scatterplot with user-variable scale ranges.

Identify geographic unit and retrieve basic data about that unit.

List geographic entities falling within any specified range of the data variable.

Time series image loop with user-controlled image change speed.

FUTURE PLANS

The number of participating agencies continues to grow, and it is expected that other agencies will join the program. The ongoing objectives of the program are:

To develop an *operational data base* that contains the federal data series that are of priority interest to the participating agencies for national policy formulation and program management. Also, to provide on-line documentation for each data element as to its source, method of collection, confidence factors, definitions, etc.

Increased operational utilization by the participating agencies.

Development of a network of agencies for data interchange.

To extend program participation to additional federal agencies in both the executive and legislative branches, and to other sectors on a demonstration project basis—especially to state, city, and local government levels.

Increased system capabilities in all categories: cartographic bases, nonmap graphic displays, statistical analysis, alternate configurations (lower performance and cost), alternative hard copy output, additional data, etc.

It is hoped that the program will move beyond demonstration of potential and the initial operation capabilities and benefits to actual employment of the system in the decision-making and management processes. Priority will also be given to establishing appropriate roles for all sectors. Toward this end, the possibility will be explored of establishing a facility operated by private industry that would provide DIDS services to all sectors on a self-supporting basis.

PRESIDENT CARTER'S MESSAGE TO CONGRESS ON LIBRARIES

Following is the press release issued by the Office of the White House Press Secretary on September 26, 1980, containing the complete text of the statement President Jimmy Carter sent to the Congress of the United States with the report of the White House Conference on Libraries and Information Services.

TO THE CONGRESS OF THE UNITED STATES:

I am pleased to transmit to you the Report of the White House Conference on Libraries and Information Services and my own recommendations on public access to information, as required by Sec. 1(d) of Public Law 93-568 of December 31, 1974.

Information is the essence of education and the lifeblood of democracy. People need accurate information to make the personal and political decisions that will shape the country's future. The production and distribution of information is a significant factor in our economy. A technological explosion is reshaping the way information is stored and communicated, while rising costs and limited resources strain the public institutions that make information accessible.

The White House Conference considered all these issues. It examined our information needs and problems and the key role of libraries in meeting them. The delegates included librarians, information specialists and community leaders. They were selected at conferences in every state and territory, through a process that involved 100,000 people. I wish to commend the National Conference on Libraries and Information Services for their key role in making the Conference a success. The Conference theme was "Bringing Information to the People." Its recommendations will help us frame an information policy for the 1980's.

The Importance of Libraries

Since the beginning of our Nation, libraries have played an important role in providing citizens with the information they need to guide our destiny. Our First Amendment rights have been strengthened by the independent status of libraries free from government control. By preserving the records of our history and culture, libraries serve as a door into our past. As a source of the information we need to direct our lives, they also serve as a door into our future. As we plan for the information requirements of the 1980's and beyond, we should acknowledge the contributions that libraries have made and ensure they remain vital.

Most libraries are local institutions, under local control. State and local governments bear the responsibility for supporting and operating public and school libraries. I agree with the White House Conference that this principle must be maintained.

At the same time, the Federal Government has assumed a special role of helping libraries provide access to information for all. The Government also provides leadership in developing new technologies and services, and encouraging resource sharing among all types of libraries. This Federal role complements the basic responsibilities of state and local governments. My Administration has worked with Congress to fulfill that role.

To ensure that library programs get the attention they deserve, we created an Office of Libraries and Learning Technologies in the new Department of Education, headed by a Deputy Assistant Secretary.

Overall Federal support for libraries has increased by almost 30% since the beginning of my Administration. We proposed improvements in the Higher Education Act to strengthen support for library research and demonstration and training programs and for college and research libraries. We supported literacy and school library and media programs through our 1978 amendments to the Elementary and Secondary Education Act.

My 1982 budget request to Congress will reflect our response to the Conference recommendations for increased budgetary support for resource sharing among libraries; research and development in information technologies; and research libraries.

The Conference recommended a new National Library and Information Services Act to redefine the Federal role. I will submit new legislation to replace the Library Services and Construction Act which will expire in 1982. This legislation will include such issues as:

Barriers to information access for the handicapped and disadvantaged;

Library networking and resource sharing;

The role of large urban libraries and research libraries as centers for library resource networks; and

New information technologies.

I urge the Congress, the library community, and the public to join in the discussion during the next year on the priorities among these important concerns.

Government Information

The Federal Government has a special responsibility to ensure that its information is made available to the people. Open government is vital to democracy. We must also recognize the constraints of national security, privacy, efficient decision making, and costs.

We are working to address these concerns in a way that increases access to information. A new office has been established in the Office of Management and Budget to develop Federal information policy. This office is working closely with the agencies, libraries, and private sector to develop a policy on the management and dissemination of information by Federal agencies. This policy will affirm the key role of the Federal depository libraries as centers where citizens can obtain free access to government publications.

The policy will also stress the special role libraries can play in helping Federal agencies disseminate information that people need. We should not create new delivery systems when libraries, with strong community bases, can do the job. The Denver Public Library is one example of a library that is working closely with several agencies to make consumer and environmental information available. I encourage and support cooperation like this. To foster such partnership, I have directed the Administrator of the General Services Administration to work with the library community and the Department of Education to select three to five Federal Information Centers and locate them together with libraries. If this cooperative effort is as successful as I expect, I will expand the program.

My Administration has also taken a number of other initiatives to improve and enhance public access to government information. For example:

We revamped the security classification system to eliminate needless initial classification and reduce the time that documents remain classified while strengthening protection for necessary secrets. About 250 million pages of documents will be released because of this change.

The Freedom of Information Act is being administered fairly. The Department of Justice has instructed agencies to release information that could legally be withheld if the release could not be clearly harmful.

Our policy on industrial innovation calls for an improvement in the dissemination of patent information, which will make over 4 million patents accessible.

The National Technical Information Service has expanded the indexing and dissemination systems available to scientists and engineers.

Increases were requested for the National Commission on Libraries and Information Sciences, an agency which has a vital leadership and coordination role in library and information science at the national level.

The Needs of the Disadvantaged

The Conference report serves as a reminder that too many of our citizens are cut off from the information available to most of us. One of the greatest barriers is functional illiteracy. To overcome this problem, I have directed the Department of Education to take the lead in coordinating Federal efforts to eliminate functional illiteracy. Their task will be to identify methods and programs of demonstrated value and to work with local education agencies, libraries, and voluntary organizations to implement these programs. Twenty percent of our Americans are functionally illiterate, and we must expand our commitment to helping these people obtain the basic skills they need.

Under my Administration, a new Basic Skills Improvement Program was authorized in 1979. Its overall objective is to bring about national improvement in student achievement in the fundamentals of education—reading, writing, speaking and mathematics.

We are working to assist disabled Americans. At my request, the broadcasting networks helped establish a pilot closed-captioning television system to permit the hearing-impaired to share the educational and entertainment shows available to everyone. In addition, the Library of Congress and the Department of Education are working to provide special materials, equipment and services for those with physical handicaps and learning disabilities.

Another frequently overlooked barrier to information is geography. Many Americans are denied access to information because of where they live, such as an Indian reservation, a Pacific Island, or an isolated area. To address these problems and those of other persons isolated from information due to their location, I am directing the Department of the Interior to analyze these issues and provide recommendations to me.

I will soon send to the Senate a protocol to the Florence Agreement of 1952 further liberalizing the exchange of books and information and reducing barriers to international understanding. The National Commission on Libraries and Information Sciences has already begun working with the International Federation of Library Associations.

The New Information and Communications Technologies

New technologies are revolutionizing the ways in which we create, store and disseminate information. For example, the text of 3,200 books can now be stored on a 12-inch videodisc which costs $20. In the library computers are replacing the card catalog. The sum of changes like these will have a major impact on our lives.

My Administration is actively encouraging the creative application of these technologies for the benefit of all individuals. As the largest user of computer technology in the world, the Federal government plays a major role in deciding how this technology is applied everywhere. We are using technology to provide government services, including information, in new and better ways. A number of agencies are actively involved in conducting or supporting research and development into new technologies and their application. We shall aggressively pursue such research. We also have a program to develop standards which will enhance our ability to transfer technology.

We have worked to remove regulations that prevent competition and constrain application of the new technologies. The Federal Communications Commission is completing a dramatic overhaul of its regulations, opening up competition and promoting diversity. Recent actions are creating 1000 new radio stations and a whole new class of community TV stations. We developed a program which has doubled minority ownership of broadcast stations. We are working with Congress to pass legislation to reduce regulation and promote competition in telecommunications. The explosion of outlets in the electronic media provides special opportunities for libraries. For example, libraries can work with cable TV systems to program public service channels. Competition will stimulate innovation, increase productivity, and make the communications industries more responsive to consumer demands.

Actions we have taken to realize the public dividend from the new technologies include:

My space policy, which is helping public service producers use satellites to cut their communication costs. The Commerce Department is responsible for this program, and I am directing them to work with the library community to make satellite and other emerging communication technologies available where it is cost-effective for networking and other purposes.

The Department of Education will support a conference of independent experts to develop an agenda for library research in the 1980's.

The library and information science communities will be encouraged to propose technology assessment studies for consideration by Federal agencies.

As our society expands use of the new information technologies, we must protect our personal privacy. Last year I proposed the Nation's first comprehensive privacy policy. Five privacy bills are now before Congress, covering medical, bank, insurance and other types of records. Their passage is an essential ingredient to an information policy of the 1980's.

The biggest challenges rest with the library and information community. These institutions are run by talented and dedicated people with strong bases in their communities. They have contributed much, and they can do even more to meet people's needs in coping with the problems we face in the 80's. I believe we have viewed libraries too narrowly. The needs of the public who must cope with our increasingly complex society can only be met by libraries actively providing access to the great variety of information they have. Libraries can provide information to individuals about jobs and education opportunities; information to families about social services and energy; and consumer information to small business on marketing and technological innovation. Americans must be able to obtain this information in convenient, accessible, community institutions like the library. To survive as community institutions, libraries must be strengthened and the public made more aware of their potential.

We expect that the libraries will help to teach people the value of energy conservation and the ways to accomplish it; help the American people protect themselves from inflation by informed purchasing; help them to see that we live in an interrelated world which requires both America's strength but also American patience and American understanding; and, help them most of all to learn that we have to look at the world as it is and not as we remembered it 25 years ago. I have every confidence that you will meet these challenges as you have others in the past. Libraries will continue to be a critical ingredient in building a stronger, a more vibrant, a more informed America that we all hope for.

JIMMY CARTER

THE WHITE HOUSE,
September 26, 1980.

Federal Agencies

FEDERAL INFORMATION CENTERS PROGRAM

Office of Consumer Affairs, Office of External Affairs,
General Services Administration, Washington, DC 20405

Donald R. Knenlein
Coordinator, Federal Information Centers Program

Federal Information Centers (FICs) are a focal point in the community for information about the federal government. Centers assist people who have questions about federal services, programs, and regulations but do not know where to turn for an answer. FIC information specialists either answer an inquirer's questions directly or perform the necessary research to locate, and put the inquirer in touch with, the expert best able to help.

However, the program is not intended to discourage the public from directly approaching a federal agency or department. FICs operate as a part of a much larger and diversified network of information programs devoted to providing information to the public on services available to them. While all centers develop a capacity to respond to a significant volume of inquiries related to state, local, and private services available in the community, FICs have a particular advantage and responsibility in providing detailed information on federal activities. Currently there are 41 FICs with an additional 43 cities connected to the nearest center by toll-free telephone tieline. Five states offer statewide toll-free service. The first pilot FIC opened in Atlanta in July 1966. The purpose of the experiment was to test the feasibility of providing the public with easy access to federal information and assistance through an efficient data and referral source that would work in conjunction with other major federal information services. In October 1969, President Richard M. Nixon directed that the pilot project be expanded to other major metropolitan areas and that the cost of the project be shared by all benefiting agencies. Consequently, the number of centers increased to the present 41, with operating costs being shared equally by 17 executive departments and agencies.

Simultaneously, in an effort to test another method of expanding this service to more of the population, toll-free telephone tielines were made available in 43 highly populated areas in close proximity to FIC cities. Together, the centers and the tielines provide service to approximately half of the U.S. population on a toll-free basis. In 1972, an experimental federal-state-local government Information Center opened in San Diego, California. The San Diego Center has been testing procedures for centralizing research and referral services for all levels of government in one jointly funded facility.

Shortly after taking office, President Jimmy Carter directed the Office of Management and Budget (OMB) to study the effectiveness of the FIC program. The study team presented its findings to the president in March 1977. The OMB report praised the high degree of responsiveness to the substantial volume and wide diversity of questions received by the FICs. The team perceived the FIC information specialists as highly competent in dealing with the public, generally knowledgeable about government programs and services, and resourceful in seeking answers to complex questions and problems.

The OMB study suggested several enhancements to the FIC program. The three major recommendations were (1) to obtain legislative authority to elevate the FICs from pilot to full program status, (2) to establish at least one FIC in each of the 22 states currently without a center, and (3) to expand toll-free service so that all U.S. residents may contact an FIC on a local-call basis.

The first recommendation was carried out in October 1978, when Carter signed PL 95–491, the Federal Information Centers Act. The act authorizes and directs the administrator of General Services to establish within the General Services Administration (GSA) a nationwide network of FICs based on the currently operating centers, to respond to requests from the public about the rules, programs, and benefits of the federal government. The bill also authorizes GSA to receive direct appropriation from Congress to fund the program, instead of distributing the cost among the benefiting agencies.

In 1980, several steps were taken toward meeting the second and third OMB study recommendations. Three new FICs were opened and the Florida, Iowa, Kansas, Nebraska, and Missouri Centers began to offer toll-free 800 telephone service to state residents. As funds become available, it is planned to extend FIC service to more of the U.S. population.

OPERATIONS

FIC operational guidelines are outlined in the GSA *Handbook,* Federal Information Center (FIC) Operations, OEA P 1035. Reference copies of this handbook are available in all FICs and in Government Depository Libraries. Within GSA, the FIC coordinator's office is a division of the Office of Consumer Affairs, located in the Office of the Assistant Administrator for External Affairs. In the GSA regions, the FICs are located in the Office of the Assistant Regional Administrator for External Affairs. The FIC manager is responsible for the day-to-day operation of the center and is supervised by the assistant regional administrator for external affairs. Policy direction and management oversight are provided by the FIC coordinator's office in Washington, D.C.

FICs are located near the main public areas of federal buildings, offering high visibility and easy access for the public. The hours of operation are generally the same as those of the major federal agencies in the area. Nationwide, the program has 195 staff members. Staffing size varies center to center, but the average full-time staff complement is four. FICs in cities that have significant bilingual population usually have staff members who speak the appropriate language. FICs also maintain a list of local interpreters who can assist in serving foreign-speaking inquirers. Seventy percent of the approximately $4.75 million budget for FY 1981 covers salaries and associated personnel costs. Another 10 percent covers communications costs, with the remainder slated for resource and reference materials, supplies, training, and travel.

The number of inquiries received by the centers has increased as the number of centers and tieline cities has grown. During FY 1980, the FICs answered over 7,600,000 inquiries. Seventy-seven percent of these inquiries were by telephone, with the remainder from visitors to the centers. Letter inquiries accounted for less than 1 percent of the total inquiry volume. Currently the centers receive about 30,000 inquiries per working day.

The range of inquiry by subject matter is broad and diverse. About 10 percent of the questions pertain to state and local governments or private organizations. Questions relate to all of the more than 120 agencies of the executive branch as well as the judicial and legislative branches of the federal government. To answer inquiries, FIC staff members must have extensive knowledge and comprehension of the functions, activities, organization, interrelationships, and overlapping jurisdictions of agencies and levels of government. They also must be able to investigate, interpret, and analyze current events, legislation, and government regulations to anticipate and respond to the information needs of the public.

Both the coordinator's office and the FIC managers publicize the services provided by the centers. The coordinator's office develops an annual, multimedia national public service campaign consisting of public service announcements for airing on radio and television stations in FIC and tieline cities. Articles describing the FIC program are placed in national publications. In addition, the FIC brochure, available in both English and Spanish, is widely distributed. Copies may be requested from any FIC or by writing the Consumer Information Center, Pueblo, Colorado 81009.

The FIC data base is entirely manually maintained and consists of a wide variety of resource and reference materials. The cornerstone of this data base is a functional index of the programs and areas of responsibility of all federal, state, and local government and private agencies. The functional subjects are listed alphabetically by key words, followed by reference to the name, address, and telephone number of the local, regional, and/or national office that has the greatest knowledge about the subject. The functional index is comprehensive enough to serve as a direct referral source in some cases, but more frequently serves as a search aid for investigating lengthier, more complex inquiries.

In addition to the functional index, the FIC uses reference publications to meet the information needs of the community. The coordinator's office supplies each center with national reference materials, brochures, fact sheets, and news releases. Each FIC obtains useful state and local government and appropriate community and private publications. FICs subscribe to at least one major newspaper and extract information useful in anticipating and answering questions. All information, regardless of the source, is verified before it is given to an inquirer.

Both the FIC managers and the coordinator's staff meet with government and private organizations that share the responsibility for providing information, advice, and assistance to the public. Through personal visits and telephone contacts, they obtain information about new resources, programs, or changes in agency organization, policy, or procedures, and they encourage other organizations to contact the FICs when new information is received. FIC managers visit tieline cities twice a year to meet with government and private groups to update the information resources for those cities.

SPECIAL PROJECTS

In addition to responding to inquiries from the public, the FIC program has been involved in numerous projects to improve service to the public. In a cooperative effort to increase the usefulness of commercial telephone directories, the FICs worked with American Telephone and Telegraph Company (AT&T) to develop a "blue pages" supplement to the telephone directories in Little Rock, Chicago, Boston, Providence, and Sacramento. Government telephone numbers are listed in the blue pages by subject as well as by organization name. Blue pages have been so well received by the public that AT&T plans to include blue pages in more city directories. FICs will continue to cooperate with local telephone companies on the development of future blue pages.

Dial-a-Reg is a project being tested in Chicago and Los Angeles in conjunction with the Office of the Federal Register. This is a daily recorded announcement in the test FICs that highlights and summarizes the most important items in that day's *Federal Register*. Daily *Federal Register*s and the Code of Federal Regulations are available to the public for their use, and complex inquiries on actions mentioned in that day's announcement can be handled by the information specialists in the Chicago and Los Angeles areas.

The FIC program is exploring the potential use of teletypewriter (TTY) or computer-assisted communications for all FICs. A TTY is currently operating in the San Francisco center for hearing-impaired residents of the Bay Area. The results of this test will help to decide the best method to expand services to the hearing-impaired.

FEDERAL INFORMATION CENTERS

For more information about the FIC program, please telephone, visit or write the center nearest you:

Alabama
Birmingham
322–8591 (toll-free tieline to Atlanta, GA)
Mobile
438–1421 (toll-free tieline to New Orleans, LA)

Alaska
Anchorage
907–271–3650
Federal Bldg. and U.S. Courthouse, 701 C St., *Anchorage* 99513

Arizona
Phoenix
602–261–3313
Federal Bldg., 230 N. First Ave., *Phoenix* 85025
Tucson
622–1511 (toll-free tieline to Phoenix)

Arkansas
Little Rock
378–6177 (toll-free tieline to Memphis, TN)

California
Los Angeles
213–688–3800
Federal Bldg., 300 N. Los Angeles St., *Los Angeles* 90012
Sacramento
916–440–3344
Federal Bldg. and U.S. Courthouse, 650 Capitol Mall, *Sacramento* 95814
San Diego
714–293–6030
Federal Bldg., 880 Front St., Rm. 1S11, *San Diego* 92188

San Francisco
415–556–6600
Federal Bldg. and U.S. Courthouse, Box 36082, 450 Golden Gate Ave., *San Francisco* 94102
San Jose
275-7422 (toll-free tieline to San Francisco)
Santa Ana
836–2386 (toll-free tieline to Los Angeles)

Colorado
Colorado Springs
471–9491 (toll-free tieline to Denver)
Denver
303–837–3602
Federal Bldg., 1961 Stout St., *Denver* 80294
Pueblo
544–9523 (toll-free tieline to Denver)

Connecticut
Hartford
527–2617 (toll-free tieline to New York, NY)
New Haven
624–4720 (toll-free tieline to New York, NY)

District of Columbia
Washington
202–755–8660
Seventh and D Sts. S.W., Rm. 5716, *Washington, D.C.* 20407

Florida
Fort Lauderdale
522–8531 (toll-free tieline to Miami)

Jacksonville
354–4756 (toll-free tieline to St. Petersburg)
Miami
305–350–4155
Federal Bldg., 51 S.W. First Ave., *Miami* 33130
Orlando
422–1800 (toll-free tieline to St. Petersburg)
St. Petersburg
813–893–3495
William C. Cramer Federal Bldg., 144 First Ave. S., *St. Petersburg* 33701
Tampa
229–7911 (toll-free tieline to St. Petersburg)
West Palm Beach
833–7566 (toll-free tieline to Miami)

Florida, North
Sarasota, Manatee, Polk, Osceola, Orange, Seminole, and Volusia counties and north
800–282–8556 (toll-free tieline to St. Petersburg)

Florida, South
Charlotte, DeSoto, Hardee, Highlands, Okeechobee, Indian River, and Brevard counties and south
800–432–6668 (toll-free tieline to Miami)

Georgia
Atlanta
404–221–6891
Federal Bldg. and U.S. Courthouse, 75 Spring St. S.W., *Atlanta* 30303

Hawaii
Honolulu
808–546–8620
Federal Bldg., Box 50091, 300 Ala Moana Blvd., *Honolulu* 96850

Illinois
Chicago
312–353–4242
Everett McKinley Dirksen Bldg., 219 S. Dearborn St., Rm. 250, *Chicago* 60604

Indiana
Gary/Hammond
883–4110 (toll-free tieline to Indianapolis)

Indianapolis
317–269–7373
Federal Bldg., 575 N. Pennsylvania, *Indianapolis* 46204

Iowa
Des Moines
515–284–4448
Federal Bldg., 210 Walnut St., *Des Moines* 50309
Other Iowa locations:
800-532-1556

Kansas
Topeka
913–295–2866
Federal Bldg. and U.S. Courthouse, 444 S.E. Quincy, *Topeka* 66683
Other Kansas locations:
800–432–2934

Kentucky
Louisville
502–582–6261
Federal Bldg., 600 Federal Pl., *Louisville* 40202

Louisiana
New Orleans
504–589–6696
U.S. Custom House, 423 Canal St., Rm. 100, *New Orleans* 70130

Maryland
Baltimore
301–962–4980
Federal Bldg., 31 Hopkins Plaza, *Baltimore* 21201

Massachusetts
Boston
617–223–7121
J.F.K. Federal Bldg., Cambridge St., Rm. E-130, *Boston* 02203

Michigan
Detroit
313–226–7016
McNamara Federal Bldg., 477 Michigan Ave., Rm. 103, *Detroit* 48226
Grand Rapids
451–2628 (toll-free tieline to Detroit)

FEDERAL INFORMATION CENTERS PROGRAM / 65

Minnesota
Minneapolis
612-349-5333
Federal Bldg. and U.S. Courthouse, 110 S. Fourth St., *Minneapolis* 55401

Missouri
Kansas City
816-374-2466
Federal Bldg., 601 E. 12 St., *Kansas City* 64106

St. Louis
314-425-4106
Federal Bldg., 1520 Market St., *St. Louis* 63103

Other Missouri locations:
800-392-7711 (toll-free tieline to St. Louis for residents within 314 area code)

800-892-5808 (toll-free tieline to Kansas City for residents within 816 and 417 area codes)

Nebraska
Omaha
402-221-3353
U.S. Post Office and Courthouse, 215 N. 17 St., *Omaha* 68102

Other Nebraska locations:
800-642-8383

New Jersey
Newark
201-645-3600
Federal Bldg., 970 Broad St., *Newark* 07102

Paterson/Passaic
523-0717 (toll-free tieline to Newark)

Trenton
396-4400 (toll-free tieline to Newark)

New Mexico
Albuquerque
505-766-3091
Federal Bldg. and U.S. Courthouse, 500 Gold Ave. S.W., *Albuquerque* 87102

Santa Fe
983-7743 (toll-free tieline to Albuquerque)

New York
Albany
463-4421 (toll-free tieline to New York, NY)

Buffalo
716-846-4010
Federal Bldg., 111 W. Huron, *Buffalo* 14202

New York
212-264-4464
Federal Bldg., 26 Federal Plaza, Rm. 1-114, *New York* 10278

Rochester
546-5075 (toll-free tieline to Buffalo)

Syracuse
476-8545 (toll-free tieline to Buffalo)

North Carolina
Charlotte
376-3600 (toll-free tieline to Atlanta, GA)

Ohio
Akron
375-5638 (toll-free tieline to Cleveland)

Cincinnati
513-684-2801
Federal Bldg., 550 Main St., *Cincinnati* 45202

Cleveland
216-522-4040
Federal Bldg., 1240 E. Ninth St., *Cleveland* 44199

Columbus
221-1014 (toll-free tieline to Cincinnati)

Dayton
223-7377 (toll-free tieline to Cincinnati)

Toledo
241-3223 (toll-free tieline to Cleveland)

Oklahoma
Oklahoma City
405-231-4868
U.S. Post Office and Courthouse, 201 N.W. Third St., *Oklahoma City* 73102

Tulsa
584-4193 (toll-free tieline to Oklahoma City)

Oregon
Portland
503-221-2222
Edith Green-Wendall Wyatt Federal Bldg., 1220 S.W. Third Ave., Rm. 109, *Portland* 97204

Pennsylvania
Allentown/Bethlehem
821-7785 (toll-free tieline to Philadelphia)
Philadelphia
215-597-7042 Federal Bldg., 600 Arch St., *Philadelphia* 19106
Pittsburgh
412-644-3456
Federal Bldg., 1000 Liberty Ave., *Pittsburgh* 15222
Scranton
346-7081 (toll-free tieline to Philadelphia)

Rhode Island
Providence
331-5565 (toll-free tieline to Boston, MA)

Tennessee
Chattanooga
265-8231 (toll-free tieline to Memphis)
Memphis
901-521-3285
Clifford Davis Federal Bldg., 167 N. Main St., *Memphis* 38103
Nashville
242-5056 (toll-free tieline to Memphis)

Texas
Austin
472-5494 (toll-free tieline to Houston)
Dallas
767-8585 (toll-free tieline to Fort Worth)
Fort Worth
817-334-3624
Lanham Federal Bldg., 819 Taylor St., *Fort Worth* 76102

Houston
713-226-5711
Federal Bldg. and U.S. Courthouse, 515 Rusk Ave., *Houston* 77208
San Antonio
224-4471 (toll-free tieline to Houston)

Utah
Ogden
399-1347 (toll-free tieline to Salt Lake City)
Salt Lake City
801-524-5353
Federal Bldg., 125 S. State St., Rm. 1205, *Salt Lake City* 84138

Virginia
Newport News
244-0480 (toll-free tieline to Norfolk)
Norfolk
804-441-3101
Federal Bldg., 200 Granby Mall, Rm. 120, *Norfolk* 23510
Richmond
643-4928 (toll-free tieline to Norfolk)
Roanoke
982-8591 (toll-free tieline to Norfolk)

Washington
Seattle
206-442-0570
Federal Bldg., 915 Second Ave., *Seattle* 98174
Tacoma
383-5230 (toll-free tieline to Seattle)

Wisconsin
Milwaukee
271-2273 (toll-free tieline to Chicago, IL)

UNITED STATES INTERNATIONAL COMMUNICATION AGENCY

Library Program Division, 1717 H St., Washington, DC 20547

Donald C. Hausrath

Regional Library Consultant,
East Asia and Pacific Region,
U.S. Embassy (Manila),
APO San Francisco, CA 96528

The International Communication Agency (USICA), headquartered in Washington, D.C., and represented in 126 countries, was established April 1, 1978 when the U.S. Information Agency was merged with the former Bureau of Educational and Cultural Affairs of the Department of State. The agency is part of the executive branch of the U.S. government and its director reports to the president of the United States and the secretary of state.

USICA's legislative authority derives from the Smith-Mundt Act of 1948, as amended, which authorizes the dissemination abroad of information about the United States, its people, culture, and policies, and the Mutual Educational and Cultural Exchange Act of 1961 (Fulbright-Hays Act), as amended, which authorizes educational and cultural exchanges between the United States and other countries.

The mission of USICA, as directed by the president of the United States, is to:

Encourage, aid, and sponsor the broadest possible exchange of people and ideas between our country and other nations . . .

Give foreign peoples the best possible understanding of our policies and our intentions, and sufficient information about American society and culture to comprehend why we have chosen certain policies over others . . .

Help ensure that our Government adequately understands foreign public opinion and culture for policy making purposes, and to assist individual Americans and institutions in learning about other nations and cultures . . .

Assist in the development and execution of a comprehensive national policy of international communications, designed to allow and encourage the flow of information and ideas among the peoples of the world . . .

Prepare for and conduct negotiations on cultural exchanges with other governments. . . .

Agency operations are organized along both functional and geographical lines. The four major functional elements are the Associate Directorates for Broadcasting (VOA), Programming (PGM), Educational and Cultural Affairs (ECA), which includes library program activities, and Management (MGT).

The largest agency element, to which one of every four agency employees reports, is the Associate Directorate for Broadcasting (VOA), whose "Voice of America" has been operating since its founder, playwright Robert E. Sherwood, named it in the early days of World War II. The "Voice" estimates its weekly audience at over 75 million—substantially *over* since these figures do not represent Chinese listeners.

The Associate Directorate for Educational and Cultural Affairs (ECA) incorporates most of the programs that were originally part of the Department of State's

Note: Data for this article was researched and collected by Marge Boone, retired USICA library program officer.

Bureau of Educational and Cultural Affairs. A major ECA activity is educational and cultural exchanges of persons. ECA annually manages the exchange of 1,500 U.S. and foreign predoctoral students and 1,200 professors and senior researchers. A wide variety of programs for students, teachers, and scholars includes the Humphrey Fellowship Program under which professionals from Third World countries receive a year's graduate training at American universities. Another program arranges visits to the United States for 2,000 foreign leaders in government, labor, mass media, science, education, and other fields. Grants-in-aids are also coordinated by ECA to private U.S. organizations such as the Asia Foundation, which receives substantial funds for book purchase and distribution to Asian institutions.

ECA supports academic programs abroad relating to the study of the United States and provides liaison between U.S. and foreign universities, academic associations, and scholars. Through ECA English-language instruction is made available at overseas posts and binational centers. ECA also publishes the journal *English Teaching Forum* and assists foreign publishers in the publication and distribution overseas of important books, adaptations, condensations, and serializations in foreign languages. Since the inception of its publishing programs in the year 1950 by its predecessor agency, USICA has assisted in the publication of more than 22,000 editions totaling more than 180 million copies. Typical titles include foreign-language versions of classics such as Eugene O'Neill's *Long Day's Journey into Night*, or modern titles such as the Daniel Boorstin trilogy, *The Americans*. USICA also cooperates with the U.S. Agency for International Development (USAID) in using PL 480 currencies for the publication of textbooks. Over 8.4 million copies of 1,500 titles have been produced through this program.

USICA LIBRARY PROGRAM

The library program, about 4 percent of the USICA budget ($459 million in 1981), was defined by the first director of USICA, Dr. John E. Reinhardt, as supporting USICA's mission by providing "foreign audiences with those books, periodicals, and other materials which embody the sustaining ideas of the American past as well as the generative energy of the present." USICA inherited from one of its predecessors, the United States Information Agency, 129 information center libraries, 15 reading rooms, including some in Eastern Europe, and library programs operating in 37 U.S. government-supported binational centers and 43 self-supporting binational centers. These overseas libraries contain about a million books. Each year the agency purchases about 22,000 periodical subscriptions and around 100,000 books for their libraries, which are used by 8.7 million visitors.

Each library is somewhat different, just as USICA activities in each country are different since they are determined by the host country's information resources and special interests shared by the United States and the host country. In size, the libraries vary from small reading rooms of a few hundred books to the largest, in Mexico City, with 31,000 volumes. Besides Mexico City, there are three other libraries with collections of over 15 thousand volumes, 13 libraries with holdings between ten and fifteen thousand volumes, and 62 with holdings of five to ten thousand. About 63 libraries maintain book collections of between one and five thousand volumes.

Besides library reference services, heavily used by the media and host government researchers, the librarians also support agency cultural program activities. For example, they work with Fulbright professors assigned to foreign universities. They prepare exhibits of materials to support guest speakers, and often maintain cooperative programs with institutions in the foreign community.

The funds for each library are allocated by the public affairs officer at each U.S. embassy. The officer is responsible for the USICA activities in the country, reporting to the ambassador and to USICA in Washington. Fixed costs consume most of the officer's budget, which averages 14 percent of the post's resources.

About 600 persons are employed in USICA libraries around the world, out of a total USICA staff of 8,671. There are 4,489 Americans and 4,182 non-Americans hired locally in foreign countries in the agency. Of the Americans in USICA, around 1,000 are assigned overseas, and 3,400 are based in the United States. About 14 percent of the non-Americans employed at USICA posts in other countries work in the library program.

Of the non-Americans in the library program, one out of two lacks a university degree. Thus, continuing education is a constant need. Training programs, as well as professional and administrative support, are provided by the Library Program Division, which employs 25 professional librarians with career status as foreign service officers. They serve both in Washington and abroad. When abroad, these librarians serve as either regional library consultants or country library directors. Presently, there are 18 foreign service librarians serving abroad. Country library directors are posted in Brazil, Mexico, Japan, Germany, and India. Regional library consultants serve a number of libraries in a region. For example, the regional library consultant in Nairobi, Kenya, visits USICA libraries in Bujumbura, Burundi; Antananarivo, Madagascar; Kigali, Rwanda; Mogadishu, Somalia Republic; Dar es Salaam, Tanzania; as well as in his or her home post. The regional library consultants make one or more trips per year to their assigned USICA and binational libraries, and, of course, work with the host country libraries and professional information and publishing organizations. At each post, the regional library consultants plan library programs, provide training, and ensure that the library meets U.S. standards and is an effective component of the post's overall program.

Foreign governments, especially legislative researchers, are increasingly using USICA libraries. Often even the smaller libraries maintain highly specialized materials. Government publications and related materials are heavily used; among those reported the most useful are those that contain legal and legislative information, for example, the *Code of Federal Regulations*, *Congressional Quarterly Weekly Report*, *National Journal*, and the definitive microfiche file of congressional materials produced by the Congressional Information Service. Pressure abroad for current congressional committee prints and related information is so high that USICA has several employees whose full-time work is devoted to acquisition of government publications. They search the Library of Congress SCORPIO file against preestablished overseas post profiles.

Specialized information needs of foreign clients have increased the need for on-line information services. U.S. interactive data bases are available in Europe and in some other parts of the world. Access to data bases in the United States from abroad has been possible for years by using the relatively costly international telephone and telex services, which charge according to the duration of the connection. The new services establish a link between a terminal and the packet-switched networks of the United States connected to time-sharing computers and data bases. These packet-switched circuits have now reached Asia, allowing USICA librarians to search more than 200 data bases. Among the more popular data bases are those in the social sciences, or those loaded with current citations to day-old newspapers or weekly magazines. These services complement the USICA-produced Foreign Affairs Data Base being developed by the USICA Agency Library, and the extensive sharing of resources with the library program from other parts of the agency.

The USICA library program and related activities, the subject of this report, is but one band in a wide array of communication activities of the agency. While these disparate mission demands would tax any organizational structure, they provide a unique reservoir of talents, products, and services enriching USICA libraries around the world.

SPECIAL DEMANDS ON THE AGENCY

Consider some of the demands on the organization. It must be as current as today's newspaper in supporting each U.S. embassy's public information requirements. It requires a responsive and flexible logistical and budgetary system to handle myriad nonrecurring needs. These include international itineraries for 600 American experts a year, individual book orders from over 150 libraries scattered from Abu Dhabi, to Ouagadougou, Upper Volta, to Zagreb, Yugoslavia, or organizing U.S. visits for 2,000 foreign leaders per year whose travel involves coordination with more than 100,000 U.S. volunteers and 90 community organizations. It must carry out its daily business in the local languages in 127 countries. It uses 39 languages, for example, in its "Voice of America" broadcasts, and publishes magazines in 22 languages. It produces films, television programs, and daily radioteletyped interpretive materials in various languages. It administers the Fulbright Scholarship program and the Humphrey Fellowships. It assists in the acquisition of American materials by foreign libraries, publishers, newspapers, television studios, and radio stations. And it is managed by constantly changing foreign service officers whose assignments rotate them from one post to another every two to four years.

The library program benefits from various agency elements and systems. For example, USICA's film and television studios produce materials used in agency libraries. Professional journalists write precis for library newsletters. USICA's communication system allows reference librarians to wire reference queries beyond the scope of a post library to the agency library in Washington. The agency library reference staff fields post reference questions with their nationwide WATS telephone contacts, through their own specialized collections, or via three on-line search systems—the Information Bank, DIALOG, and ORBIT. Responses to reference questions are wired back via the same system. If printed materials are required, they are airshipped by official mail. This service encourages users abroad to consider USICA's libraries a neighborhood resource.

AREA-WIDE PROJECTS

Five geographic area offices are the principal agency contacts with its overseas posts. Besides providing broad managerial oversight to the posts and programs abroad, they often coordinate area-wide library programs. For example, the European area office recently completed a study of its libraries, concluding that as a group they needed a strengthened reference collection and that USICA librarians needed reference training. A zero-based budget "package" was proposed that eventually funded a million-dollar upgrading of the European area reference collections and provided a two-week intensive training program for the European reference librarians held at Catholic University in Washington, D.C. This program proved so successful that other geographic area offices borrowed the program. A list of basic reference tools, jointly developed by USICA and the Library of Congress, assisted the development of USICA reference collections around the world. A core collection of circulating books also was developed and funded in the same fashion.

Another example of an area-wide project is the "International Flow of Information: A Trans-Pacific Perspective" conference and study tour held in 1979. Sponsored by USICA, the Center for the Book of the Library of Congress, and the Graduate School of Library Studies of the University of Hawaii, it brought together publishers, librarians, information and media specialists, and government officials from Australia, Burma, Hong Kong, Indonesia, Japan, Malaysia, New Zealand, the Philippines, Singapore, and the United States. The participants, who included a quorum of the national librarians in the Pacific region, explored issues related to the flow of information between Asia and other nations, emphasizing the two-way flow between Asia and the United States. The focus was on the barriers (perceived and real) to the international exchange of information and discovering ways to overcome those barriers. Topics included language, trade and economic restraints, the effects of national and international copyright, government agreements and restraints, the dissemination of information through the press and other media, international publishing, the impacts and uses of new technologies, Universal Bibliographic Control, Universal Availability of Publications, and other international cooperative efforts. After the initial meeting in Hawaii, the participants met with their counterparts in Los Angeles, New York, and Washington, D.C.; they were debriefed at the Library of Congress, and finally held a program with the International Relations Round Table of the American Library Association at their annual convention in Dallas. A follow-up meeting of many of the participants was held at the joint Australia–New Zealand Library Association meeting in 1981 in Christchurch, New Zealand.

Many U.S. publishers visited Singapore the following year to open the largest book fair ever held there, sponsored by USICA at the U.S. embassy. The publishers discussed pricing, marketing, and copyright issues. This meeting was followed by U.S. publishers meeting their counterparts at the Manila Forum on International Book Publishing Practices and first International Book Fair held August 1980, and the February 1981 USICA-sponsored book publishing conference held in Bangkok, Thailand.

A typical single-country workshop involving librarians was held in Shanghai and Peking in 1980, jointly sponsored by USICA and the newly founded China Society of Library Science. More than 300 librarians from leading institutions throughout China's 29 provinces and autonomous regions gathered for their first national instructional activity in 30 years.

THE WIRELESS FILE

The Press and Publications Service of USICA oversees a radioteletype network called the wireless file. A daily transmission of 16,000 to 18,000 words is produced of important policy statements and interpretive material on current issues of international interest. It is sent to 159 USICA posts in either English, French, Spanish, or Arabic. Besides its use as background information for U.S. embassy personnel, the wireless file is distributed to foreign leaders and used by the local media. And, of course, it is a basic tool for reference use. A current project modernizes this concept, which was inaugurated in 1946. Data will be stored electronically and pulled up as needed. Materials older than three months will be transferred to microfiche. Citations to both the on-line and microfiche collections are being inserted into a dedicated data base. Minicomputers at U.S. embassies around the world maintain the system.

The present open circuit and leased teletype lines used for wireless file transmission are being replaced by data circuits; already these rapid, economical circuits are in use in 25 embassies and 15 branch posts. This number will continue to increase rapidly over the next five to ten years. However, the state of technology in less developed areas will force the continued use of radioteletype equipment.

Agency librarians publish a number of specialized newsletters alerting client groups—such as economists, government decision makers, professors in areas related to American studies, researchers and journalists—to recently arrived significant articles, books, and videotapes in their fields. Librarians write the majority of the abstracts to meet their own specialized client needs. But assisting this service are writers who biweekly abstract approximately 20 articles selected from major U.S. periodicals commonly found in agency libraries. These are also distributed on the wireless file.

The wireless file is employed to speed reviewing and ordering library books. Agency librarians receive a biweekly offering of book reviews extracted from current library journals. Posts respond to these offerings by return cable, cutting weeks off the arrival date. Of course, posts can write or cable requests for any American book.

PGM MEDIA PRODUCTS

The Associate Directorate for Programming (PGM) produces and acquires media products used abroad. Besides the use of films and videotapes in USICA-sponsored seminars, or broadcast from foreign stations, many of their media products are used in agency libraries. In fact, in some, more nonprint materials are used than printed materials. Over 80 USICA libraries catalog videocassettes into their collection, where they are available for individual or group viewing. A typical library maintains between 50 and 100 videocassettes, constantly changing them as PGM issues new materials. About one film a week is produced by PGM in its Washington studios; around 170 a year are purchased. PGM contracts use of the Public Broadcasting Service's television library. Typical videotapes used in USICA libraries include important political speeches and press conferences, and titles as disparate as *Solar Housing USA*, *Modern American Dance Troupes*, *U.S. Foreign Policy: The Impact of Public Opinion*, and *Paul Samuelson on World Economic Problems*. Videotapes as well as printed materials are airshipped to requesting libraries.

CONCLUSION

Little known in the United States, the overseas USICA library program is a valued part of the cultural scene in many overseas cities.

Prime ministers, postmasters, and pop artists use the libraries. Students, of course, regard them as a treasure house in developing countries where a single book costs weeks of work. The variety, the currency, and the extraordinary quality of the materials available in the USICA library make it a "corner drugstore" of today's issues and of information on the United States and its culture. Recently, a U.S. tourist visiting Nepal dropped into the Katmandu USICA library. He was delighted to find a month-old issue of *Harper's Magazine* on display, and sat down to browse. As he returned it, he recalls, he wondered, as a taxpayer, how useful it was to have a current issue of *Harper's* in this far-away corner of the world. Then, he reports, it was immediately picked up by a Nepalese reader.

For much of the world, the USICA library serves to bridge cultural, economic, and political barriers. It allows patrons, as one ambassador describes it, "to look across the frontiers and see what the scientists, artists, poets, and political leaders are thinking and doing."

THE COPYRIGHT OFFICE: DEVELOPMENTS IN 1980

Library of Congress, Washington, DC 20559
202-287-8700

Susan Robinson
Writer/Editor, Information and Reference Division

In 1980 the Copyright Office continued to develop the new policies, regulations, and systems necessary to carry out its responsibilities under the copyright law. On January 1, 1978, a completely new copyright statute (Title 17 of the U.S. Code) came into effect, superseding the Copyright Act of 1909 as amended, and making important changes in the copyright system.

Instead of the former dual system of protecting works under the common law before they were published, and under the federal statute after publication, the new law establishes a single federal system of copyright for all works, published or unpublished. Copyright protection begins from the moment the work is fixed in some tangible medium of expression and in most instances lasts for the life of the author plus 50 years after the author's death. The existence of copyright in a work therefore is not contingent on registration in the Copyright Office or the exercise of any other formalities.

However, all works protected are eligible for registration in the Copyright Office. Registration is voluntary but it is a prerequisite to the initiation of an infringement suit. There are substantial advantages attached to registration and in FY 1980 registrations reached an all-time high of 464,743.

Although registration is voluntary, the law does contain a mandatory deposit requirement for all works published in the United States with a notice of copyright. In 1980 the Deposit and Acquisitions Section of the Copyright Office continued to enforce these requirements, obtaining many new acquisitions for the collections of the Library of Congress. With severe reductions in funds available for acquisitions, the enforcement of the mandatory deposit requirement is an increasingly important source of materials for the Library of Congress.

Under the new law, the Licensing Division of the Copyright Office administers the compulsory licensing systems for secondary transmissions by cable television and public performances on jukeboxes. From 1978 to 1980 the Licensing Division collected and invested over $42,000,000 in cable and jukebox royalty fees for subsequent distribution to copyright owners by the Copyright Royalty Tribunal. The Copyright Royalty Tribunal in late 1980 set new rates for jukebox licensing fees, cable fees, and mechanical royalty rates paid to writers and publishers of songs. The Licensing Division had the responsibility for notifying all the parties involved in the several compulsory licensing systems of these changes in rates and certain new procedures.

The Copyright Office also maintains a national copyright information service. The Information and Reference Division responded to a rising workload in 1980, assisting a record number of visitors and replying to correspondence. Answers to questions, informational circulars and copies of the law, regulations, and application forms may be obtained free of charge by writing to the Copyright Office, Library of Congress, Washington, D.C. 20559, or by calling 202-287-8700 between 8:30 A.M. and 5:00 P.M. (eastern standard time) on weekdays.

SPECIAL PROJECTS

The copyright law assigns the Copyright Office several special projects that require reports to be made to Congress. In January 1980 the Copyright Office submitted to Congress its *Public Broadcasting Report* on the voluntary licensing agreements that were made concerning the use of nondramatic literary works by public broadcast stations.

In 1980 the Copyright Office also completed preparations for a public hearing to be held in early 1981 on the effect of the phaseout of the "manufacturing clause" (section 601 of Title 17 of the U.S. Code). This clause, a significant and controversial feature of American copyright law since 1891, presently requires that certain nondramatic literary works by U.S. citizens must be manufactured either in the United States or in Canada in order to enjoy the full protection of the copyright law. This limitation is presently scheduled to expire on July 1, 1982. At the request of Congress, the Copyright Office has begun a study of the impact of the elimination of this clause on the U.S. book manufacturing and printing industries.

As a part of the five-year review of photocopying practices required by section 108 (i) of the law, the Copyright Office continued to consult with the advisory committee established in 1978. The advisory committee provides to these deliberations input that is representative of the interests of authors, publishers, information industries, libraries, and users of information. The register of copyrights must report on the effectiveness of the photocopying provisions in the law in balancing the rights of creators and the needs of users of copyrighted works. In 1980 the Copyright Office let a contract for the collection of data to provide detailed statistical information on photocopying activities. Additionally, regional hearings were held in 1980 in Chicago, Illinois; Washington, D.C.; Houston, Texas; and Anaheim, California; the fifth and final hearing was scheduled to be held in New York City in January 1981.

The Copyright Office continued to advise and consult with the Committee to Negotiate Guidelines for Off-the-Air Videotaping for Educational Users, an ad hoc committee established by Representative Robert Kastenmeier, chairman of the House Judiciary Subcommittee on Courts, Civil Liberties, and the Administration of Justice. The committee met on four occasions in FY 1980; its goal is to develop proposals for guidelines on fair use for broadcast audiovisual works, a continuing concern of educators and librarians.

MAJOR CHANGES AT THE COPYRIGHT OFFICE

The Copyright Office was faced with two major events in 1980—the appointment of a new register of copyrights and a move to Capitol Hill.

New Register of Copyrights Appointed

On May 13, 1980, Librarian of Congress Daniel Boorstin announced the appointment of David L. Ladd as register of copyrights, effective June 2, 1980, to succeed Barbara A. Ringer, who retired from federal service on May 30, 1980, after completing a career of distinguished service to the Copyright Office and the Library of Congress.

Barbara Ringer, register of copyrights from 1973 to 1980, is widely known for her achievements in the field of copyright. Throughout her career she was closely involved with the general revision of the U.S. copyright law. She played a leading role in organizing preliminary studies and drafts and in steering through Congress the bill that culminated in the enactment of the Copyright Act of 1976.

As a leading specialist in international copyright law, Barbara Ringer represented the United States at many international conferences. Before her retirement she received numerous honors and awards, including the library's highest award for distinguished service.

David Ladd came to the Copyright Office with extensive experience in the practice of patent, trademark, and copyright law. From 1961 to 1963, as U.S. Commissioner of Patents, he presided over a comprehensive reorganization of the Patent and Trademark Office that included initiatives in research for documentation and information retrieval.

Mr. Ladd came to the Copyright Office from the University of Miami in Coral Gables, Florida, where he was professor of law and co-director of the John M. Olin Fellowship Program in the Law and Economics Center at the university. He is the first person to have served both as commissioner of patents and register of copyrights.

The Copyright Office Returns to Capitol Hill

A second significant change in 1980 was the move of the Copyright Office from Arlington, Virginia, to its new quarters in the James Madison Memorial Building of the Library of Congress. This was accomplished in September 1980 on the basis of planning that began years ago when the Copyright Office was included as part of the general design for construction of the Madison Building. Particularly noteworthy was the transfer of more than 40,000,000 cards comprising the Copyright Card Catalog (one of the world's largest card catalogs) from Arlington to the new buliding.

The return to Capitol Hill adjacent to the other buildings of the Library of Congress has already begun to further the working partnership between the library and the Copyright Office.

LEGISLATIVE DEVELOPMENTS

Despite the enactment of the comprehensive revision legislation, there continues to be substantial congressional activity in the copyright field. The proposals reflect concerns with the organization of the office itself, technological developments, and judicial interpretation of the act.

Bills concerning copyright issues that were considered by Congress include establishing a limited performance right in sound recordings through a compulsory license that would require payments to performers and producers of copyrighted works (H.R. 997); providing an exemption to certain groups from liability for royalties from the performance of musical works (H.R. 6857, H.R. 7448, H.R. 6262, S. 2082); proposing tax incentives in the fields of the arts and humanities (H.R. 5650, H.R. 8038); and establishing a National Periodicals Center or System (Part D, Title II of PL 96-374, Ninety-sixth Congress, Second Session [1980]).

H.R. 6933

Of immediate concern to the new register and to the Library of Congress was a bill before the Ninety-sixth Congress, H.R. 6933, whose principal purpose was to amend the patent and trademark laws. Section 9 of the bill, however, as reported to the House of Representatives by the Committee on the Judiciary on September 9, 1980, provided that the comptroller general was to submit to the Congress and the president no later than July 1, 1981, a report analyzing the efficiency of the Copyright Office and the Copyright Royalty Tribunal and making recommendations as to whether these two entities should be merged with an independent Patent and Trademark Office.

The bill was then referred to the House Committee on Government Operations, before whose Subcommittee on Legislation and National Security the librarian of Congress, Daniel Boorstin, and the register, David Ladd, appeared on September 17, 1980.

Dr. Boorstin's statement to the subcommittee emphasized that the responsibility of the Library of Congress, as carried out by the Copyright Office, for protecting the works of writers, artists, composers, and other creative persons is a function compatible with its mission to house and service the nation's intellectual resources and that the proposed merger "would not serve the creators of intellectual property as well as has the Library of Congress in its more than 110 years of stewardship." He asked that section 9 of H.R. 6933, providing for the study, be deleted from the bill, explaining the close cooperation between the Copyright Office and other parts of the Library of Congress: "The Copyright Office participates in the top management councils of the Library: the Register of Copyrights is also the Assistant Librarian of Congress for Copyright Services and reports to the Librarian of Congress rather than to any intermediate level of management; and the Library, drawing upon the sophisticated and concerned support of the scholarly and library community, as well as the legal community, backs the Copyright Office splendidly." Mr. Ladd referred to the integration of the Copyright Office's record-keeping function, including its cataloging, with the national bibliographic role of the Library of Congress as well as other common tasks.

On September 18, 1980, the subcommittee, by unanimous vote, deleted section 9 from H.R. 6933. The bill, with the deletion of the provision in question, was subsequently enacted.

The Computer Software Copyright Act of 1980

The issue of liability for computer uses of copyrighted works was not resolved before passage of the new copyright law in 1976. Because of this, Congress directed the National Commission on New Technological Uses of Copyrighted Works (CONTU) to study the emerging patterns in the computer field and, based on their findings, to recommend definitive copyright provisions to deal with the situation. In the interim, section 117 of the statute was intended neither to cut off any rights existing under the act of 1909, nor to create any new rights that might be denied under the 1909 act or under applicable common law principles. In 1978, CONTU issued its final report, which included proposals to amend the copyright law. H.R. 6934, Ninety-sixth Congress, Second Session (1980), entitled the "Computer Software Copyright Act of 1980" and introduced by Representative Robert Kastenmeier, adopted many of CONTU's proposals.

The House Judiciary Subcommittee conducted public hearings on this bill in April and May of 1980. The bill was later merged by the House Judiciary Committee with H.R. 6933, Ninety-sixth Congress, Second Session (1980), which pertains primarily to patent and trademark law. As H.R. 6933, the bill was passed by both houses in November 1980, and signed into law by President Carter on December 12, 1980.

The bill amended section 101 of the act to add a specific definition of "computer programs" and amended section 117 to provide authorization for making copies or adaptations of computer programs in limited cases and under certain conditions. The bill also provided copyright protection for transfers of computer software by lease, sale, or other exchange. The house report accompanying the bill stated that the new law was not intended to restrict additional legal protection that states might provide for software through unfair competition or trade secret laws.

COPYRIGHT REGULATIONS

A significant portion of the office's regulatory activity since the new copyright act came into effect has been devoted to the regulation implementing section 115, which provides for a compulsory license for making and distributing phonorecords. The compulsory license permits the use of a copyrighted work without the consent of the copyright owner if certain conditions are met and royalties paid. Section 115 directs the Copyright Office to issue regulations governing the content and filing of certain notices and statements of account under this section. After public hearings in 1978 and 1979, the Copyright Office issued its final regulations (37 CFR Part 201), which took effect December 12, 1980.

Much of the controversy in connection with this issue was directed at complex accounting issues in the payment of statutory royalties by record companies to songwriters or copyright holders. The Copyright Office determined that a nine-month accounting period would result in full and prompt payment of royalties, without excessive overpayments. The Copyright Office undertook studies to determine the economic effect of its guidelines before the regulations were issued.

Under section 407 of the copyright law, the owner of copyright or of the exclusive right of publication in a work published with notice of copyright in the United States must deposit two copies of the work (or, in the case of sound recordings, two phonorecords), with some exemptions in certain categories, in the Copyright Office for the use or disposition of the Library of Congress. The law requires that the deposit be made within three months after first publication with notice in the United States. The mandatory deposit requirement applies also to works published with notice of copyright in the United States after first publication in a foreign country. In July 1980, the Copyright Office announced that it had decided to resume a policy of enforcing the deposit requirements against foreign books and other printed works published in the United States with notice of copyright.

Secton 111 prescribes conditions under which cable systems may obtain a compulsory license to retransmit copyrighted works. One of the conditions is the semiannual filing by cable systems of statements of account. On July 3, 1980, the Copyright Office issued revised final regulations adopting certain technical and clarifying amendments relating to cable statements of account.

COPYRIGHT OFFICE PUBLICATIONS

One of the most important recent scholarly publications of the Copyright Office is the four-volume work, issued in 1980, entitled *Decisions of the United States Courts Involving Copyright and Literary Property, 1789-1909*, with an analytical index. The first three volumes, compiled and edited under the direction of Wilma S. Davis, contained the text of judicial and administrative decisions concerning copyright and literary property that interpreted the copyright law of the states and of the federal government prior to 1909. The fourth volume, prepared by Mark A. Lillis, provides access to legal opinion with reference to more than 300 pertinent categories, together with indexes to the titles of the works identified in the decisions reported and to the names of the more than 300 participating judges and some 450 notable persons in the world of literature, art, and music mentioned in the cases. The entire four-volume set, of value to lawyer and scholar alike, is on sale by the Superintendent of Documents, U.S. Government Printing Office. This new set forms a part of the large series of volumes now covering the period 1789-1976.

INTERNATIONAL ACTIVITIES

As part of its ongoing interest in the area of multilateral copyright relationships, the Copyright Office began planning for a series of studies of the impact that membership in the Berne Union would have on the U.S. copyright system. The studies are to emphasize the relationship of Berne to commercial and noncommercial copyright interests in the United States.

Under the terms of the 1979 bilateral trade agreement between the United States and the People's Republic of China, the two countries have pledged to provide protection to the copyrights of each other's nationals. Chinese efforts to implement this agreement were furthered by a visit in 1980 to the Copyright Office by members of the China National Publications Import Corporation. China has also extended an invitation to the U.S. government for a delegation of governmental copyright experts to visit Beijing in spring 1981. The Copyright Office awaits with great interest the results of the Chinese efforts to develop a domestic copyright system.

The international protection of copyrighted works in automated information systems continues to be of major interest in the international community; the Copyright Office was represented at two international conferences in Geneva on this topic: the Expert Group on Legal Protection of Computer Software, and the Desirability and Feasibility of an International Treaty on the Protection of Computer Software.

THE NATIONAL COMMISSION ON LIBRARIES AND INFORMATION SCIENCE

1717 K St. N.W., Suite 601, Washington, DC 20036
202-653-6252

Toni Carbo Bearman
Executive Director

Douglas S. Price
Deputy Director

The National Commission on Libraries and Information Science (NCLIS) was established by PL 91-345 in 1970 as a permanent, independent agency in the executive branch, reporting directly to both the president and Congress. Its authorized functions include appraising the adequacies and deficiences of current library/information services, studying library/information needs and analyzing the means by which these needs may be met, promoting research and development activities to improve library/information services, developing overall plans for meeting library/information needs of the nation, advising all levels of government and private agencies on library and information services, and advising the president and Congress on the implementation of national information policy.

WHCOLIS-RELATED ACTIVITIES

Much of the commission's activity during 1980 arose from, or was related to, the first White House Conference on Library and Information Services (WHCOLIS), which was held in mid-November 1979. The first order of business was completing and submitting to the president, within the required 120 days, the report of the conference. The multimedia report (audio- and videotape, microfilm, and paper) was submitted on schedule, and the president appointed a high-level interagency task force to review the recommendations and recommend responses to the president. In late September, the president transmitted the report of the conference to Congress with a message emphasizing four major points: the importance of libraries (emphasizing increased budgetary support for resource sharing, research and development, and research libraries); new legislation for library and information services; government information (affirming the key role of depository libraries and initiating co-location of Federal Information Centers with libraries); the needs of the disadvantaged (emphasizing combating functional illiteracy and minimizing barriers to information access); and the new information and communications technologies (encouraging their application). [The complete text of President Carter's report is reprinted in the Special Reports Section of Part 1—*Ed.*] The commission moved promptly to respond appropriately to the initiatives contained in the president's message. In addition to submitting a request for a supplemental appropriation for FY 1981 and a revised larger request for FY 1982 (which were disallowed by the Office of Management and Budget), NCLIS is actively seeking funding from other agencies and institutions to assist it in the many activities of implementation needed to maintain the momentum engendered by the White House Conference and the president's message.

Meanwhile, NCLIS had moved ahead in following up on several of the White House Conference resolutions. The one that involved the largest number of people was convening the first meeting of an ad hoc committee (now called the white house conference on Library and Information Services Taskforce (whcLIST).

After an intensive three days in Minneapolis, whcLIST agreed on a governance structure consisting of four officers chosen at large and five board members, elected on a regional basis. The 91 attendees reviewed the 64 resolutions from WHCOLIS and made recommendations concerning tasks to be undertaken to accomplish the goals of each resolution, which groups should act as agents for the tasks, and what time frame should be established for each task. The steering committee plans to meet during the American Library Association midwinter meeting, and the full whcLIST hopes to meet again in 1981. NCLIS served as a facilitator in organizing the follow-up meeting on whcLIST, and the commission, having served as a catalyst, is now in full support of whcLIST's desire to function as a separate, independent group.

The White House Conference also provided the impetus for NCLIS to initiate several other activities, some of which had been under consideration for some time, but deferred until the results of the conference were available. Three new task forces began their activities during 1980. The first of these is the Task Force on Community Information and Referral Services. This task force is based on the premise that, if the library is to become the first place in the community to which people turn when seeking information or services, it must provide the library user at all socioeconomic and cultural levels with information and, where appropriate, referral to sources (e.g., governmental, community, neighborhood, or voluntary organizations) that can provide answers and assistance to meet their needs. The task force is seeking to define appropriate roles for libraries in the provision of community information and referral services and to define ways in which libraries can move toward fulfillment of these roles. The task force met three times during 1980, in conjunction with regular NCLIS meetings, and will continue its efforts through 1981.

The second task force, which held its first meeting in late October, is the Task Force on the Role of the Special Library in Nationwide Networks and Cooperative Programs. This task force will examine ways of making the underutilized and underrated resources of the nation's special libraries available to the emerging nationwide network and of making the resources of the network available to the special libraries. An unusual feature of the task force is that the commission is supporting expenses only for commissioners and staff. The Special Libraries Association is paying the expenses of other members.

In early November, a third newly formed task force, the Task Force on Library and Information Services to Cultural Minorities, held its first meeting. This task force is charged with exploring the current status of library and information service programs in support of the needs and desires as expressed by minority groups; developing programs designed to encourage ethnic groups in local communities to cooperate in planning, delivery, and evaluation of library programs; determining the strength of existing collections in libraries; and developing criteria and methods for expanding and improving cultural minority materials for library and information services.

Also in response to concerns about better use of federal library and information resources expressed by the White House Conference, NCLIS undertook in 1980, in cooperation with the Library of Congress and the Federal Library Committee, an 18-month study of intergovernmental library resources and services around the country. Its purpose is to propose ways to improve coordination of federal libraries and information resources and services to meet both national and local needs. This project has been undertaken, in part, in response to several resolutions of the White House Conference and the NCLIS program document *Toward a National Program for Library and Information Services: Goals for Action*, which strongly emphasized the important contributions federal libraries and information services can make and the need to minimize overlapping and duplication.

OTHER ACTIVITIES

While activities engendered by the White House Conference occupied much of the commission's attention during 1980, its regular responsibilities were not neglected. The ongoing Task Force on Public/Private Sector Relations, established to make a significant contribution to the delineation of the proper roles of government and private organizations with respect to the generation and dissemination of scientific, technical, business, and other information, submitted to the commission at its December meeting an interim report and expects to complete its recommendations by mid-1981. The task force has identified eight principles involved in the interaction among the three sectors—private enterprise, not-for-profit organizations, and government. The final report from this task force is expected to be a document of considerable interest to the library and information community.

NCLIS also continued its efforts in the international arena by agreeing, at the request of the American Library Association, which was representing many of the major library and information associations in the United States, to pay approximately one-half of the U.S. national membership dues to the International Federation of Library Associations (IFLA). This commitment broadens the international activity begun by the commission's earlier support of the Universal Availability of Publications program. The International Cooperation Planning Group, chaired by Robert

Chartrand, completed its efforts and reported to the commission recommending the establishment of a task force on international cooperation. This effort was initially approved, but budget constraints forced NCLIS to defer the initiation of this effort, pending obtaining additional funding.

In July, on the tenth anniversary of the signing of PL 91-345 establishing the commission, NCLIS was finally able to hold a meeting at which day-to-day business took a back seat to thinking about the evolving roles and goals of the commission. Two days of intensive interaction among the commissioners produced a restructuring of commission committees; a list of proposed projects, which will be ranked in order by priority to provide an agenda for the coming years; suggestions for streamlining internal procedures; and a better understanding of the commission's current and potential roles. Many of the recommendations, particularly those pertaining to internal procedures, have already been—or are in the process of being—implemented.

Through an unusual agreement between the commission and the U.S. Department of Agriculture's Science and Education Administration (SEA), Gerald J. Sophar, executive officer of SEA's Technical Information System (TIS), has been placed on loan to the commission for an indefinite period. The purpose of this is to provide a neutral focal point for encouraging other federal information-oriented agencies to follow SEA's lead to focus useful scientific, technical and social information to the small businessman, the farmer and local community groups. The program was started at TIS in 1978 in response to a congressional mandate to SEA in new authorizing legislation (Farm Bill 1977) that it should place greater emphasis than in the past on the transfer of the results of federally supported research to the people of the United States. SEA/TIS linked its new program to two conferences: The White House Conference on Small Business, and the White House Conference on Library and Information Services. This program uses a public library to transfer the results of research (e.g., Denver Public Library's Regional Energy/Environment Information Center) and incorporates a training program for community libraries in cooperation with Case Western Reserve's School of Library Science to acquaint the public and community librarians with the needs of small businesses, farms, and local community groups. In addition, it provides training on how to access the information and data that, until now, has been essentially available to large enterprises only. This program may serve as a prototype for the revitalization of the public library as an essential link between the federal government's research efforts and the public.

At the end of June, Alphonse F. Trezza, who had been the executive director of NCLIS since 1974, left the commission to join the Library of Congress staff. After an extensive search effort, chaired by Bessie B. Moore, vice chairman of NCLIS, the commission selected Dr. Toni Carbo Bearman as the new executive director. Dr. Bearman, who has had 19 years experience in the library/information field, began working at the commission in mid-November. Between Mr. Trezza's departure and Dr. Bearman's arrival, Colonel Andrew A. Aines, a former commissioner, served as acting executive director, on loan from the Department of Energy, Office of Scientific and Technical Information.

With the new guidance provided by the White House Conference and the president's message, the new priorities developed at the commission retreat, and the new staff leadership, the commission is looking forward to a renewed effort for serving the new administration, the Congress, and the people of the United States.

DEPOSITORY LIBRARY PROGRAM

Bernadine Abbott Hoduski
Professional Staff Member for Library and Distribution Services,
U.S. Congress, Joint Committee on Printing, S 151 U.S. Capitol,
Washington, DC 20510
202-224-5953

Those libraries that are designated to receive U.S. government publications are called depository libraries. Depositories are required by 44 U.S.C. section 1911 to "make Government publications available for the free use of the general public." They are a major avenue of information dissemination by federal departments and agencies, and members of Congress frequently respond to inquires from constituents by referring them to the depository library in their district.

Sections 1902 and 1903 of title 44 of the United States Code (U.S.C. 44) provide that all government publications printed at the U.S. Government Printing Office (GPO) and elsewhere, with few exceptions, are to be included in the depository program. Excepted are government publications determined by their issuing components to be required for official use only or for strictly administrative or operational purposes that have no public interest or educational value, and publications classified for reasons of national security.

Selective depository libraries choose publications according to the needs of their users. They choose these publications in advance from such categories as the *U.S. Geological Survey Water Supply Papers*, environmental impact statements, annual reports of agencies, rules and regulations, court decisions, and scientific and technical reports. The categories may contain one publication a year or many publications. Any citizen can ask that a depository obtain a government publication for his or her use either through selection or interlibrary loan.

According to title 44, section 1912, "Not more than two depository libraries in each State and the Commonwealth of Puerto Rico may be designated as regional depositories, and shall receive from the Superintendent of Documents copies of all new and revised Government publications authorized for distribution to depository libraries." Section 1912 goes on to outline the additional duties of a regional depository to "retain at least one copy of all Government publications either in printed or facsimile form (except those authorized to be discarded by the Superintendent of Documents) and within the region served will provide interlibrary loan, reference service, and assistance for depository libraries in the disposal of unwanted Government publications."

DESIGNATION OF DEPOSITORY LIBRARIES

As of February 1981, there are 1,344 depository libraries. They include such diverse institutions as Georgia Institute of Technology, Detroit Public Library, Montana State Library, the National Library of Medicine, and the Nevada Supreme Court Library. Libraries are designated in a variety of ways:

> Members of the House of Representatives may designate two per congressional district.
>
> Senators may designate two per state.
>
> Resident commissioner of Puerto Rico may designate two.
>
> The governors of Guam and American Samoa may designate one each.

The governor of the Virgin Islands may designate two (one for the island of St. Thomas and one for the island of St. Croix).

The mayor of the District of Columbia may designate two.

Libraries in the following categories may request designation: land grant colleges; law schools; state libraries; academies of the Air Force, Coast Guard, Merchant Marine, Military, and Naval services; executive departments; independent agencies; major bureaus and divisions of departments of the U.S. Government.

In addition, the District of Columbia Public Library and the American Antiquarian Society Library were designated under special legislation. For a list of depositories, see the appendix to the *Government Manual*.

ADMINISTRATION OF THE DEPOSITORY PROGRAM

Under chapter 19 of title 44, the superintendent of documents is given administrative responsibility for the Depository Library Program. The Joint Committee on Printing of the U.S. Congress has oversight responsibility. The cost of the depository program is borne by appropriations to the legislative branch of government. It costs Congress an average of $12,000 per year for each depository. This does not include the cost of cataloging and indexing publications sent to depositories. A depository library must make a considerable investment in space, staff, equipment, and supplies to service the publications, at an estimated cost of $10 per publication. The Detroit Public Library spends $35,000 annually to maintain its depository collection.

Under U.S.C. 44, sections 1710 and 1711, the superintendent of documents is responsible for a comprehensive index and catalog of all government publications. The superintendent of documents can fulfill this responsibility only with the assistance of the federal agencies. Under title 44 "the Public Printer shall, immediately upon its publication, deliver . . . a copy of every document printed at the Government Printing Office" to the superintendent of documents. The head of each executive department, independent agency and establishment of the Government shall deliver . . . a copy of every document issued or published by the department, bureau or office not confidential in character" to the superintendent of documents.

In 1976 the staff of the superintendent of documents began inputting these cataloging records into the Ohio College Library Center (OCLC) computerized cooperative cataloging network. Thousands of library users now have on-line access to these cataloging records. The computer tapes of this data are returned to GPO for the publication of the *Monthly Catalog of United States Government Publications*. The *Monthly Catalog* tapes are then sold to other libraries and library networks by the Library of Congress. This enables users of other on-line networks to have access to this data. In order to make it easy for the users to know which documents are depository, a black dot or an item number is printed with each cataloging record in the *Monthly Catalog* printed or tape data base.

The staff of the superintendent of documents (SuDoc) and the Library of Congress (LC) work together to make sure that the cataloging records meet international cataloging standards as given in the *Anglo-American Cataloguing Rules* and the MARC formats. LC has designated SuDoc the center of responsibility for the cataloging of federal publications. SuDoc records have the same status as LC records. SuDoc in turn is working toward a cooperative cataloging program with other federal libraries and cataloging services.

HISTORY OF DEPOSITORY PROGRAM

The depository program started in 1813 when the Thirteenth Congress decided that 200 copies of certain documents should be distributed to state and territorial governments and to certain academic institutions and historical societies, such as the American Antiquarian Society Library in Worcester, Massachusetts, which was designated in 1814. The system of designation by representatives and senators was formalized by joint resolutions of the Congress in 1857 and 1859. The program was assigned to the secretary of the Department of the Interior, which not only sent out documents but maintained a collection of documents. Boston Public Library and the Worcester Public Library were designated in 1859 by members of the House. Harvard College Library was designated by a senator in 1860. After passage of the 1895 Printing Act, responsibility for the program and the collection of documents was transferred to the superintendent of documents in the U.S. Government Printing Office.

In 1913 Congress passed a law preventing the depository designations from being part of the spoils system. Once a library is designated by a member of Congress, that library cannot lose its status unless it fails to live up to its obligations as stated in title 44 or chooses to relinquish its privilege.

In 1962 the Depository Library Act was passed. It increased congressional members' designations from one to two; provided for the designation of more federal libraries as depositories, set up a system of regional and selective depositories, directed GPO to include non-GPO produced publications in the depository system, and allowed selective depositories to discard certain publications after five years with the permission of the governing regional depository.

Federal Libraries

LIBRARY OF CONGRESS

Washington, DC 20540
202-287-5000

James W. McClung
Public Information Specialist

In 1980, the Library of Congress (LC) moved rapidly ahead in the occupancy of the new James Madison Memorial Building; made plans for the freezing of the library's existing card catalogs and the implementation of the second edition of the *Anglo-American Cataloguing Rules* (*AACR 2*) to take place the first working day of 1981; continued to consolidate its policies governing the growth, preservation, and use of library materials through the Collections Development Office; and carried out many active programs of service to the Congress, to the creative artist through copyright, to the scholar and the public at large, and to the library community.

JAMES MADISON MEMORIAL BUILDING

Although the first library work unit moved into the new Madison Building at the end of 1979, this past year witnessed a real increase in the number of staff members housed there and the symbolic opening of the building on April 24, 1980, at an impressive dedication ceremony on the library's one hundred eightieth birthday. A distinguished audience of members of Congress, representatives of the library community, and LC officials and architects responsible for the 25-year project heard Sen. Harry F. Byrd of Virginia describe the aptness of putting Madison's name on the new building, "for the Library of Congress was in the first instance an idea in the mind of Madison, and it was he who saw to its rebuilding when it had been destroyed" in 1814.

By the end of 1980, over half of the staff eventually scheduled to relocate had moved into the Madison building, and 85 percent occupancy was expected by the end of April 1981. Major organizational units to move included the Congressional Research Service and the Copyright Office (totaling together over 1,500 staff members). With the move of the Geography and Map Division in February and March from suburban Virginia—a task that involved the transfer of some 3.5 million sheets and volumes of maps and atlases—the first special collection occupied space in the building and the first reading room was opened to the public. Early 1981 will see the move of another major staff unit—Processing Services—and the beginning of a series of moves of large special collections of law, manuscript, pictorial, serial, and music materials to be completed in 1982.

COLLECTIONS DEVELOPMENT OFFICE

In the conviction that collection building that ignores the bibliographic control and organization, the housing and preservation, and ultimately the servicing of materials is unrealistic and detrimental, this office of the library, completing its first full year of work in 1980, made strides in the review of policies and the issuance of guidelines to coordinate a library-wide collections development plan. Toward this end, the office, working with several committees on which it is represented and with other library units, has reviewed LC's microfilming policies, serials acquisitions in light of rising costs, cataloging priorities (including investigating what is called "batch cataloging" for large quantities of items that do not lend themselves to individual cataloging), and retention policies for duplicate and superseded works. In addition, special studies were begun on the library's acquisitions in the fields of U.S. local history, U.S. state publications, and publications issued by and about the many ethnic groups in the United States, and a questionnaire about these materials was sent to state libraries and historical societies and to selected university and public libraries. Using the findings of the questionnaire and working with groups such as the Assembly of State Librarians, the Collections Development Office will be able to frame the library's acquisitions policy in these areas with an eye to coordination and to sharing responsibility with other institutions.

The office is also investigating the use of the library's Copyright Deposit Collection, an increased preservation capability, further coordination of collections development policies with the other national libraries and members of the Research Libraries Group, and the revision of the library's acquisitions policy statements. One such set of guidelines—that for manuscripts—has been approved. Other areas of concern addressed by the Collections Development Office are a review of discard policies, improved bibliographical control of microforms, and custodial assignments and responsibilities within the various divisions of the library that maintain their own collections.

NATIONAL LIBRARY SERVICE FOR THE BLIND AND PHYSICALLY HANDICAPPED

The quality of library services to the blind and physically handicapped is continually upgraded by the National Library Service for the Blind and Physically Handicapped (NLS/BPH) through research and development, automation, quality control, and public education by means of publications, user surveys, and other outreach programs. Projects in 1980 included a study of alternatives to current braille production—including an examination of new technology for computer production of high-grade braille, production of a prototype disc-cassette playback machine, training for the use of the new Kurzweil Reading Machine print-to-braille system, and cassette-braille technology.

NLS/BPH has inaugurated a new automated mailing list system for subscriptions to large-print, flexible-disc, and braille publications. New reading materials available through this program include *Analog* and *Isaac Asimov's Science Fiction Magazine*; and *Foreign Affairs, Personnel and Guidance Journal, QST, Social Worker*, and *Writer* are now available as flexible-disc, direct-circulation magazines.

AMERICAN FOLKLIFE CENTER

Since its creation in 1976, the American Folklife Center has been increasingly active in the areas of field work, publications and exhibitions, and programs intended to acquaint the public with American folklore, customs, and music. The center continued to focus on developing project archives and publications from materials gathered during field projects. Newly completed publications included *Arizona Folklife Survey, Maritime Folklife Resources*, and *Buckaroos in Paradise: Cowboy Life in Northern Nevada*, the last of which was a catalog based on the center's Paradise Valley (Nevada) folklife survey, for an exhibition that opened in 1980 at the Smithsonian Institution's Museum of American History. Other publications were *Ethnic Broadcasting in the United States*, the results of a survey conducted by Theodore Grame, and numerous bibliographic and finding aids issued by the center's Archive of Folk Song, among them *American Graffiti, The Use of Computers in Folklore and Folk Music, Cowboy Songs, Arkansas Folklife,* and *Rhymes of Children.* Publications in preparation include "Ethnic Recordings in America: A Neglected Heritage," a photo-essay entitled "Blue Ridge Harvest," and a double-disc, long-playing record, "Children of the Heav'nly King," an album of sermons and religious songs and stories from the Blue Ridge area.

In addition to completing several older projects, the center undertook, through its consultants program, to assist the Rocky Mountain Continental Divide Foundation in Colorado in its plans for an outdoor museum of high-altitude life and work and the Michigan Department of Natural Resources and Michigan State University Museum in their organization of a study of waterfowling traditions in the Point Mouillee area of that state.

Work of the Federal Cylinder Project, begun in 1979 to preserve several thousand cylinder recordings, principally of Native American songs and stories, continued in 1980. The documentary aspects of the project were aided by the development of a MARC Coding Manual for the bibliographic control of information relating to the cylinder collection.

Outdoor concerts, workshops on the arts of paper cutting and making rag rugs, and a symposium that brought together state and regional folk cultural coordinators are all a part of the center's ongoing work. Plans for the coming months include several documentary film presentations, workshops on bookbinding and the art of Easter egg decoration, another series of outdoor summer concerts, and continued planning for a major exhibition on the American cowboy scheduled to open at the Library of Congress in late spring 1982.

STAFF, BUDGET, AND SERVICES

For FY 1981, the Library of Congress is operating on an appropriation of $176,844,000, based on a continuing resolution (PL 96-369) that funds library operations through June 15, 1981; over 5,300 people were in the library's employ at year's end. Congress also passed and sent to the president for his signature a bill (PL 96-269) renaming the library's older buildings the Library of Congress Thomas Jefferson Building (for the original building completed in 1897) and the Library of Congress John Adams Building (for the library annex completed in the 1930s). Together with the James Madison Memorial Building, the Jefferson and Adams Buildings honor the three presidents involved in the early establishment of the Library of Congress.

In FY 1980, more than 907,429 readers used the various public reading rooms of the library, except law, and nearly 650,000 volumes were circulated to readers from the general collections; nearly 170,000 items were loaned outside the Library of Congress. The Law Library responded to 235,925 research requests from all sources and circulated 366,077 items in Law Library reading rooms; 4,244 items were loaned from the law collections. The Congressional Research Service (CRS) responded in 1980 more than 340,000 times to the legislative, oversight, and representational needs of the Congress and opened an experimental Information Distribution Center—so successful that it became permanent—in the Senate to provide self-service distribution of CRS reports, issue briefs, and other prepared materials on about 75 current topics of high interest. Two CRS publications became available through the U.S. Government Printing Office by year's end: *Major Legislation of Congress,* a computer-produced monthly summary of the most important legislative issues, and *CRS Studies in the Public Domain,* a semiannual list of all CRS research products that have been printed by the Congress and are available either as committee prints, House or Senate documents, or insertions in the *Congressional*

Record. The Copyright Office reported for fiscal year 1980 an all-time high in the number of registrations—464,743. A new register of copyrights, David L. Ladd, joined the LC staff on June 2, 1980. [A more complete report on the activities of the Copyright Office is included in the Federal Agencies section of Part 1—*Ed.*]

COLLECTIONS

The collections of the Library of Congress increased to nearly 77 million items in FY 1980, with especially strong rates of growth in the areas of phonorecords, photographs, and microfiche. Notable acquisitions augmented the library's collections in materials from the People's Republic of China and in holdings of music scores and memorabilia, personal papers of notable Americans, prints, photographs, drawings, and rare books. The library's major acquisition of 1979—the transfer of the Lessing Rosenwald Collection—was completed with the last and very substantial portion of Mr. Rosenwald's collection, including 5,000 reference books and books not given in his lifetime, arriving at the library by mid-1980. In May, a symposium on the illustrated book was held in memory of Mr. Rosenwald's generosity. Other special acquisitions in FY 1980 included the Stanley Edgar Hyman Papers and additions to the Margaret Mead Papers and music manuscripts or papers of George Gershwin, Béla Bartók, Arnold Schoenberg, and Richard Rodgers, as well as a collection of material documenting the career of American soprano Dorothea Dix Lawrence. The Prints and Photographs Division added works in various media to its collections by artists Walter Allner, Pierre Bonnard, Howard Brodie, Jim Dine, David Levine, Pablo Picasso, Edward Sorel, and Saul Steinberg, among others, and received by transfer over 82,000 drawings and printed samples of trademark designs registered for protection in the U.S. Patent Office in the period 1870-1910.

The major gift of 1980 was made by Hans P. and Hanni Kraus, who presented to the library a unique and remarkable collection relating to the life and explorations of Sir Francis Drake. The 60 items in the collection include maps, manuscripts, printed books, medals, and portraits. The collection is the second major gift that Mr. and Mrs. Kraus have made to the library, the first a donation in 1970 of 162 manuscripts relating to the history and culture of Spanish America in the colonial period (1492-1819). The Drake Collection has been praised as one that "draws together much otherwise scattered material into a coherent record which enables the story of Drake's life to be seen as a whole."

CATALOGING AND NETWORKING

Cooperation and planning for the future continued to characterize the work of Processing Services cataloging divisions in 1980. A considerable amount of time was spent planning the January 2, 1981, freezing of the library's existing card catalogs, and the development of what are known as "add-on catalogs" until such time as it becomes possible for the library's staff and users to rely more completely on the machine-readable bibliographic file. Concurrent with the freezing of the catalogs, the library adopted the second edition of the *Anglo-American Cataloguing Rules* and held discussions with various foreign national libraries and other cooperating libraries to ensure compatibility in the transition to the new code. Several staff members also served as faculty in a series of seven regional institutes on *AACR 2* conducted by the American Library Association's Resources and Technical Services Division, its Council of Regional Groups, and the Library of Congress. The library has also agreed to train catalogers from the National

Library of Medicine and the National Agricultural Library to standardize the cataloging among the three national libraries.

Year's end saw two major steps forward for the *National Union Catalog*. With only a small group of senior staff left to edit the final segment of the catalog in January 1981, the National Union Catalog Publication Project was disbanded following completion of its 14-year mission—the editing of a catalog of pre-1956 imprints that will, when the final volumes are published in late 1981, fill 755 volumes. Looking to the future, the library announced plans to publish the *National Union Catalog* in a register and index format once the bibliographic data is available in machine-readable form and has accordingly asked for institutional comments on the proposal from the library community. LC projects that the new catalog will allow for broader coverage of materials in terms of the numbers of languages included and will be available on a more timely basis.

Coming up to its tenth anniversary, the Cataloging in Publication Division (CIP) has completed cataloging data for more than 180,000 titles submitted by the over 2,000 publishers participating in the CIP program. Looking to 1981, the division, with funding provided by the Council on Library Resources, Inc., has planned a survey of the nation's libraries regarding their use of CIP products and services and prepared a set of guidelines for providing CIP data for multinational publications to be implemented early in the new year.

A reorganization in Processing Services early in 1980 led to the creation of the Office of the Director for Processing Systems, Networks and Automation Planning, with Henriette D. Avram named the first incumbent to this position. With her appointment, the Network Development Office was transferred from the jurisdiction of the Associate Librarian for National Programs, and the function for maintenance of the MARC communication formats, with the accompanying liaison efforts, was moved from the Automated Systems Office to Mrs. Avram's new office. [For a more complete report on the library's networking activities, see "Library Networking in the United States, 1980" in the Special Reports section of Part 1—*Ed.*]

EXHIBITS AND PUBLICATIONS HIGHLIGHTS

Major exhibitions of 1980 included "Autochromes: Color Photography Comes of Age," a collection of striking turn-of-the-century photographs made by the unique process of color photograph printing developed by Louis Lumière, and "Ten First Street, Southeast: Congress Builds a Library," a display of several hundred items depicting the construction and decoration of the Thomas Jefferson Building. The autochromes display will become a Library of Congress traveling exhibit in 1981. Other exhibits mounted in 1980 were "Belgium . . . Shall Constitute an Independent State," part of the *Belgium Today* celebration of the one hundred fiftieth anniversary of Belgian independence; "Inside Our Homes, Outside Our Windows," a display of more than 150 contemporary photographs documenting aspects of ethnic community life in Chicago; the thirty-seventh annual White House News Photographers Association show of award-winning pictures and films taken in 1979; and "Creativity: Its Many Faces," a display of items reflecting the imaginative spirit that was opened on the occasion of a symposium on creativity and the first meeting of the library's newly appointed Council of Scholars. Catalogs were published to accompany the exhibits on the Thomas Jefferson Building, Belgian independence, the Chicago photographs, and creativity.

Other Library of Congress publications in 1980 included *Arab-World Newspapers in the Library of Congress*, *The Audience for Children's Books*, *The Best of Children's Books—1964-1978*, *A Century of Photographs, 1846-1946*, *Facsimiles of Maps and*

Atlases, John Paul Jones' Memoir of the American Revolution, Las Casas as a Bishop (a bilingual edition of his holograph petition in the Kraus collection), *Members of Congress: A Checklist of Their Papers in the Manuscript Division, The Portuguese Manuscripts Collection of the Library of Congress,* and *University of Malawi Publications: A Guide,* the latest in the Maktaba Afrikana series prepared by the library's African Section. These and other LC publications are listed in *Library of Congress Publications in Print.* The catalog, which includes complete ordering information, may be obtained by writing to the Library of Congress, Central Services Division, Washington, DC 20540.

THE CENTER FOR THE BOOK IN THE LIBRARY OF CONGRESS

Washington, DC 20540

John Y. Cole

Executive Director

"To keep the book flourishing" is the purpose of the Center for the Book in the Library of Congress (LC). Established in October 1977 by PL 95–129, the center exists to help organize, focus, and dramatize our nation's interest in books, reading, and the printed word. At a planning meeting held shortly after the approval of PL 95–129, Librarian of Congress Daniel J. Boorstin explained why the Center for the Book should be at the Library of Congress:

> As the national library of a great free republic, we have a special interest to see that books do not go unread, that they are read by people of all ages and conditions, that books are not buried in their own dross, not lost from neglect or obscured from us by specious alternatives and synthetic substitutes. As the national library of the most technologically advanced nation on earth, we have a special duty, too, to see that the book is the useful, illuminating servant of all other technologies, and that all other technologies become the effective, illuminating acolytes of the book.

The Center for the Book serves as a catalyst among authors, publishers, booksellers, librarians, educators, business leaders, scholars, and readers—everyone who has or should have an interest in books and reading. Working with other organizations, the center strives to

Heighten the general public's "book awareness"

Effectively use other media to promote books and reading

Stimulate the study of books

Encourage the international flow of books and printed materials

Improve the quality of book production

With help from a large national advisory board that includes representatives from the book, educational, and business communities, the center carries out an active program of lectures, symposia, projects, and publications. George C. McGhee, former ambassador to Turkey and to the Federal Republic of Germany, is board chairman. The center's interests include the educational and cultural role of the book, nationally and internationally; the history of books and printing; the future of the book, especially as it relates to new technologies and to other media; authorship and writing; the printing, publishing, care, and preservation of books; access to and use of books and printed materials; reading; and literacy.

While LC provides administrative support, as authorized by PL 95-129, the center's program and publications are supported primarily by tax-deductible contributions from individuals and organizations. True to its catalytic function, the center has a full-time staff of only two people. During its first three years of existence, the Center for the Book received donations from 35 individuals and corporations. The major unrestricted gifts have come from Mrs. Charles W. Engelhard, McGraw-Hill, Inc., and Time, Inc. Other notable contributions were from Franklin Books, Inc. (to support programs that promote the book internationally), from Exxon Education Foundation, and from the U.S. National Institute of Education (to support symposia on textbooks and on literacy). Principal Center for the Book programs and projects are outlined below.

READING DEVELOPMENT AND PROMOTION

The center's April 1978 symposium "Television, the Book, and the Classroom," sponsored with the U.S. Office of Education, brought two revolutionary technologies—television and the book—together to explore their complementary features. The symposium helped inspire the U.S. Office of Education's research program on critical television viewing skills and led directly to the Library of Congress/CBS Television "Read More about It" project. This project provides information—both on the air and in prepared lists—about books related to certain CBS network presentations. Immediately following the telecast, performers from the program make 30-second spot announcements that encourage viewers to go to their local libraries and bookstores for books about the subject of the program. The lists are published before the telecasts in the American Library Association's *Booklist*, the American Booksellers Association's *Newswire*, and other library and trade publications. "Read More about It" has been well received: *TV Guide* called it "a welcome idea for those who believe that television can and should be the natural ally of reading" and in October 1980 the project received an achievement award from the American Council for Better Broadcasts. *Television, the Book, and the Classroom*, a volume based on the symposium proceedings, may be purchased for $4.95 (postage included) from the Information Office, Library of Congress, Washington, DC 20540.

"Books Make a Difference," an oral history project scheduled for completion in mid-1981, is another reading promotion endeavor. Citizens in over 50 communities throughout the United States are being interviewed about books—and other reading—that helped shape their lives. Excerpts from the interviews are being made available to libraries, bookstores, and the media for use in reading promotion projects at the community level.

Friends of Libraries USA and the Center for the Book hosted a forum in early 1981 entitled "Good Ideas for Friends' Groups." A major discussion topic was the most effective way for friends' groups to become involved with projects such as "Read More about It" and "Books Make a Difference."

The Book Industry Study Group, Inc. (BISG) and the Center for the Book presented an October 1978 program that examined the results of BISG's survey of adult reading in the United States. Some of the survey findings, e.g., that readers are active people, that pleasure is one of the prime motivations for reading, and that reading seems to decline rapidly after age 50, may form the basis for future Center for the Book projects. *Reading in America 1978*, a volume based on this program that also includes a summary of the survey, is available for $4.95 (postage included) from the Library of Congress Information Office.

In autumn 1981 the center will host a national symposium, "Reading and Successful Living: The Family-School Partnership." The purpose is to highlight the importance of the family-school partnership in reading development and to provide program ideas for the symposium's other sponsors: the National Parent-Teacher Association, the International Reading Association, the American Association of School Administrators, and the American Association of School Librarians.

THE BOOK IN SOCIETY

The Center for the Book is concerned about the role of the book and the printed word in our society—past, present, and future. On the historical side, one of its most important programs is the Engelhard Lecture on the Book, a commissioned, public lecture by a prominent scholar. The Engelhard lecturers thus far have been Nicolas Barker and Ian Willison of the British Library; Elizabeth Eisenstein of the University of Michigan; librarian, collector, and scholar Philip Hofer; Edwin Wolf II of the Library Company of Philadelphia; and Princeton University professor Robert Darnton. Engelhard lectures are published in LC's *Quarterly Journal* and eventually will be gathered together in a separate volume sponsored by the Center for the Book. For six months in 1979 Engelhard lecturer Elizabeth Eisenstein served as the center's first resident consultant.

The center also sponsors other lectures, as well as symposia and specific projects concerned with the relationship of books and printing to the development of our society. Lecturers have included Mirjam Foot of the British Library, author and collector Anthony Hobson, and typographers and book designers John Dreyfus and Hans Schmoller. The center's 1980 symposium "Rosenwald Symposium on the Illustrated Book" honored the magnificent collection given to the Library of Congress by Lessing J. Rosenwald and paid special attention to the collection's scholarly potential. Ten scholarly papers were commissioned for the July 1980 meeting "Literacy in Historical Perspective," which brought historians and U.S. government policymakers together to learn from each other. The January 1981 symposium celebrating the completion of the 755-volume *National Union Catalog: Pre-1956 Imprints* focused on the scholarly uses of this unique bibliographical tool. With help from the American Printing History Association, the center is helping to plan an inventory of printing and publishing archives throughout the United States. Finally, the center has sponsored publication of *The Circle of Knowledge*, a catalog of an important LC exhibit about encyclopedias (available for $2.50, postage included, from the Library of Congress Information Office).

What is "the future of the book" in our electronic age? This is a question inevitably faced by speakers participating in Center for the Book lectures or symposia dealing with the role of books and reading in today's society. Answers to the question are varied and complex but, not unexpectedly, they tend to be so positive on behalf of the book that the question usually is changed to: What shape will "the book of the future" take?

Major symposia have addressed "broadcasting books to young audiences" on radio and television, the role of textbooks in American society, and the public responsibilities of the American book community. Volumes based on two of these meetings, *The Textbook in American Society* and *Responsibilities of the American Book Community,* are available for $4.95 and $7.95 respectively (postage included) from the Library of Congress Information Office. Public lectures about the book in contemporary society have included "The Book" (Barbara Tuchman), "The Audience for Children's

Books" (Elaine Moss and Barbara Rollock), and "State of the Book World 1980" (Alfred Kazin, Dan Lacy, and Ernest Boyer). In early 1981 the center hosted a forum at which publishers, paper manufacturers, and research librarians exchanged views about producing paper for book longevity.

THE INTERNATIONAL ROLE OF THE BOOK

The Charter of the Book, set forth in 1972 during UNESCO's International Book Year, stresses the importance of the free flow of books between countries and the essential role of books in promoting international understanding. The international side of the center's program is carried out in the spirit of these principles. Symposia have included "The Book in Mexico," "Japanese Literature in Translation," and "The International Flow of Information: A Trans-Pacific Perspective," and in 1979 typographer and book designer Fernand Baudin presented a public lecture, "Belgian Books 1830–1980." The symposium "The International Flow of Information: A Trans-Pacific Perspective," held in Hawaii, was followed by a visit to Los Angeles, New York, Washington, D.C., and Corsicana and Dallas, Texas, by 17 symposium participants from 12 Pacific-rim nations. This visit, the programs in each city, and a follow-up meeting in New Zealand in early 1981 were organized by the Center for the Book and sponsored by the U.S. International Communication Agency. Another major project is the compilation, under the auspices of the Center for the Book, of a directory of international book programs sponsored by the U.S. government and by selected private organizations. Finally, the center is participating in the planning for UNESCO's World Congress on Books, which will be held in June 1982.

NATIONAL LIBRARY OF MEDICINE

8600 Rockville Pike,
Bethesda, MD 20209
301-496-6308

Robert B. Mehnert

Public Information Officer

The day May 22, 1980 marked a milestone in the history of the National Library of Medicine (NLM), as its new building, the Lister Hill Center, was formally dedicated. Previously separated divisions of the library have now come together for the first time, creating a significant opportunity for mutually beneficial interaction.

A major element in the new building is the Lister Hill National Center for Biomedical Communications, the research and development component of NLM. This division began organizationally at NLM in 1968, the result of the same congressional resolution that authorized the building. Initially housed within the existing library building, the center has pioneered in the application of the latest computer and communications technology to the problems of information transfer. In addition to the research and development program, the new building also houses the closely related programs of the National Medical Audiovisual Center (NMAC). Originally a part of the Centers for Disease Control in Atlanta, Georgia, NMAC was transferred organizationally to the library in 1967. However, because of space limitations in Bethesda, NMAC remained in Atlanta until 1980.

Other library divisions in the new building include programs that either began or were greatly expanded after the original NLM building was occupied in 1962—including Extramural Programs (first authorized in 1965) and the Toxicology Information Program (1966). The MEDLARS operation—the computers and the network management personnel—are also part of the new facility.

At the dedication ceremony on May 22, some 200 invited guests participated in a full day of activities, highlighted by an afternoon address by Patricia R. Harris, secretary of Health and Human Services. Former Senator Lister Hill himself attended and heard tributes to his leadership as the Senate's "Statesman for Health." A member of Congress for 47 years, he sponsored many of the most important pieces of health legislation enacted in this century. Among others, he cosponsored the legislation that in 1956 created the National Library of Medicine; and in 1962, he gave the keynote address at the dedication of the library building. The audience for the dedication was an impressive array of leaders in the health field: medical educators, librarians, information scientists, the NLM Board of Regents, directors of the International MEDLARS centers, officials from the Department of Health and Human Services, and friends from the library and health-science community.

Significant progress was made in 1980 on the development of a new automation system—MEDLARS III. After the basic principles of the new system were approved by the library's Board of Regents, the concept was presented at a series of meetings with members of the health-sciences community to introduce NLM's plans and solicit their views. By the end of the year, detailed functional specifications were complete and a team of systems analysts had been assembled to lay out the actual development and implementation. When operating, MEDLARS III will greatly improve NLM's internal technical processing of the biomedical literature and also provide expanded bibliographic services to health-science libraries throughout the network. In this latter regard, MEDLARS III will provide new capabilities to help the nation's health-science libraries create bibliographic records, retrieve bibliographic and text information, have access to national holdings and location information, and order documents on interlibrary loan.

In addition to the wide range of general and specialized bibliographic publications regularly issued by NLM, two noteworthy monographs appeared with the library's imprint in 1980. The first was the collected essays on the occasion of the one hundredth anniversary of the library's most important bibliographic publication: *Centenary of Index Medicus, 1879–1979,* edited by John B. Blake, chief of the History of Medicine Division. The second publication, *A Review of the United States Role in International Biomedical Research and Communications: International Health and Foreign Policy,* was written by Mary E. Corning, NLM assistant director for International Programs. Both are available from the Superintendent of Documents, U.S. Government Printing Office.

Several important appointments to the NLM staff were made in 1980: James W. Woods was selected as director of the National Medical Audiovisual Center, and Henry W. Riecken was appointed senior program adviser to the NLM director. Three new regents were named to four-year terms on the library's Board of Regents: Gwendolyn S. Cruzat, William D. Mayer, and Charles E. Molnar.

LIBRARY OPERATIONS

NLM's nationwide MEDLARS network, which provides the capability of on-line interactive searching of bibliographic data from terminals in institutions in the U.S. and around the world, continued to expand in 1980. There are now almost 1,300 MEDLINE centers in this country—at hospitals, medical schools and universities, research institutions, and commercial organizations. The Swiss Academy of Medicine became an international MEDLARS partner in June and is now regularly accessing NLM's computers in Bethesda.

Over 1.8 million searches were performed on MEDLINE and NLM's other on-line data bases in 1980. A new data base, POPLINE, was added this year. POPLINE contains about 70,000 references to the literature of population and family planning. Altogether, there are more than 4 million references to journal articles, books, and audiovisual materials in NLM's computerized files.

Late in 1979 the library announced a moratorium on adding new institutional users to the MEDLARS/MEDLINE bibliographic retrieval network because of severe strains on NLM's computers. The moratorium was partially lifted in April 1980, when new users were accepted with the understanding that they would be restricted to accessing the network's backup facility at the State University of New York in Albany. The imminent installation of a new, larger computer system at NLM allowed the moratorium to be ended completely as of August 1. All MEDLARS processing—both publications production and on-line searching—is now being done on two IBM 370/168 computers. The upgraded computer system has increased threefold the amount of work that can be handled by MEDLARS.

Several key indicators of level and quality of service improved in the fiscal year ending September 30, 1980. Although the demand for interlibrary loans declined slightly from last year, there was significant improvement in the quality of document delivery services: During the last month of the fiscal year, the fulfillment rate for lending original materials rose to 88 percent, exceeding the rate for photocopy (87 percent). The potential fulfillment rate (the rate that could be achieved except for items that were out on loan or in the bindery) was 97 percent for that month, reflecting a very healthy state of NLM's monograph collection. Turnaround time was also improved: 86 percent of photocopied loans were sent out within four days (compared with 83 percent last year); original loans supplied within four days improved even more, from 51 percent in 1979 to 68 percent in 1980.

Productivity in cataloging and serial processing also improved significantly. Completed cataloging (including historical items) rose by almost 20 percent to more than 19,000 pieces; serial items processed increased by 6.5 percent to more than 185,000. These increases are even more remarkable in view of the fact that both Cataloging and Serial Records were without section heads for the entire fiscal year. In general, however, restrictions in personnel hiring, combined with heavy turnover of staff in certain areas, has strained in NLM's capacity to provide services. [Selected NLM library services statistics are shown in Table 1.]

The Regional Medical Library (RML) program, established by NLM in the 1960s, continues to play a vital role in providing information services to health professionals across the country. The RML program is a national network of 11 regional libraries, more than 100 resource libraries, and approximately 3,000 basic unit libraries (e.g., hospital libraries) coordinated by the National Library of Medicine. Each of the 11 RMLs coordinates information delivery services within its own region and cooperates with libraries throughout the network to provide nearly 2 million interlibrary loans annually. The RMLs also promote network participation through consultation, training, workshops, and continuing education programs. During 1980, nearly $3 million was awarded by NLM to the regional and subcontracting resource libraries to operate RML programs.

TABLE 1   SELECTED STATISTICS, 1980*

Collection (book and nonbook)	2,694,090
Serial titles received	22,753
Titles cataloged	19,347
Items indexed for MEDLARS	266,730
Circulation requests filled	348,580
For interlibrary loan	182,366
For readers	166,214
Reference requests	45,212
Computerized searches (all data bases)	1,811,813
On-line	1,250,372
Off-line	561,441

*For the year ending September 30, 1980.

LISTER HILL NATIONAL CENTER FOR BIOMEDICAL COMMUNICATIONS

The Lister Hill Center performs research and development to create new, or modify existing, biomedical communication systems and networks. Emphasis at the center is on experimental programs rather than on operating proved systems. With the facilities provided by the new building, the center is carrying out more research and development with its own staff and laboratories, although collaboration with the outside biomedical science and technology communities will continue.

The Integrated Library System (ILS), under development by the Lister Hill Center since 1978, became available to the library community in 1980. The ILS is a computer-based system that can be used by health-science libraries of all sizes to improve their services, to manage their collections better, and to promote resource sharing. The first version of the Integrated Library System is available through the National Technical Information Service for a licensing fee of $2,000. Although ILS can be implemented on computers costing as little as $25,000, equipment for a medium-sized library can cost $70,000 or more.

There are four basic elements of the ILS (Version 1.0). The first is a Master Bibliographic File, the data elements for which can be specified by the library using the system. It is also possible to create a master file using data from other bibliographic source tapes, such as Library of Congress or OCLC. The Circulation Subsystem includes bar code or manual check-in/check-out capabilities. Both patrons and collection items can be identified by a wide range of entry points (for example, identification numbers, personal name, call number, and title). The Serials Check-in Subsystem allows the local creation of bar codes directly from the Master Bibliographic File (MBF) and the production of routing slips. Thus, the MBF is updated upon check-in and the serial issue is immediately available for circulation. The Online Catalog Access Subsystem allows searching of the MBF through the use of a variety of entry points, including call number, ISSN, ISBN, author, and title. Future enhancements of the ILS include serials control, acquisitions, cataloging, authority control, generalized network access, and patron interface.

A new program begun by the Lister Hill Center in 1980 is to design, develop, and evaluate an experimental system that will electronically store, retrieve, and display documents acquired by the library. The system will be developed by concurrently pursuing three research projects: document capture, data transfer and storage, and document display. The document capture project will analyze and implement techniques to scan paper documents electronically and to digitize the electrical signals generated in scanning. The data transfer and storage project will seek ways to format and store the resulting stream of digitized information on magnetic and optical discs. The document display project will develop methods for displaying retrieved documents both electronically and on paper. Using compression techniques, it is estimated that more than 500,000 journal pages can be stored on one high-density optical disc. Expanding the storage with a "jukebox," or disc-pack system containing 1,000 discs, will provide an on-line storage capacity of 3 to 4 million journal issues.

The Lister Hill Center is continuing the development and evaluation of its "knowledge bases" in such areas as hepatitis, peptic ulcer, and human genetics. This program has been described in the *Bowker Annual* in previous years.

NATIONAL MEDICAL AUDIOVISUAL CENTER

The National Medical Audiovisual Center (NMAC) is the component of the National Library of Medicine with primary responsibility for planning and administering a national program to improve the quality and use of audiovisual learning materials in health professional education and practice. NMAC programs were curtailed in 1980 because of the considerable task of packing and moving staff and equipment from Atlanta to Bethesda. However, the physical integration of NMAC facilities, programs, and expertise with those already existing at NLM will create new opportunities for improving services to NLM constituents.

Despite the staff time and effort devoted to relocating the center, many audiovisual production projects were completed. Twenty-one videotapes were finished, including programs in the Leaders in American Medicine and in the Distinguished Leaders in Nursing series. In addition, a 20-minute film highlighting NLM's history was produced and shown to those attending the dedication of the Lister Hill Center building.

The audiovisual loan service, suspended from January through March 1980, was resumed for 16mm films only in April and operated by a contractor in Atlanta. The videocassettes were shipped to Bethesda and will be available on interlibrary loan from NLM beginning in 1981. For the year, 17,500 items (down 60 percent from last year) were shipped in response to requests for loans. An aggressive acquisitions program to bring the collection up to date and publication of a new catalog in 1981 are expected to return use of these materials to the pre-1980 level.

The NMAC Educational Training and Consultation Program designs, conducts, and evaluates faculty development workshops and seminars. In FY 1980, 485 health professionals participated in 21 workshops conducted by NMAC and the 9 field training centers on such subjects as developing instructional materials, television production techniques, and basic photography for health professionals.

TOXICOLOGY INFORMATION PROGRAM

The objectives of NLM's Toxicology Information Program are to create computer-based toxicology data bases from the scientific literature and from the files of collaborating industrial, academic, and governmental organizations and to establish and operate toxicology information services for the scientific community. TOXLINE (Toxicology Information Online), the largest data base created by the program, was restructured into three files in 1980: the on-line TOXLINE (references from 1977 forward), the off-line TOXBACK 74 (a backfile of citations published from 1974 to 1976), and the off-line TOXBACK 65 (pre-1974 citations). In addition to this restructuring, another component subfile has been added to TOXLINE. The Toxicology Document and Data Depository (TD3) has citations to government reports, along with associated abstracts, key words, and ordering information. The number of searches done on TOXLINE this year was 86,000, an increase of more than 20,000 from 1979.

A new data base, the Laboratory Animal Data Bank (LADB), became available in January 1980. Unlike NLM's other data bases, which are operated on the library's MEDLARS computers, LADB is available only through the computer of a contractor—the Battelle-Columbus Laboratories. The new data base is an interagency project and provides base-line biomedical data from experimental control animals of species and strains commonly used in laboratory research and testing. These unpublished data are contributed voluntarily by industry, government agencies, and various teaching and research institutions. At the end of FY 1980, LADB contained almost 900,000 observations from more than 27,000 animals of 66 species or strains.

The Toxicology Information Program operates a literature search service in toxicology through the Toxicology Information Response Center (TIRC) at the Oak Ridge National Laboratory. The number of specialized searches completed by TIRC in 1980 was 546, almost double last year's number. The center also publishes reviews and annotated bibliographies.

GRANT PROGRAMS

In FY 1980 the National Library of Medicine, through its Extramural Programs, awarded 164 grants and contracts totaling $9,925,000. These awards are made under the Medical Library Assistance Act and are used to improve biomedical library resources, conduct research related to health-science communication, train experts in the integration of computerized techniques and the health sciences, and support scientific publications. The year 1980 marked the fifteenth anniversary of the passage of the act. In the intervening years over 4,000 grant awards ($118 million) have been made by the library.

There was a special emphasis on the Computers-in-Medicine Program this year. This program supports computer sciences research in knowledge representation, data base management, and clinical decision making. Congress designated $1.3 million in special funding for the program in 1980, allowing 10 new research projects to be funded.

TECHNICAL INFORMATION SYSTEMS/ NATIONAL AGRICULTURAL LIBRARY

U.S. Department of Agriculture
Beltsville, MD 20705
301-344-3778

Eugene M. Farkas
Chief, Educational Resources Division

An expanded education and training program for current and potential users of its agricultural information systems and services has been initiated by the Technical Information Systems/National Agricultural Library (TIS/NAL) to ensure broader public awareness of its resources and responsibilities.

The planning of the education program—in cooperation with state land-grant and other universities—coincided with a continuing general growth in both services and audiences experienced by Technical Information Systems in 1980. Located in the National Agricultural Library (NAL) building, Beltsville, Maryland, TIS was established in 1978 as a part of the Science and Education Administration (SEA), U.S. Department of Agriculture (USDA). Library resources were combined with a number of research-related data bases and with educational and other outreach activities to give TIS comprehensive information collection and dissemination capabilities.

EDUCATION AND NEW TRAINING PROGRAM

The initial phase of the new training plan consists of a series of basic-level workshops emphasizing on-line access to CRIS (current research information) and AGRICOLA (agricultural literature) as well as profiling for CALS (current awareness literature service). Several advanced-level data-base classes were also projected for 1981. Librarians and technical information specialists are the primary participants.

In support of these increased educational efforts, a 20-minute videotape, *The Information Cycle,* describing TIS operations and services has been produced and is being distributed on a loan basis to libraries, federal and state agencies, state cooperative extension services, educational institutions, and other interested groups. Publications issued for use in general outreach programs include the *TIS Guide to Services, Food and Nutrition Center, AGRICOLA* (on the use of the data base), and 35 quick bibliographies on subjects of current concern to the public, such as energy, volcanic ash, acid rain, minimum tillage, small farms, and nutrition and aging.

A new TIS demonstration center, the Educational Resources Room, was established in downtown Washington, D.C. A display of multimedia resources available from the TIS Food and Nutrition Information Center marked the opening of the new facility. TIS training sessions will be held there using the latest computer and audiovisual tools and techniques. In addition, Agricultural On-Line Access (AGRICOLA) demonstrations were held throughout the United States in cooperation with land-grant colleges and universities and professional societies.

NUTRITION INFORMATION

The Food and Nutrition Information Center reached nearly 1.5 million persons in FY 1980 through its audiovisual lending program with films, tapes, slides, and other educational aids shown in classrooms and before citizen groups. Requests for reference services tripled from 565 to 1,546 with schools, state departments of education, universities and colleges, private industry, hospitals, Congress, and other government agencies as major users. Outreach and demonstrations of on-line computer searching increased contacts with over 4,000 dietitians and nutritionists. Fifty-nine presentations were given, and three bibliographies prepared on *Food Guides* and *Dietary Guidelines, Nutrition and Aging,* and *Maternal and Infant Nutrition.*

Major new programs designed to collect and provide technical information on alternate energy sources, aquaculture, and human nutrition also were initiated by TIS in 1980 in response to current and anticipated public concerns. In support of these and other new areas of emphasis, the library expanded and refined its bibliographic and research data bases principally through creation of new subfiles and subject categories.

NEW EXTENSION, 4-H SUBFILES

Some 60–75,000 4-H and other state extension popular publications produced and used by the nation's state extension services in their educational programs are being included in the NAL's master bibliographic data base as new subfiles titled "4-H" and "CES" with citations and abstracts. The state extension services, SEA extension, and SEA Technical Information Systems are working together on this massive project, which will ensure mutual accessibility for the first time to state publications among all states and by the federal government. The project is designed to reduce or eliminate duplication of effort and to encourage more efficient use of resources at both the federal and state levels. The submission of 4-H and youth publications for the north-central states was to be completed by January 1, 1981, and additions of adult publications finished by July 1982.

Approximately 54,300 requests for information, a 26 percent increase over 1979, were answered by TIS librarians using automated literature searches and other information sources. Researchers both in this country and abroad accounted for 59 percent of all inquiries, including increased requests from developing countries. Policymakers, consulting firms, farmers, and the general public also asked for assistance, along with a growing number of scholars and librarians. Topics on which information was most frequently requested were agricultural statistics of all kinds, pest control, wind and solar energy, alcohol fuels, agricultural machinery and equipment, and forest management and production. Special information research projects in support of USDA programs included small farms, evaluation of agricultural research, hazardous wastes, nutrition research, structures of agriculture, forest biomass, alcohol fuels, energy conservation, and aquaculture.

DOCUMENT DELIVERY

A significant improvement in the efficiency of its document delivery service was recorded by TIS in FY 1980, when over 80 percent of requested items were processed and on their way in five or fewer working days from the time of initial receipt of request. A sampling indicated that from June 1 through August 31, 1980, an average of 83.5 percent of all requests received were completed in the five-day period compared with an average of 64.2 percent completed in the same three-month period in 1979. TIS receives 300,000 requests each year and considers the service efficient if 80 percent are processed in five or fewer working days. In FY 1980 3,500 more requests were handled than in FY 1979 and with less staff.

After three years of planning and development, data on the Nursery and Seed Trade Catalog Collection have become available to the TIS staff on-line using PRIME. Data from the 1978 U.S. files have been fed into the computer and the following search capabilities are possible: alphabetical listing of U.S. companies; geographical listing by state; type of business (wholesale, nursery, seedsman, etc., or any combination); and holdings. The automated file will be updated with 1979 and 1980 holdings. There are no plans to enter records prior to 1978.

CITATIONS FOR AGRIS

As part of its expanded program for cooperation with AGRIS (International Information Systems for the Agriculture Sciences and Technology), TIS increased its contribution of citations for U.S. imprints from 12,000 input sheets annually in FYs 1976–1977 to 48,989, 51,019, and 50,000 compatible machine-records for 1978–1980, respectively, thus making the United States by far the most prolific of the AGRIS participants. Development of computer compatibility is the result of cooperative agreements with Agency for International Development and is also enabling TIS to incorporate selected AGRIS citations for non-U.S. imprints with the AGRICOLA file, beginning in 1981.

TIS has worked closely in the past few years to aid the land-grant colleges and Tuskegee Institute libraries in updating and improving their services. These include the distribution of duplicate books and journal pieces, the introduction of on-line bibliographic searchings, and the free distribution of photocopies of journal articles to agricultural researchers upon request. In the fall of 1978, the NAL sponsored a meeting in Huntsville, Alabama, with the library directors and was able to bring the agricultural research directors into a three-day discussion of agricultural information needs. Those activities are now culminating through incorporation of the land-grant library directors, meetings of the group twice yearly beginning in 1979, and proposed federal legislation to aid these local agricultural library-information services to develop.

COOPERATIVE EDUCATION

A pioneering cooperative education program begun with New Mexico Highlands University six years ago has resulted in the creation of eight positions in TIS through which nine students of mostly Hispanic background learned about library and information science. Each of the students spent two six-month periods at Beltsville rotating through the various TIS units. Expansion of the program to other minority groups such as blacks, American Indians, and Orientals has been proposed for the immediate future.

The donation of the personal library of the late Charles E. Kellogg, internationally renowned soil scientist, marked a significant addition to the special historical collections presently held by the NAL. The Kellogg collection, one of the finest and largest of its kind in the world, includes soil science publications, manuscripts, slides, and unpublished journals.

Over 620 visitors, including 180 from foreign countries, were given tours of, or briefings at, the NAL building from May through November 1980. This is more than double the 295 persons, including 139 from other countries, who visited the building to learn about TIS during all of 1979. TIS missions and services were explained to scientists, librarians, technical information specialists, and nutritionists from the People's Republic of China (31), the Philippines, Brazil, Israel, Bulgaria, Bangladesh, India, Yugoslavia, New Zealand, Australia, Guadeloupe, Germany, England, France, Pakistan, Botswana, Dominican Republic, Spain, Saudi Arabia, Madagascar, and other countries.

TIS/NAL OFFICERS

Admin. Richard A. Farley; *Assoc. Admin.* Samuel T. Waters; *Chief, Educational Resources Div.* Eugene M. Farkas; *Chief, Info. Services Div.* John R. Myers; *Chief, Lib. Operations Div.* Wallace C. Olsen.

National Associations

AMERICAN LIBRARY ASSOCIATION
50 E. Huron St., Chicago, IL 60611
312-944-6780

Peggy Sullivan
President

Characterizing one year in the life of an association as diverse and complex as the American Library Association is always difficult, but it certainly requires more perspective than can be attained within a few weeks after the end of that year. The library press, with its comments on a down-to-business council (ALA's policy-making body), a highly successful annual conference, and several interesting projects, provides some clues. The attitudes of members and potential members provide others. During 1980, ALA's Planning Committee reviewed the recent survey of membership, which had been conducted to determine what members' goals and priorities were for the association, and identified five major priorities plus a few of less moment. This report is organized according to those priorities.

LEGISLATION/FUNDING

Competition for the federal dollar occupies much of the energy of any association concerned, as is ALA, with educational and other activities in the public sector. But legislative concerns extend far beyond the search for support. In a series of efforts extending from the November 1979 White House Conference on Libraries and Information Services, the Committee on Legislation drafted and council passed at the 1980 midwinter meeting an 18-point legislative program calling for full funding of library and education programs already established by the federal government, a national periodicals system, favorable postal and telecommunication rates, and passage of a national library and information services act. Some points were lost almost as soon as they were articulated, notably the request for the post of Assistant Secretary for Library and Information Sciences in the Education Department, and most, like the critical request for full funding, reflected the need to implement and build on programs already in place but not sufficiently supported to be as useful as they were intended to be. Recognition of the need for adequate financial support came up repeatedly in many parts of the association's program of action, including the theme of National Library Week in 1980: "America's greatest bargain . . . the library."

As Eileen Cooke, Associate Executive Director of ALA and a registered lobbyist, observed when the executive board discussed the high priority the membership had placed on legislation and funding, activity is a means to achievement of association goals, not an end in itself. The fact that members supported this strongly by their responses to the survey, by their legislative lobbying efforts at every level of government, and by their support of ALA's Washington office, indicates their commitment to continuing and expanding the support that makes librarianship and the ALA forceful and effective in American society.

ACCESS TO INFORMATION FOR EVERYONE

Thomas J. Galvin, ALA's president for 1979–1980, chose to stress an information agenda for the 1980s as the theme for his presidential year. An information agenda colloquium preceded the annual conference, attracting new information scholars, administrators, and scientists to the New York University Bobst Library to discuss papers written by Louis M. Branscomb of International Business Machines, Douglass Cater of the Aspen Institute, and Benjamin Compaine of Harvard. An overview of the colloquium was presented at the opening session of the annual conference.

Funded projects, as well as many ongoing programs of ALA and its membership units, related to the concern about access to information for everyone. One of ALA's smallest divisions, the Association of Specialized and Cooperative Library Agencies (ASCLA) and its Library Service to Prisoners Section, conducted a joint project with five other groups on improving jail library service. Focusing on the special library needs of people in jail, often for short periods of time but with critical information needs, the project offered a National Institute on Library Service to Jail Populations in Huntsville, Texas, in March 1980. One hundred and one participants from 36 states and the Virgin Islands, many representing public library service to jails and others representing correctional workers, participated. The project, reported in a handsome brochure available from ASCLA, left a legacy in its publications: *Workshops for Jail Library Service: A Planning Manual* and *The Jail Library: A Guide for Planning and Improving Services.* Connie House served as training project director for one year.

Since 1973, ALA's Office for Library Service to the Disadvantaged has been active in the area of provision of library service to those with special needs. In 1980, by action of ALA Council, the name of the office was changed to reflect more accurately its role. It is now the Office for Library Outreach Services. Jean E. Coleman continues as its director.

The ALA/NEH/CbN Project, funded by a grant of $199,000 from the National Endowment for the Humanities, developed a national program to enhance the ability of public libraries to create, develop, and implement humanities programs for the adult communities they serve. Courses by Newspaper were integrated into public library programs. Eleven libraries received grants, conducted 129 programs at more than 30 sites, and contributed reports that will be available in a casebook to stimulate further programs.

ALA's own distribution of information takes many forms. ALA Publishing Services produced 28 monographs and 18 pamphlets in 1980, notably the landmark one-volume *ALA World Encyclopedia of Library and Information Service,* edited by Robert Wedgeworth, Donald E. Stewart, and Joel Lee of the ALA staff. Two anniversaries were observed during the year: *Booklist*'s seventy-fifth birthday as a major reviewing journal, and the fiftieth anniversary of one of ALA's largest and hardest working committees, the Reference and Subscription Books Committee, whose members regularly review major reference books for publication in *Booklist.*

American Libraries, a membership perquisite and also available by subscription, reached an all-time high circulation of 39,112 in 1980. One encouraging sign of the times was the 28 percent increase over 1979 of the job notices published in its "Leads" section.

A new format made it possible for the *ALA Handbook of Organization and Membership Directory* to be available in one publication. This annual publication was welcomed by members and other users in late 1980.

Library Technology Reports continued its program of publication, reporting to the consumer market of libraries on microform readers, photocopiers, computer print terminals, audio headphones, and word processing equipment.

INTELLECTUAL FREEDOM

Continued emphasis on the rights guaranteed by the U.S. Constitution's First Amendment formed the program of ALA's Office of Intellectual Freedom (OIF) and its Intellectual Freedom Committee (IFC). In response to the growing number of intellectual freedom problems encountered in elementary and secondary schools, the IFC received the $5,000 Bailey K. Howard–World Book Encyclopedia–ALA Goals Award to organize and conduct national meetings of leaders in public education who will plan the development and funding of program packages and workshops for educational administrators to increase the understanding of censorship problems and to strengthen intellectual freedom in schools.

The Library Bill of Rights occasionally requires a thorough review and revision. The ALA Council adopted a new revision at the 1980 midwinter meeting, and the IFC began the task of preparing for a similar revision of the several interpretive statements that accompany the Library Bill of Rights.

It is a mistake to focus too narrowly on the activities of the OIF and the IFC when discussing ALA's responsibility and action in the area of intellectual freedom. Educational benefits, the publishing program, enhancement of administrative skills, and many of the association's other services prevent the development of some cases of violation of intellectual freedom and offer the support that individual librarians need to continue their own support of intellectual freedom.

PUBLIC RELATIONS

There are necessarily many facets to the association's public relations program: its relations with its own members and potential members, its commitment to stimulate public awareness about libraries, and the assistance it offers to others in that same effort. ALA's continued support of National Library Week (NLW) is a major part of this effort. The production of handsome graphics for NLW, as well as other media promotions, extends the impact of the NLW well beyond the traditional seven days in April. The production of book lists, the announcement of awards, and the provision of workshops and other events concerning public relations are all part of the association's overall program in this area.

PROFESSIONAL AND STAFF DEVELOPMENT

By any measure, ALA's annual conference is its major continuing contribution to the development of library staff members throughout the country. The highest attendance ever recorded, 14,566, distinguished the 1980 conference in New York City from June 28 through July 4. More than 1,900 meetings and 727 booths with 4,935 registered exhibitors vied for their time and attention. The programs of ALA's various divisions are major attractions at the conference, and a wide range of topics and program formats combine to attract participants and to frustrate the ALA Committee on Streamlining ALA Conferences, charged with considering problems of scheduling unrestricted meeting requests during midwinter and annual meetings.

The second national conference sponsored by an ALA division, the first being the Association of College and Research Libraries' 1977 conference in Boston, was "80 and Beyond," sponsored by the American Association of School Librarians (AASL) in Louisville, Kentucky, in late September. It was judged a success when 2,549 people registered for it, many of them not among AASL's 4,770 members, and representing school librarians at the building level, as distinct from supervisors, administrators, and library educators, who make up a large part of active AASL membership. The second AASL conference is now being planned for the Southwest in the fall of 1982, and others are scheduled for 1984 and 1986.

Among other membership units' continuing education activities in planning stages or in progress are a pilot program by the American Library Trustee Association to give support to a limited number of states interested in special workshops and/or seminars in trustee education; 14 institutes sponsored by the Resources and Technical Services Division concerning implementation of the revised *Anglo-American Cataloguing Rules*, with Library of Congress staff members serving as instructors, and more than 1,500 librarians already having completed the institutes to be concluded in June 1981; Library History Seminar VI, cosponsored by the Library History Round Table at the University of Texas at Austin early in 1980.

ALA's significant role in the accreditation of master's degree programs in librarianship is carried out by the Committee on Accreditation, which reported in 1980 that 69 master's degree programs were now accredited, seven of them in Canada, the rest in the United States. The committee revised the standards for accreditation several years ago and conducts periodic orientations for prospective visitors to library education sites to maintain the quality of its efforts.

The J. Morris Jones Award of $5,000 went to ALA's Office for Library Personnel Resources Advisory Committee and ALA's Committee on the Status of Women in Librarianship to develop resources that will enable library workers to document pay inequities based on the concept of equal pay for equal work and to advise library workers about methods of alleviating pay inequities. In programs such as this, staff development is clearly the goal.

OTHER PRIORITIES

In addition to the five priorities mentioned above, ALA members referred to cooperation and networking, research, the development of standards and guidelines, and international relations as areas of concern and activity for the association.

International relations activities cut across various membership groups within ALA and across other concerns as well. The association delayed the U.S.-U.S.S.R. library seminar planned for the fall of 1980 when the foreign relations program of the U.S.S.R. continued to present cause for concern about human rights.

When the International Federation of Library Associations and Institutions (IFLA) met for the first time in the Philippines, a Third World nation, the U.S. delegation of 90 members was the second largest attending this meeting, which also recorded the second highest attendance of its history in 1980. The association's official representatives were Peggy Sullivan, president; Robert W. Wedgeworth, executive director, Russell Shank, chair of the International Relations Committee, and Jane Wilson, International Relations officer. Wilson and 25 other IFLA participants embarked on a tour of libraries in the People's Republic of China after the Manila meeting. Jean Lowrie, former ALA president, serves as a member of the IFLA board.

In November, Thomas J. Galvin, immediate past president of ALA, became the association's new representative to the U.S. National Commission for UNESCO.

The two-way street that international relations provides is evident in the number of international visitors who visit the United States, often including ALA headquarters in their stops and using the amenities offered by Jane Wilson in planning their tours. Notable in 1980 was the ten-member delegation of college and university librarians from the

People's Republic of China led by Shi Guoheng, librarian of Qinghua University in Beijing.

The Association of Library Service to Children (ALSC), with a long tradition of international relations activities, continued them with sponsorship of the Arbuthnot Honor Lecture. The 1980 lecturer was Horst Kunze, director emeritus, Deutsche Staatsbibliothek, Berlin, on the topic, "German Children's Literature from its Beginning to the Nineteenth Century: A Historical Perspective," at the University of Wisconsin–Milwaukee. ALSC members participate annually in the selection of the lecturer, the topic, and the site. ALSC President Amy Kellman presented a paper at another international meeting, the biennial congress of the International Board on Books for Young People, in Prague, Czechoslovakia. The topic was library service to preschool children.

In a new approach to standards and evaluation of services, the Public Library Association published *A Planning Process for Public Libraries* in April 1980, and promptly followed it up with plans for continuing education programs based on the concepts stated in the publication. These programs were scheduled in conjunction with a number of state library association conferences in the fall of 1980, and there are more to come.

NOTES AND NAMES

ALA's headquarters has been in Chicago for most of its 105 years of existence, and as 1980 came to a close there were plans for the imminent move into space in a new 56-story building erected on ALA property next to its longtime 50 East Huron Street address. The new headquarters will be income-producing for the association, with rental receipts being channeled into ALA activities after the initial investment in adequate space is recovered.

Membership dues, which now comprise about one-fourth of the association's budget, were raised in 1980, but some promotional tactics were introduced to provide discounts for new members and to encourage them to try ALA membership as a bargain before getting involved in its activities and thus, it is hoped, hooked on the values of membership. At the end of 1980, membership included 32,323 personal members, 5,707 of them new, compared with 32,723 at the same point in 1979. Organization members at the same time numbered 2,894, including 130 new members for an ALA membership total of 35,217.

Carolyn Field and Arthur Plotnik represent ALA on the board of The American Book Awards (TABA). This effort to maintain the awards is a cooperative one among librarians, publishers, and others interested in books and reading. ALA members also participated in the voting for TABA-winning books.

A chapter relations officer charged with the responsibility to improve communications and cooperation among ALA and its 51 chapters (one for each state plus the District of Columbia) has been recommended for some time. In March, Patricia Scarry became the first chapter relations officer at ALA headquarters.

Bessie Boehm Moore, longtime library trustee and vice chair of the National Commission on Libraries and Information Science, received honorary membership in ALA during the annual conference in June. Her commitment to libraries and her services to the association were thus recognized with ALA's highest honor.

Officers of the association for 1980–1981 are: Peggy Sullivan, president; Elizabeth W. (Betty) Stone, vice-president/president-elect; Herbert Biblo, treasurer, and Robert W. Wedgeworth, executive director.

AMERICAN NATIONAL STANDARDS COMMITTEE Z39: LIBRARY AND INFORMATION SCIENCES AND RELATED PUBLISHING PRACTICES AND INTERNATIONAL ORGANIZATION FOR STANDARDIZATION TECHNICAL COMMITTEE 46—DOCUMENTATION

U.S. Department of Commerce, National Bureau of Standards
Admin. E-120, Washington, DC 20234
301-921-3402

James L. Wood
Chairman

Robert W. Frase
Executive Director

The American National Standards Committee Z39: Library and Information Sciences and Related Publishing Practices has the principal responsibility in the United States for developing and promoting standards for information systems, products, and services. Committee Z39 was established in 1939 by the American Standards Association, predecessor of the American National Standards Institute (ANSI). The Council of National Library and Information Associations serves as the Z39 Secretariat and is responsible to ANSI for the work of Z39.

The American National Standards, developed and promulgated by Z39 and published by ANSI, are intended to benefit both producers and consumers of information. Although compliance with Z39 standards is voluntary, Z39 encourages their adoption when appropriate in library, publishing, document delivery, information dissemination, and information and data handling systems.

Z39 participates in the development of international standards for libraries, documentation and information centers, indexing and abstracting services, and publishing through its membership in the International Organization for Standardization, Technical Committee 46: Documentation.

Z39 ACTIVITIES DURING 1980

New Standards

Z39.32-1981 Information on Microfiche Headers.
Z39.42-1980 Serial Holdings Statements at the Summary Level.
Z39.43-1980 Identification Code for the Book Industry.

Revisions of Published Standards

Z39.15-1980 Title Leaves of a Book (revision of Z39.15-1971).
Z39.19-1980 Guidelines for Thesaurus Structure, Construction, and Use (revision of Z39.19-1974).

Z39.21-1980 Book Numbering (revision of Z39.21-1973).
Z39.22-1981 Proof Corrections (revision of Z39.22-1974).

Published Standards Being Revised

Z39.1-1977 Periodicals: Format and Arrangement.
Z39.4-1974 Basic Criteria for Indexes.
Z39.5-1969 (R1974) Abbreviation of Titles of Periodicals.
Z39.7-1974 Library Statistics.
Z39.18-1974 Guidelines for Format and Production of Scientific and Technical Reports.
Z39.20-1974 Criteria for Price Indexes for Library Materials.
Z39.23-1974 Technical Report Number (STRN).
Z39.25-1975 Romanization of Hebrew.
Z39.26-1975 Advertising of Micropublications.

Standards for Review in 1981

Z39.24-1976 System for the Romanization of Slavic Cyrillic Characters.
Z39.27-1976 Structure for the Identification of Countries of the World for Information Interchange.
Z39.31-1976 Format for Scientific and Technical Translations.

Other Published Standards

Z39.2-1979 Bibliographic Information Interchange on Magnetic Tape.
Z39.6-1965 (R1977) Trade Catalogs.
Z39.8-1977 Compiling Book Publishing Statistics.
Z39.10-1977 (R1977) Directories of Libraries and Information Centers.
Z39.11-1972 (R1978) System for the Romanization of Japanese.
Z39.12-1972 (R1978) System for the Romanization of Arabic.
Z39.13-1979 Describing Books in Advertisements, Catalogs, Promotional Materials, and Book Jackets.
Z39.14-1979 Writing Abstracts.
Z39.16-1979 Preparation of Scientific Papers for Written or Oral Presentation.
Z39.29-1977 Bibliographic References.
Z39.33-1977 Development of Identification Codes for Use by the Bibliographic Community.
Z39.34-1977 Synoptics.
Z39.35-1979 System for the Romanization of Lao, Khmer, and Pali.
Z39.37-1979 System for the Romanization of Armenian.
Z39.39-1979 Compiling Newspaper and Periodical Publishing Statistics.
Z39.40-1979 Compiling U.S. Microform Publishing Statistics.
Z39.41-1979 Book Spine Formats.

New Standards in Process

New standards being prepared by Z39 subcommittees include: *Single Copy Standard Order Form* by Z39/SC 36, Peter Jacobs, BroDart, Inc., chairperson; *Romanization of Yiddish* by Z39/SC 5, Herbert Zafron, Hebrew Union College, chairperson; *Serials Claim Form* by Z39/SC 42, Lois Upham, Library School, University of Southern Mississippi, chairperson; *Multiple Copy Standard Order Form* by Z39/SC 36, Peter Jacobs, BroDart, Inc., chairperson; *Language Codes* by Z39/SC C, Arlene

Schwartz, ILLINET Bibliographic Data Base Service, chairperson; *Computer-to-Computer Protocol* by Z39/SC D, David C. Hartmann, Network Development Office, Library of Congress, chairperson; *Serial Holdings Statements at the Detailed Level* by Z39/SC E, Susan Brynteson, Director, University of Delaware Library, chairperson; *Serial Publication Patterns* by Z39/SC F, Gerald R. Lowell, F. W. Faxon Co., Inc., chairperson; *Terms and Symbols Used in Form Functional Areas of Interactive Retrieval Systems* by Z39/SC G, Pauline Cochrane, Syracuse University, School of Information Studies, chairperson; *Patent Data Element Identification and Application Numbering* by Z39/SC H, Philip J. Pollick, Chemical Abstracts Service, chairperson; *Bibliographic Data Source File Identification* by Z39/SC J, John G. Mulvihill, American Geological Institute, chairperson; *Romanization* by Z39/SC L, Charles W. Husbands, Harvard University Library, chairperson; *Coded Character Sets for Bibliographic Information Interchange* by Z39/SC N, Charles T. Payne, University of Chicago Library, chairperson; and *Library Item and Patron Identification Code* by Z39/SC O, Howard Harris, Maryland State Board for Higher Education, chairperson.

CHANGES IN MEMBERSHIP

During the year, four computerized library networks, the AMIGOS Bibliographic Council, Inc., INCOLSA (Indiana Cooperative Library Service Authority), OHIONET, and the Pittsburgh Regional Library Center, became Z39 voting members. Also joining Z39 as a voting member was the F. W. Faxon Co. Two members, the American Business Press and the Council on Library Resources, Inc. resigned their membership.

By the year's end, a total of 32 academic, public, and governmental libraries and commercial organizations had become Z39 Information Members.

OTHER ACTIVITIES

The 1980 annual business meeting was held on April 30 in the Whittall Pavilion at the Library of Congress. Fifty individuals representing member organizations, the Executive Council and its committees and the Z39 subcommittees attended. The Executive Council met twice on April 29 and September 23.

Executive Council committees were expanded by the appointment of Henriette D. Avram, Director, Processing Systems, Networks and Automation Planning, Library of Congress, to the International Committee, and Toni Carbo Bearman, Executive Director, National Commission on Libraries and Information Science; Samuel B. Beatty, Executive Director, American Society for Information Science; David R. Bender, Executive Director, Special Libraries Association; Patricia W. Berger, Head Librarian, National Bureau of Standards; John E. Creps, Jr., Executive Director, Engineering Index, Inc.; H. Joanne Harrar, Director, University Libraries, University of Maryland at College Park (representative of the Association of Research Libraries); John G. Lorenz, Alphonse Trezza, Library of Congress, and Robert Wedgeworth, Executive Director, American Library Association, to the Finance Committee. Mr. Lorenz was also appointed vice chairperson of the Finance Committee and Z39 treasurer. During 1980 the Finance Committee met on April 16, May 29, and September 4.

The Z39 membership amended the bylaws to strengthen the Executive Council by increasing the number of councillors from six to nine, adding the position of past chairperson, and changing the vice chairperson to vice chairperson–chairperson-elect. The membership also approved instituting a participating members fee system for the purposes of financing Z39 operations beginning in 1981, appointment of a Z39 treasurer, and providing for honorary memberships for individuals who have made outstanding contributions in the areas of library, information science, and publishing standards.

To help publicize Z39, 4,000 copies of a brochure were printed, describing the purpose, program, and standards of Z39. At year's end, the supply was exhausted and a revised edition was in press. Z39 had tabletop exhibits at the annual meetings of the National Federation of Abstracting and Indexing Services in Washington, D.C., the American Library Association in New York City, and the American Society for Information Science in Anaheim, California.

In May, Z39 became a member of the U.S. National Committee for the UNESCO General Information Program. This committee serves as the central coordinating body of the U.S. national information community and is responsible for representing and promoting its needs, interests, and views with respect to the UNESCO General Information Program.

Four issues of the *Voice of Z39* were published during the year and distributed to a mailing list of approximately 1,200.

FUNDING

Financial support for Z39's 1980 operations came from the Council on Library Resources, the National Commission on Libraries and Information Science, the National Science Foundation, the American Library Association, other Z39 member organizations, Z39 Information Members, and several nonmember organizations. The library division of the National Bureau of Standards continued its contribution-in-kind by providing Z39 with office space, equipment, and supporting services. Many subcommittee members contributed by not seeking reimbursement of expenses incurred while working on their draft standards.

Z39 OFFICERS

The Z39 Executive Council at the beginning of 1980 consisted of: *Chpn.* James L. Wood, Director, Bibliographical Operations, Chemical Abstracts Service, Box 3012, Columbus, OH 43210. 614-421-6940, ext. 2062; *V-Chpn.* Sally H. McCallum, Network Development Office, Library of Congress, Washington, DC 20540. 202-287-5137; *Councillors Representing Libraries:* Glyn T. Evans, Director of Library Services, State University of New York, Central Administration, State University Plaza, Albany, NY 12246. 518-474-1430; James E. Rush, President, James E. Rush Associates, 2223 Carriage Rd., Powell, OH 43065. 614-881-5948; *Councillors Representing Information Services:* Ben-Ami Lipetz, Dean, School of Library and Information Science, State University of New York at Albany, 1400 Washington Ave., Albany, NY 12222. 518-455-6288; Robert S. Tannehill, Jr., Library Manager, Chemical Abstracts Service, Box 3012, Columbus, OH 43210. 614-421-6940, ext. 2028; *Councillors Representing Publishing:* Robert F. Asleson, President, United States Operations, Information Handling Services, 15 Inverness Way E., Englewood, CO 80150. 303-779-0600, ext. 5353; Sandra K. Paul, SKP Associates, 160 Fifth Ave., Suite 806, New York, NY 10010. 212-675-7804; *Secretariat Rep.* John T. Corrigan, C.F.X., Council of National Library and Information Associations, Catholic Library Association, 461 W. Lancaster Ave., Haverford, PA 19041. 215-649-5251; *Exec. Dir.* Robert W. Frase, ANSC Z39, National Bureau of Standards, Administration Bldg., Rm. E-120, Washington, DC 20234. 301-921-3402.

In April, Z39 members elected Carol A. Nemeyer (Associate Librarian for National Programs, Library of Congress, Washington, DC 20540. 202-287-6587) to replace James E. Rush as Councillor Representing Libraries, and W. Theodore Brandhorst (Director of the ERIC Processing and Research Facility, 4833 Rugby Ave., Suite 303, Bethesda, MD 20014. 301-656-9723) to replace Robert S. Tannehill, Jr., as Councillor Representing Information Services. Glyn T. Evans, Councillor Representing Libraries, resigned in April and James E. Rush was appointed to complete his term.

INTERNATIONAL STANDARDIZATION ACTIVITIES

Z39 participates in the development of international standards for libraries, documentation and information centers, indexing and abstracting services, and publishing through its membership in the International Organization for Standardization, Technical Committee 46: Documentation (ISO/TC 46). ISO/TC 46 is one of 1,940 technical bodies within ISO engaged in developing international standards to facilitate the exchange of goods and services and to develop mutual cooperation in the sphere of intellectual, scientific, technological, and economic activities. Since its establishment in 1947, TC 46 has produced 27 ISO standards.

The Plenary Assembly, which meets every two years, is the governing body of TC 46. Delegates to the assembly represent member bodies (national standards organizations) that participate in the work of TC 46. The secretariat of TC 46, which is held by the Deutsches Institut für Normung (DIN) is responsible to the ISO council and to the members of the technical committee for TC 46 activities. An elected steering committee, on which the United States presently serves, assists the secretariat to plan and program the work of TC 46 and its subcommittees and working groups between meetings of the Plenary Assembly.

The program of work of TC 46 is conducted by six subcommittees, each of which is served by a secretariat in one of the national standards organizations. Most of the TC 46 subcommittees also have working groups. Table 1 lists the TC 46 subcommittees and working groups, showing the status of their U.S. participation and the national standards organization holding the secretariat of each.

The last Plenary Assembly meeting was held in Warsaw, Poland, April 24–25,

TABLE 1   ISO/TC 46 SUBCOMMITTEES AND WORKING GROUPS

Subcommittees and Working Groups	Status of U.S. Participation	Secretariat
SC 2: Conversion of Written Languages	O	France
SC 3: Terminology of Documentation	O	West Germany
SC 4: Automation in Documentation	P	Sweden
WG 1: Character Sets	P (C)	
WG 3: Bibliographic Filing Principles	P	
WG 4: Format Structure	P	
WG 5: Application Level Protocols	P	
SC 5: Mono- and Multi-lingual Thesauri and Related Indexing Practices	O	West Germany
SC 6: Bibliographic Data Elements	P	Canada
WG 1: Data Element Directory	P	
WG 2: Codes and Numbering Systems	P (C)	
SC 7: Presentation of Publications	O	France

O = Observer (wants to be kept informed).
P = Participating Member (participates in work).
P (C) = Participating, holding convenorship.

1979, and the next meeting is scheduled for Nanking, Peoples Republic of China, March 30–April 3, 1981. During the Plenary Assembly most of the subcommittees and working groups also hold meetings.

Z39 comments and votes on TC 46 proposals many times each year at various stages in the development or revision of ISO standards:

on subcommittee drafts

on Draft Proposals (DPs)—through ANSI

on Draft International Standards (DISs)—through ANSI

There is frequently a close relationship between American and International Standards. In important instances they are the same, as for example, Bibliographic Information Interchange on Magnetic Tape (Z39.2 and ISO 2709); the International Standard Serial Number (Z39.9 and ISO 3297); and the International Standard Book Number (Z39.21 and ISO 2108).

ISO/TC 46 published standards are sold in the United States by the American National Standards Institute, 1430 Broadway, New York, NY 10018. In addition to the individual ISO/TC 46 published standards, ANSI also has for sale a 500-page compilation of the texts of 56 ISO/TC 46 and related ISO standards covering the fields of bibliographic references and descriptions, abstracts and indexing; presentation of documents; conversion of written languages; document copying; microforms; bibliographic control; libraries and information systems; mechanization and automation in documentation; classifications and controlled language for information storage and retrieval; and terminology (principles): *ISO Standards Handbook I—Information Transfer* (1977).

ASSOCIATION OF AMERICAN PUBLISHERS

One Park Ave., New York, NY 10016
212-689-8920

1707 L St. N.W., Washington, DC 20036
202-293-2585

Gregory V. Gore

Staff Director, Public Relations Division

During 1980, the Association of American Publishers (AAP) developed some important new initiatives and reinforced continuing ones. At its annual meeting in May, incoming Chairman Leo N. Albert of Prentice-Hall, Inc., denounced illiteracy as "the cruelest censor of them all." In an address reprinted in the *Congressional Record*, Albert promised to lead a vigorous attack on illiteracy on both domestic and international fronts. In this regard, AAP renewed its efforts to have the federal campaign against illiteracy strengthened and coordinated through the Federal Interagency Committee on Education (FICE). AAP also announced its support for Project Read, a program to expose some 2,000 District of Columbia public school students to 30-minute daily "nonstop reading" by providing them with attractively displayed and easily accessible paperback books.

The American Book Awards were presented on May 1, 1980, for the first time, to books written, translated, or designed by U.S. citizens and published during 1979 by U.S. publishers. The culmination of more than a year of planning by representatives from the trade publishing, bookstore, library, and writing communities (under the auspices of the AAP), the American Book Awards were conceived as an entirely new national awards program to cover the broad spectrum of American publishing and to recognize books of distinction, exemplary achievement, and literary merit.

Altogether, 147 books were honored as American Book Award nominees. These books were chosen from among the more than 40,000 books published in hardcover and paperback during 1979. From the nominees, 33 books were honored with the American Book Award. The authors whose books won received a check for $1,000 and a three-dimensional wall sculpture created especially for the American Book Awards by the distinguished American artist Louise Nevelson.

For its second year, the program will retain many first-year features, but the cumbersome voting procedure will be changed so that the panels that choose the nominees will select the winners. The number of awards will also be reduced from 33 to 18. Esther Margolis (Newmarket Press) is 1980 board chair for the 1981 program.

In the international area, AAP was host to 15 Chinese publishers and publishing executives who represented the China National Publications Import Corporation (CNPIC) and the China National Publishing Administration (CNPA). The delegation visited publishing houses in New York, Boston, Washington, Chicago, and San Francisco. Committees of publishers in each city sponsored dinners, tours, and meetings.

In response to a request from the People's Republic of China, and in cooperation with the U.S. International Communications Agency and CNPIC, AAP organized an exhibit of 15,000 American books to be displayed simultaneously in six cities in China in May 1981. In addition, there will be a 300-volume "America Through American Eyes" centerpiece exhibit, similar to the one displayed at the 1979 Moscow Book Fair. The Chinese also requested 5,000 titles from the public sector to be included in the main exhibit.

The Thor Power Tool Company decision and ruling by the U.S. Supreme Court held that publishers could no longer depreciate unsold books for tax purposes while continuing to sell them at regular prices. AAP quickly assumed leadership of a Washington initiative aimed first at delaying the application of the ruling and, eventually, at obtaining exemption from it for the publishing industry.

In the copyright area, seven publishers, with AAP support, brought a major lawsuit against the Gnomon Corporation, a commercial copying establishment, citing among other things its policy of creating anthologies for use on college campuses in lieu of textbooks. These anthologies represented multiple photocopies of copyrighted materials reproduced and sold without prior permission from copyright holders. The lawsuit ended with a court-ordered consent decree precluding Gnomon from such multiple photo-copying and other unauthorized photocopying. Similar legal proceedings are pending against other commercial copying establishments.

AAP witnesses—publishers and staff—appeared before Senate and House committees, as well as federal administrative bodies, to testify on such matters as education, postal rates, literacy and basic skills, and testing.

ORGANIZATION

The association, whose membership comprises some 350 companies, is the major voice of the book publishing industry in the United States. AAP was founded in 1970 as the result of the merger of the American Book Publishers Council and the American Educational Publishers Institute.

AAP members publish the great majority of printed materials sold to American schools, colleges, libraries, and bookstores and by direct mail to homes. All regions of the country are represented. Member firms publish hardcover and paperback books: textbooks, general trade, reference, religious and technical, scientific and medical, professional and scholarly, and journals. AAP members also produce a range of other educational materials, including classroom periodicals, maps, globes, films and filmstrips, audio- and videotapes, records, slides, transparencies, and test materials.

Association policies are established by an elected 29-member board of directors representing large and small firms from many geographic locations. Leo Albert (Prentice-Hall) is chairman of the board for FY 1980/81. AAP President Townsend Hoopes, chief operating officer, is responsible for managing the AAP within the framework of basic policies set by the board. A staff of approximately 35 professional and nonprofessional personnel is located in two offices, New York and Washington.

The AAP operates under an organizational plan that ensures central direction of association affairs as "core" activities and gives important initiatives to the seven AAP divisions, each covering a major product line or distinct method of distribution of the industry. Each AAP division annually elects a chairperson and establishes committees to plan and implement independent projects. Marketing, promotion, research projects, and relations with other associations concerned with mutual problems are central features of divisional programs.

CORE COMMITTEES

Core activities include matters related to copyright, freedom to read, postal rates and regulations, statistical surveys, book distribution, public information, press relations, communications, international freedom to publish, and education for publishing.

The Copyright Committee safeguards and promotes the proprietary rights of authors and publishers domestically and internationally. It closely monitors copyright activity in the United States and abroad. It prepares congressional testimony for appropriate AAP spokespersons, assigns representatives to attend national and international copyright meetings, and sponsors seminars on copyright matters. Charles Butts (Houghton Mifflin) chairs this committee.

The committee plays an active role in disseminating information about the 1978 copyright law by providing speakers to address publisher, librarian, and educator groups and preparing and distributing printed information. Over 2,500 copies of its publication *Photocopying by Academic, Public and Non-Profit Research Libraries* have been distributed. The Copyright Committee maintains liaison with the U.S. Copyright Office and informs publishers of new and proposed regulations that relate to their activities. It participates in negotiations concerning copyright-related policy to be followed by users of copyrighted material.

The Freedom to Read Committee is concerned with protecting freedoms guaranteed by the First Amendment. It analyzes individual cases of attempted censorship by Congress, state legislatures, federal, state, or municipal governments, local school boards, or any other institution. Its action may take the form of a legal brief in support of a position against censorship, testimony before appropriate legislative committees, or public statements and communications protesting any attempt to limit freedom of communication. The committee works closely with other organizations that support its goals. The committee collaborated with the AAP School Division on a national study of some 5,000 school administrators and school librarians aimed at providing information on how to anticipate and counter censorship. Guidelines useful to publishers, educators, and librarians will be developed from the information gathered. The results will be made public in 1981. Anthony Schulte (Random House/Knopf) is chairman.

The Postal Committee monitors the activities of the U.S. Postal Service, the Postal Rate Commission, and congressional committees having responsibility for postal matters. It presents the publisher's point of view to those in policymaking positions through direct testimony, by economic analyses of proposed postal programs, and through a variety of other means. George Larie (Doubleday) is chairman.

The International Freedom to Publish Committee is the only body formed by a major group of publishers in any country for the specific purpose of protecting and expanding the freedom of written communication. The committee monitors the general status of freedom to publish and discusses problems of restriction with the U.S. government, other governments, and international organizations. When appropriate, it makes recommendations to these organizations and issues public statements.

During the year the committee has investigated violations of free expression in Argentina, Iran, Peru, Poland, South Africa, Taiwan, Uruguay, the USSR, and Yugoslavia. The committee has waged an active campaign urging U.S. ratification of the International Human Rights Covenants. It has developed a written set of "Recommendations for AAP Participation in International Book Fairs," and it is now planning, together with the Fund for Free Expression, a centerpiece book exhibit for China. John Macrae III (Dutton) chairs this committee.

The Book Distribution Task Force was created in 1976 to foster the development and implementation of more efficient book distribution systems for all book publishers. The task force, for the second year in succession, surveyed publishers' base line book distribution costs and also the current usage in the industry of computers and computer software programs. The task force also distributed a proposed standardized invoice form for publisher invoices and issues a "Glossary of Book Publishing Terms" to help publishers and their customers understand one another's language used in the distribution process. Publishers and other concerned individuals and organizations are kept informed of technological and standardization developments by periodic bulletins. Robert Follett (Follett) chairs the task force.

The Education for Publishing Program, implemented by AAP in 1978 after a three-year exploration and study of the education and training needs of the book publishing industry, works to promote and advance the continuing education development of employees already in the industry; to help attract, prepare, and educate new talent to enter the industry; and to help inform the public about the book publishing industry. This mission is being carried out by informing and guiding educational and training institutions in providing authoritative and useful courses on book publishing; initiating and sponsoring professional development courses on book publishing for industry employees; encouraging and assisting in the development and improvement of in-house training programs conducted by member companies; and by creating and providing career and other information about the industry.

During 1980, an Entry-Level Job Clearinghouse was established to assist newcomers in entering the industry. A Publishing Education Information Service was started in 1979 within the Education for Publishing Program. The service is a research, referral, and communication resource for publishers, educators, and serious students seeking information about book publishing. A collection of over 300 books about publishing, 40 periodicals dealing with the industry, and archival material are available, by appointment, in the service office library.

The Communications Task Force, established in 1979 at the recommendation of AAP immediate past chairman Alexander Hoffman (Doubleday), has as its primary aim the achievement of better understanding of the basic facts about book publishing by various publics: the publishing community itself; its immediate constituencies—authors, booksellers, librarians, educators, and book reviewers and reporters assigned to the publishing industry; suppliers—printers, binders, paper manufacturers, and financiers; government in its various manifestations—legislatures, regulatory bodies, executive agencies, and the Library of Congress and its Copyright Office; the book-reading public; and the public at large. Byron Hollinshead (Oxford University Press) chairs this committee.

DIVISIONS

General Publishing Division

The General Publishing Division (GPD), chaired by Thomas J. McCormack (St. Martin's Press), represents publishers of fiction, nonfiction, children's literature, and religious books. It maintains close cooperation with members of AAP's Mass Market Paperback and Professional and Scholarly Publishing divisions on areas of mutual concern. Among the division's responsibilities, in cooperation with the Mass Market Paperback Division, is the sponsorship of the American Book Awards program. As noted, the awards, which made their debut in the spring of 1980, are given annually for books in categories reflecting the major areas of interest of the book-reading public.

Through its committee structure, the GPD sponsors seminars, conferences, research, and publications on a wide range of areas of interest to its members. It maintains active liaison (through joint committees) with the American Booksellers Association, American Library Association, and Special Libraries Association, and it cosponsors with them activities of interest to the members of those organizations. For example, through its Libraries Committee, the division helped to organize Book Industry Tours for librarians during the June 1980 American Library Association conference in San Francisco.

The Marketing Group of the GPD presented a full-day program on the uses of computer-generated information for sales and marketing managers. With the American Booksellers Association, the group has cosponsored a pilot study on category best-seller lists.

An active group of smaller publishers is focused within the GPD. It plans programs and publications of particular interest to the growing number of smaller publishers within all divisions of AAP. The group sponsored a successful regional seminar in Berkeley, California, in 1980 and a program in New York City on the Economics of Publishing.

Mass Market Paperback Division

The Mass Market Paperback Division, chaired by Ken Collins (CBS-Fawcett), is concerned with making the paperback book an integral part of the educational and leisure reading of Americans today. Through the media, book fairs, and exhibits, the industry makes every effort possible to emphasize that paperback books provide easy accessibility to all kinds of personal and professional reading. The division worked closely with the General Publishing Division to establish the American Book Awards program.

In addition, the division is concerned with the mass paperback industry's marketing, production, and distribution problems. Its focus is on problems on the national and international levels. Separate divisional committees address themselves to the problems of financial planning, industry statistics, operational management, advertising and promotion, production, and freight and postal concerns. The division represents the industry at both the ABA and the National Association of College Stores (NACS) annual meetings.

The division implemented a Rack Clearance Center in January—a clearinghouse for requests from wholesalers, jobbers, distributors, and rack manufacturers for financial reimbursement for rack installations. The division also launched a public relations campaign to the book trade in an effort to counteract the growing problem of stripped mass paperback books. A "Campus Paperback Bestseller List," initiated three years ago, is compiled monthly from the *Chronicle of Higher Education* and distributed to college bookstores and newspapers.

College Division

The College Division, chaired by Howard Aksen (Harper & Row), is directly concerned with all aspects of the marketing, production, and distribution of textbooks to the postsecondary education field. It pays special attention to maintaining good relations between the publishing industry and college faculty, bookstore managers, and college students. In order to develop and maintain strong relations with the college student, the division has established the AAP Student Service, a public relations program featuring a series of publications specifically directed to the college student. They include "How to Get the Most Out of Your Textbook," "How to Prepare Successfully for Examinations," "How to Improve Your Reading Skills," "How to Build Your Writing Skills," and "How to Get the Most out of a College Education." A new study skills publication, "How to Read Technical Textbooks," was recently published. The division has developed several publications directed to college faculty, including an audiovisual slide show and the pamphlet "An Author's Guide to Academic Publishing."

The division maintains close relations with college bookstores through the NACS-College Division Liaison Committee. The committee recently updated a publication for college bookstore managers on "Textbook Questions and Answers." The committee cosponsors annually an Advanced Financial Management Seminar for college store managers in the spring.

The College Division's Marketing Committee has sponsored a Rely on Your Textbook advertising program with posters and news releases to campus newspapers and college bookstores. The division published in April an updated and enlarged "College Textbook Survey," which was undertaken to examine the attitudes of college bookstores, students, and faculty toward textbooks. It is hoped that the "Survey" will help publishers understand the college textbook market of the 1980s.

Professional and Scholarly Publishing Division

The Professional and Scholarly Publishing Division (PSP) is primarily concerned with the production, marketing, and distribution of technical, scientific, medical, and scholarly books and journals. Many of these publications are aimed, essentially although not exclusively, at the practicing engineer, scientist, and businessperson. To this end the division monitors relevant government activity and policies, levels of funding, and related matters; it provides for a continuous exchange of information and experience through seminars in journal publishing, marketing, sales, new technology, and copyright; and maintains relations with other professional associations, including the International Group of Scientific, Technical and Medical Publishers, government agencies, and industrial research groups. Professional societies and university presses play an integral role in divisional activities.

In 1980, an experimental committee of looseleaf publishers was added to the division and, accordingly, the annual PSP Awards program was expanded to include their publications. The Government Relations Committee monitored the courses of various pieces of legislation and participated in developing AAP's position thereon, such as the National Periodical Center and the Thor Power Tool case. The Marketing Committee developed a presentation on how to sell professional books for presentation at the American Booksellers Association and other booksellers' meetings, and is developing a basic stock list to assist the smaller and larger bookseller to begin a professional books section or to supplement an existing one. The Journals Committee followed the legislative development of the National Periodicals System and conducted an extensive program of seminars and workshops. Other standing committees are statistics and public relations. The division's ninth annual meeting addressed the financial aspects of professional and scholarly publishing.

School Division

The School Division is concerned with the production, marketing, and distribution of textbooks and instructional materials for kindergarten through twelfth grade. It is governed by a ten-member executive committee who serve three-year rotating terms and is currently chaired by E. E. Wanous (South-Western). The division works to improve instructional programs and to seek increased levels of funding. It also sponsors seminars and conferences on topics of interest to educators and publishers.

Activities in the 50 state legislatures relative to schools and educational publishing are very important to school publishers. The division retains legislative advocates in key states to monitor legislative activities and to represent the interests of educational publishers at educational conferences. Liaison committees have also been organized to meet with state boards of education and members of the state legislatures in the 22 adoption states, as well as selected open territory states, to review laws and regulations concerning the selection and adoption of instructional materials and to seek increased funding.

Other standing committees of the division include Social Issues, Research, Order Flow Improvement, Textbook Specifications, Depositories, Public Relations, Statistics Review, Testing, and Right to Read.

The Right to Read Committee is working with the Office of Basic Skills in the Department of Education on a survey of basic skills needs in the secondary schools, and its findings will be widely disseminated to publishers and educators. The Public Relations Committee works to acquaint parents, school board members, and others with some of the concerns of educational publishers. Public service ads and public service radio spots are distributed; the latest conveys the fact that "for every dollar we spend on education, less than one penny goes for school books." Publications like the *Parents' Guide to More Effective Schools* and the *Teachers Advisory Bulletin on Instructional Materials* are also part of the grass-roots public information campaign of the division.

International Division

The International Division, formed to recognize the rising importance of foreign markets for U.S. books, focuses on those issues that affect marketing of books to other countries and the ever-growing complexities of the international marketplace. Kenneth T. Hurst (Prentice-Hall International) chairs this division, which represents the entire spectrum of publishing in both size of firm and product line.

Among the priorities of the division are improving trade relations with the third world and sharing professional skills via workshops; developing a strong relationship with U.S. government agencies (U.S. International Communication Agency and the State and Commerce departments) interested in promoting the book abroad through national fairs and exhibits; promoting respect for international copyright; developing the professional skills of members through seminars and workshops; developing international sales statistics; and promoting attendance and active participation in international book fairs.

In an effort to serve its members outside the New York area, the division held its first regional seminars in Boston, Chicago, and California. A delegation traveled to Singapore, New Delhi, Australia, and New Zealand to hold seminars and to meet with representatives of those publishing communities. Continuing its efforts to combat piracy around the world, the division formed a Piracy Committee.

In 1980, the division held its first annual meeting, whose theme was The Challenge of the Eighties. The division also assisted in the organization of a major exhibit of American books to be held in the People's Republic of China in 1981.

Direct Marketing/Book Club Division

The Direct Marketing/Book Club Division, led by chairman Richard Spaulding (Scholastic, Inc.), is actively concerned with the marketing and distribution of books through direct response and book clubs. It works closely with the AAP Postal Committee to study the effects of new postal rates and regulations and monitors new developments. The division's Marketing Committee sponsored seminars during the year; for example, Electronic Technology: Friend or Foe of Publishing and Special Sales. Other issues of concern were privacy legislation and copyright.

AWARDS

On May 1, 1980, under AAP auspices, the first American Book Awards were presented to 33 books at a ceremony in New York City's Seventh Regiment Armory. The National Medal for Literature, endowed by the Guinzburg Fund in honor of Harold K. Guinzburg, founder of the Viking Press, was presented to Eudora Welty at the event. The medal, which will continue to be given under the auspices of the American Book Awards program, carries a $15,000 stipend.

The association presented the fifth annual Curtis G. Benjamin Award for Creative Publishing during the AAP annual meeting banquet in May. This year's recipient, Ursula Nordstrom (Harper & Row), was cited for her accomplishments as a leading editor of children's books for more than 40 years. The Professional and Scholarly Publishing Division completed the fourth year of its awards program, recognizing the best books and journals in its field.

The first annual Stephen Greene Memorial Education Grant, honoring the Vermont publisher killed in a plane crash en route to the 1979 American Booksellers Convention in Los Angeles, was presented to Jennifer Aliber, an Amherst College English major. After graduation from the Radcliffe Publishing Procedures course, she joined the MIT Press as an editorial assistant.

LIAISON WITH OTHER ASSOCIATIONS

The AAP has effective working relations with a large number of professional associations and agencies having allied interests. These include the American Booksellers Association, American Council on Education, American Library Association, Book

Industry Study Group, Book Manufacturers Institute, Children's Book Council, Council of the Great Cities Schools, Association of Media Producers, Information Industry Association, International Publishers Association, International Reading Association, National Association of College Stores, National Council of Teachers of English, National Education Association, P.E.N. American Center, Publishers Publicity Association, Publishers Library Marketing Group, Special Libraries Association, and UNESCO.

PUBLICATIONS

Although some AAP publications are circulated to members only, many are available to nonmembers.

The *AAP Newsletter* provides a periodic report to members on issues of concern to the publishing industry. The *Capital Letter*, issued monthly, offers news of federal government actions relating to the book community. *Publishing Abstracts* provides concise summaries of book publishing information from 500 newspapers and 4,000 periodicals, plus key information from AAP-sponsored events. Newsletters are prepared by the College, International, School, General Publishing, Mass Market Paperback, and Professional and Scholarly Publishing divisions and the Education for Publishing Program. Periodic bulletins are published by the Book Distribution Task Force.

The AAP also publishes industry statistics on sales and operating expenses and a report on compensation and personnel practices in the industry. The annual *AAP Exhibits Directory* lists more than 800 book fairs and association meetings. A publications list is available from the AAP on request.

ASSOCIATION OF RESEARCH LIBRARIES OFFICE OF MANAGEMENT STUDIES

1527 New Hampshire Ave. N.W.,
Washington, DC 20036

Maxine K. Sitts

Information Services Specialist

During 1980, the Office of Management Studies (OMS), Association of Research Libraries (ARL), marked its tenth year of operation devoted to developing strategies and tools to improve the performance of academic and research libraries. Aware of the challenges of managing complex library systems in a changing university setting amid a climate of inflation and limited resources, members of the association founded the office in 1970 to provide them with management support and specialized resources and techniques geared for large research library settings. Three basic OMS strategies have evolved during this period.

The first—the assisted self-study approach of the Academic Library Program—introduces organizational planning, problem solving, and change through an analytical process that heavily involves the library staff. These self-studies examine the demands and pressures of both the external environment and the internal library situation and devise improvements in library programs and operations.

The second strategy is to develop better management information on academic library operations, problems, and approaches through a clearinghouse called the Systems and Procedures Exchange Center (SPEC). The center periodically surveys member libraries and makes available results of these surveys as well as illustrative documents from responding libraries. The center operates on the belief that a more comprehensive understanding of the range of possible institutional approaches and responses will better equip libraries to address issues.

The third strategy relates to the way academic libraries identify, promote, and develop managerial talent within their organizations. The OMS Training Program is committed to helping academic libraries equip staffs with the skills, concepts, and leadership needed to improve performance. The focus of this training is on dealing more successfully with the human dimension of large, complex organizations.

THE ACADEMIC LIBRARY PROGRAM

Funded for five years in 1979, the Academic Library Program (ALP) has allowed the office to offer self-study opportunities to a greater number of academic libraries. On one front, currently operating studies such as the Management Review and Analysis Program (MRAP) and the Collection Analysis Project (CAP) were redesigned so that libraries can conduct smaller scope, individual modules, as well as complete self-studies. Whereas a full self-study may take anywhere from 9 to 15 months, many modules can be done in 6 to 12 weeks, at a reduced cost and with lesser use of staff resources. On a second front, the office, with support from the Lilly Foundation, designed a new Planning Program for Small Academic Libraries (PPSAL) that opens up the assisted self-study approach to academic libraries with staffs of less than 20. Although the Lilly Grant concentrated the initial use of this planning program in the Indiana area, it is now being used at mid- and small-sized libraries across the country. The third main development during 1979-1980 involved the design of two new self-studies—in the areas of preservation and public services. These studies are geared for larger research and academic libraries, and are being made available for the first time in 1981.

Support for the Academic Library Program continues to come from the Council on Library Resources, the Andrew W. Mellon Foundation, the Lilly Endowment, and the Association of Research Libraries.

Management Review and Analysis Program (MRAP)

MRAP was the first study developed by the OMS and is designed to review management procedures and policies of libraries with 50 or more on staff. Over the past years, 25 libraries—mainly large research institutions—have conducted an MRAP self-study, and individual reports are available from the office. To make the components of this program accessible to a wider range of libraries, during the past year the office has offered individual modules in the areas of planning, budgeting, policy making, management information, supervision and leadership, organization, personnel practices, staff development, and executive leadership.

Collection Analysis Project (CAP)

This study, designed to help academic libraries assess their collection development practices and policies, was employed by five libraries during 1979-1980. It is available to both large research libraries and libraries with smaller collections. Individual modules are now available in the areas of collection history and description; collection objectives and policies; materials fund allocation; organization and staffing of collection development functions; collection assessment; preservation; and resource sharing. CAP has been funded by the Andrew W. Mellon Foundation.

Organizational Screening Program

Newly implemented in 1979 as a way for libraries to quickly assess one particular area of concern, this program has been employed by two libraries over the past two years, for such purposes as the reorganization of reference facilities and a review of the library's overall organizational structure.

Academic Library Development Program (ALDP)

The Academic Library Development Program, designed under a separate grant from the Council on Library Resources, has been employed by three libraries in the past two years. Geared to mid-sized academic libraries with staffs of 20 or more, ALDP also has been modularized, and libraries can choose to assess the specific areas of operations, services, management practices, facilities, or technological applications.

Planning Program for Small Academic Libraries

During 1979-1980 21 libraries conducted this study. The program, supported by the Lilly Endowment, Inc., enables the library with a staff of less than 20 to articulate an active role in the academic community and to develop a plan for improving its capacity to participate fully in instructional and research programs. The office has received grants from the Lilly Endowment to design and implement the program in 20 libraries in Indiana and neighboring states.

Preservation Planning Program

Funded by a $151,924 grant from the National Endowment for the Humanities, this program was developed and designed during 1979-1980. It is providing a self-study procedure, technical manuals, and resource materials to libraries interested in studying and improving their internal preservation practices. The self-study helps libraries determine internal priorities as well as assess the potential impact of emerging national and regional developments on internal collections, acquisitions, and retention and binding policies. The program is being tested by three libraries during 1981, and is then to be made generally available.

Public Services Improvement Program

Now being tested in a research library, this program provides a way of involving library staff in a systematic review of the relationships among public services, user expectations, university support, the collections, and staff capabilities.

Consultant Training Program (CTP)

The first class of 20 outstanding, mid-career librarians was selected in 1979 and trained in an intensive two-week consultation skills workshop and practicum during 1979-1980. Several have been given either self-study or training assignments, and four of the participants are currently acting as principal consultants for OMS projects. A second class of 20 consultants was chosen from 159 applicants in 1981, following regional interviews conducted by the CTP Advisory Committee members, OMS staff, and the first class of consultants. Primary criteria for selecting participants included five years of library operational experience, and demonstrated communication, decision-making, and problem-solving skills.

THE OFFICE PROGRAM OF INFORMATION COLLECTION AND DISSEMINATION

This program concentrates on facilitating and improving the exchange of ideas and materials among ARL members. In addition to providing a mechanism for information exchange, the program provides synthesis and analysis of selected current issues and trends for ARL library administrators. Over its eight years of operation, the program has stressed the importance of communication among institutions to improve library operations and management, and has sought to expand the ways in which this communication can occur.

Following an emphasis in 1978 on technological developments and automation planning, the Information Program during 1979 focused on the staffing and management issues involved in implementing major change. Surveys and publications centered around two personnel-related themes: the development and evaluation of library staff, and organizational communication.

In 1980, the Systems and Procedures Exchange Center (SPEC) conducted surveys and issued publications in areas including implementation of the *Anglo-American Cataloguing Rules (AACR 2)*, library materials and cost studies, and retrospective conversion. A continuation grant of $29,500 from the H. W. Wilson Foundation allowed SPEC to continue disseminating complimentary materials to accredited library schools through December 1981. A Collaborative Research/Writing Program, which enables outstanding librarians to work with OMS staff in authoring publications, was initiated with two participants writing in the areas of internal communication and academic compensation systems. The areas of Staff Development, Organization, and Planning were covered in a series of *Resource Notebooks* issued in 1979 under a grant from the H. W. Wilson Foundation. Published in three-ring loose-leaf binders, the notebooks are designed to assist academic libraries in examining a particular aspect of management or operation. A new series covering performance appraisal, budgeting, and training of supervisors is planned for 1981-1982.

THE OFFICE PROGRAM OF ORGANIZATIONAL TRAINING AND STAFF DEVELOPMENT

At a time when the need for management skills training has obtained a high level of recognition, the OMS program of organizational training and staff development stands out as a continuing, focused program tailored specifically for academic libraries. All OMS training activities and programs are devoted to developing better supervisory and management practices and start with the recognition that more and better training of individuals is an essential building block for improving library performance.

The three Library Management Skills Institutes conducted in 1979 attracted 100 participants. In 1980, four Management Skills Institutes were held, with 145 participants. There were three general sessions and one targeted for theological librarians. These training events follow a basic format which actively engages participants in problem solving, case studies, small group discussions, and lectures concerning managerial concepts and techniques. Each participant receives a notebook with resources for further investigation of the topics covered in the institutes. Also, training staff are available for consultation on work-related problems.

Twenty-seven special-focus workshops were conducted in 1979 and 15 in 1980. These training events included one- or two-day programs conducted at libraries that focused on specific needs identified by the host libraries, descriptive presentations of

OMS programs, and OMS staff presentations at library conferences. Topics included supervisory skills, performance appraisal, public services, organizational analysis, problem solving, cooperative collection development, ownership and distribution of machine-based bibliographic records, and communication.

In the past, OMS has provided training and workshop assistance to specialized groups of librarians including Japanese bibliographers and music librarians. In 1979 the office was invited to assist a group of theological librarians in designing and operating a management training program tailored to the particular needs of their libraries. This program, financed by a grant from the Rockefeller Brothers Foundation, attracted 55 theological librarians to a five-day event held on the Princeton University campus.

The Training Program continues to make available selected management films and accompanying training materials to subscribing libraries. These libraries share the cost of acquiring the films, and OMS contributes the efforts required to screen and select films, develop training materials, maintain the collection, and schedule the use of the films. Twelve films are currently available, and in 1979 and 1980, two films were acquired: "After All: You're the Supervisor," and "Helping: A Growing Dimension of Management."

In 1981, four Management Skills Institutes will be held, three basic sessions and one advanced session, designed for those who hold management positions or who have attended previous sessions. Also planned are a series of one-day workshops on resources available to library managers.

As established by the Association of Research Libraries, the office receives counsel from an OMS Advisory Committee, an Academic Library Program Advisory Committee, and other project-related advisory groups. Principal support has come from the Council on Library Resources, ARL membership dues, and the sale of publications and services. Among its regular publications are an annual report (free) and a monthly series of SPEC kits/flyers (available by subscription). The OMS staff consists of Duane E. Webster, director, Jeffrey J. Gardner, associate, Maureen S. Schechter, training program specialist, and Maxine K. Sitts, information services specialist.

Part 2
Legislation, Funding, and Grants

Note: In view of the budget cuts being initiated by the Reagan administration (as we are going to press), readers are advised to contact the Washington office of the ALA, AAP, or IIA for the latest information on the status of federally funded projects—*Ed.*

LEGISLATION AFFECTING LIBRARIANSHIP IN 1980

Eileen D. Cooke
Director, ALA Washington Office

Carol C. Henderson
Deputy Director, ALA Washington Office

The year following the White House Conference on Library and Information Services was one of substantial achievement, yet the tide-turning November election results tended to overshadow the rest. The new Reagan administration will have a Republican majority in the Senate for the first time in a quarter of a century, and may well have a working majority in the House.

Strong library support in Congress has always come from both sides of the aisle, but the effects of this massive and unpredicted shift to the right on federal assistance to libraries is as yet unclear. What is clear is that a number of longtime congressional leaders and dependable library supporters went down to defeat—among them Senate Appropriations Committee Chair Warren Magnuson (D-Wash.), Senator Jacob Javits (R-N.Y.), House Majority Whip John Brademas (D-Ind.), and House Administration Chair Frank Thompson (D-N.J.).

The Carter administration gave a cordial reception to the White House Conference recommendations, setting an Interagency Task Force to work on them and issuing a presidential message with a number of specific commitments. Although the fate of the Department of Education under the Reagan administration is uncertain, 1980 saw the elevation of its Office of Libraries and Learning Technologies with the appointment of a deputy assistant secretary. In an atmosphere of election-year budget cutting fervor, library program funding held steady with one notable exception—the amount for interlibrary cooperation and networking more than doubled.

Higher Education Act (HEA) library programs were updated and expanded in the Education Amendments of 1980, including a compromise version of the highly controversial National Periodical Center. Congress and the administration almost went to court over the issue of legislative veto of regulations, an issue that hinged partly on the narrow question of the eligibility of gymnasium equipment for school library and equipment funds. Congress passed a federal information policy measure with the somewhat misleading title "Paperwork Reduction Act," but did not pass a revision of Title 44 government document printing and distribution. Other legislation introduced but not acted on included a major revision of the Library Services and Construction Act (LSCA)—the National Library and Information Services Act based on White House Conference resolutions.

FUNDING

Compared with other education and social programs, federal library grant programs came through the administration's budget revision and the congressional budget and appropriations process remarkably well in this past year of balanced-budget fever. At several key points along this way, the White House Conference on Library and Information Services provided the needed impetus.

President Carter submitted his FY 1981 budget to Congress in January, then

TABLE 1 FUNDS FOR LIBRARY AND RELATED PROGRAMS

Programs	FY 1980 Appropriation	FY 1981 Authorization	Carter Revised FY 1981 Budget	FY 1981 Appropriation[a]
Library Programs				
ESEA Title IV-B: School Libraries	$171,000,000[b]	Necessary sums	$171,000,000[b]	$171,000,000[b]
GPO Superintendent of Documents	23,000,000	44 USC 301	26,200,000	23,400,000
Higher Education Act: Title II	11,988,000	$140,000,000	12,988,000	12,155,000
Title II-A: College Library Resources	4,988,000	84,000,000	4,988,000	4,988,000
Title II-B: Training	667,000	23,976,000	500,000	667,000
II-B: Demonstrations	333,000	12,024,000	500,000	500,000
II-C: Research Libraries	6,000,000	20,000,000	7,000,000	6,000,000
Library of Congress	181,264,000	2 USC 131-170	196,526,000	176,844,000
Library Services and Construction Act	67,500,000	170,000,000	74,500,000	74,500,000
Title I: Library Services	62,500,000	150,000,000	62,500,000	62,500,000
Title II: Public Library Construction	(0)	Necessary sums	(0)	(0)
Title III: Interlibrary Cooperation	5,000,000	20,000,000	12,000,000	12,000,000
Medical Library Assistance Act	9,925,000	18,500,000	9,831,000	9,831,000
National Commission on Libraries and Information Science	686,000	750,000	691,000	691,000
National Library of Medicine	34,075,000	40 USC 275	34,558,000	34,899,000
USDA SEA Technical Information Systems	7,985,000	7 USC 2204	8,686,000	8,541,000
Library-Related Programs				
Adult Education Act	100,000,000[b]	270,000,000	120,000,000[b]	120,000,000[b]
Community Schools	3,138,000	55,000,000	3,138,000	10,000,000
Consumers Education	3,617,000	5,000,000	3,617,000	3,617,000
Corporation for Public Broadcasting	172,000,000[c]	Formula-based	172,000,000[c]	172,000,000[c]
Education for Handicapped Children (state grants)	874,500,000[b]	Formula-based	922,000,000[b]	922,000,000[b]
Education Information Centers	3,000,000	40,000,000		3,000,000
Education TV Programming	6,000,000	Necessary sums	6,000,000	6,000,000

ESEA Title I: Educationally Disadvantaged Children	3,215,593,000[b]	3,536,772,000[b]	3,514,772,000[b]
ESEA Title II: Basic Skills Improvement	35,000,000	40,000,000	35,000,000
ESEA Title IV-C: Educational Innovation and Support	197,400,000[b]	96,000,000[b]	142,400,000[b]
ESEA Title IV-D: Guidance, Counseling, Testing	(0)	Necessary sums	(0)
ESEA Title VII: Bilingual Education	166,963,000	50,000,000	174,963,000
ESEA Title IX: Ethnic Heritage Studies	3,000,000	999,000,000	3,000,000
Gifted & Talented Children	6,280,000	15,000,000	6,280,000
HEA Title I-A: Community Service	9,000,000	35,000,000	9,000,000
HEA Title III: Developing Institutions	110,000,000	40,000,000	120,000,000
HEA Title VII: Construction and Renovation	39,000,000	120,000,000	26,000,000
HEA Title IX: A & B Graduate/Professional Educational Opportunity	8,850,000	580,000,000	11,000,000
Indian Education Act	75,900,000	Necessary sums	81,680,000
Metric Education	1,840,000	Necessary sums	1,840,000
National Center for Educational Statistics	9,947,000	20,000,000	9,947,000
National Endowment for the Arts	154,610,000	30,000,000	158,560,000
National Endowment for the Humanities	150,100,000	175,000,000	151,299,000
National Historical Publications and Records Committee	4,000,000	170,000,000	4,000,000
National Institute of Education	74,114,000	4,000,000	74,114,000
NDEA Title VI: Foreign Language Development	17,000,000	125,000,000	21,800,000
Postsecondary Education Improvement Fund	13,500,000	75,000,000	13,500,000
Public Telecommunications Facilities	23,705,000	75,000,000	25,705,000
Teacher Centers	13,000,000	40,000,000	13,000,000
Telecommunications Demonstrations	(0)	100,000,000	(0)
Women's Education Equity	10,000,000	1,000,000	10,000,000
		80,000,000	

[a]Most of these programs funded only through June 5, 1981, by a continuing resolution, H.J. Res. 644. Exceptions are USDA, Indian Education, and Arts and Humanities Endowments programs, funded for the entire 1981 fiscal year.
[b]Advance funded program.
[c]CPB funded two years in advance.

changed his mind and decided the worsening economy required a balanced budget after all, and sent Congress a revised budget in March. No changes were made in the recommendations for major library grant programs despite the fact that the revised budget contained $648 million in cuts in other education programs for FY 1981 and $430 million in proposed rescisions or withholding of FY 1980 education funds. See Table 1 for budget and appropriations figures for library and related programs.

Not to be outdone in an election year, Congress, with great difficulty and way behind its own schedule, passed its own version of a balanced budget with teeth in it. However, economic developments turned both these paper balances into substantial deficits as the year progressed. The first congressional budget resolution for FY 1981 was passed June 12, a month behind schedule. Usually this resolution sets nonbinding targets for congressional spending, but through a complex process called "reconciliation," the resolution (H. Con. Res. 307) in effect set ceilings and required authorizing and appropriations committees to make legislative adjustments to programs to stay within the budget resolution. The omnibus reconciliation bill that resulted did not receive final congressional approval until December 3. Action on the second congressional budget resolution (H. Con. Res. 448), designed to set binding ceilings, was not completed until November 20, long after the September 15 deadline.

Delays in the budget process and a reluctance to have deficit spending become a campaign issue threw appropriations bills off schedule as well, with the result that many government agencies were funded at the last minute by a continuing resolution, normally an emergency stopgap measure. As approved by Congress December 16, the resolution (H. J. Res. 644) continues funding for library programs only through June 5, 1981, at the level passed by the House in the regular appropriations bill (H.R. 7998). For three programs the amounts are the same as the previous year and the budget recommendation: for the Elementary and Secondary Education Act (ESEA) IV-B school library program, $171 million; for the Higher Education Act II-A college library program, $4.9 million; and for Library Services and Construction Act Title I library services, $62.5 million.

There was a major increase in LSCA III interlibrary cooperation activities—$12 million as requested by President Carter compared with $5 million in FY 1980. The budget request for the HEA II-B library training and research and demonstration program was $1 million, but it was to be split evenly, instead of $667,000 for training and $333,000 for demonstrations as in 1980. Congress restored training to $667,000 while leaving demonstrations at $500,000 for a net gain of $167,000. The budget recommendation for the HEA II-C research library program was $7 million, compared with the previous year's $6 million; Congress left it at $6 million.

Both the Department of Agriculture's Technical Information Systems (formerly the National Agricultural Library) and the National Library of Medicine received slight increases over the previous year, while the Medical Library Assistance Act was down marginally. The Library of Congress, hard hit by Congress's effort to cut its own budget, received $176.8 million, $4.4 million less than the FY 1980 funding level. Coupled with inflation, this cut unavoidably reduces both the library's purchasing power and the level of national services it provides. By reference to the Commerce Department funding bill (H.R. 7584), the continuing resolution included $550,000 for "installation of computer terminals at Patent Depository libraries and/or improvements to patent search files." Some 35 libraries receive current issues of U.S. patents by requesting depository status and meeting the conditions established by the Patent and Trademark Office in the Commerce Department.

ARTS AND HUMANITIES

A five-year extension of the National Foundation on the Arts and Humanities Act and the Museum Services Act was signed into law by President Carter on December 4. The measure, S. 1386 (now PL 96-496), makes some minor changes, but is essentially a straight extension of existing arts, humanities, and museum programs. Authorization levels increase over the period FY 1981-1985 from $175 million to $306 million for the National Endowment for the Arts, from $170 million to $299 million for the National Endowment for the Humanities, and from $25 million to $45 million for the Institute of Museum Services.

COPYRIGHT

The Copyright Office held four regional public hearings during the year (with the fifth and last scheduled for New York City in January 1981) to elicit comments on the extent to which section 108 (reproduction by libraries and archives) of the Copyright Act of 1976 has achieved the intended balance between the rights of creators and the needs of users of copyrighted works that are reproduced by certain libraries and archives. The hearings will contribute to the five-year reviews required by section 108(i), the first of which must be sent to Congress by January 1, 1983. The Copyright Office also awarded a contract to King Research, Inc., of Rockville, Maryland, to do a survey of libraries, publishers, and users in preparation for the first five-year review.

In a separate development, the 1976 Copyright Law (PL 94-553) would be clearly applied to computer programs under a provision of H.R. 6933, now PL 96-517, a bill signed by the president December 12, which makes numerous amendments to the patent laws. Section 117 of PL 94-553 disclaimed any intent to modify the preexisting copyright law for computer programs. The patent law amendments have been used as the vehicle to delete Section 117, as recommended by the National Commission on New Technological Uses of Copyrighted Works.

Meanwhile, the negotiating committee to develop guidelines on fair use for broadcast audiovisual works continued to meet through the year, although progress has been agonizingly slow. Established in April 1979 by Representative Robert Kastenmeier (D-Wisc.), chair of the House Judiciary Subcommittee on Courts, Civil Liberties, and the Administration of Justice, with the cooperation of the Register of Copyrights, the negotiating committee is cochaired by Eileen Cooke of the American Library Association (ALA) Washington Office, and Leonard Wasser of the Writers Guild of America, East. [See the report from the Copyright Office on its activities during 1980 in the Federal Agencies section of Part 1—*Ed.*]

DEPARTMENT OF EDUCATION

May 4 marked the official beginning of the Department of Education and the inauguration of the Office of Libraries and Learning Technologies (OLLT), whose director is at a higher level in the bureaucracy than before. Dick Hays, who headed the Office of Libraries and Learning Resources in the old Office of Education, was appointed deputy assistant secretary for OLLT, serving under F. James Rutherford, assistant secretary for educational research and improvement.

Placement of libraries within the new department was difficult and controversial as different sectors of the education community and various assistant secretary–designates vied for one or another piece of the library pie. The White House Conference resolution for an assistant secretary of library and information services, and the attempts by ALA and other organizations to see that recommendation implemented, were undoubtedly instrumental in keeping the library programs together. Secretary of Education Shirley Hufstedler did the next best thing by providing a deputy assistant secretary, and by placing libraries under Research and Improvement, which appropriately combined libraries with educational technology, research, statistics, dissemination, school improvement and basic skills, and museum services. The 50 or so programs administered by Assistant Secretary Rutherford had a FY 1980 budget of $504 million, of which library programs comprised $250 million.

ESEA TITLE IV REGULATIONS

Final regulations for the Elementary and Secondary Education Act Title IV programs as published in the April 7 *Federal Register* (pp. 23602-23629) were disapproved by Congress in May. At issue was the definition of "instructional equipment" eligible for IV-B School Library Resources and Instructional Materials funding. The earlier proposed regulations excluded band instruments and gymnasium equipment, generating a storm of protest from music educators and a congressional hearing on the subject of band instruments. The final regulations allowed the acquisition of musical instruments under certain conditions, but specifically allowed physical education equipment as well.

The secretary of education, however, turned to the Justice Department for advice. The attorney general, in a June 6 opinion, declared unconstitutional section 431 of the General Education Provisions Act under which Congress disapproved the ESEA IV regulations and three other sets of Education Department regulations. The Education Department prepared to implement the rulings, and it looked for a time as if these narrow disagreements would escalate into a major confrontation over the larger issue of the legislative veto, requiring resolution in the courts. The House Elementary, Secondary, and Vocational Education Subcommittee held a hearing on the situation on September 18.

Meanwhile the secretary of education worked out resolutions to the disapproved regulations on other than constitutional grounds. Concerning the IV-B program, the Education Department accepted the congressional criticism of the regulations and published in the September 3 *Federal Register* (pp. 58362-58363), an amendment prohibiting local educational agencies from using IV-B funds for physical education.

FEDERAL INFORMATION POLICY AND PAPERWORK REDUCTION

President Carter signed into law on December 11 H.R. 6410 (now PL 96-511), the Paperwork Reduction Act, a measure designed to reduce federal paperwork requirements and duplications, and to consolidate statistical policy activities with information management in the Office of Management and Budget (OMB).

The major provisions of PL 96-511 include (1) establishment of an Office of Information and Regulatory Affairs within OMB to provide overall direction in the development and implementation of federal information policies, principles, standards, and guidelines, including direction over the review and approval of information collection requests, the reduction of the paperwork burden, federal statistical activities, records management activities, privacy of records, interagency sharing of information, and acquisition and use of automatic data processing and other technology for managing information resources; (2) designation by each agency head of a senior official who reports directly to the agency head and who is responsible for carrying out efficient, effective, and economical information management activities; and (3) establishment within the new Office of Information and Regulatory Affairs of a Federal Information Locator System to serve as the register of all information collection requests. For carrying out the act, $8 million would be authorized for FY 1981.

The vagueness of some provisions and the broad authority granted OMB concerned many groups, including ALA. The Senate Governmental Affairs Committee report on the bill (S. Rept. 96-930) addressed these concerns and directed OMB to maximize public access to the information the federal government collects, and to consult with other federal agencies concerned with developing government-wide information policies, such as the Government Printing Office and the Library of Congress, as well as the National Commission on Libraries and Information Science, the Joint Committee on Printing, and the Federal Library Committee.

A policy proposed in the form of a draft circular by the Office of Management and Budget titled "Improved Management and Dissemination of Federal Information" was published in the June 9 *Federal Register* (pp. 38461-38463). The policy directly addresses such issues as (1) the principles on which government policy regarding public access to federally financed information is based; (2) the relative roles of the Government Printing Office, the National Technical Information Service, and other public and private sector providers of government information; (3) conditions that have diminished public access to federal information, or have increased costs to the taxpayer; and (4) the responsibilities of the agencies in making their information more readily accessible to the public.

At year's end no final circular had been published, but the combined approach of this proposed policy and the Paperwork Reduction Act was viewed by the Carter Administration as preferable to the provisions of the Title 44 revision bill, H.R. 5424, covered elsewhere in this report.

HIGHER EDUCATION ACT EXTENSION

The major library legislation enacted during the year was part of the Higher Education Act, revised and extended for five years by the Education Amendments of 1980 (H.R. 5192). Although the bill was passed by lopsided majorities in both the House (in November 1979) and the Senate (on June 24), House-Senate conferees had difficulty reconciling the two versions. Then further opposition to the conference agreement surfaced in the Senate budget committee on the ground that the bill exceeded the spending levels in the Senate budget resolution. In a real pre-election cliffhanger, the Senate rejected the conference agreement (H. Rept. 96-1251) by a vote of 43-45 on September 4. Conferees managed to reach a new agreement that lowered the cost of the student loan programs and reduced many of the authorization levels, but made no changes in Title II library programs. This second conference agreement (H. Rept. 96-1337) was approved by both chambers and signed into law October 3, the date Congress recessed before the election (PL 96-374). Title II library provisions are summarized below.

HEA II-A, College Library Resources. The basic grant for each eligible institution is renamed "Resource Development Grant," and the maximum raised from $5,000 to $10,000. Need criteria had been considered by Congress earlier, but were *not* added. Authorization levels are $10 million for FY 1981, $30 million for each of fiscal years 1982, 1983, and 1984, and $35 million for FY 1985. The purpose is expanded to include "establishment and maintenance of networks for sharing library resources," as well as acquisition of library materials. Maintenance of effort is no longer required for total library purposes, only for library materials expenditures. Waivers of maintenance of effort are restricted to "very unusual circumstances," mainly "acts of God." Supplemental grants are deleted; special purpose grants moved to Part B.

HEA II-B, Library Training, Research, and Development. Authorizations are $10 million for FY 1981, $30 million for each of fiscal years 1982, 1983, and 1984, and $35 million for FY 1985, to be divided equally among an expanded, three-part program:

1. *Library Career Training.* Grants for fellowships and traineeships (which must receive at least 50 percent of the training funds), institutes, and "to establish, develop, or expand programs of library and information science, including new techniques of information transfer and communication technology."
2. *Research and Demonstrations.* Grants "for research and demonstration projects related to the improvement of libraries, training in librarianship, and information technology, and for the dissemination of information derived from such projects."
3. *Special Purpose Grants.* Transferred from II-A and expanded. Grants would assist higher education institutions to meet special national or regional library or information science needs; establish and strengthen joint-use library facilities, resources, or equipment; service their communities; and, with other library institutions, improve academic library services. Special purpose grants are not restricted to acquisition of library materials.

HEA II-C, Strengthening Research Library Resources. Continued essentially unchanged, with authorization levels of $10 million for FY 1981, and $15 million for each of the succeeding four years. The regional balance requirement is loosened from the former "shall . . . achieve regional balance" to "shall endeavor to achieve broad and equitable geographical distribution." The Senate Labor and Human Resources Committee provided some direction on future grants. According to S. Rept. 96-733, the "Committee believes that at least twice as many grants as are currently being made should be awarded" and it "encourages the Secretary to take care to see that the same small number of institutions do not continue to receive grants year after year."

HEA II-D, National Periodical System. This new program authorizes a nonprofit National Periodical System Corporation to "assess the feasibility and advisability of a national system and, if feasible and advisable, design such a system to provide reliable and timely document delivery from a comprehensive collection of periodical literature." The presidentially appointed board is to "be equitably representative of the needs and interests of the Government, academic and research communities, libraries, publishers, the information community, authors, and the public." A system design must be submitted to Congress by December 31, 1981, and would require a congressional resolution of approval before implementation. Authorizations are $750,000 for FY 1981, $750,000 for FY 1982, and such sums as necessary for the succeeding three years. No funds could be appropriated for II-D unless II-A, B, and C are funded at FY 1979 levels—that is, $9.9 million for II-A, $3 million for II-B, and $6 million for II-C.

This version of II-D comes from the Senate bill (S. 1839), and was developed as a compromise proposal by Senator Jacob Javits (R-N.Y.). Apparently referring to intense lobbying against the House-passed National Periodical Center by the information industry, the publishers, and some representatives of scholarly society publishers, Senator Javits at the February 28 education subcommittee markup said he had "rarely run into a buzz saw like this one." The Senate report (S. Rept. 96-733) called it "one of the most controversial issues to confront the Committee."

Other HEA provisions of interest to librarians include Title I education outreach and information service programs, Title VI international education programs, Title

VII academic facilities construction assistance, and a new Title XI urban grant university program.

POSTAL LEGISLATION

The Senate once again failed to act on pending postal legislation (H.R. 826) that would have corrected several inconsistencies in the complex statute establishing the fourth-class library postal rate. At present, a publisher may send a book to a school or library at the library rate, but the school or library must pay a higher rate to return a book to the publisher. A textbook may be sent library rate, but the teacher's guide that accompanies it may not be sent library rate. A books-by-mail listing may be refused library rate if a postal official thinks it looks more like an ineligible catalog than an eligible bibliography. Catalogs of audiovisual materials may be sent library rate, but not catalogs of books, and so on. The House passed similar legislation in both the Ninety-fifth and Ninety-sixth Congresses. The postal measure was approved by the Senate Governmental Affairs Committee in May, but never made it to the Senate floor for a vote. Had it done so, it would have faced an attempt by the committee's ranking minority member, Senator Charles Percy (R-Ill.), to delete the library rate provisions on the grounds that they were "frivolous" and too expensive.

PUBLIC LIBRARY AND NETWORKING LEGISLATION

Two pieces of library legislation were introduced during the year in response to the recommendations of the White House Conference on Library and Information Services—one a replacement for the Library Services and Construction Act, which expires in FY 1982, the other an amendment to it. Both were introduced by New York legislators who will not be returning to the Ninety-seventh Congress.

The National Library and Information Services Act (S. 2859) was introduced June 20 by Senator Jacob Javits (R-N.Y.) with several cosponsors. The bill was a major revision of Javits's National Library Act (S. 1124), a study bill developed before the White House Conference. The major provisions of S. 2858 are as follows:

1. to expand the responsibilities of the Department of Education in providing support for coordinated library and information services nationally and internationally;
2. to provide funding for networks linking publicly funded libraries and participating private libraries;
3. to authorize federal matching funds to support public library services;
4. to provide matching funds to spur public library construction and renovation;
5. to authorize federal grants to meet the special needs of library users, such as rural residents, the functionally illiterate, the handicapped, and the disadvantaged;
6. to support state planning and public awareness programs and the training of local personnel in library skills.

The National Library Resources Sharing Act (H.R. 7602) was introduced June 17 by Representative Elizabeth Holtzman (D-N.Y.). It has four provisions:

1. to amend the LSCA to provide assistance to state library agencies for long-range planning for library services;
2. to set aside 15 percent of LSCA III interlibrary cooperation funding for grants to regional and national library networks;
3. to allow libraries to receive preferential telecommunications rates;

4. to establish an assistant secretary for library and information services in the Department of Education.

[See the Special Reports section of Part 1 for a report by Henriette Avram on the status of library networking in the United States in 1980—*Ed.*]

REVENUE SHARING

A three-year extension of the revenue sharing program to provide general-purpose fiscal assistance to local and state governments has a new wrinkle that could affect funding for categorical library grant programs. The measure (H.R. 7112) continued revenue sharing as is for local governments, providing $4.6 billion in entitlement payments annually.

The state revenue sharing program was discontinued for one year (FY 1981), then reinstated at the current level of $2.3 billion per year. However, this is an authorization level, subject to the congressional appropriations process. Previously the states received automatic entitlement payments. The kicker is that in order to get the state share, state governments would have to agree to refund or decline to receive an equal amount of categorical grant assistance. Categorical grant programs eligible for such a trade-off would be specifed by regulations.

The 1976 renewal legislation for revenue sharing directed the Advisory Commission on Intergovernmental Relations (ACIR), a bipartisan body established by Congress to advise on intergovernmental problems, to do a series of studies. One of those studies, "Federal Involvement in Libraries," was issued in June 1980 and gives a detailed history of federal assistance to libraries and a useful analysis of the political dynamics of federal involvement. A limited number of single copies are available on written request to ACIR, Washington, DC 20575. The report is also available for $2.50 from GPO (*The Federal Role in the Federal System: The Dynamics of Growth*, vol. 8, "Federal Involvement in Libraries." Order No. 052-004-00079-9, Superintendent of Documents, Washington, DC 20402).

TAXATION—*THOR POWER TOOL* DECISION

The Supreme Court decision in *Thor Power Tool Co.* v. *The Commissioner of Internal Revenue* (439 U.S. 522 [1979]) was implemented for all kinds of businesses by an Internal Revenue Service ruling and applied to the 1979 and 1980 tax years as well as tax years in the future. The ruling prevents businesses from writing down the value of their inventories to a nominal level and taking a tax deduction for a business loss—formerly a common practice—unless the inventory is sold below cost or destroyed. The effects of this ruling on publishers in turn affect libraries.

Libraries that previously purchased holdings from publishers' backlists may find such items destroyed by publishers to avoid higher taxes. Publications that sell slowly over several years may be produced less often in the future. Several bills and amendments to prevent the retroactive implementation of the ruling were initiated, but did not reach final passage. The Senate-passed version of a general funding measure (H. J. Res. 637) included an amendment sponsored by Senator Daniel Moynihan (D-N.Y.) that would have exempted from the ruling publishers or small businesses forced to change accounting methods, but the amendment was dropped in conference. Senator Moynihan plans to introduce a similar exemption for publishers in early 1981.

TITLE 44 REVISION

Circumstances combined to stall, for this Congress at least, and perhaps for some time to come, an ambitious rewrite of Title 44 of the U.S. Code covering government printing and document distribution. The bill, H.R. 5424, had been in the legislative pipeline for two years, but died at the end of the Ninety-sixth Congress. The measure's main proponent, Representative Frank Thompson (D–N.J.), Chair of the House Administration Committee, was tainted by the "Abscam" scandal and lost his reelection bid. Disagreement over the best way to update the existing law led to jurisdictional fragmentation, with three House committees reporting differing versions of the bill, and no further action. Nor was there any action on the Senate version, S. 1436.

The report on H.R. 5424 (H. Rept. 96-836) is in three parts. Part 1 was issued by the House Administration Committee March 19. Part 2, from the House Rules Committee June 16, made one technical amendment to the bill. Part 3 was issued, also on June 16, by the Government Operations Committee, and substituted an entirely new text. This version (as Part 3, the latest version) deleted several important library provisions contained in the House Administration Committee bill: (1) creation of a comprehensive collection of government publications, (2) authorization of support services for depository libraries, and (3) making audiovisual materials and machine-readable data files available to depositories. In addition, the Government Operations Committee version would have removed all scientific and technical publications distributed by law from being considered government publications.

WHITE HOUSE CONFERENCE IMPLEMENTATION

President Carter on September 26 submitted to Congress the report of the November 1979 White House Conference on Library and Information Services (WHCLIS) together with his response to the WHCLIS recommendations. Among other things, he said, "I believe we have viewed libraries too narrowly. The needs of the public who must cope with our increasingly complex society can only be met by libraries actively providing access to the great variety of information they have. . . . To survive as community institutions, libraries must be strengthened and the public made more aware of their potential."

Among the more specific commitments were the following:

1. to request increased funding for library resource sharing, research and development in information technologies, and research libraries;
2. to submit new legislation to replace the Library Services and Construction Act due to expire in 1982;
3. to affirm the key role of government document depository libraries;
4. to support federal agency information dissemination through libraries;
5. to locate several Federal Information Centers together with libraries;
6. to direct the Education Department to coordinate federal efforts to eliminate functional illiteracy, including working with libraries;
7. to direct the Interior Department to recommend ways to overcome geographical barriers to information;
8. to send to the Senate a protocol to the Florence Agreement of 1952 further liberalizing the international exchange of materials;
9. to aggressively pursue research and development into new information technologies and their application, and appropriate standards;

TABLE 2 STATUS OF LEGISLATION OF INTEREST TO LIBRARIANS
(96th Congress, 2nd Session Convened January 22, 1980 Adjourned December 16, 1980)

Legislation	House Introduced	Hearings	Reported by Subcommittee	Committee Report Number	Floor Action	Senate Introduced	Hearings	Reported by Subcommittee	Committee Report Number	Floor Action	Conference Report	Final Passage	Public Law
American Folklife Center (at LC)	HR 7805			none	X	HR 7805			none	X	none	X	PL 96-522
Arts and Humanities Endowments extension	HR 7153	X		937	X	S 1386	X	X	557	X	none	X	PL 96-496
Communications Act Revision	HR 6121		X	1252	X	S 2827							
Congressional Budget Ceilings, FY 1981	H. Con. Res. 448	X		1463	X	S. Con. Res. 119	X		921	X	1469	X	
Congressional Budget Reconciliation	HR 7765	X		1167	X	S 2885			none	X	1479	X	PL 96-499
Criminal Code Revision	HR 6915	X		1396		S 1722	X		553				
ESEA IV regs—disapproval resolution	S. Con. Res. 91					S. Con. Res. 91			769	X		X	
Higher Education Act extension	HR 5192	X	X	520	X	S 1839	X	X	733	X	1337	X	PL 96-374
Information Science and Technology Act	HR 8395												
International Exchange of Government Publications	HR 7302	X		1063	X								
National Library & Info. Services Act						S 2859							

LEGISLATION AFFECTING LIBRARIANSHIP IN 1980 / 139

National Library Resources Sharing Act	HR 7602						
NSF Authorization and Scientific and Technical Equal Opportunity Act	HR 7115	X	999	X	S 568	X	X	713	X	1474	X	PL 96-516
Paperwork Reduction Act	HR 6410	X	835	X	S 1411	X		930	X	none	X	PL 96-511
Patent Law Amendments	HR 6933	X	1307	X	S 2446, 1679	X		617	X	none	X	PL 96-517
Postal Service Act	HR 79	X	126	X	S 2558, HR 826	X		776				
Public Works and Economic Development Act extension	S 3152		none	X	S 3152	X		none	X	none	X	PL 96-506
Revenue Sharing extension	HR 7112	X	1277	X	S 2574	X		1009	X	none	X	PL 96-604
Tax Incentive—Manuscript Donations	HR 2498, 7391				S 1078, 3175							
Tax on inventory (*Thor Power Tool v. IRS*)	HR 7390, etc.											
Title 44 Revision	HR 5424	X	836	X	S 2805, HR 3755	X						
Youth Act	HR 6711	X	1034	X	S 1436	X						
					S 2385	X	X	991				
Appropriations, FY 1981												
Continuing Resolution	H. J. Res. 610		1327	X	H. J. Res. 610	X		none	X	1443	X	PL 96-369
Further Continuing Resolution	H. J. Res. 637		1484	X	H. J. Res. 637	X		none	X	1536	X	
Further Continuing Resolution	H. J. Res. 644			X		X			X	none		
Agriculture	HR 7591	X	1095	X	HR 7591	X	X	1030	X	1519	X	PL 96-536
HUD and Independent Agencies	HR 7631	X	1114	X	HR 7631	X	X	926	X	1476	X	PL 96-528
Interior & Related Agencies	HR 7724	X	1147	X	HR 7724	X	X	985	X	1470	X	PL 96-526
Labor-HEW	HR 7998	X	1244	X	HR 7998	X						
Legislative Branch	HR 7593	X	1098	X	HR 7593	X						
State, Justice, Commerce	HR 7584	X	1091	X	HR 7584	X	X	949	X	1472	X	vetoed
Treasury, Postal Service	HR 7583	X	1090	X	HR 7583	X	X	955	X			PL 96-514

For bills, reports, and laws write: House and Senate Documents Rooms, U.S. Capitol, Washington, DC 20515 and 20510, respectively.

10. to direct the Commerce Department to work with the library community to make satellite and other emerging communication technologies more available;
11. to support a conference of independent experts to develop an agenda for library research in the 1980s;
12. to encourage the library and information science communities to propose technology assessment studies for consideration by federal agencies.

[The complete text of President Carter's report is reprinted in the Special Reports section of Part 1—*Ed.*]

In May, Stuart Eizenstat, assistant to the president for domestic affairs and policy, had named a 13-member interagency task force to study and analyze the White House Conference report to provide guidance for the president's response. Dick Hays, deputy assistant secretary for libraries and learning technologies in the Department of Education, chaired the interagency task force, which included representatives of the White House, the Office of Management and Budget, the Commerce Department, the National Endowment for the Humanities, the Library of Congress, the National Science Foundation, and the International Communications Agency. In March the report of the White House Conference was officially presented to the president in ceremonies in Washington, DC.

The first meeting of the Ad Hoc Committee on Implementation of the White House Conference on Library and Information Services Resolutions took place September 15–17, 1980, in Minneapolis. Established by resolutions passed by the White House Conference delegates, the group was informally termed "The Committee of 118" because it consists of two delegates from each of the states and territories, the District of Columbia, federal libraries, and Native Americans.

The committee heard from several government officials, including a live phone message from Stuart Eizenstat. Members elected a steering committee, which announced its intent to issue a newsletter, seek funding for its operations, and begin work on the 117 specific action steps identified by the committee to advance the White House Conference recommendations.

Signed into law under a Republican president (Gerald Ford) and funded under a Democratic one (Jimmy Carter), the White House Conference on Library and Information Services has enjoyed bipartisan support throughout its history. It will undoubtedly leave an imprint on the planning and delivery of library and information services at the federal, state, and local levels for years to come. Often its effects will be difficult to measure, but it has already had a definite impact on several legislative and related events.

Pressure from White House Conference delegates kept federal library programs from being cut in the development of the original Carter budget for FY 1981. Again when the budget was being revised in March, congressional leaders—White House Conference memories fresh in their minds—successfully urged that library programs not be cut.

The White House Conference process also influenced the internal organization of the Department of Education. Although the delegates' recommendation of an assistant secretary for library and information services was not followed, an attempt to split the library programs among several departmental units was headed off, and a deputy assistant secretary was appointed.

Two pieces of legislation were introduced as a direct result of the White House Conference recommendations on public libraries and networking. These bills by Senator Javits and Representative Holtzman are discussed elsewhere in this article.

In addition, the Carter administration discussed its reaction to the White House Conference at the American Library Association's annual conference in June in New York City, with a presidential message and major speeches by Stuart Eizenstat and F. James Rutherford. Finally, the ALA Council passed a legislative program based on the conference recommendations.

OTHER LEGISLATIVE ACTIVITY

For the second year in a row, National Library Week Legislative Day was the date for an Oversight Hearing on Federal Library Programs. Held on April 15 by the House Elementary, Secondary, and Vocational Education Subcommittee and the Postsecondary Education Subcommittee, the hearing concentrated on the need for adequate funding of the LSCA, ESEA, and HEA library programs.

Measures that died at the end of the Ninety-sixth Congress include a major Carter administrative initiative, the Youth Act, and major revisions of the Communications Act of 1934 and the Criminal Code. Another casualty was legislation to restore a tax incentive for the donation of artistic and literary creations to libraries and museums. One bill was introduced late in the session by Representative George Brown (D-Calif.), Chair of the House Science, Research, and Technology Subcommittee, as a trial balloon for further action in the Ninety-seventh Congress—the Information Science and Technology Act of 1980 (H.R. 8395), which would establish an independent Institute for Information Policy and Research. (For the status of legislation of interest to libraries as of December 16, 1980, see Table 2.)

LEGISLATION AFFECTING PUBLISHING IN 1980

Washington Staff, AAP*

The year 1980 was dominated by political campaigns and the elections and will be remembered as much for the proposals not enacted as for the legislation that became law. Publishers were in the same boat as other groups who found the Ninety-sixth Congress more inclined to debate than to action. For example, for the first time in history, the new fiscal year dawned on October 1 without a single appropriations bill having been enacted into law. As a matter of fact, when the Ninety-sixth Congress finally expired on December 16, five routine appropriations bills were still unenacted, including the funding for education.

Also on the pigeonhole side of the ledger were these proposals that had started on their way through Congress but had fallen by the wayside: revision of the criminal code, postal reforms, youth initiative, revision of the Government Printing Act, amendments to the Small Business Act to include publishers, and postponement of the effect of the Thor Power Tool decision on inventory accounting. Several items, however, were added to the statute books. One of them, a new higher education bill, strengthened the provisions for college and research libraries and created a commission to study the establishment of a National Periodical System.

*The AAP general Washington staff includes Richard P. Kleeman, Roy H. Millenson, Diane Rennert, and Carol A. Risher, all of whom contributed to this article.

EDUCATION AND LIBRARY AFFAIRS

Funding

Education and library programs once again found themselves orphans of the storm. The Carter budget submitted in March 1980 for the most part provided no increase for book programs. In addition, congressional inaction on appropriations legislation forced education and library programs once again to rely on a stopgap "continuing resolution" that ensured a flow of funding only through June 5, 1981—the federal fiscal year ends on September 30.

Under terms of the continuing resolution, FY 1981 funds for Library Services (LSCA I) remained at the 1980 level of $62.5 million; Instructional Materials and School Library Services (ESEA-IV-B) stood at $171 million, also the 1980 level; the Inexpensive Book Distribution remained at the 1980 level of $6.5 million; College Libraries rested at the 1980 level of $4.988 million; Assistance to Medical Libraries (III-J. PHSA) was reduced to $9.831 million and Research Libraries were increased to $7 million, $1 million over the previous year. However, it must be emphasized that these figures are not absolutely assured because, as mentioned above, Congress must renew spending authority by June 5. In addition, both the outgoing Carter administration and the incoming Reagan administration are expected to submit further budget revisions and rescissions early in 1981.

In the closing days of the session, the 1.7 million volume National Agricultural Library received $8.541 million, a modest increase over the $7.835 million appropriated for FY 1980.

New Legislation

On October 3, 1980, the president signed the Education Amendments of 1980 (PL 96-374) revising and extending through FY 1985 the Higher Education Act. A number of provisions hold particular interest for the library community. Part A of Title II of the Higher Education Act doubled college library grants from $5,000 to $10,000. However, unless appropriations are increased to accommodate this doubling of resource development grants, the newly enacted higher authorization will have no practical effect.

Part B ("Library Training, Research and Development") of Title II consolidated research and demonstration into a single program, with a new emphasis on information transfer techniques and communications technology. Also, the special purpose grants program was moved from Part A to Part B. Because the new law provides that Part B funds will be evenly divided between library career training, research and demonstrations, and special-purpose grants, each of these programs is assured in future years of some share of the Part B appropriation, unless the appropriations bill declares otherwise.

Also of great interest to the publishing industry during 1980 were efforts to create a National Periodical Center as part of the Higher Education Act. The House version of this bill included legislation to create an actual periodical center to house retrospective copies of all published periodicals and to supply photocopies to libraries around the country. The Senate version, which ultimately passed, created a National Periodical System Corporation to study the advisability and feasibility of creating a national periodical system. The corporation would complete its study and, if the project were found to be advisable and feasible, would design a National Periodical System. The system designed could not be implemented without a joint congressional resolution supporting such implementation.

The publishing industry worked closely with the library community from the outset to help create a National Periodical Center, while making sure that no publications would be adversely affected. The revised language ultimately enacted into law provides for study of the effect of such a system on publishers as well as on libraries.

H.R. 6933, the Software Act of 1980, was passed by Congress. This law provides copyright protection for computer software and amends the U.S. copyright law to make such protection clear.

Other Activities

On September 26, President Carter transmitted to Congress his Report on the White House Conference on Library and Information Services, commenting on the resolutions adopted at the November 1979 conference and adding his own recommendations. [This report is reprinted in its entirety in the Special Reports section of Part 1—*Ed.*] He stressed the importance of libraries, urged congressional and public discussion of the proposed National Library and Information Services Act that had been endorsed by the conference, cited the federal responsibility for access to information, indicated the continuing concern of his administration to meet the needs of the disadvantaged, and stressed the role of new information and communication technologies.

On February 8, ten national organizations had joined AAP in urging a coordinated and strengthened federal effort against illiteracy. The pledges received from the secretary of education and other federal officials that such an effort would be undertaken were climaxed by President Carter's pronouncement, in his September 26 comments on the White House Conference on Library and Information Services, that he had "directed the Department of Education to take the lead in coordinating federal efforts to eliminate functional illiteracy." Despite this array of declarations, no coordination effort was undertaken. However, the National Institute of Education did begin studies in the area of basic skills and literacy.

On April 7, the U.S. Office of Education (now the Department of Education) issued its regulations on Title IV-B ("Instructional Material and School Library Resources") of the Elementary and Secondary Education Act. Included was a provision that for the first time permitted IV-B funds to be used for the purchase of athletic equipment, thus diluting the IV-B money available for library books, texts, and other academic instructional materials and equipment.

The next month Congress unanimously adopted a resolution of disapproval (S. Con. Res. 91) under authority of the General Education Provisions Act and based on the contention that the regulation was inconsistent with the law. Secretary of Education Shirley Hufstedler at first denied the authority of Congress to disapprove the IV-B regulation, but, after considerable controversy, on July 23, in a letter to House Education and Labor Committee Chairman Carl Perkins, agreed that the provision was not in line with the meaning of the statute and pledged to remove it. This was subsequently done when a new regulation was published on September 3; that change, however, did not become effective until November 4.

POSTAL LEGISLATION

A significant postal bill was introduced in the House of Representatives on the first day of the Ninety-sixth Congress in 1979. Its major features included a substantial increase in public service appropriations (from $920 million to $1.1 billion for FY 1980, with additional increments through FY 1982), as well as an extension of the phasing of postal rates for Special Rate Fourth Class (the book rate) and all other classes with the exception of First Class and Parcel Post, for an additional two years. Additionally, the measure would have permitted sending teaching aids, catalogs of books and eligible educational materials, both to and from qualifying institutions at the preferred library rate (present legislation covers only shipments to such institutions). The bill passed the House by an overwhelming vote but never reached the Senate floor.

POSTAL RATE INCREASE

On the broad front of postal rates for book shipments, AAP has engaged in defending before the independent Postal Rate Commission a favorable rate proposal put forth by the U.S. Postal Service (USPS). Under the USPS proposal, the rate for books and records would increase by only 0.6 percent while overall postal rate increases would average 28 percent effect (including a 20-cent First Class letter rate). AAP argued before the Postal Rate Commission in behalf of the modest increase. A decision is expected in early 1981.

CONCENTRATION IN BOOK PUBLISHING

The Competition Review Act of 1979 introduced in the first session of the Ninety-sixth Congress, which would have mandated a commission study of competition and concentration in various basic industries, and of federal policies promoting or inhibiting competition, died at the end of the Congress. Senator Howard Metzenbaum (D-Ohio) held one day of hearings on the subject of concentration in book publishing, at which AAP testified. No legislative activity ensued, however.

LOBBY LEGISLATION

Lobby reform bills were introduced in both houses. AAP has consistently opposed two provisions of such measures: One would require disclosure of the dues paid by each individual member of a trade association, if a certain fraction of association funds is used by lobbying activities, and the other was the grass-roots provision, dealing with citizens' right to petition the government. The House bill never reached the floor for debate, and when the two provisions mentioned above were eliminated during consideration by the Senate Judiciary Committee, the bill's sponsor, Senator Lawton Chiles (D-Fla.), withdrew his support.

Since the Congress has been grappling with lobby reform since 1976, it was thought that if the legislation were defeated in 1980, there might not be another strong push to enact it in 1981. However, the switch to Republican control of the Senate makes it difficult to predict prospects for such legislation.

SMALL BUSINESS LOANS TO PUBLISHERS

Senator Robert Morgan (D-N.C.), subsequently defeated in his reelection bid, introduced a bill in 1980 that would prohibit the Small Business Administration (SBA) from denying financial assistance to media concerns, including book publishers, which are currently excluded from the SBA loan program.

Until January 1978, SBA categorically refused financial assistance to all enterprises involved in the dissemination of "ideas and values." This policy was adopted by SBA without mandate from Congress in the belief that the agency would thus avoid any appearance of governmental interference with freedom of expression. On January 27, 1978, however, the SBA modified its policy to allow loans to concerns operating in the electronic media (radio and TV), but the print media (books, newspapers, magazines, etc.) continue to be excluded.

The SBA has stated that its intent is to "avoid government interference, or the appearance thereof, with the constitutionally protected freedoms of speech and press." AAP and other spokesmen for the print media contend that present SBA regulations are inconsistent and that, in fact, the disparate treatment accorded the various "opinion molders" raises precisely those constitutional questions that the SBA has ostensibly tried to avoid.

Morgan held a hearing in the summer of 1980 on his bill at which both the SBA and AAP testified. On October 8, 1980, the SBA published in the *Federal Register* an advance notice of proposed rule making to invite public comment on how present regulations might be amended. As stated in its testimony before Congress, the SBA continues to favor a regulatory rather than a legislative approach to accomplishing such change. In its notice in the *Federal Register* the SBA outlined seven broad steps it would be willing to take to lessen the eligibility standards for "media concerns."

In its reply, AAP noted: "It is hardly consistent with the First Amendment that there should be any restrictions on loans or loan guarantees to 'opinion molders.' It is the contention of AAP that loans and loan guarantees should be made available to all enterprises, whether or not an opinion molder, so long as the activity is not otherwise unlawful." Subsequent to the advance notice, the SBA will publish proposed rules, on which AAP will comment.

THOR POWER TOOL DECISION

A bill that sought to alleviate the potentially disastrous effect for book publishers of two IRS rulings was introduced by Senator Gaylord Nelson (D-Wisc.) on June 10, 1980. A companion bill was introduced in the House by Representative Barber Conable (R-N.Y.).

The IRS issued the ruling (Revenue Ruling 80-60 and Revenue Procedure 80-5) in February 1980 in the wake of a 1979 Supreme Court decision that would make compulsory certain inventory accounting changes retroactive to 1979. Nelson's bill would have relieved taxpayers who were unaware of this inventory accounting dispute until the IRS rulings were published, and who might face a severe one-time adjustment for past write-offs of "excess" inventory.

Although the Court decision and the IRS rulings were not directed toward publishers and book inventories, the effect of extending these procedures to all taxpayers, retroactively to 1979, could have a severe impact on publishers and possibly force destruction of large numbers of slow-selling books.

Prior to the November elections, Nelson's bill was included in the proposed $39 billion general tax cut proposal, which was never acted upon. Subsequent to the elections and during the lame duck session, the Senate Finance Committee, prodded by Senator Daniel Patrick Moynihan (D-N.Y.), reported out a proposal to provide a refund for books, maps, sheet music, monographs, and periodicals from retroactive application to 1979 tax returns of the *Thor Power Tool* decision. The proposal was attached to a miscellaneous House-passed bill, but never was called up for consideration by the full Senate and thus died with Congress.

Meanwhile, Moynihan worked closely with a representative group of publishers to seek remedial legislation in the Ninety-seventh Congress.

GPO REORGANIZATION

A bill to reorganize the Government Printing Office (GPO) and do away with the Joint Committee on Printing was introduced in 1980. Bills to accomplish these ends were simultaneously introduced in both houses of Congress. Joint hearings were held in July 1979. In response to tremendous opposition, the House bill was redrafted into a totally new piece of legislation. This bill wended its way through the second session of Congress until March 19, 1980, when the Committee on House Administration completed work on it. At that time both the Rules Committee and the Committee on Government Operations asserted jurisdiction over the bill and were given 90 days to take action. The delay, the fact that there was no Senate counterpart to this bill, and the fact that the chairman of the Committee on House Administration stepped down as a result of the "Abscam" inquiry were all factors contributing to the death of this measure. Revision of Title 44 and improvement of government printing, binding, distribution, and disposal of government documents are worthy objectives and new bills will probably surface during the Ninety-seventh Congress. In the meantime the Joint Committee on Printing is attempting through a series of regulations to revise the operations of government printing and binding in an effort to achieve by regulation what was not accomplished by statute.

CRIMINAL CODE; UNANNOUNCED SEARCHES

Paradoxically, the bill that appeared in late 1979 to have its best chance of enactment in a dozen years—revision of the Federal Criminal Code—did not pass Congress, while the measure on which there appeared to be lack of consensus—to protect editorial premises from unannounced searches without subpoenas—was enacted in a limited version.

The criminal code revision fell victim to its enormous scope and complexity and, as the *New York Times* pointed out editorially, to extremism: It was too repressive for extreme libertarians and too permissive for extreme conservatives. Although neither house passed a version of the measure, it came close to floor action in both, and then failed for lack of time, which became essential when conservatives promised to propose dozens of floor amendments.

If the bill returns in the Ninety-seventh Congress—as many expect—it will be handled by a different cast of characters: Senator Strom Thurmond (R-S.C.), new chairman of the Judiciary Committee in the now Republican-controlled Senate, has retained jurisdiction over the code for the full committee. While a staunch conservative, Thurmond had agreed to the compromise bill worked out in the committee under its then chairman Senator Edward M. Kennedy (D-Mass.). But Thurmond's deal with Kennedy doubtless will collapse with the change in Senate control, and a code coming from the new Judiciary Committee is sure to bear a far more conservative stamp. In the House, meanwhile, although Representative Peter Rodino (D-N.J.) remains chairman of the Judiciary Committee, Representative Robert Drinan, the liberal Democrat from Massachusetts who managed to push the code along despite opposition from both extremes, will not be on the scene. Father Drinan retired from Congress to return to clerical duties under papal order.

Publishers' interest in the criminal code involved chiefly the provisions with First Amendment implications, such as federal definitions of and restrictions on so-called obscenity. In these areas also it is expected that any new version of the code emanating from the Ninety-seventh Congress will be more restrictive and less acceptable to freedom-to-publish advocates than the measure that advanced far in the last Congress, and civil liberties coalitions no doubt will once again do battle on the measure.

The antisearch measure, entitled "Privacy Protection Act of 1980," adopted the Carter administration approach of protecting from search or seizure without subpoena (except under unusual circumstances) "work product materials" possessed for eventual public dissemination via print or electronic media (including books). While less broad than many organizations—including AAP—had favored, this measure, acclaimed by President Carter as providing "vital safeguards for our free press," does appear to shield those involved in First Amendment-protected activities from unwarranted searches by federal officials. It was intended to reverse the 1978 U.S. Supreme Court decision (*Zurcher* v. *Stanford Daily*), which upheld a police search of the Stanford University campus newspaper offices. Subsequent to enactment of the law, the Carter administration Justice Department promulgated implementing regulations.

"NAMES OF AGENTS" BILL

Another measure closely watched by the publishing community and others concerned with constitutional rights was not enacted by Congress, notwithstanding strong support by powerful groups and individuals. The bill would have made it a crime to disclose the identities of covert CIA agents or informers. AAP and other groups following the legislation did not disagree with its aim of protecting the lives of U.S. agents, but contended that, as worded, the measure did not afford protection to legitimate journalists and authors who had obtained their information from unclassified sources. This measure also is expected to be reintroduced and intensively pushed in the new Congress.

LEGISLATION AFFECTING THE INFORMATION INDUSTRY, 1980

Robert S. Willard

Vice President, Government Relations,
Information Industry Association

The Ninety-sixth Congress, which had begun its two-year life in January 1979 with promises of being an "oversight Congress," concluded its life in December 1980, two months later than planned, with a number of major accomplishments to its credit, but also with a number of tasks left undone. It also ended its existence having witnessed one of the largest electoral revolutions in congressional history. The Republicans had seized not only the White House, but also, by a 53–47 majority, the U.S. Senate; in the House, with 74 new Republican members, the minority party looked enthusiastically ahead to the 1982 elections in hopes they could repeat the Senate experience.

The shifts in power brought about by the U.S. electorate in November reflected a dissatisfaction with government's "business as usual" approach. In fact, 1980 was a time in which nothing was as usual, and the ubiquitous medium of television never let this fact be avoided. Through nightly reminders, viewers shared the anguish of U.S. hostages in Teheran. Television also brought viewers bits and pieces of the presidential campaign from before the results of the Iowa caucus to the summer spectaculars in Detroit and New York City to the on-again, off-again debates through the election-eve concession speech of President Carter. The tawdriness of politics (and the questionableness of enforcement tactics) were on the screen when Federal Bureau of Investigation Abscam tapes clearly showed money passing hands from one government official to another. Energy, inflation,

Note: The opinions expressed in this article are those of the author and do not necessarily represent those of the Information Industry Association.

unemployment, shortages, natural disasters: these were the subjects on the minds of the American people and on the mind of the U.S. Congress.

In this context, the subject of information policy was not one of the burning issues in the minds of the legislators, but nevertheless, as in the past few years, there were a great number of bills (more than 1,000) pertaining to some aspect of information introduced; a number of these became law. In a draft report entitled *Information Policy: Public Laws from the 96th Congress* (unpublished as of February 1981), nearly five dozen laws are described in the following categories: energy; food, health, and education; taxes, pensions, and welfare; finance, trade, and small business; the courts and justice; information management; and confidentiality, disclosure, and right of privacy. In some of these laws, the information component is small, perhaps a section requiring a study and dissemination of the results; in others, the entire bill may be focused on an information issue.

It would not be feasible to discuss each of the laws covered in the draft report. Instead, this article will attempt to describe some of the major legislative efforts that occurred in 1980, whether resulting in law or not, that drew the attention of the information industry. Such legislation can be analyzed in five categories. First, there are those proposals that mandate or encourage the government to become involved in the information marketplace, thus possibly competing with other providers in that marketplace. Second, there are measures aimed at protecting the economic value of information resources. Government rules affecting the transport of information, or communications, comprise the third category. Fourth are those legislative items that address civil liberty issues in the information arena, specifically privacy and First Amendment rights. Finally, the fifth category contains those proposals that assign a regulatory role to the government that may be an incentive or an impediment to flows of information.

GOVERNMENT COMPETITION

Frequently, a government information program will be developed to make some sort of information available to the population in order to meet some perceived public need. Often, however, this information is being injected into a marketplace that is already being served by one or more nongovernmental information providers. Unless the government enters this marketplace carefully, i.e., operating in a way that does not exploit the government's built-in competitive advantages, it runs the risk of forcing the other participants out of the marketplace. In order to encourage diversity of information, the government must always avoid such market disruption.

Congress had the opportunity to come to grips with this fundamental information policy issue in the proposal to rewrite Title 44 of the United States Code, which deals with the Government Printing Office (GPO), the Superintendent of Documents, the Depository Library System, and other related subjects. Here was clearly the chance to draw appropriate boundaries on the behavior of various distributors, public sector and private sector, of government information. More than a year of effort had gone into developing this bill, which would have replaced the turn-of-the-century legislation that currently governs GPO. For a number of reasons, however, the legislation that addressed these issues (H.R. 5424) died before receiving consideration by the full House of Representatives. When the House Administration Committee favorably reported the bill, two other House committees, Government Operations and Rules, claimed jurisdiction on certain aspects of the bill. Each committee held hearings; significant opposition was voiced by those who were troubled by the labor provisions and those who felt the new bill would cost significantly more than the current law. Both committees reported the bill without recommendation but with amendments. As a result of the lack of consensus on the part of the committees, no further action was taken; the bill died when Congress adjourned.

Another proposal affecting the information marketplace did receive full consideration by the Congress, and the Congress, responding to concerns raised by the information and publishing communities, including the academic press, postponed a final decision until further analysis could be performed. The issue was the establishment of a government corporation to provide document delivery of journal articles, a National Periodical Center (NPC). The issue was included in the massive Higher Education bill (H.R. 5192) which had passed the full House in November 1979. The House bill would authorize establishment and funding (to the tune of $15 million annually) of NPC. However, no funds would become available unless the other library support programs in the Higher Education Act were funded at certain, predefined levels; this provision, known as a "trigger mechanism," was included to guarantee that NPC operations would not drain funds away from other necessary programs.

The Senate held extensive hearings on the bill including one session on NPC. After much consideration, the Senate decided to establish the government corporation, calling it the National Periodical System Corporation (NPSC), but to restrict its authority to determining the advisability and feasibility of a federal role in document delivery. If advisable and feasible, NPSC would then be authorized to design the operation, but this design could not be implemented until it was approved by both houses of Congress. When the conference committee of members of the House and Senate met to iron out the differences between the two bills, the Senate language on NPSC prevailed but the House trigger mechanism was also included. In light of current funding trends on other library programs, it does not seem likely that even the small amount ($750,000) required for the feasibility study will be authorized in the near future.

The Worldwide Information and Trade System (WITS), a centralized database of international trade opportunities and capabilities, was a third major program that posed the threat of government competition in the information marketplace. There was no bill before Congress authorizing WITS; instead, there was a request for funds in the Department of Commerce's appropriations material. In the previous year, Commerce had asked for $5 million and the Congress had approved $4 million along with explicit instructions to Commerce not to compete with the private information industry. However, representatives of the industry testified before the appropriations committees, expressing their concern that Commerce Department action had not fully conformed with the congressional directive. Responding to this pressure, the department put forth a new proposal that appeared to address many of the concerns of the industry: Commerce would actively collect, through a formal Request for Information (RFI), descriptions of private-sector information products and services that could aid exporters; using this knowledge, it would design a system that would use private-sector information to the maximum extent practicable and would collect and distribute only trade information that was not currently available from private-sector sources; it would pass this design before an independent advisory body comprised of private-sector information producers and users for review and approval; and "sunset" provisions would allow for periodic review in future years to determine if any government data could be replaced by private-sector products and services developed since the RFI was issued. The Congress explicitly endorsed this approach and then (apparently for cost-cutting reasons alone) appropriated $3 million for WITS.

PROPRIETARY RIGHTS

One of the most difficult areas of public policy in the information age is establishing the statutory basis for protecting the economic value of information products. In a time of ready access to photocopiers and tape recorders, unauthorized copying of information in printed or electronic form is a simple, usually undetectable task. The complexity of these issues is reflected in the inability of the Senate to approve S. 240, the Federal Computer Systems Protection Act. Although unanimously approved by a Senate subcommittee in 1979, no further action took place during the remainder of the Ninety-sixth Congress on this simple bill, which would have established federal penalties for unauthorized access to or damage of government computers or computers used in interstate trade or banking.

However, the Congress did approve in its final days a significant amendment to the Copyright Act of 1976 concerning computers. The Computer Software Copyright Act, H.R. 6934, was introduced in March 1980 and received widespread support. It added to the definitions in the Copyright Act a definition of "computer program" and wrote a new section 117 that described allowable copying of computer programs, essentially for execution purposes or for archival or backup purposes. Meanwhile, much attention was being focused on the Patent and Trademark policy of the country. Numerous proposals ebbed and flowed into another bill, H.R. 6933: Should the Patent and Trademark Office be independent of the Department of Commerce? Should the Copyright Office be independent of the Library of Congress? What should the ownership rights be with regard to inventions paid for by federal money? When many of these issues were resolved, the language of the computer copyright act was also added to H.R. 6933 by the Judiciary Committee in the House. Therefore, although the computer copyright provisions were noncontroversial, their fate rested with the outcome of the larger, much more controversial bill. Weeks of political jockeying, involving some of the most powerful members of both the House and Senate, ensued and it was only in the final weeks of the Congress, when many observers had given up any hope of passage, that H.R. 6933 was finally approved by both houses. The president signed PL 96-517 on December 12.

COMMUNICATIONS

Although some legislation affecting the Communications Act of 1934 was passed in 1980 (for example, affecting Hawaii's status in relation to the other states or dealing with labor practices of broadcasters), the major rewrite of the act that had been hoped for as the Ninety-sixth Congress began did not come to fruition. Nor did the less ambitious attempt to address only that part of the act dealing with common carrier (telephone) meet with any greater success. However, throughout the year, much attention was focused on the attempts of both the House and Senate Communications subcommittees to bring the Communications Act up to date with the realities of a competitive telecommunications marketplace.

These attempts were complicated by a number of external forces. In April, the Federal Communications Commission (FCC) announced its decision in the proceeding known as *Computer Inquiry II*. (The decision was modified, but not substantively, in the fall.) In the decision, FCC tried to come to grips with the evolving information technologies that made the boundary between computing and communicating very hard to discern. Defining two categories of communications services, "basic" and "enhanced," FCC ruled that it need not regulate the latter. However, it did require the largest communications company, American Telephone and Telegraph (AT&T), to set up a separate subsidiary if it wished to offer any enhanced communications services. Meanwhile, a massive antitrust suit against AT&T, initiated by the Justice Department during the Ford administration, was rapidly coming to its trial phase.

The legislation in the House, H.R. 6121, certainly dealt with what types of services AT&T could market. It also dealt with some of the same questions about how AT&T should be organized that the antitrust trial judge would be considering. In this light, despite a favorable report by the Commerce Committee, the Judiciary Committee requested an opportunity to consider the bill. After a few days of hearings, the Judiciary Committee reported the bill unfavorably with regard to its immediate consideration but without prejudice to its future treatment in the next Congress.

CIVIL LIBERTIES

Despite a significant amount of pressure from the Carter administration, very little legislation affecting personal privacy was dealt with by the Ninety-sixth Congress. In fact, only one bill, S. 1790, the Privacy Protection Act of 1980, was passed by both houses and became law. This law was directed at providing protection for the work product of journalists; it effectively reversed the Supreme Court decision *Zurcher* v. *Stanford Daily*, which held that police searches of newsrooms were allowed, and also directed the attorney general to develop guidelines for obtaining documentary material in the possession of a person when that person is not suspected of an offense under investigation.

The only other privacy legislation that made much progress was a bill addressing the privacy of medical records, H.R. 5935. This bill had been considered and reported favorably by at least two House committees, but when it was brought up on the House floor in the waning days of the Ninety-sixth Congress it was defeated. The bill was brought up "under suspension," a parliamentary tool for noncontroversial bills: No amendments are allowed and the bill must receive two-thirds of the votes to be passed. Members of the House felt the bill was too important to be handled as a suspension in the final days of the Congress, and it did not receive a two-thirds affirmative vote.

A civil liberties issue affecting information and the right to trial was addressed in S. 1482, the Classified Information Procedures Act, which was passed by the Congress and became PL 96-456. This law deals with the issue of "graymail," a circumstance that develops when a defendant in a trial claims he must introduce classified information into evidence or else he cannot get a fair trial. The government is then faced with the dilemma of either ceasing prosecution or risking the release of classified material. This new law, however, establishes clear procedures for handling such material in the courts.

REGULATION OF INFORMATION FLOWS

The final area of information policy legislation in 1980 encompasses those measures that impede or encourage the flows of information. For example, the question of flows of information across international boundaries received heightened attention. Hearings were held on the subject of transborder data flow by the House Government Operations Committee. Just before the end of the Ninety-sixth Congress, legislation aimed at improving the organizational framework within the Executive Office of the president and the State Department for dealing with international information policy was introduced (H.R. 8443). The bill was introduced for discussion purposes, not actual consideration, and it is likely the same or a similar bill will be introduced in the Ninety-seventh Congress.

Congress also aimed at the flow of information it requires of the executive branch.

Nearly every major piece of legislation includes some provision requiring a report to Congress. H.R. 6686, which became PL 96-470, reverses this situation somewhat, for as its name implies, the Congressional Reports Elimination Act of 1980 identifies a number of "required" reports that are no longer required.

Perhaps the most significant information policy bill of the Ninety-sixth Congress is one that also, ostensibly, is aimed at flows of information, specifically those of the citizens to the government. The Paperwork Reduction Act of 1980, PL 96-511, does indeed require a measurable (25 percent) reduction in the burden of federal collections of information before FY 1984. But it also addresses information issues far beyond paperwork control.

The law establishes within the Office of Management and Budget (OMB) an Office of Information and Regulatory Affairs. Further, it assigns a number of functions to the director of OMB: "The Director shall develop and implement Federal information policies, principles, standards, and guidelines and shall provide direction and oversee the review and approval of information collection requests, the reduction of the paperwork burden, Federal statistical activities, records management activities, privacy of records, interagency sharing of information, and acquisition and use of automatic data processing telecommunications, and other technology for managing information resources." This law becomes effective April 1, 1981, so it is still too early to determine how it will be implemented. It certainly appears likely, however, that future observers will identify PL 96-511 as the most important information policy bill to be passed by the Ninety-sixth Congress.

CONCLUSION

The information policy legislation mentioned above comprises some of the highlights of the year 1980, but it is by no means exhaustive. Such a treatment would expand the length of this article three- or fourfold. However, the breadth of legislative subjects included in the rubric "information policy" is evident in the measures described. It should be equally evident that the number and importance of these measures will increase as we more fully enter the information age.

Funding Programs and Grant-Making Agencies

COUNCIL ON LIBRARY RESOURCES, INC.

One Dupont Circle, Suite 620, Washington, DC 20036
202-296-4757

Nancy E. Gwinn
Program Officer

As a privately operated foundation, the Council on Library Resources, Inc. (CLR) employs a variety of approaches to help find solutions to the generic problems of libraries, especially those of academic and research libraries. A principal activity is the awarding of grants to institutions and individuals for projects that fall within the council's areas of interest, which include bibliographic services, library operations and services, library resources and their preservation, and professional education and training. The council also establishes and administers programs of its own and may seek qualified persons or organizations to carry out projects or perform research under specific CLR guidelines.

Increasingly the council performs a catalytic role in bringing individuals and organizations together to define problems and determine priorities for action. This has typified much of the early activity of CLR's Bibliographic Service Development Program, for example, and will also be used in a new program, currently on the drawing board, for professional education and training for research librarians.

The fiscal year that concluded June 30, 1980, was busy in terms of grant activity and council-administered projects. Sixty-nine grants and contracts and 15 fellowships were active, including new awards of $1,216,000. An underlying theme within every area of interest is the need for purposeful research and analysis. The council has always welcomed proposals for research projects that promise to provide the profession with needed information, whether the topic be bibliographic control, collection development, management, library instruction, or preservation. In the coming year, the council also hopes to continue targeting specific issues worthy of exploration and to involve a broad spectrum of investigators in their analysis.

Warren J. Haas is president of CLR, and Mary Agnes Thompson is secretary and treasurer. During 1980, the CLR board of directors conferred the title of Director Emeritus on two of its members: Lyman H. Butterfield, former editor-in-chief of the *Adams Papers* at the Massachusetts Historical Society, and Frederick Hard, president emeritus of Scripps College.

BIBLIOGRAPHIC SERVICES

The council's Bibliographic Service Development Program (BSDP) was initiated in 1978 to work toward the provision of effective bibliographic services that will meet the existing and future needs of scholarship and research, toward the improvement of bibliographic products, and toward the purposeful control of costs in individual libraries. A recent review of the first two years of the program revealed substantial progress in several areas. As of September 30, 1980, over $1,117,000 of the $5 million project had been used for grants and contracts, for consultants, and to support expenses of committees, task forces, and review groups.

Many BSDP projects are directed toward defining and putting into place pieces of a comprehensive nationwide bibliographic record service, most likely to be composed of the existing major data bases. The sharing of bibliographic records and products, an important component of such a service, requires the development of standards, particularly if exchanges occur in a machine-readable environment.

In 1979, the BSDP formed a Joint Committee on Bibliographic Standards, composed of technical experts from the major shared cataloging systems, research libraries, the Library of Congress (LC), the national libraries of medicine and agriculture, the National Library of Canada, and CLR. Its first task was to assist in the selection of options, provided under the new second edition of the *Anglo-American Cataloguing Rules (AACR 2)*, for the machine-based bibliographic services in the United States. The committee continues to advise the Library of Congress on matters of interpretation and on the creation of manuals that will guide application of the new rules to specialized categories of material, such as newspapers, maps, microforms, and rare books. In addition, Sue A. Dodd, data librarian at the University of North Carolina, received a CLR grant to complete a manual for cataloging machine-readable data files.

Several specific standards are receiving attention. The BSDP established a MARC Format Review Committee to work with a Library of Congress consultant to resolve problems with the MARC communications format, a standard that dictates how machine-readable bibliographic records are organized for purposes of exchange. CLR is also supporting work at the University of Illinois to identify growth trends and statistical relationships among elements of the MARC data base. The council has hired consultants to prepare position papers on two other standards: institution identification codes and detailed bibliographic holdings statements.

Much of the year has been devoted to a study commissioned by CLR of the impacts of linking the major bibliographic data bases (the Ohio College Library Center [OCLC], the Washington Library Network [WLN], and the Research Libraries Information Network) with each other and with the Library of Congress. The contractor, Battelle-Columbus Laboratories, completed its work in August 1980 and recommended that the organizations develop on-line links using automatic translation of requests and responses. The recommendation was based on an analysis of the economic and service benefits to libraries and their users of linking for three library options: interlibrary loan, shared cataloging of current monographs, and reference searching. An interactive computer model called BIBLINK was developed to compare methods of exchange. Along with other tools provided in the report, Battelle recommends that BIBLINK be used to examine other link alternatives and to reassess those used in the study as new data becomes available. The report also suggests the formation of two committees, one to work on communications standards and the other on applications standards.

Participants at a CLR-sponsored meeting in September 1979 agreed that a single, comprehensive name authority file, as a basis for a nationwide service, should be established, beginning with the integration of existing files at several institutions. The following March, CLR awarded a grant to the Research Libraries Group (RLG) and the Washington Library Network (WLN) for the first phase of a two-year project that will provide the organizations with the technical capacity to support a nationwide shared authority file system. When all phases are complete, each network will continue to operate its own system, but will be able to share authority records. CLR grants are enabling the Library of Congress to help establish telecommunications requirements for the project and to convert over 100,000 heavily used name authority records—an important foundation for the service—from manual to machine-readable form. All of these organizations participate, with others, in a CLR-established Task Force on a Name Authority File Service to ensure that the projects are consistent with other on-going activities and to spell out requirements in such areas as data collection, file maintenance, on-line and off-line access, standards, financing, and management. The BSDP is also starting to explore the problems associated with developing authority files for subject terms.

Throughout this activity, the BSDP is attempting to identify the kinds of bibliographic products and services needed by libraries and their users. As one step, OCLC and RLG recently completed a CLR-funded study of the approaches, problems, and priorities involved in the issue of on-line patron access to bibliographic data bases. To assist in the project and to help plan future work, this past summer the council brought together 30 individuals from institutions that are operating or actively planning on-line catalogs for public use. The project report has been published by the council. Another series of meetings, involving representatives of some of the multistate bibliographic networks (SOLINET, NELINET, WLN, and AMIGOS), has been held at the council's invitation to discuss the emerging role of these organizations in the nationwide system.

The council's long-standing interest and involvement in the CONSER (Conversion of Serials) project, a cooperative file-building effort that has resulted in a national serials data base, continues as part of the BSDP. The council funded and managed CONSER in its early stages, but management has now been assumed by OCLC. CLR continues to furnish funds to support telecommunications costs for some of the CONSER participants. In FY 1980, CLR provided partial support for the conversion of the union list of serials of the Boston Theological Institute to machine-readable form through the CONSER project. Completion of the two-year project, also supported by the Lilly Endowment and the Arthur Vining Davis Foundation, will add over 6,700 unique theological serial titles to the nationwide data base.

LIBRARY OPERATIONS AND SERVICES

Libraries are involved in a major transformation that is moving them from roles as self-contained repositories to that of windows on an increasingly interdependent and complex bibliographic world. The activities of the BSDP emphasize the manner in which automation is changing the nature of the environment within which libraries function. To manage in a constructive manner the necessary changes in library operations and services that must accompany these new developments has become a critical requirement in many libraries. Recent council programs have supported work toward helping individual academic libraries improve management practices. The past year also saw the publication of two CLR-supported books concerning building, planning, and furnishing: *Furnishing the Library Interior* (New York: Marcel Dekker, 1980) by William S. Pierce, facilities planning officer of the Pennsylvania State University Libraries, and *Mason on Library Buildings* (Metuchen, N.J.: Scarecrow Press, 1980) by Ellsworth Mason, head of special collections, University of Colorado Libraries.

The council's principal focus in terms of improving library management continues to be through support of the Office of Management Studies (OMS) of the Association of Research Libraries (ARL). Having just completed its first energetic decade, the office has clearly become a key element in the total effort to improve management and fiscal practices in academic and research libraries.

The office's major activity is the development of assisted self-studies for use, with consultative help, by academic libraries of every size. Collected under the general title of the Academic Library Program, the studies provide tools and procedures for libraries to examine their environment, assess operational implications, and devise improvements in programs and activities. The Management Review and Analysis Program for large academic libraries, the Academic Library Development Program for mid-sized libraries, and the Planning Program for Small Academic Libraries help institutions examine their overall settings and practices. Other programs look at specific matters, such as collection management or, in a program currently on the drawing board, preservation.

Council funds are supporting a Consultant Training Program to provide up to 100 librarians with training that will enable them to act as consultants to libraries wishing to engage in an Academic Library Program study. A first group of 20 academic librarians was selected to participate in a two-week workshop in September 1979 followed by an internship on a project guided by an OMS staff member. The second group of trainees will be selected in early 1981.

In June 1980, a grant was awarded to the Society of American Archivists for a project designed to establish a system of self-study and peer evaluation for archives. Participation would be voluntary and would be undertaken with the aim of determining how well a repository has directed its resources toward fulfilling the goals and objectives it has set for itself. The society has been concerned about the recent increase in the number of archival agencies and their relative quality, particularly those institutions that might not realize the commitment necessary for an adequate program.

Other new grants of FY 1980 included support for teaching faculty attendance at conferences at Earlham College and the University of Wisconsin-Parkside on the topic of bibliographic instruction and for the Fifth Assembly of State Librarians, held at the Library of Congress in April 1980.

LIBRARY RESOURCES AND THEIR PRESERVATION

In his overview of scholarly and research services in the new *ALA World Encyclopedia of Library and Information Services*, David H. Stam, director of research libraries of the New York Public Library, states that "collecting and preservation should remain the most important functions of research libraries." Growing financial constraints and inflationary pressures have highlighted the issues involved, however, and in recent years have led to increasing concern for the future of these functions, the importance of which Stam goes on to explain:

> In a general way large research libraries often play an active role in shaping the direction of scholarship itself through their decisions about what is important to preserve for posterity and what is chaff to be discarded. By determining what is retained and made accessible from the human record, research libraries often have the power to determine new directions in scholarship, or at the least to affect the extent of those directions.*

The collection development function is important to libraries of all types, and all need assistance in using their limited resources to full effect. This past year the council funded a proposal from the Associated Colleges of the Midwest (ACM) to extend

---

*David H. Stam, "Scholarly and Research Services," *ALA World Encyclopedia of Library and Information Services* (Chicago: American Library Association, 1980), p. 497.

the utility of research on collection use and efficiency of acquisitions policies to the general management of small libraries. Using three ACM member libraries as test sites, project staff tested inexpensive and easily implemented methodologies for gathering data on collection use and developed guidelines to assist librarians in analyzing and using study results. A manual has been drafted that can be used by any small academic library to conduct similar studies. The ARL Office of Management Studies is completing plans to test the manual in several environments, after which the work will be published.

During the past year, two other CLR-supported guides to library resources in foreign countries were published: *Australian and New Zealand Library Resources* (London: Mansell and Melbourne: D. W. Thorpe, 1979) by Robert B. Downs, dean of library administration emeritus, University of Illinois, and *A Guide to British Government Publications* (New York: H. W. Wilson, 1980) by Frank Rodgers, library director at the University of Miami.

Such guides will be of little use, however, if the material to which they direct the searcher has crumbled to dust and vanished. The majority of materials published since the mid-nineteenth century have been printed on paper with a high acid content—an internal self-destruct mechanism—and their life span is short. While some paper manufacturers now use alkaline processes, their numbers are few, and publishers do not place a priority on use of their papers.

To attempt to encourage more widespread use of acid-free and durable papers, the council has been supporting work of a Committee on Production Guidelines for Book Longevity, which has been meeting for a year and a half. The committee's aim is to establish a basic set of guidelines to assure reasonable permanence and acceptable durability of printed materials and to consider the relation of the guidelines to the ways in which books are used. In essence, the committee is seeking to raise awareness of the problem among all those concerned and to develop practical, realistic methods of dealing with it.

Two other modest CLR-supported projects focus on other aspects of the preservation issue. Early in 1980, CLR joined other funding agencies to match an NEH (National Endowment for the Humanities) Challenge Grant in support of a library conservation program at Southern Illinois University at Carbondale. The university library has set up a conservation laboratory, headed by a trained conservator, and is developing training programs, workshops, and other activities to assist libraries and other institutions throughout Illinois and the region. CLR has also awarded a small grant to the University of Wyoming to support direct editorial costs associated with producing the fledgling newsletter *Conservation Administration News*, edited by the university's library director.

PROFESSIONAL EDUCATION AND TRAINING

During the past year the council held discussions with a variety of people on the topic of requirements of research librarians for professional education and training. As the fiscal year closed, the CLR board of directors authorized the staff to expand the council's program in this area. Subsequently, the council received grants of $650,000 and $450,000 respectively from the Andrew W. Mellon Foundation and the Carnegie Corporation of New York to meet about 60 percent of the initial costs of a three-year effort. Among the goals of the new program are these:

Recruit to academic and research librarianship an appropriate share of the best and brightest college graduates and provide them with a rigorous and stimulating basic professional education.

Identify in the present ranks of librarians those who, by their skills and other qualities, show clear promise for professional leadership and then provide them with exceptional opportunities for additional training.

Focus the attention of librarians and others who should be concerned on the fundamental issues now facing research libraries.

Raise the quality of and make more pertinent the research related to library matters and increase the involvement of librarians and others outside the profession in the research process.

Promote more effective communication between practitioners and library school educators.

Influence the content and structure of professional education for research librarianship to enhance its pertinence to present and projected concerns of academic and research libraries.

Continue to press for improvement in library management with special attention to capitalizing fully on professional staff skills.

An advisory committee has been appointed to consider methods and priorities important to the goals. John McDonald, director of libraries at the University of Connecticut, chairs the committee. Other members are Rutherford Rogers, Yale University library director; Robert Vosper, chair of the CLR board committee on professional education; Margot McBurney, library director at Queens University and chair of the ARL professional education committee; Russell Bidlack, dean of the University of Michigan library school; and William Gerberding, president of the University of Washington.

Prospects are strong that activities like those described below may be included.

Development by a very few schools of an intensive basic professional education program specifically for academic research librarianship, to include a structured internship.

Funding of a special effort to recruit into research librarianship a larger portion of the most promising college graduates.

Creation of a new management fellows program for individuals recently named to policy-level positions, who, chosen competitively, would spend a substantial amount of time with specialists in several fields to probe the substance of research libraries now and in the future.

Operation of an annual invitational "frontiers" conference involving librarians, scholars, educators, university officers, and others to consider in depth one or more specific topics of great importance to research libraries.

Support for research by library educators and others on major issues of direct pertinence to research library operations and management.

The central theme of all projected activities is to provide distinctive opportunities for professional growth for exceptional research librarians, present as well as prospective.

One of the council's ongoing professional development programs, the Academic Library Management Intern Program, will continue as part of the professional education effort. For the 1980–1981 academic year, five midcareer librarians were selected to work closely with the directors and top administrative staffs of five large university libraries, as follows:

Beverlee A. French, reference librarian, Biomedical Library, University of California, San Diego, will intern with John McDonald, University of Connecticut.

Kathleen Gunning, head of reference, Brown University Library, has been assigned to work with Joseph H. Treyz, University of Wisconsin-Madison.

Kathleen Moretto, assistant director, Yale University Music Library, will spend her year with James F. Govan, University of North Carolina.

Maxine H. Reneker, personnel/business librarian at the University of Colorado Libraries, will work with Patricia Battin, Columbia University.

Charlene E. Renner, automated records librarian, University of Illinois at Urbana-Champaign, will intern with Joseph Rosenthal, University of California, Berkeley.

For the last three years, under contract with the National Library of Medicine, the council has also administered a Health Sciences Library Management Intern Program, modeled after the academic library program. The 1980–1981 year is the final one for this program, and the following librarians were chosen as the last class of interns.

Robert J. Sekerak, director, Hospital Library Development Services and reference librarian, Charles A. Dana Medical Library, University of Vermont, will intern with L. Yvonne Wulff at the University of Michigan.

Kenneth E. Weeks, assistant to the university librarian, University of California, San Francisco, has been assigned to work with C. Robin LeSueur of the Francis A. Countway Library of Medicine, Harvard University.

Joan Zenan, medical librarian, Savitt Medical Library, University of Nevada, will intern with Rachel Goldstein at Columbia University.

Another grant made in the past year was directed toward providing enriching experiences for students in the throes of professional education. A grant to Wright State University is supporting the costs of internships in national agencies or institutions for students enrolled in the Department of History's program in Archival and Historical Administration. Required to give 300 hours of service, the students will probably work in such agencies as the National Archives, the National Trust for Historic Preservation, or the Folger Shakespeare Library.

INTERNATIONAL PROGRAMS

The nightly news provides a constant reminder of how events all over the world affect the daily well-being of American citizens. Electronic systems allow instant communication, and transmission of information has become a global enterprise. Libraries continue to have their place in the organization and transmission of information in international, as well as national arenas. From its beginning, the council has not hesitated to keep informed about, participate in, and support programs designed to facilitate worldwide understanding of and agreements on vital issues affecting libraries and information transfer.

In the past 22 years, CLR has made grants of more than $1.6 million to projects of international scope. In FY 1980, major new programs have been specifically supported by generous grants to the council from the Exxon Education Foundation.

In the past decade, the primary channel of council support has been the International Federation of Library Associations and Institutions (IFLA). Since 1971, four sequential council grants have supported the work of the IFLA secretariat as it managed a restructuring and expansion of IFLA's professional program. The current grant primarily supports the work of IFLA's professional activities coordinator, who oversees eight divisions and 41 sections and round tables, as well as monitoring IFLA-UNESCO contracts and representing IFLA at important international meetings. For the same time period, CLR has been supporting efforts of the IFLA International Office for Universal Bibliographic Control, which is working toward development of a worldwide system for the control and exchange of bibliographic information.

A new grant was awarded this year to IFLA for special projects in the areas of copyright of bibliographic records and files; conversion of copyrighted library materials for use by handicapped readers; and conservation of materials with emphasis on prospective aspects of the problem. Another new grant went to the International Council on Archives for projects related to worldwide preservation and use of archival sources, with special attention to Third World countries.

CLR-SUPPORTED PROJECTS, 1979–1980

NEW GRANTS AND CONTRACTS

Associated Colleges of the Midwest	
Manual to guide study of collection use in small academic libraries	$ 39,830
Boston Theological Institute	
Two-year serial cataloging project	8,890
Earlham College	
Fourth Conference on Bibliographic Instruction	4,400
International Council on Archives	
Special projects	30,000
International Federation of Library Associations and Institutions	
Special projects	70,000
Library of Congress	
Fifth Assembly of State Librarians	14,250
Foster Mohrhardt	
Travel grant to chair IFLA Program Management Committee	7,000
National Commission on Libraries and Information Science	
Partial support for library school students to attend White House Conference on Library and Information Services	10,000
Plainedge Public Library	
Research to determine reasons for nonuse of public libraries	29,250
Society of American Archivists	
Pilot project for self-study and peer review of archives	18,670
Southern Illinois University at Carbondale	
Library conservation program	15,000
University of Wisconsin-Parkside	
Bibliographic instruction conference	1,200
University of Wyoming	
Support of *Conservation Administration News*	2,000
Wright State University	
Internships for masters degree students in archival and historical administration	2,500
Total	$252,990

NEW COUNCIL-ADMINISTERED PROGRAM GRANTS AND CONTRACTS

Academic Library Management Intern Program, 1980–1981	$111,639
Bibliographic Service Department Program	
American Association of Law Libraries	
LAWNET planning meeting	2,500

COUNCIL ON LIBRARY RESOURCES, INC. / 161

Pauline Atherton	
Travel grant to attend ISO/TC 46/SC4/WG5 meeting in Rome	1,000
Battelle Memorial Institute-Columbus Laboratories	
Study of linking of bibliographic utilities	233,112
Howard Harris and Patricia Harris	
Position paper on an institution identification code standard	2,700
Institute for Research in Social Science, University of North Carolina, Chapel Hill	
Machine-readable data files cataloging manual	5,524
Library of Congress	
Conversion of retrospective name authority files	220,000
Travel costs re the nationwide authority file service project	17,000
OCLC, Inc.	
On-line patron access to bibliographic data bases (joint project with RLG)	8,150
Rensselaer Polytechnic Institute	
Planning a thesaurus for the fields of art and architecture	10,000
Research Libraries Group	
On-line patron access to bibliographic data bases (joint project with OCLC)	8,150
Toward formation of a nationwide authority file service (joint project with WLN)	168,651
University of Illinois, Urbana-Champaign	
MARC data base statistics	23,463
Washington Library Network	
Toward the formation of a nationwide authority file service (joint project with RLG)	149,666
Travel important to profession for foreign visitors	
Johnston L. Abukutsa, University of Nairobi	
A study of user education programs in the United States	1,500
J. E. Traue, Wellington, New Zealand	
Visits to U.S. research libraries	500
Total	$963,555

ONGOING GRANTS AND CONTRACTS

American Association of Law Libraries ($20,000—1968)
American Library Association
  Ethnic and sexual composition/salary survey for librarians ($13,856—1977)
  Secretariat for the U.S. National Committee for the UNESCO General Information Program ($2,500—1978)
Association of Research Libraries
  Academic Library Program ($326,500—1978)
Council of National Library and Information Associations, Inc.
  Continued support of the American National Standards Committee Z-39 ($30,000—1979)
Robert B. Downs
  Preparation of second edition of *British Library Resources* ($3,000—1979)
Earlham College
  Periodical list for *Choice* ($7,500—1975)

International Federation of Library Associations and Institutions
  Professional activities of the secretariat ($174,000—1975; $75,000—1979)
  International Office for Universal Bibliographic Control ($150,000—1977)
Iowa State University
  Mechanized indexing procedures applied to production of subject-enhanced keyword index ($1,926—1977)
MIDLNET
  Toward salary of a technical advisory ($22,778—1977)
National Association of State Universities and Land-Grant Colleges, Office for Advancement of Public Negro Colleges
  Status report on libraries of black public colleges ($4,000—1978)
Carl M. Spaulding
  Travel grant to chair meetings of new standards group within National Micrographics Associations ($2,000—1979)
State University of New York at Binghamton
  Meeting on retrospective collection development ($2,675—1978)
University of California, Berkeley
  National shelflist measurement project ($20,000—1978)
University of California, Los Angeles
  Third edition of *Handbook of Data Processing for Libraries* ($14,500—1978)
University of Connecticut
  New England Academic Librarians' Writing Seminar ($20,610—1976)
University of Kentucky
  Preparation of "Leaders in American Academic Librarianship, 1925-75" ($10,000—1979)

CLR PUBLICATIONS FREE UPON REQUEST

24th Annual Report (Washington, DC, 1980).
CLR Recent Developments (Washington, DC, 1973-   ).
CLR Program Guidelines (brochure).

LIBRARY SERVICES AND CONSTRUCTION ACT

State and Public Library Service Branch Staff,*
Division of Library Programs,
Office of Libraries and Learning Technologies, ED

The Library Services and Construction Act (LSCA) is the only federal program designed to assist the states in developing and improving public library services and promoting interlibrary cooperation. Originally enacted in 1956 and intended to assist states in extending library services to rural areas, it has grown into a multipurpose program that will be celebrating its twenty-fifth anniversary in 1981. Funding in FY 1980 for

*Written by Nathan Cohen, Clarence Fogelstrom, Dorothy Kittel, Evaline Neff, and Trish Skaptason; Robert Klassen, Acting Branch Chief.

public library services provided $62.5 million to the states under Title I and $5 million for interlibrary cooperation projects under Title III. No funds have been appropriated for public library construction, Title II, since FY 1973.

The LSCA program funds are administered by the 57 state and territorial library administrative agencies, each of which submitted a three-year basic state plan for fiscal years 1980, 1981, and 1982 and annually submits both a long-range program for library development based on the state's assessed needs and an annual program. These documents outline a state's goals, objectives, priorities, and activities for specified periods of time. Furthermore, they provide assurances to the U.S. Department of Education that specific requirements will be met annually in the state-federal agreement signed by both parties.

All qualifying documents are developed by the state in consultation with the branch program officers. A statewide advisory council assists the state library administrative agency in developing and reviewing the documents. The council is broadly representative of all types of libraries and library user groups. A minimum of one-third of each council's membership is comprised of general users of public library services.

TITLE I—PUBLIC LIBRARY SERVICES

The Public Library Services Program provides funds to encourage and strengthen state library administrative agencies in extending public library services to areas without such services and improving library services where they are defined as inadequate by state standards. These funds support efforts to make public libraries more accessible to persons who, by reason of distance, residence, physical handicap, or other disadvantaged circumstance, might not have access to the informational or educational services available in the public library. Included among the designated target groups are the state institutionalized population, the rural and urban disadvantaged, and those who have limited English-speaking ability. The state library administrative agencies have reported that these services reach 30 million disadvantaged, 5 million persons of limited English-speaking ability, 2.2 million elderly, 1.2 million physically handicapped, and 723,000 state institutionalized persons.

Under the provision for Major Urban Resource Libraries (MURL), those funds appropriated above $60 million are reserved for the state library to allocate to urban public libraries. That portion of funds from the excess over $60 million is based on the ratio of the state's urban population to the state's entire population. Each state is then allowed to apportion not more than 50 percent of its MURL allocation to its major urban libraries located in cities with a population of 100,000 or more and whose collections serve defined regional areas in the state. The $2.5 million program has been operative at this level since FY 1979 and reinforces another Title I priority to strengthen metropolitan public libraries as national or regional resource centers. [See Table 1 for the state allotments and matching requirements for FY 1981.]

In addition, Title I is to strengthen state library administrative agencies. In FY 1978 $5.1 million or 8.8 percent of the Title I funds was used for these purposes. It should be noted that Title I funds are being spent increasingly for projects that involve long-term, ongoing activities and less for short-term demonstrations. A recent evaluation study of Title I by Applied Management Sciences noted over 56 percent of the LSCA projects could be classified in this category. The study also found that 44 percent of all Title I projects have some form of interlibrary cooperation involved in their services or in the acquisition of materials.

TABLE 1 LSCA TITLE I, PUBLIC LIBRARY SERVICES, STATE ALLOTMENTS AND MATCHING REQUIREMENTS, FY 1981

States and Outlying Areas	Total Federal Allotment	Total State and Local Matching	$60 Million Level	MURL
Alabama	$1,072,405	$ 712,557	$1,030,382	$ 42,023
Alaska	296,180	601,335	291,547	4,633
Arizona	755,316	650,446	728,567	26,749
Arkansas	707,109	448,675	682,682	24,427
California	5,421,793	6,979,381	5,170,261	251,532
Colorado	833,242	867,599	802,739	30,503
Connecticut	929,188	1,256,623	894,063	35,125
Delaware	336,664	417,512	330,081	6,583
District of Columbia	357,024	613,677	349,460	7,564
Florida	2,226,797	2,035,831	2,129,167	97,630
Georgia	1,387,622	1,045,949	1,330,415	57,207
Hawaii	411,081	521,498	400,913	10,168
Idaho	406,401	314,807	396,459	9,942
Illinois	2,829,852	3,692,047	2,703,173	126,679
Indiana	1,460,635	1,387,717	1,399,911	60,724
Iowa	880,045	849,603	847,288	32,757
Kansas	749,231	774,216	722,775	26,456
Kentucky	1,016,710	739,872	977,369	39,341
Louisiana	1,130,909	806,242	1,086,068	44,841
Maine	455,544	318,401	443,235	12,309
Maryland	1,170,691	1,394,926	1,123,933	46,758
Massachusetts	1,550,496	1,664,300	1,485,443	65,053
Michigan	2,348,484	2,630,283	2,244,992	103,492
Minnesota	1,141,673	1,125,351	1,096,313	45,360
Mississippi	763,740	416,875	736,585	27,155
Missouri	1,334,267	1,179,897	1,279,630	54,637
Montana	382,531	307,336	373,739	8,792
Nebraska	567,168	534,557	549,482	17,686
Nevada	355,853	463,142	348,346	7,507
New Hampshire	403,358	350,301	393,562	9,796
New Jersey	1,912,048	2,565,816	1,829,579	82,469
New Mexico	484,327	343,300	470,631	13,696
New York	4,352,816	5,194,927	4,152,776	200,040
North Carolina	1,503,693	1,106,885	1,440,895	62,798
North Dakota	352,811	303,948	345,450	7,361
Ohio	2,711,441	2,706,023	2,590,466	120,975
Oklahoma	865,302	706,260	833,255	32,047
Oregon	773,803	762,435	746,163	27,640
Pennsylvania	2,952,709	2,943,276	2,820,112	132,597
Rhode Island	418,101	392,330	407,595	10,506
South Carolina	879,109	589,990	846,397	32,712
South Dakota	361,470	258,016	353,692	7,778
Tennessee	1,213,984	850,966	1,165,141	48,843
Texas	3,253,183	3,014,993	3,106,113	147,070
Utah	508,197	369,821	493,351	14,846
Vermont	313,965	226,422	308,475	5,490
Virginia	1,411,492	1,363,757	1,353,135	58,357
Washington	1,087,616	1,260,432	1,044,860	42,756
West Virginia	635,500	471,450	614,522	20,978
Wisconsin	1,295,889	1,212,607	1,243,101	52,788
Wyoming	299,456	337,956	294,665	4,791
American Samoa	47,044	23,029	46,705	339
Guam	62,442	32,167	61,361	1,081

TABLE 1 LSCA TITLE I, PUBLIC LIBRARY SERVICES,
STATE ALLOTMENTS AND MATCHING REQUIREMENTS, FY 1981 (cont.)

States and Outlying Areas	Total Federal Allotment	Total State and Local Matching	$60 Million Level	MURL
Northern Mariana Islands	43,674	22,856	43,497	177
Puerto Rico	950,016	489,402	913,888	36,128
Trust Territory	65,695	0	64,457	1,238
Virgin Islands	62,208	32,047	61,138	1,070
Total	$62,500,000	$62,682,067	$60,000,000	$2,500,000

Estimated distribution of $62,500,000 with a minimum allotment of $200,000 to the 50 states, the District of Columbia, and Puerto Rico and $40,000, to the other outlying areas; the remainder distributed on the basis of the total resident population July 1, 1978, for the 50 states and the District of Columbia, and 1976 data for Puerto Rico and the other outlying areas. Required matching expenditures were computed on the basis of the FY 1980–1981 "federal share" percentages.

The same study also noted that over one-third of all public libraries in the United States have received at least one direct Title I grant since 1965. Yet they estimate that only 6 percent of all public libraries failed to receive at least one direct benefit from the Title I program.

Services to the Handicapped

Services to the physically handicapped are defined in LSCA as "the providing of library services, through public or other nonprofit libraries, agencies, or organizations, to physically handicapped persons (including the blind and other visually handicapped) certified by competent authority as unable to read or to use conventional printed materials as a result of physical limitations." In practice, library services to the disabled are of a broader nature and encompass the entire handicapped community, including parents, relatives, teachers, and others who are involved with the handicapped. One of the significant outcomes of this LSCA priority is the increased public awareness of needs and problems and the fostering of some new approaches to service.

According to the FY 1979 reports, $3.7 million in LSCA funds was used in conjunction with $10.3 million in state and local funds to support library projects serving 1.2 million handicapped persons, of whom approximately 270,000 are legally blind. Most of the states used a combination of federal and state funds; fewer than ten states used only LSCA funds for these service projects. Here are some examples of service activities for the blind:

1. *Statewide program.* The Kentucky Library for the Blind and Physically Handicapped produced its newsletter on a flexible disc, formed talking book discussion groups, held workshops for the staff on services to the blind and the deaf, and had a sculptor demonstrate soft stone carving and whittling for the blind. At the local level, the Lexington (Kentucky) Public Library's service for the deaf produced signed programs, a teletype communication system, and captioned films on deafness, and promoted services for the deaf during Deaf Heritage Week.
2. *Use of technology.* The most sophisticated technological application continues to be the Kurzweil Reading Machine, a device that scans ordinary printed materials and reads them aloud in synthetic English speech. The machine is easily operated by push-button controls and enables a blind person to "read" the

printed materials independently for the first time. An increasing number of libraries used LSCA funds to purchase these machines.
3. *Outreach activities.* Mail or outreach visits by librarians and volunteers deliver talking books along with the playback equipment needed to read them. Many state libraries supported taping projects to record materials to satisfy the special needs of the blind, such as foreign language courses. For example, Utah provided recording services for all textbook requirements needed in studying foreign language by blind students.
4. *Radio reading.* This activity involves the use by blind patrons of specially adapted receivers loaned by the library that pick up daily broadcasts, often consisting of the reading of newspapers, book discussion groups, grocery store ads, and other items of local interest. Eleven states (Arizona, Connecticut, Idaho, Indiana, Massachusetts, Nebraska, New York, Oklahoma, Tennessee, Utah, and Washington) provided these radio reading services through their public libraries.

Services to the Institutionalized

One of the groups specifically named in the act for special attention are those persons residing in state-supported institutions. These include inmates, patients, or residents of penal institutions, reformatories, residential training schools, orphanages, residential schools for handicapped persons, and other institutions or hospitals operated or substantially supported by the state.

The manner in which states administer the LSCA services to state-supported institutions is varied. Some states establish formulas based on institutional population and make grants directly to individual institutions; some states provide indirect services to the institutions such as book ordering and processing, consultant services, and training of library personnel; some states make grants to the nearest public library in return for library services rendered to an inmate population; other states conduct a competition and fund the most innovative project; and a number of states support, in whole or in part, the salary of librarians who are working in the libraries within the state institutions.

In FY 1979 $3.4 million in LSCA funds was used in projects totaling $15.5 million with combined state and local funds to reach 723,000 persons living in state institutions.

Basic areas of expenditure are:

1. *Salaries and wages.* In FY 1979 more than $5.7 million in combined federal and state funds was used for salary support of staff within the institutional setting as well as for statewide consultants for institutional services.
2. *Audiovisual materials.* The calming features of audiovisual presentations are generally recognized and deemed beneficial by institutional librarians and staff. States reported that there have been successful projects on the use of multiple listening posts for music. For those persons with physical, developmental, or emotional blocks that preclude the use of standard book materials, the states reported high success with key expenditures for audiovisual materials.
3. *Books and other print materials.* With LSCA support, many libraries moved away from relying on expected donation of materials and developed better collection development policies. Also, with the increasing emphasis on moving residents into mainstream activities and away from state institutions to private

group homes and halfway houses, the institutional libraries purchased more materials on prerelease and coping skills.
4. *Cooperative programs.* A number of states reported cooperative programs between the state institutional library and the public library located in the community in which a group home or halfway house was located. Reports indicated that literacy classes, language lessons, and drug and alcohol prevention programming were supported with Title I funds. Some state institutions had no permanent library and relied on the public library or the state library to furnish materials. There were also reports of local public libraries providing librarians to visit the institution on a part-time basis to either run the library or help users choose books. Some institutions had deposit collections on loan from the local public library with the functions of circulation carried out by inmates or patients.

Services to Persons of Limited English-Speaking Ability

The Education Amendments of 1974 required the states under Title I of LSCA to add criteria in their needs assessments and state plans to ensure that priority would be given to programs and projects serving areas with high concentrations of persons of limited English-speaking ability.

In FY 1979 nearly $2.2 million in LSCA funds was applied to $3.5 million state and local funds supporting 67 projects in 34 states and territories serving an estimated five million persons of limited English-speaking ability. Ninety-two percent of the funds was used to provide cultural and library services to the Hispanic population. A few interesting examples of these activities are noted below:

1. *Training.* California's Chicano Resource Center provided training on how to serve bilingual communities.
2. *All-purpose center.* The Miami-Dade (Florida) Public Library's Hispanic Branch sponsored lectures, language classes, art exhibits, film showings, and story hours for children. Their specialized reference collection was also used extensively as a source of information on Latin American affairs.
3. *Job information and adult learning.* The Centro Hispano de Information at the Brooklyn Public Library had an outreach project to bilingual communities with emphasis on job information and adult independent learners programs.
4. *Language exchange program.* In a Norwalk, Connecticut, project native Spanish speakers who were learning English, and those who wanted to learn Spanish, helped each other by talking for half an hour in Spanish and another half hour in English through topically programmed talk sessions.

Services to the Aging

Although a new Title IV, Older Readers Services, was added to LSCA in 1973, no specific appropriation was made. However, many projects supporting public library services to older readers are supported under Title I.

In FY 1979 there were 19 identifiable projects funded under Title I that were specifically designed for the aging using $460,000 in LSCA funds and totaling $775,000 when combined with state and local funds. Our projections, however, are that nearly $1.1 million in LSCA funds was used in all LSCA projects to reach an estimated 2.2 million persons over age 65.

Funds have been used to purchase talking books, large-print materials, magnifiers, and bookmobiles and to pay for services such as home delivery, film programs, special seminars, and outreach services to nursing homes, nutrition centers, and senior day care centers. Some examples follow:

1. *Staff assistance.* Laurens and Lexington (South Carolina) counties provided two librarians to work full time with the programming for the aging.
2. *Homebound services.* The Snyder (Pennsylvania) County library program called Volunteers Insuring Shut-Ins the Opportunity to Read (VISITOR) and the James Brown Library (Williamsport, Pennsylvania) program called Bringing Reading to Aging through Volunteer Organization (BRAVO) both relied on volunteers to provide homebound library services. In the BRAVO program, cooperation with other social service agencies working with the aging was also stressed.
3. *Cooperative programs.* The Brooklyn (New York) SAGE project, an already successful outreach program, found that it added 150–250 older readers when it "piggybacked" onto such programs as "Friendly Visitor" and "Meals on Wheels." Other efforts to serve the visually handicapped older readers were reported through cooperation with the Library of Congress network of 159 regional and subregional libraries for the blind and physically handicapped.
4. *Information programs.* The Gray and Growing programs by the Baltimore County Public Library deal with improving the perceived value of life through presentations on health, arts and crafts, and reminiscences of early days in the area. Seminars (such as one on crime prevention sponsored by the New York Public Library, the Senior Citizens Crime Prevention Program, the New York City Foundation for Senior Citizens, Inc., and the Department for Aging of the City of New York) have received good community support.

Major Urban Resource Libraries (MURL)

This program activity concluded its second year of operation in FY 1980 with a $2.5 million allotment. These funds were used to enhance the role of the large urban public library (serving 100,000 population or more) as a regional resource library in the respective states. The nine states without urban centers (Delaware, Maine, Montana, New Hampshire, North Dakota, South Dakota, Vermont, West Virginia, and Wyoming) spent their proportionate share of the $2.5 million for purposes consistent with general Title I activities.

Activities funded with the FY 1980 MURL allotments have included Ohio College Library Center (OCLC) costs, computer searches, courier services, the purchase of reference materials for regional and statewide interlibrary loan purposes, and basic collection development to shore up the statewide and regional responsibilities to share these resources.

TITLE II—PUBLIC LIBRARY CONSTRUCTION

LSCA Title II funds for public library construction were last appropriated in FY 1973 with these funds being obligated by FY 1975. During the five-year period from FY 1976 to FY 1980 in which funds have not been available, 45 construction projects have been administered under Title II authority, utilizing $8.5 million in transfer funds from other federal programs. (See Table 2.) Federal funds for the 45 projects represented 41 percent of the total cost of the projects. Of the 45 projects, 36 were funded

TABLE 2 LSCA TITLE II, CONSTRUCTION, FY 1965–1980

Fiscal Year	Number Library Projects Approved	Federal	Local and State[a]	Total
1965	363	$ 29,864	$ 62,851	$ 92,715
1966	364	29,778	62,483	92,261
1967	278	24,583	52,107	76,690
1968	284	27,429	66,137	93,566
1969	211	22,257	69,500	91,757
1970	65	5,095	16,989	22,084
1971	114	8,571	34,427	42,998
1972	131	9,533	30,646	40,179
1973	52	2,606	15,360	17,966
1974	99	10,787[b]	44,570	55,357
1975	65	4,048[c]	26,776	30,824
Total LSCA	2,026	174,551	481,846	656,397
Appalachia	0	14,300[d]	0	14,300
Subtotal	2,026	$188,851	$481,846	$670,697
1976[e]	11	1,606	938	2,544
1977[e]	5	851	3,432	4,283
1978[e]	13	2,094	1,021	3,115
1979[e]	9	2,281	2,516	4,797
1980[e]	7	1,626	4,307	5,933
Subtotal	45	$ 8,458	$ 12,214	$ 20,672
Total	2,071	$197,309	$494,060	$691,369

[a] Budgeted amounts as reported by states.
[b] 1973 appropriation released in FY 1974.
[c] Carryover funds from FY 1973 appropriation not obligated in FY 1974.
[d] Funds from the Appalachian Regional Development Act that were allocated to LSCA-administered projects are listed separately from LSCA funds. Since projects also included LSCA funds, the number of projects and local/state matching funds for these projects are included above.
[e] Although LSCA federal funds were not available for projects after FY 1975, all projects for FY 1976–1980 were administered under the LSCA administrative authority, but funded from other federal programs. Of the 45 projects approved since FY 1976, 36 received funds from the Appalachian Regional Development Act program in the amount of $6.8 million.

from the Appalachian Regional Development Act program in the amount of $6.8 million.

In FY 1980 eight projects were funded under the Title II authority, receiving $1,626,143 in federal funds. (See Table 3.) All of these funds were from the Appalachian Regional Development Act program except for $31,706 from the U.S. Department of Energy.

An emerging development in library construction in recent years has been the introduction of passive solar energy systems. One of the projects funded in FY 1980 was the Mount Airy (North Carolina) Public Library, which was designed to utilize the latest knowledge of solar techniques. Substantial savings in energy consumption are projected for the building.

Other federal funding programs that provide for public library construction include General Revenue Sharing (Title I of the State and Local Fiscal Assistance Act of 1972) and the Community Development Block Grants (Title I of the Housing and Com-

TABLE 3 PUBLIC LIBRARY CONSTRUCTION PROJECTS ADMINISTERED UNDER THE LIBRARY SERVICES AND CONSTRUCTION ACT, TITLE II, WITH APPALACHIAN REGIONAL DEVELOPMENT ACT FUNDS, FY 1980

	Funding by Source		
Name and Location	Federal ARDA	Local/State	Total
Royston Public Library Royston, Georgia	$ 80,000	$ 250,000	$ 330,000
Dalton Regional Library Dalton, Georgia	450,000	1,537,500	1,987,500
Heard County Public Library Franklin, Georgia	65,000	225,334	290,334
Mars Hill Library Mars Hill, North Carolina	77,687	77,688	155,375
Mount Airy Public Library Mount Airy, North Carolina	331,706[a]	918,294	1,250,000
McDowell County Public Library Welch, West Virginia	250,000	797,000	1,047,000
Martinsburg-Berkeley County Library Martinsburg, West Virginia	346,750	431, 250	778,000
Taylor County Public Library[b] Grafton, West Virginia	25,000	69,429	94,429
Total	$1,626,143	$4,306,495	$5,932,638

[a]Includes $31,706 from the Department of Energy.
[b]The Taylor County Public Library project was originally approved in FY 1979 and funded as follows: Federal ARDA—$250,425, Local/State—$245,825, for a total of $496,250. The amounts represent funding increases to the FY 1979 project.

munity Development Act of 1974). Data on funding levels for libraries for these two programs are not available.

Federal loan assistance for public library construction is available for communities under 10,000 population from the Community Facilities Loans program administered by the Department of Agriculture. This program has provided for 34 low-interest loans to libraries in the amount of $4.9 million from 1974 to 1980. The program has been amended to include eligibility for communities of up to 20,000 population.

Additional historical information about LSCA Title II is detailed in a recent publication, "Public Library Construction, 1965–1978." National data, along with state breakouts, are examined in the areas of construction costs, population served, number and type of project, floor area, seating capacity, and book-volume capacity. Copies are available on request from the U.S. Department of Education, Office of Libraries and Learning Technologies, Washington, DC 20202.

TITLE III—INTERLIBRARY COOPERATION

The Interlibrary Cooperation Program was enacted in 1966 to improve the effectiveness of the entire country's system of libraries through cooperative library activities among public libraries, college and university libraries, school libraries, and special libraries. Projects approved by the state library agencies are funded when the resources of two or more different types of libraries are joined in providing improved library services to the clients served by each.

In FY 1980 approximately 175 projects were funded at the $5 million level un-

TABLE 4 LSCA TITLE III EXPENDITURE PATTERNS,
FY 1980
(Based on the latest annual reports of
56 states and territories)

Category	No. of States
Interlibrary loan and reference networks	38
Multi-state organizations	29
Union lists/catalogs	25
Continuing education	23
Use of computers	15
Preparation of special subject lists or directories	9
Planning for interlibrary cooperation	9
In-state regional multitype cooperative systems	8
Processing centers	5
Automated circulation systems	6
Delivery systems	3

der the 11 categories identified in Table 4. Although no state or local matching funds are required, 14 states expended nearly $7 million to carry out their LSCA project activities. Some key state efforts supported by FY 1979 funds are noted below:

1. *Minnesota.* The Minnesota State Library continued to provide some support for MINITEX. It also used Title III funds along with state monies to establish seven multicounty, multitype library systems covering the entire state. Participants in each system developed plans to provide for sharing resources among all participating libraries and developed a delivery system, a bibliographic data base, a communications system, and a long-range plan for the statewide effort.
2. *Louisiana.* The Louisiana State Library continued to support a statewide data base for Library of Congress card numbers and a teletype communication network. A statewide library system had been formed initially under Title III and is now gradually being taken over by state and local funds. Each year an attempt is made to establish a new system and in FY 1979 the Heartland Library and Information Service Network received a major grant to begin system services.
3. *Wyoming.* The Wyoming State Library installed a statewide automated circulation system. It is also tied to the OCLC interlibrary loan subsystem, improving access immeasurably to materials within and outside the state.
4. *Tennessee.* Over the past six years, the Tennessee State Library provided two-year grants to Vanderbilt University, Memphis Public Library, and the University of Tennessee to place their library holdings into the SOLINET data base.

A 1978 evaluation study of LSCA III by Applied Management Sciences noted that the program is a major driving force behind the development of multitype library cooperatives and networking in the country today. Use of LSCA III, along with LSCA I, has resulted in greater centralization of planning and administration of library services at the state and regional levels. Title III is also credited as a major influence on state legislatures in modifying or passing legislation favoring cooperation and networking.

The study also found that over 62 percent of the states were able to install or upgrade telecommunications linkages among public, academic, and special libraries be-

TABLE 5 LSCA TITLE III, INTERLIBRARY COOPERATION, STATE ALLOTMENTS AND MATCHING REQUIREMENTS, FY 1981

States and Outlying Areas	Federal Allotment	States and Outlying Areas	Federal Allotment
Alabama	$205,908	New Hampshire	$ 78,673
Alaska	58,291	New Jersey	365,586
Arizona	145,606	New Mexico	94,071
Arkansas	136,439	New York	829,755
California	1,033,046	North Carolina	287,928
Colorado	160,426	North Dakota	69,061
Connecticut	178,672	Ohio	517,609
Delaware	65,990	Oklahoma	166,523
District of Columbia	69,862	Oregon	149,122
Florida	425,443	Pennsylvania	563,492
Georgia	265,854	Rhode Island	81,477
Hawaii	80,142	South Carolina	169,149
Idaho	79,252	South Dakota	70,707
Illinois	540,128	Tennessee	232,833
Indiana	279,739	Texas	620,634
Iowa	169,327	Utah	98,611
Kansas	144,449	Vermont	61,673
Kentucky	195,316	Virginia	270,393
Louisiana	217,034	Washington	208,801
Maine	88,598	West Virginia	122,821
Maryland	224,600	Wisconsin	248,409
Massachusetts	296,828	Wyoming	58,914
Michigan	448,585	American Samoa	11,340
Minnesota	219,081	Guam	14,268
Mississippi	147,208	Northern Marianas	10,699
Missouri	255,707	Puerto Rico	182,633
Montana	74,713	Trust Territory	14,886
Nebraska	109,826	Virgin Islands	14,223
Nevada	69,639		
	Total	$12,000,000*	

*Tabulation of $12,000,000 with a federal "minimum" allotment of $40,000 to the 50 states, the District of Columbia, and Puerto Rico; $10,000 to the other outlying areas. The balance is listed on the basis of total resident population July 1, 1978, for the 50 states and the District of Columbia; 1976 data for Puerto Rico and the other outlying areas.

cause of Title III. More than 75 percent of the states also actively participated in intrastate and multistate library networks.

Although program shortcomings were cited in the report, the states were unanimous in their feeling that increased funding levels should be sought. In the states, it was noted, library cooperation and networking have become accepted modes of improving library services and achieving increased efficiency and economies. [Table 5 shows the state allotments under LSCA Title III for FY 1981.]

ELEMENTARY AND SECONDARY EDUCATION ACT, TITLE IV, PART B—INSTRUCTIONAL MATERIALS AND SCHOOL LIBRARY RESOURCES

Beatrice Simmons

*Education Program Specialist, School Media Resources Branch,
Division of Library Programs,
Office of Libraries and Learning Technologies, ED*

The Elementary and Secondary Education Act (ESEA), Title IV, Part B, as amended, Instructional Materials and School Library Resources, provides funds to the states, seven extrastate jurisdictions, and the Bureau of Indian Affairs, Department of Interior, for the acquisition of school library resources, textbooks, and other printed and published materials; and for the acquisition of instructional materials and equipment to be used in providing education in academic subjects. These benefits are for the use of children in public and private nonprofit elementary and secondary schools. Funds are also provided to state education agencies for program administration.

Amounts allotted to states and other jurisdictions for fiscal years 1978, 1979, and 1980 were $154,497,324, $167,500,000, and $180,000,000, respectively. Table 1 shows the allotments for 1981. Funds are allotted to the states, Puerto Rico, and the District of Columbia on the basis of the number of children aged five to seventeen, as compared with the total number of children in all states and jurisdictions. One percent of the amount available under Title IV-B is reserved for American Samoa, Guam, the Virgin Islands, the Trust Territory of the Pacific Islands, and the Northern Mariana Islands, and for schools conducted by the Department of the Interior for Indian children.

Title IV, Part B, is administered cooperatively in the Department of Education with Part C of Title IV. Staff in the programs review the state plans and their annual amendments, prepare regulations and administrative memoranda, conduct conferences, review state and local Title IV programs, and provide technical assistance. The review and monitoring of state and local programs for Part B is on a triennial cycle.

Part B funds are distributed among local educational agencies (LEAs) according to the enrollments in public and private schools within the school districts of those agencies, except that higher per-pupil amounts are provided to LEAs whose tax effort for children is substantially greater than the state average tax effort for education, but whose per-pupil expenditures (excluding ESEA Title I funds) are no greater than the state average per-pupil expenditure, and to LEAs with the largest number or percentage of children whose education imposes a higher than average cost per child. Examples of children whose education imposes a higher than average cost per child are children from low-income families, children who are handicapped, and children living in sparsely populated areas. Table 2 shows the number of states and the various types of high-cost children identified in fiscal years 1978, 1979, and 1980.

Staff of participating LEAs in consultation with appropriate private school officials choose the program purposes for which they wish to use their allocation. Table 3 shows the purposes for which funds were expended in FY 1978 and 1979.

Educational trends, population infusion, and electronic devices are affecting choices in instructional materials, instructional equipment, and the nature of the program of service. There is widespread use of microcomputers to teach mathematics,

TABLE 1 ALLOTMENTS UNDER ESEA TITLE IV-B, AS AMENDED (PL 95-561) FOR PROGRAM YEAR 1981

State or Area	Amount	State or Area	Amount
Alabama	$ 2,955,906	New Jersey	$ 5,537,996
Alaska	366,892	New Mexico	1,031,452
Arizona	1,855,229	New York	13,142,357
Arkansas	1,657,938	North Carolina	4,285,025
California	16,188,256	North Dakota	512,265
Colorado	2,042,136	Ohio	8,345,068
Connecticut	2,325,958	Oklahoma	2,076,749
Delaware	449,962	Oregon	1,775,620
District of Columbia	467,268	Pennsylvania	8,587,356
Florida	5,818,357	Puerto Rico	3,004,363
Georgia	4,084,272	Rhode Island	695,711
Hawaii	695,711	South Carolina	2,360,571
Idaho	702,633	South Dakota	536,493
Illinois	8,663,503	Tennessee	3,291,647
Indiana	4,264,257	Texas	10,300,673
Iowa	2,229,044	Utah	1,121,444
Kansas	1,692,550	Vermont	387,660
Kentucky	2,710,157	Virginia	3,914,671
Louisiana	3,364,333	Washington	2,834,762
Maine	858,389	West Virginia	1,391,422
Maryland	3,225,883	Wisconsin	3,675,845
Massachusetts	4,291,947	Wyoming	325,357
Michigan	7,431,299	American Samoa	120,725
Minnesota	3,163,580	Guam	360,005
Mississippi	2,066,365	Northern Marianas	53,461
Missouri	3,596,236	Trust Territory	363,650
Montana	616,102	Virgin Islands	336,140
Nebraska	1,190,669	Bureau of Indian Affairs	
Nevada	519,187	(Department of the Interior)	459,088
New Hampshire	678,405		
Total			$171,000,000*

*Distribution of $171,000,000 with 1 percent ($1,693,069) of the amount reserved for the Insular Areas and the Bureau of Indian Affairs, and the balance distributed on the basis of the 5–17 population for the 50 states, District of Columbia, and Puerto Rico, with distribution made on the total public and nonpublic elementary and secondary school enrollment, fall 1978 for the areas.

science, and economics. The increased use of software is affecting microcomputer utilization in other areas of the curriculum as well. A more realistic use of television equipment is emerging as students become participants rather than observers. Many students plan, write, and produce a variety of programs. Visible spin-offs are improved language and oral communications and "turned on" students. Computer literacy for the gifted and talented enables students to learn new ways to apply existing talent through computer interaction. It also allows students and teaching staff to develop skills in computer literacy by providing strong instructional support in math, science, social studies, and English. The influx of immigrants over the past two years has caused LEAs to examine their learning materials to determine what is needed to teach children from such diverse backgrounds in a productive learning situation.

There is greater involvement of professional staff, including librarians, media specialists, and teachers, in planning for the use of ESEA Title IV-B funds. More emphasis is being placed on needs assessment, the specificity of instructional objectives,

TABLE 2 ESEA TITLE IV—B: HIGH-COST CHILDREN FACTORS SELECTED BY STATES, FY 1978, 1979, 1980

	Number of States		
	1978	1979	1980
Aid for dependent children	2	2	1
Basic skills (reading, mathematics)	4-R 3-M	3	8
Bilingual	26	25	16
Critical subjects (other than reading and mathematics)	1	2	0
Free lunch	2	1	2
Gifted and talented	16	12	12
Guidance (includes potential dropouts)	3	3	3
Handicapped, exceptional children, special education	20	19	17
Hawaiian English program	1	—	0
Institutionalized children (includes foster homes, facilities for the neglected and delinquent, schools for deaf and blind, and mentally handicapped)	10	10	9
Low achievers	1	5	*
Low income	35	34	36†
Migrant	3	2	0
Minorities	1	2	2
Primary mental health project	1	—	—
Small schools	9	16	14
Sparsity (isolation, rural, transportation)	29	28	28
Special needs	1	2	4
Vocational education	1	1	0

*Included in Basic skills.
†Includes three states in which children classified as ESEA I are eligible, but not participating in that program.

and activities to implement objectives with follow-up evaluation strategies. Funds are being targeted toward definite identified needs, resulting in long-range planning and impact on the educational process.

In progress, in the Office of Libraries and Learning Technologies, is the "Beltway Videodisc Project." This is a cooperative demonstration shared among three federal programs: Educational Technology Development Branch, School Media Resources Branch (Part B), and the Basic Skills Program. The project takes advantage of the revolution in information and communication technologies by supplying three schools

TABLE 3 ESEA TITLE IV-B FUNDS, BY PROGRAM PURPOSE, FY 1978 AND 1979

Purpose	1978	Percent	1979	Percent
Administration	$ 4,860,876	3.7	$ 6,735,329	4.5
School library resources/other instructional materials	65,965,586	50.2	79,213,448	53.0
Textbooks	3,344,559	2.5	4,341,736	2.7
Instructional equipment	41,233,644	31.3	45,586,626	30.1
Minor remodeling	1,085,799	0.8	447,673	0.3
Testing	2,524,768	2.0	3,969,442	2.6
Counseling and guidance	12,578,592	9.5	10,290,927	6.8
Total	$131,593,824	100	$150,585,181	100

in each of the local entities: Maryland, Virginia, and the District of Columbia, with the newest developments in videodiscs, telecommunications, and microcomputers.

The first phase of the project is an awareness phase during which students will increase their basic skills, teachers will be trained in the use of technology in the teaching of basic skills, and administrators will become informed of the cost benefits of this application of technology to basic skills education and will provide guidance for widespread adoption of successful technology.

Some of the questions addressed by the second phase of the Beltway Project are (1) what can technology teach best in the area of basic skills? (2) how can technology be used in the diagnostic and prescriptive development of educational strategies for teaching all children? (3) what are the staffing and staff development requirements for the effective uses of technology in schools? (4) what are the management requirements for the uses of high technology in basic skills education? The answers to such questions will determine the cost-effectiveness of such systems, monetarily and instructionally.

The third phase will be devoted to dissemination and training efforts designed to allow the cooperating schools to move out to other schools within their regions and states to train other staff in the techniques required to implement these learning experiences. The Educational Technology Development Branch will support these outreach activities.

Certain publications that may be of interest to teachers and librarians are the *Aids to Media Selection for Students and Teachers*, currently under revision; the revised *Questions and Answers about Title IV, Part B of the Elementary and Secondary Education Act*; and the federal regulations interpreting the amended ESEA Title IV. Requests for these publications should be directed to Office of Libraries and Learning Technologies, U.S. Department of Education, 400 Maryland Avenue S.W., Washington, DC 20202.

HIGHER EDUCATION ACT, TITLE II-A, COLLEGE LIBRARY RESOURCES

Beth A. Phillips
Education Program Specialist

Frank A. Stevens
*Chief, Library Education and Postsecondary Resources Branch,
Division of Library Programs,
Office of Libraries and Learning Technologies, ED*

The College Library Resources Program under Title II-A of the Higher Education Act of 1965, as amended, supports the improvement of library resources in institutions of higher education and certain other eligible library agencies. Since the inception of the program in 1966, approximately 2,600 institutions of higher education have particpated annually, and 39,091 awards totaling $190.6 million for basic, supplemental, and special purpose grants have been made. (The appropriation level for Title II-A since 1973 has permitted the funding of only basic grant awards.)

In FY 1981, Congress reauthorized the Title II-A program until FY 1985 by enacting the Education Amendments of 1980. The new legislation establishes a Resource Development Grant, rescinds the supplemental grant, and moves the special purpose grant to Title II, Part B. The Resource Development Grant is designed to assist in the acquisition of library materials such as books, periodicals, documents, magnetic tapes, phonograph records, audiovisual materials, and other related library materials, including initial binding. The legislation also expands the purpose of the Title II-A grant. In addition to using grant funds for acquisition activities, institutions may also use them to pursue eligible networking activities for the purpose of resource sharing. Other changes introduced by the amendments include the revision of the maintenance-of-effort requirements so that (1) the only variable involved is the library materials expenditures, and (2) expenditures may be calculated through actual expenditures on library materials *or* the average annual expenditure per full-time equivalent student. Finally, the waiver of the maintenance-of-effort requirement is limited to "very unusual" circumstances.

Eligible applicants include public and private nonprofit institutions of higher education, combinations of these institutions, branches of institutions of higher edu-

TABLE 1 HIGHER EDUCATION ACT, TITLE II-A, COLLEGE LIBRARY RESOURCES, FY 1980

State or Area	No. of Grants	1980 Obligations	State or Area	No. of Grants	1980 Obligations
Alabama	59	$112,100	Nevada	8	$ 15,200
Alaska	11	20,900	New Hampshire	24	44,300
Arizona	26	49,000	New Jersey	46	87,400
Arkansas	25	47,500	New Mexico	20	38,000
California	192	363,700	New York	196	371,150
Colorado	25	51,300	North Carolina	96	182,400
Connecticut	39	74,100	North Dakota	16	30,400
Delaware	10	19,000	Ohio	105	199,500
District of Columbia	14	26,600	Oklahoma	38	72,200
Florida	79	150,100	Oregon	35	66,500
Georgia	72	136,800	Pennsylvania	147	279,300
Hawaii	12	22,800	Rhode Island	14	26,600
Idaho	9	17,100	South Carolina	51	96,900
Illinois	111	210,900	South Dakota	20	37,700
Indiana	49	92,270	Tennessee	48	91,200
Iowa	56	106,400	Texas	114	216,600
Kansas	44	83,600	Utah	9	17,100
Kentucky	35	66,500	Vermont	20	36,700
Louisiana	24	45,600	Virginia	74	140,600
Maine	26	49,400	Washington	42	79,800
Maryland	45	87,400	West Virginia	24	45,100
Massachusetts	98	185,550	Wisconsin	76	144,400
Michigan	80	152,000	Wyoming	8	15,200
Minnesota	51	96,000	Guam	1	1,900
Mississippi	42	79,800	Puerto Rico	31	58,500
Missouri	53	100,700	Trust Territories	2	3,800
Montana	17	32,000	Virgin Islands	2	3,800
Nebraska	24	45,600			
			Total	2,595	$4,926,270

TABLE 2 HIGHER EDUCATION ACT, TITLE II-A,
COLLEGE LIBRARY RESOURCES, FY 1966–1980

FY	Appropriation	Basic	Supplemental	Special Purpose	Obligations
1966	$10,000,000	1,830	—	—	$ 8,400,000
1967	25,000,000	1,983	1,266	132	24,500,000
1968	25,000,000	2,111	1,524	60	24,900,000
1969	25,000,000	2,224	1,747	77	24,900,000
1970	12,500,000	2,201	1,783	—	9,816,000
1971	9,900,000	548	531	115	9,900,000
1972	11,000,000	504	494	21	10,993,000
1973	12,500,000	2,061	—	65	12,500,000
1974	9,975,000	2,377	—	—	9,960,000
1975	9,975,000	2,569	—	—	9,957,416
1976	9,975,000	2,560	—	—	9,958,754
1977	9,975,000	2,600	—	—	9,946,484
1978	9,975,000	2,568	—	—	9,963,611
1979	9,975,000	2,520	—	—	9,903,201
1980	4,988,000	2,595	—	—	4,926,970

cation, and nonprofit library institutions whose primary function is to provide library and information services to students, faculty, and researchers of higher education on a formal cooperative basis.

Funding for FY 1980 provided a grant of $1,900 for each eligible institution. Grantees were located in every state, the District of Columbia, Puerto Rico, the Virgin Islands, and the Trust Territories. A total of 2,595 grant awards was made to institutions of higher education including 34 nonprofit library institutions and 20 combinations of institutions of higher education.

Congress also reauthorized the Title II-C, Strengthening Research Library Resources Programs. This program is designed to aid the major research libraries in the collection and dissemination of research materials. The legislation specifically prohibits a library from receiving funding from both Title II-A and II-C in the same fiscal year.

In FY 1980, $4.9 million was awarded to 2,595 institutions. Notification of the grant awards was made on March 31, 1980. (See Table 1 for the number of awards and total funding by state. Table 2 traces the funding history of Title II-A by fiscal year from 1966 to date.)

HIGHER EDUCATION ACT, TITLE II-B, LIBRARY EDUCATION

Frank A. Stevens

*Chief, Library Education and Postsecondary Resources Branch,
Division of Library Programs,
Office of Libraries and Learning Technologies, ED*

Janice Owens

*Program Assistant, Library Education and
Postsecondary Resources Branch*

Title II-B (Library Training) of the Higher Education Act of 1965, as amended (20 U.S.C. 1021, 1032), authorizes a program of federal financial assistance to institutions of higher education and other library organizations and agencies to assist in training persons in librarianship and to establish, develop, and expand programs of library and information science, including new techniques of information transfer and communication technology. Grants are made for fellowships and traineeships at the associate, bachelor, master, post master, and doctoral levels for training in librarianship. Grants may also be used to assist in covering the costs of institutes or courses of training or study to upgrade the competencies of persons serving in all types of libraries, information centers, or instructional materials centers offering library and information services, and those serving as educators.

In FY 1974, the Title II-B Training Program Regulations were revised primarily for the purpose of establishing explicitly the evaluation criteria and the corresponding point-scoring system governing the selection and rejection of proposals. The regulations were published in final form in the *Federal Register* on May 17, 1974 (45 CFR 132). On April 3, 1980, proposed revisions in program selection criteria were published in the *Federal Register* to reflect the requirements of the Education Division General Administrative Requirements (EDGAR), which mandated the inclusion of certain standard criteria in all discretionary programs. On October 3, 1980, Title II-B was reauthorized by the Education Amendments of 1980 (P.L. 96-374), with no major changes other than to introduce a new program goal—"new techniques of information transfer and communication technology." Program regulations are a part of the application package that is provided on request to all interested parties at the time of the annual program announcement.

FELLOWSHIP PROGRAM

The entire FY 1980 appropriation of $667,000 was awarded for fellowships. Thirty-two library and information science education programs received 101 (17 doctoral, 5 post-master, 72 master, and 7 associate) fellowship awards. The order of priorities for fellowship training levels in FY 80 was as follows: master, associate, post-master, doctoral, and bachelor. Stipend levels varied depending on level of study, length of program, and degree of related prior experience, within a range of $1,750 to $4,700 per fellow plus dependency allowance as permitted. Additionally, grantee institutions receive an institutional allowance of up to $3,000 per fellow.

The selection of persons as fellowship recipients is, and has been throughout the history of the program, the responsibility of the grantee institution. However, such

TABLE 1 LIBRARY EDUCATION FELLOWSHIP/TRAINEESHIP PROGRAM, FY 1966–1980

Academic Year	Institutions	Doctoral	Post-master	Master	Bachelor	Assoc.	Total	FY
1966/67	24	52	25	62	—	—	139	1966
1967/68	38	116	58	327	—	—	501	1967
1968/69	51	168	47	494	—	—	709	1968
1969/70	56	193	30	379	—	—	602	1969
1970/71	48	171	15	200	+ 20[a]	—	406	1970
1971/72	20	116	6	—	+ 20[a]	—	142	1971
1972/73	15	39	3	+ 20[a]	—	—	62	1972
1973/74	34	21	4	145 + 14[a]	—	20	204	1973
1974/75	50	21	3	168 + 3[a]	—	5	200	1974
1975/76	22	27	6	94	—	—	127	1975
1976/77	12	5	3	43	—	—	51	1976
1977/78	37	18	3	134	—	5	160	1977
1978/79	33	25	9	139	10	5	188	1978
1979/80	36	19	4	134	2	3	162	1979
1980/81	32	17	5	72	—	7	101	1980
Total		1008	221	2,391 + 37[a]	12 + 40[a]	45	3,754	

[a]Indicates traineeships.

selection and program operation must be consistent with the grant application on which award of funds was based.

Key factors given substantial consideration in the review process were the extent to which the fellowship program award would increase opportunities for minority groups and/or economically disadvantaged persons to enter the library profession and the extent to which the fellowship program award could prepare librarians to work more responsively with the disadvantaged and develop viable alternatives to traditional library service patterns. Table 1 represents a review of the fellowship program since it began in 1966.

Fellowship grants were awarded in FY 1980 to the institutions shown in Table 2. A more detailed analysis of these awards is contained in a booklet available on request from the Library Education and Postsecondary Resources Branch, Division of Library Programs, Office of Libraries and Learning Technologies, 400 Maryland Ave. S.W., Washington, DC 20202.

INSTITUTE PROGRAM

The institute program provides long- and short-term training and retraining opportunities for librarians, media specialists, information scientists, and persons desiring to enter these professions. Many institutes have given experienced practitioners the opportunity to update and advance their skills in a given subject. Institute programs have been supported since FY 1968 under the Higher Education Act of 1965 and since FY 1973 under further amendments included in the Education Amendments of 1972. However, due to the limited appropriation in FY 1980, no institute applications were requested.

In FY 1971, the program was redirected to allow it to focus on certain critical and priority areas. The priorities through FY 1979 were:

1. To attract minority and/or economically deprived persons in librarianship as professionals and paraprofessionals.

TABLE 1 SUBJECT CATEGORIES OF FUNDING ACTIONS, HEAD, TITLE II-B, LIBRARY RESEARCH AND DEMONSTRATION PROGRAM, FY 1967–1980

Subject Category	FY/67–FY/69	FY/70	FY/71	FY/72	FY/73	FY/74	FY/75	FY/76	FY/77	FY/78	FY/79	FY/80	Total
Education and training	20	3	0	2	3	5	5	6	4	0	1	0	49
Functional development reader services, processing (including acquisitions, cataloging, classification, etc.)	27	8	0	0	4	5	7	4	3	4	3	1	66
Institutional cooperation to serve special target groups	4	5	5	15	10	8	2	4	2	6	4	1	66
Planning and development	22	4	10	12	6	2	4	3	4	4	3	1	75
Technology: ADP, microfilm, hardware, etc.	25	10	3	2	1	0	1	2	5	3	1	1	54
Total	98	30	18	31	24	20	19	19	18	17	12	4	310

Funding Actions during Each Fiscal Year

TABLE 2 TOTAL OBLIGATIONS AND NUMBER OF PROJECTS FUNDED, HEA, TITLE II-B, LIBRARY RESEARCH AND DEMONSTRATION, FY 1967–1980

FY	Obligation	No. of Projects
1967	$ 3,381,052	38
1968	2,020,942	21
1969	2,986,264	39
1970	2,160,622	30
1971	2,170,274	18
1972	2,748,953	31
1973	1,784,741	24
1974	1,418,433	20
1975	999,338	19
1976	999,918	19
1977	995,193	18
1978	998,904	17
1979	980,563	12
1980	319,877	4
Total	$23,965,074	310

deafness at Gallaudet College was awarded in 1979. The center opened in 1980 and serves the public, the hearing impaired, and professionals seeking information on deafness.

A project to conduct a state-of-the-art survey on public library services to the blind and physically handicapped was funded in 1978 and completed in 1980. The study found that while public library service to hearing-impaired persons appears to be in great need of improvement, public library resources, services, and facilities for visually and mobility impaired persons also need upgrading.

In October 1980, OLLT, in cooperation with the Fund for Improvement of Postsecondary Education, sponsored a project that will develop new methods of teaching on-line searching of computerized data bases.

A project to produce a guide for disseminating information on current automation alternatives for libraries was funded in 1978 and completed in 1980. The guide provides suggestions reflecting librarians' experience for determining requirements, estimating costs, writing specifications, negotiating contracts, and installing automated systems. Automated systems and services for acquisitions, cataloging, circulation, reference, and serials are described.

A project to conduct a "Networks for Networkers" conference for experts, operators, and evaluators to examine the state of the art of networking was funded in 1978 and held in 1979. Conference results were published in 1980 in *Networks for Networkers*, which covers the network revolution, national policy and network development, network technology and standards, network governance and funding, and network users and services.

The first phase of a study of the information needs and patterns of 2400 representative New England households was funded in 1979 and completed in 1980. Respondents listed libraries ninth in the order of 13 information sources consulted. First and second in ranking were the respondent's own experience and something learned from a friend or neighbor. In December 1980 a contract was awarded to conduct phase

TABLE 3 LIBRARY RESEARCH AND DEMONSTRATION PROGRAM, HEA, TITLE II-B, GRANTEES AND CONTRACTORS

Grantee or Contractor	FY/67-FY/69	FY/70	FY/71	FY/72	FY/73	FY/74	FY/75	FY/76	FY/77	FY/78	FY/79	FY/80	Total
Universities and colleges	57	11	7	13	13	9	8	11	11	11	10	1	162
Nonprofit organizations	25	8	3	6	1	7	6	4	3	3	1	3	70
Profit organizations	9	5	0	2	0	0	0	1	0	0	1	0	18
Public libraries	1	0	1	2	3	3	1	0	0	1	0	0	12
Government agencies	2	2	3	3	0	0	0	0	0	0	0	0	10
Local school districts	3	2	2	2	4	1	0	0	0	0	0	0	14
State and municipal governments	1	2	2	3	3	0	4	3	4	2	0	0	24
Total	98	30	18	31	24	20	19	19	18	17	12	4	310

TABLE 4 FUNDED PROJECTS, FY 1980, HEA TITLE II-B,
LIBRARY RESEARCH AND DEMONSTRATION

Institution and Principal Investigator	Project Title	Funds Awarded
Bibliographic Center for Research, Denver, Colo. Joan Segal	New Methods of Teaching Online Searching of Computerized Databases	$ 57,125
Contract Research Corporation Caren von Hipple	Libraries in Literacy	49,151
King Research Nancy DeWath	1981–1982 Library Human Resources: Study of Supply and Demand	176,151
North Texas State University James A. Kitchens	Evaluation and Assessment of the Olney Community Library	36,619

II of the project. Phase II will result in an evaluation methodology to determine the optimum design and performance of library information networks that provide citizens' consumer information. This will be the first comprehensive study to link citizens' (consumer) information needs with networks.

ADDITIONAL INFORMATION

The Directory of Library Research and Demonstration Projects, 1966–1975 and *Abstracts* for FY 76, FY 77, FY 78, and FY 79 are available upon request from the Department of Education, Office of Libraries and Learning Technologies, Library Research and Demonstration Branch, 400 Maryland Ave. S.W., ROB #3, Rm. 3319A, Washington, DC 20202, or by calling 202-245-2993.

All project reports are generally made available to the Education Resources Information Center (ERIC). As the material becomes available, it is announced in ERIC's monthly *Resources in Education* (Superintendent of Documents, U.S. Government Printing Office, Washington, DC 20402). The announcement includes an abstract, price of the report in hard copy or microfiche, and order instructions.

HOW TO APPLY

Requests for proposals (RFPs), how to obtain them, and projects for which bids are sought are announced in *Commerce Business Daily*, the daily journal in which U.S. government contracts are advertised. The RFP outlines the background, purpose, and scope of the project, delineates tasks, explains how to apply, and defines the selection criteria by which proposals will be judged.

HIGHER EDUCATION ACT, TITLE II-C
STRENGTHENING RESEARCH LIBRARY RESOURCES

Frank A. Stevens
Chief, Library Education and Postsecondary Resources Branch,
Division of Library Programs,
Office of Libraries and Learning Technologies, ED

Title II-C of the Higher Education Act (HEA) of 1965, as amended, Strengthening Research Library Resources Program, authorizes federal financial assistance to major research libraries for the purpose of promoting research and education of higher quality by providing financial aid to help maintain and strengthen their collections, and to make these collections available to researchers and scholars beyond their primary users and to other libraries whose users have need for research materials.

The Title II-C program was enacted through the Education Amendments of 1976 on October 12, 1976, in recognition of the fact that the major research libraries of the nation represent the bibliographic foundation of our research resources and that financial stringency and increased costs have severely reduced their capabilities for resource sharing.

Major research libraries are those whose collections make a significant contribution to higher education and research, are broadly based, are recognized as having national or international significance for scholarly research, are of a unique nature, not widely held, and are of such importance that substantial demands are made on the institution by researchers and scholars outside its primary clientele. They include institutions of higher education, public libraries, state libraries, and private nonprofit independent research libraries.

It is estimated that approximately 200 libraries fall within this definition, and the Title II-C program is authorized to make up to 150 grants annually to assist them. Specific criteria have been established by regulation, published in the *Federal Register* on December 28, 1977, measuring significance as a major research library and measuring appropriateness of projects. Additionally, criteria were also established in the regulations to ensure reasonable regional allocation of grant funds throughout the nation. These criteria were proposed for revision in the *Federal Register* for April 3, 1980, in order to meet the requirements of the new Education Division General Administrative Requirements (EDGAR), which mandated several standard selection criteria for all discretionary programs. These revised criteria do not significantly alter the selection criteria of the current regulations, but they do alter significantly the cri-

TABLE 1 PROGRAM FUNDING RECORD, HEA, TITLE II-C, STRENGTHENING RESEARCH LIBRARY RESOURCES, FY 1977–1980

Fiscal Year	Authorization	Appropriation	Expenditures
1977	$10,000,000	0	0
1978	15,000,000	$5,000,000	$4,999,996
1979	20,000,000	6,000,000	6,000,000
1980	20,000,000*	6,000,000	5,992,268

*Continuing resolution.

TABLE 2   ANALYSIS OF APPLICATIONS,
HEA, TITLE II-C, FY 1980

Category	Amounts ($)
Number of proposals received	71
Amount of funds requested	17,291,842
Number of proposals supported	22*
Applicants by type of library	
Institutions of higher education	58
Independent research libraries	2
Public libraries	4
State libraries	1
Museums	2
Other	4

*Four of these proposals were jointly sponsored, directly benefiting seven additional institutions.

terion point ratio between the institutional-significance criteria and the nature-of-the-project criteria. These revised criteria will be in effect for the FY 1981 grant cycle and were published in the *Federal Register* on December 24, 1980. A major, more thorough revision of the program regulations is planned for FY 1982.

The authorizing legislation prohibits any institution from receiving a grant under HEA, Title II-A, College Library Resources Program, and Title II-C during the same fiscal year.

Announcement of the closing date for receipt of applications is published annually in the Federal Register. Application packages are available on request to all interested parties at the time of program announcement.

TABLE 3   NUMBER OF APPLICATIONS AND AWARDS, BY REGION,
HEA, TITLE II-C, 1980

Region	No. of Applications	No. of Awards
I: New England (Connecticut, Maine, Massachusetts, New Hampshire, Rhode Island, Vermont)	5	3
II: New York, Puerto Rico, Virgin Islands	8	3
III: Middle Atlantic states (Delaware, District of Columbia, Maryland, New Jersey, Pennsylvania, West Virginia)	8	2
IV: Southeastern states (Alabama, Florida, Georgia, Kentucky, Mississippi, North Carolina, South Carolina, Tennessee, Virginia)	9	2
V: Great Lakes states (Indiana, Michigan, Ohio)	7	1
VI: Midwest (Illinois, Iowa, Minnesota, Missouri, Wisconsin)	11	4
VII: Southwestern states (Arizona, Arkansas, Louisiana, New Mexico, Oklahoma, Texas)	8	2
VIII: Mountain Plains states (Colorado, Kansas, Montana, Nebraska, Nevada, North Dakota, South Dakota, Utah, Wyoming)	5	2
IX: Pacific Northwest states (Alaska, Idaho, Oregon, Washington)	3	1
X: California, Hawaii, American Samoa, Guam	7	2

Funds provided may be used for the acquisition of books and other library materials; bindings, repairing, and preserving books and other library materials; cataloging, abstracting, and making available guides of library collections; distributing materials and bibliographic information to users beyond primary clientele; acquisition of equipment and supplies; communication expenses; and hiring necessary additional staff to carry out funded activities. Each institution is limited to one application, which may include more than one project. The length of a project cannot exceed three years.

Fiscal Year 1980 was the third year of program operations. Table 1 provides the program funding record. Seventy-one applications were received in FY 1980, requesting over $17 million. Table 2 provides an analysis of the FY 1980 applications by type of applicant. Table 3 indicates the Title II-C designated regional areas and the number of applications and awards for each region.

Six million dollars was available for award in FY 1980. In order to achieve maximum program impact, 22 grants were awarded—the highest being $995,781 and the

TABLE 4   ANALYSIS OF GRANT AWARDS BY MAJOR ACTIVITY, HEA, TITLE II-C, FY 1980

Institution	Collection Development	Preservation	Bibliographic Control and Access
American Museum of Natural History	$119,544	—	$118,275
University of Arizona	79,650	—	122,899
Brown University	55,307	—	217,164
University of California at Berkeley	—	—	995,781
University of Chicago (continuation)	18,611	$ 4,000	56,429
University of Chicago (new)	175,000	—	—
Colorado State University	—	—	236,356
Cornell University	54,484	—	185,929
Duke University	250,000	—	—
Harvard College	—	396,657	—
Henry E. Huntington Library and Art Gallery	—	251,551	—
University of Illinois at Urbana-Champaign	64,920	—	—
University of Kansas	—	—	136,967
University of Michigan	—	—	606,000
Missouri Botanical Garden	—	—	244,571
New York State Education Department	—	—	305,849
University of North Carolina at Chapel Hill	—	—	321,445
University of Pennsylvania	—	41,250	126,489
Princeton University	—	—	153,661
University of Texas at Austin	21,546	—	153,454
University of Washington	—	—	150,000
Yale University	—	95,461	195,474
Total	$839,062	$788,919	$4,326,743

Note: The nature of the Title II-C program is such that the grants do not conveniently break down into detailed categories of program activities. Further, some grants include more than one project. Therefore, this table analyzes each grant by the amount of funding for three general program activities: collection development, preservation, and bibliographic control and access.

lowest $64,920. Eighteen grants were awarded to institutions of higher education, three to independent research libraries, and one to a state library. Table 4 lists the institutions that received FY 1980 grant awards and the major program activities to be undertaken. A more complete project description is contained in the publication *FY/80 Abstracts: Strengthening Research Library Resources Program*, which is available on request from the Office of Libraries and Learning Technologies, Division of Library Programs, Library Education and Postsecondary Resources Branch, 400 Maryland Avenue S.W., Washington, DC 20202. Like the earlier slates of grants awarded in FY 1978 and 1979, this third slate indicates a wide range of activities and subject matter emphasizing collection development, preservation, and resource sharing.

NATIONAL ENDOWMENT FOR THE HUMANITIES SUPPORT FOR LIBRARIES, 1980

Washington, DC 20506
202-724-0386

The National Endowment for the Humanities (NEH) is an independent federal grant-making agency created by Congress in 1965 to support projects of research, education, and public activity in the humanities. According to the legislation that established the Endowment, the humanities include, but are not limited to, the following fields: history, philosophy, languages, literature, linguistics, archaeology, jurisprudence, history and criticism of the arts, ethics, comparative religion, and those aspects of the social sciences employing historical or philosophical approaches. This last category includes cultural athropology, sociology, political theory, international relations, and other subjects concerned with questions of value.

The Endowment's grant-making operations are conducted through five major divisions. The Division of Research Grants provides support for group projects of research in the humanities, for research resources, for the preparation of important research tools, and for the editing of significant humanistic texts. The Division of Fellowships, through several programs, provides stipends that enable individual scholars, teachers, and members of nonacademic professions to study areas of the humanities that may be directly and fruitfully related to the work they characteristically perform. The Division of Education Programs supports projects and programs through which institutions endeavor to renew and strengthen the impact of teaching in the humanities at all levels. The Division of Public Programs—through projects in the media, projects involving individual academic humanists, and projects of nonacademic public institutions such as libraries, museums, and historical organizations—seeks to encourage broad national dissemination and increased understanding of the humanities. The Division of Special Programs is designed to fund innovative projects that do not fall into specific categories established in the existing divisions. Finally, the Division of State Programs makes grants to citizens' committees in each state to provide support for local humanities projects.

Other projects are eligible for support through the Office of Planning and Policy Assessment and through a program of Challenge Grants.

CATEGORIES OF SUPPORT

The NEH seeks to cooperate with libraries in strengthening the general public's knowledge and use of the humanities through its various programs. These programs are:

Division of Public Programs

Libraries Humanities Projects awards grants for projects that draw upon those humanistic resources in libraries that are designed to serve the general adult public. The specific goals of the library program are to strengthen programs that stimulate and respond to public interest in the humanities; to enhance the ability of library staff to plan and implement these programs; and to increase the public's awareness and use of a library's existing humanities resources.

Librarians are encouraged to replicate, combine formats, or create entirely new approaches to humanities programming. The following lists a few project ideas that are eligible for support.

A library can sponsor programs on humanities themes that draw on the library's book, magazine, audiovisual, and staff resources. The theme may be related directly to the humanities disciplines or provide a humanistic perspective on a popular community topic or issue.

Libraries could work with community groups to plan and present programs for the public using and publicizing the library's humanities resources. Such projects could include humanities workshops for community and group leaders or the preparation of special print materials or displays on library holdings.

A library can attempt to increase the use of humanities resources by planning programs in conjunction with television programs or exhibitions developed by other community institutions.

A library may plan projects that strengthen professional staff expertise in the humanities as well as provide humanities programming for the public. These could include workshops on the humanities disciplines, reference training, or programming ideas in preparation for a public humanities program.

A state library, library association, or large library system could produce "packaged" programs that would include specially prepared humanities materials, scholars and experts in the humanities as speakers, and special activities designed for use in local public libraries.

A library can plan a formal or informal sequential educational program for the adult public on a humanities topic or issue of interest to the community.

A library may develop a new concept or theme for public programming: investigating the history of a community's peoples and institutions; exploring the relationship between a community's values and the technology of an advanced society; relating the humanities to library services and human needs; reaching audiences who do not normally use the library or the humanities; or combining humanities programming with new trends in library service.

Any nonprofit library may apply. Libraries may submit proposals individually or in cooperation with other community organizations. Academic and school libraries are also eligible if the proposed project is aimed at the adult public.

Education Division

Libraries may receive grants directly or be part of a larger university effort to develop new curricula or educational materials. Grants directly to libraries are usually in support of humanities institutes, in which scholars use the library's resources as part of a program of study with experts on the theme of the institute and simultaneous development of new curricula for the participant's home institution. The Folger Shakespeare Library and the Newberry Library are recent grantees.

Fellowships Division

Through its program of Fellowships Support to Centers for Advanced Study, this division provides funds to independent research libraries for stipends to resident scholars. In 1980, the Newberry Library, the Huntington Library, and the American Antiquarian Society were among the centers that housed NEH fellows.

Research Division

The Research Resources Program focuses on making raw research materials more accessible to scholars. It meets this goal through projects that address national problems in the archival and library field, through projects that serve as models in systems development and library automation, and through processing grants that are used to catalog, inventory, or otherwise gain bibliographic control of significant research collections.

The Research Resources Program also helps to develop collections by providing funds either to microfilm materials in foreign repositories so that they will be available in the United States or to collect data through oral history techniques. Responsibility for applications to prepare bibliographies, indexes, guides to various kinds of source materials, and similar finding aids has been transferred from the Research Tools to the Research Resources Program. The latter also has a small additional amount of funding available to support projects in the area of conservation and preservation that will benefit more than a single institution.

Division of Special Programs

The Endowment supports a selected number of projects in which humanities scholars work directly with public organizations and institutions in order to join humanistic knowledge with effective dissemination formats—especially to sectors of the society not usually involved in humanistic study. Libraries and library organizations either working alone or in conjunction with other institutions are among those who may receive support for such projects.

Challenge Grants

Libraries are also eligible for support under the Endowment's program of Challenge Grants, now in its fourth year of funding. Challenge Grants are designed to stimulate increased support for humanities institutions from private citizens, business and labor organizations, state and local governments, and civic and other groups by offering one federal dollar for every three raised in the private sector. Challenge Grants are intended to be a means by which institutions can better finance their humanities operations and more effectively serve their respective clientele; they should help secure long-term financial stability and economic independence. To those ends, funds may cover a variety of costs: to help in fund-raising plans and development efforts; for general expenses; to defray deficits; to cover increased costs and the renovation of facilities; for acquisition of equipment and materials; for maintenance, preservation, and conservation of collections; and for other management and administrative expenses.

TABLE 2 FELLOWSHIPS FOR TRAINING IN LIBRARY AND INFORMATION SCIENCE, ACADEMIC YEAR 1980–1981

Institution	Project Director	No.	Level*	Amount
Arkansas				
University of Arkansas, Fayetteville 72701	David V. Loertscher	2	M	$12,600
California				
University of California, Los Angeles, 405 Hilgard Ave., Los Angeles 90024	Cheryl Metoyer-Duran	1	M	6,300
University of Southern California, Los Angeles 90007	Edward J. Kazlauskas	4	M	25,200
Florida				
Florida State University, Tallahassee 32306	Harold Goldstein	4	M (2) D (2)	29,200
Georgia				
Atlanta University, 223 Chestnut St. S.W., Atlanta 30314	Lorene B. Brown	1	M	6,300
Illinois				
Northern Illinois University, DeKalb 60115	Henry C. Dequin	5	PM	40,150
University of Illinois, 410 David Kinley Hall, Urbana 61801	Charles H. Davis	6	M (3) D (3)	44,100
Indiana				
Ball State University, Muncie 47306	Marina E. Axeen	2	M	12,600
Indiana University, Bloomington 47402	Bernard M. Fry	4	M	25,200
Kentucky				
University of Kentucky, 461 Patterson Office Tower, Lexington 40506	Timothy Sineath	1	M	6,300
Maryland				
University of Maryland, College Park 20742	Kieth C. Wright	2	M	12,600
Massachusetts				
Simmons College, 300 The Fenway, Boston 02115	Ching-chih Chen	2	D	16,600
Michigan				
University of Michigan, 580 Union Dr., Ann Arbor 48109	Russell E. Bidlack	7	M (4) D (3)	48,900
Mississippi				
Coahoma Junior College, Rte. 1, Box 616, Clarksdale 38614	McKinley C. Martin	7	AA	34,150
University of Southern Mississippi, Southern Sta., Box 5146, Hattiesburg 39401	Onva K. Boshears, Jr.	2	M	12,600
New York				
CUNY, Queens College, 65-30 Kissena Blvd., Flushing 11367	Richard J. Hyman	4	M	25,200
Columbia University, Box 20, Low Memorial Library, New York 10027	Richard L. Darling	3	M	19,200

TABLE 2 FELLOWSHIPS FOR TRAINING IN LIBRARY AND INFORMATION SCIENCE, ACADEMIC YEAR 1980–1981 (cont.)

Institution	Project Director	No.	Level*	Amount
Pratt Institute, DeKalb Ave. & Hall St., Brooklyn 11205	Rhoda Garoogian	1	M	6,300
St. John's University, Grand Central & Utopia Pkwys., Jamaica 11439	Fr. Jovian P. Lang	3	M	19,200
SUNY at Albany, 1400 Washington Ave., Albany 12222	Richard S. Halsey	1	M	6,300
SUNY at Buffalo, 201 Bell Hall, Buffalo 14260	George S. Bobinski	1	M	6,300
North Carolina Appalachian State University, Boone 28608	Alice P. Naylor	2	M	12,600
North Carolina Central University, 1801 Fayetteville St., Durham 27707	Annette L. Phinazee	3	M	19,200
Ohio Case Western Reserve University, Cleveland 44106	James E. Rogers	4	M (2) D (2)	29,200
Oklahoma University of Oklahoma, 1000 Asp Ave., Norman 73019	Taylor C. Anthony	5	M	31,200
Oregon University of Oregon, Eugene 97403	Dorothy M. Latham	2	M	12,600
Pennsylvania University of Pittsburgh, 1028 Cathedral of Learning, Pittsburgh 15260	Patricia B. Pond	5	M (3) D (2)	35,800
Tennessee Vanderbilt University, Box 501, Peabody College, Nashville 37203	Edwin S. Gleaves	2	M	12,600
Texas North Texas State University, N.T. Box 13796, Denton 76203	James L. Thomas	3	M (2) D (1)	21,000
Texas Woman's University, Box 22905, T.W.U. Sta., Denton 76204	Brooke E. Sheldon	6	M (4) D (2)	41,800
University of Texas, Box 7576, University Sta., Austin 78712	C. G. Sparks	4	M	25,200
Washington University of Washington, Seattle 98195	Peter Hiatt	2	M	10,500

*D = doctoral, P = post-master, M = master, BS = bachelor of science, A = associate of arts.

TABLE 3 LIBRARY TRAINING INSTITUTE PROGRAM ENROLLMENT DATA, FY 1968-1979

Academic Year	Participants	Institutes	FY
1968/69	2,084	66	1968
1969/70	3,101	91	1969
1970/71	1,347	46	1970
1971/72	1,557	38	1971
1972/73	684	17	1972
1973/74	1,301 + 45[a]	26 + 3[a]	1973
1974/75	1,339 + 35[a]	30 + 2[a]	1974
1975/76	1,244 + 35[a]	26 + 2[a]	1975
1976/77	120	5	1976
1977/78	802 + 112[a]	22 + 3[a]	1977
1978/79	1,101 + 100[a]	24 + 1[a]	1978
1979/80	1,081	24	1979
Total	16,088	426	

[a]Traineeship program.

2. To train professionals in service to the disadvantaged, including the aged and the handicapped.
3. To present alternatives for recruitment, training, and utilization of library personnel and manpower.
4. To foster and develop innovative practice to reform and revitalize the traditional system of library and information service.
5. To retrain librarians to master new skills needed to support key areas, such as the Right to Read campaign, drug abuse education, enviornmental and ecological education, early childhood education, career education, management (planning, evaluation, and needs assessment), human relations and social interaction, service to the institutionalized, community learning center programs, service to foster the quality of life, intellectual freedom, and institute planning.
6. To train those who teach other trainers.
7. To train library trustees, school administrators, and other persons with administrative, supervisory, and advisory responsibility for library, media, and information services, such as boards of education, state advisory councils, etc.
8. To train and retrain persons in law librarianship.

Table 3 is a history of the institute awards.

HIGHER EDUCATION ACT, TITLE II-B, LIBRARY RESEARCH AND DEMONSTRATION PROGRAM

Adrienne Chute

Project Officer
Library Research and Demonstration Branch
Division of Library Programs
Office of Libraries and Learning Technologies

The Library Research and Demonstration Program (LRDP) of the Office of Libraries and Learning Technologies (OLLT) awards and administers grants and contracts for research and demonstration projects to improve training in librarianship, to improve information technology, and to disseminate information derived from LRDP projects. The 1980 Amendments to the Higher Education Act of 1965 reauthorized and modified the program to include support for research into more economical and efficient information delivery, cooperative efforts (such as networking), developmental projects, and improvement of information technology. The new act also extends program eligibility to profit-making organizations.

FUNDED PROJECTS

The projects highlighted in this article include projects funded in 1980 and others of note that were completed in 1980. The article describes planning efforts and projects that illustrate program trends in the areas of library services for the disabled, information technology, and networking and cooperation. Tables 1-4 supply statistical information on Library Research and Demonstration Program trends.

In December 1980, a contract was awarded for compiling a library and information service agenda for the 1980s. This agenda of project ideas will assist the Department of Education and other agencies and organizations in targeting research funds toward the most critical needs. The project is expected to be completed in December 1981.

In October 1980, OLLT, in cooperation with the National Center for Educational Statistics, awarded a contract to assess human resources supply-and-demand conditions in the field of librarianship and project them to 1990. The study will develop current employment and labor force estimates, identify and discuss factors affecting employment levels and staffing patterns in libraries, and assess prospective supply-and-demand conditions through 1990.

A project to prepare a planning guide for public libraries, funded in 1977, was completed in 1980. It describes a participatory planning process to guide librarians and community representatives. The planning process sets goals and objectives tailored to local needs. Each library's individual goals and objectives become the standards that particular library will strive to reach. The planning process also designs strategies to achieve local standards, and inaugurates planning cycles, which continuously adjust to changing community conditions.

The results of a contract "Libraries in Literacy," funded in 1979, will be available in May of 1981. This project will produce the first national survey of libraries' activities in literacy education and will identify the characteristics conducive to the implementation of literacy education by libraries.

A grant for the design and installation of a national information center on

Office of Planning and Policy Assessment

As an aid in understanding national needs in the humanities and designing new or improved programs to meet such needs, this office of the Endowment supports—through its Planning and Assessment Studies Program—projects in the following areas: collection and analysis of data assessing the status of and trends and resources in important sectors of humanistic activity; and research into and development of tools aiding evaluation and policy analysis of programs in humanities organizations, including libraries.

NATIONAL SCIENCE FOUNDATION SUPPORT FOR INFORMATION SCIENCE RESEARCH

1800 G St. N.W., Washington, DC 20550
202-357-9554

Sarah N. Rhodes

Division of Information Science and Technology

The National Science Foundation (NSF) is an independent agency of the federal government established by Congress in 1950 to promote the progress of science. The NSF, through its Division of Information Science and Technology (IST), supports basic and applied research in information science, information technology, and the economic and social impacts of information use. The objectives of the program are to obtain a deeper understanding of the structure, organization, transfer, and use of information; to investigate the societal and economic impact of information technology, including computers and telecommunications; and to accelerate appropriate application of scientific and engineering advances in information technology.

Information science studies the structure of information and its transfer. Research includes topics such as the optimal organization of information collections, the relationship between form and content for natural language information, the evaluation of statistical theories of information, and the automatic recognition of patterns of information in text, image, and numerical files. Since information systems involve users, research also is focused on how people represent knowledge and information internally, how they recognize patterns of information, and how they systematically abstract from the information presented to their senses those messages that are most pertinent.

Information technology is concerned with the technical means available for effecting the exchange of information. Emphasis is on research related to new applications of advanced technology, the application of information science theory to the design of information systems, and instrumentation for information science.

The growth of machine-accessible information and the new microelectronic and telecommunications media provide incentive for greater effort to understand the role of information in the economy, and its potential impact on all segments of society. Important research topics include investigations of possible trade-offs between the information labor force and information capital and other aspects related to productivity, problems of aggregation encountered in modeling information flows, and the criteria by which models of the information economy can be validated. Regarding societal impacts, research focuses on the effects of information technology on the work force, the impact of public policies affecting the communications and information industries, the potential of advanced information technology applications for education and training, and the relationship between the individual and mass communication systems.

In order to enhance the development of information science and contribute to the scientific vitality of the field, IST has established Special Research Initiation Awards for New Investigators as part of its program of research support. These awards are offered only to principal investigators who have earned a doctoral degree in a field related to information science, including the information, computer, cognitive, and mathematical sciences, linguistics, and electrical engineering, and have held the doctorate for no more than five years.

SUBMISSION AND REVIEW OF PROPOSALS

Proposals may be submitted by academic institutions, by nonprofit and profit-making organizations, or by groups of such organizations. Joint proposals that bring a coordinated range of expertise and research skills to bear on complex problems are particularly encouraged. In the selection of projects to be supported, preference is given to research that is fundamental and general, and to applied research concerned with scientific and technical information rather than, for example, business information or mass communication. The development of hardware is beyond the scope of this program, as are projects to develop, implement, or evaluate information systems except for those dealing with generalizations that go beyond the particular information systems involved.

A program announcement, *Research in Information Science* (NSF-79-68), which also provides information on how to submit a proposal, is available from the Division of Information Science and Technology. Potential applicants are encouraged to discuss their research ideas with IST staff, in person, or by letter or telephone.

Except for proposals for Special Research Initiation Awards, for which deadlines are announced, research proposals may be submitted at any time. Review generally requires six to eight months, and proposed activities should be scheduled with that in mind. Proposals are reviewed by NSF staff and external reviewers selected for their knowledge and expertise in topics addressed by the proposals. The award of NSF grants is discretionary. In general, projects are supported in order of merit to the extent permitted by available funds. The principal criteria by which a research proposal is evaluated are the technical adequacy of the investigators and their institutional base, the adequacy of the research design, the scientific significance of the proposed project, its utility or relevance, and its implications for the scientific potential of the field.

NSF plans to award approximately $6.1 million for information science research in FY 1981.

DISSEMINATION OF RESULTS

The foundation encourages grantees and contractors to present their research results at appropriate professional meetings and to publish in scientific journals. Copies of final technical reports are made available through the National Technical Information Service of the U.S. Department of Commerce. In addition, summaries of awards are available through the Smithsonian Science Information Exchange. Annual lists of awards and bibliographies of reports from completed projects are available from IST.

Table 1 lists the grants and contracts for research in information science

TABLE 1 NSF AWARDS FOR INFORMATION SCIENCE RESEARCH, FY 1980

Principal Investigator(s)/ Institution	Proposal Title	Duration (months)	Amount ($)
Jeffrey Ullman Department of Air Force & Stanford University	Implementation of a Simple User Model by a Relational Data Base	24	49,487
Stephen Grossberg Boston University	Decision-Making and Information Processing in Real-Time Network Models	36	157,990
James Anderson Brown University	Cognitive Applications of Matrix Memory Models	12	44,602
Howard Wainer Bureau of Social Science Research	Social Science Applications of Dynamic Multivariate Displays	12	40,728
Lotfi A. Zadeh University of California, Berkeley	A Theory of Approximate Reasoning	12	29,500
Louis E. Narens University of California, Irvine	Problems in the Theory of Measurement that Pertain to Information Concepts	36	111,264
Wesley W. Chu University of California, Los Angeles	File Allocation and Query Optimization for Distributed Data Bases	24	112,220
Judea Pearl and Norman C. Dalkey University of California, Los Angeles	Studies in the Organization of Information Structures	18	39,174
W. D. Haseman Carnegie-Mellon University	Distributed Data Base Design	6	39,211
Zellig Harris Columbia University	Information Correlates of Basic Language Structures	24	74,989
Ralph M. Weischedel University of Delaware	Natural Language Processing Systems and Ill-Formed Input	24	136,681
H. Russell Bernard University of Florida	Degradation of Accuracy in Social Network Data	—	19,403
Alec Peters The Franklin Institute Research Laboratories	Support for Coordination of Scientific and Technical Information Activities	7	50,000
David S. Becker IIT Research Institute	An Augmented English Dictionary for Information Retrieval	12	83,285
William B. Rouse University of Illinois, Urbana-Champaign	Modeling of Human Behavior in Seeking and Generating Information	24	144,120
Martha E. Williams University of Illinois, Urbana-Champaign	Automatic Duplicate Detection of Journal Articles Appearing in Multiple Data Bases—A Feasibility Study	24	269,303
Madan L. Puri Indiana University	Problems in Decision-Making and Information Retrieval Studied with Techniques of Fuzzy Sets and Systems	36	112,690

TABLE 1 NSF AWARDS FOR INFORMATION SCIENCE RESEARCH, FY 1980 (cont.)

Principal Investigator(s)/ Institution	Proposal Title	Duration (months)	Amount ($)
Elliot Noma Institute for Scientific Information	Citation-Based Measures of Interactivity and Similarity	12	38,188
Donald J. Hillman Lehigh University	A Theoretical Basis for Knowledge Management	24	123,551
John J. O'Connor Lehigh University	Citing Statements: Recognition by Computer and Use to Improve Full-Text Retrieval	24	115,447
Carol C. McDonough University of Lowell	A Simultaneous Equation Model of the Demand for Academic and Professional Journals	12	25,342
Jack Minker and Barry E. Jacobs University of Maryland	Applications of Logic and Theorem Proving to Data Bases	36	207,835
Richard S. Marcus and J. Francis Reintjes Massachusetts Institute of Technology	Investigations of Computer-Aided Document Search Strategies	24	155,360
J. Francis Reintjes Massachusetts Institute of Technology	Investigation of Electronic Interlibrary Resource-Sharing Networks	12	95,000
Whitman A. Richards Massachusetts Institute of Technology	Natural Computation and Control	12	234,196
Manfred Kochen University of Michigan	Dynamics in the Organization of Scientific Specialties	24	134,782
Murray Turoff New Jersey Institute of Technology	Electronic Information Exchange Test Facility	—	2,000
Jean-Claude Falmagne New York University	Probabilistic Measurement Theoretic Models of Information Processing	31	156,909
Fritz Machlup New York University	Information Science: An Analysis of Methodological Issues and Interdisciplinary Relationships	12	39,973
Mitchell L. Moss New York University	Publication of Proceedings of a Conference on Telecommunications and Productivity	12	9,976
Naomi Sager New York University	Computer-Based Investigation into the Structure of Information	24	274,645
Thomas L. Isenhour University of North Carolina	Computer Applications to Analytical Chemistry	12	66,500
Kenneth R. Mount Northwestern University	Message Spaces and Computing Time for Allocation Mechanisms	24	78,409
Neal K. Kaske OCLC, Inc.	Development of Generalized Algorithm to Determine Terminal Requirements for On-Line Catalogs in Libraries	12	97,902

TABLE 1   NSF AWARDS FOR INFORMATION SCIENCE RESEARCH, FY 1980 (cont.)

Principal Investigator(s)/ Institution	Proposal Title	Duration (months)	Amount ($)
K. S. Fu Purdue University	Research on Error-Correcting Techniques in Automated Information Processing	36	151,794
F. F. Leimkuhler Purdue University	Analysis and Application of Information Productivity Models	24	108,099
F. F. Leimkuhler Purdue University	Analysis and Application of Information Productivity Models	—	1,819
John Moyne Queens College of CUNY	Language and Human Information Processing	15	91,140
Donald A. Dunn Stanford University	Economics of Computer Communication Networks	12	166,458
Donald E. Knuth Stanford University	Theoretical Basis for Development of Document Preparation Systems	24	338,707
Michael McGill Syracuse University	A Study of the Impact of Representations in Information Retrieval Systems	24	155,613
Starr Roxanne Hiltz Upsala College	Workshop to Compare and Synthesize Evaluations of Computer-Based Information Exchange	6	43,711
George P. Huber University of Wisconsin, Madison	A Study of the Distribution, Processing, and Use of Scientific and Technical Information in Research Organizations	12	91,214
William D. Haseman University of Wisconsin, Milwaukee	Distributed Data Base Design	18	243,651
Roger Schank Yale University	Theoretical Foundations of Natural Language Processing	24	183,785
D. Stott Parker University of California, Los Angeles	Data Semantics and Logical Data Base Design	24	57,489
Caroline M. Eastman Florida State University	Multiple Attribute Retrieval Techniques for Tree-Structured Information	12	24,063
Karen J. Neff Hofstra University	Research on Automated Natural Language Generation	24	110,633
Donna J. Brown University of Illinois, Urbana	Storage and Access Costs in Data Structures for Information Retrieval Problems	24	62,663
Sowmitri Swamy University of Illinois, Urbana	Access Time versus Storage Space in Information Retrieval Systems	24	59,829
Bruce A. Whitehead University of Louisville	Representation and Processing of Spatially Structured Information in Cognition	24	77,840
W. Bruce Croft University of Massachusetts, Amherst	A Generalized Model of Document Retrieval	24	61,740

TABLE 1   NSF AWARDS FOR INFORMATION SCIENCE RESEARCH, FY 1980 (cont.)

Principal Investigator(s)/ Institution	Proposal Title	Duration (months)	Amount ($)
Janet Pierrehumbert Massachusetts Institute of Technology	The Use of Intonation in Automatic Speech Understanding	24	43,701
Matthew B. Koll National Bureau of Standards	Refinement and Use of Concept Similarities in Information Retrieval	12	35,498
Carla S. Ellis University of Oregon	Concurrency in the Access and Manipulation of Information Structures	24	62,500
Karen H. Chase Pennsylvania State University	Completions of Relations and Embedded Joint Dependencies in Relational Data Bases: A Study Using Boolean Matrices	12	36,630
James F. Allen University of Rochester	Recognizing Intent in Natural Language	24	80,000
Sargue N. Srihari State University of New York at Buffalo	Contextual Algorithms for Text Recognition	24	55,800
David S. Warren State University of New York at Stony Brook	Montague Grammar and Data Base	24	79,902
Elaine Rich University of Texas, Austin	Individual User Modeling in Computer Systems	24	56,315
Michael Tanenhaus Wayne State University	Lexical Ambiguity Resolution in Discourse	24	38,977

awarded by the foundation in FY 1980. Most of these awards were supported entirely by the Division of Information Science and Technology, but a few were funded jointly by IST and other NSF divisions, including the Division of Mathematical and Computer Sciences (MCS), the Division of Behavioral and Neural Sciences (BNS), the Division of Social and Economic Sciences (SES), the Division of Policy Research and Analysis (PRA), and the Division of Chemistry (CHE).

NATIONAL HISTORICAL PUBLICATIONS AND RECORDS COMMISSION

General Services Administration
National Archives and Records Service
Washington, DC 20408
202-724-1083

In 1934, Congress established the National Historical Publications Commission to make plans, estimates, and recommendations for the publication of important historical documents and to work with various public and private institutions in gathering, annotating, and publishing papers and records of national historical significance.

The commission was inactive until 1950 when, at the urging of President Truman, Congress provided funds for a small professional staff. In 1964, the commission's publications program was strengthened by the enactment of PL 88–383, which allows the Administrator of General Services, on recommendation of the commission, to make allocations to federal agencies and grants to state and local agencies as well as to nonprofit organizations and institutions for collecting, editing, and publishing significant historical documents.

On December 22, 1974, President Gerald R. Ford signed PL 93536, which changed the commission's name to the National Historical Publications and Records Commission (NHPRC). With new funds—the annual authorization was increased from $2,000,000 to the present level of $4,000,000—the commission was to assist agencies and institutions in all states and territories in gathering, arranging, describing, and preserving significant papers and records.

The commission has also sponsored publication of the *Guide to Archives and Manuscripts in the United States* (1961), and has published a *Directory of Archives and Manuscript Repositories in the United States* (1978), the first publication from the commission's national Historical Records Inventory; the bibliographic volumes *Writings on American History;* an important survey by Walter Rundell, Jr., *In Pursuit of American History: Research and Training in the United States;* and an analysis of historical editing, *The Publication of American Historical Manuscripts,* edited by Fred Shelley and Leslie Dunlap.

Representation on the commission is fixed by law to include a member of the federal judiciary, one member from each house of Congress, two presidential appointees, the Librarian of Congress or an alternate, the secretary of defense or an alternate, the secretary of state or an alternate, and two members each of the American Historical Association, the Organization of American Historians, the American Association for State and Local History, and the Society of American Archivists. The Archivist of the United States serves as chairperson.

The commission's grants for both the publications and records programs usually require the contribution of nonfederal funds in a matching or cost-sharing plan.

PUBLICATIONS PROGRAM

Many of the commission's publications grants in FY 1980 went to help support continuing projects such as *The Papers of Daniel Webster* ($14,850 grant to Dartmouth College), *The Papers of Carlos Montezuma* ($20,000 to Klein Independent School District, Spring, Texas), *Freedmen in Southern Society, 1861–67* ($79,100 to the

University of Maryland), *The Henry Clay Papers* ($26,856 to the University of Kentucky), and *The Papers of James Madison* ($54,588 to the University of Virginia).

Volumes from commission-sponsored projects that were published during the year include volume 1 of *The Papers of Andrew Jackson* (University of Tennessee Press), volume 3 of *The Papers of John Marshall* (University of North Carolina Press), volumes 7 and 8 of *The Papers of Ulysses S. Grant* (Southern Illinois University Press), volumes 8 and 9 of *The Booker T. Washington Papers* (University of Illinois Press), and volumes 32-34 of *The Papers of Woodrow Wilson* (Princeton University Press). Among microform publications completed during the year were *The Letters and Papers of Richard Rush* (29 reels, Nassau Community College, New York), *The Correspondence of Lydia Maria Child* (97 microfiche cards, University of Massachusetts), and *The Papers of Louis Dembitz Brandeis at the University of Louisville* (184 reels, University of Louisville).

New publication grants included $35,730 to the State Historical Society of Wisconsin and the University of Wisconsin for a microfilm edition of the papers of nationally prominent progressives from that state; $5,817 to the University of Nebraska for a comprehensive microform edition of the papers of botanist Charles E. Bessey; $16,645 to the University of New Mexico for a comprehensive microform and selective five-volume printed edition of the papers of Diego de Vargas, governor and recolonizer of New Mexico (1690–1704); $25,802 to the University of Louisville for a microfilm edition of the papers of pioneer filmmaker D. W. Griffith; and $22,103 to the University of California for a comprehensive microfilm and selective two-volume book edition of the papers of social reformer and anarchist Emma Goldman.

In all, during FY 1980 the commission provided 75 grants, averaging $29,000 each, to historical editing projects at universities, historical societies, libraries, and state and federal agencies from New England to California. It also made available to university and other nonprofit presses subvention grants to help in publishing the editions sponsored by the commission. Moreover, the commission is participating in a committee to promote higher quality book production standards, and is now making plans to sponsor a large conference on the use of word processing in documentary editing. It continues to offer editing fellowships and to conduct an annual historical editing institute. Its research staff continues to provide reference materials from the National Archives, the Library of Congress, and other institutions to editors of commission-sponsored projects, and to offer guidance on a wide range of research questions.

But even with the great advances of the historical editing field in the last decades, problems still persist, especially the question of financial support for large-scale editions. Funds from federal grant-making agencies, such as the commission, are not expected to keep pace with rising editorial and production costs for some of the major comprehensive projects.

On March 20, 1980, the Andrew W. Mellon Foundation announced a grant of $425,000 to the commission in support of five documentary editions of the Founding Fathers: The Adams Family, Benjamin Franklin, Thomas Jefferson, James Madison, and George Washington. The grant is intended to support the projects for three years while the editors and sponsoring institutions develop long-term financial bases.

In addition to the support provided to these five projects, the foundation has also made available the sum of $25,000 to undertake a study examining some of the problems now facing long-term editions. The study will not only assist private foundations and federal funding agencies such as the commission and the National Endowment for the Humanities in directing their future programs, but will provide much-needed information and direction for editors, prospective editors, and all others interested in this field.

As the contours of editing change, as new technology, new subjects, and new methods shape historical editing in the 1980s, the commission remains committed to the same standards of scholarly excellence that have characterized the work of documentary editors over the past three decades.

RECORDS PROGRAM

The records grant program supports a variety of activities relating to preservation of historical records and their preparation for use by researchers. Survey and accessioning, appraisal, arrangement and description, preparation of guides and other finding aids, microfilming, and training are among the items that regularly appear in proposals to the commission. The records program does not at this time support projects relating to newspapers, rare books or published items (except where these are incidental parts of collections of historical records), or oral history interviewing or transcribing. Emphasis is on the information in records rather than on the artifact value of the items; thus microfilming or other means of copying fragile records is usually preferred to the much more expensive restoration of individual documents.

The commission strongly endorses standard archival techniques, especially in arrangement and description of historical records, and has supported several projects that foster the awareness of these techniques, including the Basic Manual Series of the Society of American Archivists and H. G. Jones's *Local Government Records: An Introduction to Their Management, Preservation and Use,* published by the American Association for State and Local History. Finally, the commission has supported several workshops on archival techniques and on conservation methods.

To carry out the historical records program, the commission relies heavily on the advice of state historical records advisory boards, made up of archivists, historical program administrators, and others interested in historical records within the state. These advisory boards, chaired by a historical record coordinator, develop priorities and preferred approaches and review records of grant proposals from the states prior to commission consideration. The head of the state's archival program is usually the state coordinator; the director of the state-funded historical society, where one exists, is also a member of the board. Many advisory boards, which have been appointed in every state except Maine, have placed local needs, especially local government records programs, among their highest priorities. State records are also often a high priority.

Although the commission wishes to respond as effectively to the needs of small and local repositories as it does to large ones, it hopes that small repositories will consider forming cooperative projects when possible. Often a cooperative program involving several institutions with common problems can be cost-effective and can more readily justify the level of resources necessary to support a professional approach.

Suggestions for Applicants

The records program distributes an introductory pamphlet, detailed "Suggestions for Applicants" that should be read by all applicants, *Annotation* (a newsletter), lists of grant projects funded in the past, and special guidelines for microform projects. At present there are three records program application deadlines each year: February 1, June 1, and October 1.

Assessing Needs, Solving Problems, Planning Programs

In its 1978 "Statement of National Needs and Preferred Approaches," the commission challenged archivists and others concerned about the fate of historical records to gather together to define key questions and develop agendas for action. The commission received reports from three such planning groups in 1980, the first from the Joint Committee on the Archives of Science and Technology addressing questions about the preservation and control of sci/tech records, the second from the United Negro College Fund focusing on the development of archival programs for historically black colleges, and the third from the Western Council of State Libraries outlining needs and developing new programs in conservation and preservation for 18 western states. Future conferences, most notably one sponsored by the George Meany Center of the AFL-CIO, and a second sponsored by the Institute for the Study of Contemporary Social Problems and the Police Foundation, will address critical questions concerning labor records and police records. The commission looks forward to assisting other groups in assessing needs, solving problems, and planning programs.

National Historical Records Inventory

In addition to its grants function, the records program administers the development of a national automated data base of information on historical records repositories and their holdings. The first publication of this program is a *Directory of Archives and Manuscript Repositories in the United States* (1978) listing basic information about the holdings of over 3,200 repositories. The directory is arranged by state and city, and as special features includes separate lists of 18 types of repositories such as local historical societies, museums, religious institutions, corporate archives, and public libraries. The commission has also developed information standards, field and tag assignments, selection codes, and editorial and indexing formats that are being used by survey projects in several states using the SPINDEX program for archival description and the production of guides. These projects, sponsored by the commission, are identifying and describing repository holdings to the collection level or below. Information about its data base design and sponsored projects is available from the commission.

New Projects

In FY 1980 the commission recommended 86 records grants totaling $1,886,016 for projects in 36 states. The average grant was $21,698. Grants were made to colleges and universities (24), private historical societies, museums, and archives (15), state agencies (11), cities and counties (10), public and special libraries (6), and to 20 other institutions. The commission received 178 requests totaling $5,373,804. Many projects received reduced outright grants or offers of reduced grants conditional on increased nonfederal funding.

The following grants are representative of those recommended during FY 1980.

Grants to Cities and Counties

City of Los Angeles, California: $34,732 to provide a consultant, an archivist, and other assistance in the development of an archival program for the city.

City of Providence, Rhode Island: $14,945 for a second phase of a project to establish an archives and records program for the city.

Grants to State Agencies

Kentucky Historical Society, Frankfort: $33,862 for the first phase of a joint project with the Kentucky State Archives to arrange, describe, and make available the papers and records of Kentucky governors, 1792–1927.

Pennsylvania Historical and Museum Commission, Harrisburg: $56,569 for the second year of its project to microfilm for preservation and research the records of municipal and county governments in Pennsylvania.

State Historical Society of Wisconsin, Madison: $84,540 for the second phase of the Midwest Archives Guide Project, an interstate cooperative project to develop common descriptive methods and a shared information base for public records in the state archives systems in Minnesota, Wisconsin, Illinois, and Indiana.

Grants to Colleges and Universities

University of Massachusetts, Amherst: $20,728 to arrange and describe the papers of prominent black educator Horace Mann Bond (1904–1972) and his family, including his father, James, and his sons, James and Julian.

Cornell University, Ithaca, New York: $78,251 for the third phase of a comprehensive survey of archives and manuscript repositories in New York. In this phase, the project will survey repository holdings in the Buffalo and Syracuse areas and will complete all work in central and western New York State. The New York survey is one of several linked with NHPRC's historical records data base program.

Temple University, Philadelphia, Pennsylvania: $43,655 (partial matching) to survey the status of newspaper photograph collections and develop recommendations for their preservation and control generally and the *Philadelphia Inquirer* collection specifically.

Grants to Private Historical Societies, Museums, and Archives

The Corcoran Gallery of Art, Washington, DC: $32,422 to assist in the planning and implementation of an archival program for the Gallery and the School of Art. The Corcoran, founded in 1869, is the oldest gallery in Washington, DC.

Western Heritage Museum, Omaha, Nebraska: $22,544 to preserve and make available the Bostwick-Frohardt Photographs Collection. This collection, which dates from 1902 through the early 1940s, documents the growth of Omaha and the activities of its citizens in political, social, urban, and rural life.

Grants to Public and Special Libraries

Grand Rapids Public Library, Grand Rapids, Michigan: $32,938 to develop a local records program for the City of Grand Rapids. Project activities include a survey and appraisal of legislation covering public records disposition, establishment of an archives for historically valuable records, and publication of a guide to the city's records.

Memphis/Shelby County Public Library and Information Center, Memphis, Tennessee: $14,616 to arrange, describe, and prepare descriptive inventories to six series of city and county records.

Other Records Project Grants

Society for Research in Child Development, Berkeley, California: $24,383 to locate, identify, preserve, and make available the records of individuals and organizations important in the field of child development prior to World War II.

New England Document Conservation Center, Andover, Massachusetts: $9,650 for conservation seminars in New York, New Jersey, and New England.

The Salvation Army, New York, New York: $24,518 to inventory and appraise the records of territorial and divisional headquarters, hospitals, homes, and service units, and to develop retention and disposition schedules for Salvation Army records.

Western Council of State Libraries, Salem, Oregon: $10,925 (plus $2,500 supplemental) for the final phase of its Western States Materials Conservation Project to determine conservation needs and propose solutions through coordinated conservation activities in 18 western states.

PUBLICATIONS OF THE COMMISSION

Annotation (the commission's triannual newsletter).
Annual Report.
Directory of Archives and Manuscript Repositories in the United States.
Fact Sheet: The National Historical Publications and Records Commission and Its Work.
Microform Guidelines.
National Historical Publications and Records Commission Subvention Program Guidelines.
Publications Catalog, 1976.
Publications Program Guidelines and Procedures: Applications and Grants.
Records Program Guidelines and Procedures: Applications and Grants.
Report to the President, 1978.
SPINDEX and Guide/Data Base: Introductory Materials.
The State Historical Records Coordinator and the State Historical Records Advisory Board: Suggested Roles and Procedures.
Suggestions for Records Program Applicants.

Part 3
Library Education, Placement, and Salaries

GUIDE TO LIBRARY PLACEMENT SOURCES

Margaret Myers
Director, Office for Library Personnel Resources,
American Library Association

This year's guide updates the listing in the 1980 *Bowker Annual* with information on new joblines, new services, and changes in contacts and groups listed previously. The sources listed primarily give assistance in obtaining professional positions, although a few indicate assistance for paraprofessionals. The latter, however, tend to be recruited primarily through local sources.

GENERAL SOURCES OF LIBRARY JOBS

Library Literature. Classified ads of library vacancies and positions wanted are carried in many of the national, regional, and state library journals and newsletters. Members of associations can sometimes list "position wanted" ads free of charge in their membership publications. Listings of positions available are regularly found in *American Libraries, Chronicle of Higher Education, College & Research Libraries Newsletter, Journal of Academic Librarianship, Library Journal, LJ/SLJ Hotline, Online, Special Libraries,* and *Wilson Library Bulletin.* State and regional library association newsletters, state library journals, and foreign library periodicals carrying such ads are listed in later sections. Newsletters such as the *Acquisitive Librarian, American Indian Libraries Newsletter, Black Caucus Newsletter,* and *CLENExchange* are beginning to carry some job ads. Some newsletters of on-line user groups are listing positions for searchers. (For a "User Group Directory" see *Online* 4:78–80 July 1980).

Newspapers. The *New York Times* Sunday Week in Review section carries a special section of ads for librarian jobs in addition to the regular classifieds. Local newspapers, particularly the larger city Sunday editions, often carry job vacancy listings in libraries, both professional and paraprofessional.

LIBRARY JOBLINES

New joblines were added during 1980 in Illinois and Texas by the Association of College and Research Libraries and the New York and Bay Area chapters of the Special Libraries Association. Library joblines or job "hotlines" give recorded telephone messages of job openings in a specific geographical area. Most tapes are changed once a week on Friday afternoon, although individual listings may sometimes be carried for several weeks. The classified section of *American Libraries* carries jobline numbers in each issue. Although the information is fairly brief and the cost of calling is borne by the individual job seeker, a jobline provides a quick and up-to-date listing of vacancies that is not usually possible with printed listings or journal ads.

Most joblines carry listings for their state or region only, although some will occasionally accept out-of-state positions if there is room on the tape. While a few will list technician and other paraprofessional positions, the majority are for professional jobs only. When calling the joblines, one might occasionally find a time when the telephone keeps ringing without any answer; this will usually mean that the tape is being changed or there are no new jobs for that period.

The following are in operation: American Society for Information Science, 202-

210 / LIBRARY EDUCATION, PLACEMENT, AND SALARIES

659-8132; Arizona State Library/JAM, 602-278-1327; Association of College and Research Libraries, 312-944-6795; British Columbia Library Association, 604-263-0014 (B.C. listings only); California Library Association, 916-443-1222 for northern California and 213-629-5627 for southern California (identical lists); California Media and Library Educators Association, 415-697-8832; Colorado State Library, 303-839-2210 (Colorado listings only, includes paraprofessional); Florida State Library, 904-488-5232 (in-state listings only); Georgia Library Association/JMRT, 404-634-5726 (5:00 P.M.–8:00 A.M. Monday through Friday; 12 noon Saturday through 8:00 A.M. Monday); Illinois Library Job Hotline, 312-828-0930 (cosponsored by the Special Libraries Association Illinois Chapter and Illinois Regional Library Council—all types of jobs listed); Maryland Library Association, 301-685-5760; Metropolitan Washington Council of Governments (D.C.), 202-223-2272; Midwest Federation of Library Associations, 517-487-5617 (also includes paraprofessional and out-of-state if room on tape; cosponsored by six state library associations—Illinois, Indiana, Michigan, Minnesota, Ohio, and Wisconsin); New England Library Board, 207-623-2286 (New England area jobs only); New Jersey Library Association/State Library, 609-695-2121; New York Library Association, 212-227-8483; North Carolina State Library, 919-733-6410 (professional jobs in North Carolina only); Ontario Library Association Job Hotline in Toronto, 416-363-3380; Oregon Library Association, 503-585-2232 (cosponsored by Oregon Educational Media Association); Pacific Northwest Library Association, 206-543-2890 (Alaska, Alberta, British Columbia, Idaho, Montana, Oregon, Washington; includes both professional and paraprofessional and other library-related jobs); Pennsylvania Cooperative Jobline, 412-362-5627 (cosponsored by the Pennsylvania Library Association, Pennsylvania Learning Resources Association, Pittsburgh Regional Library Center, Special Libraries Association–Philadelphia Chapter, Medical Library Association–Philadelphia and Pittsburgh groups, American Society for Information Science–Delaware Valley Chapter, Pennsylvania School Librarians Association [also accepts paraprofessional out-of-state listings]); Special Libraries Association, New York Chapter, 212-753-7247; Special Libraries Association, San Francisco Bay Chapter, 408-737-2365; Special Libraries Association, Southern California Chapter, 213-795-2145; Texas State Library Jobline, 512-475-0408; University of South Carolina College of Librarianship, 803-777-8443; Virginia Library Association Jobline, 804-355-0384. Delaware jobs are listed on the New Jersey, Pennsylvania, and Maryland joblines.

For those employers who wish to place vacancy listings on the jobline recordings, the following numbers can be called: Arizona, 602-269-2535; ASIS, 202-659-3644; California, 916-447-8541; Colorado, 303-839-2174; District of Columbia, 202-223-6800, ext. 344; Florida, 904-487-2651; Georgia, 404-329-6872; New England, 207-622-4733; New Jersey, 609-292-6237; New York, 212-227-8032; New York/SLA, 212-790-0639; North Carolina, 919-733-2570; Pennsylvania, 412-362-6400; San Francisco/SLA, 408-738-7177; Southern California/SLA, 213-446-8251, ext. 32; Texas, 512-475-4110; Virginia, 804-770-5572.

Write: British Columbia Library Association, Box 46378, Sta. G, Vancouver, B.C., V6R 4G6, Canada; California Media and Library Educators Association, 1575 Old Bayshore Hwy., Suite 204, Burlingame, CA 94010; Colorado State Library Jobline, 1362 Lincoln, Denver, CO 80203; Maryland Library Association, 115 W. Franklin St., Baltimore, MD 21201; Oregon Library Association JOBLINE, Oregon State Library, Salem, OR 97310; PNLA Jobline, c/o Pacific Northwest Bibliographic Center, University of Washington, 253 Suzzalo Library FM-25, Seattle, WA 98195; University of South Carolina, College of Librarianship Placement, Columbia, SC 29208 (no geographical restrictions).

For the Midwest Federation Jobline, employers should send listings to their own state association executive secretary, who will refer these to the Michigan Library Association where the recording equipment is housed. There is a $5 fee to be paid by the employer for each listing. Paraprofessional positions are also accepted. For the Illinois Library Job Hotline, contact Illinois Regional Library Council, 425 N. Michigan Ave., Chicago, IL 60611, 312-828-0928. An employer fee of $20 is charged to list the position for two weeks.

SPECIALIZED LIBRARY ASSOCIATIONS AND GROUPS

American Association of Law Libraries, 53 W. Jackson Blvd., Chicago, IL 60604, 312-939-4764. Placement service is available without charge. Lists of openings and personnel available are published several times per year in a newsletter distributed to membership. Applicants are referred to placement officers for employment counseling.

American Libraries, c/o J. W. Grey, 50 E. Huron St., Chicago, IL 60611. "Career LEADS EXPRESS": advance galleys (three to four weeks) of job listings to be published in next issue of *American Libraries*. Early notice of some 40 to 60 "Positions Open" sent about the fourteenth of each month; does not include editorial corrections, late changes, and the majority of "Late Job Notices," as they appear in the regular *AL* LEADS section. For each month, send $2 check made out to *AL* EXPRESS; self-addressed, standard business-size envelope (4 x 9), and 15¢ postage on envelope.

Consultants Keyword Clearinghouse (CKC). A new *American Libraries* service that helps match professionals offering library/information expertise with institutions seeking it. Published quarterly, CKC appears in the Career LEADS section of the January, April, June, and October issues of *AL*. Rates: $3/line—classified; $30/inch—display. Inquiries should be made to J. W. Grey, LEADS editor, *American Libraries*, 50 E. Huron St., Chicago, IL 60611, 312-944-6780, ext. 326.

American Library Association, 50 E. Huron St., Chicago, IL 60611, 312-944-6780. A placement service is provided at each annual conference (June or July) and midwinter meeting (January). Handouts on interviewing, preparing a résumé, and other job-seeking information are available from the ALA Office for Library Personnel Resources.

American Library Association, Association of College and Research Libraries, Fast Job Listing Service, 50 E. Huron St., Chicago, IL 60611, 312-944-6780. Monthly circular listing job openings received in ACRL office during previous four weeks (supplements listings that will continue to appear in *C&RL News*). $5 to ACRL members requesting service (indicate ALA/ACRL membership number); $10 to nonmembers. Renewable each six months. Jobline recorded telephone message updated each Friday lists current job openings. Phone 312-944-6795 for listing. Employers who wish to have a listing for two weeks should send check for $25 (ACRL members) or $30 (non-ACRL members).

American Library Association (ALA) Black Caucus, c/o Dean Virginia Lacy Jones, Atlanta University School of Library Service, Atlanta, GA 30314. Although not a placement service, a data bank of black librarians is maintained, and employers do request information on possible candidates.

ALA Social Responsibilities Round Table, Rhode Island Affiliate, c/o Marcia Hershoff, 228 W. School St., Woonsocket, RI 02895. SRRT Jobline appears monthly in *Rhode Island Library Association Bulletin*, listing positions in southeast New England, including paraprofessional and part-time jobs. Job seekers desiring copy of most recent monthly Jobline send self-addressed, stamped envelope. Groups of envelopes may also be sent. To post a notice, contact Elizabeth Rogers, 150 Empire St., Providence, RI 02903.

American Society for Information Science, 1010 16 St. N.W., Suite 210, Washington, DC 20036, 202-659-3644. There is an active placement service operated at ASIS annual meetings (usually October) and midyear meetings (usually May) (locales change). All conference attendees (both ASIS members and nonmembers), as well as ASIS members who cannot attend the conference, are eligible to use the service to list or find jobs. Job listings are also accepted from employers who cannot attend the conference, interviews are arranged, and special seminars are given. During the rest of the year, current job openings are listed on the ASIS Jobline, 202-659-8132. Seventeen of the ASIS chapters have placement officers who further assist members in finding jobs.

The ASIS Jobline operates 24 hours a day, seven days a week. Brief descriptions—including contact information—of current job openings around the country are recorded every Friday noon. New jobs are listed first, starting with overseas or West Coast jobs and working back toward jobs in the Washington, DC, area. Thereafter, jobs still available from the preceding week's recordings are listed. The average tape length is seven minutes. The number to call is 202-659-8132.

American Theological Library Association, c/o Office of the Executive Secretary, Lutheran Theological Seminary, 7301 Germantown Ave., Philadelphia, PA 19119. Free to members; $5 filing fee for nonmembers for listing up to two years or until employment is secured. Application forms should be requested. Referrals are made throughout the year. Although not large in numbers, openings are representative of the size of the association.

Art Libraries Society/North American (ARLIS/NA), c/o Executive Secretary, 143 Bowling Green Place, Iowa City, IA 52240. Art librarian and slide curator jobs are listed in the newsletter (5 times a year).

Associated Information Managers, 316 Pennsylvania Ave. S.E., Suite 502, Washington, DC 20003, 202-544-1969. AIM Career Clearinghouse lists positions open on a biweekly basis in conjunction with the AIM Network. Position applicants send résumé and cover letter to AIM, which forwards materials to employers. Open to AIM members only. Employers may list positions free of charge.

Association for Educational Communication & Technology, Placement Service, 1126 16 St. N.W., Washington, DC 20036, 202-833-4180. Positions available are listed in the monthly *AECT Bulletin* by code number and state; responses to ads are forwarded by the association to the appropriate employer/employee. A placement center operates at annual conferences. Available also to nonmembers; request application.

Council of Library/Media Technical Assistants, c/o Richard Taylor, Editor, Wilbur Wright College, 3400 N. Austin Ave., Chicago, IL 60634. *COLT Newsletter* appears 11 times a year and will accept listings for library/media technical assistant positions. However, correspondence relating to jobs cannot be handled.

Information Exchange System for Minority Personnel (IESMP, Inc.), Box 668, Fort Valley, GA 31030. Nonprofit organization designed to recruit minority librarians for EEO/AA employers. *Informer*, quarterly newsletter. Write for membership categories, services, and fees.

Medical Library Association, 919 N. Michigan Ave., Suite 3208, Chicago, IL 60611, 312-266-2456. Monthly *MLA News* lists positions wanted and positions available in its "Employment Opportunities" column (up to 20 free lines for MLA members plus $2 per line over this, or $3 per line for nonmembers). MLA members may request advance mailings of "Employment Opportunities" at no charge for six months; this service is available to nonmembers for a prepaid fee of $25. Also offers placement service at annual conference each summer.

Music Library Association, Placement Director, Karen K. Miller, The Cleveland

GUIDE TO LIBRARY PLACEMENT SOURCES / 213

Institute of Music, 11021 East Boulevard, Cleveland, OH 44106. Registration fee of $7 per year (September through August). MLA members who register receive the *Job List*.

National Registry for Librarians, 40 W. Adams St., Chicago, IL 60603, 312-793-4904. Established as a professional placement service in 1965, the registry is a centralized nationwide clearinghouse for professional librarians and employers. There are no registration, referral, or placement fees for this service. Librarians seeking professional employment complete an application form. Employers also complete job order forms that describe their vacancies. Copies of all applications meeting the employer's selection criteria are forwarded to allow the employer to contact the applicant directly. The registry does not maintain a file of school credits or personal references, nor does it make any recommendations. The registry does not maintain or distribute vacancy lists.

Online, Inc., c/o John Edward Evans, I. D. Weeks Library, University of South Dakota, Vermillion, SD 57069, 605-677-5371. "Jobline" column in *Online* and *Database* lists position announcements in field of on-line searching. Jobline also distributes biweekly placement lists. Applicants must provide stamped, self-addressed no. 10 business-size envelopes. Several envelopes may be sent at one time to ensure continuing service. Due to deadlines, not all jobs appear in the journals, but all announcements are reported in the biweekly lists.

Reforma, National Association of Spanish-Speaking Librarians in the U.S., Editor, Luis Herrera, El Paso Public Library, 501 N. Oregon, El Paso, TX 79901. Quarterly newsletter lists and invites listings, especially those for bilingual and minority librarians. For listing of Spanish-speaking/Spanish-surnamed professionals, request "Quien es Quien: A Who's Who of Spanish-Heritage Librarians in the U. S." (1980) for $3 from Arizona Center for Educational Research and Development, College of Education, Rm. 311, University of Arizona, Tucson, AZ 85721. The *Amoxcalli* quarterly newsletter of the Reforma El Paso Chapter lists job openings also. Contact chapter at Box 2064, El Paso, TX 79951.

Society of American Archivists, 330 S. Wells, Suite 810, Chicago, IL 60606, 312-922-0140. The *SAA Newsletter* is sent (to members only) six times annually and lists jobs and applicants, as well as details of professional meetings and courses in archival administration.

Special Libraries Association, 235 Park Ave. S., New York, NY 10003, 212-477-9250. In addition to the Conference Employment Clearing House, a monthly listing of positions wanted and available, *Employment Opportunities*, is available free for six months to SLA members who request this in writing. Most SLA chapters also have employment chairpersons who act as referral persons for employers and job seekers. The official newsletter of the association, *SpeciaList*, carries classified advertising 12 times a year.

Theresa M. Burke Employment Agency, 25 W. 39 St., New York, NY 10018, 212-398-9250. A licensed, professional employment agency that has specialized for over 30 years in the recruitment of library and information personnel for academic, public, and special libraries. Staffed by employment counselors who have training and experience in both library service and personnel recruitment. Presently the majority of openings are in special libraries in the northeast and require subject backgrounds and/or specific kinds of experience. Fees are paid by the employer.

STATE LIBRARY AGENCIES

In addition to the joblines mentioned previously, some of the state library agencies issue lists of job openings within their areas. These include Indiana (on request);

214 / LIBRARY EDUCATION, PLACEMENT, AND SALARIES

Minnesota (*Position Openings in Minnesota and Adjoining States*, semi-mo., sent to public and academic libraries); Mississippi (job vacancy list, mo.); Ohio (*Library Opportunities in Ohio*, mo., sent to accredited library education programs and interested individuals upon request); Pennsylvania ("Positions Open"); Texas (*Texas Placement News*, bi-mo., free).

On occasion, when vacancy postings are available, state library newsletters or journals will list these, such as Alabama (*Cottonboll*, bi-mo.); California (CLASS newsletters); Indiana (*Focus on Indiana Libraries*); Louisiana (*Library Communique*, mo.); Massachusetts (*Massachusetts Position Vacancies*, mo., sent to all public libraries in-state and to interested individuals on a one-time basis); Missouri (*Show-Me Libraries*, mo.); Nebraska (*Overtones*, 13 times a year); New Hampshire (*Granite State Libraries*, bi-mo.); New Mexico (*Hitchhiker*, w., newsletter); Oklahoma (*ODL Source*, mo.); Utah (*Horsefeathers*, mo.); Virginia (*News*, mo.); and Wyoming (*Outrider*, mo.).

Many state library agencies will refer applicants informally when vacancies are known to exist, but do not have formal placement services. The following states primarily make referrals to public libraries only: Alabama, Connecticut, Georgia, Idaho, Louisiana, South Carolina (institutional also), Tennessee, and Vermont. Those who refer applicants to all types of libraries are Delaware, Florida, Maryland, Massachusetts, Mississippi, Missouri, Montana, Nebraska, Nevada (largely public and academic), New Hampshire, New Mexico, North Dakota, Ohio, Oklahoma, Rhode Island, South Dakota, Utah, West Virginia (public, academic, special), and Wyoming. The Missouri State Library offers a formal placement service, matching interests and qualifications of registered job applicants with positions available in Missouri libraries. Addresses of the state agencies are found in the *Bowker Annual* or *American Library Directory*.

STATE AND REGIONAL LIBRARY ASSOCIATIONS

State and regional library associations will often make referrals, run ads in association newsletters, or operate a placement service at annual conferences, in addition to the joblines sponsored by some groups. Referral of applicants when jobs are known is done by the following associations: Arkansas, Delaware (also for Delaware listings, call the Maryland, New Jersey, or Pennsylvania joblines), Hawaii, Louisiana, Michigan, Nevada, South Dakota, Tennessee, Texas, and Wisconsin. Although listings are infrequent, job vacancies are placed in the following association newsletters or journals when available: Alaska (*Newspoke*, 6 times a year; *Sourdough*, 4 times a year); Georgia (*Georgia Librarian*); Indiana (*Focus on Indiana Libraries*, 6 times a year); Iowa (*Catalyst*, 6 times a year); Kansas (*KLA Newsletter*, 3 times a year); Massachusetts (*Bay State Librarian*, 3 times a year; *Bay State Letter*, 10 times a year); Minnesota (*MLA Newsletter*, 10 times a year); Mountain Plains (*MPLA Newsletter*, bi-mo., lists vacancies and position-wanted ads for individual and institutional members or area library school students); Nevada (*Highroller*, 6 times a year); New Hampshire (*NHLA Newsletter*, 6 times a year; *Granite State Libraries*); New Jersey (*New Jersey Libraries*, 8 times a year); New Mexico (shares notices via state library's *Hitchhiker*, w.); New York (*NYLA Bulletin*, 10 times a year); Oklahoma (*The Oklahoma Librarian; President's Newsletter*); Pennsylvania (*PLA Bulletin*, mo.); Rhode Island (*Bulletin*, mo.); Vermont (*VLA News*, Box 803, Burlington, VT 05402, 10 times a year); Virginia (*Virginia Librarian*, q.); West Virginia (*West Virginia Libraries*); and Wyoming (*Roundup*, q.). The Southeastern Librarian lists jobs in that geographical area.

At their annual conference the following associations have indicated some type of placement service, although it may only consist of bulletin board postings: Alabama,

Indiana, Kansas, Louisiana, Maryland, Mountain Plains, New Jersey, New York, Texas, and Vermont.

The following associations have indicated they have no placement service at this time: Minnesota, Mississippi, Montana, New Mexico, North Dakota, Oklahoma, Pacific Northwest, Tennessee, and Wyoming. State and regional association addresses are found in the *Bowker Annual*.

LIBRARY EDUCATION PROGRAMS

Library education programs offer some type of service for their current students as well as alumni. Of the ALA-accredited programs, the following handle placement activities through the library school: British Columbia, Columbia, Dalhousie, Denver, Drexel, Emory, Geneseo, Hawaii, Illinois, Long Island, Louisiana, Michigan, Minnesota, Missouri, Pittsburgh, Pratt, Queens, Texas-Austin, Toronto, Western Ontario, and Wisconsin-Madison.

The central university placement center handles activities for the following schools: Alabama A&M, Brigham Young, Case Western, North Carolina, Peabody/Vanderbilt, Southern California, South Florida, and UCLA. However, in most cases, faculty in the library school will still do informal counseling regarding job seeking.

In some schools, the placement services are handled in a cooperative manner; in most cases the university placement center sends out credentials while the library school posts or compiles the job listings. Schools utilizing both sources include Alabama, Arizona, Ball State, Buffalo, Catholic, Chicago, Clarion State, Denver, Emporia, Florida State, Geneseo, Indiana, Iowa, Kent, Maryland, North Carolina Central, North Texas, Northern Illinois, Oklahoma, Peabody/Vanderbilt, Pratt, Queens, Rhode Island, San Jose, Simmons, South Carolina, South Florida, Southern Connecticut, Southern Mississippi, Syracuse, Tennessee, Texas Woman's, Washington, Western Michigan, and Wisconsin-Milwaukee.

In sending out placement credentials, schools vary as to whether they distribute these free, charge a general registration fee, or request a fee for each file or credentials sent out.

Those schools that have indicated that they post job vacancy notices for review but do not issue printed lists are Alabama, Alabama A&M, Ball State, British Columbia, Catholic, Chicago, Emory, Emporia, Florida State, Hawaii, Kent, Louisiana, Maryland, North Carolina Central, Northern Illinois, Peabody/Vanderbilt, Queens, San Jose, Simmons, South Carolina, South Florida, Southern California, Southern Mississippi, Syracuse, Tennessee, Texas Woman's, Toronto, UCLA, Washington, Western Michigan, and Western Ontario. (Notices of positions open reported to schools are sent out to graduates on the school's placement mailing list as they are received.)

In addition to job vacancy postings, some schools issue a printed listing of positions open that is distributed primarily to students and alumni and only occasionally available to others. The following schools issue listings free to students and alumni *only* unless indicated otherwise: Arizona (every two weeks, $6 per year for alumni, $12 per year for nonalumni); Brigham Young; Buffalo (mo. newsletter; service to all area professionals upon request for academic year); California; California-Berkeley (alumni receive 10 per year out-of-state listings if registered; $25 fee for service, also a jobline, call 415-642-1716 to list positions); Case Western (alumni $10 for six lists); Clarion State (free to students and alumni); Columbia (alumni six issues, $2); Dalhousie ($5 per year for students, alumni, and others); Denver (alumni $8 per year); Drexel (free in office; by mail to students and alumni who supply self-addressed, stamped envelopes—12 for six months);

Geneseo (free in office; by mail only to students and alumni who send self-addressed, stamped envelopes); Illinois (free in office; by mail to anyone who sends no. 10 self-addressed, stamped envelopes); Indiana (others may send self-addressed, stamped envelopes); Iowa (students and alumni as part of $10 registration fee); Long Island (no charge); Michigan (free for one year following graduation, all other graduates, $5 per year for 12 issues); Minnesota (if 28¢ self-addressed envelopes are supplied); Missouri (Library Vacancy Roster, tri-w. printout, 50¢ per issue, with minimum of 5 issues, to anyone); North Carolina (subscription fee of $10 per year); North Texas State ($5 for six months, students and alumni); Peabody/Vanderbilt (students and alumni if registered for fee); Pittsburgh (others for $3 for six months); Pratt (alumni, weekly during spring, fall, and summer sessions; others, renew every three months); Southern Connecticut; Syracuse (listings sent out by university service twice a month, 8 months per year, 50¢ per issue. Available to anyone requesting); Texas–Austin; Western Michigan ($7.50 for 26 weeks to anyone, issued by University Placement Services); Wisconsin–Madison (subscription $5 per year for 12 issues, to anyone); Wisconsin–Milwaukee (monthly to SLS graduates registering with Department of Placement and Career Development).

As the job market has tightened, a number of schools are providing job hunting seminars and short courses or more actively trying to help graduates obtain positions. Most schools will offer at least an annual or semiannual discussion on placement, often with outside speakers representing different types of libraries or recent graduates relating experiences. Some additional programs offered by schools include Ball State (job hunting, résumé writing, videotaped job interview role-playing sessions); Brigham Young (students write résumé that is critiqued in basic administration class); British Columbia ("Employment Week" in spring term with employers invited to interview); Buffalo (assists laid-off local employees; sends list of graduates to major libraries in the United States; operates SDI service; résumé seminar and follow-up critique, strategy sessions for conference job seeking; "Put a Buffalo in Your Library" buttons); California–Berkeley (career awareness workshops on résumés, interview, and job search); Columbia (alumni/ student career day; sessions on résumé writing, interviewing, job counseling during the spring; edge-notched card service); Dalhousie (sessions on job searching, etc., with critiquing of résumés); Denver (résumé writing in administration course, interview workshop, profile of students so job listings can be sent matching interests, Career Day for students/alumni, career awareness workshop with university placement personnel, individual counseling, postings); Drexel (job search workshops: résumés, cover letters, interviewing; individual job counseling by appointment available to students and alumni); Emory (job strategy meeting each term, résumé assistance and job counseling); Hawaii (workshop each semester, computer-based placement file); Illinois (résumé writing, interview role playing in library administration class, counseling/critiquing for individuals in library school placement office, computer-based placement profiles for students and alumni, job search workshops by university-wide placement service); Indiana (convocation on job search, seminar on résumé writing, interview role playing in course work, critique of individual résumés and letters); Iowa (job strategy and résumé writing session each term, individual counseling); Kent (annual placement workshops, résumé writing, interviewing, strategies); Michigan (seminar sessions on job hunting, résumé writing, interviewing and search strategies); and Minnesota (résumé writing, individual counseling, interview techniques). The following also offer additional programs: North Carolina (workshop on résumé preparation, job seeking strategy, interview techniques; students may do mock interview on videotape with critique); North Carolina Central (seminars, counseling); Peabody/Vanderbilt (regular seminars on library marketplace, résumé preparation, interviews, etc.); Pittsburgh (individual counseling, preconference strategy sessions, placement colloquium sessions, day-long workshops covering search strategy, résumés, and other means of access, interview techniques); Pratt (job clinics throughout the year, book of résumés sent to employers); Rhode Island (résumés critiqued in library administration course, jobs seminar annually); Simmons (series of four programs each semester); South Carolina (seminars on job search and résumé writing offered as part of curriculum); South Florida (part-time administrative assistant recruits minority students and identified placement possibilities); Southern Connecticut (ETP Annual Job Workshop); Southern Mississippi (placement seminar); Syracuse (job strategy workshops, career possibilities colloquium series); Toronto (publishes annual placement and salary survey in Canadian Library Association's *Feliciter;* conducts periodic career-awareness workshops involving outside speakers; job counseling); UCLA (compiles "Job Hunting Handbook"); Washington (job search strategy and interviewing discussions, postings); Western Ontario (job search strategy workshops); Wisconsin-Madison (job finding programs, résumé writing); Wisconsin-Milwaukee (Job Fair with interview role playing and résumé writing).

Employers will often list jobs with schools only in their particular geographical area; some library schools will give information to nonalumni regarding their specific locales, but are *not* staffed to handle mail requests and advice is usually given in person. Schools that have indicated they will allow librarians in their areas to view listings are Alabama, Alabama A&M, Arizona, Ball State, Brigham Young, British Columbia, Buffalo, Case Western, Catholic, Chicago, Dalhousie, Denver, Drexel, Emory, Emporia, Florida State, Geneseo, Illinois, Indiana, Iowa, Kent, Louisiana, North Texas, Peabody/Vanderbilt, Pittsburgh, Pratt, Queens, Rhode Island, San Jose, South Carolina, Southern California, Southern Connecticut, Southern Mississippi, Syracuse, Tennessee, Texas-Austin, Texas Woman's, Toronto, UCLA, Washington, Western Michigan, Western Ontario, Wisconsin-Madison, and Wisconsin-Milwaukee.

A list of accredited program addresses can be requested from ALA or found in the *Bowker Annual.* Individuals interested in placement services of other library education programs should contact the schools directly.

FEDERAL LIBRARY JOBS

The first step in obtaining employment in a federal library is to become listed on the Librarian's Register, which is a subset of files maintained by the U.S. Office of Personnel Management (OPM) in order to match federal job applicants with federal job vacancies (Washington Area Office [SSS], Box 52, Washington, DC 20044). Applicants should obtain a Qualifications Information Statement for Professional Librarian Positions (QI-1410), a Federal Employment Application Instructions and Forms Pamphlet (OPM form 1282), and an Occupational Supplement for Professional Librarian Positions (OPM form 1203-B) from any Federal Job Information Center. (Federal Job Information Centers are located in many cities across the country. They are listed under "U.S. Government" in major metropolitan area telephone directories. A *Federal Job Information Centers Directory* is available from OPM.)

One is considered for all grades for which one is qualified and indicates one will accept. As vacancies occur, applications will be evaluated in relation to an agency's specific requirements, and the best qualified candidates are referred for consideration. Eligibility will remain in effect for one year; updated information must be submitted to remain eligible after this time.

Applications are accepted only when the register is "open." The frequency with which, and the length of time, the register is open depends on the size of the inventory. The inventory is judged to be too low when a significant proportion of applicants who are qualified for positions decline them. This so-called declination rate is reversed by opening the register, thereby expanding the applicant pool.

In recent years the register has been opened once each year. It was open June 2-30 in 1980. It generally remains open approximately two weeks, with advance notice going to all local Federal Job Information Centers. The centers have current information on vacancies in the "Competition Notice for Professional Librarian Positions" (CN-1410), for Grades GS-7 through GS-12 and "Senior Level Positions, Announcement 408," for Grades GS-13 through GS-15.

Applicants who are most likely to be successful are those with training and experience in the fields of medical librarianship, law librarianship, engineering, the sciences, and audiovisual materials. Expertise in computerized library systems is extremely valuable. Over half the vacancies occur in the Washington area. Most librarian positions are in three agencies—Army, Navy, and Veterans Administration.

The examiner does not select those to be hired, but does play the crucial role in weighing the relative experience of those on the register. When selecting the most qualified candidates, whose forms are then forwarded to the hiring agency, the examiner must consider many factors simultaneously: work experience, education (formal and informal), geographical preference, etc. Any information that should be considered must be on these forms and must not be left for someone to discover during the interview stage. Chances are that the applicant may never reach the interview stage if pertinent experience or education is not explained at the outset.

In addition to filing the appropriate forms, applicants also can attempt to make personal contact directly with federal agencies in which they are interested. The *Federal Times* and the Sunday *Washington Post* sometimes list federal library openings. In addition, there are some "excepted" agencies that are not required to hire through the usual OPM channels. While these agencies may require the standard forms, they maintain their own employee selection policies and procedures. Government establishments with positions outside the competitive civil service include Energy Research and Development Administration; Board of Governors of the Federal Reserve System; Central Intelligence Agency; Department of Medicine and Surgery; Federal Bureau of Investigation; Foreign Service of the United States; National Science Foundation; National Security Agency; Central Examining Office; Tennessee Valley Authority; U.S. Nuclear Regulatory Commission; U.S. Postal Service; Judicial Branch of the Government; Legislative Branch of the Government; U.S. Mission to the United Nations; World Bank and IFC; International Monetary Fund; Organization of American States; Pan American Health Organization; and United Nations Secretariat.

In addition, the Library of Congress operates its own independent merit selection system. Thus, applicants for positions at the library should submit an SF-171, Personal Qualifcations Statement, to the Recruitment and Placement Officer, Library of Congress, 10 First St. S.E., G-114, Washington, DC 20540. Persons who apply for specific vacancies by Posting Number enhance their prospects for consideration.

General information on applying for federal jobs can be found in the *Occupational Outlook Quarterly*, Winter 1977 pp. 2-9 ("Working for U.S."); *The Uncle Sam Connection* by James E. Hawkins (Follett, 1978, 168 pp., $4.95); *How to Get a Federal Job and Advance*, 4th ed., by David Waelde (Fedhelp Publications, Capitol Hill, Box 9004, Dept. GOF, Washington, DC 20003); and *The Washington Job-Hunter*, Box 57339, Washington, DC 20037 (6 issues for $15, 12 issues for $27).

ADDITIONAL GENERAL AND SPECIALIZED JOB SOURCES

School Libraries. School librarians often find that the channels for locating positions in education are of more value than the usual library ones, e.g., contacting county or city school superintendent offices. The National Center for Information on Careers in Education is no longer in operation. A list of commercial teacher agencies may be obtained from the National Association of Teachers Agencies, c/o Elwood Q. Taylor, 1825 K St. N.W., Suite 706, Washington, DC 20006.

Affirmative Action Register, 8356 Olive Blvd., St. Louis, MO 63132. The goal is to "provide female, minority and handicapped candidates with an opportunity to learn of professional and managerial positions throughout the nation and to assist employers in implementing their Affirmative Action Programs." Free distribution of monthly bulletin is made to leading businesses, industrial and academic institutions, and over 4,000 agencies that recruit qualified minorities and women, as well as to all known female, minority, and handicapped professional organizations, placement offices, newspapers, magazines, rehabilitation facilities, and over 8,000 federal, state, and local governmental employment units. Individual mail subscriptions are available for $15 per year. Librarian listings are in most every issue. Sent free to libraries on request.

American Association of Junior Colleges Career Staffing Center, 621 Duke St., Box 298, Alexandria, VA 22314, 703-548-8020. Persons interested in junior or community college positions complete a registration form and submit with a $30 yearly fee. Condensed personnel information is sent to deans who make direct contact with individuals in whom they are interested; in addition, vacancy listings are distributed to registrants in the spring and fall.

Catalyst, 14 E. 60 St., New York, NY 10022. A national nonprofit organization dedicated to expanding career opportunities for women, through publications, local resource center listings, and a library that serves as a clearinghouse for all information concerning women and work, careers, and career education.

The Chronicle of Higher Education (published weekly during the academic year, 1333 New Hampshire Ave. N.W., Washington, DC 20036) is receiving more classified ads for library openings than previously, although many are at the administrative level; *Academe* (bulletin of the American Association of University Professors, One DuPont Circle, Washington, DC 20036) also lists librarian jobs at times, as well as *Change: The Magazine of Learning* (NBW Tower, New Rochelle, NY 10801; published by Heldref Publications, the publishing division of the nonprofit Helen Dwight Reid Educational Foundation).

Educational Information Service, Box 662, Newton Lower Falls, MA 02162. Instant Alert service for $24 sends individual 12 notices of openings on same day EIS hears of job. Publishes lists of faculty and administrative education openings (library jobs only a small portion, however). Send for lists of other services and fees.

Federal Research Service, Box 1059, Vienna, VA 22180, 703-281-0200. Published every other Wednesday, the *FCO Report* is a compilation of current vacancies in federal government agencies. Subscription rates are $21 for six biweekly reports; send for information on rates for longer periods. Since this includes all types of positions in the government, it is likely that only a small percentage are librarian vacancies.

OVERSEAS

Opportunities for employment in foreign countries are limited and immigration policies of individual countries should be investigated. Employment for Americans is virtually limited to U.S. government libraries, libraries of U.S. firms doing worldwide business, and American schools abroad. Library journals from other countries will sometimes list vacancy notices (e.g., *Quidunc* [Australia], *British Columbia Library Association Reporter, Canadian Library Journal, Feliciter, Library Association Record, Times Literary Supplement, Ontario Library Review*, and *Times Higher Education Supplement*). Some persons have obtained jobs by contacting foreign publishers or vendors directly. Non-U.S. government jobs usually call for foreign language fluency.

Although they do not specifically discuss librarian positions, several general brochures may be of help in providing further addresses: "American Students and Teachers Abroad: Sources of Information about Overseas Study, Teaching, Work, Travel" and "Federal Jobs Overseas" from Superintendent of Documents, U.S. Government Printing Office, Washington, DC 20402, for $1 and 30¢ respectively.

Action, P305, Washington, DC 20525. An umbrella agency that includes the Peace Corps and Vista. Will sometimes need librarians in developing nations and host communities in the United States. For further information, call toll-free 800-424-8580 and ask for Recruitment. Recruiting offices in many large cities.

Council for International Exchange of Scholars, Suite 300, 11 DuPont Circle, Washington, DC 20036, 202-833-4950. Administers U.S. government Fulbright awards for university lecturing and advanced research abroad; usually six to eight awards per year are made to specialists in library science. Open to U.S. citizens with university or college teaching experience. Request registration forms to receive spring announcement for academic year to start 12 to 18 months later.

Department of Defense, c/o Director, Dept. of Defense Dependent Schools, OAS (M&RA), Rm. 152, Hoffman I, 2461 Eisenhower Ave., Alexandria, VA 22331. Overall management and operational responsibilities for the education of dependents of active duty military personnel and DOD civilians who are stationed overseas, including recruitment of teaching personnel, are assigned to this agency. For application brochures, write to above address specifying "Attention: Recruitment."

Educational Information Service, Box 662, Newton Lower Falls, MA 02162. Instant Alert service for $24 will send individual 12 notices of overseas openings on same day EIS learns of opening (library jobs only a small portion, however). Send for free details of other services.

Home Country Employment Registry, National Association for Foreign Student Affairs, 1860 19 St. N.W., Washington, DC 20009. Services are offered to U.S.-educated foreign students to assist them in locating employment in their home countries following completion of their studies.

International Association of School Librarianship, c/o School of Librarianship, Western Michigan University, Kalamazoo, MI 49008. Informal contacts might be established through this group.

International School Services, Box 5910, Princeton, NJ 08540. Private, nonprofit organization established to provide educational services for American schools overseas, other than Department of Defense schools. These are American elementary and secondary schools enrolling children of business and diplomatic families living away from their homeland. ISS seeks to register men and women interested in working abroad in education who meet basic professional standards of training and experience. Specialists, guidance counselors, department heads, librarians, supervisors, and administrators normally will need one or more advanced degrees in the appropriate field as well as professional experience commensurate with positions sought.

U.S. International Communication Agency (formerly USIA) will occasionally seek librarians with MLS, four years' experience for regional library consultant positions. Candidates must have proven administrative ability, skills to coordinate the overseas

USICA library program with other information functions of USICA in various cities worldwide. Relevant experience might include cooperative library program development, community outreach, public affairs, project management, personnel training. USICA maintains more than 139 libraries in over 82 countries, with 1 million books and 660 local library staff worldwide. Libraries provide reference service and material about the United States for foreign audiences. Five-year U.S. citizenship is required; overseas allowances and differentials where applicable, vacation leave, term life insurance, medical and retirement programs. Send standard U.S. Government Form 171 to Employment Branch, ICA, Washington, DC 20547. All types of jobs within ICA are announced through a recording (202-724-9864 or 9865). However, chances of librarian positions being announced are slim.

Overseas—Special Programs

ALA Black Caucus has a librarian exchange program with Africa. Contact E. J. Josey, New York State Education Department, Cultural Education Center, Rm. 10C47, Empire State Plaza, Albany, NY 12230.

International Exchanges. Most exchanges are handled by direct negotiation between interested parties. A few libraries, such as the Chicago Public Library, have established exchange programs for their own staff. In order to facilitate exchange arrangements, the *IFLA Journal* (issued February, May, August, and November) provides a listing of persons wishing to exchange positions *outside* their own country. All listings must include the following information: full name, address, present position, qualifications (with year of obtaining), language, abilities, preferred country/city/library and type of position. Send to IFLA Secretariat, Netherlands Congress Building, Box 82128, 2508 EC, The Hague, Netherlands.

USING INFORMATION SKILLS IN NONLIBRARY SETTINGS

A great deal of interest has been shown in "alternative careers" or in using information skills in a variety of ways in nonlibrary settings. These jobs are not usually found through the regular library placement sources, although many library schools are trying to generate such listings for their students and alumni. Job listings that do exist may not call specifically for "librarians" by that title, so that ingenuity may be needed to search out jobs where information management skills are needed. Some librarians are working on a free-lance basis by offering services to businesses, alternative schools, community agencies, legislators, etc.; these opportunities are usually not found in advertisements but created by developing contacts and publicity over a period of time. A number of information-brokering business firms have developed from individual free-lance experiences. Small companies or other organizations often need one-time service for organizing files or collections, bibliographic research for special projects, indexing or abstracting, compilation of directories, and consulting services. Bibliographic networks and on-line data base companies are using librarians as information managers, trainers, researchers, systems and database analysts, on-line services managers, etc. Jobs in this area are sometimes found in library network newsletters or other data processing journals. Classifieds in *Publishers Weekly* may lead to information-related positions.

Librarians can be found working in law firms as litigation case supervisors (organizing and analyzing records needed for specific legal cases); with publishers as sales representatives, marketing directors, editors, and computer services experts; with community agencies as adult education coordinators, volunteer administrators, grants writers, etc.

Information on existing information services or methods for using information skills in nonlibrary settings can be found in *Wilson Library Bulletin* (49): 440–445, February 1975; *Special Libraries* (67): 243–250, May/June 1976; *ASIS Bulletin* (2): 10–20, February 1976; *RQ* (18): 177–179, Winter 1978; *New York Times*, December 12, 1979 "Careers" section; *Show-Me Libraries* (31): 5–8, May 1980; and *Savvy*, January 1981, pp. 20–23. The *Canadian Library Journal* (34), no. 2, April 1977, has an entire issue on alternative librarianship. Syracuse University School of Information Studies, 113 Euclid Ave., Syracuse, NY 13210, has available *Proceedings of the Information Broker/Free-Lance Librarian Workshop*, April 1976 for $5, and *Alternative Careers in Information/Library Services: Summary of Proceedings of a Workshop*, July 1977, for $5.50. The *Directory of Fee-Based Information Services 1980-1981* lists information brokers, freelance librarians, independent information specialists, and institutions that provide services for a fee. Individuals do not need to pay to have listings; directory is available for $6.95 prepaid from Information Alternative, Box 657, Woodstock, NY 12498. It is supplemented by *The Journal of Fee-Based Information Services* (bi-mo.; $11 one-year subscription to institutions, $9 to others). Issues include new listings, changes of address, announcements, feature articles, and an exchange column.

What Else You Can Do with a Library Degree, edited by Betty-Carol Sellen, is published by Neal-Schuman Publishers and Gaylord Brothers, Inc. (Box 4901, Syracuse, NY 13221) for $14.95 plus 25¢ postage. Other publications include *Fee-Based Information Services: A Study of a Growing Industry* by Richard W. Boss and Lorig Marinjian (New York, Bowker, 1980, $20) and *Information Brokering: A State-of-the-Art Report* by Gary M. Kaplan (Emerald Valley Publishing Co., 2715 Terrace View Dr., Eugene, OR 97405. Write for current list of other titles in a series The Business of Information). Directories such as *Information Sources 1980-81: The Membership Directory of the Information Industry Association, Library Resources Market Place 1980,* and *Information Industry Market Place 1981* might provide leads of possible organizations in which information skills can be applied.

"A National Profile of Information Professionals" by Donald W. King et al. (*Bulletin of the American Society for Information Science* (6): 18–22, August 1980) gives the results of a 1980 study funded by the National Science Foundation and carried out by the University of Pittsburgh School of Library and Information Science and King Research, Inc. *Information Professionals in the United States: Their Function and Distribution* will be based on the study and published in 1981 by Marcel Dekker.

JOB HUNTING IN GENERAL

Wherever information needs to be organized and presented to patrons in an effective, efficient, and service-oriented fashion, the skills of professional librarians can be applied, whether or not they are in traditional library settings. However, it will take considerable investment of time, energy, imagination, and money on the part of an individual before a satisfying position is created or obtained, in a conventional library or another type of information service. Usually, no one method or source of job hunting can be used alone. Public and school library certification requirements often vary from state to state; contact the state library agency for such information in a particular state. Certification requirements are summarized in *Certification of Public Libraries in the U.S.*, 3rd. ed., 1979, from the ALA Library Administration and Management Association ($3). A summary of school library/media certification requirements by state is found in *School Library Journal* (24): 38–50, April 1978 or *Requirements for Certification 1980-81*, 45th ed., by Elizabeth H. Woellner (University of Chicago Press, 1980). Civil service requirements whether on a local, county, or state level often add another layer of procedures to the job search. Some civil service jurisdictions require written and/or oral examinations; others assign a ranking based on a review of credentials. Jobs are usually filled from the top candidates on a qualified list of applicants. Since the exams are held only at certain time periods and a variety of jobs can be filled from a single list of applicants (e.g., all Librarian I positions regardless of type of function), it is important to check whether a library in which one is interested falls under civil service procedures.

If one wishes a position in a specific subject area or in a particular geographical location, remember those reference skills to ferret information from directories and other tools regarding local industries, schools, subject collections, etc. Working as a substitute librarian or in temporary positions while looking for a regular job can provide valuable contacts and experience. Part-time jobs are not always advertised, but often found by canvassing local libraries and leaving applications. Some students have pooled resources to hire a clipping service for a specific time period in order to get classified librarian ads for a particular geographical area.

For information on other job hunting and personnel matters, please request a checklist of personnel materials available from the ALA Office for Library Personnel Resources, 50 E. Huron St., Chicago, IL 60611.

RECENT LIBRARY PERSONNEL SURVEYS

Margaret Myers

Director, American Library Association
Office for Library Personnel Resources

Library personnel statistics are often collected for specific types of libraries or positions, for particular geographical areas, or at different time periods and by a variety of organizations or associations. Therefore, administrators, staff members, and others who seek comparative data for setting compensation structures or negotiating salaries, establishing affirmative action goals, determining staffing patterns, or other purposes often have difficulty in knowing where to turn for current statistical data on library personnel. This article attempts to summarize selected sources of information, particularly for salary surveys and affirmative action data. The author welcomes information on additional resources not covered.

SALARY INFORMATION

In using salary data for comparative purposes, it is important to ascertain when the information was collected, what constituted the sample, and whether the positions surveyed match those with which one wishes to make comparisons. Geographic location, size of organization, job scope, or type of library will often influence the pay level of a particular job.

Librarians are beginning to document discrepancies in pay in comparison with other professions having similar requirements, such as level of education, experience, and responsibilities. Occupations and professions that have a high proportion of female

Note: For an overview of other 1980 research related to libraries and librarianship, see the article by Mary Jo Lynch in the Library Research and Statistics section of Part 4—*Ed.*

workers have historically had substantially lower salaries than those fields that are predominantly male. Because librarianship is a predominantly female profession, library workers have often suffered depressed wages. Some librarians have achieved upgrading of salaries using the concept of "equal pay for work of equal value" or "comparable wages for comparable work." The American Library Association (ALA) Committee on the Status of Women in Librarianship and the ALA Office for Library Personnel Resources (OLPR) are currently developing an information/resource kit for use by librarians who are attempting to achieve pay equity.

ACADEMIC LIBRARY SURVEYS

The only regularly updated salary data for academic libraries is compiled from the annual survey of the Association of Research Libraries (ARL). This provides information on the average, median, and beginning professional salaries in ARL libraries. In addition, tables detail the numbers of staff and average salaries for 18 positions in ARL libraries, from directors to professionals with under five years of experience. Tables also display the distribution of these positions by sex, minority group, geographical location (see Table 1), and size and type of institution. The latest *ARL Annual Salary 1979-80*, published in December 1980, is available from the Association of Research Libraries, 1527 New Hampshire Ave. N.W., Washington, DC 20036 for $3 (ARL members) or $5 (nonmembers).

Occasional surveys of academic libraries by region have been conducted by the big ten universities, *Academe* (December 1978), and the Association of College and Research Libraries (1976). Several state associations (e.g., Ohio, Louisiana) also publish recommended guidelines on occasion.

In 1978 and 1979, the College and University Personnel Association (11 Dupont-Circle, Suite 1201, Washington, DC 20036) conducted a survey, "Women and Minorities in Administration of Higher Education Institutions," which will be published in spring 1981 and should include some salary data for head librarians.

Salary data for selected positions (director, branch/department head, beginning professionals) also will be available in spring 1981 in the ALA Office for Library Personnel Resources report *Racial, Ethnic, and Sexual Composition of Library Staff in Academic and Public Libraries*.

PUBLIC LIBRARY SURVEYS

Statistics of Public Libraries in the U.S. and Canada Serving 100,000 Population or More is a biennial survey conducted since 1958 by the Fort Wayne and Allen County (Indiana) Public Library. It gives salary information for director, assistant director, and beginning professional positions in large public libraries. The next survey will be undertaken in early 1981.

Since 1972, the *Library Journal* has published an analysis of the Fort Wayne information to show relationships between the sex of the director, geographic area, population served, per capita support, and beginning librarian salaries (see "Sex, Salaries, & Library Support—1979," by Kathleen M. Heim and Carolyn Kacena, *Library Journal* 105 [January 1, 1980]: 17-22, or 1980 *Bowker Annual*, pp. 334-344.

A compilation of salary data for public libraries, systems, and state agencies in West-North-Central States (North Dakota, South Dakota, Nebraska, Kansas, Minnesota, Iowa, Missouri) has been conducted by Carl Sandstedt, Director, St. Charles City-County Library (425 Spencer Rd., Box 529, St. Peters, MO 63376; send a self-addressed stamped envelope if requesting survey results). The "1981 Salary Survey"

TABLE 1 AVERAGE SALARIES OF ARL UNIVERSITY LIBRARIANS BY REGION

Position	Northeast New England (8)*	Northeast Middle Atlantic (14)	North Central East N. Central† (15)	North Central West N. Central (7)	South East S. Central (4)	South West S. Central (8)	South South Atlantic (14)	West Mountain (7)	West Pacific (12)	Canada‡ (10)
Director	$47,315	$50,626	$50,216	$49,914	$42,666	$43,662	$45,823	$45,275	$50,318	$44,990
Associate director	33,431	38,290	35,289	34,316	27,901	31,235	37,347	34,008	43,003	36,571
Assistant director	29,052	30,751	32,217	29,328	24,894	27,841	28,430	27,995	35,977	33,144
Medical law head	40,570	42,747	36,314	37,021	30,012	31,285	39,601	37,350	41,373	29,856
Branch head	24,836	23,586	23,363	20,138	19,823	18,669	21,908	21,348	25,997	25,398
Subject specialist	21,383	20,967	20,110	20,549	16,211	17,417	19,013	20,753	25,453	20,215
Functional specialist	20,441	22,039	19,975	23,989	16,701	20,012	19,350	22,149	23,829	22,606
Dept. head										
Reference	23,276	23,464	20,981	21,523	21,678	22,282	24,009	22,697	27,280	25,735
Cataloging	24,024	22,539	24,185	20,252	20,035	24,057	23,525	24,075	27,868	25,756
Serials	21,047	21,498	21,140	19,697	19,059	20,322	21,934	21,922	27,151	20,280
Documents/maps	24,136	20,225	21,252	19,731	15,705	18,907	19,335	20,671	27,627	22,987
Circulation	18,692	21,015	19,560	22,133	17,186	19,738	21,026	20,457	24,625	23,656
Special collection	32,252	25,311	22,430	23,665	22,240	21,323	24,783	23,904	29,837	25,002
Other	22,653	22,047	22,789	20,431	19,255	21,197	22,034	20,731	27,102	23,886
Other										
Over 15 yrs. exper.	19,669	21,180	21,172	20,042	17,575	19,108	19,637	21,040	25,938	23,399
10–15 yrs. exper.	19,057	19,517	19,105	19,271	18,030	19,060	18,930	19,110	22,689	20,932
5–10 yrs. exper.	17,093	17,298	17,232	16,781	15,632	17,052	17,585	17,451	19,480	19,095
Under 5 yrs. exper.	14,815	14,837	14,561	14,524	13,341	14,303	14,769	15,186	17,305	16,363

*The number in parentheses below each of the column heads indicates the number of ARL libraries included.
†Excludes Chicago.
‡Canadian salaries expressed in U.S. dollars.
Source: *ARL Annual Salary Survey 1979–1980* (Washington, DC: Association of Research Libraries, December 1980), p. 28.

TABLE 2 AVERAGE SALARIES FOR
PUBLIC LIBRARIES WITH BUDGETS
OVER $2,200,000—WEST-NORTH-
CENTRAL STATES, 1981

Position	Salary
Director	$44,065
Assistant director	$34,537
Top scale department head	$29,452
Starting MLS	$14,205
Starting sub-professional	$10,507
Starting clerical	$ 7,872
Hourly shelver	$ 3.15

Source: Preliminary data, *1981 Salary Survey: West-North-Central States* (St. Peters, MO: St. Charles City-County Library, 1981).
Note: The full survey gives data for other sizes of libraries as well as low and high ranges of salary data.

gives data for directors, assistant directors, department heads, starting MLS, and several support positions by size of library. (See Table 2.)

The Memphis Public Library compiles an annual salary survey for public libraries in the southeastern and southwestern states, which gives information for a variety of positions in individual libraries as well as low and high ranges and the average and median salaries by size of institution. Individual copies of the 1981 survey can be obtained by sending a self-addressed, stamped envelope to Robert Croneberger, Memphis-Shelby County Public Library & Information Center, 1850 Peabody St., Memphis, TN 38104.

Some state library associations or agencies collect salary data for their individual states or provide recommended guidelines based on studying existing salaries. Some examples are "Salary and Fringe Benefit Survey of Wisconsin Public Libraries, 1980" (Wisconsin Association of Public Libraries); "New Jersey Library Association 1981 Recommended Minimum Salaries for Public Libraries" (*New Jersey Libraries* 18 [November 1980]): 3–6); "Recommended Job Classifications and Salary Goals for Ohio, 1979–80" (Ohio Library Association); "Salary Standards for South Carolina Public Libraries" (South Carolina Library Association, October 1979); "Louisiana Library Association Public Library Section Suggested Position and Pay Plan 1979–80" (May 1980); and "Public Library Personnel Report: Data for Massachusetts FY 1979" (Boston: Massachusetts Board of Library Commissioners, October 1979). The Rhode Island Library Association has conducted a salary survey of public libraries that will be published in early 1981.

The ALA OLPR report mentioned previously will also contain salary data for selected positions in public libraries.

SCHOOL LIBRARY SURVEYS

The Educational Research Service (ERS) 1800 N. Kent St., Arlington, VA 22209) conducts an annual "National Survey of Salaries and Wages in Public Schools," which includes some salary data for school librarians. The three volumes include *Salaries Paid Professional Personnel in Public Schools, Scheduled Salaries for Profes-*

sional *Personnel in Public Schools* and *Wages and Salaries Paid Support Personnel in Public Schools*. The 1980-1981 survey to be published in March 1981 by ERS will be available for $24 for each volume. Data are given for geographical areas and individual school systems, as well as total number of persons enrolled and per pupil expenditure. In 1979-1980, the mean salaries paid public school librarians was $16,764.

SPECIAL LIBRARY SURVEYS

Since 1967, the Special Libraries Association has conducted a salary survey every three years, which has been reported in *Special Libraries*. Figures are shown by type of institution, number of persons supervised, education level, subject field, years of experience, geographical area, and so forth. The latest triennial survey was reported in *Special Libraries* 70 (December 1979): 559-589. Annual updates using a sample of 25 percent of the membership are conducted between the larger surveys (see *Special Libraries* 71 [December 1980]: 541-542).

The *Law Library Journal* regularly reports on surveys of law librarians. The spring 1980 issue (73: 451-497) included salaries of head law librarians in the United States by size of library and salaries of full-time professional law librarians. Surveys of regional law librarian groups were also reported in the *Law Library Journal*, that is, the Greater Philadelphia Law Library Association in spring 1980 (73: 498-505), and Southern California, summer 1979 (72: 526-533). The American Association of Law Libraries Private Law Libraries Special Interest Section reported on its 1979 survey in the winter 1980 journal (73: 218-226).

A survey of New England Hospital Libraries was published in *Hospital Libraries*, spring 1980 (5: 3-5), giving salary information by type and size of hospital. In the fall of 1979, the mean salary of a full-time hospital library director was $14,000.

STATE LIBRARY AGENCY SALARY DATA

The ALA Association of Specialized and Cooperative Library Agencies compiles an annual survey of state library agency salaries for the chief officers of state library agencies. This gives the minimum and maximum for a variety of positions: state librarian, assistant director, director of reference services or reader services, consultants, specialists, and beginning professionals. The latest report, dated December 1980, is available from ALA/ASCLA, 50 E. Huron St., Chicago, IL 60611.

The *State Salary Survey*, published annually since 1973, gives salary ranges for 31 occupational groups, including library services. Beginning librarian, senior librarian, and library services director salary ranges are given for each state. The latest edition, August 1, 1980, is available from the U.S. Office of Personnel Management, Office of Intergovernmental Personnel Programs (Box 14184, Washington, DC 20044). (Some data from this edition are shown in Table 3.)

TABLE 3   MEAN SALARIES, STATE LIBRARY SURVEY (AUGUST 1, 1980)

	Beginning Librarian	Senior Librarian	Library Services Director
Mean minimum salary	$13,128	$16,366	$27,070
Mean maximum salary	$17,744	$22,349	$33,859

Source: *State Salary Survey, August 1, 1980*. Washington, DC: U.S. Office of Personnel Management, 1980.

TABLE 4 FACULTY SALARIES, ALA ACCREDITED PROGRAMS, 1979–1980

Faculty Rank and Term of Appointment	AALS Member Schools Average	Median
Professors (fiscal year)	$36,308	$36,369
Professors (academic year)	29,194	28,500
Assoc. professors (fiscal year)	30,531	30,519
Assoc. professors (academic year)	22,985	22,750
Asst. professors (fiscal year)	23,538	23,422
Asst. professors (academic year)	19,052	18,688
Instructors (fiscal year)	14,925	14,925
Instructors (academic year)	15,623	16,085
Lecturers (fiscal year)	21,134	20,249
Lecturers (academic year)	21,432	21,389

Source: *1980 Association of American Library Schools Library Education Statistical Report* (State College, PA: AALS, October 1980), p. F-27.

OTHER POSITIONS

Other surveys exist for particular types of positions. The annual survey reporting on placements and salaries of new MLS graduates from ALA accredited programs has been published in *Library Journal* since 1951 and is reprinted each year in the

TABLE 5 DEGREES AND CERTIFICATES AWARDED BY U.S. LIBRARY

Ethnic Group	S	Assoc. of Arts No.	Col.[1]	Row[2]	Bachelor's No.	Col.	Row	Non-Accred. MA No.	Col.	Row
White	F	131	72.0%	2.7%	256	88.3%	5.4%	224	72.3%	4.7%
	M	16	8.8	.3	15	5.2	.3	63	20.3	1.3
	T	147	80.8	3.1	271	93.4	5.7	287	92.6	6.0
American Indian/ Alaskan Native	F	—	—	—	—	—	—	1	.3	14.3
	M	—	—	—	—	—	—	—	—	—
	T	—	—	—	—	—	—	1	.3	14.3
Asian/ Pacific Islander	F	7	3.8	4.0	—	—	—	3	1.0	1.7
	M	—	—	—	2	.7	1.2	1	.3	.6
	T	7	3.8	4.0	2	.7	1.2	4	1.3	2.3
Black	F	22	12.1	7.8	13	4.5	4.6	17	5.5	6.0
	M	1	.5	.4	1	.3	.4	1	.3	.4
	T	23	12.6	8.5	14	4.8	5.0	18	5.8	6.4
Hispanic	F	4	2.2	4.3	3	1.0	3.2	—	—	—
	M	1	.5	1.1	—	—	—	—	—	—
	T	5	2.7	5.3	3	1.0	3.2	—	—	—
Total	F	164	90.1	3.1	272	93.8	5.1	245	79.0	4.6
	M	18	9.9	.3	18	6.2	.3	65	21.0	1.2
	T	182	100	3.4	290	100	5.4	310	100	5.8

Source: *Degrees and Certificates Awarded by U.S. Library Education Programs, 1976–1979* (Chicago: Amer-
[1]Col. = % of the column., i.e., % of the workfor
[2]Row = % of the row, i.e., % of ethnic group by sex

Bowker Annual. [The report on 1979 graduates immediately follows this article—*Ed.*] The data for 1980 graduates will be published in a 1981 summer issue of *Library Journal.*

Since 1973, reports by Russell E. Bidlack on library school faculty salaries have appeared annually in the *Journal of Education for Librarianship.* The 1979–1980 data have been included in the *1980 Association of American Library Schools Library Education Statistical Report* (471 Park La., State College, PA 16801; $15). (Some of the 1979–1980 data are shown in Table 4.)

In 1979, the journal *Online* surveyed its subscription list to determine salaries paid to on-line searchers in various types of libraries (e.g., corporate, academic, government, public) (see *Online* 3 [July 1979]: 51–53). However, there are no plans to repeat this survey. Salaries paid to librarians in charge of technical documentation in data processing outfits are found with data processing salaries in the "1980 Salary Survey" in *Datamation* 26 (February 1980): 110–118.

Profiles of members by various library and information science associations have resulted in some salary data in the last year. However, care must be taken if profile data are considered in setting compensation. Since individuals are surveyed rather than institutions, there may be a limited number of persons in any given type of position and this may not provide a large enough sample for comparative purposes. Surveys of association members are found in "A Profile of ALA Personal Members" by Leigh S. Estabrook and Kathleen M. Heim (*American Libraries* 43 [Fall 1980]: 527–535); "Profile of ASIS Membership" by Donald W. King, Cheri Krauser, and Virginia M. Sague (*Bulletin of the American Society for Information Science* 6 (Aug. 1980): 9–17; "AIM Profiles the Information Management Professional" (*The Information Manager* 2

EDUCATION PROGRAMS, 1978–1979

ALA-Accred. MA			6th Yr. Cert.			Ph.D.			Total		
No.	Col.	Row	No.	Col.	Row	No.	Col.	Row	No.	Col.	Row
3179	72.3%	66.7%	54	62.1%	1.1%	25	44.6%	.5%	3869	72.7%	81.1%
769	17.5	16.1	12	13.8	.3	24	42.9	.5	899	16.9	18.9
3948	89.7	82.8	66	75.9	1.4	49	87.5	1.0	4768	89.7	100
3	.1	42.9	—	—	—	—	—	—	4	.1	57.1
1	0.0	14.3	1	1.1	14.3	1	1.8	14.3	3	.1	42.9
4	.1	57.1	1	1.1	14.3	1	1.8	14.3	7	.1	100
122	2.8	70.5	3	3.4	1.7	2	3.6	1.2	137	2.6	79.2
32	.7	18.5	—	—	—	1	1.8	.6	36	.7	20.8
154	3.5	89.0	3	3.4	1.7	3	5.4	1.7	173	3.2	100
179	4.1	63.5	10	11.5	3.5	2	3.6	.7	243	4.6	86.2
30	.7	10.6	5	5.7	1.8	1	1.8	.4	39	.7	13.8
209	4.8	74.1	15	17.2	5.3	3	5.4	1.1	282	5.3	100
62	1.4	66.0	1	1.1	1.1	—	—	—	70	1.3	74.5
22	.5	23.4	1	1.1	1.1	—	—	—	24	.5	25.5
84	1.9	89.4	2	2.3	2.1	—	—	—	94	1.8	100
3545	80.6	66.6	68	78.2	1.3	29	51.8	.5	4323	81.2	81.2
854	19.4	16.0	19	21.8	.4	27	48.2	.5	1001	18.8	18.8
4399	100	82.6	87	100	1.6	56	100	1.1	5324	100	100

ican Library Association Office for Library Personnel Resources, 1980), p. 4.

[Spring 1980]: 32-33); and "Survey of the Archival Profession—1979" by Ann Morgan Campbell (*The American Archivist* 43 [Fall 1980]: 527-535).

AFFIRMATIVE ACTION DATA

Since 1973/1974, the American Library Association Office for Library Personnel Resources has surveyed library education programs asking them to report the numbers and types of degrees and certificates they awarded and the ethnicity and sex of the degree recipients. These data are compiled for libraries to use in their affirmative action plans. Employers are required to determine to what extent minorities and women are underutilized on their staffs; information is needed on the composition of the library labor force so that comparison of an individual library's staff can be made with the appropriate labor markets.

The degrees and certificates awarded in 1978-1979 are reported in Table 5. For a full report, request *Degrees and Certificates Awarded by U.S. Library Education Programs, 1976-79* from ALA/OLPR.

In 1980, a sample of 1,233 public and academic libraries was surveyed to collect additional data for use by libraries in their affirmative action plans. This report, *The Racial, Ethnic, and Sexual Composition of Library Staff in Public and Academic Libraries*, will be available from ALA/OLPR in spring 1981. (Data from this survey are shown in Table 6.)

ADDITIONAL PERSONNEL DATA

The National Center for Education Statistics (NCES) regularly provides staffing statistics in its survey data. Recently published NCES data for fall 1978-1979 showed 58,413 full-time equivalent staff in academic libraries; 23,675 were professionals. [See the full report on the results of the NCES 1978-1979 survey of academic libraries in the Library Research and Statistics section of Part 4—*Ed.*] The 1978 survey of public school libraries and media centers indicated 84,238 full-time equivalent staff employed, 96 percent of which was certified staff. From 1978 data collected by NCES, to be published in 1981, public library professional staff showed a 10 percent increase, from 36,135 in 1976 to 38,702 in 1978. Technical, clerical, and other staff increased 11 percent from 1974 to 1978 and numbered 48,000 (full-time equivalent).

TABLE 6 RACIAL, ETHNIC, AND SEXUAL COMPOSITION OF LIBRARY STAFF IN ACADEMIC AND PUBLIC LIBRARIES

Racial/Ethnic Group	Percent
American Indian	.2
Asian/Pacific Islander	4.0
Black	5.8
Hispanic	1.8
White	88.2
Total	100.0
Male	28.0
Female	72.0
Total	100.0

Source: *The Racial, Ethnic and Sexual Composition of Library Staff in Academic and Public Libraries* (Chicago: American Library Association Office for Library Personnel Resources, 1981).

New data on the job market should be available at the end of a two-year project begun in 1980 by King Research, Inc , "1981–82 Library Human Resources: Study of Supply and Demand," which will update the U.S. Bureau of Labor Statistics report *Library Manpower* published in 1975. King Research also was involved in the Occupational Survey of Information Professionals, which was completed in 1980. [See the full report on the results of this survey immediately following "Placements and Salaries, 1979: Wide Horizons—*Ed.*]

PLACEMENTS AND SALARIES, 1979: WIDER HORIZONS

Carol L. Learmont

Associate Dean, School of Library Service, Columbia University, New York

This is the twenty-ninth annual report on placements and salaries of graduates of American Library Association (ALA) accredited library school programs. For the 1979 report of the 67 eligible schools, 61 completed the questionnaire in whole or in part. Each geographical area is well represented, and the Northeast, Southeast, and West are fully represented. [See Table 1.]

In 1979 the average beginning level salary was $13,127, based on 2,119 known full-time professional salaries of both men and women [Tables 2 and 3]. Salaries and opportunities in 1979 appeared to be strongest in the category of "Other Libraries and Library Agencies," [see Table 4] which includes many positions in the nontraditional areas of the information world. There seem to be fewer recent graduates of accredited programs in the market than ever before. This fact, plus the clear effort being made by many schools to educate for the new information age and to seek out nontraditional uses of library training and skills, is making the job picture a somewhat brighter one.

THE JOB MARKET

Forty-seven schools reported no major difficulties in placing 1979 graduates, while eight schools reported major or some difficulties in making placements. This is an improvement over 1978, when 13 schools had major or some placement difficulties. Several of the placement officers felt that placements in 1979 took somewhat longer and that more interviews were required than ever before. There is still a scarcity of people with backgrounds in science, engineering, mathematics, business and management, and languages. Frequent mention was made of a need for people interested in cataloging. Several schools noted that graduates are taking considerable time locating just the right job. The addition of laboratory work in information science courses is important and has made graduates more attractive to employers. At the same time, some schools feel that more employers than ever before are hiring on a temporary or part-time basis. In both 1977 and 1978, 169 temporary professional placements were reported; in 1979 there were 189. This may be a trend, or it may reflect more accurate knowledge of individual posts.

Note: Adapted from *Library Journal*, November 1, 1980.

232 / LIBRARY EDUCATION, PLACEMENT, AND SALARIES

TABLE 1 STATUS OF 1979 GRADUATES, SPRING 1980

	No. of Graduates			Not in Lib. Positions			Empl. Not Known			Permanent Prof. Placements			Temp. Prof. Placements			Nonprof. Library Placements			Total in Lib. Positions		
	Women	Men	Total	Women	Men	Total	Women	Men	Total	Women	Men	Total	Women	Men	Total	Women	Men	Total	Women	Men	Total
United States	3,835	897	4,732	478	138	616	852	194	1,046	2,212	508	2,720	136	19	155	157	38	195	2,505	565	3,070
Northeast	1,466	315	1,781	150	43	193	406	81	487	807	173	980	46	5	51	57	13	70	910	191	1,101
Southeast	596	131	727	51	9	60	163	32	195	364	87	451	8	1	9	10	2	12	382	90	472
Midwest	955	225	1,180	135	44	179	109	27	136	647	141	788	24	2	26	40	11	51	711	154	865
Southwest	312	66	378	52	5	57	59	18	77	173	41	214	15	0	15	13	2	15	201	43	244
West	506	160	666	90	37	127	115	36	151	221	66	287	43	11	54	37	10	47	301	87	388
Canada	300	107	407	51	24	75	26	5	31	193	74	267	30	4	34	0	0	0	223	78	301
All Schools	4,135	1,004	5,139	529	162	691	878	199	1,077	2,405	582	2,987	166	23	189	157	38	195	2,728	643	3,371

TABLE 2 PLACEMENTS AND SALARIES OF 1979 GRADUATES—SUMMARY BY REGION

	Place-ments	Salaries			Low Salary			High Salary			Average Salary			Median Salary		
		Women	Men	Total	Women	Men	Total	Women	Men	Total	Women	Men	Total	Women	Men	Total
United States	2,565	1,612	381	1,993	5,000	6,700	5,000	32,200	40,000	40,000	12,872	13,630	13,016	12,758	13,049	12,760
Northeast	827	594	132	726	6,864	7,680	6,864	32,200	40,000	40,000	13,001	13,868	13,146	12,889	13,181	12,694
Southeast	450	258	63	321	5,000	6,700	5,000	21,600	24,000	24,000	12,448	12,968	12,561	12,299	12,599	12,387
Midwest	763	462	108	570	7,200	8,541	7,200	27,000	26,700	27,000	12,768	13,377	12,853	12,696	12,451	12,604
Southwest	202	104	24	128	9,010	9,000	9,000	22,116	18,000	22,116	12,804	13,283	12,962	12,554	12,875	12,650
West	323	194	54	248	8,100	8,300	8,100	24,732	21,600	24,732	13,357	14,556	13,725	13,284	14,357	13,838
Canada	272	97	29	126	9,600	9,000	9,000	22,694	26,000	26,000	15,010	15,454	15,010	15,133	14,525	14,967
All Schools	2,837	1,709	410	2,119	5,000	6,700	5,000	32,200	40,000	40,000	12,987	13,696	13,127	12,885	13,103	12,883

Salaries for 1979 graduates improved over those for 1978, but fell far below the increase in the cost of living. The 1979 salaries increased at the rate of 4.8 percent, compared with 5.3 percent in 1978, 6.5 percent in 1977, and 5.2 percent in 1976. In 1979 the average (mean) beginning salary for all graduates was $13,127; for women, $12,987 (increased by five percent from 1978); and for men, $13,696 (a nine percent increase). Median salaries were $12,883 for all graduates, $12,885 for women, and $13,103 for men (Table 8). For new graduates with prior experience in a form relevant for salary purposes, the average beginning salary was $13,701 (down from $13,856 in 1978); without experience, $12,127 (up from $11,153 in 1978); see Table 13.

PLACEMENTS

The 61 responding schools awarded first professional degrees to 5,139 graduates in 1979 (Table 1). This was 303 fewer than the 5,442 degrees awarded by 62 schools in 1978. One school did not report in 1978, while six schools did not report in 1979. The graduates of those schools would increase the total number of 1979 graduates, but even so, the drop is significant and continues the trend noted last year. In 1979 the average number of graduates per school reporting was 84; in 1978 the average was 88; and in 1977 the average was 103. Apparently, fewer beginning librarians are in the job market.

Table 1 shows permanent and temporary professional placements, as well as nonprofessional library placements and totals for the three. These are library or information-related positions. Table 1 also shows the number of graduates reported who were not in library positions or whose employment status was unknown at the beginning of April 1980. Thirteen percent were known not to be in library positions, compared with 14 percent reported for 1978 graduates. In April 1980 the whereabouts of 21 percent were unknown, compared with 23 percent in April 1979. Sixty-five percent of the 1979 graduates were known to be employed either in professional or nonprofessional positions in libraries or information-related work, compared with 62 percent of the 1978 graduates. Fifty-eight percent of the 1979 graduates were employed in permanent professional positions, compared with 56 percent of the 1978 graduates. Employment distribution for 2,119 of the 5,139 graduates is shown in Table 4 and Table 12. These are full-time professional placements and exclude part-time placements.

Some placement officers were able to estimate the number of graduates unemployed after three months, four months, and six months. Thirty-six schools recorded at least partial figures. The median for those unemployed after three months was 23 percent; after four months, 14 percent; and after six months, eight percent.

In 1979 six percent of all known library and related placements were in nonprofessional positions (Table 1). In 1978 five percent were in that category, and in 1977, three percent. About six percent of the women and six percent of the men were in nonprofessional positions, compared with five percent of the women and five percent of the men in 1978, and three percent of the women and two percent of the men in 1977.

School and college and university placements dropped in 1979. Public library placement increased slightly. Other libraries and library agencies continued to show an increase (Table 5).

U.S. and Canadian placement comparisons appear in Table 6. Table 7, showing special placements, is self-explanatory.

DEMAND AND SUPPLY

Fifty schools indicated a total of 48,230 vacant positions reported to them. These included posts at all levels, and many of the positions were listed simultaneously at the

234 / LIBRARY EDUCATION, PLACEMENT, AND SALARIES

TABLE 3 PLACEMENTS AND SALARIES OF 1979 GRADUATES

	Place-ments	Salaries			Low Salary			High Salary			Average Salary			Median Salary		
		Women	Men	Total	Women	Men	Total	Women	Men	Total	Women	Men	Total	Women	Men	Total
Alabama	52	31	6	37	$9,500	$9,000	$9,000	$17,000	$16,700	$17,000	$12,679	$12,218	$12,604	$13,000	$11,750	$13,000
Alabama A&M	15	0	0	0	0	0	0	0	0	0	0	0	0	0	0	0
Albany	45	30	5	35	9,000	9,665	9,000	18,000	18,000	18,000	12,760	13,660	12,889	12,400	12,600	12,500
Arizona	53	0	0	0	0	0	0	0	0	0	0	0	0	0	0	0
Atlanta	38	26	7	33	9,797	12,303	9,797	18,000	17,035	18,000	12,425	12,903	12,526	12,300	12,927	12,303
Brigham Young	28	4	9	13	10,000	9,845	9,845	15,288	17,784	17,784	12,527	12,957	12,785	12,550	12,000	12,500
British Columbia	59	6	0	6	9,600		9,600	21,000		21,000	14,500		14,500	15,700		15,700
Buffalo	42	30	7	37	10,000	10,000	10,000	28,000	17,400	28,000	13,923	14,000	13,934	13,000	13,500	13,500
California (Berk.)	36	25	11	36	8,316	12,000	8,316	16,320	19,992	19,992	13,541	16,164	14,338	13,800	16,200	14,088
California (LA)	47	33	5	38	8,250	14,000	8,250	18,200	17,600	17,600	13,175	15,504	13,499	13,000	15,000	13,200
Case Western	57	19	4	23	8,724	11,092	8,724	21,324	12,996	21,324	12,992	12,145	12,845	12,648	11,751	12,648
Catholic	56	44	9	53	9,500	9,500	9,500	25,000	24,703	25,000	15,561	17,154	16,357	15,000	15,900	15,000
Chicago	18	0	0	0	0	0	0	0	0	0	0	0	0	0	0	0
Clarion	10	4	1	5	6,864	9,500	6,864	12,950	9,500	12,950	9,978	9,500	9,683	9,550	9,500	9,500
Columbia	58	46	11	57	8,500	11,500	8,500	17,000	16,000	17,000	12,623	12,855	12,668	12,544	12,303	12,500
Dalhousie	20	0	0	0	10,000		10,000	16,000		16,000						
Denver	41	34	6	40	9,400	9,000	8,600	22,157	17,220	22,157	13,173	13,348	13,320	13,000	13,500	13,457
Drexel	82	59	10	69	8,600	11,500	8,600	26,000	28,080	28,080	12,907	16,411	13,444	12,800	13,684	13,000
Emory	43	36	6	42	8,800	12,200	8,800	17,500	17,800	17,800	11,985	14,210	12,303	11,800	14,100	11,860
Florida State	46	33	12	45	8,400	9,152	8,400	17,500	13,996	17,500	12,099	10,844	11,764	12,200	10,946	12,000
Geneseo	53	30	1	31	9,000	9,000	9,000	15,250	11,600	15,250	11,000	11,000	11,000	10,500	10,300	10,400
Hawaii	30	17	3	20	9,802	13,752	9,802	21,000	15,600	21,000	13,282	14,450	13,457	12,480	14,000	13,143
Illinois	66	42	15	57	9,360	10,000	9,360	19,000	17,400	19,000	12,308	12,615	12,389	11,940	12,220	14,088
Indiana	84	36	12	48	8,000	9,800	8,000	16,935	16,200	16,935	11,720	12,378	11,881	12,000	11,832	12,000
Iowa	29	16	3	19	9,000	12,960	9,000	18,000	13,248	18,000	12,143	13,069	12,289	12,187	13,000	12,236
Kent State	94	67	17	84	9,000	8,541	8,541	22,000	22,500	22,500	13,076	14,185	13,288	12,450	13,780	12,500
Kentucky	46	15	5	20	5,000	6,700	5,000	14,700	13,500	14,700	10,940	11,412	11,294	11,500	12,000	11,750

Louisiana State	41	31	6		9,010	9,000	9,000	17,600	14,500	17,600	12,106	12,571	12,194	11,615	13,000	12,000
Long Island	26	22	4	37	8,300	11,000	8,300	16,566	17,000	17,000	12,392	14,223	12,674	12,600	14,446	12,850
Maryland	29	12	3	26	12,000	8,600	8,600	15,200	17,735	17,735	12,766	13,445	12,912	13,600	13,167	13,383
Michigan	115	80	11	15	7,200	10,000	7,200	27,000	26,700	27,000	13,300	14,000	13,400	12,800	12,700	12,800
Minnesota	44	39	5	91	7,200	10,700	7,200	21,990	25,590	25,590	14,212	15,134	14,317	14,232	12,500	14,215
Missouri	37	24	9	44	9,240	10,272	9,240	18,200	17,035	18,200	11,755	12,970	14,362	11,500	12,024	11,550
Montreal	52	0	0	33	0	0	0	0	0	0	0	0	0	0	0	0
North Carolina	34	26	7	0	9,000	8,500	8,500	19,000	24,000	24,000	12,272	14,173	12,675	11,800	13,812	12,144
North Carolina Central	24	10	4	33	8,500	11,000	8,500	16,440	18,255	18,255	12,535	13,439	12,776	12,600	12,250	12,500
North Texas State	34	11	4	14	11,300	11,200	11,200	15,600	18,000	18,000	12,524	13,566	12,876	12,000	12,500	12,000
Peabody	73	36	6	17	7,000	9,000	7,000	21,600	20,000	21,600	12,568	13,857	12,778	12,000	13,000	12,000
Pittsburgh	0	36	7	43	8,000	10,000	8,000	27,000	23,000	27,000	12,867	14,771	13,178	12,720	13,200	12,720
Pratt	24	12	7	43	11,000	11,000	11,000	17,000	21,000	21,000	14,528	13,628	14,142	14,800	12,850	14,000
Queens	18	15	9	21	8,000	10,000	8,000	32,200	16,000	32,200	14,435	16,533	15,480	15,720	17,000	14,000
Rhode Island	30	21	3	18	10,000	10,025	10,000	20,000	17,035	20,000	12,833	12,660	12,794	12,000	10,700	14,000
Rosary	73	46	6	27	8,000	10,000	8,000	24,000	14,200	24,000	12,188	11,750	11,084	12,300	10,800	11,600
Rutgers	80	61	4	50	8,000	9,500	9,500	22,800	16,000	22,800	14,472	12,208	0	14,000	12,000	11,800
St. Johns	11	7	16	77	9,500	10,500	10,500	15,000	17,035	15,000	12,355	10,500	0	12,000	10,500	0
San Jose	44	11	1	8	11,500	10,500	10,500	16,500	10,500	16,500	13,000	13,000	12,125	11,500	12,000	12,000
Simmons	179	108	4	15	8,100	8,300	8,100	23,000	17,500	23,000	14,040	14,040	0	12,800	12,005	12,375
South Carolina	20	16	28	136	8,181	7,680	7,680	17,736	40,000	17,736	12,176	14,712	12,557	13,642	12,000	13,500
Southern California	31	27	4	20	10,000	10,600	10,000	24,000	16,000	24,000	13,274	14,709	13,162	0	0	0
Southern Connecticut	36	31	5	31	9,300	9,980	10,100	19,000	17,000	19,000	13,896	14,380	13,968	12,700	13,100	13,000
South Florida	20	16	4	36	10,400	10,500	9,300	18,600	18,600	18,600	12,986	13,696	13,084	12,450	12,303	12,450
Syracuse	48	26	6	20	10,000	10,000	10,400	29,000	29,000	29,000	12,864	13,380	12,987	13,275	20,500	13,475
Tennessee	39	13	1	32	8,000	13,500	10,000	21,600	17,000	21,600	13,455	19,334	14,558	12,000	13,500	12,750
Texas (Austin)	36	27	9	14	10,000	11,000	8,000	16,200	16,000	16,200	13,289	13,500	13,304	13,100	12,500	13,100
Texas Woman's	38	35	3	36	9,500	12,500	10,000	22,116	14,500	22,116	12,970	13,827	13,228	13,500	12,500	13,500
Toronto	56	44	6	38	11,500	13,500	9,500	22,694	26,000	22,694	13,616	13,167	13,548	15,300	15,000	15,200
Washington	66	43	12	50	10,000	10,500	11,500	24,732	21,600	24,732	15,658	16,255	15,729	12,896	15,854	13,430
Western Michigan	31	13	2	55	10,000	9,000	10,000	15,000	18,000	15,000	14,261	16,320	14,710	13,500	11,500	13,100
Western Ontario	85	47	6	19	9,600	9,000	9,000	22,000	22,000	22,000	11,929	13,833	12,607	14,400	14,050	12,500
Wisconsin (Madison)	77	50	23	70	10,000	10,500	10,000	22,665	16,000	22,665	14,873	14,652	14,800	12,300	12,800	14,000
Wisconsin (Milwaukee)	38	30	14	64	9,500	13,000	9,500	22,500	25,000	25,000	12,721	12,871	12,754	14,500	14,500	12,500
			8	38							14,868	15,575	15,017			14,500

PLACEMENTS AND SALARIES, 1979 / 235

TABLE 4 PLACEMENTS BY TYPE OF LIBRARY

Schools	Public Women	Public Men	Public Total	Elementary & Secondary Women	Elementary & Secondary Men	Elementary & Secondary Total	College & University Women	College & University Men	College & University Total	Other Women	Other Men	Other Total	Total Women	Total Men	Total
Alabama	14	6	20	18	0	18	6	3	9	4	1	5	42	10	52
Alabama A&M	0	0	0	13	2	15	0	0	0	0	0	0	13	2	15
Albany	5	2	7	9	1	10	11	0	11	15	2	17	40	5	45
Arizona	23	4	27	7	2	9	11	2	13	3	1	4	44	9	53
Atlanta	10	3	13	9	0	9	7	4	11	4	1	5	30	8	38
Brigham Young	7	3	10	0	3	3	1	3	4	5	6	11	13	15	28
British Columbia	17	3	20	2	3	5	2	7	9	20	5	25	41	18	59
Buffalo	7	0	7	7	1	8	8	3	11	12	4	16	34	8	42
California (Berk.)	3	2	5	3	0	3	6	5	11	13	4	17	25	11	36
California (LA)	11	0	11	2	2	4	14	0	14	14	6	20	41	6	47
Case Western	14	2	16	4	0	4	9	5	14	17	6	23	44	13	57
Catholic	3	1	4	5	0	5	4	1	5	33	9	42	45	11	56
Chicago	4	1	5	4	0	4	4	2	5	5	3	8	13	5	18
Clarion	4	0	4	0	0	0	0	2	2	0	0	0	8	2	10
Columbia	9	3	12	3	0	3	11	7	18	23	2	25	46	12	58
Dalhousie	3	1	4	8	0	8	7	1	8	7	1	8	18	2	20
Denver	11	3	14	5	1	6	6	0	6	13	2	15	35	6	41
Drexel	8	3	11	11	1	12	15	3	18	34	7	41	68	14	82
Emory	5	2	7	4	1	5	16	2	18	12	1	13	37	6	43
Florida State	10	4	14	10	1	11	11	5	16	3	2	5	34	12	46
Geneseo	12	0	12	8	1	9	9	2	11	17	4	21	46	7	53
Hawaii	5	0	5	3	0	3	4	2	6	6	4	10	23	7	30
Illinois	15	4	19	9	1	10	21	11	32	10	2	12	49	17	66
Indiana	30	2	32	3	0	3	22	8	30	7	5	12	68	16	84
Iowa	8	2	10	10	1	11	4	1	5	3	0	3	25	4	29
Kent State	43	2	45	21	5	26	4	6	10	8	5	13	76	18	94

School													
Kentucky	7	5	12	7	0	7	14	6	20	7	0	7	35	11	46
Louisiana State	7	0	7	13	0	13	3	5	8	12	1	13	35	6	41
Long Island	5	2	7	10	1	11	0	0	0	7	1	8	22	4	26
Maryland	5	0	5	7	1	8	3	1	4	11	1	12	26	3	29
Michigan	26	2	28	21	3	24	20	7	27	35	1	36	102	13	115
Minnesota	13	2	15	6	1	7	6	1	7	14	4	15	39	5	44
Missouri	10	3	13	4	0	4	10	2	12	4	4	8	28	9	37
Montana	10	3	13	1	1	2	0	10	20	13	1	17	34	18	52
North Carolina	10	2	12	3	0	3	8	4	12	6	1	7	27	7	34
North Carolina Central	1	2	3	7	0	7	9	1	10	3	1	4	20	4	24
North Texas State	10	4	14	6	0	6	6	3	9	5	2	7	27	7	34
Peabody	13	4	17	14	0	14	21	8	29	10	3	13	58	15	73
Pratt	1	1	2	3	0	3	3	3	6	8	3	11	15	9	24
Queens	2	1	3	1	0	1	1	0	1	11	5	13	15	3	18
Rhode Island	8	3	11	7	1	8	2	3	5	4	2	6	21	9	30
Rosary	23	1	24	11	2	13	9	2	11	23	2	25	66	7	73
Rutgers	12	7	19	5	1	6	13	6	19	34	2	36	64	16	80
St. Johns	2	1	3	2	0	3	1	0	1	4	0	4	9	2	11
San Jose	9	2	11	8	0	8	10	4	14	8	3	11	35	9	44
Simmons	53	5	58	15	0	15	41	23	64	33	9	42	142	37	179
South Carolina	0	3	3	12	2	12	2	0	2	2	1	3	16	4	20
Southern California	11	0	11	2	0	2	4	0	4	10	4	14	27	4	31
Southern Connecticut	11	1	12	12	2	12	4	2	6	4	2	6	31	5	36
South Florida	5	2	7	5	0	5	2	1	3	4	1	5	16	4	20
Syracuse	5	2	7	11	0	11	10	2	12	14	4	18	40	8	48
Tennessee	7	1	8	14	0	14	6	1	7	10	0	10	37	2	39
Texas (Austin)	7	3	10	6	2	8	6	4	10	8	0	8	27	9	36
Texas Woman's	7	2	9	20	1	21	6	0	6	2	0	2	35	3	38
Toronto	17	0	17	3	1	4	4	4	8	24	3	27	48	8	56
Washington	12	4	16	15	1	16	14	6	18	10	6	16	51	15	66
Western Michigan	7	0	7	6	2	8	6	9	12	3	1	4	22	9	31
Western Ontario	12	8	20	6	2	8	15	9	24	23	10	33	56	29	85
Wisconsin (Madison)	25	5	30	11	2	13	16	6	22	9	3	12	61	16	77
Wisconsin (Milwaukee)	6	4	10	10	1	11	4	2	6	10	1	11	30	8	38
Total	**640**	**138**	**778**	**459**	**49**	**508**	**503**	**213**	**716**	**673**	**162**	**835**	**2,275**	**562**	**2,837**

238 / LIBRARY EDUCATION, PLACEMENT, AND SALARIES

TABLE 5 PLACEMENTS BY TYPE OF LIBRARY, 1951-1979

Year	Public	School	College & Universities	Other Library Agencies*	Total
1951-1955**	2,076 (33%)	1,424 (23%)	1,774 (28%)	1,000 (16%)	6,264
1956-1960**	2,057 (33)	1,287 (20)	1,878 (30)	1,105 (17)	6,327
1961-1965	2,876 (30)	1,979 (20)	3,167 (33)	1,600 (17)	9,622
1966-1970	4,773 (28)	3,969 (23)	5,834 (34)	2,456 (15)	17,032
1971	999 (29)	924 (26)	1,067 (30)	513 (15)	3,503
1972	1,117 (30)	987 (26)	1,073 (29)	574 (15)	3,751
1973	1,180 (31)	969 (25)	1,017 (26)	712 (18)	3,878
1974	1,132 (31)	893 (24)	952 (26)	691 (19)	3,668
1975	994 (30)	813 (24)	847 (25)	714 (21)	3,368
1976	764 (27.1)	655 (23.2)	741 (26.3)	657 (23.2)	2,817
1977	846 (28.4)	673 (22.6)	771 (25.9)	687 (23.1)	2,977
1978	779 (26.1)	590 (19.8)	819 (27.4)	798 (26.7)	2,986
1979	778 (27.4)	508 (17.9)	716 (25.3)	835 (29.4)	2,837

*From 1951 through 1966 these tabulations were for "special and other placements" in all kinds of libraries. Beginning with 1967, these figures include only placements in library agencies that do not clearly belong to one of the other three groups.

**Figures for individual years are reported in preceding articles in this series.

various schools. In 1978, 45 schools reported a total of 36,902 positions. The average number reported per school in 1979 was 965, compared to 820 in 1978 and 900 in 1977.

Nineteen schools reported increases in vacancy listings ranging from one to 100 percent; the median was 15 percent. Twenty-five schools reported no significant changes from 1978. Five schools reported a decline, ranging from 8 to 35 percent. Five placement officers reported major difficulty in placing 1979 graduates; three reported some difficulty; and 47 reported no major difficulty. Five placement officers felt that they had more difficulty placing graduates in 1979 than in 1978; 19 felt they had less difficulty; and 36 felt they had about the same amount of difficulty both years.

The continuing upward trend in the "Other Libraries and Library Agencies" category, which includes nontraditional areas and special libraries, is significant and clearly continues to be an important growth area. The predicted drop in school and college and university placements is reflected in the figures for 1979, while public library placements appear to be holding firm.

SALARIES

The salary statistics reported here include only full-time annual salaries and exclude such variables as vacations and other fringe benefits, which may be part of the total compensation. They do not reflect differences in hours worked per week. Such

TABLE 6 U.S. AND CANADIAN PLACEMENTS COMPARED
(Percents May Not Total 100 Because of Rounding)

	Placements	Public Libraries	School Libraries	College & University Libraries	Other Lib. & Library Agencies
All Schools	2,837	778 (27.4%)	508 (17.9%)	716 (25.3%)	835 (29.4%)
Women	2,275	640 (28.1)	459 (20.2)	503 (22.1)	673 (29.6)
Men	562	138 (24.6)	49 (8.7)	213 (37.9)	162 (28.8)
U.S. Schools	2,565	704 (27.4)	489 (19.1)	647 (25.2)	725 (28.3)
Women	2,078	581 (28.0)	447 (21.5)	464 (22.3)	586 (28.2)
Men	487	123 (25.3)	42 (8.6)	183 (37.6)	139 (28.5)
Canadian Schools	272	74 (27.2)	19 (7.0)	69 (25.4)	110 (40.4)
Women	197	59 (29.9)	12 (6.1)	39 (19.8)	87 (44.2)
Men	75	15 (20.0)	7 (9.3)	30 (40.0)	23 (30.7)

TABLE 7 SPECIAL PLACEMENTS*

	Women	Men	Total
Government jurisdiction (U.S. and Canada)			
Other government agencies (except USVA hospitals)	42	5	47
State and Provincial libraries	42	13	55
National libraries	25	9	34
Armed Services libraries (domestic)	7	1	8
Overseas agencies (incl. Armed Services)	7	1	8
Total government jurisdiction	123	29	152
Library science			
Advanced study	19	16	35
Teaching	27	6	33
Total library science	46	22	68
Audiovisual and media centers	109	27	136
Children's services—public libraries	125	7	132
Children's services—school libraries	115	14	129
Law	94	18	112
Youth services—school libraries	91	15	106
Science and technology	86	16	102
Medicine (incl. nursing schools)	77	13	90
Business and finance (banking business administration)	66	14	80
Communications industry (advertising, newspaper, publishing, radio & TV, etc.)	51	8	59
Information science services	47	11	58
Youth services (public libraries)	52	5	57
Research & development	38	8	46
Systems analysis; automation	28	12	40
Hospitals (incl. USVA hospitals)	35	4	39
Rare books, manuscripts, archives	20	16	36
Social sciences	21	14	35
Outreach activities and services	29	2	31
Art and museum	25	1	26
Religion (seminaries, theological schools)	17	8	25
Music	18	4	22
Networks and consortia	18	3	21
Historical agencies	14	5	19
Freelance	12	2	14
Bookstore	10	2	12
Children's services—other	11	1	12
Professional associations	8	2	10
Youth services—other	10	—	10
Correctional institutions	6	3	9
Centers for Spanish-speaking	5	3	8
Architecture	6	—	6
Geneological	4	2	6
International agencies	5	1	6
Maps	4	1	5
Government agencies (not U.S. and Canada)	1	3	4
Services to the blind	3	1	4
Consulting	2	1	3
International relations	3	—	3
Manufacturing	2	1	3
Theatre & motion pictures	2	1	3
Documents & government publications	1	1	2
Labor unions	1	1	2
Records management	2	—	2
Women's organizations	2	—	2
Internship	1	—	1
Information brokers	1	—	1
Mathematics	—	1	1
Total Special Placements	**1,447**	**303**	**1,750**

*Includes special placements in all types of libraries, not limited to the "other libraries and library agencies" shown in Table 4.

TABLE 8   SALARY DATA SUMMARIZED

	Women	Men	Total
Average (Mean salary)	$12,987	$13,696	$13,127
Median Salary	12,885	13,103	12,883
Individual Salary Range	5000-32,000	6700-40,000	5000-40,000

information might provide more precise comparability, but such data is probably beyond the needs of most library schools and the profession. In any case, the validity of the analysis presented here rests on comparable statistics collected since 1951.

Of the 61 schools reporting, 57 supplied some salary data. Not every school could provide all the information requested, nor could they supply it for all employed graduates. The schools were asked to exclude atypical salaries, such as those for which the stipend includes both compensation and living allowances, those for graduates from outside North America who return to employment in their home countries, and all salaries for part-time employment. With these exclusions added to the number of salaries not known or reported, we have known salary information for 2,119 of the 1979 graduates (1,709 women and 410 men). This represents 75 percent of the known placements and 41 percent of all graduates reported, a larger percentage of known placements than in 1978 (69 percent), and a larger percentage of the total known 1978 graduates (38 percent). Salary data as reported in the 57 schools are given in Tables 2 and 3 and summarized in Table 8.

Average (Mean) Salaries

The 1979 average salary for all graduates was $13,127, an increase of $600 (4.8 percent) over the 1978 average of $12,527. Annual changes in average salaries since 1967 are shown in Table 9, which also includes a beginning salary index figure that may be compared with the Annual Cost of Living Index (COL) reports issued by the U.S. government.

The COL index for 1979 was 217.7, an increase of 22.4 points over the 1978 figure of 195.3, a gain of 11 percent. The comparable increase in the beginning salary index is three percent, eight points below the increase in the cost of living.

The range in reported average salaries of all 1979 graduates is wide, from $9683 to $16,357, a difference of $6,674. For women the range in average salaries was from $9,978 to $15,658, with a difference of $5,680; for men the range was $9,500 to $19,334, a $9,834

TABLE 9   AVERAGE SALARY INDEX FOR STARTING LIBRARY POSITIONS, 1967-1979

Year	Library Schools	Fifth-Year Graduates	Average Beginning Salary	Increase in Average	Beginning Index
1967	40	4,030	$ 7,305	—	—
1968	42	4,625	7,650	$355	105
1969	45	4,970	8,161	501	112
1970	48	5,569	8,611	450	118
1971	47	5,670	8,846	235	121
1972	48	6,079	9,248	402	126
1973	53	6,336	9,423	175	128
1974	52	6,370	10,000	617	135
1975	51	6,010	10,594	554	145
1976	53	5,415	11,149	555	153
1977	53	5,467	11,894	745	163
1978	62	5,442	12,527	633	168
1979	61	5,139	13,127	600	173

difference. In the 55 schools that reported average salaries for both men and women, the women's average was highest in 11 schools, the men's average was highest in 42, and the average was the same in two.

Table 12 summarizes the salaries offered to men and women in different types of libraries and library-related agencies. The average men's salary is higher than the average women's salary in every category but public libraries, continuing the familiar pattern.

Median Salaries

In 1979 the median for all graduates was $12,883, an increase of $1,004 over the 1978 median salary of $11,879. The median salary for women was $12,885; for men, $13,103. Many of the schools reporting figures in this category do not report complete figures, which skews the final result slightly. In 24 of the 55 schools reporting, the median salary for women was higher than that for men; in 29 schools it was lower; in one school it was the same; and one school reported no men.

Salary Range

The 1979 range of individual salaries offered to new graduates again shows the expected large gap between the lowest and the highest because of such variables as education and experience [Tables 10, 11, 12, and 13]. The range in 1979 (Table 8) was from a low of $5,000 to a high of $40,000, a difference of $35,000. The low salary was received by

TABLE 10 HIGH SALARIES BY TYPE OF LIBRARY

	Public			School			College & Univ.			Other Libraries & Lib. Agencies		
	Women	Men	Total	Women	Men	Total	Women	Men	Total	Women	Men	Total
$ 7000	—	—	—	—	—	—	—	—	—	1	—	—
8000	—	—	—	—	—	—	—	1	—	—	—	—
9000	—	1	—	—	1	1	—	1	1	—	—	—
10,000	—	7	—	1	1	1	2	1	2	—	3	1
11,000	2	2	1	—	3	—	2	1	1	1	3	1
12,000	10	7	7	2	2	1	8	6	4	1	6	2
13,000	9	9	7	3	3	2	8	7	5	4	1	1
14,000	7	7	8	6	2	5	9	5	7	5	3	2
15,000	10	5	12	7	2	7	2	8	5	5	1	2
16,000	5	2	6	5	—	4	3	5	5	6	5	7
17,000	4	1	4	10	3	12	3	4	5	13	10	15
18,000	1	2	3	3	1	4	4	2	6	5	1	4
19,000	2	—	2	3	—	3	2	1	3	2	—	2
20,000	1	—	1	3	—	3	3	1	3	1	2	2
21,000	2	1	3	3	—	2	2	—	2	2	3	3
22,000	—	—	—	5	2	3	2	—	2	2	1	2
23,000	1	—	1	—	1	1	—	—	—	—	1	1
24,000	—	—	—	—	—	—	1	—	1	2	2	3
25,000	—	—	—	—	3	2	—	—	—	1	—	1
26,000	—	—	—	—	1	1	—	—	—	1	1	1
27,000	—	—	—	1	—	1	—	—	—	1	—	1
28,000	—	—	—	1	—	1	—	—	—	—	1	1
29,000	—	—	—	—	—	—	—	1	1	—	—	—
30,000	—	—	—	—	—	—	—	—	—	—	—	—
31,000	—	—	—	—	—	—	—	—	—	—	—	—
32,000	—	—	—	—	—	—	—	—	—	1	—	1
33,000	—	—	—	—	—	—	—	—	—	—	—	—
34,000	—	—	—	—	—	—	—	—	—	—	—	—
35,000	—	—	—	—	—	—	—	—	—	—	—	—
36,000	—	—	—	—	—	—	—	—	—	—	—	—
37,000	—	—	—	—	—	—	—	—	—	—	—	—
38,000	—	—	—	—	—	—	—	—	—	—	—	—
39,000	—	—	—	—	—	—	—	—	—	—	—	—
40,000	—	—	—	—	—	—	—	—	—	—	1	1

TABLE 11 LOW SALARIES BY TYPE OF LIBRARY

	Public			School			College & Univ.			Other Libraries & Lib. Agencies		
	Women	Men	Total	Women	Men	Total	Women	Men	Total	Women	Men	Total
$ 5000	—	—	—	1	—	1	—	—	—	—	—	—
6000	1	—	1	—	—	—	—	1	1	—	—	—
7000	1	—	1	1	—	1	1	—	1	3	1	4
8000	8	2	9	4	—	4	4	3	6	2	—	2
9000	16	7	15	11	1	12	5	6	8	10	1	10
10,000	16	13	19	17	1	17	26	6	24	15	7	17
11,000	3	7	4	5	5	6	8	6	9	15	12	15
12,000	5	10	4	4	2	3	4	12	3	8	11	6
13,000	1	5	1	3	3	3	1	7	1	1	4	—
14,000	3	—	2	3	3	3	1	—	—	—	5	—
15,000	1	1	—	1	1	1	1	—	—	—	2	—
16,000	—	—	—	—	1	—	—	1	—	—	—	—
17,000	—	—	—	2	3	2	—	1	—	—	1	—
18,000	—	—	—	—	1	—	—	—	—	—	—	—
19,000	—	—	—	—	—	—	—	—	—	—	—	—
20,000	—	—	—	—	—	—	—	—	—	—	—	—
21,000	—	—	—	—	—	—	—	—	—	—	—	—
22,000	—	—	—	—	—	—	—	—	—	—	—	—
23,000	—	—	—	—	1	—	—	—	—	—	—	—
24,000	—	—	—	—	—	—	—	—	—	—	1	—
25,000	—	—	—	—	2	—	—	—	—	—	—	—
26,000	—	—	—	—	1	—	—	—	—	—	—	—
27,000	—	—	—	—	—	—	—	—	—	—	—	—
28,000	—	—	—	—	—	—	—	—	—	—	—	—
29,000	—	—	—	—	—	—	—	1	—	—	—	—

a woman school librarian in a seminary. The high salary was received by the male president of a library-related agency.

High Salaries

In 1979 the range of high salaries was from $12,950 to $40,000, a difference of $27,050. Forty-two salaries were $20,000 or more (25 women, 17 men). The median high salary for all graduates was $19,992. For women it was $18,440; for men, $17,600. For the sixth year women show the highest median. The median high salary was $18,000 in 1978, with a range of salary from $12,000 to $34,000. Twenty-eight salaries were over $20,000 in 1978 (15 women, 13 men). Distribution of high salaries by type of library is outlined in Table 10 and in a different context in Table 11.

In 1979 the category of "Other Libraries and Library Agencies" accounted for the majority of high salaries reported, with 44 percent, up from 36 percent in 1978. School libraries accounted for 28 percent, down from 36 percent in 1978. Academic libraries were down to 18 percent from 22 percent in 1978. Public libraries were up to 10 percent from a drop to 7 percent in 1978. As in 1978, media specialists and school librarians, information specialists (especially in special libraries), and administrative positions were most frequently mentioned as receiving the highest salaries. Other specialties mentioned several times were reference, medicine, law, and automation. The positions were fairly scattered geographically, with Texas, New York, and California leading the field. The primary reasons given for high salaries were previous experience and knowledge of a specific subject field. Many people receive degrees and continue on in the posts previously held or in the same organization. This is especially common in the school library field. Civil service, corporate support, and special needs for information specialists were responsible for some of the high salaries.

TABLE 12 COMPARISON OF SALARIES BY TYPE OF LIBRARY

	Place-ments	Salaries Known Women	Salaries Known Men	Salaries Known Total	Low Salary Women	Low Salary Men	Low Salary Total	High Salary Women	High Salary Men	High Salary Total	Average Salary Women	Average Salary Men	Average Salary Total	Median Salary Women	Median Salary Men	Median Salary Total
Public Libraries																
United States	704	451	106	557	$6,864	$8,300	$6,864	$23,000	$21,000	$23,000	$12,190	$12,179	$12,218	$12,109	$11,971	$12,146
Northeast	184	140	29	169	6,864	9,500	6,864	23,000	15,744	23,000	12,204	11,979	12,102	12,076	11,804	12,070
Southeast	116	67	26	93	8,707	9,000	8,707	18,000	18,255	18,255	11,764	12,501	12,094	11,879	12,181	11,959
Midwest	254	171	29	200	7,200	8,541	7,200	21,861	15,650	21,861	11,754	11,936	11,912	11,710	11,715	11,852
Southwest	67	22	10	32	9,010	9,000	9,000	14,500	18,000	18,000	12,467	11,859	12,148	12,006	11,988	12,275
West	83	51	12	63	8,100	8,300	8,100	17,644	18,000	18,000	12,353	13,060	13,261	13,264	12,721	13,059
Canada	74	29	7	36	10,000	11,000	10,000	21,000	17,000	21,000	15,617	14,142	15,663	15,883	14,050	15,752
All	778	480	113	593	6,864	8,300	6,864	23,000	21,000	23,000	12,381	12,223	12,410	12,319	12,019	12,346
School Libraries																
United States	489	342	30	372	5,000	9,845	5,000	28,000	25,700	28,000	13,612	15,448	13,742	13,274	15,182	13,369
Northeast	129	103	8	111	8,300	10,025	8,300	28,000	23,000	28,000	13,438	15,295	13,872	13,247	15,292	13,570
Southeast	120	69	2	71	5,000	11,500	5,000	20,000	17,800	20,000	13,024	14,650	13,155	12,991	14,650	13,115
Midwest	134	95	15	110	8,000	11,300	8,000	27,000	25,700	27,000	14,377	17,017	14,552	14,034	16,481	14,125
Southwest	57	42	3	45	9,200	11,500	9,200	22,116	14,808	22,116	13,672	13,827	13,662	12,277	13,827	12,364
West	49	33	2	35	9,400	9,845	9,400	21,000	13,000	21,000	13,608	11,422	13,130	13,047	11,422	12,709
Canada	19	8	3	11	10,000	16,500	10,000	22,000	26,000	26,000	17,160	22,625	18,577	17,308	21,250	17,500
All	508	350	33	383	5,000	9,845	5,000	28,000	26,000	28,000	13,745	16,022	13,928	13,426	15,688	13,528
College/Univ. Libs.																
United States	647	349	135	484	7,800	6,700	6,700	24,000	29,000	29,000	12,545	13,295	12,517	12,302	13,205	12,237
Northeast	194	120	48	168	8,700	8,600	8,600	21,850	29,000	29,000	12,508	14,059	12,349	12,350	14,071	11,895
Southeast	137	72	25	97	8,400	6,700	6,700	21,600	20,000	21,600	12,116	12,915	11,992	11,800	13,078	12,023
Midwest	193	96	40	136	7,800	9,000	7,800	22,665	18,000	22,665	12,466	12,664	12,440	12,333	12,177	12,173
Southwest	46	18	10	28	10,500	11,000	10,500	20,000	16,000	20,000	12,615	13,291	13,079	11,994	13,200	12,562
West	77	43	12	55	8,250	10,500	8,250	24,000	17,500	24,000	13,531	13,502	13,516	13,248	13,543	13,231
Canada	69	16	11	27	9,600	9,000	9,000	22,694	17,000	22,694	15,474	13,741	14,616	15,000	13,500	14,225
All	716	365	146	511	7,800	6,700	6,700	24,000	29,000	29,000	12,662	13,316	12,600	12,410	13,219	12,315
Other Libraries/Agencies																
United States	725	470	110	580	7,000	7,680	7,000	32,000	40,000	32,000	13,448	14,400	13,681	13,249	14,402	13,283
Northeast	320	231	47	278	8,000	7,680	7,680	32,000	40,000	40,000	13,781	15,560	13,982	13,657	15,519	13,582
Southeast	77	50	10	60	7,000	10,500	7,000	21,600	24,000	24,000	13,253	14,220	13,343	13,054	14,217	12,942
Midwest	182	100	24	124	7,000	10,400	7,000	24,000	22,125	24,000	12,826	12,886	13,132	12,578	12,591	12,927
Southwest	32	22	1	23	9,000	12,000	9,000	18,000	12,000	18,000	13,491	12,000	13,521	12,893	12,000	12,893
West	114	67	28	95	9,996	10,600	9,996	24,732	21,600	24,732	13,989	14,843	14,533	13,872	15,408	14,017
Canada	110	44	8	52	9,600	12,000	9,600	20,000	18,000	20,000	14,936	15,086	14,874	14,917	15,014	14,917
All	835	514	118	632	7,000	7,680	7,000	32,000	40,000	40,000	13,532	14,431	13,749	13,344	14,430	13,379

TABLE 13 EFFECTS OF EXPERIENCE ON SALARIES

	Salaries without Previous Experience (45 Schools)			Salaries with Previous Experience (46 Schools)		
	Women	Men	All	Women	Men	All
Number of Positions	611	166	777	664	156	820
Range of Low Salaries	$5,000-14,000	$6,700-14,600	$5,000-11,900	$8,000-19,136	$8,600-26,700	$8,000-26,700
Mean (Average)	9,442	10,776	9,270	10,895	12,889	10,778
Median	9,500	10,600	9,500	10,140	12,500	10,000
Range of High Salaries	9,500-21,600	6,700-24,000	9,500-24,000	12,950-32,000	11,500-26,700	11,500-32,000
Mean (Average)	15,036	14,616	16,069	19,226	18,139	19,897
Median	15,000	15,000	16,000	18,166	17,035	18,228
Range of Average Salaries	7,966-15,247	6,700-17,800	7,650-15,144	11,971-21,500	11,000-26,700	12,000-22,458
Mean (Average)	11,935	12,386	12,014	14,368	15,126	14,309
Median	11,937	12,375	12,127	13,600	14,550	13,701

Low Salaries

Lowest beginning salaries offered to 1979 graduates ranged from $5,000 to $14,000 with $9,000 as the median low salary for all graduates. In 1978 the low salaries ranged from $5,000 to $15,000, with $8,500 as the median low for all graduates. Of the 55 schools reporting low salaries for both men and women, seven reported higher low salaries for women, and 38 reported higher low salaries for men.

Public libraries again accounted for the majority of low salaries—40 percent—slightly better than in 1978, when they accounted for 41 percent and for 45 percent in 1977. Academic libraries accounted for 25 percent, up from 22 percent in 1978. Special libraries accounted for 21 percent, less than the 22 percent in 1978. School libraries accounted for 14 percent of the total, less than the 15.5 percent in 1978 and 16 percent in 1977.

There was no significant pattern in the geographical location of the positions. New York with 14 and Texas with 6 led the other states and Canada. The positions cited most often were reference, cataloging, and librarian, presumably in a small operation. The reason most commonly given for acceptance of the salary was geographical preference, followed by family commitments.

Distribution of low salaries is shown in Table 11 and Table 12.

NEXT YEAR?

Twenty-four placement officers see no change in the number of vacancies reported so far in 1980; six predict a decrease; and 22 feel that there is an increase. Forty-three schools expect that 1980 graduates will have the same amount of difficulty finding professional positions as did the 1979 graduates unless we have a severe recession. Seven expect less difficulty, and ten expect more difficulty, especially in California, but the failure of Proposition 9 to pass may modify this.

The responses to a question about types of libraries that are noticeably increasing or decreasing in the number of vacancies are summarized as follows:

Number of schools that think positions are:

	Increasing	Decreasing
Public libraries	12	9
School libraries	4	18
Academic libraries	16	6
Other libraries and library agencies	27	2

The solid increase seen in the "Other Libraries and Library Agencies" category is attributed to schools' making a special effort to find jobs for graduates in information management; an improved faculty strength in the special library area, which makes for better contacts in the field; and a feeling that business and industry recognize their information needs and are creating jobs and filling vacancies. Decreases are attributed to tight budgets, loss of federal funds, lower enrollments, and to a reluctance or refusal to fill vacancies as they occur.

Placement officers are surprisingly optimistic about academic library opportunities, but stress the need there for people with an interest in management and computers, or with a strong subject specialty. Thirty-three schools expect that salaries for 1980 graduates will be better than those offered to 1979 graduates. Estimates range from "slightly" to $2,000, with most estimates in the $1,000 to $1,500 range. Eighteen schools predict no change in 1980.

As has been true for the past few years, graduates with undergraduate backgrounds in science and technology (most particularly), mathematics, engineering, business, and languages are in demand. Graduates with such backgrounds should have a wider choice of jobs than other graduates.

With fewer beginners in the marketplace, there may be more and better opportunities in every type of library. Many graduates are finding positions out of their home states, and one Texas school reported many good opportunities in Texas for beginners. Many graduates are also finding permanent professional opportunities as the result of intern programs and part-time or full-time work while attending library school. Prospects for 1980 and the years following look very exciting and promising for the creative and well prepared graduate.

THE INFORMATION PROFESSION: AN OCCUPATIONAL SURVEY

Anthony Debons

Professor of Information Science, University of Pittsburgh

The basic assumption underlying all information science programs in colleges and universities is that there is a need for personnel who can be identified as information personnel. Another assumption is that such personnel possess skills through education and experience that are applied in the exercise of professional responsibilities. These assumptions are validated by employment data from those who have completed the information science programs. But what do such personnel do and where are they employed? This report attempts to provide an answer to these questions.

In 1972, the University of Pittsburgh sent out approximately 6,000 questionnaires to potential employers of information professionals, namely, industrial concerns, government agencies, research and development organizations, defense contractors, and professional associations. Response to the survey was poor; however, the study did reveal that the need for information professionals trained at the baccalaureate level is greater than for those trained at the masters and doctorate levels. The study highlighted the sampling problems that can arise when respondents are confronted with unconventional and poorly defined occupational areas.

In 1976, the University of Pittsburgh hosted a conference of high-level representatives from government, industry, and academia to attack the conceptual and technical problems uncovered in the 1972 study and to outline an approach for further study of the occupational composition of information professionals. They recommended a five-year program undertaken in three stages.

Stage 1: *Determination of Functions.* The objective was to identify those working as information professionals by reference to the functions they perform rather than to their qualifications or job classification and/or titles.

Stage 2: *Establish Personal Profiles.* The intent is to gather personal data, education, training, career patterns, and so forth, on samples drawn from the population of information professionals identified in Stage 1.

Stage 3: *Need Projections*. The intent of this stage is to analyze the data gathered in Stage 2 to ascertain what gaps exist in the education and training of information professionals and how these might be addressed, and to make projections on which manpower planning and allocation of educational resources can be based.

In 1978, the Division of Information Science and Technology, National Science Foundation (NSF), approved a grant for conducting Stage 1 of this program with Helene Ebenfield of NSF as the project monitor. At the University of Pittsburgh, Anthony Debons, as principal investigator; Una Mansfield, as project manager; and Donald Shirey, as associate principal investigator, were responsible for the development of the concept of the study and dissemination of the findings. Donald W. King (King Research Inc., Rockville, Md.) was responsible for the development of the questionnaire, the conducting of the survey, and the analysis of the data. Among the many professionals who contributed to the support of the study was Glen Harmon, who developed an initial assessment of the data, part of which is included in this report.

Several aspects of the conceptualization of the study are important to the understanding of the findings.

First, the investigators outlined basic postulates on which the various functions describing the information professionals could be established.

Information professionals are concerned with information systems.

Information systems are environments (i.e., organizations, institutions) of people, technology, and procedures that facilitate (a) the generation of new knowledge, (b) use of knowledge, and (c) transfer of knowledge for the purpose of solving problems and making decisions. Retrieval of documents, storage of records, indexing, cataloging, and so forth, are considered components of such systems.

Information is the result of a human process, of which one can find evidence in a physical record—the record being the commodity.

Information systems facilitate the human processes through the acquisition, use, and dissemination (transfer) of the commodities, but their essential objective is problem solving and decision making.

Based on these postulates, the following definition of an information professional was established: An information professional may be differentiated from other professionals who may also work with data by the fact that she/he is concerned with the content and therefore with the cognitive/intellectual operations performed on the data by the end-user.

Five main classifications of function were proposed for the study:

People who *analyze* the requirements and then design/implement such systems (information systems analysts and designers)

People who help end-users in their jobs through the use of such systems (data/information preparation on behalf of others; searching for data/information on behalf of others)

People who manage such systems (managing information operations, programs, services or data bases)

People who research such systems

People who train others to use such systems

TABLE 1 INFORMATION PROFESSIONALS BY SECTOR OF EMPLOYMENT

Sector	Number	Percent
Industry	1,161,500	71
State & local government	370,500	22
Federal government	78,900	5
Colleges & universities	30,100	2
Total	1,641,000	100

Source: Occupational Survey of Information Professionals, 1980.

Questionnaires were mailed to 2,358 individuals representing industry, state and local government, federal government, and colleges and universities. Of these, 1,193 responses were received for analysis. The responses were analyzed by function, by subunit, by occupational title (how the information professional is classified in terms of job title and education) and by work field (why and for what general purpose the functions are carried out). There were 1,641,000 information professionals so identified.

Table 1 shows the number and percentage of professionals reported from each sector of employment.

Table 2 shows the number and percentage of information professionals by primary information function performed. A total of 1,493 occupational titles were associated with the functions identified in Table 2.

Table 3 presents the number of professionals by work field and by sector of employment.

The data from the study indicate (1) that the information profession is one of the largest occupational areas in the United States and that information professionals are not identified with any particular institution or organizational unit (for example, only 2 percent of all information professionals is employed by colleges and universities, 71 percent in industry and business, 22 percent by state and local government, and 5 percent by the federal government), and (2) that although information professionals work in different types of organizations with diverse concepts, technologies, and cli-

TABLE 2 INFORMATION PROFESSIONALS BY PRIMARY INFORMATION FUNCTION PERFORMED

Information Functions	Number	Percent
Management of information	273,900	17
Data & information preparation	213,500	13
Data & information analysis	257,100	15
Searching for data/information	92,000	6
Information systems analysis	285,800	16
Information systems design	103,400	6
Operational information functions	272,700	17
Education/training of info. workers	42,800	3
Information research & development	20,700	1
Other information functions	5,700	1
Function not specified	93,400	6
Total	1,641,000	100

Source: Occupational Survey of Information Professionals, 1980.

TABLE 3 INFORMATION PROFESSIONALS BY WORK FIELD AND BY SECTOR OF EMPLOYMENT

Work field	Industry	State/Local Govt.	Federal Govt.	Colleges and Universities	Total
Computer	594,700	42,700	38,100	7,500	683,000
Education/training	15,500	107,600	1,200	7,600	131,900
Financial	46,300	21,100	300	1,300	69,000
Information services	83,800	53,600	12,400	700	150,500
Library	74,500	69,900	5,600	9,800	159,800
Management support	115,900	36,800	13,600	1,400	167,700
Research	96,900	20,600	5,800	1,500	124,800
Statistical	1,400	2,400	—	100	3,900
Technical publications	35,200	2,400	1,300	100	39,000
Other	6,700	5,600	300	100	12,700
Unspecified	90,600	7,800	300	—	98,700
Total	1,161,500	370,500	78,900	30,100	1,641,000

Source: Occupational Survey of Information Professionals, 1980.

entele, they share a set of common concerns associated with the concepts basic to information flow (e.g., general systems paradigm).

The implications of the data to institutions are diverse and their importance has to be judged in terms of their impact on (1) the creation of job titles that clearly delineate the nature of the functions performed, (2) the formation of career ladders that ensure the importance and complexity of function to institutional objectives, and (3) the changing of the present curriculum in academic institutions to ensure effective and adequate preparation for the functions identified. There seems little doubt as to the reality of the information profession in the community of professions. The acceptance of the profession, however, may be another matter and one that is based on the recognition that information professionals perform distinct functions that serve other professional groups well.

Present efforts in extending this reseach program along the lines indicated are now being pursued.

ACCREDITED LIBRARY SCHOOLS

This list of graduate schools accredited by the American Library Association was issued in October 1980. A list of more than 400 institutions offering both accredited and nonaccredited programs in librarianship appears in the thirty-third edition of the *American Library Directory* (Bowker, 1980).

NORTHEAST: CT; DC; MA; MD; NJ; NY; PA; RI

Catholic University of America, Grad. Dept. of Lib. and Info. Science, Washington, DC 20064. Elizabeth W. Stone, Chpn. 202-635-5085.

Clarion State College, School of Lib. Science, Clarion, PA 16214. Elizabeth A. Rupert, Dean. 814-226-2271.

Columbia University, School of Lib. Service, New York, NY 10027. Richard L. Darling, Dean. 212-280-2291.

Drexel University, School of Lib. and Info. Science, Philadelphia, PA 19104. Guy Garrison, Dean. 215-895-2474.

Long Island University, C. W. Post Center, Palmer Grad. Lib. School, Greenvale, NY 11548. John T. Gillespie, Acting Dean. 516-299-2855/2856.

Pratt Institute, Grad. School of Lib. and Info. Science, Brooklyn, NY 11205. Nasser Sharify, Dean. 212-636-3702.

Queens College, City University of New York, Grad. School of Lib. and Info. Studies, Flushing, NY 11367. Richard J. Hyman, Dir. 212-520-7194.

Rutgers University, Grad. School of Lib. and Info. Studies, New Brunswick, NJ 08903. Thomas H. Mott, Jr., Dean. 201-933-7500.

St. John's University, Div. of Lib. and Info. Science, Jamaica, NY 11439. Mildred Lowe, Acting Dir. 212-969-8000, ext. 200.

Simmons College, School of Lib. Science, Boston, MA 02115. Robert D. Stueart, Dean. 617-738-2225.

Southern Connecticut State College, Div. of Lib. Science and Instructional Technology, New Haven, CT 06515. Emanuel T. Prostano, Dir. 203-397-4532.

State University of New York at Albany, School of Lib. and Info. Science, Albany, NY 12222. Richard S. Halsey, Dean. 518-455-6288.

State University of New York at Buffalo, School of Info. and Lib. Studies, Buffalo, NY 14260. George S. Bobinski, Dean. 716-636-2411.

State University of New York, College of Arts and Science, Geneseo, School of Lib. and Info. Science, Geneseo, NY 14454. John E. Kephart, Interim Dean. 716-245-5322.

Syracuse University, School of Info. Studies, Syracuse, NY 13210. Robert S. Taylor, Dean. 315-423-2911.

University of Maryland, College of Lib. and Info. Services, College Park, MD 20742. Michael M. Reynolds, Dean. 301-454-5441.

University of Pittsburgh, School of Lib. and Info. Science, Pittsburgh, PA 15260. Thomas J. Galvin, Dean. 412-624-5230.

University of Rhode Island, Grad. Lib. School, Kingston, RI 02881. Bernard S. Schlessinger, Dean. 401-792-2878/2947.

SOUTHEAST: AL; FL; GA; KY; MS; NC; SC; TN

Alabama Agricultural and Mechanical University, School of Lib. Media, Normal, AL 35762. Howard G. Ball, Dean. 205-859-7216.

Atlanta University, School of Lib. and Info. Studies, Atlanta, GA 30314. Virginia Lacy Jones, Dean. 404-681-0251, ext. 230.

Emory University, Div. of Libnshp., Atlanta, GA 30322. A. Venable Lawson, Dir. 404-329-6840.

Florida State University, School of Lib. Science, Tallahassee, FL 32306. Harold Goldstein, Dean. 904-644-5775.

North Carolina Central University, School of Lib. Science, Durham, NC 27707. Annette L. Phinazee, Dean. 919-683-6485.

University of Alabama, Grad. School of Lib. Service, University, AL 35486. James D. Ramer, Dean. 205-348-4610.

University of Kentucky, College of Lib. Science, Lexington, KY 40506. Timothy W. Sineath, Dean. 606-258-8876.

University of North Carolina, School of Lib. Science, Chapel Hill, NC 27514. Edward G. Holley, Dean. 919-933-8366.

University of South Carolina, College of Libnshp., Columbia, SC 29208. F. William Summers, Dean. 803-777-3858.

University of South Florida, Grad. Dept. of Lib., Media and Info. Studies, Tampa, FL 33620. John A. McCrossan, Chpn. 813-974-2557 or 2100.

University of Southern Mississippi, School of Lib. Service, Hattiesburg, MS 39401.

Onva K. Bushears, Jr., Dean. 601-266-7168.

University of Tennessee, Knoxville, Grad. School of Lib. and Info. Science, Knoxville, TN 37916. Ann E. Prentice, Dir. 615-974-2148.

Vanderbilt University, George Peabody College for Teachers, Dept. of Lib. Science, Nashville, TN. 37203. Edwin S. Gleaves, Chpn. 615-327-8037.

MIDWEST: IA; IL; IN; KS; MI: MN; MO; OH; WI

Ball State University, Dept. of Lib. Science, Muncie, IN 47306. Doris W. Cox, Chpn. 317-285-7180/7189.

Case Western Reserve University, School of Lib. Science, Cleveland, OH 44106. Edward T. O'Neill, Dean. 216-368-3500.

Emporia State University, School of Lib. Science, Emporia, KS 66801. J. W. Maucker, Interim Dir. 316-343-1200, ext. 203/204.

Indiana University, Grad. Lib. School, Bloomington, IN 47401. Herbert S. White, Dean. 812-337-2848.

Kent State University, School of Lib. Science, Kent, OH 44242. A. Robert Rogers, Dean. 216-672-2782/7988.

Northern Illinois University, Dept. of Lib. Science, DeKalb, IL 60115. Sylvia G. Faibisoff, Chpn. 815-753-1735.

Rosary College, Grad. School of Lib. Science, River Forest, IL 60305. Sister M. Lauretta McCusker, O.P., Dean. 312-366-2490.

University of Chicago, Grad. Lib. School, Chicago, IL 60637. W. Boyd Rayward, Dean. 312-753-3482.

University of Illinois, Grad. School of Lib. Science, 410 David Kinley Hall, Urbana, IL 61801. Charles H. Davis, Dean. 217-333-3280.

University of Iowa, School of Lib. Science, Iowa City, IA 52242. Carl F. Orgren, Acting Dir. 319-353-3644.

University of Michigan, School of Lib. Science, Ann Arbor, MI 48109. Russell E. Bidlack, Dean. 313-764-9376.

University of Minnesota, Lib. School, 117 Pleasant St. S.E., Minneapolis, MN 55455. Wesley C. Simonton, Dir. 612-373-3100.

University of Missouri, Columbia, School of Lib. and Info. Science, Columbia, MO 65211. Edward P. Miller, Dean. 314-882-4546.

University of Wisconsin—Madison, Lib. School, Madison, WI 53706. Charles A. Bunge, Dir. 608-263-2900.

University of Wisconsin—Milwaukee, School of Lib. Science, Milwaukee, WI 53201. Mohammed M. Aman, Dean. 414-963-4707.

Wayne State University, Div. of Lib. Science, Detroit, MI 48202. Robert E. Booth, Dir. 313-577-1825.

Western Michigan University, School of Libnshp., Kalamazoo, MI 49008. Jean Lowrie, Dir. 616-383-1849.

SOUTHWEST: AZ; LA; OK; TX

Louisiana State University, Grad. School of Lib. Science, Baton Rouge, LA 70803. Jane R. Carter, Dean. 504-388-3158.

North Texas State University, School of Lib. and Info. Sciences, Denton, TX 76203. Dewey E. Carroll, Dean. 817-788-2445.

Texas Woman's University, School of Lib. Science, Denton, TX 76204. Brooke E. Sheldon, Dir. 817-387-2418.

University of Arizona, Grad. Lib. School, Tucson, AZ 85721. Ellen Altman, Dir. 602-626-3565.

University of Oklahoma, School of Lib. Science, Norman, OK 73019. James S. Healey, Dir. 405-325-3921.

University of Texas at Austin, Grad. School of Lib. Science, Austin, TX 78712. C. Glenn Sparks, Dean. 512-471-3821.

WEST: CA; CO; HI; UT; WA

Brigham Young University, School of Lib. and Info. Sciences, Provo, UT 84602. Maurice P. Marchant, Dir. 801-378-2976.

San Jose State University, Div. of Lib. Science, San Jose, CA 95192. Leslie H. Janke, Dir. 408-277-2292.

University of California, Berkeley, School of Lib. and Info. Studies, Berkeley, CA 94720. Michael K. Buckland, Dean. 415-642-1464.

University of California, Los Angeles, Grad. School of Lib. and Info. Science, Los Angeles, CA 90024; Robert M. Hayes, Dean. 213-825-4351.

University of Denver, Grad. School of Libnshp. and Info. Management, Denver, CO 80208. Bernard M. Franckowiak, Dean. 303-753-2557.

University of Hawaii, Grad. School of Lib. Studies, Honolulu, HI 96822. Ira W. Harris, Dean. 808-948-7321.

University of Southern California, School of Lib. Science, University Park, Los Angeles, CA 90007. Roger C. Greer, Dean. 213-743-2548.

University of Washington, School of Libnshp., Seattle, WA 98195. Peter Hiatt, Dir. 206-543-1794.

CANADA

Dalhousie University, School of Lib. Service, Halifax, N.S. B3H 4H8. Norman Horrocks, Dir. 902-424-3656.

McGill University, Grad. School of Lib. Science, Montreal, P.Q. H3A 1Y1. Vivian Sessions, Dir. 514-392-5947.

Université de Montréal, Ecole de bibliothéconomie, Montréal, P.Q. H3C 3J7. Daniel Reicher, Dir. 514-343-6044.

University of Alberta, Faculty of Lib. Science, Edmonton, Alta. T6G 2J4. William Kurmey, Dean. 403-432-4578.

University of British Columbia, School of Libnshp., Vancouver, B.C. V6T 1W5. Roy B. Stokes, Dir. 604-228-2404.

University of Toronto, Faculty of Lib. Science, Toronto, Ont. M5S 1A1. Katherine H. Packer, Dean. 416-978-3234.

University of Western Ontario, School of Lib. and Info. Science, London, Ont. N6A 5B9. William J. Cameron, Dean. 519-679-3542.

LIBRARY SCHOLARSHIP SOURCES

For a more complete list of the scholarships, fellowships, and assistantships offered for library study, see *Financial Assistance for Library Education* published biannually by the American Library Association.

American Library Association. Two scholarships of $3,000. The David H. Clift Scholarship is given to a varying number of U.S. or Canadian citizens who have been admitted to an accredited library school. For information, write to: Staff Liaison, David H. Clift Scholarship Jury, ALA, 50 E. Huron St., Chicago, IL 60611; the Louise Giles Minority Scholarship is given to a varying number of minority students who are U.S. or Canadian citizens and have been admitted to an accredited library school. For information, write to: Staff Liaison, Louise Giles Minority Scholarship Jury, ALA, 50 E. Huron St., Chicago, IL 60611.

American-Scandinavian Foundation. Fellowships and grants for 25 to 30 students, in amounts from $500 to $5,500, for advanced study in Denmark, Finland, Iceland, Norway, or Sweden. For information, write to: Exchange Division, American-Scandinavian Foundation, 127 E. 73 St., New York, NY 10021.

Beta Phi Mu. Three scholarships: (1) $1,500 each for a varying number of persons accepted in an ALA-accredited library program; (2) $750 each for a varying number of Beta Phi Mu members for continuing education; (3) the Harold Lancour Scholarship for Foreign Study, $750 each for a varying number of students for graduate study in a foreign country related to the applicant's work or schooling. For information, write to: Exec. Secy., Beta Phi Mu, Graduate School of Library and Information Science, University of Pittsburgh, Pittsburgh, PA 15260.

Canadian Library Association. Howard V. Phalin-World Book Graduate Scholarship in Library Science. A $2,500 maximum scholarship for a Canadian citizen or landed immigrant to attend an accredited library school in Canada or the United States. H. W. Wilson Scholarship of $2,000 and Elizabeth Dafoe Scholarship of $1,750 for a Canadian citizen or landed immigrant to attend an accredited Canadian library school. For information, write to: Scholarships and Awards Committee, Canadian Library Association, 151 Sparks St., Ottawa, Ont. K1P 5E3, Canada.

Catholic Library Association. Rev. Andrew L. Bouwhuis Scholarship of $1,500 for a person with a B.A. degree who has been accepted in an accredited library school. (Award based on financial need and proficiency.) World Book-Childcraft Awards. One scholarship of a total of $1,000 to be distributed among no more than four recipients for a program of continuing education. Open to CLA members only. For information, write to: Scholarship Committee, Catholic Library Association, 461 W. Lancaster Ave., Haverford, PA 19401.

Fulbright Awards. Fellowships and grants of varying amounts for university lecturing or advanced research abroad to candidates with a Ph.D. and library and teaching or research experience. Foreign language proficiency required in some instances. For information, write to: Council for International Exchange of Scholars, Suite 300, 11 Dupont Circle, Washington, DC 20036.

Information Exchange System for Minority Personnel. Scholarship of $500, intended for minority students, for graduate study. For information, write to: Dorothy M. Haith, Chpn., Clara Stanton Jones School, Box 91, Raleigh, NC 27602.

Medical Library Association. (1) Varying number of scholarships of $2,000 each for minority students, for graduate study in medical librarianship. (2) Grants of varying amounts for continuing education for medical librarians with an MLS and two years' professional experience. Open to MLA members only. For information, write to: Scholarship Committee, Medical Library Association, Suite 3208, 919 N. Michigan Ave., Chicago, IL 60611.

The Frederic G. Melcher Scholarship (administered by Association of Library Service to Children, ALA). Scholarship of $4,000 for a U.S. or Canadian citizen admitted to an accredited library school who plans to work with children in school or public libraries. For information, write to: Exec. Secy., Association of Library Service to Children, ALA, 50 E. Huron St., Chicago, IL 60611.

Mountain Plains Library Association. Seven grants of $500 each for residents of the association area. Open only to MPLA members with at least two years of membership. For information, write to: Joseph R. Edelen, Jr., MPLA Exec.

Secy., University of South Dakota Library, Vermillion, SD 57069.

Natural Sciences and Engineering Research Council. Ten scholarships of $8,500 each for postgraduate study in science librarianship and documentation for a Canadian citizen or landed immigrant with a bachelor's degree in science or engineering. For information, write to: J. H. Danis, Scholarships Officer, Natural Sciences and Engineering Research Council, Ottawa, Ont. K1A OR6 Canada.

New England Library Association. A varying number of scholarships in varying amounts. For information, write to: NELA Scholarship Chair, NELA, Upper Walpole Rd., Walpole, NH 03608.

Special Libraries Association. Three $3,000 scholarships for U.S. or Canadian citizens, accepted by an ALA-accredited library education program who show an aptitude for and interest in special libraries. One $1,000 scholarship for a U.S. or Canadian citizen with an MLS and an interest in special libraries who has been accepted in an ALA-accredited Ph.D. program. For information, write to: Scholarship Committee, SLA, 235 Park Ave. S., New York, NY 10003. Three scholarships of $2,000 each for minority students with an interest in special libraries. Open to U.S. or Canadian citizens only. For information, write to: Positive Action Program for Minority Groups, c/o SLA.

LIBRARY SCHOLARSHIP AND AWARD RECIPIENTS, 1980

AALS Research Grant Award—$1,500. For a project that reflects the goals and objectives of the Association of American Library Schools (AALS). *Offered by:* AALS. *Winners:* Kay Vandergrift, Columbia Univ., for "Educational Competency of the School Media Specialist: An Investigation into the Nature and Extent of Library School Responses"; Kerry Johnson and Marilyn D. White, Univ. of Maryland, for "An Investigation of the Relationship of Cognitive Studies to Person and Role Variables in Library and Information Science."

AASL Distinguished Library Service Award for School Administrators. For a unique and sustained contribution toward furthering the role of the library and its development in elementary and/or secondary education. *Offered by:* ALA American Association of School Librarians. *Winner:* Arthur S. Alford, Supt., Pitt County Public Schools, Greenville, NC; Kermit Keenum, Supt., Cobb County Public Schools, Marietta, GA.

AASL/Encyclopaedia Britannica School Library Media Program of the Year Award—$5,000. For outstanding school media programs. *Offered by:* ALA American Association of School Librarians and the Encyclopaedia Britannica Co. *Winner:* Irvine (CA) Unified School District.

AASL President's Award—$2,000. For demonstrating excellence and providing an outstanding national or international contribution to school librarianship and school library development. *Offered by:* ALA, American Association of School Librarians. *Donor:* Baker & Taylor. *Winner:* Mary Gaver.

ACRL Academic/Research Librarian of the Year Award—$2,000 (equally divided). For an outstanding national or international contribution to academic and research librarianship and library development. *Offered by:* ALA, Association of College and Research Libraries. *Donor:* Baker & Taylor. *Winner:* Evan Ira Farber, Libn., Earlham College.

ALA Honorary Life Membership Award. *Offered by:* American Library Association. *Winner:* Bessie Boehm Moore.

ASCLA Exceptional Service Award. For exceptional service to ASCLA or any of its component areas of service, namely, services to patients, the home-bound, medical, nursing, and other professional staff in hospitals, and inmates, demonstrating professional leadership, effective interpretation of program, pioneering activity, or significant research or experimental projects. *Offered by:* Association of Specialized & Cooperative Library Agencies. *Winner:* Margaret Cheeseman, Univ. of Wisconsin–Madison Lib. School.

Alabama Public Library Service Graduate Scholarships (Full-Time)—$5,000. For Alabama residents admitted to an ALA-accredited library school and interested in a career in public librarianship. *Offered by:* Alabama Public Lib. Service. *Winners:* Annesse S. Sankey and Sherrie Marquita Jones.

Alabama Public Library Service Graduate Scholarships (Part-Time)—$500. For an Alabama public librarian admitted to an ALA-accredited library school program and demonstrating a commitment to public library service. *Winners:* Linda Dotzheimer, George David Lilly, Angela Jane Weir, and Nancy Sims Woosley.

Armed Forces Librarians Achievement Citation. For significant contributions to the development of armed forces library service and to organizations encouraging an interest in libraries and reading. *Offered by:* Armed Forces Librarians Section, ALA Public Library Association. *Winner:* Arlene Luster, PACAF command libn., Hickam Air Force Base, Hawaii.

Beta Phi Mu Award—$500. For distinguished service to education for librarianship. *Offered by:* ALA Awards Committee. *Donor:* Beta Phi Mu Library Science Honorary Association. *Winner:* Virginia Lacy Jones, Dean, School of Lib. and Info. Studies, Atlanta Univ.

CASLIS Award for Special Librarianship in Canada. *Offered by:* Canadian Assn. of Special Libraries and Information Services. *Winner:* Beryl L. Anderson, Lib. Documentation Centre, National Lib., Ottawa, Canada.

CIS/GODORT/ALA Documents to the People Award—$1,000. For effectively encouraging the use of federal documents in support of library services. *Offered by:* ALA Government Documents Round Table. *Donor:* Congressional Information Service, Inc. *Winner:* Sandra Faull.

CLA Outstanding Service to Librarianship Award. *Offered by:* Canadian Library Association. *Winner:* Jessie Mifflin, St. John's, Newfoundland.

CLR Fellowships. For a list of the recipients for the 1979–1980 academic year, see the report from the Council on Library Resources, Inc., in CLTA Merit Award. *Offered by:* Canadian Library Trustee Assn. *Winner:* N. Ray Wright, Newfoundland Public Libs. Bd., Canada.

CSLA Award for Outstanding Congregational Librarian. For distinguished service to the congregation and/or community through devotion to the congregational library. *Offered by:* Church and Synagogue Library Association. *Winner:* Lois Patterson, Libn., Jarvis Memorial United Methodist Church, Greenville, NC.

CSLA Award for Outstanding Congregational Library. For responding in creative and innovative ways to the library's mission of reaching and serving the congregation and/or the wider community. *Offered by:* Church and Synagogue Library Association. *Winner:* First Christian Church, New Castle, PA (Eileen McEwen, Libn.).

CSLA Award for Outstanding Contribution to Librarianship. For providing inspiration, guidance, leadership, or resources to enrich the field of church or synagogue librarianship. *Offered by:* Church and Synagogue Library Association. *Winner:* Evelyn Ling, Akron, OH.

CSLA Distinguished Service Award. *Offered by:* Canadian School Librarians Assn. *Winner:* Onésime Tremblay, General Dir., Roman Catholic Separate School Bd., Sudbury, Ont., Canada.

Francis Joseph Campbell Citation. For an outstanding contribution to the advancement of library service to the blind. *Offered by:* Section on Library Service to the Blind and Physically Handicapped of the Association of Specialized and Cooperative Library Agencies. *Winner:* Bernard Krebs, former lib. dir., Jewish Guild for the Blind.

David H. Clift Scholarship—$3,000. For a worthy student to begin a program of library education at the graduate level. *Offered by:* ALA Awards Committee, Standing Committee on Library Education. *Winners:* Rebecca Rose Malek, New Orleans, LA; Mary Ruth Spirito, Hamden, CT.

Elizabeth Dafoe Scholarship—$1,750. For a Canadian citizen or landed immigrant to attend an accredited Canadian library school. *Offered by:* Canadian Library Association. *Winner:* Heather Kirkpatrick, Saskatoon, Sask., Canada.

John Cotton Dana Award (formerly SLA Special Citation). For exceptional support and encouragement of special librarianship. *Offered by:* Special Libraries Association. *Winner:* Not awarded in 1980.

Melvil Dewey Medal. For recent creative professional achievement of a high order, particularly in library management, library training, cataloging and classification, and the tools and techniques of librarianship. *Offered by:* ALA Awards Committee. *Donor:* Forest Press. *Winner:* Robert D. Stueart, Dean and Professor, Grad. School of Lib. and Info. Science, Simmons College, Boston.

Ida and George Eliot Prize—$100. For an essay published in any journal in the preceding calendar year which has been judged most effective in furthering medical librarianship. *Offered by:* Medical Library Association. *Winner:* Eloise C. Foster.

Facts on File Award—$1,000. For an individual who has made current affairs more meaningful to adults. *Winner:* Harva Sheeler, Jones, Day, Reavis & Pogue Law Firm, Washington, DC.

Louise Giles Minority Scholarship—$3,000. for a worthy student who is a U.S. or Canadian citizen and is also a member of a principal minority group. *Offered by:* ALA Awards Committee, Office for Library Personnel Resources Advisory Committee. *Winners:* Lorraine H. Bigman, Tsaile, AZ; Donna Jean Kennedy, Sacramento, CA.

Murray Gottlieb Prize—$100. For the best unpublished essay submitted by a medical librarian on the history of some aspect of health sciences or a detailed description of a library exhibit. *Offered by:* Medical Library Association. *Winner:* Judith A. Ouermeir.

Grolier Foundation Award—$1,000. For an unusual contribution to the stimulation and guidance of reading by children and young people through high school age, for continuing service, or one particular contribution of lasting value. *Offered by:* ALA Awards Committee. *Donor:* Grolier Foundation. *Winner:* Mabel Williams.

Grolier National Library Week Award—$1,000. For the best plan for a public relations program. *Awarded by:* National Library Week Committee of the American Library Association. *Donor:* Grolier Educational Corp. *Winner:*

South Carolina Lib. Assn., for a consumer campaign entitled "Libraries—South Carolina's Greatest Bargain."

Bailey K. Howard-World Book Encyclopedia-ALA Goal Award—$5,000. To support programs that recognize, advance, and implement the goals and objectives of the American Library Association. *Donor:* World Book-Childcraft International, Inc. *Winner:* ALA Intellectual Freedom Committee.

John Phillip Imroth Memorial Award for Intellectual Freedom—$500. For a notable contribution to intellectual freedom and remarkable personal courage. *Offered by:* ALA Intellectual Freedom Round Table. *Donor:* Intellectual Freedom Round Table. *Winner:* Elizabeth A. Phillips, North Ferrisburgh, VT.

Information Industry Association Hall of Fame Award. For leadership and innovation in furthering the progress of the information industry. *Offered by:* Information Industry Association. *Winner:* Samuel P. Wolpert, Founder and Pres., Predicasts.

Information Product of the Year Award. For excellence in product innovations and development of a product introduced within the past five years. *Offered by:* Information Industry Association. *Winner:* Research Publications, Woodbridge, CT, for "U.S. Patents on Microfilm."

Information Technology of the Year Award. For a technology that impacted the information industry. *Offered by:* Information Industry Association. *Winner:* MINI MARC, Informatics, Inc., Rockville, MD.

JMRT Professional Development Grant. *See* 3M Company Professional Development Grant.

J. Morris Jones-World Book Encyclopedia-ALA Goal Award—$5,000. To support programs that recognize, advance, and implement the goals and objectives of the American Library Association. *Donor:* World Book-Childcraft International, Inc. *Winner:* ALA Office for Lib. Personnel Resources Advisory Committee and the Committee on the Status of Women in Librarianship for the project "Equal Pay for Work of Equal Value: An Action Approach."

William T. Knox Outstanding Information of the Year Award. For excellence in managing information resources or for a distinctive contribution to the information management field. *Offered by:* Associated Information Managers. *Winner:* Benjamin H. Weil, Sr. Staff Advisor, Exxon Research and Engineering Co., Linden, NJ.

LITA Award for Achievement in Library and Information Technology. For distinguished leadership, notable development or application of technology, superior accomplishments in research or education or original contributions to the literature of the field. *Offered by:* Library and Information Technology Association. *Winner:* Henriette D. Avram, Dir. for Processing Systems, Networks and Automation Planning, Lib. of Congress.

LRRT Research Award—$500. To encourage excellence in library research. *Offered by:* ALA Library Research Round Table. *Winner:* George P. M. D'Elia, Asst. Prof., Lib. School, Univ. of Minnesota, for "The Development and Testing of a Conceptual Model of Public Library User Behavior."

Joseph W. Lippincott Award—$1,000. For distinguished service to the profession of librarianship, such service to include outstanding participation in the activities of professional library associations, notable published professional writing, or other significant activity on behalf of the profession and its aims. *Offered by:* ALA Awards Committee. *Donor:* Joseph W. Lippincott. *Winner:* E. J. Josey, Chief, Bureau of Specialist Lib. Services, NY State Education Dept.

Margaret Mann Citation. For outstanding professional achievement in the area of cataloging and classification. *Offered by:* ALA Resources and Technical Services Division/Cataloging and Classification Section. *Winner:* Peter Ronald Lewis, British Lib.

Allie Beth Martin Award—$2,000. For an outstanding librarian. *Offered by:* ALA Public Library Association. *Donor:* Baker & Taylor. *Winner:* Mary Louise Rheay.

Frederic G. Melcher Scholarship—$4,000. For young people who wish to enter the field of library service to children. *Offered by:* ALA Association for Library Service to Children. *Winners:* Kathleen Duffy, Millville, NJ; Martha Ruff, Baltimore, MD.

Isadore Gilbert Mudge Citation. For a distinguished contribution to reference librarianship. *Offered by:* Reference and Adult Services Division of American Library Association. *Winner:* Hylda Kamisar, Head, Reference Section, Lib. of Congress National Lib. Service for the Blind and Physically Handicapped.

Music Library Association Prizes—$50. For the best book-length bibliography or research tool, for the best article-length bibliography or article on music librarianship by an author not beyond the age of 40, and for the best review of a book or score published in *Notes*. *Offered by:* Music Library Association *Winners:* Maurice Hinson (best book), Michael D. Williams (best article), and Jurgen Thym (best review).

National Library Service Resources Section Publication Award. Presented to the author/authors of an outstanding monograph, published article, or original paper on acquisitions pertaining to college or university libraries. *Offered by:* ALA Resources and Technical Services Division, Resources Section. *Donor:* Arnold Santos and National Library Service, Inc. *Winner:* Charles Osborn.

Shirley Olofson Memorial Award. For individuals to attend their second annual conference of ALA. *Offered by:* ALA Junior Members Round Table. *Winners:* Larayne J. Dallas, Paul Burton Drake, Amy Fleischman, Barbara Ellen Fritchman, Marc Galbraith, Donna J. Helmer, Patricia Matthes, Sally Ann Robertson, Lucy B. Sheerr, and Jane Anne Snider.

Howard V. Phalin-World Book Graduate Scholarship in Library Science—$2,500 (maximum). For a Canadian citizen or landed immigrant to attend an accredited library school in Canada or the United States. *Offered by:* Canadian Library Association. *Winner:* Monika Langer, Montreal, P.Q., Canada.

Esther J. Piercy Award. For contribution to librarianship in the field of technical services by younger members of the profession. *Offered by:* ALA Resources and Technical Services Division. *Winner:* Nancy B. Olson, Mankato (MN) State Univ. Lib.

RTSD Resources Section Scholarship—$1,000. *Offered by:* ALA Resources and Technical Services Division. *Winners:* Charles B. Osburn, for *Academic Research and Library Resources: Changing Patterns in America* (Greenwood).

Rittenhouse Award—$200. For the best unpublished paper on medical librarianship submitted by a student enrolled in, or having been enrolled in, a course for credit in an ALA-accredited library school, or a trainee in an internship program in medical librarianship. *Offered by:* Medical Library Association. *Winner:* Anne R. Sawyer.

SLA Hall of Fame. For an extended and sustained period of distinguished service to the Special Libraries Association in all spheres of its activities. *Offered by:* Special Libraries Association. *Winners:* Rosemary R. Demarest, Charles H. Stevens, and Elizabeth R. Usher.

SLA Honorary Member. In recognition of contribution to or support of librarianship. *Offered by:* Special Libraries Association. *Winner:* Ralph H. Parker.

SLA Minority Stipends—$1,500. For students with financial need who show potential for special librarianship. *Offered by:* Special Libraries Association. *Winners:* Kathy Jenkins, Washington, DC; Amy Lee, Seattle, WA; Mae Woodley, Brooklyn, NY.

SLA Professional Award. For a significant achievement or contribution to librarianship which advances the stated objectives of the Special Libraries Association. *Offered by:* Special Libraries Association. *Winner:* Not awarded in 1980.

SLA Scholarships—$3,000. For students with financial need who show potential for special librarianship. *Offered by:* Special Libraries Association. *Winners:* Patricia Dangler, Largo, FL; Susan K. Smith, Springfield, NY; Mary Sarah Welna, Arlington, VA.

Charles Scribner's Sons Award—$3,250. To attend ALA's annual conference. *Offered by:* ALA Association for Library Service to Children. *Donor:* Charles Scribner's Sons. *Winners:* Virginia Opocensky, Monica Carollo, Susan L. Avitabile, Debra Ann McLeod, Josephine Campa, and Lucy Cutler.

Ralph R. Shaw Award for Library Literature—$500. For an outstanding contribution to library literature issued during the three years preceding the presentation. *Offered by:* ALA Awards Committee. *Donor:* Scarecrow Press. *Winner:* Rhea Rubin, for *Using Bibliotherapy: A Guide to Theory and Practice* (Oryx) and *A Bibliotherapy Sourcebook* (Oryx).

3M Company Professional Development Grant—$5,000. To encourage professional development and participation of new librarians in ALA and JMRT activities. To cover expenses for recipients attending the ALA San Francisco conference. *Offered by:* ALA Junior Members Round Table. *Winners:* Jeannie Dixon, Gary Freiburger, and Mary Jo P. Godwin.

Trustee Citations. For distinguished service to library development whether on the local, state, or national level. *Offered by:* ALA American Library Trustee Association. *Donor:* ALA. *Winners:* Dorothy C. Hevelone, Beatrice, NE; Howard Lipton, St. Clair Shores, MI.

H. W. Wilson Co. Award—$500. For the best paper published in *Special Libraries* in 1977. *Offered by:* Special Libraries Association. *Winner:* Herbert S. White, for "Cost-Effectiveness and Cost-Benefit Determination in Special Libraries."

H. W. Wilson Library Periodical Award—$500. To a periodical published by a local, state, or regional library, library group, or library association in the United States or Canada which has made an outstanding contribution to librarianship. *Offered by:* ALA Awards Committee. *Donor:* H. W. Wilson Co. *Winner: PLA Bulletin* (Pennsylvania Lib. Assn.), edited by Barbara Casini.

H. W. Wilson Library Recruitment Award—$1,000. Presented to any local, state, or regional library association, any library school, or any other appropriate group concerned with recruitment to the profession. *Offered by:* ALA Awards Committee. *Donor:* H. W. Wilson Co. *Winner:* Hana Cipris, Hamilton, Ont., Canada.

H. W. Wilson Library Staff Development Grant—$250. *Offered by:* ALA Awards Committee. *Winner:* Southern Univ., Shreveport, LA.

Wittenborn Award. For the best paper on an art librarianship topic by a current MLS student. *Offered by:* Art Libraries Society of North America. *Winner:* Barbara C. Polowy, Syracuse Univ. (NY).

Part 4
Research and Statistics

Library Research and Statistics

RESEARCH ON LIBRARIES AND LIBRARIANSHIP IN 1980: AN OVERVIEW

Mary Jo Lynch
Director, ALA Office for Research

The topic receiving prime attention in 1980 was library personnel. For some time the library community has urged the National Center for Education Statistics to update a study conducted in 1972–1973 by the Bureau of Labor Statistics (BLS) that led to the publication, in 1975, of *Library Manpower: A Study of Demand and Supply* (BLS Bulletin 1982). That study projected supply and demand to 1985. In April 1980 the National Center for Education Statistics together with the Office of Libraries and Learning Technologies of the Office of Education issued a Request for Proposal (RFP) for "1981–1982 Library Human Resources: A Study of Supply and Demand." This study, to be conducted by King Research, will be both an update and an expansion of the earlier work by BLS. Using data obtained from surveys of library employers and library schools and mathematical projections based on econometric models, the study will assess current supply and demand conditions in the field of librarianship and project them to 1990.

King Research was also involved in related work completed in 1980—the Occupational Survey of Information Professionals (OSIP). As described in this article last year [see *Bowker Annual, 1980*, p. 362], the study first identified and defined the functions performed by information professionals and then sent questionnaires to public- and private-sector employers asking how many such persons were employed. [For a full report on the results of the survey, see the article by Anthony Debons in Part 3—*Ed.*]

Released early in 1981 [and reprinted in "Recent Library Personnel Surveys" in Part 3 of this volume] are the results of the study "Racial, Ethnic and Sexual Composition of Library Staffs in Academic and Public Libraries" conducted by the American Library Association (ALA), Office for Library Personnel Resources (OLPR), with the help of funds from the Council on Library Resources. For some time OLPR has collected information about the sexual and ethnic status of graduates of library education programs but similar information was not available for the total profession, thus hampering affirmative action planning. To gather this information a questionnaire was sent to personnel officers in a random sample of public and academic libraries. Besides asking about the total number of professional librarians by sex and in each of the five racial/ethnic categories used by federal agencies, the questionnaire also asked for information about sex, racial/ethnic status, and salary for three different positions: director, department head, and beginning professional.

A closer look at librarians, at least those who are members of ALA, is provided by the results of a survey conducted for ALA's Committee on the Status of Women in Librarianship (COSWL) by Leigh Estabrook and Kathleen Heim supported in part by a Bailey K. Howard ALA Goals award of $5,000. Last spring a seven-page questionnaire was sent to a random sample of 3,000 ALA members asking questions about such factors as race, sex, salary, type of position held, number of people supervised, number of years in the position. A summary of initial findings appeared in the December 1980 issue of *American Libraries*. In addition to showing differences in the career patterns of men and women, the results provide a description of the ALA membership that was not previously available. A comparable picture of the American Society for Information Science (ASIS) membership is provided by a survey taken in the fall of 1979. Results appeared in the August 1980 issue of the *Bulletin of the American Society for Information Science*.

Supplying an impressive amount of background information for the personnel picture of the future is the first edition of the *Library Education Statistical Report* published by the American Association of Library Schools (AALS). This compilation, which covers faculty, students, curriculum, income and expenditures, and continuing professional education, was produced cooperatively by members of AALS under the direction of the AALS Library Education Statistics Committee chaired by Gary Purcell. AALS intends to produce such a report annually in the future. [Some of the data from the 1980 report are included in "Recent Library Personnel Surveys" in Part 3—*Ed.*]

LIBRARY EFFECTIVENESS

The effectiveness of library service was another topic that received attention in 1980. The final report on Paul Kantor's National Science Foundation—sponsored study—"Levels of Output Related to Costs of Operation of Scientific and Technical Libraries" (the LORCOST project) was released in the spring. This two-year study "explored the possibility of gathering quantitative data on the service rendered by scientific and technical libraries, integrating it into mathematical models of the cost-benefit relation, and providing a base for estimation of national levels of activity." Kantor based his analysis on data collected at and by 73 participating libraries. The report, which presents the results of the study through detailed formulas, plots, and tables, also explores the issue of fair pricing of library services and describes a method for analyzing the availability of reference service.

Kantor presented a paper on the topic in June at the preconference "Library Effectiveness: A State of the Art" sponsored by ALA's Library Administration and Management Association (LAMA). Before the preconference, LAMA published a volume of 24 papers to be presented at the conference, 16 of which are empirical, 3 are purely theoretical, and 5 are a mixture of the two.

Also connected with ALA's New York conference was the preconference "Research: The How and Why of It" sponsored by three ALA divisions: the Association for Library Service to Children (ALSC), the Public Library Association (PLA), and the Young Adult Services Division (YASD). Intended "to give librarians with little or no formal training in research methods practical experience in designing small-scale research," the preconference was planned for "coordinators, supervisors, specialists and other librarians working with children and young adults." Papers presented at the preconference by Jane Robbins, Mary Jo Lynch, and Boyd Rayward will be published in a 1981 issue of *Top of the News*.

TECHNICAL SERVICES

Planning for the implementation of the *Anglo-American Cataloguing Rules*, 2nd ed. (*ACCR 2*) has prompted systematic data gathering and analysis at many libraries in recent years. During 1979 this process was coordinated, for 72 university libraries, by King Research under contract to the Association of Research Libraries

(ARL). The results were published this year in *Alternatives for Future Library Catalogs: A Cost Model* by Robert R. V. Wiederkehr, which documents "the development of a computer model designed to identify and estimate the costs of producing and maintaining alternative catalog formats." As the first chapter indicates, the study team and participating libraries labored under severe time constraints, which became especially burdensome when the model turned out to be much more complex than anticipated. Despite these problems the resulting model has been very useful to some participants and the process of developing it has focused attention on both the multiplicity of factors that must be taken into account in planning future catalogs and the fact that data needed to assess the impact of these factors accurately is sadly lacking.

A study to provide data in a related area was conducted by Battelle Columbus Laboratories for the Council on Library Resources. A report, "Linking the Bibliographic Utilities: Benefits and Costs," describes Battelle's analysis of the economic and service benefits to libraries and their users from the linking of four bibliographic utilities—the Library of Congress, OCLC, the Research Libraries Information Network (RLIN), and the Washington Library Network (WLN)—to perform three library operations: shared cataloging of current monographs, interlibrary loan, and reference searching. A computer-based simulation model, BIBLINK, was developed for this project and will be used in the future by Battelle and others to experiment with different assumptions and data.

The Council on Library Resources also supported a number of activities conducted jointly by OCLC and RLIN regarding on-line public access to library bibliographic data bases. A survey was taken of 35 organizations known to be operating or developing public access systems and an issue analysis paper was prepared for discussion at a working session attended by representatives of 25 libraries, bibliographic utilities, and library networks in the United States and Canada. Four areas were identified where important questions need to be answered as soon as possible. The areas were: (1) analyzing user requirements and behavior, (2) monitoring existing public access systems, (3) developing methods for cost management, and (4) developing distributed computing and system links. Research on these topics may be expected in the future.

ACADEMIC LIBRARIES

Future research on questions related to academic libraries will be facilitated by the publication of *ACRL Statistics* in 1980. In a pilot project, the Association of College and Research Libraries (ACRL) gathered data on 98 of the 103 "non-ARL university libraries" in North America. ACRL used the same questionnarie that ARL uses for its annual statistical survey and produced a report that invites comparison of institutions, although the introduction warns that this should be done cautiously. ACRL hopes to conduct the survey at periodic intervals.

College librarians concerned about the development of useful collections will be interested in the results of a library collection use study sponsored by the Associated Colleges of the Midwest with funding from the Council on Library Resources. This project, managed by Mary Kane Trochim at Lake Forest College, had two objectives: to compile a meaningful body of information about how the collection is used in the three test libraries (Lake Forest College, Knox College, and St. Olaf College) and to produce a manual that can be used by small academic libraries to perform similar work. Building on existing studies of collection use at larger academic institutions, the project staff devised routines for collecting data, analyzing it, and presenting the results so that they can be used by decision makers at the local level. Data involved a circulation sample, a stack sample, and a shelf list sample. An important feature of the study was the active involvement of faculty members in interpreting the data gathered. The draft manual is being tested in other institutions and will be published in the near future.

PUBLIC LIBRARIES

Public libraries received a different kind of attention in 1980. This year saw formal publication of Malcolm Getz's *Public Libraries: An Economic View* (Johns Hopkins) distributed in draft form last year to participants in the White House Conference on Libraries and Information Services. Supported by grants from the Book-of-the-Month Club and the Scherman Foundation to the National Bureau of Economic Research, Getz interviewed librarians in 31 large library systems. He also examined library service and use among the branches of the New York Public Library. In his "study of the strategic decisions that shape the provision of public library service in the U.S.," Getz concentrates on comparing services offered, labor costs, allocation of resources, and use of innovations. The study uses statistical methodologies common to economists and explains them for the lay reader. It concludes with suggestions as to how public libraries can survive the "hard times" that have come to them.

A different approach to dealing with these hard times was taken by the Plainedge Public Library in Massapequa, New York. Director Joseph Eisner received a Council on Library Resources grant to support the study "Motivational Research Project to Determine Reasons for Nonuse of Public Libraries." Psychologist Ernest Dichter conducted in-depth interviews with both users and nonusers. Findings will be used by the Plainedge Public Library to expand a service program that is already recognized nationwide for innovative services. A report of the findings of Dichter's study and what Plainedge decides to do with them will be available in 1981.

Candidates for interviews in the Plainedge project were selected through telephone interviews that used an instrument developed by George D'Elia to separate public library users from nonusers as well as to distinguish between two different kinds of nonusers: (1) those who have user characteristics, yet are not users and (2) those who do not have user characteristics. D'Elia's work on related issues is described in the paper "The Development and Testing of a Conceptual Model of Public Library User Behavior," which won the $500 Library Research Round Table (LRRT) Research Development award in 1980. The paper was published in the October issue of *Library Quarterly*.

In April, ALA published *A Planning Process for Public Libraries* prepared for the Public Library Association (PLA) by Gene Palmour and his associates at King Research. This manual, the result of a two-year designing and field-testing project funded by the Office of Libraries and Learning Technologies, adapts corporate planning methods to the public library setting. The recommended planning process features systematic data gathering and analysis, development of locally determined goals and objectives, and measurement of the degree to which objectives are achieved.

FEDERAL SUPPORT

The year 1980 was both good and bad for federal support of library-related research. The Higher Education Act was reauthorized with substantial funding approved for the Title II-B Library Research and Development Program. Appropriations will still be a battle each year, however, and libraries lost some of their traditional congressional allies in the 1980 election. Responsibility for the Research and Development program moved into the new Department of Education with the Office of Libraries and Learning Technologies. Since President Reagan has indicated a desire to abolish the Department of Education, it is unclear what the future of this program will be. A hopeful note was sounded toward the end of the year when the Office of Libraries and Learning Technologies went ahead with plans to have a group of experts prepare an agenda for library and information science research in the 1980s. Cuadra Associates was awarded a contract to coordinate this work, which will be of major importance to the library community.

Finally, 1980 saw the publication of *Research Methods in Librarianship: Techniques and Interpretation* by Charles H. Busha and Stephen P. Harter (New York: Academic Press). In most other disciplines several comprehensive monographs about research methodology are available from commercial publishers. This is a first for librarianship and may be one indication that research in librarianship is finally coming of age.

RECENT DEVELOPMENTS IN LIBRARY STATISTICAL ACTIVITIES

Susanne Henderson

Chair, Statistics Section,
ALA Library Administration and Management Association
and
Systems Analyst,
Office of Central Reference,
Central Intelligence Agency

Interest in the area of library statistical activities continues to grow. The national economy and its effect on the library community in particular has made library service statistics an increasingly important tool for library administrators. This need for statistics has resulted in numerous workshops, seminars, etc., on statistical applications in libraries as well as an influx of articles describing measures, research, surveys, and evaluation of library information services. The following will update the American Library Association (ALA) activities in the area of library statistics and report on the status of significant statistical projects.

ALA LAMA STATISTICS SECTION

The ALA Library Administration and Management Association (LAMA) Statistics Section has the responsibility within ALA for all matters pertaining to the needs for and uses of statistical measurement of library resources, services, and facilities, regardless of type of library or functional activity. The section works with other organizations, agencies, and associations in planning and advising in areas of library statistical concerns; recommends and/or prepares guidelines, standards, and tools to be used in statistical activities; and recommends definitions, procedures, and policies concerning library statistics.

During 1980 the various standing committees of the section turned their emphasis from the *Handbook of Standard Terminology for Reporting Information about Libraries* to an intensive review of the new American National Standards Committee (ANSC) Z39.7 Standard on Library Statistics (the status of both of these projects is discussed later in this article). While each committee is concentrating on those sections of the standard that correspond with its area of responsibility, the section as a whole has sponsored programs and discussion sessions on the standard at the last three ALA annual conferences and plans another program at the 1981 annual conference in San Francisco.

The names of the Statistics Section Standing Committees and their 1980–1981 chairs are listed here both as a point of contact for those interested in further information on ALA activities in statistics and also to illustrate the attempt that the Statistics Section has made to cover all types of libraries..

Committee	*Chairperson*
Coordinating	Susanne Henderson Central Intelligence Agency
Development, Organization, Planning, and Programming	Janis C. Keene Tulsa City-County Library
Circulation	Mary Frances Collins University of Illinois
College and University Libraries	Harold A. Olsen San Jose State University
Nonprint Media	Evelyn M. King Texas A&M University
Personnel	Mary Lou Harkness University of South Florida
Public Libraries	John W. Sondheim Johnson County Library (Shawnee Mission, KS)
Reference	Florence J. Wilson George Mason University
School Library Media Centers	Noreen R. Michaud Simsbury (CT) High School
State Library Agencies	Edith M. Hart Arizona State Library Extension Services
Technical Services	Doris Brown DePaul University

NATIONAL CENTER FOR EDUCATION STATISTICS (NCES)

"The purpose of the Center shall be to collect and disseminate statistics and other data related to education in the United States and in other nations. The Center shall . . . collect, collate, and, from time to time, report full and complete statistics on the conditions of education in the United States; conduct and publish reports on specialized analyses of the meaning and significance of such activities; . . . and review and report on education activities in foreign countries." (Section 406(b) of the General Education Provisions Act, as amended [20 U.S.C. 1221e-1])

The center now falls under the new U.S. Department of Education within its Office of Educational Research and Improvement. Of the many activities/surveys, etc., that

NCES has been involved in during 1980 the following stand out as being of particular interest to the library community: The publication of the *Directory of Library Networks and Cooperative Library Organizations* and the initiation of two new surveys—Survey of Research Libraries and Survey of Library Human Resources. Both of these are exciting prospects and will (particularly the human resources survey) fill a void of comparable statistical information on libraries.

Further information about the center's statistical program and a catalog of NCES publications may be obtained from the Statistical Information Office, National Center for Education Statistics, 400 Maryland Ave. S.W. (1001 Presidential Bldg.), Washington, DC 20202.

HANDBOOK OF STANDARD TERMINOLOGY FOR RECORDING AND REPORTING INFORMATION ABOUT LIBRARIES

The ALA Office of Research revised version of the *Handbook* was sent to NCES in September 1980 and is now in the publication process. It is anticipated that the first published edition will be a "field review" edition for two reasons:

1. The *Handbook* has been in progress much too long (since 1977). Librarians are anxious to see it and the ALA Statistics Section believes it is no longer productive to examine drafts that have not been exposed to field review.
2. The *Handbook* needs to be used in the field so that future editions can incorporate changes based on feedback from practitioners.

The *Handbook* is a substantial accomplishment and provides the library community with a solid framework upon which a coordinated and comprehensive data-gathering program can be built. The library community anxiously awaits its arrival.

AMERICAN NATIONAL STANDARDS COMMITTEE Z39.7

The American National Standards Subcommittee on Library Statistics has been working since the end of 1977 with the ALA Statistics Section and NCES on a revision of the 1968 Standard. As mentioned earlier, drafts of this standard have been discussed at the last three ALA annual conferences and it is hoped that a new draft will be available for discussion at the 1981 ALA annual conference in San Francisco.

The revised standard has as its goals to provide figures for an accountability both within the library and to funding agencies, for an understanding of collections as intellectual resources that transcend formal differences, and for understanding and analysis of library performance and outputs as goals and products of inputs. A major goal is widespread adoption of the same categories and definitions by the many different agencies that now impose an excessive burden on libraries by requesting statistics based on different definitions and aggregations.

As with the *Handbook*, it is hoped that the standard can be field tested soon.

CHARACTERISTICS OF THE U.S. POPULATION SERVED BY LIBRARIES

Nadine Edles
Division of Statistical Services, Statistical Information Branch,
National Center for Education Statistics,
U.S. Department of Education

	Number	Percent
Total U.S. population (July 1, 1979)[a]	220,415,000	100.0
Resident population of 50 states and D.C.	219,930,000	99.8
Armed forces overseas	485,000	0.2
Resident population of U.S. outlying areas (1970)[b]	3,022,000	—
U.S. population, five years and over, including armed forces abroad (July 1, 1979)[c]	204,618,000	100.0
5–9 years	16,493,000	8.1
10–14 years	18,063,000	8.8
15–19 years	20,919,000	10.2
20–24 years	20,738,000	10.1
25–64 years	103,972,000	50.8
Age 65 and over	24,433,000	11.9
Public and nonpublic school enrollment (fall 1980)[d]	57,750,000	100.0
Kindergarten through grade 8	31,165,000	54.0
Grades 9–12	14,885,000	25.8
Higher education, total enrollment	11,700,000	20.3
Nonpublic school enrollment[e]	7,680,000	13.3
Kindergarten through grade 8	3,605,000	6.2
Grades 9–12	1,525,000	2.6
Higher education, total enrollment	2,550,000	4.4
Educational status of population aged 25 and over		
Total aged 25 and over (March 1979)[f]	123,019,000	—
With four or more years of college	19,332,000	15.7
With one to three years of college	17,379,000	14.1
With four years of high school or more	81,092,000	65.9
With less than four years of high school	41,928,000	34.1
Residence in and outside metropolitan areas		
Total noninstitutional population (April 1978)[g]	213,500,000	100.0
Nonmetropolitan areas	70,400,000	33.0
Metropolitan areas	143,000,000	67.0
In central cities	59,700,000	28.0
Outside central areas	83,300,000	39.0

CHARACTERISTICS OF THE U.S. POPULATION SERVED BY LIBRARIES (cont.)

	Number	Percent
Employment status		
Total civilian noninstitutional population 16 years old and over (October 1979)[h]	162,375,000	—
Civilian labor force, total	103,474,000	100.0
Employed	97,293,000	94.0
Unemployed	6,182,000	6.0
Occupational groups		
Employed persons, 16 years old and over (October 1979)[h]	97,293,000	100.0
Professional and technical workers	14,929,000	15.3
Managers and administrators, except farm	10,648,000	10.9
Clerical workers	17,825,000	18.3
Sales workers	6,247,000	6.4
Craftsmen and kindred workers	12,974,000	13.3
Operatives	14,550,000	14.9
Service workers	12,977,000	13.3
Farm workers and nonfarm laborers	7,369,000	7.6
Total faculty and students served by college and university libraries (fall 1980)	12,530,000	100.0
Faculty	830,000	6.6
Students, total enrollment	11,700,000	93.4

[a] As of July 1, 1978, estimates of the Bureau of the Census, U.S. Department of Commerce. Armed forces overseas includes forces stationed in outlying areas of the United States. *Current Population Reports*, Series P-25, September 1979.

[b] As of April 1, 1970, Puerto Rico, Guam, Virgin Islands, American Samoa, Canal Zone, and the Trust Territory of the Pacific Islands. Includes members of the armed forces overseas stationed in these outlying areas. U.S. Census of Population, *Number of Inhabitants*, PC(1), 1970, A53–A58.

[c] As of July 1, 1978, age data are Series II estimates by the Bureau of the Census, U.S. Department of Commerce. *Current Population Reports*, P-25, no. 704, July 1977, *Projections of the Population of the United States: 1977 to 2050*.

[d] As of Fall 1978, estimates of the U.S. Department of Education, National Center for Education Statistics, Back-to-School press release, August 31, 1980.

[e] A segment of public and nonpublic school enrollment reported above. Percentages for nonpublic school enrollment are based on the total figure for public and nonpublic school enrollment.

[f] As of March 1977, Bureau of the Census, U.S. Department of Commerce. Unpublished data.

[g] Bureau of the Census, U.S. Department of Commerce, *Statistical Abstract of the United States*. 1979 edition in process. Due to rounding, details will not add up to total.

[h] U.S. Department of Labor, Bureau of Labor Statistics, "The Employment Situation: October 1979" (press release). Details will not add to total because of independent seasonal adjustment.

As of Fall 1979, estimates of the U.S. Department of Education, National Center for Education Statistics, Back-to-School press release, August 31, 1980. Faculty includes full-time and part-time staff with the rank of instructor or above and junior staff, such as graduate assistants, who provide instruction in colleges, universities, and professional schools.

NUMBER OF LIBRARIES IN THE UNITED STATES AND CANADA

Statistics are from the thirty-third edition of the *American Library Directory*, edited by Jaques Cattell Press (Bowker, 1980). Data are exclusive of elementary and secondary school libraries. The directory does not list small public libraries. Law libraries with fewer than 10,000 volumes are included only if they specialize in a specific field. The count of these libraries, shown separately under the Summary section below, is from the Bowker Company's mailing lists. In addition to listing and describing some 31,600 individual libraries, the thirty-third edition of the *ALD* lists over 350 library consortia, including processing and purchasing centers and other specialized organizations.

LIBRARIES IN THE UNITED STATES

A. Public libraries 8,717
   Public libraries with branches 1,115
   Public library branches .. 5,936
   Total public libraries (including branches) 14,653*
B. Junior college libraries ... 1,191
   Departmental 27
   Departmental medicine 7
   Departmental religious 3
   University and college ... 1,911
   Departmental 1,489
   Departmental law ... 123
   Departmental medicine 128
   Departmental religious 18
   Total academic libraries .. 4,618*
C. Armed forces
   Air Force 135
     Medical 19
   Army 182
     Law 3
     Medical 25
   Navy 168
     Law 1
     Medical 19
   Total armed forces libraries 485*
D. Government libraries 1,260
   Law 385
   Medical 229
   Total government libraries 1,260*
E. Special libraries 4,645*
F. Law libraries 417*
G. Medical libraries 1,674*
H. Religious libraries 913*
   Total law (including academic, armed forces and government) 929
   Total medical (including academic, armed forces and government) 2,101
   Total religious (including academic) 934
   Total special (including all law, medical and religious) 8,609
   Total libraries counted (*) 28,665

LIBRARIES IN REGIONS ADMINISTERED BY THE UNITED STATES

A. Public libraries 13
   Public libraries with branches 4
   Public library branches .. 15
   Total public libraries (including branches) ... 28*
B. Junior college libraries ... 8
   University and college libraries 27
   Departmental 14
     Departmental law ... 1
   Total academic libraries .. 49*

C. Armed forces
   Air Force 1
   Army 1
   Navy 4
   Total armed forces 6*
D. Government libraries 15
   Law 6
   Medical 1
   Total government libraries 15*
E. Special libraries 12*
F. Medical libraries 3*
   Total libraries counted (*) 113

LIBRARIES IN CANADA

A. Public libraries 639
   Public libraries with
     branches 112
   Public library branches .. 804
   Total public libraries
     (including branches) ... 1,443*
B. Junior college libraries ... 111
   Departmental 1

   Departmental
     medicine 1
   University and college ... 148
   Departmental 212
     Departmental law ... 16
     Departmental
       medicine 27
     Departmental
       religious 6
   Total academic libraries .. 471*
C. Government libraries 226*
D. Special libraries 467*
E. Law libraries 23*
F. Medical libraries 129*
G. Religious libraries 54*
   Total libraries counted (*) 2,813

SUMMARY

Total U.S. libraries 28,665
Total libraries administered by
   the United States 113
Total Canadian libraries 2,813
Grand total libraries listed ... 31,591

*Note: Numbers followed by an asterisk are added to find "Total libraries counted" for each of the three geographic areas (United States, U.S.-administered regions, and Canada). The sum of the three totals is the "Grand total libraries listed" in the *ALD* (shown in the Summary). For details on the count of libraries, see the preface to the thirty-third edition of the *ALD*—*Ed.*

PUBLIC AND ACADEMIC LIBRARY ACQUISITION EXPENDITURES

Every two years the R. R. Bowker Company compiles statistics on library acquisition expenditures from information reported in the *American Library Directory*. The statistics given here are based on information from the 33rd edition of the directory (1980), which was compiled from questionnaire responses received between fall 1979 and spring 1980. In most cases the statistics reflect expenditures for the 1978-1979 period.

The total number of public libraries listed in the 33rd edition of the *ALD* is 8,717, while the total for academic libraries is 4,618. Not included in the *ALD* are public libraries with annual incomes of less than $2,000 or book funds of less than $500 (of which there are an estimated 2,500 libraries) or law libraries of less than 10,000 volumes (of which there are approximately 330).

UNDERSTANDING THE TABLES

Number of Libraries includes only those libraries in the *ALD* that reported either annual income or acquisition expenditures (8,037 public libraries; 2,413 academic libraries). Those libraries that did not report acquisition expenditures but did report annual income are included in the count, although they are not reflected in the columns of acquisition expenditure figures.

Total Acquisition Expenditures for a given state is almost always greater than (in a few cases equal to) the sum of the Categories of Expenditure. This is because the Total Acquisition Expenditures amount also includes the expenditures of libraries that did not itemize by category.

Categories of Expenditure. Figures in these columns represent only those libraries that itemized expenditures. Libraries that reported a total acquisition expenditure amount but did not itemize are only represented in the Total Acquisition Expenditures column.

Unspecified includes monies reported as not specifically books, periodicals, AV, microform, or binding (e.g., library materials) or any of the categories in combination. When libraries report only Total Acquisition Expenditures without itemizing by category, the total amount is *not* reflected as unspecified.

Estimated Percent of Acquisitions is based on a comparison of the total expenditures for each of the categories and the total of all of the categories, i.e., the total amount spent on books in the United States was compared with the sum of all of the categories of expenditure. The reader should note, therefore, that the percentages are not based on the figures in the Total Acquisition Expenditures column.

PUBLIC AND ACADEMIC LIBRARY ACQUISITION EXPENDITURES / 275

TABLE 1 PUBLIC LIBRARY ACQUISITION EXPENDITURES

State	Number of Libraries	Total Acquisition Expenditures	Books	Periodicals	Audiovisual	Microform	Binding	Unspecified
Alabama	138	$ 4,469,065	$ 1,474,580	$ 173,030	$ 148,940	$ 254,930	$ 36,327	$ 164,140
Alaska	22	992,272	329,142	119,060	75,100	160,100	14,590	—
Arizona	74	3,647,604	1,741,673	165,143	122,483	42,320	55,615	110,737
Arkansas	46	1,930,732	459,130	38,216	6,141	1,459	8,971	13,569
California	184	38,533,254	25,893,505	2,192,879	952,139	213,425	303,210	179,954
Colorado	122	9,971,430	2,448,254	259,957	98,755	20,967	62,992	353,559
Connecticut	165	6,321,715	2,052,596	247,503	192,579	12,629	54,504	95,169
Delaware	24	618,270	416,798	117,432	52,395	2,000	—	—
District of Columbia	1	815,100	647,600	114,500	53,000	—	—	—
Florida	129	5,338,591	2,354,010	273,307	294,081	57,296	50,362	43,400
Georgia	52	5,059,864	2,343,433	271,995	264,105	120,423	98,580	5,918
Hawaii	1	1,327,145	—	—	—	—	—	—
Idaho	100	1,454,696	617,833	67,584	51,726	7,212	4,844	4,591
Illinois	563	37,131,537	8,859,953	1,549,606	1,288,801	653,710	245,164	454,963
Indiana	223	7,290,287	4,160,173	482,881	513,351	67,280	137,781	80,757
Iowa	489	5,850,787	1,705,158	223,468	193,034	49,757	21,826	4,160
Kansas	304	6,192,208	2,026,345	273,025	92,285	32,899	33,358	—
Kentucky	107	15,277,741	2,452,090	148,558	328,591	15,807	36,441	21,349
Louisiana	68	5,509,053	1,559,188	261,814	164,030	15,479	58,721	534,435
Maine	164	2,765,996	744,037	101,638	30,925	16,103	11,852	10,723
Maryland	31	14,670,292	3,772,413	259,892	436,632	18,048	79,600	988,117
Massachusetts	346	11,291,409	5,421,566	537,933	441,784	132,348	128,000	2,181,139
Michigan	367	15,876,598	6,140,375	727,819	684,563	121,384	138,568	76,245
Minnesota	134	9,677,799	3,593,396	425,381	516,364	55,712	89,142	29
Mississippi	51	1,968,952	1,128,860	124,388	94,182	25,668	18,016	31,000
Missouri	122	12,139,967	3,279,023	313,410	237,140	272,064	93,505	298,800
Montana	75	894,614	500,700	40,840	27,534	400	3,230	102,662
Nebraska	241	4,789,573	786,137	82,869	138,472	32,005	21,268	17,473
Nevada	23	1,143,777	275,923	34,089	20,750	13,673	6,007	402,696
New Hampshire	216	3,232,829	1,060,242	35,548	88,732	4,692	6,750	12,712
New Jersey	309	19,596,090	6,984,922	947,302	616,501	160,922	83,298	208,846
New Mexico	46	1,405,975	535,452	63,259	13,129	1,104	4,540	—

TABLE 1 PUBLIC LIBRARY ACQUISITION EXPENDITURES (cont.)

State	Number of Libraries	Total Acquisition Expenditures	Books	Periodicals	Audiovisual	Microform	Binding	Unspecified
New York	719	23,531,673	17,760,718	1,968,985	811,116	197,036	309,021	2,533,503
North Carolina	131	4,382,827	1,636,940	266,197	185,505	21,253	33,174	93,418
North Dakota	55	640,718	396,683	27,436	71,483	7,800	1,800	—
Ohio	250	28,080,847	10,403,314	1,250,985	1,367,491	87,823	307,792	161,311
Oklahoma	84	3,526,875	1,243,423	229,511	184,568	37,734	36,003	6,468
Oregon	97	2,551,534	1,559,336	147,899	64,012	5,700	7,815	54,804
Pennsylvania	424	8,647,110	4,242,096	886,860	282,175	154,115	73,261	2,909,634
Rhode Island	47	856,204	492,920	55,586	18,598	12,021	16,274	17,659
South Carolina	40	1,904,883	970,666	64,285	80,734	5,767	25,514	265,268
South Dakota	70	858,677	401,756	75,848	95,548	28,184	10,123	4,679
Tennessee	94	2,770,329	1,827,978	229,935	298,098	31,295	25,994	306,005
Texas	359	11,411,398	17,342,085	1,467,427	802,460	50,196	331,377	2,013,904
Utah	46	2,253,563	659,580	32,646	74,860	2,500	42,675	—
Vermont	175	793,074	336,562	36,945	18,018	4,951	3,309	11,787
Virginia	81	7,769,895	3,636,466	455,707	274,922	117,513	90,206	227,811
Washington	65	11,218,946	3,161,732	464,851	459,786	28,447	23,943	204,416
West Virginia	77	1,488,594	787,882	58,354	212,123	2,850	13,251	116,750
Wisconsin	320	9,752,421	2,877,886	405,577	372,025	30,796	40,918	100,635
Wyoming	22	642,073	328,115	35,196	36,098	3,000	9,900	—
Pacific Islands	2	100,715	127,323	34,926	65,085	1,000	2,000	—
Puerto Rico	1	2,278,660	—	—	—	—	—	—
Virgin Islands	1	90,000	—	—	—	—	—	—
Total U.S.	8,037	$382,736,238	$165,957,968	$18,869,482	$14,012,949	$3,411,797	$3,311,412	$15,424,195
Estimated % of Acquisitions			75	8.5	6.3	1.5	1.5	7

TABLE 2 COLLEGE AND UNIVERSITY LIBRARY ACQUISITION EXPENDITURES

State	Number of Libraries	Total Acquisition Expenditures	Books	Periodicals	Categories of Expenditure Audiovisual	Microform	Binding	Unspecified
Alabama	44	$ 5,474,871	$ 1,973,280	$ 1,035,309	$ 119,163	$ 121,017	$ 159,979	$ 1,190,026
Alaska	7	1,782,694	486,326	173,012	23,445	34,703	16,418	—
Arizona	17	4,680,822	1,244,157	734,686	74,408	27,700	100,317	—
Arkansas	24	3,115,641	1,140,399	531,236	47,000	77,584	76,051	463,271
California	178	44,943,094	15,995,522	10,416,914	1,036,233	928,988	2,609,933	5,164,731
Colorado	29	4,636,719	2,219,752	2,416,507	285,990	132,132	240,659	403,544
Connecticut	36	5,746,848	1,930,984	1,283,940	35,629	86,320	371,533	—
Delaware	8	3,159,077	891,755	543,760	5,800	5,242	98,187	—
District of Columbia	12	1,368,518	1,767,648	1,103,853	28,006	100,340	193,934	606,274
Florida	74	16,429,666	11,847,182	4,530,412	856,257	1,006,627	969,164	901,601
Georgia	59	8,950,621	3,442,884	3,056,031	126,143	165,731	497,434	257,350
Hawaii	13	1,928,695	1,040,103	131,950	67,717	72,951	154,400	649,100
Idaho	8	418,581	834,213	594,264	71,388	30,971	39,708	—
Illinois	104	19,088,862	6,262,327	4,503,533	579,824	201,561	988,291	1,529,668
Indiana	47	13,555,190	3,619,526	2,957,744	119,284	51,458	539,289	2,002,806
Iowa	46	5,496,000	1,528,724	2,501,012	68,924	163,930	355,378	189,240
Kansas	47	3,284,520	2,448,944	2,040,305	132,903	313,419	228,182	3,000
Kentucky	38	5,087,353	2,469,641	1,732,023	76,750	53,517	249,662	76,590
Louisiana	25	3,388,941	2,273,571	1,836,452	56,411	161,837	351,635	915,680
Maine	26	1,958,957	606,028	359,334	21,730	19,175	47,120	17,000
Maryland	41	3,043,121	33,752	1,287,873	107,548	122,754	262,240	32,309
Massachusetts	84	9,065,191	5,122,610	3,935,042	275,816	201,338	1,212,973	4,267,974
Michigan	75	19,527,904	3,774,158	2,666,912	266,418	194,566	633,098	3,433,210
Minnesota	47	3,818,177	2,694,977	1,996,127	119,954	55,100	296,977	207,194
Mississippi	41	3,536,352	1,051,880	912,515	104,714	174,709	178,436	11,800
Missouri	57	7,635,330	2,901,168	3,308,946	239,164	283,520	372,811	16,442
Montana	11	591,859	247,791	359,295	9,593	1,540	17,000	—
Nebraska	22	2,915,002	1,720,610	1,382,116	122,832	79,132	140,339	175,290
Nevada	6	2,231,873	411,004	356,142	9,855	800	59,999	—
New Hampshire	20	2,518,122	948,471	541,285	44,278	133,813	75,192	628,923
New Jersey	51	4,720,226	4,154,255	2,431,823	362,927	254,364	378,248	4,373,884
New Mexico	21	2,291,258	1,011,051	471,760	36,318	13,922	137,854	80,321

TABLE 2 COLLEGE AND UNIVERSITY LIBRARY ACQUISITION EXPENDITURES (cont.)

State	Number of Libraries	Total Acquisition Expenditures	Books	Periodicals	Audiovisual	Microform	Binding	Unspecified
New York	169	27,655,358	11,914,842	7,078,700	501,747	635,948	1,323,018	2,882,630
North Carolina	103	17,353,428	4,116,954	3,536,736	255,919	111,215	561,683	2,226,365
North Dakota	14	840,284	680,126	533,613	33,771	13,092	36,463	150,000
Ohio	96	11,802,055	6,031,988	4,786,889	246,640	285,043	838,678	1,513,249
Oklahoma	43	3,151,402	1,021,867	1,299,887	54,527	83,803	141,729	1,040,084
Oregon	35	6,337,957	1,989,362	2,250,307	112,628	145,228	219,279	—
Pennsylvania	137	19,489,719	6,897,438	6,443,622	301,010	625,895	970,636	514,140
Rhode Island	14	2,721,536	893,060	925,046	12,282	25,562	152,006	44,626
South Carolina	49	4,221,632	2,123,830	1,687,066	87,208	72,939	227,696	113,101
South Dakota	15	1,074,975	420,872	326,908	33,738	14,950	38,541	—
Tennessee	51	12,416,235	2,832,498	3,000,061	192,027	208,765	427,828	728,587
Texas	126	20,754,939	11,763,810	6,527,831	817,557	376,135	954,660	3,184,625
Utah	10	1,587,577	1,114,919	492,900	70,273	5,500	121,735	5,000
Vermont	17	473,882	935,982	661,185	25,258	31,415	86,816	1,252
Virginia	68	8,988,067	3,964,052	2,464,810	245,865	175,452	341,649	15,000
Washington	40	7,695,761	3,521,050	3,508,331	343,292	43,793	506,021	13,039
West Virginia	19	1,328,793	537,611	386,293	63,816	62,603	32,930	26,611
Wisconsin	62	6,831,560	4,080,033	3,649,887	253,663	92,920	402,288	71,024
Wyoming	7	972,778	418,895	479,475	31,036	2,706	40,224	6,812
Pacific Islands	3	76,800	19,666	3,480	3,299	—	—	—
Puerto Rico	17	830,971	574,341	323,980	123,555	5,097	44,994	112,500
Total U.S.	2,413	$372,995,794	$153,947,797	$122,493,120	$9,341,548	$8,288,822	$19,521,315	$40,230,873
Estimated % of Acquisitions			43.5	34.6	2.6	2.3	5.5	11.4

HEALTH SCIENCES LIBRARIES IN THE UNITED STATES: SURVEY III, 1979

Susan Crawford
*Director, Division of Library and Archival Services,
American Medical Association*

Alan M. Rees
*Professor, School of Library and Information Science,
Case Western Reserve University*

Health sciences libraries as focal institutions for biomedical communication exist within a complex and dynamic environment. The collection and analysis of data within reasonable time intervals and covering the entire universe of health sciences libraries are essential for effective management and planning. At the level of the individual library, normative data provide the basis for formulation of standards and criteria to measure the quality of collections and the effectiveness of library services. At the aggregate level, whether national, state, or local, information on the nature and distribution of library resources, personnel, and services is essential for the orderly development of consortia, networks, and nationwide library systems.

The field of health sciences librarianship has fared better than most areas of library practice in the accumulation and analysis of significant data. Early surveys covered select populations such as medical school libraries,[1] medical society libraries,[2] and hospital libraries.[3] The first comprehensive survey, covering medical school, medical society, and allied health training program libraries was conducted by the Committee on Surveys and Statistics (COMSAS) of the Medical Library Association in 1965.[4-6]

However, it was not until 1969 that the entire universe of health sciences libraries in the United States was covered in a single survey by Crawford, with grant support from the National Library of Medicine. This was followed by a second survey of the universe in 1973, which generated 17 papers and monographs analyzing the significance of data in addition to the publication of the *Directory of Health Sciences Libraries* in the United States in 1969 and 1973.[7-9] Data bases for health sciences libraries in the United States are summarized in Table 1.

Due to the rapid obsolescence of the data, it was planned that surveys of the universe of health sciences libraries should be conducted at five-year intervals. Since 1973, great changes have taken place including demographic shifts in sponsoring organizations and advances in library technology. The explosive growth of on-line data base searching and the increased use of bibliographic records have been accompanied by inflation, copyright restrictions, and the proliferation of consortia and networks. Moreover, changes in the patterns of health care delivery and planning have led to the creation of many libraries in entirely new contexts such as health maintenance organizations. To document and analyze the changing library scene, the National Library of Medicine awarded a grant in 1978 to Case Western Reserve University to design and implement a third survey of Health Sciences Libraries in the United States.

OBJECTIVES OF THE SURVEY

To create a machine-readable format compatible with the national data base developed in the 1969 and 1973 surveys.

TABLE 1 DATA BASES FOR HEALTH SCIENCES LIBRARIES IN THE UNITED STATES

Type of Health-Related Organization	Years of Surveys	Published Data (Reference Nos.)*	Machine-Readable Data
Medical schools	1962, 1965, 1969, 1973, 1979	1, 4, 10, 11	1969, 1973, 1979
Medical societies	1964, 1965, 1969, 1973, 1979	2, 12	1969, 1973, 1979
Hospitals	1964, 1969, 1973, 1979	3, 13	1969, 1973, 1979
Educational programs in allied health sciences	1969, 1973, 1979	14	1969, 1973, 1979
Voluntary health organizations	1969, 1973, 1979	12	1969, 1973, 1979
Business–industrial organizations	1969, 1973, 1979	15	1969, 1973, 1979
Federal, state, municipal government organizations	1969, 1973, 1979	16	1969, 1973, 1979
Regional medical libraries	1969, 1973, 1979	16	1973, 1979
Outpatient group practice clinics	1969, 1973, 1979	15	1969, 1973, 1979
Health maintenance organizations	1979		1979
Health planning organizations	1979		1979
Area health education centers	1979		1979

*Numbers refer to journals, articles, and monographs in the list of references at the end of this article. References to published data for the 1979 survey are not available at the time of printing.

To publish a directory displaying salient data for each library listed.

To publish an analytic monograph entitled *Health Sciences Libraries in the United States: Three Decades of Progress, 1950–1980*, utilizing the survey data gathered over almost three decades.

SURVEY METHODOLOGY

The sequence of tasks involved the following:

Construction of the survey population

Design and pretesting of the survey instrument

Mailing and follow-up procedures

Data encoding and entry

Preliminary analysis of the data

Design of computer programs for computer typesetting and analysis

Printing of *Directory of Health Sciences Libraries*

Construction of the Survey Population

As in the two previous surveys, all health-related institutions in the United States were queried to determine whether a library exists and, if so, to elicit relevant data. Authoritative sources, such as the American Medical Association, the American Dental Association, the National League for Nursing, and the American Dietetic Association, were contacted to identify health-related organizations. The American Hospital Association provided a computer tape with names and addresses of all hospitals in the United States. Printed directories were also consulted extensively. A special effort was made to include health planning organizations, area health education centers, health maintenance organizations, health systems agencies as well as pharmaceutical companies, foundations, professional associations, medical societies, and government agencies. Names and addresses were also derived from the 1973 *Directory of Health Science Libraries*, lists from regional medical libraries, the roster of MEDLINE Centers in the United States, and the listing of institutional members of the Medical Library Association. These addresses were matched and merged by computer into a master list of 12,630 unique names and addresses.

Design and Pretesting of the Survey Instrument

The questionnaire was designed to yield information on library facilities, personnel, resources, cataloging practices, reference services including data base searching, circulation transactions, photocopying, interlibrary loan and borrowing, participation in networks and consortia, and the existence of special programs such as patient education and clinical librarianship. Personnel with expertise in library planning, management, and technical operations were consulted with regard to the content of the questionnaire. A twelve-page questionnaire was constructed containing more than one hundred questions together with definitions of all terms used.

The survey instrument was critiqued at a meeting of the Project Advisory Committee held in Chicago in October 1978. A second draft of the questionnaire was presented in December 1978 in ten libraries in each of the following states: Illinois, Ohio, California, and Nevada. A third draft of the questionnaire was reviewed by the president and directors of the Medical Library Association and by technical staff of the Council on Library Resources and the National Library of Medicine.

Mailing and Follow-up Procedures

The first mailing was made in February 1979 to 12,630 health-related organizations. This yielded a response of 3,125 replies (24.75 percent), which, when analyzed, resulted in the identification of 1,710 libraries. After the initial list was edited to eliminate duplicates and returns, a second mailing of 6,200 was sent in May 1979. Two subsequent mailings were made in July and September. These four mailings resulted in the identification of only 2,110 libraries and it was clear that the universe was far from complete. A telephone canvas indicated that many of the questionnaires mailed did not reach the libraries, particularly in organizations such as Veterans Administration hospitals. Moreover, many librarians indicated some resistance to completing yet another questionnaire since "they were surveyed to death"; and yet others felt that the detailed instrument was not relevant to their scale of library operation.

To secure the maximum response from libraries, an abbreviated questionnaire was mailed in December 1979 to 1,278 institutions that prima facie seemed to have a high probability of possessing a library. These institutions included those in the 1973 directory that had not responded to the questionnaire in 1979. This final mailing was highly successful and yielded an additional 800 libraries. A battery of telephone calls gathered data for an additional 95 libraries producing a total of 2,775 libraries reporting data.

Data Encoding and Entry

Questionnaires were edited for consistency and standardized by field for keypunching. A machine-readable record was created that provided the basis for the computer typesetting programs for statistical analysis.

Preliminary Analysis of the Data

The 1979 *Directory of Health Sciences Libraries* is intended to provide an inventory of health sciences libraries in the United States and only a very limited analysis has been performed, specifically to generate Tables 2-7. Detailed analyses including correlation of variables, time series analysis, and variance due to quantitative differences will be made in a companion volume, *Health Sciences Libraries in the United States: Three Decades of Progress, 1950-1980*, to appear in 1981.

Design of Computer Programs for Computer Typesetting and Analysis

Two separate programs were designed: one to store the data to be manipulated for statistical analysis, and the other for publication of the directory.

The complexity of the questionnaire and the ambiguity of many responses necessitated evaluating and editing each completed questionnaire before information could be keyed into the computer.

Printing of *Directory of Health Sciences Libraries*

Actual production of the 1979 directory was not undertaken until the raw data had been corrected and amended to incorporate late responses. The Ecotran-Chi Corporation with its Mandec and Digitype Divisions was instrumental in executing the necessary programming activities.

RESULTS OF THE SURVEY

As did the two previous surveys, the third survey defines a library as a collection that meets two of the following criteria: 25 serial titles, 500 monographs, and some personnel (professional and/or clerical). However, many institutions reported "libraries" that did not exactly match these criteria. In some instances, the essential data were missing, the budget was of a size that implied a minimal level of monograph and journal acquisitions, or the library was newly established and had not yet reached the defined threshold. Each return was scrutinized to examine circumstantial evidence of the existence of a library; for example, membership in a library consortium or the employment of library personnel. In this manner, if a professional librarian was employed, the library was included, whether or not one of the other two criteria was reported. This decision is justified on the assumption that the existence of paid professional staff implies some minimal budget for resources, maintenance, and services. In such cases it was necessary to "read between the lines" to identify emerging libraries aspiring to meet minimal standards.

If it becomes a national priority to make library resources available to larger numbers of health care professionals, particularly in remote areas, it will be necessary to consolidate and extend the minimal resources of a large number of these marginal libraries located mainly in community hospitals. These underdeveloped libraries, struggling to survive, constitute the essential building blocks for future networking and resource sharing. Every effort has, therefore, been made to include nascent, developing libraries since they represent in many instances the only access that many health professionals have to library resources and services. Pending further analysis of the geographical location and distribution of library resources, we estimate that some 420 of the 2,775 libraries listed in the 1979 directory do not strictly meet the defined criteria.

The Universe of Health Sciences Libraries

The number of libraries in 1979 as compared with 1969 and 1973 is shown in Table 2. There is a decrease in the number of libraries from 3,155 in 1969 to 2,775 in

TABLE 2 THE UNIVERSE
OF HEALTH SCIENCES
LIBRARIES IN THE
UNITED STATES
1969, 1973, AND 1979

Year	Total
1969	3,155
1973	2,984
1979	2,775

1979, which represents a decline of some 400 libraries or 12 percent. Preliminary analysis of the data showed a trend toward discontinuation of smaller libraries and amalgamation of others, especially among allied health training programs, hospitals, and professional societies. At the same time, there is greater sharing of resources and services as reflected by the proliferation of consortia and networks.

Geographic Distribution

As indicated in the 1980 census, the United States has experienced a major shift in population during the past ten years, from the northeastern to the southern, southwestern, and northwestern states. Tables 3 and 4 indicate the distribution of libraries

TABLE 3 HEALTH SCIENCES LIBRARIES BY LOCATION, 1979

State	Number	State	Number
Alabama	31	Nebraska	17
Alaska	3	Nevada	12
Arizona	22	New Hampshire	10
Arkansas	18	New Jersey	84
California	248	New Mexico	13
Colorado	38	New York	251
Connecticut	55	North Carolina	47
Delaware	11	North Dakota	15
District of Columbia	34	Ohio	138
Florida	83	Oklahoma	27
Georgia	55	Oregon	22
Hawaii	9	Pennsylvania	197
Idaho	9	Rhode Island	17
Illinois	177	South Carolina	22
Indiana	73	South Dakota	14
Iowa	35	Tennessee	42
Kansas	38	Texas	112
Kentucky	27	Utah	9
Louisiana	39	Vermont	10
Maine	25	Virginia	51
Maryland	74	Washington	41
Massachusetts	119	West Virginia	23
Michigan	118	Wisconsin	84
Minnesota	57	Wyoming	10
Mississippi	20		
Missouri	70	Canal Zone	5
Montana	10	Puerto Rico	4
	Total	2,775	

TABLE 4 STATES WITH LARGEST NUMBER OF HEALTH SCIENCES LIBRARIES, 1973 AND 1979: BY RANK ORDER DISTRIBUTION

Rank Order 1973	Number of Libraries	Rank Order 1979	Number of Libraries
1. New York	322	1. New York	251
2. California	258	2. California	248
3. Pennsylvania	205	3. Pennsylvania	197
4. Illinois	175	4. Illinois	177
5. Ohio	139	5. Ohio	138
6. Massachusetts	128	6. Massachusetts	119
7. Michigan	126	7. Michigan	118
8. Texas	118	8. Texas	112
9. New Jersey	101	9. New Jersey and Wisconsin	84/84
Total	1,572	Total	1,528

by state and rank order of the nine states with the largest number of libraries. Although the ordering has remained constant, there has been a change in the distribution of libraries. New York, for example, still has the most libraries, but shows a decrease of 22 percent from 322 to 251 libraries. In 1973, New York had 64 more health sciences libraries than California, but by 1979, the difference was only three libraries. Thus, the migration of population appears to be correlated with the migration of health sciences organizations.

Libraries by Type of Sponsoring Organization

Libraries classified by type of sponsoring organization are shown in Table 5. In 1979, there were 124 medical school libraries, up from 101 in 1969, an increase of 23 percent. The number of hospital libraries, however, has decreased from 2,002 to 1,802 or 10 percent since 1969. Three new types of libraries have emerged since the last survey—those of health maintenance organizations, area health education centers, and health planning organizations. These libraries, which support new structures for health

TABLE 5 HEALTH SCIENCES LIBRARIES BY TYPE OF SPONSORING ORGANIZATION, 1979

Sponsoring Organization	Number
Medical schools	124
Professional & vocational schools (excluding medical schools)	182
Business & industrial organizations	70
Research organizations	72
Societies & foundations	41
Hospitals	1,802
Area health education centers	83
Health maintenance organizations	32
Health planning organizations	28
Other	341
Total	2,775

TABLE 6 HEALTH SCIENCES
LIBRARY PERSONNEL: 1969,
1973, AND 1979

Year	Total*
1969	9,245
1973	10,277
1979	9,302

*Includes professional and nonprofessional staff. The 1969 data represent the total number of personnel, part- or full-time; the 1973 and 1979 data represent the number of full-time equivalents.

care delivery and planning, total 143. Libraries are born and they die—the data tell of the evolution over the years.

Library Manpower

The total numbers of health sciences library personnel for 1969, 1973, and 1979 are compared in Table 6. These figures reflect a decrease of 975 in full-time equivalent personnel between 1973 and 1979. We do not know whether this increase is in the number of trained professionals or nonprofessionals. More in-depth analysis is required to determine whether there is an effect of automation here, so that fewer but better trained staff are required.

Book and Journal Resources

In Table 7, the total book and journal resources of all health sciences libraries in the United States are compared for 1973 and 1979. There is an increase of some four million bound volumes (14 percent) in books and bound journals. There is also a slight decrease of some 6,000 (1 percent) in total current serial titles subscribed to by libraries. We appear to be buying more books and fewer journals.

FURTHER ANALYSES

Data from the three surveys indicate that the ecology of health sciences libraries is obviously dynamic and changing. These analyses, however, are preliminary and will be further refined. In particular, we are interested in investigating the factors underlying some of the observations, e.g., the consistent decrease in number of health sciences libraries. What are the dynamics underlying these changes and what are the implica-

TABLE 7 HEALTH SCIENCES LIBRARY RESOURCES:
1973 AND 1979

Resource Category	Total 1973	Total 1979
Bound volumes (monographs & serials)	30,519,759	34,706,434
Current serial titles	736,588	732,408
Nonprint materials	—	1,136,711

tions for resource and service sharing? Are there health personnel that are underserved or is this a reflection of the effectiveness of the network/consortia system? The decrease in current subscriptions also generates a number of questions of significance to both libraries and the publishing industry. Are health sciences libraries indeed cutting down on the number of journals they buy? If so, why, and what is being cut? The factors contributing to these changes are undoubtedly complex and multiple, and require further analyses. These and other questions will be addressed by the investigators in a forthcoming monograph.

NOTES

1. H. Bloomquist, "The Status and Needs of Medical School Libraries in the United States," *Journal of Medical Education* 38 (March 1963): 145-163.
2. S. Crawford, D. Michel, and C. Waligorski, "The Contemporary Medical Society Library," *Bulletin of the Medical Library Association* 53 (April 1965): 178-195.
3. R. H. Giesler and H. Yast, "A Survey of Current Hospital Library Resources," *Hospitals* 38 (June 1964): 55-57.
4. Medical Library Association, Committee on Surveys and Statistics, "Library Statistics of Schools in the Health Sciences," *Bulletin of the Medical Library Association* 54 (July 1966): 207-229 (Part I); 55 (April 1967): 178-190 (Part II).
5. Medical Library Association, "Library Statistics of Veterinary Schools," *Bulletin of the Medical Library Association* 55 (April 1967): 201-206.
6. Medical Library Association, "Health Science Libraries of National, State and Local Organizations," *Bulletin of the Medical Library Association* 55 (April 1967): 191-200.
7. F. Schick and S. Crawford, *Directory of Health Sciences Libraries in the United States* (Chicago: American Medical Association, 1970).
8. S. Crawford, "Health Sciences Libraries in the 1960s: An Overview," *Bulletin of the Medical Library Association* 60 (April 1972): 4-12.
9. S. Crawford and G. Dandurand, *Directory of Health Sciences Libraries in the United States* (Chicago: American Medical Association, 1974).
10. A. M. Rees, "Medical School Libraries, 1961-71," *Bulletin of the Medical Library Association* 60 (April 1972): 13-18.
11. S. Crawford, "Medical School Libraries in the United States, 1960 through 1975," *Journal of the American Medical Association* 237 (January 1977): 464-468.
12. S. Crawford, "Health Sciences Libraries of Professional Societies, Voluntary Health Organizations and Foundations," *Bulletin of the Medical Library Association* 60 (April 1972): 38-45.
13. J. D. Miller, "Health Sciences Libraries in Hospitals," *Bulletin of the Medical Library Association* 60 (April 1972): 19-28.
14. T. Samore, S. Crawford, and G. Dandurand, "Libraries Service Educational Programs in the Allied Health Professions and Occupations," *Bulletin of the Medical Library Association* 60 (April 1972): 29-37.
15. S. Crawford, "Health Sciences Libraries in Outpatient Group Practice Clinics and Business and Industrial Organizations," *Bulletin of the Medical Library Association* 60 (April 1972): 46-49.
16. P. Vaillancourt, "Health Science Libraries of Federal, State, County, and Municipal Governments and Regional Libraries of the National Library of Medicine," *Bulletin of the Medical Library Association* 60 (April 1972): 50-56.

NCES SURVEY OF COLLEGE AND UNIVERSITY LIBRARIES, 1978-1979

Theodore Samore
Professor, School of Library Science, University of Wisconsin-Milwaukee

College and university libraries continue to rely on statistical reports on academic libraries published by the National Center for Education Statistics (NCES) of the U.S. Department of Education. The two most recent reports are *Library Statistics of Colleges and Universities, 1976: Institutional Data* (a joint effort of NCES and the University of Illinois Graduate School of Library Science), published in 1979; and *Library Statistics of Colleges and Universities, 1977: Institutional Data* (a joint effort of NCES and Indiana State University, Department of Library Science), published in 1980.

As in previous surveys conducted by NCES, the two reports list the collections, staff, and expenditures of over 3,000 individual U.S. academic libraries and joint library systems. In addition, a separate table provides useful indexes for each institution, such as the amount of money spent per student and per faculty member for library expenses and the number of volumes held per full-time equivalent (FTE) student. These indexes have not been used by academic library administrators as they should be for purposes of comparison and as indicators of adequate library service. One unusual statistic from the 1977 report is the fact that 38 academic institutions reported having no library whatsoever (there were 57 such reported in the 1976 report).

The most recent NCES survey of academic libraries took place in the fall of 1979. Although most of the data has been tabulated, publication of the findings will not occur until middle or late 1981. (NCES will conduct the next survey of academic libraries in fall 1981.) Mr. Richard M. Beazley, of NCES, has generously made available some of the preliminary tables. These tables include data on circulation, reference transactions, collections, operating expenditures, and staff.

It should be remembered that NCES classifies all academic institutions, whether publicly or privately controlled, into four types:

1. *University.* An institution that: (a) gives considerable stress to graduate instruction, (b) confers undergraduate and graduate degrees in a variety of liberal arts fields, and (c) has at least two professional schools that are not exclusively technological.
2. *Four-year institution with graduate programs.* A four-year institution, not classified as a university, offering programs leading to graduate or other post-baccalaureate degrees, including first-professional degrees.
3. *Four-year institution with no graduate programs.* A four-year institution, not classified as a university, offering no degrees beyond the baccalaureate.
4. *Two-year institution.* An institution offering at least two but fewer than four years of college-level education.

Most of the tables described below include both control and type in their breakdown of statistical data.

Table 1 summarizes circulation data for all types of libraries by control and size of enrollment. During 1978-1979, 201 million items were circulated to academic library users, which represents an increase of almost 3 percent over the figure for 1976-1977.

TABLE 1 CIRCULATION OF MATERIALS TO LIBRARY USERS (EXCLUDING DIAL ACCESS MATERIALS), COLLEGE AND UNIVERSITY LIBRARIES, 1978-1979*

Institution	Total Public & Private	Public Total	Public Median	Public Mean	Private Total	Private Median	Private Mean
All types	201,286,280	136,395,929	30,368	93,166	64,890,351	14,897	39,161
10,000 or more	100,462,150	86,216,026	195,488	326,575	14,246,124	345,037	459,552
5,000 to 9,999	39,032,731	26,017,471	57,011	85,303	13,015,260	97,819	178,291
1,000 to 4,999	46,014,105	22,116,281	19,184	31,959	23,897,824	31,331	44,419
500 to 999	9,484,084	1,612,637	7,547	10,609	7,871,447	15,000	19,198
Fewer than 500	6,293,210	433,514	5,087	8,500	5,859,696	5,098	9,685
Universities	80,494,687	56,379,367	403,085	587,285	24,115,320	248,000	371,004
10,000 or more	67,444,955	54,257,544	489,355	661,677	13,187,411	374,410	507,208
5,000 to 9,999	11,865,472	2,057,343	162,356	158,257	9,808,129	223,996	316,391
1,000 to 4,999	1,184,260	64,480	0	0	1,119,780	106,106	139,972
4-yr. insts. with grad. students	74,221,111	49,587,280	89,767	133,658	24,633,831	19,500	37,666
10,000 or more	24,611,921	23,553,208	212,575	261,702	1,058,713	111,970	211,742
5,000 to 9,999	19,419,508	16,503,860	109,518	133,095	2,915,648	52,960	85,754
1,000 to 4,999	23,772,587	9,233,246	48,119	65,484	14,539,341	36,320	53,257
500 to 999	2,999,975	179,325	28,278	25,617	2,820,650	19,601	28,206
Fewer than 500	3,417,120	117,641	10,621	13,071	3,299,479	6,857	13,634
4-yr. insts. w/out grad. students	18,020,830	3,663,308	32,199	42,596	14,357,522	15,382	21,590
10,000 or more	143,655	143,655	0	0	0	0	0
5,000 to 9,999	311,160	157,943	86,284	78,971	153,217	5,561	30,643
1,000 to 4,999	10,930,469	3,006,452	36,274	44,872	7,924,017	28,050	35,855
500 to 999	4,701,240	259,486	15,569	23,589	4,441,754	16,380	19,228
Fewer than 500	1,934,306	95,772	7,600	19,154	1,838,534	5,500	8,839
2-yr. insts.	28,549,652	26,765,974	16,848	29,380	1,783,678	2,956	6,533
10,000 or more	8,261,619	8,261,619	78,167	90,787	0	0	0
5,000 to 9,999	7,436,591	7,298,325	37,258	43,965	138,266	48,500	46,088
1,000 to 4,999	10,126,789	9,812,103	14,703	20,314	314,686	4,853	8,741
500 to 999	1,782,869	1,173,826	7,512	8,759	609,043	5,144	7,709
Fewer than 500	941,784	220,101	4,500	5,948	721,683	2,100	4,656

*Source: National Center for Education Statistics, Department of Education. Unpublished data from the Survey of College and University Libraries, fall 1979.

Also reported (but not included in Table 1) was this fact: the number of total hours the main academic library is open per typical week varies from less than 20 (11 academic libraries reported this) to those open 140 hours or more (31 so reported). Encouragingly, almost half of all main academic libraries reported that they were open between 60 and 79 hours per week; and an almost equal number reported that the main library was open seven days per week.

Furthermore, the number of reference and directional transactions that take place during a typical week in 3,000 academic libraries is staggering—almost 2,250,000. A reference transaction is defined as:

> an information contact which involves the use, recommendation, interpretation, or instruction in the use of one or more information sources, or knowledge of such sources, by a member of the reference/information staff. Information sources include:
> 1. print and nonprint materials;
> 2. machine readable data bases (including computer assisted instruction);
> 3. library bibliographic records, excluding circulation records;
> 4. other libraries and institutions; and
> 5. persons both inside and outside the library.

A directional transaction is defined as:

> an information contact which facilitates the use of the library in which the contact occurs, and its environ, and which may involve the use of sources describing that library, such as schedules, floor plans, handbooks, and policy statements. Examples of directional transactions are:
> 1. directions for locating facilities such as restrooms, carrels, and telephones;
> 2. directions for locating library staff and users;
> 3. directions for locating materials for which the user has a call number;
> 4. supplying materials such as paper and pencils; and
> 5. assisting users with the operation of machines.

Incidentally, directional transactions outnumbered reference transactions during the typical week mentioned above by a quarter of a million.

Table 2 presents summary data for bookstock volumes added during 1978–1979 and bookstock volumes held at the end of the year while Table 3 presents the same kind

TABLE 2 VOLUMES OF BOOKSTOCK ADDED DURING YEAR AND VOLUMES OF BOOKSTOCK HELD AT END OF YEAR, COLLEGE AND UNIVERSITY LIBRARIES, 1978–1979*

Institution	Vols. Added Total	Vols. Added Median	Vols. Held Total	Vols. Held Median
All types	21,606,527	2,503	519,849,274	59,095
10,000 or more	9,631,571	22,488	238,824,903	468,644
5,000 to 9,999	4,379,957	6,579	102,899,079	146,461
1,000 to 4,999	5,419,995	2,993	123,743,402	66,913
500 to 999	1,193,166	1,676	31,803,768	44,200
Fewer than 500	981,838	986	22,578,122	22,156
Universities	8,502,905	40,857	233,121,670	1,076,005
10,000 or more	6,800,202	54,493	181,153,493	1,287,101
5,000 to 9,999	1,549,342	20,726	47,602,222	602,203
1,000 to 4,999	153,361	13,242	4,365,955	380,078
4-yr. insts. with grad. students	8,156,611	4,725	182,731,277	123,488
10,000 or more	2,315,877	21,591	48,661,009	458,477
5,000 to 9,999	2,152,398	11,991	44,907,384	257,321
1,000 to 4,999	2,924,829	5,389	69,170,672	138,122
500 to 999	308,122	2,470	8,115,812	63,932
Fewer than 500	455,385	1,284	11,876,400	34,041
4-yr. insts. w/out grad. students	2,517,107	2,534	61,542,710	72,000
10,000 or more	29,530	0	340,140	0
5,000 to 9,999	124,344	3,631	672,329	70,929
1,000 to 4,999	1,351,710	3,950	33,698,520	100,664
500 to 999	661,010	2,437	19,356,559	76,873
Fewer than 500	350,513	1,310	7,475,162	28,076
2-yr. insts.	2,429,904	1,513	42,453,617	28,920
10,000 or more	485,962	3,888	8,670,261	84,625
5,000 to 9,999	553,873	2,791	9,717,144	51,408
1,000 to 4,999	990,095	1,642	16,508,255	29,375
500 to 999	244,034	991	4,331,397	20,282
Fewer than 500	175,940	630	3,226,560	14,532

*Source: National Center for Education Statistics, Department of Education. Unpublished data from the Survey of College and University Libraries, fall 1979.

TABLE 3 TITLES OF BOOKSTOCK ADDED DURING YEAR AND TITLES OF BOOKSTOCK HELD AT END OF YEAR, COLLEGE AND UNIVERSITY LIBRARIES, 1978–1979*

Institution	Titles Added Total	Titles Added Median	Titles Held Total	Titles Held Median
All types	14,507,091	2,008	340,256,103	47,863
10,000 or more	5,879,090	14,274	139,497,585	305,426
5,000 to 9,999	2,888,289	4,912	67,060,275	107,059
1,000 to 4,999	4,013,894	2,342	90,874,384	51,276
500 to 999	949,334	1,354	25,180,872	34,406
Fewer than 500	776,484	807	17,642,987	18,481
Universities	4,837,350	22,500	129,582,815	584,384
10,000 or more	3,897,468	29,110	100,083,170	663,821
5,000 to 9,999	850,750	13,482	26,904,417	385,038
1,000 to 4,999	89,132	7,217	2,595,228	237,918
4-yr. insts. with grad. students	5,616,755	3,400	125,701,110	90,316
10,000 or more	1,582,516	14,567	32,085,308	313,130
5,000 to 9,999	1,476,473	8,647	31,238,849	182,475
1,000 to 4,999	2,019,783	3,895	47,885,845	99,421
500 to 999	213,775	1,748	5,817,121	37,895
Fewer than 500	324,208	909	8,673,987	23,652
4-yr. insts. w/out grad. students	2,030,014	2,100	48,580,999	58,620
10,000 or more	21,386	0	233,331	0
5,000 to 9,999	105,902	2,727	563,203	48,920
1,000 to 4,999	1,066,818	3,163	25,996,391	78,390
500 to 999	540,901	1,996	15,637,974	61,656
Fewer than 500	295,007	1,050	6,150,100	22,173
2-yr. insts.	2,022,972	1,301	36,391,179	25,500
10,000 or more	377,720	3,216	7,095,776	69,581
5,000 to 9,999	455,164	2,239	8,353,806	44,844
1,000 to 4,999	838,161	1,362	14,396,920	25,955
500 to 999	194,658	846	3,725,777	17,483
Fewer than 500	157,269	559	2,818,900	12,252

*Source: National Center for Education Statistics, Department of Education. Unpublished data from the Survey of College and University Libraries, fall 1979.

of data for book titles. A bookstock volume includes bound periodicals and is defined thusly: "For reporting purposes, a volume is a physical unit of any printed, typewritten, handwritten, mimeographed, or processed work contained in one binding or portfolio, hardbound or paper bound, which has been cataloged, classified, or made ready for use." A title is defined as "a publication which forms a separate bibliographic whole, whether issued in one or several volumes, reels, discs, slides, or parts." Of course, Table 3 reports only bookstock titles, including periodicals.

A comparison of Tables 2 and 3 is instructive. It shows that the median number of titles acquired by all academic libraries during 1978–1979 was a mere 2,008; the median number for volumes was 2,503. Furthermore, the total number of titles held by all academic libraries at the end of the year was over 340 million while the total number of volumes held was 520 million. A rough computation shows that each title represents approximately 1.5 physical volumes. And this ratio appears to be constant throughout.

Table 4 summarizes the distribution of operating expenditures by purpose for over 3,000 academic libraries. These libraries spent over $1,500,000,000 during 1978–1979, an increase of 19 percent over two years ago (for 1976–1977, the amount was $1,260,000,000). Although this seems a respectable increase, it far from matched the rate of inflation for the same period. Staffing costs took 60 percent of total expenditures.

And the gap between book and periodical expenditures is narrowing appreciably. In 1974–1975, academic libraries spent $73,000,000 more on books than on periodicals; in 1978–1979 the difference was $44,000,000. At this rate, in three or four years expenditures for periodicals will equal—if not surpass—those for books.

Table 5 provides a breakdown of library operating expenditures according to the number of institutions that spend anywhere from less than $10,000 to over $2,000,000. Surprisingly, 96 academic libraries spent less than $10,000; at the other end, 152 spent $2,000,000 or more. Harvard University alone spent over $15,000,000.

Table 6 lists operating expenditures by state. As expected, California ranks first ($177 million) and New York second ($138 million); Texas is third with $83 million and Illinois fourth with $81 million. The ranking pretty much coincides with the rankings of these states in population.

Table 7 presents a breakdown of academic library staff by sex and by classification (professional and nonprofessional). Females constitute 83 percent of the total nonprofessional staff of all academic libraries and 63 percent of the total professional staff; these percentages have remained relatively constant over the years. The total number of staff increased by 1,325 over two years ago, an increase of a little over 2 percent.

Table 8 identifies the number of full-time equivalent (FTE) librarians for all types of academic institutions, both public and private. Almost 21,000 librarians, excluding administrators, were employed out of a total professional staff of 23,675. University libraries alone employed over one-third of all FTE librarians.

Table 9 provides statistical measures of hours of student assistance in academic libraries. These hours totaled almost 40,000,000 during 1978–1979, an appreciable increase of over 8 percent. This help cost academic libraries $80,000,000 (see Table 4) but it should be noted that Table 9 includes hours of student assistance not charged to library budgets.

Table 10 ranks the 50 largest academic libraries by the number of volumes held as of fall 1977. Except for the fact that Michigan and California–Berkeley are neck and neck for fourth place, the rankings remain pretty much the same as in previous years.

An examination of these NCES reports—and others—stretching back to 1967 indicate three major trends in academic library collections, expenditures, and staff. First, library collections are increasing at a markedly slower rate; indeed, there appears to be a steady decline in the number of books being added each year, particularly since 1974–1975. If this trend continues, academic libraries could eventually approach a "steady state" where the number of books added each year barely covers the number of books withdrawn or missing each year. More encouraging, however, is the considerable increases in the acquisition of book titles on microform and in the number of government publications.

Second, expenditures continue to rise, but nowhere near enough to offset inflation. Furthermore, staffing expenditures are taking bigger bits out of the total operating expenditures. Over a 15-year span (1965–1979) the percent of library expenditures devoted to staffing increased by almost 10 percent with a commensurate decrease in the percent of expenditures devoted to library materials. Persistent inflation will only aggravate this trend.

TABLE 4 TOTAL OPERATING EXPENDITURES AND DISTRIBUTION OF EXPENDITURES (IN THOUSANDS OF DOLLARS) OF COLLEGE AND UNIVERSITY LIBRARIES, 1978–1979*

Institution	Total	Salaries & Wages[a]	Fringe Benefits	Student Wages[b]	Books	Periodicals	Microforms	AV	Other Materials	Binding & Rebinding	Other
Public											
All types	$1,012,537	$482,975	$79,432	$52,486	$146,975	$118,120	$14,685	$13,726	$6,588	$16,140	$81,409
10,000 or more	616,157	286,685	48,089	37,103	87,502	79,363	8,301	4,585	3,013	11,522	49,995
5,000 to 9,999	196,138	95,551	15,734	8,611	30,199	20,397	3,121	3,797	1,778	2,406	14,544
1,000 to 4,999	179,390	90,926	14,103	6,080	26,175	16,138	2,971	4,435	1,337	2,021	15,203
500 to 999	14,873	7,361	1,146	582	2,082	1,394	200	623	124	112	1,247
Fewer than 500	5,980	2,452	360	110	1,017	829	92	285	335	79	420
Universities	395,536	177,941	28,172	24,453	56,979	58,919	5,147	1,271	2,311	8,484	31,859
10,000 or more	374,680	169,092	26,903	23,457	53,522	55,246	5,037	1,162	1,801	8,141	30,319
5,000 to 9,999	18,637	7,671	1,031	825	3,119	3,526	85	92	509	327	1,452
1,000 to 4,999	2,218	1,177	238	171	339	147	24	17	0	16	88
4-yr. insts. with grad. students	384,640	174,628	30,995	20,321	62,681	48,663	6,457	4,027	2,327	6,568	27,971
10,000 or more	179,223	81,264	15,217	11,111	28,587	22,228	2,684	1,441	727	3,225	12,738
5,000 to 9,999	120,585	54,095	9,469	5,996	21,543	14,913	2,493	1,592	806	1,890	7,788
1,000 to 4,999	78,784	37,035	5,897	2,977	11,905	10,226	1,228	745	474	1,346	6,952
500 to 999	2,823	1,202	245	200	190	632	8	59	0	48	240
Fewer than 500	3,224	1,032	167	37	457	664	45	190	319	60	253
4-yr. insts. w/out grad. students	30,312	14,998	2,315	1,039	5,286	2,685	651	475	227	402	2,236
10,000 or more	1,652	845	105	65	338	108	59	24	31	10	66
5,000 to 9,999	1,038	604	183	53	91	46	12	10	19	10	9
1,000 to 4,999	25,367	12,538	1,879	873	4,381	2,342	529	354	159	346	1,966
500 to 999	1,719	757	102	37	335	165	39	70	16	23	174
Fewer than 500	537	253	46	10	141	24	12	18	1	13	20
2-yr. insts.	202,049	115,408	17,951	6,672	22,029	7,853	2,430	7,953	1,724	685	19,342
10,000 or more	60,602	35,483	5,864	2,469	5,056	1,781	521	1,958	453	146	6,871
5,000 to 9,999	55,877	33,180	5,051	1,736	5,447	1,912	531	2,104	443	179	5,296
1,000 to 4,999	73,021	40,176	6,089	2,058	9,551	3,424	1,191	3,319	705	313	6,196
500 to 999	10,331	5,402	800	346	1,557	597	153	494	108	41	833
Fewer than 500	2,218	1,167	147	63	419	141	35	77	15	6	147

Private									
All types	489,527	227,111	34,873	27,042	77,482	61,074	5,400	3,397	2,704	9,129	41,314
10,000 or more	132,941	63,499	11,611	6,106	18,607	16,785	1,104	269	397	2,743	11,821
5,000 to 9,999	114,518	53,295	8,191	4,945	17,050	16,538	1,016	463	669	2,266	10,085
1,000 to 4,999	160,271	70,460	10,215	10,799	28,106	19,836	2,439	1,619	823	2,804	13,170
500 to 999	46,248	22,123	2,687	3,335	7,981	4,640	557	591	367	726	3,242
Fewer than 500	35,550	17,735	2,170	1,857	5,739	3,274	284	455	449	592	2,996
Universities	224,198	105,369	17,811	9,892	32,141	30,869	1,814	487	943	4,664	20,209
10,000 or more	128,263	61,287	11,268	5,907	17,912	16,087	1,044	254	365	2,673	11,466
5,000 to 9,999	86,104	39,821	5,958	3,473	12,405	13,218	634	202	532	1,791	8,070
1,000 to 4,999	9,831	4,261	585	512	1,825	1,564	136	31	46	199	673
4-yr. insts. with											
grad. students	167,295	75,431	11,269	9,771	27,443	21,517	2,502	1,556	1,051	3,033	13,722
10,000 or more	4,677	2,212	342	199	695	698	60	15	32	69	355
5,000 to 9,999	25,203	11,637	1,999	1,336	4,069	3,208	338	229	68	465	1,854
1,000 to 4,999	99,626	43,370	6,433	6,440	16,640	13,345	1,761	952	470	1,782	8,433
500 to 999	16,361	7,717	995	997	2,667	1,987	194	179	181	294	1,150
Fewer than 500	21,428	10,495	1,500	799	3,371	2,279	149	181	300	422	1,930
4-yr. insts. w/out											
grad. students	86,448	39,855	5,162	6,726	16,106	8,036	934	1,003	551	1,355	6,719
10,000 or more	0	0	0	0	0	0	0	0	0	0	0
5,000 to 9,999	1,760	975	155	64	368	67	12	10	10	4	96
1,000 to 4,999	48,640	21,662	3,051	3,744	9,314	4,819	487	550	292	807	3,915
500 to 999	26,570	12,555	1,516	2,137	4,767	2,448	325	314	152	412	1,943
Fewer than 500	9,478	4,663	440	782	1,657	703	110	128	96	132	765
2-yr. insts.	11,587	6,456	631	654	1,792	652	151	352	159	77	664
10,000 or more	0	0	0	0	0	0	0	0	0	0	0
5,000 to 9,999	1,450	862	79	72	208	46	32	23	59	5	65
1,000 to 4,999	2,175	1,167	146	104	327	109	55	86	15	16	150
500 to 999	3,317	1,851	176	202	547	205	38	97	33	19	149
Fewer than 500	4,645	2,576	230	276	710	292	25	146	52	38	300
Total, public & private	$1,502,064	$710,086	$114,306	$79,528	$224,457	$179,194	$20,085	$17,124	$9,292	$25,269	$122,722

[a]Includes salary equivalents of contributed services staff.
[b]Wages of students serving on an hourly basis, charged to the library.
Source: National Center for Education Statistics, Department of Education. Unpublished data from the Survey of College and University Libraries, fall 1979.

TABLE 5 DISTRIBUTION OF COLLEGES AND UNIVERSITIES, BY LIBRARY OPERATING EXPENDITURES, 1978–1979*

Institution	Total	Less Than $10,000	$10,000 to $19,999	$20,000 to $49,999	$50,000 to $99,999	$100,000 to $199,999	$200,000 to $499,999	$500,000 to $999,999	$1,000,000 to $1,999,999	$2,000,000 or more
Public										
All types	1,464	1	3	66	223	328	399	187	143	114
10,000 or more	264	0	0	0	0	0	42	43	72	107
5,000 to 9,999	305	0	0	0	2	28	128	86	57	4
1,000 to 4,999	692	0	2	16	129	258	216	55	13	3
500 to 999	152	1	1	32	72	35	9	2	0	0
Fewer than 500	51	0	0	18	20	7	4	1	1	0
Universities	96	0	0	0	0	0	0	2	19	75
10,000 or more	82	0	0	0	0	0	0	0	9	73
5,000 to 9,999	13	0	0	0	0	0	0	2	10	1
1,000 to 4,999	1	0	0	0	0	0	0	0	0	1
4-yr. insts. with grad. students	371	0	0	0	2	17	87	125	102	38
10,000 or more	90	0	0	0	0	0	0	8	49	33
5,000 to 9,999	124	0	0	0	0	0	11	66	44	3
1,000 to 4,999	141	0	0	0	1	12	70	48	8	2
500 to 999	7	0	0	0	0	2	3	2	0	0
Fewer than 500	9	0	0	0	1	3	3	1	1	0
4-yr. insts. w/out grad. students	86	0	0	2	6	17	49	6	6	0
10,000 or more	1	0	0	0	0	0	0	0	0	0
5,000 to 9,999	2	0	0	0	0	0	1	1	0	0
1,000 to 4,999	67	0	0	1	2	11	43	5	5	0
500 to 999	11	0	0	0	1	6	4	0	0	0
Fewer than 500	5	0	0	0	3	0	1	0	1	0
2-yr. insts.	911	1	3	64	215	294	263	54	16	1
10,000 or more	91	0	0	0	0	0	42	35	13	1
5,000 to 9,999	166	0	0	0	2	28	116	17	3	0
1,000 to 4,999	483	0	2	15	126	235	103	2	0	0
500 to 999	134	1	1	32	71	27	2	0	0	0
Fewer than 500	37	0	0	17	16	4	0	0	0	0

NCES SURVEY OF COLLEGE AND UNIVERSITY LIBRARIES / 295

	Total									Private
All types	1,657	95	126	245	363	373	286	95	36	38
10,000 or more	31	0	0	1	0	0	0	1	10	19
5,000 to 9,999	73	0	0	0	53	1	16	24	18	14
1,000 to 4,999	538	1	6	18	141	166	222	59	8	5
500 to 999	410	9	24	42	169	152	38	4	0	0
Fewer than 500	605	85	96	184	0	54	10	7	0	0
Universities	65	0	0	0	0	0	2	7	22	34
10,000 or more	26	0	0	0	0	0	0	0	7	19
5,000 to 9,999	31	0	0	0	0	0	0	5	13	13
1,000 to 4,999	8	0	0	0	0	0	2	2	2	2
4-yr. insts. with grad. students	654	27	38	60	120	141	178	72	14	4
10,000 or more	5	0	0	1	0	0	0	1	3	0
5,000 to 9,999	34	0	0	0	0	0	11	17	5	1
1,000 to 4,999	273	0	0	2	14	68	136	44	6	3
500 to 999	100	1	1	10	27	35	23	3	0	0
Fewer than 500	242	26	37	47	79	38	8	7	0	0
4-yr. insts. w/out grad. students	665	22	32	97	174	223	102	15	0	0
10,000 or more	0	0	0	0	0	0	0	0	0	0
5,000 to 9,999	5	0	0	0	0	1	3	1	0	0
1,000 to 4,999	221	0	1	5	25	93	84	13	0	0
500 to 999	231	0	3	12	86	115	14	1	0	0
Fewer than 500	208	22	28	80	63	14	1	0	0	0
2-yr. insts.	273	46	56	88	69	9	4	1	0	0
10,000 or more	0	0	0	0	0	0	0	0	0	0
5,000 to 9,999	3	0	0	0	0	0	2	1	0	0
1,000 to 4,999	36	1	5	11	14	5	0	0	0	0
500 to 999	79	8	20	20	28	2	2	0	0	0
Fewer than 500	155	37	31	57	27	2	1	0	0	0
Total, public & private	3,121	96	129	311	586	701	685	282	179	152

Source: National Center for Education Statistics, Department of Education. Unpublished data from the Survey of College and University Libraries, fall 1979.

TABLE 6 OPERATING EXPENDITURES OF COLLEGE AND UNIVERSITY LIBRARIES (IN THOUSANDS OF DOLLARS) BY STATE OR AREA, 1978–1979*

State or Area	Total	Salaries & Wages[a]	Fringe Benefits	Student Wages[b]	Books	Periodicals	Microforms	AV	Other Materials	Binding & Rebinding	Other
Aggregate U.S.	$1,502,064	$710,086	$114,306	$79,528	$224,457	$179,194	$20,085	$17,124	$9,292	$25,269	$122,722
States & D.C.	1,484,922	699,801	113,012	78,939	222,419	177,661	19,953	16,947	9,149	25,060	121,982
Alabama	19,105	8,811	796	1,070	3,305	2,887	280	238	101	348	1,269
Alaska	4,225	2,162	416	254	782	251	72	24	2	24	236
Arizona	17,084	6,944	1,110	888	3,794	1,999	292	229	195	345	1,287
Arkansas	9,349	3,658	577	635	1,854	1,375	205	103	18	152	772
California	177,690	85,910	17,415	11,947	23,527	17,298	1,700	1,489	1,078	3,115	14,212
Colorado	18,467	9,100	1,120	841	2,604	2,492	194	326	57	316	1,417
Connecticut	26,747	13,575	1,876	1,020	3,842	2,871	353	190	363	452	2,204
Delaware	3,779	1,598	302	163	837	499	63	29	8	90	191
District of Columbia	19,063	9,359	1,657	990	2,550	2,117	261	133	3	242	1,752
Florida	49,301	20,026	3,314	1,721	10,970	5,125	1,415	1,549	1,000	1,041	3,140
Georgia	27,847	11,965	1,874	1,221	4,877	4,278	364	241	88	621	2,318
Hawaii	7,618	3,531	766	295	1,054	852	72	70	1	136	841
Idaho	5,957	2,718	436	296	1,150	640	85	98	68	57	409
Illinois	81,632	39,992	4,877	4,898	10,566	9,377	549	904	568	1,251	8,651
Indiana	31,114	14,640	1,606	2,236	4,526	4,312	244	228	338	607	2,377
Iowa	20,024	8,896	1,568	1,251	3,135	2,853	255	223	92	418	1,333
Kansas	16,057	6,902	909	1,062	2,614	2,358	134	205	60	251	1,562
Kentucky	19,188	9,065	1,146	1,172	3,247	2,328	194	133	31	325	1,547
Louisiana	19,390	9,305	1,023	767	3,567	2,432	244	117	46	419	1,469
Maine	5,566	2,448	373	294	1,039	762	49	12	117	76	396
Maryland	26,905	14,204	1,794	1,083	3,289	3,166	257	286	68	390	2,366
Massachusetts	66,630	32,670	4,325	2,766	9,403	8,280	1,050	781	533	1,276	5,545
Michigan	50,225	23,896	4,546	3,485	6,578	5,577	668	572	217	733	3,951
Minnesota	25,606	12,530	2,044	2,245	3,208	2,615	127	317	264	387	1,870
Mississippi	12,792	5,438	853	691	2,258	1,683	316	238	176	216	924
Missouri	26,966	12,230	1,536	1,611	4,009	4,081	516	312	171	487	2,013
Montana	4,006	1,841	249	309	420	762	32	47	28	56	261
Nebraska	11,586	4,883	604	583	2,121	1,697	90	172	73	225	1,138

Nevada	4,455	2,238	277	190	726	608	42	46	10	95	223
New Hampshire	7,788	3,347	558	321	1,140	1,215	175	65	68	86	813
New Jersey	39,754	21,041	3,379	1,356	7,223	3,035	319	458	120	550	2,273
New Mexico	9,293	4,275	673	411	1,490	1,288	115	97	24	171	750
New York	138,075	70,252	15,137	5,029	18,979	14,660	1,448	873	855	2,179	8,664
North Carolina	46,082	21,010	3,344	1,947	8,745	5,091	874	859	343	681	3,188
North Dakota	3,895	1,625	150	153	888	601	20	32	13	58	355
Ohio	57,275	26,154	4,911	3,396	7,451	7,233	1,123	440	229	832	5,506
Oklahoma	16,203	6,412	725	1,205	2,834	2,364	656	270	92	226	1,419
Oregon	17,649	8,372	1,442	861	2,052	2,609	228	206	45	270	1,563
Pennsylvania	71,437	35,360	6,930	3,421	9,129	9,004	970	566	233	1,327	4,498
Rhode Island	8,269	3,774	695	460	1,284	1,103	83	51	12	173	635
South Carolina	16,596	7,454	1,090	548	3,044	2,358	415	165	30	297	1,195
South Dakota	4,039	1,738	235	209	628	665	29	40	15	71	410
Tennessee	24,600	11,345	1,228	1,371	3,402	3,571	375	484	48	496	2,280
Texas	83,564	36,780	4,200	4,578	13,707	10,514	1,352	1,487	750	1,388	8,809
Utah	15,048	6,549	762	1,259	2,382	2,207	74	151	6	255	1,403
Vermont	4,942	2,075	333	270	951	703	54	31	13	93	418
Virginia	37,995	17,011	1,889	1,715	5,984	4,717	571	338	121	611	5,039
Washington	32,176	15,304	2,861	1,993	3,179	3,551	536	444	208	552	3,549
West Virginia	7,510	3,855	284	348	1,100	975	137	173	48	101	488
Wisconsin	31,825	14,373	2,727	2,060	4,464	4,072	272	365	96	460	2,936
Wyoming	2,535	1,157	69	41	413	548	5	42	6	37	117
U.S. service schools	5,847	3,438	293	139	774	710	76	13	25	112	267
Outlying areas:	11,295	6,847	1,001	449	1,264	823	57	164	118	97	474
American Samoa	69	43	6	0	9	2	0	5	0	0	3
Canal Zone	162	61	12	39	10	3	3	10	0	6	19
Guam	406	259	28	0	91	0	0	0	0	0	27
Puerto Rico	10,356	6,369	938	388	1,085	779	52	145	106	88	406
Trust Territory	32	14	0	0	8	2	1	4	1	0	3
Virgin Islands	270	101	18	23	61	37	0	0	10	4	17

[a]Includes salary equivalents of contributed services staff.
[b]Wages of students serving on an hourly basis, charged to the library.
Source: National Center for Education Statistics, Department of Education. Unpublished data from the Survey of College and University Libraries, fall 1979.

TABLE 7 PROFESSIONAL AND NONPROFESSIONAL STAFF IN COLLEGE AND UNIVERSITY LIBRARIES, FALL 1979*

Institution	All Staff Total	All Staff Men	All Staff Women	Professional Staff (FTE) Total	Professional Staff (FTE) Men No.	Professional Staff (FTE) Men % of Total	Professional Staff (FTE) Women No.	Professional Staff (FTE) Women % of Total	Nonprofessional Staff (FTE) Total	Nonprofessional Staff (FTE) Men No.	Nonprofessional Staff (FTE) Men % of Total	Nonprofessional Staff (FTE) Women No.	Nonprofessional Staff (FTE) Women % of Total
Public													
All types	38,307.5	9,401.0	28,906.5	14,889.3	5,716.3	38.4	9,173.0	61.6	23,418.2	3,684.7	15.7	19,733.5	84.3
10,000 or more	22,759.8	5,643.9	17,115.9	8,419.6	3,233.5	38.4	5,186.1	61.6	14,340.2	2,410.4	16.8	11,929.8	83.2
5,000 to 9,999	7,378.9	1,781.4	5,597.5	2,939.4	1,169.0	39.8	1,770.4	60.2	4,439.5	612.4	13.8	3,827.1	86.2
1,000 to 4,999	7,366.7	1,794.4	5,572.3	3,125.8	1,177.2	37.7	1,948.6	62.3	4,240.9	617.2	14.6	3,623.7	85.4
500 to 999	590.7	135.6	455.1	304.7	104.1	34.2	200.6	65.8	286.0	31.5	11.0	254.5	89.0
Fewer than 500	211.4	45.7	165.7	99.8	32.5	32.6	67.3	67.4	111.6	13.2	11.8	98.4	88.2
Universities	14,655.1	3,525.7	11,129.4	5,216.8	1,966.7	37.7	3,250.1	62.3	9,438.3	1,559.0	16.5	7,879.3	83.5
10,000 or more	13,936.8	3,364.3	10,572.5	4,960.8	1,854.1	37.4	3,106.7	62.6	8,976.0	1,510.2	16.8	7,465.8	83.2
5,000 to 9,999	665.3	142.4	552.9	239.0	102.6	42.9	136.4	57.1	426.3	39.8	9.3	386.5	90.7
1,000 to 4,999	53.0	19.0	34.0	17.0	10.0	58.8	7.0	41.2	36.0	9.0	25.0	27.0	75.0
4-yr. insts. with grad. students	13,774.6	3,196.5	10,578.1	5,597.2	2,097.5	37.5	3,499.7	62.5	8,177.4	1,099.0	13.4	7,078.4	86.6
10,000 or more	6,330.0	1,565.7	4,764.3	2,514.2	991.5	39.4	1,522.7	60.6	3,815.8	574.2	15.0	3,241.6	85.0
5,000 to 9,999	4,251.3	923.9	3,327.4	1,755.3	653.4	37.2	1,101.9	62.8	2,496.0	270.5	10.8	2,225.5	89.2
1,000 to 4,999	3,007.6	661.9	2,345.7	1,248.8	421.6	33.8	827.2	66.2	1,758.8	240.3	13.7	1,518.5	86.3
500 to 999	92.9	20.0	72.9	42.4	15.0	35.4	27.4	64.6	50.5	5.0	9.9	45.5	90.1
Fewer than 500	92.8	25.0	67.8	36.5	16.0	43.8	20.5	56.2	56.3	9.0	16.0	47.3	84.0
4-yr. insts. w/out grad. students	1,217.4	316.3	901.1	508.0	207.8	40.9	300.2	59.1	709.4	108.5	15.3	600.9	84.7
10,000 or more	74.0	15.0	59.0	21.5	8.0	37.2	13.5	62.8	52.5	7.0	13.3	45.5	86.7
5,000 to 9,999	41.4	19.0	22.4	17.4	8.0	46.0	9.4	54.0	24.0	11.0	45.8	13.0	54.2
1,000 to 4,999	1,014.9	259.7	755.2	421.6	173.4	41.1	248.2	58.9	593.3	86.3	14.5	507.0	85.5
500 to 999	65.8	18.0	47.8	36.1	14.0	38.8	22.1	61.2	29.7	4.0	13.5	25.7	86.5
Fewer than 500	21.3	4.6	16.7	11.4	4.4	38.6	7.0	61.4	9.9	.2	2.0	9.7	98.0
2-yr. insts.	8,660.4	2,362.5	6,297.9	3,567.3	1,444.3	40.5	2,123.0	59.5	5,093.1	918.2	18.0	4,174.9	82.0
10,000 or more	2,419.0	698.9	1,720.1	923.1	379.9	41.2	543.2	58.8	1,495.9	319.0	21.3	1,176.9	78.7
5,000 to 9,999	2,420.9	696.1	1,724.8	927.7	405.0	43.7	522.7	56.3	1,493.2	291.1	19.5	1,202.1	80.5
1,000 to 4,999	3,291.2	853.8	2,437.4	1,438.4	572.2	39.8	866.2	60.2	1,852.8	281.6	15.2	1,571.2	84.8
500 to 999	432.0	97.6	334.4	226.2	75.1	33.2	151.1	66.8	205.8	22.5	10.9	183.3	89.1
Fewer than 500	97.3	16.1	81.2	51.9	12.1	23.3	39.8	76.7	45.4	4.0	8.8	41.4	91.2

NCES SURVEY OF COLLEGE AND UNIVERSITY LIBRARIES / 299

Private												
All types	20,105.3	5,225.6	14,879.7	8,785.9	3,008.3	34.2	5,777.6	65.8	11,319.4	2,217.3	19.6	9,102.1	80.4
10,000 or more	4,701.2	1,573.9	3,127.3	1,686.9	669.6	39.7	1,017.3	60.3	3,014.3	904.3	30.0	2,110.0	70.0
5,000 to 9,999	4,857.8	1,348.2	3,509.6	1,744.2	624.6	35.8	1,119.6	64.2	3,113.6	723.6	23.2	2,390.0	76.8
1,000 to 4,999	6,697.9	1,434.6	5,263.3	3,133.0	1,034.2	33.0	2,098.8	67.0	3,564.9	400.4	11.2	3,164.5	88.8
500 to 999	2,131.5	412.4	1,719.1	1,191.8	317.6	26.6	874.2	73.4	939.7	94.8	10.1	844.9	89.9
Fewer than 500	1,716.9	456.5	1,260.4	1,030.0	362.3	35.2	667.7	64.8	686.9	94.2	13.7	592.7	86.3
Universities	8,455.0	2,593.1	5,861.9	2,962.1	1,126.6	38.0	1,835.5	62.0	5,492.9	1,466.5	26.7	4,026.4	73.3
10,000 or more	4,441.9	1,504.8	2,937.1	1,580.6	633.9	40.1	946.7	59.9	2,861.3	870.9	30.4	1,990.4	69.6
5,000 to 9,999	3,631.2	981.6	2,649.6	1,219.8	436.2	35.8	783.6	64.2	2,411.4	545.4	22.6	1,866.0	77.4
1,000 to 4,999	381.9	106.7	275.2	161.7	56.5	34.9	105.2	65.1	220.2	50.2	22.8	170.0	77.2
4-yr. insts. with grad. students	6,990.1	1,671.0	5,319.1	3,252.3	1,137.6	35.0	2,114.7	65.0	3,737.8	533.4	14.3	3,204.4	85.7
10,000 or more	259.3	69.1	190.2	106.3	35.7	33.6	70.6	66.4	153.0	33.4	21.8	119.6	78.2
5,000 to 9,999	1,050.9	293.1	757.8	431.0	147.0	34.1	284.0	65.9	619.9	146.1	23.6	473.8	76.4
1,000 to 4,999	4,081.5	856.3	3,225.2	1,857.6	623.6	33.6	1,234.0	66.4	2,223.9	232.7	10.5	1,991.2	89.5
500 to 999	668.1	156.2	511.9	345.8	101.6	29.4	244.2	70.6	322.3	54.6	16.9	267.7	83.1
Fewer than 500	930.3	296.3	634.0	511.6	229.7	44.9	281.9	55.1	418.7	66.6	15.9	352.1	84.1
4-yr. insts. w/out grad. students	3,991.6	822.9	3,168.7	2,159.9	648.9	30.0	1,511.0	70.0	1,831.7	174.0	9.5	1,657.7	90.5
10,000 or more	.0	.0	.0	.0	.0	.0	.0	.0	.0	.0	.0	.0	.0
5,000 to 9,999	97.0	36.4	60.6	58.0	21.4	36.9	36.6	63.1	39.0	15.0	38.5	24.0	61.5
1,000 to 4,999	2,105.7	436.0	1,669.7	1,046.0	333.6	31.9	712.4	68.1	1,059.7	102.4	9.7	957.3	90.3
500 to 999	1,277.0	229.7	1,047.3	733.0	193.3	26.4	539.7	73.6	544.0	36.4	6.7	507.6	93.3
Fewer than 500	511.9	120.8	391.1	322.9	100.6	31.2	222.3	68.8	189.0	20.2	10.7	168.8	89.3
2-yr. insts.	668.6	138.6	530.0	411.6	95.2	23.1	316.4	76.9	257.0	43.4	16.9	213.6	83.1
10,000 or more	.0	.0	.0	.0	.0	.0	.0	.0	.0	.0	.0	.0	.0
5,000 to 9,999	78.7	37.1	41.6	35.4	20.0	56.5	15.4	43.5	43.3	17.1	39.5	26.2	60.5
1,000 to 4,999	128.8	35.6	93.2	67.7	20.5	30.3	47.2	69.7	61.1	15.1	24.7	46.0	75.3
500 to 999	186.4	26.5	159.9	113.0	22.7	20.1	90.3	79.9	73.4	3.8	5.2	69.6	94.8
Fewer than 500	274.7	39.4	235.3	195.5	32.0	16.4	163.5	83.6	79.2	7.4	9.3	71.8	90.7
Total, public & private	58,412.8	14,626.6	43,786.2	23,675.2	8,724.6	36.9	14,950.6	63.1	34,737.6	5,902.0	17.0	28,835.6	83.0

Source: National Center for Education Statistics, Department of Education. Unpublished data from the Survey of College and University Libraries, fall 1979.

TABLE 8 NUMBER OF FULL-TIME EQUIVALENT LIBRARIANS IN COLLEGE AND UNIVERSITY LIBRARIES, FALL 1979[a]*

Institution	Total Public & Private	Public Total	Public Median	Public Mean	Private Total	Private Median	Private Mean
All types	20,948.0	13,134.5	4.0	8.9	7,813.5	2.2	4.7
10,000 or more	8,968.5	7,458.3	21.3	28.2	1,510.2	33.0	48.7
5,000 to 9,999	4,197.1	2,628.1	7.0	8.6	1,569.0	14.0	21.4
1,000 to 4,999	5,466.4	2,696.7	3.0	3.8	2,769.7	4.0	5.1
500 to 999	1,300.6	257.6	1.0	1.6	1,043.0	2.2	2.5
Fewer than 500	1,015.4	93.8	1.0	1.8	921.6	1.0	1.5
Universities	7,410.0	4,717.5	41.0	49.1	2,692.5	28.6	41.4
10,000 or more	5,898.4	4,478.9	49.0	54.6	1,419.5	47.4	54.5
5,000 to 9,999	1,347.5	224.6	17.5	17.2	1,122.9	22.0	36.2
1,000 to 4,999	164.1	14.0	.0	.0	150.1	14.0	18.7
4-yr. insts. with grad. students	7,838.5	4,971.2	11.0	13.3	2,867.3	3.0	4.3
10,000 or more	2,284.7	2,194.0	24.0	24.3	90.7	13.0	18.1
5,000 to 9,999	1,968.2	1,586.8	12.0	12.7	381.4	9.3	11.2
1,000 to 4,999	2,764.6	1,119.0	7.0	7.9	1,645.6	5.0	6.0
500 to 999	333.9	35.4	5.0	5.0	298.5	2.8	2.9
Fewer than 500	487.1	36.0	2.0	4.0	451.1	1.0	1.8
4-yr. insts. w/out grad. students	2,334.5	455.3	4.0	5.2	1,879.2	2.5	2.8
10,000 or more	21.5	21.5	.0	.0	.0	.0	.0
5,000 to 9,999	56.8	16.4	9.4	8.2	40.4	2.0	8.0
1,000 to 4,999	1,288.8	372.8	5.0	5.5	916.0	4.0	4.1
500 to 999	670.5	34.1	3.0	3.1	636.4	3.0	2.7
Fewer than 500	296.9	10.5	2.0	2.1	286.4	1.0	1.3
2-yr. insts.	3,365.0	2,990.5	2.5	3.2	374.5	1.0	1.3
10,000 or more	763.9	763.9	6.7	8.3	.0	.0	.0
5,000 to 9,999	824.6	800.3	4.1	4.8	24.3	7.7	8.1
1,000 to 4,999	1,248.9	1,190.9	2.0	2.4	58.0	1.5	1.6
500 to 999	296.2	188.1	1.0	1.4	108.1	1.0	1.3
Fewer than 500	231.4	47.3	1.0	1.2	184.1	1.0	1.1

[a] Includes administrators and "other" professionals; includes contributed services staff.
*Source: National Center for Education Statistics, Department of Education. Unpublished data from the Survey of College and University Libraries, fall 1979.

Third, staffing itself has reached a point of near equilibrium. Despite respectable increases in services (circulation, interlibrary lending, on-line reference, etc.) and more students, the number of FTE library staff increased only 2.8 percent between fall 1975 and fall 1979 (56,800 to 58,400). And most of this negligible increase was in nonprofessional staff. The future seems to offer little encouragement.

TABLE 9   HOURS OF STUDENT ASSISTANCE IN COLLEGE AND UNIVERSITY LIBRARIES, 1978–1979[a]*

Institution	Total Public & Private	Public Total	Public Median	Public Mean	Private Total	Private Median	Private Mean
All types	39,549,806	26,121,108	5,580	17,842	13,428,698	3,451	8,104
10,000 or more	18,741,206	16,196,908	42,307	61,351	2,544,308	63,467	82,074
5,000 to 9,999	7,407,908	5,246,855	12,207	17,202	2,161,053	21,456	29,603
1,000 to 4,999	9,849,882	4,137,204	3,629	5,978	5,712,678	7,545	10,618
500 to 999	2,268,516	464,187	1,301	3,053	1,804,329	3,525	4,400
Fewer than 500	1,282,284	75,954	900	1,489	1,206,330	942	1,993
Universities	14,051,498	10,002,444	90,460	104,192	4,049,054	46,140	62,293
10,000 or more	11,906,400	9,527,486	97,574	116,188	2,378,914	92,854	91,496
5,000 to 9,999	1,873,840	406,493	30,225	31,268	1,467,347	42,998	47,333
1,000 to 4,999	271,258	68,465	0	0	202,793	17,532	25,349
4-yr. insts. with grad. students	15,370,920	10,283,692	19,691	27,718	5,087,228	4,221	7,778
10,000 or more	5,125,357	4,959,963	45,903	55,110	165,394	25,399	33,078
5,000 to 9,999	4,146,895	3,529,700	24,401	28,465	617,195	14,651	18,152
1,000 to 4,999	5,182,856	1,704,964	9,414	12,091	3,477,892	9,130	12,739
500 to 999	475,706	71,692	5,515	10,241	404,014	3,471	4,040
Fewer than 500	440,106	17,373	544	1,930	422,733	820	1,746
4-yr. insts. w/out grad. students	4,516,027	796,464	7,409	9,261	3,719,563	4,031	5,593
10,000 or more	54,972	54,972	0	0	0	0	0
5,000 to 9,999	78,102	18,333	10,120	9,166	59,769	9,705	11,953
1,000 to 4,999	2,641,315	667,760	8,466	9,966	1,973,555	6,897	8,930
500 to 999	1,259,025	46,065	3,438	4,187	1,212,960	4,392	5,250
Fewer than 500	482,613	9,334	935	1,866	473,279	1,350	2,275
2-yr. insts.	5,611,361	5,038,508	2,972	5,530	572,853	600	2,098
10,000 or more	1,654,487	1,654,487	11,862	18,181	0	0	0
5,000 to 9,999	1,309,071	1,292,329	6,000	7,785	16,742	3,000	5,580
1,000 to 4,999	1,754,453	1,696,015	2,294	3,511	58,438	1,333	1,623
500 to 999	533,785	346,430	1,241	2,585	187,355	1,320	2,371
Fewer than 500	359,565	49,247	751	1,331	310,318	348	2,002

[a] Includes hours of student assistance not charged to library budgets.
Source: National Center for Education Statistics, Department of Education. Unpublished data from the Survey of College and University Libraries, fall 1979.

TABLE 10 COLLECTIONS AND OPERATING EXPENDITURES OF 50 COLLEGE AND UNIVERSITY LIBRARIES WITH THE LARGEST NUMBER OF VOLUMES, FALL 1977

Institution or Branch in Rank Order	Vols. at End of Year	Vols. Added During Year	Total Lib. Operating Expenditures	Salaries, Wages, & Fringe Benefits	Books & Other Lib. Materials	Binding & Rebinding	Other
1. Harvard Univ.	9,547,576	191,878	$14,362,801	$9,101,183	$3,262,000	$436,701	$1,562,917
2. Yale Univ.	6,884,604	203,825	11,225,498	7,177,888	2,434,317	226,631	1,386,662
3. Univ. of Illinois, Urbana	5,494,786	142,626	7,353,119	4,551,833	2,210,425	160,264	430,597
4. Univ. of Michigan, Ann Arbor	4,917,381	149,210	9,336,782	6,176,489	2,341,978	207,954	610,361
5. Univ. of California, Berkeley	4,917,330	149,277	11,779,605	8,590,185	2,255,075	278,315	656,030
6. Columbia Univ., Main Div.	4,716,162	118,586	8,247,083	6,454,647	1,640,032	152,404	0
7. Stanford Univ.	4,170,325	133,157	11,178,908	6,401,918	2,882,493	270,318	1,624,179
8. Univ. of California, Los Angeles	3,908,053	122,893	11,746,071	8,087,531	2,022,313	417,977	1,218,250
9. Univ. of Chicago	3,886,130	138,352	6,155,418	3,187,603	1,394,989	169,036	1,403,790
10. Univ. of Texas, Austin	3,713,821	225,768	9,319,210	4,990,945	3,794,931	106,092	427,242
11. Univ. of Minnesota, Minneapolis-St. Paul	3,363,576	80,194	7,818,661	5,666,699	1,593,057	136,685	422,220
12. Indiana Univ., Bloomington	3,242,300	139,635	5,860,362	3,921,886	1,410,504	137,520	390,452
13. Univ. of Wisconsin-Madison	3,238,152	105,289	7,661,913	4,913,903	1,850,693	149,285	748,032
14. Cornell Univ., Endowed Colleges	3,184,941	86,364	5,844,929	3,600,065	1,601,945	125,282	517,637
15. Ohio State Univ., Main Campus	3,126,131	127,849	6,664,995	4,482,013	1,630,840	24,679	527,463
16. Princeton Univ.	2,910,461	101,083	5,935,330	3,836,014	1,612,961	103,344	383,011
17. Univ. of Pennsylvania	2,784,260	92,640	5,945,355	4,072,832	1,306,108	177,081	389,334
18. Duke Univ.	2,712,405	100,262	4,055,977	2,498,105	1,195,819	97,470	264,583
19. Northwestern Univ.	2,544,896	72,907	4,956,369	3,302,689	1,413,940	177,761	121,979
20. Univ. of Washington	2,381,642	116,301	8,484,423	5,543,265	2,090,513	308,413	542,232
21. Univ. of North Carolina, Chapel Hill	2,274,173	89,186	5,677,100	3,413,984	1,782,396	120,777	359,943
22. New York Univ.	2,251,948	110,062	5,328,244	3,494,305	1,416,532	116,841	300,566

23. Johns Hopkins Univ.	2,091,315	50,745	4,087,453	2,293,571	1,142,713	42,796	608,373
24. Univ. of Virginia, Main Campus	2,081,003	94,437	5,456,663	2,954,943	1,847,513	127,815	526,392
25. Univ. of Iowa	2,055,581	101,933	4,949,661	2,705,362	1,950,932	126,046	167,321
26. Univ. of Utah	1,944,566	110,239	3,655,064	2,032,162	1,191,117	71,462	360,323
27. Univ. of Missouri, Columbia	1,882,394	48,734	3,084,075	1,623,271	1,105,077	85,428	270,299
28. Univ. of Florida	1,852,841	47,266	4,186,513	3,170,822	700,647	56,008	259,036
29. Univ. of Kansas, Main Campus	1,849,096	78,919	3,829,537	2,113,943	1,331,169	68,298	316,127
30. Univ. of Southern California	1,784,192	66,770	4,402,131	2,699,974	1,260,882	98,676	342,599
31. Michigan State Univ.	1,773,033	59,654	4,642,167	2,736,970	1,365,252	106,380	433,565
32. Univ. of Pittsburgh, Main Campus	1,769,669	91,892	4,824,606	3,020,341	1,319,418	109,759	375,082
33. Brown Univ.	1,732,829	61,474	2,634,182	1,595,292	717,001	76,879	245,010
34. Univ. of Georgia	1,719,178	100,074	4,649,684	2,315,894	1,831,403	170,843	331,544
35. Wayne State Univ.	1,704,848	41,551	4,651,605	2,795,272	1,118,310	78,226	659,797
36. Univ. of Rochester	1,684,154	60,297	3,442,441	2,099,760	989,686	94,090	258,905
37. Syracuse Univ., Main Campus	1,678,402	98,117	3,347,673	1,973,067	1,001,685	56,459	316,462
38. Massachusetts Institute of Technology	1,669,840	71,305	3,475,824	2,346,375	849,192	52,314	227,943
39. Louisiana State Univ. & A&M	1,659,954	59,567	3,499,310	1,900,486	1,312,720	91,197	194,907
40. Case Western Reserve Univ.	1,586,157	28,800	3,208,192	1,842,588	787,550	57,998	520,056
41. Southern Illinois Univ., Carbondale	1,514,677	54,749	5,393,452	3,358,447	1,459,947	80,000	495,058
42. Univ. of Hawaii, Manoa	1,504,632	71,961	4,397,774	3,001,418	1,065,497	104,482	226,377
43. State Univ. of New York, Buffalo, Main Campus	1,497,377	64,351	4,354,840	2,871,657	852,121	119,907	511,155
44. Pennsylvania State Univ., Main Campus	1,467,610	53,399	5,958,957	4,121,435	1,307,250	113,241	417,031
45. Univ. of Colorado, Boulder	1,420,986	51,762	3,479,889	2,350,968	916,669	70,000	142,252
46. Brigham Young Univ., Main Campus	1,334,581	52,360	*	*	*	*	*
47. Emory Univ.	1,244,249	50,875	3,578,612	1,631,366	1,616,327	94,002	236,917
48. Univ. of Maryland, College Park Campus	1,231,540	60,488	5,457,680	3,435,002	1,233,212	138,332	651,134
49. Univ. of Connecticut, Main Campus	1,131,026	61,487	2,949,762	1,554,612	1,186,816	70,520	137,814
50. Washington Univ.	1,092,099	31,991	3,692,064	2,287,093	1,035,534	70,283	299,154

*Data not provided.

ACADEMIC LIBRARY BUILDINGS IN 1980

Barbara Livingston
Assistant Editor, *Library Journal*

Bette-Lee Fox
Associate Editor, *Library Journal*

Deborah Waithe
Assistant Editor, *Library Journal*

 Library Journal's survey of academic library construction and remodeling projects includes libraries completed in the period from July 1, 1979 to June 30, 1980. All data is reported directly from the libraries and their architects. Identification of building projects was once again aided by a questionnaire mailed to every academic library listed in the *American Library Directory;* in addition the news pages of the library press were scoured for mentions of building projects. Again this year, the trend toward the inclusion of libraries in building complexes or in shared space makes a clear comparison, in terms of square foot costs or total dollar value, impractical.

 This year only a handful of new building projects cost over $1 million. In 1976, when the total number of all building projects was roughly similar to 1980's, all of the 15 new libraries reported were over $1 million projects, ranging up to the leader for the year, the University of Arizona at Tucson, at over $12 million.

Note: Reprinted from *Library Journal,* December 1, 1980.

TABLE 1 ACADEMIC LIBRARIES, 1970–1980

	1970	1971	1972	1973	1974	1975	1976	1977	1978-1979	1980
New Libraries	41	33	17	17	21	18	15	6	38	14
Additions	9	6	2	1	9	2	5	5	8	2
Additions plus Renovation	16	10	3	3	10	5	8	7	22	11
TOTALS	66	49	22	21	40	25	28	18	66	27
Combined Additions and Addition plus Renovation	25	16	5	4	19	7	13	12	30	13
Percentage of Combined A and A & R	37.87	32.65	22.72	19.04	47.50	28.00	46.42	66.63	45.45	48.15

TABLE 2 NEW LIBRARIES

Name of Institution	Project Cost	Gross Area	Assignable	Non-Assignable	Sq. Ft. Cost	Building Cost	Equipment Cost	Book Capacity	Seating Capacity	Notes
Indiana Univ. Northwest, Gary	$8,500,000	111,700	100,000	11,700	$58.00	$6,500,000	$1,000,000	550,000	1,000	
Univ. of North Florida, Jacksonville	5,600,000	120,000	80,090	39,910	42.19	5,063,500	300,000	n/a	n/a	Planned completely by library staff
Los Angeles Trade-Technical Coll.	4,946,800	82,338	61,516	20,822	48.40	3,984,900	961,900	117,000	766	
West Virginia Univ., Morgantown	4,390,689	66,413	56,260	10,153	55.67	3,697,168	427,000	300,000	700	
Milwaukee Sch. of Engineering, Wis.	4,000,000	56,895	41,050	15,845	56.63	3,222,043	313,173	70,000	332	
John Brown Univ., Siloam Springs, Ark.	n/a	58,000	n/a	n/a	53.45	3,100,000	n/a	120,000	600	*Complex housing library plus other depts., student servs., art gallery
Christopher Newport Coll., Newport News, Va.	1,059,943	16,000	14,000	2,000	53.32	853,259	141,439	70,050	201	
Music School, Univ. of Louisville (Belknap Campus), Ky.	875,700	15,000	12,000	3,000	56.42		100,000	60,000	165	*Part of School of Music complex

TABLE 2 NEW LIBRARIES (cont.)

Name of Institution	Project Cost	Gross Area	Assignable	Non-Assignable	Sq. Ft. Cost	Building Cost	Equipment Cost	Book Capacity	Seating Capacity	Notes
Florida State University Music Library, Tallahassee	866,500	18,000	15,509	2,491	42.00	756,000	74,964*	5,586**	250	*Includes $25,000 sound equipment **in linear feet
Univ. of Washington, Seattle	685,000	8,563	7,560	1,003	60.02	514,000	140,000*	40,168	125	*Includes book detection system & emergency announcement closing system Part of Coll. of Design
Iowa State Univ., Ames	158,924	3,264	1,958	1,306	39.32	128,340	1,488	12,000	65	
California Sch. of Professional Psychology, Fresno	82,135	2,400	1,200	1,200	31.30	75,135	6,000	12,500	20	
Univ. of Texas, Fine Arts Library, Austin	*	55,000	49,000	6,000	n/a	n/a	208,300*	186,000	560	*Library occupies top 3 levels of Admin. Bldg. part of 5-bldg. complex ($44,000,000) **Library only
Hebrew Union Coll., Jewish Inst. of Religion, New York City	*	30,000	21,000	9,000	n/a	n/a	200,000	150,000	148	*Part of educational complex

TABLE 3 ADDITIONS

Name of Institution	Project Cost	Gross Area	Assignable	Non-Assignable	Sq. Ft. Cost	Building Cost	Equipment Cost	Book Capacity	Seating Capacity	Notes
Stanford Univ., Calif.	$14,700,000	180,820	131,280	49,540	$51.00	$9,235,229	$1,480,000	1,191,140	1137	Addition doubles size of existing bldg.
Kennesaw Coll., Marietta, Ga.	4,357,401	97,595	n/a	n/a	41.65	4,082,401	275,000	300,000	1000	

TABLE 4 ADDITION PLUS RENOVATION

Name of Institution		Project Cost	Gross Area	Assignable	Non-Assignable	Sq. Ft. Cost	Building Cost	Equipment Cost	Book Capacity	Seating Capacity	Notes
Univ. of Vermont, Burlington	Total	$4,642,000	166,948	130,265	36,683	$54.28	$3,911,541	$370,459	1,100,000	1,580	
State Agricultural Coll., Canton, N.Y.	New	4,282,000	72,065	57,765	14,300						
	Renovated	360,000	94,883	72,500	22,383						
St. Lawrence Univ., Canton, N.Y.	Total	4,200,000	96,000	72,960	23,040	35.41	3,400,000	450,000	598,600	674	
	New	3,658,550	53,000	40,280	12,720	56.04	2,970,000	383,000	191,500	611	
	Renovated	541,450	43,000	32,680	10,320	10.00	430,000	67,000	407,100	63	
West Georgia Coll., Carrollton	Total	3,766,806	108,119	85,133	22,986	28.89	3,118,863	176,694	450,000*	1,000	*Plus compact storage system
	New	2,392,009	43,669	34,385	9,284	44.14	1,942,354	82,440	200,000	400	
	Renovated	1,374,797	64,450	50,748	13,702	18.38	1,176,509	94,254	250,000	600	
Appalachian State Univ., Boone, N.C.	Total	3,328,000	141,630	113,302	28,328	19.45	2,762,441	300,000	661,000	1,676	
	New		56,214	44,970	11,244	42.91	2,412,441		276,000	691	
	Renovated		85,416	68,332	17,084	4.10	350,000		385,000	985	
Univ. of Tulsa, Okla.	Total	3,303,167	127,104	112,010	15,094	24.11	3,061,968	241,199	1,170,014	659	
	New	3,181,254	65,794	57,297	8,497	44.69	2,940,055	241,199	853,505	250	
	Renovated	121,913	61,310	54,716	6,594	2.00	121,913	0	316,509	409	
Pittsburgh State Univ., Pa.	Total	2,406,605	74,500	58,806	15,694	32.30	1,970,347	436,258	387,545	707	
	New		45,250	35,064	10,186					417	
	Renovated		29,250	23,742	5,508					290	
Univ. of Santa Clara, Calif.	Total	1,800,000	78,698					127,762	825,670	576	
	New		36,450						480,270	184	
	Renovated		42,248						345,400	184	
Concord Coll., Athens, W.Va.	Total	1,571,889	40,672	32,134	8,538	25.15	1,430,000	141,889	172,000	350	
	New		12,448	11,146	1,302						
	Renovated		28,224	20,988	7,236						
Univ. of Minnesota Technical Coll., Crookston	Total	1,118,150	17,759	12,648	5,111	45.91	815,390	145,000	40,000	132	
	New		10,250	6,660	3,590	63.00	645,750		40,000	112	
	Renovated		7,509	5,988	1,521	30.00	169,640		0	20	
Azusa Pacific Coll., Calif.	Total	910,045	20,367	20,190	177	41.34	842,045	68,000	90,000	243	
	New	827,045	11,291	11,190	101	67.93	767,045	60,000	10,000	131	
	Renovated	83,000	9,076	9,000	76	8.26	75,000	8,000	80,000	112	
Univ. of Guam, Mangilao	Total	718,065	28,136	22,194	5,942	23.27	654,782	35,000	350,000	215	
	New		8,454	6,613	1,841						
	Renovated		19,682	15,581	4,101						

TABLE 5 RENOVATION ONLY

Name of Institution	Project Cost	Gross Area	Assignable	Non-Assignable	Sq. Ft. Cost	Building Cost	Equipment Cost	Book Capacity	Seating Capacity	Notes
West Virginia Univ., Morgantown	$1,955,290	31,458	21,410	10,048	$54.00	$1,690,290	$265,000	70,000	238	
Hebrew Coll., Brookline, Mass.	600,000	4,500	3,700	8,000	111.11	500,000	40,000	24,000	48	
Univ. of Toledo, Ward Canaday Center, Ohio	226,000	9,055	9,055	0	21.31	193,000	33,000	16,000*	12	*Plus 1344 archival boxes
Trinity Univ., Library & Education Center, San Antonio, Tex.	153,216	4,755	4,314	441	32.22	153,216	n/a	25,000	60	
Hawaii Pacific Coll., Honolulu	33,242	4,000	4,000	0	5.13	20,513	12,729	25,000	67	
Center for Biblical Studies, Modesto, Calif.	8,000	4,000	4,000	0	1.63	6,500	1,500	2,500	50	
International Univ., Independence, Mo.	2,500	3,000	2,000	1,000	n/a	n/a	n/a	15,000	10	

TABLE 6 NEW LAW LIBRARIES

Name of Institution	Project Cost	Gross Area	Assignable	Non-Assignable	Sq. Ft. Cost	Building Cost	Equipment Cost	Book Capacity	Seating Capacity	Notes
Tarlton Law Library, Univ. of Texas, Austin	$10,100,000*	223,352	167,439	55,913	$38.56*	$8,600,000*	$1,500,000*	522,107	1200	*Costs apply to entire bldg. of which law library occupies part
Golden Gate Univ., San Francisco	9,000,000*	27,600	25,416	2,184	36.00	993,600	n/a	160,000	365	*Costs apply to entire 6-story bldg. of which library occupies 2 floors
Loyola Univ., Chicago	4,500,000*	48,000	42,000	6,000	n/a	n/a	n/a	150,000	265	*New 5-story law bldg. housing library on 2 floors

TABLE 7 NEW ACADEMIC BUILDINGS NOT PREVIOUSLY REPORTED

Name of Institution	Project Cost	Gross Area	Assignable	Non-Assignable	Sq. Ft. Cost	Building Cost	Equipment Cost	Book Capacity	Seating Capacity
Carthage Coll., Kenosha, Wis. (1977)*	$8,000	620	483	137	$12.90	n/a	n/a	n/a	n/a
Univ. of Alabama in Huntsville (1978)	1,291,039	38,731	22,961	15,770	31.22	$1,209,193	$81,846	200,000	200-360
Western Illinois Univ., Macomb (1978)	12,500,000	222,300	157,542	64,758	43.70	9,735,000	1,200,000	1,000,000	2,000
Univ. of Connecticut, Storrs (1978)	18,605,500	397,000	293,524	103,476	46.87	14,155,000	2,255,500	3,000,000	2,996
American Univ., Washington (1979)	7,800,000	112,500	90,000	22,500	n/a	n/a	910,000	450,000	1,355

*(date of building completion)

PUBLIC LIBRARY BUILDINGS IN 1980

Barbara Livingston
Assistant Editor, *Library Journal*

Bette-Lee Fox
Associate Editor, *Library Journal*

Deborah Waithe
Assistant Editor, *Library Journal*

    This year's crop of public library building projects shows a continued decline in the number of new buildings and indications of growing inflation in construction and related costs. There are other indications, however, which warn against too close reliance on the statistics. First, with the disappearance of federal funding under LSCA Title I, there has apparently been a loss of communication between some state library agencies and individual public libraries, and state agencies are in some cases having difficulty in getting the questionnaires for these tables out to all the libraries which should have them.

    Scattered reports also indicate that some canny builders and planners have been able to take advantage of the slump in construction to save money on their projects. Also among the unknowns is the extent to which the new emphasis on energy-saving construction has run up the cost of individual buildings or their equipment.

    As in previous years, buildings which were reported too late for this compilation will be added to next year's record. Information on libraries which were missed is therefore welcome and will assist in making the statistical record more nearly complete.

Note: Reprinted from *Library Journal*, December 1, 1980.

TABLE 1 NEW PUBLIC LIBRARY BUILDINGS CONSTRUCTED DURING YEAR ENDING JUNE 30, 1980

Symbol Code: B—Branch Library; BS—Branch & System Headquarters; M—Main Library; MS—Main & System Headquarters; S—System Headquarters; SC—School District; NA—Not Available

Community	Pop in M	Code	Project Cost	Gross Sq. Ft.	Const. Cost	Sq. Ft. Cost	Equip. Cost	Site Cost	Other Costs	Vols.	Reader Seats	Fed. Funds	State Funds	Local Funds	Gift Funds	Notes
ALABAMA																
Birmingham	12	B	$198,000	5,080	$167,038	$32.88	$16,437	owned	$14,525	30,000	26	$198,000	0	0	0	Library/recreation center
Evergreen	16	M	440,000	5,000	325,000	47.00	60,000	$30,000	25,000	40,000	48	0	0	$400,000	0	
Graysville	5	M	152,760	4,836	115,397	23.86	12,650	4,110	20,603	10,000	32	0	0	152,760	0	
Montgomery	4	B	184,000	4,500	177,000	39.33	7,000	owned	n/a	15,000	20	0	0	177,000	$7,000	
Red Bay	3	M	168,000	4,400	115,000	26.14	12,000	35,000	6,000	20,000	20	0	0	51,000	117,000	
Roanoke	8	M	134,039	3,000	97,600	32.53	17,879	10,000	8,560	25,000	20	134,039	0	0	0	
Talladega	35	M	541,678	13,500	44,522	32.93	60,401	owned	36,755	70,200	104	0	0	531,678	10,000	
ARIZONA																
Litchfield Park	3	M	204,681	4,000	177,681	44.00	12,000	owned	15,000	15,000	n/a	50	0	0	204,681	Library occupies 76% of bldg.
Tucson	50	B	501,278	11,735	387,410	64.87	49,191	38,000	26,677	35,000	52	0	0	501,278	0	
CALIFORNIA																
Roseville	24	M	2,310,000	30,000	1,850,000	61.66	200,000	owned	260,000	100,000	100	2,310,000	0	0	0	Circular design with 2 outdoor reading areas, meeting & story hour rooms
FLORIDA																
Ft. Lauderdale	8	B	295,113	7,500	253,995	33.86	29,868	owned	11,250	10,000	95	295,113	0	0	0	Library-in-Action for disadvantaged
Miami	n/a	B	2,945,600	52,600	2,264,567	43.05	390,133	96,000	194,900	175,000	280	0	0	2,945,600	0	
Pompano Beach	14	B	452,407	10,000	376,967	37.70	40,240	7,500	27,700	15,000	90	368,407	84,000	0	0	Library-in-Action for disadvantaged
GEORGIA																
Atlanta	607	MS	18,920,000	245,000	13,400,000	55.00	2,900,000	owned	2,600,000	1,000,000	700	0	0	18,920,000	0	
Dalton	16	B	184,000	4,000	150,000	37.50	24,000	owned	10,000	n/a	24	144,000	20,000	20,000	0	
Stockbridge	3	B	331,826	10,000	254,953	50.78	10,000	50,000	16,873	21,900	40	0	112,200	30,100	189,526	5000 sq. ft enclosed & floor for future

TABLE 1 NEW PUBLIC LIBRARY BUILDINGS CONSTRUCTED DURING YEAR ENDING JUNE 30, 1980 (cont.)

Community	Pop in M	Code	Project Cost	Gross Sq. Ft.	Const. Cost	Sq. Ft. Cost	Equip. Cost	Site Cost	Other Costs	Vols.	Reader Seats	Fed. Funds	State Funds	Local Funds	Gift Funds	Notes
IDAHO																
American Falls	5	M	234,817	5,650	207,653	36.75	14,800	owned	12,325	45,000	24	0	104,000	130,777	0	Purchased used bookmobile, placed it on city property
Macon	2	M	4,000	240	n/a	n/a	n/a	n/a	n/a	2,000	0	0	0	4,000	n/a	
INDIANA																
Decatur	17	M	768,971	13,850	620,062	n/a	n/a	37,069	58,000	100,000	160	0	0	753,971	15,000	
Portage	25	B	1,000,000	10,000	821,000	80.15	95,000	30,000	54,000	55,000	60	0	0	1,000,000	0	
Valparaiso	50	MS	1,700,000	20,000	1,229,000	61.45	196,000	65,000	210,000	150,000	135	0	0	1,700,000	0	
IOWA																
Avoca	2	M	153,853	2,400	121,200	55.00	17,770	owned	14,883	15,000	21	6,000	0	2,621	132,732	$12,500 not accounted for in funding
Riceville	3	M	115,000	3,600	98,500	n/a	4,000	6,000	2,600	n/a	n/a	n/a	n/a	17,000	n/a	Leases space to city in exchange for utilities & insurance
KANSAS																
Coffeyville	25	M	531,929	14,972	410,017	35.52	35,432	owned	86,480	92,000	87	531,929	0	0	0	2-step semicircular theater for storyhours. Activity corner has sink
Olathe	37	M	1,600,000	24,833	1,383,156	55.69	103,619	owned	113,225	100,000	183	0	0	1,600,000	0	Indian limestone exterior, copper roof, energy efficient
LOUISIANA																
Bayou Sorrell	1	B	79,000	1,365	79,000	57.87	0	0	7,900	6,000	9	0	0	79,000	10,000	
Donaldsonville	12	MS	940,118	12,644	598,533	47.34	119,794	151,000	70,791	50,000	68	0	0	940,118	0	Timber pile/reinforced concrete foundation; steel frame & columns

PUBLIC LIBRARY BUILDINGS IN 1980 / 313

Gonzales	30	B	$1,204,748	18,450	$983,384	$53.30	$146,860	owned	$74,504	90,000	102	0	0	$1,204,748	0	Concrete block exterior walls; 4-ply built-up roof
Grosse Tete	1	B	72,214	1,440	69,714	48.41	0	n/a	6,971	7,000	12	0	0	72,214	0	
Maringouin	2	B	108,571	2,300	104,571	45.46	0	n/a	10,457	8,000	14	0	0	108,571	12,000	
New Orleans	n/a	B	790,128	90,514	551,909	58.00	105,689	$91,153	41,377	55,000	65	0	0	790,128	0	
Rosedale	1	B	72,214	1,440	69,714	48.41	0	n/a	6,971	7,000	15	0	0	72,214	7,000	
MARYLAND																
Clinton	45	B	1,667,046	25,682	1,351,365	52.62	167,139	owned	148,542	120,000	144	0	0	1,667,046	0	Solar power
Westminster	19	MS	1,843,090	40,000	1,464,808	36.62	128,100	156,250	93,932	101,000	100	0	0	1,843,090	0	
MASSACHUSETTS																
Framingham	66	M	4,520,000	53,000	3,500,000	66.04	356,000	0	664,000	200,000	345	4,500,000	0	20,000	0	Near senior citizen center & art museum
MICHIGAN																
Mt. Clemens	627	MS	1,978,545	29,412	1,717,221	58.39	119,843	owned	141,481	250,000	176	1,978,545	0	0	0	First floor of projected 2-story 75,000 sq. ft. bldg.
Sterling Heights	108	M	2,300,000	32,150	2,000,000	62.50	198,500	owned	100,000	140,000	202	1,600,000	0	721,000	0	
MINNESOTA																
Howard Lake	2	B	24,058	5,120	190,000	37.16	16,558	24,000	135,000	18,000	23	5,000	0	230,145	8,913	Library/Community Center
St. Francis	5	B	137,241	1,970	111,169	56.43	16,012	owned	10,060	8,100	20	0	0	137,241	0	Pre-engineered structure; contains auto license office
MISSISSIPPI																
Baldwyn	3	B	$265,000	4,045	$196,447	$48.57	$40,140	$15,000	$13,413	17,500	22	0	$132,000	$82,500	$50,000	
Greenwood	41	MS	694,348	16,000	494,508	30.91	80,169	90,000	29,671	117,000	175	0	200,000	450,035	44,313	Space for expansion
Horn Lake	4	B	206,400	3,944	144,592	36.66	25,953	24,000	11,855	14,000	23	0	99,200	107,200	0	
Myrtle	3	B	10,450	640	9,800	15.31	650	n/a	n/a	5,500	10	0	0	8,450	2,000	In metal building shared by Fire Dept.
Pachuta	3	B	42,336	2,503	38,200	15.27	1,011	3,000	125	5,800	12	0	0	38,836	3,500	Most building materials were donated
Raleigh	1	B	160,051	3,700	129,963	35.13	20,466	owned	9,623	12,000	24	0	80,019	80,032	0	Combined library—city hall

314 / LIBRARY RESEARCH AND STATISTICS

TABLE 1 NEW PUBLIC LIBRARY BUILDINGS CONSTRUCTED DURING YEAR ENDING JUNE 30, 1980 (cont.)

Community	Pop in M	Code	Project Cost	Gross Sq. Ft.	Const. Cost	Sq. Ft. Cost	Equip. Cost	Site Cost	Other Costs	Vols.	Reader Seats	Fed. Funds	State Funds	Local Funds	Gift Funds	Notes
Rosedale	2	B	177,734	3,094	129,930	41.99	23,049	9,000	15,755	14,000	18	0	88,867	76,367	12,500	Easy expansion possible; energy efficient
Tylertown	2	B	234,936	4,295	183,533	42.73	31,559	8,500	11,344	18,000	29	0	117,468	116,468	1,000	Space to expand
Vardaman	1	B	125,379	2,565	85,559	33.36	18,442	10,000	11,378	11,700	18	0	62,689	62,690	0	Energy efficient
Woodville	2	B	292,005	5,000	233,259	46.65	30,307	10,000	18,349	22,000	24	$150,000	90,880	48,807	0	
NEBRASKA																
Ainsworth	4	M	176,920	3,640	147,376	40.49	16,989	owned	12,556	22,200	36	0	0	163,300	13,620	
NEVADA																
Zephyr Cove	5	B	322,918	4,300	292,250	59.64	8,668	owned	22,000	20,000	29	0	0	254,168	68,750	Plans to add 1000 sq. ft. meeting room, 1981
NEW HAMPSHIRE																
Wolfeboro	10	M	645,000	10,500	484,000	46.09	60,800	owned	60,200	40,000	64	600,000	0	45,000	0	
NEW JERSEY																
Florham Park	9	M	580,000	6,350	350,000	55.03	48,000	owned	182,000	40,000	56	0	0	550,000	30,000	In Williamsburg Colonial style to match rest of municipal complex
NEW MEXICO																
Las Cruces	9	M	2,166,787	28,000	1,552,610	55.45	141,000	322,420	150,757	140,000	207	2,166,787	0	0	0	Passive solar design; 65% recession into the ground for energy conservation
NEW YORK																
Elmira	102	M	2,974,621	49,229	2,472,543	50.00	232,957	66,500	202,621	322,671	143	50,000	0	2,474,621	0	$50,000 not accounted for in funding
Flushing	20	B	451,159	7,500	401,159	53.00	50,000	n/a	n/a	27,000	104	0	0	401,159	0	
Martinsburg	1	M	94,000	3,750	86,500	23.00	n/a	owned	7,500	6,000	60	0	10,000	0	84,000	
New City	31	M	1,761,697	20,900	1,271,275	60.00	84,711	120,000	285,711	120,000	108	0	0	1,761,697	0	

PUBLIC LIBRARY BUILDINGS IN 1980 / 315

New Rochelle	75	M	5,200,000	71,367	4,200,000	58.00	476,000	owned	500,000	250,000	310	0	0	5,200,000	0	Recycled structure incorporated in new bldg.
Rockaway Park	2	B	646,318	7,500	472,118	62.94	50,000	90,500	33,700	27,000	104	0	0	646,318	0	
NORTH CAROLINA																
Andrews	6	B	220,000	4,890	178,000	36.40	28,000	owned	14,000	25,000	60	110,000	0	85,000	25,000	Georgian with porch & columns
Durham	151	MS	3,250,000	65,000	2,463,000	37.90	300,000	250,000	235,000	260,894	410	0	0	3,000,000	250,000	
Four Oaks	2	MS	100,000	2,280	75,000	29.00	20,000	5,000	0	5,000	24	0	0	15,000	85,000	
Oakboro	10	B	n/a	1,350	n/a	n/a	n/a	n/a	n/a	6,000	25	0	0	0	all	Skylight is helpful in winter, but too hot in summer
Sanford	31	M	1,173,546	20,000	838,185	58.00	101,635	120,000	113,726	100,000	96	743,000	0	180,546	250,000	
Sherrills Ford	2	M	79,000	1,375	n/a	57.45	9,600	3,500	0	5,800	24	0	0	79,000	3,500	Good use of space and materials, economical and easy to supervise with minimum personnel
OHIO																
Canton	232	MS	6,774,231	118,113	5,392,373	45.00	334,998	448,500	568,360	500,000	244	4,185,900	0	992,294	1,561,037	Constructed of reinforced steel; heated & cooled by solar energy
PENNSYLVANIA																
Bellwood	8	M	173,419	6,000	139,060	23.78	19,249	6,500	8,610	26,000	32	8,000	0	0	165,419	One-story library Strong emphasis on energy conservation & AV equipment
Exton	283	M	4,051,419	52,600	3,219,305	61.21	323,894	163,100	345,120	250,000	250	244,150	0	3,806,769	0	
Philadelphia	42	B	$620,000	$7,500	$502,000	$66.93	$27,000	$19,000	72,000	52,500	52	0	0	$620,000	0	
Philadelphia	26	B	315,000	4,614	269,800	58.47	21,000	1,500	22,700	15,500	50	$313,500	0	1,500	0	
Wayne	29	M	1,530,087	21,350	1,110,266	52.00	135,332	150,000	134,489	85,000	160	70,000	0	1,365,000	$94,587	
SOUTH DAKOTA																
Gregory	4	M	60,000	3,000	60,000	20.00	10,000	10,000	0	25,000	28	0	0	5,750	54,250	Labor and money donated by the community
Milbank	10	M	396,780	7,525	343,197	48.74	27,844	owned	25,739	36,000	31	255,500	0	141,280	0	Single floor, wide open

TABLE 1   NEW PUBLIC LIBRARY BUILDINGS CONSTRUCTED DURING YEAR ENDING JUNE 30, 1980 (cont.)

Community	Pop in M	Code	Project Cost	Gross Sq. Ft.	Const. Cost	Sq. Ft. Cost	Equip. Cost	Site Cost	Other Costs	Vols.	Reader Seats	Fed. Funds	State Funds	Local Funds	Gift Funds	Notes
TENNESSEE																
Bartlett	40	B	603,830	13,500	522,000	38.67	48,300	owned	33,530	66,600	120	0	0	603,830	0	Brick exterior, concrete block interior
Rogersville	40	M	671,038	11,000	519,699	47.00	65,000	50,000	36,339	20,000	64	592,038	0	76,000	3,000	Neighborhood Facilities Center housing library, Senior Citizens Center & Emergency Operating Center; building half intended size due to inflation
TEXAS																
Houston	30	B	465,750	6,500	350,000	53.84	60,000	owned	55,750	40,000	60	0	0	465,750	0	Adult Learning Center in cooperation with Houston Community College
Hurst	33	M	1,517,811	25,614	1,161,171	45.30	201,297	60,000	95,343	85,000	118	170,337	0	1,347,474	0	
VIRGINIA																
Front Royal	20	M	617,000	10,800	525,855	48.33	51,475	15,001	24,669	90,000	60	4,200	0	159,000	453,800	
Madison Heights	16	B	296,750	8,000	241,750	32.18	16,000	25,000	14,000	36,000	24	9,000	0	258,750	29,000	
Radford	14	M	382,000	8,750	347,000	39.66	35,000	owned	n/a	48,000	54	0	0	347,000	35,000	
WASHINGTON																
Belfair	6.5	B	306,243	3,600	259,564	72.10	16,830	owned	29,849	10,000	20	0	0	306,243	0	
Blaine	3	B	31,977	1,152	28,043	24.34	3,934	owned	n/a	11,000	12	27,843	0	2,714	1,420	
Sumner	10	B	400,000	6,688	335,000	50.09	30,000	owned	35,000	26,000	35	380,000	0	20,000	0	
WEST VIRGINIA																
Belington	2	M	20,858	480	13,958	29.08	3,900	3,900	0	4,000	8	0	17,858	3,000	0	
Charleston	5	B	75,123	1,250	62,143	49.71	6,584	4,896	1,500	6,000	16	0	15,500	59,623	0	
Lesage	2	M	21,379	480	14,479	30.16	3,900	3,000	0	4,000	8	0	18,379	3,000	0	
Morgantown	2	M	20,836	480	13,936	29.03	3,900	3,000	0	4,000	8	0	17,836	3,000	0	
Poca	1	M	21,281	480	14,381	29.96	3,900	3,000	0	4,000	8	0	18,281	3,000	0	
WYOMING																
Lyman	3	B	102,000	1,600	98,000	61.25	6,750	owned	4,000	5,000	16	83,000	0	15,000	0	Stick built, brick & cedar veneer with hip roof

TABLE 2 PUBLIC LIBRARY BUILDINGS ADDITIONS, REMODELINGS, AND RENOVATIONS

Community	Pop in M	Code	Project Cost	Gross Sq. Ft.	Const. Cost	Sq. Ft. Cost	Equip. Cost	Site Cost	Other Costs	Vols.	Reader Seats	Fed. Funds	State Funds	Local Funds	Gift Funds	Notes
ALABAMA																
Birmingham	6	B	$114,047	2,200	$86,125	$39.15	$14,032	$7,000	$6,890	25,000	24	$100,000	0	$14,047	0	Birmingham Beautification Board Award—1980
Decatur	156	MS	214,279	5,000	175,545	35.11	18,274	owned	20,460	17,000	34	120,000	0	0	$94,279	Most of labor & materials & all funds donated locally
Florala	4	M	24,000	1,600	24,000	15.00	n/a	owned	0	9,000	n/a	0	0	0	24,000	
ALASKA																
Seward	3	M	32,009	1,875	29,384	15.67	2,000	owned	625	25,000	39	0	$27,000	5,009	0	Sprinkler system installed over entire 4,000 sq. ft. basement
CONNECTICUT																
New Canaan	20	M	2,007,835	33,600	1,612,207	47.98	200,138	owned	195,490	140,000*	173	0	72,000	1,935,835	0	*Eventually will hold 200,000
Rocky Hill	16	M	850,000	18,112	705,495	46.93	65,905	owned	78,600	n/a	109	0	72,000	778,000	0	
DELAWARE																
Milton	4	B	203,186	4,700	144,600	30.77	18,187	28,000	12,399	20,000	35	58,586	0	144,600	0	
GEORGIA																
Ellaville	3	B	111,200	2,400	81,091	33.79	19,500	owned	10,609	11,000	16	0	69,100	39,825	5,275	
IDAHO																
Post Falls	8	M	130,152	3,710	112,626	35.08	0	owned	17,523	16,000	30	0	66,000	64,152	0	
ILLINOIS																
Morton Grove	26	M	761,779	9,089	597,969	65.79	18,527	100,000	45,283	4,000	12	6,939	0	740,011	14,829	
Westmont	14	M	245,335	8,120	201,573	24.82	19,878	owned	23,884	45,000	60	20,000	0	225,335	0	
Wilmette	30	M	553,870	18,906	339,081	17.94	164,700	owned	50,089	63,961	6	0	0	552,170	1,700	
INDIANA																
DeMotte	10	B	122,033	4,500	15,691	26.87	29,366	73,000	3,976	30,000	40	0	0	122,033	0	
Greensburg	12	M	48,765	6,080	n/a	8.02	n/a	n/a	9,150	5,000	12	0	0	47,755	10,160	Remodeled church
Jeffersonville	53	M	87,113	4,064	87,113	21.43	292	n/a	5,025	n/a	n/a	0	0	87,113	0	
Rolling Prairie	3	B	58,040	1,800	41,800	32.00	4,000	10,000	2,240	12,000	20	0	0	58,040	0	
IOWA																
Churdan	1	MS	55,000	2,590	46,000	17.76	0	0	8,300	20,000	20	0	5,000	10,000	40,000	
Gilman	1	M	21,504	1,008	21,504	21.33	5,250	10,000	0	10,000	38	0	0	0	21,504	
Massena	2	M	8,288	675	6,750	10.00	1,538	owned	0	4,000	10	800	0	3,042	4,446	

318 / LIBRARY RESEARCH AND STATISTICS

TABLE 2 PUBLIC LIBRARY BUILDINGS ADDITIONS, REMODELINGS, AND RENOVATIONS (cont.)

Community	Pop in M	Code	Project Cost	Gross Sq. Ft.	Const. Cost	Sq. Ft. Cost	Equip. Cost	Site Cost	Other Costs	Vols.	Reader Seats	Fed. Funds	State Funds	Local Funds	Gift Funds	Notes
KENTUCKY																
Dixon	15	M	225,530	4,800	176,460	46.98	26,821	12,500	9,749	30,000	30	35,000	113,636	64,394	12,500	Converted elementary school, sharing with Senior Citizens Center & County Meeting Room
LOUISIANA																
Jennings	32	BS	102,393	6,700	82,566	12.32	13,956	owned	5,871	31,000	41	0	0	102,393	0	Former post office
MARYLAND																
College Park	18	B	626	0	0	0	626	owned	0	10,500	20	0	0	0	0	Air conditioned space in renovated public school
Edgewood	n/a	B	288,200	7,420	242,400	32.67	30,141	owned	15,659	40,000	34	0	0	288,200	0	
Hagerstown	217	M	483,080	6,746	427,445	63.36	27,161	owned	28,474	3,600	38	0	409,167	0	73,913	
Rock Hall	3	B	0	693	0	0	0	0	0	5,000	8	0	0	0	0	All work was donated; all equipment used or borrowed
Salisbury	62	MS	$1,989,200	50,250	$1,609,700	$32.03	$162,100	$77,200	$140,200	175,000	200	0	$1,754,000	$235,200	0	
MASSACHUSETTS																
Dracut	23	M	691,356	12,000	562,562	46.88	42,174	owned	86,620	50,000	106	$609,000	4,000	70,000	$8,356	
Falmouth	25	M	1,174,367	30,000	985,887	32.87	58,351	owned	130,129	180,000	122	936,000	0	237,267	1,000	
West Springfield	27	M	730,491	20,000	605,046	30.25	29,304	owned	96,141	76,000	130	687,000	0	38,546	4,945	
MICHIGAN																
Adrian	20	M	490,430	19,000	176,941	9.31	66,724	246,765	0	100,000	104	306,016	0	0	184,414	Converted department store; story-well and tree house
Ann Arbor	22	B	110,841	1,600	92,791	57.99	10,540	owned	7,510	15,000	16	0	0	110,841	0	
Auburn	7	B	40,930	960	18,540	19.31	1,090	20,500	800	6,600	13	0	0	34,930	6,000	Modular, double-wide unit was a former bank branch donated & transported

PUBLIC LIBRARY BUILDINGS IN 1980 / 319

Edmore	4	M	69,262	2,774	38,777	25.00	2,000	27,000	1,485	12,000	20	0	0	21,734	47,528
Evart	4	M	47,293	1,584	42,583	26.89	2,441	0	2,269	n/a	n/a	0	0	19,878	27,415
Indian River	2	M	24,100	1,780	21,945	13.54	2,000		155	30,000	10	0	0	1,200	22,900
Northville	20	M	410,000	6,100	410,000	67.00	0	owned	0	40,000	40	120,000	0	0	290,000	Auditorium seats 100
MISSISSIPPI														
Caledonia	1	B	44,365	2,760	24,050	8.71	3,614	15,000	1,701	9,200	24	500	19,714	3,000	21,151
Cleveland	48	MS	325,000	4,200	208,337	49.60	43,322	35,757	37,584	45,000	40	0	162,500	0	162,500	Labor was donated
Drew	3	B	122,200	2,420	94,647	39.11	19,881	owned	7,672	20,000	23	0	61,100	0	61,100
Indianola	36	MS	415,000	10,058	294,982	27.28	48,538	owned	71,480	50,000	52	0	200,000	5,000	210,000
Kiln	3	B	33,547	1,200	3,489	2.91	5,058	25,000	0	1,200	12	25,000	0	0	8,547
NEBRASKA														
Gibbon	2	M	2,000	1,224	1,975	1.63	25	owned	0	7,000	14	0	0	2,000	0	High school shop class did remodeling. Future Business Leaders of America paid for carpet. Friends of library donated rest of funds
NEW HAMPSHIRE														
Bedford	10	M	159,300	6,000	132,300	22.05	19,000	n/a	8,000	60,000	52	74,000	0	0	85,300
Merrimack	16	M	590,191	12,880	458,467	35.59	56,535	owned	60,490	50,000	97	20,000	0	0	555,157
Peterborough	5	M	410,889	11,951	315,444	26.39	25,000	50,000	20,445	56,000	48	0	0	15,034	193,000
Washington	1	M	59,500	715	53,700	75.00	4,075	325	1,400	7,500	21	0	0	217,889	59,175	325
NEW YORK														
Brighton	35	M	750,000	13,500	607,202	45.00	95,000	41,500	6,298	70,000	96	0	0	20,000	730,000	Converted school
North Merrick	17	M	58,000	10,000	23,500	5.80	27,000	owned	7,500	60,000	n/a	0	0	0	58,000
NORTH CAROLINA														
Gatesville	8	B	11,950	1,600	8,065	5.04	3,885	owned	0	12,000	14	0	0	5,975	5,975	Converted bank branch building
King	9	B	125,000	3,254	25,493	7.83	19,360	79,600	547	13,000	30	25,000	0	50,000	50,000
PENNSYLVANIA														
Havertown	57	M	1,430,000	30,700	1,260,000	41.04	70,000	owned	100,000	150,000	120	0	0	0	1,430,000	Many energy efficient design features
Oil City	15	M	760,092	13,500	682,766	50.58	27,218	37,033	13,075	77,000	100	37,033	0	723,059	0	Heritage room for local historical and genealogical materials

TABLE 2 PUBLIC LIBRARY BUILDINGS ADDITIONS, REMODELINGS, AND RENOVATIONS (cont.)

Community	Pop in M	Code	Project Cost	Gross Sq. Ft.	Const. Cost	Sq. Ft. Cost	Equip. Cost	Site Cost	Other Costs	Vols.	Reader Seats	Fed. Funds	State Funds	Local Funds	Gift Funds	Notes
SOUTH CAROLINA																
Calhoun Falls	2	B	30,730	1,053	28,984	27.53	1,746	owned	0	5,000	12	0	10,000	2,000	18,730	Renovated 2-room clapboard house
TEXAS																
Houston	59	B	1,105,000	15,000	900,000	60.00	100,000	owned	105,000	65,000	68	735,000	0	370,000	0	
VERMONT																
Castleton	3	MS	85,570	4,201	74,446	17.72	645	owned	9,285	15,000	n/a	1,194	0	84,376	535	Renovated schoolhouse; all funding sources not available
North Hero	2	M	46,250	3,000	46,250	15.40	750	owned	0	4,000	17	750	2,163	2,500	2,400	
Townshend	1	M	17,200	1,330	15,500	11.65	1,700	owned	0	2,000	20	6,900	1,100	8,200	1,000	Includes exit ramp for the handicapped
VIRGINIA																
Louisa	16	B	77,640	2,570	14,631	5.69	5,507	56,752	750	15,000	25	48,000	0	29,640	0	Remodeled Girl Scout Lodge
WASHINGTON																
Silverdale	10	B	280,000	3,940	207,265	53.00	29,000	23,000	20,735	20,000	36	267,000	0	3,000	10,000	Remodeled garage now housing computer central hardware for automated circulation system
Spokane	81	S	73,178	880	69,978	79.52	n/a	n/a	3,200	n/a	n/a	0	0	73,178	0	
WEST VIRGINIA																
Hillsboro	2	M	19,871	480	14,071	29.31	2,800	3,000	0	4,000	8	0	16,871	3,000	0	
Paden City	5	B	55,713	1,250	50,713	40.57	5,000	owned	0	6,000	16	0	17,000	38,713	0	

TABLE 3 LEASED PUBLIC LIBRARY BUILDING SPACE

Community	Pop in M	Code	Project Cost	Gross Sq. Ft.	Const. Cost	Sq. Ft. Cost	Equip. Cost	Site Cost	Other Costs	Vols.	Reader Seats	Fed. Funds	State Funds	Local Funds	Gift Funds	Notes
Arroyo Grande, Calif.	28	B	$839,750	12,000	$750,000	$62.50	$86,000	$3,750	0	50,000	104	$839,750	0	0	0	
Chatom, Ala.	3	M	28,274	900	22,823	25.36	5,451	owned	0	6,000	10	0	$2,798	$22,823	$2,653	
Elizabeth, W.Va.	4	M	160,000	4,800	146,466	30.51	5,424	n/a	$8,110	18,000	44	0	128,000	32,000	0	
Fairfield, Ohio	30	B	225,000	3,400	200,000	60.00	8,600	n/a	0	25,000	50	0	0	225,000	2,000	
Hart, Mich.	6	M	67,820	2,534	55,000	21.70	7,820	n/a	5,000	40,000	20	0	0	54,220	13,600	
Holt, Mich.	15	B	66,873	3,200	50,840	15.88	0	n/a	0	12,000	36	0	0	66,873	0	
Jeanerette, La.	8	B	441,699	5,988	373,681	62.40	34,135	*	33,883	30,100	43	0	0	441,699	0	*99-year lease
Maggie Valley, N.C.	2	B	10,289	800	10,000	12.50	829*	n/a	0	2,700	9	0	0	829	10,000	*excludes shelving
Mobile, Ala.	58	B	165,355	9,000	136,980	15.22	28,375	n/a	n/a	55,000	75	0	0	30,355	135,000	
Mt. Hope, W.Va.	5	B	57,437	1,250	48,741	38.99	7,146	leased	1,550	6,000	24	0	50,050	7,387	0	
Owings Mill, Md.	10	B	55,856	4,000	16,927	4.23	15,329	n/a	23,600	15,000	4	0	0	55,856	0	
Spokane, Wash.	41	BS	377,000*	7,670	250,000*	45.63	27,000	100,000	n/a	30,000	61	0	0	0	0	*Estimated
What Cheer, Iowa	2	MS	40,000	n/a	n/a	n/a	0	n/a	n/a	4,500	0	0	5,000	0	16,300	
Winter Park, Fla.	24	M	1,312,000	20,000	890,000	44.50	70,130	300,000	51,870	90,000	164	940,000	0	300,000	72,000	

TABLE 4 SIX-YEAR COST SUMMARY—PUBLIC LIBRARY BUILDINGS
(For 1969 through 1973 data, see p. 3518 of December 1, 1973 *Library Journal*, or p. 263 of 1974 *Bowker Annual*)

	Fiscal 1975	Fiscal 1976	Fiscal 1977	Fiscal 1978	Fiscal 1979	Fiscal 1980
Number of new bldgs.	125	187	142	135	165	90
Number of ARR's (1)	87	90	69	83	99	61
Sq. ft., new bldgs.	1,474,751	1,817,272	2,100,016	1,355,130	2,794,667	1,568,476
Sq. ft., ARR's	586,854	980,338	585,635	624,755	853,875	462,102
New bldgs:						
Construction cost	$47,860,591	$66,374,466	$85,986,538	$54,508,361	$92,015,718	$70,311,893
Equipment cost	5,982,891	8,212,051	10,727,160	7,433,541	12,672,493	9,043,108
Site cost	4,264,214	5,266,693	8,401,254	5,508,018	2,816,422	2,943,999
Other costs	5,417,981	7,858,816	9,442,938	6,712,240	8,106,465	8,785,624
Total—Project cost	63,625,677	87,712,026	114,557,890	74,162,160	115,611,098	91,084,624
ARR's—Project cost	17,220,607	36,966,911	17,144,009	16,773,136	28,877,686	19,614,720
New & ARR Project cost	$80,846,284	$124,678,937	$131,701,899	$90,935,296	$144,488,784	$110,699,344
Fund Sources:						
Federal, new bldgs.	$8,599,789	$23,030,416	$19,226,511	$13,304,652	$62,713,111	$22,234,338
Federal, ARR's	2,294,804	4,323,509	1,149,718	4,046,901	18,107,556	4,239,718
Federal, total	$11,524,593	$27,353,925	$20,376,229	$17,351,553	$80,820,667	$26,474,056
State, new bldgs.	$1,955,815	$5,241,537	$5,757,047	$5,803,920	$13,797,410	$1,289,677
State, ARR's	823,164	2,264,815	1,381,725	1,095,665	1,282,911	3,082,351
State, total	$2,778,979	$7,506,352	$7,138,772	$6,899,585	$15,080,321	$4,372,028
Local, new bldgs.	$46,813,074	$50,501,926	$82,266,956	$47,193,528	$69,244,923	$60,451,371
Local, ARR's	12,049,376	26,900,408	13,286,234	10,364,429	9,299,527	8,705,258
Local, total	$58,862,450	$77,402,334	$95,553,190	$57,557,957	$78,544,450	$69,156,629
Gift, new bldgs.	$6,256,999	$8,938,147	$7,307,376	$7,860,060	$11,390,586	$4,034,548
Gift, ARR's	1,423,263	3,478,179	1,326,332	1,266,141	1,282,911	3,560,915
Gift, total	$7,680,262	$12,416,326	$8,633,708	$9,126,201	$12,763,497	$7,595,463
Total funds used	$80,846,284	$124,678,937	$131,701,899	$90,935,296	$106,298,268	$107,598,176

(1) Additions, Remodelings and Renovations

TABLE 5 CANADA—PUBLIC LIBRARY BUILDINGS

Community	Pop in M	Code	Project Cost	Gross Sq. Ft.	Const. Cost	Sq. Ft. Cost	Equip. Cost	Site Cost	Other Costs	Vols.	Reader Seats	Fed. Funds	Province Funds	Local Funds	Gift Funds	Notes
ALBERTA																
Blairmore	3	M	$416,422	3,600	$331,857	$92.18	$14,000	owned	$30,565	15,000	60	$181,211	$90,606	$99,606	$47,000	Pine log bldg. for "heritage" look
Eckville	2	B	38,053	1,440	33,260	26.43	4,793	owned	0	4,000	12	0	3,105	34,948	0	
Seba Beach	1	M	31,354	800	30,031	37.54	1,323	owned	0	4,000	9	0	12,542	18,812	0	
MANITOBA																
Minnedosa	4	M	97,700	2,600	95,000	36.54	2,700	owned	0	25,000	15	0	8,000	45,500	41,500	
QUEBEC																
Boucherville	30	M	1,226,500	18,000	902,500	48.00	135,000	$119,000	70,000	90,000	162	0	797,225	429,275	0	Located in a shopping center, costs absorbed by center owner.
Brossard	47	M	54,500	13,500	n/a	n/a	52,900	leased	1,600	100,000	131	0	0	54,500	0	
Montreal-Nord	50	M	1,223,000	14,500	743,000	51.20	275,000	155,000 (owned)	50,000	100,000	117	0	269,000	954,000	0	First automated library in province; CRT screen used for circulation control & technical svcs.

Book Trade Research and Statistics

U.S. BOOK TITLE OUTPUT— A ONE HUNDRED-YEAR OVERVIEW

Dorothy B. Hokkanen

The United States book industry has been recording data on book title output since 1880. Prior to that time there was no single source of comparable year-to-year figures, and the few that were collected are of questionable reliability today. This study, therefore, will be limited to the years, beginning in 1880, since the R. R. Bowker Company has been collecting data annually and recording them in *Publishers Weekly* magazine.

The period which marks the beginning of this study was characterized by two conditions which do not prevail today and which are very significant in analyzing the book industry of that time.

First, it was not until 1891 that the United States felt it valuable to be a party to any international copyright agreements. This meant that American publishers formerly were free to reprint foreign books, without any legal obligation to compensate the foreign author or publisher. Though this practice benefited publishers who were able to print and sell popular English books inexpensively, it impeded the development of American authors since they received little or no encouragement from the American publishers who were interested chiefly in reprinting English books. Furthermore, in the absence of any international copyright agreements, American authors were frequently not paid when their works were reprinted and sold abroad.

The second characteristic of the early years of recorded book statistics was the integration of book publishing and printing, both in terms of operations and of record-keeping. Most publishers at that time had their own printing presses, and the recorded figure for a given year included any book titles printed in this country whether or not the plates were made in the United States. It also included bound books that were imported for distribution here. This practice lasted until after 1930. By 1940 data on imported books were collected and reported separately, and production totals included only titles published by United States companies.

Note: Reprinted, with revisions by C. B. Grannis, from the July 1970 issue of *Printing and Publishing* magazine, published by Printing and Publishing Industries Division, U.S. Dept. of Commerce, Washington, DC 20230. The original article, written by Dorothy B. Hokkanen, commodity industry specialist in the Printing and Publishing Industries Division of the U.S. Dept. of Commerce in 1970, was entitled "American Book Title Output—A Ninety-Year Overview." The author's explanations of book industry title data remain true in 1980, except for information provided with Table 3.

WHAT IS A BOOK?

The clear definition of what constitutes a book is another ambiguity which has made data less than comparable over much of the period. Pamphlets were included in book data without being separately identified through 1913. From 1913 to 1919 they were counted separately but not broken down by subject. From 1920 to 1928 they were included in the totals and also identified by separate category. Since 1928 they have been excluded completely.

Even when the data made the distinction between a book and a pamphlet, the problem of interpreting the data remained. No clear definition of a "pamphlet" existed before 1940. At this time it was determined that a pamphlet was a publication of less than 50 pages in length or one costing less than fifty cents. This definition was later changed to include any publication of 64 pages or less, regardless of price. The Bowker Company made another change in 1959, in order to conform with the international definition used by UNESCO, which was to include titles of 49 pages or more within the book category.

Finally, another change made in 1967 tended to increase international comparability. Previously, each volume in a multivolume set was counted as a separate unit if each volume was sold separately. Beginning in 1967 each volume was counted separately only if each volume in the set had a different title and formed a separate and complete unit. This is the definition that is still used today.

The classification of books by subject matter has also undergone a number of changes since 1890, but these are relatively easy to follow. Categories of fiction, juvenile books, religion, biography, education, language, travel, medicine, poetry and drama, literature, history, law, natural sciences, fine arts, sports, and philosophy have remained virtually unchanged over the entire period. The category "political and social" was redefined several times since 1880 and is now represented by the "sociology and economics" category. The "useful arts" category of 1880 was changed to "technical and military books," and later to "technology." "Domestic and rural," a category in 1880, was separated into two categories—"agriculture and gardening" and "domestic economy," as the original category became too broad. "Domestic economy" finally became "home economics," and "agriculture and gardening" was simplified to "agriculture." "Humor and satire" was dropped in the early 1900s and placed in a miscellaneous category. Reference works were added as a separate category between 1900 and 1910 and later dropped. A separate category was created for business between 1910 and 1920. The changes in these classification systems and a study of the number of book titles published in each field are valuable guides to the broad trends in publishing, reading, and the general interests of the American public.

GROWTH OF TITLE OUTPUT

In the eight decades between 1880 and 1960, book title output grew at an annual average rate of about 2.5 percent. [See Tables 1 and 2.] During that period the most impressive growth in a single decade occurred between 1900 and 1910, the latter year marking the culmination of more than thirty years of steady growth. Output began to decline after 1910 and reached its lowest point of the century in 1920, as a direct result of the United States involvement in World War I. Prosperity returned for the book industry in the twenties, along with the prosperity of the general economy, only to decline again in the aftermath of the Depression. Growth resumed in the mid-thirties and continued until the United States entered World War II. Following the war, book

TABLE 1 U.S. BOOK PRODUCTION: TITLES PUBLISHED, 1880-1979

Year	Total	New Books	New Editions	Year	Total	New Books	New Editions
1979[a]	45,182	36,112	9,070	1929	10,187	8,342	1,845
1978	41,216	31,802	9,414	1928	9,176	7,614	1,562
1977	42,780	33,292	9,488	1927	8,899	7,450	1,449
1976	41,698	32,352	9,346	1926	8,359	6,832	1,527
1975	39,372	30,004	9,368	1925	8,173	6,680	1,493
1974	40,896	30,575	10,271	1924	7,538	6,380	1,158
1973	39,951	28,140	11,811	1923	7,178	6,257	921
1972	38,053	26,868	11,185	1922	6,863	5,998	865
1971	37,692	25,526	12,166	1921	6,446	5,438	1,008
1970[b]	36,071	24,288	11,783	1920	6,187	5,101	1,086
1969	29,579	21,787	7,792	1919	8,594	7,625	969
1968	30,387	23,321	7,066	1918	9,237	8,085	1,152
1967[c]	28,762	21,877	6,885	1917	10,060	8,849	1,211
1966	30,050	21,819	8,231	1916	10,445	9,160	1,285
1965	28,595	20,234	8,361	1915	9,734	8,349	1,385
1964	28,451	20,542	7,909	1914	12,010	10,175	1,835
1963	25,784	19,057	6,727	1913[d]	12,230	10,607	1,623
1962	21,904	16,448	5,456	1912	10,903	10,135	768
1961	18,060	14,238	3,822	1911	11,223	10,440	783
1960	15,012	12,069	2,943	1910	13,470	11,671	1,799
1959	14,876	12,017	2,859	1909	10,901	10,193	708
1958	13,462	11,012	2,450	1908	9,254	8,745	509
1957	13,142	10,561	2,581	1907	9,620	8,925	695
1956	12,538	10,007	2,531	1906	7,139	6,724	415
1955	12,589	10,226	2,363	1905	8,112	7,514	598
1954	11,901	9,690	2,211	1904	8,291	6,971	1,320
1953	12,050	9,724	2,326	1903	7,865	5,793	2,072
1952	11,840	9,399	2,441	1902	7,833	5,485	2,348
1951	11,255	8,765	2,490	1901	8,141	5,496	2,645
1950	11,022	8,634	2,388	1900	6,356	4,490	1,866
1949	10,892	8,460	2,432	1899	5,321	4,749	572
1948	9,897	7,807	2,090	1898	4,886	4,332	554
1947	9,182	7,243	1,939	1897	4,928	4,171	757
1946	7,735	6,170	1,565	1896	5,703	5,189	514
1945	6,548	5,386	1,162	1895	5,469	5,101	368
1944	6,970	5,807	1,163	1894	4,484	3,837	647
1943	8,325	6,764	1,561	1893	5,134	4,281	853
1942	9,525	7,786	1,739	1892	4,862	4,074	788
1941	11,112	9,337	1,775	1891	4,665	—	—
1940	11,328	9,515	1,813	1890	4,559	—	—
1939	10,640	9,015	1,625	1889	4,014	—	—
1938	11,067	9,464	1,603	1888	4,631	—	—
1937	10,912	9,273	1,639	1887	4,437	—	—
1936	10,436	8,584	1,852	1886	4,676	—	—
1935	8,766	6,914	1,852	1885	4,030	—	—
1934	8,198	6,788	1,410	1884	4,088	—	—
1933	8,092	6,813	1,279	1883	3,481	—	—
1932	9,035	7,556	1,479	1882	3,472	—	—
1931	10,307	8,506	1,801	1881	2,991	—	—
1930	10,027	8,134	1,893	1880	2,076	—	—

[a] For explanation of 1979 and 1980 figures, see the article, "Book Title Output and Average Prices, 1980 Preliminary Figures" later in this section of Part 4 of the *Bowker Annual*.

[b] A significant rise in the number of titles reported for 1970 may not be due as much to more books being published as to better reporting.

[c] The decline in title output from 1966 to 1967 indicated in this table does not mean a decline in American book production output as such; rather it reflects a revision which was made in the method of counting at the beginning of 1967. See text.

[d] These data do not include pamphlets after 1912. From 1880 to 1912 pamphlets are included.

Source: R. R. Bowker Company, New York.

TABLE 2   BOOK TITLE OUTPUT BY SUBJECT, 1880–1960, FOR 10-YEAR INTERVALS*

Classification	1960	1950	1940	1930	1920	1910	1900	1890	1880
Agriculture, gardening	156	152	139	74	67	200	76	29	43
Biography	879	603	647	792	285	644	274	213	151
Business	305	250	402	210	168	150	—	—	—
Education	348	256	349	240	111	423	641	399	131
Fiction	2,440	1,907	1,736	2,103	1,123	1,539	1,278	1,118	292
Fine Arts	470	357	222	230	100	245	167	135	44
Games, sports	286	188	182	142	60	145	51	82	32
General literature, essays and criticism	726	591	536	539	301	2,042	543	183	106
Geography, travel	466	288	308	385	166	599	192	162	115
History	865	516	853	431	539	565	257	153	72
Home economics	197	193	94	55	28	132	a	a	a
Juvenile	1,725	1,059	984	935	477	1,010	527	408	270
Law	394	298	202	75	109	678	543	458	62
Medicine, hygiene	520	443	472	318	207	544	218	117	114
Music	98	113	124	62	49	100	—	—	24
Philology	228	148	319	215	195	200	b	b	b
Philosophy, ethics	480	340	110	295	242	265	101	11	22
Poetry, drama	492	531	738	696	453	752	400	168	111
Religion	1,104	727	843	834	504	943	448	467	239
Science	1,089	706	403	462	231	711	184	93	56
Sociology, economics	754	515	876	523	396	784	269	183	99
Technical, military	698	497	611	351	352	707	153	133	63
Miscellaneous	282	345	88	60	24	42	34	42	30
Total	15,012	11,022	11,328	10,027	6,187	13,420	6,356	4,559	2,076

*Included pamphlets before 1920.
[a] Included with "Agriculture and Gardening" before 1910.
[b] Included with "Education" before 1910.
Source: R. R. Bowker Company, New York.
Note: Changes in classifications since 1960 make it impractical to include 1970 figures in Table 2. See Table 3.

production began to soar, and growth has continued to the present virtually without interruption.

THE SIXTIES

The decade of the sixties in particular was characterized by an unprecedented growth of book titles, averaging 7.8 percent per year from 1960 to 1969. From 15,012 new titles and editions reported in 1960, the total more than doubled to 30,387 in 1968, before dropping slightly in 1969. [See footnote to Table 3, regarding 1970 book production statistics.]

The trend of book title output in the sixties followed a predictable pattern. In a decade of unprecedented national wealth and personal propserity, Americans have had the leisure time to pursue a wide variety of interests through reading, as well as the

TABLE 3 BOOK TITLE OUTPUT BY SUBJECT, 1970–1979

Classification with Dewey Decimal Numbers	1970	1971	1972	1973[a]	1974	1975	1976[b]	1977	1978	1979
Agriculture [630–639; 712–719]	265	324	390	382	391	456	600	594	552	538
Art [700–711; 720–779]	1,169	1,246	1,470	1,377	1,525	1,561	1,681	1,795	1,483	2,021
Biography [920–929]	1,536[c]	1,797[c]	1,986	2,325	2,197	1,968	2,085	2,104	1,891	2,042
Business [650–659]	797	700	684	762	925	820	983	1,077	1,248	1,362
Education [370–379]	1,178	1,250	1,292	1,618	1,161	1,038	1,078	1,194	1,063	1,121
Fiction	3,137	3,430	3,260	3,688	3,562	3,805	3,836	3,681	3,693	3,264
General works [000–099]	846	1,012	1,048	1,187	1,191	1,113	1,261	1,448	1,310	1,471
History [900–909; 930–999]	1,995	1,978	1,629	1,598	1,292	1,823	2,295	2,022	2,016	2,160
Home economics [640–649]	321	477	596	669	828	728	806	795	845	897
Juveniles	2,640	2,223	2,526	2,042	2,592	2,292	2,478	2,918	2,909	3,052
Language [400–499]	472	536	479	458	441	438	523	556	458	560
Law [340–349]	604	661	716	756	1,031	915	861	948	1,065	1,218
Literature [800–810; 813–820; 823–899]	3,085	2,986	2,525	2,307	2,285	1,904	1,694	1,866	1,800	1,749
Medicine [610–619]	1,476	1,655	1,839	2,002	2,281	2,282	2,587	2,833	2,788	3,257
Music [780–789]	404	402	402	336	273	305	366	373	439	389
Philosophy, psychology [100–199]	1,280	1,354	1,164	1,406	1,368	1,374	1,386	1,372	1,367	1,377
Poetry, drama [811; 812; 821; 822]	1,474	1,494	1,484	1,917	1,626	1,501	1,582	1,437	1,297	1,361
Religion [200–299]	1,788	1,567	1,705	1,826	1,851	1,778	2,058	2,121	2,180	2,325
Science [500–599]	2,358	2,697	2,586	2,714	3,049	2,942	2,852	3,015	2,877	3,156
Sociology, economics [300–339; 350–369; 380–399]	5,912	6,095	6,415	6,565	6,640	6,590	6,993	6,814	6,465	7,715
Sports, recreation [790–799]	799	890	941	1,082	1,132	1,225	1,224	1,119	1,160	1,122
Technology [600–609; 620–629; 660–699]	1,141	1,309	1,425	1,347	1,593	1,720	1,888	2,218	1,896	2,391
Travel [910–919]	1,394	1,609	1,491	1,587	1,612	794	581	480	414	634
Total	36,071	37,692	38,053	39,951	40,846	39,372	41,698	42,780	41,216	45,182

[a] Data beginning in 1973 are derived by Bowker from Library of Congress MARC data primarily, consistent with *Weekly Record* listings. Not counted are U.S. government publications, or publications of many other governmental units, or university theses —categories which, by some estimates, may total 30,000 to 40,000 titles per year. Also not counted are large numbers of paperback mass market fiction books not recorded by the Library of Congress and noted only in part by *Weekly Record*; therefore, for the later seventies, it is estimated that mass market paperbacks, particularly fiction, may be undercounted by as many as 2,000 to 2,500 titles that, if counted, would raise the above totals accordingly.

[b] Beginning in 1976, some improvement in arriving at final title counts has been effected by extending the amount of time devoted to counting the books of a given year; *PW* therefore issues both "preliminary" figures in February or March and "final" figures in August or September. The figures for 1976–1979 above are "final," as reported in *Publishers Weekly*.

[c] This figure includes biographies placed in other classes by the Library of Congress.

money to spend on books. Federal aid to education made more textbooks available to more students than ever before. Federal aid also supported libraries which, in turn, support the book industry. A record number of college students and graduates have created a reading public whose demand for more reading matter stimulated the industry and encouraged authors. . . .

[The trends of the seventies are perhaps less easily related to the title output data presented in Tables 1 and 3. The more recent figures do not fully reflect the continuing mass market paperback revolution, but do seem to reflect population and library growth in the decade of the seventies.—*C. B. Grannis.*]

BOOK TITLE OUTPUT AND AVERAGE PRICES, 1980 PRELIMINARY FIGURES

Chandler B. Grannis
Contributing Editor, *Publishers Weekly*

Preliminary figures based on listings of 1980 publications, in R. R. Bowker's *Weekly Record*, indicate declining title output in most categories (Table 1–4) and a continuing rise in average per-volume prices (Tables 5, 6, 7, and 8).

No details about mass market paperback output or prices can be presented here because only 372 such volumes have yet been tabulated, out of a likely actual total of 10 times that many. The 372 titles are included, however, in the figures in Tables 1, 3, and 4, showing title output, translations, and imports. The uncounted paperbacks, if included, would probably raise the overall title count by as much as 3,000; how this would be divided by categories remains to be seen.

Final figures regarding books issued in 1980, including, it is hoped, a comprehensive tabulation of mass market paperbacks, will be published in *Publishers Weekly* in the summer, after additional listing of 1980 books has been completed by *Weekly Record*.

Leaving aside the mass market paperbacks—which were almost but not quite as scantily listed in the 1979 preliminary report as in this one—the 1980 title output appears to be lower in most categories compared with 1979. Comparing the two "preliminary" columns of Table 1 will show strong declines in output of new fiction, sociology-economics, science, religion, among other fields.

Table 2, consisting mainly of "trade" or "quality" paperbacks, suggests more moderate declines.

As expected, price averages appear to be increasing. In Table 5, as in Table 1, the columns that are to be compared most realistically are those headed "Preliminary," and in Table 5 they indicate an overall average per-volume price rise from $22.80 in 1979 to $23.57 in 1980. The 1979 figure would be lower had it not been for an unusual

Note: Adapted from *Publishers Weekly*, March 13, 1981, where the article was entitled "1980 Title Output and Average Prices: Preliminary Figures."

TABLE 1 AMERICAN BOOK TITLE OUTPUT—1979 AND 1980
(From Weekly Record Listings of Domestic and Imported Hardbound and Paperbound Books)

Categories with Dewey Decimal Numbers	1979 titles (preliminary) New Books	1979 titles (preliminary) New Editions	1979 titles (preliminary) Totals	1979 titles (final)* New Books	1979 titles (final)* New Editions	1979 titles (final)* Totals	1980 titles (preliminary) New Books	1980 titles (preliminary) New Editions	1980 titles (preliminary) Totals
Agriculture (630-639; 712-719)	340	92	432	432	106	538	290	67	357
Art (700-711; 720-779)	1,369	243	1,612	1,718	303	2,021	1,165	201	1,366
†Biography	1,281	396	1,677	1,557	485	2,042	1,152	402	1,554
Business (650-659)	912	260	1,172	1,057	305	1,362	724	221	945
Education (370-379)	802	154	956	952	169	1,121	699	109	808
Fiction	2,065	786	2,851	2,313	951	3,264	1,616	769	2,385
General Works (000-099)	953	185	1,138	1,248	223	1,471	1,119	164	1,283
History (900-909; 930-999)	1,245	502	1,747	1,546	614	2,160	1,238	562	1,800
Home Economics (640-649)	607	109	716	767	130	897	637	83	720
Juveniles	2,337	286	2,623	2,704	348	3,052	2,306	242	2,548
Language (400-499)	333	110	443	435	125	560	350	78	428
Law (340-349)	726	274	1,000	873	345	1,218	594	223	817
Literature (800-810; 813-820; 823-899)	1,084	381	1,465	1,298	451	1,749	1,066	319	1,385
Medicine (610-619)	2,123	533	2,656	2,609	648	3,257	1,970	503	2,473
Music (780-789)	173	138	311	219	170	389	179	105	284
Philosophy, Psychology (100-199)	899	248	1,147	1,082	295	1,377	889	273	1,162
Poetry, Drama (811; 812; 821; 822)	875	218	1,093	1,084	277	1,361	770	173	943
Religion (200-299)	1,555	392	1,947	1,861	464	2,325	1,310	354	1,664
Science (500-599)	2,082	521	2,603	2,563	593	3,156	1,817	440	2,257
Sociology, Economics (300-339; 350-369; 380-399)	5,165	1,069	6,234	6,422	1,293	7,715	4,628	1,061	5,689
Sports, Recreation (790-799)	780	167	947	931	191	1,122	634	132	766
Technology (600-609; 620-629; 660-699)	1,530	399	1,929	1,922	469	2,391	1,378	306	1,684
Travel (910-919)	421	102	523	519	115	634	346	73	419
Total	**29,657**	**7,565**	**37,222**	**36,112**	**9,070**	**45,182**	**26,877**	**6,860**	**33,737**

*It is estimated that mass market paperback fiction may be undercounted by as many as 2,500 titles that, if counted, would raise these totals accordingly.
†Dewey Decimal Numbers omitted because biographies counted here come from many Dewey classifications.

TABLE 2 PAPERBACKS OTHER THAN MASS MARKET—1979 AND 1980
(From *Weekly Record* Listings of Domestic and Imported Books)

Categories	1979 titles (prelim.) New Bks.	New Eds.	Totals	1979 titles (final) New Bks.	New Eds.	Totals	1980 titles (prelim.) New Bks.	New Eds.	Totals
Fiction	205	112	317	256	125	381	212	127	339
Nonfiction	6,901	1,657	8,558	8,671	1,905	10,576	6,627	1,462	8,089
Total	7,106	1,769	8,875	8,927	2,030	10,957	6,839	1,589	8,428

number of extremely high-priced social and economic reports in that year—materials priced at $350, $495, and similar levels—which skewed the sociology-economics average upward to a degree not so far repeated in 1980.

It is in order to deal with this sort of problem that *PW* instituted the Table 6 calculations, showing what the average prices in certain major Dewey Decimal categories would be if prices over $80 were eliminated. It is obvious here that the pattern of price increases, 1978–1980, is reasonably consistent. In this table the preliminary averages, totaling $18.95 for 1979 and rising to $21.71 for 1980, indicate an average increase of about 14.5%.

Table 8, using an informal yet not unreliable data base (ads in *PW*'s Fall Annoucement issues) quite different from that of *Weekly Record*, also indicates expected price increases. The average per volume for novels was up about 12.6%, the median, up about 15.6%; for biography, etc., the per-volume average increased 7.1%, the median, 7.5%; and for volumes of history, the per-volume average rose 17.6% and the median, 16%.

SOURCES OF DATA ON TITLES AND PRICES

Certain points about the *Weekly Record* data should be kept in mind:

Sources of *Weekly Record* listings are (1) books catalogued by the *WR* staff and (2) data distributed in MARC II tapes by the Library of Congress and then selected and augmented by *WR*.

TABLE 3 ENGLISH TRANSLATIONS—1979 AND 1980
(From *Weekly Record* Listings of Domestic and Imported Hardbound and Paperbound Books)

Original Language	1979 titles (prelim.) Totals	1979 titles (final) Totals	1980 titles (prelim.) Totals
French	272	315	194
German	241	300	185
Italian	51	60	44
Oriental	61	75	40
Russian	131	159	86
Scandinavian	27	35	27
Spanish	54	61	33
Other	531	655	490
Total	1,368	1,660	1,099

TABLE 4 BOOK IMPORTS—1979 AND 1980
(From *Weekly Record* Listings of Domestic and Imported Hardbound and Paperbound Books)

Category	1979 titles (prelim.) New Books	New Editions	Totals	1979 titles (final) New Books	New Editions	Totals	1980 titles (prelim.) New Books	New Editions	Totals
Agriculture	84	7	91	107	10	117	64	9	73
Art	149	21	170	206	24	230	113	8	121
Biography	126	14	140	156	17	173	90	10	100
Business	44	13	57	61	18	79	44	12	56
Education	131	4	135	162	7	169	85	5	90
Fiction	44	9	53	62	9	71	43	4	47
General Works	113	8	121	139	11	150	86	4	90
History	196	24	220	271	28	299	195	24	219
Home Economics	30	3	33	48	3	51	33	2	35
Juveniles	28	1	29	42	1	43	46	2	48
Language	91	11	102	122	15	137	97	12	109
Law	61	13	74	75	16	91	58	16	74
Literature	139	13	152	178	16	194	117	9	126
Medicine	325	52	377	475	65	540	386	59	445
Music	19	8	27	25	9	34	24	2	26
Philosophy, Psychology	97	9	106	142	10	152	144	10	154
Poetry, Drama	97	9	106	129	10	139	78	8	86
Religion	109	6	115	129	7	136	62	7	69
Science	613	51	664	829	61	890	643	55	698
Sociology, Economics	861	50	911	1,168	68	1,236	729	36	765
Sports, Recreation	91	10	101	115	10	125	54	4	58
Technology	209	37	246	282	46	328	215	30	245
Travel	50	6	56	67	7	74	39	3	42
Total	**3,707**	**379**	**4,086**	**4,990**	**468**	**5,458**	**3,445**	**331**	**3,776**

Not counted are U. S. government publications; publications of many other units of government; and university theses.

Known to be underreported are (1) undetermined numbers of textbooks, some of which do not become available for the *WR* or MARC systems, and (2) paperbacks, especially mass market paperbacks; among the latter, fiction may be undercounted by as many as 2,000 titles. *WR* does catalogue many paperbacks not catalogued by the Library of Congress, but some others do not come to Bowker's attention. Publishers are urgently requested to address their titles each month to *Weekly Record*, R. R. Bowker Co., 1180 Avenue of the Americas, New York, NY 10036.

It is important to note that the *WR* title count of "new editions" does not include reissues and new printings; these are not really new or revised editions and cannot be so counted.

TABLE 5 AVERAGE PER-VOLUME OF HARDCOVER BOOKS—1979 AND 1980
(From Weekly Record Listings of Domestic and Imported Books)

Categories with Dewey Decimal Numbers	1979 volumes (preliminary) Total volumes	1979 volumes (preliminary) Total prices	1979 volumes (preliminary) Average prices	1979 volumes (final) Total volumes	1979 volumes (final) Total prices	1979 volumes (final) Average prices	1980 volumes (preliminary) Total volumes	1980 volumes (preliminary) Total prices	1980 volumes (preliminary) Average prices
Agriculture (630-639; 712-719)	332	$ 6,586.31	$19.84	419	$ 8,775.25	$20.94	272	6,687.51	24.59
Art (700-711; 720-779)	1,110	23,832.23	21.47	1,399	30,713.67	21.95	916	24,401.16	26.64
*Biography	1,376	23,448.68	17.04	1,675	29,345.96	17.52	1,273	24,853.54	19.52
Business (650-659)	930	21,494.78	23.11	1,077	24,891.70	23.11	719	16,202.89	22.54
Education (370-379)	613	9,112.04	14.86	706	10,660.19	15.10	514	8,612.06	16.75
Fiction	1,722	19,495.18	11.32	2,027	24,294.73	11.99	1,814	22,323.96	12.31
General Works (000-099)	783	21,920.07	27.99	989	28,241.18	28.56	879	25,216.16	28.69
History (900-909; 930-999)	1,362	25,816.69	18.95	1,685	33,343.83	19.79	1,431	32,273.73	22.55
Home Economics (640-649)	441	5,248.36	11.90	552	6,595.37	11.95	432	5,651.37	13.08
Juveniles	2,605	18,583.88	7.13	3,002	21,423.88	7.14	2,477	20,326.66	8.21
Language (400-499)	290	5,455.01	18.81	356	6,498.02	18.25	251	5,196.99	20.71
Law (340-349)	733	20,241.68	27.61	891	26,229.98	29.44	579	18,313.92	31.63
Literature (800-810; 813-820; 823-899)	1,060	17,910.49	16.90	1,290	22,752.61	17.64	1,050	19,450.66	18.52
Medicine (610-619)	2,045	56,702.58	27.73	2,554	74,760.49	29.27	1,924	61,700.91	32.07
Music (780-789)	228	4,220.39	18.51	289	5,471.18	18.93	221	4,623.14	20.92
Philosophy, Psychology (100-199)	851	14,422.04	16.95	1,024	18,408.39	17.98	841	17,892.16	21.27
Poetry, Drama (811; 812; 821; 822)	708	11,118.69	15.70	868	13,744.01	15.83	617	10,560.84	17.12
Religion (200-299)	1,078	14,850.53	13.78	1,286	19,071.84	14.83	917	16,260.74	17.73
Science (500-599)	2,067	59,143.98	28.61	2,525	77,243.53	30.59	1,764	61,976.25	35.13
Sociology, Economics (300-339; 350-369; 380-399)	4,606	192,187.97	41.73	5,656	246,449.93	43.57	4,131	135,174.74	32.72
Sports, Recreation (790-799)	634	8,616.80	13.59	750	10,409.68	13.88	509	7,794.59	15.31
Technology (600-609); 620-629; 660-699)	1,475	38,454.17	26.07	1,838	51,140.20	27.82	1,276	40,935.91	32.08
Travel (910-919)	288	4,342.34	15.08	342	5,135.38	15.02	214	3,419.34	15.98
Total	27,337	$623,204.89	$22.80	33,200	$795,601.00	$23.96	25,021	$589,849.23	23.57

*Dewey Decimal Numbers omitted because biographies counted here come from many Dewey classifications.

TABLE 6 AVERAGE PER-VOLUME PRICES OF HARDCOVER BOOKS, ELIMINATING ALL VOLUMES PRICED AT $81 OR MORE*

Dewey Classifications	1978 (final)	1979 (prelim.)	1979 (final)	1980 (prelim.)
General Works (000-999)	$20.34	$19.83	$21.06	$23.40
Philos., Psychol. (100-199)	15.10	16.62	17.50	19.50
Religion (200-299)	13.29	12.90	13.01	15.32
Soc., Econ., Law, Educ. (300-399)	16.95	18.15	18.69	20.31
Languages (400-499)	17.01	18.25	18.07	19.54
Science (500-599)	25.21	26.61	27.77	31.04
All Classifications (000-999)	$18.01	$18.95	$19.63	$21.71

*Compare indicated categories with Table 5.

TABLE 7 AVERAGE PER-VOLUME PRICES OF TRADE PAPERBACKS—1979 AND 1980
(From Weekly Record Listings of Domestic and Imported Books)

	1979 volumes (preliminary)			1979 volumes (final)			1980 volumes (preliminary)		
Category	Total volumes	Total prices	Average prices	Total volumes	Total prices	Average volumes	Total volumes	Total prices	Average prices
Agriculture	95	$ 623.62	$6.56	117	$ 795.42	$6.80	88	$ 746.77	$8.49
Art	511	4,282.10	8.38	634	5,278.15	8.33	455	4,093.11	9.00
Biography	253	1,448.10	5.72	314	1,771.00	5.64	262	1,700.97	6.49
Business	232	1,985.06	8.56	277	2,476.61	8.94	225	2,282.11	10.14
Education	333	2,303.36	6.92	404	2,790.26	6.91	291	2,352.44	8.08
Fiction	322	1,355.05	4.21	388	1,715.05	4.42	344	2,005.91	5.83

TABLE 8 AVERAGE AND MEDIAN PRICES, THREE CATEGORIES
PW FALL ANNOUNCEMENT ADS, 1972–1980

Category	Vols.	Avg. $	Med. $	Vols.	Avg. $	Med. $
General Works	353	2,351.46	6.66	480	3,107.03	6.47	409	3,237.08	7.91

	Vols.	Total $	Avg.		Vols.	Total $	Avg.		Vols.	Total $	Avg.
General Works	353	2,351.46	6.66		480	3,107.03	6.47		409	3,237.08	7.91
History	379	2,479.83	6.54		474	3,160.86	6.67		369	2,704.14	7.33
Home Economics	267	1,432.47	5.37		337	1,845.41	5.48		287	1,783.67	6.21
Juveniles	348	1,100.59	3.16		413	1,333.96	3.23		395	1,361.20	3.45
Language	153	1,152.89	7.54		205	1,544.48	7.53		179	1,509.98	8.44
Law	288	3,319.94	11.53		361	4,217.19	11.68		246	2,591.69	10.54
Literature	387	2,478.28	6.40		447	2,903.81	6.50		339	2,460.08	7.26
Medicine	570	5,390.69	9.46		667	6,372.84	9.55		541	6,084.33	11.25
Music	79	683.70	8.65		97	889.40	9.17		63	547.30	8.69
Philosophy, Psychology	279	1,810.30	6.49		340	2,229.09	6.56		319	2,387.24	7.48
Poetry, Drama	396	1,660.93	4.19		504	2,123.38	4.21		342	1,678.49	4.91
Religion	867	3,929.74	4.53		1,038	4,769.13	4.59		739	4,464.92	6.04
Science	516	5,791.78	11.22		614	7,049.89	11.48		493	6,292.39	12.76
Sociology, Economics	1,590	12,139.99	7.64		2,036	16,424.23	8.07		1,565	14,518.20	9.28
Sports, Recreation	300	1,824.00	6.08		360	2,203.43	6.12		256	1,785.39	6.97
Technology	456	4,015.57	8.81		556	5,135.22	9.24		412	5,261.35	12.77
Travel	235	1,384.24	5.89		294	1,756.59	5.97		206	1,352.45	6.57
Total	**9,209**	**$64,943.69**	**$7.05**		**11,357**	**$81,892.43**	**$7.21**		**8,825**	**$73,201.21**	**$8.29**

Novels, except Mystery, Western, SF, Gothic: Average & Median Prices	Avg.	Med.	Biography, Memoirs, Letters: Average & Median Prices	Avg.	Med.	History, including Pictorial, but not Art books: Average & Median Prices	Avg.	Med.
1980—317 vols./42 pubs.	$11.73	$11.50	1980—130 vols./56 pubs.	$17.05	$15.00	1980—154 vols./57 pubs.	$19.85	$18.50
1979—291 vols./43 pubs.	$10.42	$9.95	1979—160 vols./67 pubs.	$15.92	$13.95	1979—219 vols./67 pubs.	$16.88	$15.95
1978—282 vols./43 pubs.	$9.63	$8.95	1978—213 vols./73 pubs.	$13.54	$12.95	1978—207 vols./85 pubs.	$15.59	$15.00
1977—233 vols./37 pubs.	$9.18	$8.95	1977—169 vols./62 pubs.	$13.12	$12.50	1977—241 vols./72 pubs.	$15.83	$15.00
1976—174 vols./34 pubs.	$8.74	$8.95	1976—130 vols./61 pubs.	$12.87	$11.95	1976—151 vols./63 pubs.	$13.96	$14.95
1975—150 vols./35 pubs.	$8.51	$7.95	1975—128 vols./53 pubs.	$12.50	$10.95	1975—178 vols./74 pubs.	$15.32	$13.95
1974—212 vols./38 pubs.	$7.68	$7.95	1974—190 vols./80 pubs.	$12.31	$10.95	1974—219 vols./74 pubs.	$12.91	$12.50
1973—225 vols./40 pubs.	$7.34	$6.95	1973—190 vols./78 pubs.	$10.67	$8.95	1973—228 vols./73 pubs.	$13.38	$12.50
1972—171 vols./37 pubs.	$6.95	$6.95	1972—170 vols./61 pubs.	$10.12	$8.95	1972—262 vols./89 pubs.	$12.30	$12.30

BOOK SALES STATISTICS: HIGHLIGHTS FROM AAP ANNUAL SURVEY, 1979

Chandler B. Grannis

The 1979 statistical report of the Association of American Publishers (AAP) was prepared by John P. Dessauer; forthcoming reports will be prepared by Touche, Ross & Company, financial consultants.

Dessauer notes that data in the medical and college text categories continue under review by the Bureau of the Census, since the "medical professional" sales reported to the 1977 census seem to have included a substantial amount of textbook sales—which was not true of the 1972 census. To "reestablish comparability," Dessauer observed, some 35 percent of the sales classified in the AAP report as medical professional (see Table 1) may have to be put into the college textbook category. Readers should make due allowance for this possibility in looking at the estimates in the table, he warns.

The sales estimates in the table, Dessauer adds, are based on the final, not the preliminary, report of the 1977 Census of Manufactures for Standard Industry Classification 2731—which means book publishing. That report was completed in the spring of 1980. AAP's 1978 figures, based on the earlier census report, have therefore been somewhat adjusted.

Dessauer also points out that, if census and AAP data are compared, it is important to remember that the census does not cover most university presses or other institutionally sponsored and not-for-profit publishing, nor the audiovisual and other media materials that are covered in the AAP study. On the other hand, AAP figures omit Sunday school materials and "certain pamphlets." The "other sales" item in Table 1 includes only sheet sales (except those to prebinders) and miscellaneous merchandise sales. Finally, Dessauer states, AAP estimates "include domestic sales and export sales only and do not cover indigenous activities of publishers' foreign subsidiaries."

A comparable table for 1980 was scheduled for release by AAP, as customary, in late spring of 1981. When this volume of the *Bowker Annual* went to press, comprehensive 1980 figures had not appeared, though early sampling reports suggested increases in dollar sales in all divisions, lesser unit increases in most divisions, and declines in unit sales in some areas. An 11-month summary by the Book Industry Study Group, for the *BISG Bulletin*, edited by John Dessauer, estimated an 11.7 percent overall increase in dollar sales over January through November of 1979, and a 3.8 percent increase in unit sales. A dollar sales decline was shown only in book club paperback sales, and there were unit sales declines in that area and in the profesisonal and elhi text categories as well. The various trade book categories showed an overall dollar increase of over 20 percent and a unit increase of over 19 percent. The impact of December sales, however, was yet to be revealed.

TABLE 1 ESTIMATED BOOK PUBLISHING INDUSTRY SALES 1972, 1977, 1978, and 1979
(Millions of Dollars)

	1972 $	1977 $	1977 % Change from 1972	1978 $	1978 % Change from 1977	1978 % Change from 1972	1979 $	1979 % Change from 1978	1979 % Change from 1972
Trade (Total)	442.0	832.4	88.3	971.4	16.7	119.8	1016.1	4.6	129.9
Adult hardbound	251.5	501.3	99.3	586.0	16.9	133.0	608.3	3.8	141.9
Adult paperbound	79.6	168.9	112.2	202.0	19.6	153.8	222.8	10.3	179.9
Juvenile hardbound	106.5	136.1	27.8	145.2	6.7	36.3	151.5	4.3	42.3
Juvenile paperbound	4.4	26.1	493.2	38.2	46.2	768.2	33.5	−12.3	661.4
Religious (Total)	117.5	250.6	113.3	275.6	10.0	134.6	295.4	7.2	151.4
Bibles, testaments, hymnals and prayerbooks	61.6	116.3	88.8	134.6	15.7	118.5	138.9	3.2	125.5
Other religious	55.9	134.3	140.3	141.0	5.0	152.2	156.5	11.0	180.0
Professional (Total)	381.0	698.2	83.3	804.6	15.2	111.2	885.1	10.0	132.3
Technical and scientific	131.8	249.3	89.2	277.5	11.3	110.6	301.1	8.5	128.5
Business and other professional	192.2	286.3	49.0	333.3	16.4	73.4	370.0	11.0	92.5
Medical	57.0	162.6	185.3	193.8	19.2	240.0	214.0	10.4	275.4
Book clubs	240.5	406.7	69.1	463.2	13.9	92.6	501.7	8.3	108.6
Mail order publications	198.9	396.4	99.3	440.4	11.1	121.4	485.8	10.3	144.2
Mass market paperback	252.8	542.5	114.6	609.0	12.3	140.9	673.3	10.6	166.3
Rack-sized	250.0	487.7	95.1	544.3	11.6	117.7	603.2	10.8	141.3
Non-rack-sized	2.8	54.8	1857.1	64.7	18.1	2210.7	70.1	8.4	2403.6
University presses	41.4	56.1	35.5	62.2	10.9	50.2	68.0	9.3	64.3
Elementary and secondary text	497.6	755.9	51.9	833.4	10.2	67.5	930.1	11.6	86.9
College text	375.3	649.7	73.1	736.5	13.4	96.2	825.6	12.1	120.0
Standardized tests	26.5	44.6	68.3	51.9	16.3	95.9	61.6	18.6	132.5
Subscription reference	278.9	294.4	5.6	341.2	15.9	22.3	383.5	12.4	37.5
AV and other media (Total)	116.2	151.3	30.2	151.2	−0.1	30.1	146.3	−3.2	25.9
Elhi	101.2	131.4	29.8	130.5	−0.7	29.0	129.6	−0.7	28.1
College	9.2	11.6	26.1	12.2	5.2	32.6	7.8	−36.5	−15.2
Other	5.8	8.3	43.1	8.5	2.4	46.6	8.9	4.2	53.5
Other sales	49.2	63.4	28.9	51.9	−18.1	5.5	59.7	15.0	21.3
Total	3017.8	5142.2	70.4	5792.5	12.7	91.9	6332.2	9.3	109.8

Source: From *AAP 1979 Industry Statistics*, New York: Association of American Publishers, 1980.

U.S. CONSUMER EXPENDITURES ON BOOKS IN 1979

John P. Dessauer
Book Industry Statistician

Estimated expenditures on books by individual and institutional consumers increased by 9.6% in 1979 to reach of new high of $7.2 billion. Unit increases totaled only 2.0%, however, and the year's record compared poorly with the 14.1% gain in dollars and 5.3% in units that had been posted in 1978.

The above conclusions and the data presented in Tables 1 and 2 are derived from analyses in *Book Industry Trends—1980*, to be released shortly by the Book Industry Study Group. The tables show comparisons for 1979 and 1978 for consumer expenditures by type of book (Table 1) and by channel of distribution (Table 2). Table 1 also includes comparative data for dollar expenditures per unit, which provide some indication of price movement during the year.

The best dollar gains among the product categories listed in Table 1 were recorded by professional and textbooks; the strongest unit advances occurred among adult trade paperbounds and juvenile hardbounds. The performance of juvenile paperbounds, a consistently volatile category, was the worst in both dollars and units. (Readers should note that the professional and college textbook expenditures shown in Table 1 are subject to possible adjustment, after a current review by the U.S. Census of Manufactures of data reported by medical publishers for 1977 is completed. As much as 8% of professional dollar sales shown may ultimately have to be shifted to the college textbook category.)

The dollar-per-unit comparison indicates that average per-unit expenditures increased by only 7.5%, substantially below the 12.7% increase posted by the Consumer Price Index during 1979. The largest increases were recorded for hardbound and paperbound religious books; the smallest gain for adult trade paperbounds. It is important to recognize that average per-unit consumer expenditures, though indicative of book price inflation, are influenced also by other factors, notably the title, binding, and price mix in a given category. For example, remainders are included in the categories in Table 1 (although they appear separately, under "other" expenditures, in Table 2), which tends to moderate increases in categories where the proportion of remainder and special sales is unusually high. Furthermore, as the entries for religious and book club expenditures per unit demonstrate, disproportionate increases or decreases in either of the subcategories of hardbound and paperbound books can substantially raise or lower the averages for the total category. In general, however, it appears that in 1979, book price inflation fell behind the overall inflation rate, a pattern that appeared to be continuing in 1980.

The data in Table 2 indicate that among distribution channels, general retailers again posted the best increase during 1979, although their 12.4% dollar and 3.8% unit gains fell behind the 15.8% dollar and the 7.8% unit pace they set in 1978. College stores achieved the least gains, with only a 2.1% dollar increase and a 6.1% unit loss in 1979, compared to a 14.1% dollar and a 1.7% unit growth in 1978. The only pleasant surprise was generated by schools, which posted an 11.6% dollar and a 4.5% unit gain, improving on their 10.5% dollar and 1.5% growth record of 1978. Elhi textbooks were

Note: Adapted from *Publishers Weekly*, January 16, 1981, where the article was entitled "Book Expenditures Rise, but Unit Sales Are Flat in 1979."

TABLE 1 U.S. DOMESTIC CONSUMER EXPENDITURES ON BOOKS, 1979 AND 1978 MILLIONS OF DOLLARS AND UNITS

	1979 Dollars	1979 Units	1978 Dollars	1978 Units	% Change Dollars	% Change Units	Dollars per Unit 1979	Dollars per Unit 1978	% Change
Trade	1586	324	1506	323	5.4	0.4	4.90	4.67	4.9
Adult Hardbound	955	126	913	128	4.6	−1.1	7.55	7.14	5.7
Adult Paperbound	355	96	326	89	9.0	7.8	3.71	3.67	1.1
Juvenile Hardbound	217	59	201	54	8.3	8.3	3.69	3.69	0.0
Juvenile Paperbound	59	43	66	52	−10.7	−17.2	1.38	1.28	7.8
Religious	464	108	432	112	7.2	−3.7	4.28	3.85	11.2
Hardbound	321	41	299	44	7.1	−6.6	7.83	6.83	14.6
Paperbound	143	67	133	69	7.5	−1.8	2.12	1.94	9.3
Professional	868	53	776	50	11.9	4.8	16.51	15.45	6.9
Hardbound	686	29	614	28	11.9	4.7	23.46	21.97	6.8
Paperbound	182	23	162	22	12.2	4.8	7.80	7.28	7.1
Book Clubs	493	221	455	231	8.3	−4.0	2.22	1.97	12.7
Hardbound	368	64	327	61	12.6	6.3	5.72	5.40	5.9
Paperbound	124	157	128	170	−2.7	−7.7	.79	.75	5.3
Mail Order Publications	499	46	452	43	10.2	5.6	10.87	10.42	4.3
Mass Market Paperback	1074	527	965	500	11.3	5.4	2.04	1.93	5.7
University Press	71	8	65	8	9.0	4.6	8.96	8.59	4.3
Hardbound	54	4	49	4	9.3	4.7	14.41	13.81	4.3
Paperbound	17	4	16	4	8.4	4.3	4.12	3.99	3.3
Elhi Text	913	261	817	252	11.7	3.9	3.49	3.25	7.4
Hardbound	504	100	440	92	14.6	8.9	5.05	4.80	5.2
Paperbound	409	161	377	160	8.4	1.1	2.53	2.36	7.2
College Text	926	92	828	89	11.8	3.1	10.08	9.30	8.4
Hardbound	716	61	636	57	12.6	5.4	11.83	11.08	6.8
Paperbound	210	31	192	32	9.1	−1.0	6.70	6.07	10.4
Subscription Reference	357	1	317	1	12.6	6.0	307.33	287.91	6.8
Total	7249	1641	6613	1608	9.6	2.0	4.42	4.11	7.5

Source: Book Industry Trends—1980.
Note: Dollars and unit data have been rounded to millions. Change percentages, however, are based on unrounded data. Some subtotals and totals may not add exactly due to rounding.

TABLE 2 CHANNELS OF U.S. DOMESTIC BOOK DISTRIBUTION
1979 AND 1978
ESTIMATED CONSUMER EXPENDITURES—MILLIONS OF DOLLARS AND UNITS

	1979 Dollars	1979 Units	1978 Dollars	1978 Units	% Change Dollars	% Change Units
General Retailers	2496	686	2222	661	12.4	3.8
College Stores	1223	189	1199	702	2.1	−6.1
Libraries and Institutions	602	72	556	70	8.2	2.3
Schools	1175	319	1053	306	11.6	4.5
Direct to Consumer	1660	320	1488	318	11.5	0.6
Other	94	54	95	52	− 1.6	4.3
Total	7249	1641	6613	1608	9.6	2.0

Source: *Book Industry Trends—1980.*

the chief contributing factor here—as their 11.7% dollar and 3.9% unit gains shown in Table 1 demonstrate.

On the whole, however, 1979 was a disappointing year for the industry, particularly with respect to unit consumption. Judging from preliminary estimates, 1980 seems likely to prove to be a better year.

PRICES OF U.S. AND FOREIGN PUBLISHED MATERIALS

Sally F. Williams

Budget and Planning Officer, Harvard College Library Harvard University,
Cambridge, MA 02138
617-495-2400

Not surprisingly, prices of library materials in 1980 continued to rise, with serial prices increasing more than monograph prices. (See Tables 1–8.) Preliminary figures for U.S. hardcover books showed a modest 3.4 percent increase while U.S. trade paperback prices showed a 17.6 percent increase and U.S. periodicals and serials prices showed a 19.4 percent increase. Do not be lulled by the low preliminary increase in hardcover monographs. The 1979 preliminary figures showed an increase of 13.4 percent but 1979 final figures revealed the increase to be 24 percent. For periodicals also the preliminary figures have been lower than final figures; in 1980 the preliminary increase of 10 percent turned into a final figure of more than 13 percent.

International price information is typically late in being reported and this handicaps U.S. libraries who need up-to-date facts for sensible budgeting. Preliminary findings indicate that the international price picture, particularly for periodicals and serials, is even worse than the domestic outlook. (See Tables 9–12.)

After steep increases of 18 and 22 percent in 1975 and 1976, British book prices stabilized in 1977 and 1978 with two consecutive increases of only 3 pecent. Figures for 1979, however, show that the average price was 17.2 percent higher than in 1978 as measured in pounds sterling.

The average price of a German book in 1979 increased 1.5 percent over the 1978 price (in marks, not dollars). While average prices in six categories decreased, average prices in the remaining 17 areas increased, with six of these increasing by 10 percent or more. Then, too, the table includes both cloth and paper editions, thus the German book index reflects a large number of inexpensive titles that many U.S. libraries might not be likely to buy.

Illustrating the zany range of price increases are the prices paid by eight libraries for Latin American books (Table 12). The low was a decrease of 46 percent (Guatemala) and the high was an increase of 128.6 percent (Panama) of 1979 prices over 1978.

But as long as the dollar continues to decline in value against foreign currencies, libraries purchasing materials from abroad get little comfort from figures that show inflation in foreign countries increasing more slowly than U.S. inflation. The dollar has declined the most in European countries that supply the bulk of library materials. Even with the recent rise in the strength of the dollar against other currencies, when one compares the value of the dollar at the close of 1980 with the value ten years ago, one sees the following: one-third the value in Switzerland, one-half the value in the Netherlands and West Germany, three-fourths the value in France and Italy. In Spain the dollar lost only 5 percent of its value. Only in Great Britain was the dollar worth more in 1980 than in 1970.

Library budgets are being stretched to the limit due to double-digit library materials inflation, decreased value of the dollar abroad, and increased volume of publishing worldwide. Therefore, materials budgets need to be carefully allocated. For just this purpose the ALA/RTSD/RS Library Materials Price Index Committee has sponsored the preparation and publication of the following tables.

The price indexes were designed to measure the rate of price changes of newly published materials against those of earlier years. The price indexes reflect price trends at the national level and are useful for comparing with local purchasing patterns. The price indexes reflect retail prices, not the cost to a particular library. The price indexes were never intended to be a substitute for information that a library might collect about its own purchases. The prices on which the indexes are based do not include discounts, vendor service charges, or other service charges. These variables naturally affect the average price for library materials paid by a particular library. However, as recent studies have shown, this does not necessarily mean that the rate of increase in prices paid by a particular library is significantly different from the rate of increase shown by the price indexes. The Library Materials Price Index Committee is very interested in pursuing correlations of individual library's prices with national prices and would like to be informed of any studies undertaken.

This year there are two significant changes in the price tables for hardcover and trade paperback books that should be noted. First, in anticipation of the revision of American National Standard Criteria for Price Indexes for Library Materials (ANSI Z39.20—1974), the three-year base period on which the U.S. price indexes have been calculated has been changed to a one-year base period. Second, the base year has been changed to 1977. These two changes will make it easier to compare with the U.S. government Consumer Price Index which also has a one-year base of 1977. The same changes will be reflected in the price tables for serials and mass-market paperbacks in the 1982 edition of the *Annual*.

As ever, readers are cautioned to use the indexes with care and note the particulars of each index. Be aware, for example, of the categories of "preliminary" and

(text continued on page 353)

TABLE 1   U.S. PERIODICALS: AVERAGE PRICES AND PRICE INDEXES, 1976-1980*
(Index Base: 1967-1969 = 100)

Subject Area	1967-1969 Average Price	1976 Average Price	1976 Index	1977 Average Price	1977 Index	1978 Average Price	1978 Index	1979 Average Price	1979 Index	1980 Average Price	1980 Index
U.S. periodicals (based on the total group of titles included in the indexes which follow)	$8.66	$22.52	260.0	$24.59	283.9	$27.58	318.5	$30.37	350.7	$34.54	398.8
Agriculture	4.68	10.75	229.7	11.58	247.4	12.48	266.7	14.16	302.6	15.24	325.6
Business and economics	7.54	16.98	225.2	18.62	246.9	21.09	279.7	22.97	304.6	25.42	337.1
Chemistry and physics	24.48	86.72	354.3	93.76	383.0	108.22	442.1	118.33	483.4	137.45	561.5
Children's periodicals	2.60	5.32	204.6	5.82	223.8	6.34	243.8	6.70	257.7	7.85	301.9
Education	6.34	16.00	252.4	17.54	276.7	19.49	307.4	21.61	340.9	23.45	369.9
Engineering	10.03	31.87	317.7	35.77	356.6	39.77	396.5	42.95	428.2	49.15	490.0
Fine and applied arts	6.71	12.42	185.1	13.72	204.5	14.82	220.9	17.42	259.6	18.67	278.2
General interest periodicals	7.28	15.24	209.3	16.19	222.4	17.26	237.1	18.28	251.1	19.87	272.9
History	6.04	11.94	197.7	12.64	209.3	13.71	227.0	14.67	242.9	15.77	261.1
Home economics	6.45	17.86	276.9	18.73	290.4	21.67	336.0	23.21	359.8	24.63	381.9
Industrial arts	6.87	12.51	182.1	14.37	209.2	15.48	225.3	17.65	256.9	20.70	301.3
Journalism and communications	5.72	15.90	278.0	16.97	296.7	19.95	348.8	23.86	417.1	27.34	478.0
Labor and industrial relations	3.01	10.33	343.2	11.24	373.4	13.24	439.9	15.74	522.9	18.84	625.9
Law	8.71	16.21	186.1	17.36	199.3	18.74	215.2	20.98	240.9	23.00	264.1
Library science	6.27	15.96	254.5	16.97	270.7	19.34	308.5	20.82	332.1	23.25	370.8
Literature and language	5.38	11.60	215.6	11.82	219.7	12.84	238.7	13.84	257.2	15.30	284.4
Math, botany, geology and general science	15.30	42.51	277.8	47.13	308.0	54.16	354.0	58.84	384.6	67.54	441.4
Medicine	19.38	47.47	244.9	51.31	264.8	57.06	294.4	63.31	326.7	73.37	378.6
Philosophy and religion	5.27	9.94	188.6	10.89	206.6	11.66	221.3	13.25	251.4	14.73	279.5
Physical education and recreation	4.89	9.27	189.6	10.00	204.5	10.79	220.7	12.27	250.9	13.83	282.8
Political science	6.18	13.09	211.8	14.83	240.0	15.62	252.8	17.47	282.7	19.30	312.3
Psychology	14.55	29.39	202.0	31.74	218.1	34.21	235.1	38.10	261.9	41.95	288.3
Sociology and anthropology	6.11	17.11	280.0	19.68	322.1	21.58	353.2	23.70	387.9	27.56	451.1
Zoology	13.39	31.34	234.1	33.69	251.6	37.05	276.7	40.15	299.9	44.58	332.9
Total number of periodicals	6,944		3,151		3,218		3,255		3,314		3,358

*Compiled by Norman B. Brown and Jane Phillips. For further comments see *Library Journal*, July 1980, "Price Indexes for 1980: U.S. Periodicals and Serial Services," by Norman B. Brown and Jane Phillips. For average prices for years prior to 1976, see previous editions of the *Bowker Annual*.

TABLE 2 U.S. SERIAL SERVICES: AVERAGE PRICES AND PRICE INDEXES, 1976–1980*†
(Index Base: 1967–1969 = 100)

	1967–1969 Average Price	1976 Average Price	1976 Index	1977 Average Price	1977 Index	1978 Average Price	1978 Index	1979 Average Price	1979 Index	1980 Average Price	1980 Index
Business	$119.76	$192.25	160.5	$216.28	180.6	$222.45	185.7	$249.05	208.0	$294.00	245.5
General and humanities	28.23	86.60	306.8	90.44	320.4	94.88	336.1	118.83	420.9	124.28	440.2
Law	60.87	113.37	186.2	126.74	208.2	137.91	226.6	158.65	260.6	184.38	302.9
Science and technology	65.23	122.69	188.1	141.16	216.4	160.61	246.2	173.96	266.7	191.35	293.3
Social sciences (excluding business and law)	65.63	136.40	207.8	145.50	221.7	153.94	234.6	169.55	258.3	190.07	289.6
Soviet translations	90.82	161.84	178.2	175.41	193.1	187.44	206.4	201.89	222.3	229.68	252.9
U.S. documents	18.37	60.36	328.6	62.88	342.3	72.52	394.8	75.87	413.0	78.87	429.3
"Wilson Index"	253.33	406.50	160.6	438.00	172.9	467.17	184.4	487.75	192.5	541.92	213.9
Combined‡	$ 72.42	$129.47	178.6	$142.27	196.5	$153.95	212.6	171.06	236.5	194.21	268.2

*Compiled by Norman B. Brown and Jane Phillips. For further comments see *Library Journal*, July 1980, "Price Indexes for 1980: U.S. Periodicals and Serial Services," by Norman B. Brown and Jane Phillips. For average prices for years prior to 1976, see previous editions of the *Bowker Annual*.
†The definition of a serial service has been taken from the *American National Standard Criteria for Price Indexes for Library Materials* (ANSI Z39.20—1974).
‡Excludes "Wilson Index."

TABLE 3 U.S. HARDCOVER BOOKS: AVERAGE PRICES AND PRICE INDEXES, 1977–1980*
(Index of 100.0 Equivalent to Average Price for 1977)

Categories with Dewey Decimal Numbers	1977 Average Price	1978 (Final) Vols.	1978 Average Price	1978 Index	1979 (Prelim.) Vols.	1979 Average Price	1979 Index	1979 (Final) Vols.	1979 Average Price	1979 Index	1980 (Prelim.) Vols.	1980 Average Price	1980 Index
Agriculture (630–639; 712–719)	$16.24	416	$17.24	106.2	332	$19.84	122.2	419	$20.94	128.9	272	$24.59	151.4
Art (700–711; 720–779)	21.24	1,017	21.11	99.4	1,110	21.47	101.1	1,399	21.95	103.3	916	26.64	125.4
Biography[1]	15.34	1,574	15.76	102.7	1,376	17.04	111.1	1,675	17.52	114.2	1,273	19.52	127.2
Business (650–659)	18.00	956	19.27	107.0	930	23.11	128.4	1,077	23.11	128.4	719	22.54	125.2
Education (370–379)	12.95	657	13.86	111.7	613	14.86	114.7	706	15.10	116.6	514	16.75	129.3
Fiction	10.09	2,254	11.27	82.3	1,722	11.32	112.2	2,027	11.99	118.8	1,814	12.31	122.0
General Works (000–099)	30.99	1,140	25.51	100.5	783	27.99	90.3	989	28.56	92.2	879	28.69	92.6
History (900–909; 930–999)	17.12	1,661	17.20	101.0	1,362	18.95	110.7	1,685	19.79	115.6	1,431	22.55	131.7
Home Economics (640–649)	11.16	495	11.27	98.9	441	11.90	106.6	552	11.95	107.1	432	13.08	117.2
Juveniles	6.65	2,961	6.58	111.4	2,605	7.13	107.2	3,002	7.14	107.4	2,477	8.21	123.4
Language (400–499)	14.96	256	16.67	96.9	290	18.81	125.7	356	18.25	122.0	251	20.71	138.4
Law (340–349)	25.04	713	24.26		733	27.61	110.3	891	29.44	117.6	579	31.63	126.3
Literature (800–810; 813–820; 823–89)	15.78	1,354	17.98	113.9	1,060	16.90	107.1	1,290	17.64	111.8	1,050	18.52	117.4

PRICES OF U.S. AND FOREIGN PUBLISHED MATERIALS / 345

Subject	1977 Avg. Price	1977 No.	1978 (final) Avg. Price	1978 (final) Index	1978 (final) No.	1979 (prelim.) Avg. Price	1979 (prelim.) Index	1979 (prelim.) No.	1979 (final) Avg. Price	1979 (final) Index	1979 (final) No.	1980 (prelim.) Avg. Price	1980 (prelim.) Index
Medicine (610–619)	24.00	2,199	25.01	104.2	2,045	27.73	115.5	2,554	29.27	122.0	1,924	32.07	133.6
Music (780–789)	20.13	361	24.68	122.6	228	18.51	92.0	289	18.93	94.0	221	20.92	103.9
Philosophy, Psychology (100–199)	14.43	968	14.75	102.2	851	16.95	117.5	1,024	17.98	124.6	841	21.27	147.4
Poetry, Drama (811; 812; 821; 822)	13.63	878	14.86	109.0	708	15.70	115.2	868	15.83	116.1	617	17.12	125.6
Religion (200–299)	12.26	1,077	13.04	106.4	1,078	13.78	112.4	1,286	14.83	121.0	917	17.73	144.6
Science (500–599)	24.88	2,331	26.20	105.3	2,067	28.61	115.0	2,525	30.59	123.0	1,764	35.13	141.2
Sociology, Economics (300–339; 350–369; 380–399)	29.88	4,663	29.66	99.3	4,606	41.73	139.6	5,656	43.57	145.8	4,131	32.72	109.5
Sports, Recreation (790–799)	12.28	732	12.96	105.5	634	13.59	110.7	750	13.88	113.0	509	15.31	124.7
Technology (600–609; 620–629; 660–699)	23.61	1,384	22.64	95.9	1,475	26.07	110.4	1,838	27.82	117.8	1,276	32.08	135.9
Travel (910–919)	18.44	250	17.12	92.8	288	15.08	81.8	342	15.02	81.4	214	15.98	86.6
Total	$19.22	30,297	$19.30	100.4	27,337	$22.80	118.6	33,200	$23.96	124.7	25,021	$23.57	122.6

*Price indexes are based on the books recorded in the "Weekly Record" of *Publishers Weekly*. 1980 (preliminary) includes items listed during 1980 with an imprint date of 1980; 1979 (final) includes items listed January 1979–June 1980 with an imprint date of 1979; 1979 (preliminary) includes items listed during 1979 with an imprint date of 1979; 1978 (final) includes items listed January 1978–June 1979 with an imprint date of 1978; 1977 includes items listed January 1, 1977–June 30, 1978 with an imprint date of 1977. (See "Book Title Output and Average Prices, 1979–1980" by Chandler B. Grannis, earlier in this section of Part 4.)

¹Includes biographies placed in other classes by the Library of Congress.

TABLE 4 U.S. MASS MARKET PAPERBACK BOOKS: AVERAGE PRICES AND PRICE INDEXES, 1977–1979*
(Index Base: 1967–1969 = 100)

Category	1967–1969 Average Price	1977 (Final) No. of Books	1977 Average Price	1977 Index	1978 (Final) No. of Books	1978 Average Price	1978 Index	1979 (Prelim.) No. of Books	1979 Average Price	1979 Index	1979 (Final) No. of Books	1979 Average Price	1979 Index
Agriculture	$ .88	5	$1.55	176.1	—	—	—	—	—	—	—	—	—
Art	.86	4	2.78	323.3	—	—	—	—	—	—	—	—	—
Biography	.93	33	1.84	197.9	88	$2.04	237.2	46	$2.61	303.5	50	$2.32	249.5
Business	1.06	7	2.06	194.3	—	—	—	—	—	—	—	—	—
Education	1.33	2	1.73	130.1	—	—	—	—	—	—	—	—	—
Fiction	.75	1,386	1.66	221.3	1,100	1.88	250.7	814	2.01	268.0	862	2.03	270.7
General works†	—	20	1.88	—	—	—	—	—	—	—	—	—	—
History	.98	35	2.06	210.2	15	2.05	209.2	13	2.35	239.8	15	2.40	244.9
Home economics†	—	15	1.93	—	—	—	—	—	—	—	—	—	—
Juveniles	.71	42	1.40	197.2	38	1.38	194.4	76	1.48	208.5	88	1.51	212.7
Language†	—	1	1.50	—	—	—	—	—	—	—	—	—	—
Law	.86	6	1.98	230.2	—	—	—	—	—	—	—	—	—
Literature	.96	10	1.98	206.3	—	—	—	—	—	—	—	—	—
Medicine	.87	51	2.04	234.5	32	2.04	234.5	31	2.39	274.7	33	2.39	274.7
Music	.83	4	2.29	276.0	—	—	—	—	—	—	—	—	—
Philosophy, psychology†	—	55	1.87	—	31	1.98	—	15	2.56	—	16	2.64	—
Poetry, drama	.92	6	2.10	228.3	—	—	—	—	—	—	—	—	—
Religion	.85	15	1.73	203.5	—	—	—	—	—	—	—	—	—
Science	.96	10	1.92	200.0	—	—	—	—	—	—	—	—	—
Sociology, economics†	—	71	1.90	—	56	2.17	—	46	2.30	—	46	2.30	—
Sports, recreation	.87	51	1.86	213.8	17	2.18	250.6	18	2.24	257.5	20	2.24	257.4
Technology	1.04	15	2.07	199.0	—	—	—	—	—	—	—	—	—
Travel†	—	9	2.07	—	—	—	—	—	—	—	—	—	—
All‡	$0.79	1,853	$1.72	217.7	1,374	$1.90	240.5	1,131	$2.06	260.8	1,215	$2.08	263.3

*See footnote to Table 3. Figures for 1978 and 1979 are limited to categories in which at least 15 titles were tabulated for 1978. Preliminary tabulations were not done for 1980, because the available sample was too small. Final figures for 1980 are scheduled for publication in *Publishers Weekly* in summer 1981.
†No base for calculation of index has been established.
‡"All" includes all items listed in "Weekly Record" including categories in which fewer than 15 titles were tabulated.

TABLE 5 U.S. TRADE (HIGHER PRICED) PAPERBACK BOOKS: AVERAGE PRICES AND PRICE INDEXES, 1977–1980
(Index Base: 1977 = 100)*

	1977 Average Price	1978 (Final) No. of Books	1978 (Final) Average Price	1978 (Final) Index	1979 (Prelim.) No. of Books	1979 (Prelim.) Average Price	1979 (Prelim.) Index	1979 (Final) No. of Books	1979 (Final) Average Price	1979 (Final) Index	1980 (Prelim.) No. of Books	1980 (Prelim.) Average Price	1980 (Prelim.) Index
Agriculture	$5.01	139	$5.86	117.0	95	$6.56	130.9	117	$6.80	135.7	88	$8.49	169.5
Art	6.27	471	6.81	108.6	511	8.38	133.6	634	8.33	132.8	455	9.00	143.5
Biography	4.91	286	4.72	96.1	253	5.72	116.5	314	5.64	114.9	262	6.49	132.2
Business	7.09	280	7.99	112.7	232	8.56	120.7	277	8.94	126.1	225	10.14	143.0
Education	5.72	410	6.68	116.8	333	6.92	121.0	404	6.91	120.8	291	8.08	141.2
Fiction	4.20	353	4.63	110.2	322	4.21	100.2	388	4.42	105.2	344	5.83	138.8
General works	6.18	342	6.67	107.9	353	6.66	107.8	480	6.47	104.7	409	7.91	128.0
History	5.81	368	5.99	103.1	379	6.54	112.6	474	6.67	114.8	369	7.33	126.2
Home economics	4.77	365	4.98	104.4	267	5.37	112.6	337	5.48	114.9	287	6.21	130.2
Juveniles	2.68	340	2.82	105.2	348	3.16	117.9	413	3.23	120.5	395	3.45	128.7
Language	7.79	203	6.18	79.3	153	7.54	96.8	205	7.53	96.7	179	8.44	108.3
Law	10.66	361	10.97	102.9	288	11.53	108.2	361	11.68	109.6	246	10.54	98.9
Literature	5.18	458	5.48	105.8	387	6.40	123.6	447	6.50	125.5	339	7.26	140.2
Medicine	7.63	556	8.31	108.9	570	9.46	124.0	667	9.55	125.2	541	11.25	147.4
Music	6.36	81	6.91	108.6	79	8.65	136.0	97	9.17	144.2	63	8.69	136.6
Philosophy, psychology	5.57	379	6.60	118.5	279	6.49	116.5	340	6.56	117.8	319	7.48	134.3
Poetry, drama	4.71	428	4.62	98.1	396	4.19	89.0	504	4.21	89.4	342	4.91	104.2
Religion	3.68	1,093	4.22	114.7	867	4.53	123.1	1,038	4.59	124.7	739	6.04	164.1
Science	8.81	550	9.49	107.7	516	11.22	127.4	614	11.48	130.3	493	12.76	144.8
Sociology, economics	6.03	1,764	6.52	108.1	1,590	7.64	126.7	2,036	8.07	133.8	1,565	9.28	153.9
Sports, recreation	4.87	413	5.42	111.3	300	6.08	124.8	360	6.12	125.7	256	6.97	143.1
Technology	7.97	518	7.55	94.7	456	8.81	110.5	556	9.24	115.9	412	12.77	160.2
Travel	5.21	164	6.02	115.5	235	5.89	113.0	294	5.97	114.6	206	6.57	126.1
Total	$5.93	10,322	$6.31	106.4	9,209	$7.05	118.9	11,357	$7.21	121.6	8,825	$8.29	139.8

*See footnote to Table 3.

TABLE 6 U.S. NONPRINT MEDIA: AVERAGE PRICES AND PRICE INDEXES, 1972–1980*
(Index Base: 1972 = 100)

Category	1972 Average Quantity	1972 Index	1976 Average Quantity	1976 Index	1977 Average Quantity	1977 Index	1978 Average Quantity	1978 Index	1979 Average Quantity	1979 Index	1980 Average Quantity	1980 Index
16mm Films												
Average rental cost per minute	$ 1.15	100	$ 1.16	100.9	$ 1.23	107	$ 1.22	106.1	$ 1.35	117.3	$ 1.41	122.6
Average color purchase cost per minute	11.95	100	12.93	108.2	13.95	116.7	12.56	105.1	13.62	113.9	12.03	100.6
Average cost of color film	241.39	100	253.42	105	308.85	127.9	350.42	145.1	328.24	135.9	279.09	115.6
Average length per film (min.)	20.2	—	19.6	—	22.14	—	27.9	—	24.1	—	23.2	—
Videocassettes												
Average purchase cost per minute	—	—	—	—	—	—	—	—	—	—	7.58	100.0
Filmstrips												
Average cost of filmstrip	12.95	100	17.18	132.7	18.60	143.6	17.43	134.6	21.42	165.4	21.74	167.8
Average cost of filmstrip set (cassette)	37.56	100	58.41	155.5	76.26	203.0	62.31	165.9	65.97	175.6	67.39	179.4
Average number of filmstrips per set	2.9	—	3.4	—	4.1	—	3.6	—	3.08	—	3.1	—
Average number of frames per filmstrip	63.3	—	62.8	—	64.2	—	58.0	—	71.8	—	67.9	—
Multimedia Kits												
Average cost per kit	51.33	100	93.63	182.4	93.65	182.4	117.38	228.7	85.70	166.9	92.71	180.6
Sound Recordings												
Average cost per disc	6.10	100	5.85	95.9	6.72	110.2	7.06	115.8	7.21	118.2	7.75	127.0
Average cost per cassette	7.81	100	12.08	157.7	10.63	136.1	12.57	161.1	12.58	161.1	9.34	119.5

*Compiled by David B. Walch. Cost analysis for the nonprint media shown in this table was based on information derived from selected issues of *Previews*. It should be noted that the years listed do not necessarily reflect the year of production. For example, the majority of films reviewed by *Previews* in 1980 were actually produced in 1979.

TABLE 7   U.S. LIBRARY MICROFILM: AVERAGE RATES
AND INDEX VALUES, 1969-1978

Negative Microfilm[1] (35mm per exposure)	1969	1972	1975	1978
Average rate	$ .0493	$ .0621	$ .0707	$ .0836
Index value	100.0	125.9	143.4	169.7
Percent + or −	0	+25.9	+17.3	+26.3
Positive Microfilm[2] (35mm per foot)				
Average rate	$ .0960	$ .0839	$ .1190	$ .1612
Index value	100.0	87.4	123.9	168.0
Percent + or −	0	−12.6	+36.6	+44.0

*Compiled by Imre T. Jarmy, Library Materials Price Index Committee, Resources Section, Resources and Technical Services Division, American Library Association, from the *Directory of Library Reprographic Services: A World Guide*, 7th edition (Microform Review, Westport, Conn., 1978), supplemented by data secured by correspondence and by telephone interviews with the staffs of the indexed libraries. These libraries are listed in the "Library Microfilm Rates" articles in the following issues of *Library Resources and Technical Services:* Winter 1967 (11:1), Summer 1969 (13:3), Summer 1970 (14:3), Winter 1974 (18:1), Fall 1977 (21:4), and Summer 1979 (23:3); in the *Newspaper and Gazette Report*, April 1978 (6:1); and in the *National Preservation Report*, April 1979 (1:1). The rates listed in the fourth edition of the *Directory* are used as base prices with an index value of 100 in computing subsequent index values.
[1]Includes 49 selected libraries for 1969; 48 for 1972; 46 for 1975; and 48 for 1978.
[2]Includes 22 selected libraries for 1969; 20 for 1972; 19 for 1975; and 19 for 1978.

TABLE 8   SELECTED U.S. DAILY NEWSPAPERS:
AVERAGE SUBSCRIPTION RATES AND INDEX
VALUES, 1969-1978*

Year	Average Rate	Index Value	% (+ or −)
1969	$34.1592	100.0	0
1972	42.7647	125.2	+25.2
1975	58.4120	171.0	+45.8
1978	76.4391	223.8	+52.8

*Compiled by Imre T. Jarmy, Library Materials Price Index Committee, Resources Section, Resources and Technical Services Division, American Library Association, from data secured by correspondence and by telephone interviews with the circulation managers and publishers of the indexed newspapers and, when necessary, by examination of the pertinent year end editions of individual issues. Data for 95 of the 133 titles indexed were available at press time. The complete list will be published in the Summer 1980 edition of *Library Resources and Technical Services*.

TABLE 9 BRITISH BOOKS BY MAJOR CATEGORIES: AVERAGE PRICES AND PRICE INDEXES, 1976–1979*
(Index Base: 1966–1967 = 100)

	1966–1967 Average Price £ p	1976 No. of Books	1976 Average Price £ p	1976 Index	1977 No. of Books	1977 Average Price £ p	1977 Index	1978 No. of Books	1978 Average Price £ p	1978 Index	1979 No. of Books	1979 Average Price £ p	1979 Index
Adult fiction	.85	3,768	2.27½	267.6	3,806	2.55	300.0	4,137	2.76	324.7	4,039	3.20	376.5
Adult nonfiction[1]	2.19	26,467	5.14½	234.9	22,806	6.40	292.2	25,826	6.54	298.6	25,038	7.70	351.6
Reference books[2]	2.66	2,417	5.16½	194.2	1,968	7.30	274.4	2,248	7.59	285.3	2,326	9.15	344.0
Children's fiction	.54	1,437	1.36½	252.8	1,204	1.44	266.7	1,337	1.54	285.2	1,441	1.86	344.4
Children's nonfiction	.67½	1,204	1.32½	196.3	1,055	1.19	176.3	1,211	1.20	177.8	1,242	1.37	203.0
All categories combined	1.84½	32,876	4.51	244.4	28,871	5.49	297.6	32,511	5.65	306.2	31,760	6.62	358.8

*Data compiled by Thomas W. Leonhardt from *Library Association Record*, March 1980.
[1]See Table 10 for breakdown by Dewey classes.
[2]Reference Books are included in the total for nonfiction.

Information note: The average annual market exchange rate for 1979 was 2.2240 U.S. dollars per pound sterling as reported by the Bureau of Statistics, International Monetary Fund in its periodical *International Finance Statistics*.

TABLE 10 BRITISH ADULT NONFICTION BOOKS: AVERAGE PRICES AND PRICE INDEXES, 1976–1979*
(Index Base: 1966–1967 = 100)

Classes	1966–1967 Average Price £ p	1976 No. of Books	1976 Average Price £ p	1976 Index	1977 No. of Books	1977 Average Price £ p	1977 Index	1978 No. of Books	1978 Average Price £ p	1978 Index	1979 No. of Books	1979 Average Price £ p	1979 Index
000	5.21	1,035	6.23½	119.7	724	8.18	157.0	938	8.44	162.0	986	12.70	243.8
100	1.86½	674	5.22	279.9	654	5.61	300.8	698	6.38	342.1	716	7.45	399.5
200	1.29½	1,135	3.06	236.3	890	3.18	245.6	1,169	2.86	220.9	1,035	4.60	355.2
300	1.47	7,627	4.88	332.0	6,125	6.28	427.2	6,598	6.24	424.5	7,114	7.03	478.2
400	.66	590	2.99½	453.8	479	3.63	550.0	796	2.75	416.7	781	2.74	415.2
500	2.99	2,302	9.04	302.3	2,159	10.95	366.2	2,244	11.72	392.0	2,163	13.78	460.9
600	2.47½	5,104	6.14	248.1	4,718	7.94	320.8	5,412	8.59	347.1	4,965	9.99	403.6
700	2.38½	2,718	4.68	196.2	2,444	5.57	233.5	2,797	5.52	231.5	2,516	6.19	259.5
800	1.03½	2,486	3.09½	299.0	2,193	3.44	332.4	2,287	3.51	339.1	2,181	4.78	461.8
900	1.69½	2,796	4.53½	267.6	2,420	4.54	267.8	2,887	4.67	275.5	2,581	4.91	289.7

*Data compiled by Thomas W. Leonhardt from *Library Association Record*, March 1980.
000 General works; Bibliographies; Librarianship
100 Philosophy; Psychology; Occultism, etc.
200 Not subdivided
300 Social Science; Politics; Economics; Law; Public Administration; Social Welfare; Education; Social Customs, etc.
400 Language; School Readers
500 General Science; Mathematics; Astronomy; Physics; Chemistry; Geology; Meteorology; Pre-history; Anthropology; General Biology; Botany; Zoology
600 Medicine; Public Safety; Engineering/Technology; Agriculture; Domestic Economy; Business Management; Printing & Book Trade; Manufactures; Building
700 Architecture; Fine Arts; Photography; Music; Entertainment; Sports, Amusements
800 General and Foreign Literature; English Literature
900 Geography; Travel; Biography; History

Information note: The average annual market exchange rate for 1979 was 2.2240 U.S. dollars per pound sterling as reported by the Bureau of Statistics, International Monetary Fund in its periodical *International Finance Statistics*.

TABLE 11. GERMAN BOOKS: AVERAGE PRICES AND PRICE INDEXES, 1976–1979*
(Index Base: 1967–1969 = 100)

	1967–1969 Average Price	1976 Average Price	1976 Index	1977 Average Price	1977 Index	1978 Average Price	1978 Index	1979 Average Price	1979 Index
General, library science, college level textbooks	DM32.66	DM54.04	165.5	DM68.47	209.6	DM61.93	189.6	DM67.57	206.9
Religion, theology	16.33	22.33	136.7	23.31	142.1	24.57	150.5	26.08	159.7
Philosophy, psychology	26.45	23.21	87.8	26.67	100.8	27.28	103.1	24.43	92.4
Law, administration	23.57	35.19	149.3	33.92	143.9	36.92	156.6	46.28	196.4
Social sciences, economics, statistics	20.07	25.72	128.2	25.97	129.4	29.13	145.1	31.73	158.1
Political and military science	16.47	24.37	148.0	22.91	139.1	21.64	131.4	27.44	166.6
Literature and linguistics	28.97	25.83	89.2	27.79	95.9	29.43	101.6	27.03	93.3
Belles lettres	5.83	6.98	119.7	6.57	112.7	7.44	127.6	7.47	128.1
Juveniles	6.09	8.24	135.3	9.07	148.9	9.26	152.1	7.85	128.9
Education	10.65	17.03	159.9	16.50	154.9	17.54	164.7	17.96	168.6
School textbooks	5.66	10.10	178.4	10.88	192.2	11.44	202.1	11.51	203.4
Fine arts	30.18	51.85	171.8	49.70	164.7	46.81	155.1	49.09	162.7
Music, dance, theatre, film, radio	23.79	27.07	113.8	28.04	117.9	28.76	120.9	25.84	108.6
History, folklore	31.24	36.99	118.4	38.79	124.2	39.75	127.2	37.29	119.4
Geography, anthropology, travel	16.26	31.20	191.9	32.20	198.0	27.46	168.9	30.49	187.5
Medicine	40.60	52.57	129.5	50.29	123.9	50.82	125.2	58.10	143.1
Natural sciences	34.73	81.77	235.4	93.45	269.1	97.02	279.4	101.75	293.0
Mathematics	25.40	32.50	128.0	29.98	118.0	30.22	119.0	34.82	137.1
Technology	21.89	42.66	194.9	42.45	193.9	57.85	264.3	55.13	251.9
Touring guides and directories	18.43	23.08	125.2	21.78	118.2	34.56	187.5	30.09	163.3
Home economics and agriculture	12.31	24.60	199.8	25.10	203.9	21.75	176.7	22.36	181.6
Sports and recreation	12.00	19.93	166.1	18.99	158.3	20.13	167.8	19.01	158.4
Miscellaneous	11.18	—	—	11.30	101.1	7.96	71.2	8.39	75.0
Total	DM18.60	DM20.52	110.3	DM21.87	117.6	DM23.28	125.2	DM23.62	127.0

*Indexes are tentative and based on average prices *unadjusted* for title production. Figures for 1979 were compiled by Thomas W. Leonhardt from *Buch und Buchhandel in Zahlen*, Frankfurt, 1980.

Information note: The average annual market exchange rate for 1979 was 1.7315 Deutsche Marks per U.S. dollar as reported by the Bureau of Statistics, International Monetary Fund in its periodical *International Finance Statistics*.

TABLE 12 LATIN AMERICAN BOOKS: NUMBER OF COPIES
AND AVERAGE COST FY 1979 AND 1980*

	Number of Books FY 1979	Number of Books FY 1980	Average Cost FY 1979	Average Cost FY 1980	% (+ or −) over 1979
Argentina[1]	4,753	3,638	$ 9.10	$12.37	+35.9
Bolivia[1]	1,302	1,495	9.61	9.27	−3.5
Brazil	7,882	8,432	8.63	7.79	−9.7
Chile[1]	1,684	1,454	10.52	13.44	+27.8
Colombia[1]	2,320	2,216	9.42	10.42	+10.6
Costa Rica	94	147	4.05	8.87	+119.0
Cuba[2]	1	—	15.00	—	—
Dominican Republic	501	163	6.86	9.88	+44.0
Ecuador	739	744	5.74	6.69	+16.5
El Salvador	71	159	7.45	7.97	+7.0
Guatemala	80	389	6.13	3.31	−46.0
Guyana	62	10	4.60	2.60	−43.5
Haiti	278	170	6.86	6.48	−5.5
Honduras	216	192	6.01	5.03	−16.3
Jamaica	257	94	3.97	3.45	−13.1
Mexico[1]	3,197	4,195	6.39	7.26	+13.6
Nicaragua	13	154	12.54	8.68	−30.8
Panama	38	12	4.16	9.41	+128.6
Paraguay[1]	322	354	8.77	8.86	−1.0
Peru[1]	3,251	2,609	6.29	6.09	−3.2
Puerto Rico	487	458	5.95	5.71	−4.0
Trinidad	55	1	4.22	17.00	—
Uruguay[1]	2,165	1,923	8.55	9.56	+11.8
Venezuela	1,552	1,440	8.98	10.57	+17.7
Other Caribbean	1,037	1,273	5.28	5.57	+5.5

*Compiled by Peter J. de la Garza, Seminars on the Acquisition of Latin American Library Materials (SALALM), Acquisition Committee, from reports on the number and cost of current monographs purchased by the libraries of Cornell University, University of Florida, University of Illinois, Library of Congress, University of Minnesota, New York Public Library, University of Texas and University of Wisconsin.
[1]Includes some binding costs.
[2]Insufficient data for meaningful comparison.

"final" in the U.S. book prices tables; for a more accurate picture, compare like categories only and do not make the mistake of comparing preliminary figures to final figures. Take note that the German book price index includes both paperback and hardcover books and this affects the price as noted earlier. Also note that this year the U.S. nonprint media price index omits costs of cassette sets since there were very few produced and sold, but has added information for video cassettes since there has been a substantial increase in production in this format.

In addition to the indexes presented here, there are two other published price indexes not sponsored by the Library Materials Price Index Committee that are of interest. These are: Hill, G. R. and Boonin, J. M., "Price Indexes, Foreign and Domestic Music," *Music Library Association Notes*, March 1981; Scott, B., "Price Index for Legal Publications," *Law Library Journal* 73: 227-229, Winter 1980.

The current members of the Library Materials Price Index Committee are Sally F. Williams, chairperson; Peter Graham, Nelson A. Piper, Thomas W. Leonhardt, and Beth Shapiro. Consultants to the committee are Noreen G. Alldredge, Hugh C. Atkinson, Norman B. Brown, Imre T. Jarmy, Dennis E. Smith, and David B. Walch.

NUMBER OF BOOK OUTLETS IN THE UNITED STATES AND CANADA

The *American Book Trade Directory* has been published by the R. R. Bowker Company since 1915. Revised annually, it features lists of booksellers, publishers, wholesalers, periodicals, reference tools, and other information about the U.S. book market as well as markets in Great Britain and Canada. The data provided in Tables 1 and 2 for the United States and Canada, the most current available, are from the 1980 edition of the directory.

The 19,132 stores of various types shown in Table 1 are located in approximately 4,766 cities in the United States, Canada, and regions administered by the United States. All "general" bookstores are assumed to carry hardbound (trade) books, paperbacks, and children's books; special effort has been made to apply this category only to bookstores for which this term can properly be applied. All "college" stores are assumed to carry college-level textbooks. The term "educational" is used for outlets handling school textbooks up to and including the high school level. The category "mail order" has been confined to those outlets that sell general trade books by mail and are not book clubs; all others operating by mail have been classifed according to the kinds of books carried. The term "antiquarian" covers dealers in old and rare books. Stores handling only secondhand books are classified by the category "used." The category "paperbacks" represents stores with stock consisting of more than an 80% holding of paperbound books. Other stores with paperback departments are listed under the major classification ("general," "department store," "stationers," etc.), with the fact that paperbacks are carried given in the entry. A bookstore that specializes in a subject to the extent of 50% of its stock has that subject designated as its major category.

TABLE 1 BOOKSTORES IN THE UNITED STATES (AND CANADA)

Antiquarian	940 (62)	Museum store and art gallery	179 (7)
Mail order—antiquarian	555 (14)	Newsdealer	138 (7)
College	2,686 (134)	Office supply	31 (2)
Department store	1,272 (116)	Paperback*	846 (38)
Drugstore	21 (3)	Religious	2,487 (174)
Educational	104 (13)	Rental	5 (0)
Export-importer	26 (1)	Science-technology	50 (6)
Foreign language	94 (22)	Special†	1,537 (193)
General	5,197 (1,046)	Stationer	150 (19)
Gift shop	79 (11)	Used	340 (12)
Juvenile	114 (15)		
Law	58 (4)	Total listed in the United States	17,218
Mail order (general)	214 (12)		
Medical	98 (3)	Total listed in Canada	1,914

*This figure does not include paperback departments of general bookstores, department stores, stationers, drugstores, or wholesalers handling paperbacks.
†Indicates stores specializing in subjects other than those specifically given in the list.

Note: In Tables 1 and 2, the Canadian figure for each category is in parentheses following the U.S. figure.

TABLE 2 WHOLESALERS IN THE UNITED STATES (AND CANADA)

General wholesalers	662 (105)	Total listed in the United States	1,032
Paperback wholesalers	370 (19)	Total listed in Canada	124

BOOK REVIEW MEDIA STATISTICS

NUMBER OF BOOKS REVIEWED BY MAJOR BOOK-REVIEWING PUBLICATIONS, 1979 AND 1980

	Adult 1979	Adult 1980	Juvenile 1979	Juvenile 1980	Young Adult 1979	Young Adult 1980	Total 1979	Total 1980
Booklist[1]	2,900	3,267	1,280	1,244	1,243	1,283	5,812	6,149
Bulletin of the Center for Children's Books	—	—	452	460	398	405	850	865
Choice[2]	6,814	6,551	—	—	—	—	6,814	6,551
Horn Book	23	51	334	324	119	117	476	492
Kirkus Services	3,938	3,971	904	915	—	—	4,842	4,886
Library Journal	6,014	6,130	—	—	—	—	6,014	6,130
New York Review of Books	550	600	—	—	—	—	550	600
New York Times Sunday Book Review	2,000	2,000	300	300	—	—	2,300	2,300
Publishers Weekly[3]	4,336	4,400	545	550	—	—	4,881	4,950
School Library Journal	—	—	2,249	2,245	272	357	2,521	2,602
Washington Post Book World	1,856	1,727	128	116	—	—	1,984	1,843

[1] All figures are for a 12-month period from September 1 to August 31, e.g., 1979 figures are for September 1, 1978–August 31, 1979. Totals include reference and subscription books. In addition, *Booklist* published reviews of nonprint materials: 1,534 in 1979; 1,216 in 1980.

[2] All figures are for a 12-month period beginning in March and ending in February, e.g., 1979 figures are for March 1979–February 1980.

[3] Includes reviews of paperback originals and reprints.

Part 5
International Reports and Statistics

International Reports

FRANKFURT BOOK FAIR, 1980

Herbert R. Lottman
International Correspondent, *Publishers Weekly*

The thirty-second Frankfurt Book Fair took place (from October 8 to 13) in an atmosphere of suspended disbelief. Publishers who had been expressing pessimism in winter, spring and summer suddenly began to act and talk as if they were not suffering the world economic crisis in general and the particular problems of their own countries' book trades. Indeed, suffering seemed to have been unequally distributed, and once again one of the chief occupations of book people during the run of the fair was to find out how the rest of the world was doing, and perhaps to take strength from the strong ones. "A good deal of the publishing process is borrowing confidence from each other," Doubleday's Sam Vaughan explained. "It may sound like a cliché, but there really is a community of the book." It was clear that varying levels of inflation and currency values from region to region were leading to a new division of labor, e.g., the United States had become the cheap and fast place to go to manufacture co-editions. "Printed in the U.S." seems likely to become as common a label as "Printed in Hong Kong."

In the absence of reliable indicators on levels of business activity from country to country, fairgoers were obliged to depend on their personal observations in the international pavilion familiarly known as *Halle Funf*, for the major trade publishers of the world outside the German language all fit neatly into this Hall 5. And here it was noticeable that leading imprints of the United States and United Kingdom—all present with display booths—had reduced their Frankfurt contingents. But in many cases the reduction kept the smaller staffs mighty busy, and gave nearly everyone the impression that the fair was a lively one. The surprise was that there were as many participants prepared to say it was a "good fair" as that it was a "quiet one." No one said it was "disappointing" because no one expected very much.

And there was the incontrovertible evidence that the fair was still growing. Official figures were: 5,216 imprints represented, 3,813 of them non-German (East or West). Last year there had been 5,045, 3,734 of them non-German. Importantly, there were 3,883 individual exhibitors against 3,533 last year, a continuation of the trend to mounting and staffing one's own booth; 1,333 imprints showed on collective stands against 1,512 last year. An extra 10,000 square meters of exhibition space had been filled in Hall 8, for a total of 80,100 square meters, allowing the fair management to give more space to exhibitors, and more space between exhibitors. The extra space certainly contributed to the feeling that the fair was quieter, and fair director Peter Weidhaas reported that traffic in the aisles and between pavilions was as brisk as ever. This time 95 countries were represented, including a number of African states showing for the

Note: Reprinted from *Publishers Weekly*, November 14, 1980, where the article was entitled "Frankfurt 1980: A Seller's Fair for the Anglo-Americans."

first time as part of the fair's theme; *that* surely contributed to the rise in all figures. An estimated 285,000 books were on view. The biggest exhibitors were West Germany (1,352 individual imprints), the United Kingdom (564), the United States (544), France (229), the Netherlands (190), Italy (178), and Switzerland (177).

One way to measure Frankfurt is by the acuteness of the shortage of hotel rooms. It was more acute than ever this year. Clearly the slicing of staff from the United States and other far-off and Deutschmark-poor nations had been offset by new exhibitors delighted to find a hotel. Cocktail party talk about the difficulty of getting a room and keeping it, or the shock of finding oneself stricken from the reservation file, was as widespread as ever.

At the fair itself, one had to be impressed by the features that make it easy to work in Frankfurt, from telephones on stands and convenient telex and photocopiers and banks to the Literary Agents Center in Hall 5, which seemed to be utilized by all the world's agents. In adjacent Hall 5a, where scientific and technical publishers of Germany and the rest of the world are centered, the International Booksellers and Librarians Center had more space (and never seemed crowded), providing similar facilities. Restaurants on the fairgrounds seemed less crowded, and somehow better, than usual. It was possible that high prices and bad business back home kept more fairgoers on sausages and apples.

One thing was clear: the center of gravity at Frankfurt had shifted perceptibly from the Anglo-American half of International Hall 5 to economically healthier countries, like Japan and parts of Scandinavia, and above all to Halls 6 and 8, where the West Germans hang their shingles. And of course the prosperous publishers besieged the American and British stands looking for hot properties, like rich tourists mobbing souvenir stands in a poor but picturesque foreign clime.

Not surprisingly, some of the poor natives found themselves shorthanded. André Schiffrin of Pantheon Books called this his best "selling fair," although in fact he would have preferred to buy more, for his list depends on foreign input. Allan Eady of Crown was happily surprised to discover that the British were buying rights as if they had no economic problems at all. (Another publishing person explained this by the fact that it was cheaper for the British to buy rights to books someone else was editing than to create their own in a period of staff cutting.) "A terrific working fair," Putnam's Peter Israel exclaimed, on the Sunday afternoon preceding Monday morning packing up. Just across the aisle Roger W. Straus, Jr., of Farrar, Straus & Giroux, was working on a Frankfurt Sunday afternoon for the first time in anyone's memory. London's André Deutsch, smack in the middle of the forlorn British, reported "the best fair I've had in years and years." Tom Maschler of Jonathan Cape was optimistic about the fair and the months that would follow it. He and others seemed to share a formula: keep a tight ship; steer away from marginal books. The British got considerable help for their Frankfurt show from a governmental subsidy that was more generous than usual, for it covered the full cost of their stands regardless of size, rather than the usual grant covering minimal stands only.

And some kinds of publishing were stronger than others. "One thing I've learned," commented Werner Linz, ex-Seabury Press, now Crossroad Publishing Company, "is that religious publishing is recessionproof." The same phrase was used the very same day about sci-tech publishing by Charles Ellis, co-managing director of Britain's Pergamon Group. Ruth Gottstein of Independent Publishers Services, which represents four-score small U.S. presses, found business as good as ever for the small and the specialized. Perhaps a healthy shakedown was under way, she said, but "quality was showing." She was one of several participants who commented that the more generous space arrangements could lead a visitor to the false impression that things were quieter this year. But Rosalie Siegel, American literary agent and scout for Scherz Verlag, felt that everyone in the American compound was busy because booths were understaffed—and she proceeded to name the missing people.

Howard Graham of Grolier and Franklin Watts was seeing fewer people, but he felt that all the important ones were on hand. "We just don't find the extra people each firm took along because it owed them a holiday." Grolier itself was operating from a minimum-sized booth because its request for a larger stand had been turned down. "Obviously things are tighter, even in Germany—but that makes the need for cooperating even greater." Graham noted, for example, that people who usually were unwilling to talk about major reference projects, because they are kept as deep secrets until they are ready to be launched, suddenly had opened up.

For an Alfredo Machado, whose Distribuidora Récord imprint in Brazil is strong on international best sellers, a Frankfurt fair couldn't be all bad when there were new titles on the market by Harold Robbins, Morris West, and even Gabriel García Márquez. When he could be talked to over the heads of publishers who crowded around his little table, Scandinavian agent Lennart Sane reported he was selling three times as much as last year. Without as many big books, and under prevailing conditions, average advances were lower, but he still expected to double his turnover.

Surprisingly, coproducers seemed to be suffering less than had been expected with the shooting up of prices in traditional printing countries and the weakness of traditional customers. Obviously some of their optimism was the result of earlier reductions in payroll and budgets; there seemed no way to go but up. Agent Tom Mori of Tokyo's Tuttle-Mori Agency reported unexpectedly good results with illustrated books; Mitchell Beazley's David Campbell said that international business wasn't bad; he was "guardedly optimistic," convinced that quality would tell, and that his firm would continue to find cheap places to print. Despite rising costs and differing rates of inflation from partner to partner, it was the best fair international copublishing consultant Ljubo Stefanović ever had. Referring to sales of the costly facsimile editions for his principal, Harcourt Brace Jovanovich's Johnson Reprint, Stefanović explained: "We're in the Rolls-Royce business, where you don't ask how much it costs."

HOW ARE PUBLISHERS FARING?

PW asked a few publishers in the most significant trading nations for thumbnail evaluations of their own publishing economies. Lionel Leventhal of Arms & Armour Press and the London Book Fair said he thought the present situation was even worse than *PW*'s October 3 survey of the British scene had reported. The strong British currency had crippled the export business that was essential to Britain's bookselling; high costs had hurt packagers who were Britain's particular contribution to international publishing. On the surface, the German book trade was still strong and book sales were satisfactory, but publishers were scanning the horizon for storm signals. Gerhard Beckmann of Munich's Steinhausen Verlag observed that overproduction of titles was proving a strain even for the efficient German bookselling system; so orders were down and books were being returned too quickly. Increased paperback production has glutted available racks without having found a market.

There were few major changes in the German scene, although one bit of news spread around the fair: Munich's Droemer had been totally absorbed by the Georg von Holtbrinck Group, which until then had been a minority partner; the patriarchal founder Willy Droemer and his top management were gone. A takeover that didn't happen involved the Bauer press group's plan to buy the Econ Verlag Group; so it stands as before, with 75 percent in the hands of educational publisher Schroedel, 25 percent with Econ's Erwin Barth von Wehrenalp.

Considering that Spain's overall economic situation is very bad (the 1 million unemployed represent 12 percent of the working-age population), the Spanish publishing industry does not look as bad as it might otherwise. According to Mario Lacruz of Argos Vergara in Barcelona, title and copy production have reached a plateau, while cover prices rise faster than the cost of living index (they have doubled in a span of four years).

It was a bad year for Italy and for Italian publishers. The rise in paper and printing has contributed to the loss of the country's competitive advantage in copublishing and, with the inevitable increases in list prices, sales have fallen off (they are way down in Turin, an industrial town particularly hurt by the problems of Fiat). Sergio Giunti of Florence's Giunti Group also pointed out that for the first time the Italian population has stopped growing, and there has been a regular decline in primary school enrollment (from 1 million pupils to 750,000 in 15 years), a decline that will continue. Still, Italian publishing lives; there have been no spectacular bankruptcies, even among the giants which are perennially on the brink.

Japan's publishers are cautious, reports Hideo Aoki of the Japan Uni agency; returns via that country's splendid distribution system continue to alarm. To listen to Turkish agent Nurcihan Kesim, the recent military takeover in her country may reduce the chronic disorder, and lead to economic growth. Kesim, who was attending her ninth Frankfurt, insists that Turkish publishers can and do export royalties (although, for practical purposes, only three houses buy significant numbers of foreign books). At the fair she sold Harold Robbins's *Goodbye Janette* (for which there is still no manuscript to show) to Altin of Istanbul for $3,500 advance. So Turkey also lives.

In fact, New York agent Roslyn Targ was obtaining record advances from a number of European countries for *Goodbye Janette*, and good money for her husband William Targ's novel *Secret Lives* (now committed to the United Kingdom's Granada, the Netherlands' Elsevier, Brazil's Récord, and Argentina's 'Emecé'). But there was no *Princess Daisy* this year. Some publishers commented that the lack of real or imagined blockbusters was healthy for books as a whole. There *was* a Princess Caroline, the young lady from Monaco whose novel a Hachette affiliate was talking up but—in the absence of a finished manuscript—not signing up.

Timo Kärnekull of Sweden's Askild & Kärnekull was showing a dummy of *The Great Royal Book of Lists* (imprisonments, assassinations, last words, etc.), and selling it around the world. Foreigners were wearing out the carpet in front of the Doubleday stand to ask foreign rights manager Jacqueline Everly about what everyone was calling "another *Kramer vs. Kramer*": *Kiss Mommy Goodbye* by Joy Fielding, a March release and a movie to come. Econ Verlag claimed two contenders for the championship: Hans Herlin's *The Devil Is on God's Side*, the first German spy novel said to be in the le Carré class, sold to Doubleday, Collins, and their counterparts elsewhere; and an autobiographical novel by Soviet poet and occasional bad boy (but usually fair-haired boy) Yevgeny Yevtushenko, for which it had acquired world rights from the Soviet copyright agency VAAP. Arthur Rosenthal of Harvard University Press was showing *The Harvard Medical School Health Letter Book*, which at home was getting what he claimed was the highest first printing (40,000 copies) in the history of university press publishing; he was "selling rights like mad."

THE VATICAN LIBRARY PROJECT

Perhaps the biggest Frankfurt book this year was not a novel or an entertainment, but a soberly packaged facsimile. The project had actually gotten under way at a previous Frankfurt fair, when Hans Weitpert of Germany's Belser and copublishing magician Ljubo Stefanović hammered out the lines of a Vatican Library reproduction unit. Weitpert had done a book on Vatican Council II, at which time he had an opportunity to examine some of the library's priceless holdings. Stefanović immediately brought in Harcourt Brace Jovanovich, whose William Granville took over, with New York editor Anne Papantonio in charge of the "Vatican project." A photographic and color-separation unit was set up just below the main reading room of the Vatican Library; an estimated $1 million went into equipping it, notably with a laser scanner (feedback will be used to improve techniques for future facsimile volumes).

The first reproduction undertaken was an eleventh-century illuminated life of Saint Benedict, a *Codex Benedictus* found at Monte Cassino monastery; a dummy and sample pages were shown at a Frankfurt fair press conference, and release is planned for next autumn. This will be followed by a fifteenth-century Ptolemaic atlas, a *Divine Comedy* illustrated by Botticelli and other major holdings among the Vatican's 60,000 illuminated manuscripts. *Codex Benedictus* will be printed in 600 copies to sell at $6,000 prepublication, $7,500 thereafter. During the fair Japan's Iwanami Shoten joined the Vatican project as well as the Harcourt Brace Jovanovich-Giunti joint venture that will produce illustrated catalogs of the entire Hermitage museum collection in Leningrad; the Harcourt *Windsor Codex* of Leonardo da Vinci drawings owned by Britain's Royal family; and the Harcourt-Giunti *Codex de France* (a new project that will publish Leonardo's drawings and notes held by the Institut de France in facsimile).

After a morning of suspense, news of the awarding of the Nobel Prize for Literature to Czeslaw Milosz reached Hall 5 via some excited phone calls. The surprise may have been greatest for Roger W. Straus, Jr., who had Milosz's most readable book, a novel called *Issa Valley*, in his forthcoming catalogue (scheduled for February 1981 publication, but now certain to be moved up to January). It happened to be Farrar, Straus & Giroux's fourth Nobel in seven years, and the firm was sitting on world English rights. Other language rights were managed by one of the fair's smallest publishing imprints, Stockholm's Bromberg (which was already getting lots of help from Isaac Bashevis Singer's Nobel of last year). When he was head of Poland's main scientific publishing house in the early years of the Communist regime, Adam Bromberg was a close friend of Milosz, who was also still resident in Poland; they continued their friendship in exile, when Milosz went from Europe to the United States and Bromberg stayed in Sweden to start a new publishing house. Bromberg woke Milosz with a predawn phone call to inform him of the prize; after the fair Bromberg was to fly to Berkeley, California, to discuss the status of Milosz's foreign rights. Meanwhile, the Swedish publisher made it known that he was selling world rights for languages other than English, but could give *Issa Valley* only to publishers who would also agree to do the author's essays and poetry.

The major parties this year were an opener given by Scherz Verlag, which covers the German-language market from a Swiss base and—every other year—sponsors a splendid bash at which the world's publishing elite has an opportunity to catch up on each other's gossip on the eve of the fair; and what has now become the traditional Friday night reception of Germany's giant Bertelsmann Group. (Like the book fair itself, Bertelsmann's party had expanded to facilitate movement.) Several other German publishers held traditional noontime or evening affairs, such as Springer-Verlag's Friday morning at the Hessischer Hof and Lübbe's Sunday dinner at the Frankfurter Hof. Traditional American parties include Harper & Row's informal get-together on Thursday and the elegant Reader's Digest Saturday night (both designed for foreigners). The Association of American Publishers brought together its own and foreign top brass. Among other parties: "An Evening with Ken Follett" on the night before the opening of the fair.

Every other year Frankfurt presents a theme, chiefly aimed at the German public and the media. This year it was "Africa—A Continent Asserts Its Identity." (The public was admitted to the fairgrounds from 2 P.M. to 6:30 P.M. each day from October 8-12.) Just before the fair opened, a symposium on African literature held in Frankfurt's City Council heard some of Africa's leading writers. There were concurrent exhibitions of modern art from Africa, documents on African religion, a black Africa film month.

At the formal opening of the fair on October 7 the first Noma prize for African literature (a check for $3,000 representing the interest on a $100,000 endowment), sponsored by Shoichi Noma, ailing president of Tokyo's giant Kodansha, and presented by his son and vice-president Koremichi Noma, went to a Senegalese woman writing in French, Mariama Bâ. Her first novel, *Une si longue lettre*, dealing with the theme of women's emancipation in a polygamous society, had already appeared in French and German, respectively with Dakar's Nouvelles Editions Africaines and Switzerland's Edition Sven Erik Bergh; the Senegalese house was handling rights and selling them as far away as Norway (to Cappelen's Sigmund Strømme), with options out to the United States and the United Kingdom. Kodansha sponsored an evening reception at the Hessischer in honor of the prizewinner, who was present.

Back at the fairgrounds, a special building was opened for Africa: a brightly lit pavilion with a bamboo shack counter restaurant for African fast food, piped African music and, occasionally, *live* African music; a large central area for readings by authors, lectures and debates; and stands of 32 African countries representing 200 imprints, showing 2,000 books, a tribute to an industry that hardly existed 20 years ago. Nigeria alone had 33 participating houses, and *The African Book Publishing Record* distributed a special Frankfurt issue containing a who's who of Africans at the fair.

Also in that pavilion were two exhibitions: a collection of Africana from publishers the world over (3,500 titles) and "Printed and Published in Africa," a display of 2,000 titles of 180 publishers on that continent, believed to be the largest such exhibition ever mounted. There was a complete catalog, and the show was to be put on the road—to UNESCO headquarters in Paris, notably. The German book trade set up a literary rights information service it was calling Society for the Promotion of African, Asian, and Latin American Literature, with sponsorship by publishers, writers, and the university establishment, and with Protestant church financing.

Inevitably, the focus on Africa focused also on South Africa, whose stand in the center of Hall 5 had been a target of anti-apartheid protests in past years. This year, by bringing a considerable number of Africans to Frankfurt, the German book trade had provided the troops with still more energetic protest, enhanced by portable loudspeakers and formal speeches by African writers. The black Africans closed down their pavilion for a one-day boycott, also in protest against the presence of South Africa. Fair director Weidhaas, who believes that the fair should be open to everybody, felt that the black African protest was a natural development, since opposition to the existence of white South Africa is *also* part of the black African story.

Because publishers from all over the world come to Frankfurt, it is the ideal meeting place for the trade as well as for international organizations of the profession. Global entities such as Time-Life and Bertelsmann consult with their far-flung representatives. Or a publisher might meet with its counterparts for a discussion of shared problems, e.g., Germany's Klett staged its now traditional International Meeting of Educational Publishers.

Each year on the morning before the fair opens the International Group of Scientific, Technical and Medical Publishers (STM, for short), representing 137 member firms in 19 countries, holds a general assembly in a ballroom of the Intercontinental—which is no longer large enough for this no-nonsense trade-oriented affair. Publisher delegates listened to an opening statement by STM chairman Dr. Günther Hauff of Georg Thieme Verlag that blasted UNESCO for having sent STM a letter criticizing it for worrying too much about copyright protection (UNESCO termed copyright a "barrier") instead of encouraging "new reproduction technology, allowing easy and inexpensive republication." STM replied to the UNESCO bureaucrats in language they probably don't often hear: "Without the legal anchor of copyright, no inventive publishing techniques and strategies could ever be developed." Privately, UNESCO's own copyright people—who after all are responsible for managing one of the two international copyright conventions—were dismayed at the attitude of the higher-ups of their organization, who seemed ready to throw over the notion of copyright—which favors developed nations—in behalf of the world organization's majority of developing nations.

MOVES AGAINST BOOK PIRACY

The International Publishers Association (IPA) held a session of its International Committee (two delegates from each member country), also at the Intercontinental, one purpose of which was to plan the execution of resolutions voted at its May congress in Stockholm. Under president Manuel Salvat, John T. Sargent of Doubleday was elected vice-president; Propicio Machado Alves of Brazil's Libros Técnicos e Cientificos became regional vice-president for Latin America, and there are plans to elect regional vice-presidents from the other areas as well. It was agreed that a watchdog committee on piracy would be set up, financial support to be solicited from publishers so that the committee could collect case histories of book pirating as a first step toward combating such practices. A new electronic media committee would be responsible for collecting and collating data on developments in the field, while a more organized effort was to be made to bring trainees from the Third World into the offices of the leading publishing nations. On the motion of Robert E. Baensch of Springer-Verlag in New York, a task force would coordinate IPA relations with the Moscow Book Fair, although it seemed clear that many major publishers, especially in the sci-tech area, were certain to participate next September despite the talk of boycott that followed the previous fair. The task force would deal with pre-fair and fair-time incidents that had been a burden on IPA's tiny Geneva secretariat in the past. It was expected that the secretariat would be reinforced to deal with the several new tasks it had been given at the Stockholm congress.

One of the most unusual Frankfurt events was the meeting of the Motovun Group that has grown out of the annual cruise off Yugoslavia's Dalmatian coast, during which publishers involved in international projects spend a sunny week brainstorming. It was one such cruise that introduced China's National Publishing Administration to the outside world in the person of the administration's deputy director Xu Liyi. And Xu was in Frankfurt this year, a guest at the Sunday morning Motovun Group breakfast in the Frankfurt Plaza, with Wang Kuochung of Shanghai Scientific and Technical Publishers and Zhu Guangxi of China Translation and Publishing Corporation.

Motovun breakfast first-timers included representatives from Thames & Hudson, Germany's Belser, Finland's Otava, Japan's Shogakukan, joining international specialists from houses such as McGraw-Hill, Harcourt Brace Jovanovich, and Mitchell Beazley, under the sponsorship of two Yugoslav publishers, Neboja Tomasević of Yugoslav Review (Revija) and Branko Juričević of Mladost. Edward E. Booher, formerly of McGraw-Hill and now a publisher's consultant, as secretary of the Motovun Group serves as a link between Yugoslav and Chinese copublishing partners and their Western colleagues. It was announced that next year's cruise in the southern Adriatic would take place from June 21 to June 28. Xu Liyi, evoking the group's joint visit to China last April, stressed that things were "different" in China now. Friends were welcome; indeed, the Chinese were prepared to organize another international publishing delegation visit. Meanwhile, Motovun had, in Booher's words, come of age. Books copublished by and among its members would henceforth bear the phrase "A Motovun Group Book" on or near the title page, with an appropriate symbol to be designed.

A contact initiated at the IPA congress in Stockholm became a takeover on the eve of the Frankfurt fair. Under its terms France's Bordas Group, a large sci-tech and educational publisher, will absorb Dutch Elsevier's French-language publishing, which operated under the Elsevier-Sequoia logo from a Belgian base. The latter list will be phased out, eliminating the trade side, leaving the illustrated reference book line, which will be published within the bosom of Bordas in Paris.

During Frankfurt's fair week, everybody else's book fair was on sale. VAAP chairman Boris Pankin was present to talk up the next Moscow fair (September 2–8, 1981); a crew from Bologna recruited for next April's Children's Book Fair, and so did Mayor Kollek for the Jerusalem fair, which will follow Bologna; the London Book Fair, skipping a year, is next scheduled for spring 1982. As for Frankfurt itself, its next fair is scheduled for October 14–19, 1981.

INTERNATIONAL AND COMPARATIVE LIBRARIANSHIP: A CURRENT ASSESSMENT

Josephine Riss Fang

Professor, Graduate School of Library and Information Science, Simmons College, Boston, MA 02115

"Librarians, archivists, information scientists and documentalists are increasingly communicating and cooperating on a national and international level. Knowledge and information, contained both in the records of the past and in the technology of the present and future, are considered of vital concern to nations and to the world community. Professionals from all countries are attempting to cope with the volume of created information and the increasing demands for specialized and sophisticated user services on the one hand, and to supply basic needs in developing countries on the other hand." With these introductory statements the new edition of an international reference work notes the growth and development of professional organizational activities, particularly in the increase in the number of international associations from 41 in 1976 to 59 in 1980, all attempting to assist professionals to carry out their tasks in a better way.*

*Taken from Josephine R. Fang and Alice H. Songe, *International Guide to Library, Archival, and Information Science Associations*, 2nd ed. (New York: R. R. Bowker, 1980), p. vii.

The theme of the forty-sixth general conference of IFLA in Manila, August 18-23, 1980, "Global Information Exchange for Greater International Understanding," reflected this heightened international awareness. We now accept the fact that librarianship and information science are disciplines that cross national boundaries. Rapid communication tools contribute to the sharing of knowledge and information transfer worldwide.

Information exchange and cooperation in the fields of science and technology have made great progress on the international level, to a large extent with the help of UNESCO. However, the areas of economics, social sciences, literature, and other fields of the humanities have not received the same attention, although they are equally important for international cooperation and mutual understanding. Due to their professional expertise in obtaining, analyzing, and disseminating information, librarians play an important role in conducting such information exchanges at all levels of communication.

Despite tremendous growth in international library and information science activities, the discipline of international and comparative librarianship is still fairly young. Choosing from among the various definitions that can be found in the literature of the profession:

"*International Librarianship* consists of activities carried out among or between governmental or non-governmental institutions, organizations, groups or individuals of two or more nations, to promote, establish, develop, maintain and evaluate library, documentation and allied services, and librarianship and the library profession generally, in any part of the world" (J. Stephen Parker, "International Librarianship—A Reconnaissance," *Journal of Librarianship* 6 [Oct. 1974]: 219-232).

"*Comparative Librarianship* is a discipline that analyses libraries, library systems, some aspects of librarianship, or library problems in two or more national, cultural, or societal environments, in terms of socio-political, economic, cultural, ideological, and historical contexts. These analyses are made for the purpose of understanding the underlying similarities and differences, with the ultimate aim of trying to arrive at valid generalizations and principles" (J. Periam Danton, *The Dimensions of Comparative Librarianship* [Chicago: American Library Association, 1973], p. 52).

Studies in the area of international librarianship are comparatively easy to identify, since they deal with activities that invite investigation and research. Research in the more complex field of comparative librarianship includes area studies that describe and analyze a given country or region; cross-national or cross-cultural studies that compare various library systems or specific aspects in two or more countries; and case studies dealing with a specific problem in two or more countries with the goal of arriving at some solution. Comparative librarianship requires exact definitions and selection of specific research methods.

CURRICULUM DEVELOPMENTS

Librarians need to find solutions to the many problems and challenges in carrying out their work. The study of international and comparative librarianship offers an opportunity to exchange information and to find solutions through research of another country's problems. Today, this field is an integral part of library and information science education and training and not merely an elective frill. International aspects should be included in all or most library and information science courses. For instance, we cannot prepare cataloging rules without considering international developments; we cannot acquire foreign publications without knowing something of the foreign book trade and national bibliographic control. Technological advances and the creation of data bases for information transfer make international awareness and knowledge imperative. Thus, a large number of library schools offer courses in international and comparative librarianship with a variety of approaches.

One example is an outline for an area study of a country. As we know, libraries do not exist in a vacuum but have been created by society for society, and therefore information on socioeconomic, cultural, and other background data of a country is vital for the understanding and evaluation of its library system and information services.

Outline of an Area Study for a Country

Background Information
Historical, political, and economic factors (including basic statistics on area, population, etc.)

Cultural background and educational system (including literacy level)

The Library System
Brief history of development

Structure (types of libraries: national, academic and research, public, school, special; prominent libraries and any outstanding collections; library statistics; national planning)

Management of libraries (classification systems in use; access to library material; services provided; technical installations)

Education for librarianship and information science (programs and schools)

Library legislation

Professional associations (including activities and publications)

Library cooperation and international activities (networks; membership in international and regional groups; participation in projects)

The Publishing Industry and the Book Trade
Brief survey, statistics, organizations, major publishers, library–book trade relations

Bibliographic control (current and retrospective national and trade bibliographies and other acquisition tools for librarians)

Summary
Main characteristics and achievements of librarianship (including information on prominent librarians, past and present)

Development trends, particularly in relation to the information industry; areas of needed research

Selected Bibliography
Annotated list of main sources of information, including general and special reference tools and journals and any further statistical data

An area study should be flexible enough to cover specific national characteristics and developments, yet it is useful to adhere to the same structured approach for each country in order to facilitate comparative investigations.

INTERNATIONAL COOPERATION

International cooperation exists today through a number of established channels and international bodies, of which we here discuss some of the most important examples.

UNESCO

An organization that is leading in the promotion and support of modern international librarianship and that has become a major force in world library affairs since its foundation in 1946 is the United Nations Educational, Scientific, and Cultural Organization (UNESCO). One of the 13 specialized agencies of the United Nations, UNESCO is an intergovernmental agency made up of 130 member states. Its work is far-reaching and has three main functions:

To encourage international intellectual cooperation

To give operational assistance to member states and

To promote peace, human rights and mutual understanding among peoples

"Since wars begin in the minds of men, it is in the minds of men that the defences of peace must be constructed," a statement from the UNESCO Constitution, which gives direction to UNESCO's activities.

An example of UNESCO's work is the so-called Florence Agreement, adopted at a convention in Florence, Italy, in 1950, which promotes the free flow of books, publications, and educational, scientific, and cultural materials so that no discriminatory customs duties and national taxation be imposed between countries. This agreement also covers audiovisual materials. As is the procedure with UNESCO's conventions, such agreements have to be ratified by the individual member states and the ratification process is a slow one. [A special report on Protocol to the Florence Agreement appears later in this section of Part 5—*Ed*.]

Another important area of UNESCO activity is the new General Information Programme (PGI), which was created in 1976 through a merger of the Universal System for Information in Science and Technology (UNISIST) program in the science sector and the National Information Systems (NATIS) program in the communications sector, which had been created in the early 1970s to build on UNESCO's earlier work on documentation, libraries, and archives, and to foster the concept of national information systems. The two programs were combined to avoid serious overlapping of activities.

PGI is an intergovernmental program under the director of the Bureau of Studies and Programmes. It has four charges:

To promote national and regional policies and plans

To promote the establishment and application of methods, norms, and standards

To further the development of information "infrastructures" (i.e., library and information services and use of modern techniques in information transfer)

To promote education and training of information providers and users

The General Information Programme deals mainly with issues of concern to policymakers in government, libraries, information centers, or schools for professional education. It is the only such worldwide program uniting developed and developing countries and governmental and independent bodies. It provides funds for many worthwhile projects, often in collaboration with other organizations, such as the International Federation of Library Associations and Institutions (IFLA) and the International Federation for Documentation (FID). The General Information Programme promises to become a significant force in international cooperation.

Some other recent UNESCO contributions were the promotion of children's books during the International Year of the Child in 1979; promotion of book production in Africa through the Regional Centre for Book Development in Africa (CREPLA); support of children's book production in Asia as well as in Latin America; and strengthening national book production everywhere. UNESCO has a long-term program of encouraging the reading habit.

International Federation of Library Associations and Institutions (IFLA)

Founded in Edinburgh, Scotland, on September 30, 1927, this independent, nongovernmental and nonprofit organization unites about 900 national library associations, libraries, library schools, and librarians in over 100 countries, as well as a number of other institutions and individuals. The objective of IFLA is to promote international understanding, cooperation, discussion, research, and development in all fields of library activity, including bibliography, information services, and the education of personnel. This objective is achieved:

- By the operation of a central secretariat (in The Hague) and of professional units
- By the organization of conferences and meetings
- By regional development
- By fostering research, study, and publication
- By collaboration with other international organizations

The structure of IFLA is as follows:

- The IFLA Council, which is the general assembly of all members and decides on resolutions through voting
- The Executive Board, which consists of seven to nine elected members, and is the governing body
- The Professional Board of about ten elected members, which gives professional guidance.

The actual professional work of IFLA is carried out by the members in some 30 sections, which are coordinated by the eight divisions:

- Regional Activities (with three regional sections: Asia, Africa, Latin America and the Caribbean)
- Management and Technology
- Special Libraries
- General Research Libraries
- Libraries Serving the General Public
- Education and Research
- Collections and Services
- Bibliographic Control

The activities of the sections vary from those concentrating on specific types of libraries, such as national libraries, children's libraries, and science and technology libraries, to those dealing with library functions and technical activities, such as cataloging, bibliography, conservation, statistics, theory, and research. In addition, there are a number of round tables, including Editors of Library Journals and Library History.

IFLA maintains two offices, in addition to its permanent headquarters in the Netherlands.

IFLA International Office for Universal Bibliographic Control (UBC). Located at the British Library, Reference Division, in London, England, with Dorothy Anderson as director, this office works toward the realization of universal bibliographic control and as a clearinghouse for bibliographic questions. UBC is a worldwide system for the exchange of bibliographic information, the object of which is to make universally and promptly available, in a form that is internationally acceptable, basic bibliographic data on all publications issued in all countries. IFLA believes that national systems cannot be planned in isolation and that each country, in planning its own system, should bear in mind both the contributions it can receive from the rest of the world and the contributions it can make. The UBC office has an active publications program, including the quarterly journal *International Cataloguing*.

IFLA Office for International Lending. Located at the British Library, Lending Division, Boston Spa, England, with Maurice Line as director, this office acts as a clearinghouse for international loan requests and promotes international lending by improving procedures and removing barriers. For example, it issues an international loan form and publishes the *Brief Guide to Centres of International Lending and Photocopying*. This office also serves as coordinating unit for a new IFLA program, Universal Availability of Publications (UAP), which was conceived by Maurice Line and aims to make all published material universally available. The groundwork for such a project has to be done nationally. UAP is considered a logical extension of UBC. [The 1980 IFLA conference is the subject of a separate article that appears later in this section of Part 5—*Ed.*]

International Federation for Documentation/Fédération Internationale de Documentation (FID)

Founded in Brussels, Belgium, by Henri La Fontaine and Paul Otlet on September 2, 1895, this independent, nongovernmental association has 312 members including 240 institutional members of national and international bodies, and is headquartered in The Hague, Netherlands. The objective of FID is to promote, through international cooperation, research in and development of documentation, which includes, among other things, the organization, storage, retrieval, dissemination, and evaluation of information, however recorded, in the fields of science, technology, social sciences, arts, and humanities. It aims to group internationally organizations and individuals interested in the problems of documentation and to coordinate their efforts; to promote the study, organization, and practice of documentation in all its forms; and to contribute to the creation of an international network of information systems.

The program of the federation includes activities through the following committees:

Classification Committee (for Universal Decimal Classification [UDC])
Research on the Theoretical Basis of Information
Linguistics in Documentation
Information for Industry
Education and Training
Classification Research
Terminology of Information and Documentation
Patent Information and Documentation
Social Sciences Documentation
Broad System of Ordering (BSO)
Task Force for Information Users

An active publications program supports among others the following serial publications: *FID News Bulletin* (12 per year) with its quarterly insert *Newsletter on Educa-*

tion and Training Programmes; R & D Projects in Documentation and Librarianship (6 per year); and *International Forum on Information and Documentation (IFID)* (4 per year), its international journal.

RESOURCES

The definitive study and textbook in the field of international and comparative librarianship has yet to be written. But there are a number of excellent sources, both serial and monograph, that provide current and retrospective information.

Journals

The names of some of the important international periodicals are listed below; full bibliographic information is readily available from standard sources.

- *Aslib Information* (particularly its "Current Awareness" listings)
- *FID News Bulletin* (with quarterly insert *Newsletter on Education and Training Programmes*)
- *IBID* (International Bibliography, Information, Documentation)
- *IFLA Journal*
- *Focus on International and Comparative Librarianship* (Library Association)
- *Inspel: International Journal of Special Libraries*
- *International Cataloguing*
- *International Classification*
- *International Forum on Information and Documentation*
- *International Library Review*
- *Journal of Library History, Philosophy and Comparative Librarianship*
- *LEADS* (ALA International Relations Round Table)
- *Library and Information Science Abstracts (LISA)* (good international coverage)
- *Library Research: An International Journal*
- *Libri: International Library Review and Communication*
- *UNESCO Book Promotion News* (1973–   )
- *UNESCO Journal of Information Science, Librarianship and Archives Administration* (formerly *UNESCO Bulletin for Libraries*)

In addition, many general and specialized professional journals carry international items such as the June issue of the *Wilson Library Bulletin*, special issues of *Library Trends*, and others.

Other Reference Sources (Monographs and Series)

- *ALA World Encyclopedia of Library and Information Services*. Chicago: American Library Association, 1980. A comprehensive source on current library and information services developments throughout the world.
- *ALA Yearbook*, 1976–   . Includes information on current international activities.
- *Bibliographical Services throughout the World 1970-74*, by Marcelle Beaudiquez. Paris: UNESCO, 1977. A standard international reference work, updated every five years.
- *The Book Trade of the World*, ed. by S. Taubert. 3 vols. New York: R. R. Bowker, Vol. 1, 1972. Vol. 2, 1976. Vol. 3, 1980.

The Bowker Annual of Library and Book Trade Information. New York: R. R. Bowker. An extensive annual reference work of international coverage.

The Development of Special Libraries as an International Phenomenon, ed. by Johan van Halm. New York: Special Libraries Association, 1978. Discusses special libraries in countries throughout the world.

Dictionarium bibliothecarii practicum: The Librarian's Practical Dictionary in Twenty Languages, by Zoltan Pipics. 5th ed. Munich: K. G. Saur, 1971.

Encyclopedia of Library and Information Science, ed. by Allen Kent et al. Vol. 1- . New York: Marcel Dekker, 1968- . Published in intervals. Extensive articles on countries and major topics.

Europa Yearbook. 21st ed. 2 vols. Detroit, MI: Gale, 1980.

Guide to Major Libraries of the World, by C. R. Steele. New York: R. R. Bowker, 1976.

Handbook for Information Systems and Services, by Pauline Atherton. New York: Unipub, 1977.

Handbook on the International Exchange of Publications, ed. by Frans Vanwijingaerden. 4th ed. Paris: UNESCO, 1978. The standard international reference work.

International Bibliography of the Book Trade and Librarianship, 1973-1975, ed. by Helga Lengenfelder and Gitta Hausen. 11th ed. New York: K. G. Saur, 1976.

International Encyclopedia of Higher Education, ed. by Asa Knowles. 10 vols. San Francisco: Jossey-Bass, 1978.

International Guide to Library, Archival and Information Science Associations, by J. R. Fang and A. H. Songe. 2d ed. New York: R.R. Bowker, 1980. Standard reference work on national and international professional organizations.

International Literary Market Place. New York: R. R. Bowker, latest edition.

Library Association. Yearbook. London, The Association, 1965–

World Guide to Higher Education: A Comparative Survey of Systems, Degrees and Qualifications. Paris, UNESCO, 1976.

World Guide to Library Schools and Training Courses in Documentation. New ed. Paris: UNESCO, 1981 (forthcoming).

World of Learning. London: Europa Verlag. Latest edition.

World Guide to Libraries/Internationales Bibliothekshandbuch. 5th ed. by Helga Lengenfelder. Munich: K. G. Saur, 1980. Standard international directory.

In addition, there are a number of useful reference works published by UNESCO and IFLA. Some of the more recent monographs that could be used as partial texts to be supplemented by further readings are:

Barefoot Librarian: Library Developments in Southeast Asia with Special Reference to Malaysia, by D. E. K. Wijasuriya et al. Hamden, CT: Linnet Books, 1975.

Comparative and International Library Science, ed. by John F. Harvey. Metuchen, NJ: Scarecrow Press, 1977.

A Handbook of Comparative Librarianship. 2nd ed. by S. Simsova and M. A. MacKee. Hamden, CT: Linnet Books, 1975. Extensive bibliographies.

National Library and Information Services: A Handbook for Planners. London: Butterworth, 1977.

Reader in Comparative Librarianship, ed. by D. J. Fosket. Englewood, CO: Information Handling Services, 1976.

Selected References for Current Information

The *ALA Yearbook 1980* (Chicago: American Library Association, 1980) contains the following useful articles:

Anderson, Dorothy, "Universal Bibliographic Control," pp. 313-314.

Bettembourg, I., "UNESCO," pp. 311-313.

Franck, Jane P., "International Relations Round Table," pp. 178-179.

Lowrie, Jean, "International Relations," pp. 174-178.

Wijnstroom, Margreet, "IFLA," pp. 159-160.

The following articles are in the *ALA World Encyclopedia of Library and Information Services* (Chicago: American Library Association, 1980):

Baker, F. W. G. "International Council of Scientific Unions," p. 258.

Brown, Kenneth R., "International Federation for Documentation (FID)," pp. 260-261.

Eggert, Johanna, "International Organization for Standardization," p. 268.

Pellowski, Anne, "UNICEF," p. 567.

Rayward, W. Boyd, "International Library and Bibliographical Organizations," pp. 264-268.

Rhoads, James B., "International Council on Archives," pp. 259-260.

Tocatlian, Jacques, "UNESCO," pp. 564-567.

Wijnstroom, Margreet, "International Federation of Library Associations and Institutions (IFLA)," pp. 261-264.

SUMMARY AND NEW DEVELOPMENTS

The involvement of U.S. librarians in international activities is increasing at all levels. Most of the national professional associations have infrastructures with sections or round tables devoted to international interests and activities. The American Library Association, for instance, maintains an International Relations Committee, an appointed, policymaking body; an International Relations Round Table, an activity-centered elected members' group; and an International Library Education Subcommittee (appointed). All these activities are coordinated by an international relations officer.

Likewise, U.S. representatives attend international meetings and serve in international professional bodies. One example of international cooperation in the educational sector was a joint meeting of educational groups of IFLA, FID, and ICA (International Council on Archives) in Frankfurt, December 12-13, 1980. This historic first meeting of about 30 representatives of the educational sectors of the three major international organizations was held at the Deutsche Bibliothek in Frankfurt, the Federal Republic of Germany, to lay the groundwork for future cooperation. The IFLA group was headed by H.-P. Geh and Paul Kaegbein (both Federal Republic of Germany), the FID/ET by Paul Wasserman (United States), and ICA by Ammadou Bousso (Senegal). UNESCO was represented by Kenneth Roberts (PGI) and FID further by the executive secretary, Kenneth Brown. Some of the resulting resolutions provided for:

    Closer cooperation for the *Newsletter on Education and Training Programmes*

    Cooperation on the "Clearinghouse on Education and Training Materials" (Wasserman)

    General support of the IFLA project "Equivalence and Reciprocity of Professional Qualifications" (Fang)

    Exploration of subject areas of mutual interest

    Consideration of potential projects and joint seminars

    Future joint meetings, particularly through regional cooperation

    Agreement to cooperate with UNESCO's PGI and other intergovernmental organizations

    Establishment of liaison officers in each group, possibly from 1982 on

Thus, international librarianship is demonstrating its vitality and has given our profession increased challenges for the future. Further research, particularly that initiated at our library and information science schools, is needed to provide the field with a solid foundation and with the tools for meaningful growth.

IFLA: SOME HIGHLIGHTS OF THE 1980 CONFERENCE

Josephine Riss Fang

Professor, Graduate School of Library and Information Science,
Simmons College, Boston, MA 02115

    The forty-sixth general conference of the International Federation of Library Associations and Institutions (IFLA) met in Manila, the Philippines, August 18–23, 1980. For the first time in IFLA's over fifty-year history, a general conference took place outside Europe and North America and on Asian soil, reflecting the growing importance of the Asian nations and IFLA's world-embracing activities. The theme of the conference was "Development of Libraries and Information Systems: Global Information Exchange for Greater Understanding." The local sponsors were the National Library of the Philippines, the Philippine Library Association, and the UNESCO National Commission of the Philippines, with Dr. Serafin D. Quiason, national librarian, and Professor Rosa M. Vallejo from the Institute of Library Science of the University of the Philippines heading the organizing committee.

    Some 1,237 delegates from 52 countries attended approximately 150 meetings held in the Philippine International Convention Center. Ninety of the delegates were from the United States and over 500 were Philippine librarians. The current president of IFLA, Else Granheim from Norway, gave the opening address and stressed that "only through knowledge can we create a better community with more equal opportunities for all." Both President Ferdinand Marcos and First Lady Imelda Romualdez Marcos of the Philippines attended the opening session and addressed the assembly. Other welcoming speeches were given by Kenneth Roberts, representing the director-general of UNESCO, and Dr. Quiason.

Each section and division offered a variety of programs, and papers were presented on a variety of topics, ranging from conservation efforts in tropical climates to access to information in various developing countries.

Among the resulting recommendations at the end of the conference were:

To conduct a study to define the needs for education and training in the South Pacific and/or Southeast Asia

To explore the feasibility of an international library school in this area

To help developing countries in the publication of professional journals

To support research in reading habits

To create a data base of ongoing and completed research projects in developing countries

To establish, as an experiment, a West African Clearinghouse for the 14 countries of the West African subregion for interlibrary loan, resource sharing, and other forms of cooperation

To prepare packaged information in multimedia formats for nonliterate populations

To establish a Round Table on the Management of Library Associations to discuss common problems and to help in making the associations more effective

These were only a few of the formulated issues, which will be brought up again at the next conference. The regional section on Latin America and the Caribbean made strong recommendations for including Spanish as one of IFLA's working languages in order to ensure greater participation by these areas.

IFLA-RELATED MEETINGS

Two other meetings related to IFLA were held in Manila in 1980: the annual meeting of the International Association of Orientalist Librarians and the UNESCO/IFLA Pre-Conference Seminar on Library Education Programmes in Developing Countries with Special Reference to Asia, held from August 11–15, 1980, with Dr. Paul Kaegbein of the University of Cologne, the Federal Republic of Germany, as course director, and participants from many countries. A result of the seminar was the following draft resolutions, which were endorsed by the IFLA Section on Library Schools and Other Training Aspects:

That a feasibility study be conducted on the need and market for education and training of paraprofessional staff in the South Pacific and/or Southeast Asia area;

That a determination be made of the need for updating the knowledge and skills of teachers in library and information science;

That consideration be given to an international and/or regional library school;

That acceptance be given to the concept of a single educational program for librarianship and information science and the desirability of including archival studies in the programs of existing and future schools of library and information science;

That support be given to the concept of regional education programs and the teaching of the new technology in the context of developing countries;

That a follow-up seminar be arranged to review progress made in the interim period;

That IFLA and UNESCO request the United Nations University in Tokyo to conduct research and development projects and programs in information systems and services.

FUTURE IFLA CONFERENCES

The schedule for proposed future IFLA meetings is as follows:

1981: Leipzig, August 17–22. Forty-seventh General Conference and Council Meeting. Theme: "National Institutions and Professional Organizations of Librarianship."

1982: Montreal, August 22–28, Queen Elizabeth Hotel. Forty-eighth General Conference. Theme: "Networks: Various Aspects and Types."

1983: Munich. General Conference and Council Meeting.

1984: Nairobi, Kenya. General Conference (tentative).

1985: New York. General Conference and Council Meeting.

1986: Tokyo, General Conference.

One of the greatest benefits that members get from attending annual conferences is to be able to interact with so many colleagues from all over the world and share with them problems and experiences in the field of librarianship and information services. In Manila a historic event took place when two librarians from the People's Republic of China were present as guests of the national librarian. They were Ms. Sizhuang Liang from Beida University Library and Mr. Zhigang Ding from the National Library of Beijing. It is hoped that the Chinese Library Association will soon join IFLA as a member. For, as Herman Liebaers, former IFLA president, said, "IFLA can be no more than the sum of its members: It exists only by virtue of their contribution—whether moral or material—and its activity can never be a one-way affair." [For a general overview of IFLA activities, see the article "International and Comparative Librarianship" earlier in this section of Part 5—*Ed.*]

LIBRARY SERVICES IN INDIA

D. R. Kalia

Chairperson, Center for Library and Information Studies,
III-C/30 Lajpat Nagar, New Delhi 110024, India

Libraries of printed books were first established in India in the middle of the nineteenth century. Previously libraries in the royal palaces and in the traditional schools attached to temples and mosques had only manuscripts inscribed on palm leaves and handmade paper. The country's manuscript collection was among the largest in the world but access was limited to the hereditary priestly class.

Note: The data in this article are based on a nationwide survey conducted by the author during 1978 and 1979.

PUBLIC LIBRARIES

Today India has a national public library system that serves a population of 632 million (mid-1977) in an area of 3.3 million square kilometers with a density of 192 persons. The urban population constitutes 23% of the total and the rural 77%, spread over 2,643 towns and 575,000 villages, making a total of 577,643 habitations. The country is divided into 21 states and 9 union territories for purposes of administration. These are further subdivided into 401 districts and 5,027 development blocks.

The national public library system envisages a national library, three regional libraries at Madras, Bombay, and Delhi, a state central library in each state, a district central library in each district, and a central block library in each development block. Each city with a population of 100,000 and above will have its own city public library system. The district public library system will have branches and deposit stations in towns and villages.

Since independence in 1947, a national library at Calcutta and two regional libraries at Madras and Bombay have been established. Today, 15 states out of 21 (71%) have state central libraries; 291 out of 401 districts (73%) have district central libraries; 1,798 development blocks out of 5,027 blocks (36%) have block libraries; 41,828 villages out of 575,936 (7%) have village libraries; and 1,280 towns out of 2,643 (48%) have town libraries. Of the 29 metropolitan cities that have a population of 400,000 and above, only four (14%)—Madras, Hyderabad, Bombay, and Delhi—have city public library systems with central libraries, branches, and deposit stations. Delhi has four bookmobiles, each with a carrying capacity of 3,000 volumes. It is estimated that only about 20% of the literate population of India has access to public library service.

LIBRARY LEGISLATION

Under the Indian constitution provision of public library service is the responsibility of the state and union territory governments. The central government can only extend financial support to them. In order to channel aid the central government established the Raja Ram Mohum Roy Library Foundation in 1972. It spends about 5 million rupees a year in grants to district, block, and village libraries.

In 1979, the ministry of education in the Department of Culture established a library section under the charge of an undersecretary to promote development of public libraries in India. Of 21 states, 13 have full-time qualified librarians as state officers to administer public library service in their respective states. Of the 9 union territories, 3 have such officers.

Madras State, now called Tamil Nadu, proved to be the most progressive in adopting library legislation as early as 1948. A statutory library authority was constituted for the capital city of Madras and for each district. Because the municipal authorities were ineffective, they were divested of the responsibility to provide public library service. A library tax was levied on property. Hyderabad State (now defunct) adopted similar legislation in 1955; Andhra Pradesh, in 1960; Mysore (now called Karnataka), in 1965; Maharashtra, in 1967; and West Bengal, in 1979.

Under the Karnataka State Public Libraries Act, a tax is levied on commodities, vehicles, one's profession, and land. The act calls for a library authority not only for the capital city of Bangalore but also for each city with a population of 100 thousand and above. In Karnataka, public library personnel are paid by state funds, thereby relieving the city and district library authorities of this financial burden.

PER CAPITA EXPENDITURES

During 1978-1979, India spent 120 million rupees, or about 50 paise per literate person, on public library service. It is estimated that public libraries presently have 58 million volumes for a literate population of 253 million, or about one book for every four persons. They add about 3 million volumes to their collections annually, which means that one volume is being added for every nine persons. The national library in Calcutta has 2 million volumes and the two regional libraries in Madras and Bombay have 300,000 volumes. On average, each state central library has 50,000 volumes; a district central library, 10,000 volumes; a block central library, 1,000 volumes; and a village library, 500 volumes.

With a few exceptions, public libraries have not received adequate attention from the state governments. State governments lack political will and commitment to legislate and impose library taxes, without which public library service cannot be universalized.

ACADEMIC AND SCHOOL LIBRARIES

India has (as of January 1, 1980) the largest number of educational institutions in the world. There are 621,500 schools (grades 1-12), out of which 477,000 (77%) are elementary schools (grades 1-5), 98,500 (16%) are secondary schools (grades 6-8), and 46,000 (7%) are higher secondary schools (grades 9-12). There are 3,667 colleges for general education, 3,276 colleges for professional education, and 1,405 other colleges, making a total of 8,348 colleges. All of these institutions offer programs of study varying from three to five years for undergraduates and two years for graduates. In addition, there are 88 traditional universities, 20 agricultural universities, and 16 other university-level institutions, making a total of 124.

When India gained its independence in 1947, only 15% of the population could read or write. In 1980, out of a total population of 632 million, 40% (or 253 million) are literate; 100 million are students (5 million in institutions of higher learning), 3 million are teachers, and 1.4 million are scientists and technicians.

ACADEMIC LIBRARIES

As of January 1, 1980, each of the 124 universities and 8,348 colleges in India has its own library. Additionally, some of the universities have departmental libraries, which may or may not be part of the central library complex. In 1953 the University Grants Commission was established to oversee the development and financing of university and college libraries. Since then over 50 universities have been provided with modern library buildings, some of which are centrally air conditioned.

As of January 1, 1980, the total number of volumes in the collections of all of the university and college libraries in India was 450 million volumes, or 9 volumes per student (35 volumes is considered desirable). (Book collections of university libraries vary between 50,000 and 600,000 volumes and those of college libraries between 10,000 and 50,000 volumes.) Annually about 10 million books are added to their collections, giving an average of one book per 3 students (2 books per student is considered desirable). During the year 1978-1979, India spent Rs. 3,300 million on higher education, out of which 155 million, or 5%, was spent on university and college libraries (10% is considered desirable).

SCHOOL LIBRARIES

As is the case in many other countries, little attention has been paid to the development of school libraries in India. There is no national or state agency to promote and finance school libraries. At present, although all of the higher secondary schools in India do have central libraries, other secondary schools only have class libraries, and elementary schools have no libraries whatsoever.

As of January 1, 1980, of the 46,000 libraries attached to higher secondary schools in India, about 20% (8,600) are managed by professionally qualified librarians; the remaining 80% are managed by schoolteachers with no library training.

The total number of volumes in the book collections of all secondary and higher secondary schools is 67 million volumes for use by 27 million students, giving an average of 2.5 volumes per student. (The average size of the higher secondary school library collection varies between 1,000 and 10,000 volumes and that of other secondary schools between 500 and 2,000 volumes.)

The total expenditure on Indian higher secondary schools during 1979–1980 was approximately Rs. 4,950 million, out of which only 100 million, or 2%, was spent on library services (5% is considered desirable). Expenditures on other secondary school libraries on the average does not exceed Rs. 500 per school, and there are no expenditures at all on library services in the elementary schools.

SPECIAL LIBRARIES

About 1,500 special libraries are in the country today, excluding those attached to educational institutions. These may be classified into the following: agricultural research libraries; art and cultural research libraries; education research and training libraries; law libraries; medical research libraries; and science and technology research libraries. Most of the special libraries are attached to departments of the Indian government, such as the Department of Atomic Energy, the Department of Space, the Department of Science and Technology, the Department of Electronics, the Council of Scientific and Industrial Research, the Defense Research and Development Organization, the Indian Council of Agricultural Research, or the Indian Council of Medical Research. Similarly, each department of each of the state governments maintains a research library for use by its officers. There are also about 300 libraries attached to private companies, and many learned societies maintain their own libraries.

READING MATERIAL

India is the seventh largest producer of books in the world, ranks third in the production of English-language titles (after the United States and the United Kingdom), and has developed a foreign market mainly for its publications in English. During 1978–1979, India's book exports were valued at Rs. 50 million.

Since English was the official language, as well as the medium of instruction at the university level under British rule, the development of modern Indian languages did not receive much attention until after independence was gained in 1947. Today, about 30,000 titles are being published in 15 regional languages (about 10,000 of which are in English). Also published are about 15,000 periodicals (3,000 of which are in English), with a total circulation of 40 million copies. A library can acquire about 10,000 new titles in modern Indian languages each year and 5,000 in English.

Unfortunately, titles in the modern Indian languages do not compare favorably with the English-language titles in terms of subject coverage. Furthermore, India continues to depend upon U. S. and British books for higher education and research, importing Rs. 100 million worth of books annually. The import of books is facilitated by the fact that India does not impose any restriction on the import of books, nor does it levy any import duty or sales tax (value added tax) on them. In fact, publishers are given a rebate on income tax by way of incentive.

NATIONAL INFORMATION SYSTEM AND AUTOMATION

In order to interlink and coordinate the large number of information sources, systems, and services in India into an integrated and effective network, the government of India has recently approved the program of National Information Systems for Science and Technology (NISSAT) as part of UNISIST (International System of Information), along with a national information policy for guidance. Basically, it is a network concept and, as such, centralized facilities are not contemplated except in a few specific areas. The major instruments for developing information centers are discipline- and project-oriented centers and regional information centers, which are multidisciplinary in nature. In addition, there would be certain centralized facilities for document supply, on-line information retrieval, and a data base on current research. So far six such centers have been established in addition to three computer-based national information centers, and about a half dozen libraries in the country have undertaken computerization of their catalogs.

LIBRARY EDUCATION AND PERSONNEL

Today there are 42 library schools in India, the second largest number in any country after the United States and India has about 30,000 qualified librarians. All of the schools offer one year bachelor's degree programs, ten have master's degree programs (one year after BLS), and nine enroll students for the Ph.D. degree. Delhi University Library School began offering the M.Phil. degree in library science as a post-MLS program in 1979. About a dozen women's polytechnical institutes conduct two-year programs leading to a diploma for undergraduates, and state library associations offer 6- to 12-month certificate programs. The total annual output of trained librarians is about 2,500.

PROTOCOL TO THE FLORENCE AGREEMENT

Robert W. Frase

Executive Director,
American National Standards Committee Z39

As one of the last acts of his administration, President Carter submitted a message to the Senate requesting approval of the Protocol to the Florence Agreement (Agreement on the Importation of Educational, Scientific, and Cultural Materials). The president's message, a supporting letter from the secretary of state, and the text of the protocol are contained in Senate Treaty Document No. 97-2, Ninety-seventh Congress, first Session. The text of the president's message reads as follows:

> With a view to receiving the advice and consent of the Senate to ratification, I transmit herewith the Protocol to the Agreement on the Importation of Educational, Scientific,

and Cultural Materials, adopted at Nairobi, Kenya, on November 26, 1976, and opened for signature at the United Nations on March 1, 1977. I also transmit for the information of the Senate, the report of the Department of State with respect to the Protocol.

The Protocol amends and expands the coverage of the Agreement on the Importation of Educational, Scientific, and Cultural Materials, which was adopted at Florence in July 1950, opened for signature on November 22, 1950, and entered into force for the United States on November 2, 1966. The purpose of the original Agreement was to facilitate the international flow of educational, scientific, and cultural materials, and generally the exchange of ideas, through the extension of duty-free treatment to a range of such educational, scientific, and cultural materials. The present Protocol substantially broadens the list of eligible products, including those for the advancement of the blind and other handicapped persons.

Ratification of the Protocol is expected to have important beneficial effects on the United States exports of products covered by the Agreement. It will also result in important benefits for the blind and handicapped in this country. I recommend, therefore, that the Senate give early and favorable consideration to the Protocol and advise and consent to its ratification.

The supporting letter to the president from the secretary of state discusses the provisions of the protocol including his recommendations with respect to several optional provisions.

OPTIONAL PROVISIONS

The optional provisions recommended by the secretary of state are as follows:

Part II—Internal Taxes

Countries adhering to this option agree not to levy any internal taxes or charges on certain materials including books and publications assigned to libraries. For the United States, this would bind only the federal government, which does not levy sales taxes in any case.

Part III—Export Taxes

Countries adhering to this option agree not to levy any export taxes on materials covered by any of the provisions of the protocol or the basic agreement.

Part IV—Provision of Foreign Exchange

Countries adhering to this option agree to provide the necessary licenses and/or foreign exchange for the importation of books and publications consigned to libraries, books adopted or recommended as higher education textbooks, books in foreign languages, and auditory and visual materials of an educational, scientific, or cultural nature imported by organizations approved by the importing country. Since the United States does not impose import licenses or limit foreign exchange, this would not change the present status of imports into the United States, but if adopted by other countries it might increase the exports of U.S. materials.

Annex A—Books, Publications and Documents liberalizes the present Annex A in the basic agreement, extending and refining the definition of books.

Annex B—Works of Art also liberalizes the provisions of the basic agreement.

Annex C1—Visual and Auditory Materials rescinds the previous requirements contained in the agreement that the items covered be of an educational, scientific, and cultural character, and that they be assigned to approved institutions. Thus, films, sound recordings, filmstrips, and slides would enter duty free under the agreement even if they were being imported for commercial purposes. Beyond the expansion resulting from the elimination of the requirements just cited, several additional categories of visual and auditory materials are added, especially microforms.

Annex E—Articles for the Blind and Other Handicapped extends the duty-free import of materials for the blind to materials specifically designed for the handicapped, provided that equivalent articles are not being manufactured in the importing country.

There are several optional provisions that the United States does not intend to adopt, namely Annex F—Sports Equipment; Annex G—Musical Instruments and Musical Equipment; and Annex H—Materials and Machines Used for the Production of Books, Publications, and Documents.

LEGISLATIVE TIMETABLE

The next step in the legislative process will be for the Senate Committee on Foreign Relations to hold hearings on whether the Senate should give its advice and consent to the protocol as an international treaty. If the Senate approves the protocol, the secretary of state has indicated that the protocol would not be deposited with the secretary-general of the United Nations and come into force in the United States until implementing legislation making the necessary changes in U.S. tariff and other laws has been approved by both houses of Congress and signed by the president.

International Statistics

U.S. BOOK EXPORTS AND IMPORTS AND INTERNATIONAL TITLE OUTPUT

Chandler B. Grannis
Contributing Editor, *Publishers Weekly*

A 1979 increase of 18.5% in the dollar value of recorded exports of books from the United States and a 15.7% increase in the dollar value of book imports, compared with 1978, are reported by the U.S. Department of Commerce, Bureau of the Census. The numbers of copies of books exported, however, increased only 6.9%, an obvious reflection of price rises. Total copies of books imported rose moderately, less than did the dollar values. (See Tables 1 and 2.)

The importance of the Canadian market is once again evident. In 1979 the dollar value of reported exports to Canada was 40.5% of all the recorded U.S. book exports, in dollars. This is a small increase from the 1978 percentage [see *Bowker Annual, 1979*, pp. 510–514].

Frustrating, however, to anyone looking for complete or nearly complete export-import data is that shipments valued below $250 are omitted, along with "low-valued exports by mail [and] low-valued and nondutiable imports by mail," to quote a footnote in the Department of Commerce report. This restriction obviously leaves out a significant amount of the book industry's foreign trade—at least 10%, some book trade economists believe. But worse is to come. According to William S. Lofquist, editor of *Printing & Publishing* (published quarterly by the Department of Commerce, Bureau of Industrial Economics), this frustration will be accentuated in the data now being accumulated for 1980. Under a new Bureau of the Census decision, the starting point for recording exports and imports has been raised to $500, effective in April 1980—not in January!

Census people, Lofquist tells *PW*, claim that the $500 starting point will leave out no more than 5% of total U.S. world trade; but this is an average, and will not state the realities of any one commodity, he observes.

Another problem with the book data is the grouping of over half the book exports under the single title, "Books, Not Elsewhere Classified," and the lumping of 80% of book imports under the equally uniformative heading "Other Books." These categories cry out for reexamination; they are hopelessly outdated.

In both areas noted here, strongly worded comments addressed to appropriate bureaus by book industry leaders and economic authorities would be necessary if useful

Note: Reprinted from *Publishers Weekly*, September 26, 1980, where the article was entitled "U.S. Export-Import Figures and International Title Output."

Editor's Note: For average prices of British, German, and Latin American books, see "Prices of U.S. and Foreign Published Materials" in the Book Trade Research and Statistics section of Part 4.

TABLE 1 U.S. BOOK EXPORTS 1977–1979
Shipments Valued at $250 or More ONLY

	TO ALL COUNTRIES: Dollar Values				TO CANADA ONLY: Dollar Values				TO ALL COUNTRIES: Units			
	1977	1978	1979	% Change 1978/79	1977	1978	1979		1977	1978	1979	% Change 1978/79
Bibles, Testaments & Other Religious Books (2703020)	$18,385,933	$20,728,789	$23,943,939	+15.5	$6,550,579	$6,313,640	$6,399,153		39,731,193	42,153,722	39,090,837	−7.3
Dictionaries & Thesauruses (2703040)	6,123,398	3,965,864	5,735,680	+44.6	1,203,844	914,692	1,273,275		1,749,640	1,040,744	1,562,092	+50.1
Encyclopedias (2703060)	24,586,694	32,294,083	29,878,607	−7.5	5,405,254	6,231,693	9,199,365		8,047,975	9,875,858	6,840,325	−30.8
Textbooks, Workbooks & Standardized Tests (2703070)	72,060,134	70,297,302	83,550,838	+18.9	39,135,076	33,387,418	38,064,696		—	—	—	—
Technical Scientific & Professional Books (2703080)	45,302,922	49,479,329	51,577,922	+4.2	12,959,201	9,843,843	12,385,527		16,173,862	16,024,867	14,846,886	−7.4
Books Not Elsewhere Classified & Pamphlets (2704000)	142,397,340	187,450,445	237,891,882	+26.9	79,221,421	87,244,510	107,881,787		34,975,663	157,759,062	180,163,203	+14.2
Children's Picture & Painting Books (7375200)	5,296,324	6,404,411	6,666,452	+4.1	4,511,016	2,562,161	2,914,796		16,340,550	—	—	—
Total Domestic Merchandise, Omitting Shipments Under $250	$314,152,745	$370,620,223	$439,245,220	+18.5	$148,988,391	$148,597,956	$178,118,599		—	—	—	+6.9

SOURCE: Extracted from U.S. Department of Commerce quarterly, *Printing and Publishing,* issues of April 1977, 1978, 1979; hitherto unpublished data supplied to *PW* by *P&P* editors.

TABLE 2 U.S. BOOK IMPORTS 1977–1979
Shipments Valued at $250 or More ONLY

	Dollar Values				Units			
	1977	1978	1979	% Change 1978/79	1977	1978	1979	% Change 1978/79
Bibles and Prayerbooks (2702520)	$ 8,490,189	$ 8,781,188	$ 6,082,482	−30.7	7,274,177	3,995,295	3,388,872	−15.3
Books, Foreign Language (2702540)	22,170,970	25,177,094	25,456,683	+ 1.1	14,832,412	14,507,863	17,373,156	+19.7
Books Not Specially Provided For, wholly or in part the work of an author who is a U.S. national or domiciliary (2701560)	3,799,617	4,678,542	3,454,528	− 26.2	2,694,209	2,244,604	1,228,169	−45.3
Other Books (2702580)	132,284,454	191,808,521	229,713,246	+19.8	117,836,144	159,326,315	183,092,783	+14.9
Toy Books and Coloring Books (7375200)	1,735,420	1,880,580	3,978,548	+111.6	—	—	—	—
Total Imports, Omitting Shipments Under $250	$168,480,630	$232,325,925	$268,685,497	+ 15.7	—	—	—	—

TABLE 3 TITLE OUTPUT, PRINCIPAL BOOK-PRODUCING COUNTRIES

	1975	1976	1977		1975	1976	1977
AFRICA				**EUROPE**			
Egypt	—	1,486	—	Austria	5,636	6,336	6,800
Nigeria	1,324	—	—	Belgium	5,848	6,414	5,964
				Bulgaria	3,669	3,813	4,088
NORTH AMERICA				Czechoslovakia	10,372	9,457	9,568
Canada	6,735	6,241	7,878	Denmark	7,068	6,783	8,021
Cuba	851	726	1,039	Finland	4,558	4,589	3,679
Mexico	5,822	4,851	—	France	—	29,371	31,673
U.S.A.*	85,287	84,542	87,780	Germany (E.)	5,800	5,792	5,844
				Germany (W.)	40,616	44,477	48,736
SOUTH AMERICA				Greece	2,613	3,935	4,981
Argentina	5,141	6,674	5,285	Hungary	8,603	9,393	9,048
Brazil	—	12,296	—	Italy	9,187	9,463	10,116
Colombia	1,272	—	—	Netherlands	12,028	12,557	13,111
Peru	1,090	925	910	Norway	4,855	5,723	4,823
				Poland	10,277	11,418	11,552
ASIA				Portugal	5,943	5,668	6,122
Burma	—	1,164	—	Romania	7,860	6,556	7,218
Hong Kong	880	1,494	1,735	Spain	23,527	24,584	24,896
India	12,708	15,802	12,885	Sweden	9,012	7,988	6,009
Indonesia	2,187	2,667	2,265	Switzerland	9,928	9,989	9,894
Iraq	595	1,588	1,758	United Kingdom	35,526	34,340	36,196
Israel	1,907	—	2,214	Yugoslavia	11,239	9,054	10,418
Japan	34,490	36,066	40,905				
Rep. Korea	10,921	13,334	13,081	**OCEANIA**			
Malaysia	1,445	1,302	1,341	Australia	1,761	2,325	3,077
Pakistan	1,143	1,081	1,331	New Zealand	1,887	1,835	1,939
Philippines	2,247	1,609	1,753				
Singapore	577	1,203	1,207	**U.S.S.R.**	**78,697**	**84,304**	**85,395**
Sri Lanka	1,153	1,140	1,201	Byeloruss S.S.R.	2,941	2,489	2,330
Thailand	2,419	2,578	3,390	Ukraine S.S.R.	8,731	9,110	8,430
Turkey	—	6,320	6,830				

SOURCES: UNESCO Statistical Yearbook 1978, published 1980 (Unipub, N.Y.); R.R. Bowker Co. data services; University Microfilms Int'l.; G.P.O. *Includes books and pamphlets issued through U.S. Government Printing Office (in 1975, 15,750; in 1976, 16,931; in 1977, estimated 15,000); also university theses (in 1975, 31,478; in 1976, 34,709; in 1977, estimated 31,000). *Not included in the U.S. figures are publications of state and local governments, publications of numerous institutions, and many reports, proceedings, lab manuals and workbooks.

changes were to be initiated, let alone adopted. But there are those in government, Lofquist points out, who would welcome such comments.

Space does not permit comment on the UNESCO figures shown here in Table 3, or on certain data that UNESCO does *not* provide. Let it be observed, however, that the title output reports omit some major publishing countries, notably China, Taiwan, and South Africa.

BRITISH BOOK PRODUCTION, 1980

In 1980 publishers in Britain issued a total of 48,158 titles, of which 37,382 were new books, and 10,776 reprints and new editions. The output of new books and new editions according to category is given in detail in Table 1. The figures have been compiled from the booklists that have appeared week by week in *The Bookseller*.

This record total represents an advance of 6,218 titles—almost 15 percent—on last year's previous record total of 41,940 (Table 2).

There is no easy explanation for this huge leap. Last year it was believed that catching up with 1978 printing delays was a contributory factor: this solution is scarcely tenable this year. Last year there was indeed an increase in the number of English-language imported books handled through British distributors: this factor recurs this year—but certainly not sufficiently to account for over 6,000 titles.

The recorded output over several years of 10 randomly chosen British trade publishers (shown in Table 3) hardly suggests a title explosion. Nevertheless, there are now over 10,000 publishers' names recorded in *British Books in Print*. It would therefore seem a probability that among those 10,000—large, medium, and pretty small—are a substantial number who have, judiciously or otherwise, decided that during a difficult time of falling print runs and sales per title the only way to maintain turnover and contribute to overheads is to increase the number of titles issued.

Given so large a leap, all the categories in Table 4 show increases. Fiction, up last year by 172 titles, is increased this year by 594 titles or 13 percent to a total of 5,145; children's books, up last year by 204, have risen by 271 titles or 8.5 percent to 3,485.

Note: Adapted from *The Bookseller* (12 Dyott St., London WC1A 1DF, England), January 3, 1981, where the article was entitled "UK Publishers' Output Leaps Again."

TABLE 1 BOOK TITLE OUTPUT, 1980

Classification	December, 1980 Total	Reprints and New Editions	Trans.	Limited Editions	January–December, 1980 Total	Reprints and New Editions	Trans.	Limited Editions
Aeronautics	8	1	—	—	194	32	4	—
Agriculture and forestry	19	4	—	—	503	120	6	—
Architecture	23	2	1	—	424	71	6	2
Art	119	9	1	2	1,408	199	37	8
Astronomy	10	3	—	—	154	37	7	—
Bibliography and library economy	48	12	—	—	804	138	—	3
Biography	65	15	3	1	1,360	362	56	3
Chemistry and physics	80	13	11	—	824	150	27	—
Children's books	141	40	2	—	3,485	604	114	2
Commerce	122	29	1	—	1,440	375	5	—
Customs, costumes, folklore	10	2	1	—	148	48	23	1
Domestic science	61	32	—	—	667	156	2	—
Education	70	9	—	—	1,258	208	2	1
Engineering	137	22	4	—	1,594	379	27	1
Entertainment	40	9	—	—	641	113	19	1
Fiction	250	132	9	—	5,145	2,074	161	10
General	42	7	—	—	489	87	10	—
Geography and archaeology	25	5	1	—	413	113	10	1
Geology and meteorology	17	1	—	—	333	43	2	—
History	138	17	2	—	1,587	357	50	2
Humour	7	—	—	—	158	30	—	—
Industry	44	4	—	—	688	139	8	—
Language	50	6	—	—	626	112	6	1
Law and public administration	114	20	—	—	1,548	347	11	—
Literature	118	26	7	—	1,185	248	70	5
Mathematics	111	26	10	—	800	175	27	—
Medical science	286	53	2	—	3,323	633	27	—
Military science	2	—	1	—	151	69	3	—
Music	54	7	3	—	444	102	12	1

BRITISH BOOK PRODUCTION, 1980 / 389

TABLE 1 BOOK TITLE OUTPUT, 1980 (cont.)

Classification	December, 1980 Total	December, 1980 Reprints and New Editions	December, 1980 Trans.	December, 1980 Limited Editions	January–December, 1980 Total	January–December, 1980 Reprints and New Editions	January–December, 1980 Trans.	January–December, 1980 Limited Editions
Natural sciences	87	14	4	—	1,278	181	14	4
Occultism	15	2	—	—	258	38	9	—
Philosophy	28	6	2	—	490	144	43	—
Photography	27	3	1	—	232	28	5	—
Plays	13	3	1	—	325	95	35	1
Poetry	51	6	6	6	786	80	54	60
Political science and economy	362	89	—	—	4,269	1,009	89	—
Psychology	81	15	3	—	807	143	4	—
Religion and theology	82	17	12	1	1,725	302	129	1
School textbooks	164	33	2	—	2,317	357	5	—
Science, general	15	2	—	—	104	19	1	—
Sociology	68	12	4	—	1,195	177	21	—
Sports and outdoor games	28	8	—	—	613	132	10	—
Stockbreeding	10	3	—	—	372	88	4	—
Trade	36	8	1	—	631	139	4	—
Travel and guidebooks	46	21	—	—	716	278	15	4
Wireless and television	19	4	—	—	246	45	4	—
Total	3,343	752	95	10	48,158	10,776	1,178	112

Note: This table shows the books recorded in December and the total for January–December with the numbers of new editions, translations and limited editions.

TABLE 2 GROWTH IN TITLE OUTPUT, 1947–1980

Year	Total	Reprints and New Editions
1947	13,046	2,441
1948	14,686	3,924
1949	17,034	5,110
1950	17,072	5,334
1951	18,066	4,938
1952	18,741	5,428
1953	18,257	5,523
1954	18,188	4,846
1955	19,962	5,770
1956	19,107	5,302
1957	20,719	5,921
1958	22,143	5,971
1959	20,690	5,522
1960	23,783	4,989
1961	24,893	6,406
1962	25,079	6,104
1963	26,023	5,656
1964	26,154	5,260
1965	26,358	5,313
1966	28,883	5,919
1967	29,619	7,060
1968	31,470	8,778
1969	32,393	9,106
1970	33,489	9,977
1971	32,538	8,975
1972	33,140	8,486
1973	35,254	9,556
1974	32,194	7,852
1975	35,608	8,361
1976	34,434	8,227
1977	36,322	8,638
1978	38,766	9,236
1979	41,940	9,086
1980	48,158	10,776

TABLE 3 BOOK TITLE OUTPUT, BY PUBLISHER, 1969, 1974, 1979, AND 1980

Publisher	1980 New Books	1980 New Editions	1980 Total	1979 New Books	1979 New Editions	1979 Total	1974 New Books	1974 New Editions	1974 Total	1969 New Books	1969 New Editions	1969 Total
Blackwell Scientific	62	35	97	32	29	61	22	13	35	34	19	53
Cape	78	3	81	80	9	89	95	11	106	121	27	148
Collins	339	112	451	393	67	460	480	234	714	324	139	463
Constable	45	9	54	39	5	44	53	5	58	46	1	47
Deutsch	91	6	97	96	2	98	90	5	95	78	13	91
Faber	124	40	164	138	61	199	142	63	205	240	89	329
M. Joseph	86	4	90	83	6	89	89	16	105	96	10	106
OUP	673	299	972	480	241	721	429	162	591	548	239	787
Routledge	227	51	278	230	39	269	168	40	208	273	46	319
Thames & Hudson	104	31	135	110	16	126	117	7	124	122	17	139
Total	1,829	590	2,419	1,681	475	2,156	1,685	556	2,241	1,882	600	2,482

TABLE 4 COMPARISON OF BOOK PRODUCTION BY SUBJECT, 1979 AND 1980

	1979	1980	+ or −
Art	1,226	1,408	+182
Biography	1,236	1,360	+124
Chemistry and physics	684	824	+140
Children's books	3,214	3,485	+271
Commerce	1,073	1,440	+367
Education	1,024	1,258	+234
Engineering	1,334	1,594	+260
Fiction	4,551	5,145	+594
History	1,421	1,587	+166
Industry	488	688	+200
Law and public administration	1,404	1,548	+144
Literature	1,161	1,185	+24
Medical science	2,510	3,323	+813
Natural sciences	1,157	1,278	+121
Political science	3,364	4,269	+905
Religion	1,509	1,725	+216
School textbooks	2,144	2,317	+173
Sociology	964	1,195	+231
Travel and guidebooks	674	716	+42

Part 6
Reference Information

Bibliographies

THE LIBRARIAN'S BOOKSHELF

Carol S. Nielsen
*Former Library Science Librarian,
University of North Carolina, Chapel Hill*

This bibliography is intended as a buying and reading guide for individual librarians and library collections. Some of the titles listed are core titles that any staff development collection might contain, others may be of more current interest only. Bibliographic tools that most libraries are likely to have for day-to-day operations have been excluded from this list.

BOOKS

General Works

The ALA Yearbook: A Review of Library Events, 1979. Chicago: American Library Association, 1980. $44.

American Library Association. Headquarters Library. *A.L.A. Publications Checklist, 1979.* Chicago, 1980. $4.50.

American Library Directory, 1980. 33rd ed. New York: R. R. Bowker, 1980. $55.63.

American Library Laws. 4th ed. Chicago: American Library Association, 1973. $40. 1st supplement, 1973-1974. 1975. $10. 2nd supplement, 1975-1976. 1977. $12.50. 3rd supplement, 1977-1979. 1980. $13.50.

Association for Educational Communications and Technology. Task Force on Definition and Technology. *Educational Technology: A Glossary of Terms.* Washington, DC: AECT, 1979. $21.

A Biographical Directory of Librarians in the United States and Canada. 5th ed. Chicago: American Library Association, 1970. $45.

Bowker Annual of Library and Book Trade Information 1980. 25th ed. New York: R. R. Bowker, 1980. $29.95.

Cole, John Y. *For Congress and the Nation: A Chronological History of the Library of Congress.* Washington, DC: U.S. Govt. Printing Office, 1979. $8.

Directory of Special Libraries and Information Centers. 5th ed. Detroit: Gale Research Co., 1979. Vols. 1-3. Vol. 1 $110; Vol. 2 $86; Vol. 3 $96.

Encyclopedia of Library and Information Science. New York: Marcel Dekker, 1968-1979. Vols. 1-29. $55 per vol.

Estabrook, Leigh, ed. *Libraries in Post-Industrial Society.* Phoenix, AZ: Oryx Press, 1977. $13.95.

Fang, Josephine Riss, and Songe, Alice H. *International Guide to Library, Archival, and Information Science Associations.* New York: R. R. Bowker, 1980. $35.

Harris, Michael, ed. *Advances in Librarianship.* New York: Academic Press, 1970- . Vol. 10, 1980. $23.

Harrod, L. M., comp. *The Librarians' Glossary and Reference Book.* 4th rev. ed. Boulder, CO: Westview, 1977. $30.

Shera, Jesse H. *An Introduction to Library Science: Basic Elements of Library Services.* Littleton, CO: Libraries Unlimited, 1976. $10.

———. Bobinski, George, and Wynar, Bohdan, eds. *Dictionary of American Library Biography*. Littleton, CO: Libraries Unlimited, 1977. $65.

Sherman, Steve. *ABC's of Library Promotion*. 2nd ed. Metuchen, NJ: Scarecrow Press, 1980. $12.

Vaillancourt, Pauline M. *International Directory of Acronyms in Library, Information and Computer Sciences*. New York: R. R. Bowker, 1980. $45.

Weibel, Kathleen, and Heim, Kathleen M. *The Role of Women in Librarianship 1876-1976: The Entry, Advancement, and Struggle for Equalization in One Profession*. Phoenix, AZ: Oryx Press, 1979. $14.95.

Administration

Breivik, Patricia, and Gibson, E. Burr. *Funding Alternatives for Libraries*. Chicago: American Library Association, 1979. $9.95.

Current Concepts in Library Management. Littleton, CO: Libraries Unlimited, 1979. $18.50.

Kemper, Robert E., and Ostrander, Richard E. *Directorship by Objectives*. Littleton, CO: Libraries Unlimited, 1977. $8.

Lancaster, F. W. *The Measurement and Evaluation of Library Services*. Washington, DC: Information Resources Press, 1977. $27.50.

Lee, Sul H., ed. *Library Budgeting: Critical Challenge for the Future*. Ann Arbor, MI: Pierian Press, 1977. $10.

———. *Emerging Trends in Library Organization: What Influences Change*. Ann Arbor, MI: Pierian Press, 1978. $11.95.

Personnel Manual: An Outline for Libraries. Chicago: American Library Association, 1977. $3.

Prentice, Ann E. *Strategies for Survival: Library Financial Management Today*. Library Journal Special Report No. 7. New York: R. R. Bowker, 1978. $5.

Archives, Conservation, and Manuscripts

Baker, John P., and Soroka, Marguerite C. *Library Conservation: Preservation in Perspective*. Stroudsburg, PA: Dowden, Hutchinson, & Ross, 1978. $45.

Brichford, Maynard J. *Appraisal and Accessioning*. SAA Basic Manual Series. Chicago: Society of American Archivists, 1977. $3 for members, $4 for nonmembers.

College and University Archives: Selected Readings. Chicago: Society of American Archivists, 1979. $11.

Falco, Nicholas. *Manual for the Organization of Manuscripts*. New York: Queensborough Public Library, 1978. $7.

Fleckner, John A. *Surveys*. SAA Basic Manual Series. Chicago: Society of American Archivists, 1977. $3 for members, $4 for nonmembers.

Gracy, David B., II. *Arrangement and Description*. SAA Basic Manual Series. Chicago: Society of American Archivists, 1977. $3 for members, $4 for nonmembers.

Holbert, Sue E. *Reference and Access*. SAA Basic Manual Series. Chicago: Society of American Archivists, 1977. $3 for members, $4 for nonmembers.

Kemp, Edward C. *Manuscript Solicitation for Libraries, Special Collections, Museums, and Archives*. Littleton, CO: Libraries Unlimited, 1978. $18.50.

McWilliams, Jerry. *The Preservation and Restoration of Sound Recordings*. Nashville, TN: American Association for State and Local History, 1979. $9.95.

Morrow, Carolyn Clark. *A Conservation Bibliography for Librarians, Archivists, and Administrators*. Troy, NY: Whitston Publishing Co., 1979. $18.50.

Swartzburg, Susan. *Preserving Library Materials: A Manual*. Metuchen, NJ: Scarecrow Press, 1980. $12.50.

Thompson, Enid T. *Local History Collections: A Manual for Librarians*. Nashville, TN: American Association for State and Local History, 1978. $5.75.

Walch, Timothy. *Security.* SAA Basic Manual Series. Chicago: Society of American Archivists, 1977. $3 for members, $4 for nonmembers.

Audiovisual

Audio-Visual Equipment Directory 1979/80. 24th ed. Fairfax, VA: National Audio-Visual Association, 1979. $28.50.

Audiovisual Market Place, 1981: A Multimedia Guide. 11th ed. New York: R. R. Bowker, 1981. $29.95.

Boyle, Deirdre, ed. *Expanding Media.* Phoenix, AZ: Oryx Press, 1977. $13.95.

Brown, James W., ed. *Educational Media Yearbook 1980.* Littleton, CO: Libraries Unlimited, 1980. $20.

Cabeceiras, James. *The Multimedia Library: Materials Selection and Use.* New York: Academic Press, 1978. $15.

Sive, Mary Robinson. *Selecting Instructional Media: A Guide to Audiovisual and Other Instructional Media Lists.* Littleton, CO: Libraries Unlimited, 1978. $13.50.

Automation and Information Retrieval

Annual Review of Information Science and Technology. Washington, DC: American Society for Information Science. White Plains, NY: Knowledge Industry Publications. Vols. 3–5 (1968–1970) and Vols. 7–9 (1972–1974). $35 per vol. Vol. 10 (1975). $27.50. Vol. 11 (1976). $35. Vols. 12–15 (1977–1980). $42.50 per vol.

Atherton, Pauline, and Christian, Roger W. *Librarians and Online Services.* White Plains, NY: Knowledge Industry Publications, 1977. $24.

Bahr, Alice H. *Automated Library Circulation Systems, 1979–1980.* White Plains, NY: Knowledge Industry Publications, 1979. $24.50.

Buying New Technology. Library Journal Special Report No. 4. New York: R. R. Bowker, 1978. $3.95 prepaid.

Clinic on Library Applications of Data Processing. University of Illinois Proceedings. Champaign, IL: University of Illinois, Grad. School of Lib. Science, Publications Office, 1963–1980 vol. $9.

Gough, Chet, and Srikantaiah, Taverekere. *Systems Analysis in Libraries: A Question and Answer Approach.* Hamden, CT: Linnet, 1978. $9.50.

Grosch, Audrey N. *Minicomputers in Libraries 1979–80.* White Plains, NY: Knowledge Industry Publications, 1979. $24.50.

Hayes, Robert M., and Becker, Joseph. *Handbook of Data Processing for Libraries.* 2nd ed. New York: Wiley, 1974. $23.75.

International On-Line Information Meeting, First, London, 1977. Oxford: Learned Information, 1978. $30.

International On-Line Information Meeting, Second, London, 1978. Oxford: Learned Information, 1979. $30.

International On-Line Information Meeting, Third, London, 1979. Oxford: Learned Information, 1980. $30.

Kent, Allen, and Galvin, Thomas J., eds. *The On-Line Revolution in Libraries.* New York: Marcel Dekker, 1978. $29.75.

King, Donald W. *Key Papers in the Design and Evaluation of Information Systems* (American Society for Information Science). White Plains, NY: Knowledge Industry Publications, 1978. $19.95.

Lancaster, F. Wilfrid, and Gallup, Emily F. *Information Retrieval On-Line.* New York: Wiley, 1973. $20.

Martin, Susan K. *Library Networks, 1978–79.* White Plains, NY: Knowledge Industry Publications, 1978. $24.50.

Watson, Peter G., ed. *Charging for Computer-Based Reference Services.* Chicago: American Library Association, 1978. $4.

White, Howard. *Reader in Machine-Readable Social Data.* Englewood, CO: Information Handling Services, 1978. $19.

Buildings, Furniture, Equipment

Bahr, Alice H. *Book Theft and Library Security Systems, 1978-79.* White Plains, NY: Knowledge Industry Publications, 1978. $24.50.

Brooks, James, and Draper, James. *Interior Designs for Libraries.* Chicago: American Library Association, 1979. pap. $12.50.

Cohen, Aaron, and Cohen, Elaine. *Designing and Space Planning for Libraries: A Behavioral Guide.* New York: R. R. Bowker, 1979. $24.95.

Hannigan, Jane A., and Estes, Glenn E. *Media Center Facilities Design.* Chicago: American Library Association, 1978. $10.50.

Lushington, Nolan, and Mills, Willis N., Jr. *Libraries Designed for Users.* Syracuse, NY: Gaylord Professional Publications, 1979. $20.

Myers, Gerald E. *Insurance Manuals for Libraries.* Chicago: American Library Association, 1977. $5.

Novak, Gloria, ed. *Running Out of Space—What Are the Alternatives?* Chicago: American Library Association, 1978. $14.

Nyren, Karl. *New Public Library Buildings.* Library Journal Special Report No. 8. New York: R. R. Bowker, 1979. $5.

Pierce, William S. *Furnishing the Library Interior.* New York: Marcel Dekker, 1980. $39.75.

Pollett, Dorothy, and Haskell, Peter C. *Sign Systems for Libraries.* New York: R. R. Bowker, 1979. $24.95.

Schell, Hal B., ed. *Reader on the Library Building.* Englewood, CO: Information Handling Services, 1975. $19.

Sourcebook of Library Technology: A Cumulative Edition of Library Technology Reports 1965-1975. Chicago: American Library Association, 1976. $75. $30 with current subscription to *Library Technology Reports.* On microfiche.

Children's and Young Adults' Services and Materials

The Arbuthnot Lectures, 1970-79. Association for Library Service to Children, American Library Association. Chicago: American Library Association, 1980. $12.50.

Braverman, Miriam. *Youth, Society and the Public Library.* Chicago: American Library Association, 1979. $15.

Briggs, Nancy E. *Children's Literature through Storytelling and Drama.* 2nd ed. Dubuque, IA: W. C. Brown, 1979. $4.95.

Broderick, Dorothy M. *Library Work with Children.* New York: H. W. Wilson, 1977. $10.

Campbell, Patricia J. *Sex Education Books for Young Adults, 1892-1979.* New York: R. R. Bowker, 1979. $15.95.

Children's Media Market Place, ed. by Deirdre Boyle and Stephen Calvert. Syracuse, NY: Gaylord Professional Publications, 1978. $15.95.

deWitt, Dorothy. *Children's Faces Looking Up.* Chicago: American Library Association, 1979. $11.

Directions for Library Service to Young Adults. Prepared by Young Adult Services Division, Services Statement Development Committee, American Library Association. Chicago: American Library Association, 1977. $2.50.

Dreyer, Sharon. *The Bookfinder: A Guide to Children's Literature about the Needs and Problems of Youth.* Minneapolis, MN: American Guidance Service, 1977. $25.

Duke, Judith S. *Children's Books and Magazines: A Market Study.* White Plains, NY: Knowledge Industry Publications, 1979. $24.95.

Fader, Daniel. *The New Hooked on Books.* New York: Putnam, 1977. $8.95.

Foster, Joan, ed. *Reader in Children's Librarianship.* Englewood, CO: Information Handling Services, 1978. $20.

Graves, Michael, et al. *Easy Reading: Book Series and Periodicals for the Less Able Reader.* Newark, DE: International Reading Association, 1979. $3.

Haviland, Virginia, ed. *Children's Literature: A Guide to Reference Sources.* Washington, DC: Library of Congress, 1966. $5.45. 1st supplement, 1972. $5.50. 2nd supplement, 1978. $7.75.

Huck, Charlotte S. *Children's Literature in the Elementary School.* 3rd ed. New York: Holt, Rinehart & Winston, 1976. $13.95.

Illustrators of Children's Books 1967-1976, comp. by Lee Kingman, Grace Allen Hogarth, and Harriet Quimby. Boston: The Horn Book, 1978. $32.50.

Kirkpatrick, D. L., ed. *Twentieth Century Children's Writers.* London: Macmillan, 1978. $40.

Martin, Betty, and Carson, Ben. *The Principal's Handbook on the School Library Media Center.* Syracuse, NY: Gaylord Professional Publications, 1978. $8.95.

Meacham, Mary. *Information Sources in Children's Literature: A Practical Reference Guide for Children's Librarians, Elementary School Teachers, and Students of Children's Literature.* Westport, CT: Greenwood Press, 1978. $18.95.

Rogers, JoAnn V., ed. *Libraries and Young Adults.* Littleton, CO: Libraries Unlimited, 1979. $15.

Sutherland, Zena, and Arbuthnot, May Hill. *Children and Books.* 5th ed. Glenview, IL: Scott, Foresman, 1977. $13.95.

Wilson, June B. *The Story Experience.* Metuchen, NJ: Scarecrow Press, 1979. $8.

College and University Libraries

Association of College and Research Libraries. *New Horizons for Academic Libraries.* Papers Presented at the ACRL 1978 National Conference. New York: K. G. Saur, 1979. $25.

Gore, Daniel, ed. *Farewell to Alexandria: Solutions to Space, Growth, and Performance Problems of Libraries.* Westport, CT: Greenwood Press, 1976. $12.50.

Johnson, Edward R. *Organization Development for Academic Libraries.* Westport, CT: Greenwood Press, 1980. $19.95.

Kent, Allen, ed. *Use of Library Materials: The University of Pittsburgh Study.* New York: Marcel Dekker, 1979. $25.

Lyle, Guy R. *The Administration of the College Library.* 4th ed. New York: H. W. Wilson, 1974. $9.

Martin, Murray S. *Budgetary Control in Academic Libraries.* Greenwich, CT: JAI Press, 1978. $21.

Osburn, Charles. *Academic Research and Library Resources: Changing Patterns in America.* Westport, CT: Greenwood Press, 1979. $18.95.

Roger, Rutherford D., and Weber, David C. *University Library Administration.* New York: H. W. Wilson, 1970. $20.

SPEC Kits. Washington, DC: Association of Research Libraries. 1973- . Nos. 1- . $7.50 for members, $15 for nonmembers. (Recent kits have been on such topics as Library Materials Costs, Indirect Cost Rates in Research Libraries, and Online Bibliographic Search Services.)

Wilkinson, Billy R. *Reader in Undergraduate Libraries.* Englewood, CO: Information Handling Services, 1978. $20.

Comparative and International Librarianship

Atherton, Pauline. *Handbook for Information Systems and Services.* New York: Unipub, 1977. $17.25.

Avicenne, Paul, ed. *Bibliographical Services throughout the World.* New York. Unipub, 1978. $20.

Benge, Ronald. *Cultural Crisis and Librar-*

ies in the Third World. Hamden, CT: Linnet Books, 1979. $17.50.

Harvey, John F., ed. Comparative and International Library Science. Metuchen, NJ: Scarecrow Press, 1977. $12.

Huq, A. A. Abdul, and Aman, Mohammed M. Librarianship and the Third World: An Annotated Bibliography of Selected Literature on Developing Nations, 1960-1975. New York: Garland, 1977. $32.

Penna. C. V., Foskett, D. J., and Sewell, P. H. National Library and Information Services: A Handbook for Planners. London: Butterworths, 1977. $16.95.

Copyright

Association for Educational Communications and Technology. Copyright and Educational Media. Washington, DC: AECT, 1977. $3.95.

Henry, Nicholas, ed. Copyright, Congress and Technology: The Public Record. Phoenix, AZ: Oryx Press, 1978. Vols. 1-5, $95.

Johnston, Donald. Copyright Handbook. New York: R. R. Bowker, 1978. $14.95.

The Librarian's Copyright Kit: What You Must Know Now. Chicago: American Library Association, 1978. $7.

Education for Librarianship

Borko, Harold, ed. Targets for Research in Library Education. Chicago: American Library Association, 1973. $10.

Conant, Ralph Wendell. The Conant Report: A Study of the Education of Librarians. Cambridge, MA: MIT Press, 1980. $17.50.

Conroy, Barbara. Library Staff Development and Continuing Education: Principles and Practices. Littleton, CO: Libraries Unlimited, 1977. $17.50.

―――. Library Staff Development Profile Pages: A Guide and Workbook for Library Self Assessment and Planning. Available from the author, Box 502, Tabernash, CO, 1979. $12.

Financial Assistance for Library Education: Academic Year 1980-81. Chicago: American Library Association, 1979. 50¢.

Library Education and Personnel Utilization: A Statement of Policy Adopted by the Council of the American Library Association, June 30, 1970. Rev. for terminology, 1976. Chicago: American Library Association, 1976. Free.

Morehead, Joe. Theory and Practice in Library Education. Littleton, CO: Libraries Unlimited, 1980. $17.50.

Reeves, William Joseph. Librarians as Professionals: The Occupation's Impact on Library Work Arrangements. Lexington, MA: Lexington Books, 1980. $19.95.

Shera, Jesse H. The Foundations of Education for Librarianship. New York: Wiley, 1972. $21.95.

Information and Society

Adkinson, Burton W. Two Centuries of Federal Information. Stroudsburg, PA: Dowden, Hutchinson, & Ross, 1978. $15.

Compaine, Benjamin. The Book Industry in Transition. White Plains, NY: Knowledge Industry Publications, 1978. $24.50.

Giuliano, Vincent, et al. Into the Information Age: A Perspective for Federal Action on Information. Chicago: American Library Association, 1979. pap. $8.

Information Industry Association. Membership Directory, 1981-82. Bethesda, MD: Information Industry Association, 1981. $21.

Information Market Place, 1981. An International Directory of Information Products and Services. New York: R. R. Bowker, 1980. $24.50.

Machlup, Fritz, and Leeson, Kenneth. Information through the Printed Word. 3 vols. New York: Praeger, 1978. $69.85.

U.S. National Commission on Libraries and Information Science. National Inventory of Library Needs, 1975. Washington, DC, 1977. $3.60.

Warnken, Kelly. *Directory of Fee Based Information Services: 1978/79.* Woodstock, NY: Information Alternative, 1978. $5.

Intellectual Freedom

Busha, C. H. *An Intellectual Freedom Primer.* Littleton, CO: Libraries Unlimited, 1977. $17.50.

Intellectual Freedom Manual. Chicago: American Library Association, 1975. $5.

Library History

Garrison, Dee. *Apostles of Culture.* New York: Macmillan Information, 1979. $14.50.

Gates, Jean Key. *Introduction to Librarianship.* 2nd ed. New York: McGraw-Hill, 1976. $11.95.

Goldstein, Harold, ed. *Milestones to the Present: Papers from Library History Seminar V.* Syracuse, NY: Gaylord, 1978. $15.

Harris, Michael H., and Davis, Donald G., Jr. *American Library History: A Bibliography.* Austin, TX: University of Texas Press, 1978. $18.

Jackson, Sidney L. *A Brief History of Libraries and Librarianship in the West.* New York: McGraw-Hill, 1974. $20.

———, et al., eds. *A Century of Service: Librarianship in the United States and Canada.* Chicago: American Library Association, 1976. $25.

Johnson, Elmer D., and Harris, Michael H. *A History of Libraries in the Western World.* 3rd ed. Metuchen, NJ: Scarecrow Press, 1976. $10.

Thomison, Dennis. *A History of the American Library Association, 1876-1972.* Chicago: American Library Association, 1978. $30.

Winckler, Paul A. *Reader in the History of Books and Printing.* Englewood, CO: Information Handling Services, 1978. $22.

Winger, Howard W., ed. *American Library History, 1876-1976. Library Trends,* July 1976. Champaign, IL: University of Illinois, Graduate School of Library Science, Publications Office, 1977. $8.

Materials Selection

Bonk, Wallace John, and Magrill, Rose Mary. *Building Library Collections.* 5th ed. Metuchen, NJ: Scarecrow Press, 1979. $10.

Broadus, Robert N. *Selecting Materials for Libraries.* New York: H. W. Wilson, 1973. $12.

Carter, Mary D., et al. *Building Library Collections.* Metuchen, NJ: Scarecrow Press, 1974. $9.

Evans, G. Edward. *Developing Library Collections.* Littleton, CO: Libraries Unlimited, 1979. $15.

Miller, Shirley. *The Vertical File and Its Satellites.* 2nd ed. Littleton, CO: Libraries Unlimited, 1979. $20.

Microforms and Computer Output Microforms

Bahr, Alice H. *Microforms: The Librarians' View, 1978-79.* 2nd ed. White Plains, NY: Knowledge Industry Publicatons, 1978. $24.50.

Catalog Use Committee, Reference and Adult Services Division, American Library Association. *Commercial COM Catalogs: How to Choose, When to Buy.* Chicago, 1978. $2.50.

Diaz, Albert J. *Microforms and Library Catalogs: A Reader.* Westport, CT: Microform Review, 1977. $20.95.

Fundamentals of Computer Output Microfilm. Silver Spring, MD: National Micrographics Association, 1974. $2.

Gabriel, Michael R. *The Microform Revolution in Libraries.* Greenwich, CT: JAI Press, 1980. $26.50.

Gaddy, Dale. *A Microform Handbook.* Silver Spring, MD: National Micrographics Association, 1974. $6.

Saffady, William. *Computer-Output Microfilm: Its Library Applications.* Chicago: American Library Association, 1978. $10.50.

———. *Micrographics.* Littleton, CO: Libraries Unlimited, 1978. $16.

Teague, Sydney. *Microform Librarianship.* 2nd ed. Boston: Butterworths, 1979. $15.95.

Networks and Interlibrary Cooperation

Getting into Networking: Guidelines for Special Libraries. Prepared by the Guidelines Subcommittee, SLA Networking Committee. New York: Special Libraries Association, 1977. $6.

Giuliano, Vincent. *A New Governance Structure for OCLC: Principles and Recommendations.* Metuchen, NJ: Scarecrow Press, 1978. $8.

Kent, Allen, and Galvin, Thomas J., eds. *Library Resource Sharing: Proceedings of the 1976 Conference on Resource Sharing in Libraries.* New York: Marcel Dekker, 1977. $29.75.

———. *The Structure and Governance of Library Networks.* New York: Marcel Dekker, 1979. $43.75.

Periodicals and Serials

Davinson, Donald. *The Periodicals Collection.* Rev. and enl. ed. London: Andre Deutsch, 1978. $16.25.

Guidelines for Handling Library Orders for Serials and Periodicals. Chicago: American Library Association, 1974. $1.95.

Katz, Bill. *Magazine Selection: How to Build a Community-Oriented Collection.* New York: R. R. Bowker, 1971. $14.95.

———, and Gellatly, Peter. *Guide to Magazine and Serial Agents.* New York: R. R. Bowker, 1975. $19.25.

Osborn, Andrew D. *Serial Publications: Their Place and Treatment in Libraries.* 2nd ed. Chicago: American Library Association, 1973. $18.

Public Libraries

Altman, Ellen, et al. *A Data Gathering and Instructional Manual for Performance Measures in Libraries.* Chicago: Celadon Press, 1976. $10.

Book Reading and Library Usage: A Study of Habits and Perceptions. Conducted for ALA. Princeton, NJ: The Gallup Organization, 1978. Available from ALA. $60.

Geddes, Andrew. *Fiscal Responsibility and the Small Public Library.* Small Libraries Publications No. 3. Chicago: American Library Association, 1978. $1.

Hanna, Patricia B. *People Make It Happen: The Possibilities of Outreach in Every Phase of Public Library Service.* Metuchen, NJ: Scarecrow Press, 1978. $7.

Performance Measures for Public Libraries. Chicago: American Library Association, 1973. $3.50.

Prentice, Ann. *Public Library Finance.* Chicago: American Library Association, 1977. $7.

Price, Paxton, P. *Future of the Main Urban Library: Report of a Conference, October 26-27, 1978.* Las Cruces, NM: Urban Libraries Council, 1978. $7.95.

Public Library Association. *The Public Library Mission Statement and Its Imperatives for Service.* Chicago: American Library Association, 1979. $1.50.

Shearer, Kenneth D., ed. *The Collection and Use of Public Library Statistics by State Agencies: A Compilation of Forms.* Chicago: American Library Association. Library Administration and Management Association, 1978. $13.50.

Sinclair, Dorothy. *Administration of the Small Public Library.* Chicago: American Library Association, 1979. $10.

Turick, Dorothy. *Community Information Services in Libraries.* Library Journal Special Report No. 5. New York: R. R. Bowker, 1978. $5.

Reference Services

Bloomberg, Marty. *Introduction to Public Services for Library Technicians.* 2nd ed. Littleton, CO: Libraries Unlimited, 1977. $11.50.

Fjallbrant, Nancy, and Stevenson, Malcolm. *User Education in Libraries.* Hamden, CT: Linnet, 1978. $12.50.

Katz, William A. *An Introduction to Reference Work.* 3rd rev. ed. New York: McGraw-Hill, 1978. 2 vols. Vol. 1, $14.95. Vol. 2, $13.95.

——, and Tarr, Andrea. *Reference and Information Services: A Reader.* Metuchen, NJ: Scarecrow Press, 1978. $12.50.

Lockwood, Deborah. *Library Instruction: A Bibliography.* Westport, CT: Greenwood Press, 1979. $16.50.

Lubans, John, ed. *Educating the Library User.* New York: R. R. Bowker, 1974. $17.95.

——. *Progress in Educating the Library User.* New York: R. R. Bowker, 1978. $16.95.

Morehead, Joe. *Introduction to United States Public Documents.* 2nd ed. Littleton, CO: Libraries Unlimited, 1978. $17.50.

Morgan, Candace, ed. *The Purposes of Reference Measurement.* Chicago: American Library Association, 1978. $2.

Murfin, Marjorie, and Wynar, Lubomyr. *Reference Service: An Annotated Bibliographic Guide.* Littleton, CO: Libraries Unlimited, 1977. $15.

Sheehy, Eugene P. *Guide to Reference Books.* 9th ed. Chicago: American Library Association, 1976. $30.

Research

Bundy, Mary Lee, and Wasserman, Paul, eds. *Reader in Research Methods in Librarianship.* Englewood, CO: Microcard Editions Books, 1970. $14.

Carpenter, Ray L. *Statistical Methods for Librarians.* Chicago: American Library Association, 1978. $12.50.

Chen, Ching-Chih, ed. *Quantitative Measurement and Dynamic Library Service.* Phoenix, AZ: Oryx Press, 1978. $16.50.

Srikantaiah, Taverekere, and Huffman, Herbert H. *Introduction to Quantitative Research Methods for Librarians.* 2nd ed. Newport Beach, CA: Headway Publications, 1977. $8.

School Libraries

Bell, Irene. *Basic Media Skills through Games.* Littleton, CO: Libraries Unlimited, 1979. $13.50.

Cole, John Y., ed. *Television, the Book, and the Classroom.* Washington, DC: Library of Congress, 1978. $4.95.

Davies, Ruth Ann. *School Library Media Program: Instructional Force for Excellence.* 3rd ed. New York: R. R. Bowker, 1979. $16.95.

Gillespie, John T., and Spirt, Diana L. *Creating a School Media Program.* New York: R. R. Bowker, 1973. $16.25.

Hart, Thomas L., ed. *Instruction in School Media Use.* Chicago: American Library Association, 1978. $8.50.

Liesener, James W. *Systematic Process for Planning Media Programs.* Chicago: American Library Association, 1976. $7.

Shapiro, Lillian L. *Serving Youth: Communication and Commitment in the High School Library.* New York: R. R. Bowker, 1975. $16.25.

Services for Special Groups

Cylke, Frank K. *Library Service for the Blind and Physically Handicapped: An International Approach.* New York: K. G. Saur, 1978. $18.

Rubin, Rhea Joyce, ed. *Bibliotherapy Sourcebook.* Phoenix, AZ: Oryx Press, 1978. $14.95.

——. *Using Bibliotherapy: A Guide to Theory and Technique.* Phoenix, AZ: Oryx Press, 1978. $10.95.

Schauder, Donald E., and Gram, Malcolm. *Libraries for the Blind: An International Study of Policies and Practices.*

Steverage, Herts., England: Peter Peregrinas, 1979. $21.50.

Strom, Maryalls G., ed. *Library Services to the Blind and Physically Handicapped.* Metuchen, NJ: Scarecrow Press, 1977. $12.

Velleman, Ruth A. *Serving Physically Disabled People: An Information Handbook for All Libraries.* New York: R. R. Bowker, 1979. $17.50.

Wright, Kieth. *Library and Information Services for Handicapped Individuals.* Littleton, CO: Libraries Unlimited, 1979. $15.

Special Libraries

Drazniowsky, Roman, comp. *Map Librarianship: Readings.* Metuchen, NJ: Scarecrow Press, 1975. $20.

Larsgaard, Mary. *Map Librarianship.* Littleton, CO: Libraries Unlimited, 1978. $18.50.

Rowley, J. E. *The Dissemination of Information.* London: Andre Deutsch, 1978. $19.25.

Strable, Edward G. *Special Libraries: A Guide for Management.* Rev. ed. New York: Special Libraries Association, 1975. $8.

Strauss, Lucille J., Shreve, Irene M., and Brown, Alberta L. *Scientific and Technical Libraries: Their Organization and Administration.* 2nd ed. New York: Wiley, 1972. $19.25.

State Libraries

The ASLA Report on Interlibrary Cooperation. 2nd ed. Chicago: Association of State Library Agencies (ALA), 1978. $15.

Simpson, Donald B. *The State Library Agencies: A Survey Project Report, 1979.* 4th ed. Chicago: Association of State Library Agencies (ALA), 1979. $15.

Technical Services

Bernhardt, Frances Simonsen. *Introduction to Library Technical Services.* New York: H. W. Wilson, 1979. $15.

Bloomberg, Marty, and Evans, G. Edward. *Introduction to Technical Services for Library Technicians.* 3rd ed. Littleton, CO: Libraries Unlimited, 1976. $8.50.

Magrill, Rose Mary, and Rinehart, Constance, comps. *Library Technical Services: A Selected Annotated Bibliography.* Westport, CT: Greenwood Press, 1977. $14.95.

Technical Services: Acquisitions

Grieder, Ted. *Acquisitions: Where, What and How.* Westport, CT: Greenwood Press, 1978. $18.95.

Orne, Jerrold. *The Language of the Foreign Book Trade.* 3rd ed. Chicago: American Library Association, 1976. $15.

Technical Services: Cataloging and Classification

Chan, Lois Mai. *Library of Congress Subject Headings: Principles and Applications.* Littleton, CO: Libraries Unlimited, 1978. $17.50.

Gorman, Michael, and Winkler, Paul W., eds. *Anglo-American Cataloging Rules.* 2nd ed. Chicago: American Library Association, 1978. $15.

Immroth, John Philip. *Immroth's Guide to the Library of Congress Classification.* Littleton, CO: Libraries Unlimited, 1980. $22.50.

Manheimer, Martha L. *OCLC: An Introduction to Searching and Input.* New York: Neal-Schuman, 1979. $8.50.

Maxwell, Margaret. *Handbook for AACR2: Explaining and Illustrating the Anglo-American Cataloguing Rules, 2nd Edition.* Chicago: American Library Association, 1980. $20.

OCLC: A Bibliography. Columbus, OH: OCLC, Inc., 1979.

Smith, Lynn S. *A Practical Approach to Serials Cataloging.* Greenwich, CT: JAI Press, 1978. $27.50.

Wellisch, Hans H. *The PRECIS Index System: Principles, Applications, and Prospects.* New York: H. W. Wilson, 1977. $12.50.

———. *Indexing and Abstracting: An International Bibliography.* Santa Barbara, CA: ABC-Clio, 1980. $22.75.

PERIODICALS

The journals listed below are titles that might normally be purchased as part of a continuing education program in a library or as subscriptions for individual librarians. Titles used primarily for selection have been excluded.

ALA Washington Newsletter
American Libraries
American Society for Information Science Bulletin
College and Research Libraries
Conservation Administration Review
Drexel Library Quarterly
IFLA Journal
International Cataloguing
International Library Review
Journal of Academic Librarianship
Journal of Education for Librarianship
Journal of Library Automation
Journal of Library History
Library Journal
Library of Congress Information Bulletin
Library Quarterly
Library Resources and Technical Services
Library Trends
Libri
Medical Library Association Bulletin
Newsletter on Intellectual Freedom
OnLine
Public Library Quarterly
RQ
RSR (Reference Services Review)
School Library Journal
School Media Quarterly
Serials Librarian
Serials Review
Special Libraries
Top of the News
U* N* A* B* A* S* H* E* D* Librarian
UNESCO Bulletin for Libraries
VOYA: Voice of Youth Advocates
Wilson Library Bulletin

BASIC PUBLICATIONS FOR THE PUBLISHER AND THE BOOK TRADE

Jean R. Peters

Librarian, R. R. Bowker Company

BIBLIOGRAPHIES OF BOOKS ABOUT BOOKS AND THE BOOK TRADE

These six books contain extensive bibliographies.

Gottlieb, Robin. *Publishing Children's Books in America, 1919–1976: An Annotated Bibliography.* New York: Children's Book Council, 1978. $15.

Lee, Marshall. *Bookmaking: The Illustrated Guide to Design/Production/Editing.* New York: R. R. Bowker, 1979. $29.50. Bibliography is divided into four parts: Part I covers books and includes a general bibliography as well as extensive coverage of books on all technical aspects of bookmaking; Part 2 lists periodicals; Part 3 lists films, filmstrips, etc.; Part 4 lists other sources.

Lehmann-Haupt, Hellmut, Wroth, Lawrence C., and Silver, Rollo. *The Book in America.* 2nd ed. New York: R. R. Bowker, 1951, o.p. Bibliography covers cultural history, bibliography, printing and bookmaking, book illustration, bookselling, and publishing.

Melcher, Daniel, and Larrick, Nancy. *Printing and Promotion Handbook.* 3rd ed. New York: McGraw-Hill, 1966. $24.95. Bibliography covers general reference, advertising, artwork, book publishing, color, copyright, copywriting, direct mail, displays, editing and proofreading, layout and design, lettering, magazine publishing, newspaper publishing, packaging, paper, photography, printing, publicity, radio and TV, shipping, typography, and visual aids.

The Reader's Adviser: A Layman's Guide to Literature. 12th ed. 3 vols. New York: R. R. Bowker, 1974–1977. $75 (3-vol. set); $29.95 (ea. vol.). Vol. 1. *The Best in American and British Fiction, Poetry, Essays, Literary Biography, Bibliography, and Reference*, ed. by Sarah L. Prakken. 1974. Chapters on "Books about Books" and "Bibliography" cover history of publishing and bookselling, practice of publishing, bookmaking, rare book collecting, trade and specialized bibliographies, book selection tools, best books, etc. Vol. 2. *The Best in American and British Drama and World Literature in English Translation*, ed. by F. J. Sypher. 1977. Vol. 3. *The Best in the Reference Literature of the World*, ed. by Jack A. Clarke. 1977.

Tanselle, G. Thomas. *Guide to the Study of United States Imprints*. 2 vols. Cambridge, MA: Belknap Press of Harvard University Press, 1971. $50. Includes sections on general studies of American printing and publishing as well as studies of individual printers and publishers.

TRADE BIBLIOGRAPHIES

American Book Publishing Record Cumulative, 1876–1949: An American National Bibliography. 15 vols. New York: R. R. Bowker, 1980. $1,975.

American Book Publishing Record Cumulative, 1950–1977: An American National Bibliography. 15 vols. New York: R. R. Bowker, 1979. $1,500.

American Book Publishing Record Five-Year Cumulatives. New York: R. R. Bowker, 1960–1964 Cumulative. 4 vols. $110. 1965–1969 Cumulative. 5 vols. $110. 1970–1974 Cumulative. 4 vols. $110. Annual vols.: 1965–1969, $45 each; 1970, o.p.; 1971, o.p.; 1972, o.p.; 1973, o.p.; 1974, $45; 1975, $45; 1976, $45; 1977, $45; 1978, $49.50; 1979, $53.

Book Publishers Directory: An Information Service Covering New and Established, Private and Special Interest, Avant-Garde and Alternative, Organization and Association, Government and Institution Presses, ed. by Elizabeth Geiser and Annie Brewer. Detroit: Gale, 1979. $110. Supplement, 1980. $45.

Books in Print. 4 vols. New York: R. R. Bowker, ann. $110.

Books in Print Supplement. New York: R. R. Bowker, ann. $53.

Books in Series in the United States. 3rd ed. New York: R. R. Bowker, 1980. $150.

British Books in Print: The Reference Catalog of Current Literature. New York: R. R. Bowker, 1980. $130 (plus duty where applicable).

Canadian Books in Print, ed. by Martha Pluscauskas. Toronto: University of Toronto Press, ann. $40.

Canadian Books in Print: Subject Index, ed. by Martha Pluscauskas. Toronto: University of Toronto Press, ann. $35.

Cumulative Book Index. New York: H. W. Wilson. Monthly with bound semiannual and larger cumulations. Service basis.

El-Hi Textbooks in Print. New York: R. R. Bowker, ann. $35.

Forthcoming Books. New York: R. R. Bowker. $32.50 a year. $7.50 single copy. Bimonthly supplement to *Books in Print*.

Large Type Books in Print. New York: R. R. Bowker, 1980. $19.95.

Paperbound Books in Print. New York: R. R. Bowker. 2 vols. per year. $70.

Publishers' Trade List Annual. New York: R. R. Bowker, ann. 6 vols. $59.

Robert, Reginald, and Burgess, M. R. *Cumulative Paperback Index, 1939–59.* Detroit: Gale, 1973. $38.

Small Press Record of Books in Print, ed. by Len Fulton. Paradise, CA: Dustbooks, 1980. $17.95.

Subject Guide to Books in Print. 2 vols. New York: R. R. Bowker, ann. $79.50.

Subject Guide to Forthcoming Books. $30 a year. $45 in combination with *Forthcoming Books.*

Turner, Mary C., ed. *Libros en Venta.* New York: R. R. Bowker, 1974. $57.50. Supplement, 1974. 1976. $35. Supplement, 1975. 1978. $35. Supplement, 1976–77. 1979. $59. A Spanish-language "Books in Print/Subject Guide."

BOOK PUBLISHING

Education and Practice

Association of American University Presses. *One Book—Five Ways: The Publishing Procedures of Five University Presses.* Los Altos, CA: William Kaufmann, 1978. $18.75. pap. $10.75.

Bailey, Herbert S., Jr. *The Art and Science of Book Publishing.* New York: Harper & Row, 1970. $10.

Bodian, Nat G. *Book Marketing Handbook: Tips and Techniques for the Sale and Promotion of Scientific, Technical, Professional, and Scholarly Books and Journals.* New York: R. R. Bowker, 1980. $45.

Bohne, Harald, and Van Ierssel, Harry. *Publishing: The Creative Business.* Toronto: University of Toronto Press, 1973. pap. $7.50.

Dessauer, John P. *Book Publishing: What It Is, What It Does.* New York: R. R. Bowker, 1974. $13.95. pap. $7.50.

Glaister, Geoffrey. *Glaister's Glossary of the Book: Terms Used in Paper-Making, Printing, Bookbinding, and Publishing.* 2nd ed., completely rev. Berkeley: University of California Press, 1979. $75.

Grannis, Chandler B. *Getting into Book Publishing.* New York: R. R. Bowker, 1979. Pamphlet, one free; in bulk 75¢ each.

Grannis, Chandler B., ed. *What Happens in Book Publishing.* 2nd ed. New York: Columbia University Press, 1967. $20.

Greenfeld, Howard. *Books: From Writer to Reader.* New York: Crown, 1976. $8.95.

Hackett, Alice Payne, and Burke, Henry James. *Eighty Years of Best Sellers, 1895–1975.* New York: R. R. Bowker, 1977. $16.25.

Peters, Jean, ed. *Bookman's Glossary.* 5th ed. New York: R. R. Bowker, 1975. $12.50.

Smith, Datus C., Jr. *A Guide to Book Publishing.* New York: R. R. Bowker, 1966. $14.25.

To Be a Publisher: A Handbook on Some Principles and Programs in Publishing Education. Prepared by the Association of American Publishers Education for Publishing Program. New York: Association of American Publishers, 1979. $10.

Analysis, Statistics, Surveys

Altbach, Philip G., and McVey, Sheila, eds. *Perspectives on Publishing.* Lexington, MA: Lexington Books, 1976. $23.95.

ANSI Standards Committee Z-39. *American National Standard for Compiling Book Publishing Statistics, Z-39.8.* New York: American National Standards Institute, 1978. $4.

Benjamin, Curtis G. *A Candid Critique of Book Publishing.* New York: R. R. Bowker, 1977. $16.50.

Bowker Annual of Library and Book Trade Information. New York: R. R. Bowker, ann. $29.95.

Bowker Lectures on Book Publishing. New York: R. R. Bowker, 1957. o.p.

Bowker Lectures on Book Publishing, New Series. New York: R. R. Bowker. 8 vols. 1973-81. $2.50 each. Vol. 1. Pilpel, Harriet F. *Obscenity and the Constitution.* 1973. Vol. 2. Ringer, Barbara A. *The Demonology of Copyright.* 1974. Vol. 3. Henne, Frances E. *The Library World and the Publishing of Children's Books.* 1975. Vol. 4. Vaughan, Samuel S. *Medium Rare: A Look at the Book and Its People.* 1976. Vol. 5. Bailey, Herbert S. *The Traditional Book in the Electronic Age.* 1977. Vol. 6. Mayer, Peter. *The Spirit of the Enterprise.* 1978. Vol. 7. De Gennaro, Richard. *Research Libraries Enter the Information Age.* 1979. Vol. 8. Dystel, Oscar. *Mass Market Publishing: More Observations, Speculations and Provocations.* 1980.

The Business of Publishing: A PW Anthology. New York: R. R. Bowker, 1976. $14.25.

Cheney, O. H. *Economic Survey of the Book Industry, 1930-31.* The Cheney Report. Reprinted. New York: R. R. Bowker, 1960. o.p.

Compaine, Benjamin. *The Book Industry in Transition: An Economic Study of Book Distribution and Marketing.* White Plains, NY: Knowledge Industry Publications, 1978. $24.95.

Dessauer, John P. *Association of American Publishers 1979 Industry Statistics.* New York: Association of American Publishers, 1980. Nonmemb. $220.

———, Doebler, Paul D., Noble, J. Kendrick, Jr., and Nordberg, E. Wayne. *Book Industry Trends—1980.* Darien, CT: Book Industry Study Group, 1980. Apply for price scale.

Fitzgerald, Frances. *America Revised: History Schoolbooks in the Twentieth Century.* Boston: Little, Brown, 1979. $9.95.

Gedin, Per. *Literature in the Marketplace,* trans. by George Bisset. Woodstock, NY: Overlook, 1977. $12.95.

Kujoth, Jean Spealman. *Book Publishing: Inside Views.* Metuchen, NJ: Scarecrow, 1971. $14.50.

Machlup, Fritz, and Leeson, Kenneth W. *Information through the Printed Word: The Dissemination of Scholarly, Scientific, and Intellectual Knowledge.* 3 vols. Vol. 1. *Book Publishing.* Vol. 2. *Journals.* Vol. 3. *Libraries.* New York: Praeger, 1978. Vol. 1, $25.95; Vol. 2, $27.95; Vol. 3, $23.95.

Nordberg, E. Wayne, and Hasan, Kazi. *Paper Availability Study.* Darien, CT: Book Industry Study Group, 1977. $300.

Smith, Roger H., ed. *The American Reading Public: A Symposium.* New York: R. R. Bowker, 1964. o.p.

Smith, Roger H. *Paperback Parnassus: The Birth, the Development, the Pending Crises of the Modern American Paperbound Book.* Boulder, CO: Westview, 1976. $18.

Yankelovich, Skelly, and White, Inc. *The 1978 Consumer Research Study on Reading and Book Purchasing.* Darien, CT: Book Industry Study Group, 1978. $1,500. To library members of BISG, $50.

History

Briggs, Asa, ed. *Essays in the History of Publishing: In Celebration of the 250th Anniversary of the House of Longman, 1724-1974.* New York: Longman, 1974. $15.

Cerf, Bennett. *At Random: The Reminiscences of Bennett Cerf.* New York: Random House, 1977. $12.95.

Haydn, Hiram. *Words & Faces.* New York: Harcourt Brace Jovanovich, 1974. $8.95.

Hodges, Sheila. *Golancz: The Story of a Publishing House.* London: Golancz, 1978. £7.50.

Kurian, George. *Directory of American Book Publishing: From Founding Fathers to Today's Conglomerates.* New York: Monarch, 1975. $25.

Lehmann-Haupt, Hellmut. *The Book in America*. 2nd ed. New York: R. R. Bowker, 1951. o.p.

Madison, Charles. *Jewish Publishing in America*. New York: Hebrew Publishing Co., 1976. $11.95.

Morpurgo, J. E. *Allen Lane: King Penguin*. London: Hutchinson, 1979. £9.95.

Mott, Frank Luther. *Golden Multitudes: The Story of Best Sellers in the United States (1662–1945)*. Reprint ed. New York: R. R. Bowker, 1960. $11.95.

Mumby, Frank A., and Norrie, Ian. *Publishing and Bookselling: A History from the Earliest Times to the Present Day*. New York: R. R. Bowker, 1974. $39.95.

Regnery, Henry. *Memoirs of a Dissident Publisher*. New York: Harcourt Brace Jovanovich, 1979. $12.95.

Schick, Frank L. *The Paperbound Book in America: The History of Paperbacks and Their European Background*. New York: R. R. Bowker, 1958. o.p.

Stern, Madeleine B. *Books and Book People in 19th-Century America*. New York: R. R. Bowker, 1978. $27.50.

Targ, William. *Indecent Pleasures*. New York: Macmillan, 1975. $14.95.

Tebbel, John. *A History of Book Publishing in the United States*. 3 vols. Vol. 1. *The Creation of an Industry, 1630–1865*. Vol. 2. *The Expansion of an Industry, 1865–1919*. Vol. 3. *The Golden Age between Two Wars, 1920–1940*. Vol. 4. *The Great Change, 1940–1980*. New York: R. R. Bowker, 1972, 1975, 1978. Vols. 1, 2, 3, $35 each; Vol. 4, $37.50.

SCHOLARLY BOOKS

Harman, Eleanor, and Montagnes, Ian, eds. *The Thesis and the Book*. Toronto: University of Toronto Press, 1976. $10. pap. $5.

Horne, David. *Boards and Buckram: Writings from "Scholarly Books in America," 1962–1969*. Hanover, NH: University Press of New England, 1980. Dist. by American University Press Services, Inc., New York. $10.

Nemeyer, Carol A. *Scholarly Reprint Publishing in the United States*. New York: R. R. Bowker, 1972. o.p.

Scholarly Communication: The Report of the National Enquiry. Baltimore: Johns Hopkins University Press, 1979. $12.95. pap. $3.95.

EDITORS, AGENTS, AUTHORS

Appelbaum, Judith, and Evans, Nancy. *How to Get Happily Published*. New York: Harper & Row, 1978. $9.95.

Berg, A. Scott. *Max Perkins: Editor of Genius*. New York: Dutton, 1978. $15.

Commins, Dorothy Berliner. *What Is an Editor? Saxe Commins at Work*. Chicago: University of Chicago Press, 1978. $10.

Henderson, Bill, ed. *The Art of Literary Publishing: Editors on Their Craft*. Yonkers, NY: Pushcart, 1980. $15.

Madison, Charles. *Irving to Irving: Author-Publisher Relations: 1800–1974*. New York: R. R. Bowker, 1974. $13.50.

Mitchell, Burroughs. *The Education of an Editor*. Garden City, NY: Doubleday, 1980. $8.95.

Reynolds, Paul R. *The Middle Man: The Adventures of a Literary Agent*. New York: Morrow, 1972. $6.95.

Strauss, Helen M. *A Talent for Luck*. New York: Random House, 1979. $12.95.

Unseld, Siegfried. *The Author and His Publisher*. Chicago: University of Chicago Press, 1980. $12.50.

Watson, Graham. *Book Society: Reminiscences of a Literary Agent*. New York: Atheneum, 1980. $10.95.

BOOK DESIGN AND PRODUCTION

Grannis, Chandler B. *The Heritage of the Graphic Arts*. New York: R. R. Bowker, 1972. $21.95.

Lee, Marshall. *Bookmaking: The Illustrated Guide to Design and Production.* 2nd ed. New York: R. R. Bowker, 1979. $29.50.

Rice, Stanley. *Book Design: Systematic Aspects.* New York: R. R. Bowker, 1978. $18.95.

―――. *Book Design: Text Format Models.* New York: R. R. Bowker, 1978. $18.95.

Strauss, Victor. *The Printing Industry: An Introduction to Its Many Branches, Processes and Products.* New York: R. R. Bowker, 1967. $32.50.

White, Jan. *Editing by Design.* New York: R. R. Bowker, 1974. $19.25.

Wilson, Adrian. *The Design of Books.* Layton, UT: Peregrine Smith, 1974. pap. $9.95.

BOOKSELLING

Anderson, Charles B., ed. *Bookselling in America and the World: A Souvenir Book Celebrating the 75th Anniversary of the American Booksellers Association.* New York: Times Books, 1975. $9.50.

―――, Smith, G. Royce, and Cobb, Sanford, eds. *Manual on Bookselling: How to Open and Run Your Own Bookstore.* New York: American Booksellers Association, 1974. Distributed by Harmony Books. $10.95. pap. $4.95.

Bliven, Bruce. *Book Traveller.* New York: Dodd, Mead, 1975. $4.95.

CENSORSHIP

de Grazia, Edward, comp. *Censorship Landmarks.* New York: R. R. Bowker, 1969. $27.50.

Ernst, Morris L., and Schwartz, Alan U. *Censorship.* New York: Macmillan, 1964. $6.95.

Haight, Anne Lyon. *Banned Books.* 4th ed. updated and enlarged by Chandler B. Grannis. New York: R. R. Bowker, 1978. $14.95.

Hentoff, Nat. *The First Freedom: The Tumultuous History of Free Speech in America.* New York: Delacorte, 1980. $9.95.

Jenkinson, Edward B. *Censors in the Classroom: The Mind Benders.* Carbondale, IL: Southern Illinois University Press, 1979. $12.50.

Moon, Eric, ed. *Book Selection and Censorship in the Sixties.* New York: R. R. Bowker, 1969. $16.95.

COPYRIGHT

Bogsch, Arpad. *The Law of Copyright under the Universal Convention.* 3rd ed. New York: R. R. Bowker, 1969. o.p.

Cambridge Research Institute. *Omnibus Copyright Revision: Comparative Analysis of the Issues.* Washington, DC: American Society for Information Science, 1973. $48.

Copyright Revision Act of 1976: Law, Explanation, Committee Reports. Chicago: Commerce Clearing House, 1976. $12.50.

Johnston, Donald F. *Copyright Handbook.* New York: R. R. Bowker, 1978. $18.50.

Wittenberg, Philip. *Protection of Literary Property.* Boston: The Writer, Inc., 1978. $12.95.

BOOK TRADE DIRECTORIES AND YEARBOOKS

American and Canadian

American Book Trade Directory, 1980. 26th ed. New York: R. R. Bowker, ann. $54.95.

Chernofsky, Jacob L., ed. *AB Bookman's Yearbook.* 2 vols. Clifton, NJ: AB Bookman's Weekly, ann. $10; free to subscribers to *AB Bookman's Weekly.*

Congrat-Butlar, Stefan, ed. *Translation & Translators: An International Directory and Guide.* New York: R. R. Bowker, 1979. $35.

Kim, Ung Chon. *Policies of Publishers.* Metuchen, NJ: Scarecrow, 1978. pap. $9.50.

Literary Market Place, 1981, with Names & Numbers. New York: R. R. Bowker, ann. $29.50. The business directory of American book publishing.

Publishers and Distributors of the United States: A Directory. New York: R. R. Bowker, 1980. $8.95.

U.S. Book Publishing Yearbook and Directory, 1980/81. White Plains, NY: Knowledge Industry Publications, 1980. $35.

Foreign and International

International ISBN Publishers Directory, 1980. New York: R. R. Bowker, 1980. $95.

International Literary Market Place 1980-81. New York: R. R. Bowker, 1980. $35.

Publishers' International Directory. 8th ed. New York: K. G. Saur, 1979. $99.

Taubert, Sigfred, ed. *The Book Trade of the World.* Vol. I. Europe and International Sections. Vol. II. U.S.A., Canada, Central and South America, Australia and New Zealand. Vol. III. Africa, Asia. New York: R. R. Bowker. Vol. I, 1972, $46.75; Vol. II, 1976, $46.75; Vol. III, 1980, $46.75.

Turner, Mary C., ed. *La Empresa del Libro en America Latina.* Buenos Aires: Bowker Editores, 1974. $21.95. A "Literary Market Place" for Latin America.

UNESCO Statistical Yearbook, 1978/79. New York: Unipub, 1980. $85.75.

Writers and Artists Yearbook. Boston: The Writer, Inc., 1980. $12. Covers the British book world.

Newspapers and Periodicals

Directory of Newspapers and Periodicals. Philadelphia: N. W. Ayer, ann. $62.

Editor and Publisher International Year Book. New York: Editor and Publisher, ann. $35.

Irregular Serials and Annuals: An International Directory. New York: R. R. Bowker, 1980. $62.50.

Magazine Industry Market Place: The Directory of American Periodical Publishing. New York: R. R. Bowker, 1980. $35.

New Serial Titles 1950-1970. New York: R. R. Bowker, 1973. 4 vols. o.p. Available on microfilm, $100; or xerographic reprint, $250.

New Serial Titles 1950-1970, Subject Guide. New York: R. R. Bowker, 1975. 2 vols. $138.50.

Sources of Serials: An International Publisher and Corporate Author Directory to Ulrich's and Irregular Serials. New York: R. R. Bowker, 1977. $52.50.

Ulrich's International Periodicals Directory. 19th ed. New York: R. R. Bowker, 1980. $69.50.

Working Press of the Nation: Newspapers, Magazines, Radio and TV, and Internal Publications. Chicago: National Research Bureau, ann. 5 vols. $198.

EDITING

Barzun, Jacques. *Simple and Direct: A Rhetoric for Writers.* New York: Harper & Row, 1976. $11.95.

Bernstein, Theodore. *The Careful Writer.* New York: Atheneum, 1965. $14.95.

Fowler, H. W. *Directory of Modern English Usage.* 2nd rev. ed. New York: Oxford University Press, 1965. $12.50.

Jordan, Lewis. *The New York Times Manual of Style and Usage.* New York: Times Books, 1976. $10.

A Manual of Style. 12th rev. ed. Chicago: University of Chicago Press, 1969. $15.

Skillin, Marjorie E., and Gay, Robert M. *Words into Type.* Rev. ed. Englewood Cliffs, NJ: Prentice-Hall, 1974. $18.95.

Strunk, William, Jr., and White, E. B. *Elements of Style.* 3rd ed. New York: Macmillan, 1978. $4.95.

Zinsser, William. *On Writing Well: An Informal Guide to Writing Nonfiction*. 2d. ed. New York: Harper & Row, 1980. $8.50.

PERIODICALS

AB Bookman's Weekly (weekly including Yearbook). Clifton, NJ: AB Bookman's Weekly. $40.

American Book Publishing Record (monthly). New York: R. R. Bowker. $25.

The American Bookseller (monthly). New York: American Booksellers Association. $12.

BP Report: On the Business of Book Publishing (weekly). White Plains, NY: Knowledge Industry Publications. $165.

Printing and Publishing: Quarterly Industry Report. Washington, DC: U.S. Department of Commerce. $5.

Publishers Weekly. New York: R. R. Bowker. $38.

Scholarly Publishing: A Journal for Authors & Publishers (quarterly). Toronto: University of Toronto Press. $17.50.

Weekly Record. New York: R. R. Bowker. $15. A weekly listing of current American book publications, providing complete cataloging information.

For a list of periodicals reviewing books, see *Literary Market Place*.

Distinguished Books

LITERARY PRIZES, 1980

ASCAP-Deems Taylor Awards—$500. *Offered by:* American Society of Composers, Authors, and Publishers. *Winners:* David Baskerville for *Music Business Handbook and Career Guide* (Sherwood Co.); Xavier Frascogna, Jr. and H. Lee Hetherington for *Successful Artist Management* (Billboard Books); William Gottlieb for *The Golden Age of Jazz* (Simon & Schuster); Samuel Lipman for *Music after Modernism* (Basic Books); Hans Moldenhauer and Rosaleen Moldenhauer for *Anton von Webern* (Knopf); Daniel Patterson for *The Shaker Spiritual* (Princeton Univ. Press); Isabel Pope and Masakata Kanazawa for *The Musical Manuscript—Montecassino 871* (Oxford Univ. Press); Nolan Porterfield for *The Life and Times of America's Blue Yodeler—Jimmie Rodgers* (Univ. of Illinois Press); Roger Sessions for *Roger Sessions on Music* (Princeton Univ. Press); Solomon Volkov and Antonina Bauis for *Testimony—The Memoirs of Dmitri Shostakovitch* (Harper & Row); Eric von Schmidt and Jim Rooney for *Baby, Let Me Follow You Down* (Anchor Books).

Academy of American Poets Fellowship—$10,000. For distinguished poetic achievement. *Winner:* Mona Van Duyn.

Jane Addams Children's Book Award. For a book promoting the cause of peace, social justice, and world community. *Offered by:* Women's International League for Peace and Freedom and the Jane Addams Peace Association. *Winner:* David Kherdian for *The Road from Home: The Story of an Armenian Childhood* (Greenwillow).

American Academy and Institute of Arts and Letters Awards in Literature—$3,000 each. *Winners:* Ann Beattie, William Dickey, Paul Fussell, Maxine Kumin, George Oppen, Robert Pinsky, Lewis Thomas, Larry Woiwode; Richard Howard (award of merit medal for poetry).

American Academy in Rome Fellowship in Creative Writing—$7,180. *Offered by:* American Academy and Institute of Arts and Letters. *Winner:* Mary Morris.

American Book Awards. *Winners:* (art/illustrated—hardcover, collection) Larry Rivers with Carol Brightman for *Drawings and Digressions* (Clarkson N. Potter); (art/illustrated—hardcover, original art) Leonard Lubin for *The Birthday of the Infanta* by Oscar Wilde (Viking); (art/illustrated—paperback) Emily Blair Chewning for *Anatomy Illustrated* (Fireside/Simon & Schuster); (autobiography—hardcover) Lauren Bacall for *By Myself* (Knopf); (autobiography—paperback) Malcolm Cowley for *—And I Worked at the Writer's Trade: Chapters of Literary History, 1918-1978* (Penguin); (biography—hardcover) Edmund Morris for *The Rise of Theodore Roosevelt* (Coward, McCann & Geoghegan); (biography—paperback) A. Scott Berg for *Max Perkins: Editor of Genius* (Pocket Books); (children's—hardcover) Joan Blos for *A Gathering of Days: A New England Girl's Journal, 1830-32* (Scribner's); (children's—paperback) Madeline L'Engle for *A Swiftly Tilting Planet* (Dell); (current interest—hardcover) Julia Child for *Julia Child and More Company* (Knopf); (current interest—

paperback) Christopher Lasch for *The Culture of Narcissism* (Warner); (first novel) William Wharton for *Birdy* (Knopf); (general fiction—hardcover) William Styron for *Sophie's Choice* (Random); (general fiction—paperback) John Irving for *The World According to Garp* (Pocket Books); (general nonfiction—hardcover) Tom Wolfe for *The Right Stuff* (Farrar, Straus & Giroux); (general nonfiction—paperback) Peter Matthiessen for *The Snow Leopard* (Bantam); (general reference books—hardcover) Elder Witt, ed., for *Congressional Quarterly's Guide to the U.S. Supreme Court* (Congressional Quarterly); (history—hardcover) Henry Kissinger for *White House Years* (Little, Brown); (history—paperback) Barbara Tuchman for *A Distant Mirror: The Calamitous 14th Century* (Ballantine); (mystery—hardcover) John D. MacDonald for *The Green Ripper* (Lippincott); (mystery—paperback) William F. Buckley, Jr. for *Stained Glass* (Warner); (poetry) Philip Levine for *Ashes* (Atheneum, paperback); (religion/inspiration—hardcover) Elaine Pagels for *The Gnostic Gospels* (Random); (religion/inspiration—paperback) Sheldon Vanauken for *A Severe Mercy* (Bantam); (science—hardcover) Douglas Hofstadter for *Gödel, Escher, Bach: An Eternal Golden Chain* (Basic Books); (science—paperback) Gary Zukav for *The Dancing Wu Li Masters: An Overview of the New Physics* (Morrow); (science fiction—hardcover) Frederik Pohl for *Jem* (St. Martin's); (science fiction—paperback) Walter Wangerin, Jr. for *The Book of the Dun Cow* (Pocket Books); (translation) Jane Gary Harris and Constance Link for *The Complete Critical Prose and Letters* by Osip E. Mandelstam (Ardis); (western) Louis L'Amour for *Bendigo Shafter* (Bantam); (book design) R. D. Scudellari, art dir., for *The Architect's Eye: American Architectural Drawings from 1799-1978* by Deborah Nevins and Robert A. M. Stern (Pantheon); (cover design) Ann Spinelli, art dir., and David Myers, designer, for *Famous Potatoes* by Joe Cottonwood (Delta/Seymour Lawrence); (jacket design) Lidia Ferrara, art dir., and Fred Marcellino, designer, for *Birdy* by William Wharton (Knopf).

American Translators Association Award. *Winner:* Jamake Highwater for *Song from the Earth* (New York Graphic Society).

Hans Christian Andersen Medal. *Winners:* Suekichi Akaba (Japan); Bohumil Riha (Czechoslovakia).

Sherwood Anderson Book Award. *Offered by:* Ohioana Library Association. *Winner:* David Wagoner for *The Hanging Garden* (Atlantic-Little, Brown).

Anisfield-Wolf Award—$1,500. For a scholarly book in the field of race relations. *Offered by:* Cleveland Foundation. *Winners:* Carol Beckwith and Tepilit Ole Saitoti for *Maasai* (Abrams).

Association of Jewish Libraries Book Awards. For outstanding contributions in the field of Jewish literature for children. *Winners:* Carol Snyder for *Ike and Mama and the Block Wedding* (Coward); (body of work award) Marilyn Hirsh.

Bancroft Prize—$4,000 each. For books of exceptional merit and distinction in American history, American diplomacy, and the international relations of the United States. *Offered by:* Columbia University. *Winners:* Robert Dallek for *Franklin D. Roosevelt and American Foreign Policy: 1932-1945* (Oxford Univ. Press); Thomas Dublin for *Women at Work: The Transformation of Work and Community in Lowell, Massachusetts, 1826-1860* (Columbia Univ. Press); Donald Worster for *Dust Bowl: The Southern Plains in the 1930s* (Oxford Univ. Press).

Mildred L. Batchelder Award—citation. Intended to encourage the translation and publication in the United States of outstanding books originally written in languages other than English. *Offered by:* ALA Association for Library Service to Children. *Winner:* E. P. Dutton, for *The Sound of the Dragon's Feet* by Aliki Zei.

Curtis G. Benjamin Award for Creative Publishing. *Winner:* Ursula Nordstrom.

Bennett Award. *Winner:* V. S. Naipaul.

Gerard and Ella Berman Award—$500. For a book of Jewish history. *Offered by:* Jewish Book Council. *Winner:* Todd M. Endelman for *The Jews of Georgian England* (Jewish Publication Society).

James Tait Black Memorial Prizes—£400 each. *Winners:* (biography) Brian Finney for *Christopher Isherwood* (Faber); (novel) William Golding for *Darkness Visible* (Faber).

Bologna Children's Book Fair. Graphic Arts Prizes. *Winners:* (children's graphics) *Vault of Heaven and Snail Shell* (Verlag Sauerlander, Switzerland); (young people's graphics) *Anno's Song Book* (Kodansha, Japan); (budding critics) *The Book of the Village* (Fabula Verlag, Federal Republic of Germany).

Books in Canada Award. *Winner:* Clark Blaise for *Lunar Attractions* (Seal Books).

Boston Globe-Horn Book Awards—$200 each. For excellence in children's literature. *Winners:* (fiction) Andrew Davies for *Conrad's War* (Crown); (nonfiction) Mario Salvadori for *Building: The Fight against Gravity* (Atheneum/ McElderry); (illustration) Chris Van Allsburg for *The Garden of Abdul Gasazi* (Houghton Mifflin).

British National Book Awards. *Winners:* (children) Colin Dann for *The Animals of Farthing Wood* (Heinemann); (novel) Penelope Lively for *Treasures of Time* (Heinemann).

John Nicholas Brown Prize. *Offered by:* Mediaeval Academy of America. *Winner:* John Monfasani for *George of Trebizond: A Biography and a Study of His Rhetoric and Logic* (Brill of Leiden).

Georg Büchner Prize. *Offered by:* The West German Academy for Language and Poetry. *Winner:* Christa Wolf.

Witter Bynner Prize. *Offered by:* American Academy and Institute of Arts and Letters. *Winner:* Pamela White Hadas.

Caldecott Medal. For the most outstanding picture book for children. *Offered by:* ALA Association for Library Service to Children. *Medal contributed by:* Daniel Melcher. *Winner:* Barbara Cooney for *Ox-Cart Man* by Donald Hall (Viking).

California Young Reader Medal Awards. *Winners:* Betsy Byars for *The Pinballs* (Harper & Row); Bill Peet for *Big Bad Bruce* (Houghton Mifflin).

Canada Council Children's Literature Prize (Canada). *Winner:* Barbara Claassen Smucker for *Days of Terror* (Clark Irwin/ Herald Press).

Canadian Library Association Book of the Year for Children Award. *Offered by:* Canadian Association of Children's Librarians. *Winner:* James Houston for *River Runners: A Tale of Hardship and Bravery* (McClelland & Stewart).

Hadley Cantril Memorial Award. *Winner:* William Ker Muir, Jr. for *Police: Streetcorner Politicians* (Univ. of Chicago Press).

Carey-Thomas Award. For a distinguished project of book publishing. *Offered by:* R. R. Bowker. *Winner:* George Braziller, for an "exceptional publishing program"; (honor citation) University of California Press for *The Plan of St. Gall* by Walter Horn and Ernest Born; (special citation) Pantheon Books for *The Architect's Eye: American Architectural Drawings from 1799-1978* by Deborah Nevins and Robert A. M. Stern.

Carnegie Medal. For the outstanding book for children written in English and first published in the United Kingdom. *Offered by:* British Library Association. *Winner:* Peter Dickinson for *Tulku* (Gollancz).

Child Study Children's Book Committee at Bank Street College Award. *Winner:* T. A. Dyer for *The Whipman Is Watching* (Houghton Mifflin).

Children's Book Guild Nonfiction Award. *Winner:* Shirley Glubok.

Children's Reading Round Table Award. *Offered by:* ALA Children's Reading Round Table. *Winner:* Yolanda Frederici.

Children's Science Book Awards. *Offered by:* The New York Academy of Sciences. *Winners:* (younger category) Karla Kuskin, author, and Marc Simont, illustrator, for *A Space Story* (Harper & Row); (older category) Mario Salvadori, author, and Saralinda Hooker and Christopher Ragus, illustrators, for *Building: The Fight against Gravity* (Atheneum/McElderry); (special award) Harry N. Abrams, Inc., "for a series of reference books which have exceedingly beautiful photographs and which are unusually affordable."

Cholmondeley Award for Poets—£500 each. For the benefit and encouragement of poets of any age, sex, or nationality. *Offered by:* Society of Authors (UK). *Winners:* George Barker, Roy Fuller, Terence Tiller.

Christopher Awards. For books distinguished for their "affirmation of the highest values of the human spirit." *Winners:* (adult books) Mary Craig for *Blessings* (Morrow); Sally Fitzgerald, ed., for *The Habit of Being: Letters of Flannery O'Connor* (Farrar, Straus & Giroux); Philip Hallie for *Lest Innocent Blood Be Shed: The Story of the Village of Le Chambon and How Goodness Happened There* (Harper & Row); Elaine Ipswitch for *Scott Was Here* (Delacorte); Edmund Morris for *The Rise of Theodore Roosevelt* (Coward, McCann & Geoghegan); Norman Myers for *The Sinking Ark* (Pergamon); Kefa Sempangi with Barbara Thompson for *A Distant Grief* (Regal); Lewis Thomas for *The Medusa and the Snail* (Viking); Gary Zukov for *The Dancing Wu Li Masters* (Morrow); (children's books) Sue Ellen Bridgers for *All Together Now* (Knopf); Catharine Edmonds, Joan Gross, Olga Litowinsky, Stephen Mooser, Pamela Morton, Barbara Beasley Murphy, Barbara Seuling, Bebe Willoughby, eds., for *The New York Kid's Book* (Doubleday); Esther Allen Peterson for *Frederick's Alligator* (Crown); Gloria Skurzynski for *What Happened in Hamelin* (Four Winds).

Frank and Ethel S. Cohen Award—$500. For an outstanding book dealing with an aspect of Jewish thought originally written in English by a U.S. or Canadian resident. *Offered by:* Jewish Book Council of the National Jewish Welfare Board. *Winner:* David Biale for *Gershom Scholem: Kabbalah and Counter History* (Harvard Univ. Press).

Commonwealth Awards for Distinguished Service in Literature. *Winners:* Gabriel García Márquez and Robert Penn Warren.

Commonwealth Poetry Prize—£250. For a first published book by a poet who comes from a Commonwealth country other than Great Britain. *Winner:* Shirley Lim (Malaysia) for *Crossing the Peninsula* (Heinemann).

de la Torre Bueno Prize. *Winner:* Jack Anderson for *The One and Only: The Ballet Russe de Monte Carlo* (Dance Horizons).

Ralph Waldo Emerson Award. *Offered by:* Phi Beta Kappa. *Winners:* Frank E. Manuel and Fritzie P. Manuel for *Utopian Thought in the Western World* (Harvard Univ. Press).

English-Speaking Union of the United States Award. *Winner:* Nuruddin Farah (Somalia) for *Sweet and Sour Milk* (Allison & Busby, London).

William and Janice Epstein Award—$500. To encourage fictional writing on Jewish themes. *Offered by:* Jewish Book Council of the National Jewish Welfare Board. *Winner:* Daniel Fuchs for *The Apathetic Bookie Joint* (Methuen).

Christopher Ewart-Biggs Memorial Prize (Great Britain). *Winner:* Francis Lyons for *Culture and Anarchy in Ireland, 1890-1939* (Oxford Univ. Press).

Geoffrey Faber Memorial Prize (Great Britain). *Winners:* George Szirtes for *Slant Door* (Secker & Warburg); Hugo Williams for *Love-Life* (Andre Deutsch).

Eleanor Farjeon Award. For distinguished services to children's books. *Offered by:* Children's Book Circle (Great Britain). *Winner:* Dorothy Butler.

Dorothy Canfield Fisher Award—scroll. For a book selected by children of Vermont. *Offered by:* Vermont State PTA and Vermont State Department of Libraries. *Winner:* David Budbill for *Bones on Black Spruce Mountain* (Dial).

Four-Leaf Clover Award. *Offered by:* Lucky Book Club. *Winner:* Carla Stevens.

R. T. French Tastemaker Awards. *Winners:* (top cookbook and basic/general) Jacques Pepin for *La Methode* (Times Books); (Europe and the Americas) Elizabeth Lambert Ortiz for *The Book of Latin American Cooking* (Knopf); (international) Walter Slezak for *My Stomach Goes Traveling* (Doubleday); (natural foods/special diet) Helen Corbitt for *Helen Corbitt's Greenhouse Cookbook* (Houghton Mifflin); (oriental) Jean Yueh for *The Great Tastes of Chinese Cooking* (Times Books); (original softcover) James Beard for *James Beard's Fowl & Game Bird Cookery* (Harcourt Brace Jovanovich); (single subject) Gaston Lenôtre for *Lenôtre's Ice Creams and Candies* (Barron's); (specialty) Helen Witty and Elizabeth Schneider for *Better Than Store-Bought* (Harper & Row).

Friends of American Writers Awards—$1,000. For natives or residents of the Middle West or books with midwestern locale, for young readers. *Winner:* (adult award) Nancy Price for *An Accomplished Woman* (Coward, McCann & Geoghegan).

Georgia Children's Book Award. *Winners:* Harry Allard, author, and James Marshall, illustrator, for *Miss Nelson Is Missing* (Scholastic).

Alexander Gode Medal. *Offered by:* American Translators Association. *Winner:* Gregory Rabassa.

Goethe House-PEN Translation Prize—$500. For the best translation from German to English. *Winner:* Joachim Neugroschel for *The Tongue Set Free: Remembrance of a European Childhood* (Seabury).

Golden Spur Awards. *Offered by:* Western Writers of America. *Winners:* (novel) William Decker for *The Holdouts* (Little, Brown); (nonfiction) Donald E. Worcester for *The Apaches: Eagles of the Southwest* (Univ. of Oklahoma Press); (short subject) James Bellah for *Jason Glendauer's Watch* (Far West Magazine).

Eva L. Gordon Award for Children's Science Literature. *Offered by:* American Nature Society. *Winner:* Ross E. Hutchins for *Look at Ants* (Dodd, Mead).

Governor-General's Award (Canada). *Winner:* Michael Ondaatje for *Rat Jelly and Other Poems* (Marion Boyars).

Grand Prix du Roman (France). *Winner:* Louis Gardel for *Fort Saganne* (Seuil).

Kate Greenaway Medal. *Offered by:* British Library Association. *Winner:* Jan Pienkowski for *Haunted House* (Heinemann).

Haskins Medal. *Offered by:* Mediaeval Academy of America. *Winner:* Kenneth M. Setton for *The Papacy and the Levant (1204-1571)* (American Philosophical Society).

Hawthornden Prize—£100 and silver medal. To an English writer under 41 years of age for the best work of imaginative literature. *Offered by:* Society of Authors (UK). *Winner:* Peter Rushforth for *Kindergarten* (Hamish Hamilton).

Hugh M. Hefner First Amendment Award. *Winner:* (book publishing) Nat Hentoff for *The First Freedom: The Tumultuous History of Free Speech in America* (Delacorte).

Ernest Hemingway Foundation Award—$6,000. For the best first book of fiction by an American writer. *Offered by:* PEN American Center. *Winner:* Alan Saperstein for *Mom Kills Kids and Self* (Macmillan/Ballantine).

Herskovits Award. *Winners:* Margaret Strobel for *Muslim Women in Mombasa* (Yale Univ. Press); Richard B. Lee for *Kung San: Men, Women, and Work in a Foraging Society* (Cambridge Univ. Press).

Sidney Hillman Foundation Book Award. *Winner:* William Shawcross for *SideShow: Nixon, Kissinger and the Destruction of Cambodia* (Simon & Schuster).

Amelia Frances Howard-Gibbon Medal. For outstanding illustration of a children's book published in Canada. *Offered by:* Canadian Library Association. *Winner:* Laszlo Gal for *The Twelve Dancing Princesses*, retold by Janet Lunn (Methuen).

William Dean Howells Medal for Fiction. *Offered by:* American Academy and Institute of Arts and Letters. *Winner:* William Maxwell for *So Long, See You Tomorrow* (Knopf).

Hugo Award. See World Science Fiction Convention Awards.

International PEN Silver Pen Award (Great Britain). *Winner:* Anne Chisolm for *Nancy Cunard* (Sidgwick & Jackson).

International Reading Association Children's Book Award. *Winner:* Ouida Sebestyan for *Words by Heart* (Little, Brown).

Iowa School of Letters Award for Short Fiction—$1,000. For a book-length collection of short stories. *Winner:* James Fetler for *Deliberate Collisions* (Univ. of Iowa Press).

Blanche F. Ittleson Prize for Research in Child Psychiatry. *Winners:* Alexander Thomas and Stella Chase for *The Dynamics of Psychological Development* (Brunner/Mazel).

Joseph Henry Jackson Award. *Offered by:* San Francisco Foundation. *Winner:* Wendy Bishop.

Leon Jolson Award—$500. For the best book on the Nazi holocaust. *Offered by:* Jewish Book Council of the National Jewish Welfare Board. *Winner:* Benjamin B. Ferencz for *Less Than Slaves: Jewish Forced Labor and the Quest for Compensation* (Harvard Univ. Press).

Juniper Prize—$1,000. *Offered by:* University of Massachusetts Press. *Winner:* Lucille Clifton for *Two-Headed Woman* (Univ. of Massachusetts Press).

Janet Heidinger Kafka Prize in Fiction by an American Woman. *Winner:* Barbara Chase-Riboud for *Sally Hemings* (Viking/Avon).

Morris J. Kaplun Memorial Award—$500. For an outstanding book on the state of Israel. *Offered by:* Jewish Book Council of the National Jewish Welfare Board. *Winner:* Emanuel Levy for *The Habima—Israel's National Theater 1917–1977; A Study of Cultural Nationalism* (Columbia Univ. Press).

Sue Kaufman Prize for First Fiction. *Offered by:* American Academy and Institute of Arts and Letters. *Winner:* Jayne Anne Phillips for *Black Tickets* (Delacorte).

Irwin Kerlan Award. For achievement in children's literature. *Offered by:* Kerlan Collection, University of Minnesota. *Winner:* Glen Rounds.

Robert Kirsch Award. *Winners:* (outstanding body of work) Wallace Stegner; (poetry) Robert Kelly for *Kill the Messenger* (Black Sparrow Press).

Coretta Scott King Award. *Offered by:* American Library Association. *Winner:* Walter Dean Meyers for *The Young Land Lords* (Viking).

Janusz Korczak Literary Award—$1,000. *Offered by:* Anti-Defamation League of B'nai B'rith. *Winners:* Hugh Franks for *Will to Live* (Routledge, London) and Zindri Mandela for *Black as I Am* (Guild of Tutors).

Lamont Poetry Selection Award. *Offered by:* Academy of American Poets. *Winner:* Michael Van Walleghen for *More Trouble with the Obvious* (Univ. of Illinois Press).

Harold Morton Landon Translation Awards. *Winners:* Saralyn R. Daly for *The Book of True Love*, by Juan Ruiz (Pennsylvania State Univ. Press) and Edmund Keeley for *Ritsos in Parentheses*, by Yannis Ritsos (Princeton Univ. Press).

Jules F. Landry Award—$1,000. For the best manuscript submitted to Louisiana State University Press in the field of southern history, biography, or literature. *Winner:* William Gillette for *Retreat from Reconstruction, 1869–1879* (Louisiana State Univ. Press).

Abraham Lincoln Award for Literature. *Winner:* John Cheever.

Locus Awards. *Winners:* (anthology) Terry Carr, ed., for *Universe 9* (Doubleday); (art or illustrated book) Wayne D. Barlowe and Ian Summers for *Barlowe's Guide to Extraterrestrials* (Workman); (artist) Michael Whelan; (fantasy novel) Patricia McKillip for *Harpist in the Wind* (Atheneum); (magazine) *The Magazine of Fantasy and Science Fiction;* (novelette) George R. R. Martin for *Sandkings* (Omni); (novella) Barry B. Longyear for *Enemy Mine* (Isaac Asimov's Science Fiction Magazine); (publisher) Ballantine/Del Rey; (related nonfiction book) Peter Nicholls, ed., for *The Science Fiction Encyclopedia* (Doubleday); (science fiction novel) John Varley for *Titan* (Berkley/Putnam); (short story) George R. R. Martin for "The Way of Cross and Dragon" (Omni); (single-author collection) Larry Niven for *Convergent Series* (Del Rey).

Los Angeles Times Book Prizes. *Winners:* (fiction) Walker Percy for *The Second Coming* (Farrar, Straus & Giroux); (general interest) Harrison Salisbury for *Without Fear or Favor* (Times Books); (history/biography) Ronald Steel for *Walter Lippmann and the American Century* (Atlantic/Little, Brown).

James Russell Lowell Prize—$1,000. *Offered by:* Modern Language Association of America. *Winner:* Barbara Lewalski for *Protestant Poetics and the Seventeenth-Century Religious Lyric* (Princeton Univ. Press).

Booker McConnell Award (Great Britain). *Winner:* William Golding for *Rites of Passage* (Faber).

Howard R. Marraro Prize in Literature. *Winner:* Nicholas J. Perella for *Midday in Italian Literature: Variations on an Archetypal Theme* (Princeton Univ. Press).

Lenore Marshall Memorial Poetry Prize—$3,500. For an outstanding book of poems published in the United States. *Offered by:* New Hope Foundation and *Saturday Review. Administered by:* Book-of-the-Month Club. *Winner:* Stanley Kunitz for *The Poems of Stanley Kunitz* (Atlantic-Little, Brown).

Somerset Maugham Award—£500. *Winners:* Humphrey Carpenter for *The Inklings* (Allen & Unwin); Max Hastings for *Bomber Command* (Michael Joseph); Christopher Reid for *Arcadia* (Oxford Univ. Press).

Frederic G. Melcher Book Award—$1,000. For the most significant contribution to religious liberalism. *Offered by:* Unitarian/Universalist General Assembly. *Winners:* Frank E. Manuel and Fritzie P. Manuel for *Utopian Thought in the Western World* (Harvard Univ. Press).

Jan Mitchell Prize in Art History—$10,000. For the author of an outstanding book on art history. *Winner:* Michael Baxandall for *The Limewood*

Sculptors of Renaissance Germany (Yale Univ. Press).

Harriet Monroe Poetry Award. *Winner:* Charles Simic.

Mother Goose Award (Great Britain). *Winner:* Reg Cartwright, illustrator, for *Mr. Potter's Pigeon* by Patrick Kinmouth (Hutchinson).

Frank Luther Mott-Kappa Tau Alpha Research Award. For the best book in journalism. *Winner:* David Halberstam for *The Powers That Be* (Knopf).

Mystery Writers of America—Edgars. *Winners:* (best mystery novel) Arthur Maling for *The Rheingold Route* (Harper & Row); (best first novel) Richard North Patterson for *The Lasko Tangent* (Norton); (best paperback) William L. DeAndrea for *The Hog Murders* (Avon); (best short story) Geoffrey Norman for "Armed and Dangerous" (Esquire); (fact crime book) Robert Lindsey for *The Falcon and the Snowman* (Simon & Schuster); (best critical/biographical study) Ralph E. Hone for *Dorothy L. Sayers: A Literary Biography* (Kent State Univ. Press); (grand master) W. R. Burnett; (juvenile novel) Joan Lowery Nixon for *The Kidnapping of Christine Lattimore* (Harcourt Brace Jovanovich).

National Arts Club Gold Medal of Honor. *Winner:* Isaac Bashevis Singer.

National Book Critics Circle Awards. *Winners:* (fiction) Shirley Hazzard for *Transit of Venus* (Viking); (general nonfiction) Ronald Steel for *Walter Lippmann and the American Century* (Atlantic-Little, Brown); (poetry) Frederick Seidel for *Sunrise* (Viking Penguin); (criticism) Helen Vendler for *Part of Nature, Part of Us: Modern American Poets* (Harvard Univ. Press).

National Council of Teachers of English Award for Excellence in Poetry for Children. *Winner:* Myra Cohn Livingston.

National Historical Society Book Prize. *Winner:* John D. Unruh, Jr. for *The Plains Across: The Overland Emigrants and the Trans-Mississippi West, 1840–1860* (Univ. of Illinois Press).

Nebula Awards. For excellence in the field of science fiction. *Offered by:* Science Fiction Writers of America. *Winners:* (novel) Arthur C. Clarke for *The Fountains of Paradise* (Harcourt Brace Jovanovich); (novella) Barry B. Longyear for *Enemy Mine* (Isaac Asimov's Science Fiction Magazine); (novelette) George R. R. Martin for *Sandkings* (Omni); (short story) Edward Bryant for "giANTS" (Analog).

Nene Award. *Winner:* Paula Danziger for *The Cat Ate My Gymsuit* (Delacorte).

Neustadt International Prize for Literature (United States). *Winner:* Joseph Skvorecky.

New Jersey Library Association Garden State Children's Book Awards. *Winners:* (easy-to-read) Peggy Parish, author, and Lynn Sweat, illustrator, for *Teach Us, Amelia Bedelia* (Greenwillow); (younger fiction) Beverly Cleary, author, and Alan Tiegreen, illustrator, for *Ramona and Her Father* (Morrow); (younger nonfiction) Tomie De Paola for *The Quicksand Book* (Holiday).

New Writers Awards. *Offered by:* Great Lakes Colleges Association. *Winners:* (fiction) Robert Bohm for *In the Americas* (Panache Books); (poetry) Eve Shelnutt for *The Love Child* (Black Sparrow Press).

New York Academy of Sciences Children's Science Book Awards. *See* Children's Science Book Awards.

New York Times Best Illustrated Children's Book Awards. *Winners:* Edward Ardizzone for *A Child's Christmas in Wales* by Dylan Thomas (David R. Godine); Guy Billout for *Stone & Steel: A Look at Engineering* (Prentice-Hall); M. B. Goffstein for *An Artist* (Harper & Row); Helme Heine for *Mr. Miller the Dog* (Atheneum/McElderry); Arnold Lobel for *The Headless Horseman Rides Tonight: More Poems to Trouble Your Sleep* by Jack Prelutsky (Greenwillow); David Macaulay for *Unbuilding* (Houghton Mifflin); Allen Say for *The Lucky Yak* by Annetta Lawson (Parnassus/Houghton Mifflin); Binette Schroeder for *The Wonderful Travels and Adventures of Baron Münchhausen*, text by Peter Nickl (Chatto & Windus Merrimack Book Service); William Steig for *Gorky Rises* (Farrar, Straus & Giroux); James Stevenson for *Howard* (Greenwillow).

New Zealand Book Award (New Zealand). *Winner:* Sylvia Ashton-Warner for *I Passed This Way* (A. H. & A. W. Reed Ltd.).

Newbery Medal. For the most distinguished contribution to literature for children. *Donor:* ALA Library Service to Children. *Medal contributed by:* Daniel Melcher. *Winner:* Joan W. Blos for *A Gathering of Days: A New England Girl's Journal, 1830-32* (Scribner's).

Nobel Prize for Literature—about $130,000. For high achievement in the field of literature. *Offered by:* Swedish Academy, Stockholm. *Winner:* Czeslaw Milosz.

Noma Award for Publishing in Africa (Japan). *Winner:* Mariama Bâ for *Une si longue lettre* (Les Nouvelles Editions Africaines—Dakar, Senegal).

Norte Prize (United States). *Winner:* Mario Szichman (Argentina) for "A las 20:25 la senora entro en la inmortalidad" (at 8:30 p.m. the lady entered immortality). Unpublished manuscript.

Eve Orpen Award for Excellence in Publishing (Canada) *Winner:* Harald Bohne.

George Orwell Award. For distinguished contributions to honesty and clarity in public language. *Offered by:* National Council of Teachers of English. *Winner:* Sheila Harty for *Hucksters in the Classroom: A Review of Industry, Propaganda in Schools* (Center for Study of Responsive Law).

Owl Prize (Japan). *Winner:* Irene Haas, illustrator, for *Carrie Hepple's Garden* by Ruth Craft (Atheneum).

PEN Translation Prize—$1,000. For the best book-length translation into English. *Donor:* Book-of-the-Month Club. *Winner:* Charles Simic for *Homage to the Lame Wolf* by Vasco Popa.

Pegasus Prize for Literature. *Winner:* Kirsten Thorup for *Baby* (Louisiana State Univ. Press).

Phi Beta Kappa Science Award. *Offered by:* Phi Beta Kappa. *Winner:* David A. Park for *The Image of Eternity: Roots of Time in the Physical World* (Univ. of Massachusetts Press).

Photographic Historical Society of New York Prize. For distinguished achievement in photographic history. *Winner:* William Crawford for *The Keepers of Light* (Morgan & Morgan).

George Polk Award in Journalism. *Winner:* William Shawcross for *Sideshow: Kissinger, Nixon and the Destruction of Cambodia* (Simon & Schuster Pocketbooks).

Prix Femina. *Winner:* Jocelyne François for *Jouenous España* (Gallimard/Mercure de France).

Prix Goncourt. *Winner:* Yves Navarre for *Jardin d'acclimatation* (Flammarion).

Prix Interallie. *Winner:* Christine Arnothy for *Toutes les chances plus une* (Grasset).

Prix Medicis. *Winner:* Jean-Luc Benoziglio for *Cabinet Portrait* (Seuil).

Prix Medicis Etranger. *Winner:* Andre Brink for *A Dry White Season* (Stock).

PSP Awards. *Offered by:* Professional and Scholarly Publishing Division of the Association of American Publishers. *Winners:* (Hawkins Award) Gerald L. Mandell, R. Gordon Douglas, and John E. Bennett for *Principles and Practices of Infectious Diseases* (Wiley); (architecture and urban planning and excellence in book design and production) Walter Horn and Ernest Born for *The Plan of St. Gall* (Univ. of California Press); (business and management) David M. Brownstone and Gorton Carruth for *Where to Find Business Information* (Wiley); (engineering) Frederick S. Merritt for *Building Engineering and Systems Design* (Van Nostrand Reinhold); (humanities) Frank E. Manuel and Fritzie P. Manuel for *Utopian Thought in the Western World* (Harvard Univ. Press); (life sciences) Robert F. Goldberger, ed., for *Biological Regulation and Development* (Plenum); (most creative & innovative new project) Matthew M. Cohen for *Instructions for Parents* (Appleton-Century-Crofts); (physical and earth sciences) Kenneth Lang and Owen Gingerich for *Sourcebook in Astronomy and Astrophysics* (Harvard Univ. Press); (technology) John E. Midwinter for *Optical Fibers for Transmission* (Wiley); (outstanding new journal of the year) Wayne Delozier, ed., for *The Journal of Experimental Learning and Simulation* (Elsevier).

Pulitzer Prizes—$1,000 each. *Offered by:* Trustees of Columbia University on the recommendation of the Advisory Board on the Pulitzer Prizes. *Winners:* (fiction) Norman Mailer for *The Executioner's Song* (Little, Brown); (general nonfiction) Douglas R. Hofstadter for *Gödel, Escher, Bach: An Eternal Golden Braid* (Basic); (biography) Edmund Morris for *The Rise of Theodore Roosevelt* (Coward, McCann & Geoghegan); (history) Leon F. Litwack for *Been in the Storm So Long: The Aftermath of Slavery* (Knopf); (poetry) Donald Rodney Justice for *Selected Poems* (Atheneum).

Trevor Reese Memorial Prize (Great Britain). *Winner:* John Lliffe for *A Modern History of Tanganyika* (Cambridge Univ. Press).

Regina Medal. For distinguished contribution to children's literature. *Offered by:* Catholic Library Association. *Winner:* Beverly Cleary.

John Llewellyn Rhys Memorial Prize—£100. For a memorable book by a British Commonwealth writer under 30. *Offered by:* John Llewellyn Rhys Memorial Trust/National Book League. *Winner:* Desmond Hogan for *The Diamonds at the Bottom of the Sea* (Hamish Hamilton).

Richard and Hinda Rosenthal Foundation Award—$2,000. For a work of fiction that is a considerable literary achievement though not necessarily a commercial success. *Offered by:* American Academy and Institute of Arts and Letters. *Winner:* Stanley Elkin for *The Living End* (Dutton).

Carl Sandburg Awards. *Offered by:* Friends of the Chicago Public Library. *Winners:* (fiction) Cyrus Colter for *Night Studies* (Swallow); (nonfiction) Ernest Samuels for *Bernard Berenson: The Making of a Connoisseur* (Harvard Univ. Press); (poetry) John Jacob for *Scatter—Selected Poems* (Wine Press).

Charles and Bertie G. Schwartz Award for Jewish Juvenile Literature. *Offered by:* National Jewish Book Awards. *Winner:* Arnost Lustig for *Dita Saxova* (Harper & Row).

Scott-Moncrieff Prize (Great Britain) *Winners:* Brian Pearce for *The Institutions of France under the Absolute Monarchy.*

Seal Books Novel Award—$50,000. *Offered by:* Seal Books (Canada). *Winner:* Tim Wynne-Jones for *Odd's End* (McClelland & Stewart).

Sequoyah Children's Book Award. *Winner:* Eleanor Clymer for *The Get-Away Car* (Dutton).

Constance Lindsay Skinner Award. *Offered by:* Women's National Book Association. *Winner:* Anne Pellowski.

Kenneth B. Smilen/Present Tense Literary Awards. *Winners:* (fiction) Philip Roth for *The Ghost Writer* (Farrar, Straus & Giroux); (general nonfiction) Philip Hallie for *Lest Innocent Blood Be Shed: The Story of the Village of Le Chambon and How Goodness Happened There* (Harper); (Judaica) Arthur Green for *Tormented Master: A Life of Rabbi Nahman of Bratslav* (Univ. of Alabama Press); (photography) Gail Rubin for *Psalmist with a Camera* (Abbeville); (scholarship) Benjamin B. Ferencz for *Less Than Slaves: Jewish Forced Labor and the Quest for Compensation* (Harvard Univ. Press).

W. H. Smith Literary Award—£1,000. To the author of a book written in English and published in the United Kingdom which makes the most significant contribution to literature. *Offered by:* W. H. Smith & Son Ltd. *Winner:* Thom Gunn for *Selected Poems 1950–1975* (Faber).

John Ben Snow Prize. *Winner:* Diantha Dow Schull for *Landmarks of Otsego County* (Syracuse Univ. Press).

Society of Midland Authors Awards. *Winners:* (biography) Nellie Snyder Yost for *Buffalo Bill: His Family, Friends, Fame and Failures* (Swallow); (fiction) William Maxwell for *So Long, See You Tomorrow* (Knopf); (history) John D. Unruh, Jr. for *The Plains Across: The Overland Emigrants and the Trans-Mississippi West, 1840–1860* (Univ. of Illinois Press); (poetry) Ralph Mills for *Living with Distance* (Boa Editions); (politics and economics) Edwin Chen for *P.B.B.: An American Tragedy* (Prentice-Hall); (psychology and sociology) J. Fred Macdonald for *Don't Touch that Dial* (Nelson-Hall); children's book) Lucinda Mays for *The Other Shore* (Atheneum).

James J. Strebig Memorial Trophy. *Offered by:* Aviation/Space Writers Association. *Winner:* Harny B. Combs for *Kill Devil Hill: Discovering the Secret of the Wright Brothers* (Houghton Mifflin).

Theatre Library Association Award. For the outstanding book on recorded performance, including motion pictures and television. *Winner:* Herbert J. Gans for *Deciding What's News: A Study of "The CBS Evening News," "The NBC Nightly News," Newsweek and Time* (Pantheon).

Irita Van Doren Award—silver bowl. For outstanding contributions to the cause of books and reading. *Offered by:* American Booksellers Association, Publishers Ad Club, and Publishers Publicity Association. *Winner:* Studs Terkel.

Harold D. Vursell Award. *Offered by:* American Academy and Institute of Arts and Letters. *Winner:* Tom Wolfe.

Wattie Award (New Zealand). *Winner:* Albert Wendt for *Leaves of the Banyan* (Longman Paul).

Walt Whitman Award—$1,000. To an unpublished poet. *Offered by:* Academy of American Poets and the Copernicus Society of America. *Winner:* Jared Carter for *Work, for the Night Is Coming* (Macmillan).

Laura Ingalls Wilder Medal. *Winner:* Dr. Seuss (Theodor Geisel).

Laurence L. Winship Award. *Winner:* Millicent Bell for *Marquand: An American Life* (Atlantic-Little, Brown).

Nero Wolfe Award for Mystery Fiction. *Winner:* Helen McCloy for *Burn This* (Dodd, Mead).

World Fantasy Awards. *Winners:* (novel) Elizabeth A. Lynn for *Watchtower* (Berkley/Putnam); (anthology/collection) Jessica Amanda Salmonson, ed., for *Amazons!* (DAW); (life achievement) Manly Wade Wellman; (short story) Elizabth A. Lynn for "The Woman Who Loved the Moon" (Amazons) and Ramsey Campbell for "Mackintosh Willy" (Shadows 2).

World Science Fiction Convention Awards. *Winners:* (John W. Campbell Award) Barry B. Longyear; (Gandulf Award) Ray Bradbury; *Hugo Awards:* (nonfiction) Peter Nichols, ed., for *The Science Fiction Encyclopedia* (Doubleday); (novel) Arthur C. Clarke for *The Fountains of Paradise* (Harcourt Brace Jovanovich); (novelette) George R. R. Martin for *Sandkings* (Omni); (novella) Barry B. Longyear for *Enemy Mine* (Isaac Asimov's Science Fiction Magazine); (short story) George R. R. Martin for "The Way of Cross and Dragon" (Omni).

Yale Series of Younger Poets. For a first volume of poetry by a promising young American poet. *Offered by:* Yale University Press. *Winner:* John Bensko for *In the Dark, the Shelves* (Yale Univ. Press).

Young Hoosier Book Award. *Winner:* Willo Davis Roberts for *Don't Hurt Laurie* (Atheneum).

Morton Dauwen Zabel Award—$2,500. For a poet of progressive, original, and experimental tendencies. *Offered by:* American Academy and Institute of Arts and Letters. *Winner:* Donald Finkel.

NOTABLE BOOKS OF 1980

This is the thirty-fourth year in which this list of distinguished books has been issued by the Notable Books Council of the Reference and Adult Services Division of the American Library Association.

Arnold, Eve. *In China.* Knopf.
Atwood, Margaret. *Life before Man.* Simon & Schuster.
Bogan, Louise. *Journey around My Room: The Autobiography of Louise Bogan.* Viking.
Calvino, Italo, comp. *Italian Folktales.* Trans. by George Martin. Helen and Kurt Wolff/HBJ.
Desai, Anita. *Clear Light of Day.* Harper.
Drabble, Margaret. *The Middle Ground.* Knopf.
Flaubert, Gustave. *The Letters of Gustave Flaubert, 1830–1857.* Selected, edited, and trans. by Francis Steegmuller. Belknap/Harvard Univ. Pr.
Gibson, Margaret. *The Butterfly Ward.* Vanguard.
Gould, Stephen Jay. *The Panda's Thumb: More Reflections in Natural History.* Norton.
Kaplan, Justin. *Walt Whitman: A Life.* Simon & Schuster.
Keneally, Thomas. *Confederates.* Harper.
Kiely, Benedict. *The State of Ireland: A Novella & Seventeen Stories.* Godine.
Kingston, Maxine Hong. *China Men.* Knopf.
Kramer, Jane. *Unsettling Europe.* Random.
Lanes, Selma G. *The Art of Maurice Sendak.* Abrams.
Lash, Joseph P. *Helen and Teacher: The Story of Helen Keller and Anne Sullivan Macy.* Delacorte/Seymour Lawrence.
Lipman, Jean, and Armstrong, Tom, eds. *American Folk Painters of Three Centuries.* Hudson Hills Pr.
Manchester, William. *Goodbye, Darkness: A Memoir of the Pacific War.* Little.
Massie, Robert K. *Peter the Great: His Life and World.* Knopf.
Meredith, William. *The Cheer.* Knopf.
Morris, Wright. *Plains Song: For Female Voices.* Harper.
Percy, Walker. *The Second Coming.* Farrar.
Pym, Barbara. *A Glass of Blessings.* Dutton.
Rubin, William, ed. *Pablo Picasso: A Retrospective.* Museum of Modern Art.

Silk, Leonard, and Silk, Mark. *The American Establishment.* Basic.

Steel, Ronald. *Walter Lippmann and the American Century.* Atlantic/Little.

Strand, Mark. *Selected Poems.* Atheneum.

Strouse, Jean. *Alice James: A Biography.* Houghton.

Toole, John Kennedy. *A Confederacy of Dunces.* Louisiana State Univ. Pr.

Troyat, Henri. *Catherine the Great.* Dutton.

Vendler, Helen. *Part of Nature, Part of Us.* Harvard Univ. Pr.

Watt, Ian. *Conrad in the Nineteenth Century.* Univ. of California Pr.

Welty, Eudora. *The Collected Stories of Eudora Welty.* Harcourt.

BEST YOUNG ADULT BOOKS OF 1980

Each year a committee of the Young Adult Services Division of the American Library Association compiles a list of best books for young adults selected on the basis of young adult appeal. These titles must meet acceptable standards of library merit and provide a variety of subjects for different tastes and a broad range of reading levels. *School Library Journal* (*SLJ*) also provides a list of best books for young adults. This year the list was compiled by Rose Moorachian and *SLJ*'s Greater Boston Area Committee of Public and School Library YA Specialists and published in the December 1980 issue of *SLJ*. The following list combines the titles selected for both lists. The notation ALA or *SLJ* following the price indicates from which list each title was taken.

Adams, Douglas. *The Hitchhiker's Guide to the Galaxy.* Harmony. $6.95. ALA.

Auel, Jean M. *Clan of the Cave Bear.* Crown. $12.95. ALA.

Bach, Alice. *Waiting for Johnny Miracle.* Harper. $8.95. ALA.

Barlowe, Wayne Douglas and Ian Summers. *Barlowe's Guide to Extraterrestrials.* Workman. $14.95. pap. $7.95. ALA.

Bode, Janet. *Kids Having Kids: The Unwed Teenage Parent.* Watts. $7.95. ALA.

Boissard, Janine. *A Matter of Feeling.* Little. $8.95. ALA, *SLJ*.

Boyle, Donald. *Brown Sugar: 80 Years of America's Black Superstars.* Harmony. $15.95. ALA.

Bradshaw, Gillian. *Hawk of May.* Simon & Schuster. $10.95. ALA.

Brancato, Robin. *Come Alive at 505.* Knopf. $7.95. ALA.

Brown, Dee. *Creek Mary's Blood.* Holt. $12.95. ALA.

Brown, Michael. *Laying Waste: The Poisoning of America by Toxic Chemicals.* Pantheon. $11.95. ALA.

Butterworth, W. E. *LeRoy and the Old Man.* Four Winds. $7.95. ALA.

Calvert, Patricia. *The Snowbird.* Scribner's. $1.75. ALA.

Carlisle, Olga. *Island in Time: A Memoir of Childhood.* Holt. $12.95. *SLJ*.

Cohen, Barbara. *Unicorns in the Rain.* Atheneum. $8.95. ALA.

Curtis, Patricia. *Animal Rights.* Four Winds. $8.95. ALA.

Demetz, Hana. *The House on Prague Street.* St. Martin's. $8.95. *SLJ*.

DeVeaux, Alexis. *Don't Explain.* Harper. $7.95. ALA.

Due, Linnea A. *High and Outside.* Harper. $9.95. ALA.

Evans, Christopher. *The Micro Millennium.* Viking. $10.95. *SLJ*.

Garfield, Brian. *The Paladin.* Simon & Schuster. $17.95. ALA.

Gwaltney, John Langston. *Dry-longso, a Self Portrait of Black America.* Random. $12.95. *SLJ.*

Hall, Lynn. *The Leaving.* Scribner's. $8.95. ALA.

Haugaard, Erik Christian. *Chase Me, Catch Nobody.* Houghton. $7.95. ALA.

Hayden, Torey. *One Child.* Putnam. $9.95. ALA, *SLJ.*

Heidish, March Moran. *Witnesses.* Houghton. $10.95. *SLJ.*

Highwater, Jamake. *The Sun, He Dies.* Lippincott. $11.95. *SLJ.*

Hogan, William. *The Quartzsite Trip.* Atheneum. $10.95. ALA, *SLJ.*

Judson, Horace Freeland. *The Search for Solutions.* Holt. $16.95. *SLJ.*

King, Stephen. *Firestarter.* Viking. $13.95. ALA.

Lee, Mildred. *The People Therein.* Houghton. $10.95. ALA.

Laure, Jason, and Ettagale, Laure. *South Africa: Coming of Age under Apartheid.* Farrar. $13.95. ALA.

LeGuin, Ursula K. *The Beginning Place.* Harper. $8.95. ALA, *SLJ.*

Lewinski, Jorge. *The Camera at War: A History of War Photography from 1848 to the Present Day.* Simon & Shuster. $17.95. *SLJ.*

MacLeish, Robert. *First Book of Eppe.* Random. $9.95. ALA.

Maiorano, Robert. *Worlds Apart: The Autobiography of a Dancer from Brooklyn.* Coward. $9.95. ALA.

Matthew, Christopher. *Long-haired Boy.* Atheneum. $9.95. ALA.

Mayerson, Evelyn. *If Birds Are Free.* Lippincott. $10.95. *SLJ.*

Miller, Frances. *The Truth Trap.* Dutton. $9.95. ALA.

Millman, Marcia. *Such a Pretty Face: Being Fat in America.* Norton. $10.95. *SLJ.*

O'Neal, Zibby. *Language of Goldfish.* Viking. $8.95. ALA.

Paterson, Katherine. *Jacob Have I Loved.* Crowell. $8.95. ALA.

Pfeffer, Susan Beth. *About David.* Delacorte. $8.95. ALA.

Platt, Colin. *The Atlas of Medieval Man.* St. Martin's. $22.50. *SLJ.*

Prince, Alison. *The Turkey's Nest.* Morrow. $7.95. ALA.

Prochnik, Leon. *Endings: Death, Glorious and Otherwise as Faced by Ten Outstanding Figures of Our Times.* Crown. $9.95. ALA.

Sagan, Carl. *Cosmos.* Random. $19.95. ALA.

Sallis, Susan. *Only Love.* Harper. $8.95. ALA.

Sargent, Pamela. *Watchstar.* Simon & Schuster, pap. $2.25. *SLJ.*

Sebestyen, Ouida. *Far from Home.* Atlantic/Little. $8.95. ALA.

Shreve, Susan. *The Masquerade.* Knopf. $7.95. ALA.

Silverberg, Robert. *Lord Valentine's Castle.* Harper. $12.50. ALA.

Spielman, Ed. *The Mighty Atom.* Viking. $10.95. ALA.

Terkel, Studs. *American Dreams: Lost and Found.* Pantheon. $14.95. ALA.

Thomas, Kurt, and Kent Hannon. *Kurt Thomas on Gymnastics.* Simon & Schuster. $19.95. pap. $8.95. ALA.

Vinge, Joan D. *The Snow Queen.* Dial. $10.95. *SLJ.*

Webb, Sheyann, and Rachel Nelson. *Selma Lord, Selma: Girlhood Memories of Civil Rights Days.* Univ. of Alabama Press. $4.95. ALA.

Wells, Rosemary. *When No One Was Looking.* Dial. $8.95. ALA.

Wolfe, Tom. *The Right Stuff.* Farrar. pap. $3.50. ALA.

Yeager, Robert C. *Seasons of Shame: The New Violence in Sports.* McGraw. $12.95. *SLJ.*

Zindel, Paul. *The Pigman's Legacy.* Harper. $8.95. ALA.

BEST CHILDREN'S BOOKS OF 1980

A list of notable children's books is selected each year by the Notable Children's Books Committee of the Association for Library Service to Children of the American Library Association. The committee is aided by suggestions from school and public children's librarians throughout the United States. The book review editors of *School Library Journal* (*SLJ*) also compile a list each year, with full annotations, of best books for children. The following list is a combination of ALA's Notable Children's Books of 1980" and *SLJ*'s selection of "Best Books 1980," published in the December 1980 issue of *SLJ*. The source of each selection is indicated by the notation ALA or *SLJ* following the price. [See the article "Literary Prizes" for Newbery, Caldecott, and other award winners—Ed.]

Anno, Mitsumasa. *Anno's Medieval World.* Adapt. from the trans. by Ursula Synge. Philomel. $9.95. ALA.

Bang, Molly. *The Grey Lady and the Strawberry Snatcher.* Four Winds. $10.95. ALA.

Briggs, K. M. *Kate Crackernuts.* Greenwillow. $9.95. *SLJ.*

Bryan, Ashley. *Beat the Story-Drum, Pum-Pum.* Atheneum. $10.95. ALA.

Bullard, Pamela, and Judith Stoia. *The Hardest Lesson: Personal Accounts of a Desegregation Crisis.* Little. $8.95. *SLJ.*

Burch, Robert. *Ida Early Comes over the Mountain.* Viking. $8.95. ALA, *SLJ.*

Byars, Betsy. *The Night Swimmers.* Illus. by Troy Howell. Delacorte. $7.95. *SLJ.*

Cherry, Mike. *Steel Beams and Iron Men.* Four Winds (Scholastic). $9.95. *SLJ.*

Chukovsky, Korney. *Good Morning, Chick.* Adapt. by Mirra Ginsburg. Illus. by Byron Barton. Greenwillow. $7.95. *SLJ.*

Clements, Bruce. *Anywhere Else But Here.* Farrar. $8.95. *SLJ.*

Cohen, Barbara. *I Am Joseph.* Illus. by Charles Milolaycak. Lothrop. $9.95. ALA.

Cole, Joanna. *A Frog's Body.* Photos by Jerome Wexler. Morrow. $6.95. ALA, *SLJ.*

Crews, Donald. *Truck.* Greenwillow. $7.95. ALA, *SLJ.*

Davies, Andrew. *Conrad's War.* Crown. $7.95. ALA, *SLJ.*

Edmonds, Walter D. *The Night Raider and Other Stories.* Little. $6.95. *SLJ.*

Fox, Paula. *A Place Apart.* Farrar. $9.95. *SLJ.*

Freedman, Russell. *Immigrant Kids.* Dutton. $9.95. ALA.

Fritz, Jean. *Where Do You Think You're Going, Christopher Columbus?* Illus. by Margot Tomes. Putnam. $7.95. ALA, *SLJ.*

Galdone, Paul. *King of the Cats: A Ghost Story by Joseph Jacobs.* Houghton/Clarion. $8.95. *SLJ.*

Giblin, James, and Dale Ferguson. *The Scarecrow Book.* Crown. $8.95. ALA.

Grimm Brothers. *The Bremen-Town Musicians.* Retold and illus. by Ilse Plume. Doubleday. $8.95. ALA.

———. *Hansel and Gretel.* Illus. by Lisbeth Zwerger. Trans. from the German by Elizabeth D. Crawford. Morrow. $7.95. ALA.

Hancock, Sibyl. *Old Blue.* Illus. by Erick Ingraham. Putnam. $6.95. ALA.

Hill, Eric. *Where's Spot?* Putnam. $6.95. ALA.

Horwitz, Elinor Lander. *On the Land: American Agriculture from Past to Present.* Atheneum. $8.95. *SLJ.*

Hurmence, Belinda. *Tough Tiffany.* Doubleday. $7.95. ALA.

Hutchins, Pat. *The Tale of Thomas Mead.* Greenwillow. $5.95. *SLJ.*

Irwin, Constance. *Strange Footprints on the Land: Vikings in America.* Harper. $8.95. *SLJ.*

Jaspersohn, William. *How the Forest Grew.* Illus. by Chuck Eckart. Greenwillow. $5.95. ALA.

Kuskin, Karla. *Dogs & Dragons, Trees & Dreams.* Harper. $8.79. ALA.

Langton, Jane. *The Fledgling.* Harper. $7.89. ALA.

L'Engle, Madeleine. *A Ring of Endless Light.* Farrar. $9.95. ALA.

Lee, Mildred. *The People Therein.* Houghton/Clarion. $10.95. *SLJ.*

Lerner, Carol. *Seasons of the Tallgrass Prairie.* Morrow. $7.95. ALA.

Lobel, Arnold. *Fables.* Harper. $8.95. ALA.

Low, Joseph. *Mice Twice.* Atheneum. $9.95. ALA.

Lowry, Lois. *Autumn Street.* Houghton. $6.95. ALA, *SLJ.*

Macaulay, David. *Unbuilding.* Houghton. $9.95. *SLJ.*

MacLachlan, Patricia. *Arthur, for the Very First Time.* Illus. by Lloyd Bloom. Harper. $8.95. ALA.

Major, Kevin. *Hold Fast.* Delacorte. $8.95. *SLJ.*

Noble, Trinka Hakes. *The Day Jimmy's Boa Ate the Wash.* Illus. by Steven Kellog. Dial. $7.95. ALA.

Moore, Lillian. *Think of Shadows.* Illus. by Deborah Robison. Atheneum. $7.95. ALA.

Oakley, Graham. *Graham Oakley's Magical Changes.* Atheneum. $12.95. ALA.

O'Neal, Zibby. *The Language of Goldfish.* Viking. $8.95. ALA, *SLJ.*

Opie, Iona and Peter Opie. *A Nursery Companion.* Oxford. $19.95 *SLJ.*

Parker, Nancy Winslow. *Poofy Loves Company.* Dodd. $7.95. ALA.

Paterson, Katherine. *Jacob Have I Loved.* Crowell. $8.95. ALA, *SLJ.*

Pelgrom, Els. *The Winter When Time Was Frozen.* Trans. from the Dutch by Maryka and Raphael Rudnik. Morrow. $8.95. ALA.

Peter and the Wolf. Adapt. from the musical tale by Sergei Prokofiev. Illus. by Erna Voigt. Godine. $10. ALA.

Pomerantz, Charlotte. *The Tamarindo Puppy and Other Poems.* Greenwillow. $7.95. ALA, *SLJ.*

Prelutsky, Jack. *The Headless Horseman Rides Tonight: More Poems to Trouble Your Sleep.* Illus. by Arnold Lobel. Greenwillow. $7.95. *SLJ.*

Pringle, Laurence. *Lives at Stake: The Science and Politics of Environmental Health.* Macmillan. $8.95. *SLJ.*

Rice, Eve. *Goodnight, Goodnight.* Greenwillow. $6.95. ALA, *SLJ.*

Rockwell, Harlow. *My Kitchen.* Greenwillow. $7.95. ALA.

Sargent, Sarah. *Weird Henry Berg.* Crown. $7.95. *SLJ.*

Sebestyen, Ouida. *Far from Home.* Atlantic (Little). $8.95. *SLJ.*

Selsam, Millicent E. *Eat the Fruit, Plant the Seed.* Morrow. $7.95. *SLJ.*

Siegel, Beatrice. *An Eye on the World: Margaret Bourke-White, Photographer.* Warne. $8.95. ALA.

Slepian, Jan. *The Alfred Summer.* Macmillan. $7.95. *SLJ.*

Stecher, Miriam B., and Alice S. Kandell. *Max, the Music-Maker.* Lothrop. $6.95. ALA.

Stevenson, James. *Howard.* Greenwillow. $7.95. *SLJ.*

———. *That Terrible Halloween Night.* Greenwillow. $7.95. ALA, *SLJ.*

Switzer, Ellen. *Our Urban Planet.* Photographs by Michael John Switzer and Jeffrey Gilbert Switzer. Atheneum. $12.95. *SLJ.*

The Three Little Pigs. Illus. by Erik Blegvad. Atheneum. $8.95. *SLJ.*

Travers, P. L. *Two Pairs of Shoes.* Illus. by Leo Dillon and Diane Dillon. Viking. $10.95. ALA.

Turner, Ann. *A Hunter Comes Home.* Crown. $7.95. ALA.

Wells, Rosemary. *When No One Was Looking.* Dial. $8.95. *SLJ.*

Westall, Robert. *Fathom Five.* Greenwillow. $7.95. *SLJ.*

Yorinks, Arthur. *Louis the Fish.* Illus. by Richard Egielski. Farrar. $9.95. *SLJ.*

Young, Ed. *High on a Hill: A Book of Chinese Riddles.* Collins. $8.95. ALA.

Zizmor, Jonathan, and Diane English. *The Doctor's Do-It-Yourself Guide to Clearer Skin.* Lippincott. $7.95. *SLJ.*

Zolotow, Charlotte. *Say It!* Illus. by James Stevenson. Greenwillow. $7.95. ALA.

BEST SELLERS OF 1980: HARDCOVER FICTION AND NONFICTION

Daisy Maryles
Senior Editor, *Publishers Weekly*

Higher unit sales for a wider spread of fiction titles than ever before, including books by veteran novelists as well as first fiction from acclaimed writers of nonfiction and a mixture of historical novels, sagas, and suspense, characterize *Publishers Weekly*'s list of top 1980 fiction best sellers. In nonfiction, the adage that politics make strange bedfellows could be applied equally to books. Unsurprisingly, in a year that saw double-digit inflation and a prime lending rate of 20 percent, many nonfiction best sellers were financial self-help books. But alongside these money salvos were cookbooks; books about the future and outer space; new books by a Watergate conspirator and former President Nixon; and books to help develop one's human potential, and about one person's cure through holistic medicine therapy.

This year's list of 1980 top fiction sellers includes six novels with sales over 200,000 copies and 24 with sales over 100,000 copies. Previously, the best fiction performance was in 1979, when 21 titles topped the 100,000-copy mark.

The unit sales for the nonfiction titles were a bit lower than in previous years, but there were many more nonfiction titles racking up six-figure unit sales. In fact, seven books with sales over 100,000 copies did not even make our list of the top 25 sellers.

The books on *PW*'s annual best seller lists, including runners-up, are based on sales figures supplied by publishers. All figures are claimed by the respective firms to reflect only 1980 U.S. trade sales—that is, sales to bookstores, wholesalers, and libraries only. There are books that appear in the listings without their copy-sales figures printed here; missing figures in such cases were submitted to *PW* in confidence, for use only in placing titles in their correct positions on a specific list.

Publishers' sales figures only reflect books shipped and billed, and are not necessarily the final net sales for the books. In a number of cases, the 1980 sales figures of the publisher will include books still on bookstore and wholesaler shelves at the end of the year, some of which are earmarked for returns.

Again, publishers continue to question the veracity of the figures that some of their colleagues quote for these lists, often suggesting that sales figures in some houses are exaggerated to get an author on an annual list (while at the same time, all pub-

Note: Adapted from *Publishers Weekly,* March 13, 1981, where the article was entitled "The Year's Bestselling Books: Hardcover Fiction and Nonfiction."

lishers attest to the correctness of their own figures). *PW* is still open to ideas for a workable, foolproof method for collecting sales figures for these lists that would be acceptable to all publishers. Short of attaining that ideal, we decided to reprint B. Dalton's 1980 bestsellers [see Bookselling & Marketing in *Publishers Weekly*, March 13, 1981]. A new James Michener novel has in recent years become a sure bet for the top position on these annual lists, and the author did not disappoint in 1980. Michener's blockbuster 1,000-page historical novel of South Africa easily outdistanced the unit sales of the other fiction best sellers. *The Covenant* sold about 553,000 copies in the last two months of 1980 and continues to hold the number 1 spot of *PW*'s weekly best seller list. Michener's last two best sellers—*Chesapeake* in 1978 and *Centennial*, published in 1974—both led *PW*'s annual lists in their year of publication.

The second best selling fiction spot for 1980 is taken by Robert Ludlum for *The Bourne Identity*, with sales of 325,000 copies. It enjoyed the lead position on *PW*'s weekly lists longer than any other novel in 1980, virtually dominating the chart from mid-March to the end of July. In 1979, Ludlum garnered the top spot on *PW*'s annual list for *The Matarese Circle* with sales of 250,000 copies.

Two first novels on the top 15 list include authors well known in nonfiction circles. In the number 9 spot, with sales of 197,000 copies is *The Fifth Horseman* by Larry Collins and Dominique Lapierre. Both had previously collaborated on best selling nonfiction works, including *Is Paris Burning?*, *Freedom at Midnight*, and *O Jerusalem*. The number 10 spot, with sales of 161,700, is taken by *The Spike*, by veteran journalists Arnaud de Borchgrave, senior editor of *Newsweek*, and Robert Moss of the London *Economist*.

The only other newcomers among authors to these annual lists among the top 15 are Cynthia Freeman with *Come Pour the Wine* and Lawrence Sanders with *The Tenth Commandment* (which earned the number 15 spot with sales of nearly 129,000 copies). However, both Freeman and Sanders are no strangers to best seller charts in general, and their previous works made weekly charts.

The remaining nine novelists on the 1980 list are all veterans. In fact Sidney Sheldon, Judith Krantz, Ken Follett, and Belva Plain enjoyed almost the same rankings in 1978 as on this year's list. Sheldon's *Rage of Angels*, number 3 best seller in 1980, had the top spot on *PW*'s weekly chart for two months. (Two years ago *Bloodline* made number 4 on the annual.) Krantz, with sales of 240,000 copies for her second novel, *Princess Daisy*, is number 4 this year. While it never topped *PW*'s list (it ran a close race in the second position), it was 1980's longest-running hardcover best seller, enjoying a spot on the list for at least 35 out of 52 weeks. Her first novel, *Scruples*, was number 5 in 1978, with sales of 210,000 copies. Follett, in the number 6 spot for his 1980 sales of *The Key to Rebecca*, took the number 10 spot in 1978 for *The Eye of the Needle*; the author also managed the number 11 position for *Triple* in 1979. Plain's first novel, *Evergreen*, sold 182,738 copies in 1978, enough for the number 6 spot. In 1980, her second novel, *Random Winds*, sold more than 199,500 copies, which gave it the number 7 rank.

Stephen King, the best selling author in the horror-suspense genre, continues to gain popularity with hardcover buyers. While his books always sold well in paperback, it was only with his third novel, *The Stand*, that he began to rank high on hardcover best seller charts. In 1979, King made number 6 on these annual charts with sales of 175,000 copies for that title; he did much better in 1980 with *Firestarter*, which sold nearly 285,000 copies.

In the early seventies, Frederick Forsyth achieved a top rank on annual best seller charts four years in a row for three novels; in fact, in 1972, he was in the number 3 and number 4 spots with *The Odessa File* and *The Day of the Jackal*, respectively.

Then Forsyth took a break from fiction writing, but happily for his fans not for too long. His fourth novel, *The Devil's Alternative*, made the 1980 list in the number 8 spot with sales of 194,500.

Erica Jong's best seller this year, *Fanny*, made the number 12 spot with sales of nearly 150,000 copies in 1980; back in 1977, she ranked number 8 with sales of 141,190 for *How to Save Your Own Life*, and her first novel, *Fear of Flying*, has been one of the best selling paperbacks in the past decade. At the same time, her status on these annual best seller charts heralds a growing trend in publishing—mass market firms entering the hardcover mainstream.

E. L. Doctorow places number 13 this year, with sales of 141,200 for *Loon Lake*. In 1975, he saw sales of 232,340 for *Ragtime*, which was enough to rank the book as the lead seller of that year.

Back in 1946, Taylor Caldwell made an annual list for the first time with sales of 221,000 for *This Side of Innocence* (it was that year's second top-selling fiction). Subsequently, she has become a familiar fixture on *PW*'s end-of-the-year charts. Her latest, *Answer as a Man*, sold 136,000 copies and came in at number 14.

THE FICTION RUNNERS-UP

For the first time in the history of these annual lists, all the fiction runners-up boasted sales of over 98,000 copies. The novelists that made the second tier included six veterans of the lists. A first novel, *The Clan of the Cave Bear*, also made the group; publisher Crown claimed its $100,000 advance was one of the largest for a first novel. New names on these end-of-the-year charts include Jeffrey Archer, Eric Van Lustbader, and Helen Van Slyke (her novel was published posthumously). For Archer and Lustbader, their latest novels represented their first major commercial successes.

In ranked order, the 10 fiction runners-up are: *The Second Lady* by Irving Wallace (NAL Books, published 10/10/80; 125,000 copies sold in 1980); *No Love Lost* by Helen Van Slyke (Lippincott & Crowell, 5/2/80; 121,419); *Kane & Abel* by Jeffrey Archer (Simon & Schuster, 5/25/80; 121,000); *The Clan of the Cave Bear* by Jean M. Auel (Crown, 9/10/80; 119,000); *The Origin: A Biographical Novel of Charles Darwin* by Irving Stone (Doubleday, 8/8/80); *The Ninja* by Eric Van Lustbader (M. Evans/Dutton, dist., 5/29/80; 114,800); *Sins of the Father* by Susan Howatch (Simon & Schuster, 6/30/80; 113,000); *Unfinished Tales* by J. R. R. Tolkien, edited by Christopher Tolkien (Houghton Mifflin, 11/18/80); *Creek Mary's Blood* by Dee Brown (Holt, Rinehart and Winston, 3/35/80; 98,150); and *Manchu* by Robert Elegant (McGraw-Hill, 10/19/80; 98,000).

THE NONFICTION BEST SELLERS

The most popular hardcover category in 1980 was of books that offered information or advice on money matters. Five of the top 15 nonfiction titles of the year dealt with this subject, as did one of the runners-up. Their total 1980 sales exceeded 1.4 million copies, thus at least assuring financial self-help for their authors.

Leading the nonfiction best seller chart is *Crisis Investing* by Douglas R. Casey, which sold 438,640 copies in 1980; it had a five-month tenure on *PW*'s weekly best seller lists last year (seven weeks as the national nonfiction leader) and is still one of the lead best sellers on the weekly charts. In the number 3 position, with sales of about 310,000 copies, is *Free to Choose;* the authors, Milton and Rose Friedman, build a case for calling for a rollback of government controls on the economy. That thought generated enough consumer interest to make the book the longest-running nonfiction best seller in 1980, since *Free to Choose* placed on *PW*'s weekly list 47 times.

Robert Allen's *Nothing Down*, number 9 in 1980, offered advice on hedging inflation by investing in real estate to at least 197,000 customers in 1980. Real estate was also the panacea in best seller number 15—Albert J. Lowry's *How to Become Financially Independent by Investing in Real Estate*, which sold 152,000 copies in 1980. It also is making a reappearance on *PW*'s annual list; in 1979 it held the number 12 spot with sales of 184,000 copies. *The Coming Currency Collapse* by Jerome F. Smith is in the number 14 spot with sales of nearly 160,000 copies and is its publisher's first best seller.

Carl Sagan's *Cosmos* secured the number 2 spot with sales of 423,000 copies and was the scarcest book around by the end of 1980 as a 13-part PBS series on the book created an unexpected deluge of customers. Sagan's earlier books, *Broca's Brain* and *The Dragons of Eden*, both placed on *PW*'s annual charts.

Gay Talese's long-awaited, much-heralded firsthand report on sex in America received an exceptional amount of press and broadcast coverage and *Thy Neighbor's Wife* perched atop *PW*'s weekly list for three months. It sold enough copies to secure the number 5 position.

The autobiography that people were most interested in reading was Shelley Winters's "tell-all," which came in at number 10. Two other autobiographies—Ingrid Bergman's and Phil Donahue's—sold in sufficient quantities to make the runners-up list. At the same time, self revelations by Gloria Swanson, Merv Griffin, and Linda Lovelace all sold over 100,000, a high sales rate that in previous years would have garnered one of the top 25 spots.

Woody Allen's most successful collection of humor pieces to date, *Side Effects*, sold 190,100 copies, enough to secure the number 11 spot. His previous collection, *Without Feathers*, was a runner-up on the 1975 end-of-year list with sales of 94,300.

A book that enjoyed a 37-week run on 1980 weekly *PW* lists, *Anatomy of an Illness*, talked about the author's successful battle with a disease that had been diagnosed as incurable; its sales earned the book the number 4 position. Alvin Toffler made a first appearance on an annual list with *The Third Wave*, number 7, which presents a look at what lies ahead in the eighties and beyond. Wayne Dyer made his fourth appearance on these annuals with *The Sky's the Limit*, which racked up sales of 213,000 copies, enough for the number 6 spot.

Two cookbooks add to the mix of 1980 top sellers: *Craig Claiborne's Gourmet Diet*, number 8 with sales of 198,000 copies; and *Betty Crocker's International Cookbook*, number 13 with sales of 166,800. Last year's number 14 nonfiction best seller, *The Fannie Farmer Cookbook*, makes a reappearance as a runner-up. Luckily for indulgers, there is also a best selling fitness book—*James Fixx's Second Book of Running*; it sold 171,900 copies in 1980, making it the number 12 best seller for the year. Fixx's *Complete Book of Running* was number 3 in 1978 with sales of over 543,400 copies.

THE NONFICTION RUNNERS-UP

This year's nonfiction runners-up demonstrate the eclectic tastes of the American reading public; their choices included sex, literary vignettes, politics, cookbooks, war memoirs, and a book of lists.

In ranked order, the 10 nonfiction runners-up are: *Men in Love* by Nancy Friday (Delacorte, published 3/31/80; 151,000 copies sold); *The Real War* by Richard Nixon (Warner Books, 5/16/80; 150,300); *The Fanny Farmer Cookbook* (Knopf, 9/19/79; 148,300 sold in 1980); *Money Dynamics for the 1980s* by Venita VanCaspel (Reston/Prentice-Hall, 9/80; 147,000); *Music for Chameleons* by Truman Capote

(Random House, 8/22/80; 130,100); *Book of Lists #2* by Irving Wallace, David Wallechinsky, Amy Wallace, and Sylvia Wallace (Morrow, 2/21/80); *Will: The Autobiography of G. Gordon Liddy* by G. Gordon Liddy (St. Martin's, 5/16/80; 125,130); *Donahue: My Own Story* by Phil Donahue & Co. (Simon & Schuster, 2/13/80; 123,000); and *Goodbye Darkness: A Memoir of the Pacific War* by William Manchester (Little, Brown, 9/17/80).

PUBLISHERS WEEKLY HARDCOVER TOP SELLERS

Fiction

1. *The Covenant* by James A. Michener (published November 24, 1980) Random House
2. *The Bourne Identity* by Robert Ludlum (March 26, 1980) Richard Marek (Putnam, dist.)
3. *Rage of Angels* by Sidney Sheldon (July 8, 1980) Morrow
4. *Princess Daisy* by Judith Krantz (March 9, 1980) Crown
5. *Firestarter* by Stephen King (September 29, 1980) Viking
6. *The Key to Rebecca* by Ken Follett (September 22, 1980) Morrow
7. *Random Winds* by Belva Plain (May 27, 1980) Delacorte
8. *The Devil's Alternative* by Frederick Forsyth (March 3, 1980) Viking
9. *The Fifth Horseman* by Larry Collins and Dominique Lapierre (August 25, 1980) Simon & Schuster
10. *The Spike* by Arnaud de Borchgrave and Robert Moss (May 1, 1980) Crown
11. *Come Pour the Wine* by Cynthia Freeman (November 27, 1980) Arbor House
12. *Fanny, Being the True History of the Adventures of Fanny Hackabout Jones* by Erica Jong (August 19, 1980) NAL Books
13. *Loon Lake* by E. L. Doctorow (September 25, 1980) Random House
14. *Answer as a Man* by Taylor Caldwell (January 12, 1981; shipped early to reach bookstores in late November) Putnam
15. *The Tenth Commandment* by Lawrence Sanders (September 19, 1980) Putnam

Nonfiction

1. *Crisis Investing: Opportunities and Profits in the Coming Great Depression* by Douglas R. Casey (July 21, 1980) Stratford Press (Harper & Row, dist.)
2. *Cosmos* by Carl Sagan (October 24, 1980) Random House
3. *Free to Choose: A Personal Statement* by Milton and Rose Friedman (January 11, 1980) Harcourt Brace Jovanovich
4. *Anatomy of an Illness as Perceived by the Patient* by Norman Cousins (September 24, 1979) Norton
5. *Thy Neighbor's Wife* by Gay Talese (May 2, 1980) Doubleday
6. *The Sky's the Limit* by Dr. Wayne W. Dyer (October 15, 1980) Simon & Schuster
7. *The Third Wave* by Alvin Toffler (March 24, 1980) Morrow
8. *Craig Claiborne's Gourmet Diet* by Craig Claiborne with Pierre Franey (June 23, 1980) Times Books
9. *Nothing Down* by Robert Allen (February 27, 1980) Simon & Schuster
10. *Shelley Also Known as Shirley* by Shelley Winters (June 19, 1980) Morrow
11. *Side Effects* by Woody Allen (September 30, 1980) Random House
12. *Jim Fixx's Second Book of Running* by James F. Fixx (April 21, 1980) Random House
13. *Betty Crocker's International Cookbook* (September 26, 1980) Random House

14. *The Coming Currency Collapse and what to do about it* by Jerome F. Smith (October 14, 1980) Books in Focus
15. *How to Become Financially Independent by Investing in Real Estate* by Albert J. Lowry (November 1977; redistributed in 1979 and marketed as a new title) Simon & Schuster

Note: Rankings on this list are determined by sales figures provided by the publishers; the numbers reflect reports of copies "shipped and billed" only and should not be regarded as net sales figures since publishers do not yet know what their final returns will be.

Part 7
Directory of Organizations

Directory of Library and Related Organizations

NATIONAL LIBRARY AND INFORMATION-INDUSTRY ASSOCIATIONS, UNITED STATES AND CANADA

AMERICAN ASSOCIATION OF LAW LIBRARIES
53 W. Jackson Blvd., Chicago, IL 60604
312-939-4764

OBJECT

"To promote librarianship, to develop and increase the usefulness of law libraries, to cultivate the science of law librarianship and to foster a spirit of cooperation among members of the profession." Established 1906. Memb. 2,850. Dues (Active) $65; (Inst.) $65; (Assoc.) $65 & $125; (Student) $10. Year. June 1 to May 31.

MEMBERSHIP

Persons officially connected with a law library or with a law section of a state or general library, separately maintained; and institutions. Associate membership available for others.

OFFICERS (JUNE 1980–JUNE 1981)

Pres. Francis Gates, Columbia Univ., Law Lib., 435 W. 116 St., New York, NY 10027; *V.P./Pres.-Elect.* Roger F. Jacobs, U.S. Supreme Court, Law Lib., One First St. N.E., Washington, DC 20543; *Secy.* Shirley R. Bysiewicz, Univ. of Connecticut, School of Law Lib., 1800 Asylum Ave., West Hartford, CT 06117; *Treas.* Joyce Malden, Municipal Reference Lib., 1004 City Hall, Chicago, IL 60602; *Past Pres.* Connie E. Bolden, Washington State Law Lib., Temple of Justice, Olympia, WA 98501.

EXECUTIVE BOARD

Officers; Sue Dyer; Mary Fisher; Anthony P. Grech; Marcia Koslov; Kathie Price; Carol West.

COMMITTEE CHAIRPERSONS (1980–1981)

Certification Board. Edgar J. Bellefontaine, Social Law Lib., 1200 Court House, Boston, MA 02108.
CONELL. Claire Engel, State Law Lib. of Montana, Capitol Bldg., Helena, MT 59601.
Constitution and Bylaws. Robert L. Oakley, Boston Univ., Pappas Law Lib., 765 Commonwealth Ave., Boston, MA 02115.
Copyright. Laura Nell Gasaway, Univ. of Oklahoma Law Lib., 300 Timberdell, Norman, OK 73019.
Education. Jill Mubarak, Univ. of Southern California, 3660 University Ave., Los Angeles, CA 90007.
Elections. Rita Dermody, Continental Bank Corporate Counsel, 231 S. LaSalle St., Chicago, IL 60693.
Exchange of Duplicates. Merle J. Slyhoff, Univ. of Pennsylvania, Biddle Law Lib., 3400 Chestnut St., Philadelphia, PA 19104.

Foreign, Comparative and International Law. Anita K. Head, Univ. of Kansas, School of Law, Lawrence, KS 66045.

Index to Foreign Legal Periodicals. Robert C. Berring, Harvard Law School Lib., Langdell Hall, Cambridge, MA 02138.

Indexing of Periodical Literature. Marlene McGuirl, Lib. of Congress/American British Div., 10 First St. S.E., Washington, DC 20540.

Joseph L. Andrews Bibliographic Award. S. Alan Holoch, Univ. of Southern California, Law Center, University Pk., Los Angeles, CA 90007.

Law Library Journal. Penelope A. Hazelton, Univ. of Maine, School of Law, Donald Garbrecht Law Lib., 246 Deering Ave., Portland, ME 04102.

Legislation and Legal Developments. Leah F. Chanin, Walter F. George School of Law, Mercer Univ., 1021 Georgia Ave., Macon, GA 31201.

Membership. Charlotte L. Levy, Brooklyn Law School, 250 Joralemon St., Brooklyn, NY 11201.

Memorials. George E. Skinner, Univ. of Arkansas, School of Law Lib., Fayetteville, AR 72701.

Nominations. Maureen McCann Moore, Dept. of Justice Lib., Washington, DC 20530.

Placement. Larry Wenger, Univ. of Virginia, Law Lib., North Grounds, Charlottesville, VA 22901.

Public Relations. Alice J. Murray, Univ. of the Pacific, McGeorge College of Law, 3282 Fifth Ave., Sacramento, CA 95817.

Recuitment. Donna M. Tuke, Friedman and Koven, 208 S. LaSalle St., Chicago, IL 60604.

Relations with Publishers and Dealers. Dick Danner, Duke Univ., School of Law Lib., Durham, NC 27706.

Scholarships and Grants. Dennis J. Stone, Gonzaga Univ., School of Law, Box 3538, 600 E. Sharp, Spokane, WA 99220.

Standards. Patricia Wyatt, Dilworth, Paxson, Kalish and Levy, 2600 Fidelity Bldg., Philadelphia, PA 19109.

Statistics. David Thomas, Brigham Young Univ., Law Lib., Provo, UT 84601.

SPECIAL-INTEREST SECTION CHAIRPERSONS

Academic Law Libraries. Reynold J. Kosek, Mercer Univ., Walter F. George School of Law, 1021 Georgia Ave., Macon, GA 31201.

Automation and Scientific Development. Robert S. Grundy, Conoco Inc. Law Lib., Suite 1614, Box 2197, Houston, TX 77001.

Contemporary Social Problems. Peter C. Schanck, Univ. of Detroit, 551 E. Jefferson, Detroit, MI 48226.

Government Documents. Michael Gehringer, U.S. Supreme Court, Lib., One First St. N.E., Washington, DC 20543.

Law Library Service to Institutional Residents. Ann Puckett, Southern Illinois Univ., School of Law Lib., Carbondale, IL 62901.

Micrographics and Audiovisual. Lynn Wishart, School of Law, Washington and Lee Univ., Lexington, VA 24450.

On-Line Bibliographic Services. Catherine Chenu-Campbell, McGeorge School of Law Lib., Univ. of the Pacific, 3282 Fifth Ave., Sacramento, CA 95817.

Private Law Libraries. Dianne C. Witkowski, Schiff, Hardin and Waite, 233 S. Wacker Dr., Suite 7200, Chicago, IL 60606.

Readers' Service. Nicholas Triffin, Univ. of Connecticut, West Hartford, CT 06117.

State, Court and County Law Libraries. Judith M. Foust, State Lib. of Pennsylvania, Education Bldg., Harrisburg, PA 17126.

Technical Services. Colleen M. Raker, Univ. of Pennsylvania, Biddle Law Lib., 3400 Chestnut St., Philadelphia, PA 19104.

REPRESENTATIVES

ABA (American Bar Association). Dan Henke.

American Correctional Association. D. A. Divilbiss.

American Library Association. Judith Wright.
American Library Association. Adult Services Committee. Inter-Library Loan Code Revision Committee. Randall Peterson.
American National Standards Institute. Committee PH-5. Larry Wenger.
American National Standards Institute. Committee Z-39. Robert L. Oakley.
American Society for Information Science. Signe Larson.
Association of American Law Schools. Earl Borgeson.
British-Irish Association of Law Libraries. Connie Bolden.
CLENE. Kathleen Price.
Canadian Association of Law Libraries. Paul Murphy.
Council of National Library and Information Associations. Al Coco; Jane Hammond.
Council of National Library and Information Associations. Ad Hoc Committee on Copyright. Laura N. Gasaway.
International Association of Law Libraries. Anita K. Head.
Library of Congress. Carleton Kenyon.
Special Libraries Association. Sally Wiant.
U.S. Copyright Office. Ellen Mahar.

AMERICAN LIBRARY ASSOCIATION
Executive Director, Robert Wedgeworth
50 E. Huron St., Chicago, IL 60611
312-944-6780

OBJECT

The American Library Association is an organization for librarians and libraries with the overarching objective of promoting and improving library service and librarianship. Memb. (Indiv.) 32,178; (Inst.) 3,079. Dues (Indiv.) $50; (Nonsalaried Libns.) $15; (Trustee & Lay Members) $20; (Student) $10; (Foreign Indiv.) $30; (Inst.) $50 & up (depending upon operating expenses of institution).

MEMBERSHIP

Any person, library, or other organization interested in library service and librarianship.

OFFICERS

Pres. Peggy A. Sullivan, Chicago Public Lib., 425 N. Michigan Ave., Chicago, IL 60611; *V.P./Pres.-Elect.* Elizabeth W. (Betty) Stone, Grad. Dept. of Lib. & Info. Science, Catholic Univ. of America, Washington, DC 20064; *Treas.* Herbert Biblo, John Crerar Lib., 35 W. 33 St., Chicago, IL 60616; *Exec. Dir.* (*Ex officio*). Robert Wedgeworth. (Address general correspondence to the executive director.)

EXECUTIVE BOARD

Officers; immediate past pres.; Thomas J. Galvin (1981); Norman Horrocks (1981); Donald H. Trottier (1981); Connie R. Dunlap (1982); Grace P. Slocum (1982); E. J. Josey (1983); Ella Gaines Yates (1983); Jane Anne Hannigan (1984); Brooke E. Sheldon (1984).

ENDOWMENT TRUSTEES

John Juergensmeyer (1981); John E. Velde (1982); William V. Jackson (1983).

DIVISIONS

See the separate entries that follow: American Assn. of School Libns.; American Lib. Trustee Assn.; Assn. for Lib. Service to Children; Assn. of College and Research Libs.; Assn. of Specialized and Cooperative Lib. Agencies; Lib. Admin. and Management Assn.; Lib. and Info. Technology Assn.; Public Lib. Assn.; Reference and Adult Services Div.; Resources and Technical Services Div.; Young Adult Services Div.

PUBLICATIONS

American Libraries (11 issues; memb.).
ALA Handbook of Organization 1980-1981 and membership directory (ann.).
ALA Yearbook (ann.; $55).
Booklist (23 issues; $32).
Choice (11 issues; $50).

ROUND TABLE CHAIRPERSONS

(ALA staff liaison is given in parentheses.)

Exhibits. Jean Mester, H. W. Wilson Co., 950 University Ave., Bronx, NY 10452 (Chris Hoy).

Federal Librarians. Mary A. Huffer, Dept. of Interior, Washington, DC 20240 (to be appointed).

Government Documents. Jeanne Isacco, Cuyahoga County Lib. System, 4510 Memphis Ave., Cleveland, OH 44144 (Bill Drewett).

Intellectual Freedom. Eli M. Oboler, University Lib., Idaho State Univ., Pocatello, ID 83209 (Henry Reichman).

International Relations. Josephine R. Fang, School of Lib. Science, Simmons College, Boston, MA 02115 (Jane Wilson).

Junior Members. Anne Hollingsworth, Texas State Lib., Box 12927, Capitol Sta., Austin, TX 78711 (Patricia Scarry).

Library History. Phyllis Dain, School of Lib. Service, Columbia Univ., New York, NY 10027 (Joel M. Lee).

Library Instruction. Lois M. Pausch, 246 Lib., Univ. of Illinois, Urbana, IL 61801 (Jeniece Guy).

Library Research. Ruth Katz, Assoc. Dir., Joyner Lib., East Carolina Univ., Greenville, NC 27834 (Mary Jo Lynch).

Map and Geography. David A. Cobb, Map and Geography Lib., Univ. of Illinois, Urbana, IL 61801 (Celeste Lavelli).

Social Responsibilities. Barbara J. Pruett, 2798 Porter St., Washington, DC 20008 (Jean E. Coleman).

Staff Organizations. Charles King, Free Public Lib., Louisville, KY 40203 (John Katzenberger).

COMMITTEE CHAIRPERSONS

Accreditation (Standing). Tom G. Watson, Univ. of the South, Sewanee, TN 37375 (Elinor Yungmeyer).

"American Libraries," Editorial Advisory Committee for (Standing). Ellis Hodgin, Dir., Robert Scott Small Lib., College of Charleston, 66 George St., Charleston, SC 29401 (Arthur Plotnik).

Awards (Standing). Janice Feye-Stukas, Office of Public Lib. and Inter-Lib. Cooperation, Dept. of Educ., 301 Hanover Bldg., St. Paul, MN 55101 (Ann M. Cunniff).

Chapter Relations (Standing). Hannah McCauley, Lib. Dir., Ohio Univ., Lancaster Branch, Lancaster, OH 43130 (Patricia Scarry).

Conference Program (Standing). Suzanne LeBarron, Bur. of Special Services, Cultural Education Center, Empire State Plaza, Albany, NY 12230 (Ruth R. Frame).

Constitution and Bylaws (Standing). Susanna Alexander, State Lib., Box 387, 308 E. High St., Jefferson City, MO 65102 (Miriam L. Hornback).

Council Orientation (Special). Alice Ihrig, 9322 S. 53 Ave., Oak Lawn, IL 60453 (Miriam L. Hornback).

Equal Rights Amendment (task force). Kay Cassell, Bethlehem Public Lib., 451 Delaware Ave., Delmar, NY 10254; and Alice B. Ihrig, 9322 S. 53 Ave., Oak Lawn, IL 60453 (Patricia Scarry).

Instruction in the Use of Libraries (Standing). Joseph A. Boisse, Samuel Paley Lib., Temple Univ., Philadelphia, PA 19122 (Andrew M. Hansen).

Intellectual Freedom (Standing, Council). Frances C. Dean, Div. of Instructional Materials, Montgomery County Public Schools, Rockville, MD 20850 (Judith F. Krug).

International Relations (Standing, Council). Russell Shank, Univ. Libn., Univ. of California, Los Angeles, CA 90024 (Jane Wilson).

Legislation (Standing, Council). Peter J. Paulson, State Lib., Cultural Education Center, Empire State Plaza, Albany, NY 12230 (Eileen D. Cooke).
Library Education (Standing, Council). Evelyn H. Daniel, School of Info. Studies, Syracuse Univ., Syracuse, NY 13210 (Margaret Myers).
Library Personnel Resources, Office for (Standing, Advisory). Patricia Pond, School of Lib. & Info. Science, Univ. of Pittsburgh, Pittsburgh, PA 15260 (Margaret Myers).
Mediation, Arbitration, and Inquiry, Staff Committee on (Standing). Robert Wedgeworth, ALA Headquarters, 50 E. Huron St., Chicago IL 60611.
Membership (Standing). Samuel Simon, Finkelstein Memorial Lib., 19 S. Madison Ave., Spring Valley, NY 10977 (Peggy Barber).
National Library Week (Standing). Jordan M. Scepanski, Central Lib., Vanderbilt Univ., Nashville, TN 37203 (Peggy Barber).
Organization (Standing, Council). Arthur Curley, New York Public Lib., Fifth Ave. & 42 St., New York, NY 10018 (Ruth R. Frame).
Outreach Services, Office for Library (Standing, Advisory). Doreitha R. Madden, Lib. Outreach Service, State Lib., Trenton, NJ 08625 (Jean E. Coleman).
Planning (Standing, Council). Judith R. Farley, 1301 Delaware Ave. S.W., Apt. N-404, Washington, DC 20024 (Ruth R. Frame).
Professional Ethics (Standing, Council). Barbara Rollock, Public Lib., 8 E. 40 St., New York, NY 10016 (Judith F. Krug).
Program Assessment Processes, Review (Special). Edward G. Holley, Dean, School of Lib. Science, Univ. of North Carolina, Chapel Hill, NC 27514 (Robert Wedgeworth).
Program Evaluation and Support (Standing, Council). Gerald R. Shields, Asst. Dean, School of Info. & Lib. Studies, State Univ. of New York, Amherst, NY 14260 (Sheldon I. Landman).

Publishing (Standing, Council). Elaine Sloan, Dean of Univ. Lib., Indiana Univ., Bloomington, IN 47405 (Donald E. Stewart).
Reference and Subscription Books Review (Standing). Robert M. Pierson, Grad. School of Lib. & Info. Science, Catholic Univ. of America, Washington, DC 20064 (Helen K. Wright).
Research (Standing). John McCrossan, Grad. Dept. of Lib. Media & Info. Studies, Univ. of South Florida, Tampa, FL 33620 (Mary Jo Lynch).
Resolutions (Standing, Council). Dale M. Bentz, 1615 E. College, Iowa City, IA 52240 (Miriam L. Hornback).
Standards (Standing). Jasper G. Schad, Box 68, Wichita State Univ., Wichita, KS 67208 (Ruth R. Frame).
Women in Librarianship, Status of (Standing, Council). Kathleen Heim, 410 David Kinley Hall, Univ. of Illinois—Champaign, Urbana, IL 61801 (Margaret Meyers).

JOINT COMMITTEE CHAIRPERSONS

American Correctional Association—ASCLA Committee on Institution Libraries. Robert F. Ensley, Senior Consultant, Lib. Development Group, State Lib., Centennial Bldg., Springfield, IL 62756.
American Federation of Labor/Congress of Industrial Organizations—ALA, Library Service to Labor Groups, RASD. ALA Chpn. to be appointed; AFL/CIO Co-Chpn. Dorothy Shields, Dept. of Educ., AFL/CIO, 815 16 St. N.W., Washington, DC 20006.
Anglo-American Cataloguing Rules Common Revision Fund. ALA Rep. Donald E. Stewart, ALA Headquarters; CLA Rep. Laurie Bowes, Canadian Lib. Assn., 151 Sparks St., Ottawa, Ont. KIP 5E3, Canada; (British) Lib. Assn. Rep. Charles Ellis, Publishing Mgr., Lib. Assn., 7 Ridgmount St., London WC1E 7AE, England.
Anglo-American Cataloguing Rules, Joint Steering Committee for Revision of.

444 / DIRECTORY OF LIBRARY AND RELATED ORGANIZATIONS

ALA Chpn. Frances Hinton, 105 W. Walnut La., Philadelphia, PA 19144.
Association for Educational Communications and Technology—AASL. AASL Chpn., Marie V. Haley, Community School Dist., Sioux City, IA 51105; AECT Chpn. Dianne de Cordova, 8 Patton Pl., Dumont, NJ 07628.
Association of American Publishers—ALA. AAP Chpn. Thomas Houston, New York Academy of Sciences, 2 E. 63 St., New York, NY 10021.
Association of American Publishers—RTSD. ALA Chpn. Susan B. Harrison, 3308 Warden Dr., Philadelphia, PA 19129; AAP Chpn. Tom Houston, New York Academy of Sciences, 2 E. 63 St., New York, NY 10021.
Children's Book Council—ALA. ALA Co-Chpn. Virginia M. Crowley, 6059-3 Monticello Dr., Montgomery, AL 36117; CBC Co-Chpn. Ann Durrell, E. P. Dutton, New York, NY 10016.
Nonbook Materials, Joint Advisory Committee on. Chpn. Nancy Williamson, Faculty of Lib. Science, Univ. of Toronto, 140 St. George St., Toronto, Ont. M5S 1A1, Canada.
Society of American Archivists—ALA Joint Committee on Library-Archives Relationships. Chpn. Ellen Dunlap, 1620 University Dr., Durham, NC 27707.
U.S. National Park Service—ALSC Joint Committee. ALSC Co-Chpn. Elizabeth Watson, Public Lib., Fitchburg, MA 01420; U.S. National Park Service Co-Chpn. Patricia M. Stanek, Cowpens Memorial Battlefield, Chesnee, SC 29323.

AMERICAN LIBRARY ASSOCIATION
AMERICAN ASSOCIATION OF SCHOOL LIBRARIANS
Executive Secretary, Alice E. Fite
Professional Assistant, Ruth E. Feathers
50 E. Huron St., Chicago, IL 60611
312-944-6780

OBJECT

The American Association of School Librarians is interested in the general improvement and extension of library media services for children and young people. AASL has specific responsibility for planning programs of study and service for the improvement and extension of library media services in elementary and secondary schools as a means of strengthening the educational program; evaluation, selection, interpretation, and utilization of media as they are used in the context of the school program; stimulation of continuous study and research in the library field and to establish criteria of evaluation; synthesis of the activities of all units of the American Library Association in areas of mutual concern; representation and interpretation of the need for the function of school libraries to other educational and lay groups; stimulation of professional growth, improvement of the status of school librarians, and encouragement of participation by members in appropriate type-of-activity divisions; and conduct activities and projects beyond the scope of type-of-activity divisions, after specific approval by the ALA Council. Established in 1951 as a separate division of ALA. Memb. 7,000.

MEMBERSHIP

Open to all libraries, school library media specialists, interested individuals and business firms with requisite membership in the ALA.

OFFICERS

Pres. D. Philip Baker, Public Schools, 195 Hillandale Ave., Stamford, CT 06902;

1st V.P./Pres.-Elect. Betty Buckingham, State Dept. of Public Instruction, Des Moines, IA 50319; *2nd V.P.* Shirley L. Aaron; *Rec. Secy.* Carolyn Markuson; *Past Pres.* Rebecca T. Bingham; *Exec. Secy.* Alice E. Fite.

BOARD OF DIRECTORS

Officers; Patricia E. Jensen, Region I (1982); Judith M. King, Region II (1983); Diane A. Ball, Region III (1981); Ruth A. Moline, Region IV (1982); Dorothy W. Blake, Region V (1981); Lotsee P. Smith, Region VI (1983); Genevieve K. Craig, Region VII (1982); *Regional Dirs. from Affiliate Assembly.* Dale W. Brown (1982); Albert H. Saley (1981); Jim Weigel (1982); *NPSS Chpn.* Pauline H. Anderson; *SS Chpn.* Jacqueline Morris; *Ex Officio Ed. School Media Quarterly.* Jack R. Luskay.

PUBLICATION

School Media Quarterly (q.; memb.; nonmemb. $15). *Ed.* Jack R. Luskay, School of Lib. Science, Clarion State College, Clarion, PA 16214.

SECTION COMMITTEES

Nonpublic Schools Section

Executive. Pauline Anderson, Andrew Mellon Lib., Choate Rosemary Hall, Wallingford, CT 06492.

Bylaws. Elva A. Harmon, 1315 E. 26 Pl., Tulsa, OK 74114.

Nominating. Evalyn S. Rogers, 821 N. Clay, Kirkwood, MO 63122.

Program—San Francisco, 1981. James P. Godfrey, Rye Country Day School, Cedar St., Rye, NY 10580.

Supervisors Section

Executive. Jacqueline Morris, 5225 Leone Pl., Indianapolis, IN 46226.

Bylaws. Wanna M. Ernst, 16 Brisbane Dr., Charleston, SC 29407.

Critical Issues Facing School Library Media Supervisors (Discussion Group). LuOuida Vinson Phillips, 4425 Gilbert Ave., Dallas, TX 75219.

Nominating—1981 Election. Rosa L. Presberry, 704 Country Village Dr., 2C, Bel Air, MD 21014.

Program—San Francisco, 1981. Elizabeth B. Day, Santa Barbara County Schools, Box 6307, 4400 Cathedral Oaks Rd., Santa Barbara, CA 93118.

Publications. Mary Oppman, Portage Township Schools, 5894 J Central Ave., Portage, IN 46368.

COMMITTEE CHAIRPERSONS

Program Coordinating. Rebecca T. Bingham, Jefferson County Public Schools, 675 River City Mall, Louisville, KY 40211.

Unit Group I—Organizational Maintenance

Unit Head. Marie V. Haley, Sioux City Community Schools, 1221 Pierce St., Sioux City, IA 51105.

Bylaws. Dorothy W. Blake, 232 Daniel Ave. S.E., Atlanta, GA 30317.

Conference Program Planning—San Francisco, 1981. Albert H. Saley, RD 1, Box 111, Blairstown, NJ 07825.

Local Arrangements—San Francisco, 1981. Elizabeth W. McDavid, 2315 Collins Ave., Pinole, CA 94564.

Nominating—1981 Election. Linda Beeler, 5838 S. Stony Island, 14 E, Chicago, IL 60637.

Resolutions. Shirley L. Aaron, School of Lib. Science, Florida State Univ., Tallahassee, FL 32306.

Unit Group II—Organizational Relationships

Unit Head. Bernice L. Yesner, 16 Sunbrook Rd., Woodbridge, CT 06525.

American Association of School Administrators—AASL (*Liaison*). Dale W. Brown, 3801 W. Braddock Rd., Alexandria, VA 22303.

American University Press Services, Inc. (*Advisory*). Dolores E. Victorian, Walt Whitman H.S., 7100 Whittier Blvd., Bethesda, MD 20034.

Association for Educational Communications and Technology—AASL (Joint). Marie V. Haley, Community School Dist., Sioux City, IA 51105 (AASL); Dianne de Cordova, 8 Patton Pl., Dumont, NJ 07628 (AECT).

International Reading Association (Liaison). Virginia Mathews, 17 Overshore Dr. W., Hamden, CT 06514.

National Congress of Parents and Teachers (Liaison). Doris Masek, 6815 N. Algonquin Ave., Chicago, IL 60646.

Unit Group III—Media Personnel Development

Unit Head. Richard J. Sorensen, State Dept. of Public Instruction, Div. of Lib. Services, Madison, WI 53702.

Library Education. Evelyn H. Daniel, School of Info. Studies, Syracuse Univ., Syracuse, NY 13210.

Networking—Interconnection of Learning Resources (Ad Hoc). Donald C. Adcock, School Dist. #41, 793 N. Main St., Glen Ellyn, IL 60137.

Professional Development. Carol Diehl, School Dist., 901 W. Washington St., New London, WI 54961.

Research. Jacqueline C. Mancall, School of Lib. & Info. Science, Drexel Univ., Philadelphia, PA 19104.

Video Communications. Carolyn Markuson, 56 Dellwood Ave., Chatham, NJ 07928.

Unit Group IV—Media Program Development

Unit Head. Wanna M. Ernst, 16 Brisbane Dr., Charleston, SC 29407.

Early Childhood Education. Christina C. Young, 1253 Girard St. N.E., Washington, DC 20017.

Evaluation of School Media Programs. E. Blanche Woolls, 270 Tennyson Ave., Pittsburgh, PA 15213.

Facilities, Media Center. Sally K. Anderson, RFD 2, Box 321, Oakland, ME 04963.

School Library Media Services to Children with Special Needs. Rosa L. Presberry, 704 Country Village Dr., 2C, Bel Air, MD 21014.

Standards Program and Implementation. Elsie L. Brumback, 201 Annandale Dr., Cary, NC 27511.

Student Involvement in the Media Center Program. Gerald Hodges, Univ. of North Carolina-Greensboro, School of Education, 47 McNutt Bldg., Greensboro, NC 27412.

Unit Group V—Public Information

Unit Head. Doris A. Hicks, City School Dist., Dept. of Learning Resources, Rochester, NY 14610.

Distinguished Library Service Award for School Administrators. David A. Russell, Dept. of Adult Education and Instruction Services, College of Education, Univ. of Wyoming, Laramie, WY 82071.

Intellectual Freedom Representation and Information. Darleen Hunter, 2541 Vernal Dr., Grove City, OH 43123.

International Relations. Lucille C. Thomas, Center for Lib., Media & Telecommunications, Bd. of Educ., 139 Livingston St., Brooklyn, NY 11221.

Legislation. Jane H. Love, 209 Commerce St., Centreville, MD 21617.

President's Award Selection, AASL/Baker & Taylor. Anne Elise Shafer, 1412 Washington St., Evanston, IL 60202.

School Library Media Program of the Year Award Selection, AASL/EB. Michael G. de Ruvo, Box 367, Roslyn, NY 11576.

COMMITTEES (SPECIAL)

AASL General Conference Planning. Jack R. Luskay, School of Lib. Science, Clarion State College, Clarion, PA 16214.

Publications Advisory. Glenn E. Estes, Grad. School of Lib. & Info. Science, Univ. of Tennessee, 804 Volunteer Blvd., Knoxville, TN 37916.

Resource Development. Antoinette Negro, 10022 Stedwick Rd., 302, Gaithersburg, MD 20760.

REPRESENTATIVES

ALA Legislation Assembly. Jane H. Love.
ALA Membership Promotion Task Force. Anne C. Ansley.
Associated Organizations for Professionals in Education. Evelyn H. Daniel.
Education U.S.A. Advisory Board. Alice E. Fite.
Educational Media Council. Alice E. Fite.
Freedom to Read Foundation. Darleen Hunter.
Library Education Assembly. Evelyn H. Daniel.
RTSD/CCS/AASL Cataloging of Children's Materials. Winifred E. Duncan.

AFFILIATE ASSEMBLY

The Affiliate Assembly is composed of the representatives and delegates of the organizations affiliated with the American Association of School Librarians. The specific purpose of this assembly is to provide a channel for communication for reporting concerns of the affiliate organizations and their membership and for reporting the actions of the American Association of School Librarians to the affiliates.

Executive Committee

Patsy R. Scales, 4A Oakwood Apts., Hallcox St., Greenville, SC 29609.

Bylaws

Gerald G. Hodges, Lib. Science/Education Technology, Univ. of North Carolina-Greensboro, Greensboro, NC 27412.

Nominating Committee—1981 Election

Sue Albertson Walker, 6065 Parkridge Dr., East Petersburg, PA 17520.

Organization Review (Ad Hoc).

Hugh Durbin, 4240 Fairoaks Dr., Columbus, OH 43214.

Affiliates

Region I. Connecticut Educational Media Assn.; Massachusetts Assn. for Educational Media; Maine Educational Media Assn.; New England Educational Media Assn.; Rhode Island Educational Media Assn.; Vermont Educational Media Assn.

Region II. Delaware Learning Resources Assn.; District of Columbia Assn. of School Libns.; Maryland Educational Media Organization; Educational Media Assn. of New Jersey; Pennsylvania School Libns. Assn.; School Lib. Media Sec., New York Lib. Assn.

Region III. Assn. for Indiana Media Educators; Illinois Assn. for Media in Education; Iowa Educational Media Assn.; Michigan Assn. for Media in Education; Minnesota Educational Media Organization; Missouri Assn. of School Libns.; Ohio Educational Lib. Media Assn.; Wisconsin School Lib. Media Assn.; School Div., Michigan Lib. Assn.

Region IV. Mountain Plains Lib. Assn., Children's & School Sec.; Colorado Educational Media Assn.; Kansas Assn. of School Libns.; North Dakota Assn. of School Libns.; South Dakota School Lib./Media Assn.; Wyoming School Lib. Media Assn.

Region V. Alabama Instructional Media Assn.; Children & School Libns. Div., Alabama Lib. Assn.; Florida Assn. for Media in Education, Inc.; Georgia Lib. Media Dept.; School and Children's Sec., Georgia Lib. Assn.; Kentucky School Media Dept.; North Carolina Assn. of School Libns.; School & Children's Sec., Southeastern Lib. Assn.; South Carolina Assn. of School Libns.; School Lib. Sec., Tennessee Education Assn.; Virginia Educational Media Assn.

Region VI. Louisiana Assn. of School Libns.; School Libs., Children, Young Adult Services, New Mexico Lib. Assn.; Oklahoma Assn. of School Lib. Media Specialists; School Libs. Div., Arizona State Lib. Assn.; School Libs. Div.,

Arkansas Lib. Assn.; Texas Assn. of School Libs.
Region VII. California Media & Lib. Educators Assn.; Hawaii Assn. of School Libs.; Idaho Educational Media Assn.; Oregon Educational Media Assn.; School Lib. Div., Idaho Lib. Assn.; School Lib./Media Div., Montana Lib. Assn.; Washington State Assn. of School Libns.

AMERICAN LIBRARY ASSOCIATION
AMERICAN LIBRARY TRUSTEE ASSOCIATION
ALTA Program Officer, Sharon L. Jordan
50 E. Huron St., Chicago, IL 60611
312-944-6780

OBJECT

The development of effective library service for all people in all types of communities and in all types of libraries; it follows that its members are concerned as policymakers with organizational patterns of service, with the development of competent personnel, the provision of adequate financing, the passage of suitable legislation, and the encouragement of citizen support for libraries. Open to all interested persons and organizations. Organized 1890. Became an ALA division 1961. Memb. 1,710. (For dues and membership year, see ALA entry.)

OFFICERS (1980-1981)

Pres. Jeanne Davies, Box 159, Deer Trail, CO 80105; *1st V.P./Pres. Elect.* Nancy Stiegemeyer, 215 Camellia Dr., Cape Girardeau, MO 63701; *2nd V.P.* Don Surratt; *Secy.*, Herbert Davis; *Council Rep./Parliamentarian.* Jean M. Coleman.

BOARD OF DIRECTORS

Officers; *Council Administrators.* Nell Henry (1981); Albert I. Mayer (1981); Sondrea Messing (1981); Marlys Mlady (1981); Charles Reid (1981); *Reg. V.Ps.* Dina Butcher (1981); Barbara D. Cooper (1981); John Hamilton (1981); Paulette Holahan (1981); Allan Kahn (1981); Arthur Kirschenbaum (1981); Lila Milford (1981); John T. Short (1981); Athalie Solloway (1982); Barbara Steigerwalt (1981); *Past Pres.* James A. Hess; *Past Pres. Ex Officio.* Ronald Dubberly (1981); *Ed. The Public Library Trustee.* Robert L. Faherty.

PUBLICATION

Public Library Trustee. Ed. Robert L. Faherty, 6908 Lamp Post La., Alexandria, VA 22306.

COMMITTEE CHAIRPERSONS

Action Development. Donald C. Earnshaw, 226 S. Douglas St., Lee's Summit, MO 64063.

ALTA Foundation Committee. Herbert Davis, Box 108, Brooklandville, MD 21022.

Awards. John T. Short, Box E, Avon, CT 06001.

Budget. Nancy Stiegemeyer, 215 Camellia Dr., Cape Girardeau, MO 63701.

Conference Program and Evaluation. Nell Henry, 109 N. Olive St., Searcy, AR 72148.

Education of Trustees. Virginia G. Young, 10 Parkway Dr., Columbia, MO 65201.

Task Force on Identity. Daniel Casey, 202 Scarboro Dr., Syracuse, NY 13209.

Intellectual Freedom. Norma J. Buzan, 3057 Betsy Ross Dr., Bloomfield Hills, MI 48013.

Legislation. Deborah Miller, 840 Rosedale La., Hoffman Estates, IL 60195.

Task Force on Liaison with Leagues of Municipalities. Norma L. Mihalevich, Box 287, Crocker, MO 65452.

Task Force on Literacy Programs. Marguerite W. Yates, 190 Windemere Rd., Lockport, NY 14094.

Task Force on Membership. Barbara S. Prentice, 1933 E. Third St., Tucson, AZ 85719.

Nominating. Charles Reid, 620 West Dr., Paramus, NJ 07652.

Task Force on Personnel Policies and Practices. Peter Cannici, 212 Howard Ave., Passaic, NJ 07055.

Publications. James A. Hess, 91 Farms Rd. Circle, East Brunswick, NJ 08816.

Publicity. Joanne C. Wisener, 860 19 Pl., Yuma, AZ 85364.

Task Force on Serving the Unserved. Fred K. Darragh, Box 86, Little Rock, AR 72203.

Speakers Bureau. Jo Anne Thorbeck, 2100 Irving S., Minneapolis, MN 55405.

State Associations. Nancy Stiegemeyer, 215 Camellia Dr., Cape Girardeau, MO 63701.

Jury on Trustee Citations. John Velde, Jr., 2003 La Brea Terr., Hollywood, CA 90046.

AMERICAN LIBRARY ASSOCIATION
ASSOCIATION FOR LIBRARY SERVICE TO CHILDREN
Executive Director, Mary Jane Anderson
50 E. Huron St., Chicago, IL 60611
312-944-6780

OBJECT

"Interested in the improvement and extension of library services to children in all types of libraries. Responsible for the evaluation and selection of book and nonbook materials for, and the improvement of techniques of, library services to children from preschool through the eighth grade or junior high school age, when such materials or techniques are intended for use in more than one type of library." Founded 1900. Memb. 4,978. (For information on dues see ALA entry.)

MEMBERSHIP

Open to anyone interested in library services to children.

OFFICERS (JULY 1980-JULY 1981)

Pres. Amy Kellman, 211 Castlegate Rd., Pittsburgh, PA 15221; *V.P.* Helen Mullen, Office of Work with Children, Free Lib. of Philadelphia, Logan Sq., Philadelphia, PA 19103; *Exec. Dir.* Mary Jane Anderson, ALSC/ALA, 50 E. Huron St., Chicago, IL 60611; *Past Pres.* Marilyn L. Miller, Assoc. Prof., School of Lib. Science, Univ. of North Carolina, Chapel Hill, NC 27514. (Address general correspondence to the executive director.)

DIRECTORS

Officers; Margaret Bush (ALA Councillor); Susan Collier; Adele Fasick; Carolyn Field; Suzanne Glazer; Beth Greggs; Harriet Quimby; Gail M. Sage; Linda Silver.

PUBLICATIONS

ALSC *Newsletter* (q.; memb.).

Top of the News (q.; memb.; $15 nonmemb.).

COMMITTEE CHAIRPERSONS

Priority Group I—Child Advocacy

Coord. Marilyn Iarusso, Office of Children's Services, New York Public Lib., 8 E. 40 St., New York, NY 10011.

Boy Scouts of America (Advisory). Frances V. Sedney, Hartford County Lib., 100 Pennsylvania Ave., Bel Air, MD 21014.

Legislation. Trevelyn Jones, 315 E. 70 St., Apt. 5B, New York, NY 10021.

Mass Media (*Liaison with*). Elizabeth Huntoon, 2046 Clifton, Chicago, IL 60614.
Organizations Serving the Child (*Liaison with*). Effie Lee Morris, 66 Cleary Ct., Apt. 1009, San Francisco, CA 94101.
U.S. National Park Service/ALS (*Joint*). Elizabeth Watson, Fitchburg Public Lib., 610 Main St., Fitchburg, MA 01420.

Priority Group II—Evaluation of Media

Coord. Gertrude B. Herman, 1425 Skyline Dr., Madison, WI 53705.
H. C. Anderson Award Nominations—1982. Elizabeth B. Murphy, 4811 43 Pl. N.W., Washington, DC 20016.
Mildred L. Batchelder Award Selection—1982. Zena B. Sutherland, 1418 E. 57 St., Chicago, IL 60637.
Mildred L. Batchelder Award Selection—1981. Virginia M. Crowley, 6059-3 Monticello Dr., Montgomery, AL 36117.
Caldecott Award. Gail M. Sage, 1721 Laguna Rd., Santa Rosa, CA 95401.
Film Evaluation. Susan Harloe, 1825 N. Edison, Stockton, CA 95204.
Filmstrip Evaluation. Hannah Zeiger, 167 Pond Brook Rd., Chestnut Hill, MA 02167.
"Multimedia Aproach to Children's Literature" Revision (*Ad Hoc*). Lynne R. Pickens, 1481 Hampton Ct., Decatur, GA 30033.
Newbery Award. Ruth I. Gordon, 609 North St., Susanville, CA 96130.
Notable Children's Books. Marilyn Kaye, College of Libnshp., Univ. of South Carolina, Columbia, SC 29208.
Print and Poster Evaluation. Alma L. Mehn, 4009 Jay La. S., Rolling Meadows, IL 60008.
Recording Evaluation. Sharon Gunn, 5301 S. University, Chicago, IL 60615.
Selection of Foreign Children's Books. Grace Ruth, 859 42 Ave., San Francisco, CA 94121.
Toys, Games and Realia Evaluation. Darrell Hildebrant, Veteran's Memorial Lib., 520 Ave. A E., Bismarck, ND 58501.

Laura Ingalls Wilder Award—1983. Spencer Shaw, School of Libnshp., Suzzalo Lib., FM-30, Univ. of Washington, Seattle, WA 98195.

Priority Group III—People Power

Coord. Betty J. Peltola, 4109 N. Ardmore, Milwaukee, WI 53211.
Arbuthnot Honor Lecture. Dudley B. Carlson, Princeton Public Lib., 65 Witherspoon St., Princeton, NJ 08540.
Continuing Education. Caroline Heilman, Vermont Dept. of Libs., State Office Bldg. Post Office, Montpelier, VT 05602.
Managing Children's Services (*Discussion Group*). Mary Somerville, 1010 La Fontenay Ct., Louisville, KY 40223.
Media Evaluation: The Group Process, Implementation (*Ad Hoc*). Bridget L. Lamont, Illinois State Lib., Development Group, Centennial Bldg., Rm. 011, Springfield, IL 62756.
Melcher Scholarship. Mary Louise Rheay, Cobb County Public Lib., 30 Atlanta St., Marietta, GA 30060.
Charles Scribner Award Selection. Mary Ann Paulin, 1205 Joliet, Marquette, MI 49855.
State and Regional Leadership (*Discussion Group*). Margaret Gillespie, Hennepin County Public Lib., 7009 York Ave. S., Edina, MN 55435.
Teachers of Children's Literature (*Discussion Group*). Ramona Mahood, Brisler Lib., Rm. 201, Dept. of Lib. Science, Memphis State Univ., Memphis, TN 38152; Bernice Yesner, 16 Sunbrook Rd., Woodbridge, CT 06525.

Priority Group IV—Social Responsibilities

Coord. Diana D. Young, North Carolina State Lib., 109 E. Jones St., Raleigh, NC 27611.
Children with Special Needs (*Library Services to*). Eliza T. Dresang, Media Services, Metropolitan School Dist., 545 W. Dayton St., Madison, WI 53703.

Disadvantaged Child (Library Services to the-Discussion Group). Brenda V. Johnson, D.C. Public Lib., Washington, DC 20001.
Intellectual Freedom. Neel Parikh, 2136 Byron St., Berkeley, CA 94702.
International Relations. Barbara Barstow, South Euclid Branch Lib., 4645 Mayfield Rd., South Euclid, OH 44121.
Preschool Services and Parent Education. Jill Locke, Farmington Community Lib., 32737 W. 12 Mile Rd., Farmington Hills, MI 48018.
Program Support Publications (Ad Hoc). Beth Babikow, Baltimore County Public Lib., 320 York Rd., Towson, MD 21204.
Social Issues in Relation to Library Materials and Services for Children (Discussion Group). Annette C. Blank, 5477 Cedonia Ave., Baltimore, MD 21206.

Priority Group V—Planning, Research, and Development

Coord. Margaret Poarch, South Hills Apts., 23, South St., Geneseo, NY 14454.
Collection of Children's Books for Adult Research (Discussion Group). Henrietta Smith, 1202 N.W. Second St., Delray Beach, FL 33444.
Local Arrangements—San Francisco 1981. Linda Perkins, 1429 Cedar St., Berkeley, CA 94702.
Membership. Nancy Bush, Dept. of Educational Media, College of Education, Univ. of South Alabama, Mobile, AL 36688.
Nominating—1980. Ethel Manheimer, 2373 Woolsey St., Berkeley CA 94705.
Organization and Bylaws. Margaret M. Kimmel, School of Lib. & Info. Sciences, Univ. of Pittsburgh, 135 N. Bellefield, Pittsburgh, PA 15260.
Program Evaluation and Support. Helen Mullen, Office of Work with Children, Free Lib. of Philadelphia, Logan Sq., Philadelphia, PA 19103.
Publications. Blanche Woolls, 270 Tennyson, Pittsburgh, PA 15213.

Research and Development. Nan Johnston, Stark County Dist. Lib., 715 Market Ave. N, Canton, OH 44702.
C. Rollins Oral History Project Task Force (Ad Hoc). Judith Davie, Box 2175, Boone, NC 28607.
Special Collections (National Planning of). Barbara Maxwell, Apt. 809A, Alden Park Manor, Wissahickon & Chelten Aves., Philadelphia, PA 19144.
"Top of the News" (Joint ALSC/YASD Editorial). Audrey Eaglen, Cuyahoga County Public Lib., 4510 Memphis Ave., Cleveland, OH 44144.

REPRESENTATIVES

AFL/CIO-ALA Committee on Library Service to Labor Groups. To be appointed.
ALA Appointments. Helen Mullen.
ALA Budget Assembly. Helen Mullen.
ALA Legislative Assembly. Trevelyn Jones.
ALA Library Education Assembly. Caroline Heilmann.
ALA San Francisco Conference (1981) Program. Amy Kellman.
ALA Philadelphia 1982 Program. Helen Mullen.
ALA Membership Promotion Task Force. Nancy Bush.
Caroline M. Hewins Scholarship. Priscilla Moulton.
International Board on Books for Young People, U.S. Section, Executive Board. Amy Kellman; Mary Jane Anderson; Barbara Barstow.
RTSD/CCS Cataloging of Children's Materials. Helen P. Gregory; Marilyn Karrenbrock.

LIAISON WITH OTHER NATIONAL ORGANIZATIONS

American Association for Gifted Children. Naomi Noyes.
American National Red Cross. Red Cross Youth. Barbara Shumer.
Big Brothers and Big Sisters of America. Helen Mullen.
Boys Clubs of America. Jane Kunstler.

Camp Fire Girls. Anitra Steele.
Child Development Associates Consortium. Mary Jane Anderson.
Child Study Association of America. Augusta Baker.
Child Welfare League of America. Ethel Ambrose.
Children's Theatre Association. Amy E. Spaulding.
Day Care and Child Development Council of America. Margaret Bush.
Girls Clubs of America. Karen Breen.
National Association for the Education of Young Children. Theresa Chekon.
National Story League. Linda Hansford.
Parents without Partners. To be appointed.
Puppeteers of America. Darrell Hildebrandt.
Salvation Army. Margaret Malm.
Society of American Magicians. Marion Peck.

AMERICAN LIBRARY ASSOCIATION
ASSOCIATION OF COLLEGE AND RESEARCH LIBRARIES
Executive Secretary, Julie A. Carroll Virgo
50 E. Huron St., Chicago, IL 60611
312-944-6780

OBJECT

"Represents research and special libraries and libraries in institutions of postsecondary education, including those of community and junior colleges, colleges, and universities." Founded 1938. Memb. 9,000. (For information on dues see ALA entry.)

OFFICERS (JULY 1980-JUNE 1981)

Pres. Millicent D. Abell, Univ. of California at San Diego, La Jolla, CA 92093; *V.P./Pres.-Elect.* David C. Weber, Stanford Univ., Stanford, CA 94025; *Past Pres.* Le Moyne W. Anderson, Colorado State Univ., Ft. Collins, CO 80521.

BOARD OF DIRECTORS

Officers; section chairs and vice-chairs; *Directors-at-Large.* William J. Studer (1981); Billy R. Wilkinson (1981); Joyce Ball (1982); George M. Bailey (1983); Imogene I. Book (1984); Sara Lou Whildin (1984).

PUBLICATIONS

ACRL Nonprint Media Publications (irreg.). *Ed.* Dwight Burlingame, Bowling Green State Univ., Bowling Green, OH 43402.

ACRL Publications in Librarianship (irreg.). *Ed.* Joe W. Kraus, Illinois State Univ., Normal, IL 61761.

Choice (11 issues; $50); *Choice Reviews on Cards* ($120). *Ed.* Jay M. Poole, 100 Riverview Center, Middletown, CT 06457.

College & Research Libraries (6 issues; memb.; nonmemb. $25). *Ed.* C. James Schmidt, Brown Univ., Providence, RI 02912.

College & Research Libraries News (11 issues; memb.; nonmemb. $5) *Ed.* George M. Eberhart, ACRL headquarters.

SECTION CHAIRPERSONS

Anthropology. Patricia Ann White, Michigan State Univ., Lansing, MI 48824.

Art. John C. Larsen, Northern Illinois Univ., DeKalb, IL 60115.

Asian and African. E. Christian Filstrup, Oriental Div., New York Public Lib., New York, NY 10018.

Bibliographic Instruction. Sharon Rogers, Univ. of Toledo, Toledo, OH 43606.

College Libraries. Willis M. Hubbard, Stephens College, Columbia, MO 65201.

Community and Junior College Libraries. Barbara Collinsworth, Macomb County Community College, Warren, MI 48093.
Education and Behaviorial Sciences. Eva L. Kiewitt, Indiana Univ., Bloomington, IN 47401.
Law and Political Science. Frances H. Hall, North Carolina Supreme Court Lib., Raleigh, NC 27611.
Rare Books and Manuscripts. Kenneth E. Carpenter, Harvard Business School, Boston, MA 02138.
Science and Technology. Thomas G. Kirk, Berea College, Berea, KY 40404.
Slavic and East European. Wojcieck Zalewski, Stanford Univ., Stanford, CA 94305.
University Libraries. Pearce S. Grove, Western Illinois Univ., Macomb, IL 61455.
Western European Specialists. Kenneth O. Jensen, Univ. of Virginia, Charlottesville, VA 22901.

DISCUSSION GROUPS

Audiovisual. David B. Walch, State Univ. of New York-Buffalo, Buffalo, NY 14222.
Cinema Librarians. Eileen Sheahan, Memphis Public Lib., Memphis, TN 38104.
Future of the Catalog in Research Libraries. James Thompson, Johns Hopkins Univ., Baltimore, MD 21218.
Librarians of Library Science Collections. JoAnn Michalak, Columbia Univ., New York, NY 10027.
Metropolitan Academic and Research Libraries. George C. Grant, Morgan State Univ., Baltimore, MD 21239.
Personnel Officers of Research Libraries. H. Lea Wells, Univ. of Tennessee, Knoxville, TN 37916.
Staff Development in Academic Research Libraries. Barbara von Wahlde, Yale Univ., New Haven, CT 06520.
Undergraduate Librarians. Barbara Kornstein, Univ. of California, Berkeley, CA 94720.

COMMITTEE CHAIRPERSONS

ACRL Academic or Research Librarian of the Year Award. David Kaser, Indiana Univ., Bloomington, IN 47405.
"ACRL Nonprint Media Publications" Editorial Bd. Dwight Burlingame, Bowling Green State Univ., Bowling Green, OH 43402.
"ACRL Publications in Librarianship" Editorial Bd. Joe W. Kraus, Illinois State Univ., Normal, IL 61761.
Academic Status. Ann Bristow Beltran, Indiana Univ., Bloomington, IN 47401.
Appointments (1981) and Nominations (1982). Keith M. Cottam, Vanderbilt Univ., Nashville, TN 37203.
Audiovisual. David H. Eyman, Juniata College, Huntingdon, PA 16652.
Budget and Finance. Richard J. Talbot, Univ. of Massachusetts, Amherst, MA 01002.
Chapters. Gary L. Menges, Univ. of Washington, Seattle, WA 98105.
"Choice" Editorial Bd. William Miller, Michigan State Univ., East Lansing, MI 48823.
"College & Research Libraries" Editorial Bd. C. James Schmidt, Brown Univ., Providence, RI 02912.
"College & Research Libraries News" Editorial Bd. Jay K. Lucker, Massachusetts Inst. of Technology, Cambridge, MA 02139.
Conference Executive—ACRL National Conference, Minneapolis 1981. Virgil F. Massman, J. J. Hill Reference Lib., St. Paul, MN 55102.
Conference Program Planning—San Francisco 1981. Millicent D. Abell, Univ. of California at San Diego, La Jolla, CA 92093.
Conference Program Planning—Philadelphia 1982. David C. Weber, Stanford Univ., Stanford, CA 94025.
Constitution and Bylaws. Mary W. George, Univ. of Michigan, Ann Arbor, MI 48109.
Continuing Education. Robert Goehlert, Indiana Univ., Bloomington, IN 47401.

Copyright Committee (Ad Hoc). Meredith Butler, State Univ. of New York-Brockport, Brockport, NY 14420.

Legislation. Keith W. Russell, Univ. of Arizona, Tucson, AZ 85721.

Membership. Judith Blight, Univ. of Lowell, Lowell, MA 01854.

Planning. David C. Weber, Stanford Univ., Stanford, CA 94025.

Publications. Lawrence J. M. Wilt, Dickinson College, Carlisle, PA 17013.

Standards and Accreditation. Patricia Ann Sacks, Muhlenberg and Cedar Crest Colleges, Allentown, PA 18104.

"Standards for College Libraries" Revision (Ad Hoc). Arthur Monke, Bowdoin College, Brunswick, ME 04011.

Supplemental Funds. Carlton C. Rochell, New York Univ., New York, NY 10012.

REPRESENTATIVES

American Association for the Advancement of Science. Thomas G. Kirk.

American Council on Education. Russell Shank.

ALA Association of Specialized and Cooperative Library Agencies, Standards for the Library Functions at the State Level Subcomittee (Ad Hoc). Jasper G. Schad.

ALA Committee on Appointments. David C. Weber.

ALA Conference Program Planning Committee (San Francisco 1981). Millicent D. Abell.

ALA Conference Program Planning Committee (Philadelphia 1982). David C. Weber.

ALA Legislation Assembly. Keith W. Russell.

ALA Membership Promotion Task Force. Judith Blight.

ALA Planning and Budget Assembly. David C. Weber.

ALA Resources and Technical Services Division. Committee on Cataloging: Description and Access. LeRoy D. Ortopan.

ALA Standing Committee on Library Education (SCOLE). Ann Bristow Beltran; JoAnn Michalak.

Association for Asian Studies, Committee on East Asian Libraries. Warren Tsuneishi.

Freedom to Read Foundation. Tom G. Watson.

LC Cataloging in Publication Advisory Group. Nancy Patton Van Zant.

AMERICAN LIBRARY ASSOCIATION
ASSOCIATION OF SPECIALIZED AND COOPERATIVE LIBRARY AGENCIES
(Formerly Association of State Library Agencies and Health and Rehabilitative Library Services Division)
Executive Secretary, Sandra M. Cooper
50 E. Huron St., Chicago, IL 60611
312-944-6780

OBJECT

To represent state library agencies, specialized library agencies, and multitype library cooperatives. Within the interests of these types of library organizations, the Association of Specialized and Cooperative Library Agencies has specific responsibility for:

1. Development and evaluation of goals and plans for state library agencies, specialized library agencies, and multitype library cooperatives to facilitate the implementation, improvement, and extension of library activities designed to foster improved user services, coordinating such activ-

ities with other appropriate ALA units.
2. Representation and interpretation of the role, functions, and services of state library agencies, specialized libraries, and library cooperatives within and outside the profession, including contact with national organizations and government agencies.
3. Development of policies, studies, and activities in matters affecting state library agencies, specialized library agencies, and multitype library cooperatives relating to (a) state and local library legislation, (b) state grants-in-aid and appropriations, and (c) relationships among state, federal, regional, and local governments, coordinating such activities with other appropriate ALA units.
4. Establishment, evaluation, and promotion of standards and service guidelines relating to the concerns of this association.
5. Identifying the interests and needs of all persons, encouraging the creation of services to meet these needs within the areas of concern of the association, and promoting the use of these services provided by state library agencies, specialized library agencies, and multitype library cooperatives.
6. Stimulating the professional growth and promoting the specialized training and continuing education of library personnel at all levels in the areas of concern of this association and encouraging membership participation in appropriate type-of-activity divisions with ALA.
7. Assisting in the coordination of activities of other units within ALA that have a bearing on the concerns of this association.
8. Granting recognition for outstanding library service within the areas of concern of this association.
9. Acting as a clearinghouse for the exchange of information and encouraging the development of materials, publications, and research within the areas of concern of this association.

BOARD OF DIRECTORS

Pres. Carmela M. Ruby, California State Lib., Box 2037, Sacramento, CA 95809; *V.P./Pres. Elect.* Anne Marie Falsone, Asst. Commissioner of Education, Colorado State Lib., 1362 Lincoln St., Denver, CO 80203; *Past Pres.* Edward Seidenberg, Lib. Development Div., Texas State Lib., Box 12927, Capitol Sta., Austin, TX 78711. *Div. Councillor.* Susan M. Haskin (1981). *Directors-at-Large.* Catherine D. Cook (1982); Robert A. Drescher (1981); Kathleen O. Mayo (1981); Lorraine D. Schaeffer (1982). *Sec. Reps.* Shirley A. Edsall, HCLS Chpn. (1981); Arlene Bansal, LSBPH Chpn. (1981); Alice L. Hagemeyer, LSDS Chpn. (1981); James E. Pletz, LSIES Chpn. (1981); Connie House, LSPS Chpn. (1981); Linda D. Crowe, MLCS Chpn. (1981); Charles A. Bolles, SLAS Chpn. (1981). *Ex Officio* (Nonvoting). *Interface Ed.* Linda Howard Mielke; *Planning, Organization and By-laws Committee Chpn.* Alan D. Lewis; *Exec. Secy.* Sandra M. Cooper.

PUBLICATION

Interface (q.; memb.; no subscriptions). *Ed.* Linda Howard Mielke, Special Community Service, Maryland State Dept. of Educ., Div. of Lib. Development and Service, Box 8717, Baltimore-Washington Airport, Baltimore, MD 21240.

COMMITTEE CHAIRPERSONS

American Correctional Association-ASCLA Committee on Institution Libraries (Joint). Robert F. Ensley, Lib. Development Group, Illinois State Lib., Centennial Bldg., Springfield, IL 62756.

Audiovisual. Leon L. Drolet, Jr., Dir., Suburban Audio Visual Service, 125 Tower Dr., Burr Ridge, IL 60521.

Awards. Richard T. Miller, Jr., Coord. for Development of Special Lib. Services, Missouri State Lib., 308 E. High St., Jefferson City, MO 65102.

Awards—Exceptional Achievement Award Jury. To be appointed.

Awards—Exceptional Service Award Jury. M. Lethene Parks, Coord. of Special Services, Pierce County Lib., 2356 Tacoma Ave. S., Tacoma, WA 98402.

Bibliotherapy. Barbara F. Allen, 8338 St. Helena Hwy., Napa, CA 94558.

Conference Program—San Francisco, 1981 (Ad Hoc). Roderick G. Swartz, State Libn., State Lib., Olympia, WA 98504.

Continuing Education. Dottie R. Hiebing, Public Lib. Consultant, Continuing Education, Div. for Lib. Services, 125 S. Webster, Madison, WI 53702.

"Interface" Editorial Policy (Ad Hoc). Alphonse F. Trezza, Dir., Intergovernmental Lib. Cooperation Project, c/o Lib. of Congress, Federal Lib. Committee, Washington, DC 20540.

International Relations. To be appointed.

International Year of Disabled Persons. Phyllis I. Dalton, 850 E. Desert Inn Rd., 1101, Las Vegas, NV 89109.

Legislation. Barbara F. Weaver, State Libn., State Lib., 185 W. State St., Trenton, NJ 08625.

Membership Promotion. Marnie M. Warner, Consultant on Outreach, Massachusetts Bd. of Lib. Commissioners, 648 Beacon St., Boston, MA 02215.

Nominating. Lorraine D. Schaeffer, State Libn., R. A. Gray Bldg., Tallahassee, FL 32301.

Planning, Organization and Bylaws. Alan D. Lewis, Asst. Dir., Office of Public Libs. and Inter-Lib. Coop., 301 Hanover Bldg., 480 Cedar St., St. Paul, MN 55101.

Publications. Sally B. Roberts, Country Scholar, Inc., Emerson Hill Rd., Rte. 127, Contoocooke, NH 03229.

Research. Galen E. Rike, Dept. of Lib. Science, Ball State Univ., Muncie, IN 47306.

Standards. Susan B. Madden, Coord. of Young Adult Services, King County Lib. System, 300 Eighth N., Seattle, WA 98109.

Standards for Library Functions at the State Level (Ad Hoc, Subcommittee). W. Lyle Eberhart, Wisconsin Dept. of Public Instruction, Div. for Lib. Services, 126 Langdon St., Madison, WI 53702.

Standards for Library Service to the Blind and Physically Handicapped (Ad Hoc, Subcommittee). Katherine M. Jackson, Head, Reference Div., Texas A&M Univ. Libs., College Station, TX 77843.

Standards for Library Services to the Deaf (Ad Hoc, Subcommittee). Lethene Parks, Pierce County Lib., 2356 Tacoma Ave. S., Tacoma, WA 98402.

REPRESENTATIVES

ALA Government Documents Round Table (GODORT). Allan S. Quinn (1981).

ALA International Relations Committee. To be appointed.

ALA Legislation Assembly. Barbara F. Weaver (1982).

ALA Legislation Committee, Copyright Subcommittee. F. William Summers (1981).

ALA Library Education Assembly. Dottie R. Hiebing (1982).

ALA Membership Promotion Task Force. Marnie M. Warner (1982).

ALA/LAMA/BES Committees for Facilities for Specialized Library Services. To be appointed.

ALA/LAMA/LOMS Programmatic Planning Discussion Group. Lesley C. Loke (1981).

ALA/LAMA/SS Statistics for State Libraries Committee. To be appointed.

ALA/LITA/ISAD Technical Standards for Automation Committee. To be appointed.

ALA/RASD Interlibrary Loan Committee. Danuta A. Nitecki (1982).

ALA/RTSD/CCS Cataloging: Description and Access Committee. To be appointed.

American Correctional Association (ACA). Robert F. Ensley.

Chief Officers of State Library Agencies (COSLA). Sandra M. Cooper.
Freedom to Read Foundation. Phyllis I. Dalton (1981).
Interagency Council on Library Resources for Nursing. Frederick Pattison; Mary A. Shopa.
Urban Libraries Council. Nettie Barcroft Taylor (1981).

SECTION CHAIRPERSONS

Health Care Libraries (HCLS). Shirley A. Edsall, Dir., Learning Resources, Wilson Memorial Hospital, 33-57 Harrison St., Johnson City, NY 13790.
Library Service to Prisoners (LSPS). Connie House, Box 1360, Kountze, TX 77625.
Library Service to the Blind and Physically Handicapped (LSBPH). Arlene Bansal, Deputy Dir., Lib. Archives and Public Records Dept., State Capitol, 1700 W. Washington, Phoenix, AZ 85007.
Library Service to the Deaf. Alice L. Hagemeyer, 2930 Craiglawn Rd., Silver Spring, MD 20904.
Library Service to the Impaired Elderly (LSIES). James E. Pletz, Senior Citizens Specialist, Public Lib., 425 N. Michigan Ave., Chicago, IL 60611.
Multitype Library Cooperation Section (MLCS). Linda D. Crowe, North Suburban Lib. System, 200 W. Dundee Rd., Wheeling, IL 60090.
State Library Agency (SLAS). Charles A. Bolles, State Lib., 325 W. State St., Boise, ID 83702.

AMERICAN LIBRARY ASSOCIATION
LIBRARY ADMINISTRATION AND MANAGEMENT ASSOCIATION
Executive Secretary, Roger H. Parent
50 E. Huron St., Chicago, IL 60611
312-944-6780

OBJECT

"The Library Administration and Management Association provides an organizational framework for encouraging the study of administrative theory, for improving the practice of administration in libraries, and for identifying and fostering administrative skill. Toward these ends, the division is responsible for all elements of general administration which are common to more than one type of library. These may include organizational structure, financial administration, personnel management and training, buildings and equipment, and public relations. LAMA meets this responsbility in the following ways:

1. Study and review of activities assigned to the division with due regard for changing developments in these activities.

2. Initiating and overseeing activities and projects appropriate to the division, including activities involving bibliography compilation, publication, study, and review of professional literature within the scope of the division.

3. Synthesis of those activities of other ALA units which have a bearing upon the responsibilities or work of the division.

4. Representation and interpretation of library administrative activities in contacts outside the library profession.

5. Aiding the professional development of librarians engaged in administration and encouragement of their participation in appropriate type-of-library divisions.

6. Planning and development of those programs of study and research in library administrative problems which are most needed by the profession." Established 1957.

OFFICERS

Pres. Mary Hall, Prince George's County Memorial Lib., 6532 Adelphi Rd., Hyattsville, MD 20782; *V.P./Pres.-Elect.* Carolyn Snyder; *Past Pres.* Dale B. Canelas; *Exec. Secy.* Roger H. Parent. (Address correspondence to the executive secretary.)

BOARD OF DIRECTORS

Officers; Barbara Conroy; Joan R. Erwin; Suzanne Henderson; Patricia Hogan; Bernard Kreissman; Margaret A. Otto. *Directors-at-Large.* Sandra Coleman; Gary Strong; Joseph Kimbrough. *Ex Officio.* Sec. v.-chpns.; exec. secy.; *LAMA Newsletter ed.*

PUBLICATIONS

Friends of the Library National Notebook (q.). *Ed.* Sandy Dolnick, 4909 N. Ardmore Ave., Milwaukee, WI 53217.
LAMA Newsletter (q.; memb.). *Ed.* Ross G. Stephen, Univ. of Wisconsin-Oshkosh, 800 Algoma Blvd., Oshkosh, WI 54901.

COMMITTEE CHAIRPERSONS

Membership. Patricia M. Paine, Fairfax County Public Lib., Springfield, VA 22151.
Nominating. Betty W. Bender, Public Lib., W. 906 Main Ave., Spokane, WA 99201.
Organization. Nancy R. McAdams, Univ. of Texas, Austin, TX 78712.
Orientation Programs. June L. Engle, Emory Univ. Div. of Libs., Atlanta, GA 30322.
Program. Elizabeth Salzer, J. Henry Meyer Memorial Lib., Stanford Univ. Libs., Stanford, CA 94305.
Publications. Dale B. Canelas, Stanford Univ. Libs., Stanford, CA 94305.
Small Libraries Publications. Kay A. Cassell, Bethlehem Public Lib., 451 Delaware Ave., Delmar, NY 12054.

DISCUSSION GROUP CHAIRPERSONS

Middle Management. Mary Trefry, 3208 N.E. 71 Terr., Gladstone, MO 64119.
Racism Sexism Awareness. To be appointed.
Women Administrators. Joanne R. Euster, J. Paul Leonard Lib., San Francisco State Univ., 1630 Holloway Ave., San Francisco, CA 94132; Patricia Olsen, Avon Township Lib., 210 W. University Dr., Rochester, MI 48062.

SECTION CHAIRPERSONS

Buildings and Equipment Section. Bernard Kreissman, Univ. of California, Davis, CA 95616.
Circulation Services Section. Patricia M. Hogan, North Suburban Lib. System, 200 W. Dundee, Wheeling, IL 60090.
Library Organization and Management Section. Margaret A. Otto, Dartmouth College Lib., Hanover, NH 02139.
Personnel Administration Section. Barbara Conroy, Box 502, Tabernash, CO 80478.
Public Relations Section. Joan Erwin, Public Lib., 10 N. Rosalind Ave., Orlando, FL 32801.
Statistics Section. Susanne Henderson, 5937 S. Second St., Arlington, VA 22204.

LAMA REPRESENTATIVES

ALA Legislation Assembly. Janice Feye-Stukas.
ALA Membership Committee. Patricia M. Paine.
Freedom to Read Foundation (FTRF). Laurence Miller.

AMERICAN LIBRARY ASSOCIATION
LIBRARY AND INFORMATION TECHNOLOGY ASSOCIATION
Program Director, Donald P. Hammer
50 E. Huron St., Chicago, IL 60611
312-944-6780

OBJECT

"The Library and Information Technology Association provides its members and, to a lesser extent, the information dissemination field as a whole, with a forum for discussion, an environment for learning, and a program for action on all phases of the development and application of automated and technological systems in the library and information sciences. Since its activities and interests are derived as responses to the needs and demands of its members, its program is flexible, varied, and encompasses many aspects of the field. Its primary concern is the design, development, and implementation of technological systems in the library and information science fields. Within that general precept, the interests of the division include such varied activities as systems development, electronic data processing, mechanized information retrieval, operations research, standards development, telecommunications, networks and collaborative efforts, management techniques, information technology and other aspects of audiovisual and video cable communications activities, and hardware applications related to all of these areas. Although it has no facilities to carry out research, it attempts to encourage its members in that activity.

Information about all of these activities is disseminated through the division's publishing program, seminars and institutes, exhibits, conference programs, and committee work. The division provides an advisory and consultative function when called upon to do so.

It regards continuing education as one of its major responsibilities and through the above channels it attempts to inform its members of current activities and trends, and it also provides retrospective information for those new to the field."

OFFICERS

Pres. S. Michael Malinconico, Assoc. Dir. for Technical and Computer Services, Public Lib., Branch Libs., 8 E. 40 St., New York, NY 10016; *V.P./Pres.-Elect.* Brigitte L. Kenney, INFOCON, Inc., 400 Plateau Pkwy., Golden, CO 80401; *Past Pres.* Barbara E. Markuson, Dir., INCOLSA, 1000 W. 42 St., Indianapolis, IN 46208.

DIRECTORS

Officers; Kenneth J. Bierman (1981); Helen Cyr (1981); Nancy L. Eaton (1983); Bonnie K. Juergens (1981); Angie W. LeClercq (1982); Marilyn J. Rehnberg (1981); *Councillor.* Ronald F. Miller (1981); *Ex Officio. Bylaws and Organization Committee Chpn.* Heike Kordish (1982); *Publications Committee Chpn.* Charles Husbands (1982); *Program Dir.* Donald P. Hammer.

PUBLICATIONS

Journal of Library Automation (JOLA) (q.; memb.; nonmemb. $15). *Ed.* Brian Aveney, Blackwell North American, 10300 S.W. Allen Blvd., Beaverton, OR 97005. For information or to send manuscripts, contact Donald P. Hammer, LITA Program Dir., ALA, 50 E. Huron St., Chicago, IL 60611.

LITA Newsletter (tri-ann.; memb.). *Ed.* Patricia Barkalow, Head, Systems, Univ. Libs., Univ. of Tennessee, Knoxville, TN 37916.

COMMITTEE CHAIRPERSONS

Awards. Jerome Pennington, Asst. Dir., Public Lib., 605 N. El Dorado, Stockton, CA 95202.

Bylaws and Organization. Heike Kor-

dish, Columbia Univ. Libs., 322 Butler Lib., New York, NY 10027.
Education. James Benson, Grad. School of Lib. Science, Univ. of Alabama, Box 6242, University, AL 35486.
Legislation and Regulation. Judith Sessions, Dir., Mount Vernon College Lib., 2100 Foxhall Rd. N.W., Washington, DC 20007.
Membership. Blanche E. Woolls, 270 Tennyson Ave., Pittsburgh, PA 15213.
Nominating. Maurice Freedman, 158 Landsdowne Ave., Westfield, NJ 07090.
Program Planning. Kaye Gapen, Asst. Dir., Technical Services, Iowa State Univ. Lib., Ames, IA 50011.
Publications. Charles Husbands, Systems Libn., OSPR Widener 88, Harvard Univ. Lib., Cambridge, MA 02138.
Representation in Machine-Readable Form of Bibliographic Information, RTSD/LITA/RASD (MARBI). Eleanor Montague, Box 5900, 340 W. Blaine, Riverside, CA 92507.
Telecommunications. Joan M. Maier, Chief, Lib. Services, Lib., Rm. 51, National Oceanic and Atmospheric Admin., 325 Broadway, Boulder, CO 80303.

DISCUSSION GROUP CHAIRPERSONS

Library Automation (COLA). Patricia H. Earnest, 2775 Mesa Verde Dr. E., Apt. U-216, Costa Mesa, CA 92626.
MARC Users. William Mathews, 73 E. Linden Ave., Englewood, NJ 07631.

SECTION CHAIRPERSON

Audio-Visual Section (AVS). Helen Cyr, 100 Glen Argyle Rd., Baltimore, MD 21212.
Information Science and Automation Section (ISAS). Bonnie K. Juergens, Box 17487, Austin, TX 78760.
Video and Cable Communications Section (VCCS). Marilyn J. Rehnberg, Special Extension Services Lib., Public Lib., 215 N. Wyman, Rockford, IL 61101.

AMERICAN LIBRARY ASSOCIATION
PUBLIC LIBRARY ASSOCIATION
Executive Secretary, Shirley C. Mills
50 E. Huron St., Chicago, IL 60611
312-944-6780

OBJECT

To advance the development, effectiveness, and financial support of public library service to the American people; to speak for the library profession at the national level on matters pertaining to public libraries; and to enrich the professional competence and opportunities of public librarians. In order to accomplish this mission, the Public Library Association has adopted the following goals:

1. Conducting and sponsoring research about how the public library can respond to changing social needs and technological developments.
2. Developing and disseminating materials useful to public libraries in interpreting public library services and needs.
3. Conducting continuing education for public librarians by programming at national and regional conferences, by publications such as the newsletter, and by other delivery methods.
4. Establishing, evaluating, and promoting goals, guidelines, and standards for public libraries.
5. Maintaining liaison with relevant national agencies and organizations engaged in public administration and human services such as National Association of Counties, Municipal League, Commission on Post-Secondary Education.

6. Maintaining liaison with other divisions and units of ALA and other library organizations such as the Association of American Library Schools and the Urban Libraries Council.
7. Define the role of the public library in service to a wide range of user and potential user groups.
8. Promoting and interpreting the public library to a changing society through legislative programs and other appropriate means.
9. Identifying legislation to improve and to equalize support of public libraries. Organized 1951. Memb. 4,238.

MEMBERSHIP

Open to all ALA members interested in the improvement and expansion of public library services to all ages in various types of communities.

OFFICERS (1980–1981)

Pres. Robert H. Rohlf, Hennepin County Lib., Edina, MN 55435; *V.P./Pres.-Elect.* Agnes M. Griffen, Montgomery County Dept. of Public Libs., Rockville, MD 20850; *Past Pres.* Ronald A. Dubberly, Public Lib., Seattle, WA 98104.

BOARD OF DIRECTORS (1980–1981)

Officers; Ervin J. Gaines; Joel Rosenfeld; Kathleen E. Mehaffey; Patricia Woodrum; Nancy Doyle Bolt; Mildred K. Smock; *Sec. Reps. AEPS Pres.* Jeanne M. Patterson; *AFLS Pres.* Marjorie E. Homeyard; *CIS Chair, Steering Committee.* Carolyn A. Anthony; *MLS Pres.* Ronald S. Kozlowski; *PLSS Pres.* Kathleen R. Imhoff; *SMLS Pres.* Patricia Hudson; *Ex Officio Public Libraries Ed.* Kenneth Shearer, Jr.; *PLA-ALA Membership Rep.* Charles M. Brown; *Past Pres. ALTA.* James A. Hess; *Exec. Secy.* Shirley Mills-Fischer; *Councillor.* Emily C. Payne.

PUBLICATIONS

Public Libraries (q.; memb.). *Ed.* Kenneth D. Shearer, Jr., 1205 LeClair St., Chapel Hill, NC 27514.
Public Library Reporter (occas.). Ed. varies. Standing orders or single order available from Order Dept., ALA, 50 Huron St., Chicago, IL 60611.

SECTION HEADS

Alternative Education Programs (AEPS). Jeanne M. Patterson.
Armed Forces Librarians (AFLS). Marjorie E. Homeyard.
Community Information (CIS). Carolyn A. Anthony.
Metropolitan Libraries (MLS). Ronald S. Kozlowski.
Public Library Systems (PLSS). Kathleen R. Imhoff.
Small and Medium-sized Libraries (SMLS). Patricia A. Hudson.

COMMITTEE CHAIRPERSONS

Audiovisual. Larry Pepper, Rolling Prairie Libs., 345 W. Eldorado, Decatur, IL 62522.
Bylaws. Leon Drolet, Suburban Audio Visual Service, 920 Barnsdale Rd., La Grange Park, IL 60525.
Cataloging Needs of Public Libraries. Mary Kaye Donahue, Hidalgo County Lib. System, 601 N. Main St., McAllen, TX 78501.
Children, Service to. Ethel N. Ambrose, Stockton-San Joaquin County Public Lib., 506 N. El Dorado St., Stockton, CA 95202.
Conference Program Coordinating. Gary M. Shirk, Acquisitions, Univ. of Minnesota Libs., Minneapolis, MN 55455.
Goals, Guidelines, and Standards for Public Libraries. Charles W. Robinson, Baltimore County Public Lib., 320 York Rd., Towson, MD 21204.
Human Services. Effie Lee Morris, 66 Cleary Ct., 1009, San Francisco, CA 94109.
Legislation. Donald J. Sager, Chicago

Public Lib., 425 N. Michigan, Chicago, IL 60611.
Allie Beth Martin Award. Frank E. Gibson, Omaha Public Lib., 215 S. 15 St., Omaha, NE 68102.
Membership. Charles M. Brown, Public Lib. of Columbus & Franklin County, 28 S. Hamilton Rd., Columbus, OH 43213.
Multi-Lingual Library Service. Yolanda Cuesta, 911 Pierce St., Albany, CA 94706.
Nominating. Helen A. Knievel, Northeastern Iowa Regional Lib. System, 619 Mulberry St., Waterloo, IA 50703.
Organization. David Snider, Casa Grande Public Lib., 405 E. Sixth St., Casa Grande, AZ 85222.
Orientation. Edward A. Howard, Evansville Public Lib., 22 S.E. Fifth St., Evansville, IN 47708.
Public Libraries Ed. Kenneth D. Shearer, 1205 LeClair St., Chapel Hill, NC 27514.
"Public Library Reporter." Caren Brown, Berkeley Heights Public Lib., 290 Plainfield Ave., Berkeley Heights, NJ 07992.
Publications. Betty J. Turock, 11 Undercliff Rd., Montclair, NJ 07042.
Research. Douglas Zweizig, King Research, Inc., 6000 Executive Blvd., Rockville, MD 20852.
State Library Association Public Library Sections. Larry T. Nix, Wisconsin Div. for Lib. Service, B 32, 4th fl., GEF-3, 125 Webster St., Madison, WI 53702.
University Press Books for Public Libraries. Claudya B. Muller, Worcester Public Lib., Snow Hill, MD 21863.

AMERICAN LIBRARY ASSOCIATION
REFERENCE AND ADULT SERVICES DIVISION
Executive Secretary, Andrew M. Hansen
50 E. Huron St., Chicago, IL 60611
312-944-6780

OBJECT

The Reference and Adult Services Division is responsible for stimulating and supporting in every type of library the delivery of reference/information services to all groups, regardless of age, and of general library services and materials to adults. This involves facilitating the development and conduct of direct service to library users, the development of programs and guidelines for service to meet the needs of these users, and assisting libraries in reaching potential users.

The specific responsibilities of RASD are:

1. Conduct of activities and projects within the division's areas of responsibility.
2. Encouragement of the development of librarians engaged in these activities, and stimulation of participation by members of appropriate type-of-library divisions.
3. Synthesis of the activities of all units within the American Library Association that have a bearing on the type of activities represented by the division.
4. Representation and interpretation of the division's activities in contacts outside the profession.
5. Planning and development of programs of study and research in these areas for the total profession.
6. Continuous study and review of the division's activities.

Formed by merger of Adult Services Division and Reference Services Division, 1972. Memb. 5,496. (For information on dues, see ALA entry.)

OFFICERS (1980–1981)

Pres. H. Joanne Harrar, Univ. of Maryland, College Park, MD 20742; *V.P./ Pres.-Elect.* Geraldine B. King, Ramsey County Public Lib., St. Paul, MN 55113; *Secy.* Mary U. Hardin, Oklahoma Dept. of Libs., Oklahoma City, OK 73105.

DIRECTORS

Officers; Sharon Anne Hogan; David F. Kohl; Margaret Thrasher; Marjorie Karlson; Thomas A. Childers; Charles A. Bunge; *Past Pres.* Nancy H. Marshall; *Ex Officio, History Sec. Chair.* Joyce Duncan Falk; *Machine-Assisted Reference Sec. Chair.* Guy T. Westmoreland; *Ed. RQ.* Helen B. Josephine; *Council of State and Regional Groups Chair.* Janice A. Hummel, South Maryland Regional Lib. Assn., LaPlata, MD 20646; *Exec. Secy.* Andrew M. Hansen. (Address general correspondence to the executive secretary.)

PUBLICATIONS

RQ (q.; memb.; nonmemb. $20). *Ed.* Helen B. Josephine, Box 246, Berkeley, CA 94701.

RASD Update (bi-mo.; memb.; nonmemb. $6). *Ed.* Della L. Giblon, Leon County Public Lib., 1940 N. Monroe St., Suite 81, Tallahassee, FL 32303.

SECTION CHAIRPERSONS

History. Joyce Duncan Falk, 2726 Cuesta Rd., Santa Barbara, CA 93105.

Machine-Assisted Reference Services (MARS). Guy T. Westmoreland, Stanford Univ. Lib., Stanford, CA 94305.

COMMITTEE CHAIRPERSONS

Adult Library Materials. Della L. Giblon, Leon County Public Lib., 1940 N. Monroe St., Suite 81, Tallahassee, FL 32303.

Adults, Services to. Peggy Glover, Free Lib. of Philadelphia, Logan Sq., Philadelphia, PA 19103.

AFL/CIO-ALA. Library Service to Labor Groups. To be appointed.

Aging Population, Library Service to. Marilee Neale, Rosenberg Lib., Galveston, TX 77550.

Bibliography. Janet M. Gilligan, International Communication Agency, 1717 H St. N.W., Washington, DC 20547.

Budget. Geraldine B. King, Ramsey County Public Lib., St. Paul, MN 55113.

Business Reference Services. James B. Taylor, Seattle Public Lib., Seattle, WA 98155.

Catalog Use. Linda Arret, Lib. of Congress, Washington, DC 20540.

Conference Program—San Francisco 1981. Cynthia B. Duncan, Old Dominion Univ., Norfolk, VA 23508.

Cooperative Reference Services. Candace D. Morgan, Oregon State Lib., Salem, OR 97310.

Dartmouth Medal. Irene Christopher, 790 Boylston St., Boston, MA 02199.

Facts on File Award. Karen L. Furlow, 117 Raspberry St., Metairie, LA 70005.

Goals and Objectives for Planning. Gary Purcell, Univ. of Tennessee, Knoxville, TN 37916.

Interlibrary Loan. Noelene P. Martin, 525 Glen Rd., State College, PA 16801.

Membership. Judith A. Tuttle, Univ. of Wisconsin, Memorial Lib., Madison, WI 53705.

Isadore Gilbert Mudge Citation. Diane C. Parker, State Univ. of New York-Buffalo, Amherst, NY 14260.

Nominating. Marilyn H. Boria, Chicago Public Lib., Chicago, IL 60611.

Notable Books Council. Jane Cumming Selvar, 15 Beech Tree La., Bronxville, NY 10708.

Organization. David F. Kohl, Undergraduate Lib., Univ. of Illinois, Urbana, IL 61801.

Outstanding Reference Sources. Deborah C. Masters, B-16 Univ. Lib., State Univ. of New York, Albany, NY 12222.

Professional Development. Eleanore R. Ficke, 11310 Fairway Ct., Reston, VA 22090.

Prototype Workshop on Performance Improvement for Reference Librarians (Ad Hoc). Tina Roose, North Suburban Lib. System, 5215 Oakton, Skokie, IL 60076.
Publications. Nancy E. Gwinn, Council on Lib. Resources, Inc., One Dupont Circle, Suite 620, Washington, DC 20036.
Spanish-speaking, Library Services to. To be appointed.
Standards. Elaine Z. Jennerich, Baylor Univ. Lib., Box 6307, Waco, TX 76706.
Wilson Indexes. Wayne Gossage, 382 W. Clinton Ave., Irvington, NY 10533.

DISCUSSION GROUP CHAIRPERSONS

Library Service to an Aging Population. Elliott E. Kanner, North Suburban Lib. System, 200 W. Dundee Rd., Wheeling, IL 60090; Marcia Piotrowski, Steger-South Chicago Heights Public Lib. Dist., South Chicago Heights, IL 60411.
Interlibrary Loan. Marilyn H. Boria, Chicago Public Lib., Chicago, IL 60611; Elaine M. Albright, Lincoln Trail Lib. System, Champaign, IL 61820.
Reference Services in Large Research Libraries. Dianne Legg, Reference Dept., Univ. of Minnesota Lib., Minneapolis, MN 55455.
Reference Services in Medium-sized Research Libraries. John M. Meador, Univ. of Utah Lib., Salt Lake City, UT 84112.
Women's Materials and Women Library Users. Pat Simon, New City Lib., N. Main St., New City, NY 10956.

REPRESENTATIVES

ALA Legislation Assembly. Virginia E. Parker, Port Washington Public Lib., Port Washington, NY 11050.
ALA Legislation Committee (Ad Hoc Copyright Subcommittee). Mary U. Hardin, Oklahoma Dept. of Libs., 200 N.E. 18 St., Oklahoma City, OK 73105.
ALA Membership Promotion Task Force. Judith A. Tuttle, Univ. of Wisconsin Lib., Madison, WI 53705.
Coalition of Adult Education Organization. Eleanore R. Ficke, 11310 Fairway Ct., Reston, VA 22090; Andrew M. Hansen, ALA, 50 E. Huron St., Chicago, IL 60611.
Freedom to Read Foundation. To be appointed.

AMERICAN LIBRARY ASSOCIATION
RESOURCES AND TECHNICAL SERVICES DIVISION
Executive Director, William I. Bunnell
50 E. Huron St., Chicago, IL 60611
312-944-6780

OBJECT

"Responsible for the following activities: acquisition, identification, cataloging, classification, reproduction, and preservation of library materials; the development and coordination of the country's library resources; and those areas of selection and evaluation involved in the acquisition of library materials and pertinent to the development of library resources. Any member of the American Library Association may elect membership in this division according to the provisions of the bylaws."

Established 1957. Memb. 6,164. (For information on dues see ALA entry.)

OFFICERS (JUNE 1980–JUNE 1981)

Pres. Karen Horny, 1915 Sherman Ave., Evanston, IL 60201; *V.P.* Charlotta Hensley, 1385 Edinboro Dr., Boulder, CO 80303; *Chpn. Council of Regional Groups.* David Gray Remington, 115-B E St. S.E., Washington, DC 20003; *Past Pres.* William A. Gosling, 4339 Berini Dr., Durham, NC 27705. (Address correspondence to the executive director.)

DIRECTORS

Officers; section chairpersons; LITA Rep.; RTSD Planning Committee Chpn.; RTSD Rep. to ALA Legislative Assembly; *LRTS* Ed.; *RTSD Newsletter* Ed.; Doris H. Clack, 1115 Frazier Ave., Tallahassee, FL 32304 (Council of Regional Groups V. Chpn.); Joseph Howard, Dir., Processing Dept., Lib. of Congress, Washington, DC 20540 (Lib. of Congress liaison); Suzanne Massonneau, Bailey Lib., Univ. of Vermont, Burlington, VT 05401; Robin N. Downes, Univ. of Houston Lib., 4800 Calhoun Blvd., Central Campus, Houston, TX 77004; Ann Eastman, 716 Burruss Dr. N.W., Blacksburg, VA 24060; Alfred Lane, 19 Barrow St., New York, NY 10014 (parliamentarian).

PUBLICATIONS

Library Resources & Technical Services (q.; memb. or $15). *Ed.* Elizabeth Tate, 11415 Farmland Dr., Rockville, MD 20852.

RTSD Newsletter (bi-mo.; memb. or *LRTS* subscription only). *Ed.* Arnold Hirshon, Box 9184, Duke Sta., Durham, NC 27706.

SECTION CHAIRPERSONS

Cataloging and Classification. Nancy J. Williamson, Univ. of Toronto, 140 St. George St., Toronto, Ont. M5S 1A1.

Preservation of Library Materials Section. Nina J. Root, American Museum of Natural History, Central Park W. & 79 St., New York, NY 10024.

Reproduction of Library Materials. Harriet K. Rebuldela, Acquisitions Dept., Univ. of Colorado Libs., Boulder, CO 80309.

Resources. Paul Mosher, Stanford Univ., Green Lib., Stanford, CA 94305.

Serials. Marcia Tuttle, Serials Dept., Univ. of North Carolina, Wilson Lib. 024-A, Chapel Hill, NC 27514.

COMMITTEE CHAIRPERSONS

Association of American Publishers/ RTSD Joint Committee. Susan B. Harrison, 3308 Warden Dr., Philadelphia, PA 19129; Tom Houston, New York Academy of Sciences, 2 E. 63 St., New York, NY 10021.

Audiovisual. Judith K. Meyers, Lakewood City Schools, 1470 Warren Rd., Lakewood, OH 44107.

Commercial Technical Services Committee. Mary Fischer Ghikas, Chicago Public Lib., 425 N. Michigan Ave., Chicago, IL 60611.

Conference Program. Karen Horny, 1915 Sherman Ave., Evanston, IL 60201 (1981).

Duplicates Exchange Union. Carol Dick Buell, Metro Technical Community College, Box 3777, Omaha, NE 68103 (1981).

Education. John M. Cohn, 7 Valley View Dr., Rockaway, NJ 07866.

Filing (Ad Hoc). Joseph Rosenthal, 245 General Lib., Univ. of California, Berkeley, CA 94720.

International Cataloging Consultation (Special). John D. Byrum, Chief, Descriptive Cataloging Div., Processing Dept., Lib. of Congress, Washington, DC 20540.

Membership. Murray S. Martin, Pennsylvania State Univ., E505 Pattee Lib., University Park, PA 16802.

Nominating. Frederick C. Lynden, 31 Ferry La., Barrington, RI 02806.

Organization and Bylaws. William A. Gosling, 4339 Berini Dr., Durham, NC 27705.

Esther J. Piercy Award Jury. Peter Spyers-Duran, 11221 Weatherby Rd., Los Alamitos, CA 90720.

Planning and Research. Susan H. Vita, 3711 Taylor St., Chevy Chase, MD 20015.

Program Evaluation and Support. Charlotta Hensley, 1385 Edinboro Dr., Boulder, CO 80303.

Public Documents RASD/RTSD/ ASLA. Gail M. Nichols, 1087 Harbor Way, Rodeo, CA 94572.

Representation in Machine-Readable Form of Bibliographic Information, RTSD/LITA/RASD (MARBI). Eleanor Montague, Box 5900, 340 W. Blaine, Riverside, CA 92507.

Technical Services Costs. Peter S.

Graham, Indiana Univ., Lib. C2, Bloomington, IN 47405.

REPRESENTATIVES

ALA Freedom to Read Foundation. Paul Cors.
ALA Government Documents Round Table. Gail M. Nichols.
ALA Legislation Assembly. Ann Heidbreder Eastman.
ALA Library and Information Technology Association. Arnold Hirschon.
ALA Membership Promotion Task Force. Murray Martin.
American National Standards Institute, Inc. (ANSI), Standards Committee Z39 on Library Work, Documentation and Related Publishing Practices. Susan H. Vita; Charlotta Hensley.
CONSER Advisory Group. Jean Cook.
Joint Steering Committee for Revision of AACR. Frances Hinton.
Universal Serials and Book Exchange, Inc. Alfred Lane.

AMERICAN LIBRARY ASSOCIATION YOUNG ADULT SERVICES DIVISION
Executive Secretary, Evelyn Shaevel
50 E. Huron St., Chicago, IL 60611
312-944-6780

OBJECT

"Interested in the improvement and extension of services to young people in all types of libraries; has specific responsibility for the evaluation, selection, interrelation and use of books and nonbook materials for young adults except when such materials are intended for only one type of library." Established 1957. Memb. 3,000 (For dues, see ALA entry.)

MEMBERSHIP

Open to anyone interest in library services to young adults.

OFFICERS (JULY 1980–JULY 1981)

Pres. Audrey Eaglen, Cuyahoga County Public Lib., 4510 Memphis Ave., Cleveland, OH 44144; *V.P./Pres.-Elect.* Evie Wilson, 8602 Champlain Ct., Apt. 85, Tampa, FL 33614; *Past Pres.* Eleanor K. Pourron, Young Adult Services, Arlington County Public Lib., 1015 Quincy St., Arlington, VA 22201; *Division Councillor.* Bruce Daniels, Dept. of State Lib. Services, 95 Davis St., Providence, RI 02908.

DIRECTORS

Susan Tait; Thomas Wm. Downen; Patty Campbell; Barbara Newmark; Joan Atkinson; Lydia LaFleur.

COMMITTEE CHAIRPERSONS

Activities. Jack Forman, 5708 Baltimore Dr., 396, La Mesa, CA 92041.
Best Books for Young Adults. Larry Rakow, Cuyahoga County Public Lib., 4510 Memphis Ave., Cleveland, OH 44144.
Education. Gerald Hodges, Lib. Science/Educational Technology, Univ. of North Carolina, Greensboro, NC 27412.
High-Interest/Low-Literacy Level Materials Evaluation. Ellin Chu, Rochester Public Lib., 115 South Ave., Rochester, NY 14604.
Intellectual Freedom Committee. Judith F. Kurman, Rte. 2, Box 325, Apt. D, Jackson, OH 45640.
Legislation Committee, Evie Wilson, 8602 Champlain Ct., Apt. 85, Tampa, FL 33614.
Library of Congress, Advisory Committee to Collection Development Section

(*Talking Books*). Eileen McMurrer, Shirlington Branch Lib., 2700 S. Arlington Mill Dr., Arlington, VA 22206.
Library Service to Young Adults in Institutions. To be appointed.
Library Services for Spanish-speaking Youth Committee. John W. Cunningham, 979 N. Fifth St., Philadelphia, PA 19123.
Local Arrangements—San Francisco 1981. Elizabeth J. Talbot, 4008 Loma Vista Ave., Oakland, CA 94619.
Media Selection and Usage. Mary Elizabeth Wendt, New York Public Lib., Office of Special Services, 8 E. 40 St., New York, NY 10016.
Membership Promotion. Barbara Newmark, Westchester Lib. System, 280 N. Central Ave., Hartsdale, NY 10530.
National Organization Serving the Young Adult Liaison. Linda Miller, Blue Island Public Lib., 2433 York St., Blue Island, IL 60406.
Nominating 1981. Alice Sedgwick, 11237 N. Solar Ave., Mequon, WI 53092.
Organization and Bylaws. Roberta Gellert, Lewis Rd., Irvington, NY 10533.
Outstanding Biographies for the College Bound. Marion Hargrove, 61 St. Andrews Rd., Severna Park, MD 21146.
Outstanding Books on the Performing Arts for the College Bound. Carolyn Hale, Chestnut Hill Lib., 8711 Germantown Ave., Philadelphia, PA 19118.
Outstanding Fiction for the College Bound. Suzanne Sullivan, John F. Kennedy Lib., Univ. of California, 5151 State University Dr., Los Angeles, CA 90032.
Outstanding Non-Fiction for the College Bound. To be appointed.
Program and Budget Development. Evie Wilson, 8602 Champlain Ct., Apt. 85, Tampa, FL 33614.
Program Development Committee. Julia Losinski, Prince George's County Memorial Lib., 6532 Adelphia Rd., Hyattsville, MD 20782.
Publishers' Liaison Committee. Mimi Kayden, Richardsville Rd., R.F.D. 2, Carmel, NY 10512.
Research Committee. Shirley Fitzgibbons, Grad. Lib., Indiana Univ., Bloomington, IN 47405.
Selected Films for Young Adults. Donna Rae Meyers, 23691 Delmere Dr., 226C, North Olmstead, OH 44070.
Television Committee. Penelope S. Jeffrey, 4733 Morningside Dr., Cleveland, OH 44109.
Top of the News Editorial Committee. Audrey Eaglen, Ed., Cuyahoga County Public Lib., 4510 Memphis Ave., Cleveland, OH 44144.

AMERICAN MERCHANT MARINE LIBRARY ASSOCIATION
(Affiliated with United Seamen's Service)
Executive Director, Mace Mavroleon
One World Trade Center, Suite 2601, New York, NY 10048

OBJECT

Provides ship and shore library service for American-flag merchant vessels, the Military Sealift Command, the Coast Guard, and other waterborne operations of the U.S. government.

OFFICERS

Chmn. of the Bd. James C. Kellogg III; *Pres./Treas.* James J. Hayes; *Secy.* Franklin K. Riley, Jr.

TRUSTEES

Edith Augenti; Ralph R. Bagley; H. A. Downing; John I. Dugan; Charles Francis; Arthur Friedberg; Richard I. Gulick; Robert E. Hart; Thomas A. King; Carolyn McKinley; Thomas J. Patterson, Jr., Andrew Rich; George J. Ryan; S. Fraser Sammis; Philip Steinberg; Paul E. Trimble, Edward Turner; C. E. Whitcomb; Adrian P. Spidle; Jeannette Spidle; Samuel Thompson.

AMERICAN SOCIETY FOR INFORMATION SCIENCE
Executive Director, Samuel B. Beatty
1010 16 St. N.W., Washington, DC 20036
202-659-3644

OBJECT

"The American Society for Information Science provides a forum for the discussion, publication, and critical analysis of work dealing with the design, management, and use of information systems and technology." Memb. (Indiv.) 4,431; (Student) 483; (Inst.) 91. Dues. (Indiv.) $55; (Student) $15; (Inst.) $300; (Sustaining Sponsor) $600.

OFFICERS

Pres. Mary C. Berger, Cuadra Associates, 1523 Sixth St., Santa Monica, CA 90401; *Pres.-Elect.* Ruth Tighe, Govt. of Northern Mariana Islands, Dept. of Educ., Saipan, GM 96950; *Treas.* Frank Slater, Univ. of Pittsburgh, G-33 Hillman Lib., Pittsburgh, PA 15260; *Past Pres.* Herbert Landau, Solar Energy Research Institute, 1617 Cole Blvd., Golden, CO 80401. (Address correspondence to the executive director.)

COUNCIL

Officers; *Chapter Assembly Councillor.* Joe Ann Clifton; *SIG Cabinet Councillor.* Bonnie C. Carroll; *Councillors-at-Large.* Toni Carbo Bearman; Charles H. Davis; Carol Johnson; Darlene Myers; Edmond J. Sawyer; Julie Carroll Virgo.

PUBLICATIONS

Note: Unless otherwise indicated, publications are available from Knowledge Industry Publications, 2 Corporate Park Dr., White Plains, NY 10604.

Annual Review of Information Science and Technology (vol. 3, 1968–vol. 10, 1975, $35 ea., memb. $28; vol. 11, 1976–vol. 15, 1980, $42.50 ea., memb. $34).

Bulletin of the American Society for Information Science (6 per year; memb. or $35 domestic, $42.50 foreign). Available directly from ASIS.

Collective Index to the Journal of the American Society for Information Science (vol. 1, 1950–vol. 25, 1974, $60 ea., memb. $42). Available from John Wiley & Sons, 605 Third Ave., New York, NY 10016.

Computer-Readable Data Bases: A Directory and Data Sourcebook 1979 ($95, memb. $76).

Cumulative Index to the Annual Review of Information Science and Technology (vols. 1–10, $35 ea., memb. $28).

Journal of the American Society for Information Science; formerly *American Documentation* (bi-mo.; memb. or $55 domestic, $60 foreign). Available from John Wiley & Sons, 605 Third Ave., New York, NY 10016.

Key Papers in the Design and Evaluation of Information Systems. Ed. by Donald W. King ($25, memb. $20).

Library and Reference Facilities in the Area of the District of Columbia (10th ed., 1979, $19.50, memb. $15.60).

Proceedings of the ASIS Annual Meetings (vol. 5, 1968–vol. 9, 1972, $15 ea., memb. $12; vol. 10, 1973–vol. 16, 1979, $19.50 ea., memb. $15.60).

COMMITTEE CHAIRPERSONS

Awards and Honors. Trudi Bellardo, College of Lib. Science, Univ. of Kentucky, Lexington, KY 40506.

Budget and Finance. Frank Slater, Univ. of Pittsburgh, G-33 Hillman Lib., Pittsburgh, PA 15260.

Conferences and Meetings. Stephanie Normann, Solar Energy Research Institute, 1617 Cole Blvd., Golden, CO 80401.

Constitution and Bylaws. Harley Baade, Shell Oil Co., Box 2463, Rm. 901, One Shell Plaza, Houston, TX 77001.

Education. Pauline V. Angione, SDC

Search Service, Suite 500, 625 N. Michigan Ave., Chicago, IL 60611.
Executive. Mary C. Berger, Cuadra Associates 1523 Sixth St., Suite 12, Santa Monica, CA 90401.
International Relations. Irene Farkas-Conn, Arthur L. Conn & Associates, Inc., 1469 E. Park Pl., Chicago, IL 60637.
Inter-Society Cooperation. Signe E. Larson, U.S. Dept. of Housing & Urban Development Lib., 451 Seventh St. S.W., Washington, DC 20410.
Marketing. Nancy Hardy, Engineering Index, Inc., 345 E. 47 St., New York, NY 10017.
Membership. Gerard O. Platau, Chemical Abstracts Service, Box 3012, Columbus, OH 43210.
Networking. Ward Shaw, Colorado Alliance of Research Libs., Denver Public Lib., Administration Center, 3840 York St., Unit 1, Denver, CO 80205.
Nominations. Herbert B. Landau, Solar Energy Research Institute, 1617 Cole Blvd., Golden, CO 80401.
Professionalism. Robert O. Stanton, Bell Telephone Laboratories, Rm. MH 6A-316, 600 Mountain Ave., Murray Hill, NJ 07974.
Public Affairs. Dennis McDonald, 3508 Valley Dr., Alexandria, VA 22302.
Publications. Joseph Kuney, Informatics, Inc., 6011 Executive Blvd., Rockville, MD 20852.
Research. Thomas Martin, Syracuse Univ., School of Information Studies, 113 Euclid Ave., Syracuse, NY 13210.
Standards. Margaret Park, Computer Center, Univ. of Georgia, Athens, GA 30602.

AMERICAN THEOLOGICAL LIBRARY ASSOCIATION
Executive Secretary, Rev. David J. Wartluft
Lutheran Theological Seminary, 7301 Germantown Ave., Philadelphia, PA 19119

OBJECT

"To bring its members into closer working relationships with each other, to support theological and religious librarianship, to improve theological libraries, and to interpret the role of such libraries in theological education, developing and implementing standards of library service, promoting research and experimental projects, encouraging cooperative programs that make resources more available, publishing and disseminating literature and research tools and aids, cooperating with organizations having similar aims and otherwise supporting and aiding theological education." Founded 1947. Memb. (Inst.) 150; (Indiv.) 460. Dues (Inst.) $50–$300, based on total library expenditure; (Indiv.) $10–$55, based on salary scale. Year. May 1–April 30.

ATLA is a member of the Council of National Library and Information Associations.

MEMBERSHIP

Persons engaged in professional library or bibliographical work in theological or religious fields and others who are interested in the work of theological librarianship.

OFFICERS (JUNE 1980-JUNE 1981)

Pres. Simeon Daly, St. Meinrad School of Theology, St. Meinrad, IN 47577; *V.P./Pres.-Elect.* Jerry Campbell, Perkins School of Theology, Southern Methodist Univ., Dallas, TX 75275; *Treas.* Robert A. Olsen, Jr., Libn., Brite Divinity School, Texas Christian Univ., Ft. Worth, TX 76129; *Newsletter Ed.* Donn Michael Farris, Divinity School Lib., Duke Univ., Durham, NC 27706.

BOARD OF DIRECTORS

John Baker-Batsel; James Dunkly; Roberta Hamburger; Norman Kansfield; Harriet V. Leonard; Sarah Lyons; Stephen L. Peterson; Elmer O'Brien; *ATS Rep.* David Schuller.

PUBLICATIONS

Newsletter (q.; memb. or $6).
Proceedings (ann.; memb.; or $10).
Religion Index One (formerly *Index to Religious Periodical Literature, 1949–*date).
Religion Index Two: Multi-Author Works.

COMMITTEE CHAIRPERSONS

ATLA Newsletter. Donn Michael Farris, Ed., Divinity School Lib., Duke Univ., Durham, NC 27706.

ATLA Representative to ANSI Z39. Warren Kissinger, 6309 Queen's Chapel Rd., Hyattsville, MD 20782.

ATLA Representative to the Council of National Library and Information Associations. James Irvine, Princeton Theologal Seminary, Box 111, Princeton, NJ 08540.

ATLA Representative to the Universal Serials and Book Exchange. USBE liaison now assigned to Library Materials Exchange Committee.

Annual Conferences. Delena Goodman, School of Theology Lib., Anderson College, Anderson, IN 46011.

Archivist. Gerald W. Gillette, Presbyterian Historical Society, 425 Lombard St., Philadelphia, PA 19147.

Bibliographic Systems. Elizabeth Chambers, Apt. 507, 807 W. Taylor Rd., DeKalb, IL 60115.

Clearinghouse on Personnel. David J. Wartluft, Lutheran Theological Seminary, 7301 Germantown Ave., Philadelphia, PA 19119.

Collection Evaluation and Development. Donald Vorp, Drew Univ. Lib., Madison, NJ 07940.

Contacts with Foundations. John Baker-Batsel, Grad. Theological Union Lib., 2451 Ridge Rd., Berkeley, CA 94709.

Library Consultation Service. John B. Trotti, Union Theological Seminary, 3401 Brook Rd., Richmond, VA 23227.

Library Materials Exchange (*formerly Periodical Exchange*). James Overbeck, Columbia Theological Seminary Lib., 701 Columbia Dr., Decatur, GA 30030.

Membership. James Pakala, Biblical Theological Seminary Lib., 200 N. Main St., Hatfield, PA 19440.

Microtext Reproduction Board. Charles Willard, Exec. Secy., Princeton Theological Seminary, Princeton, NJ 08540; Maria Grossmann, Andover-Harvard Lib., 45 Francis Ave., Cambridge, MA 02138.

Nominating. Roland Kircher, Wesley Theological Seminary Lib., 4400 Massachusetts Ave. N.W., Washington, DC 20016.

Periodical Indexing Board. R. Grant Bracewell, Emmanual College Lib., 75 Queen's Pk., Toronto, Ont. M5S 1K7, Canada.

Preservation of Theological Materials, (*Ad Hoc*). Andrew Scrimgeour, Iliff School of Theology Lib., 2201 S. University, Denver, CO 80210.

Publication. James Dunkly, Nashotah House Lib., Nashotah, WI 53058.

Reader Services. Sara Mobley, Pitts Theological Lib., Emory Univ., Atlanta, GA 30322.

Relationships with Learned Societies. Andrew Scrimgeour, Iliff School of Theology Lib., 2201 S. University, Denver, CO 80210.

Standards of Accreditation. Stephen E. Peterson, Yale Divinity School Lib., 409 Prospect St., New Haven, CT 06510.

Statistician and Liaison with ALA Statistics Coordinating Committee. David Green, Grad. Theological Union, 2451 Ridge Rd., Berkeley, CA 94709.

Systems and Standards. Doralyn Hickey, Reporter, School of Lib. & Info. Sciences, North Texas State Univ., Denton, TX 76203.

ART LIBRARIES SOCIETY OF NORTH AMERICA (ARLIS/NA)

c/o Pamela J. Barry, Executive Secretary,
143 Bowling Green Pl., Iowa City, IA 52242
319-351-2078

OBJECT

"To promote art librarianship, particularly by acting as a forum for the interchange of information and materials on the visual arts." Established 1972. Memb. 1,200. Dues. (Inst.) $50; (Indiv.) $25; (Assoc.) $15; (Sustaining) $150; (Sponsoring) $500. Year. Jan. 1–Dec. 31.

MEMBERSHIP

Open and encouraged for all those interested in visual librarianship, whether they be professional librarians, students, library assistants, art book publishers, art book dealers, art historians, archivists, architects, slide and photograph curators, or retired associates in these fields.

OFFICERS (JAN. 1981–JAN. 1982)

Chpn. Karen Muller, Ryerson & Burnham Libs., Art Institute of Chicago, Michigan Ave. & Adams St., Chicago, IL 60603; *Past Pres.* Wolfgang Freitag, Harvard Univ., Fogg Art Museum Lib., Cambridge, MA 02138; *Treas.* Theresa Cederholm, Fine Arts Research, Boston Public Lib., Boston, MA 02117. (Address correspondence to executive secretary.)

COMMITTEES

(Direct correspondence to headquarters.)
Art Book Publishing Awards.
Cataloging Advisory Committee.
Education.
Exhibition Catalogs.
Iconography.
Nominating Committee.
Publications.
Standards.
George Wittenborn Memorial Award.

EXECUTIVE BOARD

The chairperson, past chairperson, chairperson-elect, secretary, treasurer, and four regional representatives (East, Midwest, West, and Canada).

PUBLICATIONS

ARLIS/NA Newsletter (bi-mo.; memb.).
Directory of Art Libraries and Art Librarians in North America (bienn.).
Directory of Members (memb.).
Guide to Primitive Art Slide Collections from Boston to Washington, DC $3.50).
NH Classification for Photography: An Alternative to TR ($2).

CHAPTERS

Allegheny; Arizona; DC-Maryland-Virginia; Georgia; Kansas-Missouri; Kentucky-Tennessee; Michigan; Mid-States; New England; New Jersey; New York; Northern California; Ohio; Southeast; Southern California; Texas; Twin Cities; Western New York.

ASSOCIATED INFORMATION MANAGERS
Executive Director, Rita Lombardo
316 Pennsylvania Ave. S.E., Suite 502
Washington, DC 20003
202-544-1969

OBJECT

To maintain a forum for emerging information managers, linking them to information sources and to other managers; to create an awareness of the value of information and its potential for increased productivity; and to improve career opportunities for information managers.

MEMBERSHIP

Information managers in industry, government, academia, or individual consultants concerned with information management. Employees of firms that market information products and/or services are also eligible for membership.

OFFICERS

Chpns. James G. Kollegger, Pres., Environmental Information Center, Inc.; Sarah Kadec, Deputy Dir., Office of Admin., Exec. Office of the President, the White House. (Address all correspondence to the executive director.)

EXECUTIVE COMMITTEE

Herbert R. Brinberg, Pres., Aspen Systems Corp.; Roberta Gardner, Dir., Info. Services, Moody's Investors Service, Inc.; Andrew P. Garvin, Chpn. & Chief Exec., FIND/SVP; Joseph H. Kuney, V.P., Informatics, Inc.; Michael D. Majcher, Mgr., Info. Resources, Xerox Corp.; Morton Meltzer, Info. Mgr., Martin Marietta Corp.

PUBLICATIONS

AIM Network (bi-weekly), newsletter.
AIM Membership Roster, annual directory.
So You Want to Be an Information Manager, Resource Kit.
Information Sources (IIA Membership Directory), a directory of information products and services.

ASSOCIATION OF ACADEMIC HEALTH SCIENCES LIBRARY DIRECTORS
Secretary, Peter Stangl, Director, Lane Library, Stanford
University Medical Center, Stanford, CA 94305

OBJECT

"To promote, in cooperation with educational institutions, other educational associations, government agencies, and other non-profit organizations, the common interests of academic health sciences libraries located in the United States and elsewhere, through publications, research, and discussion of problems of mutual interest and concern, and to advance the efficient and effective operation of academic health sciences libraries for the benefit of faculty, students, administrators, and practitioners."

MEMBERSHIP

Regular membership is available to nonprofit educational institutions operating a school of health sciences that has full or provisional accreditation by the Association of American Medical Colleges. Annual dues $50. Regular members shall be represented by the chief administrative officer of the member institution's health sciences library.

Associate membership (and nonvoting representation) is available to organizations having an interest in the purposes and activities of the association.

OFFICERS (JUNE 1980–JUNE 1981)

Pres. C. Robin Lesueur, Countway Lib. of Medicine, Harvard Univ., 10 Shattuck St., Boston, MA 02115; *Pres.-Elect.* Virginia H. Holtz, Middleton Health Sciences Lib., Univ. of Wisconsin, 1305 Linden Dr., Madison, WI 53706; *Past Pres.* Samuel Hitt, Health Sciences Lib., Univ. of North Carolina, Chapel Hill, NC 27514; *Secy.-Treas.* Peter Stangl, Lane Medical Lib., Stanford Univ., Stanford, CA 94305.

BOARD OF DIRECTORS (JUNE 1980–JUNE 1981)

Officers; Glenn L. Brudvig, Bio-Medical Lib., Univ. of Minnesota, Diehl Hall, Minneapolis, MN 55455; Nelson J. Gilman, Norris Medical Lib., Univ. of Southern California, 2025 Zonal Ave., Los Angeles, CA 90033.

COMMITTEE CHAIRPERSONS

Advisory Committee on Annual Statistics for Medical School Libraries. Richard A. Lyders.
Audit Committee. Thomas D. Higdon.
Bylaws Committee. Rose Hogan.
Committee on Information Control and Technology. James F. Williams II.
Committee on the Development of Standards and Guidelines. Jean Miller.
Medical Education Committee. Henry L. Lemkau, Jr.
Newsletter Advisory Committee. Richard B. Frederickson.
Nominating Committee. Raymond A. Palmer.
Program Committee. Richard B. Frederickson.

MEETINGS

An annual business meeting is held in conjunction with the annual meeting of the Medical Library Association in June. Annual membership meeting and program is held in conjunction with the annual meeting of the Association of American Medical Colleges in October.

ASSOCIATION OF AMERICAN LIBRARY SCHOOLS
Executive Secretary, Janet Phillips
471 Park La., State College, PA 16801
814-238-0254

OBJECT

"To advance education for librarianship." Founded 1915. Memb. 790. Dues (Inst.) $125; (Assoc. Inst.) $75; (Indiv.) $25; (Assoc. Indiv.) $20. Year. Sept. 1980–Aug. 1981.

MEMBERSHIP

Any library school with a program accredited by the ALA Committee on Accreditation may become an institutional member; any educator who is employed full time for a full academic year in a library school with an accredited program may become a personal member.

Any school that offers a graduate degree in librarianship or a cognate field but whose program is not accredited by the ALA Committee on Accreditation may become an associate institutional member; any part-time faculty member or doctoral student of a library school with an accredited program or any full-time faculty member employed for a full academic year at other schools that offer graduate degrees in librarianship or cognate fields may become an associate personal member.

OFFICERS
(FEBRUARY 1981–JANUARY 1982)

Pres. Harold Goldstein, Lib. School, Florida State Univ., Tallahassee, FL 32306; *Past Pres.* Charles Bunge, Lib. School, Univ. of Wisconsin, Madison, WI 53706. (Address correspondence to the executive secretary.)

DIRECTORS

John Clemons (Emory); Jane R. Carter (Louisiana State); Marcy Murphy (Western Michigan).

PUBLICATION

Journal of Education for Librarianship (5 issues per year; $18).

COMMITTEE CHAIRPERSON

Conference. Margaret Monroe, Prof., Lib. School, Univ. of Wisconsin, Madison, WI 53706.
Continuing Education. Joan C. Durrance, Lecturer, School of Lib. Science, Univ. of Michigan, Ann Arbor, MI 48109.
Editorial Board. Charles D. Patterson, Prof., Grad. School of Lib. Science, Louisiana State Univ., Baton Rouge, LA 70803.
Legislation. Herbert S. White, Prof., Grad. Lib. School, Indiana Univ., Bloomington, IN 47401.
Nominating. June L. Engle, Asst. Prof., Div. of Libnshp., Emory Univ., Atlanta, GA 30322.
Research. Pauline Wilson, Assoc. Prof., Grad. School of Lib. & Info. Science, Univ. of Tennessee, Knoxville, TN 37916.

REPRESENTATIVES

ALA SCOLE. Jane R. Carter (Louisiana).
Council of Communication Societies. Guy Garrison (Drexel).
IFLA. Sarah K. Vann (Hawaii); Josephine Fang (Simmons).
Organization of American States. Margaret Goggin (Denver).

ASSOCIATION OF JEWISH LIBRARIES
c/o National Foundation for Jewish Culture
122 E. 42 St., Rm. 408, New York, NY 10017

OBJECT

"To promote and improve library services and professional standards in all Jewish libraries and collections of Judaica; to serve as a center of dissemination of Jewish library information and guidance; to encourage the estabishment of Jewish libraries and collections of Judaica; to promote publication of literature which will be of assistance to Jewish librarianship; to encourage people to enter the field of librarianship." Organized 1966 from the merger of the Jewish Librarians Association and the Jewish Library Association. Memb. 600. Dues. (Inst.) $18; (Indiv.) $10. Year. Calendar.

OFFICERS (JUNE 1980–JUNE 1982)

Pres. Barbara Y. Leff, Stephen S. Wise Temple, 15500 Stephen S. Wise Dr., Los Angeles, CA 90024; *Treas.* Mary G. Brand, Rabbi Alexander S. Gross Hebrew Academy Jr.-Sr. Lib., 2842 Pine Tree Dr., 6, Miami Beach, FL 33140; *Corres. Secy.* Edith Lubetski, Hedi Steinberg Lib., Yeshiva Univ., 245 Lexington Ave., New York, NY 10016; *Rec. Secy.* Linda P. Lerman, Boston Theological Inst., 151 North St., C, Newton, MA 02160.

PUBLICATIONS

AJL Bulletin (bienn.) *Ed.* Irene S. Levin, 48 Georgia St., Valley Stream, NY 11580.

Membership Kit.
Proceedings.

DIVISIONS

Research and Special Libraries. Edith Degani, Jewish Theological Seminary of America, 3080 Broadway, New York, NY 10027.

Synagogue School and Center Libraries. Rita C. Frischer, Sinai Temple Lib., 10400 Wilshire Blvd., Los Angeles, CA 90024.

ASSOCIATION OF RESEARCH LIBRARIES
Executive Director, Shirley Echelman
1527 New Hampshire Ave. N.W., Washington, DC 20036
202-232-2466

OBJECT

"To initiate and develop plans for strengthening research library resources and services in support of higher education and research." Established 1932 by the chief librarians of 43 research libraries. Memb. (Inst.) 111. Dues (ann.) $3,000. Year. Jan.–Dec.

MEMBERSHIP

Membership is institutional.

OFFICERS (OCT. 1980–OCT. 1981)

Pres. Jay K. Lucker, Dir., Massachusetts Institute of Technology Libs., Cambridge, MA 02139; *V.P.* Millicent D. Abell, Libn., Univ. of California, San Diego Lib., La Jolla, CA 92037; *Exec. Committee Member-at-Large.* Irene B. Hoadley, Dir., Texas A&M Univ. Libs., College Station, TX 77843; *Exec. Dir.* (effective May 15, 1981). (Address general correspondence to the executive director.)

BOARD OF DIRECTORS

Sterling J. Albrecht, Brigham Young Univ.; Charles Churchwell, Washington Univ.; James F. Govan, Univ. of North Carolina; Donald Koepp, Princeton Univ.; Margot B. McBurney, Queen's Univ.; Eldred Smith, Univ. of Minnesota; James F. Wyatt, Univ. of Rochester.

PUBLICATIONS

ARL Annual Salary Survey (ann.; memb. or $5).
ARL Library Statistics (ann.; memb. or $5).
ARL Minutes (s.-ann.; memb. or $7.50 ea.).
ARL Newsletter (approx. 6 per year; memb. or $12).
76 United Statesiana. Seventy-six works of American scholarship relating to America as published during two centuries from the Revolutionary era of the United States through the nation's bicentennial year. Ed. by Edward C. Lathem ($7.50; $5.75 paper to nonmembs.).
13 Colonial Americana. Ed. by Edward C. Lathem ($7.50).
(the above two titles are distributed by the Univ. of Virginia Press.)
Our Cultural Heritage: Whence Salvation? Louis B. Wright; *The Uses of the Past,* Gordan N. Ray; remarks to the eighty-ninth membership meeting of the association ($2).

COMMITTEE CHAIRPERSONS

African Acquisitions. Hans Panofsky, Northwestern Univ. Lib., Evanston, IL 60210.
ARL/CRL Joint Committee on Expanded Access to Journal Collections. C. James Schmidt, Brown Univ. Lib., Providence, RI 02912.

ARL Statistics. Richard J. Talbot, Univ. of Massachusetts Libs., Amherst, MA 01002.

Center for Chinese Research Materials. Philip McNiff, Boston Public Lib., Boston, MA 02117.

East Asian Acquisitions. Warren Tsuneishi, Lib. of Congress, Washington, DC 20540.

Foreign Newspapers on Microfilm. Joseph E. Jeffs, Georgetown Univ. Lib., Washington, DC 20007.

Interlibrary Loan. Kenneth G. Peterson, Southern Illinois Univ. Lib., Carbondale, IL 62901.

Latin American Acquisitions. Carl W. Deal, Univ. of Illinois Lib., Urbana, IL 61803.

Middle Eastern Acquisitions. David Partington, Harvard Univ. Lib., Cambridge, MA 02138.

Nominations. ARL Vice-President.

Office of Management Studies. Irene Hoadley, Texas A&M Univ. Lib., College Station, TX 77843.

Preservation of Research Library Materials. David Stam, New York Public Lib., New York, NY 10018.

South Asia Acquisitions. Louis Jacob, Lib. of Congress, Washington, DC 20540.

Southeast Asia Acquisitions. Charles Bryant, Yale Univ. Lib., New Haven, CT 06520.

Western European Acquisitions. Howard Sullivan, Wayne State Univ. Lib., Detroit, MI 48202.

TASK FORCE CHAIRPERSONS

Bibliographic Control. James Govan, Univ. of North Carolina Libs., Chapel Hill, NC 27515.

Library Education. Margot B. McBurney, Queen's Univ. Lib., Kingston, Ont. K7L 5C4, Canada.

ARL MEMBERSHIP 1980

Nonuniversity Libraries

Boston Public Lib.; Center for Research Libs.; John Crerar Lib.; Lib. of Congress; Linda Hall Lib.; National Agricultural Lib.; National Lib. of Canada; National Lib. of Medicine; New York Public Lib.; New York State Lib.; Newberry Lib.; Smithsonian Institution Libs.

University Libraries

Alabama; Alberta; Arizona; Arizona State; Boston; Brigham Young; British Columbia; Brown; California (Berkeley); California (Davis); California (Los Angeles); California (Riverside); California (San Diego); California (Santa Barbara); Case Western Reserve; Chicago; Cincinnati; Colorado; Colorado State; Columbia; Connecticut; Cornell; Dartmouth; Duke; Emory; Florida; Florida State; Georgetown; Georgia; Guelph; Harvard; Hawaii; Houston; Howard; Illinois; Indiana; Iowa; Iowa State; Johns Hopkins; Kansas; Kent State; Kentucky; Louisiana State; McGill; McMaster; Maryland; Massachusetts; Massachusetts Institute of Technology; Miami; Michigan; Michigan State; Minnesota; Missouri; Nebraska; New Mexico; New York; North Carolina; Northwestern; Notre Dame; Ohio State; Oklahoma; Oklahoma State; Oregon; Pennsylvania; Pennsylvania State; Pittsburgh; Princeton; Purdue; Queen's (Kingston, Canada); Rice; Rochester; Rutgers; Saskatchewan; South Carolina; Southern California; Southern Illinois; Stanford; SUNY (Albany); SUNY (Buffalo); SUNY (Stony Brook); Syracuse; Temple; Tennessee; Texas; Texas A&M; Toronto; Tulane; Utah; Vanderbilt; Virginia; Virginia Polytechnic; Washington; Washington (St. Louis); Washington State; Wayne State; Western Ontario; Wisconsin; Yale; York.

ASSOCIATION OF VISUAL SCIENCE LIBRARIANS
c/o F. Eleanor Warner, Librarian, New England College of Optometry,
420 Beacon St., Boston, MA 02115

OBJECT

"To foster collective and individual acquisition and dissemination of visual science information, to improve services for all persons seeking such information, and to develop standards for libraries to which members are attached." Founded 1968. Memb. (U.S.) 31; (foreign) 11. Annual meeting held in December in connection with the American Academy of Optometry; Boston, MA (1978); Long Beach, CA (1979); Chicago, IL (1980).

OFFICER

Chpn. F. Eleanor Warner, Libn., New England College of Optometry, 420 Beacon St., Boston, MA 02115.

PUBLICATIONS

PhD Theses in Physiological Optics (irreg.).
Standards for Vision Science Libraries.
Vision Union List of Serials (irreg.).

BETA PHI MU
(International Library Science Honor Society)
Executive Secretary, Blanche Woolls
School of Library and Information Science
University of Pittsburgh, Pittsburgh, PA 15260

OBJECT

"To recognize high scholarship in the study of librarianship, and to sponsor appropriate professional and scholarly projects." Founded at the University of Illinois in 1948. Memb. 17,500.

MEMBERSHIP

Open to graduates of library school programs accredited by the American Library Association who fulfill the following requirements: complete the course requirements leading to a fifth-year or other advanced degree in librarianship with a scholastic average of A—(e.g., 4.75 where A equal 5 points, 3.75 where A equals 4 points, etc.)—this provision shall also apply to planned programs of advanced study beyond the fifth year that do not culminate in a degree but that require full-time study for one or more academic years; receive a letter of recommendation from their respective library schools attesting to their demonstrated fitness of successful professional careers. Former graduates of accredited library schools are also eligible on the same basis.

OFFICERS

Pres. Mary Alice Hunt, Assoc. Prof., School of Lib. Science, Florida State Univ., Tallahassee, FL 32306; *V.P./Pres.-Elect.* Robert D. Stueart, Dean, School of Lib. Science, Simmons College, Boston, MA 02115; *Past Pres.* George M. Bailey, Assoc. Dir. of Libs., Claremont Colleges, Claremont, CA 91711; *Treas.* Marilyn P. Whitmore, Univ. Archivist, Hillman Lib., Univ. of Pittsburgh, Pittsburgh, PA 15260; *Exec. Secy.* Blanche Woolls, Prof., School of Lib. & Info. Science, Univ. of Pittsburgh, Pittsburgh, PA 15260; *Admin. Secy.* Mary Y. Tomaino, School of Lib. & Info. Science, Univ. of Pittsburgh, Pittsburgh, PA 15260.

DIRECTORS

George L. Hebben, 2925 B Ave. W., Plainwell, MI 49080 (Kappa Chapter—Western Michigan Univ./1981); Arnulfo

D. Trejo, Grad. Lib. School, Univ. of Arizona, Tucson, AZ 85721 (Beta Pi Chapter—Univ. of Arizona/1981); Marion L. Mullen, 124 Pattison St., Syracuse, NY 13203 (Pi Lambda Sigma Chapter—Syracuse Univ./1982); Elizabeth Snapp, The Lib.—Texas Woman's Univ., Denton, TX 76204 (Beta Lambda Chapter—Texas Woman's Univ. and North Texas State Univ./1982); Carol Penka, 200 Main Lib., Univ. of Illinois, Urbana, IL 61801 (Alpha Chapter—Univ. of Illinois/1983); Mary Jane Kahao, Grad. School of Lib. Science Lib., Louisiana State Univ., Baton Rouge, LA 70803 (Beta Zeta Chapter—Louisiana State Univ./1983). *Directors-at-Large.* Diane Thompson, Coord. of Children's Services, Pierce County Lib., Tacoma, WA 98402 (1982); Anthony Miele, Dir., State Agency, Public Lib. Services, Montgomery, AL 36130 (1981).

PUBLICATIONS

Newsletter (bienn.)

Beta Phi Mu sponsors a modern Chapbook series. These small volumes, issued in limited editions, are intended to create a beautiful combination of text and format in the interest of the graphic arts and are available to members only. In January 1980, the 14th in the Chapbook series was published by the society, *A Book for a Sixpence: The Circulating Library in America*, by David Kaser.

CHAPTERS

Alpha. Univ. of Illinois, Grad. School of Lib. Science, Urbana, IL 61801; *Beta.* Univ. of Southern California, School of Lib. Science, University Park, Los Angeles, CA 90007; *Gamma.* Florida State Univ., School of Lib. Science, Tallahassee, FL 32306; *Delta* (Inactive). Loughborough College of Further Education, School of Libnshp., Loughborough, England; *Epsilon.* Univ. of North Carolina, School of Lib. Science, Chapel Hill, NC 27514; *Zeta.* Atlanta Univ., School of Lib. & Info. Studies, Atlanta, GA 30314; *Theta.* Pratt Institute, Grad. School of Lib. & Info. Science, Brooklyn, NY 11205; *Iota.* Catholic Univ. of America, Grad. Dept. of Lib. & Info. Science, Washington, DC 20064, and Univ. of Maryland, College of Lib. & Info. Services, College Park, MD 20742; *Kappa.* Western Michigan Univ., School of Libnshp., Kalamazoo, MI 49008; *Lambda.* Univ. of Oklahoma, School of Lib. Science, Norman, OK 73019; *Mu.* Univ. of Michigan, School of Lib. Science, Ann Arbor, MI 48109; *Nu.* Columbia Univ., School of Lib. Service, New York, NY 10027; *Xi.* Univ. of Hawaii, Grad. School of Lib. Studies, Honolulu, HI 96822; *Omicron.* Rutgers Univ., Grad. School of Lib. & Info. Studies, New Brunswick, NJ 08903; *Pi.* Univ. of Pittsburgh, School of Lib. & Info. Science, Pittsburgh, PA 15260; *Rho.* Kent State Univ., School of Lib. Science, Kent, OH 44242; *Sigma.* Drexel Univ., School of Lib. & Info. Science, Philadelphia, PA 19104; *Tau.* State Univ. of New York at Geneseo, School of Lib. & Info. Science, College of Arts and Science, Geneseo, NY 14454; *Upsilon.* Univ. of Kentucky, College of Lib. Science, Lexington, KY 40506; *Phi.* Univ. of Denver, Grad. School of Libnshp., Denver, CO 80208; *Pi Lambda Sigma.* Syracuse Univ., School of Info. Studies, Syracuse, NY 13210; *Chi.* Indiana Univ., Grad. Lib. School, Bloomington, IN 47401; *Psi.* Univ. of Missouri, Columbia, School of Lib. & Info. Science, Columbia, MO 65211; *Omega.* San Jose State Univ., Div. of Lib. Science, San Jose, CA 95192; *Beta Alpha.* Queens College, City College of New York, Grad. School of Lib. & Info. Studies, Flushing, NY 11367; *Beta Beta.* Simmons College, School of Lib. Science, Boston, MA 02115; *Beta Delta.* State Univ. of New York-Buffalo, School of Info. & Lib. Studies, Buffalo, NY 14260; *Beta Epsilon.* Emporia State Univ., School of Lib. Science, Emporia, KS 66801; *Beta Zeta.* Louisiana State Univ., Grad. School of Lib. Science, Baton Rouge, LA 70803; *Beta Eta.* Univ. of Texas at Austin, Grad. School of Lib. Science, Austin, TX 78712;

Beta Theta. Brigham Young Univ., School of Lib. & Info. Science, Provo, UT 84602; *Beta Iota.* Univ. of Rhode Island, Grad. Lib. School, Kingston, RI 02881; *Beta Kappa.* Univ. of Alabama, Grad. School of Lib. Service, University, AL 35486; *Beta Lambda.* North Texas State Univ., School of Lib. & Info. Science, Denton, TX 76203, and Texas Woman's Univ., School of Lib. Science, Denton, TX 76204; *Beta Mu.* Long Island Univ., Palmer Grad. Lib. School, C. W. Post Center, Greenvale, NY 11548; *Beta Nu.* St. John's Univ., Div. of Lib. & Info. Science, Jamaica, NY 11439; *Beta Xi.* North Carolina Central Univ., School of Lib. Science, Durham, NC 27707; *Beta Omicron.* Univ. of Tennessee, Knoxville, Grad. School of Lib. & Info. Science, Knoxville, TN 37916; *Beta Pi.* Univ. of Arizona, Grad. Lib. School, Tucson, AZ 85721; *Beta Rho.* Univ. of Wisconsin-Milwaukee, School of Lib. Science, Milwaukee, WI 53201 (installed May 21, 1978); *Beta Sigma.* Clarion State College, School of Lib. Science, Clarion, PA 16214 (installed May 9, 1980); *Beta Tau.* Wayne State Univ., Div. of Lib. Science, Detroit, MI 48202 (installed June 5, 1979); *Beta Upsilon.* Alabama A&M Univ., School of Lib. Media, Normal, AL 35762 (installed Oct. 4, 1980); *Beta Phi.* Univ. of South Florida, Grad. Dept. of Lib., Media & Info. Studies, Tampa, FL 33620 (installed June 6, 1980); *Beta Chi.* Southern Connecticut State College (to be installed).

BIBLIOGRAPHICAL SOCIETY OF AMERICA
Executive Secretary, Caroline F. Schimmel
Box 397, Grand Central Sta., New York, NY 10017

OBJECT

"To promote bibliographical research and to issue bibliographical publications." Organized 1904. Memb. 1,500. Dues. $20. Year. Calendar.

OFFICERS (JAN. 1980–JAN. 1982)

Pres. Marcus A. McCorison, American Antiquarian Society, Salisbury St. & Park Ave., Worcester, MA 01609; *1st V.P.* G. Thomas Tanselle, Guggenheim Memorial Foundation, 96 Park Ave., New York, NY 10016; *2nd V.P.* William B. Todd, Parlin Hall 110, Univ. of Texas, Austin, TX 78712; *Treas.* Frank S. Streeter, 141 E. 72 St., New York NY 10021; *Secy.* James M. Wells, Newberry Lib., 60 W. Walton Pl., Chicago, IL 60610.

COUNCIL

Officers; Katharine Pantzer; Charles A. Ryscamp; P. W. Filby; William B. Todd; Andrew B. Myers; Lola L. Szladits.

PUBLICATION

Papers (q.; memb.). *Ed.* William B. Todd, Parlin Hall, Univ. of Texas, Austin, TX 78712. *Book Review Ed.* Kenneth Carpenter, Baker Lib., Harvard Univ., Cambridge, MA 02163.

COMMITTEE CHAIRPERSON

Publications. Stephen R. Parks, Yale Univ. Lib., New Haven, CT 06520.

CANADIAN ASSOCIATION FOR INFORMATION SCIENCE (ASSOCIATION CANADIENNE DES SCIENCES DE L'INFORMATION)
Secretariat/Secrétariat, Box 776, Sta. G, Calgary, Alta. T3A 2G6, Canada

OBJECT

Brings together individuals and organizations concerned with the production, manipulation, storage, retrieval, and dissemination of information with emphasis on the application of modern technologies in these areas. CAIS is dedicated to enhancing the activity of the information transfer process, utilizing the vehicles of research, development, application, and education, and serves as a forum for dialogue and exchange of ideas concerned with the theory and practice of all factors involved in the communication of information. Dues. (Inst.) $75; (Regular) $25; (Student) $10.

MEMBERSHIP

Institutions and all individuals interested in information science and who are involved in the gathering, the organization, and the dissemination of information (computer scientists, documentalists, information scientists, librarians, journalists, sociologists, psychologists, linguists, administrators, etc.) can become members of the Canadian Association for Information Science.

OFFICERS

Pres. Fred Matthews; *V.P.* Margaret Telfer; *Secy.* Ellen Pearson; *Treas.* Monique Lecavalier.

DIRECTORS

F. Groen, C. Bregaint; *Past Pres.* A. MacDonald.

PUBLICATIONS

CAIS Bulletin (q.; free with membership).
The Canadian Conference of Information Science: Proceedings (ann.; 9th ann., 1981, $16.50).
The Canadian Journal of Information Science (ann.; nonmemb. $12).

CANADIAN LIBRARY ASSOCIATION
Executive Director, Paul Kitchen
151 Sparks St., Ottawa, Ont. K1P 5E3, Canada
613-232-9625

OBJECT

To develop high standards of librarianship and of library and information service. CLA develops standards for public, university, school, and college libraries and library technician programs; offers library school scholarships and book awards; carries on international liaison with other library associations; and makes representation to government and official commissions. Founded in Hamilton in 1946, CLA is a nonprofit voluntary organization governed by an elected council and board of directors. Memb. (Indiv.) 4,070; (Inst.) 1,000. Dues (Indiv.) $40.00 & $63.00, depending on salary; (Inst.) $36.50 & up, depending on budget. Year. July 1–June 30.

MEMBERSHIP

Open to individuals, institutions, and groups interested in librarianship and in library and information services.

OFFICERS (1980-1981)

Pres. Alan MacDonald, Dir. of Libs., Univ. of Calgary, Calgary, Alta. T2N 1N4; *1st V.P./Pres.-Elect.* Marianne Scott, Dir. of Libs., McGill Univ. Libs., Montreal, P.Q. H3A 1Y1; *2nd V.P.* Beth Barlow, Government Pubns., Lib., Univ. of Saskatchewan, Saskatoon, Sask. S7N 0W0; *Treas.* Françoise Hébert, Dir. CNIB, Toronto, Ont. M4G 3E8; *Past Pres.* Erik Spicer, Parliamentary Libn., Lib. of Parliament, Ottawa, Ont. K1A 0A9. (Address general correspondence to the executive director.)

BOARD OF DIRECTORS

Officers; division presidents.

COUNCIL

Officers; division presidents; councillors, including representatives of ASTED and provincial/regional library associations.

COUNCILLORS-AT-LARGE

To June 30, 1981; Penelope Marshall; Pat Noonan.

To June 30, 1982; Sheila Laidlaw; Ken Haycock.

To June 30, 1983; Marie Zielinska; Gordon Ray.

PUBLICATIONS

Canadian Library Journal (6 issues; memb. or nonmemb. subscribers, Canada $15, U.S. $17 [Can.], international $20 [Can.]).

CM: Canadian Materials for Schools and Libraries. (4/year; $15).

DIVISION CHAIRPERSONS

Canadian Association of College and University Libraries. Calvin Evans, Asst. Libn., Public Services, Univ. of Alberta, Edmonton, Alta. T6G 2J8.

Canadian Association of Public Libraries. Patricia Cavill, Asst. Libn., Saskatchewan Provincial Lib., Regina, Sask. S4P 3V7.

Canadian Association of Special Libraries and Information Services. Marilyn Schafer, Mgr., Eastern Canada, Infomart, Ottawa, Ont. K1P 6A4.

Canadian Library Trustees' Association. Donald Harvey, Trustee, Newfoundland Public Libs. Bd., St. John's, Nfld. A1C 2H2.

Canadian School Library Association. Ted Monkhouse, Educational Media Consultant, Lib., Wellington County Bd. of Educ., Guelph, Ont. N1E 2S9.

ASSOCIATION REPRESENTATIVES

Association pour l'Avancement des Sciences et des Techniques de la Documentation (ASTED). Lise Brousseau, Dir.-Gen., ASTED, 360 rue le Moyne, Montreal, P.Q. H2Y 1Y3.

Atlantic Provinces Library Association. Ann Nevill, Health Sciences Lib., W. K. Kellogg Health Sciences Lib., Dalhousie Univ., Halifax, N.S. B3H 4H7.

British Columbia Library Association. Mary Beth MacDonald, McPherson Lib., Univ. of Victoria, Victoria, B.C. V8W 2K3.

Library Association of Alberta. Heather-Belle Dowling, County of Strathcona Municipal Lib., Sherwood Park, Alta. T8A 3J4.

Manitoba Library Association. William Birdsall, Admin. Offices, Univ. of Manitoba Libs., Winnipeg, Man. R3T 2N2.

Ontario Library Association. Jean Orpwood, Deputy Chief Libn., North York Public Lib., Willowdale, Ont. M2J 4S4.

Quebec Library Association. Marie-Louise Simon, Municipal Lib., Ville St. Laurent, P.Q. H4L 2H2.

Saskatchewan Library Association. Karen Labuik, Wapiti Regional Lib., Prince Albert, Sask. S6V 1B7.

CATHOLIC LIBRARY ASSOCIATION
Executive Director, Matthew R. Wilt
461 W. Lancaster Ave., Haverford, PA 19041
215-649-5250

OBJECT

"The promotion and encouragement of Catholic literature and library work through cooperation, publications, education and information." Founded 1921. Memb. 3,280. Dues $20–$500. Year. July 1980–June 1981.

OFFICERS (APRIL 1979–APRIL 1981)

Pres. Sister Franz Lang, OP, Barry College Lib., Miami, FL 33161; *V.P.* Kelly Fitzpatrick, Mt. St. Mary's College, Emmitsburg, MD 21727; *Past Pres.* Sister Mary Arthur Hoagland, IHM, Office of the Superintendent of Schools, Philadelphia, PA 19103. (Address general correspondence to the executive director.)

EXECUTIVE BOARD

Officers; Rev. Robert P. Cawley, Central Assn. of the Miraculous Medal, Philadelphia, PA 19144; Brother DeSales Pergola, OSF, St. Francis Prep School, Fresh Meadows, NY 11363; Mary A. Grant, Nazareth H.S. Media Center, Brooklyn, NY 11203; Brother Emmett Corry, OSF, St. John's Univ., Jamaica, NY 11439; Sister Teresa Rigel, CSJ, Red Cloud Indian School, Pine Ridge, SD 57770; Irma C. Godfrey, 6247 Westway Pl., St. Louis, MO 63109.

PUBLICATIONS

Catholic Library World (10 issues; memb. or $20).
The Catholic Periodical and Literature Index (subscription).

COMMITTEE CHAIRPERSONS

Advisory Council. Kelly Fitzpatrick, Mt. St. Mary's College, Emmitsburg, MD 21727.
AASL Standards Committee. Sister Mary Arthur Hoagland, IHM, Office of the Superintendent of Schools, Philadelphia, PA 19103.
ANSI-Z39. Richard A. Davis, Rosary College, River Forest, IL 60305.
Catholic Health Association of the U.S. Pamela Kay Drayson, St. Mary's Hospital, Kansas City, MO 64108.
Catholic Library World Editorial. Sister Marie Melton, RSM, St. John's Univ., Jamaica, NY 11439.
The Catholic Periodical and Literature Index. Arnold M. Rzepecki, Sacred Heart Seminary College Lib., Detroit, MI 48206.
Catholic Press Association. John T. Corrigan, CFX, CLA Headquarters, 461 W. Lancaster Ave., Haverford, PA 19041.
Constitution and Bylaws. Sister Margaret Huyck, CSJ, Lib. Consultant, New Orleans, LA 70122.
Continuing Education. Sister Mary Dennis Lynch, SHCJ, Rosemont College, Rosemont, PA 19010.
Continuing Library Education Network Exchange (CLENE). Sister Mary Dennis Lynch, SHCJ, Rosemont College, Rosemont, PA 19010.
Council of National Library and Information Association (CNLIA). Matthew R. Wilt, Exec. Dir., CLA Headquarters, 461 W. Lancaster Ave., Haverford, PA 19041; Brother Emmett Corry, OSF, St. John's Univ., Jamaica, NY 11439.
Elections. Mary Mountain, LaSalle College H.S., Philadelphia, PA 19118.
Finance. Arnold M. Rzepecki, Sacred Heart Seminary College Lib., Detroit, MI 48206.
Membership/Unit Coord. Jane F. Hindman, CLA Headquarters, 461 W. Lancaster Ave., Haverford, PA 19041.
Nominations. James C. Cox, Loyola Univ. Medical Center Lib., Maywood, IL 60153.
Program Coord. John T. Corrigan,

CFX, CLA Headquarters, 461 W. Lancaster Ave., Haverford, PA 19041.
Public Relations. Sister Mary Margaret Cribben, RSM, Villanova College, Villanova, PA 19085.
Publications. Sister Mary Field, OP, Rosary College Lib., River Forest, IL 60305.
Regina Medal. Sister Barbara Anne Kilpatrick, St. Vincent de Paul School, Nashville, TN 37208.
Scholarship. Sister Jane Marie Barbour, CDP, Our Lady of the Lake Univ. of San Antonio, San Antonio, TX 78285.
Special Libraries Association. Mary-Jo DiMuccio, Sunnyvale Public Lib., Sunnyvale, CA 94087.
Universal Serials and Book Exchange (USBE). Sister Therese Marie Gaudreau, SND, Trinity College, Washington, DC 20017.

SECTION CHAIRPERSONS

Archives. Rev. John B. DeMayo, St. Charles Seminary Lib., Overbrook, Philadelphia, PA 19151.

Children's Libraries. Sally Anne Thompson, 7015 E. San Miguel, Paradise Valley, AZ 85253.
College, University, Seminary Libraries. Sister Therese Marie Gaudreau, SND, Trinity College, Washington, DC 20017.
High School Libraries. Reverend Timothy Buyansky, OSB, Benedictine H.S. Lib., Cleveland, OH 44104.
Library Education. Rev. Jovian P. Lang, OFM, St. John's Univ., Jamaica, NY 11439.
Parish/Community Libraries. Sister Mary Agnes Sullivan, OP, St. Agnes Convent, Memphis, TN 38117.
Public Libraries. Margaret Long, Public Lib. of Cincinnati, Cincinnati, OH 45202.

ROUND TABLE CHAIRPERSONS

Cataloging and Classification Round Table. Tina-Karen Weiner, La Salle College, Philadelphia, PA 19141.
Health Sciences Round Table. Pamela Kay Drayson, St. Mary's Hospital, Kansas City, MO 64108.

CHIEF OFFICERS OF STATE LIBRARY AGENCIES
Anthony W. Miele, Director, Alabama Public Library Service
6030 Monticello Dr., Montgomery, AL 36109

OBJECT

The object of COSLA is to provide "a means for cooperative action among its state and territorial members to strengthen the work of the respective state and territorial agencies. Its purpose is to provide a continuing mechanism for dealing with the problems faced by the heads of these agencies which are responsible for state and territorial library development."

MEMBERSHIP

The Chief Officers of State Library Agencies is an independent organization of the men and women who head the state and territorial agencies responsible for library development. Its membership consists solely of the top library officers of the 50 states and one territory, variously designated as state librarian, director, commissioner, or executive secretary.

OFFICERS (NOV. 1980–NOV. 1982)

Chpn. W. Lyle Eberhart, Administrator, Wisconsin Dept. of Public Instruction, General Exec. Facility III, 125 S. Webster St., Madison, WI 53702; *V. Chpn.* Patricia Klinck, State Libn., Vermont Dept. of Libs., c/o State Office Bldg., Montpelier, VT 05602; *Secy.* Marcia Lowell, State Libn., Oregon State Lib., Salem, OR 97310; *Treas.* Cliff Lange, State Libn., New Mexico State Lib., Box 1629, Sante

Fe, NM 87501; *ALA Affiliation.* Sandra Cooper, ALA, Exec. Secy. ASCLA.

DIRECTORS

Officers; immediate past chairperson: William G. Asp, Dir., Dept. of Educ., Office of Public Libs. and Interlib. Cooperation, 301 Hanover Bldg., 480 Cedar St., St. Paul, MN 55101; two elected members: Barbara Weaver, Dir., State Dept. of Educ., Div. of State Lib. and History, 185 W. State St., Trenton, NJ 08625; Barratt Wilkins, State Libn., State Lib. of Florida, R. A. Gray Bldg., Tallahassee, FL 32301.

COMMITTEE CHAIRPERSONS

Continuing Education. Barbara Weaver, State Libn., New Jersey State Lib.

Legislation. Robert Clark, Jr., Oklahoma Dept. of Libs.

Liaison with ALA and Other National Library-Related Organizations. Joe Forsee, Dir., Div. of Public Lib. Services, Georgia.

Liaison with Library of Congress. Russell Davis, Utah State Lib. Commission.

Liaison with Library of Congress, Division for Blind and Physically Handicapped. Russell Davis, Utah State Lib. Commission.

Liaison with National Commission on Libraries and Information Science. Lyle Eberhart, Wisconsin Dept. of Public Instruction.

Liaison with U.S. Department of Education. Frank Scannell, State Libn., Michigan Dept. of Educ.

Liaison with National Center for Education Statistics. Barratt Wilkins, State Libn., Florida State Lib.

Network Development. Ann Marie Falsone, State Libn., Colorado Dept. of Educ.

Statewide Planning and Organization Committee. Gary Nichols, Maine State Libn.

Outlaying State/Territorial Library Agencies. Henry Chang, Territorial Libn., Virgin Islands.

CHINESE-AMERICAN LIBRARIANS ASSOCIATION
Executive Director, Tze-chung Li
Rosary College Graduate School of Library Science
River Forest, IL 60305

OBJECT

"(1) To enhance communication among Chinese-American librarians as well as between Chinese-American librarians and other librarians; (2) to serve as a forum for discussion of mutual problems and professional concerns among Chinese-American librarians; (3) to promote Sino-American librarianship and library services; and (4) to provide a vehicle whereby Chinese-American librarians may cooperate with other associations and organizations having similar or allied interest."

MEMBERSHIP

Membership is open to everyone who is interested in the association's goals and activities. Memb. 340. Dues (Regular) $15; (Student and Nonsalaried) $7.50; (Inst.) $45; (Permanent) $150.

OFFICERS (JUNE 1980–JUNE 1981)

Pres. Lee-hsia Ting, Assoc. Prof., Western Illinois Univ., Macomb, IL 61455; *V.P./Pres.-Elect.* David T. Liu, Libn., Pharr Memorial Lib., Pharr, TX 78577;

Treas. Sally C. Tseng, Libn., Univ. of Nebraska, Lincoln, NE 68510; *Secy.* William W. Wan, Libn., Texas Woman's Univ., Denton, TX 76204; *Exec. Dir.* Tzechung Li, Prof., Rosary College Grad. School of Lib. Science, River Forest, IL 60305.

PUBLICATIONS

Directory of Chinese American Librarians in the United States, 1976 ($5; memb. $2.50).
Journal of Library and Information Science (2/year; memb. or $15).
Membership Directory, 1980 ($1.50).
Newsletter (3/year; memb.).

COMMITTEE CHAIRPERSONS

Annual Program. David T. Liu, Pharr Memorial Lib., Pharr, TX 78577.
Awards. Hwa-wei Lee, Ohio Univ., Athens, OH 45701.
Membership. Ophelia Y. Lo, University Microfilms, Ann Arbor, MI 48104.
Nominating. John Yung-hsiang Lai, Harvard-Yenching Lib., Cambridge, MA 02138.
Publicatons. Bessie K. Hahn, Johns Hopkins Univ., Baltimore, MD 21218.

CHAPTER CHAIRPERSONS

California. Eunice C. Ting, Univ. of California, Los Angeles, CA 90049.
Mid-Atlantic. Chang C. Lee, Behrend College, Pennsylvania State Univ., Erie, PA 16563.
Mid-West. Roy Chang, Western Illinois Univ. Lib., Macomb, IL 61455.
Northwest. Marjorie H. Li, Rutgers Univ., New Brunswick, NJ 08903.
Southwest. William Wan, Texas Woman's Univ. Lib., Denton, TX 76201.

JOURNAL OFFICERS

Margaret Fung, National Taiwan Normal Univ., Taipei, Taiwan; Chen-ku Wang, National Central Lib., Taipei, Taiwan; John Yung-hsiang Lai, Harvard-Yenching Lib., Cambridge, MA 02138.

DISTINGUISHED SERVICE AWARDS

The first distinguished service award was presented to Dr. Ernst Wolff on June 30, 1980.

CHURCH AND SYNAGOGUE LIBRARY ASSOCIATION
Executive Secretary, Dorothy J. Rodda
Box 1130, Bryn Mawr, PA 19010

OBJECT

"To act as a unifying core for the many existing church and synagogue libraries; to provide the opportunity for a mutual sharing of practices and problems; to inspire and encourage a sense of purpose and mission among church and synagogue librarians; to study and guide the development of church and synagogue librarianship toward recognition as a formal branch of the library profession." Founded 1967. Memb. 1,300. Dues (Contributing) $100; (Inst.) $75; (Affiliated) $25; (Church or Synagogue) $20; (Indiv.) $10. Year. July 1980–June 1981.

OFFICERS (JULY 1980–JUNE 1981)

Pres. Robert Dvorak, Gordon-Conwell Theological Seminary, South Hamilton, MA 01982; *1st V.P.* Elsie E. Lehman, 1051 College Ave., Harrisonburg, VA 22801; *2nd V.P.* Joyce L. White, 713 W. Ash St., Salina, KS 67401; *Treas.* Bruce B. Bruce, 1809 W. Hovey, Normal, IL 61761; *Past Pres.* Alma V. Lowance, 1717 Bellevue Ave., A-826, Richmond, VA 23227;

Publns. Dir. and Bulletin Ed. William H. Gentz, 300 E. 34 St., Apt. 9C, New York, NY 10016.

EXECUTIVE BOARD

Officers; committee chairpersons.

PUBLICATIONS

Church and Synagogue Libraries (bimo.; memb. or $15, Can. $18). Ed. William H. Gentz. Book reviews, ads, $130 for fullpage, camera-ready ad, one-time rate.
CSLA Guide No. 1. Setting Up a Library: How to Begin or Begin Again ($2.50).
CSLA Guide No. 2, rev. 2nd ed. Promotion Planning All Year 'Round ($4.50).
CSLA Guide No. 3, rev. ed. Workshop Planning ($6.50).
CSLA Guide No. 4, rev. ed. Selecting Library Materials ($2.50).
CSLA Guide No. 5. Cataloging Books Step by Step ($2.50).
CSLA Guide No. 6. Standards for Church and Synagogue Libraries ($3.75).
CSLA Guide No. 7. Classifying Church or Synogogue Library Materials ($2.50).
CSLA Guide No. 8. Subject Headings for Church or Synagogue Libraries ($3.50).
CSLA Guide No. 9. A Policy and Procedure Manual for Church and Synagogue Libraries ($3.75).
Church and Synagogue Library Resources: Annotated Bibliography ($2.50).
A Basic Book List for Church Libraries: Annotated Bibliography ($1.75).
Helping Children Through Books: Annotated Bibliography ($3.75).
The Family Uses the Library. Leaflet (5¢; $3.75/100).
The Teacher and the Library—Partners in Religious Education. Leaflet (10¢; $7/100).
Promotion and Publicity for a Congregational Library. Sound slide set ($75; rental fee $10).

COMMITTEE CHAIRPERSONS

Awards. Rachel Kohl.
Chapters. Fay W. Grosse.
Continuing Education. Elsie E. Lehman.
Fund Raising. Ruth Turner.
Library Services. Judith Stromdahl.
Membership. Lois Seyfrit.
Nominations and Elections. Alma Lowance.
Public Relations. Maryann J. Dotts.
Sites. Sherry D. Fleet.

CONTINUING LIBRARY EDUCATION NETWORK AND EXCHANGE (CLENE), INC.
Executive Director, Eleanore R. Ficke
620 Michigan Ave. N.E., Washington, DC 20064
202-635-5825

OBJECT

The basic missions of CLENE, Inc., are (1) to provide equal access to continuing education opportunities, available in sufficient quantity and quality over a substantial period of time to ensure library and information science personnel and organizations the competency to deliver quality library and information services to all; (2) to create an awareness and a sense of need for continuing education of library personnel on the part of employers and individuals as a means of responding to societal and technological change. Founded 1975. Mem. 390. Dues (Indiv.) $15; (Inst./Assoc.) $35–$100; (State Agency) $750–$3,000 according to population. Year. Twelve months from date of entry.

MEMBERSHIP

CLENE, Inc., welcomes as members: institutions—libraries, information centers, data banks, schools and departments of library, media, and information science—any organization concerned with continuing education; professional associations in library, media, information science, and allied disciplines; local, state, regional and national associations; individuals; state library and educational agencies; consortia.

OFFICERS (JUNE 1980-JUNE 1981)

Pres. Suzanne H. Mahmoodi, OPLIC, 301 Hanover Bldg., 480 Cedar St., St. Paul, MN 55101; *Pres.-Elect.* Janet L. Blumberg, Chief, Consultant Services Div., Washington State Lib., AJ-11, Olympia, WA 98504; *Secy.* Susan K. Schmidt, Exec. Dir., Southwestern Lib. Assn., Box 23713, TWU Sta., Denton, TX 76204; *Treas.* Dottie Hiebing, Public Lib. Consultant-Continuing Education, Div. for Lib. Services, 126 Langdon, Madison, WI 53706; *Past Pres.* James A. Nelson, Dept. of Lib. & Archives, Box 537, Frankfort, KY 40601.

BOARD OF DIRECTORS

Officers; Judith J. Field, Flint Public Lib., 1026 E. Kearsley St., Flint, MI 48502; Margaret Knox Goggin, 6151 S. Kearney St., Englewood, CO 80111; Donald Haynes, State Libn., Virginia State Lib., Richmond, VA 23219; Marcia Lowell, State Lib., Oregon State Lib., Salem, OR 97310; Margaret Myers, Dir., Office for Lib. Personnel Resources, American Lib. Assn., 50 E. Huron St., Chicago, IL 60611; Garland Strother, Asst. Libn., St. Charles Parish Lib., Box 975, Luling, LA 70070; Sandra S. Stephan, Specialist in Staff Development and Continuing Education, Div. of Lib. Development and Services, Maryland State Dept. of Educ., 200 W. Baltimore St., Baltimore, MD 21201; Celia C. Suarez, Dir. of Lib. Services, Miami-Dade Community College, North Campus Lib., 11380 N.W. 27 Ave., Miami, FL 33167; Dan Tonkery, Assoc. Univ. Libn., Univ. of California, Univ. Research Lib., 405 Hilgard Ave., Los Angeles, CA 90024; Susan S. Whittle, Public Lib. Consultant, State Lib. of Florida, R. A. Gray Bldg., Tallahassee, FL 32301.

PUBLICATIONS

CLENExchange (6/year). Newsletter $6 (nonmemb.).
Continuing Education Communicator (mo.). $10 (Indiv.); $15 (Institutional nonmemb.).
Directory of Continuing Education Opportunities (1979) (ann.). $22.80.
Model Continuing Education Recognition System in Library and Information Science 1979 (June) $29.80.
Proceedings of CLENE Assembly I: Self-Assessment (January 1976). $4.25 (memb.); $5 (nonmemb.).
Proceedings of CLENE Assembly II: Updating and Skills for Ourselves (July 1976).
Proceedings of CLENE Assembly III. (February 1977).
Who's Who in Continuing Education: Human Resources in Continuing Library, Information, Media Education (Sept. 1979). $30.

Concept Papers

#1 *Developing CE Learning Materials.* Sheldon and Woolls (1977). $4.25 (memb.); $5 (nonmemb.).
#2 *Guide to Planning and Teaching CE Courses.* Washtien (1975). $4.25 (memb.); $5 (nonmemb.).
#3 *Planning & Evaluating Library Training Programs.* Sheldon (1976). $4.25 (memb.); $5 (nonmemb.).
#4 *Helping Adults to Learn.* Knox (1976) (out of print).
#5 *Continuing Library Education: Needs Assessment & Model Programs.* Virgo, Dunkel, Angione (1977). $10.20 (memb.); $12 (nonmemb.).
#6 *Recognition for Your Continuing Education Accomplishments.* James Nelson (June 1979).
Annotated Bibliography of Recent Continuing Education Literature (1976). $4.25 (memb.); $5 (nonmemb.).
Continuing Education Resource Book (1977). $2.55 (memb.); $3 (nonmemb.).
Continuing Education Planning Inventory: A Self-Evaluation Checklist (1977). $1.70 (memb.); $2 (nonmemb.).

Guidelines for Relevant Groups Involved in Home Study Programs (1977). $4.25 (memb.); $5 (nonmemb.).

COMMITTEES

Assembly Planning Committee.
By-laws Committee.
Committee on Committees.
Finance Committee.
Long-Range Planning Committee.
Membership Committee.
Nominating Committee.
Project Development Committee.
Publications Committee.
Task Force on the Recognition System.

COUNCIL FOR COMPUTERIZED LIBRARY NETWORKS
President, Robin J. Braithwaite, Manager of Marketing,
University of Toronto Library, Toronto, Ont. M5S 1A5, Canada
416-978-7171

OBJECT

"CCLN serves several purposes. It disseminates information concerning on-line library networks; collates information provided by members; and organizes and coordinates professional development activities. In addition, it acts as a change agent by promoting dialogue within the library profession and among professional groups working in allied fields; participating in planning of the national network; informing the private sector of members' problems with existing technology and needs for new solutions; and making research and development recommendations to the federal government and foundations to facilitate support of state, regional, national, and international networking efforts." Dues. (Inst.) $200.

MEMBERSHIP

CCLN has two types of membership: Network Members and Associate Members. Network Members represent on-line computerized library networks that provide services on a nonprofit basis to administratively independent libraries for a state, region, or multistate area in North America. New applicants are admitted to membership upon a two-thirds vote of current Network Members. Each Network Member has one representative with one vote at business meetings who is eligible to serve on the Executive Committee, and be appointed a program officer. Each Network Member represents its local and regional library members.

Associate Members represent individual libraries using services provided by a CCLN Network Member.

Two other types of CCLN membership are being reviewed: Affiliate Members and Educational Members. The former would include those suppliers of services, systems, or data bases that are of use or interest to Network Members. Educational Members would include accredited institutions offering advanced degrees in library or information science.

OFFICERS

Pres. Robin J. Braithwaite (1980–1981), Mgr. of Marketing, Univ. of Toronto Lib. Automation Systems, 130 S. St. George St., Suite 8003, Toronto, Ont. M5S 1A5, Canada; *Secy.* James G. Schoenung (1979–1981), Exec. Dir., PALINET/ULC, 3420 Walnut St., Philadelphia, PA 19104; *Treas.* Peter J. Paulson, Dir., New York State Interlib. Loan Network—NYSILL, New York State Lib., Cultural Education Center, Albany, NY 12238. (Address correspondence to the president.)

PUBLICATIONS

CCLN News (q.; memb.).
News Flash Current Awareness Service (irreg.; memb.).
Network Technology Reports (planned).
Resources Surveys (planned).

CCLN MEMBERSHIP

AMIGOS Bibliographic Council; Bibliographic Center for Research (BCR); California Lib. Authority for Systems and Services (CLASS); Cooperative College Lib. Center (CCLC); Five Associated Univ. Libs. (FAUL); Illinois Lib. & Info. Network (ILLINET); Indiana Cooperative Lib. Services Authority (INCOLSA); Michigan Lib. Consortium (MLC); Midwest Region Lib. Network (MIDLNET); Minnesota Interlib. Telecommunications Exchange (MINITEX); New England Lib. Info. Network (NELINET); New York State Interlib. Loan Network (NYSILL); OCLC, Inc.; OHIONET; PALINET and Union Lib. Catalogue of Pennsylvania (PALINET/ULC); Pittsburgh Regional Lib. Center (PRLC); Research Libs. Group (RLG); Southeastern Lib. Network (SOLINET); State Univ. of New York (SUNY); Univ. of Toronto Lib. Automation Systems (UTLAS); Washington Lib. Network (WLN); Wisconsin Lib. Consortium (WLC).

COUNCIL OF NATIONAL LIBRARY AND INFORMATION ASSOCIATIONS, INC.
461 W. Lancaster, Ave., Haverford, PA 19041
215-649-5251

OBJECT

To provide a central agency for cooperation among library associations and other professional organizations of the United States and Canada in promoting matters of common interest.

MEMBERSHIP

Open to national library associations and organizations with related interests of the United States and Canada. American Assn. of Law Libs.; American Lib. Assn.; American Society of Indexers; American Theological Lib. Assn.; Art Libs. Society/North America; Assn. of Jewish Libs.; Catholic Lib. Assn.; Church and Synagogue Lib. Assn.; Council of Planning Libns.; Lib. Binding Institute; Lib. Public Relations Council; Lutheran Lib. Assn.; Medical Lib. Assn.; Music Lib. Assn.; National Federation of Abstracting and Indexing Services; Society of American Archivists; Special Libs. Assn.; Theatre Lib. Assn.

OFFICERS (JULY 1980–JUNE 1981)

Chpn. Richard M. Buck, PARC, New York Public Lib., 111 Amsterdam Ave., New York, NY 10023; *V. Chpn.* John T. Corrigan, CFX, Catholic Lib. Assn., 461 W. Lancaster Ave., Haverford, PA 19041; *Past Chpn.* Jane L. Hammond, Law Lib., Myron Taylor Hall, Cornell Univ., Ithaca, NY 14853; *Secy.-Treas.* Barbara Preschel, 400 E. 56 St., New York, NY 10022. (Address correspondence to chairperson at 461 W. Lancaster Ave., Haverford, PA 19041.)

DIRECTORS

Robert DeCandido, New York Public Lib., Research Lib., Fifth Ave. & 42 St., New York, NY 10018 (July 1980–June 1983); Mary M. Cope, City College Lib., City Univ. of New York, 135 St. & Convent Ave., New York, NY 10031 (July 1978–June 1981); Vivian Hewitt, Carnegie Endowment for International Peace, 30 Rockefeller Plaza, New York, NY 10020 (July 1979–June 1982).

COUNCIL OF PLANNING LIBRARIANS, PUBLICATIONS OFFICE
1313 E. 60 St., Chicago, IL 60637

OBJECT

To provide a special interest group in the field of city and regional planning for libraries and librarians, faculty, professional planners, university, government, and private planning organizations; to provide an opportunity for exchange among those interested in problems of library organization and research and in the dissemination of information about city and regional planning; to sponsor programs of service to the planning profession and librarianship; to advise on library organization for new planning programs; to aid and support administrators, faculty, and librarians in their efforts to educate the public and their appointed or elected representatives to the necessity for strong library programs in support of planning. Founded 1960. Memb. 200. Dues. $35 (Inst.); $10 (Indiv.). Year. July 1–June 30.

MEMBERSHIP

Open to any individual or institution that supports the purpose of the council upon written application and payment of dues to the treasurer.

OFFICERS (1980–1981)

Pres. Patricia Coatsworth, Libn., Merriam Center Lib., 1313 E. 60 St., Chicago, IL 60637; *V.P./Pres.-Elect.* Katharina Richter, City of Tucson Planning Dept., Box 27210, Tucson, AZ 85726; *Secy.* Chris Hail, Frances Loeb Lib., Gund Hall, Harvard Univ., Cambridge, MA 02138; *Treas.* Gary Scales, RR 2, Box 293, Louisville, TN 37777; *Member-at-Large.* Monica Welch, Canadian Housing Info. Center, Central Mortgage Housing Corp., Montreal Rd., Ottawa, Ont. K1A 0P7, Canada; *Ed. Publications Program.* James Hecimovich, 1313 E. 60 St., Chicago, IL 60637.

PUBLICATIONS

CPL Bibliographies approx. 30 bibliographies published per year). May be purchased on standing order subscription or by individual issue. Subscription rates on request.

#1–3. *Comprehensive Index to Exchange Bibliographies*, No. 1-1565, 3-vol. set ($25). Subject Index (119 pp., $12). Author Index (100 pp., $10). Numerical Index (89 pp., $9).

#4. *Planning Principles for Transportation Systems.* Dominick Gatto (16 pp., $3.50).

#5. *Futures Planning in Management*, Roger Evered (52 pp., $7).

#6. *Effects of Environmental Regulations on Housing Costs*, David E. Dowall and Jesse Mingilton (67 pp., $7).

#7. *Land Banking*, Claudia Michniewicz (13 pp., $3.50).

#8. *Opposition to Volunteerism.* Doris B. Gold (21 pp., $3.50).

#9. *Tax Incremental Financing*, Debra L. Allen and Jack R. Huddleston (13 pp., $3.50).

#10. *Primary Source Materials on Environmental Impact Studies*, Catharine Askow (23 pp., $3.50).

#11. *Historic Preservation in the Pacific Northwest: A Bibliography of Sources 1947–1978*, Lawrence N. Crumb (63 pp., $7).

#12. *Community Goals and Goal Formulation: A Reference*, George E. Bowen (29 pp., $3.50).

#13. *Discrimination in Housing*, Robert E. Ansley, Jr. (75 pp., $10).

#14. *Urban Recreation Planning: A Selected Bibliography*, Seymour M. Gold (15 pp., $3.50).

#15. *Interracial Housing Since 1970: From Activism to Affirmative Marketing*, Dudley Onderdonk III (30 pp., $3.50).

#16. *Wind Energy Planning: A Bibliography*, Toru Otawa (31 pp., $3.50).

#17. *German City Planning History: 1871-1945*, John R. Mullin (43 pp., $7).
#18. *Government Regulations and the Cost of Housing: A Partially Annotated Bibliography*, Anne McGowan (13 pp., $3.50).
#19. *Methods of Handling Complaints against the Police*, Edwana D. Collins (32 pp., $5).
#20. *Mobile Home Resource List*, Carol B. Meeks (24 pp., $3.50).

COUNCIL ON LIBRARY RESOURCES, INC.
Secretary-Treasurer, Mary Agnes Thompson,
One Dupont Circle, Suite 620, Washington, DC 20036
202-296-4757

OBJECT

A private operating foundation, the council seeks to assist in finding solutions to the problems of libraries, particulary academic and research libraries. In pursuit of this aim, the council makes grants to and contracts with other organizations and individuals. The Ford Foundation established CLR in 1956 and has since contributed $31.5 million to its support. CLR receives support from other foundations as well; the Andrew W. Mellon Foundation and the Carnegie Corporation of New York granted $1.5 million to CLR in 1977. The council's current program interests include establishment of a computerized system of national bibliographic control, library management and institutional development, professional education, collection building, and analysis and planning.

MEMBERSHIP

Members constitute the council's board of directors. Limited to 20.

OFFICERS

Pres. Warren J. Haas; *Secy.-Treas.* Mary Agnes Thompson. (Address correspondence to headquarters.)

PUBLICATIONS

Annual Report.
CLR Recent Developments.

EDUCATIONAL FILM LIBRARY ASSOCIATION
Executive Director, Nadine Covert
43 W. 61 St., New York, NY 10023
212-246-4533

OBJECT

"To promote the production, distribution and utilization of educational films and other audio-visual materials." Incorporated 1943. Memb. 1,800. Dues (Inst.) $80-$175; (Commercial Organizations) $200; (Indiv.) $35. Year. July-June.

OFFICERS

Pres. William Murray (1978-1981), Dir., Media Services, Aurora Public Schools, 1085 Peoria St., Aurora, CO 80011; *Pres.-Elect.* Stephen Hess (1979-1982), Dir., Educational Media Center, Univ. of Utah, 207 Milton Bennion Hall, Salt Lake City, UT 84112; *Treas.* Nadine Covert (Ex Officio), Exec. Dir., EFLA, 43 W. 61 St., New York, NY 10023; *Secy.* Lillian Katz (1979-1981), Port Washington Public Lib., 245 Main St., Port Washington, NY 11050.

BOARD OF DIRECTORS

Officers; Helen Cyr (1979-1982), Audio Visual Dept., Enoch Pratt Free Lib., 400

Cathedral St., Baltimore, MD 21201; Frances Dean (1979–1982), Dir., Instructional Materials Div., Montgomery County Public Schools, 850 Hungerford Dr., Rm. 55, Rockville, MD 20850; Clifford J. Ehlinger (1980–1983), Dir., Div. of Media, Grant Wood Area Education Agency, 4401 Sixth St. S.W., Cedar Rapids, IA 52401; Jerry Hostetler (1978–1981), Asst. Dir., Media Learning Resources Service, Southern Illinois Univ., Carbondale, IL 62901; Angie Leclercq (1980–1983), Head, Undergraduate Lib., Univ. of Tennessee, 1015 Volunteer Blvd., Knoxville, TN 37916; Connie McCarthy (1980–1983), Head, Audiovisual Services, Connecticut State Lib., 231 Capitol Ave., Hartford, CT 06115.

PUBLICATIONS

EFLA Bulletin (q.).
EFLA Evaluations. (5/year).
American Film Festival Program Guide (ann.).
Sightlines (q.). *Ed.* Nadine Covert.
Write for list of other books and pamphlets.

FEDERAL LIBRARY COMMITTEE
Library of Congress, Washington, DC 20540
202-287-6055

OBJECT

"For the purpose of concentrating the intellectual resources present in the federal library and library related information community: To achieve better utilization of library resources and facilities; to provide more effective planning, development, and operation of federal libraries; to promote an optimum exchange of experience, skill, and resources; to promote more effective service to the nation at large. Secretariat efforts and the work groups are organized to: Consider policies and problems relating to federal libraries; evaluate existing federal library programs and resources; determine priorities among library issues requiring attention; examine the organization and policies for acquiring, preserving, and making information available; study the need for a potential of technological innovation in library practices; and study library budgeting and staffing problems, including the recruiting, education, training, and remuneration of librarians." Founded 1965. Memb. (Federal Libs.) 2,600; (Federal Libns.) 4,000. Year. Oct 1–Sept. 30.

MEMBERSHIP

Libn. of Congress, Dir. of the National Agricultural Lib., Dir. of the National Lib. of Medicine, representatives from each of the other executive departments, and delegates from the National Aeronautics and Space Admin., the National Science Foundation, the Smithsonian Institution, the U.S. Supreme Court, International Communication Agency, the Veterans Admin., and the Office of Presidential Libs. Six members will be selected on a rotation basis by the permanent members of the committee from independent agencies, boards, committees, and commissions. These rotating members will serve two-year terms. Ten regional members shall be selected on a rotating basis by the permanent members of the committee to represent federal libraries following the geographic pattern developed by the Federal Regional Councils. These rotating regional members will serve two-year terms. The ten regional members, one from each of the ten federal regions, shall be voting members. In addition to the permanent representative from DOD, one nonvoting member shall be selected from each of the three services (U.S. Army, U.S. Navy, U.S. Air Force). These service members, who will serve for two years, will be selected by the permanent Department of Defense member from a slate provided by the Federal Library Committee. The membership in each service shall be rotated equitably among the special service, technical, and academic and school libraries in that service. DOD shall continue to have one voting member in the committee. The DOD representative may poll the three service members for their opinions before reaching a decision concerning the vote. A representative of the Office of Management and Budget, designated by the budget director and others appointed by the chairperson, will meet with the committee as observers.

OFFICERS

Chpn. Carol Nemeyer, Assoc. Libn. for National Programs, Lib. of Congress, Washington, DC 20540. *Exec. Dir.* James P. Riley.

PUBLICATIONS

Annual Report (Oct.).
FLC Newsletter (irreg.).

FEDLINK NETWORK OFFICE
Coordinator, Lucinda Leonard
Federal Library Committee, Library of Congress, Washington, DC 20540
202-287-6454

OBJECT

The Federal Library and Information Network (FEDLINK) is an FLC operating cooperative program, established to minimize costs and enhance services through the use of on-line data base services for shared cataloging, interlibrary loan, acquisitions, and information retrieval. FEDLINK was established to:

1. Expedite and facilitate on-line data base services among federal libraries and information centers.
2. Develop plans for the expansion of such services to federal libraries and information centers.
3. Promote cooperation and utilization of the full potential of networks and technologies to institutions and provide for formal relationships between library and information networks and the FEDLINK membership.
4. To serve as the major federal library and information cooperative system in the emerging national library and information service network.
5. Promote education, research, and training in network services and new library and information technology for the benefit of federal libraries and information centers.

MEMBERSHIP

FEDLINK membership is nationwide and is made up of over 400 libraries, information centers, and systems that participate in automated functions through OCLC, Inc., or similar systems and services sponsored and coordinated by FLC.

INFORMATION INDUSTRY ASSOCIATION
President, Paul G. Zurkowski
316 Pennsylvania Ave. S.E., Suite 502, Washington, DC 20003
202-544-1969

MEMBERSHIP

For details on membership and dues, write to the association headquarters. Memb. Over 150.

STAFF

Pres. Paul G. Zurkowski; *V.P., Government Relations.* Robert S. Willard; *Mgr., Meetings and Admin.* Helena M. Strauch; *AIM Exec. Dir.* Rita Lombardo.

BOARD OF DIRECTORS

Chpn. Thomas A. Grogan, McGraw-Hill; *V. Chpn.* Roy K. Campbell, Dun & Bradstreet; *Secy.* Paul G. Zurkowski, Info. Industry Assn.; *Treas.* Norman M. Wellen, Business International Corp.; *Past Chpn.* Robert F. Asleson, Info. Handling Services; William A. Beltz, Bureau of National Affairs; J. Christopher Burns, Washington Post Co.; Carlos A. Cuadra, Cuadra Associates, Inc.; William L. Dunn, Dow Jones Info. Services; Elizabeth B. Eddison, Warner-Eddison Assocs.; Andrew P. Garvin, FIND/SVP; James G. Kollegger, Environment Info. Center, Inc.; Jerome S. Rubin, Mead Data Central; William J. Senter, Xerox Publishing Group; Roger K. Summit, Lockheed Info. Systems; Loene Trubkin, Data Courier, Inc.

PUBLICATIONS

The Information Resource: Policy, Background, and Issues—An Infostructure Handbook (1980).
Information Sources (3rd ed., 1980).

LUTHERAN CHURCH LIBRARY ASSOCIATION
122 W. Franklin Ave., Minneapolis, MN 55404
612-870-3623
Executive Secretary, E. T. (Wilma) Jensen
(Home address: 3620 Fairlawn Dr., Minnetonka, MN 55404
612-473-5965)

OBJECT

"To promote the growth of church libraries by publishing a quarterly journal, *Lutheran Libraries;* furnishing booklists; assisting member libraries with technical problems; providing meetings for mutual encouragement, assistance, and exchange of ideas among members." Founded 1958. Memb. 1,800. Dues. $8, $15, $25, $100, $500, $1,000. Year. Jan.–Jan.

OFFICERS (JAN. 1981–JAN. 1983)

Pres. Esther Damkoehler, Libn., Hope Lutheran Lib., Milwaukee, WI (7822 Eagle St., Wauwatosa, WI 53213); *V.P.* Marlys Johnson, 4709 Oregon Ave. N., Minneapolis, MN 55428; *Secy.* Vivian Thoreson, American Lutheran Church Women, 422 S. Fifth St., Minneapolis, MN 55415; *Treas.* Mrs. G. Frank (Jane) Johnson, 2930 S. Hwy. 101, Wayzata, MN 55391. (Address correspondence to the executive secretary.)

EXECUTIVE BOARD

Elaine Hanson; Mary Jordan; Charles Mann; Larraine Pike; Solveig Bartz, Daniel Brumm.

ADVISORY BOARD

Chpn. Gary Klammer; Rev. Rolf Aaseng; Mrs. H. O. Egertson; Mrs. Donald Gauerke; Mrs. Harold Groff; Rev. James Gunther; Rev. A. B. Hanson; Malvin Lundeen; Mary Egdahl; Rev. A. C. Paul; Don Rosenberg; Stanley Sandberg; Les Schmidt; Aron Valleskey.

PUBLICATION

Lutheran Libraries (q.; memb., nonmemb. $8). *Ed.* Erwin E. John, 6450 Warren St., Minneapolis, MN 55435.

COMMITTEE CHAIRPERSONS

Budget. Rev. Carl Manfred, Normandale Lutheran Church, 6100 Normandale Rd., Minneapolis, MN 55436.

Finance. Mrs. Lloyd (Betty) LeDell, Libn., Grace Lutheran of Deephaven, 15800 Sunset Rd., Minnetonka, MN 55343.

Library Services Board. Mrs. Forrest (Juanita) Carpenter, Libn., Rte. 1, Prior Lake, MN 55372.

Publications Board. Rev. Carl Weller, Augsburg Publishing House, 426 S. Fifth St., Minneapolis, MN 55415.

MEDICAL LIBRARY ASSOCIATION
Executive Director, Shirley Echelman
919 N. Michigan Ave., Chicago, IL 60611
312-266-2456

OBJECT

Founded in 1898 and incorporated in 1934, its major purpose is to foster medical and allied scientific libraries, to promote the educational and professional growth of health sciences librarians, and to exchange medical literature among the members. Through its programs and publications, MLA encourages professional development of its membership, whose foremost concern is for the dissemination of health sciences information for those in research, education, and patient care. Memb. (Inst.) 1,350. (Indiv.) 3,680. Dues. (Inst.) Subscriptions up to 199 $75, 200-299 $100, 300-599 $125, 600-999 $150, 1,000+ $175; (Indiv.) $45. Year. From month of payment.

MEMBERSHIP

Open to those working in or interested in medical libraries.

OFFICERS

Pres. Gertrude Lamb, Hartford Hospital, Health Science Libs., Hartford, CT 06115; *Past Pres.* Lois Ann Colaianni, Health Sciences Info. Center, Cedars-Sinai Medical Center, Los Angeles, CA 90048; *Pres.-Elect.* Charles W. Sargent, Texas Technical Univ., Lib. Health Sciences Center, Lubbock, TX 79430.

DIRECTORS

Jean K. Miller; Beatrix Robinow; John A. Timour; Naomi C. Broering; Arlee May; Eloise C. Foster; Lucretia McClure.

PUBLICATIONS

Bulletin (q.; $45).

Index to Audiovisual Serials in the Health Sciences (4/year; $18).

Current Catalog Proof Sheets (Option A, w., $45); (Option B, mo., $39).

MLA News (mo.; $15/year).

Vital Notes (3/year; $20).

STANDING COMMITTEE CHAIRPERSONS

Audiovisual Standards and Practices Committee. Carmel C. Bush, TALON Regional Medical Lib. Program, 5323 Harry Hines Blvd., Dallas, TX 75235.

Bibliographic and Information Services Assessment Committee. Michele R. Chatfield, FDA, Bureau of Foods, 200 C St. S.W., HFF-39, Washington, DC 20204.

"Bulletin" Consulting Editors Panel. Gloria Werner, Biomedical Lib., Center for the Health Sciences, Univ. of California, Los Angeles, CA 90024.

Bylaws Committee. Jacqueline L. Picciano, American Journal of Nursing Co., 10 Columbus Circle, New York, NY 10019.

Certification and Recertification Appeals Panel. Lucretia McClure, Univ. of Rochester, School of Medicine/Dentistry, Edward G. Miner Lib., 601 Elmwood Ave., Rochester, NY 14642.

Certification Eligibility Committee. Virginia L. Algermissen, Texas A&M Univ., Medical Sciences Lib., Box HJ, College Station, TX 77843.

Certification Examination Review Committee. William D. Walker, Medical Lib. Center of New York, 17 E. 102 St., New York, NY 10029.

Committee on Committees. Charles W. Sargent, Texas Technical Univ., Lib., Health Sciences Center, Lubbock, TX 79430.

Continuing Education Committee. Alison Bunting, UCLA Biomedical Lib., Center for the Health Sciences, Los Angeles, CA 90024.

Copyright. Dean Schmidt, Medical Lib., Univ. of Missouri, M-210 Medical Center, Columbia, MO 65212.

Editorial Committee for the Bulletin. Justine Roberts, Univ. of California-San Francisco, Lib. Systems Office, San Francisco, CA 94143.

Editorial Committee for the MLA News. Virginia Massey Bowden, Univ. of Texas, Health Sciences Center at San Antonio, 7703 Floyd Curl Dr., San Antonio, TX 78284.

Elections Committee. Charles W. Sargent, Texas Technical Univ., Lib., Health Sciences Center, Lubbock, TX 79430.

Exchange Committee. Joan S. Zenan, Health Sciences Lib., Columbia Univ., 701 W. 168 St., New York, NY 10032.

Executive Committee. Gertrude Lamb, Hartford Hospital, Health Science Libs., Hartford, CT 06115.

Finance. Jean K. Miller, Univ. of Texas, Health Science Center at Dallas Lib., 5323 Harry Hines Blvd., Dallas, TX 75235.

Health Sciences Library Technicians Committee. Judith Hodges, Tennessee Hospital Assn., 500 Interstate Blvd. S., Nashville, TN 37210.

Honors and Awards Committee. Dana McDonald, Southern Illinois Univ., School of Medicine Lib., 801 N. Rutledge St., Springfield, IL 62702. *Janet Doe Lectureship Subcommittee.* Erich Meyerhoff, Cornell Univ. Medical College, New York, NY 10021. *Eliot Prize Subcommittee.* Michael Fineman, Univ. of California-Irvine, Medical Center Lib., 101 City Dr. S., Orange, CA 92668. *Gottlieb Prize Subcommittee.* Agnes Roach, Lib. Consultant, 340 W. Diversey Pkwy., Chicago, IL 60657. *Rittenhouse Award Subcommittee.* Dana McDonald, Southern Illinois Univ., School of Medicine Lib., 801 N. Rutledge St., Springfield, IL 62702.

Hospital Library Standards and Practices Committee. Jane A. Lambremont, Univ. of North Carolina, Health Science Center Lib., Chapel Hill, NC 27514.

International Cooperation Committee. C. Robin LeSeuer, Countway Lib. of Medicine, 10 Shattuck St., Boston, MA 02115.

Interlibrary Loan and Resource Sharing Standards and Practices Committee. Patricia Jones, Univ. of Illinois at the Medical Center, Lib. of the Health Sciences, Box 7509, Chicago, IL 60680.

Legislation. Mary M. Horres, Health Sciences Lib., 223-H, Univ. of North Carolina, Chapel Hill, NC 27514.

Library Standards and Practices. James E. Raper, Jr., Medical Lib. Center of New York, 17 E. 102 St., New York, NY 10029.

MLA/NLM Liaison Committee. Jean K. Miller, Health Sciences Center at Dallas, Lib., Univ. of Texas, 5323 Harry Hines Blvd., Dallas, TX 75235.

Membership Committee. Gail A. Yo-

kote, UCLA Biomedical Lib., Center for the Health Sciences, Los Angeles, CA 90024.
National Issues Advisory Council. Lois Ann Colaianni, Health Sciences Info. Center, Cedars-Sinai Medical Center, Box 48956, Los Angeles, CA 90048.
1981 National Program Committee. Frances Groen, Medical Lib., McGill Univ., 3655 Drummond St., Montreal, P.Q. H3G 1Y6, Canada.
1982 National Program Committee. Alison Bunting, Biomedical Lib., Univ. of California, Center for the Health Sciences, Los Angeles, CA 90024.
1983 National Program Committee. Richard Lyders, Texas Medical Center Lib., 1133 M. D. Anderson Blvd., Houston, TX 77030.
Nominating Committee. Charles W. Sargent, Texas Technical Univ., Lib., Health Sciences Center, Lubbock, TX 79430.
Oral History Committee. Nancy Whitten Zinn, Lib., Univ. of California, San Francisco, CA 94143.
Program and Convention Committee. Thomas D. Higdon, Univ. of Arizona, Arizona Health Sciences Center Lib., Tucson, AZ 85724.
Publication Panel. Virginia H. Holtx, W. S. Middleton Health Sciences Lib., Univ. of Wisconsin, 1305 Linden Dr., Madison, WI 53562.
Recertification Committee. Shirley Edsall, Wilson Memorial Hospital, 33-57 Harrison St., Johnson City, NY 13790.
Scholarship Committee. Jo Anne Boorkman, Univ. of North Carolina, Health Sciences Lib., 223H, Chapel Hill, NC 27514.
Status and Economic Interests of Health Sciences Library Personnel Committee. Rachael K. Goldstein, Columbia Univ., Health Sciences Lib., 701 W. 168 St., New York, NY 10032.
Surveys and Statistics Committee. Ching-chih Chen, Simmons College, School of Lib. & Info. Science, 300 The Fenway, Boston, MA 02115.

"Vital Notes" Participatory Panel. Donald L. Potts, Medical Lib. Center of New York, New York, NY 10029.

AD HOC COMMITTEES

For the International Exchange and Redistribution of Library Materials. Janis Sharp, Personnel Libn., Houston Academy of Medicine, Texas Medical Center Lib., Jesse H. Jones Lib. Bldg., Houston, TX 77030.
"Handbook" Consultants Panel. Louise Darling, Biomedical Lib., Univ. of California, Los Angeles, CA 90024.
MLA/HeSCA Joint Committee to Develop Guidelines for Audiovisual Facilities in Health Sciences Libraries. Gloria H. Hurwitz, Coord., Learning Resources Facilities, MCV Box 62, Richmond, VA 23298.
On MLA Group Structure Implementation. Ursula H. Poland, Schaffer Lib. of Health Sciences, Albany Medical College, Albany, NY 12208.
Study Group on MLA's Role in the Educational Process for Health Sciences Librarians. Phyllis S. Mirsky, Reference Sec., National Lib. of Medicine, 8600 Rockville Pike, Bethesda, MD 20209.
To Develop a Statement of Goals of the Medical Library Association. Virginia H. Holtz, Middleton Health Sciences Lib., Univ. of Wisconsin, Madison, WI 53706.
To Develop and Implement an AACR2 Training Program. Sally Sinn, Acting Head, Cataloging Sec., National Lib. of Medicine, 8600 Rockville Pike, Bethesda, MD 20209.
To Develop Criteria for Hospital Library Consultants. Judith Messerle, St. Joseph Hospital Lib., Alton, IL 62002.
To Examine the Certification and Recertification Process. Beatrix Robinow, McMaster Univ., Hamilton, Ont. L8N 3Z5, Canada.
To Recommend Additional Sources of Income for MLA. Rose Hogan, Medical and Health Science Lib., Univ. of Arkansas, 4301 W. Markham St., Little Rock, AR 72201.

MUSIC LIBRARY ASSOCIATION
2017 Walnut St., Philadelphia, PA 19103
215-569-3948

OBJECT

"To promote the establishment, growth, and use of music libraries; to encourage the collection of music and musical literature in libraries; to further studies in musical bibliography; to increase efficiency in music library service and administration." Founded 1931. Memb. about 1,700. Dues. (Inst.) $31; (Indiv.) $24; (Student) $12. Year. Sept. 1–Aug. 31.

OFFICERS

Pres. Donald W. Krummel, Grad. Lib. School, Univ. of Illinois, Urbana, IL 61801; *Past Pres.* Ruth Watanabe, Sibley Music Lib., Eastman School of Music, Rochester, NY 14604; *Secy.* George R. Hill, Music Dept., Baruch College/CUNY, 17 Lexington Ave., New York, NY 10010; *Treas.* Shirley Emanuel, 522 10 St. N.W., Washington, DC 20002; *Ed. of "Notes."* William McClellan, Music Lib., Music Bldg., Univ. of Illinois, Urbana, IL 61801.

DIRECTORS

Officers; Olga Booth; Garrett H. Bowles; Margaret LaSpinoso; Kathleen J. Moretto; Charles Simpson; John W. Tanno.

PUBLICATIONS

Music Cataloging Bulletin (mo.; $12).
MLA Index Series (irreg.; price varies according to size).
MLA Newsletter (q.; free to memb.).
MLA Technical Reports (irreg.; price varies according to size).
Notes (q.; inst. subscription $31; nonmemb. subscription $21).

COMMITTEE CHAIRPERSONS

Audio-Visual. Arne J. Arneson, Music Lib., Univ. of Colorado, Boulder, CO 80302.
Automation. Garrett H. Bowles, Music Lib., Univ. of California at San Diego, La Jolla, CA 92093.
Basic Music Collection. Pauline S. Bayne, Music Lib., Univ. of Tennessee, Knoxville, TN 37916.
Cataloging and Classification. Judith Kaufman, Music Lib., State Univ. of New York, Stony Brook, NY 11794.
Constitutional Revision. Geraldine Ostrove, Lib., New England Conservatory of Music, Boston, MA 02115.
Education. Kathryn P. Logan, Music Lib., Univ. of North Carolina, Chapel Hill, NC 27514.
Legislation. Susan T. Sommer, Music Div., New York Public Lib., 111 Amsterdam Ave., New York, NY 10023.
Microforms. Stuart Milligan, Sibley Music Lib., Eastman School of Music, Rochester, NY 14604.
Music Library Administration. Brenda Chasen Goldman, Music Lib., Tufts Univ., Medford, MA 02155.
Public Library. Donna Mendro, Dallas Public Lib., Dallas, TX 75201.
Publications. Linda Solow, Music Lib., Massachusetts Institute of Technology, Cambridge, MA 02139.
Selection and Acquisition. Katherine Holum, Music Lib., Univ. of Minnesota, Minneapolis, MN 55455.

NATIONAL LIBRARIANS ASSOCIATION
Executive Director, Peter Dollard
Box 586, Alma, MI 48801
517-463-7111, ext. 332

OBJECT

"To promote librarianship, to develop and increase the usefulness of libraries, to cultivate the science of librarianship, to protect the interest of professionally qualified librarians, and to perform other functions necessary for the betterment of the profession of librarianship. It functions as an association of librarians, rather than as an association of libraries." Established 1975. Memb. 550. Dues. $15 per year; $25 for 2 years; (Students and Retired and Unemployed Librarians) $7.50. Year. July 1–June 30.

MEMBERSHIP

Any person interested in librarianship and libraries who holds a graduate degree in library science may become a member upon election by the executive board and payment of the annual dues. The executive board may authorize exceptions to the degree requirements to applicants who present evidence of outstanding contributions to the profession. Student membership is available to those graduate students enrolled full time at any accredited library school.

OFFICERS (JULY 1, 1980–JUNE 30, 1981)

Pres. Norman Tanis, California State Univ. at Northridge, Northridge, CA 91330; *Immed. Past Pres.* June Stratton, Box 1204, South Bend, IN 46624. (Address all correspondence to the executive director.)

PUBLICATION

NLA Newsletter: The National Librarian (q.; 1 year $12, 2 years $22, 3 years $30).

COMMITTEE CHAIRPERSONS

Certification Standards. David Perkins, California State Univ., Northridge, CA 91330.

Professional Education. John Colson, 813 Somonauk St., Sycamore, IL 60178.

Professional Welfare. Julio A. Martinez, San Diego State Univ. Lib., San Diego, CA 92181.

NATIONAL MICROGRAPHICS ASSOCIATION
Executive Director, O. Gordon Banks
8719 Colesville Rd., Silver Spring, MD 20910
301-587-8202

OBJECT

The National Micrographics Association (NMA) is the trade and professional association that represents the manufacturers, vendors, and professional users of micrographic equipment and software. The purpose of the association is to promote the lawful interests of the micrographic industry in the direction of good business ethics; the liberal discussion of subjects pertaining to the industry and its relationship to other information management technologies, technological improvement, and research; standardization; the methods of manufacturing and marketing; and the education of the consumer in the use of information management systems.

Founded 1943. Memb. 10,000. Dues. (Indiv.) $60. Year. July 1, 1980-June 30, 1981.

OFFICERS

Pres. B. J. Cassin, 3000 Sand Hill, Suite 210, Bldg. 3, Menlo Park, CA 94025; *V.P.* John C. Marken, Bell & Howell Co., Micro Photo Div., Drawer E, Old Mansfield Rd., Wooster, OH 44691; *Treas.* Marilyn Courtot, Office of the Secy. of the Senate, U.S. Capitol, RM. S-221, Washington, DC 20510. (Address general correspondence to the executive director.)

PUBLICATIONS

Journal of Micrographics (mo.; memb. and subscriptions). *Ed.* Ellen T. Meyer. Book reviews included; product review included. Ads accepted.

SOCIETY OF AMERICAN ARCHIVISTS
330 S. Wells St., Suite 810, Chicago, IL 60606
Executive Director, Ann Morgan Campbell
312-922-0140

OBJECT

"To promote sound principles of archival economy and to facilitate cooperation among archivists and archival agencies." Founded 1936. Memb. 3,800. Dues (Indiv.) $45-$75, graduated according to salary; (Student) $30 with a two-year maximum on student membership; (Inst.) $50; (Sustaining) $100.

OFFICERS (OCT. 1980-SEPT. 1981)

Pres. Ruth W. Helmuth, Case Western Reserve Univ., Cleveland, OH 44106; *V.P./Pres.-Elect.* Edward Weldon, National Archives and Records Service, Washington, DC 20408; *Treas.* Mary Lynn McCree, Univ. of Illinois at Chicago Circle, Chicago, IL 60680.

COUNCIL

Edmund Berkeley, Jr.; Lynn Bonfield; Shonnie Finnegan; Meyer H. Fishbein; Robert Gordon; Richard Lytle; Paul McCarthy, Jr.; Virginia C. Purdy.

STAFF

Exec. Dir. Ann Morgan Campbell; *Dir. Administrative Services.* Joyce E. Gianatasio; *Membership Asst.* Bernice Brack; *Bookkeeper.* Andrea Giannattasio; *Publns. Asst.* Kathleen Kelly Hajek; *Program Officer.* Thomas C. Pardo; *Newsletter Ed./Program Officer.* Deborah Risteen; *Program Officer.* Mary Lynn Ritzenthaler; *Program Asst.* Linda Ziemer.

PUBLICATIONS

The American Archivist (q.; $30). *Ed.* Virginia C. Purdy, National Archives and Records Service (NN), Washington, DC 20408. Book reviews and related correspondence should be addressed to the editor. Rates for B/W ads: full-page, $200; half-page, $125; outside back cover, $300; half-page minimum insertion; 10% discount for four consecutive insertions; 15% agency commission.

SAA Newsletter. (6/year; memb.) *Ed.* Deborah Risteen, SAA, 300 S. Wells, Suite 810, Chicago, IL 60606. Rates for B/W ads: full-page, $300; half-page, $175; quarter-page, $90; eighth-page, $50.

PROFESSIONAL AFFINITY GROUPS (PAGs) AND CHAIRS

Acquisition. Charles Schultz, Texas A&M Univ., College Station, TX 77843.
Aural and Graphic Records. Diane Vogt-O'Connor, Cranbrook Academy of

Art Lib., Box 801, Bloomfield Hills, MI 48013.
Business Archives. Linda Edgerly, 103 W. 75 St., Apt. 3B, New York, NY 10023.
College and University Archives. Helen Slotkin, Institute Archives, 14N-118, Massachusetts Institute of Technology, Cambridge, MA 02139.
Conservation. Howard Lowell, 1310 Franklin St., 202, Denver, CO 80218.
Description. Eleanor McKay, Brister Lib., Memphis State Univ., Memphis, TN 38152.

Government Records. Sue E. Holbert, Minnesota Historical Society, 1500 Mississippi St., St. Paul, MN 55101.
Manuscript Repositories. Clifton Jones, 906 Cordova St., Dallas, TX 75223.
Reference, Access and Outreach. Karyl Winn, Univ. of Washington Lib., FM-25, Seattle, WA 98195.
Religious Archives. Sister M. Felicitas Powers, Box 10490, Baltimore, MD 21209.
Theme Collections. Olha Della Cava, 131 Sylvan Ave., Leonia, NJ 07605.

SPECIAL LIBRARIES ASSOCIATION
Executive Director, David R. Bender
235 Park Ave. S., New York, NY 10003
212-477-9250

OBJECT

"To provide an association of individuals and organizations having a professional, scientific or technical interest in library and information science, especially as these are applied in the recording, retrieval and dissemination of knowledge and information in areas such as the physical, biological, technical and social sciences and the humanities; and to promote and improve the communication, dissemination and use of such information and knowledge for the benefit of libraries or other educational organizations." Organized 1909. Memb. 11,500. Dues. (Sustaining) $250; (Indiv.) $55; (Student) $12. Year. Jan.-Dec. and July-June.

OFFICERS (JUNE 1980-JUNE 1981)

Pres. James B. Dodd, Georgia Inst. of Technology, Atlanta, GA 30332; *Pres.-Elect.* George H. Ginader, 45 S. Main, Cranbury, NJ 08512; *Div. Cabinet Chpn.* Ruth S. Smith, Institute for Defense Analyses, 400 Army-Navy Dr., Arlington, VA 22202; *Div. Cabinet Chpn.-Elect.* Julie H. Bichteler, Univ. of Texas at Austin, Grad. School of Lib. Science, Box 7576, University Sta., Austin, TX 78712; *Chap.*

Cabinet Chpn. Didi Pancake, Univ. of Virginia, Clark Hall, Charlottesville, VA 22901; *Chap. Cabinet Chpn.-Elect.* Jane Dysart, Royal Bank of Canada, Royal Bank Plaza, Toronto, Ont. M5J 2J5, Canada; *Treas.* Dorothy Kasman, Coopers & Lybrand, 1251 Ave. of the Americas, New York, NY 10020; *Past. Pres.* Joseph M. Dagnese, Purdue Univ. Libs., West Lafayette, IN 47907.

DIRECTORS

Beryl L. Anderson (1978–81); Pat Molholt (1978–81); Jack Leister (1979–82); Mary Vasilakis (1979–1982); Jacqueline J. Desoer (1980–83); Sandra K. Hall (1980–83).

PUBLICATIONS

Special Libraries (q.) and *SpeciaList* (mo.). Cannot be ordered separately ($36 for both; add $5 postage outside the U.S., including Canada). *Ed.* Nancy M. Viggiano.

COMMITTEE CHAIRPERSONS

Awards. Vivian D. Hewitt, Carnegie Endowment for International Peace, 30 Rockefeller Plaza, New York, NY 10020.

Consultation Service. Carol L. Vantine, General Mills, Inc., JFB Technical Center, 9000 Plymouth Ave. N., Minneapolis, MN 55427.
Copyright Law Implementation. Efren W. Gonzalez, Bristol-Myers Products, 1350 Liberty Ave., Hillside, NJ 07207.
Education. Laura N. Gasaway, Univ. of Oklahoma, Law Lib., 300 Timberdell, Norman, OK 73019.
Government Information Services. Charles Olsen, International Monetary Fund and World Bank, Washington, DC 20431.
Networking. James Webster, State Univ. of New York-Buffalo, Science and Engineering Lib., Buffalo, NY 15260.
Nominating (for spring 1982 election). Richard Funkhouser, Purdue Univ., Math Science Lib., West Lafayette, IN 47907.
Positive Action Program for Minority Groups. Gloria H. Broaddus, Babcock & Wilcox Co., Power Generation Group Technical Lib., 20 S. VanBuren Ave., Barberton, OH 44203.

Publications. David E. King, Standard Education Corp., 200 W. Monroe St., Chicago, IL 60606.
Publisher Relations. James B. Poteat, Television Info. Office, 745 Fifth Ave., New York, NY 10022.
Research. Fred W. Roper, Univ. of North Carolina, School of Lib. Science, Manning Hall 026-A, Chapel Hill, NC 27514.
Scholarship. Minnie G. Thurston, Offshore Power Systems Lib., Box 8000, Jacksonville, FL 32211.
Standards. Audrey N. Grosch, Univ. of Minnesota, S-34 Wilson Lib., Lib. Systems Dept., Minneapolis, MN 55455.
Statistics. Beth Ainsley, Georgia Power Co., 270 Peachtree St. N.W., Atlanta, GA 30302.
Student Relations Officer. Linda C. Smith, Univ. of Illinois, Grad. School of Lib. Science, 410 Kinley Hall, Urbana, IL 61801.
H. W. Wilson Co. Award. William C. Petru, Hewlett-Packard Co., 1501 Page Mill Rd., Palo Alto, CA 94304.

THEATRE LIBRARY ASSOCIATION
Secretary-Treasurer, Richard M. Buck
111 Amsterdam Ave., New York, NY 10023

OBJECT

"To further the interests of collecting, preserving, and using theatre, cinema, and performing arts materials in libraries, museums, and private collections." Founded 1937. Memb. 500. Dues. (Indiv.) $15; (Inst.) $20. Year. Jan. 1–Dec. 31, 1981.

OFFICERS (1980–1981)

Pres. Brooks McNamara, Grad. Drama Dept., School of the Arts, New York Univ., 61 W. Fourth St., Rm. 300, New York, NY 10012; *V.P.* Louis A. Rachow, Walter Hampden-Edwin Booth Theatre Collection and Lib., The Players, 16 Gramercy Pk., New York, NY 10003; *Secy.-Treas.* Richard M. Buck, Asst. to the Chief, Performing Arts Research Center, New York Public Lib. at Lincoln Center, 111 Amsterdam Ave., New York, NY 10023; *Rec. Secy.* Geraldine Duclow, Libn.-in-Charge, Theatre Arts Collection, Free Lib. of Philadelphia, Logan Sq., Philadelphia, PA 19103. (Address correspondence, except *Broadside*, to the secretary-treasurer. Address *Broadside* correspondence to V.P. Louis A. Rachow, ed.)

EXECUTIVE BOARD

Officers: William Appleton; Mary Ashe; Laraine Correll; Babette Craven; Geraldine Duclow; Robert C. Eason, Jr.; Mary Ann Jensen; Brigitte Kueppers;

Frank C. P. McGlinn; Martha Mahard; Sally Thomas Pavetti; *Ex Officio.* Lee Ash; Mary C. Henderson; Dorothy L. Swerdlove; Don B. Wilmeth; *Honorary.* Rosamond Gilder.

COMMITTEE CHAIRPERSONS

Awards. William Appleton.
Nominations. Louis A. Rachow.

Program and Special Events. Richard M. Buck.
Publications. Louis A. Rachow.

PUBLICATIONS

Broadside (q.; memb.).
Performing Arts Resources (ann.; memb.).

UNIVERSAL SERIALS AND BOOK EXCHANGE, INC.
Executive Director, Alice Dulany Ball
3335 V St. N.E., Washington, DC 20018
202-529-2555

OBJECT

"To promote the distribution and interchange of books, periodicals, and other scholarly materials among libraries and other educational and scientific institutions of the United States, and between them and libraries and institutions of other countries." Organized 1948. Memb. year—libraries: Jan. 1–Dec. 31 or July 1–June 30. Memb. year—associations: Jan. 1–Dec. 31.

MEMBERSHIP

Membership in USBE is open to any library that serves a constituency and is an institution or part of an institution or organization. The USBE corporation includes a representative from each member library and from each of a group of sponsoring organizations listed below.

OFFICERS

Pres. Margaret A. Otto, Libn. of the College, Dartmouth College, Hanover, NH 03755; *V.P./Pres.-Elect.* H. Joanne Harrar, Dir. of Libs., Univ. of Maryland, College Park, MD 20742; *Secy.* Nina W. Matheson, Asst. Dir., Health Info. Management Studies, Assn. of American Medical Colleges, One Dupont Circle N.W., Washington, DC 20036; *Treas.* Juanita S. Doares, Assoc. Dir., College Management and Development, New York Public Lib., New York, NY 10017; *Past Pres.* Ralph H. Hopp, Dir., Institute of Technology Libs., Univ. of Minnesota, Minneapolis, MN 55455.

MEMBERS OF THE BOARD

Executive director; Virginia Boucher, Head, Interlib. Cooperation, Univ. of Colorado, Boulder, CO 80309; Anne C. Edmond, Libn., Mount Holyoke College, South Hadley, MA 01075; Nathan Einhorn, Chief, Exchange and Gift Div., Lib. of Congress, Washington, DC 20540; Jay K. Lucker, Dir. of Libs., Massachusetts Institute of Technology, Cambridge, MA 02139; Susan K. Martin, Dir., Milton S. Eisenhower Lib., Johns Hopkins Univ., Baltimore, MD 21218; Ryburn M. Ross, Asst. Univ. Libn. for Technical and Automated Services, Cornell Univ. Libs., Ithaca, NY 14853.

SPONSORING MEMBERS

Alabama Lib. Assn.; Alaska Lib. Assn.; American Assn. of Law Libs.; American Council of Learned Societies; American Society for Info. Science; American Lib. Assn.; American Theological Lib. Assn.; Arizona State Lib. Assn.; Assn. of American Lib. Schools; Assn. of Jewish Libs.; Assn. of Research Libs.; Assn. of Special Libs. of the Philippines; Associazione Italiana Biblioteche; British Columbia Lib. Assn.; California Lib. Assn.; Catholic Lib. Assn.; Colorado Lib. Assn.; District of Columbia Lib. Assn.; Ethiopian Lib. Assn.; Federal Lib. Committee; Federation of Indian Lib. Assns.; Florida Lib. Assn.; Idaho Lib. Assn.; Interamerican Assn. of Agricultural Libns. and Documentalists; Jordan Lib. Assn.; Kenya Lib. Assn.; Lib. of Congress; Maryland Lib. Assn.; Medical Lib. Assn.; Michigan Lib. Assn.; Music Lib. Assn.; National Academy of Sciences; National Agricultural Lib.; National Lib. of Medicine; New Jersey Lib. Assn.; North Carolina Lib. Assn.; Pennsylvania Lib. Assn.; Philippine Lib. Assn.; Smithsonian Institution; Social Science Research Council; South African Lib. Assn.; Southeastern Lib. Assn.; Special Libs. Assn.; Special Libs. Assn. of Japan; Theatre Lib. Assn.; Uganda Lib. Assn.; Vereinigung Osterreichischer Bibliothekare.

STATE, PROVINCIAL, AND REGIONAL LIBRARY ASSOCIATIONS

The associations in this section are organized under three headings: United States, Canada, and Regional Associations. Both the United States and Canada are represented under Regional Associations. Unless otherwise specified, correspondence is to be addressed to the secretary or executive secretary named in the library association entry.

UNITED STATES

Alabama

Memb. 1,143. Founded 1904. Term of Office. Apr. 1980–Apr. 1981. Publication. *The Alabama Librarian* (6 per year). *Ed.* Neil Snider, Sta. 12, Livingston 35470.

Pres. Dallas Baillio, Dir., Mobile Public Lib., 701 Government St., Mobile 36602; *1st V.P./Pres. Elect.* Julia Rotenberry, 249 Highland St. N., Montevallo 35115; *2nd V.P.* Frances F. Davis, 1912 Washington St., Tuskegee Institute, Tuskegee 36088; *Secy.* Miriam Pace, 6033 Monticello Dr., Montgomery 36130; *Treas.* Pat Moore, 613 Winwood Dr., Birmingham 35226; *ALA Chapter Councillor.* James Ramer, Dean, Graduate School of Library Service, Univ. of Alabama, Box 6242, University 35486.

Address correspondence to the executive secretary, Alabama Lib. Assn., Box BY, University 35486.

Alaska

Memb. (Indiv.) 276; (Inst.) 27. Term of Office. Mar. 1980–Mar. 1981. Publications. *Sourdough* (q.); *Newspoke* (bi-mo.).

Pres. Sharon West, Elmer Rasmuson Lib., Univ. of Alaska, Fairbanks 99701; *V.P./Pres.-Elect.* Mollie Bynum, Box 8722, Anchorage 99508; *Secy.* Ila Jean Reiersen, Anchorage Municipal Libs., 427 F St., Anchorage 99501; *Treas.* Errol Locker, 217 E. 11 St., Anchorage 99501.

Arizona

Memb. 1,050. Term of Office. Oct. 1, 1980–Oct. 1, 1981. Publication. *ASLA Newsletter* (mo.). *Ed.* Mitzi Rinehart, Maricopa County Lib., 3375 W. Durango, Phoenix 85009.

Pres. William Morris, 1336 E. Lawrence La., Phoenix 85020; *Pres.-Elect.* Maggie Nation, Flagstaff Public Lib., 11 W. Cherry, Flagstaff 86001; *Secy.* Sandra

Steffey Lobeck, Yuma Elementary School Dist. 1, 450 Sixth St., Yuma 85364; *Treas.* Marge Goble, 6418 W. Colter St., Glendale 85301.

Arkansas

Memb. 1,150. Term of Office. Oct. 1980–Sept. 1981. Publication. *Arkansas Libraries* (q.).

Pres. Phyllis Burkett, 1006 W. Arch, Searcy 72143; *Exec. Secy.* Jo Jones, Box 2275, Little Rock 72203.

California

Memb. (Indiv.) 3,000; (Inst.) 178; (Business) 70. Term of Office. Jan. 1–Dec. 31, 1981. Publication. *The CLA Newsletter* (mo.).

Pres. Regina Minudri, Berkeley Public Lib., 2090 Kittredge St., Berkeley 94704; *V.P./Pres. Elect.* Carol Aronoff, Santa Monica Public Lib., 1343 Sixth St., Santa Monica 90401; *Treas.* William F. McCoy, Univ. of California Lib., Davis 95616; *ALA Chapter Councillor.* Gilbert W. McNamee, San Francisco Public Lib., Business Branch, 530 Kearny St., San Francisco 94108.

Address correspondence to Stefan B. Moses, Exec Dir., California Lib. Assn., 717 K St., Suite 300, Sacramento 95814.

Colorado

Term of Office. Nov. 1980–Oct. 1981. Publication. *Colorado Libraries* (q.). *Ed.* Terry Hubbard, Colorado State Univ. Libs., Fort Collins 80523; *Adv. Mgr.* Richard Beeler, Colorado State Univ. Libs., Fort Collins, 80523.

Pres. David Price, Aurora Public Lib., Admin. Services, 1470 S. Havana, Aurora 80012; *Exec. Secy.* Milinda Walker, 3920 S. Truckee Ct., Aurora 80013.

Connecticut

Memb. 1,000. Term of Office, July 1, 1980–July 1, 1981. Publications. *CLA MEMO* (newsletter, 10 per year). *Ed.* Joyce Reid, Windsor Public Lib., 323 Broad St., Windsor 06095; *Connecticut Libraries* (q.). *Ed.* Frank Ferro, New Britain Public Lib., 20 High St., New Britain 06050. *Adv. Mgr.* Andy Bacon, North Haven Lib., 17 Elm St., North Haven 06473.

Pres. Nancy Kline, Univ. of Connecticut Lib., U-5H, Storrs 06268; *V.P./Pres.- Elect.* Vince Juliano, Waterford Public Lib., 49 Rope Ferry Rd., Waterford 06385; *Treas.* Carol Hutchinson, Fairfield Public Lib., 1080 Old Post Rd., Fairfield 06430; *Secy.* Jeanne Simpson, Connecticut Lib. Assn., State Lib., Rm. L-216, 231 Capitol Ave., Hartford 06115.

Delaware

Memb. (Indiv.) 224; (Inst.) 22. Term of Office. May 1980–May 1981. Publication. *DLA Bulletin* (4 per year).

Pres. Jean Trumbore, Morris Lib., Univ. of Delaware, Newark 19711; *V.P./Pres. Elect.* Dick Humphreys, Delaware Law School, Concord Pike, Wilmington 19803; *Secy.* Phyllis Rust, 102 Haven Lake Ave., Milford 19963; *Treas.* Anthony Grillo, Dupont Technical Lib., 2010 Delaware Ave., Wilmington 19806.

Address correspondence to the Delaware Lib. Assn., Box 1843, Wilmington 19899.

District of Columbia

Memb. 950. Term of Office. May 1980– May 1981. Publication. *Intercom* (mo.). *Co-Eds.* Mary Feldman, U.S. Dept. of Transportation, Lib. Services Div., 400 Seventh St. S.W., Washington, DC 20540; Jacque-Lynne Schulman, George Washington Univ., Himmelfarb Health Sciences Lib., 2300 Eye St. N.W., Washington, DC 20037.

Pres. Murray Howder, National Clearinghouse for Bilingual Education, 1300 Wilson Blvd., Suite B2-11, Rosslyn, VA 22209; *Pres.-Elect.* Martha Bowman, George Washington Univ. Lib., 2130 H St. N.W., Washington, DC 20052; *Secy.* Judith Sessions, Mount Vernon College

Lib., 2100 Foxhall Rd. N.W., Washington, DC 20007; *Treas.* Betty Bogart, Bogart-Brociner Assoc., Inc., 47 Williams Dr., Annapolis, MD 21401.

Florida

Memb. (Indiv.) 800; (In-state inst.) 50; (Out-of-state inst.) 30. Term of Office. May 1980–May 1981.
Pres. Samuel F. Morrison, Asst. Dir., Broward County Lib., Box 5463, Fort Lauderdale 33310; *V.P./Pres.-Elect.* Ada Seltzer, Univ. of South Florida Medical Center Lib., 12901 N. 30 St., Tampa 33612; *Secy.* Joyce Wente, Coral Springs Branch (Broward County Lib.), 9571 W. Sample Rd., Coral Springs 33065; *Treas.* Mabel Shaw, Tallahassee Community College, 444 Appleyard Dr., Tallahassee 32304.

Georgia

Memb. 750. Term of Office. Oct. 1979–Oct. 1981. Publication. *Georgia Librarian* (q.). *Ed.* Wanda Calhoun, Augusta/Richmond County Public Lib., Augusta 30902.
Pres. Carlton J. Thaxton, Dir. Lake Blackshear Regional Lib., 307 E. Lamar St., Americus 31709; *1st V.P./Pres.-Elect.* Charles E. Beard, Dir. of Libs., West Georgia College, Carrollton 30117; *2nd V.P.* Anne C. Ansley, Consultant, Media Field Services, State Dept. of Educ., 156 Trinity Ave. S.W., Atlanta 30303; *Treas.* Frank R. Lewis, Libn., LaGrange College, LaGrange 30240; *Secy.* Marjorie J. Clark, Head Libn., North Georgia College, Dahlonega 30533; *Exec. Secy.* Ann W. Morton, Box 833, Tucker 30084.

Hawaii

Memb. 483. Term of Office. Mar. 1980–Mar. 1981. Publications. *Hawaii Library Association Journal* (bienn.); *Hawaii Library Association Newsletter* (5 per year); *HLA Membership Directory* (ann.); *Directory of Libraries & Information Sources in Hawaii & the Pacific Islands* (irreg.); *Index to Periodicals of Hawaii; Hawaii Legends Index.*
Pres. Lucretia Fudge, Program Coord., Maui Regional Lib., Wailuku, Maui; *V.P./Pres. Elect.* Stella Watanabe, Chief Libn., Hickam AFB, Honolulu; *Secy.* Janet Fujii, Children's Libn., Kaimuki Reg. Lib., Honolulu 96816; *Treas.* Rex Frandsen, Libn. Archivist, BYU-HC, Laie 96762.
Address correspondence to Hawaii Lib. Assn., Box 4441, Honolulu 96813.

Idaho

Memb. 364. Term of Office. June 1, 1980–May 31, 1981. Publication. *The Idaho Librarian* (q.). *Ed.* Doug Birdsall.
Pres. Helen Rambo, Riley Lib., Northwest Nazarene College, Nampa 83651; *V.P./Pres.-Elect.* Sam Sayre, Idaho State Univ. Lib., Pocatello 83209; *Secy.* Elaine Leppert, Caldwell Public Lib., 1010 Dearborn, Caldwell 83605; *Treas.* Lynn Baird, Univ. of Idaho Lib., Serials Dept., Moscow 83843.

Illinois

Memb. 3,470. Term of Office. Oct. 1980–Dec. 1981. Publications. *ILA Reporter* (s. ann.); *Q* (newsletter, 6 per year).
Pres. Robert R. McClarren, 1560 Oakwood Pl., Deerfield 60015; *V.P./Pres.-Elect.* Clayton Highum, Dir., Illinois Wesleyan Univ. Lib., Bloomington 61701; *Exec. Secy.* Judith Coate Burnison, 425 N. Michigan Ave., Suite 1304, Chicago 60611; *Treas.* Stanley D. Moreo, 104 King Arthur Ct., Apt. 3, Collinsville 62234.

Indiana

Memb. (Life) 59; (Indiv.) 1,185; (Inst.) 240. Term of Office. Nov. 1980–Nov. 1981. Publication. *Focus on Indiana Libraries* (6 per year, $6). *Ed.* Elbert L. Watson.
Pres. Mary Bishop, Crawfordsville Public Lib., 222 S. Washington, Crawfordsville 47933; *V.P./Pres.-Elect.* Robert Y. Coward, Franklin College Lib., Franklin 46131; *Secy.* Betty C. Martin, Vigo County Public Lib., One Library Sq., Terre Haute 47807; *Treas.* Leslie R. Galbraith, Chris-

tian Theological Seminary, 1000 W. 42 St., Indianapolis 46208; *Exec. Dir.* Elbert L. Watson, Indiana Lib. Assn., 1100 W. 42 St., Indianapolis 46208.

Address correspondence to the executive director.

Iowa

Memb. 1,540. Term of Office. Jan. 1981–Jan. 1982. Publication. *The Catalyst* (bi-mo.). *Ed.* Naomi Stovall, 921 Insurance Exchange Bldg., Des Moines 50309.

Pres. Beverly Lind, Admin., Northeastern Iowa Regional Lib. System, 619 Mulberry St., Waterloo 50703.

Kansas

Memb. 950. Term of Office. July 1980–June 1981. Publications. *KLA Newsletter* (q.); *KLA Membership Directory* (ann.).

Pres. Dan Masoni, Emporia Public Lib., 110 E. Sixth Ave., Emporia 66801; *V.P./Pres.-Elect.* Virginia Quiring, Farrell Lib., Kansas State Univ., Manhattan 66506; *Secy.* Rebecca Hinton, Topeka Public Lib., 1515 W. Tenth, Topeka 66604; *Treas.* Ron Fingerson, School of Lib. Science, Emporia State Univ., Emporia 66801.

Kentucky

Memb. 1,160. Term of Office. Jan.–Dec. 1981. Publication. *Kentucky Libraries* (q.).

Pres. Sara Leech, Medical Center Lib., Univ. of Kentucky, Lexington 40506; *V.P.* Betty Delius, Dir., Bellarmine College, Louisville 40205; *Secy.* Harold Gordon, Paul Sawyier Lib., Frankfort 40601.

Louisiana

Memb. (Indiv.) 1,404; (Inst.) 84. Term of Office. July 1980–June 1981. Publication. *LLA Bulletin* (q.).

Pres. F. Landon Greaves, Box 302, SLU Sta., Hammond 70402; *1st V.P./Pres.-Elect.* Ben Brady, 3945 Drusilla Dr., Baton Rouge 70809; *2nd V.P.* Patsy Perritt, 1187 Stanford Ave., Baton Rouge 70808; *Secy.* Doyle Sanders, 4135 Inwood Rd., Shreveport 71109; *Exec. Dir.* Chris Thomas, Box 131, Baton Rouge 70821; *Parliamentarian.* Anna Perrault, 5609 Valley Forge Dr., Baton Rouge 70808.

Address corespondence to the executive director.

Maine

Memb. 700. Term of Office. (*Pres.* & *V.P.*). Spring 1980–Spring 1982. Publication. *Downeast Libraries* (4 per year); *Monthly Memo* (12 per year).

Pres. Claire Lambert, Jesup Memorial Lib., 355 Main St., Bar Harbor 04609; *V.P.* Schuyler Mott, Paris Hill, Paris 04271; *Secy.* Richard Sibley, Waterville Public Lib., Waterville 04901; *Treas.* Jonathan Burns, Portland Public Lib., 5 Monument Sq., Portland 04101.

Address correspondence to Maine Lib. Assn., c/o Maine Municipal Assn., Local Government Center, Community Dr., Augusta 04330.

Maryland

Memb. Approx. 900. Term of Office. June 1, 1980–June 1, 1981.

Pres. Dallas Shaffer, Prince George's County Memorial Lib., 6532 Adelphia Rd., Hyattsville 20782; *1st V.P.* Sandy Stephan, Maryland State Dept. of Educ., Div. of Lib. Development & Services, 200 W. Baltimore St., Baltimore 21201; *2nd V.P.* Claudia Sumler, Kent County Lib., Box 386, Chestertown 21620; *Treas.* Robert Greenfield, Maryland Lib. Assn., 115 W. Franklin St., Baltimore 21201.

Massachusetts

Memb. (Indiv.) 1,500; (Inst.) 200. Term of Office. July 1979–June 1981. Publication. *Bay State Librarian* (3 per year). *Co-Eds.* Gary Sorkin, Bd. of Lib. Commissioners, 648 Beacon St., Boston 02215; Robin Robinson-Sorkin, Lowell City Lib., Lowell 01852.

Pres. Bruce Baker, Western Regional Public Lib. System, Springfield 01103; *V.P.* Ann Montgomery Smith, Bd. of Lib.

Commissioners, 648 Beacon St., Boston 02215; *Rec. Secy.* Helen Harding, Gale Free Lib., Holden 01520; *Treas.* Thomas Jewell, Waltham Public Lib., Waltham 02154; *Exec. Secy.* Patricia Demit, Massachusetts Lib. Assn., Box 7, Nahant 01908. Address correspondence to the executive secretary.

Michigan

Memb. (Indiv.) 2,200; (Inst.) 100. Term of Office. Nov. 1, 1980–Oct. 31, 1981. Publications. *Michigan Librarian* (2 per year); *Michigan Librarian Newsletter* (8 per year).
Pres. Howard Lipton, 22504 Statler, St. Clair Shores 48081; *Exec. Dir.* Frances H. Pletz, 226 W. Washtenaw, Lansing 48933.

Minnesota

Memb. 950. Term of Office (*Pres.* and *V.P.*) Nov. 1, 1980–Oct. 31, 1981; *Secy.* Nov. 1, 1980–Oct. 31, 1982; *Treas.* Nov. 1, 1979–Oct. 31, 1981. Publication. *MLA Newsletter* (10 per year).
Pres. Patricia Harpole, Minnesota Historical Society, 690 Cedar St., St. Paul 55101; *V.P./Pres.-Elect.* Mary Wagner, Dept. of Lib. Science, College of St. Catherine, 2004 Randolph Ave., St. Paul 55105; *Treas.* Charles O. Richardson, Goodhue County National Bank Bldg., Red Wing 55066; *Exec. Dir.* Adele Panzer Morris, 16491 Fishing Ave., Rosemount 55068. Address correspondence to the executive director.

Mississippi

Memb. 1,250. Term of Office. Jan. 1981–Dec. 1981. Publication. *Mississippi Libraries* (q.).
Pres. Savan Tynes, Biloxi Public Schools, 213 Miramar Ave., Biloxi, 39530; *V.P./Pres.-Elect.* Jack C. Mulkey, Jackson Metropolitan Lib. System, 301 N. State St., Jackson 39201; *Secy.* Myra Macon, School of Lib. Science, Univ. of Mississippi, University 38677; *Treas.* Kay Miller, Cook Memorial Lib., Univ. of Southern Mississippi, Southern Sta., Box 5053, Hattiesburg 39401; *Exec. Secy.* Kay Mitchell, Box 4710, Jackson 39216. Address correspondence to the executive secretary.

Missouri

Memb. 1,324. Term of Office. Sept. 30, 1980–Sept. 30, 1981. Publication. *Missouri Library Association Newsletter* (6 per year).
Pres. Philip Tompkins, Assoc. Dir., UMKC Libs., 5100 Rockhill Rd., Kansas City 64110; *V.P./Pres.-Elect.* Sallie Henderson, Scenic Regional Lib., 11 S. Washington Ave., Union 63084; *Treas.* Valerie Darst, 626 Taylor St., Moberly 65270; *Secy.* Charlaine Ezell, 821 E. Walnut, Apt. 200, Columbia 65201.

Montana

Memb. 555. Term of Office. June 1980–June 1981. Publication. *MLA President's Newsletter* (4–6 per year).
Pres. Richard Gercken, Great Falls Public Lib., Great Falls 59401; *V.P./Pres.-Elect.* Erling Oelz, Univ. of Montana Lib., Missoula 59812; *Secy.* Esther Dean, Rosebud County Lib., Forsyth 59327.

Nebraska

Memb. 985. Term of Office. Oct. 1980–Oct. 1981. Publication. *NLA Quarterly.*
Pres. Dean Waddel, 5911 Earl Dr., Lincoln 68505; *V.P./Pres.-Elect.* Vern Haselwood, 9919 Pasadena, Omaha 68124; *Secy.* Gale Kosalka, 5003 Sunset Dr., Ralston 68127; *Treas.* Charles Grasmick, 2306 Country Club, Omaha 68104. *Exec. Secy.* Ray Means, Dir., Alumni Memorial Lib., Creighton Univ., 2500 California St., Omaha 68178. Address correspondence to the executive secretary.

Nevada

Memb. 250. Term of Office. Jan. 1, 1981–Dec. 31, 1981. Publication. *Highroller* (6 per year).
Pres. Martha Gould, Washoe County

Lib., Box 2151, Reno 89505; *V.P./Pres.-Elect.* Dean Allen, Clark County School Dist., Curriculum Lib., Las Vegas 89101; *Exec. Secy.* Joyce Lee, Nevada State Lib., Capitol Complex, 401 N. Carson St., Carson City 89710; *Treas.* Wendy Muchmore, Washoe County Lib., Box 2151, Reno 89505.

New Hampshire

Memb. 318. Term of Office. May 1980–May 1981. Publication. *NHLA Newsletter* (bi-mo.).

Pres. Benette Pizzimenti, Concord Public Lib., Concord 03301; *1st V.P.* Carol Nelson, 43 Lyndon St., Concord 03301; *2nd V.P.* John Hallahan, Manchester City Lib., 405 Pine St., Manchester 03104; *Secy.* vacant; *Treas.* Joe Considine, New England College Lib., Henniker 03242.

New Jersey

Memb. 1,600. Term of Office. May 1980–May 1981. Publication. *New Jersey Libraries* (8 per year).

Pres. Dorothy Jones, Dir., East Orange Public Lib., 21 S. Arlington, East Orange 07018; *V.P./Pres.-Elect.* June Adams, Dir., Somerset County Lib., Admin. Bldg., Somerville 08876; *2nd V.P.* Silva Barsumyan, Dir., Union City Public Lib., 324 43 St., Union City 07087; *Past Pres.* Drew Burns, Dir., Wayne Public Lib., 475 Valley Rd., Wayne 07470; *Rec. Secy.* Sara Eggers, Dir., Old Bridge Public Lib., 1 Old Bridge Plaza, Old Bridge 08857; *Corres. Secy.* Susan White, Princeton Univ., Firestone Lib., Princeton 08540; *Treas.* Rowland Bennett, Dir., Maplewood Memorial Lib., 51 Baker St., Maplewood 07040; *Exec. Secy.* Abagail Dahl-Hansen Studdiford, New Jersey Lib. Assn., 221 Boulevard, Passaic 07055.

Address correspondence to the executive secretary.

New Mexico

Memb. 5,001. Term of Office. Apr. 1980–Apr. 1981. Publication. *New Mexico Library Association Newsletter. Ed.* Laurel Drew, Albuquerque Public Lib., 501 Copper N.W., Albuquerque 87102.

Pres. Joseph D. Sabatini, Albuquerque Public Lib., 501 Copper N.W., Albuquerque 87102; *1st V.P./Pres.-Elect.* Jeanne N. Winkles, Lovington Public Lib., 103 N. First St., Lovington 88260; *2nd V.P.* Benjamin T. Wakashige, Box 682, Zuni 87327; *Secy.* Barbara J. Hutchinson, New Mexico State Univ. Lib., Box 3475, Las Cruces 88003; *Treas.* Cecil Clotfelter, Golden Lib., Eastern New Mexico Univ., Portales 88130.

New York

Memb. 4,500. Term of Office. Oct. 1980–Nov. 1981. Publication. *NYLA Bulletin* (10 per year, Sept.–June). *Ed.* Diana J. Dean.

Pres. Patricia Mautino, Curriculum Resource Center, Oswego County BOCES, Mexico 13114; *1st V.P.* Linda Bretz, Monroe County Lib. System, 115 South Ave., Rochester 14604; *2nd V.P.* Jacqueline Miller, Yonkers Public Lib., 70 S. Broadway, Yonkers 10701; *Exec. Dir.* Dadie Perlov, CAE, New York Lib. Assn., 15 Park Row, Suite 434, New York 10038.

Address correspondence to the executive directory.

North Carolina

Memb. 2,500. Term of Office. Oct. 1979–Sept. 1981. Publication. *North Carolina Libraries* (q., $10). *Ed.* Jonathan A. Lindsey, Carlyle Campbell Lib., Meredith College, Raleigh 27611.

Pres. H. William O'Shea, Dir., Wake County Public Libs., 104 Fayetteville St., Raleigh 27601; *1st V.P./Pres.-Elect.* Mertys W. Bell, Dean of Learning Resources, Guilford Technical Institute, Box 309, Jamestown 27282; *2nd V.P.* Philip W. Ritter, Dir., Central North Carolina Regional Lib., 342 S. Spring St., Burlington 27215; *Secy.* David Harrington, Educational Materials Coord., Rowan County Schools, Box 1348, Salisbury 28144; *Treas.* W. Robert Pollard, Head of Reference, D. H. Hill Lib., North Carolina State Univ.,

Raleigh 27607; *Dir. 1.* Carol A. Southerland, Libn., Williamston H.S., Rte. 2, Box 70, Williamston 27892; *Dir. 2.* Emily S. Boyce, Prof., Dept. of Lib. Science, East Carolina Univ., Greenville 27834.

North Dakota

Memb. (Indiv.) 350; (Inst.) 30. Term of Office (*Pres., V.P.,* and *Pres.-Elect.*). Oct. 1979–Oct. 1981. Publication. *The Good Stuff* (q.). *Ed.* Janet Crawford, Mandan Public Lib., Mandan 58554.

Pres. Tom Jones, Dir., Veterans Memorial Public Lib., 520 Ave. A. E., Bismarck 58501; *V.P./Pres.-Elect.* Ron Rudser, Minot State College Lib., Minot 58701; *Secy.* Marilyn Guttromson, North Dakota Legislative Council Lib., Capitol, Bismarck 58505; *Treas.* Cheryl Bailey, Mary College Lib., Bismarck 58501.

Ohio

Memb. (Indiv.) 1,933; (Inst.) 189. Term of Office. Oct. 1980–Oct. 1981. Publications. *Ohio Library Association Bulletin* (q.); *Ohio Libraries: Newsletter of the Ohio Library Association* (8 per year).

Pres. Nancy Wareham, Cleveland Area Metropolitan Lib. System, Cleveland 44106; *V.P./Pres.-Elect.* John Wallach, Dayton Montgomery County Public Lib., Dayton 45402; *Secy.* Linda Blaha, Cuyahoga County Public Lib., Parma Regional Branch, Cleveland 44129; *Exec. Dir.,* A. Chapman Parsons, 40 S. Third St., Suite 409, Columbus 43215.

Address correspondence to the executive director.

Oklahoma

Memb. (Indiv.) 550; (Inst.) 18. Term of Office. July 1, 1980–June 30, 1981. Publication. *Oklahoma Librarian* (bi-mo.).

Pres. Aarone Corwin, 9217 Nawassa, Midwest City 73130; *V.P./Pres.-Elect.* John Walker, East Central Univ., Linscheid Lib., Ada 74820; *Secy.* Sandra Ellison, Oklahoma Dept. of Libs., 200 N.E. 18, Oklahoma City 73105; *Treas.* Norman Nelson, Oklahoma State Univ. Lib., Stillwater 74078; *Exec. Secy.* Peggy Augustine, Central Lib., 400 Civic Center, Tulsa 74103.

Address correspondence to the executive secretary.

Oregon

Memb. (Indiv.) 765; (Inst.) 54. Term of Office. Apr. 1980–Apr. 1981. Publication. *Oregon Library News* (mo.). *Ed.* Nadine Purcell, Lib. Processing Center, 1915 Hazel St., Medford 97501.

Pres. James Meeks, Eugene Public Lib., 100 W. 13 Ave., Eugene 97401; *V.P./Pres.-Elect.* Carol Ventgen, Coos Bay Public Lib., 525 W. Anderson, Coos Bay 97420; *Secy.* June Knudson, Hood River County Lib., 502 State St., Hood River 97301; *Treas.* Martin Stephenson, Corvallis Public Lib., 645 N.W. Monroe, Corvallis 97330.

Pennsylvania

Memb. 2,000. Term of Office. Oct. 1980–Oct. 1981. Publication. *PLA Bulletin* (mo.).

Pres. Scott Bruntjen, Pittsburgh Regional Lib. Center, 100 Woodland Rd., Pittsburgh 15232; *Exec. Dir.* Nancy L. Blundon, Pennsylania Lib. Assn., 100 Woodland Rd., Pittsburgh 15232.

Puerto Rico

Memb. 300. Term of Office. Jan. 1980–Dec. 1982. Publications. *Boletín* (s. ann.); *Cuadernos Bibliotecológicos* (irreg.); *Informa* (mo.); *Cuadernos Bibliográficos* (irreg.).

Pres. Jorge Encarnación; *V.P.* Luisa Vigo Cepeda; *Secy.* Leticia P. Encarnación.

Address correspondence to the Sociedad de Bibliotecarios de Puerto Rico, Apdo. 22898, U.P.R. Sta., Rio Piedras 00931.

Rhode Island

Memb. (Indiv.) 560; (Inst.) 33.Term of Office. Nov. 1980–Oct. 1981. Publication. *Rhode Island Library Association Bulletin* (mo.). *Ed.* Shelley Schlessinger.

Pres. Beth I. Perry, Rhode Island College Lib., Providence 02908; *V.P.* Anne T. Parent, Cranston Public Lib., Cranston 02905; *Secy.* Sally P. Grucan, Rhode Island Historical Society Lib., Providence 02906; *Treas.* Catherine Mello Alves, East Providence Public Lib., East Providence 02915; *Member-at-Large.* David I. Panciera, Westerly Public Lib., Westerly 02891; *N.E.L.A. Councillor.* Constance E. Lachowicz, South Kingstown Public Lib. System, Peace Dale 02883; *A.L.A. Councillor.* Margaret A. Pitsenberger, Providence Public Lib., Providence 02903.

St. Croix

Memb. 29. Term of Office. Apr. 1980–May 1981. Publications. *SCLA Newsletter* (q.); *Studies in Virgin Islands Librarianship* (irreg.).
Pres. Mary Bandyk, Frederiksted Lib., Lagoon St. Complex #3, Frederiksted 00840; *V.P.* Corrine Brodhurst, Box 6554, Christiansted 00820; *Treas.* Mary Bleecker, College of the Virgin Islands, Box 84, Kingshill 00850; *Secy.* Helen Laurence, Public Lib., 49–50 King St., Christiansted 00820; *Bd. Members.* Ena Henderson, Jane Kelley, Sylvia Trout.

South Carolina

Memb. 1,025. Term of Office. Jan.–Dec. 1981. Publication. *The South Carolina Librarian* (s. ann.). *Ed.* Laurance Mitlin, Dacus Lib., Winthrop College, Rock Hill 29733; *News and Views of South Carolina Library Association* (bi-mo.). *Ed.* John Sukovich, Wessels Lib., Newberry College, Newberry 29108.
Pres. F. William Summers, College of Librarianship, Univ. of South Carolina, Columbia 29208; *V.P./Pres.-Elect.* Gerda Belknap, Richland County Public Lib., 1400 Sumter St., Columbia 29201; *2nd V.P.* Pat Scales, Greenville Middle School, Greenville 29615; *Treas.* Donna Nance, Thomas Cooper Lib., Univ. of South Carolina, Columbia 29208; *Secy.* Neal Martin, Francis Marion College Lib., Florence 29501; *Exec. Secy.* Louise Whitmore, Rte. 3, 160 Irwin Rd., Lexington 29072.

South Dakota

Memb. (Indiv.) 427; (Inst.) 69. Term of Office. Oct. 1980–Oct. 1981. Publications. *Book Mark* (bi-mo.); *Newsletter.* Ed. Phil Brown, H. M. Briggs Lib., South Dakota State Univ., Brookings 57006.
Pres. Dora Ann Jones, E. Y. Berry Lib., Black Hills State College, Spearfish 57783; *Pres.-Elect.* Stephen K. Ooten, 1051 Ninth S.W., Huron 57350; *Secy.* Jerry Bowman, 21 Fifth St. S.E., No. 4, Watertown 57201; *Treas.* Rosalie Umphrey, 281½ Upper Valley Rd., Spearfish 57783.

Tennessee

Memb. 1,365. Term of Office. May 1980–May 1981. Publication. *Tennessee Librarian* (q.).
Pres. Wilma Tice, Coord. of Lib. Services, Metropolitan Public Schools, 2301 Tenth Ave. S., Nashville 37204; *V.P./Pres.-Elect.* Ruth Ann Vaden, Trustee, Reelfoot Regional Lib. Center, Martin 38237; *Treas.* Mary Glenn Hearne, Head, Nashville Rm., Nashville Public Lib., Nashville 37203; *Exec. Secy.* Betty Nance, Box 120085, Nashville 37212.

Texas

Term of Office. Apr. 1980–Apr. 1981.
Pres. Ray C. Janeway, Dir., Texas Tech Univ. Lib., Lubbock 79409; *Pres.-Elect.* Leroy R. Johnson, Dir., Institutional Services, Fort Worth Institutional Service Dept., 3210 W. Lancaster, Fort Worth 76107; *Continuing Exec. Dir.* Jerre Hetherington, TLA Office, 8989 Westheimer, Suite 108, Houston 77063.

Utah

Memb. 650. Term of Office (*Pres.* and *V.Ps.*) Mar. 1980–Mar. 1981. Publications. *Utah Libraries* (bienn.); *ULA Newsletter* (irreg.).
Pres. J. Dennis Day, Dir., Salt Lake City Public Lib., 205 E. Fifth St., Salt Lake City 84111; *1st V.P.* Blaine Hall,

Brigham Young Univ., Provo 84602; *2nd V.P.* Jane Peterson, Office of Legislative Research, Utah State Capitol Bldg., Salt Lake City 84111; *Exec. Secy.* Gerald A. Buttars, Utah State Lib. Commission, 2150 S. 300 W., Salt Lake City 84115; *ALA Chapter Councillor.* Nathan Smith, Lib. School, Brigham Young Univ., Provo 84602.

Vermont

Memb. 490. Term of Office. Jan.–Dec. 1981. Publication. *VLA News* (q.).

Pres. Edward Scott, Castleton State College Lib., Castleton 05735; *V.P./Pres.-Elect.* Maxie Ewins, Fletcher Free Lib., Burlington 05401; *Secy.* Ann Turner, Libn., Norwich Univ., Northfield 05663; *Treas.* Marjorie Zunder, Head, Technical Processes, Vermont Dept. of Libs., Montpelier 05602.

Virginia

Memb. 1,067. Term of Office. Dec. 1980–Nov. 1981. Publication. *Virginia Librarian Newsletter* (5 per year).

Pres. Betty Ragsdale, Blue Ridge Regional Lib., Martinsville 24112; *V.P./Pres.-Elect.* H. Gordon Bechanan, 111 Yorkshire Ct., Blacksburgh 24060; *Secy.* Fran Freimarck, Pamunkey Regional Lib., Box 119, Hanover 23069; *Treas.* Donald J. Kenney, Virginia Polytechnic Institute and State Univ., Blacksburg 24061.

Washington

Memb. (Indiv.) 940; (Inst.) 31. Term of Office. Aug. 1979–July 1981. Publications. *Highlights* (bi-mo.); *Password* (bi-mo.).

Pres. Verda R. Hansberry, Seattle Public Lib., Seattle 98104; *1st V.P./Pres.-Elect.* Anthony M. Wilson, Highline Community College, Midway 98031; *2nd V.P.* June Pinnell, Bellingham Public Lib., Bellingham 98225; *Secy.* Zay Pribble Washington Regional Lib. for the Blind and Physically Handicapped, 811 Harrison St., Seattle 98129; *Treas.* Marion J. Otteraaen, Longview Public Lib., Longview 98632.

West Virginia

Memb. (Indiv.) 1,100; (Inst.) 42. Term of Office. Dec. 1980–Nov. 1981. Publication. *West Virginia Libraries* (q.).

Pres. Judy Rule, Cabell County Public Lib., Huntington 25701; *1st V.P./Pres.-Elect.* Ellen Wilkerson, Box 436, Hamlin 25523; *2nd V.P.* Maureen Conley, West Virginia Univ., Medical Center Lib., Morgantown 26505; *Treas.* Dave Childers, West Virginia Lib. Commission, Science & Culture Center, Charleston 25305; *ALA Councillor.* Jo Ellen Flagg, Kanawha County Public Lib., 123 Capitol St., Charleston 25301.

Wisconsin

Memb. 2,000. Term of Office. Jan. 1981–Dec. 1981. Publication. *WLA Newsletter* (bi-mo.).

Pres. John J. Jax, Univ. of Wisconsin-Stout, Pierce Lib., Menomonie 54751; *V.P.* Vida Stanton, Univ. of Milwaukee, School of Lib. Science, Mitchell Hall, Milwaukee 53201; *Admin. Secy.* Bonnie Lynne Robinson, Wisconsin Lib. Assn., 1922 University Ave., Madison 53705.

Wyoming

Memb. (Indiv.) 378; (Inst.) 20; (Sub.) 11. Term of Office. Apr. 1980–Apr. 1981. Publication. *Wyoming Library Roundup* (q.). *Ed.* Linn Rounds, Wyoming State Lib., Cheyenne 82002.

Pres. Lisa Kinney, Albany County Lib., 405 Grand Ave., Laramie 82070; *V.P./Pres.-Elect.* Paul Knoblich, George Amos Memorial Lib., Gillette 82716; *Exec. Secy.* Irene Nakako, Rock Springs Public Lib., Rock Springs 82901.

CANADA

Alberta

Memb. (Indiv.) 309; (Inst.) 79; (Trustee) 36. Term of Office. May 1980–May 1981. Publication. *Letter of the L.A.A.* (mo.).

Pres. Heather-Belle Dowling, Dir., County Strathcona Municipal Lib., 2001

Sherwood Dr., Sherwood Park T8A 3J4; *1st V.P./Pres.-Elect.* B. J. Busch, Head, Education Lib., Univ. of Alberta, Edmonton T6G 2G5; *2nd V.P.* Duncan Rand, Chief Libn., Lethbridge Public Lib., 810 Fifth Ave. S., Lethbridge T1J 4C4; *Treas.* Ann Austin, Libn., Varsity Branch, Calgary Public Lib., 4616 Varsity Dr. N.W., Calgary T3A 1V7; *Hon. Secy.* Donna Gordon, Public Services Lib., Energy and Natural Resources, 9th fl., Petroleum Plaza S., 9915 108 St., Edmonton T5K 2C9.

Address correspondence to the president, Box 1357, Edmonton T5J 2N2.

British Columbia

Memb. 565. Term of Office. June 1, 1980–May 31, 1981. *The Reporter* (6 per year). *Ed.* John Black.

Pres. Mary Beth MacDonald; *V.P.* Ted Dobb; *Secy.* Ellen Heaney; *Treas.* Paul Cook.

Address correspondence to BCLA, Box 46378, Sta. G, Vancouver V6R 4G6.

Manitoba

Memb. 300. Term of Office. Sept. 1980–Sept. 1981. Publication. *Manitoba Library Association Bulletin* (q.).

Pres. Bill Birdsall, Admin. Offices, Elizabeth Dafoe Lib., Univ. of Manitoba, Winnipeg R3T 2N2; *1st V.P.* Virginia Davis, School Lib. Services, Box 1, 1181 Portage Ave., Winnipeg R3G 0T3; *2nd V.P.* Paul Nielson, Instructor, Lib. Technician Program, Red River, Community College, 2055 Notre Dame Ave., Winnipeg R3H 0J6; *Treas.* Hugh Larimer, Reference Dept., Elizabeth Dafoe Lib., Univ. of Manitoba, Winnipeg R3T 2N2; *Corres. Secy.* Joan Turnbull, Henderson Branch, Winnipeg Public Lib., 1044 Henderson Hwy., Winnipeg R2M 2K5; *Rec. Secy.* Barbara Kerfoot, Learning Resources Centre, Red River Community College, 2055 Notre Dame Ave., Winnipeg R3H 1J9; *Past Pres.* Carolynne Scott, Calgary Public Lib., 616 MacLeod Trail S.E., Calgary, Alberta.

Address correspondence to Manitoba Lib. Assn., c/o E. MacMillan, 6 Fermor Ave., Winnipeg R2M 0Y2.

Ontario

Memb. 2,400. Term of Office. Nov. 1, 1980–Oct. 31, 1981. Publications. *Focus* (bi-mo.); *Expression* (bi-mo.); *The Reviewing Librarian* (q.); *The Revolting Librarian* (q.).

Pres. Jean Orpwood; *V.P.* Barbara Smith; *Secy.* Shirley Edgar; *Treas.* Jane Moore; *Exec. Dir.* Diane Wheatley; *Past Pres.* Kenneth R. Frost.

Address correspondence to Ontario Library Assn., Suite 402, 73 Richmond St. W., Toronto M6S 1N6.

Quebec

Memb. (Indiv.) 192; (Inst.) 68; (Commercial) 8. Term of Office. May 1980–May 1981. Publication. *ABQ/QLA Bulletin*.

Pres. Marie-Louise Simon, Bibliothèque municipale, 1380 De l'Eglise, Saint Laurent H4L 2H2; *V.P.* Anne Galler, 5667 Merrimac St., Cote St. Luc; *Treas.* Françoise Brais, Editions Héritage, 300 r. Arran, St. Lambert; *English Secy.* Sharon Huffman, Reginald J. P. Dawson Lib., 1967 Graham Blvd., Mount Royal H3R 1G9; *French Secy.* Madeleine Fink, Bibliothèque municipale, 490 r. Mercille, St. Lambert J4P 2L5.

Saskatchewan

Memb. 270. Term of Office. July 1, 1980–June 30, 1981. Publication. *Saskatchewan Library Forum* (5 per year).

Pres. Karen Labuik, Wapiti Regional Lib., 145 12 St. E., Prince Albert S6V 1B7; *V.P.* Rowena Lunn, Chinook Regional Lib., 1240 Chaplin St. W., Swiss Current S9H 0G8; *Secy.* Donna Wells, Frances Morrison Public Lib., 311 23 St. E., Saskatoon S7K 0J6; *Treas.* Catherine Macauley, Regina Public Lib., 2311 12 Ave., Regina S4P 0N3.

Address correspondence to the secretary, Box 3388, Regina S4P 3H1.

REGIONAL

Atlantic Provinces: N.B., Nfld., N.S., P.E.I.

Memb. (Indiv.) 310; (Inst.) 185. Term of Office. May 1980-Apr. 1981. Publication. *APLA Bulletin* (bi-mo.).

Pres. Lorraine McQueen; *Pres.-Elect.* Ann Neville; *V.P. Nova Scotia.* Iain Bates; *V.P. Prince Edward Island.* Pam Forsyth; *V.P. Newfoundland.* Barbara Eddy; *V.P. New Brunswick.* Claude Potvin; *Secy.* Susan Whiteside; *Treas.* Betty Sutherland.

Address correspondence to Atlantic Provinces Lib. Assn., c/o School of Lib. Service, Dalhousie Univ., Halifax B3H 4H8, Nova Scotia.

Middle Atlantic: DE, MD, NJ, PA, WV

Term of Office. Jan. 1981-Jan. 1982.

Pres. Jane E. Hukill, Brandywine College Lib., Box 7139, Concord Pike, Wilmington, DE 19803; *V.P.* Nicholas Winowich, Kanawha County Public Lib., 123 Capitol St., Charleston, WV 25301; *Secy.-Treas.* Richard Parsons, Baltimore County Public Lib., 320 York Rd., Towson, MD 21204.

Midwest: IL, IN, IA, MI, MN, OH, WI

Term of Office. Oct. 1979-Oct. 1983.

Pres. Robert H. Donahugh, Dir., Public Lib. of Youngstown and Mahoning County, 305 Wick Ave., Youngstown, OH 44503; *V.P.* Walter D. Morrill, Box 287, Duggan Lib., Hanover College, Hanover, IN 47243; *Secy.* Joseph Kimbrough, Dir., Minneapolis Public Lib. & Info. Center, 300 Nicollet Mall, Minneapolis, MN 55401; *Treas.* Frances Pletz, Michigan Lib. Assn., 226 W. Washtenaw, Lansing, MI 48933.

Address correspondence to the president, Midwest Federation of Lib. Assns.

Mountain Plains: CO, KS, NE, NV, ND, SD, UT, WY

Publication. *MPLA Newsletter* (bi-mo.).

Pres. Jane Kolbe, Dir., Sioux Falls College Lib., Sioux Falls, SD 57101; *V.P./Pres.-Elect.* Dorothy Middleton, East High School, 2800 E. Pershing Blvd., Cheyenne, WY 82001; *Secy.* Carol White, Univ. of Wyoming Libs., Laramie, WY 82070; *Exec. Secy.* Joe Edelen, Head, Technical Services, Univ. of South Dakota Lib., Vermillion, SD 57069.

New England: CT, MA, ME, NH, RI, VT

Term of Office. Oct. 1980-Sept. 1981. Publications. *NELA Newsletter* (6 per year). *Ed.* Brenda Claflin, Faxon Lib., 1073 New Britain Ave., West Hartford, CT 06110; *A Guide to Newspaper Indexes in New England; The Genealogists' Handbook for New England Research.*

Pres. Norma Creaghe, Geisel Lib., St. Anselm College, Manchester, NH 03102; *V.P./Pres.-Elect.* Stanley Brown, Dartmouth College Lib., Hanover, NH 03755; *Treas.* Clifton Giles, Univ. of Southern Maine, Gorham, ME 04038; *Secy.* Lucy Sheerr, Fernald Lib. Colby-Sawyer College, New London, NH 03257; *Dirs.* John Jackson, Mary Cheney Lib., Manchester, CT 06040; Denis Lorenz, West Hartford Public Lib., 20 S. Main St., Hartford, CT 06107; *Past Pres.* Edward Chenevert, Portland Public Lib., 5 Monument Sq., Portland, ME 04101; *Exec. Secy.* Lee MacDuffie, Upper Walpole Rd., Walpole, NH 03608.

Address correspondence to the executive secretary.

Pacific Northwest: AK, ID, MT, OR, WA, Alta., B.C.

Memb. 949 (active); 317 (subscribers). Term of Office. (*Pres.* and *1st V.P.*) Oct. 1980-Oct. 1981. Publication. *PNLA Quarterly.*

Pres. William F. Hayes, Boise Public Lib., 715 Capitol Blvd., Boise, ID 83702; *1st V.P.* Joy Scudamore, Greater Vancouver Lib. Federation, 1105 Commercial Dr., Vancouver, B.C. V5L 3X3; *2nd V.P.* Donna Selle, Washington County Cooperative Lib. Services, Box 5129, Aloha, OR 97005; *Secy.* Audrey Kolb, Alaska State Lib./Northern Region, 1215 Cowles, Fairbanks, AK 99701; *Treas.* Kay Salmon, Corvallis Public Lib., Corvallis, OR 97103.

Southeastern: AL, FL, GA, KY, MS, NC, SC, TN, VA, WV

Memb. 2,900. Term of Office. Nov. 1980–Nov. 1982. Publication. *The Southeastern Librarian* (q.).

Pres. Paul H. Spence, Pres., Univ. College Lib., Univ. of Alabama, Birmingham, AL 35294; *V.P./Pres.-Elect.* Barratt Wilkins, State Libn., State Lib. of Florida, Tallahassee, FL 32304; *Secy.* Joseph F. Boykin, Dir., Univ. of North Carolina Lib., Charlotte, NC 28223; *Treas.* Annette L. Phinazee, Dean, School of Lib. Science, North Carolina Central Univ., Durham, NC 27709; *Exec. Secy.* Ann W. Morton, Box 987, Tucker, GA 30084.

Address correspondence to the executive secretary.

Southwestern: AZ, AR, LA, NM, OK, TX

Memb. (Indiv.) 1,658; (Inst.) 231. Term of Office. Oct. 1980–Nov. 1982. Publication. *SWLA Newsletter* (bi-mo.).

Pres. Robert L. Clark, Jr., Dir., Oklahoma Dept. of Libs., 200 N.E. 18 St., Oklahoma City, OK 73150; *Pres.-Elect.* Dorlyn Hickey, Dept. of Lib. Science, North Texas State Univ., Denton, TX 76204; *Rep.-at-Large.* Pat Woodrum, Dir., Tulsa City-County Lib., 400 Civic Center, Tulsa, OK 74103; *Exec. Dir.* Susan K. Schmidt, Box 23713, TWU Sta., Denton, TX 76204.

STATE LIBRARY AGENCIES

The state library administrative agency in each of the states has the latest information on state plans for the use of federal funds under the Library Services and Construction Act. The directors, addresses, and telephone numbers of the state agencies are listed below.

Alabama

Anthony W. Miele, Dir., Alabama Public Lib. Service, 6030 Monticello Dr., Montgomery 36130. Tel: 205-277-7330.

Alaska

Richard B. Engen, Dir., Lib. & Museums, Dept. of Educ., Pouch G., State Office Bldg., Juneau 99811. Tel: 907-465-2910.

Arizona

Sharon G. Womack, Acting Dir., Dept. of Lib., Archives and Public Records, 3rd fl. Capitol, Phoenix 85007. Tel: 602-255-4035.

Arkansas

Frances Nix, State Lib., Arkansas State Lib., One Capitol Mall, Little Rock 72201. Tel: 501-371-1526.

California
Gary E. Strong, State Lib., California State Lib., Box 2037, Sacramento 95809. Tel: 916-445-2585 or 4027.

Colorado
Anne Marie Falsone, Deputy State Lib., Colorado State Lib., 1326 Lincoln St., Denver 80203. Tel: 303-839-3695.

Connecticut
Clarence R. Walters, State Libn., Connecticut State Lib., 231 Capitol Ave., Hartford 06115. Tel: 203-566-4192 or 4301.

Delaware
Sylvia Short, Dir., Delaware Div. of Libs., Dept. of Community Affairs and Economic Development, Box 639, Dover 19901. Tel: 302-736-4748.

District of Columbia
Hardy R. Franklin, Dir., Dist. of Columbia Public Lib., 901 G St., N.W., Washington 20001. Tel: 202-727-1101.

Florida
Barratt Wilkins, State Libn., State Lib. of Florida, R.A. Gray Bldg., Tallahassee 32304. Tel: 904-487-2651.

Georgia
Joe B. Forsee, Dir., Div. of Public Lib. Services, 156 Trinity Ave., S.W., Atlanta 30303. Tel: 404-656-2461.

Hawaii
Ruth S. Itamura, Asst. Superintendent/State Libn., Div. of Lib. Services, Dept. of Educ., Box 2360, Honolulu 96804. Tel: 808-548-2431 (through overseas operator 8-556-0220).

Idaho
Charles M. Bolles, State Libn., Idaho State Lib., 325 W. State St., Boise 83702. Tel: 208-334-2150.

Illinois
Kathryn J. Gesterfield, Dir., Illinois State Lib., Centennial Memorial Bldg., Springfield 62756. Tel: 217-782-2994.

Indiana
C. Ray Ewick, Dir., Indiana State Lib., 140 N. Senate Ave., Indianapolis 46204. Tel: 317-232-3692.

Iowa
Barry L. Porter, Dir., State Lib. Commission of Iowa, Des Moines 50319. Tel: 515-281-4105.

Kansas
Ernestine Gilliland, State Libn., Kansas State Lib., 3rd fl., State Capitol, Topeka 66612. Tel: 913-296-3296.

Kentucky
James A. Nelson, State Libn., Kentucky Dept. of Lib. and Archives, Box 537, Frankfort 40602. Tel: 502-564-7910.

Louisiana
Thomas F. Jaques, State Libn., Louisiana State Lib., Box 131, Baton Rouge 70821. Tel: 504-342-4923.

Maine
J. Gary Nichols, State Libn., Maine State Lib., Cultural Bldg., State House Sta. 64, Augusta 04333. Tel: 207-289-3561.

Maryland
Nettie B. Taylor, Asst. State Superintendent for Libs., Div. of Lib. Development and Services, State Dept. of Educ., 200 W. Baltimore St., Baltimore 21201. Tel: 301-659-2000.

Massachusetts
Roland Piggford, Interim Dir., Massachusetts Bd. of Lib. Commissioners, 648 Beacon St., Boston 02215. Tel: 617-267-9400.

Michigan
Francis X. Scannell, State Libn., Michigan State Lib., 735 E. Michigan Ave., Lansing 48913. Tel: 517-373-1580.

Minnesota
William Asp, Dir., Lib. Div., Dept. of Educ., 301 Hanover Bldg., 480 Cedar St., St. Paul 55101. Tel: 612-296-2821.

Mississippi
David M. Woodburn, Acting Dir., Mississippi Lib. Comm., 1100 State Office Building, Box 3260, Jackson 39207. Tel: 601-354-6369.

Missouri
Charles O'Halloran, State Libn., Missouri State Lib., Box 387, Jefferson City 65102. Tel: 314-751-2751.

Montana
Alma Jacobs, State Libn., Montana State Lib., 930 E. Lyndale Ave., Helena 59601. Tel: 406-449-3004.

Nebraska
John L. Kopischke, Dir., Nebraska Lib. Commission, Lincoln 68509. Tel: 402-471-2045.

Nevada
Joseph J. Anderson, State Libn., Nevada State Lib., Capitol Complex, Carson City 89710. Tel: 702-885-5130.

New Hampshire
Avis M. Duckworth, State Libn., New Hampshire State Lib., 20 Park St., Concord 03301. Tel: 603-271-2392.

New Jersey
Barbara F. Weaver, Asst. Commissioner of Educ., Div. of State Lib. Archives and History, 185 W. State St., Trenton 08625. Tel: 609-292-6200.

New Mexico
Clifford E. Lange, Dir., New Mexico State Lib., 300 Don Gaspar St., Santa Fe 87503. Tel: 505-827-2033.

New York
Joseph F. Shubert, State Libn./Asst. Commissioner for Libs., Room 10C34, C.E.C., Empire State Plaza, Albany 12230. Tel: 518-474-5930.

North Carolina
David Neil McKay, Dir./State Libn., Dept. of Cultural Resources, Division of State Library, 109 E. Jones St., Raleigh 27611. Tel: 919-733-2570.

North Dakota
Richard J. Wolfert, State Libn., North Dakota State Lib., Bismarck 58505. Tel: 701-224-2492.

Ohio
Richard M. Cheski, Dir., State Lib. of Ohio, 65 S. Front St., Columbus 43215. Tel: 614-466-2693 or 2694.

Oklahoma
Robert L. Clark, Jr., Dir., Oklahoma Dept. of Libs., 200 N.E. 18 St., Oklahoma City 73105. Tel: 405-521-2502.

Oregon
Marcia Lowell, State Libn., Oregon State Lib., Salem 97310. Tel: 503-378-4367.

Pennsylvania
Elliot L. Shelkrot, State Libn., State Lib. of Pennsylvania, Box 1601, Harrisburg 17105. Tel: 717-787-2646.

Puerto Rico
Blanca N. Rivera de Ponce, Dir., Public Lib. Div., Dept. of Educ., Apartado 859, Hato Rey 00919. Tel: 809-753-9191 or 754-0750 (through overseas operator at 472-6620).

Rhode Island

Bruce E. Daniels, Deputy Dir., Dept. of State Lib. Services, 95 Davis St., Providence 02908. Tel: 401-277-2726.

South Carolina

Betty E. Callaham, State Libn., South Carolina State Lib., 1500 Senate St., Box 11469, Columbia 29211. 803-758-3181.

South Dakota

Robert Beamer, Acting State Libn., South Dakota State Lib., State Lib. Bldg., Pierre 57501. Tel: 605-773-3131.

Tennessee

Katheryn C. Culbertson, State Libn. and Archivist, Tennessee State Lib. and Archives, 403 Seventh Ave., N., Nashville 37219. Tel: 615-741-2451.

Texas

Dorman H. Winfrey, Dir.-Libn., Texas State Lib., Box 12927, Capitol Sta., Austin 78711. Tel: 512-475-2166.

Utah

Russell L. Davis, Dir., Utah State Lib., 2150 S. 300 West, Suite 16, Salt Lake City 84115. Tel: 801-533-5875.

Vermont

Patricia E. Klinck, State Libn., State of Vermont, Dept. of Libs., c/o State Office Bldg. Post Office, Montpelier 05602. Tel: 802-828-3261 ext. 3265.

Virginia

Donald R. Haynes, State Libn., Virginia State Lib., Richmond 23219. Tel: 804-786-2332.

Washington

Roderick G. Swartz, State Libn., Washington State Lib., Olympia 98504. Tel: 206-753-5592.

West Virginia

Frederic J. Glazer, Exec. Secy., Science and Cultural Center, West Virginia Lib. Commission, Charleston 25305. Tel: 304-348-2041.

Wisconsin

W. Lyle Eberhart, Asst. Superintendent, Div. for Library Services, Dept. of Public Instruction, 125 S. Webster St., Madison 53702. Tel: 608-266-2205.

Wyoming

Wayne H. Johnson, State Libn., Wyoming State Lib., Barnett Bldg., Cheyenne 82002. Tel: 307-777-7281.

American Samoa

Linette A. Hunter, Program Dir., Office of Lib. Services, Dept. of Educ., Box 1329, Pago Pago 96799. Tel: 633-5869 (through overseas operator).

Guam

Magdalena S. Taitano, Libn., Nieves M. Flores Memorial Lib., Box 652, Agana 96910. Tel: 472-6417 (through overseas operator).

Northern Mariana Islands

Augustine C. Castro, Dir. of Lib. Services, Commonwealth of the Northern Mariana Islands, Saipan 96950. Tel: 6534 (through overseas operator).

Pacific Islands (Trust Territory of)

Harold Crouch, Chief of Federal Programs, Dept. of Educ., Saipan, Mariana Islands 96950.

Virgin Islands

Henry C. Chang, Dir., Libs. and Museums, Dept. of Conservation and Cultural Affairs, Government of the Virgin Islands, Box 390, Charlotte Amalie, St. Thomas 00801. Tel: 809-774-3407 (through overseas operator at 472-6620).

STATE SCHOOL LIBRARY MEDIA ASSOCIATIONS

Alabama
Alabama Lib. Assn., Div. of Children's and School Libns. Memb. 480. Term of Office. Apr. 1980–Apr. 1981 Publication. *ALACS*.
Pres. Joan L. Atkinson, 183 Woodland Hills, Tuscaloosa 35401.

Alaska
[See entry under State, Provincial, and Regional Library Associations—*Ed.*]

Arizona
School Lib. Div., Arizona State Lib. Assn. Memb. 400. Term of Office. Sept. 1980–Sept. 1981. Publication. *ASLA Newsletter*.
Pres. Karen Whitney, 8247 W. Vale Dr., Phoenix 85033; *Pres.-Elect.* Marguerite Pasquale, 934 N. Venice Ave., Tucson 85711; *Secy.* Betty Gilbert, 4429 W. Rovey, Glendale 85301; *Treas.* Jane Cox, 4628 E. Calle Tuberia, Phoenix 85018.

Arkansas
School Lib. Div., Arkansas Lib. Assn. Memb. 294. Term of Office. Jan.–Dec. 1981.
Chpn. Betty Kerns, 15 Sherrill Heights, Little Rock 72202.

California
California Media and Lib. Educators Assn. (CMLEA), Suite 204, 1575 Old Bayshore Hwy., Burlingame 94010. Tel. 415-692-2350. Job Hotline. 415-697-8832. Memb. 1,500. Term of Office. June 1980–May 1981. Publication. *CMLEA Journal* (s. ann.).
Pres. Curtis May, Dir., Lib. Services, San Mateo County Schools, 333 Main St., Redwood City 94063; *Pres.-Elect.* Marian D. Copeland, IMC Coord., Rialto Unified School Dist., 182 E. Walnut Ave., Rialto 92376; *Past Pres.* Lucy Gregor, Scholastic, Inc., 15 Park Vista, Irvine 92714; *Secy.*

Ron McBeath, Dir., Instructional Resources Center, San Jose State Univ., San Jose 95192; *Treas.* Kathy Pabst, 10806 Via Cascabel, San Diego 92124.

Colorado
Colorado Educational Media Assn. Memb. 680. Term of Office. Feb. 1981–Feb. 1982. Publication. *The Medium* (mo.).
Pres. Randall W. Donahoo, St. Vrain Valley School RE 1J, 395 S. Pratt Pkwy., Longmont 80501.

Connecticut
Connecticut Educational Media Assn. Term of Office. May 1980–May 1981.
Officers to be elected. Address correspondence to Admin. Secy., Anne Weimann, 25 Elmwood Ave., Trumbull 06611. Tel. 203-372-2260.

Delaware
Delaware School Lib. Media Assn. Memb. 116. Term of Office. Nov. 1980–Nov. 1981. Publication. *DSLMA Newsletter*.
Pres. Alice J. Thornton, Ogletown Middle School, Chestnut Hill Rd., Newark 19713; *V.P.* Vacant; *Secy.* Mary Lou Hess, Ursuline Academy, 1106 Pennsylvania Ave., Wilmington 19806; *Treas.* Patricia Robertson, Conrad Jr. H.S., Jackson Ave. & Boxwood Rd., Wilmington 19804.

District of Columbia
D.C. Assn. of School Libns. Memb. 150. Term of Office. Aug. 1980–Aug. 1981. Publication. *Newsletter* (3 per year).
Pres. Janice Spencer, Shepherd Elementary School, 14 St. & Kalmia Rd. N.W., Washington 20012; *V.P./Pres.-Elect.* Gwendolyn Cogdell, Jefferson Junior H.S., Eighth & H Sts. S.W., Washington 20024; *Secy.* DeLesta Cross, Seaton School, Tenth St. & RI Ave. N.W., Wash-

ington 20001; *Treas.* Ellen Amy, Fletcher-Johnson School, Benning & C Sts. N.E., Washington 20002. *Immed. Past Pres.* Edna Becton, Randall H.S., Eye St. & Delaware Ave. S.W., Washington 20024.

Florida

Florida Assn. for Media in Education, Inc. Memb. 1,400. Term of Office. Oct. 1980–Oct. 1981. Publication. *Florida Media Quarterly* (q.).

Pres. Shirley L. Aaron, Assoc. Prof., School of Lib. Science, Florida State Univ., Tallahassee 32306; *V.P.* Patricia S. Deniston, Dir. of Learning Resources, Polk Community College, 999 Ave. H N.E., Winter Haven 33660; *Pres.-Elect.* Ronald Slawson, 4618 N.W. 41 Pl., Gainesville 32601; *Secy.* Nancy Young, 8310 N.W. Fourth Pl., Gainesville 32601; *Treas.* Diane Johnson, 9659 86 Ave., North Seminole 33543.

Georgia

School and Children's Lib. Div. of the Georgia Lib. Assn. Term of Office. Oct. 1979–Oct. 1981.

Chpn. Kathy Brock, Rte. 1, Box 130A, Bremen 30110.

Hawaii

Hawaii Assn. of School Libns. Memb. 240. Term of Office. Apr. 1980–Apr. 1981. Publication. *The Golden Key* (biann.).

Pres. Penny Boyne, Mid-Pacific Institute, 2445 Kaala St., Honolulu 96822; *V.P.* Ruth Petrowski, Koko Head Elementary School, 189 Lunalilo Home Rd., Honolulu 96825.

Idaho

School Libs. Div. of the Idaho Lib. Assn. Term of Office. May 1980–May 1981. Publication. Column in *The Idaho Librarian* (q.).

Chpn. Vera Kenyon, Libn., Wilder Public Schools, Wilder 83676; *Chpn.-Elect.* Vaughn Overlie, Libn., Genessee Public Schools, Genessee 83832.

Illinois

Illinois Assn. for Media in Education (IAME). (Formerly Illinois Assn. of School Libns.) Memb. 750. Term of Office. Jan. 1981–Dec. 1981. Publication. *IAME News for You* (q.). *Ed.* Charles Rusiewski, 207 E. Chester, Nashville 62263.

Pres. Carolyn Rohrer, 324 Carmelhead La., Palatine 60193.

Indiana

Assn. for Indiana Media Educators. Memb. 950. Term of Office (Pres.). Apr. 24, 1980–Apr. 30, 1981. Publication. *Indiana Media Journal.*

Pres. Lavon Hart, 1230 S. Clinton St., Fort Wayne 46802; *Exec. Secy.* James Thompson, Indiana State Univ., STW 1205, Terre Haute 47809.

Iowa

Iowa Educational Media Assn. Memb. 700. Term of Office. Apr. 1980–Apr. 1981. Publication. *Iowa Media Message* (q.) *Ed.* Roger Volker, 321 Curtiss Hall, Iowa State Univ., Ames 50011.

Pres. Bill Oglesby, C215 East Hall, Univ. of Iowa, Iowa City 52242; *Pres.-Elect.* Eleanor Blanks, Roosevelt H.S., 4419 Center St., Des Moines 50312; *Secy.* Linda Waddle, Cedar Falls H.S., Tenth & Division, Cedar Falls 50613; *Treas.* Norma Whipple, North Scott J.H.S., 205 S. Fifth St., Eldridge 52748.

Kansas

Kansas Assn. of School Libns. Memb. 800. Term of Office. July 1980–June 1981. Publication. *KASL Newsletter* (s. ann.).

Pres. Louise Tilson, 940 N. Wichita, Ulysses 67880.

Kentucky

Kentucky School Media Assn. Memb. 625. Term of Office. Oct. 1980–Oct. 1981. Publication. *KSMA Newsletter.*

Pres. Patricia J. Mize, Rte. 1, Calhoun 42327; *Pres.-Elect.* James R. Connor, Rte. 12, Box 7, London 40741; *Secy.* Barbara L.

Eichholz, Rte. 3, Madisonville 42431; *Treas.* Mary Faye Carr, 929 Rogersyille Rd., Radcliff 40160.

Louisiana

Louisiana Assn. of School Libns., c/o Louisiana Lib. Assn., Box 131, Baton Rouge 70821. Memb. 395. Term of Office. July 1, 1980–June 30, 1981.

Pres. Alex Kropog, Rte. 1, Box 173, Holden 70744; *1st V.P./Pres.-Elect.* Vivian Hurst, 404 Parent St., New Roads 70760; *2nd V.P.* Genevieve M. Wheeler, 1205 Chimney Wood La., New Orleans 70126; *Secy.* Kathryn Derveloy, Rte. 2, Box 491, Springfield 70462; *Treas.* Ina Sarkies, Rte. 3, Box 498, New Iberia 70560.

Maine

Maine Educational Media Assn. Memb. 160. Term of Office. Oct. 1980–Sept. 1982. Publication. *Mediacy* (q.).

Pres. Lucille Emory, Mount Blue H.S., School Dist. No. 9, Farmington 04938; *Pres.-Elect.* Jeff Small, Box 979, Caribou 04736; *V.P.* Jo Coyne, Medonak Valley H.S., Waldoboro 04572; *Secy.* Sue Chapman, Libn., Gray-New Gloucester H.S., Gray 04039; *Treas.* Edna Mae Bayliss, Lot 25, West Village Park, Monmouth 04259.

Maryland

Maryland Educational Media Organization. Memb. 760. Term of Office. Oct. 1980–Oct. 1981. Publication. *MEMO-Random* (newsletter, q.).

Pres. Harry Bock, Prince Georges County Public School, Palmer Park Service, 8437 Landover Rd., Landover 20785; *Pres.-Elect.* Walker Jung, 1942 Sunberry Rd., Dundalk 21222; *Secy.* Jack Burroughs, 6605 Weaver Ct., Laurel 20810; *Treas.* Margaret Denman, Box 056, Westminster 21157; *Past Pres.* Jane Love, George Fox Middle School, Outing Ave., Pasadena 21122.

Massachusetts

Massachusetts Assn. for Educational Media. Memb. 630. Term of Office. June 1, 1980–May 31, 1981. Publication. *Media Forum* (q.).

Pres. James M. Donovan, 9 Eel River Circle, Plymouth 02360; *Pres.-Elect.* Marion Dubrawski, 21 Gladstone St., East Boston 02128; *Secy.* Edna Kotomski, 28 Strathmore Rd., Worcester 01604; *Treas.* Stephen W. Scharl, 6 Hillside Apts., Palmer 01069.

Michigan

Michigan Assn. for Media in Education (MAME), Bur. of School Services, Univ. of Michigan, 401 S. Fourth St., Ann Arbor 48109. Memb. 1,250. Term of Office. 1 year. Publication. *Media Spectrum* (q.).

Pres. Ruth Fitzgerald, 4151 Louis Dr., Flint 48507; *Pres.-Elect.* Margaret Grazier, 17565 Pennington, Detroit 48221; *V.P.* Archie E. Watson, R.R. 2, Box 78, Lawton 49065; *Past Pres.* Edward Howard, 14861 18 Ave., Marne 49435; *Treas.* Les Hotchkiss, 15426 Bealfred, Fenton 48430; *Secy.* Charles St. Louis, 3565 Green St., Muskegon 49444.

Minnesota

Minnesota Educational Media Organization. Memb. 1,200. Term of Office. May 1981–May 1982. Publication. *Minnesota Media*.

Pres. Donald E. Overlie, Owatonna H.S., Owatonna 55060; *Secy.* Mick Briscoe, 500 E. Third St., Morris 56267. *Past Pres.* Saundra S. Hustad, 590 N. Owasso Blvd., St. Paul 55112.

Mississippi

Mississippi Assn. of Media Educators. Memb. 70. Term of Office. Mar. 1980–Mar. 1981. Publication. *MAME* (newsletter, bi-ann.).

Pres. Dale Sellers, Mississippi Gulf Coast Junior College, Perkinston Campus, Perkinston 39573; *Pres.-Elect.* Joan Haynie, Mississippi ETV, Drawer 1101, Jackson 39205; *V.P.* Joseph L. Ellison, Media Center, Jackson State Univ., Jackson 39206; *Secy.* Irene Eaves, 88 Bellair

Dr., Vicksburg 39180; *Treas.* Carolyn Reed, Southern Sta., Box 8214, Hattiesburg 39401.

Missouri

Missouri Assn. of School Libns. Memb. 600. Term of Office. Sept. 1–Aug. 31. Publication. *MASL Newsletter* (4 per year). *Ed.* Mary Reinert, Rte. 3, Nevada 64772.

Pres. Katy Burr, 5 Summersweet La., Ballwin 63011.

Address correspondence to MASL, c/o MLA Exec. Office, 402 S. Fifth St., Columbia 65201.

Montana

Montana School Lib. Media, Div. of Montana Lib. Assn. Memb. 170. Term of Office. May 1980–May 1981. Publication. *Newsletter* (q.).

Chpn. Bruce McIntyre, Office of Public Instruction, Rm. 106, State Capitol, Helena 59601.

Address general correspondence to MSL/MA, c/o Montana Lib. Assn., Montana State Lib., 930 E. Lyndale Ave., Helena 59601.

Nebraska

Nebraska Educational Media Assn. Memb. 400. Term of Office. July 1, 1980–June 30, 1981. Publication. *NEMA Newsletter* (4 per year). *Ed.* Cliff Lowell, Box 485, Holdrege 68949.

Pres. Jim Titterington, Univ. of Nebraska-Lincoln, 421 Nebraska Hall, Lincoln 68522; *Pres.-Elect.* Steve Davis, 322 E. 28, Kearney 68847.

Nevada

Nevada Assn. of School Libns. Memb. 55. Term of Office. Jan. 1, 1981–Dec. 31, 1982.

Chpn. Lynn Ossolinski, Box 5049, Incline Village 89450.

New Hampshire

New Hampshire Educational Media Assn. Memb. 140. Term of Office. May 1980–May 1981. Publication. *ON—LINE* (irreg.).

Pres. Barbara Broderick, Somersworth H.S., Memorial Dr., Somersworth 03878; *1st V.P.* Carol Shelton, Cardigan Mountain School, Canaan 03741; *2nd V.P.* Shelley Lochhead, Hopkinton H.S., Hopkinton 03229; *Treas.* Germaine Schmanska, Lebanon H.S., Lebanon 03766; *Rec. Secy.* Nancy Kantar, Memorial School, Bow 03301; *Corres. Secy.* Marcia Burch, Jr. H.S., Claremont 03743. Address correspondence to NHEMA, 103 N. State St., Concord, NH 03301.

New Jersey

Educational Media Assn. of New Jersey (EMAnj). (Organized Apr. 1977 through merger of New Jersey School Media Assn. and New Jersey Assn. of Educational Communication Technology.) Memb. 1,200. Term of Office. May 1980–Apr. 1981. Publications. *Signal Tab* (newsletter, mo.); *Emanations* (journal, q.).

Pres. Anne Ida King, 3-25 Dorothy St., Fair Lawn 07410; *Pres.-Elect.* Ethel Kutteroff, R.R. 1, M56, Chester 07930; *V.P.* Mary Jane McNally, 249 Belleville Ave., Apt. 43A, Bloomfield 07003; *Rec. Secy.* Jean Rappaport, 156 Bradford St., New Providence 07974; *Corres. Secy.* Alice Domineske, 14 Hinsdale La., Willingboro 08046; *Treas.* Robert Bonardi, 2284 Alpine St., Union 07083.

New Mexico

New Mexico Media Assn. Memb. 100. Term of Office. Apr. 1980–Apr. 1981. Publication. *New Mexico Media News* (bimo.).

Pres. K. Nova Duhrsen, 908 W. Conway, Las Cruces 88001.

New York

School Lib. Media Sec., New York Lib. Assn., 15 Park Row, Suite 434, New York 10038. Memb. 875. Term of Office. Nov. 1980–Nov. 1981. Publications. Participates in *NYLA Bulletin* (mo. except July and Aug.); *SLMS Gram* (s. ann.).

Pres. Carol Kearney, Dir., School Libs., Buffalo City School System, Buffalo 14202; *1st V.P. & Pres.-Elect.* Mary Joan Egan, Lib. Media Dir., Burnt Hills Ballston Lake Central School Dist., Ballston Lake 12019; *2nd V.P.* Rod Jaros, Dir., Lib. Media Services, Horace Greeley H.S., Chappaqua 10514; *Past Pres.* Evelyn Daniel, School of Info. Studies, Syracuse Univ., Syracuse 13210; *Secy.* Barbara Riley, Lib. Media Specialist, Elliot R. Hughes Lib., New Hartford Central Schools, New Hartford 13413; *Treas.* Barbara Jones, Project Dir., School Lib. System, BOCES, Mexico 13114; *SLMS Publications.* Rod Jaros, Chappaqua 10514.

North Carolina

North Carolina Assn. of School Libns. Memb. 900. Term of Office. Oct. 1979–Oct. 1981.

Chpn. Arabelle Shockley, Coord., School Media Services, Winston-Salem/Forsyth County Schools, Winston-Salem 27102; *Chpn.-Elect.* Paula Fennell, Consultant, Div. of Educational Media, Dept. of Public Instruction, Raleigh 27611; *Secy.-Treas.* Jeanette Smith, Dir., Media Services, Forsyth County Day School, Lewisville 27023.

North Dakota

North Dakota Lib. Assn., School Sec. Memb. 84. Term of Office. 1 year. Publication. *North Dakota Media Newsletter* (q.).

Pres. Lorraine Dvorak, Rte. 4, Mandan 58554.

Ohio

Ohio Educational Lib. Media Assn. Memb. 1,800. Term of Office. Oct. 1980–Oct. 1981. Publication. *Ohio Media Spectrum* (q.).

Pres. Betty Wolford, Princeton Jr. H.S., 11157 Chester Rd., Cincinnati 45246; *1st V.P.* Darlene Hunter, Grove City H.S., 4665 Hoover Rd., Grove City 43123; *2nd V.P.* Ralph Carder, Fairborn City Schools, 312 E. Whittier Ave., Fairborn 45324; *Secy.* Mary Behm, 1223 E. River St., Elyria 44035; *Treas.* Betty Carter, 9562 Friar Tuck Dr., West Chester 45069.

Oklahoma

Oklahoma Assn. of School Lib. Media Specialists. Memb. 600. Term of Office. July 1, 1980–June 30, 1981. Publications. "School Library News" column in *Oklahoma Librarian* (q.); "Library Resources" section in *Oklahoma Educator* (mo.).

Chpn. Judy Tirey, Will Rogers Elementary, Edmond 73034; *V. Chpn./Chpn.-Elect.* Pamela Brooks, Eastwood H.S., Tulsa 74145; *Secy.* Jan Voss, Enid Elementary Field Libn., Enid 73701; *Treas.* Charlene Johnson, Pawnee H.S., Pawnee 74058.

Oregon

Oregon Educational Media Assn. Memb. 800. Term of Office. Oct. 1, 1980–Sept. 30, 1981. Publication. *Interchange.*

Pres. Phil Corson, Dist. Media Coord., North Clackamas School Dist., 11250 S.E. 27 Ave., Milwaukie 97222; *Pres.-Elect.* Ruth Stiehl, Oregon State Univ., Education Hall III, Corvallis 97331.

Pennsylvania

Pennsylvania School Libns. Assn. Memb. 1,300. Term of Office. July 1, 1980–June 30, 1982. Publications. *Learning and Media* (4 per year); *027.8* (4 per year).

Pres. Sue A. Walker, 6065 Parkridge Dr., East Petersburg 17520; *V.P./Pres.-Elect.* Anna Harkins, 5630 Glen Hill Dr., Bethel Park 15102; *Secy.* Linda Cook, R.D. 1, Box 170, Guys Mills 16327; *Treas.* Roberta Ireland, 631B Waupelani Dr., State College 16801; *Past Pres.* Celeste DiCarlo, 327 Ridge Point Circle, A-23, Bridgeville 15017.

Rhode Island

Rhode Island Educational Media Assn. Memb. 300. Term of Office. June 1979–June 1981. Publications. *RIEMA Newsletter* (9 per yr.); *Media News* (2 per year).

Address correspondence c/o RIEMA, 5 Whitwell Pl., Newport 02840.
Pres. Rita Stein; *Pres.-Elect.* James Kenny; *Secy.* Lillian Desrosiers; *Treas.* Raymond Amache.

South Carolina

South Carolina Assn. of School Libns. Memb. 600. Term of Office. Apr. 1981–Apr. 1982. Publication. *Media Messenger* (5 per year).
Pres. Alleene Holland, 501 Nottingham Rd., Columbia 29210.

South Dakota

South Dakota School Lib. Media Assn., Sec. of the South Dakota Lib. Assn. and South Dakota Education Assn. Term of Office. Oct. 1980–Oct. 1981.
Pres. Pat Cook, Middle School, Vermillion 57069; *Pres.-Elect.* Ray Novak, Baltic Schools, Baltic 57003; *Secy.* Margaret Maxon, Huron Senior H.S., Huron 57350; *Treas.* Donna Duenwald, Box 493, Platte 57369.

Tennessee

Tennessee Education Assn., School Lib. Sec., 598 James Robertson Pkwy., Nashville 37219. Term of Office. June 1980–June 1981.
Chpn. Margaret Lewis, 709 Holly Ave., South Pittsburg 37380.

Texas

Texas Assn. of School Libns. Memb. 1,800. Term of Office. Apr. 1980–Apr. 1981. Publication. *Media Matters* (2 per year).
Chpn. Linda Garrett, 725 Winifred, Garland 75041; *Chpn.-Elect.* Pam Johnson, Box 26, Rio Vista 76093; *Secy.* Lois McCulley, One Vera Ct., Wichita Falls 76310; *Treas.* Elizabeth Haynes, 10165 Bermuda, El Paso 79925.

Utah

Utah Lib. Assn., School Sec. Memb. 130. Term of Office. Mar. 1980–Mar. 1981. Publications. *Horsefeathers* (newsletter, mo.); *Utah Libraries* (journal, q.).
Chpn. Margaret P. Sargent, 6822 Pine View Circle, Salt Lake City 84121; *V. Chpn.* Mary Jensen, 1125 N. University, Provo 84601; *Secy.-Treas.* Gwen Nutting, 4653 Fortuna Way, Salt Lake City 84117.

Vermont

Vermont Educational Media Assn. Memb. 135. Term of Office. May 1980–May 1981. Publication *VEMA News* (q.).
Pres. William H. Bugbee, Barre Town Elementary School, R.F.D. 2, Barre 05641; *V.P./Pres.-Elect.* Pat Mraz, Champlain Valley H.S., Hinesburg 05461; *Secy.* Fran McKinney, South Royalton H.S., South Royalton 05068; *Treas.* Richard Hurd, Barre City School, Barre 05641.

Virginia

Virginia Educational Media Assn. (VEMA). Term of Office. Nov. 1980–Nov. 1981.
Pres. Barbara Booker, Dir., Media Services, Charlottesville City Schools, Rte. 6, Box 267, Charlottesville 22901.

Washington

Washington Lib. Media Assn. Memb. 700. Term of Office. Jan. 1, 1981–Dec. 31, 1981. Publication. *The Medium* (q.); *The Newsletter* (irreg.).
Pres. Hester Davidson, 3818 N.E. 178 St., Seattle 98155; *Pres.-Elect.* Dave Wagar, 12907 63 N.E., Kirkland 98033; *V.P.* Don Riecks, 21221 Fifth Ave. S., Seattle 98148; *Secy.* Alice Barnard, 4556 52 N.E., Seattle 98105; *Treas.* Bruce Eyer, 212 S. 29 Ave., Yakima 98902.

West Virginia

School Libns. Dept., West Virginia Education Assn. Memb. 6. Term of Office. Nov. 1979–Nov. 1981. Publication. *Newsletter WVSL* (ann.).
Pres. Marilyn Jean Moellendick, 3315 Smith St., Parkersburg 26101; *Pres.-Elect.* Barbara G. Ball, 1010 Kilgore Ave., Cul-

loden 25510; *Secy.-Treas.* Linda Adkins, Box 33, Comfort 25049.

Wisconsin

Wisconsin School Lib. Media Assn., Div. of Wisconsin Lib. Assn. Term of Office. Jan. 1981-Dec. 1981. Publication. *WLA Newsletter* (6 per year). *Ed.* Bonnie Lynne Robinson.

Pres. Eleanor Hoehn, Wauwatosa West H.S., 11400 W. Center St., Wauwatosa 53222; *V.P./Pres.-Elect.* Carol Stanke, Maplewood Jr. H.S., Midway Rd., Menasha 54952; *Secy.* Gloria Barclay, Arrowhead H.S., Hartland 53029; *Financial Advisor.* Glenn Thompson, Univ. of Wisconsin-Eau Claire, Eau Claire 54701; *Past Pres.* Carol Diehl, School Dist. of New London, 901 W. Washington St., New London 54961.

Wyoming

Wyoming School Lib. Media Assn. Memb. 25. Term of Office. May 1980-Apr. 1981.

Chpn. Debbie Proctor, 359 Foothills, Gillette 82716; *Secy.* Vickie Hoff, 511½ 13 St., Rawlins 82301.

STATE SUPERVISORS OF SCHOOL LIBRARY MEDIA SERVICES

Alabama

Ruth H. Johnson and Hallie A. Jordan, Educational Specialists, Lib. Media Services, 111 Coliseum Blvd., Montgomery 36193. Tel: 205-832-5810.

Alaska

Frances M. Leon, Alaska State Lib., Pouch G, Juneau 99811. Tel: 907-465-2919.

Arizona

Mary Choncoff, Libn. and Learning Resources Coord., ESEA IV-B, State Dept. of Educ., 1535 W. Jefferson, Phoenix 85007. Tel: 602-255-5271.

Arkansas

Betty J. Morgan, Specialist, Lib. Services, State Dept. of Educ., Arch Ford Bldg., Capitol Grounds, Little Rock 72201. Tel: 501-371-1861.

California

Gerald W. Hamrin, ESEA Title IV-B Program Administrator, State Dept. of Educ., 721 Capitol Mall, Sacramento 95814. Tel: 916-445-7456.

Colorado

Jerry L. Terrill, Senior Consultant, ESEA Title IV, State Dept. of Educ., 201 E. Colfax, Denver 80203. Tel: 303-839-2234.

Connecticut

Betty V. Billman, Instructional Media Consultant, and Robert G. Hale, Sr., Instructional Television Consultant, State Dept. of Educ., Box 2219, Hartford 06115. Tel: 203-566-5409.

Delaware

Richard L. Krueger, Supv., Lib. Media Services, and ESEA Title IV-B, State Dept. of Public Instruction, John G. Townsend Bldg., Box 1402, Dover 19901. Tel: 302-736-4667.

District of Columbia

Olive De Bruler, Dir., Dept. of Lib. Science, Public Schools of the District of

Columbia, 801 Seventh St. S.W., Washington 20024. Tel: 202-724-4952.

Florida

Eloise T. Groover, Administrator, School Lib. Media Services, State Dept. of Educ., Knott Bldg., Tallahassee 32301. Tel: 904-488-0095.

Georgia

Nancy P. Hove, Coord., Media Field Services, State Dept. of Educ., 156 Trinity Ave. S.W., Atlanta 30303. Tel: 404-656-2418.

Hawaii

Patsy Izumo, Dir., Multimedia Services Branch, State Dept. of Educ., 641 18 Ave., Honolulu 96816. Tel: 808-732-5535.

Idaho

Agatha TeMaat, Consultant, Educational Media (Instructional TV), State Dept. of Educ., Len B. Jordan Bldg., Boise 83720. Tel: 208-384-2113.

Illinois

Marie Rose Sivak, Education Consultant, Lib. Media Services, State Bd. of Educ., 100 N. First St., Springfield 62777. Tel: 217-782-2826.

Indiana

Phyllis Land, Dir., Div. of Instructional Media, State Dept. of Public Instruction, Indianapolis 46204. Tel: 317-927-0296.

Iowa

Betty Jo Buckingham, Consultant, Education Media, State Dept. of Public Instruction, Des Moines 50319. Tel: 515-281-3707.

Kansas

Position vacant. Write to Kansas State Dept. of Educ., 120 E. Tenth, Topeka 66612. Tel: 913-296-3434.

Kentucky

Judy L. Cooper, Program Mgr. for School Media Services, State Dept. of Educ., 1830 Capital Plaza Tower, Frankfort 40601. Tel: 502-564-2106.

Louisiana

James S. Cookston, State Supv. of School Libs., State Dept. of Educ., Rm. 602, Education Bldg., Box 44064, Baton Rouge 70804. Tel: 504-342-3399.

Maine

John W. Boynton, Coord., Media Services, Maine State Lib., LMA Bldg., State House Sta. 64, Augusta 04333. Tel: 207-289-2956.

Maryland

Paula Montgomery, Chief, School Media Services Branch, Div. of Lib. Development and Services, State Dept. of Educ., 200 W. Baltimore St., Baltimore 21201. Tel: 301-796-8300, ext. 264.

Massachusetts

Raymond L. Gehling, Jr., Coord., Lib. and Learning Resources, ESEA Title IV-B, Curriculum Services, Dept. of Educ., 31 St. James Ave., Boston 02116. Tel: 617-727-5742.

Michigan

Francis Scannell, State Dept. of Educ., State Lib. Services, Box 30007, Lansing 48909. Tel: 517-374-9630.

Minnesota

Robert H. Miller, Supv., Educational Media Unit, State Dept. of Educ., Capitol Square Bldg., St. Paul 55101. Tel: 612-296-6114.

Mississippi

Yvonne C. Dyson, State Dept. of Educ., Educational Media Services, Box 771, Jackson 39205. Tel: 601-354-6864.

Missouri

Jo Albers, Lib. Supv., Dept. of Elementary and Secondary Educ., Box 480, Jefferson City 65102. Tel: 314-751-4445.

Montana

Bruce MacIntyre and Deb Carlson, Lib. Media Consultants, State Dept. of Public Instruction, Helena 59601. Tel: 406-449-2468 (MacIntyre) and 406-449-2438 (Carlson).

Nebraska

John Courtney, Media Consultant, ESEA Title IV, State Dept. of Educ., Box 94987, 301 Centennial Mall S., Lincoln 68509. Tel: 402-471-2481.

Nevada

William F. Arensdorf, Chpn., Instructional Materials and Equipment, State Dept. of Educ., Capitol Complex, Carson City 89710. Tel: 702-885-5700, ext. 214.

New Hampshire

Reginald A. Comeau, Consultant, Educ. Media Services, Libs. and Learning Resources, Div. of Instruction, 64 N. Main St., Concord 03301. Tel: 603-271-2401.

New Jersey

Anne Voss, Coord., School and College Media Services, State Dept. of Educ., Trenton 08625. Tel: 609-292-6256.

New Mexico

Dolores Dietz, Coord., ESEA Title IV-B, Libs. and Learning Resources, State Dept. of Educ., Santa Fe 87503. Tel: 505-827-5441.

New York

Lore Scurrah, Chief, Bur. of School Libs., and Coord., ESEA Title IV-B, Bur. of School Libs., State Educ. Dept., Albany 12234. Tel: 518-474-2468.

North Carolina

Elsie L. Brumback, Dir., Div. of Educational Media, State Dept. of Public Instruction, Raleigh 27611. Tel: 919-733-3193.

North Dakota

Patricia Herbel, Coord., Lib. Services and Elementary Curriculum, Dept. of Public Instruction, Bismarck 58505. Tel: 701-224-2281.

Ohio

Theresa M. Fredericka, Lib. Media Consultant, State Dept. of Educ., 65 S. Front St., Rm. 1005, Columbus 43215. Tel: 614-466-2761.

Oklahoma

Carla Kitzmiller, Clarice Roads, and Barbara Spriestersbach, Coords., Lib. and Learning Resources Div., State Dept. of Educ., Oklahoma City 73105. Tel: 405-521-2956.

Oregon

Lyle Wirtanen, Consultant, School Lib. Resources, ESEA Title IV-B, State Dept. of Educ., Salem 97310. Tel: 503-378-5600.

Pennsylvania

Joan P. Diana, Chief, School Lib. Media Div., Bur. of Curriculum Services, State Dept. of Educ., Box 911, 333 Market St., Harrisburg 17108. Tel: 717-783-9230.

Rhode Island

Rita Stein, Consultant, ESEA Title IV-B and School Lib. Resources, State Dept. of Educ., 235 Promenade St., Providence 02908. Tel: 401-277-2617.

South Carolina

Margaret W. Ehrhardt, Consultant, Lib. Services, State Dept. of Educ., Rutledge Bldg., Rm. 706, Columbia 29201. Tel: 803-758-3696.

South Dakota

James O. Hansen, State Superintendent, Div. of Elementary and Secondary Education, Richard F. Kneip Bldg., Pierre 57501. Tel: 605-773-3243.

Tennessee

Christine Brown, Dir., School Lib. Resources, 115 Cordell Hull Bldg., Nashville 37219. Tel: 615-741-1896.

Texas

Mary R. Boyvey, Learning Resources Program Dir., Instructional Resources Div., Texas Education Agency, Austin 78701. Tel: 512-475-6465.

Utah

John E. Gillespie, Jr., Coord., Media Production Sec., Curriculum and Instruction Div., State Office of Educ., 250 E. Fifth S., Salt Lake City 84111. Tel: 801-533-5573.

Leroy R. Lindeman, Administrator, Curriculum and Instruction Div., State Office of Educ., 250 E. Fifth S., Salt Lake City 84111. Tel: 801-533-5550.

Kenneth Neal, Media Utilization Specialist, Curriculum and Instruction Div., State Office of Educ., 250 E. Fifth S., Salt Lake City 84111. Tel: 801-533-6040.

Robert Nohavec, Instructional Design and Media Management Specialist, Curriculum and Instruction Div., State Office of Educ., 250 E. Fifth S., Salt Lake City 84111. Tel: 801-533-5572.

Dorothy Wardrop, Coord., Curriculum Development, Curriculum and Instruction Div., State Office of Educ., 250 E. Fifth S., Salt Lake City 84111. Tel: 801-533-5572.

Vermont

Jean D. Battey, School Lib. Media Coord., ESEA Title IV-B, Div. of Federal Assistance, State Dept. of Educ., Montpelier 05602. Tel: 802-828-3124.

Virginia

Mary Stuart Mason, Supv., School Libs. and Textbooks, State Dept. of Educ., Box 6Q, Richmond 23216. Tel: 804-786-7705.

Washington

Nancy Motomatsu, Supv., Learning Resources Services, Office of State Superintendent of Public Instruction, Olympia 98504. Tel: 206-753-6723.

West Virginia

Carolyn R. Skidmore, Coord., and Susannah G. Dunn, Supv., Libs. and Learning Resources, 1900 Washington St., Rm. 346, Charleston 25305. Tel: 304-348-3925.

Wisconsin

Dianne McAfee Williams, Dir., Bur. of Instructional Media Programs, State Dept. of Public Instruction, Madison 53702. Tel: 608-266-1965.

Wyoming

Jack Prince, Coord., Instructional Resources, State Dept. of Educ., Hathaway Bldg., Cheyenne 82002. Tel: 307-777-7411.

American Samoa

Linette Alapa Hunter, Program Dir., Lib. Services, Office of Lib. Services, Dept. of Educ., Pago Pago 96799.

Pacific Islands (Trust Territory of)

Tomokichy Aisek, Supv., Lib. Services, Dept. of Educ., Truk, Caroline Islands 96942.

Augustine Castro, Dir., Lib. Services, Dept. of Educ., Saipan, Mariana Islands 96950.

Tamar Jordan, Supv., Lib. Services, Dept. of Educ., Majuor, Marshall Islands 96960.

Puerto Rico

Blanca N. Rivera de Ponce, Dir., Public Lib. Div., Dept. of Educ., Hato Rey 00919. Tel: 809-753-9191; 754-0750.

Virgin Islands

Beulah Harrigan, Acting Dir., L.S.I.M. Dept. of Educ., St. Thomas 00801.

INTERNATIONAL LIBRARY ASSOCIATIONS

INTER-AMERICAN ASSOCIATION OF AGRICULTURAL LIBRARIANS AND DOCUMENTALISTS
IICA-CIDIA, Turrialba, Costa Rica

OBJECT

"To serve as liaison among the agricultural librarians and documentalists of the Americas and other parts of the world; to promote the exchange of information and experiences through technical publications and meetings; to promote the improvement of library services in the field of agriculture and related sciences; to encourage the improvement of the professional level of the librarians and documentalists in the field of agriculture in Latin America."

OFFICERS

Pres. Fernando Monge, Centro Internacional de Agricultura Tropical, Cali, Colombia; *V.P.* Yone Chastinet, BINAGRI (Biblioteca Nacional de Agricultura), Brasília, DF, Brazil; *Exec. Secy.* Ana Maria Paz de Erickson, IICA-CIDIA, Turrialba, Costa Rica. (Address correspondence to the executive secretary.)

PUBLICATIONS

Boletín Informativo (q.).
Boletín Especial (irreg.).
Revista AIBDA (2 per year).
Proceedings. Tercera Reunión Interamericana de Bibliotecarios y Documentalistas Agrícolas, Buenos Aires, Argentina, April 10–14, 1972 (U.S. price: $10 including postage).
Proceedings. Cuarta Reunión Interamericana de Bibliotecarios y Documentalistas Agrícolas, Mexico, D.F., April 8–11, 1975 (U.S. price: Memb. $5 including postage; nonmemb. $10 including postage).
Proceedings. Quinta Reunión Interamericana de Bibliotecarios y Documentalistas Agrícolas, San Jose, Costa Rica, April 10–14, 1978 (U.S. price: Memb. $10 plus postage; nonmemb. $15 plus postage).

INTERNATIONAL ASSOCIATION OF AGRICULTURAL LIBRARIANS AND DOCUMENTALISTS
MAFF, Central Veterinary Laboratory,
New Haw, Weybridge, Surrey KT15 3NB, England

OBJECT

"The Association shall, internationally and nationally, promote agricultural library science and documentation as well as the professional interest of agricultural librarians and documentalists." Founded 1955. Memb. 525. Dues. (Inst.) $26; (Indiv.) $13.

OFFICERS

Pres. P. Aries, France; *V.Ps.* H. Haendler, Germany; M.S. Malugani, Costa Rica; *Secy.-Treas.* D. E. Gray, UK; *Ed.* R. Farley, USA.

EXECUTIVE COMMITTEE

H. Buntrock, Luxembourg; S. Contour, France; G. de Bruyn, Netherlands; A. L. Geisendorf, Switzerland; K. Harada, Italy; F. C. Hirst, UK; M. J. MacIntosh, Canada; J. C. Sisan, Philippines; A. T. Yaikova, USSR; representatives of National Assns. of Agricultural Libns. and Documentalists.

PUBLICATION

Quarterly Bulletin of the IAALD (memb.).

AMERICAN MEMBERSHIP

By individuals or institutions.

INTERNATIONAL ASSOCIATION OF LAW LIBRARIES
Vanderbilt Law Library, Nashville, TN 37203, USA

OBJECT

"To promote on a cooperative, nonprofit, and fraternal basis the work of individuals, libraries, and other institutions and agencies concerned with the acquisition and bibliographic processing of legal materials collected on a multinational basis, and to facilitate the research and other uses of such materials on a worldwide basis." Founded 1959. Memb. over 600 in 64 countries.

OFFICERS (1980-1983)

Pres. Igor I. Kavass, Vanderbilt Univ., Law School Lib., Nashville, TN 37203, USA; *1st V.P.* Klaus Menzinger, Bibliothek für Rechtswissenschaft der Universität Freiburg, D-7800 Freiburg, Fed. Rep. of Germany; *2nd V.P.* Ivan Sipkov, Lib. of Congress, Washington, DC 20540, USA; *Secy.* Adolf Sprudzs, Law School Lib., Univ. of Chicago, 1121 E. 60 St., Chicago, IL 60637, USA; *Treas.* Arno Liivak, Rutgers Univ., Law Lib., Camden, NJ 08102, USA.

BOARD MEMBERS (1980-1983)

Officers: Robert F. Brian, Australia; Myrna Feliciano, Philippines; Eric Gaskell; Belgium; Lajos Nagy, Hungary; Fernando de Trazegnies, Peru; Yoshiro Tsuno, Japan; Christian Wiktor, Canada; Shaikha Zakaria, Malaysia.

SERVICES

1. The dissemination of professional information through the *International Journal of Law Libraries* through continuous contacts with the affiliated national groups of law librarians and through work within other international organizations, such as IFLA and FID.
2. Continuing education through the one-week IALL Seminars in International Law Librarianship annually.
3. The preparation of special literature for law librarians, such as the *European Law Libraries Guide,* and of introductions to basic foreign legal literature.
4. Direct personal contacts and exchanges between IALL members.

IALL REPRESENTATIVES

A liaison between the law librarians of their regions and the IALL administration is being appointed for every country or major area.

PUBLICATION

International Journal of Law Libraries (formerly *IALL Bulletin*) (3 per year). *Ed. in Chief.* Arno Liivak, Rutgers Univ. Law Lib., Camden, NJ 08102, USA; *Assoc. Ed. in Chief.* Ivan Sipkov, Law Lib., Lib. of Congress, Washington, DC 20540, USA.

INTERNATIONAL ASSOCIATION OF METROPOLITAN CITY LIBRARIES
c/o P. J. Th. Schoots, Director, Gemeentebibliothek Rotterdam,
Nieŭwe Markt 1, NL-3001 Rotterdam, Netherlands

OBJECT

"The Association was founded to assist the worldwide flow of information and knowledge by promoting practical collaboration in the exchange of books, exhibitions, staff, and information." Memb. 97.

OFFICERS

Pres. Pieter J. van Swigchem, Openbare Bibliothek, Bilderdijkstraat 1-7, The Hague, Netherlands; *Secy.-Treas.* Piet J. Th. Schoots, Gemeentebibliothek, Nieŭwe Markt 1, NL-3001 Rotterdam, Netherlands; *Past Pres.* Juergen Eyssen, Stadtbibliothek Hildesheimer Str. 12, D-3000 Hannover 1, Fed. Rep. of Germany. (Address correspondence to the secretary-treasurer.)

PROGRAM

A research team and correspondents are engaged in drawing up a practical code of recommended practice in international city library cooperation and in formulating objectives, standards, and performance measures for metropolitan city libraries.

PUBLICATIONS

Review of the Three Year Research and Exchange Programme 1968-1971.
Annual International Statistics of City Libraries (INTAMEL).

INTERNATIONAL ASSOCIATION OF MUSIC LIBRARIES, ARCHIVES AND DOCUMENTATION CENTRES (IAML)
Musikaliska akademiens bibliotek
Nybrokajen 11, S-111 48 Stockholm, Sweden

OBJECT

To promote the activities of music libraries, archives, and documentation centers and to strengthen the cooperation among them, to promote the availability of all publications and documents relating to music and further their bibliographical control, to encourage the development of standards in all areas that concern the association, and to support the protection and preservation of musical documents of the past and the present. Memb. 1,800.

OFFICERS (AUG. 1980-MAY 1983)

Pres. Brian Redfern, School of Libnshp., Polytechnic of North London, 207-225 Essex Rd., London N1 3PN, England; *Past Pres.* Barry S. Brook, City Univ. of New York, 33 W. 42 St., New York, NY 10036, USA; *V.P.s.* Maria Calderisi, National Lib., Music Div., Ottawa K1A 0N4, Canada; János Kárpáti, Lib. of the Liszt Ferenc Academy of Music, Box 206, H-1391 Budapest, Hungary; Nanna Schiødt, Svanevaenget 20, DK-2100 København Ø, Denmark; Heinz Werner, Berliner Stadtbibliothek, Breite Strasse 32-34, DDR-102 Berlin, German Democratic Rep.; *Secy.-Gen.* Anders Lönn, Musikaliska akademiens bibliotek, Nybrokajen 11, S-111 48 Stockholm, Sweden; *Treas.* Wolfgang Rehm, Heinrich-Schütz Allee 29, D-3500 Kassel, Fed. Rep. of Germany.

PUBLICATION

Fontes Artis Musicae (4 per year, memb.).

COMMISSION CHAIRPERSONS

Bibliographical Research. François Lesure, Dépt. de la Musique, Bibliothèque Nationale, 2 r. Louvois, F-75002 Paris, France.

Broadcasting Music Libraries. Bengt Kyhlberg, Sveriges Radio, S-10510 Stockholm, Sweden.

Cataloging. Brian Redfern, School of Libnshp., Polytechnic of North London, 207-225 Essex Rd., London N1 3PN, England.

Education and Training. Don L. Roberts, Music Lib., Northwestern Univ., Evanston, IL 60201, USA.

International Inventory of Musical Sources. Kurt von Fischer, Laubholzstr. 46, CH-8703 Erlebach ZH, Switzerland.

International Repertory of Music Literature. Barry S. Brook, RILM Center, City Univ. of New York, 33 W. 42 St., New York, NY 10036, USA.

International Repertory of Musical Iconography. Barry S. Brook, Research Center for Musical Iconography, City Univ. of New York, 33 W. 42 St., New York, NY 10036, USA.

Libraries of Conservatories and Colleges of Music. Anthony Hodges, Royal Northern College of Music, 124 Oxford Rd., Manchester M13 9RD, England.

Music Information Centers. James Murdoch, Australia Music Centre, Box N9, Sydney NSW 2000, Australia.

Public Music Libraries. Eric Cooper, London Borough of Enfield, Music Dept., Town Hall, Green Lanes, Palmers Green, London N13 4XD, England.

Record Libraries. Claes Cnattingius, Sveriges Riksradio, Grammofonarkivet, S-10510 Stockholm, Sweden.

Research Music Libraries. Rudolf Elvers, Westendallee 65, D-1000 Berlin 19, Fed. Rep. of Germany.

US BRANCH

Pres. Harold E. Samuel, Music Lib., Yale Univ., 98 Wall St., New Haven, CT 06520; *Secy.-Treas.* Don L. Roberts, Music Lib., Northwestern Univ., Evanston, IL 60201.

UK BRANCH

Pres. John May, 5 Hotham Rd., London SW15 1QN; *Hon. Secy.* Susan M. Clegg, Birmingham School of Music, Paradise Circus, Birmingham B3 3HG; *Hon. Treas.* Ruth Davies, The Lib., CCAT, Collier Rd., Cambridge CB1 2AJ.

PUBLICATION

BRIO. Eds. Clifford Bartlett, BBC Music Lib., Yalding House, London W1N 6AJ, and Malcolm Jones, Birmingham Public Lib., 2020 Seventh Ave. N., Birmingham, AL 35203 (2 per year; memb.).

INTERNATIONAL ASSOCIATION OF ORIENTALIST LIBRARIANS (IAOL)
c/o Graduate School of Library Studies, Univ. of Hawaii at Manoa,
2550 The Mall, Honolulu, Hawaii 96822

OBJECT

"To promote better communication among Orientalist librarians and libraries, and others in related fields, throughout the world; to provide a forum for the discussion of problems of common interest; to improve international cooperation among institutions holding research resources for Oriental Studies." The term Orient here specifies the Middle East, East Asia, and the South and Southeast Asia regions.

Founded in 1967 at the twenty-seventh International Congress of Orientalists in Ann Arbor, Michigan. The parent organization changed its name at the thirtieth Congress in Mexico City, 1976, to the International Congress of Human Sciences in Asia and North Africa (ICHSANA).

OFFICERS

Pres. G. Raymond Nunn; *Secy.-Treas.* John E. Leide; *Ed.* Eloise Van Niel.

PUBLICATION

International Association of Orientalist Librarians Bulletin (s.ann., memb.).

INTERNATIONAL ASSOCIATION OF SOUND ARCHIVES
c/o David Lance, Keeper, Dept. of Sound Records,
Imperial War Museum, Lambeth Rd., London SE1 6HZ, England

OBJECT

IASA is a UNESCO-affiliated organization that functions as a medium for international cooperation between archives and other institutions that preserve recorded sound documents. The association is involved in such fields as the preservation, organization, and use of sound recordings; techniques of recording and methods of reproducing sound; the international exchange of literature and information; and in all subjects relating to professional sound archive work.

MEMBERSHIP

Open to all categories of archives, institutions, and individuals who preserve sound recordings or have a serious interest in the purposes or welfare of IASA.

OFFICERS (1978-1981)

Pres. Rolf Schuursma, Stichting Film en Wetenschap, Hengereldstr. 29, Utrecht, Netherlands. *V. Ps.* Marie-France Calas, Phonothèque Nationale, 19 r. Richelieu, 75084 Paris Cedex, France. Tor Kummen, Norsk RikskringKasting, Bjornstjerne Bjornsons, Plass 1, Oslo 3, Norway. Dietrich Schüller, Phonogrammarchiv der Österreichischen Akademie der Wissenschaften, Liebiggasse 5, A-1010 Vienna, Austria. *Ed.* Ann Briegleb, Ethnomusicology Archive, Music Dept., Univ. of California, Los Angeles, CA 90024, USA. *Assoc. Ed.* Frank Gillis, Archives of Traditional Music, Indiana Univ., Bloomington, IN 47401, USA. *Secy.* David Lance, Dept. of Sound Records, Imperial War Museum, Lambeth Rd., London SE1 6HZ, England. *Treas.* Ulf Scharlau, Süddentscher Rundfunk, Postfach 837, 7000 Stuttgart 1, Fed. Rep. of Germany.

PUBLICATIONS

An Archive Approach to Oral History.
Directory of IASA Member Archives.
Phonographic Bulletin (3 per year; memb. or subscription).

INTERNATIONAL COUNCIL ON ARCHIVES
Secretariat, 60 r. des Francs-Bourgeois
F-75003 Paris, France

OBJECT

"To establish, maintain, and strengthen relations among archivists of all lands, and among all professional and other agencies or institutions concerned with the custody, organization, or administration of archives, public or private, wheresoever located." Established 1948. Memb. 690 (representing 109 countries). Dues. (Indiv.)

$25; (Inst.) $40; (Archives Assns.) $100; (Central Archives Directorates) $150 minimum, computed on the basis of GNP and GNO per capita.

OFFICERS

Pres. Oscar Gauye; *V.P.s.* Dagfinn Mannsåker; Ms. Soemartini; *Exec. Secy.* C. Kesckeméti; *Treas.* Alfred Wagner. (Address all correspondence to the executive secretary.)

PUBLICATIONS

Archivium (ann.; memb. or subscription to Verlag Dokumentation München, Possenbacher Str. 2, Postfach 71 1009, D-8 Munich 71, Fed. Rep. of Germany).

ICA Bulletin (s. ann.; memb., or U.S. $3).

Microfilm Bulletin (subscriptions to Centro Nacional de Microfilm, Serrano 15, Madrid 6, Spain).

ADPA—Archives and Automation (ann. £3 memb.; subscriptions to L. Bell, Public Record Office, Chancery La., London WC2A 1LR, England).

Guides to the Sources of the History of Nations (Latin American Series, 11 vols. pub.; African Series, 10 vols. pub; Asian Series, 3 vols. pub.).

Archival Handbooks (6 vols. pub.).

INTERNATIONAL FEDERATION FOR DOCUMENTATION
Box 30115, 2500 GC The Hague, Netherlands

OBJECT

To group internationally organizations and individuals interested in the problems of documentation and to coordinate their efforts; to promote the study, organization, and practice of documentation in all its forms, and to contribute to the creation of an international network of information systems.

PROGRAM

The program of the federation includes activities for which the following committees have been established: Central Classification Committee (for UDC); Research on the Theoretical Basis of Information; Linguistics in Documentation; Information for Industry; Education and Training; Classification Research; Terminology of Information and Documentation; Patent Information and Documentation; Social Sciences Documentation; Informetrics. It also includes the BSO Panel (Broad System of Ordering).

OFFICERS

Pres. Ricardo A. Gietz, CAICYT, Moreno 431/33, 1091 Buenos Aires, Argentina; *V.P.s.* S. Fujiwara, Univ. of Tokyo Lib., 3-1, Hongo 7-chome, Bunkyo-ku, Tokyo, Japan; M. W. Hill, Science Reference Lib., British Lib., 25 Southhampton Bldgs., Chancery La., London, England; A. I. Mikhailov, VINITI, Baltijskaja ul. 14, Moscow A219, USSR; *Treas.* Herbert S. White, Grad. Lib. School, Indiana Univ., Bloomington, IN 47405, USA; *Councillors.* Margarita Almada de Ascencio, Mexico City, Mexico; M. Brandreth, Ottawa, Canada; Emilia Currás, Madrid, Spain; I. Essaid, Baghdad, Iraq; C. Keren, Tel-Aviv, Israel; A. van der Laan, The Hague, Netherlands; P. Lázár, Budapest, Hungary; E.-J. Frhr. von Ledebur, Bonn, Fed. Rep. of Germany; S. S. Ljungberg, Södertälje, Sweden; Raimundo N. Fialho Mussi, Brasília, Brazil; V. Stefánik, Bratislava, Czechoslovakia; Mu'azu H. Wali, Lagos, Nigeria; *Belgian Member.* Monique Jucquois-Delpierre, La

Hulpe, Belgium; *Secy.-Gen.* K. R. Brown, The Hague, Netherlands; *Pres., FID/CLA.* P. de Souza Moraes, Rio de Janeiro, Brazil; *Pres., FID/CAO.* B. L. Burton, Hong Kong; *Pres., FID/CAF.* Canute P. M. Khamala, Nairobi, Kenya. (Address correspondence to the secretary-general.)

PUBLICATIONS

FID News Bulletin (mo.) with supplements on document reproduction (q.).
Newsletter on Education and Training Programmes for Specialized Information Personnel (q.).
International Forum on Information and Documentation (q.).
R & D Projects in Documentation and Librarianship (bi-mo.).
FID Directory (bienn.).
FID Publications (ann.).
FID Annual Report (ann.).
Proceedings of congresses; Universal Decimal Classification editions; manuals; directories; bibliographies on information science, documentation, reproduction, mechanization, linguistics, training, and classification.

MEMBERSHIP

Approved by the FID Council; ratification by the FID General Assembly.

AMERICAN MEMBERSHIP

National Academy of Sciences-National Research Council.

INTERNATIONAL FEDERATION OF FILM ARCHIVES
Secretariat, Coudenberg 70, B-1000 Brussels, Belgium

OBJECT

"To facilitate communication and cooperation between its members, and to promote the exchange of films and information; to maintain a code of archive practice calculated to satisfy all national film industries, and to encourage industries to assist in the work of the Federation's members; to advise its members on all matters of interest to them, especially the preservation and study of films; to give every possible assistance and encouragement to new film archives and to those interested in creating them." Founded in Paris, 1938. 64 members in 45 countries.

EXECUTIVE COMMITTEE
(JUNE 1979-JUNE 1981)

Pres. Wolfgang Klaue, DDR; *V.Ps.* Eileen Bowser, USA; David Francis, UK; Vladimir Pogacic, Yugoslavia; *Secy.-Gen.* Robert Daudelin, Canada; *Treas.* Jan de Vaal, Netherlands. (Address correspondence to B. Van der Elst, executive secretary, at headquarters address.)

COMMITTEE MEMBERS

Cosme Alves-Netto, Brazil; Todor Andreykov, Bulgaria; Raymond Borde, France; Freddy Buache, Switzerland; Jon Stenklev, Norway.

PUBLICATIONS

Film Preservation (available in English, French, and German).
The Preservation and Restoration of Colour and Sound in Films.
Film Cataloging.
Study on the Usage of Computers for Film Cataloging.
Handbook for Film Archives.
International Index to Film and Television Periodicals (cards service).
International Index to Film Periodicals (cumulative volumes).

Preservation of Film Posters.
Guidelines for Describing Unpublished Script Materials.
Annual Bibliography of FIAF Members' Publications.
Proceedings of the FIAF Varna Symposium—1977: L'Influence du Cinema Sovietique Muet Sur le Cinema Mondial/ The Influence of Silent Soviet Cinema on World Cinema.

INTERNATIONAL FEDERATION OF LIBRARY ASSOCIATIONS AND INSTITUTIONS (IFLA)
Netherlands Congress Bldg., Box 82128,
2508 EC The Hague, Netherlands

OBJECT

"To promote international understanding, cooperation, discussion, research, and development in all fields of library activity, including bibliography, information services, and the education of library personnel, and to provide a body through which librarianship can be represented in matters of international interest." Founded 1927. Memb. (Lib. Assns.) 151; (Inst.) 752; (Aff.) 87; in 111 countries.

OFFICERS AND EXECUTIVE BOARD

Pres. Else Granheim, Dir., Norwegian Directorate for Public and School Libs., Oslo, Norway; *1st V.P.* G. Pflug, Dir.-Gen., Deutsche Bibliothek, Frankfurt/Main, Fed. Rep. of Germany; *2nd V.P.* Ludmilla Gvishiani, Dir., State Lib. of Foreign Literature, Moscow, USSR; *Treas.* Marie-Louise Bossuat, Dir., Bibliographical Centre of the National Lib., Paris, France; *Exec. Bd.* G. Rückl, Dir., Central Lib. Institute, Berlin, DDR; E. R. S. Fifoot, Bodley's Libn., Bodleian Lib., Oxford, UK; Jean Lowrie, Dir., School of Libnshp., Western Michigan Univ., Kalamazoo, MI, USA; J. S. Soosai, Rubber Research Institute of Malaysia, Kuala Lumpur, Malaysia; *Ex Officio Member.* H. P. Geh, Chpn., Professional Bd., Dir., Württembergische Landesbibliothek, Stuttgart, Fed. Rep. of Germany; *Secy.-Gen.* Margreet Wijnstroom, IFLA headquarters; *Dir.,* IFLA International Office for Universal Bibliographic Control. D. Anderson, c/o Reference Div., British Lib., London, UK; *Dir.,* IFLA Office for International Lending. M. B. Line, c/o British Lib. Lending Div., Boston Spa, Wetherby, West Yorkshire, UK; *Publications Officer.* W. R. H. Koops, Univ. Libn., Groningen, Netherlands; *Professional Coord.* A. L. van Wesemael, IFLA headquarters.

PUBLICATIONS

IFLA Annual.
IFLA Journal (q.).
IFLA Directory (ann.).
IFLA Publications Series.
International Cataloguing (q.).

AMERICAN MEMBERSHIP

American Assn. of Law Libs.; American Lib. Assn.; Art Libs. Society of North America; Assn. of American Lib. Schools; Assn. of Research Libs.; Assn. of Music Libs.; International Assn. of Law Libs.; International Assn. of Orientalist Libns.; International Assn. of School Libns.; Medical Lib. Assn.; Special Libs. Assn. *Institutional Members:* There are 134 libraries and related institutions that are institutional members or affiliates of IFLA in the United States (out of a total of 903), and 37 Personal Affiliates (out of a total of 87).

INTERNATIONAL INSTITUTE FOR CHILDREN'S LITERATURE AND READING RESEARCH
Mayerhofg. 6, A-1040 Vienna, Austria

OBJECT

"To create an international center of work and coordination; to take over the tasks of a documentations center of juvenile literature and reading education; to mediate between the individual countries and circles dealing with children's books and reading." Established Apr. 7, 1965. Dues. Austrian schillings 250 (with a subscription to *Bookbird*); Austrian schillings 270 (with a subscription to *Bookbird* and *Jugend und Buch*).

PROGRAM

Promotion of international research in field and collection and evaluation of results of such research; international bibliography of technical literature on juvenile reading; meetings and exhibitions; compilation and publication of recommendation lists; advisory service; concrete studies on juvenile literature; collaboration with publishers; reading research.

OFFICERS

Pres. Adolf März; *Hon. Pres.* Josef Stummvoll; *V.P.* Otwald Kropatsch; *Dir.* Lucia Binder; *V.-Dir.* Viktor Böhm. (Address all inquiries to director at headquarters address.)

PUBLICATIONS

Bookbird (q.; memb. or Austrian schillings 250 [approx. $14]).

Jugend und Buch (memb. or Austrian schillings 120 [approx. $7]).

Schriften zur Jugendlektüre (series of books and brochures dealing with questions on juvenile literature and literary education in German).

INTERNATIONAL ORGANIZATION FOR STANDARDIZATION
ISO Central Secretariat
1 r. de Varembé, Case postale 56, CH-1211 Geneva 20, Switzerland

OBJECT

To promote the development of standards in the world in order to facilitate the international exchange of goods and services and to develop mutual cooperation in the spheres of intellectual, scientific, technological, and economic activity.

OFFICERS

Pres. Henri-Durand, France; *V.P.* Ralph Hennessy, Canada; *Secy.-Gen.* Olle Sturen, Sweden.

TECHNICAL WORK

The technical work of ISO is carried out by over 160 technical committees. These include:

TC 46—Documentation (Secretariat, DIN Deutsches Institut für Normung, 4-10, Burggrafenstr., Postfach 1107, D-1000 Berlin 30, Germany). Scope: Standardization of practices relating to libraries, documentation and information centers, indexing and abstracting services, archives, information science, and publishing.

TC 37—Terminology (Principles & Co-

ordination) (Secretariat, Osterreichisches Normungsinstitut, Leopoldgasse 4, A-1020 Vienna, Austria). Scope: Standardization of methods for setting up and coordinating national and international standardized terminologies.

TC 97—Computers & Information Processing (Secretariat, American National Standards Institute ANSI, 1430 Broadway, New York, NY 10018, USA). Scope: Standardization in the area of computers and associated information processing systems and peripheral equipment, devices, and media related thereto.

PUBLICATIONS

Catalogue (ann.).
Memento (ann.).
Annual Review.
Bulletin (mo.).
Liaisons.
Member Bodies.

FOREIGN LIBRARY ASSOCIATIONS

The following list of regional and national foreign library associations is a selective one. For a more complete list with detailed information, see *International Guide to Library, Archival, and Information Science Associations* by Josephine Riss Fang and Alice H. Songe (R. R. Bowker, 1980). The *Guide* also provides information on international associations, some of which are described in detail in the article on "International Library Associations" that appears earlier in Part 7 of this volume. A more complete list of foreign and international library associations also can be found in *International Literary Market Place* (R. R. Bowker), an annual publication.

REGIONAL

Africa

International Assn. for the Development of Documentation, Libs. and Archives in Africa, Secy. E. K. W. Dadzie, Box 375, Dakar, Senegal.

Standing Conference of African Lib. Schools, c/o School of Libns., Archivists and Documentalists, Univ. of Dakar, B.P. 3252, Dakar, Senegal.

Standing Conference of African Univ. Libns. Eastern Area (SCAULEA), c/o Univ. Libn., Univ. of Nairobi, Kenya.

Standing Conference of African Univ. Libns. Western Area (SCAULWA), c/o S. C. Nwoye, Univ. Libn., Univ. of Nigeria, Nsukka.

Standing Conference of East African Libns., c/o Tanzania Lib. Assn., Box 2645, Dar-es-Salaam, Tanzania.

The Americas

Assn. of Caribbean Univ., Research and Institutional Libs. (Asociación de Bibliotecas Universitarias, de Investigación e Institucionales del Caribe), Secy. A. Jerrerson, Apdo. Postal S, Estación de la Universidad, San Juan, PR 00931.

Latin American Assn. of Schools of Lib. and Info. Science (Asociación Latinoamericana de Escuelas de Bibliotecologia y Ciencias de la Información), Colegio de Bibliotecologia, Universidad Nacional Autónoma de México, México 20, D.F., Mexico.

Seminar on the Acquisition of Latin American Lib. Materials, SALALM Secretariat, Benson Latin American Collection, Univ. of Texas at Austin, SHR 1-108, Austin, TX 78712.

Asia

Congress of Southeast Asian Libns. (CONSAL), Chpn. Patricia Lim, c/o Singapore Lib. Assn., National Lib., Stamford Rd., Singapore 6, Republic of Singapore.

British Commonwealth of Nations

Commonwealth Lib. Assn., Exec. Secy., Box 534, Kingston 10, Jamaica.

Standing Conference on Lib. Materials on Africa (SCOLMA), c/o Secy. P. M. Larby, Institute of Commonwealth Studies, 27 Russell Sq., London WC1B 5DS, England.

Europe

LIBER (Ligue des Bibliothèques Européennes de Recherche), Assn. of European Research Libs., c/o K. W. Humphreys, European Univ. Institute, Badia Fiesolana, Via dei Roccettini 5, San Domenico di Fiesole, Florence, Italy.

Scandinavian Assn. of Research Libns. (Nordiska Vetenskapliga Bibliotekarieförbundet), c/o Avdelingsbibliotekar Per Morten Bryhn, Universitetsbiblioteket, Drammensveien 42, N-Oslo 2, Norway.

NATIONAL

Afghanistan

Afghan Lib. Assn. (Anjuman Kitab-Khana-I), Exec. Secy. Eidi M. Khoursand, Box 3142, Kabul.

Argentina

Argentine Assn. of Scientific and Technical Libs. and Info. Centers (Asociación Argentina de Bibliotecas y Centros de Información Científicos y Técnicos), Santa Fe 1145, Buenos Aires, Exec. Secy. Olga E. Veronelli.

Australia

Australian School Lib. Assn., c/o Secy., Box 80, Balmain N.S.W. 2041.

Lib. Assn. of Australia, Science Centre, Exec. Dir. Gordon Bower, 35 Clarence St., Sydney, N.S.W.

Lib. Automated Systems Info. Exchange (LASIE), Pres. Dorothy Peake, Box 602, Lane Cove 2066, N.S.W.

State Libns. Council of Australia, Pres. K. A. R. Horn, Lib. Council of Victoria, 328 Swanston St., Melbourne, Vic. 3000.

Austria

Assn. of Austrian Libns. (Vereinigung Österreichischer Bibliothekare—VÖB), Pres. Franz Kroller, c/o Österreichische Nationalbibliothek, A-1014 Vienna.

Assn. of Austrian Public Libs. and Libns. (Verband Österreichischer Volsbüchereien und Volksbibliothekare), Exec. Secy. Rudolf Müller. Langegasse 37, A-1080 Vienna.

Austrian Society for Documentation and Infor. (Österreichische Gesellschaft für Dokumentation und Information—ÖGDI), Exec. Secy. Bruno Hofer, c/o ON, Österreichisches Normungsinstitut, Leopoldsgasse 4, POB 130, A-1027 Vienna.

Belgium

Assn. of Libns. and Documentalists of the State Institute of Social Studies (Association des Bibliothécaires—Documentalistes de l'Institut d'Etudes Sociales de l'Etat), Secy. Claire Gerard, 26 r. de l'Abbaye, B-1050 Brussels.

Assn. of Theological Libns. (Vereniging van Religieus-Wetenschappelijke Bibliothécarissen), Minderbroederstr. 5, B-3800 St. Truiden, Exec. Secy. K. Van de Casteele, Elsbos 16, B-2520 Edegem.

Belgian Assn. for Documentation (Belgische Vereniging voor Documentatie—BVD/Association Belge de Documentation—ABD), Secy.-Gen. Jeanine Dardenne, Box 110, 1040 Brussels 26.

Belgian Assn. of Archivists and Libns.

(Association des Archivistes et Bibliothécaires de Belgique/Vereniging van Archivarissen en Bibliothécarissen van België), Exec. Secy. T. Verschaffel, Bibliothèque Royale Albert I, 4 bd. de l'Empereur, B-1000 Brussels.

National Assn. of French-Speaking Libns. (Association nationale des Bibliothécaires d'Expression française), Exec. Secy. Ch. Massaux, Bibliothèque Central de la Ville de Bruxelles, Palais du Midi, av. de Stalingrad 55A, 1000 Brussels.

Flemish Assn. of Libns., Archivists, and Documentalists (Vlaamse Vereniging van Bibliotheek-, Archief-, en Documentatie-personeel—VVBADP), Exec. Secy. J. Bogaert, Box 59, Goudbloemstraat 10-12, 2000 Antwerp.

Bolivia

Bolivian Lib. Assn. (Asociación Boliviana de Bibliotecarios), Pres. Efraín V. Sánchez, Casilla 992, Cochabamba.

Brazil

Assn. of Brazilian Archivists (Associação dos Arquivis tas Brasileiros), Praça de Botafogo, 186, Sala B-217, Rio de Janeiro.

Brazilian Federation of Lib. Assns. (Federação Brasileira de Associações de Bibliotecários), c/o Pres. Elizabeth Maria Ramos de Carvalho, rua Humberto de Campos 366, ap. 1302, 22430 Rio de Janeiro, R.J.

Bulgaria

Lib. Sec. at the Trade Union of the Workers in the Polygraphic Industry and Cultural Institutions (Bibliotečna Sekcjica pri Zentralnija Komitet na Profsăjuza na Rabotnicite ot Poligrafičeskata Promišlenost i Kulturnite Instituti), Pres. Nikola Červenkov, Zdanov Str. 7, Sofia.

Canada

ASTED, Inc. (Association pour l'Avancement des Sciences et des Techniques de la Documentation/Association for the Advancement of the Science and Technology of Documentation), Dir.-Gen. Arthur Boudrais, 360 r. Le Moyne, Montreal, P.Q. H2Y 1Y3.

Bibliographical Society of Canada (La Société Bibliographique du Canada), Secy.-Treas. Marion D. Cameron, Box 1878, Guelph, Ont. N1H 7A1.

Canadian Assn. for Information Science (L'Association Canadienne des Sciences de l'Information), Pres. Alan H. MacDonald, Box 776, Sta. G, Calgary, Alta. T3A 2G6.

Canadian Assn. of Lib. Schools (Association Canadienne des Écoles des Bibliothécaires), Pres. Gerald Prodrick, School of Lib. and Info. Science, Univ. of Western Ontario, London, Ont. N6A 558.

Canadian Council of Lib. Schools (Conseil Canadienne des Écoles Bibliothéconomie) (CCLS/CCEB), Pres. Daniel Reicher, Dir., École de bibliothéconomie, Univ. de Montréal, Montréal, P.Q. H3C 3J7.

Canadian Lib. Assn., Exec. Dir. Paul Kitchen, 151 Sparks St., Ottawa, Ont. K1P 5E3. (For detailed information on the Canadian Lib. Assn. and its divisions, see "National Library and Information Industry Associations, U.S. and Canada"; for information on the library associations of the provinces of Canada, see "State, Provincial, and Regional Library Associations.")

Chile

Chilean Lib. Assn. (Colegio de Bibliotecarios de Chile), Exec. Secy. Elisa Dominguez, Diagonal Paraguay 383, Torre 11, Apdo. 122, Casilla 3741, Santiago.

China, People's Republic of

China Society of Lib. Science (CSLS) (Zhongguo Tushuguan Xuehui), Secy.-Gen. Tan Xiangjin, 7 Wenjinjie Beijing (Peking).

Chinese Science and Technology Info. Assn. (Zhongguo Kexue Jishu Qingbao

Xuehui), Dir. Wu Heng Heping Li, Beijing (Peking).

Colombia

Colombian Academy of Libns. (Colegio Colombiano de Bibliotecarios—(CCB), Apdo. Aéreo 1307, Medellin.
Colombian Assn. of Libns. (Asociación Colombiana de Bibliotecarios—(ASCOLBI), Apdo. Aéreo 30993, Bogotá, D.E.

Costa Rica

Assn. of Costa Rican Libns. (Asociación Costarricense de Bibliotecarios), Apdo. Postal 3308, San José.

Cyprus

Lib. Assn. of Cyprus (Kypriakos Synthesmos Vivliothicarion), c/o Pedagogical Academy, Box 1039, Nikosia.

Czechoslovakia

Assn. of Slovak Libns. and Documentalists (Zväz slovenských knihovníkov a informatikov), Pres. Vít Rak; Exec. Secy. Bohuchval Šmid, Michalská 1, 885 17 Bratislava.
Central Lib. Council of the Czechoslovak Socialist Republic (Ústřední knihovnická rada ČSR), Pres. Jaroslav Lipovský, c/o Ministry of Culture of the ČSR, Valdštejnská 30, Prague 1-Malá Strana.

Denmark

The Archives Society (Arkivforeningen), Exec. Secy. Dan Tørning, Rigsarkivet, Rigsdagsgården 9, DK-1218 Copenhagen K.
Assn. of Danish Research Libs. (Danmarks Forskningsbiblioteksforening), Pres. Palle Birkelund, c/o Rigsbibliotekarembedet, Christians Brygge 8, DK-1219 Copenhagen K.
Assn. of Danish School Libs. (Danmarks Skolebiblioteksforening), Exec. Secy. Niels Jacobsen, Vejlemosevej 21, DK-2840 Holte.

Danish Assn. of Music Libs., Danish Sec. of AIBM (Dansk Musikbiblioteksforening, Dansk sektion of AIBM), c/o Secy., Irlandsvej 90, KD-2300 Copenhagen K.
Danish Lib. Assn. (Danmarks Biblioteksforening), Pres. K. J. Mortensen, Trekronergade 15, DK-2500 Valby-Copenhagen.

Dominican Republic

Dominican Lib. Assn. (Asociación Dominicana de Bibliotecarios/ASOD-OBI), c/o Biblioteca Nacional, Plaza de la Cultura, Santo Domingo, Pres. Prospero J. Mella Chavier; Secy.-Gen. Veronica Regus de Tosca.

Ecuador

Ecuadorian Lib. Assn. (Asociación Ecuatoriana de Bibliotecarios—AEB), Exec. Secy. Elizabeth Carrion, Casa de la Cultura Ecuatoriana, Casilla 87, Quito.

Egypt

See United Arab Republic.

El Salvador

El Salvador Lib. Assn. (Asociación de Bibliotecarios de El Salvador), c/o Secy.-Gen. Edgar Antonio Pérez Borja, Urbanización Gerardo Barrios Polígono, "B" No. 5, San Salvador, C.A.

Ethiopia

Ethiopian Lib. Assn. (ELA) (Ye Ethiopia Betemetsahft Serategnot Mahber), Exec. Secy. Asrat Tilahun, Box 30530, Addis Ababa.

Finland

Assn. of Research and Univ. Libns. (Tieteellisten Kirjastojen Virkailijat-Vetenskapliga Bibliotekens Tjänstemannaförening R.Y.), Exec. Secy. Anneli Arjasto, c/o Museovirasto, Neryanderinkatu 13, 00100 Helsinki 10.
Finnish Assn. for Documentation (Suo-

men Kirjallisuupalvelun Seura-Samfundet for Litteraturjanst i Finland), c/o Marjatta Okko, Pres., State Institute of Geology, Otaniemi.

Finnish Libns. Assn. (Suomen Kirjastonhoitajat-Finlands Bibliotekarier R.Y.), Exec. Secy. Kari Turunen, Cygnaeuksenkatu 4B11, SF-00100 Helsinki 10.

Finnish Lib. Assn. (Suomen Kirjastoseura-Finlands Biblioteksförening), Exec. Secy. Hilkka M. Kauppi, Museokatu 18, SF-00100 Helsinki 10.

France

Assn. of French Archivists (Association des archivistes français, Exec. Secys. Mme Rey-Courtel and Mlle. Etienne, 60 r. des Francs-Bourgeois, F-75141 Paris, CEDEX 03.

Assn. of France Info. Scientists and Special Libns. (Association Française des Documentalistes et des Bibliotécaires Spécialisés—ADBS), Exec. Secy. Y. Rosenfeld, 5, av. Franco russe, 75007 Paris.

Assn. of French Libns. (Association des Bibliothécaires Français), Exec. Secy. Jean-Marc Léri, 65 r. de Richelieu, F-75002 Paris.

Assn. of French Theological Libs. (Association des Bibliothèques ecclésiastiques de France), Exec. Secy. Paul-Marie Guillaume, 6 r. du Regard, F-75006 Paris.

German Democratic Republic

Lib. Assn. of the German Democratic Republic (Bibliotheksverband der Deutschen Demokratischen Republik), Exec. Secy. Wilfried Kern, Hermann-Matern-Str. 57, DDR-1040 Berlin.

Germany, Federal Republic of

German Assn. for Documentation (Deutsche Gesellschaft für Dokumentation, e.V.—DGD), Exec. Secy. Jürgen Scheele, Westendstr. 19, D-6000 Frankfurt am Main 1.

Assn. of German Archivists (Verein deutscher Archivare—VdA), Exec. Secy. Volker Buchholtz, Hessisches Staatsarchiv, Schloss, D-6100 Darmstadt.

Assn. of German Libns. (Verein deutscher Bibliothekare, e.V.—VDB), Pres. Herman Havekost, Postfach 506, Holzgartenstrasse 16, Universitätsbibliothek, D-7000 Stuttgart 1.

Working Group of Univ. Libs. (Arbeitsgemeinschaft der Hochschulbibliotheken), Chpn. G. Weigand, c/o Universitaetsbibliothek Kiel, Olshausenstrasse 29, D-2300 Kiel 1.

Working Group of Art Libs. (Arbeitsgemeinschaft der Kunstbibliotheken), Exec. Secy. Albert Schug, Kunst- und Museumsbibliothek der Stadt Köln, Kattenbug 18-24, D-5000 Köln 1.

Ghana

Ghana Lib. Assn., Exec. Secy. P. Amonoo, Box 4105, Accra.

Greece

Greek Lib. Assn. (Enosis Ellenon Bibliothakarion), Box 2118, Athens-124.

Guatemala

Lib. Assn. of Guatemala (Asociación Bibliotecológica Guatemalteca), c/o Dir., Biblioteca Nacional de Guatemala, 5a Av. 7-26, Zona 1, Guatemala, C.A.

Guyana

Guyana Lib. Assn. (GLA), Exec. Secy. Pamela Dos Ramos, c/o 76/77 Main St., Box 110, Georgetown.

Honduras

Assn. of Libns. and Archivists of Honduras (Asociación de Bibliotecarios y Archivistas de Honduras), Secy.-Gen. Juan Angel Ayes R., 3 Av. 4 y 5 C., no. 416, Comayagüela, DC, Tegucigalpa.

Hong Kong

Hong Kong Lib. Assn., Pres. R. W. Frenier, c/o Lib., Univ. of Hong Kong, Pofulam Rd., Hong Kong.

Hungary

Assn. of Hungarian Libns. (Magyar Könyvtárosok Egyesülete), Secy. D. Kovács, Box 486, H-1827 Budapest.
Info. Science Society (Tájékoztatási Tudományos Társaság—MTESZ/TTT), c/o Pál Gágyor, Kossuth ter 6-8, Budapest 1055.

Iceland

Icelandic Lib. Assn. (Bókavaröaféiag Íslands), Pres. Th. Thorvaldsóttir, Box 7050, 127 Reykjavík.

India

Indian Assn. of Special Libs. and Info. Centres (IASLIC), Exec. Secy. S. M. Ganguly, P-291. CIT Scheme 6M, Kankurgachi Calcutta 700 054.
Indian Lib. Assn. (ILA), Secy. O. P. Trikha, Delhi Public Lib., S. P. Mukerji Marg, Delhi 110006.
Punjab Lib. Assn., 233 Model Town, Jullundur City-3.

Indonesia

Indonesian Lib. Assn. (Ikatan Pustakawan Indonesia—IPI), Pres. K. Sukarman; Secy. John P. Rompas, Jalan Merdeka Selatan 11, Belakang, Jakarta-Pusant.

Iran

Iranian Lib. Assn., Exec. Secy. M. Niknam Vazifeh, Box 11-1391, Tehran.

Iraq

Iraqi Lib. Assn., Exec. Secy. N. Kamalal-Deen, Box 4081, Baghdad-Adhamya.

Ireland, Republic of

Irish Assn. for Documentation and Info. Services (IADIS), Exec. Secy. Alf Mac-Lochlainn, National Lib. of Ireland, Dublin 2.
Irish Assn. of School Libns. (Cumann Leabharlannaithe Scoile-CLS), Headquarters: The Lib., Univ. College, Dublin 4, Exec. Secy. Sister Mary Columban, Loreto Convent, Foxrock Co., Dublin.
Lib. Assn. of Ireland (Cumann Leabharlann Na h-Éireann), Pres. S. Bohan; Hon. Secy. N. Hardiman, Thomas Prior House, Merrion Rd., Dublin 4.

Israel

Israel Lib. Assn. (ILA) (Irgun Safrane Israel), Secy. R. Porath, Box 7067, Jerusalem.

Italy

Federation of Italian Public Libs. (Federazione Italiana delle Biblioteche Popolari—FIBP), c/o la Società Umanitaria, Via Davario 7, Cap. N., I-20122 Milan.
Italian Libs. Assn. (Associazione Italiana Biblioteche—AIB), Secy. A. M. Caproni, c/o Istituto di Patologia del Libro, Via Milano 76, 00184 Rome.
National Assn. for Public and Academic Libs. (Ente Nazionale per le Biblioteche Popolari e Scholastiche), Via Michele Mercati 4, I-00197 Rome.
National Assn. of Italian Archivists (Associazione Nazionale Archivistica Italiana—ANAI), Secy. Antonio Dentoni-Litta, Via di Ponziano, 15, 00152 Rome.

Ivory Coast

Assn. for the Development of Documentation, Libs. and Archives of the Ivory Coast (Association pour le Développement de la Documentation, des Bibliothèques et Archives de la Côte d'Ivoire), c/o Bibliothèque Nationale, B.P. 20915 Abidjan.

Jamaica

Jamaica Lib. Assn. (JLA), Secy. A. Chambers, Box 58, Kingston 5.

Japan

Japan Documentation Society (Nippon Dokumentêsyon Kyôkai—NIPDOK), Exec. Secy. Tsunetaka Ueda, Sasaki

Bldg., 5-7 Koisikawa 2-chome, Bunkyô-ku, Tokyo 112.
Japan Lib. Assn. (JLA) (Nippon Toshokan Kyôkai), Exec. Secy. H. Kurihara, 1-10 1-chome, Taishido, Setagaya-ku, Tokyo 154.
Japan Special Lib. Assn. (Senmon Toshokan Kyôgikai—SENTOKYO), Exec. Secy. Yasunosuke Morita, c/o National Diet Lib., 1-10-1 Nagata-cho, Chiyoda-ku, Tokyo 100.

Jordan

Jordan Lib. Assn. (JLA), Pres. Anwar Akroush; Secy. Najib Shurbaji; Treas. Butros Hashweh, Box 6289, Amman.

Korea, Democratic People's Republic of

Lib. Assn. of the Democratic People's Republic of Korea, Secy. Li Geug, Central Lib., Box 109, Pyongyang.

Korea, Republic of

Korean Lib. Assn. (Hanguk Tosogwan Hyophoe), Exec. Secy. Dae Kwon Park, 100, 1-Ka, Hoehyun-Dong, Chung-Ku, Box 2041, Seoul.

Laos

Laos Lib. Assn. (Association des Bibliothécaires Laotiens), Direction de la Bibliothèque Nationale, Ministry of Education, Box 704, Vientiane.

Lebanon

Lebanese Lib. Assn. (LLA), Exec. Secy. I. Sadaka, National Lib., p. de l'Etoile, Beirut.

Malaysia

Lib. Assn. of Malaysia (Persatuan Perpustakaan Malaysia—PPM), Secy. Chew Wing, Box 2545, Kuala Lumpur.

Mauritania

Mauritanian Assn. of Libns., Archivists, and Documentalists (Association Mauritanienne des Bibliothécaires, des Archivistes et des Documentalistes—AMBAD), c/o Pres. Oumar Diouwara, Dir., National Lib., Nouakchott.

Mexico

Assn. of Libns. of Higher Education and Research Institutions (Asociación de Bibliotecarios de Instituciónes de Ensenãnza Superior e Investigación—ABIESI), Pres. Elsa Barberena, Apdo. Postal 5-611, México 5, D.F.
Mexican Assn. of Libns. (Asociación Mexicana de Bibliotecarios, A.C.), Pres. Ana Mari Magaloni de Bustamante, Apdo. 27-102, México 7, D.F.

Netherlands

Assn. of Archivists in the Netherlands (Vereniging van Archivarissen in Nederlan—VAN), Exec. Secy. Léon Hustinx, Hoeflaan 65, 5223 JJ 's-Hertogenbosch.
Assn. of Theological Libns. (Vereniging voor het Theologisch Bibliothecariaat), Exec. Secy. R. T. M. Van Dijk, Doddendaal 20, Nijmegen.
Assn. of Univ. Libs. and the Royal Lib. (UKB-Samenwerkingsverband van de Universiteits- en Hogeschoolbibliotheken en de Koninklijke Bibliotheek), Exec. Secy. J. L. M. van Dijk, c/o Bibliotheek Rijksuniversiteit Limburg, Postbus 616, 6200 MD Maastricht.
Dutch Lib. Assn. (Nederlandse Vereniging van Bibliothecarissen, Documentalisten en Literatuuronderzoekers—NVB), Secy. G. van Dijk, c/o Provinciale Bibliotheek van Zeeland, Abdij 9, 4331 BK Middelburg.
Netherlands Assn. of Business Archivists (Nederlandse Vereniging van Bedrijfsarchivarissen—NVBV), Secy. C. L. Groenland, Aalsburg 25 26-6602 WD Wijchen.

New Zealand

New Zealand Lib. Assn. (NZLA), Pres. I. W. Malcolm, 10 Park St., Box 12-212, Wellington 1.

Nicaragua

Assn. of Univ. and Special Libs. of Nicaragua (Asociación de Bibliotecas Universitarias 6 Especializadas de Nicaragua—ABUEN), Secy. Cecilie Aguilar Briceño, Biblioteca Central, Universidad Nacional Autónoma de Nicaragua, Apdo. No. 68, León.

Nigeria

Nigerian Lib. Assn. (NLA), c/o Hon. Secy. E. O. Ejiko, P.M.B. 12655, Lagos.

Norway

Assn. of Archivists (Arkivarforeningen), Secy.-Treas. Atle Steinar Nilsen, Postboks 10, Kringsjå, Oslo 8.

Assn. of Norwegian Research Libns. (Norske Forskningebibliotekarers Forening—NFF), Secy. G. Langland, Malerhaugveien 20, Oslo 6.

Norwegian Lib. Assn. (Norsk Bibliotekforening—NBF), Secy.-Treas. G. Langland, Malerhaugveien 20, Oslo 6.

Pakistan

Pakistan Lib. Assn. (PLA), Exec. Secy. A. H. Siddiqui, c/o Pakistan Institute of Development Economics, Univ. Campus, Box 1091, Islamabad.

Society for the Promotion and Improvement of Libs. (SPIL), Exec. Secy. Akhtar Hamid, Al-Majeed, Hamdard Centre, Nazimabad, Karachi-18.

Panama

Panama Assn. of Libns. (Asociación Panameña de Bibliotecarios), c/o Apdo. 2444, Panama, Republic of Panama.

Papua New Guinea

Papua New Guinea Lib. Assn. (PNGLA), Exec. Secy. Patricia Mehegan, Box 5368, Boroko, P.N.G.

Paraguay

Paraguayan Assn. of Univ. Libns. (Asociación de Bibliotecarios Universitarios del Paraguay—ABUP), c/o Yoshiko M. de Freundorfer, Head, Escuela de Bibliotecologia, Universidad Nacional de Asunción, Asunción.

Peru

Assn. of Peruvian Archivists (Asociación Peruana de Archiveros), Archivo General de la Nación, C. Mañuel Cuadros, Palacio de Justicia, Apdo. 1802, Lima.

Assn. of Peruvian Libns. (Asociación Peruana de Bibliotecarios), Exec. Secy. Amparo Geraldino de Orban, Apdo. 3760, Lima.

Lib. Group for the Integration of Socio-Economic Info. (Agrupación de Bibliotecas para la Integración del la Información Socio-Económica—ABIISE), Dir. Isabel Olivera Rivarola, Apdo. 2874, Lima 100.

Philippines

Assn. of Special Libs. of the Philippines (ASLP), Pres. Susima Lazo Gonzales, Box 4118, Manila.

Philippine Lib. Assn. Inc. (PLAI), Pres. Filomena M. Tann, c/o National Lib., Teodoro M. Kalaw St., Manila.

Poland

Polish Libns. Assn. (Stowarzyszenie Bibliotekarzy, Polskich—SBP), Pres. Witold Stankiewicz; Gen. Secy. L. Toś, ul. Konopczyńskiego 5/7, 00953 Warsaw.

Portugal

Portuguese Assn. of Libns., Archivists, and Documentalists (Associação Portuguesa de Bibliotecários Arquivistas e Documentalistas—BAD), Exec. Secy. Paula Stubs Lacerda, Rua Ocidental ao Campo Grande 83, 1700 Lisbon.

Rhodesia

See Zimbabwe.

Romania, Socialist Republic of

Assn. of Libns. in the Socialist Republic of Romania (Asociatia Bibliotecarilor din

Republica Socialista Romania/Association des Bibliothécaires de la République Socialiste de Roumanie), Pres. G. Botez, Biblioteca Centrala de Stat, Strada Ion Ghica 4, 7001 8 Bucharest.

Scotland

See United Kingdom.

Senegal

Senegal Assn. for the Development of Documentation, Libs., Archives and Museums (Commission des Bibliothèques de l'ASDBAM, Association Sénégalaise pour le Développement de la Documentation, des Bibliothèques, des Archives et des Musées), Gen. Secy. R. Ba, B.P. 375, Dakar.

Sierra Leone

Sierra Leone Lib. Assn. (SLLA), c/o Secy. F. Thorpe, Sierra Leone Lib. Bd., Rokell St., Freetown.

Singapore

Lib. Assn. of Singapore (LAS), Hon. Secy. A. W. K. Ng, c/o National Lib., Stamford Rd., Singapore 0617.

South Africa

South African Indian Lib. Assn. (SAILA), c/o Secy., SAILA, 7 Ascot St., Durban.

Spain

National Assn. of Libns., Archivists and Archeologists (Asociación Nacional de Bibliotecarios, Archiveros, Arqueólogus y Documentalists), Exec. Secy. C. Iniguez, Paseo de Calvo Sotelo 22, Apdo. 14281, Madrid 1.

Sri Lanka (Ceylon)

Sri Lanka Lib. Assn. (SLLA), Exec. Secy. N. A. T. de Silva, c/o Univ. of Colombo, Race Course, Reid Ave., Colombo 7.

Sudan

Sudan Lib. Assn. (SLA), Exec. Secy. Mohamed Omar, Box 1361, Khartoum.

Sweden

Assn. of Special Research Libs. (Sveriges Vetenskapliga Specialbiblioteks Förening —SVSF), Pres. W. Odelberg, c/o Statens Psykologisk-Pedagogiska Bibliothek, Box 23099, 10435 Stockholm.

Swedish Assn. of Archivists (Svenska Arkivasamfundet), Rikjsarkivet, Fack, S-100, 26 Stockholm.

Swedish Assn. of Univ. and Research Libs. (Svenska Bibliotekariesamfundet— SBS), c/o Secy. Birgit Nilsson, Libn., Sveriges Lantbrucks-universitetsbibliotek, Ultunabiblioteket, S-750 Uppsala.

Swedish Council of Research Libs. (Forskningsbiblioteksrådet—FBR), Exec. Secy. Karin Melin-Fravolini, Box 6404, S-113 82 Stockholm 6.

Swedish Lib. Assn. (Sveriges Allmänna Biblioteksförening—SAB), Pres. B. Martinsson, Box 1706, S-221 01, Lund.

Swedish Society for Technical Documentation (Tekniska Litteratursällskapet —TLS), Secy. Birgitta Levin, Box 5073, S-10242 Stockholm 5.

Union of Univ. and Research Libs. (Vetenskapliga Bibliotekens Tjänstemannaförening—VBT), Pres. Bo Strenström, Box 50 S-13101, Nacka 1.

Switzerland

Assn. of Swiss Archivists (Vereinigung Schweizerischer Archivare—VSA), c/o Pres. Walter Lendi, Staatsarchivar, Staatsarchiv St. Gallen, Regierungsgebäude, CH-9001, St. Gallen.

Assn. of Swiss Libns. (Vereinigung Schweizerischer Bibliothekare/Association des Bibliothécaires Suisses/Associazione dei Bibliotecari Svizzeri—VSB/ ABS), Exec. Secy. W. Treichler, Hallwylstrasse 15, CH-3003 Bern.

Swiss Assn. of Documentation (Schweizerische Vereinigung für Dokumentation/Association Suisse de Documentation—SVD/ASD), Secy.-Treas. W. Bruderer, BID GD PTT 3030 Berne.

Tanzania

Tanzania Lib. Assn., Exec. Secy. T. E. Mlaki, Box 2645, Dar-es-Salaam.

Trinidad and Tobago

Lib. Assn. of Trinidad and Tobago (LATT), Secy. L. Elliott, Box 1177, Port of Spain, Trinidad.

Tunisia

Tunisian Assn. of Documentalists, Libns. and Archivists (Association Tunisienne des Documentalistes, Bibliothécaires et Archivistes), Exec. Secy. Rudha Tlili, 43 rue de la Liberté, Le Bardo.

Turkey

Turkish Libns. Assn. (Türk Kütüphaneciler Derneği—TKD), Exec. Secy. Nejat Sefercioglu, Necatibey Caddesi 19/22, P.K. 175, Yenisehir, Ankara.

Uganda

Uganda Lib. Assn. (ULA), Exec. Secy. I. M. Kigongo-Bukenya, Dip. Lib., D.P.A. (Mak), Box 5894, Kampala.

Uganda Schools Lib. Assn. (USLA), Exec. Secy. J. W. Nabembezi, Box 7014, Kampala.

Union of Soviet Socialist Republics

USSR Lib. Council, Pres. N. S. Kartashov, Lenin State Lib., 3 Prospect Kalinina, 101 000 Moscow.

United Arab Republic

Egyptian Lib. and Archives Assn. (ELAA), Exec. Secy. Ahmed M. Mansour, c/o Lib. of Fine Arts, 24 El-Matbâa, Al-Ahlia, Boulaq, Cario.

Egyptian School Lib. Assn. (ESLA), Exec. Secy. M. Alabasiri, 35 Algalaa St., Cairo.

United Kingdom

ASLIB (Association of Special Libraries and Information Bureaux), Dir.-Gen. Basil Saunders, 3 Belgrave Sq., London SW1X 8PL.

Assn. of British Theological and Philosophical Libs. (ABTAPL), Hon. Secy. Mary Elliott, King's College Lib., Strand, London WC2R 2LS.

Bibliographical Society, Hon. Secy. M. M. Foot, The Rooms of the British Academy, Burlington House, Piccadilly, London W1V 0NS.

British and Irish Assn. Of Law Libns. (BIALL), Exec. Secy. D. M. Blake, Libn., Harding Law Lib., Univ. of Birmingham, Box 363, Birmingham B15 2TT.

The Lib. Assn., Exec. Secy. Keith Lawrey, 7 Ridgmount St., London WC1E 7AE.

Private Libs. Assn. (PLA), Exec. Secy. Frank Broomhead, Ravelston, South View Rd., Pinner, Middlesex.

School Lib. Assn. (SLA), Chpn. Don H. Rogers, Victoria House, 29-31 George St., Oxford OX1 2AY.

Scottish Lib. Assn. (SLA), Hon. Secy. M. C. Hood, The Mitchell Lib., North St., Glasgow G3 7DN.

Society of Archivists (SA), Exec. Secy. C. M. Short, South Yorkshire County Record Office, Cultural Activities Centre, 56 Ellin St., Sheffield SI 4PL.

The Standing Conference of National and Univ. Libs. (SCONUL), Exec. Secy. A. J. Loveday, Secretariat and Registered Office, 102 Euston St., London NW1 2HA.

Welsh Lib. Assn., Exec. Secy. Geoffrey Thomas, Gwynedd Lib. Service, Maesincla, Caernarfon Gwynedd, North Wales.

Uruguay

Lib. and Archive Science Assn. of Uruguay (Agrupación Bibliotecológica del Uruguay—ABU), Pres. Luis Alberto Musso, Cerro Largo 1666, Montevideo.

Venezuela

Assn. of Venezuelan Libns. and Archivists (Colegio de Bibliotecólogos y Archivólogos de Venezuela—COL-BAV), Exec. Secy. M. Hermoso, Apdo. 6283, Caracas 101.

Wales.

See United Kingdom.

Yugoslavia

Croatian Lib. Assn. (Hrvatsko bibliotekarsko društvo—HBD), Pres. Vera Mudri-Škunca; Exec. Secy. Nada Gomercić, National and Univ. Lib., Marulicev trg 21, YU-41000 Zagreb.

Lib. Assn. of Bosnia and Herzegovina (Društvo Bibliotekara Bosne i Hercegovine—DB BiH), Exec. Secy. Fahrudin Kalender, Obala 42, YU-71000 Sarajevo.

Society of Libns. in Slovenia (Društvo bibliotekarjev Slovenije—DBS), Exec. Secy. Majda Armeni, Turjaška 1, YU-61000 Ljubljana.

Society of Libns. of Macedonia (Društvo na bibliotekarite na SR Makedonija), c/o Bulevar "Goce Delčev", b b, YU-91000 Skopje.

Union of Lib. Workers of Serbia (Savez Bibliotečkih Radnika Srbije), Exec. Secy. Branka Popović, Skerlićeva 1, YU-11000 Belgrade.

Union of Libns. Assns. of Yugoslavia (Sveza društev bibliotekarjev Jugoslavije), Exec. Secy. Božika Zdravković, Ramiz Sadiku b b, YU-38000 Priština.

Zaire

Zairian Assn. of Archivists, Libns. and Documentalists (Association Zairoise des Archivistes, Bibliothécaires et Documentalistes—AZABDO), Exec. Secy. Mulamba Mukunya, Box 805, Kinshasa X1, Zaire.

Zambia

Zambia Lib. Assn. (ZLA), Box 32839, Lusaka.

Zimbabwe (formerly Rhodesia)

Zimbabwe Lib. Assn.—ZLA (formerly Rhodesia Lib. Assn.), Hon. Secy. B. L. B. Mushonga, Box 3133, Salisbury.

Directory of Book Trade and Related Organizations

BOOK TRADE ASSOCIATIONS, UNITED STATES AND CANADA

For more extensive information on the associations listed in this section, see the annual issues of the *Literary Market Place* (Bowker).

Advertising Typographers Assn. of America, Inc., 461 Eighth Ave., New York, NY 10001. 212-594-0685.

American Booksellers Assn., Inc., 122 E. 42 St., New York, NY 10168. 212-867-9060. *Pres.* Joan Ripley; *Exec. Dir.* G. Roysce Smith.

American Institute of Graphic Arts, 1059 Third Ave., near 63 St., New York, NY 10021. 212-752-0813. *Pres.* James K. Fogleman; *Exec. Dir.* Caroline W. Hightower.

American Medical Publishers Assn. *Pres.* G. James Gallagher, Williams & Wilkins Co., Baltimore, MD 21202. 301-528-4211; *Secy.-Treas.* Mercedes Bierman, Wiley Medical, John Wiley & Sons, Inc., 605 Third Ave., New York, NY 10158. 212-867-9800; *Pres.-Elect.* Jerry Newman, Medical Examination Publishing Co., Inc., 969 Stewart Ave., Garden City, NY 11530. 516-222-2277.

American Printing History Assn., Box 4922, Grand Central Sta., New York, NY 10163. *Pres. & Ed., APHA Newsletter.* Catherine T. Brody, New York City Technical College Lib., 300 Jay St., Brooklyn, NY 11201. 212-643-3802; *V.P.s* Jack Golden, Philip Grushkin, E. H. "Pat" Taylor; *Secy.* Jean Peters; *Treas.* Philip Sperling; *Ed., Printing History.* Susan Thompson. (Address correspondence to APHA, Box 4922, except Newsletter matters, which go directly to Catherine Brody.)

American Society for Information Science (ASIS), 1010 16 St. N.W., Washington, DC 20036. 202-659-3644.

American Society of Indexers, 235 Park Ave. S., 8 fl., New York, NY 10003. *Pres.* George I. Lewicky, H. W. Wilson Co., 950 University Ave., Bronx, NY 10452. 212-588-8400.

American Society of Journalists & Authors, 1501 Broadway, New York, NY 10036. 212-997-0947.

American Society of Magazine Photographers (ASMP), 205 Lexington Ave., New York, NY 10016. 212-889-9144. *Dir.* Stuart Kahan.

American Society of Picture Professionals, Inc., Box 5283, Grand Central Sta., New York, NY 10017. *Pres.* Margaret Mathews. 212-972-6396; *Secy.* Alice Lundoff. 212-888-3595.

American Translators Assn., 109 Croton Ave., Ossining, NY 10562. 914-941-1500. *Pres.* Thomas R. Bauman; *Staff Administrator.* Rosemary Malia.

Antiquarian Booksellers Assn. of America, Inc., 50 Rockefeller Plaza, New York, NY 10020. 212-757-9395. *Pres.* John H. Jenkins; *V.P.* Elisabeth Woodburn; *Secy.* Louis Weinstein; *Treas.* Harvey W. Brewer; *Admin. Asst.* Janice M. Farina.

549

Assn. of American Publishers, One Park Ave., New York, NY 10016. 212-689-8920. *Pres.* Townsend Hoopes; *V.P.s* Thomas D. McKee, Robert Rasmussen; *Staff Dirs.* Phyllis Ball, Gregory V. Gore, Parker B. Ladd, Mary E. McNulty, Saundra L. Smith; *Washington Office.* 1707 L St. N.W., Washington, DC 20336. 202-293-2585; *V.P.* Richard P. Kleeman; *Staff Dirs.* Roy H. Millenson, Diane G. Rennert, Carol A. Risher; *Chpn.* Leo N. Albert, Prentice-Hall; *V.Chpn.* Martin P. Levin, Times Mirror; *Secy.* Alexander Burke, McGraw-Hill; *Treas.* George Grune, Reader's Digest.

Assn. of American University Presses, One Park Ave., New York, NY 10016. 212-889-6040. *Pres.* Morris Philipson, Dir., Univ. of Chicago Press, Chicago, IL 60637. 312-753-3344; *Exec. Dir.* Richard Koffler.

Assn. of Canadian Publishers, 70 The Esplanade E., Toronto, Ont. M5E 1R2, Canada. 416-361-1408. *Pres.* Malcolm Lester; *V.P.* Rob Sanders; *Treas.* Harry Van Ierssel; *Exec. Dir.* Phyllis Yaffe.

Assn. of Jewish Book Publishers, House of Living Judaism, 838 Fifth Ave., New York, NY 10021. *Pres.* Jacob Steinberg, Bobbs-Merrill Co., One Pennsylvania Plaza, New York, NY 10001. 212-947-2540. (Address correspondence to the president.)

Bibliographical Society of America. *See* the preceding section, Directory of Organizations, under National Library & Information-Industry Associations, United States and Canada, for detailed information.

Book Industry Study Group, Inc., Box 2062, Darien, CT 06820. 203-655-2473. *Chpn.* DeWitt C. Baker; *V.Chpn.* Howard Willets, Jr.; *Treas.* George Q. Nichols; *Secy.* Hendrik Edelman; *Managing Agent.* John P. Dessauer, Inc.

Book League of New York. *Pres.* Alfred Lane, Columbia Univ. Lib., New York, NY 10027. 212-280-3532; *Treas.* A. C. Frasca, Jr., Freshet Press Inc., 90 Hamilton Rd., Rockville Centre, NY 11570. 506-766-3011.

Book Manufacturers Institute, 111 Prospect St., Stamford, CT 06901. 203-324-9670. *Pres.* Robert R. Hackford, Maple Vail Book Manufacturing Group, 187 Clinton St., Binghamton, NY 13902; *Exec. V.P.* Douglas E. Horner.

Book Publicists of Southern California, 9255 Sunset Blvd., Suite 515, West Hollywood, CA 90069. 213-858-7112. *Pres.* Irwin Zucker; *V.P.* Steve Fiske; *Secy.* Nancy Sayles; *Treas.* Bruce Merrin.

Book Week Headquarters, Children's Book Council, Inc., 67 Irving Pl., New York, NY 10003. 212-254-2666. *Exec. Dir.* John Donovan; *Chpn, 1981 Book Week Committee.* Sandra Jordan, Farrar, Straus & Giroux, Inc., 19 Union Sq. W., New York, NY 10003. 212-741-6900.

The Bookbinders' Guild of New York, c/o *Secy.* Thomas Snyder, Dikeman Laminating, 181 Sargeant Ave., Clifton, NJ 07013. 201-473-5696; *Pres.* Alice Sanchez Claypool, The Book Press, 757 Third Ave., New York, NY 10017; *V.P.* Sam Green, Murray Printing Co., 60 E. 42 St., New York, NY 10165; *Treas.* Gene Sanchez, William Morrow & Co., 105 Madison Ave., New York, NY 10016; *Asst. Secy.* Joel Moss, A. Horowitz & Son, Box 1308, 300 Fairfield Ave., Fairfield, NJ 07006.

Bookbuilders of Boston, Inc., c/o *Pres.* Terry Ann McGarry, Houghton Mifflin Co., One Beacon St., Boston, MA 02107. 617-725-5612; *1st V.P.* Richard Darcy, Arcata Book Group, 275 Hancock St., North Quincy, MA 02171. 617-328-3700.

Bookbuilders of Southern California, 5225 Wilshire Blvd., Suite 316, Los Angeles, CA 90036. *Pres.* Casimira Kostecki, Goodyear Publishing Co., 1640 Fifth St., Santa Monica, CA 90401; *V.P.* Larry Cooke, Arcata Book Group, 7120 Hayvenhurst, Van Nuys, CA 91406; *Secy.* Sally Kostal, Goodyear Publishing Co., 1640 Fifth St., Santa Monica, CA 90401.

Bookbuilders West, c/o *Pres.* Eva M. Strock, 170 Ninth St., San Francisco, CA 94103. 415-922-6341; *V.P.* Bill Cartwright, Arcata Book Group, 985 University Ave., Los Gatos, CA 95030. 408-395-6131; *Secy.* Sharon Hawkes, Annual Reviews, Inc., 4139 El Camino Way, Palo Alto, CA 94306. 415-493-4400; *Treas.* Bill Ketron, Arcata Book Group, 985 University Ave., Los Gatos, CA 95030. 408-395-6131.

Booksellers Assn. of Philadelphia, c/o Catholic Lib. Assn., 461 W. Lancaster Ave., Haverford, PA 19041. 215-649-5250. *Pres.* Ernie Saxton, Chilton Book Co., 201 King of Prussia Rd., Radnor, PA 19087. 215-687-8200; *V.P.* Nellie Anderson, Penn Center Books, Suburban Sta. Bldg., 16 St. & Kennedy Blvd., Philadelphia, PA 19103. 215-563-0868; *Secy.* Linda Fein, Free Lib. of Philadelphia, Logan Sq., Philadelphia, PA 19103. 215-686-5322; *Treas.* Matthew R. Wilt, Catholic Lib. Assn., 461 W. Lancaster Ave., Haverford, PA 19041. 215-649-5250.

Brotherhood of Book Travelers, c/o *Pres.* Bebe Cole, 101 Second St., Garden City, NY 11530; *Treas.* Dick Clunan, George Braziller, Inc.; *Secy.* Lou Cohen, St. Martin's Press, Inc.

Canadian Book Publishers' Council, 45 Charles St. E., Suite 701, Toronto, Ont. M4Y 1S2, Canada. 416-964-7231. *Pres.* Peter J. Waldock, Penguin Books Canada, Ltd.; *1st V.P.* Ronald D. Besse, Gage Publishing, Ltd.; *2nd V.P.* Rachel Mansfield, McGraw-Hill Ryerson, Ltd.; *Exec. Dir.* Jacqueline Nestmann-Hushion; *Member Organizations.* The School Group, The College Group, The Trade Group, The Paperback Group.

Canadian Booksellers Assn., 56 The Esplanade, Suite 400, Toronto, Ont. M5E 1A7, Canada. 416-361-1529. *Exec. Dir.* Bernard E. Rath; *Convention Mgr.* Irene Read.

Chicago Book Clinic, 410 S. Michigan Ave., Suite 433, Chicago, IL 60605. 312-663-9860. *Pres.* Richard T. Congdon; *Exec. V.P.* Stuart J. Murphy, Edit, Inc.; *Treas.* Richard G. Young, Synthegraphics Corp.

Chicago Publishers Assn., c/o *Pres.* Robbert J. R. Follett, Follett Publishing Co., 1010 W. Washington Blvd., Chicago, IL 60607. 312-666-4300.

The Children's Book Council, 67 Irving Pl., New York, NY 10003. 212-254-2666. *Exec. Dir.* John Donovan; *Assoc. Dir.* Paula Quint; *Asst. Dirs.* Christine Stanicki, Peter Dews; *Pres.* Norma Jean Sawicki, Ed. in Chief & Dir. Children's Book Dept., Crown Publishers, Inc., One Park Ave., New York, NY 10016. 212-532-9200.

Christian Booksellers Assn., Box 200, 2620 Venetucci Blvd., Colorado Springs, CO 80901. 303-576-7880. *Exec. V.P.* John T. Bass.

Connecticut Book Publishers Assn., c/o *Pres.* Alex M. Yudkin, Associated Booksellers, 147 McKinley Ave., Bridgeport, CT 06606; *V.P.* Richard Dunn; *Treas.* John Atkin.

The Copyright Society of the U.S.A., New York Univ. School of Law, 40 Washington Sq. S., New York, NY 10012. 212-598-2280/2210. *Pres.* Stanley Rothenberg; *Secy.* Jerold Couture; *Exec. Dir.* Alan Latman; *Asst.* Kate McKay.

Council on Interracial Books for Children, Inc., 1841 Broadway, New York, NY 10023. 212-757-5339. *Dir.* Bradford Chambers; *Pres.* Beryle Banfield; *V.P.s* Albert V. Schwartz, Frieda Zames, Katie Cumbo, Marylou Byler; *Managing Ed., Interracial Books for Children Bulletin.* Ruth Charnes; *Bk. Review Coord.* Lyla Hoffman; *Dir., CIBC Racism & Sexism Resource Center for Educators.* Robert B. Moore; *Secy.* Elsa Velasquez.

Edition Bookbinders of New York, Inc., Box 124, Fort Lee, NJ 07024. 201-947-7289. *Exec. Secy.* Morton Windman; *Pres.* Sam Goldman, Publishers Book Bindery; *V.P.* Robert G. Luburg, Tapley-Rutter Co.; *Treas.* Martin Blumberg, American Book-Stratford Press.

Educational Paperback Assn., c/o *Pres.* Allan Hartley, H. P. Koppelmann, 140 Van Block Ave., Hartford, CT 06101.

Evangelical Christian Publishers Assn., Box 1568, West Chester, PA 19380. 215-696-0285. *Exec. Dir.* C. E. Andrew.

Fourth Avenue Booksellers, *Perm. Secy.* Stanley Gilman, Box 456, New York, NY 10003.

Graphic Artists Guild, 30 E. 20 St., Rm. 405, New York, NY 10003. 212-982-9298. *Pres.* Gerald McConnell.

Guild of Book Workers, 663 Fifth Ave., New York, NY 10022. 212-757-6454. *Pres.* Caroline F. Schimmel.

Information Industry Assn. *See* "National Library and Information-Industry Associations" earlier in Part 7—*Ed.*

International Assn. of Book Publishing Consultants, c/o Joseph Marks, 485 Fifth Ave., New York, NY 10017. 212-867-6341.

International Assn. of Printing House Craftsmen, Inc., 7599 Kenwood Rd., Cincinnati, OH 45236. 513-891-0611. *Pres.* Ralph G. Pike; *Exec. V.P.* John A. Davies.

International Copyright Information Center (INCINC), Assn. of American Publishers, 1707 L St. N.W., Suite 480, Washington, DC 20036. 202-293-2585. *Dir.* Carol A. Risher.

International Standard Book Numbering Agency (ISBN), 1180 Ave. of the Americas, New York, NY 10036. 212-764-3384. *Exec. Dir.* Emery I. Koltay; *Officers.* Beatrice Jacobson, Leigh C. Yuster, Gary Ink.

JWB Jewish Book Council, 15 E. 26 St., New York, NY 10010. 212-532-4949. *Pres.* Robert Gordis.

Library Binding Institute, 50 Congress St., Suite 633, Boston, MA 02109. 617-227-7450. *Exec. Dir.* Dudley A. Weiss;

Public Relations *Dir.* Beverly Adamonis.

Magazine & Paperback Marketing Institute (MPMI), 344 Main St., Suite 205, Mt. Kisco, NY 10549. 914-666-6788. *Exec. V.P.* Woodford Bankson, Jr.

Metropolitan Lithographers Assn., 123 E. 62 St., New York, NY 10021. 212-759-0966. *Pres.* Ralph Mazzocco; *Exec. Dir.* Albert N. Greco.

Midwest Book Travelers Assn., c/o *Pres.* Paul Dimmitt, Wybel Associates; *V.P.* Ted Heinecken, Heinecken Associates; *Secy.* Peter Muehr, Grosset & Dunlap; *Treas.* Robert Rainer, Rainer Associates; *Bd. of Dirs.* Robert Gurney, Harper & Row; Wm. S. Holland, Hayden Book Co.; John Strohmayer, Holt, Rinehart & Winston.

Minnesota Book Publishers Roundtable, c/o *Pres.* John N. Dwyer, Liturgical Press, Collegeville, MN 56301. 612-363-2220; *V.P.* Susan Stan, Lerner Publications Co., 241 First Ave. N., Minneapolis, MN 55401; *Secy.-Treas.* Norton Stillman, Nodin Press, Inc., 519 N. Third St., Minneapolis, MN 55401.

National Assn. of College Stores, 528 E. Lorain St., Oberlin, OH 44074. 216-775-1561. *Pres.* Robert W. Bell, Lehigh Univ. Bookstore, Bethlehem, PA 18015; *Exec. Dir.* Garis Distelhorst.

National Council of Churches of Christ in the U.S.A., Div. of Education and Ministry, 475 Riverside Dr., New York, NY 10115. 212-870-2271/2272.

National Micrographics Assn. For detailed information, *see* National Library and Information-Industry Associations, United States and Canada, earlier in Part 7—*Ed.*

New England Small Press Assn. (NESPA), 45 Hillcrest Pl., Amherst, MA 01002. *Dirs.* William R. Darling, Diane Kruchkow.

New Mexico Book League, 8632 Horacio Pl. N.E., Albuquerque, NM 87111. 505-299-8940. *Exec. Dir.* Dwight A. Myers;

Pres. Ruth Wuori; *V.P.* Drew Harrington; *Treas.* Frank N. Skinner; *Ed.* Carol A. Myers.

New York Rights & Permissions Group, c/o *Chpn.* Dorothy McKittrick Harris, Reader's Digest General Books, 750 Third Ave., New York, NY 10017. 212-972-3762.

New York State Small Press Assn., c/o The Promise of Learnings, Inc., Box 1264, Radio City Sta., New York, NY 10019. 212-586-4235. *Exec. Dir.* Janey Tannenbaum; *Gen. Mgr.* Jim Mele.

Northern California Booksellers Assn., c/o *Pres.* Larry Alperstein, Books Plus, 3910 24 St., San Francisco, CA 94114. 415-863-8150.

Periodical & Book Assn. of America, Inc., 205 E. 42 St., New York, NY 10017. 212-486-9777. *Exec. Dir.* Joseph Greco.

Periodical Distributors of Canada. *Pres.* Gerald Benjamin, 425 Guy St., Montreal, P.Q. H3J 1T1, Canada. 514-931-4221; *Secy.* Jim Neill, 120 Sinnott Rd., Scarborough, Ont., Canada. 416-752-8720.

Philadelphia Book Clinic, *Secy-Treas.* Thomas Colaiezzi, Lea & Febiger, 600 Washington Sq., Philadelphia, PA 19106. 215-925-8700.

Pi Beta Alpha (formerly Professional Bookmen of America, Inc.), 1215 Farwell Dr., Madison, WI 53704. *Pres.* Clinton L. Strand; *Exec. Sec.* Charles L. Schmalbach.

Printing Industries of Metropolitan New York, Inc., 461 Eighth Ave., New York, NY 10001. 212-279-2100. *Pres.* James J. Conner III; *Dir., Public Relations.* Daniel Soskin.

Proofreaders Club of New York, c/o *Pres.* Allan Treshan, 38-15 149 St., Flushing, NY 11354. 212-461-8509.

Publishers' Ad Club, c/o *Secy.* Susan Ball, William Morrow & Co., Inc., 105 Madison Ave., New York, NY 10016. 212-889-3050; *Pres.* Bridget Marion, Farrar, Straus & Giroux, 19 Union Sq. W., New York, NY 10003. 212-741-6919; *V.P.* Peter Minichiello, Pocket Books, 1230 Ave. of the Americas, New York, NY 10020. 212-246-2121; *Treas.* Pat Cool, Dell Publishing Co., One Dag Hammarskjold Plaza, New York, NY 10017. 212-832-7300.

Publishers' Alliance, Box 3, Glen Ridge, NJ 07028. 201-429-8757. *Exec. Secy.* Linda P. Grant.

Publishers' Library Promotion Group, *Pres.* Neal Porter, Scribner Book Companies, 597 Fifth Ave., New York, NY 10017. 212-486-2669; *V.P.* Jim Roginski, Putnam Publishing Group, 200 Madison Ave., New York, NY 10016. 212-576-8975; *Treas.* Sigi Friedman, Simon & Schuster, 1230 Ave. of the Americas, New York, NY 10016. 212-245-6400.

Publishers' Publicity Assn., Inc., c/o *Pres.* Barbara J. Hendra, Barbara Hendra Associates, Inc, Suite 1101, Empire State Bldg., 350 Fifth Ave., New York, NY 10118. 212-947-9898; *V.P.* Diane Glynn, Berkley Books, 200 Madison Ave., New York, NY 10016. 212-686-9820; *Secy.* Selden Sutton, Little, Brown & Co., 747 Third Ave., New York, NY 10017. 212-688-8380; *Treas.* Eileen Prescott, Eileen Prescott Co., 733 Third Ave., New York, NY 10017. 212-682-2268.

The Religion Publishing Group, c/o Eve F. Roshevsky, Doubleday & Co., 245 Park Ave., New York 10017. 212-953-4673. *Pres.* John A. Hollar, Fortress Press, 2900 Queen La., Philadelphia, PA 19129; *Secy.-Treas.* Eve F. Roshevsky.

Research and Engineering Council of the Graphic Arts Industry, Inc., 4351 Garden City Dr., Suite 503, Landover, MD 20785. 301-577-5400. *Pres.* Harold A. Molz; *1st V.P., Finance and Membership.* Gilbert Bachman; *2nd V.P. and Secy.* Donald H. Laux; *Managing Dir.* Deforest D. Choha.

Société de Développement du Livre et du Périodique, 1151 r. Alexandre-DeSève,

Montreal, P.Q. H2L 2T7, Canada. 514-524-7528. *Pres.* Yves Dubé; *Directeur General.* Thomas Déri; Association des Editeurs Canadiens, *Pres.* M. René Bonenfant; Association des Libraires du Québec, *Pres.* Pierre Renaud; Société Canadienne Française de Protection du Droit d'Auteur, *Pres.* Pierre Tisseyre; Société des Editeurs de Manuels Scolaires du Québec, *Pres.* Pierre Tisseyre.

Society of Authors' Representatives, Inc., 40 E. 49 St., New York, NY 10017. 212-548-6333. *Pres.* Peter Shepherd; *Exec. Secy.* Jeanne Boose.

Society of Photographer & Artist Representatives, Inc. (SPAR), Box 845, New York, NY 10022. 212-628-9148. *Pres.* Fran Milsop.

Society of Photographers in Communication. *See* American Society of Magazine Photographers (ASMP).

Southern California Booksellers Assn., c/o *Pres.* Miriam Bass, Vroman's Book Store, 695 E. Colorado, Pasadena, CA 91101. 213-449-5320; *V.P.* Jan Sparks, "Jan, The Book Merchant," 13175 Mindanao Way, Marina del Rey, CA 90291. 213-823-8466; *Secy.* Roberta Whitehead, Northridge Books, Northridge, CA 91324. 213-349-5484; *Treas.* Joe Chevalier, Chevalier's Books, 126 N. Larchmont, Los Angeles, CA 90004. 213-465-1334.

Standard Address Number (SAN) Agency. *See* International Standard Book Numbering Agency.

Technical Assn. of the Pulp & Paper Industry (TAPPI), One Dunwoody Pk., Atlanta, GA 30338. 404-394-6130. *Pres.* W. O. Kroeschell; *V.P.* Sherwood G. Holt; *Exec. Dir.* Philip E. Nethercut; *Treas.* W. L. Cullison.

Translation Research Institute, 5914 Pulaski Ave., Philadelphia, PA 19144. 215-848-7084. *Dir.* Charles Parsons.

West Coast Bookmen's Assn., 27 McNear Dr., San Rafael, CA 94901. *Pres.* Robert Wilkins; *Secy.-Treas.* Phillip R. Ventura, 1521 Verde Vista Dr., Monterey Park, CA 91754.

Western Book Publishers Assn., Box 4242, San Francisco, CA 94101.

Women's National Book Assn., c/o *National Pres.* Mary Glenn Hearne, Dir., The Nashville Room, Public Lib. of Nashville and Davidson County, Eighth Ave. N. and Union, Nashville, TN 37203. 615-244-4700, ext. 68 (office); *V.P./Pres.-Elect.* Sylvia Cross, 19824 Septo St., Chatsworth, CA 91311. 213-886-8448 (home); *Secy.* Cathy Rentschler, H. W. Wilson Co., 950 University Ave., Bronx, NY 10452. 212-588-8400, ext. 257 (office); *Treas.* Patricia A. Hodge, RSM, Lib. Dir., Trinity College, Colchester Ave., Burlington, VT 05401. 802-864-0337, ext. 343 (office); *Past Pres.* Ann Heidbreder Eastman, College of Arts and Science, Virginia Polytechnic Institute and State Univ., Blacksburg, VA 24061. 703-961-6390 (office). NATIONAL COMMITTEE CHAIRS: *Dir., Public Affairs.* Cosette Kies, Dept. of Lib. Science, George Peabody College of Vanderbilt Univ., Nashville, TN 37203. 615-327-8038 (office); *Asst. Secy.* Joan Cunliffe, TABA/AAP, One Park Ave., New York, NY 10016. 212-689-8920; *Ed., The Bookwoman.* Jean K. Crawford, Abington Press, 201 Eighth Ave. S., Nashville, TN 37202. 615-749-6422 (office); *Review Ed., The Bookwoman.* Mary V. Gaver, 300 Virginia Ave., Danville, VA 24541. 804-799-6746; *Membership Chpn.* Anne J. Richter, 55 N. Mountain Ave., A-2, Montclair, NJ 07042. 201-746-5166 (office). November–May: 140 Seaman Ave., Opa-Locka, FL 33054. 305-681-3281; *UN/NGO Rep.* Clare Friedland, 36 E. 36 St., New York, NY 10016. 212-685-6205; *Finance Chpn.* Sandra K. Paul, SKP Associates, 160 Fifth Ave., New York, NY 10010. 212-675-7804 (office). CHAPTER PRESIDENTS: *Binghamton.* Frances Kisling, 307 June St., Endicott, NY 13769. 607-785-5984; *Boston.*

Frances Mulcahy, 39 Leavitt St., Hingham, MA 02043. 617-749-4794; *Cleveland.* Kathalee Grant, Independence Public Lib., 7121 Valley View Dr., Independence, OH 44131. 216-447-0160; *Detroit.* Olga Pobutsky, 16815 Parkside, Detroit, MI 48221. 313-863-1389; *Los Angeles.* Carole Garland, Pinnacle Books, Inc., One Century Plaza, 2029 Century Park E., Los Angeles, CA 90067. 213-552-9111 (office); *Nashville.* Janice Sanford, Nolensville, TN 37135. 615-776-2428; *New York.* Margaret Klee Lichtenberg, Grosset & Dunlap, 51 Madison Ave., New York, NY 10016. 212-689-9200; *San Francisco.* Adele Horwitz, Presidio Press, 31 Pamaron Way, Novato, CA 94947. 415-883-1323 (office); *Washington, DC/Baltimore, MD.* Nancy C. Essig, Johns Hopkins Univ. Press, Baltimore, MD 21218. 301-338-7851 (office).

INTERNATIONAL AND FOREIGN BOOK TRADE ASSOCIATIONS

For Canadian book trade associations, see the preceding section on Book Trade Associations, United States and Canada. For a more extensive list of book trade organizations outside the United States and Canada, with more detailed information, consult *International Literary Market Place* (R. R. Bowker). An annual publication, it also provides extensive lists of major bookstores and publishers in each country.

INTERNATIONAL

Antiquarian Booksellers Assn. (International), 154 Buckingham Palace Rd., London SW1W 9TZ, England.

International Booksellers Federation (IBF), Grunangergasse 4, A-1010 Vienna 1, Austria. *Secy.-Gen.* Gerhard Prosser.

International League of Antiquarian Booksellers, 5 Bloomsbury St., London WC1B 3QE, England. *Pres.* Stanley Crowe.

International Publishers Assn., 3 av. de Miremont, CH-1206 Geneva, Switzerland. *Secy.-Gen.* J. Alexis Koutchoumow.

NATIONAL

Argentina

Cámara Argentina de Editores de Libros (Council of Argentine Book Publishers), Talcahuano 374, p. 3, Of. 7, Buenos Aires 1013.

Cámara Argentina de Publicaciones (Argentine Publications Assn.), Reconquista 1011, p. 6, 1003 Buenos Aires. *Pres.* Modesto Ederra.

Cámara Argentina del Libro (Argentine Book Assn.), Av. Belgrano 1580, p. 6, 1093 Buenos Aires. *Pres.* Eustasio A. Garcia.

Federación Argentina de Librerías, Papelerías y Actividades Afines (Federation of Bookstores, Stationers and Related Activities), España 848, Losario, Santa Fé.

Australia

Assn. of Australian Univ. Presses, c/o Univ. of Queensland Press, Box 42, St. Lucia, Qld. 4068. *Pres.* Frank W. Thompson.

Australian Book Publishers Assn., 163 Clarence St., Sydney, N.S.W. 2000.

Australian Booksellers Assn., Box 3254, Sydney, N.S.W. 2001.

Wholesale Booksellers Assn. of Australia, c/o Book Supplies Pty. Ltd., 55 York St., Sydney, N.S.W. 2000. *Secy.* David Joel.

Austria

Hauptverband der graphischen Unternehmungen Österreichs (Austrian Graphical Assn.), Grünangergasse 4, A-1010 Vienna 1.

Hauptverband des österreichischen Buchhandels (Austrian Publishers and Booksellers Assn.), Grünangergasse 4, A-1010 Vienna. *Secy.* Gerhard Prosser.

Osterreichischer Verlegerverband (Assn. of Austrian Publishers), Grünangergasse 4, A-1010 Vienna. *Secy.* Gerhard Prosser.

Verband der Antiquare Österreichs (Austrian Antiquarian Booksellers Assn.), Grünangergasse 4, A-1010 Vienna. *Secy.* Gerhard Prosser.

Belgium

Cercle Belge de la Librairie (Belgian Booksellers Assn.), r. du Luxembourg 5, bte. 1, B-1040 Brussels.

Fédération des Editeurs Belges (Belgian Publishers Assn.), 111 av. du Parc, B-1060 Brussels. *Dir.* J. De Raeymaeker.

Syndicat Belge de la Librairie Ancienne et Moderne (Belgian Assn. of Antiquarian and Modern Booksellers), r. du Chêne 21, B-1000 Brussels.

Vereniging ter Bevordering van het Vlaamse Boekwezen (Assn. for the Promotion of Flemish Books), Frankrijklei 93, B-2000 Antwerp. *Secy.* A. Wouters. Member organizations: Algemene Vlaamse Boekverkopersbond; Uitgeversbond-Vereniging van Uitgevers van Nederlandstalige Boeken at the same address; and Bond-Alleenverkopers van Nederlandstalige Boeken (book importers), De Smethlaan 4, B-1980 Tervuren. *Secy.* J. van den Berg.

Bolivia

Cámara Boliviana del Libro (Bolivian Booksellers Assn.), Box 682, La Paz. *Pres. Lic.* Javier Gisbert.

Brazil

Associação Brasileira de Livreiros Antiquarios (Brazilian Assn. of Antiquarian Booksellers), Rua do Rosario 135-137, Rio de Janeiro.

Associação Brasileira do Livro (Brazilian Booksellers Assn.), Av. 13 de Maio 23, andar 16, Rio de Janeiro. *Dir.* Alberjano Torres.

Cámara Brasileira do Livro (Brazilian Book Assn.), Av. Ipiranga 1267, andar 10, São Paulo. *Secy.* Jose Gorayeb.

Sindicato Nacional dos Editores de Livros (Brazilian Book Publishers Assn.), Av. Rio Branco 37, andar 15, Salas 1503/6 e 1510/12, 20097 Rio de Janeiro. *Exec. Secy.* Maria Helena Geordane.

Bulgaria

Drzavno Obedinenie Bulgarska Kniga (State Bulgarian Book Assn.), pl. Slavejkov 11, Sofia.

Soyuz Knigoizdatelite i Knizharite (Union of Publishers and Booksellers), vu Solum 4, Sofia.

Burma

Burmese Publishers Union, 146 Bogyoke Market, Rangoon.

Chile

Cámara Chilena del Libro, Av. Bulnes 188, Casilla 2787, Santiago. *Secy.* A. Newman.

Colombia

Cámara Colombiana de la Industria Editorial (Colombian Publishers Council), Cr. 7a, No. 17-51, Of. 409-410, Apdo. áereo 8998, Bogotá. *Exec. Secy.* Hipólito Hincapié.

Czechoslovakia

Ministerstvo Kultury CSR, Odbor Knižni Kultury (Ministry of Culture CSR, Dept. for Publishing and Book Trade), Staré Mésto, námesti Perštyně 1, 117 65 Prague 1.

Denmark

Danske Antikvarboghandlerforening (Danish Antiquarian Booksellers Assn.), Silkegade 11, DK-1113 Copenhagen.

Danske Boghandleres Bogimport A/S (Danish Booksellers Bookimport Ltd.),

Herlev Hovedgade 199, Box 546, DK-2730 Herlev. *Dir.* Hans Pedersen.
Danske Boghandlerforening (Danish Booksellers Assn.), Boghandlernes Hus, Siljangade 6, DK-2300 Copenhagen S. *Secy.* Elisabeth Brodersen.
Danske Forlaeggerforening (Danish Publishers Assn.), Købmagergade 11, DK-1150 Copenhagen K. *Dir.* Erik V. Krustrup.

Ecuador

Sociedad de Libreros del Ecuador (Booksellers Society of Ecuador), C. Bolivar 268 y Venezuela, Of. 501, p. 5, Quito. *Secy.* Eduardo Ruiz G.

Finland

Kirja-ja Paperikauppojen Liittory (Finnish Booksellers and Stationers Assn.), Pieni Roobertinkatu 13 B 26, SF-00130 Helsinki 13, *Secy.* Pentti Kuopio.
Suomen Antikvariaattiyhdistys Finska Antikvariatforeningen (Finnish Antiquarian Booksellers Assn.), P. Makasiininkatu 6, Helsinki 13.
Suomen Kustannusyhdistys (Publishers Assn. of Finland), Eerikinkatu 14B, 00100 Helsinki 10. *Secy.-Gen.* Unto Lappi.

France

Cercle de la Librairie (Booksellers Circle), 117 bd. St.-Germain, F-75279 Paris, Cedex 06.
Fédération française des Syndicats de Libraires (French Booksellers Assn.), 117 bd. St.-Germain, F-75279 Paris, Cedex 06.
Office de Promotion de l'Edition Française (Promotion Office of French Publishing), 117 bd. St.-Germain, F-75279 Paris, Cedex 06. *Managing Dir.* Gustave Girardot; *Secy.-Gen.* Marc Franconie; *Asst. Dir.* Pierre-Dominique Parent.
Syndicat National de la Librairie ancienne et moderne (Assn. of Antiquarian and Modern Booksellers), 117 bd. St.-Germain, F-75006 Paris. *Secy.* G. Fleury.
Syndicat National de l'Edition (French Publishers Assn.), 117 bd. St.-Germain, F-75279 Paris, Cedex 06. *Secy.* Pierre Fredet.
Syndicat National des Importateurs et Exportateurs de Livres (National French Assn. of Book Importers and Exporters), 117 bd. St.-Germain, F-75279 Paris, Cedex 06.

Germany (Democratic Republic of)

Börsenverein der Deutschen Buchhandler zu Leipzig (Assn. of GDR Publishers and Booksellers in Leipzig), Gerichtsweg 26, 7010 Leipzig.

Germany (Federal Republic of)

Börsenverein des deutschen Buchhandels (German Publishers and Booksellers Assn.), Grosser Hirschgraben 17–21, Box 2404, D-6000 Frankfurt am Main 1. *Secy.* Hans-Karl von Kupsch.
Bundeverband der Deutschen Versandbuchhändler e.V. (National Federation of German Mail-Order Booksellers), Rheinstr. 30/32, D-6200 Wiesbaden.
Landesverband der Buchhändler und Verleger in Niedersachsen e.V. (Provincial Federation of Booksellers and Publishers in Lower Saxony), Hausmannstr. 2, D-3000 Hannover 1. *Managing Dir.* Wolfgang Grimpe.
Verband Bayerischer Verlage und Buchhandlungen e.V. (Bavarian Publishers & Booksellers Federation), Thierschstr. 17, D-8000 Munich 22. *Secy.* F. Nosske.
Verband deutscher Antiquare e.V. (German Antiquarian Booksellers Assn.), Zum Talblick 2, D-6246 Glashütten im Taunus.
Verband deutscher Bühnenverleger e.V. (Federation of German Theatrical Publishers), Bundesallee 23, D-1000 Berlin 31.
Verband Deutscher Buch-, Zeitungs- und Zeitschriften-Grossisten e.V. (Federation of German Wholesalers of Books, Newspapers and Periodicals), Classen-Kappelmann-Str. 24, D-5000 Cologne 41.
Vereinigung evangelischer Buchhändler (Assn. of Protestant Booksellers), Lehenstr. 31, D-7000 Stuttgart 1.

Ghana

Ghana Booksellers Assn., Box 7869, Accra.

Great Britain
See United Kingdom.

Greece
Syllogos Ekdoton kai Vivliopolon Athinon (Assn. of Publishers and Booksellers Assns. of Athens), Themistocleus 54 Str., Athens.

Syllogos Ekdoton Vivliopolon (Greek Publishers Assn.), 22-24 Har. Trikoupi St., Athens.

Hong Kong
Hong Kong Booksellers & Stationers Assn., Man Wah House, Kowloon.

Hungary
Magyar Könyvkiadók és Könyvterjesztök Egyesülése (Hungarian Publishers and Booksellers Assn.), Vörösmarty tér 1, 1051 Budapest. *Pres.* György Bernát.

Iceland
Iceland Publishers Assn., Laufasvegi 12, 101 Reykjavik. *Pres.* Oliver Steinn Jóhannesson, Strandgötu 31, 220 Hafnarfjörður. *Gen. Mgr.* Gísli Ólafsson.

India
All-India Booksellers and Publishers Assn., 17L Connaught Pl., New Delhi 1. *Pres.* Mohan Lal Choudary.

All-India Hindi Publishers Assns., 3625 Subhash Marg, 110 002 New Delhi.

Bombay Booksellers & Publishers Assn., c/o Bhadkamkar Marg, Navjivan Cooperative Housing Society, Bldg. 3, 6th fl., Office 25, Bombay 400 008.

Booksellers & Publishers Assn. of South India, c/o Higginbothams, Ltd., 814, Anna Salai, Mount Rd., Madras 600 002.

Delhi State Booksellers & Publishers Assn., c/o The Students' Stores, Box 1511, 110 006 Delhi. *Pres.* Devendra Sharma.

Federation of Indian Publishers, M-138, Connaught Circus, New Delhi 110 001. *Pres.* G. A. Vazirani; *Exec. Secy.* M. C. Minocha.

Indian Assn. of Univ. Presses, Calcutta Univ. Press, Calcutta. *Secy.* S. Kanjilal.

Publishers Assn. of India, 14-18 Calicut St., Ballard Estate, Bombay 400 038. *Chmn.* P. S. Jayasinghe.

Indonesia
Ikatan Penerbit Indonesia (IKAPI) (Assn. of Indonesian Book Publishers), Jalan Pengarengan 32, Jakarta Pusat III/4. *Pres.* Ismid Hadad.

Ireland (Republic of)
CLE/Irish Book Publishers Assn., 55 Dame St., Dublin 2. *Secy.* Hilary Kennedy.

Israel
Book & Printing Center of the Israel Export Institute, Box 29732, 29 Hamered St., Tel Aviv 68125. *Dir.* Shlomo Erel.

Book Publishers Assn. of Israel, Box 20123, 29 Carlebach St., Tel Aviv. *Exec. Dir.* Benjamin Sella; *International Promotion and Literary Rights Dept. Dir.* Lorna Soifer.

Italy
Associazione Italiana degli Editori di Musica (Italian Assn. of Music Publishers) Piazza del Liberty 2, I-20121 Milan.

Associazione Italiana Editori (Italian Publishers Assn.), Via delle Erbe 2, I-20121 Milan. *Secy.* Archille Ormezzano.

Associazione Librai Antiquari d'Italia (Antiquarian Booksellers Assn. of Italy), Via Jacopo Nardi 6, I-50132 Florence. *Pres.* Renzo Rizzi.

Associazione Librai Italiani (Italian Booksellers Assn.), Piazza G. G. Belli 2, I-00153 Rome.

Jamaica
Booksellers Assn. of Jamaica, c/o Sangster's Book Stores, Ltd., Box 366, 97 Harbour St., Kingston.

Japan
Antiquarian Booksellers Assn. of Japan, 29 San-ei-cho, Shinjuku-ku, Tokyo 160.

Books-on-Japan-in-English Club, Shinnichibo Bldg., 2-1 Sarugaku-cho 1-chome, Chiyoda-ku, Tokyo 101.

Japan Book Importers Assn., Rm. 302, Aizawa Bldg., 20-3 Nihonbashi, 1-chome, Chuoku, Tokyo 103. *Secy.* Kazushige Terakubo.

Japan Book Publishers Assn., 6 Fukuromachi, Shinjuku-ku, Tokyo 162. *Secy.* S. Sasaki.

Japan Booksellers Federation, 1-2 Surugadai, Kanda, Chiyoda-ku, Tokyo 101.

Textbook Publishers Assn. of Japan (Kyokasho Kyokai), 20-2 Honshiocho Shinjuku-ku, Tokyo 160. *Secy.* Masae Kusaka.

Kenya

Kenya Publishers Assn., Box 72532, Nairobi.

Korea (Republic of)

Korean Publishers Assn., 105-2 Sagandong, Chongno-ku, Seoul 110. *Secy.* Kyung-hoon Lee.

Luxembourg

Confédération du Commerce Luxembourgeois-Groupement Papetiers-Libraires (Confederation of Retailers, Group for Stationers and Booksellers), 23, Centre Allée-Scheffer, Luxembourg. *Pres.* Pierre Ernster; *Secy.* Fernand Kass.

Malaysia

Malaysian Book Publishers Assn., Box 335, Kuala Lumpur 01-02. *Hon. Secy.* J. B. Ho.

Mexico

Instituto Mexicano del Libro A.C. (Mexican Book Institute), Paseo de la Reforma 95, Dept. 1024, México 4 D.F. *Secy.-Gen.* Isabel Ruiz González.

Morocco

Association des Libraires du Maroc (Assn. of Booksellers of Morocco), 67 r. de Foucauld, Casablanca.

Netherlands

Koninklijke Nederlandse Uitgeversbond (Royal Dutch Publishers Assn.), Nieuwe Zijds Voorburgwal 44, 1012 SB Amsterdam. *Secy.* R. M. Vrij; *Managing Dir.* A. Th. Hulskamp.

Nederlandsche Vereeniging van Antiquaren (Antiquarian Booksellers Assn. of the Netherlands), Nieuwe Spiegelstra. 40, 1017-DG Amsterdam. *Pres.* A. Gerits.

Nederlandse Boekverkopersbond (Booksellers Assn. of the Netherlands), Waalsdorperweg 119, 2597-HS The Hague. *Secy.* P. J. de Groot.

Vereeniging ter bevordering van de belangen des Boekhandels (Dutch Book Trade Assn.), Lassusstraat 9, Amsterdam Z. *Secy.* M. van Vollenhoven-Nagel.

New Zealand

Book Publishers Assn. of New Zealand, Box 78071, Grey Lynn, Auckland 2. *Pres.* D. J. Heap; *Dir.* Gerard Reid.

Booksellers Assn. of New Zealand, Inc., Box 11-377, Wellington. *Dir.* Kate Fortune.

Nigeria

Nigerian Publishers Assn., c/o P.M.B. 5164, Ibadan.

Norway

Norsk Antikvarbokhandlerforening (Norwegian Antiquarian Booksellers Assn.), Ullevalsveien 1, Oslo 1.

Norske Bokhandlerforening (Norwegian Booksellers Assn.), Øvre Vollgate 15, Oslo 1.

Norsk Bokhandler-Medhjelper-Forening (Norwegian Book Trade Employees Assn.), Øvre Vollgate 15, Oslo 1.

Norske Forleggerforening (Norwegian Publishers Assn.), Øvre Vollgate 15, Oslo 1. *Dir.* Tor Solumsmoen.

Norsk Musikkforleggerforening (Norwegian Music Publishers Assn.), Box 1499 Vika, Oslo 1.

Pakistan

Pakistan Publishers and Booksellers Assn., YMCA Bldg., Shahra-e-Quaid-e-Azam, Lahore.

Paraguay

Cámara Paraguaya del Libro (Paraguayan Publishers Assn.), Libreria Internacional S.A., Estrella 721, Asunción.

Peru

Cámara Peruana del Libro (Peruvian Publishers Assn.), Apdo. 10253, Lima 100. *Pres.* Andrés Carbone O.

Philippines

Philippine Book Dealers Assn., c/o Philippine Education Co., Quezon Ave. & Banawe, Metro Manila. *Pres.* Jose C. Benedicto.

Philippine Educational Publishers Assn., 927 Quezon Ave., Quezon City 3008, Metro Manila. *Pres.* Jesus Ernesto R. Sibal.

Poland

Polskie Towarzystwo Wydawców Ksiaźek (Polish Publishers Assn.), ul. Mazowiecka 2/4, 00-048 Warsaw.

Stowarzyszenie Ksiegarzy Polskich Zarząd Główny (Assn. of Polish Booksellers), ul. Mokotowska 4/6, 00-641 Warsaw. *Pres.* Tadeusz Hussak.

Portugal

Associação Portuguesa dos Editores e Livreiros (Portuguese Assn. of Publishers and Booksellers), Largo de Andaluz 16, 1, Esq., 1000 Lisboa.

Romania

Centrala editorială (Romanian Publishing Center), Piata Scînteii 1, R-71341 Bucharest. *Gen. Dir.* Gheorghe Trandafir.

Singapore

Singapore Book Publishers Assn., Box 846, Colombo Court Post Office, Singapore 0617. *Secy.* Lena U Wen Lim.

South Africa (Republic of)

Associated Booksellers of Southern Africa, One Meerendal, Nightingale Way, Pinelands 7405. *Secy.* P. G. van Rooyen.

Book Trade Assn. of South Africa, Box 105, Parow 7500.

Book Trade Assn. of South Africa, Box 337, Bergvlei 2012.

Overseas Publishers Representatives Assn. of South Africa, Box 21342, Marshalltown 2107, Johannesburg. *Secy.* P. Hardingham.

South African Publishers Assn., Box 123, Kenwyn 7790. *Secy.* P. G. van Rooyen.

Spain

Federacion de Gremios de Editores de España (Spanish Federation of Publishers Assns.), General Pardiñas, 29 Madrid 1. *Pres.* Juan Salvat; *1st V.P.* Francisco Pérez González; *Secy.-Gen.* Raúl Rispa.

Gremi d'Editors de Catalunya (Assn. of Catalonian Publishers), Mallorca, 272-274, Barcelona 37. *Pres.* Antoni Comas Baldellou.

Gremio Nacional de Libreros (Assn. of Spanish Booksellers), Fernandez de la Hoz 12, Madrid 4.

Gremio Sindical de Libreros de Barcelona (Assn. of Barcelona Booksellers), C. Mallorca 272-276, Barcelona 9.

Instituto Nacional del Libro Español (Spanish Publishers and Booksellers Institute), Santiago Rusiñol 8-10, Madrid 3. *Dir.* Juan Pedro Cortés Camacho.

Sri Lanka

Booksellers Assn. of Sri Lanka, Box 244, Colombo 2. *Secy.* W. L. Mendis.

Sri Lanka Publishers Assn., 61 Sangaraja Mawatha, Colombo 10. *Secy.-Gen.* Eamon Kariyakarawana.

Sweden

Svenska Antikvariatföreningen, c/o Rönnells, Birger Jarlsgatan 32, S-11429 Stockholm.

Svenska Bokförlaggareföreningen

(Swedish Publishers Assn.), Srearägen 52, S-111 34 Stockholm. *Managing Dir.* Jonas Modig.

Svenska Bokhandlareföreningen, Div. of Bok-, Pappers- och Kontorsvaruförbundet (Swedish Booksellers Assn., Div. of the Swedish Federation of Book, Stationery and Office Supplies Dealers), Skeppargatan 27, S-114 52 Stockholm. *Secy.* Per Nordenson.

Svenska Tryckeriföreningen (Swedish Printing Industries Federation), Blasieholmsgatan 4A, Box 16383, S-10327 Stockholm. *Managing Dir.* Per Gålmark.

Switzerland

Schweizerischer Buchhändler- und Verleger-Verband (Swiss German-Language Booksellers and Publishers Assn.), Bellerivestr. 3, CH-8008 Zurich. *Managing Dir.* Peter Oprecht.

Società Editori della Svizzera Italiana (Publishers Assn. for the Italian-Speaking Part of Switzerland), Box 282, Viale Portone 4, CH-6501 Bellinzona.

Société des Libraires et Editeurs de la Suisse Romande (Assn. of Swiss French-Language Booksellers and Publishers), 2 av. Agassiz, CH-1001 Lausanne. *Secy.* Robert Junod.

Vereinigung der Buchantiquare und Kupferstichhändler der Schweiz (Assn. of Swiss Antiquarians and Print Dealers), c/o Markus Krebser, Bälliz 64, CH-3601 Thun.

Thailand

Publishers and Booksellers Assn. of Thailand, c/o *Secy.* Plearnpit Praepanich Praepittaya L.P., 115/10 Soi Asoke, Sukhumvit Rd., Bangkok.

Tunisia

Syndicat des Libraires de Tunisie (Tunisian Booksellers Assn.), 10 av. de France, Tunis.

Turkey

Editòrler Derneği (Publishers Assn.), Ankara Caddesi 60, Istanbul.

United Kingdom

Assn. of Learned and Professional Society Publishers, R. J. Millson, 30 Austenwood Close, Chalfont St., Peter Gerrards Cross, Bucks., SL9 9DE.

Booksellers Assn. of Great Britain & Ireland, 154 Buckingham Palace Rd., London SW1W 9TZ. *Dir.* G. R. Davies.

Educational Publishers Council, 19 Bedford Sq., London WC1B 3HJ. *Dir.* John R. M. Davies.

National Book League, Book House, East Hill, London SW18. *Dir.* Martyn Goff, O.B.E.

National Federation of Retail Newsagents, 2 Bridewell Pl., London EC4V 6AR.

Publishers Assn., 19 Bedford Sq., London WC1B 3HJ. *Secy./Chief Exec.* Clive Bradley.

Uruguay

Asociación de Libreros del Uruguay (Uruguayan Booksellers Assn.), Av. Uruguay 1325, Montevideo.

Cámara Uruguaya del Libro (Uruguayan Publishing Council), Carlos Roxlo 1446, p. 1, Apdo. 2, Montevideo. *Secy.* Arnaldo Medone.

Yugoslavia

Association of Yugoslav Publishers and Booksellers, Kneza Miloša str. 25, Box 883, Belgrade. *Pres.* Branko Juričević.

Zambia

Booksellers Assn. of Zambia, Box 139, Ndola.

Zimbabwe

Advertising Media Assn., c/o Associated Chambers of Commerce of Zimbabwe Rhodesia, Box 1934, Salisbury.

Booksellers Assn. of Zimbabwe, Box 1934, Salisbury. *Hon. Secy.* L. Craven.

Calendar, 1981–1982

The list below contains information regarding place and date of association meetings or promotional events that are national or international in scope. Information is as of January 1981. For further details, contact the association directly. Addresses of library and book trade associations are listed in Part 7 of this *Bowker Annual*. For additional information on book trade and promotional events, see the *1980 Exhibits Directory*, published by the Association of American Publishers; *Chase's Calendar of Annual Events*, published by the Apple Tree Press, Box 1012, Flint, MI 49501; *Literary Market Place* and *International Literary Market Place*, published by R. R. Bowker; *Publishers Weekly* "Calendar," appearing in each issue; and *Library Journal's* "Calendar" feature, appearing in each semimonthly issue.

1981

May

3–6	Association of American Publishers	Key Biscayne, FL
4–7	National Computer Conference	Chicago, IL
7–8	Association of Research Libraries	New York, NY
20–25	Warsaw International Book Fair	Warsaw, Poland
23–26	American Booksellers Association	Atlanta, GA
5/29–6/4	Medical Library Association	Montreal, Canada
28–31	Association of American University Presses	San Francisco, CA
*	International Book Festival	Nice, France

June

13–18	Special Libraries Association	Atlanta, GA
6/28–7/1	American Association of Law Libraries	Washington, DC
6/28–7/4	American Library Association	San Francisco, CA
6/28–7/4	Theatre Library Association	San Francisco, CA
*	American Theological Library Association	St. Louis, MO
*	Church and Synagogue Library Association	St. Louis, MO

July

2–7	National Education Association	Minneapolis, MN
18–21	Canadian Booksellers Association	Vancouver, BC, Canada

August

1–5	International Association of Printing House Craftsmen	Boston, MA
17–22	International Federation of Library Associations and Institutions	Leipzig, German Democratic Republic

September

2–8	Moscow International Book Fair	Moscow, USSR
9/30–10/3	Association of College and Research Libraries	Minneapolis, MN

*To be announced.

October

25-30	American Society for Information Science	Washington, DC
28-29	Association of Research Libraries	Washington, DC
14-19	Frankfurt Book Fair	Frankfurt, Federal Republic of Germany
4-6	London Book Fair	London, England

November

1-4	Book Manufacturers Institute	Marco Island, FL

December

27-30	Modern Language Association	New York, NY

1982

January

17-23	International Association of Printing House Craftsmen	*
22-29	American Library Association	Denver, CO
28-31	Special Libraries Association	Louisville, KY

March

14-21	Leipzig Spring Fair	Leipzig, German Democratic Republic

April

2-5	National Science Teachers Association	Chicago, IL
7-9	Pubmart	New York, NY
11-15	National Association of College Stores	Boston, MA
12-15	Catholic Library Association	Chicago, IL
14-17	National Council of Teachers of Math	Toronto, Canada
26-30	International Reading Association	Chicago, IL

May

2-7	Association for Educational Communications and Technology	Dallas, TX
5-7	Association of Research Libraries	Scottsdale, AZ
9-12	Association of American Publishers	Marco Island, FL
19-24	International Book Fair	Warsaw, Poland
21-24	Association of American University Presses	Minneapolis, MN
5/29-6/1	American Booksellers Association	Anaheim, CA

June

7-10	National Computer Conference (AFIPS)	New York, NY
11-17	American Association of Law Libraries	Detroit, MI
12-17	Medical Library Association	Anaheim, CA
5-10	Special Libraries Association	Detroit, MI

*To be announced.

July

10–16	American Library Association	Philadelphia, PA

August

22–28	International Federal of Library Associations and Institutions	Montreal, Canada

October

6–11	Frankfurt Book Fair	Frankfurt, Federal Republic of Germany
17–21	American Society for Information Science	Columbus, OH
*	Association of Research Libraries	*
*	International Book Fair	Belgrade, Yugoslavia

November

18–28	National Council of Teachers of English	Washington, DC
24–27	National Council for the Social Studies	Boston, MA

December

27–30	Modern Language Association	New York, NY

*To be announced.

Five-Year Cumulative Index

The following is a five-year cumulative index, referring users directly to pages in the 1977–1981 editions of the *Bowker Annual;* to find references to editions before 1977, see the cumulative indexes which appeared in 1976, 1971, and 1965.

All important articles and charts appearing in the 1977–1981 editions are analytically treated in this cumulative index. Therefore, it is unnecessary to refer to the individual indexes of the 1977–1980 volumes. The following items have not been analytically treated in this cumulative index: Library associations, state, regional and provincial; State library agencies; School library associations, state; School library supervisors, state; Library associations meetings (calendar); and Educational associations meetings (calendar).

A

AACR 2, see *Anglo-American Cataloguing Rules*
AAHPER, see American Alliance for Health, Physical Education and Recreation
AAIS, see Automated Agricultural Information Systems
AALL, see American Association of Law Libraries
AALS, see Association of American Library Schools
AAP, see Association of American Publishers
"AAP Annual Industry Sales Statistics," 79:317; 77:313
AAP Exhibits Directory, 81:120
AAP Newsletter, 81:120; 80:133, 139; 79:110
AASL, see American Library Association, American Association of School Librarians
AAUP, see Association of American University Presses
ABA, see American Booksellers Association
ABA Basic Book List, 80:113; 79:111–112
ABA Book Buyer's Handbook, 80:112; 79:111; 77:86
ABA Educational Bulletin, 77:87
ABA Hardbound Basic Book List, 77:86
ABA Newswire, 80:112–113; 79:111; 77:87
ABA Paperback Basic Book List, 77:86
ABA Sidelines Directory, 80:113; 79:112; 77:86
ABA Trends, 77:86

ACRL, see American Library Association, Association of College and Research Libraries
AECT, see Association for Educational Communications and Technology
AGECON, 77:44
AGRICOLA, see Agricultural On-Line Access Data Base
AGRICOLA Users Guide, 80:111
AGRIS, see International Information Systems for the Agriculture Sciences and Technology
AIBDA, see Inter-American Association of Agricultural Librarians and Documentalists
AID, see Agency for International Development
AIIC, see International Association of Conference Interpreters
AIM, see Associated Information Managers
AIM Career Clearinghouse, 80:152
AIM Membership Roster, 80:152
AIM Network, 80:152
AIT, see Inter-American Association of Translators
AJL, see Association of Jewish Libraries
ALA, see American Library Association
ALA-AASL-Scholastic Magazines National Poster Contest, 80:123
ALA Handbook of Organization and Membership Directory, 81:103
ALA Personnel Organization and Procedures Manual, 77:57
"ALA Satellite Seminar on Copyright," 80:117

565

ALA's for ERA, **80**:118
ALA Washington Newsletter, **77**:117
ALA World Encyclopedia of Library and Information Services, **81**:103
ALA Yearbook, **77**:54
ALDP, *see* Academic Library Development Program
ALIN, *see* Agricultural Libraries Information Network
ALSC, *see* American Library Association, Association for Library Service to Children
ALTA, *see* American Library Association, American Library Trustee Association; American Literary Translators Association
AMIGOS bibliographic data base, **81**:20
ANSC, *see* American National Standards Committee Z39
ANSI, *see* American National Standards Institute
AOI, *see* Accent on Information
APIF, *see* Automated Process Information File data base
APIN, *see* Automatic Processing of Scientific Information (Poland)
ARL, *see* Association of Research Libraries
ARL Newsletter, **80**:143
ARL Statistics, 1976–1977, **78**:87
ARLIS/NA, *see* Art Libraries Society of North America
ASCLA, *see* American Library Association, Association of Specialized and Cooperative Library Agencies
ASCLA Exceptional Service Award, **79**:84
ASIS, *see* American Society for Information Science
ASIS Jobline, **81**:212; **80**:310; **79**:260; **78**:346–347; **77**:372
ASLA, *see* American Library Association, Association of State Library Agencies
ASLA Report on Interlibrary Cooperation, **79**:84; **78**:83; **77**:55, 74, 77, 78
ATA, *see* American Translators Association
ATA Chronicle, **79**:389–390
ATLA, *see* American Theological Library Association
ATLF, *see* Association of Literary Translators of France
AVLINE, **78**:75
Abdul Huq, A. M., **80**:493
Abell, Penny, **77**:3

"About Books," **80**:124; **79**:87; **78**:86; **77**:61
About Foundations: How to Find the Facts You Need to Get a Grant, **78**:180; **77**:215
Abstracts: Strengthening Research Library Resources Program, **80**:242; **79**:166; **78**:86
Academe, **78**:352
Academic Library Development Program, CLR support, **81**:156; **80**:266; **78**:171, 172; **77**:210
Academic Library Management Intern Program, **81**:158; **80**:268; **79**:190; **77**:207–208
Academic Library Program, **81**:121, 122, 156; **80**:266–267; **79**:90, 91–92, 189
Academic Research and Library Resources, **80**:362
Academy of Sciences (USSR), libraries, **79**:375–376
Accent on Information, **80**:63
Accreditation, *see* American Library Association, Committee on Accreditation; Library schools, accredited
Acquisitions, *see* Libraries, acquisitions
Action, placement services, **81**:220; **80**:318; **79**:266; **78**:353; **77**:378
Actualité terminologique, **79**:391
Ad Hoc Committee on Copyright, **81**:21
Ad Hoc Committee on Implementation of WHCOLIS Resolutions, **81**:140
Adult Education Act, extension, **79**:126
Adult Illiteracy in the United States, **80**:362
Adult learning centers, **77**:307
Advanced Study Program for Librarians, **78**:172
Advisory Committee for a National Preservation Program (ad hoc), **78**:174
Advisory Committee on Libraries and Information Services, **81**:32
Affirmative Action Register, placement services, **81**:219; **80**:317; **79**:265; **78**:352; **77**:377–378
"Africa—A Continent Asserts Its Identity," **81**:364
African Book Publishing Record, **81**:364
After Babel, **79**:393
Age Discrimination in Employment Act, **79**:125
Agency for International Development, **78**:405; **77**:441
Agents, literary, *see* Literary agents and authors
Agreement of Toronto, **77**:113–114

Agricultural Economics data base, *see* Agricultural On-Line Access Data Base
"Agricultural Information Users and Their Needs," **80:**110
Agricultural Libraries Information Network, **79:**76
Agricultural On-Line Access Data Base, **80:**111; **79:**77; **77:**44
Agriculture of the American Indian: A Selected Bibliography, **80:**111
Aids to Media Selection for Students and Teachers, **79:**148; **77:**185
Aje, Simeon B., **77:**416
Akwesasne Library and Cultural Center, **78:**56
Alabama A & M, School of Library Media, placement, **77:**372
Alldredge, Noreen G., **79:**332; **78:**307, 316
Allen, Raye Virginia, **79:**61; **78:**62
Allyn & Bacon, sues Wiley, **80:**42
Alpha Beta Alpha, **78:**363; **77:**405
Alternatives for Future Library Catalogs: A Cost Model, **81:**265
Aman, Mohammed M., **80:**493
Ambach, Gordon, **78:**26
"America through American Eyes," **81:**113; **80:**135
American Alliance for Health, Physical Education and Recreation, research and information center, **80:**63
American Archivist, **79:**95
American Association of Junior Colleges Career Staffing Center, placement services, **81:**219; **80:**316-317; **79:**265; **78:**352; **77:**377
American Association of Language Specialists, **79:**389
American Association of Law Libraries, **81:**439-441; **80:**563-564; **79:**445-446; **78:**443-444; **77:**478-479
 placement services, **81:**211; **80:**309; **79:**259; **78:**346; **77:**372
 special interest sections, **80:**402
American Association of School Librarians, *see* American Library Association, American Association of School Librarians
American Bibliography of Agricultural Economics, **77:**44
American Book Awards, **81:**44, 112-113, 119; **80:**39, 113, 132, 136
 ALA representation, **81:**106
American Bookseller, **80:**112; **79:**111
American Booksellers Association, **80:**112-114; **79:**111-114; **77:**86-89
 annual meeting, **80:**39
 BISG support, **80:**443
 Convention and Trade Exhibit, **79:**114; **77:**88
 see also Booksellers School
American Chemical Society, placement services, **80:**309; **79:**259; **78:**346; **77:**372
American Folklife Center, **81:**86-87; **80:**96; **79:**60; **78:**61-62, 68-71; **77:**36-37
 Federal Cylinder Project, **81:**87
 see also Chicago Ethnic Arts Project; South-Central Georgia Folklife Project
American Foundation for the Blind, Commission on Standards of Accreditation of Services for the Blind, *see* Commission on Standards of Accreditation of Services for the Blind
American Heritage Dictionary, censorship, **77:**17
"American Issues Forum," **77:**60
American Libraries, **81:**103; **80:**117; **79:**80; **78:**81; **77:**371
 article competition, **77:**54
 placement services, **80:**309; **79:**259; **78:**345
 placements, **81:**209, 211
American Library Association, **81:**102-106; 441-444; **80:**115-124, 565-568; **79:**79-87, 446-450; **78:**79-86, 445-448; **77:**51-61, 117, 480-484
 American Association of School Librarians, **81:**444-448; **80:**119, 568-572; **79:**83, 451-454; **78:**22, 82, 448-451; **77:**18, 54-55, 484-487
 Affiliates Assembly, **79:**36
 national conference, **80:**34
 President's Award, **78:**82
 Promotion and Recognition of Secondary School Media Programs Committee, **80:**119
 representation in NCLIS, **78:**27
American Library Trustee Association, **81:**448-449; **80:**119-120, 572-573; **79:**83, 454-455; **78:**82, 451-452; **77:**55, 487-488
 Honor Awards, **78:**82
 annual conference, **81:**104; **80:**116-117, 121; **79:**79; **78:**80-81
 book industry tours, **81:**116
 Association for Library Service to Children, **81:**449-452; **80:**120, 573-576; **79:**36, 83-84, 455-458; **78:**23, 82-83, 452-457

American Library Association (Cont.)
international relations, **81**:106
symposium on "Books and Broadcasting for Children," **80**:28-29
WHCOLIS resolution, **81**:34
Association of College and Research Libraries, **81**:452-454; **80**:120, 576-579; **79**:87-91, 459-461; **78**:82, 455-457; **77**:5, 55, 488-490
Committee on University Library Standards (with ARL), **78**:88
Fast Job Listing Service, **81**:211
Internship Project, **78**:82
national conference, **80**:120; **79**:24, 83, 88-89; **78**:82
placement services, **80**:309; **79**:259
Association of Specialized and Cooperative Library Agencies, **81**:454-457; **80**:120-121, 579-582; **79**:84, 461-464
background history, **80**:58-59
formed from ASLA and HRLSD, **79**:24
grant from OE, **80**:120
Library Service to the Deaf Section, **80**:59
Association of State Library Agencies
merged into ASCLA, **79**:84
merger with HRLSD, **78**:83; **77**:80
see also American Library Association, Association of Specialized and Cooperative Library Agencies
Black Caucus
librarian exchange program, **80**:319; **79**:267; **78**:354; **77**:379
placement services, **81**:211; **80**:310, 319; **79**:259; **77**:372
building plans, **77**:53
centennial, **79**:190; **77**:10, 17
Centennial Conference, **77**:53
Children's Services Division, **77**:493-495
Committee on Accreditation, **80**:119; **79**:80; **78**:81; **77**:53
see also Library schools, accredited
Committee on Legislation, **81**:102
Committee on Program Evaluation and Support, **77**:51
Committee on the Status of Women in Librarianship, **81**:263; **79**:82-83; **78**:31
council, **78**:31
Standing Committee on Library Education, **78**:84
divisions, autonomy, **81**:35
dues and membership, **78**:80; **77**:52-53
filmmaking, **78**:28-29; **77**:51-52
finances, **78**:79; **77**:51-52
Freedom to Read Committee, **78**:30
Freedom to Read Foundation, **81**:30, 37; **80**:27, 118; **79**:82; **78**:30
cooperation with ALA, Intellectual Freedom Committee, **78**:85
Government Documents Round Table, **79**:86
headquarters, **81**:106
Health and Rehabilitative Library Services Division, **78**:83, 459-461
merged into ASCLA, **79**:84; **77**:56, 495-497
merger with ASLA, **78**:83; **77**:80
see also American Library Association, Association of Specialized and Cooperative Library Agencies
honorary memberships, **79**:79
Independent Schools Section, **79**:36
information agenda colloquium, **81**:103
Intellectual Freedom Committee, **79**:28; **78**:30; **77**:59
conflicting scheduling, **81**:30
international relations, **81**:105-106; **78**:85-86; **77**:59
International Relations Committee, **79**:82
International Relations Office, **80**:491
International Relations Round Table, program on IFLA activities, **80**:115
Junior Members Round Table, **79**:86
Library Administration and Management Association, **81**:457-458; **80**:121, 582-583; **79**:84, 464-466
Committee on Sexism and Racism Awareness, **80**:121
name change from LAD, **79**:84
publications, **80**:121
Statistics Coordinating Committee, **80**:363
Statistics Section, **81**:267-268; **80**:121, 364-366
Library Administration Division, **78**:463-464; **77**:57, 498-500
see also Library Administration and Management Association, *above*
Library and Information Technology Association, **81**:459-460; **80**:121, 583-585; **79**:24, 84-85, 466-467
Video Cable Communications Sections, **80**:121
workshops on automation, **81**:28
Library Education Division, **77**:57-58, 500-501

disbanded, **79:**24, 82; **78:**84
see also American Library Association, council, Standing Committee on Library Education
Library History Round Table, **80:**122
Library History Seminar VI, **81:**105
Library Research Round Table award, **79:**41
Machine Assisted Reference Section, **79:**16; **77:**58
midwinter meeting, **80:**32–33, 117; **79:**79
multitype library cooperation, **78:**83
Office for Library Outreach Services, **81:**103
Office for Library Personnel Resources, **80:**123; **79:**86; **78:**86; **77:**60
Office for Library Service to the Disadvantaged, **80:**123; **79:**86; **78:**86; **77:**60
  Library Service for American Indian People, **80:**123
  name changed to Office for Library Outreach Services, **81:**103
Office for Research, **79:**37; **77:**60
Office of Intellectual Freedom, **81:**104; **80:**118–119; **79:**81; **78:**29, 85
  Intellectual Freedom Committee, **81:**104
placement services, **81:**211; **80:**309; **79:**259; **78:**346
preconferences, **81:**264
see also American Library Association, annual conference
Public Information Office, **80:**123–124; **79:**87; **78:**86; **77:**60–61
Public Library Association, **81:**460–462; **80:**121–122, 585–587; **79:**85, 467–469; **78:**84, 464–466; **77:**58, 501–502
  Metropolitan Libraries Section, **78:**84
  Mission Statement, **78:**267
  Small and Medium-Sized Libraries Section, **78:**84
publishing services, **81:**103; **80:**117–118; **79:**79–80; **78:**81
Reference and Adult Services Division, **81:**462–464; **80:**122, 587–589; **79:**85, 469–471; **78:**84, 466–468; **77:**58, 502–504
  History Section, Local History Committee, **80:**122
  Machine Assisted Reference Section, **78:**14, 84
Resolution on Prejudice, Stereotyping, and Discrimination and the Library Bill of Rights, **79:**81–82

Resources and Technical Services Division, **81:**464–466; **80:**122, 589–591; **79:**85, 471–473; **78:**84, 468–470; **77:**58–59, 504–506
  Library Materials Price Index Committee, **81:**341; **80:**455; **77:**332
  workshops on *AACR 2*, **81:**28
satellite teleconference on copyright law, **79:**32
services for the handicapped, **80:**58–59
Social Responsibilities Round Table
  placement services, **80:**310; **79:**259; **78:**346; **77:**372
  SRRT Jobline, **81:**211
  Task Force on Women, **81:**35
special citation for D. J. Urquhart, **79:**79
Standing Committee on Library Education, **79:**24
  Continuing Education Center, **81:**27
statistical activities, **80:**363–366
survey of libraries and readers, *see* Gallup Organization, reader survey
teleconference on copyright, **79:**81
Young Adult Services Division, **81:**466–467; **80:**122, 591–593; **79:**36, 85–86, 473–475; **78:**25, 85, 470–471; **77:**59, 506–508
  High Interest-Low Reading Level Materials Evaluation Committee, **78:**85
  Intellectual Freedom Committee, **78:**85
  Legislation Committee, **78:**85
  miniconferences, **80:**35
  Reevaluation of YASD Goals and Objectives Committee, **78:**85
  support of youth's rights, **80:**35
Youth Services Divisions, **80:**34
American Library Society, **78:**471–472; **77:**508
American Library Trustee Association, *see* American Library Association, American Library Trustee Association
American Literary Translators Association, **79:**395
American Merchant Marine Library Association, **81:**467; **80:**593; **79:**475; **78:**472; **77:**509
American National Standards Committee X12, Business Data Interchange, liaison with ANSC Z39, **80:**127
American National Standards Committee Z39, **81:**107–112; **80:**124–132, 266,

American National Standards Committee Z39 (Cont.)
  369-370; **79:**98-100; **78:**102-108; **77:**65-70, 207
  annual meeting, **81:**109; **80:**127; **79:**100
  code for periodicals and serials, **79:**67
  funding, **81:**110; **80:**127-128; **79:**99, 187
  international activities, **80:**129-132
  member organizations, **78:**105-108
  participation in ISO/TC 46, **79:**104
  reevaluation, **78:**44-45
  reorganized, **79:**98-99
  Subcommittee 20, Standard for Price Indexes for Library Materials, **80:**370
American National Standards Committee Z39: Recommended Future Directions, **79:**51
American National Standards Committee Z39.7, **81:**269
American National Standards Institute, **81:**107
  standards for building adaptation, **80:**56
American Overseas Library Technical Assistance, **80:**493
American Printing House for the Blind, materials for the blind, **80:**61
American Society for Information Science, **81:**468-469; **80:**593-594; **79:**475-476; **78:**473-474; **77:**509-510
  placement services, **81:**212; **80:**310; **79:**259-260; **78:**346-347; **77:**372
American Theological Library Association, **81:**469-470; **80:**595-596; **79:**476-478; **78:**474-475; **77:**510-511
  placement services, **81:**212; **80:**310; **79:**260; **78:**347; **77:**372
American Translators Association, **79:**387, 389
America's Library of Classics, **80:**40
Anderson, Charles B., **77:**87
Anglo-American Cataloguing Rules, **81:**14, 88, 154; **80:**15, 122, 265, 360-361; **79:**62, 85, 87; **78:**65, 84, **77:**39, 54, 58
  institutes, **81:**105
Antiquarian book trade associations, *see* Book trade associations
Applebaum, Edmond L., **79:**58
Aquaculture and Hydroponics: A Bibliography, **80:**111
Architectural and Transportation Barriers Compliance Board, **80:**54, 56

Architectural Barriers Act, 1968, **79:**144
Archives, **80:**259-263; **79:**96-98
  bibliography, **81:**398-399; **79:**574
  conservation and preservation, *see* Library materials, conservation and preservation
  manuscript donations, **80:**185
  National Historical Publications and Records Commission support, **79:**178
  national inventory, **81:**204
  national program needs, **79:**182-183
  planning programs, **81:**203-204
  standard techniques, **81:**203; **79:**180
  TIS/NAL archival film record, **79:**78
  see also International Council on Archives; International Federation of Film Archives; Society of American Archivists
Archivists, education and training, **79:**97
Army Library, Pentagon, **78:**76-78
Art Libraries Society of North America, **81:**471; **80:**596-597; **79:**478-479; **78:**476; **77:**511-512
  placement services, **81:**212; **80:**310; **79:**260; **78:**347; **77:** 372-373
Art of Translation, **79:**389
Arts, Humanities, and Cultural Affairs Act, **77:**105
Asbury, Barbara N., **79:**303; **78:**281; **77:**282
Ashley Books, sues CBS, **80:**42
Asia Foundation, **80:**689-690; **79:**567-568; **78:**405-406; **77:**441-442
Asian American Librarians Caucus, placements, **77:**373
Asociación Mexicana de Bibliotecarios, **77:**426
Associated Information Managers, **81:**472; **80:**597-598
  placement services, **81:**212
Association canadienne des sciences de l'information, **79:**486
Association for Educational Communication & Technology, placement services, **81:**212; **80:**310; **79:**260; **78:**27; **77:**373
Association for Library Service to Children, *see* American Library Association, Association for Library Service to Children
Association of Academic Health Sciences Library Directors, **81:**472-473; **80:**598; **79:**479-480

Association of American Library Schools, 81:473–474; 80:599; 79:480–481; 78:477; 77:512–513
  IFLA status, 79:24
Association of American Publishers, 81: 112–120; 80:132–140; 79:104–110; 78:89–94; 77:81–86
  annual meeting, 80:39
  BISG support, 80:443
  Book Distribution Task Force, 80:135
  Book Industry Tours, 81:116
  College Division, 81:117; 80:137
  Communications Task Force, 80:135–136
  cooperation with other associations, 80:139
  Copyright Clearance Center, see Copyright Clearance Center
  copyright guidelines, 79:15
  core committees, 81:114–116; 80:134–136; 78:12, 123–124; 77:82–83
  Direct Marketing/Book Club Division, 81:119
  Education for Publishing Committee, 80:133; 77:387–388
  Education for Publishing Program, 80:135
  Entry-Level Job Clearing House, 81:115–116
  Freedom to Read Committee, 80:134
  General Publishing Division, 81:116; 80:136; 79:107; 78:91; 77:83
    Marketing Group, 81:116
  International Division, 81:118–119; 80:138–139; 79:109; 78:93–94; 77:85
    annual meeting, 1st, 81:119
  International Freedom to Publish Committee, 80:134–135
  liaison with ABA, 79:112
  liaison with other associations, 81:119–120
  Management Audit Team, technology watch, 80:133
  Mass Market Paperback Division, 81:116–117
    Convenience Store Workshop, 80:136–137; 79:108
    Rack Clearance Center, 81:117; 79:108
  Postal Committee, 80:114, 134–135
  Professional and Scholarly Publishing Division, 81:117–118; 80:137–138
  publications, 81:120
  Publishing Education Information Service, 81:115–116
  School Division, 81:118; 80:138
    Right to Read Committee, 81:118
  small publishers conference, 80:39
  Smaller Publishers Group, 80:133
  sues Gnomon Corp., 81:22
  support of NACS seminars, 78:96
  Technical, Scientific and Medical Division, see above, under Professional and Scholarly Publishing Division
  see also Booksellers School
Association of American University Presses
  annual convention, 80:39
  BISG support, 80:443
Association of College and Research Libraries, see American Library Association, Association of College and Research Libraries
Association of Jewish Libraries, 81:474–475; 80:600; 78:478; 77:513–514
Association of Literary Translators of France, 79:392
Association of Research Libraries, 81:475–476; 80:140–145, 600–602; 79:481–482; 78:87–88, 478–480; 77:61–62, 514–515
  Center for Chinese Research Materials, 80:144; 78:88
  commissions dissolved, 77:61
  Committee on Interlibrary Loan, 77:63
  membership, 77:61
  Office of Management Studies, 81:120–124; 80:144; 79:90–93; 78:88, 179; 77:209
    Academic Library Development Program, see Academic Library Development Program; Academic Library Program
    Collection Analysis Project, see Collection Analysis Project
    Consultant Training Program, see Consultant Training Program
    MRAP, see Management Review and Analysis Program
    Management Skills Institute, see Management Skills Institute
    Office Program of Information Collection and Dissemination, 81:123
    Office Program of Organizational Training and Staff Development, 81:123
    Organizational Screening Program,

Association of Research Libraries (Cont.)
  see Organizational Screening Program
  Planning Program for Small Academic Libraries, see Planning Program for Small Academic Libraries
  Preservation Planning Program, see Preservation Planning Program
  Public Services Improvement Program, see Public Services Improvement Program
  Training Film Program, see Training Film Program
  Training Program, 81:124
  see also Systems and Procedures Exchange Center
  programs and projects, 80:143-144
    see also Academic Library Program; Collection Analysis Project; Library Cost Model Project
  Task Force on Statistics, 80:143; 78:179
Association of Specialized and Cooperative Library Agencies, see American Library Association, Association of Specialized and Cooperative Library Agencies
Association of State Library Agencies, see American Library Association, Association of Specialized and Cooperative Library Agencies
Association of Visual Science Librarians, 81:477; 80:602; 79:483; 78:480; 77:516
Associations, book trade, see Book trade associations
Associations, education, see names of specific associations
Associations, information science, see names of specific associations
Associations, library, see Library associations
Associations, publishers, see Book trade associations; also names of associations, e.g., Association of American Publishers
Associations, translators, see Translators associations
Atkinson, Hugh C., 79:332; 78:307, 316, 317; 77:331
Audiovisual materials, 78:221
  bibliographic control, 79:52
  bibliography, 81:399; 80:523; 79:574; 78:566
  copying, 79:43
  copyright protection, 81:77
  fair use of broadcast works, 80:185; 79:71-92
  import duties, 77:111-112
  off-air videotaping, 81:74; 80:192, 200
  prices and price indexes, 79:340-341
  videocassettes, 80:117
  see also American Library Association, Library and Information Technology Association, Video Cable Communications Section; Microforms; Phonorecords, licensing; Videodisc technology
Audiovisual Resources in Food and Nutrition, 80:110
Audiovisual Serials in Health Science, 79:74
Auel, Jean, 80:41
Australian and New Zealand Library Resources, 81:157
Authority files, see Bibliographic control, authority files
Authors, see Literary agents and authors
"Author's Guide to Academic Publishing," 81:117; 79:108
Automated Agricultural Information Systems, 79:76
Automated Process Information File data base, 77:39
Automatic Processing of Scientific Information (Poland), 79:369
Automation in libraries, see Bibliographic data bases; Cataloging and classification; Information services; Libraries, automated circulation systems; Libraries, computerized functions
Availability of Media in Library Schools, 77:58
Avram, Henriette D., 81:46
Awards, library, 81:254-259; 80:349; 79:415-420; 78:415-417; 77:390-393
Awards, literary, 81:44, 415-426; 80:539-548; 79:421-432; 78:418-432; 77:457-466
  see also Best sellers; Books, best books; Books, best books, juvenile; Books, best books, young adult
Awards, publishing
  PSP awards, 81:118
  see also names of specific awards, e.g., Benjamin, Curtis G., Award

B

BALLOTS, 81:19, 79:14, 187
BAS, see Books-Across-the-Sea

BCR, *see* Bibliographic Center for Research
BIA, *see* U.S., Bureau of Indian Affairs
BIBDATA, 77:429
BIBLINK, 81:154, 265
BIOETHICSLINE, 79:73
BISG, *see* Book Industry Study Group Inc.
BISG Bulletin, 80:445
BLA, see *Bibliographies and Literature of Agriculture*
BLAISE, *see* British Library, Automated Information Service
BLAMS, *see* Braintree Librarians and Media Specialists
BLR and DD, *see* British Library, Research and Development Department
BMI, *see* Book Manufacturers Institute
BOCES, *see* Board of Cooperative Educational Services
BRS, *see* Bibliographic Retrieval Services
BSDP, *see* Council on Library Resources, Bibliographic Service Development Program
Bâ, Mariama, 81:364
Babel: An International Journal of Translation, 79:389
Baer, Mark H., 77:3, 62
Bahamas: Public Library Service, 79:351
Bailey K. Howard-World Book Encyclopedia-ALA Goals Award, to IFC, 81:104
Baker, John F., 81:42
Barnouw, Erik, 79:59; 78:66
Barrow, W. J., Research Laboratory, 78:174; 77:210
Basic Skills Improvement Program, 81:58
Batchelder Award, 78:82–83
Bearman, Toni Carbo, 81:78
"Behind the Scenes of College Publishing," 79:108; 78:92
Bender, David R., 80:167
Benjamin, Curtis G., Award, 81:119; 80:139; 79:110
Best sellers, 81:431–436; 80:554–560; 79:433–437; 78:432–436; 77:466–476
"What Americans Are Reading," 79:87
see also Books, best books
Beta Phi Mu, 81:477–479; 80:603–604; 79:483–485; 78:360–362; 77:406
Distinguished Service Award, 78:362
grant to *The Speaker*, 78:29
Betamax case, 80:72
Bibliografía Mexicana, 77:427
Bibliographic Center for Research, 79:14

Bibliographic control
  authority files, 81:48, 154–155; 79:52; 78:43; 77:26
  international, 79:187–188
  nationwide, 81:17; 79:186; 78:170; 77:206
  nonprint media, 78:45
  Pakistan, 78:383–384
  serial publications, 79:186; 77:206
  standards, 81:48, 107–108, 154–155; 80:265–266; 79:187; 78:13
  see also Audiovisual materials, bibliographic control; Cataloging and classification; International Federation of Library Associations and Institutions, International Office for Universal Bibliographic Control; Libraries, automated circulation systems; Universal bibliographic control
Bibliographic data bases, 78:77–78; 77:5, 44
  AAP concerns, 80:135
  access, on-line, 81:265
  archival bases, national, 79:181
  Australia, 77:429
  cooperative ventures, 79:187
  copyright status, 78:52
  health sciences libraries, 81:280
  interlocking, 81:16–17
  linking, 81:47–48, 154; 80:265
  NAL, 81:99–100
  national, 80:82; 79:185–186; 78:169
  serials, 79:68
  see also National Library Network (proposed)
  nonprint media, 77:26
  patron access, on-line, 81:155
  periodicals, 81:155; 79:31
  special education materials, 80:61
  standards, *see* Bibliographic control, standards
  subject access, 78:170
  USSR, 79:374
  see also Data bases; Information services; Networks; *also* names of specific bases, e.g., HISTLINE
Bibliographic Retrieval Services, 80:66, 67
Bibliographic Retrieval Services User Council, 79:16
Bibliographic Service Development Program, CLR funding, 81:17
Bibliographic services, *see* Council on Library Resources, Bibliographic Service Development Program; Information services; Networks

Bibliographical Society of America, **81**:479; **80**:605; **79**:485; **78**:481; **77**:516
Bibliographies, bibliography, **81**:407–409; **80**:533–534; **79**:583–584; **78**:575–576
Bibliographies and Literature of Agriculture, **80**:111
Bibliography of Bibliographies, **80**:122
Bibliography of Humanistic Reading for Grade Levels 1–8, **80**:123
Bibliography on Professionalism (NLA), **80**:160
Bicknell v. *Vergennes Union High School,* **81**:37
Bidlack, Russell E., **77**:53
Biosis Previews, **77**:429
Black Experience: A Bibliography of Bibliographies, **79**:85
Blake, John B., **81**:94
Blume, Judy, **80**:32
Board of Cooperative Educational Services, **80**:30; **78**:32
 copyright infringement, **79**:16, 32, 43
Bock, D. Joleen, **80**:441; **79**:314; **78**:299; **77**:306
Bodner, Deborah, **78**:102; **77**:65
Bologna Children's Book Fair, **80**:40
Booher, Edward E., **78**:395
Book clubs, **80**:139
Book design, *see* Books, design and production
Book exchanges, *see* Book programs; Universal Serials and Book Exchange, Inc.
Book exports, **81**:384–387; **80**:510–514; **79**:410; **78**:401–405; **77**:450
 AAP concerns, **78**:93–94
 India, **81**:380
Book fairs, **80**:40; **78**:394
 dates, **80**:695–698 *passim;* **79**:593–594; **78**:581–582
 see also Frankfurt Book Fair
Book gift certificate programs, **77**:88–89
Book imports, **81**:332, 384–387; **80**:449, 510–514; **79**:325, 411; **78**:310, 401–405; **77**:452
 India, **81**:380–381
 see also Florence Agreement Protocol
Book Industries Study Alert, **80**:445
Book Industry Distributions Systems Alert, **80**:445
Book Industry Study Group, Inc., **80**:443–446; **79**:38, 61; **77**:60
Book Industry Trends, **80**:444, 445, 475
"Book Is a Loving Gift," **79**:107

Book Manufacturers Institute, BISG support, **80**:443
Book outlets, *see* Bookstores
Book programs, **80**:689–694; **79**:567–572; **78**:405–411; **77**:441-449
 federal funding, **79**:127; **78**:119
 see also names of programs, e.g., Asia Foundation; Give-a-Book Certificate Program; Reading is FUNdamental
Book publishing, *see* Publishing
Book review media, **81**:355; **80**:477; **79**:331; **78**:314; **77**:328
Book sales, **81**:45; **80**:37
 direct marketing, **80**:139; **79**:109–110
 statistics, **81**:336; **80**:471; **79**:317–321; **78**:303–306; **77**:313–318, 319–327
 wholesale, **80**:476
 see also Books, consumer expenditures; Paperback books, Sales; Textbooks, sales
Book stores, *see* Bookstores
Book trade
 bibliography, **81**:407–414; **80**:444–445, 532–538; **79**:583–588; **78**:575–580; **77**:611–615
 directories and yearbooks, **81**:412–413; **80**:537; **79**:587–588; **78**:579
 international, **81**:118–119; **80**:40, 138–139
 statistics, *see* Book exports; Book imports; Book sales; Book trade, surveys; Books, consumer expenditures; Books, prices and price indexes; Publishing statistics
 surveys, **80**:443–446
  bibliography, **80**:535–536
 see also Books, design and production; Bookselling; Publishing
Book trade associations, **81**:549–555; **80**:39–40, 676–682; **79**:555–560; **78**:550–555; **77**:582-587
 AAP liaisons, **79**:110
 cooperation, **78**:91
 foreign, **81**:555–561; **80**:682–689; **79**:560–567; **78**:556–563; **77**:587–595
 relations with ABA, **79**:113
 international, **81**:555
 meetings, **81**:562–564; **80**:114, 695–698; **79**:593–594; **78**:581–582; **77**:621–623
 see also names of specific associations, e.g., American Booksellers Association, Association of American Publishers

Booklist, **79:**80; **78:**81; **77:**54
Bookmobiles, **81:**11-12; **80:**11
Books
 automatic ordering, **80:**37
 best books, **81:**426-427; **80:**549-550; **79:**438-439; **78:**436-437; **77:**470-471
  juvenile, **81:**429-431; **80:**552-554; **79:**439-442; **78:**437-439; **77:**472-475
  young adult, **81:**427-428; **80:**550-552; **79:**442-444; **78:**439-441; **77:**475-477
  see also Awards, literary; Best sellers
 consumer expenditures, **81:**338-340
 definition, **81:**325
 design and production, bibliography, **81:**411-412; **80:**536; **79:**586; **78:**578
 distribution, *see* Publishing, distribution of books
 international flow, **79:**61
 international importance, **81:**93
 library bindings, **78:**99-102
 mailing statistics, **77:**328-329
 pirating, **81:**365-366
 postal rates, *see* Postal rates; U.S., Postal Service
 prices and price indexes, **81:**42, 329, 331, 333-335, 344-347; **80:**446-453, 458, 459, 460; **79:**326, 337; **78:**310, 313, 320-326; **77:**335
  Germany, **81:**352; **80:**454, 455, 465; **79:**344; **78:**325; **77:**340
  Great Britain, **81:**350, 351; **80:**454, 463, 464; **79:**342, 343; **78:**323-324; **77:**338, 339
  Latin America, **81:**353; **80:**454, 466; **79:**345; **78:**326; **77:**341
  see also Library materials, prices and price indexes; Paperback books, prices and price indexes
 rare books, security, **78:**88
 sales, *see* Book sales
 title output, *see* Publishing statistics, title output
 translations, **80:**449
 see also Paperback books; Textbooks
Books-Across-the-Sea, **79:**569-570; **77:**443-444
"Books and Broadcasting for Children," symposium, **80:**28-29, 120
"Books and Bucks," **78:**92
Books as Gifts, AAP Program, **78:**91
"Books Make a Difference," **81:**91
Booksellers
 continuing education, **80:**113; **79:**112
 small independent, **81:**42
 see also American Booksellers Association
Booksellers associations, *see* Book trade associations
Booksellers School, **80:**113; **79:**112; **78:**96; **77:**87
Bookselling
 backlists, **80:**37
 bibliography, **81:**412; **80:**536-537; **79:**586-587; **78:**560; **77:**614
 cost ratios, **80:**37
 financial problems, **80:**114-115
 standard account numbers, **77:**88
Bookselling in America and the World, **77:**87
Bookstores
 college, **81:**117; **80:**137; **79:**108; **78:**94-99
 expenditures, *see* Books, consumer expenditures
 financial survey by ABA, **79:**113-114
 number of, U.S. and Canada, **81:**354-355; **80:**476-477; **79:**329-330; **78:**313-314; **77:**327-328
 returns to publishers, **81:**41
"Bookweek U.S.A.," **77:**89
Boonin, J. M., **80:**455
Boorstin, Daniel J., **77:**3, 21
Booth, Larry, **78:**174
Bordas Group, takes over Elsevier French language publishing, **81:**366
Born, Gerald, **77:**77
Börsenblatt, **80:**483
Börsenverein peace prize, **78:**392, 396
Boss, Richard, **80:**361
Boultbee, Paul G., **79:**350
Bowden, Russell, **79:**360
Bowe, Frank, **80:**55
Bowker, R. R., Data Services Department, **78:**306-307
Braintree Librarians and Media Specialists, **78:**26
Braunagel, Judith S., **80:**363
Brief Guide to Centres of International Lending and Photocopying, **81:**371
Brigham Young University, Language and Intercultural Research Center, **79:**391
"Bringing Books and Teachers Together," **79:**107
British Library, **79:**360, 364
 Automated Information Service, **79:**364
 Lending Division, **79:**361-362

British Library (Cont.)
  Library Management Research Unit, **80:** 454; **79:**364
  Research and Development Department, **79:**362, 363, 364
British Library Association, International and Comparative Librarianship Group, **80:**491
British National Bibliography, **78:**324
Broadcasting stations, *see* Telecommunications, broadcasting stations
Broderick, John C., **79:**59
Bronze Hugo, **79:**81
Brother, Shirley A., **80:**204
Brower, Reuben A., **79:**390
Burchinal, Lee G., **78:**161; **77:**201
Burke, Theresa M., Employment Agency, **81:**213; **80:**307; **79:**257; **78:**344; **77:**371
Business Week, Information Processing Department, **80:**155
Byam, Milton, **78:**28

C

CAIN, **77:**44
CAIS, *see* Canadian Association for Information Science
CALA, *see* Chinese-American Librarians Association
CALS, *see* Current Awareness Literature Service
CANCERPROJ, **77:**42
CAP, *see* Collection Analysis Project; Cooperative Acquisitions Program
CARDS, *see* Card Automated Reproduction Demand System
C & RL News, **79:**89
CATLINE, **80:**106
CCC, *see* Copyright Clearance Center
CCLN, *see* Council for Computerized Library Networks
CCNBC, *see* Committee for the Coordination of National Bibliographic Control
CCRM, *see* Association of Research Libraries, Center for Chinese Research Materials
CETA, *see* Comprehensive Employment and Training Act
CHEMLINE, **80:**107; **79:**74; **78:**74
CIP, *see* Library of Congress, Cataloguing in Publication Program

CKC, *see* Consultants Keyword Clearinghouse
CLA, *see* Canadian Library Association; Catholic Library Association
CLAM, *see* Consortium of Library Automation in Mississippi
CLASS, *see* California Library Authority for Systems and Services
CLENE, *see* Continuing Library Education Network and Exchange
CLENE Exchange, **77:**385
CLR, *see* Council on Library Resources
CL Systems, Inc., **79:**18
CNLA, *see* Council of National Library and Information Associations
CNLIA, *see* Council of National Library and Information Associations
CNPIC, *see* China National Publications Import Corporation
COA, *see* American Library Association, Committee on Accreditation
COLT, *see* Council on Library/Media Technical Assistants
COM, *see* Computer Output Microfilm
COMARC, **79:**62, 187; **78:**63–64, 169
COMSAS, *see* Medical Library Association, Committee on Surveys and Statistics
COMSEARCH Printouts, **80:**276; **79:**195; **78:**180
COMSTAC, *see* Commission on Standards of Accreditation of Services for the Blind
CONACyT, *see* Consejo Nacional de Ciencia y Tecnologia
CONSER, *see* Conversion of Serials
CONTU, *see* National Commission on New Technological Uses of Copyrighted Works
COPES, *see* American Library Association, Committee on Program Evaluation and Support
COR, *see* Council of Regions
COSLA, *see* Chief Officers of State Library Agencies
COSWL, *see* American Library Association, Committee on the Status of Women in Librarianship
CPB, *see* Corporation for Public Broadcasting
CPL, *see* Council of Planning Librarians
CRIS, *see* Current Research Information System
CRS, *see* Library of Congress, Congressional Research Service

CSD, *see* American Library Association, Children's Services Division
CSLA, *see* Church and Synagogue Library Association
CTP, *see* Consultant Training Program
CTS, *see* Communications Technology Satellite
CUSS, *see* Cooperative Union Serials System
Cable television, *see* Telecommunications, cable television
Caldecott Medal, **79**:83; **78**:32, 82
California, Proposition 13, *see* Proposition 13
California Library Association, **80**:7; **79**:40
California Library Authority for Systems and Services, **81**:21; **79**:14, 15; **77**:8
California State Library, **79**:40
Call the Darkness Light, **80**:485
Campbell, Ann Morgan, **79**:94
Campbell, Francis Joseph, Award, **79**:84
Campbell, Henry C., **79**:355
"Campus Paperback Best-Seller List," **80**:137
Canada Council, Translation Prize, **79**:392
Canadian Association for Information Science (Association Canadienne des Sciences de l'Information), **81**:480; **80**:605-606; **79**:486
Canadian Institute for Scientific and Technical Information, **79**:356
Canadian International Development Agency, grant to IFLA, **77**:511
Canadian Library Association, **81**:480-481; **80**:606-607; **79**:486-488; **78**:481-482; **77**:516-518
  Intellectual Freedom Fund, **80**:32
  joint activities with Association pour l'avancement des sciences et des techniques de la documentation (ASTED), **79**:359
Canadian library associations, *see* Library associations, Canada; *also* Canadian Library Association; Canadian Association for Information Science
Canadiana, **79**:356
Capital Letter, **81**:120; **80**:139; **79**:110
Capital Provision for University Libraries, **79**:362
Captain Kangaroo, **79**:35-36
Card Automated Reproduction Demand System, **79**:64
"Career LEADS EXPRESS," job listings, **81**:211

Carnegie-Mellon University, belletristic translation program, **79**:392
Carrie, **80**:32
Carter, Jimmy
  message to Congress on libraries, **81**:56-59
  statement on White House Conference, **77**:29-30
  statement sent to ALA, July 1976, **77**:20-21
Carter, Yvonne B., **77**:183
Case, Sara, **77**:99
Cataloging and classification, **81**:14-15, 264-265; **80**:15-16; **79**:17
  bibliography, **81**:406-407; **80**:531-532; **79**:581-582; **78**:572-573; **77**:608-609
  cooperative cataloging, **79**:62; **78**:63, 372
  costs of catalogs, **80**:361
  on-line OCLC system, **80**:165, 166
  subject headings, **79**:63
  see also Bibliographic control; CATLINE; Libraries, computerized functions; Library of Congress, Cataloging in Publication program, and similar headings
Cataloging in Publication, *see* Library of Congress, Cataloging in Publication Program
Cataloging-Indexing, *see* CAIN
Catalyst, placement services, **81**:219; **80**:317; **79**:265-266; **78**:352; **77**:378
Catholic Library Association, **81**:482-483; **80**:607-609; **79**:488-489; **78**:483-484; **77**:518-519
Censorship, *see* Intellectual freedom
Centenary of Index Medicus, 1879-1979, **81**:94
Center for Discovery, Columbus and Franklin Counties, Ohio, **79**:31
Center for Research in Iranian Studies, **77**:419-420
Center for the Book, **81**:90-93; **80**:95, 190; **79**:61; **78**:61, 67-68, 111, 116, 120
  international role, **81**:93
  see also Englehard Lecture on the Book
Center for the Book in the Library of Congress, **79**:61
Centers of Research Programs, **77**:197, 198-199
Central Catalog of the German Democratic Republic, **79**:383
Central Research Agricultural Library (USSR), **79**:375

Central Research Medical Library (USSR), 79:375
Centrale des bibliothèques, 79:358
Centre de Recherche et de Documentation des Institutiones Chretienne, 78:533; 77:419–420
Certification of Public Libraries in the U.S., 81:222
Certified Library Binders, 78:100
Cervenka, Zdenen, 78:397
Chambers, Bradford, 77:18
Change: The Magazine of Learning, job listings, 81:219
Channeled Information Network, 79:15
Chaplin, A. H., 77:412
Charter of the Book, 81:93
Cheatham, Bertha M., 81:33; 80:28; 79:28; 78:22; 77:14
Chen, Ching-Chih, 80:360
Chermayeff, Ivan, 80:485
Chesapeake Bay Center for Environmental Studies, 77:48
Chicago Ethnic Arts Program, 78:71
Chicago Public Library, Indian Library Services, 78:56
Chief Officers of State Library Agencies, 81:483–484; 80:609–610; 79:489–490; 78:484–485; 77:71–75, 519–520
Child Abuse and Pornography Bill, 78:30
Child pornography, 78:29–30, 124
  see also Obscenity legislation
Children's Book Council, liaison with ABA, 79:112
Children's books, see Books, best books, juvenile
Children's Services Division, see American Library Association, Children's Services Division
"Child's Place," 80:30
China National Publications Import Corporation, 81:113
China National Publishing Administration, 81:113
Chinese-American Librarians Association, 81:484–485; 80:610; 79:490–491
Chinese Cooperative Catalog, 79:64
Choice, 79:89; 78:82; 77:5, 54
Chronicle of Higher Education, 81:117
  job listings, 81:219
  placement services, 80:316; 79:265; 78:352; 77:377
Church and Synagogue Library Association, 81:485–486; 80:611; 79:491–492; 78:485–486; 77:520–521
Chute, Adrienne, 81:184

Circle of Knowledge, 81:92
"Citizen Information Seeking Patterns: A New England Study," 80:360
Citizens Budget Commission, NYC, 81:10
Civil rights, legislation, 81:151; 79:125
Civil Rights Act, Title VII, amended, 79:125
Clan of the Cave Bear, 80:41
Clarkson College, Educational Resource Center, 81:38
Classified Information Procedures Act, 81:151
Clearinghouse for Information about Expensive Acquisitions, 77:91
Clearinghouse Memorandum, 80:63
Cline, Hugh, 80:361
Closer Look, 80:61
Codex Benedictus, 81:363
Codex de France, 81:363
Cohen, Nathan M., 81:162; 80:204; 77:172
Cole, John Y., 81:90; 78:67
Coleman, Sonja, 79:33; 78:30
  wins John Phillip Immroth Award, 79:27
Collection Analysis Project, 81:121–122; 80:144, 266
Collection, Use, and Care of Historical Documents, 78:174
College and Research Libraries, 79:89
College and Research Library News, 77:55
College and university libraries
  acquisitions, 81:274–278, 289–290; 80:9–10, 267, 378–379; 79:11, 285–286; 78:241–242; 77:262–263
  additions and renovations, 81:306–308; 80:432, 435, 436–437, 438; 78:295, 297; 77:304–305
  Bahamas, 79:352–353
  bibliography, 81:401; 80:526; 79:577; 78:568; 77:254–255, 602
  Canada, 79:357–358
  circulation, 81:287–288
  collection use, 81:265
  construction, 81:304–309; 80:431–440; 78:293–298; 77:299–305
  Egypt, 80:503
  expenditures, 81:277–278, 292–297; 80:378–379; 79:285–286; 77:267–268
  German Democratic Republic, 79:381
  India, 81:379
  management, see Association of Research Libraries, Office of Management Studies; Library directors; Library management; Library trustees

Mexico, 77:424
NCES survey, 81:287-303
operating expenses, 81:291, 292-297, 302-303; 78:244-245
Pakistan, 78:382
personnel, 77:265, 267, 268
  consulting services, 81:291, 298-301; 79:90
  continuing education, 80:268; 79:90
  faculty status, 79:23, 90; 77:4
  salaries, 78:244-245, 247, 339, 340
  student assistants, 81:291, 301
Poland, 79:369
reference services, 81:288-289
salaries and wages, 81:292-293, 296-297
services for the handicapped, 80:62
statistics, see Library statistics, college and university libraries
USSR, 79:374-375
United Kingdom, 79:361-362
use of resources, 80:236
see also Research libraries; Two-year college libraries
College bookstores, see Bookstores, college
College Entrance Examination Board, Office of Library Independent Study and Guidance Projects, 77:209
College Guide for Students with Disabilities, 80:62
College Library Centre, Quebec, 79:358
College Library Program, 79:189; 78:172-173; 77:197, 199, 208
College Store Journal, 78:95
"Colloquium on the Bicentennial of Medicine in the U.S.," 77:41
Colton, Flora D., 77:599
Columbia University
  Gold Medal, 79:395
  Translation Center, 79:392
Commerce Information Retrieval Service, 80:153
Commission on Standards of Accreditation of Services for the Blind, 80:104
Committee for the Coordination of National Bibliographic Control, 79:186; 78:170; 77:27, 206
Committee on Production Guidelines for Book Longevity, 81:157
Commonwealth Schoolbook Fund, 79:570
Communications Act of 1934, revision, 81:150; 80:201; 79:123; 78:118

Communications Technology Satellite, 79:75; 78:74; 77:43
Community college libraries, see Two-year college libraries
Community Colleges, Public Libraries and the Humanities, 79:85
Comparative Evaluation of Alternative Systems for the Provision of Effective Access to Periodical Literature, 80:81-82
Comparative librarianship, defined, 81:267
Competition Review Act, 1979, 81:144; 80:192
Comprehensive Employment and Training Act, 81:25; 80:20; 79:21, 30, 123; 78:15-16, 23, 27-28, 116; 77:13, 15, 105
Computer-Assisted Instruction Network, 77:43
Computer Catalog Center, see Library of Congress, Computer Catalog Center
Computer-created works, copyright status, 78:53; 77:32-33
Computer Inquiry II, 81:150
Computer Network Protocol for Library and Information Science Applications, 79:51
Computer Output Microfilm, 81:14; 80:16; 79:17; 78:14; 77:210
Computer software, copyright status, 78:52; 77:31-32
Computer Software Copyright Act, 81:150; 80:76-77
Concept Paper Series, 77:385
Concordiat, 79:393
Conference on Literary Translation, NYC, 79:391
Conference on Resolution of Copyright Issues, 77:27
Conference on Security and Cooperation in Europe, 78:126
Confidential Bulletin, 78:95
Congdon and Lattès, 80:41
Congrat-Butler, Stefan, 79:384, 395
Congressional Chatauqua on Information, 80:153
Congressional Reports Elimination Act, 81:152
Connecticut State Board of Education and Services for the Blind, children's programs, 78:24
Consejo Nacional de Ciencia y Tecnologia, 77:423, 427

Conservation of Library materials, *see* Library materials, conservation and preservation
Consortium of Library Automation in Mississippi, **79**:16
Consortium of Rhode Island Academic and Research Libraries, **80**:14
Consultant Training Program, **81**:122, 156
Consultants Keyword Clearinghouse, placement services, **81**:211
Consumer Research Study on Reading and Book Purchasing, **80**:444
Continuing education, *see* Continuing Library Education Network and Exchange; Education for librarianship; Library personnel, continuing education
Continuing Education Center, *see* American Library Association, Standing Committee on Continuing Education, Continuing Education Center
Continuing Education Data Base, **77**:386
Continuing Library Education Network and Exchange, **81**:486-488; **80**:19, 612-613; **79**:20, 492-493; **78**:17; **77**:6, 24, 74-75, 384
  continuing education service, **81**:28
Contributions of collected works, copyright status, **77**:169-170
Convenience Store Workshop, *see* Association of American Publishers, Mass Market Paperback Division, Convenience Store Workshop
Conversion of Serials, **81**:17, 155; **80**:266; **79**:14, 63-64, 187; **78**:169; **77**:45, 206
Cooke, Eileen D., **81**:127; **80**:175; **79**:117; **78**:111; **77**:99, 412
Cooper-Hewitt Museum, **77**:48
Cooperation, library, *see* Library cooperation
Cooperative Acquisitions Program, **77**:90
Cooperative College Register, placement services, **80**:317; **79**:266; **78**:352
Cooperative MARC, *see* COMARC
Cooperative Union Serials System, **79**:357
Coordinated Acquisitions Program, **77**:90, 91
Coordinated Plan of Research Work in Library Science, **79**:373
Copyright, **81**:22-23, 40, 131, 150; **80**:13-14, 70-73, 185; **79**:15-16, 32, 42-49; **78**:12-13, 31-32, 116-117, 123-124; **77**:37-38, 63-64, 101, 113-115, 116-171
  AAP activities, **81**:114; **80**:134; **79**:105-106; **78**:90
  ALA action, **77**:52
  ARL activities, **78**:87
  bibliography, **81**:402, 412; **80**:526, 537; **79**:577, 578; **78**:568, 579; **77**:614
  CONTU guidelines, **78**:53
  classroom reproduction, **77**:131-137
  computer-created works, *see* Computer-created works, copyright status
  computer software, **81**:150
  computer uses, **77**:156
  Congressional reports, **77**:125-158
  disposition of copy or phonorecord, **77**:147-149
  duration, **77**:116, 160, 165
  fair use, **80**:71-72; **77**:37, 116, 119, 130-139, 167-169
  fair use for broadcast works, **81**:131
  IPA concerns, **80**:496
  infringement, **77**:123
  international, **81**:324; **80**:72
  international implications, **81**:22-23; **78**:125
  LC activities, **78**:66
  legislation, **81**:75-76; **80**:72; **77**:124-125
  liability, **77**:117
  library copying, **77**:121-122, 139-146
    see also Photocopying
  manufacturing clause, **81**:74; **77**:115, 116-117, 166-167
  off-air videotaping, **80**:192
  performances and displays, 149-155
  Philippines, **78**:125
  registration, **80**:72
  reproduction rights, **77**:126-130
  reversionary rights, **77**:165-166
  rights of owners, **77**:119, 126, 160
  royalties, double taxation, **77**:112-113
  Software Act of 1980, **81**:143
  text of Public Law 94-553, **77**:625-686
  UNESCO attitude, **81**:365
  unauthorized importation, **77**:158
  United Kingdom, **79**:366
  unpublished works, **77**:116
  works protected, **77**:118-119
  see also American Library Association, teleconference on copyright; Books, pirating; Computer-created works; Data bases, copyright protection; Libraries, copying of copyrighted works; Off-Air Taping Conference;

Photocopying; U.S., Copyright Office
Copyright Clearance Center, **81**:22; **80**:14, 42; **79**:45, 70–71; **78**:12–13, 34, 37–40, 53
 IIA participation, **80**:154
Copyright Revision Act, **80**:140
Copyright Royalty Tribunal, **78**:123–124; **77**:37
 merger with U.S. Copyright Office, **81**:75
Cornerstones, **79**:81
Corporation for Public Broadcasting, federal funding, **79**:123; **78**:118
Cost-Benefit Model of Some Critical Library Operations in Terms of Use of Materials, **79**:37
Cost of Library Materials: Price Trends of Publications, **77**:331
Council for Computerized Library Networks, **81**:488–489; **80**:145–149, 613–614; **77**:94–96
Council for International Exchange of Scholars, placement services, **81**:220; **80**:318; **79**:266; **78**:353; **77**:378
Council of Europe, Strasbourg
 collaboration with LIBER, **78**:370–371
 Meeting of Experts on Shared Cataloging, **78**:372
Council of National Library and Information Associations, **81**:489; **80**:614–615; **79**:493–494; **78**:486; **77**:66, 521
Council of Planning Librarians, **81**:490–491; **80**:615–616; **79**:494; **78**:486–487; **77**:522
Council of Regions, **77**:94–95
Council on Library/Media Technical Assistants, **78**:488; **77**:523–524
 placement services, **81**:212; **80**:310; **79**:260; **78**:347; **77**:373
Council on Library Resources, **81**:153–162, 491; **80**:81, 264–271, 616; **79**:185–194, 494–495; **78**:168–178, 487–488; **77**:205–214; 523–524
 Academic Library Management Intern Program, *see* Academic Library Management Intern Program
 Bibliographic Service Development Program, **81**:47–48, 153–155; **80**:265–266
  Joint Committee on Bibliographic Standards, **81**:154; **80**:265
  MARC Format Review Committee, **81**:154

 development plan for NPC, **79**:45, 589–592
 fellowship program, **80**:269; **79**:190–191
 grant recipients, **81**:160–162; **80**:270–271; **79**:191–194; **78**:173–174, 175–178; **77**:211–214
 Health Sciences Library Management, *see* Health Sciences Library Management
 Health Sciences Management Intern Program, *see* Health Sciences Management Intern Program
 international programs, **81**:159–160
 support to international organizations, **80**:491
Craft and Context of Translation, **79**:390
Crawford, Susan, **81**:279
Croxton, F. E., **79**:58
Cultural Institutions Program, **77**:197
Cummings, Martin M., **77**:41
Current Awareness Literature Service, **80**:110; **79**:77
Current Research Information System, **79**:77
Cuyahoga County Public Library, grant from Louise Brown Foundation, **81**:36
Cylke, Frank Kurt, **80**:99

D

DEC VAX 11/780 minicomputer, **81**:53
DIDS, *see* Decision Information Display System
DIST, *see* National Science Foundation, Division of Information Science and Technology
DSI, *see* National Science Foundation, Division of Science Information
Danton, J. Periam, **81**:367; **80**:493; **77**:3
Darien Book Aid Plan, Inc., **80**:690–691; **79**:568–569; **78**:406–407; **77**:442–443
Darling, Richard L., **79**:231; **78**:329; **77**:345
Data bases
 commercial searching, **80**:66–67
 copyright protection, **81**:22, 76–77; **80**:200; **77**:32
 machine-readable, government, **80**:85–86
 microforms, **80**:143
 NTIS, **80**:85

Data bases (Cont.)
  national, for archives and manuscripts, 80:261
  on-line searching, 81:186; 80:67
  research, 80:252
  special education materials, 80:60–61
  toxicology, 80:107
  see also Bibliographic data bases; Foundation Center, data bases; Libraries, computerized functions; also names of bases, e.g., RTECS
Datamation, salary survey, 81:229
Debons, Anthony, 81:246; 80:362, 370
Decent Interval, 81:44
Decision Information Display System, 81:52–55
Decisions of the United States Courts Involving Copyright and Literary Property, 81:77
Definitions for Library Statistics, 80:363
Delos, 79:391
Denver Quarterly, translation award, 79:393
Department of Education, see U.S., Department of Education
Depository Library System, legislation, 81:148–149
Depository libraries, 81:82–84
  law libraries, 79:122
  USSR, 79:373–374
  see also Government publications
Design and Planning of National Information System, 80:492
Design Criteria: New Public Building Accessibility, 80:56
Dessauer, John P., 81:338; 80:443, 444, 467, 473; 79:327; 78:303, 307, 311; 77:313
Developing CE Learning Materials, 77:385
"Development and Testing of a Conceptual Model of Public Library User Behavior," 81:266
"Development of Libraries and Information Systems: Global Information Exchange for Greater Understanding," 81:375
DeWath, Nancy, 79:40
Dewey Decimal Classification, 77:39
Dial-a-Reg, 81:62–63; 80:76
Dial Law Information Service, 81:4
Dimensions of Comparative Librarianship, 81:367; 80:493
Directions for Library Service to Young Adults, 79:85

Directory of Archives and Manuscript Repositories in the United States, 80:259, 261; 79:98, 178
Directory of Asian and African Librarians in North America, 79:89
Directory of Fee-Based Information Services, 80:69; 79:268
Directory of Friends of Libraries Groups in the U.S., 79:84
Directory of Government Documents Collections and Librarians, 79:86
Directory of Health Sciences Libraries, 81:282
Directory of Library Reprographic Services: A World Guide, 77:342
Directory of Library Research and Demonstration Projects, 81:188; 80:232
Directory of Literacy and Adult Learning Programs, 80:123
Dockstader, Ray, 78:68
Documentary material, see Archives
Dodd, Sue A., 81:154
Dodson, James T., 77:94
Doebler, Paul D., 80:443, 444
Dog Day Afternoon, 80:31
Dollard, Peter, 80:156
Dougherty, Richard M., 80:268
Downs, Robert B., 81:157
Downs, Robert B., Award, 81:30; 79:27, 33, 81
Drennan, Henry T., 80:232
Duchac, Kenneth, 78:28
Dunlap, Connie, 77:3
Dunlap, Leslie, 80:259; 79:179

E

ECA, see U.S., International Communication Agency, Associate Directorate for Educational and Cultural Affairs
ECER data base, 80:61
EFLA, see Educational Film Library Association
ELA, see Egyptian Library Association
EMIS, see Extension Management Information System
EOP, see Information Management and Services Division, EOP
EPSIPLEPSYLINE, 77:42
ERA, see Equal Rights Amendment
ERIC, see Educational Resources Information Center
ESEA, see Elementary and Secondary Education Act

ESU, *see* English-Speaking Union of the United States
EURONET, **77:**9
Eastern Michigan University, Project LOEX, *see* Project LOEX
Eastman, Ann H., **77:**387
Editing, bibliography, **81:**411, 413–414; **80:** 538; **79:**588; **78:**580; **77:**615
Edles, Nadine, **81:**270; **80:**371
Education
  bilingual programs, **81:**39–40
    see also Library services for persons of limited English-speaking ability, bilingual programs
  school discipline, **81:**39
Education and Human Development, Inc., **80:**233
Education Amendments, **79:**35, 126, 150
Education for All Handicapped Children Act, **80:**54; **78:**24
Education for Bookselling, **78:**95–96
  see also Booksellers School
Education for librarianship, **81:**26–28
  Bahamas, **79:**353–354
  bibliography, **81:**402; **80:**526–527; **79:** 577–578; **78:**212, 568–569; **77:**602–603
  CLR support, **81:**157–159; **80:**268–269; **78:**172
  Canada, **79:**358–359
  China, **81:**23
  continuing education, **80:**19–20; **79:**20–22, 90; **78:**17–18; **77:**6, 63
    see also College and university libraries, personnel, continuing education; Library personnel, continuing education
  Egypt, **80:**505–506
  German Democratic Republic, **79:**381–382
  HEA support, **81:**179–183; **79:**151–160; **78:**144–152
  India, **81:**381
  international aspects, **81:**367–368, 376–377
  internships, **81:**24
  M.L.S. as job requirement, **78:**16
  Mexico, **77:**425
  Pakistan, **78:**384
  Poland, **79:**370–371
  training in service to the handicapped, **80:**64–65
  USSR, **79:**376
  United Kingdom, **79:**363–364
  see also Archivists, education and training; Higher Education Act, Title II-B; Library personnel, continuing education; Library personnel, training programs; Library schools; Research libraries, personnel, continuing education
Education for Publishing, **77:**387–388
  see also Association of American Publishers, Publishing Education Information Service; Publishers, continuing education
Educational Broadcast Facilities program, moved to Department of Commerce, **79:**123; **78:**118
Educational Broadcasting Facilities and Telecommunications Demonstration Act, **77:**101, 103
Educational Film Library Association, **81:**491–492; **80:**617; **79:**495; **78:** 489; **77:**524
Educational Information Service
  Alert Service, **81:**219
  overseas job openings, **81:**220
  placement services, **80:**317, 318; **79:**266
Educational Paperback Association, **80:** 39
Educational Resources Information Center, **77:**429
  Clearinghouse on Handicapped and Gifted Children, **80:**61
Effective Access to Periodical Literature, **79:**186
Eggert, Joanna, **77:**416
Egyptian Books in Print, **80:**504
Egyptian Library Association, **80:**505
Egyptian National Bibliography, **80:**504
Egyptian National Library, **80:**502
Eisner, Joseph, grant from CLR, **81:**266
Eizenstat, Stuart, **81:**140
El Hadi, Mohamed M., **80:**501
Eldridge, Marie, **77:**247
Elections, effect on libraries, **81:**33, 39
  see also Legislation affecting libraries
Electronic Alternative to Communication through Paper-Based Journals, **79:** 38
Elementary and Secondary Education Act
  Title II, Basic Skills Improvement, **79:** 127
  Title IV, **81:**132
  Title IV-B, Instructional Materials and School Library Resources, **81:**5, 33, 143, 173–176; **80:**189, 190, 218–220; **79:**35, 119, 126–127

Elementary and Secondary Education Act (Cont.)
  allotments by state, **81**:174; **80**:219
  band instruments, **80**:187
  High-cost children allotments, **80**:220
  program purpose allotments, **80**:220
  Title IV-B, School Libraries and Learning Resources, **79**:117, 146–149; **78**:111, 112, 119, 139–141; **77**:183–186
  Title IV-D, **80**:31
Emergency Building Temperature Restrictions Regulations, **80**:185–186
"Emerging Role of the State Library Agency," **77**:77
Emerson, Katherine, **80**:364
Energy conservation, *see* Libraries, energy conservation
Engelke, Hans, **78**:84
Englehard Lecture on the Book, **81**:92; **78**:66–67
  see also Center for the Book
English-Speaking Union of the United States, **80**:691–692; **79**:569–570; **78**:407–408; **77**:443–444
  see also Books-Across-the-Sea; Commonwealth Schoolbook Fund
Environmental Protection Agency, *see* U.S., Environmental Protection Agency
Equal Access, **80**:120
Equal Employment Opportunity Commission, **79**:25
Equal Pay for Equal Work: Women in Special Libraries, **77**:62
Equal Rights Amendment, **81**:29; **80**:21, 118; **79**:24–25, 82–83; **78**:31
  ALA support, **81**:35; **80**:32–33; **79**:32–33
  SLA and non-ratifying states, **80**:170
Equivalences, **79**:391
Erteschik, Ann M., **77**:172
"Essentials or Desiderata of the Bibliographic Record as Discovered by Research," **80**:361
Establishing a Legislative Framework for the Implementation of NATIS, **80**:492
Estabrook, Leigh, **81**:263
Exceptional Child Education Resources, **80**:61
Exhibitions, library, *see* "76 United Statesiana"
Extension Management Information System, **79**:77

F

FAMULUS, **80**:110
FCC, *see* U.S., Federal Communications Commission
FEDLINK Network Office, **81**:493
FIAF, *see* International Federation of Film Archives
FIC, *see* Federal Information Centers
FID, *see* International Federation for Documentation
FIT, *see* International Federation of Translators
FLC, *see* Federal Library Committee
FNIC, *see* Food and Nutrition Information Center
FNIERC, *see* Food and Nutrition Information and Education Resources Center
FTRF, *see* American Library Association, Freedom to Read Foundation
Fact Sheet on Libraries in Islamic Countries, **80**:493
"Family Reader," **79**:87
Fang, Josephine Riss, **81**:366, 375–377; **78**:376; **77**:412
Farkas, Eugene M., **81**:98; **80**:109; **79**:76
Federal Communications Commission, *see* U.S., Federal Communications Commission
Federal Computer Systems Protection Act, **81**:150; **80**:200
Federal Government Printing and Publishing: Policy Issues, **80**:197
Federal Job Information Centers Directory, **81**:217
Federal Information Centers, **81**:60–66; **80**:73–79; **79**:123–124
  list, **81**:63–66; **80**:76–79
Federal Information Centers Act, **81**:61; **80**:74
Federal libraries, *see* National libraries; Parliamentary libraries
Federal Library and Information Network, *see* FEDLINK Network Office
Federal Library Committee, **81**:492–493; **80**:617–618; **79**:496; **78**:489–490; **77**:524–525
Federal Libraries and Information Services Pre-White House Conference, **80**:44, 45
Federal Programs for Libraries, **80**:213; **79**:141–142

Federal Register, **81**:62, 132; **80**:76, 239; **79**:71, 150, 151, 161, 162, 164
Federal Research Service, placement services, **81**:219; **80**:317; **79**:266; **78**:352
Federal Software Exchange Center, **80**:86
Fellowships, *see* Council on Library Resources, fellowship program; Grants, information science; Grants, library; Scholarships
Financial Assistance for Library Education, **77**:388
Finzi, John, **79**:58
"First Amendment Implications of Secondary Information Services," **80**:155
"First Encounter with Brazilian Literature," **79**:394
Fisher, Sheldon Z., **80**:221; **79**:149; **78**:142; **77**:186
Fite, Alice, **81**:33
Five Borough Users Group, NY, **81**:10
Florence Agreement Protocol, **81**:58, 381–383; **78**:125–126; **77**:110–113
Florida Library Information Network, **79**:15
Fogelstrom, Clarence, **81**:162; **80**:204
Folk-Songs of America, **80**:96
Folklife and Fieldwork, **80**:96
Folklife and the Federal Government, **79**:60
Folklife Center News, **79**:60
Food and Nutrition Information and Education Resources Center, **79**:77–78; **77**:44
Food and Nutrition Information Center, **81**:99; **80**:110
Ford, Gerald R., statement on White House Conference, **77**:29
Foreign library associations, *see* Library associations, foreign
Forever, **80**:32
Forked Tongue, **79**:391
Fort Pierce (Florida) Bureau, **77**:48.44, **81**:44
Foundation Annual Reports: What They Are and How to Use Them, **77**:215
Foundation Center, **80**:271–276; **79**:194–195; **78**:178–182, 185; **77**:214–215, 228
 computer analysis of grants, **79**:200–205
 data bases, **80**:277–278

 field offices and cooperating libraries, **80**:272–275; **79**:196–199
 publications, **80**:276
Foundation Center National Data Book, **80**:276, 278; **79**:195, 200; **78**:179
Foundation Center Source Book Profiles, **80**:276; **79**:195; **78**:179; **77**:215
Foundation directory, **80**:276; **79**:195; **78**:179, 186, 189; **77**:224
Foundation Directory Data Bank, **77**:224
Foundation for the Promotion of the Translation of Dutch Literary Works, **79**:388
Foundation Grants index, **80**:276, 277; **79**:195, 200; **78**:179–180, 186, 189; **77**:218
Foundation Grants to Individuals, **80**:276; **79**:195; **78**:179
Foundations, with stated interest in libraries, **79**:205–207
Fox, Bette-Lee, **81**:304, 310; **80**:410, 431
Franciscan Vocation Office, placements, **77**:378
Franck, Jane P., **77**:416
Frankfurt Book Fair, **81**:359–366; **80**:40, 481–489; **79**:395–405; **78**:387, 380; **77**:432–437
Frankie, Suzanne, **77**:61
Franklin Book Programs, **78**:408–409; **77**:444–446
Frantz, Jack, **77**:3
Frase, Robert W., **81**:107, 381; **80**:124; **79**:98; **78**:119; **77**:107, 328
Freedom House/Books, USA, **80**:692–693; **79**:570–571; **78**:409–410; **77**:446
Freedom of Information Act, **81**:57; **78**:21
Freedom of speech, *see* Intellectual freedom
Freedom to publish, *see* Intellectual freedom
Freedom to read, *see* Intellectual freedom
Freedom to Read Foundation, *see* American Library Association, Freedom to Read Foundation
Freer Gallery of Art, **77**:48
Friends of Libraries, USA, **80**:121
Friends of the Library National Notebook, **79**:84
Frisch, Max, **77**:436
Fritz, Curtis L., **81**:52
Furnishing the Library Interior, **81**:155

G

GODORT, *see* American Library Association, Government Documents Round Table
GPD, *see* Association of American Publishers, General Publishing Division
GPO, *see* Government Printing Office
GRA&I, *see* Government Reports Announcements & Index
GRS, *see* General Revenue Sharing
Gaines, Ervin, **78**:25
Gallup Organization, reader survey, **79**:39, 80
Galvin, Hoyt R., **78**:281; **77**:282
Galvin, Thomas J., **81**:105; **80**:115; **79**:303
Garrison, Guy, **80**:359
Garrison, William, **80**:86
Geddes, Andrew, **80**:120
Gelfand, Morris A., **77**:3, 90
Gell, Marilyn K., **80**:43, 46
General Education Provisions Act, **81**:143
General Revenue Sharing, **81**:136; **79**:29
  statistics, **80**:243–245
  support for libraries, **80**:242–245
Georgia Governor's Conference on Libraries, **78**:80
German Book Trade Peace Prize, **80**:489; **77**:436
German Library (Deutsche Bücherei), **79**:380, 381
German National Bibliography (GDR), **79**:383
German State Library (Deutsche Staatsbibliothek), **79**:380, 381
Getz, Malcolm, **81**:266
Give-a-Book Certificate Program, **80**:113; **79**:113; **78**:98
Givens, Johnnie, **77**:3
Gnomon Corporation, copyright infringement, **81**:40, 44, 133
Gode, Alexander, Medal, **79**:390
Goethe House-PEN Translation Prize, **79**:392
Goldhor, Herbert, **80**:392; **78**:215
Goldwater, Barry, **80**:40
Gonzalez, Efren, **77**:63
Gordon, Sol, **78**:85
Gore, Gregory V., **81**:112
Gosling, Jean O., **78**:293; **77**:299
Goudy, Frank William, **80**:242
Government Advisory Committee on International Book and Library Programs, **77**:447–448
Government information, *see* U.S., government information
Government Inventions for Licensing, **80**:85
Government Printing Office, **81**:145–146
  coordinates cataloging with LC, **81**:83–84; **79**:63
  legislation, **81**:148–149
  superintendent of documents, **81**:83
Government Printing Reorganization Act, **80**:191
Government publications
  access, **81**:84
  indexing, **81**:83
Government Publications: Their Role in the National Program for Library and Information Services, **80**:83
Government Reports Announcements & Index, **80**:85
Governors' Conferences on Library and Information Science, *see* State library agencies, pre-White House conferences
Grand Rapids, Mich., Public Library, oral history project, **78**:56
Grannis, Chandler B., **81**:324, 329, 336, 384; **80**:37, 446, 510; **79**:317, 321, 409; **78**:303, 306, 317, 401; **77**:313, 319, 449
Grant proposals, **78**:162–163, 186, 189, 192–193
  archival projects, **79**:181
  Foundation Center manuals, **79**:195–196
  foundation grants, **80**:282–284
  HEA grants, **81**:188
  HEA, Title II-C, **80**:240
  information science research, **80**:254; **79**:173
  NHPRC, **81**:203; **80**:260–261
  NSF, **81**:196; **80**:254; **79**:173
Grants, information science
  NSF awards, **81**:197–200; **80**:255–258; **79**:174–178
Grants, library
  for archival work, **79**:97
  CLR grants, **81**:153, 154–155, 156, 160–162; **80**:270–271; **79**:86, 189, 191–194; **78**:173–174, 175–178; **77**:53–54, 66, 205–214
  challenge grants, **81**:194–195; **79**:168
  ESEA grants, **81**:142
  FTRF grants, **80**:119

foundation grants, **81**:8; **80**:277–285; **79**: 12, 199–207, 201–202, 207–228; **78**: 193–208; **77**:215–244
  computer analysis, **80**:278–285
  HEA grants, **81**:133–135, 184–188, 189–192; **80**:140–141, 221–222, 239–242; **79**:149–151, 151–160, 160–163, 164–166; **78**:142–144, 153–156; **77**:186–188
  LSCA grants, **81**:142; **80**:205–213, 213–216; **79**:133–146; **78**:127–139; **77**:172–183
  NEA grants, **77**:105
  NEH grants, **81**:192–195; **80**:246–251; **79**:167–171; **78**:157–161; **77**:53, 62, 105, 196–200
  NHPRC grants, **81**:201–203, 204–205; **80**:259–261, 262–263; **79**:179, 181–182
  NLM grants, **81**:98; **80**:109; **79**:75; **78**:75; **77**:44
  NSF grants, **77**:105
  statistics, **80**:279–282, 283, 284–285; **78**:183–193; **77**:217–227
  U.S. Department of State grants, **77**:62
  see also Council on Library Resources; Elementary and Secondary Education Act; Foundation Center; Grant proposals; Higher Education Act; Library Funding; Library Services and Construction Act; National Endowment for the Humanities; National Library of Medicine; National Historical Publications and Records Commission; National Science Foundation; Scholarships
Green, Joseph, **80**:380; **79**:289; **78**:266; **77**:269
Green Thumb, **80**:91
Greenaway, Emerson, **80**:59
Greene, Graham, **80**:485
Greene, Stephen, Memorial Education Grant, **81**:119
Griffin, Richard E., **80**:167
Grosser, Alfred, **80**:489
Grosset & Dunlap, sues Stratenmeyer Syndicate and S & S, **80**:42
Guide to Archives and Manuscripts in the United States, **80**:259; **79**:178
Guide to British Government Publications, **81**:157
Guide to Manuscripts in the National Agricultural Library, **80**:111
Guide to Planning and Teaching CE Courses, **77**:385
Guidelines for Audiovisual Materials and Services for Large Public Libraries, **77**:58
Guidelines for Classroom Copying in Not-for-Profit Educational Institutions, **77**:119, 132–135, 161
Guidelines for Collection Development, **80**:122
Guidelines for Educational Use of Music, **77**:119, 136–137
"Guidelines for Selection of Representatives to International Conferences, Meetings and Assignments," **80**:115
Guidelines for the Evaluation of Library Collections, **79**:85
Guidelines for the Formulation of Collection Policies, **79**:85
Guidelines for the Subject Analysis of Audio-Visual Materials, **79**:85
Guidelines for the Weeding of Library Collections, **79**:85
Guild of Professional Translators, **79**:392
Gulbenkian, Calouste, Foundation Prize, **79**:395
Gwinn, Nancy E., **81**:153; **80**:264; **79**:185; **78**:168; **77**:205

H

HEA, *see* Higher Education Act
HEW, *see* U.S., Department of Health, Education and Welfare
HISTLINE, **79**:72–73
HRLSD, *see* American Library Association, Association of Specialized and Cooperative Library Agencies
Hafter, Ruth F., **80**:361
Hagemeyer, Alice, **80**:58
Hagger, Jean, **77**:428
Hamilton, L. Clark, **78**:63
Handbook of Comparative Librarianship, **80**:493
Handbook of Standard Terminology for Reporting Information about Libraries, **81**:268, 269; **80**:364
Handicapped persons, *see* American Library Association, Association of Specialized and Cooperative Library Agencies; Education for All Handicapped Children Act; Library services for the blind; Library

Handicapped persons (Cont.)
  services for the disadvantaged; Library services for the handicapped
Handicapping America: Barriers to Disabled People, **80**:55-56
Harman, David, **80**:362
Harvard Studies in Comparative Literature, 1959, **79**:390
Hasan, Kazi, **80**:444
Hausrath, Donald C., **81**:67
Health and Planning Administration, **79**:72
Health and Rehabilitative Library Services Division, *see* American Library Association, Association of Specialized and Cooperative Library Agencies
Health sciences libraries, *see* Medical libraries
Health Sciences Libraries in the United States: Three Decades of Progress, **81**:282
Health Sciences Library Management, CLR support, **80**:268-269
Health Sciences Management Intern Program, **79**:190
Heim, Kathleen, **81**:263; **80**:334
Helping Adults to Learn, **77**:385
Henderson, Carol C., **81**:127; **80**:175; **79**:117; **78**:111
Henderson, Susanne, **81**:267
Henke, Esther, **77**:3
Hepatitis Knowledge Base, **80**:108
Hess, James A., **80**:120
"High Interest/Low Reading Level Information Packet," **80**:122
Higher Education Act
  extension, **81**:133-135, 142; **80**:177, 182
  library programs updated, **81**:127
  Title I, Education Outreach Program, **80**:177; **77**:103-104
  Title II, College and Research Library Assistance, and Library Training and Research, **80**:189; **77**:13
  Title II-A, College Library Resources, **81**:133-134, 142, 176-178; **80**:176, 177, 189, 221-223; **79**:119, 149-151; **78**:111, 112, 119, 142-144; **77**:186-188
  Title II-B, Library Education, **81**:179-183; **80**:223-232; **79**:151-160; **77**:188-192
  Title II-B, Library Research and Demonstration Program, **81**:5, 184-188; **80**:176, 177, 232-238, 359, 360; **79**:160-163; **78**:111, 112, 153-156; **77**:192-195
  funded projects, **80**:238
  Institute programs, **78**:148, 152
  sponsoring organizations, **80**:237
  Title II-B, Library Training, Research, and Development, **81**:130, 134, 142; **80**:176, 177, 232, 356, 360; **78**:111, 112, 144-152
  institute programs, **78**:148, 152
  see also Education for librarianship
  Title II-C, Strengthening Research Library Resources, **81**:5, 134, 136, 189-192; **80**:140-141, 176, 177, 189, 239-242; **79**:122, 150, 164-166; **78**:111, 112
  Title II-D, National Periodical System, **81**:134, 142-143, 189-190, 191, 198
  Title IV-A, Educational Equipment, **78**:111, 112
  Title VII, Construction, Reconstruction and Renovation of Academic Facilities, **80**:177-178
  Title XI, Urban Grant University Program, **80**:182
Hill, G. R., **80**:455
Hirschberg, Vera, **80**:43
Hirshhorn Museum and Sculpture Garden, **77**:48
Historical records, *see* Archives
Hochgesand, Karl, **77**:416
Hoduski, Bernadine Abbott, **81**:82
Hokkanen, Dorothy B., **81**:324
Holmes, James, **79**:391
Home Country Employment Registry, placement services, **81**:220; **80**:318; **79**:267; **78**:353; **77**:378
Horton, Forest, **80**:151
Hospital libraries, German Democratic Republic, **79**:380
Hospital Literature Index, **79**:74
Housing and Community Development block grants, **78**:136, 137
"How to Build Your Writing Skills," **81**:117; **80**:137; **79**:108; **77**:84
How to Comply with the Emergency Building Temperature Restrictions, **80**:186
How to Get the Most out of a College Education, **81**:117; **80**:137; **79**:108
"How to Get the Most Out of Your Textbook," **81**:117; **80**:137; **79**:108; **77**:84

"How to Improve Your Reading Skills," 81:117; 80:137; 79:108; 77:84
"How to Prepare Successfully for Examinations," 81:117; 80:137; 79:108; 77:84
"How to Read Technical Textbooks," 81:117
Howard, Joseph H., 79:58
Hughey, Elizabeth H., 80:204; 79:133; 78:127; 77:172
Humphrey Fellowship Program, 81:68
Humphreys, Kenneth W., 78:370
Hunt, James B., 78:15
Hunter, Carmen St. John, 80:362
Huntoon, Elizabeth, 80:28

I

IAALD, see International Association of Agricultural Librarians and Documentalists
IALL, see International Association of Law Libraries
IAOL, see International Association of Orientalist Librarians
IASA, see International Association of Sound Archives
IBBY, see International Board of Books for Young People
ICA, see International Council on Archives
ICLG, see British Library Association, International and Comparative Librarianship Group
ICSU, see International Council of Scientific Unions
IES, see International Exchange Service
IESMP, see Information Exchange System for Minority Personnel
IFC, see American Library Association, Office of Intellectual Freedom, Intellectual Freedom Committee
IFC, see American Library Association, Intellectual Freedom Committee
IFLA, see International Federation of Library Associations and Institutions
IIA, see Information Industry Association
ILIC, see International Library Information Center, Pittsburgh
ILS, see Lister Hill National Center for Biomedical Communications, Integrated Library System

INMARSAT, see International Maritime Satellite Organization
INTAMEL, see International Association of Metropolitan City Libraries
IPA, see International Publishers Association
IPA Publishing News, 80:495
IRC, see American Library Association, International Relations Committee
ISAD, see American Library Association, Library and Information Technology Association
ISBN, see International Standard Book Numbers
ISDP, see International Serials Data System
ISDS, see International Serials Data System
ISI, see Institute for Scientific Information
ISO, see International Organization for Standardization
ISO/TC46, see International Organization for Standardization, Technical Committee 46: Documentation
ISSN, see International Standard Serial Number
IST, see National Science Foundation, Division of Information Science and Technology
ITU, see International Telecommunication Union
IUTS, see Interuniversity Transit System
IYC, see International Year of the Child
IYL, see International Youth Library
Ihrig, Alice B., 80:47
Illinois Library and Information Network, 79:15
Illiteracy, see Literacy programs
Immroth, John Phillip, Memorial Award, 79:33
In Pursuit of American History, 80:259; 79:178–179
Incorporated Linguist, 79:390
Index Medicus, 80:105; 78:72; 77:42
Index to Festschriften in Librarianship, 78:173
Index Translationum, 79:388
Indexing, computerized, 78:170
Indian Scientific Translators Association, 79:390
Indiana Cooperative Library Services Authority, 79:15

590 / CUMULATIVE INDEX

Indians, American, *see* Library services for American Indian people
Individual Self-Planned Learning in America, **79**:39
Inexpensive Book Distribution Program, *see* Reading Is FUNdamental, Inexpensive Book Distribution Program
Information, scientific and technical, *see* Scientific and technical information
"Information Agenda for the 1980's Colloquium," **81**:13; **80**:116
"Information and the American Citizen," **80**:116
Information brokers, **80**:12, 66-69
  regional networks, **80**:13
  rates, **80**:68-69
Information centers, federal, *see* Federal Information Centers
Information Cycle, **81**:99
Information Exchange System for Minority Personnel, placement services, **81**:212; **80**:310; **79**:260
Information flow, **81**:151-152, 202-203
  international, **81**:367, 381-383
  see also Books, international flow; Publishing, distribution of books
Information Industry Association, **81**:494; **80**:149-155, 618-619
  annual conference, 1980, **80**:154-155
  Associated Information Managers, **80**:152
  committees, **80**:153-155
  Hall of Fame Award, **80**:151
  programs and projects, **80**:151-153
Information industry associations, **81**:439-504, 555-561
Information Management and Services Division, EOP, **79**:46-49
  EOP Library, **79**:48
  functions, **79**:47
  organization, **79**:47
  Records Management Office, **79**:48
  White House Information Center, **79**:47-48
Information Manager, **80**:155
Information Market Place, **80**:69
Information Needs of Urban Residents, **80**:236
Information policy legislation, *see* Legislation affecting information industry
Information Policy: Public Laws from the 96th Congress, **81**:148
Information Resource: Policy, Background and Issues, **80**:151

Information Science and Automation Division, *see* American Library Association, Library and Information Technology Association
Information Science Program Announcement, **78**:161
Information science research, **78**:161-162
  NSF support, **81**:195-200, 251-258
  see also Grants, information science
Information services, **81**:49-50
  access, **81**:58, 103
  bibliography, **81**:399, 402-403; **80**:69, 523-524; **79**:575; **78**:566-567; **77**:600
  CLR services, **80**:265-266
  citizen-to-government flow, **80**:202
  citizens' needs, **80**:236
  communication between systems, **78**:44; **77**:26
  computer program copying, **81**:150
  document delivery, **81**:12, 100, 149; **80**:198
  Egypt, **80**:503-504
  exporting, **80**:198-199
  for the blind, **80**:101
  government competition, **81**:148-149; **80**:197-200
  international, **81**:58; **80**:154, 202-203, 490-494
  legislation, *see* Legislation affecting information industry
  Library of Congress, **78**:62
  management uses, **80**:68
  minicomputer systems, **78**:74-75, 78
  NLM, **78**:73-74; **77**:42
  NSF support, **78**:161-167; **77**:201-203
  on-demand, **80**:66-69
  Pakistan, **78**:381-386
  personnel
    continuing education, **77**:384-387
    job openings, **80**:152
    salaries, **80**:151
    surveys, **81**:246-249, 263; **80**:362-363, 370
    training, **81**:367-368; **80**:225-227; **79**:152-160, 161-163, 359
    see also Library personnel
  research, *see* Grants, information science
  surveys, **80**:151
  telecommunications facilities, **77**:101, 103
  user needs, **81**:186, 188
  see also Council for Computerized Library Networks; Federal Informa-

tion Centers; Information Industry Association; Library cooperation; U.S., Information Clearinghouses
Information Sources, **80**:151
Information technology, **81**:12-14, 38-39, 58-59; **80**:253-254
bibliography, **81**:399
NTIA policies, **80**:90-91
viewdata, **80**:91
see also Information science research; Information services; Libraries, automated circulation systems; Libraries, computerized functions; Library cooperation
Information World, **80**:155
Informer, **80**:63
Inside Our Home, Outside Our Windows, **80**:96
Institute for Scientific Information, **78**:34-40
Institute for Telecommunications Sciences, *see* National Telecommunications and Information Administration, Institute for Telecommunications Sciences
Intellectual freedom, **81**:29-30, 36-38; **80**:27, 31-32, 41-42; **79**:27-28, 33-34, 81-82; **78**:19-21, 28-30; **77**:12, 15-17
AAP concerns, **81**:114-115; **79**:106; **78**:90-91
ALA activities, **78**:85
Alfred Grosser address, **80**:489
bibliography, **81**:403, 412; **80**:527, 537; **79**:578, 587; **78**:569, 578-579; **77**:603, 614
see also American Library Association, Intellectual Freedom Committee; American Library Association, Office for Intellectual Freedom; Association of American Publishers, Freedom to Read Committee; Association of American Publishers, International Freedom to Publish Committee
Interagency Committee on Telecommunications Applications, **80**:89
Inter-American Association of Agricultural Librarians and Documentalists, **81**:529; **80**:656; **79**:533-534; **78**:528; **77**:561
Inter-American Association of Translators, **79**:393
Interface, **79**:84

Intergovernmental Conference on the Planning of Documentation, Library and Archives Infrastructures, **80**:491-492
Interlibrary loan, **80**:30; **78**:87; **77**:9
audiovisual statistics, **78**:75
Canada, **79**:358
international, **80**:144
NLM services, **80**:106; **79**:73
NYSILL subsystem, **80**:13
OCLC subsystem, **81**:20; **80**:166
periodicals, **78**:44
photocopies, **78**:33
statistics, **78**:75, 253, 262
see also Libraries, automated circulation systems
International Association of Agricultural Librarians and Documentalists, **81**:529-530; **80**:656-657; **79**:534; **78**:529; **77**:562
International Association of Conference Interpreters, **79**:388
International Association of Law Libraries, **81**:530; **80**:657; **79**:534-535; **78**:529-530; **77**:562-563
International Association of Metropolitan City Libraries, **81**:531; **80**:657-658; **79**:535-536; **78**:580; **77**:563
International Association of Music Libraries, Archives and Documentation Centres, **81**:531-532; **80**:658-659; **79**:536-537; **78**:530-531; **77**:563-564
International Association of Orientalist Librarians, **81**:532-533
UNESCO/IFLA Pre-Conference Seminar on Library Education Programmes in Developing Countries, **81**:376
International Association of Poets, Playwrights, Editors, Essayists, and Novelists, American Center, *see* P.E.N. American Center
International Association of School Librarianship, placement services, **81**:220; **80**:318; **79**:267; **78**:353; **77**:378
International Association of Sound Archives, **81**:533; **80**:659-660; **79**:537; **78**:531-532; **77**:564-565
International Board of Books for Young People, translators' honor list, **79**:394
International book programs, *see* names of specific book programs

International Community of Booksellers Association, Book Promotion Seminar, **77:**436
International Council of Scientific Unions, **79:**66
International Council of Theological Library Associations, **80:**660-661; **79:** 538-539; **78:**532-533; **77:**565-566
International Council on Archives, **81:**533-534; **80:**490, 491, 660; **79:**538; **78:** 533; **77:**566
  CLR support, **79:**188; **78:**175; **77:**566
  joint meeting of educational groups of IFLA, FID, **81:**374-375
International Development Cooperation Act, **80:**203
International Exchange Service, **77:**48-49
International Federation for Documentation, **81:**371-372, 534-535; **80:**661-662; **79:**539-540; **78:**534; **77:**566-567
  joint meeting of educational groups of IFLA, ICA, **81:**374-375
International Federation of Film Archives, **81:**535-536; **80:**662-663; **79:**540; **78:** 535; **77:**567-568
International Federation of Library Associations and Institutions, **81:**370-371, 536; **80:**663-664; **79:**541; **78:** 367-370, 379-380, 535-536; **77:**210, 211, 568
  CLR support, **81:**159-160; **80:**267; **78:** 174-175
  Children's Section, **78:**174-175
  contributions to comparative librarianship, **80:**490, 491
  Division of Management and Technology, Section of Library Statistics, **77:**416
  fiftieth anniversary, **78:**367-368
  general conference, **81:**105, 367, 375-377; **80:**388, 389, 390, 391, 392, 394; **79:**359; **78:**394-395; **77:**412, 415-416
  Hospital Libraries Section, **78:**10
  International Office for Universal Bibliographic Control, **81:**370-371; **79:** 188, 367; **78:**175
  joint meeting of educational groups of FID, ICA, **81:**374-375
  Office for International Lending, **81:**371; **79:**367
  Parliamentary Library Section, **80:**508
  Professional Board, **78:**368-369
  reorganization, **77:**409-412
  Special Libraries Division, **80:**171
  Statistics Section, **79:**349-350; **78:**374-376; **77:**416
International Federation of Translators (UNESCO), **79:**387, 388
"International Flow of Information: A Trans-Pacific Perspective," **81:**70-71
International Guide to Library, Archival and Information Science Associations, **77:**412
International Group of Scientific, Technical, and Medical Publishers, meeting, **81:**365; **80:**487-488; **79:**404; **78:**394-395; **77:**436
International Human Rights Covenants, **81:**115
International Illiteracy Day, **79:**127-128
International Information Systems for the Agriculture Sciences and Technology, cooperation with TIS, **81:** 100-101
International Institute for Children's Literature and Reading Research, **81:** 537; **80:**664; **79:**541-542; **78:**536; **77:**569
International librarianship, defined, **81:**367
International library associations, *see* Library associations, international
International Library Information Center, Pittsburgh, **80:**493
International Library Statistics Standard, **77:**417
International Maritime Satellite Organization, **80:**88
International Meeting of Educational Publishers, Frankfurt, **78:**392
International News and Notes, **79:**110
International Organization for Standardization, **81:**537-538; **80:**664-665; **79:**542; **78:**537; **77:**569-570
  cooperation with IFLA, **77:**416-417
  "International Library Statistics Standards," **78:**375-376
  Technical Committee 46: Documentation, **81:**111; **80:**129-132; **79:**100-104; **78:**46, 102-108; **77:**46, 66
  approves draft ISSN standard, **79:**67
  plenary assembly, **80:**130; **79:**103-104
  steering committee, **80:**130-131
  U.S. participation, **79:**104
International Prize of the Seven, **79:**403
International Publishers Association, **80:** 495-501; **77:**436
  committee meetings, **80:**487-488

congress, Stockholm, **80:**488, 497–499
Freedom to Publish Committee, **80:**488
International Committee, **81:**365
organization and membership, **80:**496–497
International Relations Round Table, *see* American Library Association, International Relations Round Table
International School Services, placement services, **81:**220; **80:**318; **79:**267; **78:**353
International Serials Data System, **79:**66–71
international incompatibility problems, **79:**69
International Standard Book Numbers, **80:**445
International Standard Serial Number, **79:**68–69, 70–71
International Symposium on Animal Health and Disease Data Banks: Proceedings, **80:**111
International System of Information, **81:**381
International Telecommunication Union, **80:**90
International Year of Disabled Persons, **80:**53
International Year of the Child, **80:**28–30; **79:**82
International Youth Library, **80:**665–666; **79:**543; **78:**537–538; **77:**570
Inter-Parliamentary Union, International Centre for Parliamentary Documentation, **80:**508
Interuniversity Transit System, **79:**357
Iowa State University, keyword indexing project, **78:**170
Island Trees, N.Y., **81:**29, 36–37; **80:**31, 119; **78:**30
Islands and Continents Translation Award, **79:**394
Issa Valley, **81:**363
Issues and Resolutions: A Summary of Pre-Conference Activities, **80:**48, 360
"Issues for Delegate Consideration," **80:**169

J

JCP, *see* U.S., Congress, Joint Committee on Printing
JMRT, *see* American Library Association, Junior Members Round Table
Jahoda, Gerald, **80:**360
Jail Library, **81:**103
James Madison Memorial Building, *see* Library of Congress, Madison, James, Memorial Building
Jansen, Guenter, **77:**3
Jármy, Imre T., **77:**342
Jarvis-Ganns Initiative, *see* Proposition 13
Jerusalem Book Fair, **80:**40
"Job Mobility of Men and Women Librarians and How It Affects Career Advancement," **80:**363
Job Search, **78:**352
Joint Committee on Printing, *see* U.S., Congress, Joint Committee on Printing
Jones, Clara S., **77:**51
Jones, J. Morris, -Bailey K. Howard—World Book Encyclopedia—ALA Goals Award, **79:**36, 83; **78:**86
Jones, Milbrey L., **79:**146
Journal des traducteurs, **79:**389
Junior college libraries, *see* Two-year college libraries
Juvenile books, *see* Books, best books, juvenile

K

Kacena, Carolyn, **80:**334
Kadec, Sarah T., **79:**46
Kalia, D. R., **81:**377
Kanevsky, B. P., **79:**372
Keller, Helen, Center, **80:**63
Kellogg, W. K., Mich.
 support of national library network, **79:**199
 support of networks, **79:**201, 203
 support of OCLC, **79:**199
Kennedy, John F., Center for the Performing Arts, *see* Library of Congress, Performing Arts Library
Kent, Allen, **80:**361; **79:**37, 38
Kettel, Dorothy A., **80:**204
Kickapoo Tribal Library, **78:**56
King, Don, **79:**38
King, Stephen, **80:**32
King Associates, Inc., **80:**48
King Research, Inc., **81:**263, 264–265, 266; **80:**48

Kissinger, Henry, **80**:485
Kittel, Dorothy, **81**:162; **77**:172
Klasen, Robert, **81**:162
Kleeman, Richard P., **78**:119
Klett, Ernst, Verlag, **80**:488
Klor, Robert M., **80**:277
Knenlein, Donald R., **81**:60; **80**:73
Knowles, Malcolm, **77**:385
Knox, Alan, **77**:385
Kocięcka, Mirosława, **79**:367
Kohout, Pavel, **80**:488
Koutchoumow, J. A., **80**:495
Krantz, Judith, **80**:41, 484
Krug, Judith, wins Downs award, **79**:27, 33
Ku Klux Klan, **80**:32
Küng, Hans, **80**:42
Kurth, William H., **77**:331
Kurzig, Carol M., **77**:215
Kurzweil Reading Machines, **81**:12, 165–166; **80**:23–24, 35; **79**:138

L

LAD, see American Library Association, Library Administration and Management Association
LAMA, see American Library Association, Library Administration and Management Association
LBI, see Library Binding Institute
LC, see Library of Congress
LED, see American Library Association, Library Education Division
LHRT, see American Library Association, Library History Round Table
LIBER, see Ligue des Bibliothèques Européennes de Recherche
LIBER Bulletin, **78**:371, 372
LIBGIS, see Library General Information Surveys
LIONS, see Library Information and Online Network
LIRC, see Brigham Young University, Language and Intercultural Research Center
LITA, see American Library Association, Library and Information Technology Association
LMC, see United Federation of Teachers, Library Media Committee
LMRU, see British Library, Library Management Research Unit
LOEX, see Project LOEX
LOIS, see Library Order Information System
LORCOST project, see "Levels of Output Related to Costs of Operation of Scientific and Technical Libraries"
LRB, see National Center for Educational Statistics, Learning Resources Branch
LRC, see School library/media services; Two-year college libraries
LSCA, see Library Services and Construction Act
LSEP, see Library Service Enhancement Program
LTA, see Library technical assistants
LTR, see *Library Technology Reports*
Laboratory Animal Data Bank, **81**:98; **80**:107; **77**:42
Ladd, David L., **80**:74–75
Language for Life, **79**:362
Lathem, Edward C., **78**:88
Latin America Translation Conference, **79**:392
Laubach Literacy International, **80**:693–694; **79**:571–572; **78**:410–411; **77**:448–449
Law libraries
  bibliography, **80**:402–403
  construction, **81**:308; **80**:440
  statistics, see Library statistics, law libraries
  see also American Association of Law Libraries; International Association of Law Libraries; Library services and programs, access
Layton, Jeanne, **81**:30, 38
Learmont, Carol L., **81**:231; **80**:321; **79**:231; **78**:329; **77**:345
Learner's Advisory Service, **77**:209
Learning resource centers, see School library/media services; Two-year college libraries
Lee, Grant, **77**:387
Lee, Joel, **81**:103
Leeson, Kenneth, **80**:38
Legislation affecting information industry, **81**:147–152; **80**:195–203
  Congressional action, **80**:197–203
    H.R. 4392, Appropriations for Departments of State, Justice, Commerce, the Judiciary, and Related Agencies, **80**:198

PL 96-39, **80:**199
S. 918, **80:**199–200
U.S. Executive Branch action, **80:**196–197
Legislation affecting libraries, **81:**5–6, 33–34, 127–144; **80:**175–187; **79:**117–126, 126–132; **78:**80, 111–118; **77:** 99–107
AAP action, **77:**412–413
ALA action, **81:**102
Bahamas, **79:**350–351
German Democratic Republic, **79:**379
India, **81:**378
research libraries, **80:**140–141
school libraries, **79:**119
statistics, **81:**128–129, 138–139
USSR, **79:**372
see also Comprehensive Employment and Training Act; Elections, effect on libraries; Elementary and Secondary Education Act; Higher Education Act; Library Services and Construction Act; Library services for the handicapped, legislation; Obscenity legislation; Proposition 13
Legislation affecting Publishing, **81:**141–147; **80:**187–195; **78:**119–126; **77:** 107–115
see also Copyright; Obscenity legislation; Postal rates, legislation
Lenin State Library, **79:**376
Leonard, Lawrence E., **80:**204
Letters of Delegates to Congress, 1774–1789, **78:**67
"Levels of Output Related to Costs of Operation of Scientific and Technical Libraries," **81:**264
Levine, Arthur J., **78:**54; **77:**31
Levy, Alix C., **80:**66
Lewis, Alfred J., **80:**401
Liaquat Memorial Library, **78:**381
"Librarian as Youth Counselor" program, **78:**25, 85
Librarians
affirmative action data, **81:**230
Australia, **77:**430
certification, **80:**161
continuing education, **77:**384–387
see also Consultant Training Program; Continuing Library Education Network and Exchange; Education for Librarianship, continuing education; Library schools, faculty; continuing education under personnel, under types of libraries
demand and supply, **81:**233, 238; **80:**324; **79:**231, 234; **78:**15, 335; **77:**347
employment, **81:**23–26, 232; **80:**17–18; **79:**18–19
grievances, **80:**160
nonlibrary, **81:**221–222; **80:**319–320
employment overseas, **81:**219–221; **80:** 317–319; **79:**266–268, 355
exchange programs, **81:**221; **80:**319; **79:**267–268; **78:**354; **77:**379
free-lance jobs, **79:**268; **78:**354–355; **77:**379
international concerns, see Libraries, international concerns
joblines, **81:**209–211; **80:**307–309; **79:**19, 257–259; **78:**345–346; **77:**371
occupational surveys, **81:**246–249; **80:** 362–363
placement services, **81:**24–25, 209–223; **80:**307–320; **79:**89–90, 257–268; **77:** 4, 370–380
see also Library schools, placements
professional status, **79:**19–20
see also College and university libraries, personnel, faculty status
rehabilitation services, **80:**62–64
salaries, **81:**225, 232, 234–235, 238, 240–245; **80:**169, 321, 324–325, 328; **79:**231–243, 244–256; **78:**87, 329, 330, 331, 332, 335–343; **77:**345–370
USSR, **79:**376
sex and salary statistics, **78:**339, 340, 341, 342; **77:**62–63
unions, see Unions
United Kingdom, **79:**366
see also Information services, personnel; Library personnel; Library technical assistants; subdivision personnel under types of libraries
"Librarians and Their Stereotype," **80:**362
"Librarian's Guide to the New Copyright Law," **77:**101
Librarianship and the Third World, **80:** 493
Librarianship in Australia, **77:**431
Libraries, **77:**21–23
accreditation, see American Library Association, Committee on Accreditation; Library schools, accredited
acquisitions, **81:**86; **80:**9–10, 378
bibliography, **81:**406; **80:**531; **79:**581; **78:**572; **77:**608

Libraries (Cont.)
see also subdivision acquisitions under types of libraries
additions and renovations, see additions and renovations under types of libraries
administration, see Library management
automated circulation systems, **81**:15–16, 38–39; **80**:16–17; **79**:17–18
see also Libraries, computerized functions
Bahamas, **79**:350–355
budgets, **77**:14–15
building regulations for the handicapped, **80**:56–57
California, **80**:6–7
Canada, **79**:355–359
cataloging and classification, see Cataloging and classification
circulation, see Libraries, automated circulation systems; Public libraries, circulation, statistics
comparative studies, bibliography, **79**:577
computerized functions, **81**:12–14, 186; **80**:14–15, 104; **79**:16–18, 63, 575; **78**:13–15
bibliography, **80**:523–524
see also Bibliographic data bases; Cataloging and classification; Libraries, automated circulation systems; Networks
construction
USSR, **79**:376–377
see also College and university libraries, construction; Law libraries, construction; Public libraries, construction; Two-year college libraries, construction
copying of copyrighted works, **79**:42–43
see also Audiovisual materials, copying; Photocopying
depository, see Depository libraries
energy conservation, **81**:11–12; **80**:10–11; **79**:12–13, 122–123, 142; **78**:4
equipment and furniture, bibliography, **81**:400; **80**:524–525; **79**:575–576; **78**:567, **77**:600–601
see also Library materials
expenditures
Bahamas, **79**:351
India, **81**:379
under LSCA Title III, **80**:217
see also College and university libraries, expenditures; Library materials, library expenditures; Public libraries, expenditures; School library/media services, expenditures
fees, **81**:13–14
fines, **80**:25
funding, see Library funding
history
bibliography, **81**:403; **80**:527–528; **79**:578; **78**:569
see also American Library Association, Library History Round Table
international concerns, **81**:366–375; **80**:490–494
Iran, **80**:27
legislation, see Legislation affecting libraries
Mexico, **77**:423–428
bibliography, **77**:426–427
NEH support, **81**:192–195
national, see National libraries; Parliamentary libraries
number of, U.S. and Canada, **81**:272–273; **80**:373–374; **79**:280–281; **78**:237; **77**:258–259
OCLC users, **80**:164, 166
personnel, see Library personnel
promotional campaigns, **78**:24–25
public relations, **80**:23
reference services, **78**:272–273
bibliography, **81**:405; **80**:529–530; **79**:579–580; **78**:570
security, **81**:30–32; **80**:25–27; **79**:25–27; **78**:4–6, 88; **77**:10–11
state, see State libraries
statistics, see Library statistics
technical services, **81**:264–265
bibliography, **81**:406–407; **80**:531–532; **79**:581–582; **78**:572; **77**:607–608
see also Cataloging and classification; Libraries, acquisitions, and similar headings
USSR, **79**:372–377
United Kingdom, resource allocation, **79**:365–366
user surveys, **81**:266; **80**:361–362; **79**:37–41; **78**:235–236; **77**:256–258
see also U.S., population served by libraries
see also College and university libraries; Depository libraries; Law libraries; Public libraries; Research libraries; School library/media services; Special libraries; Two-year college libraries

"Libraries and Information Services in the USSR," **78**:85-86
"Libraries for All: One World of Information, Culture and Learning," **78**: 367
Libraries General Information Series, **77**: 247
Libraries in International Development, **80**:491
"Libraries in Literacy," **81**:184
Library Acquisitions: A Look into the Future, **80**:444
Library Act (Bibliotheksverordnung), **79**: 379
Library administration, *see* Library management
Library Administration and Management Association, *see* American Library Association, Library Administration and Management Association
Library Administration Division, *see* American Library Association, Library Administration Division
Library agencies, state, *see* State library agencies
Library and Information Center of the Higher Technical School, Wrocław, **79**:369
Library and Information Technology Association, *see* American Library Association, Library and Information Technology Association
Library Association (U.K.), Commission on Manpower, **79**:363
Library Association of Australia, biennial conference, **80**:115
Library Association of Australia, Library Associates of the Association, **77**: 430, 431
Library Association of the German Democratic Republic, **79**:383
Library Association Record, **80**:454
Library associations, **81**:28-29; **79**:24; **78**:18
  Bahamas, **79**:354
  Canada, **79**:359
    provincial, **81**:512-514; **80**:640-641; **79**:517-518
    see also names of library associations in sections on Library associations, foreign; Library associations, national; Library associations, regional
  continuing education programs, **80**:19
  dues, **81**:28-29
  dues, **81**:28-29
  foreign, **81**:538-548; **80**:666-675; **79**: 544-554; **78**:538-549; **77**:571-581
  international, **81**:529-538; **80**:490-491, 656-666; **79**:533-543; **78**:376-381, 528-538; **77**:561-570
  meetings, **81**:29, 562-564; **80**:695-698; **79**:593-594; **78**:617-621; **77**:581-582
    see also subdivisions meetings, conferences, etc., under names of associations
  mergers, **81**:29
  Mexico, **77**:426
  national, **81**:439-504; **80**:563-631; **79**: 445-508; **78**:443-502; **77**:412-415, 478-537
  new, **81**:23
  Pakistan, **78**:385
  placement services, **81**:214-215; **80**:309-311, 312; **79**:259-261, 261-262; **78**: 346-349; **77**:370-374
  regional, U.S. and Canada, **81**:514-515; **80**:641-642; **79**:518-520; **78**:379, 512-514
  SLA student groups, **80**:168-169
  state and provincial, **78**:502-512
  state and territorial, **81**:504-512; **80**:631-640; **79**:509-517
  state, regional, and provincial, **77**:538-548
    see also School library/media associations, state
Library Bill of Rights, **81**:30, 104; **80**:27, 34-35, 119
Library Binding Institute, **78**:99-102
Library bindings, *see* Books, library bindings
Library Career Consultants, **77**:371
Library Connection, **78**:174
Library cooperation, **78**:11-12; **77**:8-10, 45, 77-78
  Bahamas, **79**:353
  bibliography, **81**:404; **80**:528; **79**:13-15, 578-579
  broadcasting media relations, **77**:21-23
  children's programs, **78**:26-27
  circulation systems, **81**:15-16
  foundation grants, **79**:200
  funding, federal, **81**:5; **78**:137-139
  international, **81**:80-81, 368-372; **80**:4, 21-22, 508; **79**:367, 377; **78**:369, 376-377; **77**:39, 210-211

Library cooperation (Cont.)
    CLR support, **78:**174-175
    SLA participation, **80:**171
    LSCA support, **81:**170-172; **80:**216-217; **79:**144-145; **78:**138
    Library of Congress, **78:**64-65
    multitype systems, **81:**21-22; **80:**14; **79:**15
    national libraries, **80:**106
    networking, **81:**16-17
    regional, **77:**4
    school/public libraries, **81:**21; **80:**30-31; **79:**15; **77:**19-20
    WHCOLIS pre-conferences, **80:**51
    see also Interlibrary loan; Libraries, international concerns; Networks
Library Cost Model Project, **80:**143
Library directors
    salaries, **79:**244-256; **77:**362, 364
    salaries and sex, **80:**337-341, 343; **77:**362, 364
    sex and per capita support, **80:**336, 338, 339; **77:**362
    see also Association of Academic Health Sciences Library Directors
Library Education Division, *see* American Library Association, Library Education Division
Library Education Statistical Report, **81:**264
"Library Effectiveness: A State of the Art," **81:**264
Library for Natural Sciences (USSR), **79:**375
Library fraternities, **78:**360-363; **77:**405-406
Library funding, **80:**7-9, 32-33, 204-217; **79:**28-29; **77:**6-8, 76
    bond issues, **81:**9
    Carter budget, **80:**188-189
    cooperative systems, **81:**21-22
    federal, **81:**127-131; **80:**4, 5-6, 20, 178-179, 189; **79:**11-12, 117-119; **78:**8; **77:**12-13, 26, 100, 270-271
    fund raising projects, **81:**8
    local, **81:**7-8; **80:**6; **78:**6-8
    public libraries, **81:**9-10, 163, 164-165; **80:**10, 204, 334-337, 385-386, 387-389, 390-391; **79:**7-12, 296-297, 298-299, 300-302
    state, **81:**6-7; **80:**6, 381-382; **79:**10, 30, 290-291; **78:**9; **77:**74, 270-271
    United Kingdom, **81:**11
    see also Elementary and Secondary Education Act; General Revenue Sharing; Grants, library; Higher Education Act; Library Services and Construction Act; State library agencies, funding; *also* "funding" under types of libraries
Library General Information Surveys, **80:**364; **79:**277; **77:**75
    current status, **80:**366-367
    II Survey of Special Libraries in State Governments, **80:**392-395
    IV Public School Library Media, **80:**395-400
Library History Round Table, *see* American Library Association, Library History Round Table
"Library in American Society," **80:**117
Library Information and Online Network, **81:**19
"Library Is Filled with Success Stories," **80:**123
Library joblines, *see* Librarians, joblines
Library legislation, *see* Legislation affecting libraries
Library literature
    bibliography, **81:**397-407; **80:**521-532, 532-533, 533-534; **79:**382, 573-582; **78:**565-573, 575-580; **77:**599-609
    comparative and international, **80:**493
    bibliography, **81:**372-374, 401-402
    Pakistan, **78:**384-385
    placement services, **81:**209; **80:**307; **79:**257; **78:**344
    see also Book trade, bibliography
Library management, **80:**18
    bibliography, **81:**398; **80:**522; **79:**574; **78:**566, 569
    CLR support, **81:**155-156, 158-159; **80:**268; **78:**171
    OMS training activity, **79:**92-93
    systems administration, **78:**84
    theological librarians, **81:**123
Library Management Research Unit, *see* British Library, Library Management Research Unit
Library Management Skills Institutes, **81:**123-124
Library Manpower: A Study of Demand and Supply, **81:**263; **77:**369
Library materials
    bibliography, **81:**403; **79:**578; **77:**603
    conservation and preservation, **81:**156-157, 203-204; **80:**26-27, 98; **79:**27, 179, 180, 260; **78:**82; **77:**210
    bibliography, **81:**398-399; **80:**522-523; **77:**608

CLR support, **81**:156–157; **80**:267–268; **78**:174
NHPRC support, **81**:203
temperature controls, **80**:186
see also Preservation Planning Program
for the deaf, **80**:58
funding, **80**:385–386, 387–389, 390–391; **79**:296–297, 298–299, 300–302
international flow, **81**:381–383
library expenditures, **81**:292–293, 296–297; **80**:375–379, 381–382; **79**:282–286, 292–293; **78**:244–245, 247, 251, 252, 254, 258, 270–271
NEH Collections Program, **79**:168
prices and price indexes, **81**:340–353; **80**:454–466; **79**:332–345
standards, **80**:370
sales, **79**:318, 319, 320
school library/media services, **80**:396, 397
special libraries, **80**:392–393, 394
user surveys, **79**:37–41
see also Audiovisual materials; Microforms; Periodicals; Serial publications
Library Materials Price Index Committee, *see* American Library Association, Resources and Technical Services Division, Library Materials Price Index Committee
Library networks, *see* Networks
Library of Congress, **81**:85–90; **80**:94–99; **79**:58–66; **78**:60–67; **77**:35–40, 205–206
acquisitions, **81**:88; **80**:97
Adams, John, Building, **81**:87
American Folklife Center, *see* American Folklife Center
American Television and Radio Archives, **78**:66
Bibliographic Systems Office, **78**:63
bicentennial activities, **77**:35
budget, **80**:96–97; **79**:59
catalog cards (printed), **78**:65
catalog closing, **80**:15
cataloging, **81**:88–89; **80**:97–98
Cataloging in Publication Program, **81**:89; **77**:39
ANSC standards, **80**:127
Center for the Book, *see* Center for the Book
Collections Development Office, **81**:85–86

Computer Catalog Center, **78**:60–61
computerized catalogs, **78**:64
Congressional Research Service, **81**:87; **80**:96, 97, 507
Cooperative MARC, *see* COMARC
coordinate cataloging with GPO, **81**:83–84
Copyright Deposit Collection, **81**:86
Copyright Office, *see* U.S., Copyright Office
Customer Information Control System, **78**:63
employment, **79**:265
exhibits, **81**:89
funding, federal, **81**:5
HEA funding, **80**:177
Hispanic Acquisitions Project, **79**:63
Information Distribution Center, **81**:87
international activities, **78**:64
Jefferson, Thomas, Building, **81**:87; **77**:36
Kennedy, John F., Center for the Performing Arts, **78**:61
Madison, James, Memorial Building, **81**:85; **80**:94; **79**:60, 126; **78**:61; **77**:35
merit selection system, **80**:316
Motion Picture, Broadcasting and Recorded Sound Division, **80**:97
as National Bibliographic Center, **80**:4, 143
National Library Service for the Blind and Physically Handicapped, **81**:86; **80**:57, 64, 99
and national networks, **78**:169
National Preservation Program, **78**:62
National Referral Center, **80**:95–96
National Serial Data Program, *see* National Serial Data Program
network activities, **81**:88–89; **80**:48–49
Network Development Office, **80**:49; **79**:61–62; **78**:63; **77**:38
Network Technical Architecture Group, *see* Network Technical Architecture Group
Office of Planning and Development, **78**:60
Office of the Director for Processing Systems, Networks and Automation Planning, **81**:89
Performing Arts Library, **80**:94; **79**:60
Processing Services, **80**:49
publications, **81**:89–90; **80**:98–99
publications and recordings, bibliography, **79**:64–65
reorganization, **79**:58–59

Library of Congress (Cont.)
  Rosenwald, Lessing J., Collection, **80**:97
  selection system, **81**:218
  services and programs, **78**:60–61, 66–67
  shelflist, **79**:63
  Smithsonian Deposit, **77**:46–47
  Task Force on Goals, Organization, and Planning, **78**:60
  users, **81**:87
  see also COMARC; CONSER; Card Automated Reproduction Demand System; Network Advisory Committee; PRECIS
Library of Congress Book Procurement Center (Pakistan), **78**:384
Library of Congress Name Headings with References, **77**:39
Library Order Information System, **79**:63
Library Orientation/Instruction Exchange, *see* Project LOEX
Library personnel, **78**:16–17; **77**:248, 251
  continuing education, **81**:25, 69; **80**:19–20, 169; **78**:17–18; **77**:384–387
    HEA Institute Program, **81**:180–183; **80**:223–224, 227, 228–232
    see also Continuing Library Education Network and Exchange; Education for librarianship, continuing education; and subdivision personnel, continuing education under types of libraries
  costs, **78**:15–16
    see also under salaries, *below*
  discrimination in employment practices, **79**:24–25; **78**:19
    see also Library personnel, minority groups; Women in librarianship
  exchange programs, **79**:23–24; **77**:79, 379–380
    see also Librarians, exchange programs
  HEA training programs, **78**:153–156
  minority groups, **81**:263; **79**:25; **77**:6, 63
    bibliography, **79**:578
    see also American Library Association, Black Caucus; Women in librarianship
  racial, ethnic, sexual composition, **81**:230
  salaries, **81**:24; **78**:251–252; **77**:272–273
    see also Librarians, salaries; Library directors, salaries; Public libraries, personnel, salaries
  salaries and sex, **80**:334–344

  statistics, **81**:263–264; **78**:244–245, 246, 249; **77**:274–275
    bibliography, **78**:212; **77**:254
  supply and demand, **81**:184
  surveys, **81**:223–231; **80**:370
    see also Librarians, occupational surveys; Library statistics
  training programs, **81**:180; **80**:223–224; **79**:152–155, 161–163; **78**:145–147, 152; **77**:393–404
    see also Comprehensive Employment and Training Act
  training institute program, **79**:155–160
  utilization, **77**:60
  volunteers, **81**:25–26; **80**:20; **79**:22; **78**:16
    NLS, **80**:101
  see also American Library Association, Office for Library Personnel Resources; Library directors; Library technical assistants; Library trustees; *also* subdivision personnel under types of libraries, e.g., Public libraries, personnel
Library Personnel Interchange, **77**:17, 379–380
Library Photocopying and the U.S. Copyright Law of 1976, **80**:170
Library planning
  Australia, **77**:430–431
  Iran, **77**:417–423
  Mexico, **77**:423–428
  Pakistan, **78**:385–386
Library Programs Worth Knowing About, **79**:142; **78**:135
Library Public Relations Council, **79**:497; **78**:490–491; **77**:526
Library Research, **79**:41
Library research and development, **81**:263–267; **80**:359–363; **79**:37–41
  bibliography, **81**:405; **80**:530; **79**:580; **78**:570–571; **77**:605
  funding, federal, **81**:266–267; **77**:192–195
  HEA funding, **81**:184–188; **80**:232–238; **79**:160–163; **78**:153–156
    see also Higher Education Act, Title II-B
  NEH support, **80**:248; **79**:167, 168; **78**:158, 159–160; **77**:198–199
  National Library System, **80**:102
  USSR, **79**:377
  United Kingdom, **79**:364
  see also Research in information science; U.S., Department of Education, conference on library research

Library Roster, **79:**265
Library scholarships, *see* Scholarships
Library schools, **80:**18-19
  accredited, **81:**27, 249-252; **80:**345-347; **79:**269-271, 358; **78:**81, 355-358; **77:**53,380-383
  see also American Library Association, Committee on Accreditation
  Australia, **77:**430-431
  continuing education programs, *see* Education for librarianship, continuing education
  degrees, certificates, etc., awarded, **81:**229
  faculty, **81:**27
  faculty salaries, **81:**228
  job-hunting seminars, **81:**216-217; **80:**314-315; **79:**263
  placement services, **81:**215-217; **80:**312-315; **79:**262-264; **78:**349-351; **77:**375-376
  placements, **81:**231-246; **80:**321-333; **79:**231-243; **78:**329, 330, 332, 333-335, 336; **77:**345-360
  programs, **80:**18-20
  programs in service to the handicapped, **80:**64-65
  two-year M.L.S., **81:**27
  see also Association of American Library Schools; Education for librarianship
Library Service Enhancement Program, **78:**172-173; **77:**208
Library Services Act (Calif.), **78:**28
Library Services and Construction Act, **81:**162-172; **80:**204-217; **79:**31, 133-146; **78:**112, 127-139; **77:**74, 76, 78, 172-183
  amendments, **78:**119-120
  CLR support, **78:**173-174
  Carter plans for replacement legislation, **80:**57
  extension, **77:**52
  school/library support, **81:**21
  Title I, Public Library Services, **81:**5, 163-165; **80:**189, 204, 205-213; **79:**117, 133, 134-142; **78:**80, 113, 119, 128-129; **77:**173-180
    allotments, **78:**130-131
    amendments, **79:**127
    budget, **80:**176
    evaluation, **79:**40-41
  Title II, Public Library Construction, **81:**168-170; **80:**213-216; **79:**142-144; **78:**113, 120, 135-137; **77:**180-181
  Title III, Interlibrary Cooperation, **81:**130, 170-172; **80:**176; **79:**117; **78:**137-139; **77:**181-182
  Title IV, Older Readers Services, **81:**167-168; **78:**113
Library services and programs, **80:**24-25; **78:**3, 4; **77:**18-19, 44-45
  access, **81:**13; **80:**4, 24; **79:**4-5, 6
  Australia, **77:**428-431
  Bahamas, **79:**350-355
  CLR programs, **77:**208-209
  effect of funding decreases, **79:**4-5, 7-9
  effectiveness, **81:**264
  Egypt, **80:**501-506
  exchange with USSR, **77:**59
  fees, **80:**15, 34; **79:**5, 40
  fines, **80:**33
  funding, federal, **81:**128-129, 142; **80:**33-34; **79:**118, 136; **78:**112, 130
  German Democratic Republic, **79:**378-383
  humanities programs, **81:**103; **80:**22-23, 36
  India, **81:**377-381
  international, CLR support, **81:**159-160; **78:**172-174
  Library of Congress, **79:**60
  LSCA allotments and matching requirements, **81:**164-165; **80:**206-207; **79:**136-137; **78:**130
  literacy programs, *see* Literacy programs
  NEH support, **81:**192-195; **80:**246-251; **78:**157-158, 160; **77:**197
  outreach programs, **80:**22-23
  Poland, **79:**367-371
  rural development, **80:**235
  special libraries, **80:**392, 394
  statewide, **77:**71, 75-77
  two-year colleges, **78:**300
  UNESCO, **81:**369
  USICA program, **81:**68-70
  United Kingdom, **79:**360-367
Library services for American Indian People, **80:**123; **78:**54-56; **77:**27
Library services for children and young adults, **81:**36; **80:**34-36; **79:**30, 35-36; **78:**22-23; **77:**14-21
  ALA divisions, **81:**36
  bibliography, **81:**400-401; **80:**525-526; **79:**576; **78:**567-568; **77:**601-602
  ESEA support, **81:**175
  IYC programs, **80:**28-30
  Iran, **80:**29
  OCLC services, **80:**167
  USSR, **79:**374

Library services for children and young adults (Cont.)
see also American Library Association, Association for Library Service to Children; American Library Association, Young Adult Services Division; International Institute for Children's Literature and Reading Research; International Youth Library
Library services for minority groups, **80**:23
Library services for persons of limited English-speaking ability, **78**:133–134; **77**:178–179
bilingual programs, **81**:36
see also Education, bilingual programs
LSCA support, **81**:167; **80**:210–211; **79**:139–140
Library services for special groups, bibliography, **81**:405–406; **80**:530–531; **79**:580; **78**:571; **77**:606
Library services for the aging, LSCA support, **81**:167–168; **80**:211–212; **79**:140–141; **78**:134; **77**:179
Library services for the blind, **80**:23–24, 61, 99–105
LSCA support, **81**:165–166; **80**:209–210; **79**:138–139
National Library Service regional libraries, **80**:102–105
state of the art survey, **81**:186
see also Information services, for the blind; Library services for the handicapped
Library services for the deaf
LSCA funding, **80**:58
national information center, **81**:184, 185; **80**:24, 58–59
school programs, **80**:61–62
see also Telecommunications, broadcasting stations, services for the handicapped
Library services for the disadvantaged, **77**:60
federal action, **80**:58
LSCA support, **80**:207–208; **79**:135, 137; **78**:129; **77**:173, 175–176
see also American Library Association, Office for Library Service to the Disadvantaged; Library services and programs, outreach programs; Library services for minority groups
Library services for the handicapped, **80**:23–24, 53–66, 99–105; **79**:7; **78**:10, 11, 24; **77**:19

ALA support, **80**:58–59
building regulations, **79**:143–144
college library services, **80**:62
HEA grant, **80**:233, 234
handicapped person defined, **80**:55
LSCA support, **81**:165–166; **80**:204, 209–210; **79**:138–139; **78**:132–133; **77**:177
legislation, **80**:54–55; **79**:125; **78**:117–118, 139
Library of Congress, **78**:62
school library/media services, **80**:60–62
state of the art survey, **81**:186
see also American Library Association, Association of Specialized and Cooperative Library Agencies; Librarians, rehabilitation services; Library of Congress, National Library Service for the Blind and Physically Handicapped; Library schools, programs in service to the handicapped; Library services for the blind; Library services for the deaf
Library services for the institutionalized
ASCLA projects, **81**:103
cooperation with public libraries, **81**:167
LSCA support, **81**:166–167; **80**:204, 208–209; **79**:137–138; **78**:131–132; **77**:176
Library services for the mentally retarded, see Library services for the handicapped
"Library Services in Support of Independent Living for the Elderly," **78**:84
Library statistics, **81**:267–269; **80**:363–371
bibliography, **78**:211–214; **77**:253–256
college and university libraries, **81**:224, 225, 265–266, 287–303; **80**:378–379, 431–440; **78**:226, 243–248; **77**:262–263, 265–268
bibliography, **78**:213
computerized, **78**:214
federal surveys, **80**:366, 367
see also Library General Information Surveys
foundation grants, **80**:278–282, 283, 284–285
health sciences libraries, **81**:279–286
international, **79**:349–350; **78**:374–376; **77**:415–417
law libraries, **80**:401–409, 440
legislation, **80**:178–181
library schools, program statistics, **81**:228, 229
NLM, **80**:107
placement figures, **81**:234–239; **80**:322–323, 326–328, 329

public libraries, **81**:224, 225, 226, 266; **80**:375-379, 380-391, 410-430; **79**:289-303
research libraries, **80**:143, 268
salaries, **81**:223-224, 225, 226, 227, 232, 234-235, 240-245; **80**:330, 332-333
school library/media services, **81**:226-227; **80**:395-400
special libraries, **81**:227; **80**:392-395
standard terminology, **80**:368-369
standards, **80**:368-369; **79**:349-350; **78**:217, 374-376
state library agencies, **81**:227
two-year college libraries, **80**:441-442
see also American Library Association, Library Administration and Management Association, Statistics Section; Association of Research Libraries, Task Force on Statistics; Elementary and Secondary Education Act; Higher Education Act; Information services, personnel, surveys; Legislation affecting libraries, statistics; Libraries, number of, U.S. and Canada; Library funding; Library personnel, surveys; Library Services and Construction Act; National Center for Education Statistics, Learning Resources Branch; U.S., population served by libraries; subdivisions construction, expenditures, personnel, etc., under types of libraries, e.g., Law libraries, construction
"Library Statistics in Nigeria," **77**:416
Library supervisors, state school, *see* School library/media services, state supervisors
Library technical assistants, **79**:21-22; **77**:4
Canada, education, **79**:358
training programs, **77**:393-404
see also Comprehensive Employment and Training Act
Library Technology Reports, **80**:118; **78**:81-82; **77**:54
Library trainees, *see* Library personnel, training programs
Library Trends, **77**:413
Library trustees, **79**:22-23
legal liability, **80**:18
training, **80**:18
Library Vacancy Roster, **77**:377
Libros, **79**:394
Lieb, Charles H., **77**:164

Ligue de Bibliothèques Européennes de Recherche, **78**:370-374
Lilly Endowment, support to ARL, **80**:144
Lind, George, **79**:278; **78**:235; **77**:256
Linden Press, **80**:41
"Linking the Bibliographic Utilities: Benefits and Costs," **81**:265
Lipscomb, Thomas, **78**:389
Lister Hill National Center for Biomedical Communications, **81**:93, 96-97; **80**:108; **79**:72, 74-75; **78**:72-75; **77**:43
construction, **80**:105; **78**:72
Integrated Library System, **81**:96
Learning Resources Center, **77**:43
Literacy programs
AAP concerns, **81**:112
federal action, **81**:143
functional illiteracy programs, **80**:58
"Literacy, Libraries Can Make It Happen," **80**:123
Literary agents and authors
bibliography, **81**:411
international center at Frankfurt, **79**:396
Literary awards, *see* Awards, literary
Literary Classics of the U.S., **80**:40
Little, Arthur D., report, **80**:81, 395
Little, Robert David, **79**:288; **78**:248, 256
Livingston, Barbara, **81**:304, 310; **80**:410-431
Lobby Reform Act, 1978, **79**:131
Lobbying, legislation, **81**:144
see also Tax reform law, lobbying restrictions
Local Government Records: An Introduction to Their Management, Preservation and Use, **80**:260
Lockert Library of Poetry in Translation, **79**:393
Lockheed, Dialorder Service, **80**:66, 67
London Book Review, **80**:41
Lorenz, John G., **80**:140
Lottman, Herbert, **81**:44, 359; **80**:481; **79**:395; **78**:387; **77**:432
Love, Mary, **77**:3
Lovejoy, Eunice, **80**:58, 99
Lutheran Church Library Association, **81**:494-495; **80**:619-620; **79**:497-498; **78**:491-492; **77**:526-527
Lynch, Mary Jo, **81**:263; **80**:359
Lynden, Frederick C., **78**:325

M

MARC, **79**:63
Australia, **77**:429

MARC Distribution Service, **77**:40
MARC Search Service, **79**:64; **77**:40
MARC Serials Editing Guide, **79**:64
MARS, *see* American Library Association, Machine Assisted Reference Section
MEDLARS, **81**:94–95; **80**:105–106; **78**:72–73; **77**:41, 429
  on-line, *see* MEDLINE
MEDLINE, **81**:95; **80**:106; **78**:72, 73; **77**:41
METRO, *see* New York Metropolitan Reference and Research Library Agency
METRO CAP Catalog, **77**:90
METRO Census of Scientific and Technical Periodicals, **77**:91
METRO Courtesy Card, **77**:92
MIDLNET, *see* Midwest Regional Library Network
MINITEX, *see* Minnesota Interlibrary Telecommunications Exchange
MLA, *see* Medical Library Association; Music Library Association
MRAP, *see* Management Review and Analysis Program
MURL, *see* Public libraries, construction, LSCA support
McClung, James W., **81**:85; **80**:94; **79**:58; **77**:35
McClure, Charles, **80**:362
Machine readable cataloging, *see* MARC
Machlup, Fritz, **79**:38
McKenna, Frank E., **80**:168, 170; **77**:63, 64
McMullen, Hayne, **77**:361
McNulty, Mary, **80**:132
Macy, Josiah J., Jr., Foundation, **77**:41
Madison, James, Memorial Building, *see* Library of Congress, Madison, James, Memorial Building
Mahar, Mary Helen, **77**:183
Male and Female under 18, **80**:27; **79**:33; **78**:30
Management Review and Analysis Program, **81**:121, 156; **80**:266; **79**:91; **78**:171; **77**:209–210
Management Skills Institute, **79**:92
Mann, Patrick, **80**:31
Manual of Procedures for Evaluation Visits and Self-Study, **77**:53
Manual on Bookselling, **80**:113; **79**:112; **77**:86, 87
Manually Maintained Serials Records, **77**:59
Manuscript donations, tax credit, **80**:185
Manuscripts, *see* Archives
Margolin, Judith B., **77**:215

Marke, Julius J., **77**:159
Market research, reader surveys, *see* Libraries, user surveys
Martin, Allie Beth, **77**:3
  Award, **80**:122
Martinson, Jean Ann, **78**:183; **77**:215
Maryland Regional Planning Council, **80**:236
Maryles, Daisy, **81**:431; **80**:554; **79**:433; **78**:432; **77**:466
Mason, Ellsworth, **81**:155
Mason on Library Buildings, **81**:155
Massachusetts, Proposition 2½, *see* Proposition 2½
Mathews, William D., **79**:50
Media Programs: District and School, **80**:396
Medical libraries
  funding, federal, **80**:189; **78**:116, 119
  number of, **81**:282–284
  personnel, **81**:285
  see also Library services and programs, access; Library statistics; Medical Library Association; National Library of Medicine
Medical Library Assistance Act, **80**:109, 176; **79**:75, 122; **78**:111, 116
Medical Library Association, **81**:495–497; **80**:620–622; **79**:498–500; **78**:492–494; **77**:527–529
  Committee on Surveys and Statistics, **81**:279
  placement services, **81**:212; **80**:310–311; **79**:260; **78**:347; **77**:373
  see also Association of Academic Health Sciences Library Directors
Medical Literature Analysis and Retrieval System, *see* MEDLARS
Medical records, privacy, **81**:151
"Meet the Computer" week, Utah, **81**:15
Meetings, *see* Book trade associations, meetings; Library associations, meetings
Mehnert, Robert B., **81**:93; **80**:105; **79**:72; **78**:72; **77**:41
"Member of Parliament: His Requirements for Information," **80**:508
Menuhin, Yehudi, **80**:489
Mergers and acquisitions (book trade), **81**:43; **80**:38–39; **79**:331–332; **78**:315; **77**:330
Meta, **79**:389
Metropolitan libraries, *see* Public libraries; Research libraries
Michigan Library Consortium, **79**:15

Microforms
　agricultural literature, **80**:111
　archival projects, **79**:179-180
　bibliographic control, **81**:86
　bibliography, **81**:403-404; **80**:528
　CLR support, **78**:174
　documentary material, **80**:259
　import duties, **77**:111-112
　machine-readable data base, **80**:143
　NPC as competition, **80**:198
　prices and price indexes, **80**:462; **77**:342
　see also Audiovisual materials; Selected Research in Microfiche
Midwest Regional Library Network, **79**:14
Milano, Albert, **77**:217-218
Miller, Ron, **77**:3
Milosz, Czeslaw, **81**:363
Minnesota Interlibrary Telecommunications Exchange, **79**:14, 15; **78**:169
Minorities, see American Library Association, Black Caucus; Librarians, affirmative action data; Telecommunications, broadcasting stations, minority ownership
Mitchell, Gwen Davis, **80**:42
Moneypenny, Philip, **77**:77
Monographs, access to, **79**:53
Monterey Institute of Foreign Studies, Calif., **79**:388
Montreal Book Fair, **80**:40
Moon, Eric, **78**:79; **77**:3, 18
Moore, Bessie Boehm, honorary membership in ALA, **81**:106
Moore, Everett, **77**:3
Moran, Leila, **77**:44
Moscow Book Fair, **80**:40, 133
"Motivational Research Project to Determine Reasons for Nonuse of Public Libraries," **81**:266
Motovun Group, **81**:365; **80**:488-489
Mt. Diablo, CA, **81**:29, 37
Ms. Magazine, **81**:37
Multiethnic I&R Service, **81**:4
Multitype library systems, see Library cooperation, multitype systems
Municipal Government Reference Sources, **79**:86
Museum Services Act, **81**:131
Museums
　federal funding, **77**:104
　NEH support, **78**:157-158
Music Library Association, **81**:498; **80**:623; **79**:500-501; **78**:494-495; **77**:529-530
　placement services, **81**:212-213; **80**:311; **79**:260; **78**:347; **77**:373

Music materials, NLS collection, **80**:101
Myers, Margaret, **81**:209, 223; **80**:307; **79**:257; **78**:344; **77**:370-380

N

NAC, see Network Advisory Committee
NACS, see National Association of College Stores
NACS Buyers Guide, **78**:95
NACS Manual of Operation, **78**:95
NACS Trade-Text Manual, **78**:95
NACSCORP, Inc., **78**:95, 97-98
NAEP, see National Assessment on Educational Progress
NAL, see National Agricultural Library; Technical Information Systems/National Agricultural Library
NARIC, see National Rehabilitation Information Center
NASIC, see Northeast Academic Science Information Center
NATIS, see National Information System
NBA/AAP Special Achievement Medal, **79**:110
NCES, see National Center for Education Statistics
NCHEMS, see National Center for Higher Education Management Systems
NCHEMS Handbook of Standard Terminology, **80**:368-369
NCLIS, see National Commission on Libraries and Information Science
NEA, see National Endowment for the Arts
NEH, see National Endowment for the Humanities
NELINET, **81**:20
NHPRC, see National Historical Publications and Records Commission
NICE, see National Information Conference and Exposition
NISSAT, see National Information Systems for Science and Technology
NLA, see National Librarians Association
NLA Newsletter, **80**:59
NLM, see National Library of Medicine
NLS, see Library of Congress, National Library Service for the Blind and Physically Handicapped
NLW, see National Library Week
NMA, see National Micrographics Association

NMAC, *see* National Medical Audiovisual Center
NNRLIS, *see* National Natural Resources Library and Information System
NOW, *see* National Organization for Women
NPA, *see* National Publications Agency
NPC, *see* National Periodicals Center (proposed)
NPSAC, *see* National Periodicals System, Advisory Committee
NSDP, *see* National Serials Data Program
NSF, *see* National Science Foundation
NSPP, *see* National Serials Pilot Project
NTIA, *see* National Telecommunications and Information Administration
NTIS, *see* National Technical Information Service
NTP, *see* National Toxicology Program
NUC, *see* National Union Catalog Publication Project
NYPL, *see* New York Public Library
NYSILL, *see* New York State Interlibrary Loan System
"Names of Agents Bill," **81:**147
Nassau Library Act, 1847, **79:**351
National Affiliation for Literacy Advance, **77:**449
National Agricultural Library, **77:**44–46
bicentennial activities, **77:**45–46
see also Technical Information Systems/ National Agricultural Library
National Agricultural Library; **77:**44–46
National Archives and Records Service, presidential records, **79:**96
see also National Historical Publications and Records Commission
National Assessment on Educational Progress, **77:**18
National Association of College Stores, annual meeting, **80:**39; **78:**96–97
BISG support, **80:**443
liaison with ABA, **79:**112
regional meetings, **78:**97
Resource Center, **78:**96
National Association of Land-Grant Colleges and Universities, Office for Advancement of Public Negro Colleges, CLR support, **79:**189–190
National bibliography, Canada, **79:**356
National bibliography, Poland, **79:**368
National Book Award in Translation, **79:**391
National Book Center of Pakistan, **78:**383, 384

National Book Awards, **79:**107, 110, 113; **78:**98
final ceremonies, **80:**39, 139
replaced by TABA, **80:**132
National Center for Education Statistics, **81:**230, 268–269, 287–303; **80:**56; **78:**211; **77:**75, 247, 253
academic library survey, **78:**243–248, 248–256
Learning Resources Branch, **80:**364; **79:**277, 288–289
see also Library General Information Surveys; *also* subdivision user surveys under Libraries and NCES surveys under School library/media services
Library Personnel Resources Survey (proposed), **80:**370
public library survey, **78:**243–256
reorganization, **77:**252
school library survey, **78:**256–265
National Center for Higher Education Management Systems, **80:**368–369
National Center on Educational Media and Materials for the Handicapped, data base, **80:**61
National Citizens Emergency Committee to Save Our Public Libraries, **81:**10–11; **80:**183; **77:**12–13
National Collection of Fine Arts/National Portrait Gallery, **77:**47
National Commission on Libraries and Information Science, **81:**17, 78–81; **80:**80–83; **79:**50–53; **78:**42–45, 125, 168, 248; **77:**13, 24–28, 30, 75, 104, 247
conducts WHCOLIS, **79:**53
grants to ANSC Z39, **79:**99
increased budget for, **81:**57
International Cooperation Planning Group, **81:**80–81
international exchange of information, **81:**58
national network action, **78:**11
staff changes, **79:**31–32
Task Force on Community Information and Referral Services, **81:**79
Task Force on Library and Information Services to Cultural Minorities, **80:**80
Task Force on Public/Private Sector Relations, **81:**80; **80:**82
IAA participation, **80:**154
Task Force on the Role of the Special Library in Nationwide Networks

and Cooperative Programs, **80**:80
Task Force to Study Z39, **78**:103-104
WHCOLIS planning, **81**:56, 57; **80**: 44-45
National Commission on New Technological Uses of Copyrighted Works, **80**:200; **79**:16; **78**:51-54, 117, 124; **77**:26, 31-34, 38, 163, 164
 final report, **79**:43-44, 124-125
National Diet Library (Japan), **80**:507
National Endowment for the Arts, **77**:105
 reauthorization, **80**:187
National Endowment for the Humanities, **81**:192-195; **80**:246-251; **79**:167-171; **78**:157-161; **77**:196-200
 College Library Program, *see* College Library Program
 Division of Education Programs, Cultural Institutions Program, **80**:247; **79**:167
 Fellowships Support to Centers for Advanced Study, **80**:247
 funds translations, **79**:393
 grant to ARL, **80**:143
 grant to OMS for conservation of library materials, **80**:266
 humanities projects, **80**:36, 246-247
 Office of Planning and Analysis, **77**:197, 200
 prison project, **81**:4
 reauthorization, **80**:187
 Research Resources Program, **80**:247-248
 support for libraries, **80**:246-251
 supports SAA workshops, **79**:97
National Energy Conservation Policy Act, **80**:122-123, 142
National Enquiry on Scholarly Communication, **80**:361
National Foundation on the Arts and Humanities Act, **81**:131
National Grass Roots Grants Program, **79**:86
National Historical Publications and Records Commission, **81**:201-206; **80**: 258-263; **79**:178-184
 Andrew Mellon grant, **81**:202
 grant to SAA, **79**:97
 initiates guide to U.S. archives, **79**:97-98
 legislation, **80**:184-185
 publications program, **81**:201-203; **80**: 259-260
 records grant program, **80**:260
National Information Conference and Exposition, **80**:152-153

National Information Policy, **77**:28
National Information System, **80**:152-153
National Information Systems for Science and Technology, **81**:381
National Institute of Handicapped Research, **80**:63
 established, **80**:54-55
National Institute on Library Service to Jail Populations, **81**:103
National Inventory of Library Needs, **78**:43, 248; **77**:247-252, 416
National Level Bibliographic Record—Books, **79**:62
National Librarians Association, **81**:499; **80**:156-162, 624; **79**:19, 501-502; **78**:495; **77**:530-531
 Grievance Referrals Committee, **80**:160
 Professional Welfare Committee, **80**:161
 programs and projects, **80**:158-159
National libraries
 Australia, **77**:429
 Canada, **79**:356
  see also National Library of Canada
 Egypt, **80**:502
 employment, **81**:217-218; **80**:315-316; **79**:264-265; **78**:351; **77**:376-377
 German Democratic Republic, **79**:380-381
  see also German Library; German State Library
 India, **81**:378
 Iran, **77**:417-423
 Japan, **80**:507
  see also National Diet Library
 Mexico, **77**:427
 Pakistan, **78**:381-382
 USSR, **79**:376
  see also Lenin State Library
 United Kingdom, *see* British Library
 U.S.
  federal funding, **79**:127
  see also Library of Congress; National Agricultural Library; National Library of Medicine; Smithsonian Institution Libraries; Technical Information Systems/National Agricultural Library
National Library Act, **80**:183, 190
National Library and Information Services Act, **81**:57, 135, 143
National library associations, *see* Library associations, national
National Library Network (proposed), **80**:30; **79**:185-186
National Library of Australia, **77**:429

National Library of Canada, **79**:356
  meetings with LC, **79**:62–63
National Library of Medicine, **81**:93–98; **80**:105–109; **79**:72–76; **78**:72–76; **77**:41–44
  card catalog closing, **80**:106
  extramural programs, **81**:98; **78**:75–76
  funding, federal, **81**:130; **80**:177, 189
  Integrated Library System, *see* Lister Hill National Center for Biomedical Communications, Integrated Library System
  Knowledge Base Program, **80**:108
  Lister Hill National Center for Biomedical Communications, *see* Lister Hill National Center for Biomedical Communications
  Regional Medical Library Program, **81**:95; **80**:109
  see also Communications Technology Satellite; Health and Planning Administration; Laboratory Animal Data Bank; National Medical Audiovisual Center; Regional Medical Library Network; TOXLINE; Toxicology Data Bank; Toxicology Information Program, Toxicology Information Response Center
National Library of Medicine Audiovisuals Catalog, **79**:74
National Library of Medicine Classification, **79**:73
National Library of Poland, **79**:368
National Library Service for the Blind and Physically Handicapped, *see* Library of Congress, National Library Service for the Blind and Physically Handicapped
National library system, Poland, **79**:368
National Library Week, **80**:123–124; **79**:87; **77**:60–61
  ALA support, **81**:104
  Legislative Day, **81**:141
National Medal for Literature, **81**:119
National Medical Audiovisual Center, **81**:97; **80**:108–109; **79**:72, 75; **78**:75; **77**:43–44
National Micrographics Association, **81**:499–500; **80**:625–626; **79**:502–503; **78**:496–497; **77**:531–532
National Museum of History and Technology, **77**:47
National Museum of Natural History, **77**:47

National Natural Resources Library and Information System, **78**:57–60
National Organization for Women, **78**:31
National Park Services libraries, *see* U.S. International Communication Agency, National Park Services Libraries
National Periodicals Center (proposed), **81**:127, 142–143; **80**:4, 12, 81, 82, 153, 177, 182, 190, 191–192, 198, 199; **79**:45, 61, 124, 186; **78**:87
  ARL concerns, **80**:141–143
  CLR plans, **79**:31
  copyright threat, **81**:22
  legislation, **81**:149
  NCLIS advisory committee, **79**:52
  technical development plan, **79**:589–592
National Periodicals Center: Technical Development Plan, **80**:81, 267–268; **79**:61, 186
National Periodicals System, **80**:81
  Advisory Committee, **80**:81
National Policy Statement on International Book and Library Activities, **77**:448
National Preservation Program, **77**:36
National Preservation Report, **80**:98
National Program Document, **77**:24–28
National Program of Library and Information Services (proposed), **79**:50–51; **77**:64
National Publications Act of 1979, **80**:183–184, 191
National Publications Agency, **80**:184, 198
National Publications Committee, **80**:183–184
National Reading Improvement Program, **78**:119
National Referral Center, *see* Library of Congress, National Referral Center
National Registry for Librarians, placement services, **81**:213; **80**:307; **79**:257; **78**:344; **77**:370
National Rehabilitation Information Center, **80**:63–64
"National Reporting on Reference Transactions," **80**:364
National Science Foundation
  Directorate for Scientific, Technological, and International Affairs, **78**:161
  Division of Information Science and Technology, **81**:195–200; **80**:251–252; **79**:172–178
  created, **79**:37

Division of Science Information, 78:161; 77:201-202
  abolished, 79:37
  grant recipients, 81:197-200; 80:255-258; 79:174-178; 78:163-167
National Science Foundation Bulletin, 77:203
National Serials Data Program, 79:66, 69-71; 78:65; 77:206
National Serials Pilot Project, 79:66
National Study Commission on Records and Documents of Federal Officials, 79:96
National Technical Information Service, 80:83-86, 127; 78:35-36, 52-53
  Advisory Committee, IIA participation, 80:154
  Federal Software Exchange Center, *see* Federal Software Exchange Center
  indexing and dissemination systems, 81:57
National Telecommunications and Information Administration, 80:86-91
  Institute for Telecommunications Sciences, 80:87
  Office of Federal Systems and Spectrum Analysis, 80:97
  Office of Policy Analysis and Development, 80:87
  Office of Telecommunications Applications, 80:87
National Union Catalog, 79:64
National Union Catalog (Canadian), 79:356
National Union Catalog of Monographs (Australia), 77:429
National Union Catalog: Pre-1956 Imprints, 81:81, 92; 79:64
National Union Catalog Publication Project, 77:39
National Zoological Park, 77:48
Nature of Translation, 79:391
Near Eastern Literature Conference, 79:393
Neely, Eugene T., 80:363
Neff, Evaline, 81:162; 80:204
Nemeyer, Carol, 79:58
Network Advisory Committee, 81:46-47; 79:11, 62, 170; 78: 11, 170; 77: 96
  Technical Architecture Group, 80:47; 78:63, 170
Network brokers, *see* Information brokers
Networks, 81:46-51; 80:11-12; 79:13-14, 31, 61-62; 77:74, 94-96, 206

administration, 78:84
Australia, 77:428-429
bibliography, 81:404; 80:528; 79:578-579
CLR support, 78:169
Canada, 79:357-358
competition, 81:17-19
computer-to-computer transmission, 79:51
cooperation, 81:18-19, 51
electronic mail, 80:110
funding, federal, 78:138
India, 81:381
LC activities, 80:98
legislation, 81:135
library services for the blind, 80:102-105
  see also Library of Congress, National Library Service for the Blind and Physically Handicapped
linking, 81:12, 265
linking, on-line, 77:39
  see also BIBLINK; Information services, communication between systems
Mexico, 77:427-428
NNRLIS services, 78:58-60
national, 81:16, 49; 80:11; 79:13; 78:11, 168-171; 77:27
school library/media services, 80:82; 78:26-27
  see also National Library Network (proposed); School library/media services, network participation
organization, 81:49-50
parliamentary libraries, 80:509
regional, 81:19-21; 80:13-14, 30; 79:14-15; 77:8-9
on-line users of OCLC, 80:163, 164
SLA involvement, 77:63
third party access, 80:13
USICA wireless file, 81:71-72
  see also Bibliographic control; Council for Computerized Library Networks; Information services; Library cooperation; National Program of Library and Information Services (proposed); *also* names of specific networks, e.g., Ohio College Library Center
"Networks for Networkers" conference, 81:186
Neubauer, Karl W., 77:416
Nevelson, Louise, 81:113
New American Library, hardcover editions, 80:41

New England Academic Librarians' Writing Seminar, 78:172
New Readers Press, 78:440; 77:448
New Streamlined English Series, 77:449
New York Board of Regents, guidelines for textbook selection, 77:16-17
"New York Is Book Country," 80:40
New York Library Association, joint meeting with Ontario Library Association, 79:359
New York Metropolitan Reference and Research Library Agency, 77:90-94
  central advisory and referral service, 77:91
New York Public Library
  budget cutbacks, 77:15
  SADPO, see Systems Analysis and Data Processing Organization
  see also Library Information and Online Network
New York State Interlibrary Loan System, 77:93
New York Times, ALA centennial supplement, 77:54
Newbery/Caldecott award banquet reevaluation, 80:35
Newbery Medal, 79:83; 78:32, 82
News about Z39, see *Voice of Z39*
News for You, 77:449
Newspapers
  bibliography, 81:413; 80:538; 79:588; 78:579; 77:615
  rates and index values, 81:349; 80:455, 462
  searches of offices, 81:146-147, 151; 80:188, 202; 79:132
  vacancy notices, 81:209; 80:307
Nida, Eugene A., 79:390
Nielsen, Carol S., 81:397; 80:521; 79:573; 78:565
Niemi vs *NBC*, 79:33-34
Nigeria Book Week, 79:82
1978 Consumer Research Study on Reading and Book Purchasing, 79:38-39
1975 Industry Statistics, 77:313
1976 Industry Statistics, 78:303
Nixon, Richard M., papers and recordings, 79:96
Nixon Historical Records Project, 79:96
Nobel Prize for Literature, 81:363
Noble, J. Kendrick, Jr., 80:445
Noma Prize for African Literature, 81:364
Non-print materials, see Audiovisual materials
Nordberg, E. Wayne, 80:443, 444

Northeast Academic Science Information Center, 77:8
Norwood, Babetta, 80:223; 79:151; 78:144
Nursery and Seed Trade Catalog Collection, 81:100
Nyren, Karl, 80:410, 431; 77:3

O

OATS, see Original Article Tear Sheet Service
OCLC, see Ohio College Library Center
OE, see U.S., Office of Education
OHIONET, 79:15
OIF, see American Library Association, Office of Intellectual Freedom
OLLT, see U.S., Department of Education, Office of Libraries and Learning Technologies
OLPR, see American Library Association, Office for Library Personnel Resources
OLSD, see American Library Association, Office for Library Service to the Disadvantaged
OMB, see U.S., Office of Management and Budget
OMS, see Association of Research Libraries, Office of Management Studies
OSIS, see National Science Foundation, Division of Science Information
OULCS, see Ontario University Libraries Cooperative System
Obscenity legislation, 80:188; 79:34; 78:124
Occupational Survey of Information Professionals, 81:246-249, 263
Off-Air Taping Conference, 80:185
Office for Library Personnel Resources, see American Library Association, Office for Library Personnel Resources
Office of Information and Regulatory Affairs, see U.S., Office of Management and Budget, Office of Information and Regulatory Affairs
Office of Libraries and Learning Technologies, see U.S., Department of Education, Office of Libraries and Learning Technologies
Office of Management and Budget, see U.S., Office of Management and Budget
Ofori, A. G. T., 78:380
Ohio College Library Center, 81:50-51;

80:11, 12-13, 162-167; 79:14; 78:58; 77:45
GPO cataloging records, 81:83
HEA support, 80:236
Interlibrary Loan Subsystem, 80:166
Research Department, 79:37
Research Library Advisory Committee, 81:19
third party use, 81:18-19
Ohio Libraries Reach Out, 80:58
Older Americans Act, 79:126
Olympia Press, 80:40
"On-Line Bibliographic Services: Where We Are, Where We're Going," 78:84
On Translation, 79:390
Online, Inc., Conference, 80:155
placement services, 81:213
Online, salary survey, 81:229
Ontario University Libraries Cooperative System, 79:357
"Organization of the Library Profession," 78:380; 77:412
Organizational Case Studies of Collection Development Policies and Practices, 80:361
Organizational Screening Program, 81:122
Original Article Tear Sheet Service, 78:52
Orne, Jerrold, 78:293; 77:66, 299
OSIP, *see* Occupational Survey of Information Professionals
Osburn, Charles, 80:362
Ospry, Bernard, 80:4
Out Island Library Act, 1909, 79:351

P

PARIS, *see* Program Resource Information System
PASTIC, *see* Pakistan Scientific and Technological Information Center
PBWG, *see* Pakistan Bibliographical Working Group
P.E.N. American Center
survey of writers, 80:37
translation committee, 79:385-386, 390
Translation Prize, 79:390
PGI, *see* UNESCO, General Information Programme
PGM, *see* U.S., International Communication Agency, Associate Directorate for Programming
PIO, *see* American Library Association, Public Information Office
PIO national poster contest, 79:87

PLA, *see* American Library Association, Public Library Association
PLATO, 77:207
PONY-U, *see* Parents of New York United
POPLINE, 81:95
PRECIS, 79:63
PSP, *see* Association of American Publishers, Professional and Scholarly Publishing Division
PSP awards, 81:118
Packer, Katherine, 77:416
Pahlavi National Library, 77:417
see also Center for Research in Iranian Studies
Pakistan Bibliographical Working Group, 78:383
Pakistan Council of National Integration, 78:382
Pakistan National Bibliography, 78:383
Pakistan Scientific and Technological Information Center, 78:383
Palmour, Gene, 81:266; 80:361
Paper Availability Study, 80:444
Paperback books, 81:43; 80:136-137; 79:107-108; 78:91-92
growth in output, 80:37
NACS depository, 78:97
prices and price indexes, 81:346-347; 80:452-453, 459, 460; 79:338, 339; 78:321-322
sales, 81:337; 80:471; 79:318, 320; 78:304-305; 77:322-323
taxation, 79:132
title output, 81:331; 80:448; 79:323; 78:308, 309
U.S. prices at Frankfurt Fair, 79:398
see also Association of American Publishers, Mass Market Paperback Division
"Paperback Power: How to Get It," 78:85
"Paperwork Reduction Act," 81:127, 132, 152; 80:202
Papier, Lawrence W., 80:233; 79:160; 78:153; 77:192
Parents as Reading Partners, 80:30
Parents' Guide to More Effective Schools, 81:118; 79:109
Parents of New York United, 78:30; 77:16
Parliamentary libraries, 80:507-509
see also Library of Congress
Patent laws, amendments, 81:131
Paul, Sandra K., 80:445
Penland, Patrick, 79:39
Pennsylvania Library Information Network, 81:20

"Perceived Values of Information Sources for Library Decision-Making," **80:** 362
Performance of Card Catalogs: A Review of Research, **80:**361
Performing Arts Library, *see* Library of Congress, Performing Arts Library
Perigord Press, **80:**40
Periodicals
 access, **80:**81; **77:**26
 see also National Periodicals System
 bibliography, **81:**404, 407, 413, 414; **80:** 528–529, 532, 538; **79:**579, 582, 588; **78:**569, 573, 579, 580; **77:**603–604, 609, 615
 for the blind, **80:**101
 copying, **78:**34–41, 37–38
 data bases, **81:**155
 prices and price indexes, **81:**342; **80:**456; **79:**335; **78:**318; **77:**333, 336, 337
 subscription sales, **78:**97
 see also National Periodicals Center (proposed); Serial publications
Perspective on Libraries, **80:**116
Peters, Jean R., **81:**407; **80:**445, 532; **79:**583; **78:**575; **77:**611
Peters, Marybeth, **80:**70; **79:**42
Phillips, Beth A., **81:**176
Phonorecords, licensing, **80:**77
Photocopying, **79:**124; **78:**43
 copyright, **81:**40, 131; **78:**52–53, 117, **77:** 33, 38, 160–163, 167–168
 fee collection, **78:**33–41
 5-year review, **81:**74; **80:**185, 192; **79:** 44–45
 information-on-demand, **78:**36–37
 intralibrary uses, **78:**33; **77:**144–146
 royalties, **78:**33–34; **77:**26
 unauthorized, **81:**113; **77:**33–41
 see also Libraries, copying of copyrighted works
Photocopying by Academic, Public and Non-Profit Research Libraries, **81:** 114; **80:**134
Photocopying by Corporate Libraries, **79:**15
Physical Disability: A Psychological Approach, **80:**55
Physical Fitness/Sports Medicine, **79:**74
Picturepages, **79:**5, 35–36
Pierce, William S., **81:**155
Pioneer Valley Union List of Serials, **80:**216
Plain Language Definitions of Microform Terminology for Order Librarians, **77:**58

Plainedge Public Library, Massapequa, N.Y., user survey, **81:**266
Planning Library Workshops and Institutes, **77:**58
Planning Process for Public Libraries, **81:** 106, 266; **80:**121
Planning Program for Small Academic Libraries, **81:**122, 156
Plotnik, Arthur, **80:**117; **77:**54
Polish Academy of Sciences, libraries, **79:** 369
Portugal Prize, **80:**392
Postal rates, **79:**128–129
 appeals cases, **79:**130
 classification, **80:**194–195; **78:**122–123
 Court of Appeals case, **80:**194
 increase, **81:**144; **80:**42, 114
 legislation, **81:**135, 143–144; **80:**184, 193–195; **79:**128, 129–130; **78:**80, 122–123; **77:**107–110
 parcel post discounts, **80:**194
 special rate fourth class, **81:**135, 143–144; **80:**193, 194
 uniform rates, **80:**194; **79:**129
 see also U.S., Postal Rate Commission; U.S., Postal Service
Postal Reform Act, **80:**201
Postal Reorganization Act, 1970, **80:**114, 194; **79:**130; **78:**122; **77:**107–110
Postal service
 AAP concerns, **81:**115
 private carriers, **80:**193–194; **79:**128–129, 130
 see also U.S., Postal Service
Postal Service Act, 1977, **78:**121
Postal Service Act, 1978, **79:**128
Postal Service Act, 1979, **80:**184, 193
Power, Mary, **79:**53; **77:**75
Preservation of library materials, *see* Library materials, conservation and preservation
Preservation Planning Program, **81:**122
Preserved Context Indexing System, *see* PRECIS
Presidential Records Act, **79:**96, 122
Presidential Records and Materials Preservation Act, 1974, **79:**96
Price, Douglas S., **80:**78; **79:**50
Price, Richard, **80:**31
"Price Index for Legal Publications," **80:**455
"Price Indexes, Foreign and Domestic Music," **80:**455
Primer of Business Terms and Phrases Related to Libraries, **79:**84

Princess Daisy, **80:**41, 484
Princeton Microfilms, **78:**36
Printed materials, copyright of graphic designs, **80:**185
Printing industry, bibliography, **78:**560
Privacy Protection Act, 1980, **81:**146–147, 151
Prizes, *see* Awards, library; Awards, literary; Grants, information science; Grants, library; Scholarships; *also* names of prizes, e.g., Martin, Allie Beth, Award; Newbery Medal
Problems of Bibliographic Access to Nonprint Media, **80:**82
Profits with Mass Paperbacks, **77:**83
Program of Fellowship Support to Centers for Advanced Study, **77:**196
Program Resource Information System, **79:**77
Programmed Logic for Automation Teaching Operations, *see* PLATO
Problèmes théoretiques de la traduction, **79:**390
Professional Services Directory (ATA), **80:**389
Progress Report on the Occupational Survey of Information Professionals, **80:**362
Project LOEX, **79:**189; **78:**173; **77:**209
Project Media Base: Bibliographic Control of Audiovisual Resources, **79:**52
Project Mediabase, **80:**82
Proposition 13, **81:**6; **80:**6–7, 33; **79:**7–9, 13
Proposition 13 Research Inventory, **79:**40
Proposition 2½, **81:**5, 6
Proteus: His Lies; His Truth, **79:**392
Providing Legal Services for Prisoners, **79:**84
Provincial library agencies, statistical publications, **78:**230
Public Broadcasting Report, **80:**74
Public Health Service Act, Title III-J, Medical Libraries, **80:**189
Public Information Office, *see* American Library Association, Public Information Office
Public libraries
acquisitions, **81:**275–276; **80:**376–377; **79:**11, 282–284; **78:**239–240; **77:**259–261
additions and renovations, **81:**317–320; **80:**422–427; **79:**303, 311–313; **78:**290–292; **77:**293–297
Bahamas, **79:**351–352
bibliography, **81:**404; **80:**529; **79:**579; **78:**569–570; **77:**604
Canada
construction, **81:**323; **80:**429
expenditures, **79:**356–357
circulation, statistics, **80:**383–384, 385–386, 387–389, 390–391; **79:**294–295, 296–297, 298–299, 300–302; **78:**253, 272–273, 276–280
construction, **81:**310–323; **80:**410–430; **79:**303–313; **78:**281–292; **77:**361–362
EDA support, **77:**104
funding, **81:**9
LSCA support, **81:**168–170; **80:**213–216; **79:**142–144; **78:**135–137; **77:**180
construction costs, **81:**322; **80:**428–429; **79:**304, 305–306, 306–309, 310, 311–313
expenditures, **80:**381–382; **79:**282–284, 290–291, 292–293; **78:**250–252, 272–273, 276–280
funding, *see* Library funding, public libraries
German Democratic Republic, **79:**379, 380
India, **81:**378
Mexico, **77:**424
NEH Public Library Program, **79:**168
Pakistan, **78:**382
personnel
number of, **80:**383–384; **79:**294–295
salaries, **79:**244–256, 292–293; **78:**270–271, 339–340, 341
work loads, **80:**385–386, 387–389, 390–391; **79:**296–297, 298–299, 300–302
see also Library personnel
planning guide, **81:**184
Poland, **79:**370
reference services, **80:**383–384; **79:**294–295
service outlets, **79:**292–293
statistics, *see* Library personnel, surveys; Library statistics, public libraries; *also* subdivisions acquisitions, additions and renovations, construction, personnel, and reference services *above*
see also circulation, expenditures, funding, personnel, reference services *under* Public libraries *above*
support and sex, **80:**334–344
USSR, **79:**373, 375
United Kingdom, **79:**360–361, 366
see also Research libraries

Public Libraries: An Economic View, **81**:266
Public Library Association, *see* American Library Association, Public Library Association
Public Library Construction, 1965-1978, **79**:144
Public Library of Columbus and Franklin County, Center for Discovery, **81**:36
Public Library Quarterly, **79**:41
"Public Library Service to Physically Handicapped Persons," **80**:360
Public records, *see* Archives
Public Services Improvement Program, **81**:122
Public Telecommunications Facilities Program, **80**:87
Public Telecommunications Financing Act, **79**:123
Public Works Employment Act, **78**:116
  Title I, Local Public Works, **78**:136, 137
Publication of American Historical Manuscripts, **80**:259; **79**:179
Publishers
  backlists, *see* Thor Power Tool Company decision
  continuing education, **81**:115-116; **80**:133, 135; **79**:106-107
    seminars overseas, **80**:499-501
  consolidations and reorganizations, **80**:44-45
  depreciation of unsold books, *see* Thor Power Tool Company decision
  discounts and returns, **81**:42
  imprints, **80**:40
  international meeting of educational publishers, **81**:365; **80**:488
  paperback imprints, *see* Paperback books
  sales, *see* Book sales
  small business loans, **81**:144-145
Publishers associations, *see* Association of American Publishers; Book trade associations
Publishing, **81**:40-41, 42-45; **80**:37-42
  Africa, **81**:364
  bibliography, **81**:409-411; **80**:534-536; **79**:584-586; **78**:576-577; **77**:612-613
  China, **81**:43-44, 113
  distribution of books, **81**:115
    AAP concerns, **79**:106; **78**:91
    BISG study, **80**:445, 475
  economic problems, **80**:42
  IPA services, **80**:495-496
  India, **81**:380-381
  international cooperation, **80**:133
  job descriptions, **77**:387
  legislation, *see* Legislation affecting publishing
  pirated editions, **80**:40
  public relations, **81**:116
  scientific and scholarly books, **79**:108
  small publishers, **80**:136
    see also Association of American Publishers, Smaller Publishers Group
  subsidiary rights, **80**:37
  taxation, *see* Paperback books, taxation
  see also Editing, bibliography
Publishing Abstracts, **81**:120
Publishing statistics, **80**:467-473; **77**:449-453
  history, **81**:324-329
  price indexes, **79**:332-345; **78**:316-326
  title output, **81**:324-329; **80**:446-453, 512-513; **79**:321-326; **78**:306, 307-326; **77**:321, 437-441, 452
    British, **81**:388-393; **80**:514-518; **79**:405-408; **78**:398-400
    international, **81**:384-387; **80**:510-514; **79**:412; **78**:401-405
    translations, **78**:309; **77**:438-439, 453, 454
  see also Book exports; Book imports; Book sales; Books, consumer expenditures; Books, international flow; Books, prices and price indexes; Paperback books; Textbooks

Q

Queensborough Public Library, budget cutbacks, **77**:15
Questions and Answers about Title IV-B, ESEA, **79**:148
Qureshi, Naimuddin, **80**:490; **78**:381

R

RASD, *see* American Library Association, Reference and Adult Services Division
R.I.C.E., **78**:36
RIF, *see* Reading Is FUNdamental
RLG, *see* Research Libraries Group
RLIN, *see* Research Libraries Information Network
RLI/WLN, *see* Research Libraries Information Network/Washington Library Network

RML, see National Library of Medicine, Regional Medical Library Program
RTECS, see Registry of Toxic Effects of Chemical Substances
RTS, see Remote Terminal System
RTSD, see American Library Association, Resources and Technical Services Division
Rack Clearance Center, see Association of American Publishers, Mass Market Paperback Division, Rack Clearance Center
Rademacher, William, 77:3
Radio stations, see Telecommunications, broadcasting stations
Raffel, Burton, 79:391
Rare books, see Books, rare books, security
Rare Books and Manuscripts Conference, 78:82
Rate Support Grant Settlement (U.K.), 79:360
Ray, Gordon N., 77:62
"Read More about It," 81:91; 80:36, 41, 95
"Reading and Successful Living: The Family-School Partnership," 81:92
Reading in America 1978, 80:95
Reading Is Fun Day, 80:190
Reading Is FUNdamental, Inexpensive Book Distribution Program, 80:189; 79:5, 127; 78:119
 see also Reading Is Fun Day
Reading, Writing and Other Communication Aids for the Handicapped, 80:57
Rebsamen, Werner, 78:99
"Recent Studies in Measurement for Better Decisions and Service in Public Libraries," 80:121
"Recommendation on the Legal Protection of Translators and Translations and the Practical Means to Improve the Status of Translators," 79:393
Recommendations for Audiovisual Materials for Small and Medium-Sized Public Libraries, 77:58
Records Management Office, see Information Management and Services Division, EOP
Rees, Alan M., 81:279
Reference aids and services, bibliography, 77:416
Reference and Adult Services Division, see American Library Association, Reference and Adult Services Division

Reference Works for Small and Medium-Sized Libraries, 80:122
Reforma, placement services, 81:213; 80:311; 79:260; 78:347; 77:373
Regional library associations, see Library associations, regional, U.S. and Canada
Regional Medical Library Network, 79:76
Register of Copyrights, see Copyright
Registry of Toxic Effects of Chemical Substances, 80:107; 78:74
Regulation of Lobbying Act, 80:192-193
Regulations Concerning International Loan for the Soviet Union's Libraries, 79:373
Rehabilitation Act, 80:54-56, 63; 79:125, 126, 143; 78:137
Reid, D. G., 79:351
Remote Terminal System, 80:53
Rennert, Diane, 78:119
"Report about Standardization Activities," 77:416
Report on Book Information Needs, 80:443; 77:416
Report on the Feasibility of an International Serials Data System, 79:67
"Report on the Study of Library Use at Pitt," 80:361
Requirements for Certification, 1980-1981, 81:222
Research in Information Science, 79:173
Research in librarianship, see Library research and development
Research in information science
 data bases, 80:252
 infometrics, 80:253
 information processing, 80:252-253
 standards and measures, 80:252
 see also Grant proposals; Grants, information science; Information technology
Research libraries
 acquisitions, 81:156-157
 funding, federal, 81:5; 79:122
 HEA support, 81:189-194; 80:140-141; 79:164-166
 LSCA support, 80:212-213
 legislation, see Legislation affecting libraries, research libraries
 NEH Research Collections Program, 79:168
 personnel, continuing education, 81:157-159
 statistics, see Association of Research Li-

Research libraries (Cont.)
    braries, Task Force on Statistics; Library statistics, research libraries
    see also Association of Research Libraries; Public libraries
Research Libraries Group, **81:**17-18; **80:**12-13; **78:**11; **77:**39
    computer link with LC, **78:**63
    network developments, **81:**16
    shared cataloging, **80:**13
Research Libraries Information Network, **81:**18-19; **79:**14
Research Libraries Information Network/Washington Library Network, **80:**11, 12, 13
"Research: The How and Why of It," **81:**264
"Resolution on Racism and Sexism Awareness," **77:**18
Resources and Technical Services Division, see American Library Association, Resources and Technical Services Division
Resources in Education, **79:**162
Responsibilities of the American Book Community, **81:**92
Revenue sharing, see General Revenue Sharing; State and Local Fiscal Assistance Act, Title I, General Revenue Sharing
Review of the United States Role in International Biomedical Research and Communications, **81:**94
Reynolds, Fred J., **79:**244
Rhodes, Sarah N., **81:**195; **80:**251; **79:**172
Riedel, Hans, **79:**378
Right to Financial Privacy Act, **80:**202
Right to Read Committee, see Association of American Publishers, School Division, Right to Read Committee; National Reading Improvement Program
"Rights of the Translators," **79:**394
Ringer, Barbara A., **80:**74
Risher, Carol A., **78:**119
Robert, William H., **80:**32
Robinson, Susan, **80:**73
Rochell, Carleton, **77:**3
Rochester Institute of Technology, Book Testing Laboratory and Bindery, **78:**99-102
Rocky Mountain Continental Divide Foundation, outdoor museum, **81:**87
Roderer, Nancy, **79:**38
Rodgers, Frank, **81:**157
Rodriguez Gallardo, Adolfo, **77:**423
Rogan, Barbara, **80:**485
Rogers, Barbara, **78:**397
Role of Libraries in America, **77:**75
Role of Publishers in the National Library Network, **80:**135
Role of the School Library Media Program in Networking, **80:**82; **79:**51
"Rosenwald Symposium on the Illustrated Book," **81:**92
Roster of Federal Libraries, **79:**265
Roster of Prospective Federal Librarians, **79:**265
Royalties, see Copyright, royalties
Rundell, Walter, Jr., **80:**259; **79:**178
Rutgers University, Research Information Services, **78:**36
Rutgers [University] Conference on Literature and the Urban Experience, **81:**4
Ryerson, Ted, **80:**83

S

SAA, see Society of American Archivists
SADPO, see Systems Analysis and Data Processing Organization
SAMANTHA, **80:**111
SAN, see Standard Address Numbering
SBA, see Small Business Administration
SBDC, see Small Business Development Center Act
SCATT system, **77:**9
SCOLE, see American Library Association, Standing Committee on Library Education
SDC, see Systems Development Corporation
SEA, see Science and Education Administration
SERLINE, **78:**73
SLA, see Special Libraries Association
"SLA Salary Survey Report," **80:**169
SLD, see International Federation of Library Associations and Institutions, Special Libraries Division
SOLINET
    mutual support system with OCLC, **80:**50-51
    Regional Support System, **81:**20
SPEC, see Systems and Procedures Exchange Center
SPEC Flyers, **79:**92

SRIM, *see* Selected Research in Microfiche
SRRT, *see* American Library Association, Social Responsibilities Round Table
STIA, *see* National Science Foundation, Directorate for Scientific, Technological, and International Affairs
STM, *see* International Group of Scientific, Technical, and Medical Publishers
St. Angelo, Douglas, **77**:77
Samore, Theodore, **81**:287; **77**:265
Sauer, Mary E., **79**:66
Saunders Paperbacks, **80**:41
Saunders Press, **80**:41
Savage, Noël, **81**:3; **80**:3; **79**:3; **78**:3; **77**:3
Savory, Theodore H., **79**:389
Schick, Frank L., **79**:349; **78**:374; **77**:247, 331, 415
Schick, Renée, **80**:66
Schoenung, James G., **80**:145
Scholarly Communication, **80**:37, 361; **78**:395
Scholarships, **81**:252–254, 254–259; **80**:349–356; **79**:271–273; **78**:358–360; **77**:388–390
  Beta Phi Mu awards, **78**:362
  CLR, **80**:269; **79**:191; **78**:172; **77**:207–208
  HEA grants, **81**:179–180; **80**:223–224, 225–227; **79**:152–155; **78**:145–147; **77**:189–190
  NEH research stipends, **80**:247; **78**:157–159; **77**:197–198
  sources, **80**:347–349
  Stephen Greene Fund, **80**:133
  see also Grants, library; *also* names of scholarships, e.g., Academic Library Management Intern Program, Council on Library Resources, fellowship program
School Libraries, **78**:352
School library/media associations, state, **81**:519–525; **80**:646–652; **79**:523–530; **78**:518–524; **77**:19–27, 552–557
School library/media services
  Bahamas, **79**:352
  bibliography, **81**:405; **80**:530; **79**:580; **78**:571; **77**:253, 605–606
  budgets, **78**:25–27
  Canada, expenditures, **79**:356–357
  circulation statistics, **78**:262
  cooperative activities, **78**:12
  ESEA support, **79**:146–149; **78**:12
  Egypt, **80**:502–503
  employment, **81**:219
  expenditures, **80**:396, 398, 399; **78**:257–260
  funding, **80**:31; **79**:127; **78**:116
    see also Elementary and Secondary Education Act
  German Democratic Republic, **79**:379
  Hawaii, **78**:27
  India, **81**:379, 380
  Mexico, **77**:424
  NCES surveys, **79**:288–289
  national networking, **79**:52
  network participation, **80**:30, 82
  Pakistan, **78**:392
  personnel, **80**:400
    placement, **80**:316; **79**:265; **78**:352
    salaries, **78**:258, 263, 339, 340, 341
    statistics, **80**:399, 400; **78**:256–265
  Poland, **79**:370
  rural communities, **80**:235
  service cutbacks, **79**:35
  services for the handicapped, **80**:60–62
  state supervisors, **81**:525–528; **80**:652–655; **79**:530–533; **78**:504–528
  statistics, *see* Library statistics, school library/media services
  United Kingdom, **79**:362–363
  see also Library cooperation, school/public libraries; School media specialists, legislation for
"School Media Centers: Focus on Issues and Trends," **80**:119
School Media Program of the Year Award, **78**:32
School media specialists, legislation for, **79**:36
Schrieber, Philip, **80**:162
Science and Education Administration, **79**:76
Science Citation Index, **77**:429
Scientific and technical information
  licensable technology, **80**:85
  NTIS collections, **80**:84
Scientific Serials in Australian Libraries, **77**:429
Scofield, Stewart, **79**:40
Scope and Coverage Manual (NLM), **78**:73–74
Scott, B., **80**:455
Scribner Awards, **78**:83
Securing a New Library Director, **80**:120
Selected Research in Microfiche, **80**:85
Serial publications
  bibliography, **81**:404; **80**:528–529; **79**:579; **78**:569; **77**:603–604

Serial publications (Cont.)
   machine-readable data base, **78:**65
   prices and price indexes, **81:**343; **80:**457; **79:**336; **78:**319; **77:**334
   see also Periodicals
Serials in Australian Libraries, Social Sciences and Humanities, **77:**429
Serov, V. V., **79:**372
Serving Physically Disabled People: An Information Handbook, **80:**60
"76 United Statesiana," **77:**62
Seward, Stephen, **79:**199; **78:**183
"Sexism: Monitor Awareness," **80:**121
Seymour, Whitney North, Jr., **80:**4
Shaffer, Mary L., **78:**76
Shaffer, Norman J., **79:**59; **77:**58
Shah of Iran, memoirs, **80:**484
Shalit, Gene, **78:**86
Shank, Russell, **79:**79; **77:**46
Shelley, Fred, **80:**259-260; **79:**179
Sharify, Nasser, **77:**417
Shearer, Kenneth D., **77:**360
Sheehan, Kathleen, **77:**15
Sheldon, Brooke, **77:**385
Shera, Jesse, **77:**361
Sheridan, Robert, **77:**3
Short Title Catalog of Eighteenth Century Printed Books in the National Library of Medicine, **80:**106-107
Shubert, Joseph F., **77:**71
Sign Language Studies, **79:**391
Silver Cindy Award, **79:**81
Simmons, Beatrice, **81:**173; **80:**218
Simpson, Donald B., **77:**3, 75, 77
Sinnot, Lorraine, **80:**361
Sitts, Maxine K., **81:**120
Skaptason, Trish, **81:**162
Slanker, Barbara O., **80:**443
Small Business Administration, **81:**144-145; **80:**153
Small Business Development Center Act, **80:**199
Smardo, Frances, **80:**29
Smith, G. Roysce, **80:**112; **79:**111; **77:**86
Smith, Linda C., **80:**392
Smith v. *U.S.*, **77:**59
Smithsonian Astrophysical Observatory, **77:**48
Smithsonian Institution Libraries, **77:**46-49
Smithsonian Radiation Libraries, **77:**48
Smithsonian Science Information Exchange, **77:**49

Smithsonian Tropical Research Institute, **77:**48
Snepp, Frank, **80:**44
Social Sciences Citation Index, **77:**429
Social service agencies, library cooperation, **78:**12
Society for Scholarly Publishing, first meeting, **80:**39
Society of American Archivists, **81:**500-501; **80:**627-628; **79:**94-98, 504-505; **78:**497-499; **77:**532-534
   Education and Professional Development Committee, **79:**97
   manuals on archival techniques, **79:**180
   meetings, **79:**95
   placement services, **81:**213; **79:**260; **78:**344; **77:** 373
   publications program, **79:**95
Society of Authors, Translators' Association, London, **79:**389
Software Act of 1980, **81:**143
Some Questions and Answers about Title IV of the Elementary and Secondary Education Act, Part B, **77:**185-186
Songe, Alice H., **78:**376; **77:**412
Sorghums and Millets Bibliography, **80:**111
South African Institute for Librarianship and Information Science, **81:**30
South-Central Georgia Folklife Project, **78:**61
Southeastern Library Association, joint conference with Southwestern Library Association, **79:**24
Southwestern Library Association, joint conference with Southeastern Library Association, **79:**24
Soviet-American Library Seminar, 1st, **80:**21, 115
Speaker, **80:**27; **79:**27-28, 33, 81; **78:**20, 23, 28-29, 85
Special libraries
   Bahamas, **79:**353
   bibliography, **81:**406; **80:**531; **79:**581; **78:**571-572; **77:**607
   CLR training activities, **80:**268-269
   construction, **77:**305
   Egypt, **80:**503
   German Democratic Republic, **79:**381
   India, **81:**380
   international associations, **78:**378-379
   Mexico, **77:**424-425
   Pakistan, **78:**382-383
   personnel, **80:**169, 393, 394

Poland, 79:369-370
serving state government agencies, 80: 392-395
statistics, see Library statistics, special libraries
USSR, 79:375
see also Law libraries; Medical libraries; Research libraries
Special Libraries Association, 81:501-502; 80:167-172; 79:506-507; 78:499-500; 77:62-65, 534-535
annual conferences, 80:170-171
boycotts non-ERA states, 80:33
China Fund, 80:171
Committee on Networking, 77:63
Committee on Positive Action Program for Minority Groups, 77:63
continuing education courses, 81:28
continuing education seminars, 77:63
copyright guidelines, 79:15
international activities, 77:64
placement services, 81:213; 80:311; 79:267; 78:347-348; 77:373
Professional Development Department, 80:169
Publishing Division, 77:387
services to members, 80:171-172
withdraws from ARL and American Federation of Information Processing Societies, 79:24
see also Library associations, SLA student groups
Spicer, Erik J., 80:507
Standard Account Numbers, 78:98
Standard Address Numbering, 80:37
Standards for Accreditation, 1972, 80:119; 77:53
Standards for Library Functions at the State Level, 77:77, 79
Standards of Librarianship in Burma, Ceylon, India, and Pakistan, 80:493
Standards of Services for the Library of Congress Network of Libraries for the Blind and Physically Handicapped, 80:120; 79:84
Starr, Kevin, 77:3
State and Local Fiscal Assistance Act, Title I, General Revenue Sharing, 80:242; 78:136, 137; 77: 106, 282
see also General Revenue Sharing
State Historical Records Boards, 79:180
State Joint Interdepartmental Library Committee (USSR), 79:372-373

State libraries, 81:26
bibliography, 81:406; 80:531; 79:581; 78:572; 77:607
State library agencies, 81:515-518; 80:642-645; 79:520-523; 78:10, 514-517; 77:71-75, 548-551
administrative responsibilities, 77:179-180
funding, 79:10
LSCA support, 81:163; 80:212; 79:141; 78:135
NCES survey, 79:287
national network support, 77:4
personnel institute, 77:385
placement services, 81:213-214; 80:311-312; 79:261; 78:348; 77:374
political pressures, 80:6
pre-White House conferences, 80:6, 44, 47-53; 79:32, 54-55, 55-56, 56-57
seminars, 78:45
state and territorial conference plans, 77:29
statistical publications, 78:218-220
support of resource libraries, 80:205
see also American Library Association, Association of Specialized and Cooperative Library Agencies; Chief Officers of State Library Agencies
State Library Agencies: A Survey Project Report, 80:120; 78:83; 77:55, 75, 80
State library associations, see Library associations, state
State Library Policy, Its Legislative and Environmental Contexts, 77:77
State school library/media associations, see School library/media associations, state
State school library supervisors, see School library/media services, state supervisors
State University of New York at Albany, library research program, 80:236
State University of New York at Binghamton, Translator Training Program, 79:391
Statistical surveys, see Library statistics
"Status of Canadian Library Statistics," 77:416
Steiner, George, 79:393
Stevens, Chuck, 77:3
Stevens, Frank A., 81:176, 189; 80:221, 223, 239; 79:149, 151, 164; 78:142, 144; 77:186, 188

Stevens, Norman D., **78**:172
Stewart, Donald E., **81**:103
Stolen Art Alert, **81**:31
Stone, Elizabeth W., **77**:384
Strikes, **81**:39; **79**:34–35
Study of the Library System of the Department of Education (Hawaii), **78**:27
"Subject Evaluation Profile for METRO Libraries," **77**:91
Suffolk Cooperative Library System, **77**:15
Sullivan, Peggy, **81**:102
Sullivan, Robert C., **78**:326
Sun, Moon, Star, **80**:485
Survey of School Media Standards, **79**:148; **77**:185
"Survey of Telefacsimile Use in Libraries of the United States," **78**:84
Surveys, statistical, *see* Library statistics
Symbols of American Libraries, **77**:40
Symposium on Media Concentration, **79**:131
Syracuse University School of Information Studies, CLR support, **78**:170
Systems Analysis and Data Processing Organization, **81**:19
Systems Analysis of Scientific and Technical Communication in the United States, **79**:38
Systems and Procedures Exchange Center, **79**:92; **77**:209
Systems Development Corporation, **80**:66, 67
    Electronic Mailbox, **80**:67

T

TAALS, *see* American Association of Language Specialists
TABA, *see* American Book Awards
TC-46, *see* International Organization for Standardization, Technical Committee 46
TEOL, **77**:566
TIRC, *see* Toxicology Information Center, Toxicology Information Response Center
TIS/NAL, *see* Technical Information Systems/National Agricultural Library
TLA, *see* Theatre Library Association
TOXLINE, **81**:97; **80**:107; **79**:74
TOX-TIPS, see *Toxicology Testing in Progress*
TRIC, **80**:63
TSM, *see* Association of American Publishers, Technical, Scientific and Medical Division
Talese, Gay, **80**:484
Tanimura, Clinton, **78**:27
Tape recordings, *see* Audiovisual materials
Tax reform law, lobbying restrictions, **77**:105–106
Teachers Advisory Bulletin on Instructional Materials, **81**:118
Teachers' unions, *see* Unions
"Teaching Design: Interlibrary Loan Basics," **78**:84
"Technical Economic Analysis of Alternatives for Access to Periodical Literature," **80**:142
Technical information, *see* Scientific and technical information
Technical, Scientific, and medical books, AAP concerns, **78**:92–93
Technical Information Systems/National Agricultural Library, **81**:98–101; **80**:109–111; **79**:76–78
  cooperative education program, **81**:101
  Educational Resources Room, **81**:99
  Food and Nutrition Information Center, *see* Food and Nutrition Information Center
  funding, federal, **81**:130; **80**:189
  NAL Kellogg collection, **81**:101
  see also Agricultural Libraries Information Network; National Agricultural Library
Telecommunications
  broadcasting stations
    assignment of frequencies, **80**:90
    copyright regulations, **81**:131; **77**:156–157, 168–169
    influence of TV on children, **79**:34, 35–36
    land mobile radio, **80**:88
    minority ownership, **81**:58; **80**:88
    programming choices, **80**:87–88
    services for the handicapped, **80**:58
  cable TV
    deregulation of, **80**:88
    public service channels, **80**:58
  closed circuit TV enlargers, **81**:12
  eavesdropping, **80**:90
  government use, **80**:87, 89–90
  international, **80**:87, 88
  international spectrum management, **80**:90
  legislation, **81**:150–151; **78**:119
  public service agencies users, **80**:89

rural services, **80**:88-89
systems reviews, **80**:90
Telecommunications Demonstration Program, **79**:123
Telephone directories, blue pages, **80**:76
Teletext, **80**:91
Television stations, *see* Telecommunications, broadcasting stations
"Television, the Book, and the Classroom," **81**:91; **80**:95; **79**:61
Textbook in American Society, **81**:92
Textbook Questions and Answers, **80**:137; **78**:92; **77**:84
Textbooks, **81**:118; **80**:37
  AAP concerns, **80**:138; **79**:109; **78**:92, 93
  college, AAP concerns, **80**:137; **79**:108
  LC, Center for the Book conference, **80**:190
  marketing, **80**:137
  sales, **79**:318, 319, 320; **78**:304, 305; **77**:316, 317, 318, 325-326
Theatre Library Association, **81**:502-503; **80**:629-630; **79**:507; **78**:501; **77**:535-536
Theory and Practice of Translation, **79**:391
Thirteen Colonial Americana, **78**:88
Thodt, Charles A., **78**:94
Thomas, John, **80**:156
Thor Power Tool Company decision, **81**:40-41, 113, 136, 145
Thy Neighbor's Wife, **80**:484, 486
Ticknor & Fields, **80**:41
Time to Heal, **80**:42
Totok, Andrew, **78**:84
Touching, **80**:42
Toward a National Library and Information Service Network: The Library Bibliographic Component, **80**:46; **78**:63; **77**:38
Toward a National Program for Library and Information Services: Goals for Action, **81**:80; **80**:80; **79**:50, 55; **78**:42-43, 45; **77**:24, 28, 77
Toward a Science of Translating, **79**:390
Toxic Substances Control Act, Inventory Candidate List, **78**:74
Toxicology Data Bank, **80**:107; **79**:74
Toxicology Information Program, Toxicology Information Response Center, **81**:97-98; **80**:107-108; **79**:72, 74; **78**:74; **77**:42
Toxicology Information On-line, *see* TOXLINE
Toxicology Research Projects Directory, **78**:74; **77**:42

Toxicology Testing-in-Progress, **78**:74; **77**:42
Trade union libraries, German Democratic Republic, **79**:379-380
Traduire, **79**:389
Training Film Program, **79**:93
Translation, **79**:384-395
Translation, **79**:392
"Translation and Its Role in Bridging Cultures," **79**:392
Translation and Translators, **79**:395
Translation: Applications and Research, **79**:393
Translation Monthly, **79**:389
Translation Review, **79**:394
Translations, books, **79**:325
"Translator Training Guidelines," **79**:389
Translators
  education, *see* State University of New York at Binghamton, Translator Training Program; University of Arkansas, M.A. in Translation; University of Texas, Dallas, Translation Center
  professional guild, **79**:387-388
  status, **79**:385-387
  wages, **79**:386
Translators associations, **79**:387
Translators' Guild of the Institute of Linguists, London, **79**:388
"Trends in Public Library Research in the 1970's," **80**:359
Trends of Developing Librarianship in the Country, 1976-1980, **79**:373
Trezza, Alphonse F., **81**:81; **80**:80; **78**:42, 46; **77**:24, 28, 75, 247, 416
Trial and Execution, **80**:485
Troiano, Richard, **80**:321
Truett, Cecily, **80**:29
Trustees, library, *see* Library trustees
Tsosie, Mary, **78**:56
Two-year college libraries
  acquisitions, **78**:241-242; **77**:262-264
  additions and renovations, **79**:315-316
  construction, **80**:441-442; **79**:314-316; **78**:299-302; **77**:306-312

U

UAP, *see* Universal Availability of Publications
UBC, *see* International Federation of Library Associations and Institutions, International Office for Universal

UBC (Cont.)
  Bibliographic Control; Universal Bibliographic Control
UGC, see University Grants Committee (U.K.)
ULC, see Urban Libraries Council
UNESCO
  General Information Programme, **81**:369; **79**:82
  Regional Center for Reading Materials in Asia, **78**:384
  Statistics Bureau, cooperation with IFLA, **77**:416–417
  support of libraries, **81**:369–370; **80**:490
  work on UNISIST, **79**:66, 67
UNESCO Bulletin for Libraries, **80**:493
UNESCO Recommendations Concerning the International Standardization of Library Statistics, **77**:417
UNESCO Statistical Yearbook, **79**:409
UNICAT/TELECAT, see Union Catalogue/Telecommunications Catalogue
UNIMARC, adopted for international exchange of data, **79**:62
UNISIST, see International System of Information
UNISIST/ICSI-Abstracting Board, **79**:66–67
UPC, see Universal Product Code
USBE, see Universal Serials and Book Exchange, Inc.
USIA, see U.S. Information Agency
USICA, see U.S., International Communication Agency
USPS, see U.S., Postal Service
UTLAS, **81**:19
  automated catalogue services, **79**:358
Understanding College Textbook Publishing for the College Student, **77**:84
Union Catalogue/Telecommunications Catalogue, **79**:357
Union List of Selected Microforms, **77**:91
Unions, **81**:26; **80**:20–21; **79**:23; **78**:18–19, 26; **77**:4–5
  LC membership, **79**:59
United Federation of Teachers, Library Media Committee, **78**:26; **77**:15
United Kingdom, Postal Office, Prestel, **79**:365
U.S.
  Army Library, see Army Library, Pentagon

Bureau of Indian Affairs, **78**:55, 59
Census of Manufactures, **80**:467, 468
Congress
  budget process and libraries, **80**:175–176
  Joint Committee on Printing, **81**:83, 145–146; **80**:83, 183–184; **79**:125
Copyright Office, **81**:73–78, 131; **80**:70–73, 185; **79**:42; **78**:66
  merger with Copyright Royalty Tribunal, **80**:75
  moves to James Madison Memorial Building, **80**:75
Copyright Royalty Tribune, see Copyright Royalty Tribune
Criminal Code, Title 44, **81**:137, 146–147, 148; **80**:183–184, 187–188, 191, 197–198; **79**:131–132
Department of Agriculture, **77**:45
  TIS/NAL, see Technical Information Systems/National Agricultural Library
Department of Commerce
  Economic Development Administration, **77**:104
  National Technical Information Service, see National Technical Information Service
  National Telecommunications and Information Administration, see National Telecommunications and Information Administration
  "Standards Information Center," **80**:199
Department of Defense
  placement services, **81**:220; **80**:318; **79**:266; **78**:353; **77**:378
Department of Education, **80**:183
  conference on library research, **80**:59
  Office of Libraries and Learning Technologies, **81**:56, 131–132
Department of Health, Education and Welfare, **77**:13
Energy and Research Development Administration, **77**:45
Environmental Protection Agency, **77**:45
Executive Office of the President, Office of Administration, divisions, see Information Management and Services Division, EOP
Federal Communications Commission, regulations, **81**:58, 150–151
General Services Information, Office of External Affairs, Office of Consumer

Affairs, see Federal Information Centers
government information, security classification, **80:**57
Government Printing Office, see Government Printing Office
Information Agency, **81:**67; **78:**354; **77:**379
Information Clearinghouses, **80:**92-93
International Communication Agency, **81:**67-72; **80:**318
  Associate Directorate for Educational and Cultural Affairs, **81:**67-68
  Associate Directorate for Programming, **81:**72
  job opportunities, **81:**220-221; **80:**318; **79:**267
  library program, **81:**68-70
  National Commission for UNESCO, **81:**105
  National Park Services Libraries, **78:**59-60
Office of Education
  Bureau of Education of the Handicapped, **80:**61
  grant to ASCLA, **80:**120
  grant to OLSD, **77:**60
  grant to PLA, **78:**84
Office of Management and Budget
  FIC studies, **80:**74
  Office of Information and Regulatory Affairs, **81:**152
Office of Personnel Management, Librarian's Register, **80:**315
patents, dissemination of information, **80:**57
population served by libraries, **81:**270-271; **80:**371-372; **79:**278-279; **78:**235-236; **77:**256-258
Postal Rate Commission, **80:**114, 194; **79:**128, 129, 131; **77:**107
  see also Postal rates
Postal Service, **81:**144; **78:**120-123
  AAP concerns, **79:**106
  electronic mail, **80:**201-202
  legislation, **79:**128-131; see also Postal legislation
  mail classification, **79:**130-131
  subsidies, **80:**42
  task forces, **79:**129
  use of ISSN as registration number, **79:**71
  see also Association of American Publishers, Postal Committee; Postal rates

President
  Committee on Employment of the Handicapped, Library Committee, **80:**59
  message to Congress on libraries, **81:**56-59
  messages on information policy, **80:**196-197
  papers and records, **79:**122; see also Archives; Presidential Records Act
Register of Copyright, **80:**70, 71, 185
5-year review, see Photocopying, 5-year review
Senate
  Education Subcommittee hearings on basic skills, **80:**190
  Senate Post Office Committee, **78:**122
  Senatorial papers, **79:**96-97
Supreme Court, obscenity decision, **77:**88
Weather Bureau, Green Thumb, **80:**91
United States Copyright Information Center, **78:**125
U.S.-Japan Conference on Libraries, **79:**82
U.S. National Inventory of Library Needs, see National Inventory of Library Needs
U.S. National Libraries Task Force on Cooperative Activities, **77:**536
U.S./U.S.S.R. Agreement for Cooperation in Medical Science and Public Health, **77:**41
United Teachers Union of Island Trees, **77:**16
Universal Availability of Publications, **80:**82; **78:**369
Universal Bibliographic Control, **80:**492; **77:**211
  see also International Federation of Library Associations and Institutions, International Office for Universal Bibliographic Control
Universal City Studios, Inc., v. *Sony Corporation of America*, **80:**71-72
Universal Copyright Convention, **77:**115
Universal Product Code, **80:**39
Universal Serials and Book Exchange, Inc., **81:**13, 503-504; **80:**630-631; **79:**508; **78:**501-502; **77:**537
University Grants Committee (U.K.), **79:**361, 362
University Microfilms, copying services, **78:**15
University of Arkansas, M.A. in Translation, **79:**393

University of California, Berkeley
  CLR grant, **80:**268
  Institute for Governmental Studies, **79:** 40
University of California, Los Angeles, online microfiche catalog, **80:**236
University of Mississippi, Department of Library Science, placement services, **79:**261
University of North Carolina, Greensboro, access to school media material, **80:** 236
University of Pittsburgh
  Graduate School of Library and Information Science, International Library Information Center and Placement Service, **78:**154
  Hillman Library, user survey, **79:**38
  Institute on Resource Sharing, **77:**6
University of Texas, Austin, National Translation Center, **79:**390
University of Texas, Dallas, Translation Center, **79:**394
Urban libraries, *see* Public libraries
Urban Libraries Council, **81:**6, 10–11; **79:**24
Use of Library Materials: The University of Pittsburgh Study, **80:**361; **79:**38

V

Van Deerlin, Lionel, **78:**118
Vatican Library Project, **81:**363–365
Vaughan, Samuel S., **77:**387
Velleman, Ruth A., **80:**53, 60
"Video Disc: Challenge and Opportunity for Publishers," **80:**488
Videocassettes, *see* Audiovisual materials, videocassettes
Videodisc technology, **79:**74–75
  biomedical uses, **80:**108
Videotape, *see* Audiovisual materials, off-air videotaping; Audiovisual materials, videocassettes
Virgo, Julie A. C., **79:**87
Visual Artists Moral Rights Amendments, 1979, **80:**200
Vocations for Social Change, **78:**352; **77:** 378
"Voice of America," **81:**67
Voice of Z39, **81:**110; **80:**127; **79:**99–100
Voight, David, **78:**61–62
Vonnegut, Kurt, Jr., **80:**485
Vosper, Robert, **78:**367

W

WHC Update, **79:**56
whcLIST, *see* White House Conference on Library and Information Services Taskforce
WARC, *see* World Administrative Radio Conference
WHCOLIS, *see* White House Conference on Library and Information Services
WHO, *see* World Health Organization
WILCO, *see* Western Interstate Library Cooperative Organization
WIPO, *see* World Intellectual Property Organization
WITS, *see* Worldwide Information and Trade System
WLN, *see* Washington Library Network
Waithe, Deborah, **81:**304, 310
Walch, Timothy, **79:**94
Wanderers, **80:**31, 32
Warneke, Ruth, **77:**58
Washington Book Fair, **80:**40
Washington Library Network, **81:**19; **79:**14, 15; **77:**8
Washington State Library, computer simulation for network planners, **80:**236
Washtien, Joe, **77:**385
Webster, Duane E., **79:**91
Wedgeworth, Robert, **81:**103, 105; **80:**115; **79:**36; **78:**25, 31; **77:**59
"Week of the Young Child," **78:**24–25
Weidhaas, Peter, **80:**481, 482; **78:**388
Weil, Ben H., **78:**33
Weinstein, Robert A., **78:**174
Weintraub, Kathryn, **80:**361
Weissman, Gloria, **78:**157; **77:**196
Western Council of State Librarians, organized, **78:**10
Western Council of State Library Agencies, planning retreat, **81:**20
Western Interstate Library Cooperative Organization, **77:**8
"What Americans Are Reading," **80:**124; **79:**87; **78:**86
What Else You Can Do with a Library Degree, **81:**222
"What Non-Print Materials Can Do for You in the Classroom," **79:**108
"Where to Turn for Help in Folklore and Folklife," **80:**96
White House Conference on Library and Information Services, **78:**3, 46–49, 80
  AAP concerns, **80:**136
  ALA activities, **80:**116; **79:**81

Conference Information Center, **80:**45
delegate preparation, **79:**55
delegates, **80:**44-45
discussion group categories, **80:**50-51
funding approved, **78:**111
influence on federal aid, **81:**5
Information Community Advisory Committee, **80:**154
library research support, **80:**360
NCLIS activities, **81:**79-80; **79:**52
pre-conference activities, **79:**31-32; **78:** 50-51
pre-conference resolutions, **80:**48-49, 360
pre-conference workshops, **79:**81
pre-conferences, *see* State library agencies, WHCOLIS pre-White House conferences
President Carter's address, **80:**45-46
President Carter's implementation, **81:** 56-59
professional associations' activity, **79:**55
recommendations, **81:**32
implementation, **81:**137, 140-141
Resolution on Library Statistical Surveys by the Federal Government, **80:**367
resolutions, **81:**34; **80:**4-5, 46-47, 80-81, 186, 190
SLA activities, **80:**169
state pre-conference meetings, *see* State library agencies, pre-White House conferences
Theme Groups, **80:**3-4, 45
themes, **80:**45
see also State library agencies, pre-White House Conferences
White House Conference on Library and Information Services Taskforce, **81:** 79; **80:**3-5, 38, 43-47, 47-48; **79:**53-57
White House Information Center, *see* Information Management and Services Division, EOP
White House Years, **80:**485
"Who We Are," **79:**190
Wiederkehr, Robert R. V., **81:**265; **80:**361
Wijnstroom, Margreet, **78:**367, 380
Wilkins, Barratt, **79:**287
Willard, Robert S., **81:**147; **80:**195
Williams, Sally F., **81:**340-353; **80:**454
Wilson, Jane, **77:**59
Wilson, Pauline, **80:**362
Windsor Codex, **81:**363
Winnick, Pauline, **80:**204; **77:**172
Wisconsin Indian Library Training Program, **78:**56

Witkins, Janis, **80:**277
Women in librarianship, **81:**24, 263; **79:**24-25, 82
see also American Library Association, Committee on the Status of Women in Librarianship; Equal Rights Amendment
Women in Scholarly Publishing, **80:**39
Wood, James L., **81:**107; **80:**124; **79:**100
Woolls, Blanche, **77:**385
Word Guild Magazine, **79:**393
Work for Hire, copyright legislation, **77:**169
Workshops for Jail Library Service, **81:**103
World Administrative Radio Conference, **80:**90
World Health Organization, NLM assistance, **80:**106
World Intellectual Property Organization, **77:**112-113
World of Translation, **79:**391
Worldwide Conference on Special Libraries, 1st, SLA participation, **80:**171
Worldwide Information and Trade System, **81:**149; **80:**153, 198, 199
"Worldwide Information Sources," **80:**171
Wright, Beatrice, **80:**55
Wright, Louis, **77:**62
Writings on American History, **80:**259; **79:**178

Y

YASD, *see* American Library Association, Young Adult Services Division
Yankelovich, Skelley, and White, **79:**38
Yates, Ella, **77:**3
"You, Your New Baby and the Library," **78:**23-24
Young adult books, *see* Books, best books, young adult
Young Adult Services Division, *see* American Library Association, Young Adult Services Division

Z

ZEIKO, **77:**566
Z39, *see* American National Standards Committee Z39
Zara, **80:**485
Zaroulis, Nancy, **80:**485
Zeitschriftenkompletierungstelle, see ZEIKO
Zurcher v. Stanford Daily, **81:**151; **80:**188, 202
Zurkowski, Paul G., **80:**149

Directory of U.S. and Canadian Libraries

This directory has been compiled for ready reference. For libraries not listed, see the *American Library Directory* (R. R. Bowker, 1980).

UNITED STATES

Univ. of Alabama
Amelia Gayle Gorgas Lib., Box S,
University, AL 35486
Tel: 205-348-5298

Alameda County Library
22777 Main St., Hayward, CA 94544
Tel: 415-881-6337

Annapolis & Anne Arundel County Public Library
5 Harry S. Truman Pkwy., Annapolis, MD 21401
Tel: 301-224-7371

Arizona State Univ. Library
Tempe, AZ 85281
Tel: 602-965-3417

Atlanta Public Library
One Margaret Mitchell Sq. N.W., Carnegie Way & Forsyth St., Atlanta, GA 30303
Tel: 404-688-4636

Baltimore County Public Library
320 York Rd., Towson, MD 21204
Tel: 301-296-8500

Boston Athenaeum
10½ Beacon St., Boston, MA 02118
Tel: 617-227-0270

Boston Public Library
666 Boylston St., Box 286, Boston, MA 02117
Tel: 617-536-5400

Boston Univ. Libraries
Mugar Memorial Lib., 771 Commonwealth Ave., Boston, MA 02215
Tel: 617-353-3710

Brigham Young Univ.
Harold B. Lee Lib., University Hill, Provo, UT 84602
Tel: 801-378-2905

Brooklyn Public Library
Grand Army Plaza, Brooklyn, NY 11238
Tel: 212-780-7712

Broward County Libraries
Box 5463, Fort Lauderdale, FL 33310
Tel: 305-972-1100

Brown Univ. Libraries
John D. Rockefeller, Jr. Lib., Providence, RI 02912
Tel: 401-863-2162

Buffalo and Erie County Public Library
Lafayette Sq., Buffalo, NY 14203
Tel: 716-856-7525

Univ. of California, Berkeley
Univ. Lib., Berkeley, CA 94720
Tel: 415-642-3773

Univ. of California, Davis
General Lib., Davis, CA 95616
Tel: 916-752-2110

Univ. of California, Los Angeles
Univ. Lib., 405 Hilgard Ave., Los Angeles, CA 90024
Tel: 213-825-1201

Univ. of California, San Diego
Univ. Libs., Mail Code C-075, La Jolla, CA 92093
Tel: 714-452-3336

Univ. of California, Santa Barbara
Campus Lib., Santa Barbara, CA 93106
Tel: 805-961-2741

Carnegie Library of Pittsburgh
4400 Forbes Ave., Pittsburgh, PA 15213
Tel: 412-622-3100

Case Western Reserve
Univ. Libs., 11161 East Blvd., Cleveland, OH 44106
Tel: 216-368-3506

Univ. of Chicago
Joseph Regenstein Lib., 1100 E. 57 St.,
  Chicago, IL 60637
Tel: 312-753-2977

Chicago Public Library
425 N. Michigan Ave., Chicago, IL 60611
Tel: 312-269-2900

Univ. of Cincinnati
Main Lib., University & Woodside,
  Cincinnati, OH 45221
Tel: 513-475-2218

Cincinnati-Hamilton County Public Library
800 Vine St., Cincinnati, OH 45202
Tel: 513-369-6000

Cleveland Public Library
325 Superior Ave., Cleveland, OH 44114
Tel: 216-623-2800

Univ. of Colorado at Boulder
Univ. Libs., Norlin Lib., M450, Boulder,
  CO 80309
Tel: 303-492-7511

Colorado State Univ.
William E. Morgan Lib., Fort Collins, CO
  80523
Tel: 303-491-5911

Columbia Univ. Libraries
535 W. 114 St., New York, NY 10027
Tel: 212-280-2241

Univ. of Connecticut Library
Storrs, CT 06268
Tel: 203-486-2219

Contra Costa County Library System
1750 Oak Park Blvd., Pleasant Hill, CA 94523
Tel: 415-944-3423

Cornell Univ. Libraries
Ithaca, NY 14853
Tel: 607-256-4144

Cuyahoga County Public Library
4510 Memphis Ave., Cleveland, OH 44144
Tel: 216-398-1800

John Crerar Library
35 W. 33 St., Chicago, IL 60616
Tel: 312-225-2526

Dallas Public Library
1954 Commerce, Dallas, TX 75201
Tel: 214-748-9071

Dartmouth College
Baker Memorial Lib., Hanover, NH 03755
Tel: 603-646-2235

Dayton-Montgomery County Public Library
215 E. Third St., Dayton, OH 45402
Tel: 513-224-1651

Denver Public Library
1357 Broadway, Denver, CO 80203
Tel: 303-573-5152, ext. 271

Detroit Public Library
5201 Woodward Ave., Detroit, MI 48202
Tel: 313-833-1000

District of Columbia Public Library
901 G St. N.W., Washington, DC 20001
Tel: 202-727-1101

Duke Univ.
William R. Perkins Lib., Durham, NC 27706
Tel: 919-684-2034

Emory Univ. Libraries
Atlanta, GA 30322
Tel: 404-329-6861

Enoch Pratt Free Library
400 Cathedral St., Baltimore, MD 21201
Tel: 301-396-5430

Fairfax County Public Library
5502 Port Royal Rd., Springfield, VA 22151
Tel: 703-321-9810

Univ. of Florida Libraries
210 Lib. W., Gainesville, FL 32611
Tel: 904-392-0341

Florida State Univ.
Robert Manning Strozier Lib., Tallahassee,
  FL 32306
Tel: 904-644-5211

Fort Worth Public Library
300 Taylor St., Fort Worth, TX 76102
Tel: 817-870-7700

Fresno County Public Library
2420 Mariposa St., Fresno, CA 93721
Tel: 209-488-3191

DIRECTORY OF U.S. AND CANADIAN LIBRARIES / 629

Georgetown Univ.
Joseph Mark Lauinger Lib., 37 and O Sts.
N.W., Washington, DC 20057
Tel: 202-625-4095

Univ. of Georgia Libraries
Athens, GA 30602
Tel: 404-542-2716

Harvard Univ. Library
Cambridge, MA 02138
Tel: 617-495-3650

Univ. of Hawaii Library
2550 The Mall, Honolulu, HI 96822
Tel: 808-948-7205

Hennepin County Library System
York Ave. S. at 70, Edina, MN 55435
Tel: 612-830-4944

Univ. of Houston
M. D. Anderson Memorial Lib., 4800
Calhoun Blvd., Houston, TX 77004
Tel: 713-749-4241

Houston Public Library
500 McKinney Ave., Houston, TX 77002
Tel: 713-224-5441

Howard Univ. Libraries
Founders Lib., 2400 Sixth St. N.W.,
Washington, DC 20059
Tel: 202-636-7253

Univ. of Illinois at Urbana-Champaign
University Lib., Wright St., 230 Lib.,
Urbana, IL 61801
Tel: 217-333-0790

Indiana Univ. Libraries
Tenth St. and Jordan Ave., Bloomington,
IN 47401
Tel: 812-337-3403

Indianapolis-Marion County Public Library
Box 211, 40 E. St. Clair St., Indianapolis,
IN 46206
Tel: 317-635-5662

Univ. of Iowa Libraries
Iowa City, IA 52242
Tel: 319-353-4450

Iowa State Univ. Library
Ames, IA 50011
Tel: 515-294-1442

Jacksonville Public Library System
Haydon Burns Lib., 122 N. Ocean St.,
Jacksonville, FL 32202
Tel: 904-633-6870

Jefferson Parish Library
Box 7490, 3420 North Causeway Blvd. at
Melvin Dewey Dr., Metairie, LA 70010
Tel: 504-834-5850

Johns Hopkins Univ.
Milton S. Eisenhower Lib., Baltimore,
MD 21218
Tel: 301-338-8325

Joint Univ. Libraries
See Vanderbilt Univ. Library

Kansas City Public Library
311 E. 12 St., Kansas City, MO 64106
Tel: 816-221-2685

Univ. of Kansas Libraries
Watson Memorial Lib., Lawrence, KS 66045
Tel: 913-864-3601

Kent State Univ. Libraries
Kent, OH 44242
Tel: 216-672-2962

Univ. of Kentucky
Margaret I. King Lib., Lexington, KY 40506
Tel: 606-257-3801

King County Library System
300 Eighth Ave. N., Seattle, WA 98109
Tel: 206-344-7465

Library of Congress
Washington, DC 20540
Tel: 202-287-5000

Los Angeles County Public Library System
Box 111, 320 W. Temple St., Los Angeles,
CA 90053
Tel: 213-974-6501

Los Angeles Public Library
630 W. Fifth St., Los Angeles, CA 90071
Tel: 213-626-7555

Louisiana State Univ. Library
Baton Rouge, LA 70803
Tel: 504-388-2217

Louisville Free Public Library
Fourth and York Sts., Louisville, KY 40203
Tel: 502-584-4154

Maricopa County Library
3375 W. Durango, Phoenix, AZ 85009
Tel: 602-269-2535

Univ. of Maryland at College Park
Univ. Libs., College Park, MD 20742
Tel: 301-454-3011

Univ. of Massachusetts at Amherst
Univ. Lib., Amherst, MA 01003
Tel: 413-545-0284

Massachusetts Institute of Technology Libraries
Rm. 14 S-216, Cambridge, MA 02139
Tel: 617-253-5651

Memphis-Shelby County Public Library
1850 Peabody Ave., Memphis, TN 38104
Tel: 901-528-2950

Univ. of Miami
Otto G. Richter Lib., Box 248214, Memorial Dr., Coral Gables, FL 33124
Tel: 305-284-3551

Miami-Dade Public Library System
One Biscayne Blvd., Miami, FL 33132
Tel: 305-579-5001

Univ. of Michigan Library
Ann Arbor, MI 48109
Tel: 313-764-9356

Michigan State Univ. Library
East Lansing, MI 48824
Tel: 517-355-2344

Milwaukee Public Library
814 W. Wisconsin Ave., Milwaukee, WI 53233
Tel: 414-278-3000

Minneapolis Public Library
300 Nicollet Mall, Minneapolis, MN 55401
Tel: 612-372-6500

Univ. of Minnesota
O. Meredith Wilson Lib., Minneapolis, MN 55455
Tel: 612-373-3097

Univ. of Missouri-Kansas City
General Lib., 5100 Rockhill Rd., Kansas City, MO 64110
Tel: 816-276-1531

Montgomery County Department of Public Libraries
99 Maryland Ave., Rockville, MD 20850
Tel: 301-279-1401

Nassau Library System
900 Jerusalem Ave., Uniondale, NY 11553
Tel: 516-292-8920

National Agricultural Library
U.S. Dept. of Agriculture, 10301 Baltimore Blvd., Beltsville, MD 20705
Tel: 301-344-3778

National Library of Medicine
8600 Rockville Pike, Bethesda, MD 20209
Tel: 301-496-6308

Univ. of Nebraska-Lincoln
Don L. Love Memorial Lib., Lincoln, NE 68588
Tel: 402-472-2526

State Univ. of New York at Albany
Univ. Lib., 1400 Washington Ave., Albany, NY 12222
Tel: 518-457-8542

State Univ. of New York at Buffalo
Univ. Libs., 432 Capen Hall, Buffalo, NY 14260
Tel: 716-636-2965

State Univ. of New York at Stony Brook
Frank Melville Jr. Memorial Lib., Stony Brook, NY 11794
Tel: 516-246-5650

New York Public Library
Astor, Lenox and Tilden Foundations Lib., Fifth Ave. and 42 St., New York, NY 10018
Tel: 212-790-6262

New York Univ.
Elmer Holmes Bobst Lib., 70 Washington Sq. S., New York, NY 10012
Tel: 212-598-2484

Newberry Library
60 W. Walton St., Chicago, IL 60610
Tel: 312-943-9090

Univ. of North Carolina at Greensboro
Walter Clinton Jackson Lib., 1000 Spring Garden St., Greensboro, NC 27412
Tel: 919-379-5880

Northwestern Univ. Library
1935 Sheridan Rd., Evanston, IL 60201
Tel: 312-492-7658

Univ. of Notre Dame
Univ. Libs., Notre Dame, IN 46556
Tel: 219-283-7317

Ohio State Univ.
William Oxley Thompson Memorial Lib., 1858 Neil Ave. Mall, Columbus, OH 43210
Tel: 614-422-6151

Univ. of Oklahoma
William Bennett Bizzell Memorial Lib., 401 W. Brooks, Norman, OK 73019
Tel: 405-325-2611

Oklahoma State Univ. Library
Stillwater, OK 74074
Tel: 405-624-6313

Omaha Public Library
212 S. 15 St., Omaha, NE 68102
Tel: 402-444-4800

Orange County Public Library
431 City Drive S., Orange, CA 92668
Tel: 714-634-7841

Univ. of Oregon Library
Eugene, OR 97403
Tel: 503-686-3056

Univ. of Pennsylvania Libraries
3420 Walnut St., Philadelphia, PA 19104
Tel: 215-243-7091

Pennsylvania State Univ.
Fred Lewis Pattee Lib., University Park, PA 16802
Tel: 814-865-0401

Free Library of Philadelphia
Logan Sq., Philadelphia, PA 19103
Tel: 215-686-5322

Phoenix Public Library
12 E. McDowell Rd., Phoenix, AZ 85004
Tel: 602-262-6451

Univ. of Pittsburgh
Hillman Lib., Pittsburgh, PA 15260
Tel: 412-624-4400

Prince George's County Memorial Library
6532 Adelphi Rd., Hyattsville, MD 20782
Tel: 301-699-3500

Princeton Univ. Library
Princeton, NJ 08540
Tel: 609-452-3180

Purdue Univ. Libraries
Stewart Center, West Lafayette, IN 47907
Tel: 317-749-2571

Queens Borough Public Library
89-11 Merrick Blvd., Jamaica, NY 11432
Tel: 212-990-0700

Rice Univ.
Fondren Lib., Box 1892, 6100 S. Main, Houston, TX 77001
Tel: 713-527-4022

Univ. of Rochester
Rush Rhees Lib., Rochester, NY 14627
Tel: 716-275-4461

Rutgers Univ. Libraries
College Ave., New Brunswick, NJ 08901
Tel: 201-932-7505

Sacramento Public Library
7000 Franklin Blvd., Suite 540, Sacramento, CA 95823
Tel: 916-440-5926

Saint Louis County Public Library
1640 S. Lindbergh Blvd., Saint Louis, MO 63131
Tel: 314-994-3300

Saint Louis Public Library
1301 Olive St., Saint Louis, MO 63103
Tel: 314-241-2288

San Antonio Public Library
203 S. St. Mary's, San Antonio, TX 78205
Tel: 512-299-7790

San Bernardino County Free Library
104 W. Fourth St., San Bernardino, CA 92415
Tel: 714-383-1734

San Diego County Public Library
5555 Overland Ave., Bldg. 15, San Diego,
 CA 92123
Tel: 714-565-5100

San Diego Public Library
820 East St., San Diego, CA 92101
Tel: 714-236-5800

San Francisco Public Library
Civic Center, San Francisco, CA 94012
Tel: 415-558-4235

San Jose Public Library
180 W. San Carlos St., San Jose,
 CA 95113
Tel: 408-277-4822

San Mateo County Public Library
25 Tower Rd., Belmont, CA 94002
Tel: 415-573-2056

Seattle Public Library
1000 Fourth Ave., Seattle, WA 98104
Tel: 206-625-2665

Smithsonian Institution Libraries
Constitution Ave. at Tenth St. N.W.,
 Washington, DC 20560
Tel: 202-381-5496

Univ. of South Carolina
Thomas Cooper Lib., 1600 Sumter St.,
 Columbia, SC 29208
Tel: 803-777-3142

Univ. of Southern California
Edward L. Doheny Memorial Lib.,
 University Park, Los Angeles, CA 90007
Tel: 213-743-6050

Stanford Univ.
University and Coordinate Libs., Stanford,
 CA 94305
Tel: 415-497-2016

Syracuse Univ. Libraries
Ernst S. Bird Lib., 222 Waverly Ave.,
 Syracuse, NY 13210
Tel: 315-423-2575

**Tampa-Hillsborough County Public
 Library System**
900 N. Ashley, Tampa, FL 33602
Tel: 813-223-8947

Temple Univ.
Samuel Paley Lib., Berks and 13 Sts.,
 Philadelphia, PA 19122
Tel: 215-787-8231

Univ. of Tennessee, Knoxville
James O. Hoskins Lib., Knoxville, TN 37916
Tel: 615-974-0111

Univ. of Texas
Mirabeau B. Lamar Lib., Box P, Austin,
 TX 78712
Tel: 512-471-3811

Texas A & M Univ. Libraries
College Station, TX 77843
Tel: 713-845-6111

Tulane Univ. of Louisiana
Howard-Tilton Memorial Lib., New Orleans,
 LA 70118
Tel: 504-865-5131

Tulsa City-County Public Library
400 Civic Center, Tulsa, OK 74103
Tel: 918-581-5221

Univ. of Utah
Marriott Lib., Salt Lake City, UT 84112
Tel: 801-581-8558

Vanderbilt Univ. Library
419 21 Ave. S., Nashville, TN 37203
Tel: 615-322-2834

Univ. of Virginia
Alderman Lib., Charlottesville, VA 22904
Tel: 804-924-3026

Virginia Polytechnic Institute
Carol M. Newman Lib., Blacksburg,
 VA 24061
Tel: 703-961-5593

Univ. of Washington Libraries
FM-25, Seattle, WA 98195
Tel: 206-543-1760

Washington State Univ. Library
Pullman, WA 99164
Tel: 509-335-4557

Washington Univ. Libraries
Skinner and Lindell Blvds., St. Louis,
 MO 63130
Tel: 314-889-5400

Wayne State Univ. Libraries
5210 Second St., Detroit, MI 48202
Tel: 313-557-4020

Univ. of Wisconsin—Milwaukee
University Lib., 2311 E. Hartford Ave.,
 Milwaukee, WI 53201
Tel: 414-963-4785

Yale Univ.
Sterling Memorial Lib., Box 1603A, Yale
 Sta., 120 Hight St., New Haven,
 CT 06520
Tel: 203-436-8335

CANADA

Univ. of Alberta Libraries
Edmonton, Alta. T6G 2J8
Tel: 403-432-3790

Bibliothèque Municipale de Québec
37 r. Ste-Angele, Quebec, P.Q. G1R 4G5
Tel: 418-694-6356

Univ. of British Columbia Library
1956 Main Mall, Vancouver, B.C. V6T 1Y3
Tel: 604-228-3871

Etobicoke Public Library
Box 501, Etobicoke, Ont. M9C 4V5
Tel: 416-248-5681

London Public Library & Art Museum
305 Queens Ave., London, Ont. N6B 3L7
Tel: 519-432-7166

McGill Univ. Libraries
3459 McTavish St., Montreal, P.Q.
 H3A 1Y1
Tel: 514-392-4948

McMaster Univ.
Mills Memorial Lib., 1280 Main St. W.,
 Hamilton, Ont. L8S 4L6
Tel: 416-525-9140

Montreal City Library
1210 Sherbrooke E., Montreal, P.Q. H2L 1L9
Tel: 514-872-5923

National Library of Canada
Lib. Documentation Center, 395
 Wellington St., Ottawa, Ont. K1A 0N4
Tel: 613-995-9481

Queen's Univ. at Kingston
Douglas Lib., Kingston, Ont. K7L 5C4
Tel: 613-547-5950

Regina Public Library
2311 12 Ave., Regina, Sask. S4P 0N3
Tel: 306-569-7615

St. Catharines Public Library
54 Church St., St. Catharines, Ont. L2R 7K2
Tel: 416-688-6103

Saskatoon Public Library
311 23 St. E., Saskatoon, Sask. S7K 0J6
Tel: 306-664-9555

Scarborough Public Library
1076 Ellesmere Rd., Scarborough, Ont.
 M1P 4P4
Tel: 416-291-1991

Toronto Public Library
40 Orchard View Blvd., Toronto, Ont.
 M4R 1B9
Tel: 416-484-8015

Univ. of Toronto Libraries
Toronto, Ont. M5S 1A5
Tel: 416-978-2294

Univ. of Western Ontario
Univ. Lib., 1151 Richmond St. N., London,
 Ont. N6A 3K7
Tel: 519-679-6191

Windsor Public Library
850 Ouellette Ave., Windsor, Ont. N9A 4M9
Tel: 519-258-8111